HANDBOOK
of
POLITICAL THEORY

Associate Editors

HANDBOOK
of
POLITICAL THEORY

Edited by

GERALD F. GAUS AND CHANDRAN KUKATHAS

 **SAGE** Publications
London ● Thousand Oaks ● New Delhi

SAGE Publications Ltd
1 Oliver's Yard
55 City Road
London EC1Y 1SP

SAGE Publications Inc.
2455 Teller Road
Thousand Oaks, California 91320

SAGE Publications India Pvt Ltd
B-42, Panchsheel Enclave
Post Box 4109
New Delhi 110 017

British Library Cataloguing in Publication data

A catalogue record for this book is available
from the British Library

ISBN 0-7619-6787-7
ISBN 0-7619-6788-5 (pbk)

Library of Congress Control Number: 2002112355

Typeset by C&M Digitals (P) Ltd., Chennai, India
Printed in Great Britain by Cromwell Press Ltd., Trowbridge, Wiltshire

Contents

Editors' Preface

In compiling this *Handbook of Political Theory* our aim has been to provide both a comprehensive mapping of the terrain of contemporary political theory and in-depth analyses. We have eschewed short encyclopaedia-like treatments in favour of essays that present not only a précis of the state of scholarship, but the contributor's own analysis of the main issues. As such, the *Handbook* should be useful to scholars as well as students – especially postgraduate students who are seeking to acquaint themselves with current scholarship in contemporary political theory.

The *Handbook* is divided into four parts. Part I focuses on different ways of doing political theory – the nature of scholarship in political theory. This first part examines, among other problems, the relation of political theory to philosophy, political science and ideology, the place of historical scholarship in the study of texts, as well as Straussian and postmodern approaches to texts. The second part offers analyses of some of the main political theories that provide a focus for contemporary scholarship, such as Marxism, liberalism, conservatism, republicanism, communitarianism and democratic, discourse and green theories. Our aim here was not to provide a list of 'isms'; these chapters present analyses of the main contributions and trends in contemporary political theory, focused on explications, and criticisms, of the dominant liberal approaches. Part III is organized around investigations of the modern state: problems of consent, authority and obligation, the welfare state, distributive justice, pluralism and the aggregation of individual judgements, social movements, nationalism, secession, ethnic rights, international relations and the place of the state in feminist and gender theory. Because the contemporary practice of political theory is so closely linked to the history of political thought, the last part of *Handbook* is devoted to studies of periods in the history of political thought, presenting discussions of the main thinkers of each period as well as current scholarship. Our aim to present thorough analyses required editorial judgements about coverage: even given the understanding of Sage Publications, and our wonderful editor, Lucy Robinson, not every period which one of the editors or associate editors thought valuable could be included. The reader will discover that Part IV provides comprehensive and rigorous treatments of the main epochs of Western political theory, as well as fascinating chapters on crucial themes in Chinese political thought and the currently important topic of modern Islamic political thought.

Because the *Handbook* contains thematic and historical chapters, detailed examinations of a theory or theorist are apt to be found in more than one chapter. We have provided cross-references and an extensive index to assist readers in locating relevant discussions.

The editors have been assisted by a team of associate editors, who have provided invaluable guidance both in early decisions about the structure of the *Handbook*, and in reading drafts and providing expert advice. Our sincere thanks to Richard Bellamy, Michael Freeden, Moria Gatens, Susan James, Percy Lehning and Martyn Thompson for taking time from their own work to assist us in the *Handbook*. All of us were, further, assisted by an Editorial Board, who provided important guidance about the structure and content of the *Handbook*, as well as lending their expert advice; again, our sincere thanks. Finally, and most importantly, we are indebted to our contributors, who took such care in researching and writing their chapters.

Gerald F. Gaus
Chandran Kukathas

Contributors and Editors

Terence Ball was formerly Professor of Political Science at the University of Minnesota and Visiting Professor at the University of California–San Diego and Oxford. He now teaches political theory at Arizona State University. He is author of *Transforming Political Discourse* (Oxford, 1988), *Reappraising Political Theory* (Oxford, 1995), and a mystery novel, *Rousseau's Ghost* (New York, 1998), as well as editor of *James Mill: Political Writings* (Cambridge, 1992), *The Federalist* (Cambridge, 2003), co-editor of *After Marx* (1984), *Jefferson: Political Writings* (1999), and *The Cambridge History of Twentieth-Century Political Thought* (Cambridge, 2003), among other books. He is also an avid sea-kayaker and master carpenter.

John Barry is Reader in Politics at Queen's University, Belfast. His main interest is in the relation between moral/political theory and the environment, with particular focus on ecofeminism, the implications of green theory for thinking about justice, and theories of political economy in relation to the environment. He is the author of *Environment and Social Theory* (Routledge, 1999) and *Rethinking Green Politics: Nature, Virtue and Progress* (Sage, 1999), winner of the UK Political Studies Association W. J. M. Mackenzie Prize for best book published in Political Science in 1999. He is a co-editor of *Citizenship, Sustainability and Environmental Research: Q Methodology and Local Exchange and Trading Systems* (Edward Elgar, 2000), *Sustaining Liberal Democracy: Ecological Challenges and Opportunities* (Palgrave, 2001), and *The International Encyclopedia of Environmental Politics* (Routledge, 2001).

Richard Bellamy is Professor of Government at the University of Essex and Academic Director of the European Consortium for Political Research (ECPR). He is the author of *Modern Italian Social Theory: Ideology and Politics from Pareto to the Present*, *Liberalism and Modern Society: An Historical Argument*, *Liberalism and Pluralism: Towards a Politics of Compromise*, and *Rethinking Liberalism*, as well as co-author of *Gramsci and the Italian State*. His edited and co-edited books include *Victorian Liberalism: Nineteenth Century Political Thought and Practice*, *Constitutionalism, Democracy and Sovereignty: American and European Perspectives*, *Constitutionalism in Transformation: European and Theoretical Perspectives*, *Citizenship and Governance in the EU*, and *The Cambridge History of Twentieth Century Political Thought*. He is co-editor of *Critical Review of Social and Political Philosophy*.

Jane Bennett is Professor of Political Science at Johns Hopkins University. She is the author of *The Enchantment of Modern Life: Attachments, Crossings, and Ethics*

(Princeton University Press, 2001), *Thoreau's Nature* (Rowman and Littlefield, 1994), and *Unthinking Faith and Enlightenment* (New York University Press, 1986). Her current project explores the role of 'matter' or materiality in the political philosophies of Theodor Adorno, Gilles Deleuze, and Bruno Latour.

James Bohman is Danforth Professor of Philosophy at Saint Louis University. He is author of *Public Deliberation: Pluralism, Complexity and Democracy* (MIT, 1996) and *New Philosophy of Social Science: Problems of Indeterminacy* (MIT, 1991). He has also recently edited books on *Deliberative Democracy* (with William Rehg) and *Perpetual Peace: Essays on Kant's Cosmopolitan Ideal* (with Matthias Lutz-Bachmann), both with MIT Press. He is currently writing a book on cosmopolitan democracy. His other interests include philosophy of social science, critical social theory and pragmatism.

Michaelle Browers is Assistant Professor of Political Science at Wake Forest University. She has studied and conducted research in Morocco, Syria, Jordan, Egypt, Lebanon, and the Occupied Territories. She has most recently co-edited a book with Charles Kurzman, entitled *An Islamic Reformation?* (Rowman and Littlefield, 2004), and completed a monograph entitled *Democracy and Civil Society in Arab Political Thought: Transcultural Possibilities.*

Chris Brown is Professor of International Relations at the London School of Economics and the author of *International Relations Theory: New Normative Approaches* (Harvester Wheatsheaf/Columbia, 1992), *Understanding International Relations* (Macmillan, 1997; 2nd edn Palgrave, 2001), and *Sovereignty, Rights and Justice* (Polity, 2002), and editor of *Political Restructuring in Europe: Ethical Perspectives* (Routledge, 1994) and (with Terry Nardin and N. J. Rengger) *International Relations in Political Thought: Texts from the Greeks to the First World War* (Cambridge, 2002).

Richard Dagger is Professor of Political Science and Philosophy at Arizona State University, where he also directs the Philosophy, Politics, and Law Program for the Barrett Honors College. His publications include *Civic Virtues: Rights, Citizenship, and Republican Liberalism* (Oxford University Press, 1997) and, with Terence Ball, *Political Ideologies and the Democratic Ideal* (Longman, 5th edn 2004). His articles on rights, republicanism, political obligation, punishment, and other topics in political and legal philosophy have appeared in the *American Political Science Review*, *Ethics*, the *American Journal of Political Science*, the *Review of Politics*, *Political Studies*, *Criminal Justice Ethics*, *Law and Philosophy*, and other scholarly journals and books.

Fred D'Agostino was educated at Amherst College, Princeton University, and the London School of Economics and has taught at the Australian National University and the University of New England, where he was Head of the School of Social Science. He presently directs the Contemporary Studies program at the University of Queensland. He is author of the books *Chomsky's System of Ideas*, *Free Public Reason*, and *Incommensurability and Commensuration: The Common Denominator*. He is now working on a collectivist epistemology drawing on ideas of Hayek, Foucault, Kuhn, and Bakhtin.

Andrew Dobson is Professor of Politics at the Open University. He is an environmental political theorist, and his publications include *Green Political Thought* (third edition, Routledge, 2000), *Justice and the Environment* (OUP, 1998), and the edited collection *Fairness and Futurity* (OUP, 1999). His most recent book is *Citizenship and the Environment* (OUP, 2003).

John S. Dryzek is Professor and Head of the Social and Political Theory Program, Research School of Social Sciences, Australian National University. His recent books include *Deliberative Democracy and Beyond: Liberals, Critics, Contestations* (Oxford, 2000), *Post-Communist Democratization: Political Discourses across Thirteen Countries* (co-authored, Cambridge, 2002), and *Green States and Social Movements: Environmentalism in the United States, United Kingdom, Germany, and Norway* (co-authored, Oxford, 2003).

Helen Dunstan is Professor of Chinese Studies at the University of Sydney. A specialist on the history of politics and political economy in eighteenth-century China, she is the author of *Conflicting Counsels to Confuse the Age: A Documentary Study of Political Economy in Qing China, 1644–1840* (Michigan, 1996) and *State or Merchant? Political Economy and Political Process in 1740s China* (Cambridge, MA, forthcoming). She is a member of the Australian Labor Party.

H. Donald Forbes is Professor of Political Science at the University of Toronto. His works include *Ethnic Conflict: Commerce, Culture, and the Contact Hypothesis* (Yale, 1997) and *Nationalism, Ethnocentrism, and Personality: Social Science and Critical Theory* (Chicago, 1985). He is the editor of *Canadian Political Thought* (Oxford, 1987). He is currently writing books about multiculturalism in Canada and researching the political thought of George Grant.

Michael Freeden is Professor of Politics at the University of Oxford and Professorial Fellow at Mansfield College, Oxford. Among his books are *The New Liberalism: An Ideology of Social Reform* (Clarendon Press, 1978), *Liberalism Divided: A Study in British Political Thought 1914–1939* (Clarendon Press, 1986), *Reappraising J. A. Hobson* (ed.) (Unwin Hyman, 1990), *Rights* (Open University Press, 1991), *Ideologies and Political Theory: A Conceptual Approach* (Clarendon Press, 1996), *Reassessing Political Ideologies: The Durability of Dissent* (ed.) (Routledge, 2001), and *A Very Short Introduction to Ideology* (Oxford University Press, 2003). His books have been translated into Italian, Japanese and Romanian. He is the founder editor of the *Journal of Political Ideologies*, and the director of the Centre for Political Ideologies at the University of Oxford.

Moira Gatens is Professor of Philosophy at the University of Sydney. She is author of *Feminism and Philosophy: Perspectives on Equality and Difference*, *Imaginary Bodies: Power, Ethics and Corporeality*, and (with G. Lloyd) *Collective Imaginings: Spinoza, Past and Present*. She is editor of *Feminist Ethics* and co-editor of *Gender and Institutions* and *Oxford Companion to Australian Feminism*. She is presently working on women's rights.

Gerald F. Gaus is Professor of Philosophy, and on the faculty of the Murphy Institute, at Tulane University. Among his books are *Value and Justification* (1990), *Justificatory Liberalism* (1996), *Social Philosophy* (1999), *Political Concepts and Political Theories* (2000), and *Contemporary Theories of Liberalism: Public Reason as a Post-Enlightenment Project* (2003). With Stanley Benn he edited *Public and Private in Social Life* (1983), and with F. B. D'Agostino edited *Public Reason* (1998). He was formerly an editor of the *Australasian Journal of Philosophy*, and is a founding editor of *Politics, Philosophy and Economics*. He is currently working on a book on principled reasoning in morals and politics.

Susan James is Professor of Philosophy at Birkbeck College, London. Her publications include *The Content of Social Explanation* (Cambridge, 1984), *Beyond Equality and Difference* (edited with Gisela Bock, Routledge, 1992), *Passion and Action: The Emotions in Early Modern Philosophy* (Oxford, 1997, 1999), *Visible Women: Essays on Feminist Legal Theory and Political Philosophy* (edited with Stephanie Palmer, Hart, 2002), *The Political Writings of Margaret Cavendish* (edited with an introduction and notes, Cambridge, 2003). She is currently writing a book about the political philosophy of Spinoza, and one on a more wide-ranging project about the emotions in political philosophy.

Jeremy Jennings is Professor of Political Theory in the Department of Political Science and International Studies at the University of Birmingham. He is the author of *Georges Sorel: the Character and Development of His Thought* (Macmillan, 1985) and *Syndicalism in France: A Study of Ideas* (Macmillan, 1990). He has edited and translated *Intellectuals in Twentieth-Century France* (Macmillan, 1993) and *Georges Sorel's Reflections on Violence*, with introduction, for the Cambridge Texts in the History of Political Thought (Cambridge, 1999, 2002). He is the editor (with Tony Kemp-Welch) of *Intellectuals in Politics: From the Dreyfus Affair to Salman Rushdie* (Routledge, 1997), and (with Simon Glendinning et al.) of *The Edinburgh Encyclopedia of Continental Philosophy* (Edinburgh, 1999) and of a four-volume collection on *Socialism* (Routledge, 2003). He has been an assistant editor of *The British Journal of Politics and International Relations* and is a founding editor of the *European Journal of Political Theory*.

John Kekes is Research Professor at the State University of New York at Albany. His most recent books are *Against Liberalism* (Cornell, 1997), *A Case for Conservatism* (Cornell, 1998), *Pluralism in Philosophy: Changing the Subject* (Cornell, 2000), and *The Art of Life* (Cornell, 2002).

David Keyt is Professor of Philosophy at the University of Washington in Seattle. He is the author of *Aristotle Politics Books V and VI* (Clarendon Press, 1999) and co-editor with Fred D. Miller, Jr of *A Companion to Aristotle's Politics* (Blackwell, 1991).

John Kilcullen is a graduate in Philosophy of the University of Toronto and of the Australian National University. He taught politics at Macquarie University for many years and is now retired. He has written on utilitarianism, on religious toleration, on the political philosophy and ethics of Antoine Arnauld and Pierre Bayle, and on the political thought of William of Ockham. He is one of a team preparing a critical edition and translation of Ockham's main political work, the *Dialogus*.

Chandran Kukathas is Maxwell Professor of Political Science at the University of Utah. He is the author of *Hayek and Modern Liberalism* (Oxford, 1989), *Rawls: A Theory of Justice and Its Critics* (with Philip Pettit, Polity, 1990), *The Liberal Archipelago: A Theory of Diversity and Freedom* (Oxford, 2003) and various books and papers on Australian politics, liberal political theory, and multiculturalism. He is a founder and co-editor of the *Journal of Political Philosophy*.

Julian Lamont is Lecturer in the Philosophy Department at the University of Queensland. His research interests include moral and political philosophy, applied ethics, economics and philosophy, political economy, business and professional ethics, and bioethics. He is the Vice-President of the International Economics and Philosophy Society. He is completing a book entitled *Income Justice* and has had articles published in *Philosophical Quarterly*, *Journal of Political Philosophy*, *Public Affairs Quarterly*, *Social Theory and Practice*, *Australasian Journal of Philosophy*, and *Journal of Applied Philosophy*. He is an associate editor of *Politics, Philosophy and Economics*.

Peter Lassman is Senior Lecturer in Political Theory in the Department of Political Science and International Studies at the University of Birmingham. His current research interests include moral pluralism and political theory, modern German political thought from Kant to Habermas (and beyond), Max Weber, John Rawls and political liberalism, and Hannah Arendt, Leo Strauss, Carl Schmitt and the Weimar intellectuals. He is the editor of *Weber: Political Writings* (1994), *Max Weber's 'Science as a Vocation'* (with Irving Velody and Herminio Martins, 1989), and *Politics and Social Theory* (1989). He is a founding editor of the *European Journal of Political Theory*.

Percy B. Lehning is Professor of Political Philosophy, Erasmus University Rotterdam. Presently his concern is to employ the techniques of contemporary analytic political theory to discuss questions of political principle raised by the process of European political integration. Some of his recent publications are *Citizenship, Social Justice and the New Europe* (edited with Albert Weale, Routledge, 1997), *Theories of Secession* (edited, Routledge, 1998), 'Towards multicultural civil society: the role of social capital and democratic citizenship' in *Government and Opposition* (1998), 'The coherence of Rawls's plea for democratic equality' in the *Critical Review of International Social and Political Philosophy* (1998), 'Rawls in the Netherlands' in the *European Journal of Political Theory* (2002), and 'European citizenship: towards a European identity' in *Law and Philosophy* (2001).

Andrew Levine is Professor of Philosophy at the University of Wisconsin–Madison. His recent publications include *A Future for Marxism?* (Pluto), *Engaging Political Philosophy: Hobbes to Rawls* (Blackwell), and *Rethinking Liberal Equality: From a 'Utopian' Point of View* (Cornell).

Eric Mack is Professor of Philosophy at Tulane University where he is also on the Faculty of the Murphy Institute. He is the author of numerous articles in scholarly journals and anthologies on topics within ethics, political philosophy, and the philosophy of law.

Fred D. Miller, Jr is Professor of Philosophy and Executive Director of the Social Philosophy and Policy Center at Bowling Green State University. He was President of the Society for Ancient Greek Philosophy from 1998 to 2002. He is the author of *Nature, Justice, and Rights in Aristotle's Politics* (Oxford, 1995), co-editor with David Keyt of *A Companion to Aristotle's Politics* (Blackwell, 1991), editor of *A History of the Philosophy of Law from the Ancient Greeks to the Scholastics*, volume 6 of *A Treatise of Legal Philosophy and General Jurisprudence* (Kluwer, forthcoming), and associate editor of the journal *Social Philosophy and Policy*.

J. Donald Moon is Professor of Government at Wesleyan University. He is the editor of *Responsibility, Rights, and Welfare: The Theory of the Welfare State* (1988) and the author of *Constructing Community: Moral Pluralism and Tragic Conflicts* (1995, 2001), and with Stephen K. White edited *What is Political Theory?* (2004). He is consulting editor for *Political Theory*.

Christopher W. Morris is Professor of Philosophy, University of Maryland, College Park. He is the author of *An Essay on the Modern State* (Cambridge, 1998), 'The very idea of popular sovereignty: we "the people" reconsidered' in *Social Philosophy and Policy* (2000), and the editor of *The Social Contract Theories: Critical Essays on Hobbes, Locke, and Rousseau* (Rowman and Littlefield, 1999).

Véronique Mottier is Swiss National Science Foundation Research Professor at the Institut d'Études Politiques et Internationales at the University of Lausanne, Switzerland and Fellow of Jesus College, Cambridge. She is co-convenor of the Standing Group on Political Theory of the European Consortium for Political Research, and Associate Editor of *Feminist Theory* and *Nouvelles Questions Féministes*. She has co-edited *Politics of Sexuality: Identity, Gender, Citizenship* (Routledge, 1998) and *Genre et politique: débats et perspectives* (Gallimard, 2000). Her main research and teaching interests are the politics of gender and sexuality, eugenics, and discourse theory.

Thomas L. Pangle holds a University Professorship in the Department of Political Science at the University of Toronto, and is a Fellow of the Royal Society of Canada. Educated at Cornell University and the University of Chicago, he has won Guggenheim, Killam–Canada Council, Carl Friedrich von Siemens, and four National Endowment for the Humanities fellowships. He has been awarded The Benton Bowl, Yale University (for contribution to education in politics) and the Robert Foster Cherry Great Teacher of the World Prize, Baylor University. He is the author of *Montesquieu's Philosophy of Liberalism* (Chicago, 1973), *The Spirit of Modern Republicanism: The Moral Vision of the American Founders and the Philosophy of Locke* (Chicago, 1988), *The Ennobling of Democracy: The Challenge of the Postmodern Age* (Johns Hopkins, 1992), *The Learning* *of Liberty: The Educational Ideas of the American Founders*, co-authored with wife Lorraine (University Press of Kansas, 1993), *Justice among Nations: On the Moral Basis of Power and Peace*, co-authored with Peter J. Ahrensdorf (University Press of Kansas, 1999), and *Political Philosophy and the God of Abraham* (Johns Hopkins, 2003).

Raymond Plant is a Labour member of the House of Lords in the British Parliament and Professor in the Law School, King's College, University of London, where he focuses on legal and political philosophy. Among his books are *Community and Ideology: An Essay in Applied Social Philosophy* (1974), *Hegel: An Introduction* (1984), *Philosophy, Politics and Citizenship: The Life and Thought of the British Idealists* (with Andrew Vincent, 1985), *Conservative Capitalism in Britain and the United States: A Critical Appraisal* (with Kenneth Hoover, 1989), *Modern Political Thought* (1991), *Hegel* (Great Philosophers Series, 1999), and *Politics, Theology and History* (2001). He has given the Stanton Lectures at Cambridge University; the Sarum Lectures at Oxford University; the Fergusson Lectures and the Scott Holland Lectures at Manchester University and the Agnes Cummings Lectures at University College Dublin. He is currently working on a book with the title *The Neo Liberal State and the Rule of Law*.

Martyn P. Thompson is Associate Professor and Director of Graduate Studies in the Department of Political Science at Tulane University. His degrees include a PhD from the London School of Economics and Political Science, and a DrPhilHabil from the University of Tuebingen. He is author, editor, or co-editor of nine books, including *Ideas of Contract in English Political Thought in the Age of John Locke*, and over 50 articles in journals such as *Political Studies*, *Political Theory*, *American Historical Review*, *Politisches Denken*, *Journal of the History of Ideas*, *Il Pensiero Politico*, *History and Theory*, and *Historical Journal*. He is the translator or co-translator from German into English of over 100 essays, articles and academic reviews. Since 1990 he has been the editor of *Politisches Denken Jahrbuch*.

Jeremy Waldron is the Maurice and Hilda Friedman Professor of Law at Columbia Law School, in the City of New York, and Director of Columbia University's Center for Law and Philosophy. A native of New Zealand, he has taught previously at Otago, Oxford, Edinburgh, Berkeley, and Princeton. He writes in the area of overlap between jurisprudence, political theory, and moral and political philosophy, and he is the author of several books, including *God, Locke, and Equality* (Cambridge, 2002), *Law and Disagreement* (Oxford, 1999), *The Dignity of Legislation* (Cambridge, 1999), and *Liberal Rights* (Cambridge, 1993). He is presently working on a project entitled 'Cosmopolitan Right'. Professor Waldron is a frequent lecturer, having delivered the second series of Seeley Lectures at Cambridge University in 1996, the Carlyle Lectures at the University of Oxford in 1999, the Spring 2000 University Lecture at Columbia, and – in the last few years – public lectures at Harvard, Princeton, Toronto, St Andrews, Auckland, Canberra, and Buenos Aires. He was elected to the American Academy of Arts and Sciences in 1998.

David Weinstein is Associate Professor of Political Science at Wake Forest University and in 2002–3 was Visiting Fellow at Mansfield College, Oxford. His books include

Equal Freedom and Utility (Cambridge, 1998) and *The New Liberalism: Reconciling Liberty and Community*, edited with Avital Simhony (Cambridge, 2001). He is currently writing two books: *The Idolatry of Dichotomies: Utilitarianism and the New Liberalism* and *Exile and Interpretation: Constructing Modern European Intellectual History*, the latter with Avihu Zakai.

David West is Senior Lecturer in Social and Political Theory in the School of Social Sciences at the Australian National University, having previously taught at the Universities of Bradford and Liverpool. After completing a doctorate on critical theories of human interests, his first book, *Authenticity and Empowerment: A Theory of Liberation*, was published by Harvester Wheatsheaf in 1990. *An Introduction to Continental Philosophy* (Polity, Cambridge and Blackwell, US) was published in 1996. His forthcoming book *Reason, Self and Sexuality* is to be published by Polity Press in 2004.

Frederick G. Whelan is Professor of Political Science at the University of Pittsburgh, where he teaches political theory. He has published *Order and Artifice in Hume's Political Philosophy* (Princeton, 1985), *Edmund Burke and India* (Pittsburgh, 1996), and *Hume and Machiavelli: Political Realism and Liberal Thought* (Lexington Books, forthcomlng).

Part I

APPROACHES TO THE STUDY OF POLITICAL THEORY

1

Ideology, Political Theory and Political Philosophy

MICHAEL FREEDEN

It has been common practice in current professional and academic circles to assign the terms 'political thought' or 'political theory' to a subdiscipline of political science in which texts, arguments and discourses obtain an existence of their own and are studied for the values and visions they contain [see further Chapter 2]. But in the broadest sense political thought refers to thinking about politics at any level of conceptualization and articulation. Far from being an arcane, esoteric or cocooned practice, it is the preliminary to, accompaniment of, and consequence of all political activity and processes. We should certainly not regard political thought as a separate area of political study, or as a rarefied, even luxurious, form of political self-indulgence – as some hard-nosed and pragmatic detractors would have it – but should recognize it as a normal and necessary aspect of the political that requires careful analysis both for what it is and for what it does.

Political thought in the broadest sense currently exhibits six strands: (1) the meticulous construction of argument; (2) the normative prescription of standards of public conduct; (3) the imaginative production of insight; (4) the genealogical exploration of provenance and change; (5) the deconstructive unpacking of paradigms; and (6) the morphological analysis of concepts and conceptual clusters. This chapter will focus mainly on the first and the last strands, but will bring the others into its orbit. Political theorists can engage in more than one of the above, though they are unlikely to engage in all. The emphasis on one or another of the strands centrally impacts on the questions: how do we identify what political thought is; and what work do we want that identification to do for us?

For most of its existence the study of political thought was constructed and packaged as a historical narrative, a sequenced story that examined the ways in which a number of outstanding individuals such as Aristotle, Hobbes or Rousseau applied their wisdom to questions of state and of human nature. In the course of that process they provided an overlapping – if not common – field of ideas, theorems and positions from which generation after generation was supposed to draw. Those individuals, with very few exceptions – Machiavelli may have been one – were philosophers who offered conceptions of the good life combined with intricate arguments and reasons for adopting rational and moral prescriptions and proposals for implementing them, some practical, some less so. Only from the late nineteenth century onwards was the production of systematic, overarching hypotheses about the structure and functions of political institutions, processes and conduct graced with an identity of its own – through pioneers such as Max Weber, Gaetano Mosca and Roberto Michels – though it was soon to be siphoned off as political sociology. As for the more mundane thinking which inevitably accompanies any conscious account, explanation or justification of a political act, that was not acknowledged as a distinct category of political thought until the behaviourism of the mid twentieth century with its studies of attitudes and beliefs. To add to these, the specific political thinking emerging from groups or masses was identified, but as a rule pejoratively dismissed through strongly individualistic, or strongly elitist, perspectives. The interest scholars evinced in it was prompted by the aggregative opinion studies of American social science on the one hand, and – on the other hand – by the focus on popular thinking that a Marxism true to its principles should have developed far earlier, but had to await the insights of Antonio Gramsci. It was Gramsci (1971) who recognized the role of the masses as well as intellectuals in shaping political ideas at all levels of social and cultural life.

All the above varieties are, however, central aspects of thinking about politics and about the state. Their detachment from each other is significant in distinguishing among a rich panoply of political ideas, their roles and shapes, but it has frequently done harm as well as good, and exaggerated the commonalties that political thinking possesses. In particular, political thought is not just straightforwardly equivalent to what people say (and write) that they think about political issues, or even what we hear (and read) them saying. It is highly sensitive to the diverse methods it employs to determine which kinds of thinking are political, and which issues are within the remit of the scholars who study political thinking. Differences in political thought have become increasingly reflective of splits and specializations among its students, and the divergence between some philosophers and some students of ideology is the most significant, and the least understood, among these.

POLITICAL PHILOSOPHY: THE GOOD, THE RIGHT AND THE VALID

Political philosophy is situated in a highly intriguing relationship to politics. On the one hand, its focus on the normative, on forms of the good life, on what is morally proper, and on the right kind of decisions, has placed it at the centre of what most contemporary academics regard as political theory: a guide, a corrective, and a justification for enlightened and civilized forms of organized social life and political institutions. On the other hand, the disciplinary constraints that apply to producing good philosophy have all too often distanced its practitioners from the actual stuff of politics and have contributed to a general sense of the estrangement of philosophy from political life. There is unsurprisingly no complete agreement on what political philosophers do, and there are great divides between, say, Anglo-American analytical philosophers and varieties of continental philosophy, a distinction that is more substantive than geographical. Analytical philosophers are not necessarily specific students of *politics*; they may often be seen as applying their general insights to the realm of politics. That is to say, political philosophers are frequently philosophers prior to their examination of the political, and they apply techniques and methods typical of philosophers rather than other students of politics.

For instance, one of their central concerns relates to what constitutes a good argument. Which of the following, for instance, would justify civil disobedience: the disregard of past promises, the lack of crucial social or material benefits, or the breaching of a categorical moral principle? A good argument in the view of analytical philosophers is one that is rational, that identifies conceptual distinctions and logical paths of reasoning, whether deductive or inductive, and that constructs coherent compatibilities among conceptual units. The producers of a good argument are concurrently expected to undertake particular thought processes that are reflexive and self-critical. Sometimes this approach also involves an appeal to intuitions (linked also to a philosophical interest in common sense arguments), the detection of which should serve as a guide to practices, although such intuitions – it is often counter-claimed – may themselves be culture-bound.

In addition, a good political argument may have an ethical, as well as an analytical, dimension; indeed for some scholars political philosophy 'is a very specific subset of moral philosophy' (Swift, 2001: 6). On this account, a worthy political argument is presented as one that enhances and promotes values that are desirable for individuals in their capacity as members of political communities. Those values delineate what is good or bad, right or wrong, for all human beings, irrespective of their distance in time (considering future or past generations) or space; the moral rights, duties and obligations (systematized as deontology) that derive from those understandings; and their political expressions. Their realization is predicated on the attainment of the reflective equilibrium proposed by John Rawls, or the free and rational communication advocated by Jürgen Habermas (1981). While in the past, issues of political obligation and authority were predominant among political philosophers, because the state was still perceived as a supreme political institution primarily providing security and stability, in recent literature political value has typically been ascribed to distributive justice [Chapter 17], to the safeguarding of individual autonomy, to fostering a sense of community [Chapter 13], to forms of deliberative democracy [Chapter 11], to beneficial kinds of pluralism [Chapter 18], and to preserving a sustainable environment [Chapter 14]. All these reflect a view of the state as enabler of human and social flourishing, though they also allow the state to be circumvented through a grand range of attempts to reaffirm the rational, contemplative individual as the source of political nous and, not infrequently, the cultural community as the locus of individual identity-cum-autonomy.

Philosophical ends are frequently characterized by the search for certainty and truth, not merely by the pursuit of methodological purity or self-critical understanding. Certainty refers to the flight from contingency and the aspiration to unshakeable knowledge (Barber, 1988: 6). That aspiration employs, sometimes unintentionally, traditional but erroneous models from the natural sciences. Here, possibly, an infelicitous coalition between philosophers and power wielders emerges, both intent upon closing debate. Indeed, it was one of the earliest and greatest of political philosophers, Plato, who prescribed the need for convergence between power and knowledge in the figure of the philosopher-king. Truth is a far more difficult issue. As Hannah Arendt pointed out, governments and politics are based on opinion, not factual truth. For her, factual truth was an essential component of the freedom of thought that political thinking required. But the truth of the philosophers was rational truth, involving axioms and theories. That truth was singular and hence apolitical (Arendt, 1968: 231, 238, 242, 246). In approaches such as these, the non-political status of truth rests on the assumption that it is knowable, and often on ostensibly unassailable foundationalist assumptions regarding human nature, whereas politics is assumed to involve fundamental contests over both the good and the right. However, for politics the rhetoric of certainty or near-certainty – as a feature of conviction rather than of knowledge – may be necessary as a preliminary to decision-making, decision-making being an ineliminable core feature of politics. A political or ideological decision is an attempt at an unequivocal choice, superimposed on an indeterminate field, a field in which no single path is unchallengeable, or one in which many paths are possible. However, not all closure of debate successfully bridges the gap between certainty and truth. Certainty is often a necessary substitute for the unattainability of truth, and it is here that the role of ideologies is both indispensable and decisive in tailoring political thinking to the requirements of the political. Alternatively, Mill's political philosophy allowed for provisional – and in that sense, relative – truths. As he claimed,

> if the lists are kept open, we may hope that if there be a better truth, it will be found when the human mind is capable of receiving it; and in the meantime we may rely on having attained such approach to truth as is possible in our own day. This is the amount of certainty attainable by a fallible being. (Mill, 1910: 83)

THE SINGULAR AND THE UNIVERSAL

The singularity of political philosophy, when inspired by ethical frameworks, is one of its great strengths. After all, a central task of political philosophers as moral philosophers has been to provide yardsticks for public conduct, so essential in areas such as the distribution of scarce goods, or the wielding of power by political leaders and decision-makers. Societies rightly rely on political philosophers to point out ways of improving social institutions, for political ethics pertains to the instilling of virtuous public practices. At the same time, the increasing democratization of politics has shifted the emphasis of scholarship from 'great men and women' philosophers to the moral claims any individual and all individuals may direct at their societies and the benefits they ought to derive from social life. Just as historians now seldom tell the story of kings and queens but have developed a keen interest in popular history, so political theorists have refocused around individual self-development, participation, citizenship, and civic virtue (Young, 1996: 479, 484–5), notions close to the concerns of contemporary liberal theory, as we shall see.

One manifestation of this has been the recent fascination of philosophers with questions of justice. Although justice is a systemic property of a well-organized society, it has been reformulated, primarily by John Rawls (1971), as establishing the correct manner of attaining fairness for individuals, through devices that ensure that ordinary persons themselves decide reasonably on the rules of justice that ought to apply to them. Intriguingly, then, singularity refers both to the universality of rational philosophical truths and to the concentration on the individual as sited at the heart of political philosophy. Consequently, the deontology of rights and duties has been predominantly assigned to individuals, and Anglo-American political philosophy has been resistant to the impingement of groups and communities on its fundamental epistemology – an inclination towards atomism that is itself ideological as well as methodological. Moreover, that approach is predicated on the assumption that the rationally exercised faculties of individuals will in crucial instances converge on common ground rather than diverge in a range of acceptable, rational and good solutions radiating out from a common core, as John Stuart Mill had indicated. The unintended elision between the plural and the singular is evident in Rawls's ambivalent observation that political philosophy cannot coerce our considered convictions, with the immediate addition: 'If we feel coerced, it may be because, when we reflect on the matter at hand, values, principles, and standards are so formulated and arranged that they are freely recognized as ones we do, or should, accept' (1993: 45). So while many contemporary political philosophers emphasize measured individual judgement rather than blanket subscription to philosophical systems such as idealism or utilitarianism, they leave open the possibility of the convergence of individual judgements in a reasonable reflective equilibrium, as well as the question of the objectivity or subjectivity of values.

Another feature of political philosophy is evident in the abstractness of its generality. Rawls has contended that abstraction is a way of continuing public discussion when shared understandings of lesser generalities have broken down. The deeper the conflict, he has argued, the higher the level of abstraction necessary to get an uncluttered view of the roots of the conflict (Rawls, 1993: 46). Abstraction may be conceptually more difficult to comprehend, but it is also a useful modelling device that proffers simplification, sets out issues in stark and concise form and is amenable to the universalization to which so many philosophers aspire. Such constructivist approaches resonate with political theories – especially social contract theory – in which the state is an artificial edifice, and morality, legitimacy or authority can therefore be subjected to thought experiments. Conversely, social philosophers such as Marx and Engels have criticized abstract philosophy. Contrasting their approach with that of German philosophy, they wrote:

> we do not set out from what men say, imagine, conceive, nor from men as narrated, thought of, imagined, conceived … We set out from real, active men, and on the basis of their real life-processes we demonstrate the development of the ideological reflexes and echoes of this life-process. (Marx and Engels, 1974: 47)

But their repudiation of the methods of philosophy converged on their particular understanding of ideology. For them, abstract philosophy was nothing more than ideology, because both were the inverted mental reflection of a distorted and alienated reality.

A MODEL OF MODERN IDEOLOGY: PATTERNED DIVERGENCES

Non-Marxist students of ideology understand their subject-matter differently. Ideologies are usefully comprehended not as defective philosophies, but rather as ubiquitous and patterned forms of thinking about politics. They are clusters of ideas, beliefs, opinions, values, and attitudes usually held by identifiable groups, that provide directives, even plans, of action for public policy-making in an endeavour to uphold, justify, change or criticize the social and political arrangements of a state or other political community. This tells us something about their functions and about the necessary services they perform for such a community. To begin with, it is unimaginable to conceive of a society that does not engage in such patterned thought, that does not have

distinguishable and recurrent ways of thinking, say, about who should be rewarded in that society and for what, about the limits to the exercise of political power, about the value of national symbols, or about its expectations of government. However, that thinking may range from the articulate and sophisticated to the clumsy and banal; it may range from the conscious and specific to the unconscious and fuzzy; and it may range from the local through the national to the international, but always as the product of groups. Ideologies, let it be emphasized, are evident in the entire field of thinking about political ends and principles, and virtually all members of a society have political views and values they promote and defend. By contrast, analytical political philosophy sites itself at a particular end of each of these spectrums. The articulateness and sophistication of philosophical arguments are non-negotiable, their intentionality and deliberation are a *sine qua non* of recognizing them as a subject-matter for investigation and respect, and their attribution to individual inspiration is a mark and condition of their standing in the profession.

On another and parallel dimension, ideologies – in discharging the above functions – compete deliberately or unintentionally over the control of political language, by means of which they attempt to wield the political power necessary to realizing their functions. Ultimately, they aim to give precise definition to the essentially contested meanings of the major political concepts. In other words, they aim to decontest those concepts and endorse one of the multiple conceptions those concepts invariably accrue but which, importantly, the concepts cannot contain simultaneously: is equality to be understood as equality of opportunity, of need, of respect, or of outcome? What relative weight do we assign, within the notion of democracy, to self-government, political equality, an idea of community, or active participation in the public domain? When confronted with a number of those decontested concepts, arranged in a particular configuration, we perceive an ideology's typical structure. Ideologies differ from one another in the particular meaning they allocate to every one of the main political concepts, in the priority they accord each concept, and in the particular position and interrelationship between each concept and the other political concepts contained within the given ideological field (Freeden, 1996: 47–95). The production of a high degree of certainty in these defining and ordering activities ensures that ideologies are integrally intertwined with politics; ideologies too are crucially locked into the process of choosing among alternative paths of action and of subsequent decision-making. So whereas a political philosopher such as Rawls contends that many hard decisions may seem to have no clear answer (1993: 57), the morphology of concepts suggests that, to the contrary, they may have many clear answers. Doubt is not one of the most obvious features of ideological discourse. In the eagerness of ideologists to establish an uncontestable framework for political decision-making, assertion will frequently replace demonstration and proof – those prerequisites of good philosophical analysis.

Ideologies may be seen as pooled resources from which a society draws, a bank of ideas that has accrued over time and that may be cashed in almost any permutation, subject only to constraints of logic (the universal) and of the culturally permissible (the local, even when it appears in a universalist guise). To be sure, new assets may be added and constructed, and some of the older bills and coins may be removed from circulation. Continuity is not unbroken, and entirely different sets of ideas may be extracted from the same pool and confront each other with immense hostility. But all this is the very fabric of politics, just as political philosophy contributes to supplying the very fabric of qualitative values and justifications that a society may require for its moral health. We usually come across ideologies in a more or less distinct and pre-structured form, such as liberalism, conservatism, socialism, feminism or fascism. That is because certain political movements or belief systems have generated enormous support from significant social groups who have subscribed to one of the overarching and dominant 'grand' ideological families. They provide their followers with a social and political identity and operate as one of the major factors in the realization of political goals. But a few notes of caution need to be sounded.

First, there is no necessary configuration of ideologies in these forms; they may well be the product of contingent historical forces that appear and vanish over time. On the other hand, some of the ideological families may reflect fundamental human understandings of the social order and its relation to human drives and hopes. Thus, traditionalism and conservatism are rooted in deep psychological motivations; whereas the desire for emancipation from the control of others has – in one of liberalism's many manifestations – always served as an impetus for the redistribution of political power. Second, any one of these ideologies is host to loose and fluid positions. There is no obvious thing called socialism, but there certainly are socialisms: Marxist, evolutionary, or guild socialisms are examples. General morphological patterns sharing core ideas and distinct ideational paths connecting the key political concepts are evident – this is after all how we access all political thinking – but ideological micro-analysis uncovers fundamental internal differences that must be acknowledged in serious scholarly investigation.

Thus socialists extol the importance of group solidarity and of interpersonal equality, but within the family of socialisms there are considerable differences over whether solidarity expresses total human interdependence, or merely empathy and altruism; and over whether equality entails differential distribution on the basis of individual needs alone or also on the basis of contribution to the public good. Third, ideologies are not mutually exclusive. They intersect and overlap with each other, creating hybrids such as libertarianism – a cross between liberalism and conservatism. Finally, a fragmentation of ideologies has accompanied the great families and has become more marked in recent decades. Alongside the full ideologies, with their total if not totalitarian solutions to social issues, there exist thin ideologies that address areas of ideological contestation, but otherwise rely on other ideologies to fill the gaps with which they do not primarily concern themselves. Nationalism is one such instance, containing no substantive theory of distributive justice [see Chapters 17, 19].

IDEOLOGICAL ANALYSIS: WHAT DOES IT EXPLORE?

If the development of qualitative normative thinking is one of the rationales of political philosophy, it is not difficult to understand why the study of ideology receives short shrift from many philosophers, and is ignored by others (witness the absence of an American Political Science Association subject section on political ideology). For it would appear that many ideologies are incapable of producing normative profundities, particularly when we follow the tendency of some scholars to identify ideologies only with the politically extreme representatives of the genre. Nonetheless, the study of ideologies is laden with sensitivity to moral standards and political values. To begin with, it explores the choices any given combination of norms and political concepts opens up or closes, which can then be appraised against whatever political arrangements are deemed desirable by the analyst. Utilitarian or deontological evaluations of political ideas benefit greatly by testing them not only against abstract logical permutations but against the concrete manifestations these ideas have already received in the world. Second, as will be argued below, the product of Anglo-American political philosophy is itself, from the perspective of ideological analysis, a specific ideological manifestation, and its normative solutions require decoding in terms of their preferences and understandings of the social world as does any ideology. Hence the role of the student of ideologies is to unpack such beliefs, account for them, and map their complexity. That analysis may well be a necessary preliminary to the endorsement by political philosophers of particular ideational permutations. Third, the study of ideology offers a different *kind* of assessment, one that examines the logical and cultural constraints that make a particular set of political concepts intelligible, attractive, or legitimate (and vice versa); and one that weighs up the implicit as well as explicit assumptions that render an ideology plausible for its consumers. This form of evaluation appears not as a normative pronouncement but as an interpretation that seeks to be intellectually appealing instead of absolutely valid or morally prescriptive.

Consequently, a much broader range of subject-matter is prone to ideological analysis and a gulf begins to open up between it and philosophical argument. No student of 'empirical' politics would wish to disregard 'imperfect' political institutions – would want, for example, to exclude the election of the American Presidency in 2000 from study and comment. Equally, no student of ideologies would wish to exclude 'imperfect', half-baked, even inconsistent or wrong political arguments and ideas from their compass, precisely because such phenomena are both typical of political thought-practices and offer insight into how societies actually work and make decisions. Nazism has little allure for philosophers, because it fails to pass muster on moral and analytical grounds. But its nature, if not its messages, attracts the curiosity of students of ideology wishing to understand the nature of dogmatism, myth-making, extremism and terror, and wanting to account for the ideational forces that propelled political action into those directions rather than others, and that might do so again. So while the disciplinary roots of political philosophy have become increasingly remote from the concerns of the social sciences, the painstaking and critical investigation of ideologies is the only area of analysis in which political ideas can receive appropriate consideration as a *direct* branch of the study of politics, rather than of philosophy or history. Only then can questions such as the following be addressed: what are the social and political functions of political ideas; how are meaningful clusters of political argument formed and made accessible; what assumptions have to hold in order for the producer of an argument to believe that his/her argument is a true, good, or valid one (rather than whether the argument *is* true, good, or valid); how does the field of political practice constrain and mould the political ideas available to a society; how does ideological change come about; how do ideologies compete over, and shape, understandings of what is and what can be in politics? All these can only be undertaken if we also consider immorality, inconsistency and bad arguments as suitable subject-matter for analysis

within the sphere of political practice. Because they exist, and arguably always will, they have a substantial bearing on human understanding, conduct and institutional processes, without which our comprehension of the political will be profoundly impoverished.

It has often been argued, following Marx, that ideologies are a sinister and exploitative form of exercising power over individuals and groups through providing them with a false view of social reality, in which they are made to adopt the norms and aims of ruling social strata. On the account offered here, although power and control remain central features of ideologies, they are far less insidious. Rather, they reflect the core of the political: the necessity of ordering, deciding and regulating the combined affairs of groups of people, and through that of enabling individuals to have a say in their own fortunes. Politics is not just about physical force and the clash of economic interests, but also about the assignment of contested meaning to social phenomena. It is not just about the use of the law, of the police, or of illegitimate forms of violence, nor is it just about the maximization of economic assets through the manipulation of markets, or about the impact of personality on public life. It is also about deciding on the range of meanings attributed to concepts such as welfare (e.g. a mechanism of social parasitism or the institutional enabling of human flourishing) or freedom (e.g. the uninhibited assertion of individual powers against others or the rational expression of self-developing choices), and about selecting which of these meanings will be accorded legitimacy and supremacy in formulating public policy. Hence the control of political language, through which the understanding of such contested political concepts is mediated, is a cardinal and typical way of capturing the high ground of the social meanings and interpretations available to a given society. This is where ideologies come in, as the devices through which political language is presented and organized for the purposes of determining those dominant meanings. They offer the maps that attach, say, the qualifiers 'democratic' and 'human right' – rather than *lèse-majesté* or 'rebellion' – to 'dissent'; or that clash over allocating the term 'terrorist' to some activities rather than others. And to make matters quite clear: without dominant meanings, however temporary, no political decisions could be made and social paralysis would ensue. In that sense, it is manifestly misleading to insist on the elimination of plural meanings, and to express concern when faced with selection processes among meanings. Domination in the hard sense of a group preventing the equal access of others to social goods is undesirable and eliminable in principle, but 'domination' in the gentle sense of ensuring that a particular set of values secures practical preference is ineluctable. To that extent, the much-trumpeted neutrality of liberalism among different conceptions of the good is both chimerical and palpably undesirable in a political society where practices have to be put into effect, unless – as some political philosophers do – one believes in the possibility as well as the desirability of a fundamental social consensus on values.

TWO PROFESSIONAL DISCIPLINES AND THEIR SUBJECT-MATTER

Before we examine other central differences between political philosophy and political ideologies, one vital distinction needs to be mentioned. The producers and formulators of ideology may differ substantially from the producers and formulators of philosophy. Ideologies are rarely created by professional thinkers; indeed, they are more likely to emanate from social sectors with a greater or lesser interest in political ideals and ends, but with an amateurish control over the units – the political concepts – from which ideologies are fashioned. These sectors include categories such as political parties, journalists, civil servants, or oppressed groups. The *students* of ideology, to the contrary – like any practitioners of a discipline – are professional or expert analysts, in this case of political thinking, language, and concepts. They cannot take the utterances and texts of the ideologists they examine as role models or examples of coherent and optimal thinking about politics (though when not engaged in their professional activities they too will be ideologists). There is therefore a fundamental dissimilarity between political ideologists and the investigators of political ideology; the latter require different techniques in order to arrive at a higher level of conceptual analysis of the explanandum, not the least because they do not have to market their products as ideational solutions to pressing political issues. That distinction does not necessarily apply to political philosophy, where students of philosophy enter into *similar* discourses to those whom they study, in an apparently seamless conversation and convergence on techniques of good argumentation. The philosopher and the student of philosophy are often one and the same thing. Consequently, political philosophers are prone to mistake the 'inferior thinking' of ideologists for the analytical thinking produced in the *study* of political ideologies and to write both off as bad philosophy (Swift, 2001: 133), and the latter as bad scholarship as well.

One important consequence of this phenomenon is that many philosophers find it difficult to distance themselves from their own methodology (for example, privileging individual agency, rational discourse, logical cohesion, and justification of arguments in relation to ethical yardsticks), especially because what is required of them is to immerse themselves into that methodology as a given set of thought practices and to emulate its best practitioners. Hence this kind of philosophy is unusually lacking in self-criticism of its own assumptions. It does not tend to query the possible limitations that its techniques may impose on understanding and interpretation, though it is superb in its subtle critique of the distinctions and clarifications made *within* its paradigms of analysis. Certainly, it refrains from engaging in the meta-theory beloved by analysts of ideology who explore the features of the thought products they examine. Those analysts would, for instance, be particularly alert to the constraints and biases any methodology sets up – whether through notions such as agency, logical cohesion or universal ethics, or through other notions – and the way in which these understandings shaped views of, and preferences for, particular forms of social and ideational activity. Even in its Marxist versions, the concept of ideology was employed in an 'unmasking' role in order to penetrate through the illusions and distortions that unreconstructed political thinking was inevitably thought to conjure up. In non-Marxist understandings of ideology the critique of ideology as masking truth has been abandoned, simply because of the uncertainty, referred to above, concerning what truth would be. But the critique of ideology as holding hidden and implicit assumptions, irrespective of their truth or falsehood status, continues to occupy centre-stage.

Clearly, a central purpose of political theory is to prescribe and to offer good solutions to problems of political organization and practices. Philosophers and ideologues agree on this end. But students of ideology do not see prescription as their aim, though their findings are intended to assist philosophers and ideologists in *their* prescriptions. As social scientists, they strive to offer a persuasive account of what the world of ideologies is like and how it relates to the world of politics. One consequence is that contemporary students of ideology display an even more heightened awareness of political language as a tool, wielded deliberately or unintentionally to attain a selection of values and ends, without which the entire political process would founder. This ought to engender a methodological scepticism and relativism, from which vantage-point any conclusions about the worlds of political ideas and action are tentative and subject to continuous review and change. While liberal political philosophers instruct us to revise individual life plans but remain committed to the constant values of liberty, human rights and human progress, students of ideology demand revised assessments of the frameworks and constraints that propel groups into preferring one combination of ideas to another. However, to endeavour to account for the features, sources and outcomes of political ideologies is by no means an endorsement of all their manifestations; it does not promote a relativism in which 'anything goes'. Indeed, local forms of thinking may share some features with each other in a kind of contingent universalism that acts as a cultural constraint on what societies may legitimately do. Political idea systems are a product of interacting, even overlapping, human minds, and also exist within differentiated geographical, historical and cultural spaces. The comparative study of ideologies has to address these problems of translation, when differences are often masked by ostensible similarities of language, while similarities are disguised by disparate ways of expression.

IS PHILOSOPHY LIBERAL PHILOSOPHY, OR EVEN LIBERAL IDEOLOGY?

The parallel to philosophical misgivings about ideologies, and their study, is a continuous attempt by students of ideology to reduce Western political philosophy, especially in recent decades, to the one ideological dimension of liberalism. Analysts of ideology point out that the story of contemporary philosophy is tantamount to that of liberalism itself, and that political philosophy in the twenty-first century has become incapable of absorbing, and reacting to, a broader spectrum of extra-liberal political thinking. Moreover, political philosophy is accused of demonstrating considerable blindness to the liberal nature of its own premises – a critique also voiced by feminists – and ignorance about the liberal traditions that spawned such positions, in a battle of ideas that began in the eighteenth century and continues to this very day. One such example is the renewed interest among political philosophers in citizenship and participatory democracy [see Chapters 11, 13]. Employing models garnered from civic republican theories of public virtue, and augmenting them with conceptions of liberty anchored in communal self-government and tailored to eliminate the arbitrary domination of one group over another, these contemporary theories are nevertheless seeped in liberal values, no less than the theories from which they seek to differ and which they aspire to correct (Pettit, 1997; Skinner, 1998; Dagger, 1997).

The ends of Anglo-American political philosophy are those at the heart of the liberal tradition: the enhancing of a particular understanding of liberty as autonomy, coupled with a conviction in the possibility

and necessity of individual self-development guaranteed through fundamental human rights, and a growing emphasis on equality. This bundle has been predominantly couched in the language of moral universalism; in Brian Barry's phrase, 'there is no distinctive liberal theory of political boundaries at the level of principle' (2001: 137). These ends have not changed over time, though the preconditions for their attainment have been variously understood even with the liberal camp and promoted also by those who should go under the label of libertarians, even individualist anarchists. As a rule, though, the core of twentieth-century liberalism constituted an appeal for the release of a flow of free, vital and spontaneous activity emanating from individuals, one that would spread across the globe not through an internal rational logic but through a successful appeal to the intellects and emotions of the oppressed and underprivileged (Hobhouse, 1911; Freeden, 2001b: 21–2). That was equated with the story of the growth of civilization itself, but it was also decisively dependent on human co-operation and the mutual guarantee of standards of human welfare and well-being. This communitarian aspect of modern liberalism preceded by an entire century the lately rediscovered emphasis on the participation of communities in 'republican' public practices, an emphasis that accentuates a greater egalitarianism than previously supplied by liberalism [see Chapter 13]. However, the otherwise strong liberal origins of that argument have been obscured because recent political philosophers have erroneously modelled liberalism as highly individualistic. One consequence is the false exclusion of 'communitarians' from the plural camp of liberalisms, under the impact of a philosophical dichotomy between liberals and communitarians that is not borne out by the complexity of liberal ideology (Taylor, 1989; Simhony and Weinstein, 2001) [see also Chapter 30]. That ideology has developed strong appeals to mutual support and collective well-being at the heart of twentieth-century welfare state thinking [see Chapter 16].

The texts and authors encompassed by the study of ideology are broader than those examined by political philosophers, but they always include those latter texts. From the perspective of analysing ideologies, philosophical texts are selective decontestations of political concepts like any other. Both political philosophers and students of ideology employ political concepts as their basic units or building blocks, and their theories embody conceptual configurations. However, the standards of argument brought into play by philosophers about the content of those concepts, and the justification for preferring a certain configuration over another, may be more rigorous and considered than those employed in more popular or mundane writings and utterances. Here is the basis of another asymmetry: while philosophers cannot profitably read many ideological texts, because those texts fail the complex qualitative tests philosophers expect to encounter, students of ideology argue that philosophical texts may be subject to varied kinds of reading. Marx may have offered a weighty critique of German philosophy and substituted for it an epistemology that presented a searching array of new questions, but he was concurrently the creator of specific understandings of liberty as emancipation from alienation; of the individual as intimately linked to the notion of species being; and of power as exploitation of one class by another. This fashioned a particular ideological understanding of the political world and became known as Marxism. Rawls may have offered a theory of justice that satisfied the requirements of rational individual choice as well as promoting the interests of all, including the least advantaged, subject to a free-standing reflective consensus that can accommodate various versions of the good life, but he is concurrently the articulator of a specific version of American liberalism that regards individuals as rational, moral, purposive and autonomous agents (which contextualist and communitarian theories wish at the very least to water down). This is a particular subset of liberal ideology, elevating procedural justice above welfare as the first virtue of a society and promoting a universal, individualistic and over-optimistically 'neutralist' view of the state (whereas state neutrality may more appositely be interpreted as an attempt at impartiality within a preferred ethical and ideological framework). Historians of political thought know that that subset has been competing with other variants of liberalism for the best part of the past century.

SIX DIFFERENCES IN SEARCH OF ELUCIDATION

Given the distinction, lacking among philosophers, between the language used by the producers and that used by the analysts of ideology, let us note some major differences between ideology and philosophy. First, ideologies are by their very rationale public forms of language, intended to be disseminated and consumed by large groups of people, and to create shared understandings that can direct political practices. As a means to control the use of political language an ideology needs a broad circulation, and it cannot be phrased in terms that are conceptually and argumentatively too complex. Not so with political philosophy, the primary qualitative test of which has now become its acceptance by professional philosophers. It tends, consequently, to

be a semi-private or restricted language, accessible only to specialists and thus bereft of wider public impact. Its scholarly significance may be in inverse ratio to its practical import, and it often requires vulgarization – in the form of a common-language ideology – in order to acquire the communicability and influence to which a mass-oriented ideology aspires. As Gerald Gaus has commented on liberalism as theory, it now tends to be 'too principled and severe a doctrine to have widespread political appeal' (2000a: 193). The emphasis of political philosophies is on the quality of their production, while the emphasis of ideologies is on the effectiveness of their consumption. So while political philosophies share decontesting and interpretive features with ideologies, their style and 'packaging' vary considerably. At the other end of the spectrum new methodologies involving discourse analysis of common language aim at including ordinary utterances as indicative of highly informative and even influential ideological patterns (Van Dijk, 1998), as befits the emphasis of the social sciences on all forms of human interaction, and as befits the increased demands for the democratic accountability of politics.

Second, ideologies are not merely directed at groups, they always are group products. As in Karl Mannheim's famous (1936) account, ideologies are *Weltanschauungen* or world views of people who share common understandings of the world, perhaps because of joint socio-economic roots, or because they have assimilated a particular set of cultural values. Some of these people are of course philosophers themselves, but that is yet again to note the ideological dimensions of political philosophy. The usual self-understanding of philosophers is that their own thought systems are the creation of exceptionally talented, or expertly trained, individuals. The production of theory tends therefore to have an individualistic bias, and this is once again linked to the belief that qualitatively superior thought cannot be produced *en masse*, but only by exceptional thinkers. The greater appeal of the study of ideologies to the social sciences is obvious. The focus of these sciences on patterns of group behaviour is mirrored in the focus of ideological analysis on the political thought-behaviour of both overlapping and competing groups. Ideologies, after all, are offered as generally sustainable solutions to group decision-making and regulation.

Third, ideologies employ a threefold use of emotion. They wrap rational discourse in varying layers of emotive idiom; they assign emotional import to their key values; and they openly recognize the centrality of emotion in socio-political interaction. This is by no means a defect, nor is it anomalous among forms of political thought. When deliberate, the emotive idiom is usually in the form of rhetoric – a linguistic device designed to appeal to the human imagination through poetic analogy, through invoking shared sentiments, and through the stirring up of passions. Philosophical rhetoric tends to the former, while many ideologies do not shy away from the latter. However, even the most rawly emotional ideology must have a minimum of logical presentation. Racist ideologies invite potential consumers into a warped and coarse sphere of myth and prejudice, but once this looking-glass world has been entered, it follows its own preposterous logic. If indeed there are subhumans who contaminate the rest of humanity (the unsubstantiated emotive postulate), they need to be removed from contact with others (a plausible logical conclusion, given the 'truth' value of the postulate). On the other hand, even the most rational and austere political philosophy will promote values to which the philosopher is deeply committed. Philosophers, like ideologists, subscribe to nonnegotiable values, though they are rarely aware of the emotional commitment this entails, one that frequently may be read between their lines. But a nonnegotiable value, in Max Weber's terms, is a type of non-instrumental rationality (1949: 34 and *passim*). Instrumental rationality will engage in cost–benefit calculations concerning the values it endorses as well as the means to promote them. Substantive rationality endorses values at whatever cost to their champions, and is sustained by an attachment that transcends the quantitative and purposive features of instrumental rationality. Thus liberalism has a fundamentally rational belief in the superiority of liberty and human rights, which means that they cannot be traded in wholesale for other values under any circumstances. Concurrently the language of liberalism has always sanctioned liberty in quasi-sacred terms, and has eulogized its worth as a supreme sign of civilization. True, some ideologists are inclined to make assertions (e.g. communism is an 'evil empire') rather than offer the kind of reflective arguments most philosophers might find convincing. Alternatively, ideologists will submit what they regard as persuasive or appealing reasons for an argument (e.g. 'immigration should be restricted in order to protect our indigenous culture from alien influences'), but these may fall outside the criteria moral philosophers prefer for what constitutes a good reason.

Most analytical philosophers will not contemplate the creation of an apparatus that can identify and study emotion as a feature of political language. For example, in discussions of political obligation and civil disobedience, recourse is had to rational and ethical models of promising and consent, or to utilitarian arguments. But these address the problem of obligation to a government as against obligation to a state, not obligation to a nation. Yet political obligation to a nation is a significant sentiment that helps constitute political identity. The reason that it cannot be addressed using the current terms of political philosophy lies in the difficulty in conceptualizing its breach. Civil disobedience is located at the point of tension between obedience to a government and obedience to the constitutive principles of a state, and its practices are well recognized as acts of rational and ethical challenge. But would principled disobedience to a nation be expressed in a refusal to speak its language or to recognize its holidays? Ideological analysis can identify alternative features of discourse that treat obligation as an act of emotional sustenance by focusing on its unconditionality *vis-à-vis* a nation, as well as on its empowering consequences for those bearing the obligation.

A fourth distinction revolves around the issues of transparency and the face value of political language. The very essence of Western philosophy lies in its cognitive and conscious nature. Whatever else philosophy is, it is an attempt to make sense of human and natural phenomena, to explain, clarify, and justify. The ultimate success of a philosophical argument is the rational persuasion of its targeted audience in its good sense. But the ultimate success of an ideology is in its mobilization of significant groups who compete ideationally in order to impact on acts of collective decision-making. It is therefore no surprise that most, if not all, ideologies delight in surrounding their arguments in the opaque and the non-transparent aura of terms such as 'natural' or 'self-evident' precisely because this captures the high ground that is immune from challenge. These are acts of conceptual decontestation devised to end the competition over which political meaning is dominant or legitimate, and 'legitimate' does not always carry with it the connotation of morally or rationally justifiable (Gaus, 2000b: 39). As Plato shrewdly remarked of the magnificent myth with its story of the metals from which the different classes are naturally constituted, it would 'carry conviction to our whole community … [and] serve to increase their loyalty to the state and to each other' (1955: 159–61). Now, of course, observations such as these have opened ideology to the accusation of manipulating people's perceptions of the world and reinforced those who regard all ideology as a method of distorting reality. It is certainly the case that some ideologies have systematically and cynically practised such manipulation and distortion, and it is likely that all ideologies press their prejudices through some form of bias. But Marxist theorists of ideology have ignored the important distinctions between distortion and interpretation, and between manipulation and control. Whereas the first of each duo is an unsavoury option, the second is a necessary consequence of the requirement to regulate, organize and rationalize the social world. The student of ideology's equivalent to the philosopher's 'unexamined life' is an uninterpreted world. It would be a world without humanly ordered patterns and decisions, a world of chaos, entropy, and paralysis, within which no individual could function adequately.

The above feature may also be seen in a different light, leading to a fifth distinction between ideology and philosophy, which relates to intentionality and unintentionality. A key consequence of the deliberateness of analytical political philosophers is that unintentional messages, whether their own or those they examine, are of no scholarly or relevant significance. A central aim of philosophy is to control and to refine language to the point where it can carry highly accurate and complex analyses, where it can do 'exactly' what its users want it to do. Scholars of ideology aspire to similar standards in controlling knowledge according to their own criteria, but they are equally interested in the unintentional meanings forged by their subject-matter, the ideological producers. And the interpretation of thought practices is crucially dependent on understanding both the intentional and the unintentional forms of expression indulged in by ideologists.

To understand that, one must appreciate some of the insights of the hermeneutical tradition and of linguistic semantics, in particular their reference to the existence of multiple readings of any given text, as the readers or consumers of that text impose their interpretations on the polysemic words, phrases and chapters they encounter [see Chapter 2]. Political terms, like any other, accrue and shed meanings over time and space, and they can be understood differentially within a given society at a specific point in time, as each consumer of the text seeks to decontest its potentially multifold meanings and thus to render it intelligible. Paul Ricoeur employed the phrase 'surplus of meaning' to account, among others, for the gap between what the author intended to say and what his or her readers understand the author to say: the 'excess of signification'. As he put it,

> there is a problem of interpretation not so much because of the incommunicability of the psychic experience of the author, but because of the very nature of the verbal intention of the text. The surpassing of the intention by the meaning signifies precisely that understanding takes place in a nonpsychological and properly semantic space, which the text has carved out by severing itself from the mental intention of the author. (Ricoeur, 1976: 76 and *passim*)

That, of course, is a major function of ideology. It imposes a logically arbitrary but culturally significant set of meanings on political reality. This provides a plausible map in relation to which political preferences can be expressed and political action can be taken. But that imposed map is incomplete, not entirely the conscious product of its designers, and its contours and details are continually rediscovered and redrawn by later travellers.

From that perspective, political ideologies contain both overt and coded messages. Overt messages are intended by their ideologue producers to mobilize mass behaviour in certain ways, but perfect control over the consumption and allocation of meaning to those messages is unattainable. In addition, the student of ideologies wishes to decipher additional meanings carried by the ideological discourse inaccessible to the original producers. When liberal supporters of votes for women demanded their inclusion in the general suffrage, they typically assumed that political equality was both necessary and sufficient for ensuring that women were treated in the same way as men. They failed to realize that one form of surplus meaning they were carrying was related to another tacit assumption: that most differences between men and women, whether desirable or undesirable, were irrelevant to the political sphere. Current readings of these early liberal feminists interpret their claims in ways that transcend their own understandings, but that central function of ideological analysis is immaterial to most Anglo-American philosophy.

A sixth distinction between ideology and philosophy returns us to what constitutes a good argument. We have noted above the criteria for a good argument to which analytical philosophers subscribe, one that is rational, logical, coherent, precise, reflexive and self-critical. For ideologists, a good argument may contain some of these elements, particularly some degree of internal rationality and a credible underpinning of the compatibility of its principal concepts. But it will not display them exclusively or optimally. Indeed, it would be futile to insist on all these features too rigidly in an ideology, as ideologies will frequently disintegrate under such scrutiny. Moreover, that would miss the point of ideologies entirely and cause us to forget what work ideologies are designed to perform. Rather, a good ideological argument is one whose morphology of conceptual decontestations can transform or preserve political practices, and such an argument is not always optimally couched in rational or precise terms. A good argument is therefore one that brings about a change in power relationships, through prescription or through the denying of transparency.

The protection necessary to stabilize an ideology's internal structure is achieved through different kinds of argumentative persuasiveness – reason, morality, and emotion – and they are engaged differentially by philosophers and ideologists. These join two further protective devices: the removal of transparency, and the resort to linguistic fiat – a method beloved by totalitarian ideologies that lock concepts into superimposed configurations. But a good ideological argument requires further features. It must be influential, it must – as we have seen – be communicable, and it must be culturally and contextually creative. This last attribute is an intriguing one. Ideologies have to be appreciated as inventive and imaginative representations of 'social reality', when invention and imagination are the raw, visionary, constructive, experimental – and yes, also the volatile or dangerous – aspects of that perennial blend of reason and emotion that emanates from the human mind (Freeden, 2001a: 5–12). That creativity is occasionally acquired at the expense of philosophical cogency and it will often be harmful and irresponsible, but the pay-off is in terms of an adaptive ability employed to shape the fortunes of societies undergoing change. Of course, some of the greatest political philosophers, Plato or Rousseau, as well as many utopians, have exhibited marvellous imaginations too. But these are now mainly valued by philosophers as metaphors or thought exercises through which to test the robustness of assumptions, premises and hypotheses, rather than as practicable reworkings of a social order.

UNDERSTANDING POLITICAL THINKING: CONTEXTS AND DECONSTRUCTIONS

Having adumbrated some of the differences between philosophy and ideology, and between philosophy and the study of ideology, one issue of fundamental importance remains with respect to the latter. A number of recent philosophical approaches and recent analyses of ideology have been mutually reinforcing. Hermeneutics and the study of interpretation have coalesced with theories of the 'essential contestability' of concepts and with poststructuralist and feminist affirmations of the social construction of meaning [see Chapter 4]. Wittgenstein, Gadamer, and others have alerted many contemporary philosophers to the language games and the contextual inputs that fashion human understanding and that conspire against a facile universalism, even if some broadly common understandings may still operate to co-ordinate human minds. Wittgenstein's notion of family resemblances has helped students of ideology to construe ideological groupings such as socialism as consisting of a complex network of similarities rather than constituting a monolithic block. Following from that, ideologies are perceived as containing overlapping and shared components, and the borders between them are considered to be permeable. Hermeneutical inputs

have focused on the malleability of texts, and on the limitless readings to which they are open through their recontextualization. Understanding is thus permanently associated with interpretation and with the particularity of spatial and temporal viewpoints, while allowing nonetheless for some diachronic and geographical similarities to persist.

Students of ideology have applied to those insights a further micro-structural examination of the conceptual components of such texts, and they have employed this approach to proclaim the vast potential ideational resources inherent in political utterances and the fluidity of internal relationships within each ideological family. They have noted that liberty may be attached to self-development and to democratic participation in one ideological variant of liberalism, but in another liberal variant liberty may be attached to unrestricted economic transactions and to large accumulations of property. They have noted how new readings of well-established political terms such as 'natural rights' have shifted alongside a transformed understanding of what (if anything!) is natural in human social conduct. While this may allow the emergence of the unpredictable, the appreciation of historical development has also alerted students of ideology to the diachronic constraints on ideologies, channelling some ideological change into recognizably stable patterns. The school of conceptual history (Koselleck, 1985; Richter, 1995) has been influential in identifying key historical periods when a struggle over the 'correct' political and social concepts occurs, and in reconstructing the meaning of such concepts over time. In parallel John Pocock (1972) has investigated the ways in which political languages have changed over time. Cultural anthropologists, on their part, have highlighted the symbolic and often non-verbal nature of ideologies, in addition to portraying them as mapping devices that impose integrated fields of meaning on political occurrences (Geertz, 1964). Ideologies were now regarded as contained in practices and in cultural symbols as well as in oral and written texts, thus extending the disciplinary boundaries from which analytical methodologies for their investigation could be extrapolated. Finally, poststructural philosophers have regarded ideology as a modernist expedient that offers a narrative necessary to preserving the social order, itself often considered to be a fiction or a social imaginary. These approaches demote the centrality and autonomy of the subject at the heart of analytical philosophy, as can be seen in Michel Foucault's treatment of discourse as a repository of power. Theorists such as Ernesto Laclau and Chantal Mouffe have emphasized the discursive nature of ideology, and the way in which it articulates a social unity in a hegemonic manner. They also point out the existence of concepts, 'empty signifiers', to which no signified, no external social phenomenon, condition or object, corresponds. On that understanding, for example, the term 'order' is an empty concept, referring to inadequate representations of social stability because no complete order can ever exist. In contradistinction to Anglo-American political philosophy, the emphasis here is on the impossibility of making truth statements, on the illusory nature of representing reality, let alone discerning essential meanings, and on the functional rather than ethical potential of thinking about politics (Laclau and Mouffe, 1985; Laclau, 1996; Norval, 2000). Slavoj Žižek (1989; 1994), drawing on Lacanian psychoanalytical theory, similarly regards ideology as an unconscious fantasmic illusion that papers over the 'real' that cannot be fathomed or represented. Other philosophical schools, emerging from diverse intellectual bases, focus on dichotomies, agonisms and contradictions arising out of incommensurability as endemic to human thought as well as to social structure, approaches that have resulted in a revival of interest in Arendt or Carl Schmitt and that are central also to some varieties of feminism (Mouffe, 2000; Nicholson, 1990; Canovan, 1992; Schmitt, 1996). These deconstructivist positions challenge the holism and integration evident in many instances of philosophical thinking about politics, but they also challenge methodologies that propose to regard conceptual, linguistic and structural interrelationships as fruitful. One result is the problematization of pluralism, not because its nod in the direction of liberal diversity conflicts with the harmonized unity of thought that is the goal of some political philosophers, but because it now exudes the aura of unmanageable, yet endemic, destructiveness – pluralism as concealing a fragmented world [see further Chapter 18].

Some poststructuralists abandon the search for norms too readily. But even among the contrary camp of Anglo-American philosophers the certainty that is assumed to accompany objective and neutral understandings of concepts is being challenged. Thus Michael Walzer (1985) has focused on the contextual and social meanings of social goods, while Ronald Dworkin has noted that most contemporary philosophers accept that conceptual definitions are substantive and normative. Taking democracy as an example, Dworkin contends against essentialist definitions that

> we still need an account of what makes one feature of a social or political arrangement essential to its character as a democracy and another feature only contingent, and once we have rejected the idea that reflection on the meaning of 'democracy' will supply that distinction, nothing else will. (2001: 11)

Ethical values have no independent status but are derivative from what makes a good and successful life, i.e. one that furthers individual interests. These observations significantly reduce the gap between philosophers and students of ideology, though they still leave open the question of whether the idea of a good life is a stable one. Even given general consensus on the primacy of well-being, the small print that fills in that conceptual category may differ markedly from case to case. Divergent ideologies can offer varying yet plausibly legitimate notions of human flourishing.

CONCLUSION

To suggest that political philosophy concerns what ought to be, while ideology concerns what is, is not just an oversimplification; it is misleading. All too often political philosophy does not offer us what ought to be, if 'ought' implies a realizable possibility, because in its dominant current guises it is excessively utopian, a label philosophers would be loath to acknowledge. It is utopian in two senses: first, it engages in thought experiments to which no reality could correspond; second, it offers purified generalities from which conflict and inconsistencies have been surgically removed (e.g. Habermas and Rawls). The uses of political philosophy are in its sharp elucidation of issues within its broader generalities. For instance, it has cast important light on problems of equalization of treatment and of life chances by offering criteria for fair and justifiable inequalities. But it would be inappropriate to describe these as *best* practice, if best practice can never be achieved. Rather, these are models of what *good* practice could be, were we to abstract a particular set of problems from contextual constraints, and were we to smooth over the frictions which any political solution attempts to eliminate. Political philosophers achieve micro-coherence by holding most 'externalities' constant. That is one of their prime methods, and it discharges vital functions: it enables the critical construction of alternatives through which to assess, and often to reject, current practice; it advances our moral sensibilities; it refines the analytical skills required for the lucid understanding and prescription of social practices; and it encourages precise thinking on the causes and consequences of human conduct.

The study of ideology, to the contrary, is not – as often portrayed – a descriptive art, but an interpretive one. It responds to the question: which rigorous interpretive paradigms are the most helpful in furthering our understanding of the nature and potential of political thought? It reconstructs existing thought practices, but from a necessarily relative perspective; and in its critical mode it offers us tools for appreciating not what ought to be, but what can be, in the domain of political practice. Some ideologies are, *contra* Karl Mannheim, utopias, but they then are consciously and deliberately utopian. Others are concrete sets of solutions, some of which are attractive, sagacious or prudent, and some of which may be shocking and ruthless in their conceptualization and stray beyond any accepted limits of decency. Many ideologies are more modest, and less precise, approximations of what political philosophers aspire to. Ideologies are, in effect, more likely than political philosophies to abstract from logical constraints than from contextual ones. Their study tells us less than the study of political philosophies when it comes to the intricacies involved in testing political thought to its limits. But it tells us much more about the fields of political thinking available to a society, and it illuminates that thinking through exploring the constraints and options that make each ideology a distinct configuration shaped by time, space and culture. The amenability of ideologies to change and diversification also accounts for the need to decontest, to impose a particular solution – logically arbitrary though culturally significant – on political practice. This recognition of the inevitable act of decontesting the essentially contestable, an act that bestows specific meaning on an unstructured multiverse of meanings, marks out the student of ideologies from the political philosopher, who performs similar decontestations but is prone to package them as general solutions to the issues at hand (as, with less elegance, does the ideologue). If political philosophers dream of drawing thinking together, students of ideology crave understanding for its fissured condition. The discipline of political theory requires both philosophical and ideological analysis, but its practitioners need to know when to employ the one and when the other, and what crucial insights each of these subdisciplines can deliver.

REFERENCES

Arendt, H. (1968) 'Truth and politics'. In H. Arendt, *Between Past and Future*. New York: Viking.

Barber, B. (1988) *The Conquest of Politics*. Princeton, NJ: Princeton University Press.

Barry, B. (2001) *Culture and Equality*. Cambridge: Polity.

Canovan, M. (1992) *Hannah Arendt*. Cambridge: Cambridge University Press.

Dagger, R. (1997) *Civic Virtues*. Oxford: Oxford University Press.

Dworkin, R. (2001) 'Political and legal Archimedeans', draft paper.

Freeden, M. (1996) *Ideologies and Political Theory: A Conceptual Approach*. Oxford: Clarendon.

Freeden, M. (2001a) 'What is special about ideologies?' *Journal of Political Ideologies*, 6: 5–12.

Freeden, M. (2001b) 'Twentieth-century liberal thought: development or transformation?' In M. Evans, ed., *The Edinburgh Companion to Contemporary Liberalism*. Edinburgh: Edinburgh University Press.

Gaus, G. F. (2000a) 'Liberalism at the end of the century'. *Journal of Political Ideologies*, 5: 179–99.

Gaus, G. F. (2000b) *Political Concepts and Political Theories*. Boulder, CO: Westview.

Geertz, C. (1964) 'Ideology as a cultural system'. In D. E. Apter, ed., *Ideology and Discontent*. New York: Free.

Gramsci, A. (1971) *Selections from Prison Notebooks*, eds Q. Hoare and G. Newell-Smith. London: Lawrence and Wishart.

Habermas, J. (1981) *The Theory of Communicative Action*. Vol. 1, *Reason and the Rationalization of Society*. Boston: Beacon.

Hobhouse, L. T. (1911) *Liberalism*. London: Williams and Norgate.

Koselleck, R. (1985) *Futures Past*. Cambridge, MA: MIT Press.

Laclau, E. (1996) 'The death and resurrection of the theory of ideology'. *Journal of Political Ideologies*, 1: 201–20.

Laclau, E. and C. Mouffe (1985) *Hegemony and Socialist Strategy*. London: Verso.

Mannheim, K. (1936) *Ideology and Utopia*. London: Routledge and Kegan Paul.

Marx, K. and F. Engels (1974) *The German Ideology*, ed. C. J. Arthur. London: Lawrence and Wishart.

Mill, J. S. (1910) *On Liberty*. London: Dent.

Mouffe, C. (2000) *The Democratic Paradox*. London: Verso.

Nicholson, L. J., ed. (1990) *Feminism/Postmodernism*. New York: Routledge.

Norval, A. (2000) 'The things we do with words: contemporary approaches to the analysis of ideology'. *British Journal of Political Science*, 30: 313–46.

Pettit, P. (1997) *Republicanism: A Theory of Freedom and Government*. Oxford: Oxford University Press.

Plato (1955) *The Republic*. Harmondsworth: Penguin.

Pocock, J. G. A. (1972) *Politics, Language and Time*. London: Methuen.

Rawls, J. (1971) *A Theory of Justice*. Oxford: Oxford University Press.

Rawls, J. (1993) *Political Liberalism*. New York: Columbia University Press.

Richter, M. (1995) *A History of Political and Social Concepts*. New York: Oxford University Press.

Ricoeur, P. (1976) *Interpretation Theory: Discourse and the Surplus of Meaning*. Fort Worth, TX: Texas Christian University Press.

Schmitt, C. (1996) *The Concept of the Political*. Chicago: University of Chicago Press.

Simhony, A. and D. Weinstein, eds (2001) *The New Liberalism: Reconciling Liberty and Community*. Cambridge: Cambridge University Press.

Skinner, Q. (1998) *Liberty before Liberalism*. Cambridge: Cambridge University Press.

Swift, A. (2001) *Political Philosophy: A Beginner's Guide for Students and Politicians*. Cambridge: Polity.

Taylor, C. (1989) 'Cross-purposes: the liberal–communitarian debate'. In N. Rosenblum, ed., *Liberalism and the Moral Life*. Cambridge, MA: Harvard University Press.

Van Dijk, T. (1998) *Ideology: A Multidisciplinary Approach*. London: Sage.

Walzer, M. (1985) *Spheres of Justice*. Oxford: Blackwell.

Weber, M. (1949) *The Methodology of the Social Sciences*. New York: Free.

Young, I. M. (1996) 'Political theory: an overview'. In Robert E. Goodin and Hans-Dieter Klingemann, eds, *A New Handbook of Political Science*. Oxford: Oxford University Press.

Žižek, S. (1989) *The Sublime Object of Ideology*. London: Verso.

Žižek, S. (1994) 'The spectre of ideology'. In S. Žižek, ed., *Mapping Ideology*. London: Verso.

2

History and the Interpretation of Texts

TERENCE BALL

Hermeneutics – the art of interpretation – takes its name from Hermes. In Greek mythology Hermes was the winged-foot messenger of the gods and something of a trickster to boot. Like the Sphinx and the Oracle at Delphi, he relayed messages from the gods in an encoded and allusive way, typically in the form of riddles, leaving it to his human hearers to interpret the meaning and significance of any message (Palmer, 1969: 13). Sometimes they got it right, and sometimes not – often with disastrous results.

Students of political theory do not attempt to decode and interpret the meaning of messages of divine origin. But we do, of necessity, attempt to understand messages sent to us by long-dead and all-too-human thinkers whose works we read and ponder and mine for meaning. Thus political theory is in important ways a backward-looking enterprise. A very considerable part of its subject-matter is its own history, which consists of classic works from Plato onward. In this respect political theory is quite unlike (say) physics. One can be a very fine physicist without ever having studied the history of physics or having read Aristotle's *Physics* or the Ionian nature philosophers or, for that matter, the works of Galileo and Newton. The same cannot be said of political theory. A student of political theory must have read, reread and reflected upon the works of Plato, Aristotle, Machiavelli, Hobbes, Locke, Rousseau, Marx, Mill and many others if she is to be competent in her chosen vocation.

But there is more than one way to read, interpret, and understand the works that comprise the canon – changing and contested as it is – of political theory. My aim in this chapter is to say something about the variety and diversity of approaches to the interpretation of texts in political theory. I shall begin by noting that interpretation is not an option but a necessity for the meaning-seeking creatures that we are. Next I shall sketch briefly the chief tenets of various 'schools' of (or, less formally, approaches to) interpretation – Marxian, 'totalitarian', Freudian, feminist, Straussian, new historical, and postmodernist – and the interpretive controversies between and among them. Along the way I shall supply several cautionary tales about how not to interpret particular passages from important thinkers. And finally I conclude by presenting and defending my own 'pluralistic' and 'problem-driven' approach to the interpretation of texts in political theory. I want throughout to emphasize two points in particular: that not all interpretations are equally valid or valuable; and that interpretations are rationally criticizable and corrigible.

THE INDISPENSABILITY OF INTERPRETATION

Interpretation comes with the territory of being human. It is an activity from which humans cannot escape. Our prehistoric ancestors interpreted the meaning of animal entrails, omens and other signs that might make their world more intelligible and perhaps portend their future. They, like modern meteorologists, attempted to forecast the weather by looking at clouds and observing the behaviour of birds and other creatures. With the coming of literacy came the primacy of the written over the spoken word. Religious people, then as now, interpret the meaning of sacred scripture. Judges, lawyers and ordinary citizens read and interpret constitutions and other texts. And students of political theory read – and adjudicate among rival interpretations of – texts in political theory.

How one interprets the meaning of any text has implications for what one does with it. Hermeneutics can be, and often is, a deadly serious – and sometimes simply deadly – business (Ball, 1987). If you doubt it, you need only think of how Torquemada and the Spanish Inquisition interpreted the Bible, or Lenin and Stalin (not to mention Mao and Pol Pot) the works of Marx, or Hitler and the Nazis the writings of Nietzsche, or Osama bin Laden and Islamic fundamentalists the Koran, to see what carnage can result from interpretations of texts taken to be foundational for mass movements. It is therefore important for students of political theory to treat the texts they study not as sacred scripture, but as the handiwork of human beings who, although fallible, have much to teach their critical readers.

The vocation of political theory is in large part defined by its perennial fascination with and attention to 'classic' works. Each generation reads them anew and from their own vantage point. These authors and their works comprise an important aspect of our political tradition, which we renew and enrich by reading, reflecting upon and criticizing these works. And yet to read and attempt to understand a work written a long time ago, perhaps in a different language, by an author whose *mentalité* differs remarkably from our own, is a daunting task. The reader finds herself in a position akin to that of an anthropologist studying an alien culture (Rorty, Schneewind and Skinner, 1984: 6–7). As readers of works by Plato and other long-dead authors, we find ourselves in an alien age or culture with whose concepts, categories, customs, and practices we are largely unfamiliar. In such situations we are often at a loss to know *what* is being said, much less why it is being said or what its meaning may be. We therefore need a 'translation' – not only of the *words* of the text but of its *meaning*. A good translation or interpretation is one that diminishes the strangeness of the text, making it more familiar and accessible to an otherwise puzzled or perplexed observer. The artifacts or texts produced in political cultures preceding and differing from our own do not readily reveal their meanings even to the most careful reader. To read a text 'over and over again', as some (e.g. Plamenatz, 1963: I, x) advise, is no doubt necessary. But it is hardly sufficient to enable us to arrive at anything like an adequate understanding of what (say) Plato meant by advocating the use of 'noble lies' or what Machiavelli meant by comparing 'fortune' (*fortuna*) to a woman who must be beaten and bullied. To try to make sense of such puzzling terms and speech acts requires that we interpret their meaning. There is no understanding without interpretation, and no interpretation without the possibility of multiple (mis)understandings.

Nor is there a neutral standpoint or Archimedean point from which to interpret and appraise any text, classic or otherwise. All interpretation implies, and originates in, some vantage point or standpoint. Every interpretation, in short, implies an interest that provides the ground for and possibility of an interpretation – a standpoint from which inquiry can begin and interpretation proceed. These interests are, moreover, multiple and varied. One's interests can be contemporary: what (for example) can Mill still teach us about liberty? Or they may be more historical: why did Mill's arguments in *On Liberty* take the form they did? Who were Mill's main targets and his intended audience? Or one's interests may be more narrowly linguistic or literary: what metaphors did Mill employ, and with what effect? Or one's interests may be logical or philosophical: is Mill's argument in *On Liberty* logically consistent? Are there gaps or lacunae in the argument? Is the argument convincing? None of these interests necessarily excludes the others. But they do dictate what will count as a problem, what constitutes an interesting or important question, and what method might be most appropriate and fruitful for answering such questions. One would not, for example, assess the logical adequacy of Mill's argument by examining the metaphors he uses. Nor would one be able to answer questions posed from a historical perspective by looking only at the logical structure of his argument.

What one's guiding interests might be – and how one goes about answering to them – is as likely as not to depend on the interpretive 'school' to which one belongs.

'SCHOOLS' OF INTERPRETATION

There are today a number of influential schools of, or approaches to, interpretation. Each takes a distinctive approach to the history of political thought, and each is highly critical of the others. Disputes between and among these schools are heated and often protracted. I want now to offer brief thumbnail sketches of several approaches to interpretation.

Marxian Interpretation

I begin by considering the Marxian approach to textual interpretation. Marx famously remarked that 'the ideas of the ruling class are in every epoch the ruling ideas' (Marx and Engels, 1947: 39). That is, the dominant or mainstream ideas of any era are those that serve the interests of the dominant class, largely by legitimating their pre-eminent position in society. So it comes as no surprise, Marxists say, that in slave-owning societies slavery is portrayed and widely regarded as normal and natural: Aristotle said so in fourth-century BC Greece, as did George Fitzhugh and other apologists for American slavery before the Civil War. In capitalist societies the free market is portrayed in the mainstream media – books, mass-circulation magazines and newspapers, television, movies – as the most normal, natural and efficient way to organize and run an economy. Other alternatives, such as socialism, are always portrayed negatively, as abnormal, unnatural and inefficient. Ideas – including those to be found in works of political theory – combine to form a more or less consistent set or system of ideas that Marx calls an 'ideology'. The point and purpose of any ideology is to lend legitimacy to the rule of the dominant class. Thus ideologies serve as smokescreens, hiding tawdry reality from a credulous public, and presenting a rosy – albeit false – picture of a society that treats all its members fairly, that rewards the deserving and punishes the undeserving, and distributes valued goods in a just and equitable manner.

For a Marxist, then, the task of textual interpretation is to get behind appearances, to uncover the reality they obscure, and to expose what Marx calls 'the *illusion of that epoch*' (1947: 30). This general approach, which is now sometimes called 'the hermeneutics of suspicion', takes no statement at face value but views it as a stratagem or move in a game whose point is to obscure reality and legitimize existing power relations. An adequate or good interpretation is one that performs the function of 'ideology critique' – that is, penetrates the veil of illusion and brings us closer to unveiling and exposing a heretofore hidden socio-economic reality. An example may serve to illustrate what this might mean in actual interpretive practice.

One particularly important Marxian interpretation of key works in political theory is C. B. Macpherson's *The Political Theory of Possessive Individualism* (1962). By 'possessive individualism' Macpherson means the political theory that serves to support and legitimize those mainstays of modern capitalism – economic self-interest and the institution of private property. He finds Hobbes and Locke, in particular, to be ideologists and apologists for capitalism *avant la lettre*. Thus Locke, for example, ceases to be the good, grey, tolerant, proto-democratic thinker we thought we knew, and becomes instead an extraordinarily clever propagandist for the then-emerging capitalist order. Macpherson makes much, for example, of Locke's discussion of private property in the *Second Treatise of Government* (1690). Locke's problem was to justify the institution of private property, particularly since the Scriptures say that God had given the earth to all mankind. How then could any individual make any portion of that common property his own? Locke famously answers that one separates one's own part from the common by mixing one's labour with it:

> 27. Though the Earth, and all inferior Creatures be common to all men, yet every Man has a *Property* in his own *Person*. This no Body has any Right to but himself. The *Labour* of his Body, and the *Work* of his hands, we may say, are properly his. Whatsoever then he removes out of the State that Nature hath provided, and left it in, he hath mixed his *Labour* with, and joyned to it something that is his own, and thereby makes it his *Property*.

Even so, Locke adds, there remain restrictions on how much one might justifiably remove from the common store – namely, one may not take more than one can 'use' without its 'spoiling'. You might make apples from a commonly owned tree your own property by expending your labour – by climbing the tree, picking the apples, sorting and washing them, etc. – but you are entitled to take no more apples than you can use without their spoiling. These 'use' and 'spoilage' limitations are overcome, however, with the introduction of *money*:

> 47. And thus came in the use of Money, some lasting thing that Men might keep without spoiling, and that by mutual consent Men would take in exchange for the truly useful, but perishable Supports of Life.

> 48. And as different degrees of Industry were apt to give Men Possessions in different Proportions, so this *Invention of Money* gave them the opportunity to continue to enlarge them.

Macpherson makes much of these passages, which he takes to represent a key juncture in Locke's justification of capitalist accumulation and ever-greater inequalities of wealth (1962: 203–11, 233–5). Macpherson's critics contend that it is anything but: that Locke was a devout Christian who had deep misgivings about money (the love of which is said in the Scriptures to be 'the root of all evil'); that the word Locke uses in paragraph 48 is not 'property' – that which is properly and by right your own – but 'possession' (which is mere fact without moral or legal import: a thief may possess your wallet but it is not properly his, i.e. his property); hence the most we may conclude is that money, and therefore presumably capital itself, is 'a human institution about whose moral status Locke felt deeply ambivalent' (Dunn, 1984: 40).

A Marxian approach to textual interpretation encounters a number of difficulties, among them the following. We have seen already that Marxists assume that the ruling ideas of an epoch are those that serve the interests of the ruling class; and since most political thinkers have belonged to an educated and literate elite, their ideas serve the ruling class. But then Marx and Engels (and Lenin, Trotsky, Bukharin, Lukács, and many other prominent Marxists) have not belonged to the class of oppressed labourers but to a learned and literate elite. By Marxian lights their ideas should serve the interests of the ruling capitalist class, not those of the labouring proletariat. How can the ideas of these Marxists serve the interests of a class to which they do not belong? All attempts (by Marx and others) to answer this question – that there are some who through will or intellect transcend their 'objective' class basis, that the workers cannot theorize for themselves because they are afflicted with 'false consciousness' whilst middle-class intellectuals are not, etc. – are merely *ad hoc* rationalizations and are clearly unsatisfactory. Moreover, how Marxists can interpret all political theories, past and present, as ideological masks concealing and justifying the domination of one class by another – and yet exempt their own theorizing as an exception to this rule – is not explained (or even explainable) in any satisfactory way. And, not least, Marxian interpretations have a formulaic, cookie-cutter quality: the interpreter has preset ideas about what she will find – namely ideological trickery or obfuscation in the service of the ruling class – and, presto, she finds it lurking in even the most innocent-sounding passages.

'Totalitarian' Interpretations

The twentieth century saw the rise to power and prominence of various totalitarian regimes and ideologies, among which fascism and communism were particularly prominent. One important and influential approach to textual interpretation views these ideologies as rooted in the thinking of earlier political theorists going as far back as Plato. These earlier theories, when put into modern political practice, allegedly produced Hitler and the Holocaust and Stalin and the Gulag. It was therefore deemed important to detect and expose the philosophical 'origins' or 'roots' of modern totalitarianism by rereading and reinterpreting earlier thinkers in light of the latter-day 'fruits' of their theorizing.

Once one begins to look for proto-totalitarian themes and tendencies in earlier theorists, they seem to be everywhere. What is Plato's perfect republic, ruled by a philosopher-king who employs censorship and 'noble lies', if not a blueprint for a Nazi regime ruled by an all-knowing *Führer*, backed by propaganda and the Big Lie, or for a Soviet-style communist utopia ruled by a Lenin or a Stalin? Much the same might be said about Machiavelli's ruthless prince or Hobbes's all-powerful Sovereign or Rousseau's all-wise Legislator. Indeed, Rousseau's *Social Contract* has come in for special censure. Rousseau's critics have viewed him as a precursor of totalitarianism for four main reasons. The first is his notion of the General Will,

which is 'always right' and 'cannot err'. The second is Rousseau's chilling assertion that would-be dissidents must be 'forced to be free'. The third is the ominous figure of the omniscient and god-like Legislator. The fourth and most frightening feature of Rousseau's ideal republic is the civil religion that supplies a religious rationale for its draconian laws and institutions. Taken together, these four features constitute a bill of indictment of Rousseau's totalitarian intentions (Talmon, 1952; Barker, 1951; Crocker, 1968).[1] Other later thinkers – particularly Hegel and Marx – have been subjected to similar criticisms.

Among the most prominent representatives of the 'totalitarian' approach to textual interpretation was the late Sir Karl Popper, whose *The Open Society and Its Enemies* (1963 [1945]) is the most sustained and systematic attempt to trace the roots of modern totalitarianism to ideas advanced by 'enemies' of 'the open society' from Plato through to Marx. An Austrian Jew who fled from the Nazis and emigrated to New Zealand in the 1930s, Popper regarded his research for and writing of *The Open Society* as his 'war effort' (1976: 115). It may be instructive to revisit Popper's *Open Society* to show how sincerely held present-day concerns can inform – or misinform – our interpretation of 'classic' works in political theory. Let us choose from the preceding rogues' gallery a single example for closer examination: Hegel's remark in *Philosophy of Right* that 'what is rational is actual and what is actual is rational' (1952: 10).

Popper quotes Hegel's remark in English translation and then glosses it as follows: 'Hegel maintain[s] that everything that is reasonable must be real, and everything that is real must be reasonable.' Thus Hegel holds that 'everything that is now real or actual exists by necessity, and must be reasonable as well as good. (Particularly good is … the existing Prussian state)' (Popper, 1963: II, 41). The Prussian state of Hegel's time was an authoritarian police state that practised censorship, arbitrary arrest and imprisonment without due process of law. That state was real; therefore, in Hegel's view, that state was rational or reasonable and thus good. In this way, Popper claims, Hegel gave his philosophical blessing to the Prussian prototype of the modern totalitarian state, and so must himself be accounted a 'totalitarian' thinker and apologist. Hegel is, in short, an 'enemy' of the 'open society'.

But is Hegel guilty as charged? The short answer is no. Let us see why. Here is Hegel's own statement in the original German: 'Was vernunftig ist, das ist wirklich; und was wirklich ist, das ist vernunftig.' The closest English equivalent is: 'What is rational is actual; and what is actual is rational.' Note that *wirklich* is translated not as 'real' but as 'actual'. In everyday German, as in English, there is ordinarily no sharp distinction between 'real' and 'actual'. Popper (whose first language was German) fails to note that Hegel was writing not in ordinary non-technical German but in a technical-philosophical idiom. He draws and maintains a sharp distinction between *wirklich* (actual) and *reell* (real). In Hegel's philosophical nomenclature an acorn (for example) is real; but it is not actual until its potential is fully actualized, that is, when it becomes a full-grown oak. In other words, Hegel uses *wirklich* to mean 'fully actualized'; he contrasts 'actual', not with unreal, but with 'potential'. Thus Hegel's (in)famous statement means something like, 'What is rational is that which fully actualizes its potential; and that which fully actualizes its potential is rational.' This is far from being the sinister statement that Popper makes it out to be and which he takes to be evidence of Hegel's 'totalitarian' tendencies.[2]

There is a larger hermeneutical lesson to be learned from Popper's (and many others') misreading of Hegel (and Plato, Rousseau, and other theorists). First, it is important to place statements in their proper context – conceptual-philosophical or otherwise. In this instance that means taking note of how Hegel uses an apparently ordinary term in a non-ordinary or technical way. Second, one should beware of any interpreter who, like Popper, has a preset thesis that he then 'proves' by selectively quoting and stitching together statements taken out of their textual and linguistic context – a penchant Popper shares, ironically, with the Marxists he so detests.

Psychoanalytic Interpretation

In *The Interpretation of Dreams*, *The Psychopathology of Everyday Life*, and other works, Sigmund Freud famously argued that our actions are often motivated by wishes, desires, or fears of which we are not consciously aware. Psychoanalytic interpretations, like Marxian ones, fall under the heading of 'the hermeneutics of suspicion'. My apparently accidental slips of the tongue (or pen), for example, may reveal to a trained psychoanalyst aspects of my 'unconscious' that are not evident to me. So too with my dreams. Suppose I dream that I am at bat in a baseball game, bottom of the ninth inning, with my team losing, all bases loaded, one ball and two strikes. Here comes the pitch. As I begin to swing, my bat suddenly turns rubbery and floppy, like one that a circus clown might swing. The ball whizzes past my ineffectual bat and I strike out, losing the game for my team, and bringing embarrassment and disgrace upon myself. How to interpret what I've dreamed? Well, if I were a baseball player who's afraid of cracking under pressure, the meaning of my dream would be

pretty transparent. But, alas, I'm not a baseball player. I'm merely a 50-something male academic. An analyst might interpret this dream as a fear of losing sexual potency, particularly when there are high expectations and lots of pressure to 'perform'. In this case, the baseball game is not a game and the limp bat is not a bat but a symbol standing for something else … Well, you get the idea.[3]

One can supply psychoanalytic interpretations not only of dreams but of all sorts of texts – including those in political theory. This has been done in the case of Machiavelli (Pitkin, 1984), Edmund Burke (Kramnick, 1977), Martin Luther (Erikson, 1958) and Mahatma Gandhi (Erikson, 1969), among others. I want to look, more particularly, at Bruce Mazlish's (1975) psychoanalytic interpretation of themes in the work of John Stuart Mill. Mill is most famous as the author of *On Liberty* (1859) in which he argues in favour of a very wide sphere of personal freedom to live one's life as one wishes, without undue interference from others, no matter how well-meaning those others may be. Now as Mill tells us in his *Autobiography*, his stern Scots father James Mill did not permit his first-born son to live and act as he wished. Young John was not allowed to associate with other children, to play games, or to do anything except to read and be exactingly examined on books assigned by his father. The elder Mill's strict educational regimen was constructed and carried out with the best of intentions. This tightly regimented upbringing produced impressive results, but also took its toll. At age 20 John suffered a mental breakdown from which he recovered only slowly and in part through the reading of romantic poetry (chiefly Wordsworth and Coleridge) of which his father heartily disapproved. From that point on Mill ceased to be his father's intellectual clone; he became a thinker with a mind of his own, and an author more prolific and more famous than his father.

Mazlish interprets *On Liberty* less as a work of liberal political theory than as a *cri de coeur* and a declaration of personal independence that is more autobiographical than analytical (perhaps that's what Nietzsche meant when he said that all theory is autobiography). This is not what Mill consciously intended; but he was led by unconscious desires to declare himself independent of his father and, some 23 years after his father's death, to justify his own independence and autonomy (Mazlish, 1975: ch. 15). As Freud theorized, sons subconsciously wish to kill their fathers and possess their mothers: this he called the 'Oedipus complex'. Mill was locked in an Oedipal struggle with his father, whom he defeated in argument. What then of his relations with his mother? Her name was Harriet. Significantly, as Mazlish notes, Mill had an illicit affair with a married woman and mother named (you guessed it)

Harriet, who after her husband died, became Harriet Taylor Mill. From a psychoanalytic perspective, this is strong stuff, and Mazlish makes the most of it (1975: 283–93).

Although often suggestive and sometimes insightful, psychoanalytic interpretations face stiff evidentiary challenges. They are open to criticisms that they are speculative, impressionistic and non-falsifiable, and mistake coincidences for causes. To the claim that Mill symbolically defeated his father and married his mother, for example, a sceptic might answer that 'Harriet' was a very common woman's name in nineteenth-century Britain (indeed Mill had a younger sister named Harriet) and that Mill's affair with and marriage to Harriet Taylor was a coincidence of no importance, symbolic or otherwise. As for Mill's motivation in writing *On Liberty*, one can note that motivations are typically multiple and varied and while Mazlish may have correctly pinpointed one source, that is largely beside the point if one wishes to understand the *aim* and *argument* of *On Liberty*. Psychoanalytic interpretations direct our attention away from the text and toward its author: which is fine, if what we wish to understand is the latter instead of the former. But textual interpretation is not the same thing as limning authorial motivation. Mill begins *On Liberty* by saying that 'The subject of this Essay is … the nature and limits of the power which can be legitimately exercised by society over the individual.' He does not say 'by fathers over sons'. To assert, as Mazlish does, that the latter is the 'real', albeit hidden, meaning is merely to speculate about Mill's motives, not to understand the argument of *On Liberty*. It is perhaps because of these evident shortcomings that psychoanalytic interpretations have by and large fallen out of favour among students of political theory.[4]

Feminist Interpretation

Feminism has had a profound and lasting impact on the way we study and interpret works in the history of political thought. A feminist perspective puts issues concerning gender at the forefront, and from that vantage point one views political theory anew and makes interesting – and sometimes appalling – discoveries [see further Chapter 21]. Such a sensibility injects a strong strain of scepticism into the study of 'classic' works. For, as Susan Okin observes, 'the great tradition of political philosophy consists, generally speaking, of writings by men, for men, and about men' (1979: 5). To study this tradition from a feminist perspective is to be struck by the extent to which the civic and legal status of women was long considered to be a subject unworthy of theoretical treatment – or perhaps merely beneath the theorists' contempt, and therefore outside the purview of historians of political thought, most of whom happen to be male. The neglect of women in the history of Western (and indeed non-Western) political thought is a silence that, to modern ears, is deafening. Feminist rereadings and reappraisals of the 'canon' of 'classic' works have made, and continue to make, startling and often unsuspected connections between phenomena as apparently disparate as a thinker's view of the family and his (yes, his) view of liberty, authority, power, equality, obligation, and other concepts in political theory.

A feminist or gender-centred approach to the history of political thought began in the 1960s when women were looking for a 'usable past', a history that connected present struggles with previous ones largely neglected by historians, most of whom were male. Feminist historians of political thought sought heroines – and heroes – who had championed the cause of women's rights and related causes. One early anthology (Schneir, 1972) included not only selections from Mary Wollstonecraft, Emma Goldman, and others, but also a section on 'Men as Feminists', which placed Friedrich Engels, John Stuart Mill, and other men in the feminist pantheon. This transgender 'popular front' sought support from all available quarters.

Several specialized studies of particular thinkers appeared during this brief period. Theorists who might roughly be labelled as 'liberal' were singled out for special attention and homage. Melissa Butler (1991) found the 'liberal roots' of feminism in Locke's 'attack on patriarchalism'. Jeremy Bentham was honoured as 'the father of feminism' (Boralevi, 1984: ch. 2) and John Stuart Mill as its 'patron saint' (Williford, 1975). This popular front was short-lived, however, for the father was exposed as a patriarch and something of a misogynist and the patron saint as a closet sinner with feet of clay (Okin, 1979: ch. 9; Pateman, 1988; 1989). The differences between outright misogynists such as Aristotle and Rousseau and their more enlightened liberal brothers were merely matters of degree, not of kind. Male theorists marginalize women by placing them outside the public or civic sphere in which men move and act politically (Elshtain, 1981). In the name of protecting the weak, men have by and large lumped women with children and idiots and have therefore accorded them decidedly less than the rights and obligations of full-fledged citizens. And nowhere are these nefarious moves more evident than in the so-called classics of political thought.

In this angrier – and arguably more accurate – second phase, feminist scholars set out to expose and criticize the misogyny lurking in the works of Plato, Aristotle, Machiavelli, Hobbes, Locke,

Rousseau, Bentham, Mill, and Marx, amongst many others. The public/private dichotomy and the concept of consent in liberal theory are a sham, the social contract is a 'fraternal' construct, and the modern welfare state is a covertly patriarchal institution (Pateman, 1989). Not only are misogyny and patriarchy present in the history of political thought, they can be found in histories of political thought written by males whose interpretations of (say) Locke reproduce the latter's sexism by failing to detect or criticize its presence (1989: ch. 5).

A third phase followed in which the ostensibly civic virtues of men were turned into vices – the hunger for power, domination, or simply showing off – that women supposedly lacked. Men are domineering, women nurturing; men competitive, women co-operative; men think and judge in abstract and universal categories, women in concrete and particular instances; and so on. A new phrase – 'maternal thinking' – was coined to cover this gently militant momism (Ruddick, 1989). On this view, men are absent fathers and domineering patriarchs; women are caring and concerned mothers speaking 'in a different voice' (Gilligan, 1982). This represents something of a return to the 'biology-is-destiny' essentialism and 'functionalism' criticized so vigorously by Okin and others. It also accepts the public/private distinction criticized by Pateman and others, upending and reifying that dichotomy so that the 'private' realm of the family is taken to be superior to the 'public' area of politics, power, aggression, and war (Elshtain, 1987). Thus was Aristotle turned on his head, and *Antigone* reread as a heroic defence of the family against an aggressive and anti-familial political realm (Elshtain, 1981; 1982).

The new 'maternal thinking' – and the new maternalists' approach to the history of political thought, in particular – did not want for critics. Against the maternalists' valorization of the private realm and the celebration of mothering, Mary Dietz (1985) and other feminist critics held out the prospect of an active and engaged civic feminism, or 'citizenship with a feminist face'. This prospect is precluded, or at least dimmed considerably, by inadequate interpretations of Aristotle and other seminal figures from whom feminists might yet learn something of value about politics and citizenship. A 'more generous reading' of Aristotle, Sophocles, and others yields political insights and civic lessons that a cartoon-like inversion cannot hope to match (1985: 29). If feminists are to learn and apply these lessons, they must engage in more nuanced textual analysis and historical interpretation. The Western political tradition is not reducible to an abattoir or a sinkhole of misogyny and other vices; it can, despite its various vices and when properly understood, be a wellspring of political wisdom.

'Straussian' Interpretation

Straussians – followers of the late Leo Strauss (1899–1973) – claim that a canon of works by Plato and a handful of other authors contains the Whole Truth about politics, a truth which is eternal, unchanging, and accessible only to the fortunate few [see further Chapter 3]. Gaining access to this truth requires a special way of reading and of interpreting what one reads.

Strauss was a Jewish refugee from Nazi Germany who emigrated to the United States and subsequently attracted an attentive and loyal band of students and followers. He brought with him the memory of the short-lived Weimar Republic and the rise to power of Hitler and his Nazi thugs. He detested modern liberalism and distrusted liberal democracy, in no small part because Hitler had come to power in a liberal-democratic regime by legal and democratic means. It was therefore unsurprising that Strauss saw the history of modern Western liberal political thought as a story of degeneration and enfeeblement. He and his followers contrasted the vigour of classical Greek and Roman political thought with the resigned *ennui* of slack-minded modern liberal thinkers. Modern liberalism is a philosophy without foundations. Having eschewed any grounding in nature or natural law, modern liberalism, from Hobbes to the present, is reduced to a spineless relativism and is therefore without the normative foundations and philosophical resources to resist the winds of twentieth-century fanaticism blowing from both right and left. The 'crisis of the West', as diagnosed by Oswald Spengler and Carl Schmitt, amongst others, has deep philosophical roots. 'The crisis of our time,' Strauss announced, 'is a consequence of the crisis of political philosophy' (1972: 41). His and his disciples' historical inquiries and textual interpretations attempted to trace the origins and diagnose if not cure the multiple maladies of liberalism, relativism, historicism and scientism that together contribute to 'the crisis of our time'. The present being bankrupt, students of political philosophy must look to the past for guidance; they must be historians but not 'historicists'. Historicism is the relativist doctrine that different ages have different, if not indeed incommensurable, *mentalités* and outlooks; accordingly, we moderns can hardly hope to understand, much less learn from, Plato and other earlier thinkers. The history of political thought, on this historicist view, becomes a vast burial ground instead of what it can and should be – a source of genuine knowledge and a reliable guide for the perplexed (Strauss, 1959).

Knowledge and guidance of the sort we require are not easy to come by, however. They require that we read these 'old books' aright – that we decipher the real meaning of the messages encoded by authors fearful of persecution and wishing to communicate with *cognoscenti* through the ages (Strauss, 1952). For philosophy is dangerous; to espouse its truths in public – in that liberal oxymoron known as the 'marketplace of ideas' – is to risk ridicule and incomprehension, or even persecution, by *hoi polloi*. To communicate with the great thinkers of antiquity is to appreciate how far we have fallen. The rot began in the seventeenth century, with the advent of modern liberalism, and that of Hobbes and Locke especially (Strauss, 1953). They disavowed the ancient wisdom and the older idea of natural law, favouring instead a view of politics founded on security and self-interest. The ancient 'philosophical' quest for the good life was transmuted into the modern 'scientific' search for safety, security, and the accommodation of competing interests.

The 'Straussian' approach to the history of political thought requires the recovery of ancient, or at any rate premodern and preliberal, knowledge of 'political things'. And this in turn requires that one read not only the classics – Plato and Aristotle, in particular – but texts and authors who show us the way back into the labyrinth, e.g. Xenophon, Alfarabi, Maimonides, and others who are rarely (if ever) included in the non-Straussian curriculum (Strauss and Cropsey, 1972; Strauss, 1983). In this way one is sensitized to, and initiated into the secrets of, political philosophy. Most philosophers have written two doctrines – an 'exoteric' one meant for consumption by the uninitiated, and a deeper 'esoteric' doctrine to be decoded and understood by those initiated into the mysteries. A 'Straussian' interpretation involves reading between the lines of the written text, so as to reveal its 'real', albeit hidden, meaning which is communicated, as it were, in a kind of invisible ink. Straussian interpretation owes much to the cabalistic tradition inaugurated by medieval rabbis and scholars, who read religious scripture as texts that had been encoded by authors fearful of persecution and wishing to be understood only by readers who were clean, pure of heart, and initiated into the inner cicle.

Straussian interpretations have been criticized on a number of grounds. One is that they rely on the sort of supposed 'insider's knowledge' that is available only to those who have been initiated into the mysteries of Straussian interpretation (and who in turn conveniently dismiss criticisms by non-Straussian outsiders as being hopelessly ignorant and uninformed). Another is that they assume, without argument or evidence, that the 'real' text does not correspond, point for point, to the written and publicly available 'exoteric' text; the real or 'esoteric' text remains hidden from public view, its meaning inaccessible to the uninitiated and unworthy.

Postmodernist Interpretation

The interpretive standpoint or perspective of postmodernism arises out of 'the postmodern condition' of fragmentation and the failure of systematic philosophies or 'grand metanarratives' such as Hegelianism and Marxism that emerged from the European Enlightenment (Lyotard, 1984).[5] Postmodernism is not a single, unified perspective; nor, still less, is it a systematic philosophy shared by all who call themselves postmodernists. This diffuse group includes Mikhail Bakhtin, Paul de Man, Roland Barthes, Jean-François Lyotard and Jacques Derrida (literary critics and semioticians), Michel Foucault (social historian and genealogist), Jacques Lacan (psychoanalyst), Gaston Bachelard (historian of science), Jean Baudrillard (cultural theorist and critic), Richard Rorty (philosopher), and William E. Connolly (political theorist), among many others. All respond, in different ways, to the postmodern condition of fragmentation, discontinuity, disillusionment, and contingency. The world is not as coherent, continuous and comprehensible as earlier (and especially Enlightenment) thinkers believed. Even our most basic beliefs are historically contingent (Rorty, 1989). *Pace* Hegel and Marx, history has no larger point or 'meaning' discernible via an overarching philosophy of history or 'grand narrative' (Lyotard, 1984). Nor is there progress in human affairs. What is called progress is more often than not an advance in some dominant group's power to oppress another. Advances in technology – in communications technology, say – increase the opportunity for surveillance and suppression (Foucault), and mass media promote one-dimensional views of truth, beauty, normality, and morality that perpetuate and legitimize the modern consumer society and those who profit from it (Baudrillard).

The postmodern sensibility is not a single, stable thing. There are, to simplify somewhat, two main versions of postmodernist interpretation. One derives largely from Nietzsche and Foucault; the other, from Derrida. I shall briefly consider the former before describing the latter.

A Foucauldian approach to interpretation seeks to expose and criticize the myriad ways in which human beings are 'normalized' or made into 'subjects', i.e. willing participants in their own subjugation (Foucault, 1980). Thus a postmodernist perspective on the interpretation of texts typically focuses on the ways in which earlier thinkers – Rousseau or Bentham, for example – contributed ideas to the *mentalité* that paved the way for the creation and legitimation of the modern surveillance society. And conversely postmodernist interpreters look for earlier thinkers who challenged or questioned or undermined these ideas. This Foucauldian approach is well represented by William Connolly's *Political Theory and Modernity* (1988). Connolly begins with the genial suggestion that one view earlier thinkers as collegial contemporaries residing down the hall from one's office. To read their works is like dropping by for a friendly chat (1988: vii). (This is perhaps the amiably unbuttoned postmodern-egalitarian equivalent to Machiavelli's 'entering the ancient courts of ancient men', minus the Florentine's somewhat stringent dress code.) The reader's questions are posed, and criticisms made, from the perspective of the present – that is, of 'modernity' and the constitution of the modern 'subject'.

Given this set of concerns Connolly proposes to reread the history of political thought in a new and presumably more fruitful way. That is, we can see who has contributed to or dissented from the project of modernity and the construction of the modern surveillance society. A postmodernist rereading relocates and realigns earlier thinkers along alto-gether different axes. A postmodernist reading of the history of political thought not only exposes heretofore unsuspected villains, it also reveals heroes who have dared to resist the pressures and processes of 'normalization'. Amongst the former are Hobbes and Rousseau. That the historical Rousseau was exceedingly critical of the historical Hobbes does not matter for a postmodernist read-ing. For we can now see them as birds of a feather, each having extended 'the gaze' ever more deeply into the inner recesses of the human psyche, thereby aiding and abetting the subjugation of modern men and women. Amongst the latter, the Marquis de Sade and Friedrich Nietzsche are particularly prominent. 'We can,' as Connolly contends, 'treat Sade as a dissident thinker whose positive formula-tions are designed to crack the foundations upon which the theories of Hobbes and Rousseau rest' (1988: 73). Whether this design was consciously formulated and put into play by the aristocratic French pornographer is, at best, doubtful; but like other postmodernist interpreters Connolly eschews any concern with such historical niceties as authorial intention.

Despite their emphasis on 'identity' and 'differ-ence', postmodernists are not at all concerned with what John Dunn (1968) has termed the 'historical identity' of works of political theory; nor are they concerned with the differences that earlier thinkers saw amongst themselves. Rousseau hardly saw himself as Hobbes's soulmate – quite the contrary, on Rousseau's own telling – but this does not deter postmodernists from lumping these theorists together as fellow labourers on and contributors to a common project. Whether, or to what extent, such second-guessing is good history or bad remains a matter of considerable controversy.

In Derrida's version of postmodernism, the aim of interpretation is to expose and criticize the arbi-trary or constructed character of claims to truth or knowledge, particularly by examining various binary oppositions or dichotomies such as knower/known, object/representation, text/interpretation, true/false – a process that Derrida (1976) calls 'deconstruction'. According to Derrida, all attempts to 'represent' reality produce, not knowledge or truth, but only different 'representations', none of which can be proven to be better or truer than any other. All social phenomena and forms of human experience – wars, revolutions, relations between the sexes, and so on – exist only through their rep-resentations or 'texts'. And just as a literary text has many possible interpretations, so, says Derrida, do these other texts admit of multiple and contradic-tory 'readings' or interpretations. And all interpre-tations of meaning are in the final analysis 'indeterminate' and 'undecidable'. As Derrida famously puts it, 'there is nothing outside the text' and even within the text its constitutive concepts or 'signifiers' have no stable meaning. Ambiguities within the text only increase with the passage of time and multiple and varied readings, until the text's signifiers float freely and playfully apart, so that the reader – not the author – constructs what-ever meaning the text may be said to have. Thus 'the death of the author' refers not to a physical fact but to an artifact of postmodernist interpretation.

Various criticisms can be levelled against a post-modernist perspective on interpretation. One is that we do sometimes wish, and legitimately so, to know whether something Marx or Mill said was *true*. We will not be helped by being told that true/false is a specious 'binary'. More perniciously, with its empha-sis on diverse, divergent and conflicting 'readings' or interpretations – there are allegedly no facts, only interpretation 'all the way down' – postmodernism is constitutionally unable to distinguish truth from falsehood and propaganda from fact. Thus – to take a particularly dramatic example – the differences, between those who recognize the reality of the Holocaust as reported by survivors and chronicled by careful historians such as Raul Hilberg, and those (mainly neo-Nazis) who deny it ever hap-pened, are, by postmodernist lights, differences of interpretation and not of truth or falsity. But, as critics of postmodernism note, some 'represen-tations' are *mis*representations – or, more bluntly, lies – that serve to conceal and/or legitimate abuses of some human beings by others. A perspective that professes to be unable to tell fact from fiction or true statements from lies is surely unsatisfactory not only from an epistemological but from a moral point of view. Finally, though not least, postmod-ernists place themselves in a logical bind. Derrida, for one, has complained, often and loudly, that some of his critics have *mis*read, *mis*interpreted, and *mis*represented his views. But how can that be, if meanings are indeterminate and authorial intentions are irrelevant in interpreting texts, including those written by Derrida?

Cambridge 'New History'

The Cambridge 'new historians' have, since the 1960s, advanced a distinctive programme of historical research and textual interpretation. Its origins may be traced in part to R. G. Collingwood's (1978 [1939]) approach to the history of philosophy (Skinner, 2001). That history, he said, was not about an eternal but finite set of questions to which different philosophers have proposed different answers. It was, rather, about historically variable problems to which particular philosophers proposed particular answers:

> If there were a permanent problem P, we could ask 'what did Kant, or Leibniz, or Berkeley, think about P?' ... But what is thought to be a permanent problem P is really a number of transitory problems p_1 p_2 p_3 ··· whose individual peculiarities are blurred by the historical myopia of the person who lumps them together under the one name P. (1978 [1939]: 69)

In contrast to those who claim that there are 'perennial' questions or problems in political theory (e.g. Tinder, 1979), Collingwood argued that the questions themselves change in subtle but significant ways. If we are to understand the meaning of something that a particular political theorist wrote, we must first understand the problem he was addressing and attempting to solve.

This Collingwoodian approach informs Peter Laslett's lengthy and learned introduction to his edition of John Locke's *Two Treatises of Government* (1960 [1690]), which restored Locke's political treatise to its political and historical context in the Exclusion Crisis of the early 1680s. Far from having his head in the clouds of philosophical abstraction, Locke was deeply involved in the radical politics of the Shaftesbury circle. By means of some brilliant historical detective work, Laslett showed that Locke's *Two Treatises* had been written nearly a decade earlier than anyone had heretofore supposed and that, far from offering a *post hoc* justification of the Glorious Revolution of 1688–9, Locke was prescribing and legitimizing just that sort of revolutionary action before the fact. Laslett's scholarly sleuthing paved the way for subsequent interpretations of Locke (Dunn, 1969; Tully, 1980; 1993; Ashcraft, 1986) in particular, and of other works of political theory more generally.

If Laslett was circumspect about articulating and defending his method of historical investigation and textual interpretation, others were not. J. G. A. Pocock (1962), John Dunn (1968; 1969; 1996), and – most especially – Quentin Skinner (1969; 2002; Tully, 1989) provided deflationary critiques of traditional 'textbook' approaches to the interpretation of works of political theory. Most of what has heretofore passed as the history of political theory has been insufficiently historical, i.e. concerned with the context and situation in which Locke and others found themselves and the problems with which they dealt [see also Chapter 30].

In his *The Political Thought of John Locke* (1969) Dunn derides psychoanalytic, Marxian, and Straussian interpretations. His is, he says, a 'historical ... account of what *Locke* was talking about, not a doctrine written (perhaps unconsciously) by him in a sort of invisible ink which becomes apparent only when held up to the light (or heat) of the twentieth-century mind'. Dunn rejects the quixotic attempts by 'a succession of determined philosophers mounting their scholastic Rosinantes and riding forth to do battle with a set of disused windmills, or solemnly and expertly flailing thin air'. Dunn's inquiry aims instead.

> to restore the windmill to its original condition, to show how, creakingly but unmistakably, the sails used to turn. Even at the level of preserving ancient monuments it is perhaps a service to recondition these hallowed targets. There seems little purpose in recording hits on a target that has no existence outside our own minds. (1969: x)

The Cambridge historians view works of political theory as forms of political action, grasping the point or meaning of which requires that one recover the intentions of the actor/author and the linguistic resources and conventions available to him or her (Skinner, 2002). A work of political theory is itself a political act or intervention consisting of a series of interconnected actions with words – 'speech acts' in J. L. Austin's sense – that are intended to produce certain effects in the reader: to warn, to persuade, to criticize, to frighten, to encourage, to console, etc. Political theorists have not, by and large, been armchair philosophers engaged in abstract thinking. They have been political actors engaged in high-level propaganda and persuasion on behalf of this or that political cause: the critique (or defence) of democracy; the critique (or defence) of royal absolutism; likewise for religious toleration, resistance and regicide, the French (or other) revolutions, capitalism, the emancipation of slaves and/or women, and so on, through a rather long list of political causes and campaigns. Textual interpretation is largely a matter of restoring a text to the historical context in which it was composed and the question(s) to which it was offered as an answer.

CONCLUSION: PLURALISTIC AND PROBLEM-DRIVEN INTERPRETATION

I come, finally and by way of conclusion, to my own view of these matters. Very briefly: I do not believe that any single method will suffice to answer all the questions we wish to ask of any work of political theory. This nudges me in the direction of eclecticism or, better perhaps, of pluralism. A plurality of approaches and methods is preferable to a more confining mono-methodology that restricts the range of questions we can ask and address. For example, I agree with the Cambridge historians about the importance, indeed the indispensability, of the contexts – intellectual, political and linguistic – in which political theorists write and their texts appear and do their work. But of course these contexts are varied and multiple, encompassing not only the context in which a text was written, but also the successive contexts in which it was received, read, interpreted, criticized, reread, and reinterpreted and perhaps put to uses very different from those the author intended. As Alan Ryan observes:

> Once the essay or book in which we are interested has been put before the public, it takes on a life of its own. Whatever the copyright laws, an author has only a limited control over his own writings. What he writes will have implications which he did not see – implications in the narrow sense of more or less logical inferences from what he says to the consequences of what he says ... Works outlive their authors, and take on lives their writers might be perturbed to see. (1984: 3–4)

Thus authorial intentions, although important, are not in every instance all-important. For certain purposes one may wish to discover, recover, and restate an author's intentions so as to show what he was trying to do in using a certain word or phrase, or constructing a particular argument in a particular way, or even composing an entire treatise. But sometimes we are less interested in Locke, say, than in what subsequent author-actors – Thomas Jefferson, for example, or some modern feminists – made of Locke's text, and quite possibly in ways that Locke would not or even could not have intended, did not foresee, and almost certainly would not have approved of. Because political actions – including the act of writing – often produce unintended consequences, a focus on authorial intention is not always appropriate or helpful.

A second feature of my view is that our interpretive inquiries are problem-driven; that is, we are likely to be less interested in authors, texts, and/or contexts *per se* than in particular *problems* that arise as we attempt to understand them. As a rule we come to Locke or Rousseau not because we want to know 'all about' them or their texts or their times, but because we are puzzled about something. Was Thomas More being serious or satirical in describing his fictional Utopia as 'the best state of the commonwealth'? Did Locke really mean to defend the property rights of a rising bourgeoisie? How are we to understand the role of the 'civil religion' in Rousseau's *Social Contract*? What are the probable sources of John Stuart Mill's feminist sympathies? What was the nature of Marx's debt to Hegel and how did it shape his view of history and human progress?

Such problems can come from any source and be of almost any sort. One might be interested in Mill because one is sympathetic to or highly critical of the liberal tradition, or because one believes that liberty is under threat and that Mill might shed some light on our modern predicament. Or one might wish to assess the (in)adequacy of the Western and liberal conception of tolerance in light of some contemporary question or issue and find it both necessary and desirable to reread and reappraise Locke on toleration and Mill on liberty. In short, the problem-driven 'context of discovery' is wide open, even as the 'context of justification' is rather more restricted.[6] The problems can come from anywhere and be addressed via a variety of strategies; but the (in)adequacy of the resulting interpretive solutions must be assessed according to more stringent scholarly criteria.

The historical study of political theory is, in sum, a problem-solving activity. It takes other interpretations as alternative solutions to some puzzle or problem, and then goes on to assess their adequacy *vis-à-vis* each other and in relation to one's own proposed solution. Interpretation is, so to speak, a kind of triangulation between the text and two (or more) interpretations of it. Hence we cannot but take others' interpretations into account, reappraising their adequacy and value. The activity of rereading, reinterpretation, and reappraisal is not incidental to the practice of political theory but is instead an indispensable – indeed a defining – feature of our craft. Political theory, perhaps more than any other vocation, takes its own past to be an essential part of its present. Its past includes not only a history of theorizing, of great (and not-so-great) books, but a history of commentary and interpretation. It is through the latter that the former are reconsidered, criticized, and re-evaluated – in short, reappraised. The seminal works of political theory are kept alive and vivid – keep their 'classic' status, so to speak – not by being worshipped at academic shrines but, on the contrary, by being carefully reinterpreted and critically reappraised from a variety of interpretive standpoints.

NOTES

1 For a critique and attempted refutation of this interpretation of Rousseau's intentions, particularly as regards his *réligion civile*, see Ball (1995: ch. 5).

2 For further criticisms of Popper's (mis)interpretation of Hegel, see Kaufmann (1972).

3 Happily, this example is drawn not from personal experience but from Hall (1966). Sadly, he adds: 'Unpleasant dreams are more numerous than pleasant ones, and as one gets older the proportion of unpleasant dreams increases' (1966: 40).

4 This judgement may prove premature, as some postmodernists practise a form of psychoanalytic interpretation borrowed from Jacques Lacan. See e.g. Zerilli (1994).

5 For a wider-ranging (and more sympathetic) discussion of postmodernism, see Jane Bennett in this volume [Chapter 4]. See further Dews (2003).

6 I borrow this distinction from Reichenbach (1962: 6–7).

REFERENCES

Ashcraft, Richard (1986) *Revolutionary Politics and Locke's Two Treatises on Government*. Princeton, NJ: Princeton University Press.

Ball, Terence (1987) 'Deadly hermeneutics; or, *Sinn* and the social scientist'. In Terence Ball, ed., *Idioms of Inquiry: Critique and Renewal in Political Science*. Albany, NY: State University of New York Press, ch. 4.

Ball, Terence (1995) *Reappraising Political Theory: Revisionist Studies in the History of Political Thought*. Oxford: Oxford University Press.

Barker, Ernest (1951) *Essays on Government*. Oxford: Oxford University Press.

Boralevi, Lea Campos (1984) *Bentham and the Oppressed*. Berlin: de Gruyter.

Butler, Melissa A. (1991) 'Early liberal roots of feminism: John Locke and the attack on patriarchy'. In Mary Lyndon Shanley and Carole Pateman, eds, *Feminist Interpretations and Political Theory*. University Park, PA: Pennsylvania State University Press.

Collingwood, R. G. (1978 [1939]) *An Autobiography*. Oxford: Oxford University Press.

Connolly, William E. (1988) *Political Theory and Modernity*. Oxford: Oxford University Press.

Crocker, Lester G. (1968) *Rousseau's Social Contract*. Cleveland: Case Western Reserve University Press.

Derrida, Jacques (1976) *Of Grammatology*, trans. Gayatrai Spivak. Baltimore: Johns Hopkins University Press.

Dews, Peter (2003) 'Postmodernism: pathologies of modernity from Nietzsche to Foucault'. In Terence Ball and Richard Bellamy, eds, *The Cambridge History of Twentieth-Century Political Thought*. Cambridge: Cambridge University Press.

Dietz, Mary G. (1985) 'Citizenship with a feminist face: the problem with maternal thinking'. *Political Theory*, 13: 19–37.

Dunn, John (1968) 'The identity of the history of ideas'. *Philosophy* (April): 85–104.

Dunn, John (1969) *The Political Thought of John Locke*. Cambridge: Cambridge University Press.

Dunn, John (1984) *Locke*. Oxford: Oxford University Press.

Dunn, John (1996) *The History of Political Theory*. Cambridge: Cambridge University Press.

Elshtain, Jean Bethke (1981) *Public Man, Private Woman*. Princeton, NJ: Princeton University Press.

Elshtain, Jean Bethke, ed. (1982) *The Family in Political Thought*. Amherst, MA: University of Massachusetts Press.

Elshtain, Jean Bethke (1987) *Women and War*. New York: Praeger.

Erikson, Erik (1958) *Young Man Luther*. New York: Norton.

Erikson, Erik (1969) *Gandhi's Truth*. New York: Norton.

Foucault, Michel (1980) *Power/Knowledge*, ed. Colin Gordon. New York: Pantheon.

Gilligan, Carol (1982) *In a Different Voice*. Cambridge, MA: Harvard University Press.

Hall, Calvin S. (1966) *The Meaning of Dreams*, 2nd edn. New York: McGraw-Hill.

Hegel, G. W. F. (1952 [1820]) *Philosophy of Right*, trans. T. M. Knox. Oxford: Oxford University Press.

Kaufmann, Walter (1972) 'The Hegel myth and its method'. In Alasdair MacIntyre, ed., *Hegel: A Collection of Critical Essays*. Garden City, NY: Anchor.

Kramnick, Isaac (1977) *The Rage of Edmund Burke*. New York: Basic.

Locke, John (1960 [1690]) *Two Treatises of Government*, ed. Peter Laslett. Cambridge: Cambridge University Press.

Lyotard, Jean-François (1984) *The Postmodern Condition: A Report on Knowledge*, trans. Geoff Bennington and Brian Massumi. Minneapolis: University of Minnesota Press.

Macpherson, C. B. (1962) *The Political Theory of Possessive Individualism*. Oxford: Oxford University Press.

Marx, Karl and Friedrich Engels (1947) *The German Ideology*. New York: International.

Mazlish, Bruce (1975) *James and John Stuart Mill: Father and Son in the Nineteenth Century*. New York: Basic.

Okin, Susan M. (1979) *Women in Western Political Thought*. Princeton, NJ: Princeton University Press.

Palmer, Richard E. (1969) *Hermeneutics: Interpretation Theory in Schleirmacher, Dilthey, Heidegger, and Gadamer*. Evanston, IL: Northwestern University Press.

Pateman, Carole (1988) *The Sexual Contract*. Stanford, CA: Stanford University Press.

Pateman, Carole (1989) *The Disorder of Women*. Stanford, CA: Stanford University Press.

Pitkin, Hanna Fenichel (1984) *Fortune is a Woman: Gender and Politics in the Thought of Niccolo Machiavelli*. Berkeley, CA: University of California Press.

Plamenatz, John (1963) *Man and Society*, 2 vols. New York: McGraw-Hill.

Pocock, J. G. A. (1962) 'The history of political thought: a methodological enquiry'. In Peter Laslett and W. G. Runciman, eds, *Philosophy, Politics and Society*, 2nd series. Oxford: Blackwell.

Popper, Karl R. (1963 [1945]) *The Open Society and Its Enemies*, 4th edn. New York: Harper and Row.

Popper, Karl R. (1976) *Unended Quest: An Intellectual Autobiography*. London: Fontana.

Reichenbach, Hans (1961) *Experience and Prediction*. Chicago: University of Chicago Press.

Rorty, Richard (1989) *Contingency, Irony, and Solidarity*. Cambridge: Cambridge University Press.

Rorty, Richard, J. B. Schneewind and Quentin Skinner, eds (1984) *Philosophy in History*. Cambridge: Cambridge University Press.

Ruddick, Sara (1989) *Maternal Thinking: Toward a Politics of Peace*. Boston: Beacon.

Ryan, Alan (1984) *Property and Political Theory*. Oxford: Blackwell.

Schneir, Miriam, ed. (1972) *Feminism: The Essential Historical Writings*. New York: Vintage.

Skinner, Quentin (1969) 'Meaning and understanding in the history of ideas'. *History and Theory*, 8: 3–53. [Reprinted with other methodological essays in Tully, 1989.]

Skinner, Quentin (2001) 'The rise of, challenge to and prospects for a Collingwoodian approach to the history of political thought'. In Dario Castiglione and Iain Hampsher-Monk, eds, *The History of Political Thought in National Context*. Cambridge: Cambridge University Press, ch. 9.

Skinner, Quentin (2002) *Visions of Politics*, 3 vols, vol. I. Cambridge: Cambridge University Press.

Strauss, Leo (1952) *Persecution and the Art of Writing*. Glencoe, IL: Free.

Strauss, Leo (1953) *Natural Right and History*. Chicago: University of Chicago Press.

Strauss, Leo (1959) *What is Political Philosophy?* Glencoe, IL: Free.

Strauss, Leo (1972) 'Political philosophy and the crisis of our time'. In George J. Graham and George W. Carey, eds, *The Post-Behavioral Era*. New York: McKay.

Strauss, Leo (1983) *Studies in Platonic Political Philosophy*, ed. Thomas M. Pangle. Chicago: University of Chicago Press.

Strauss, Leo and Joseph Cropsey, eds (1972) *History of Political Philosophy*, 2nd edn. Chicago: Rand McNally.

Talmon, J. L. (1952) *The Origins of Totalitarian Democracy*. London: Secker and Warburg.

Tinder, Glenn E. (1979) *Political Thinking: The Perennial Questions*, 3rd edn. Boston: Little, Brown.

Tully, James (1980) *A Discourse on Property: John Locke and His Adversaries*. Cambridge: Cambridge University Press.

Tully, James, ed. (1989) *Meaning and Context: Quentin Skinner and His Critics*. Princeton, NJ: Princeton University Press.

Tully, James (1993) *An Approach to Political Philosophy: Locke in Contexts*. Cambridge: Cambridge University Press.

Williford, Miriam (1975) 'Bentham on the rights of women'. *Journal of the History of Ideas*, 36: 167–76.

Zerilli, Linda (1994) *Signifying Woman: Culture and Chaos in Rousseau, Burke and Mill*. Ithaca, NY: Cornell University Press.

3

Straussian Approaches to the Study of Politics

THOMAS L. PANGLE

THE ORIGINATING IMPULSE AND AGENDA

The studies that fall under this rubric take their inspiration from Leo Strauss's (1899–1973) critique of twentieth-century political thought and action. Born into a Jewish orthodox community in rural Wilhelminian Germany, Strauss was initially drawn to the Marburg neo-Kantian school. There he encountered a purportedly rigorous foundation for progressive liberal constitutionalism, and an interpretation of Judaism as being or as culminating in 'the religion of reason'. But Strauss soon found himself unable to deny the devastating power of Nietzsche's, and then Heidegger's and Rosenzweig's, ruthless exposure of the groundlessness, and hence the ultimately nihilistic and degrading spiritual consequences, of the claims of Western rationalism (1965: 7–8, 11, 15, 21; 1983: chs 1, 7, 15).

The 'Crisis of the West'

In this light, the Great Tradition of Western rationalism stands revealed as in the last stages of terminal illness. For that tradition lived through the mutually invigorating dialogue between competing versions of the claim to ascend from subjective cultural opinion to objective verifiable knowledge of final moral Truth. All such purported 'truths', and the very attempt to ascend toward such truth, have become incredible. Western humanism is left defended only by 'theories of justice' that explicitly abandon all pretensions to foundational and permanent truth. These 'theories' are thus at bottom indistinguishable

from subtle ideology defending beloved inherited (and admittedly transient) cultural prejudices. No sooner had World War II ended than the defeat of fascism, and the hoped-for defeat or neutralization of Marxism, was authoritatively interpreted as the victory of a dogmatic historicist relativism, issuing the following fiat: 'thou shalt embrace and serve secular individualistic and egalitarian norms which are ultimately unjustified and unjustifiable, but which reign historically, for the foreseeable future, on account of economic, technological, and military power' (Bloom, 1975; Strauss, 1971: introduction; 1989: chs 1, 2).

Strauss was incapable of surrendering his intellectual integrity to this 'manifest and deliberate collectivization or coordination of thought' (Strauss and Kojève, 1991: 27). Moreover, he anticipated the 'postmodernist' recognition that this questionably 'liberal' historicist relativism lacked any coherent defence against the more honestly authoritarian counter-commands of militant illiberal religious orthodoxy (cf. Strauss, 1965, with Owen, 2001) [see further Chapter 4].

Strauss's Response

Strauss came to grips with the crisis by launching a vast research project to explore meticulously the possibility of recovering, from the greatest rationalist political philosophers of the past, an objectively defensible conception of and standard for intellectual freedom and civic dignity. His initial studies of Spinoza, Hobbes, and Calvin (Strauss, 1930) uncovered, as the root of the 'crisis', reason's apparently insuperable failure to dispose of the 'fundamental alternative' posed by the claimed experiential testimony of miraculous divine revelation, validating the comprehensive 'supra-rational' laws elaborated in sacred Scriptures. Following Spinoza, Strauss termed this all-embracing challenge 'the theologico-political problem', and this problem, Strauss wrote late in his life, 'has remained *the* theme of my studies' (1965; 1996: III, 8).

The rediscovery of classical rationalism and of 'esoteric writing'

Increasing dissatisfaction with Spinoza's arguments against Maimonides helped propel Strauss back to a startling encounter with the medieval rationalism elaborated in the Arab-speaking world by Alfarabi and his successors. There Strauss discovered a forgotten re-enactment of authentic classical political philosophy – a re-enactment that exposed the shallowness and naïveté of all accepted scholarly interpretations of the classics. Alfarabi, Avicenna, Averroës, Halevi, and Maimonides taught Strauss to recognize that the Socratic enterprise is centred on a mode of conversational argumentation ('dialectic') which, while forging an impregnable[1] foundation for philosophy or science, exposes the theoretical way of life to persecution – a persecution that is understandable, since Socratic or 'zetetic' scepticism threatens to corrode grounding opinions essential to healthy, especially republican, civic spirit. The practical response is 'Socratic rhetoric': an intricate theory of communication, oral and written, by which otherwise potentially subversive philosophic inquiry is carried on through painstakingly wrought veils that contribute to enhancing and deepening civic life, while they entice the most capable young toward radical questioning.

It thus transpires that all conventional scholarly interpretations of classical political philosophy fail to appreciate the self-consciously strategic relation of that philosophy to its historical context. Strauss suggests that the obfuscation of the nature of 'esoteric writing' (and hence of the true, radical substance of classical philosophy) began to occur through the tradition of Christian Platonism and scholasticism. But complete ignorance has set in, he observes, only under the reign of the twin (and contradictory) late modern dogmas: on the one hand, the 'taking for granted' of 'the essential harmony between thought and society or between intellectual progress and social progress'; and, on the other hand, the unquestioned assumption that all thought, even philosophy, is determined and decisively limited by its historical epoch.[2]

Ancients versus moderns

Strauss's recovery of the lost genuine theory and practice of classical political rationalism (which 'is liberal in the original sense of the term') enables a restoration of the true meaning of the 'great alternative' seen in modern rationalism and modern 'liberalism' (1968: x and chs 1–3). The 'moderns', beginning with Machiavelli, having lost sight of the hidden core of Socratism, launched a very different 'project', with a different kind of 'esoteric writing'. The 'moderns' employed partially disguised propagandistic rhetoric to promulgate new doctrines of justice and virtue aimed at a cultural revolution that would transform the world so as to make secular reason actually rule society (1958: 172–3, 295–8; 1971: 166–79; 1995: introduction). But this 'Enlightenment' required or consisted in a drastic 'lowering of the goals' of both republicanism and philosophy. On the one hand, civic virtue has become chiefly if not simply instrumental to the pursuit of a freedom conceived as 'individuality' that is 'unredeemed and unjustified' – and that is in fact consumed by what Max Weber 'rightly identified' as the 'spirit of capitalism': unlimited material gain achieved by endless acquisitive labour, or 'the joyless quest for joy' (1971: 5–6, 60, 246–51, 294, 323). On the other hand, philosophy, which was 'originally' the 'humanizing quest for the eternal order', has 'since the seventeenth century' become 'thoroughly politicized', 'a weapon and hence an instrument' (1971: 34).

Strauss expresses his deep admiration for the 'intrepidity of thought', the 'grandeur of vision', the 'graceful subtlety of speech', and the profound political astuteness or 'public spirit' that characterize the great modern project, at least in its philosophic originators (1958: 13, 120–2, 207–8, 218, 252–3, 289–90; 1971: 177, 206–7). He readily acknowledges the magnitude of the project's world-historical achievements. But he argues that modernity, taken as a whole in all its unfolding richness, represents an estrangement from 'erotic' human nature as revealed or confirmed by Socratic dialectics (1959: 55; 1971: 175–6, 201–2). Strauss's complex diagnosis of the roots or causes points a path through the crisis – 'the tentative or experimental' revival of Socratic political philosophy – and our own original application, to our unprecedented form of society, of the Aristotelian political science and liberal education that was the fullest civic expression of Socratic philosophy (1964: 11; 1968: chs 1 and 2).

AN ARISTOTELIAN SCIENCE OF MODERN POLITICS: THE THEORETICAL FRAMEWORK

The Straussian philosophy of social science[3] begins from the civic premise that a responsible science of politics should be concerned to promote political health or fitness. But then political *philosophy* must guide, rather than be separated from, sound political *science*. For political philosophy pursues the essential questions, what is civic health, what is justice or the common good, what is human flourishing? Yet this pursuit in its proper form – the model for which is Plato's *Laws* together with Aristotle's paired *Ethics* and *Politics* – takes its bearings by first listening with docility to, and then questioning, clarifying, and critically deepening (and thus defending) the 'political *wisdom*' of respected and experienced citizens. For sound guiding principles of civic action are known, if not perfectly known, to reflective 'common sense', prior to and independent of theoretical science or philosophy. Strauss goes so far as to declare that 'the sphere governed by prudence' is 'in principle self-sufficient'. He immediately concedes, however, that in fact this sphere is ceaselessly breached by perplexing assaults from 'false doctrines' that claim to provide answers to questions that are 'the most important questions' – about the coherence of justice and about humanity's situation and fate within the whole. These questions 'are not stated, let alone answered, with sufficient clarity by practical wisdom itself'. It is the need to have these questions, and the challenges that raise them, disposed of that makes 'practical *wisdom*' dependent, *de facto* though not *de jure* on political philosophy as 'practical *science*'.

'The Pit beneath the Natural Cave'

Beginning in the medieval period, and reaching a pitch in our time, this defensive task takes on a new complexity unknown to the classics. As Strauss puts it, revising a famous Platonic metaphor, the emergence of 'pseudo-philosophy' has cast the human spirit into 'a pit beneath the natural cave' (1952: 154–8). The cultural revolution effected by 'modern' political philosophy has immensely deepened this problem, by making it appear that theory must be the *source*, as well as the guide, of practical norms. As a result, common sense has been pervasively contaminated by a parade of competing, philosophic or theoretical, moral doctrines (Hobbes, Locke, Rousseau, Smith, Kant, Hegel, Marx, utilitarianism, etc.). The successive failure of these leaves common sense, in our time, sliding into still more self-alienating enthralment to the historicist-relativistic 'scientific study of politics', which looks to mathematized and materialistic physics and biology as a model, or as a source of 'method' and 'epistemology'. This move is not without reason, since 'mathematical science' is the sole part of modern rationalism that has not undergone disgraceful self-destruction. Yet 'social science' goes

widely astray in so far as it looks to modern science as anything more than a subordinate, if (within its proper narrow bounds) marvellously effective, tool for gathering and establishing correlations among quantifiable data [see further Chapter 5]. For the modern scientific method in all its versions has no eyes to see what is in fact the critical factor in all human 'behaviour': humanity's passionate concern with *to kalon* – with self-respect, with dignity, with the human as a rational and thus free being capable of dedication, devotion, and even sacrifice, for the sake of causes perceived as just and as thereby partaking of transcendent or eternal value.

The *Politeia* or Regime

This moral core of the human as the 'political animal' (Aristotle, *Politics*, Book 3, ch. 6) is the deepest source of the contest that keeps politics ceaselessly in motion. For, as we learn vividly in Book 3 of Aristotle's *Politics*, the moral virtues, distilled in the *Ethics* as the core of true dignity, manifest themselves politically in forms distorted by passions – evil, crass, and sublime. The claim to uphold and advance some notion of justice, of fairness and the common good, is always at the heart of political action; but this claim is always put forth, justice is always in practice defined, in a partisan and biased spirit. Political life is riven by competition among adherents of conflicting 'regimes' (*politeiai*) – democracy and oligarchy and aristocracy and monarchy and theocracy and so forth, in their various versions and even mixtures. What is at stake becomes evident only when one recognizes, with Aristotle, that each 'regime' stands for, and as it gains victory imposes, a specific moral ranking of the various human types and their excellences (the priests, the warriors, the proletarians, the yeoman farmers, the merchants and businessmen, etc., etc.). The ranking is clearly expressed by the degree of civic authority or share in rule assigned to each human class or type by each of the competing regimes. Each such ranking, each 'regime', lays a claim to justice that implies a more or less severe moral condemnation of contrasting and competing 'regimes' and their rankings. The regime, as the outcome of the struggle over which human type or types will be morally preponderant, shapes the 'way of life' in each society more than any other formative factor except for nature itself. The contest among competing aspirants to define the regime is then the supremely important contest in human existence, and a political science worthy of the name must keep this most fundamental political fact squarely in view (Strauss, 1959: 33–6; 1964: 30–5, 45–9; 1971: 135–45). One may make the same point by declaring that genuine social science is political science – and its self-conscious subordinates, political economy, political psychology, political history, etc. All social sciences, in our time, which claim autonomy from political science fundamentally misunderstand the nature of human society.

A sound science of humanity will make the conflict over the regime, or among competing regimes, or among competing versions of the existing regime, its cynosure. It will view the regime contest in the light of the 'best regime simply', the regime that would be dedicated to the maximum possible human fulfilment. It will do so knowing that, while the best regime must be articulated as a standard, it cannot be regarded as a practical goal. In fact, the full articulation of the best regime reveals it to be itself riven by insoluble tensions – above all, between the highest, intellectual virtues and the civic virtues. These tensions clarify the limitations on all political life, and make precise the intractability of human nature (Bartlett, 1994; Bruell, 1994; Strauss, 1959: 34–5; 1964: ch. 2; Strauss and Kojève, 1991: 187–8). None of the actual forms of democracy, oligarchy, monarchy, tyranny, theocracy, etc. (and mixtures thereof) stand for more than a partial and dimly perceived version of justice and the good life. Yet each, by the same token, is defined above all by its dedication to some dim conception of the just and good life. The political scientist's proper role in the conflict among regimes and over the regime is neither that of a partisan nor that of a neutral 'scientific' observer engaging in merely 'comparative' politics. The political scientist's proper role is that of an unofficial umpire or judge. The best example of such a political science as applied to modern democracy may be said to be Tocqueville's *Democracy in America* [see further Chapter 5].

The gravest dangers for any particular regime are always those least noted by its partisans because those dangers are inherent in the unchecked supremacy of the regime's own favourite and dominant moral spirit – and because, as a consequence, those who dare to prescribe the needed antidotes will almost inevitably be suspected of being 'anti-regime' (Aristotle, *Politics*, Book 5, ch. 9 end). Now since the political scientist, as a loyal citizen, will exert his chastising scientific efforts first and foremost on his own regime, in its competing strands and in controversy with its most serious international and historical competitors, this means that the genuine political scientist will almost inevitably incur moral opprobrium in his own community.

In modern democracy, the courageously loyal political scientist will, imitating Tocqueville, limn the democratic dangers to democracy by reminding of aristocracy's and monarchy's contrasting moral and spiritual and civic strengths. He will not allow it to be forgotten that democracy 'is meant to be an aristocracy which has broadened into a universal aristocracy'; that 'liberal education is the ladder by which we try to ascend from mass democracy to democracy as originally meant'. He will endure, even as a badge of pride, the odium that attends the democratic political scientist who, if he is the genuine article, relentlessly points, in a reformist spirit, to the dangers inherent in the unchecked advance of the treasured moral principles of equality and individual liberty and popular sovereignty and economic 'growth': in Strauss's lapidary words, 'we are not permitted to be flatterers of democracy precisely because we are friends and allies of democracy' (1968: 4–5, 10–25).[4]

AN ARISTOTELIAN SCIENCE OF MODERN POLITICS: THE EXECUTION

The grounding expressions of Straussian neo-Aristotelian political science are necessarily polemical: in our epoch, common sense has first to be sprung free from the thought control exercised by the established intelligentsia of left and right. Leading the way are Strauss's dissection of Max Weber's 'nihilist' self-contradictions, and Herbert J. Storing's exposure of the debilitating incoherences in the Nobel laureate Herbert Simon's theory of decision and management (Storing, 1962: ch. 2; Strauss, 1971: ch. 2). But, while this kind of foundational criticism has continued, expanding to meet new manifestations of the relativistic and historicist 'scientific study' of politics (Ceaser, 1990; Mansfield, 1978; 1991: chs 1 and 11), there has been erected on these foundations a substantial literature exemplifying an alternative analysis, including the proper employment of the new quantitative tools modern science makes available.

Political Economy

A constructive sequel to Storing's critique of Simon is Steven E. Rhoads's (1985) sympathetic analysis of 'the economist's view of the world'. This book delineates the moral as well as empirical strengths of microeconomic, welfare economic, and benefit–cost analyses, while showing precisely how those very strengths risk hypertrophic distortion of their subject matter if they do not submit to governance by political philosophy, and especially by moral, cultural, and psychological categories made available in Straussian explications of Plato, Rousseau, and Tocqueville (for illuminating specific applications, see Rhoads, 1993). In general, Straussian engagement with contemporary economic thinking has insisted on the need for continual re-encounter with the texts of the philosophic founders of modern 'political economy' (Hobbes, Locke, Montesquieu, Hume, Smith, Ferguson, etc.), on the grounds that in those texts alone can one find, and truly test the cogency of, justifications for the most basic (and controversial, nay deeply problematic) moral commitments uncritically and often unconsciously at work in contemporary economics and so-called 'rational choice' (e.g. Danford, 1980; Lerner, 1987: ch. 6; Nichols and Wright, 1990: chs 1–3, 5, 10; Shulsky, 1991b). In this enterprise, and in the retrieval, from the ashen hands of conventional historicist scholarship, of the true but half-hidden positions of thinkers such as Locke, there is some overlap between Straussian and the most sophisticated Marxist scholarship (Macpherson, 1962; 1973; Strauss, 1983: ch. 13).

Political Psychology

Horwitz's searing critique of Lasswell's Freudian-inspired science of leadership 'personality' (Storing, 1962: ch. 4) has been carried forward in Straussian criticism of the application of scientific-psychological 'personality' typologies to the American presidency. Truly empirical psychology of leadership, Straussians contend, has to rise to the difficult challenge of evaluating the virtues and vices, the *moral character*, of leaders as leaders; for character is the true phenomenon underlying and generating the epiphenomena of 'personality' and 'style' with which contemporary political psychology is (to its discredit) obsessed. And acutely significant in this regard is painstaking analysis of the meaning and role played by the longing for eternity that expresses itself as the love of fame (Bessette and Tulis, 1981: chs 8–9; Frisch and Stevens, 1971; McNamara, 1999; Ruderman, 1997a; 1997b).

H. Donald Forbes's (1985) work has shown how the Straussian-inspired deployment of the Platonic regime psychology adumbrated in the eighth book of Plato's *Republic* can provide the basis for a sound critical revision of the Frankfurt school's political personality studies and their implications. Forbes's later (1997) work on ethnic conflict, testing systematically the famous 'contact hypothesis' (roughly speaking, the hypothesis that increased familiar intermingling between ethnic groups promotes greater mutual acceptance), is exemplary of Straussian employment of quantitative methods, where appropriate, in the execution of a political psychology and sociology whose horizon is explicitly Montesquieuian in human breadth and moral depth.

The Science of Regimes

The Straussian approach subordinates, however, the study of quantifiable mass effects, opinion, and 'behaviour' to the scrutiny of writings, speeches, and recorded utterances, authored by leaders at various levels but especially at the highest, when they are engaged in turning points of action – and in the formative past of a regime or nation as much as or more than in the immediate present. The working hypothesis is that the conceptions shaping the evolution of a political society's way of life are most visibly in play where those with access to rule, or seeking such access, articulate and fight over moral goals, principles, and priorities, in response to defining problems and crises.

Communist regimes

The paramountcy, as shaping causal forces, of struggles over the regime holds even in tyrannic regimes. Straussian analysis stresses the supreme importance of the need never to lose sight of the moral inferiority of tyrannies, despite the partial and disquieting advantages they may possess. But even tyrants cannot escape the natural and overriding human need for justification. Straussian study of the inner workings of tyrannies focuses here on the (often Byzantine) contests among aspirants to embody the regime's leading human qualities. These competitions take on a new, characteristic complexity in modernity, in as much as tyranny manifests itself in a new, distinctly modern, form: modern tyranny tends to be 'ideological', or to understand itself as guided by some comprehensive theoretical analysis of the human situation. The struggle over the regime is therefore simultaneously a struggle over what is to be the orthodox interpretation of the justifying ideological theory. This characteristic of modern tyranny was exhibited most powerfully in communism. Paradigmatic Straussian studies are Victor Baras's (1975) account of the crucial stages in Ulbricht's, and thereby East Germany's, career of self-definition; Myron Rush's (1958; 1965; 1974; 1993) analyses of the evolution of the post-Stalinist Soviet and East European regimes, centring on the succession struggles in the leadership; and Charles H. Fairbanks's (1993; 1995a; 1995b; 1997) explorations of the reasons for the decline, fall and aftermath of the Soviet Union.[5]

International relations

Straussian study of foreign policy and international relations (including international law) has been rooted in a revolution in Thucydidean interpretation, bringing out the close kinship between Thucydides and the Socratics. The predominant pre-Straussian notion of Thucydides among political theorists is expressed in Michael Walzer's still-influential treatment (1977: ch. 1), which dismisses Thucydides as representative of a 'realism' whose 'purpose' is to make moral 'discourse about particular cases appear to be idle chatter'. Strauss and his followers have executed sustained exegesis in arguing that, on the contrary, Thucydides' central theme is an exploration, unrivalled in its depth and lack of sentimentality, of the true meaning and full force of justice in political speech and action at its peak (Bolotin, 1987; Bruell, 1974; Orwin, 1994; Strauss, 1964: ch. 3). Straussian Thucydidean studies have exposed contemporary so-called 'realist' and 'neorealist' international theory as unrealistic in its failure to take into account how drastically foreign policy and international behaviour varies with the varying regimes and their competing moral outlooks (Ahrensdorf, 1997; Forde, 1995; Hassner, 1995; Pangle and Ahrensdorf, 1999: chs 7–8; Shulsky, 1991a) [see further Chapter 22]. As an antistrophe, we find a line of sympathetic but sceptical Straussian examinations of the strengths and weaknesses of modern philosophic, especially Kantian, international idealism – in practice as well as in theory (Forde, 1998; Hassner, 1961; 1997; Knippenberg, 1989; Pangle and Ahrensdorf, 1999: ch. 6; Plattner, 1984; Tarcov, 1984b; 1989a; 1989b). Last but not least, Francis Fukuyama (1992), inspired by Strauss, but breaking with him, has made famous the provocative thesis that Strauss's dialogic antagonist, Alexandre Kojève, in fact set forth the true (Hegelian) philosophic account that explains the world-historical meaning of the fall of Soviet communism and thus the fated dispensation of the centuries upon which we are entering.[6]

The American Regime

At the heart of American politics, in the Straussian view, is the Constitution and its evolution – viewed as the working out of the basic principles enunciated in the Revolution and above all in the Declaration of Independence. To discover the Constitution's full meaning as the basic law of the regime is to achieve clarity about the overarching moral goals, the way of life, the human types, that the Constitution fosters – and, conversely, those that it discourages. Now the study of the Founding epoch is especially revealing in these regards – and not only because we may observe the foundations in the act of being laid. In the American case the Founding was blessed with leaders – and opponents – of unusual wisdom and articulateness. Not only do these men of action speak for themselves, but they point us with some explicitness to their philosophic teachers, above all (though by no means exclusively) Locke and Montesquieu. The Founding is of course not the end, it is only the pregnant beginning of the story. But the Founding sets the horizon within which move subsequent developments – even when they verge on 'refoundings' (the Jeffersonian and Jacksonian movements, the struggles over slavery and race, the response to the Great Depression, the Cold War). The Founding exhibits unsolved and even insoluble problems that keep the regime in disquieting motion. The scientist of American government will continually miss the deep (and contestable) presuppositions and entailments of the system he is studying if he fails constantly to recur to a meticulous and meditative reflection on the writings and especially the debates of the Founding period, situating them in contrast with the great alternative philosophies of republicanism ancient and modern [see further Chapter 13].[7]

This means, to be sure, that the neo-Aristotelian political scientist will soon become aware of a deep and half-hidden complexity in the nature of the 'regime' under the conditions of modern political life – shaped as that life is, largely though by no means completely, by modern political theory. For one can say that it is the deliberate intention of modern political philosophy to try to truncate the regime character of politics: to replace reliance on human character, and therefore overt encouragement of specific character traits, with reliance on institutions, and on the minimal modifications of human behaviour and outlook required by a civic virtue that is principally 'self-interest rightly understood'. Paradoxically, the aim constantly pursued, with enormous political and legal energy, by modern liberal politics at its deepest or most self-conscious is the depoliticization of human existence. The modern liberal regime seeks to submerge its own regime character: the distinctive way of life and the restricted range of human types forcibly encouraged by liberal democracy are meant to appear to be the product of an openness to the greatest diversity of ways and types. But the distinctive human ways and characteristics actually fostered – tolerance, competitive and acquisitive entrepreneurial talent, the privatization of religious and moral demands, egalitarianism and individualism, etc. – have never been sufficient to provide the civic virtue needed in a republican form of government, even in a liberal republican form. And the various complex institutional arrangements suggested by a succession of great modern theorists (federalism, representation, separation of powers, the party system, etc.) have never gone as far as intended in obviating the need for statesmanship of a high order as well as a public spirited citizenry. So a major and persisting problematic of Straussian study has been the investigation and explanation of how precisely the modern liberal project has had to be modified, or has had to modify itself, in an attempt to incorporate essential or abiding demands of humanity's political nature, made most visible in classical republican life and thought (see esp. Diamond, 1992: ch. 21; Mansfield, 1965a; 1965b; 1971; 1978: ch. 1; 1991: Part Three).

The judiciary

Straussian approaches to American government are distinguished by the importance given to the observation that the higher judiciary, in the American system, is uniquely delegated to deliver a publicly reasoned justification of the laws through which, above all else, the regime evolves. An Aristotelian perspective on the regime context spotlights, however, the deeply problematic fact that this is an essentially aristocratic function uneasily situated within, and meant to temper, a basically democratic regime. The practice of 'judicial review' therefore requires a delicate and circumspect judicial prudence. The most fruitful focus of study of the American judiciary is, accordingly, not the 'judicial behaviour' so fashionable in 'scientific studies' (seeking to discover the sub-jurisprudential and therefore supposedly more predictable sources of judicial decisions) but rather judicial *reasoning* linked to judicial *statesmanship*. The task of sound political scientific study of the judiciary is that of examining the strengths and weaknesses of the *arguments*, in light of their civic implications and effects (discerned partly by looking to later political and legal consequences). This entails simultaneous evaluative scrutiny of the dialogue between the judicial pronouncements and the words and deeds of the various legislatures and executives (Landy and Levin, 1995; Melnick, 1983; 1994; Rabkin, 1989). Of the greatest importance are some of the earliest opinions, especially by Marshall (in sharp contrast to Taney's *Dred Scott* decision): these not only laid the groundwork of American constitutional jurisprudence, but were compelled to take far less for granted than is the case with contemporary jurisprudence. Straussians, led by Walter Berns, are not hesitant to argue the superior wisdom of those early opinions – especially as regards their grasp of the nature of judicial review, of the meaning of original intent, of the legal and political status of religion, and of the reasons that justify (and thus define) freedom of speech as well as other basic rights (Berns, 1957; 1984: chs 2 and 15; 1987; Brubaker, 1987; Canavan, 1971; Clor, 1969; Faulkner, 1968; Frisch and Stevens, 1971; Malbin, 1981).

The executive

A natural leitmotif of Straussian study of American politics is critical evaluation of those presidents and would-be presidents in the course of whose careers the regime has undergone severe and often transformative testing. Here are illuminated the evolving potentials and limits of the office, and its relation to the rest of the constitutional regime. A distinctive theme of the Straussian study of presidential *selection* has been a quest to recover or discover institutional and civic resources that might help check the regime's proclivity to drift toward more narrowly power-centred, and more demagogic, conceptions of the presidency. Part of this effort has been the retrieval and development of the Hamiltonian understanding of the presidency as a responsible republican substitute for monarchy. Looming large here are accounts, especially Harvey C. Mansfield's, of the evolution of the modern constitutional executive out of the struggle of the great philosophers to 'tame' Machiavelli's conception of 'the prince' – and to find a substitute for Aristotelian monarchy, as developed especially by Marsilius of Padua [on Marsilius, see further Chapter 25]. In unpacking this dimension of the evolution of modern constitutional theory, light is shed not only on the nature of the presidency (as well as parliamentary leadership), but also on some of the conundrums of the modern philosophers' attempts to overcome the limitations of the rule of law and institutionalized rationality (Bessette and Tulis, 1981; Diamond, 1992: chs 4 and 15; Flaumenhaff, 1992; Frisch and Stevens, 1971; Mansfield, 1989; 1991: chs 2–5 and 9; 1996: ch. 13; McNamara, 1999: chs 3 and 4; Milkis, 1993: chs 3–6; Stourzh, 1970; Storing, 1995: chs 18–22; Tarcov, 1990).

Straussians by no means ignore the enormous role played by the more anonymous and undramatic lower echelons of the modern executive – 'bureaucratic' politics or 'public administration'. But Straussian approaches typically protest against, and try to repair, the scholarly tendency to pay insufficient heed to how much the natures of bureaucracies are decisively differentiated by the distinctive moral goals set by the particular regime – and by political struggles over defining the regime – in which bureaucratic politics operate (Fairbanks, 1987; 1993: 53–6; Melnick, 2000; Shulsky, 1991a: ch. 6). Following Storing's lead, Straussian study of public administration in the American regime looks for ways to foster a distinctly American version of a 'higher' or 'senior' civil service akin to that of the United Kingdom: bureaucrats responsive to the commands of the elected government, who yet pose a moral counterweight because they are endowed with an ethos not of mere technical competence and 'neutrality', but of self-conscious responsibility to and for the overarching national interest (Lawler, Schaefer and Schaefer, 1997; Storing, 1995: chs 13–17).

The legislative branch and political parties

Paradigmatic for the Straussian perspective on Congress is Joseph Bessette's (1994) insistence on the *deliberative* nature of legislative bodies. This approach opposes the fashionable analytic tendency to reduce congressional deliberations to 'decisions' that express nothing more than the outcome of the perhaps quantifiable sum of the vectors of the tug and pull of interest-group struggle and the drive for re-election. Without by any means denying the strength of these powerful forces, Straussian analysis lays out the manifold evidence for a process in which reasoning in quest of compromises that serve the common good can supervene to mediate and to elevate the ever-active, narrow and self-serving interest struggle (Landy and Levin, 1995; Melnick, 1983; 1994). The broad-based political parties are shown to be major contributors to the deliberative dimension of the interest-group struggle, and one can characterize Straussian political science as evincing unusually high respect for the two-party system in the United States, and even for rather unpopular practices (such as party-controlled redistricting) and institutions (such as the electoral college) that arguably help maintain or strengthen the major parties.[8] Wilson Carey McWilliams (2000) and others have highlighted the importance of parties in fostering an otherwise weak and threatened 'fraternal', local or decentralized, and participatory dimension of democracy. Harry V. Jaffa's interpretation (1965: ch. 1) of the evolution of party realignment has shown how the two-party system, strangely unforeseen at the Founding, is rooted in (though surely not wholly explained by) the irrepressible if usually muted and, on the whole, healthy continuation of regime differences, or of fundamental debate over the regime. This same analysis serves to underline the important function played in American civic development by dissenters from the existing regime (Storing, 1962: ch. 3 and 319, 323; 1995: chs 12, 13; Fairbanks, 1997).

The contribution made by dissenters

Indeed, radical 'unofficial' opposition, and the moral challenges it forces upon the reigning regime, are spotlighted in the Straussian optic both as shapers of regime evolution and, even when the dissent fails, as uniquely revealing indicators of the nature of the regime. It is no accident that the biggest work of Straussian study of American political thought is Storing's seven-volume *Complete Anti-Federalist* (1981), or that the single most influential volume of Straussian 'American politics' is Jaffa's (1959) account of the intellectual evolution of the two great radicals, Douglas and Lincoln – and their decisive debates, in which and through which the American regime was transformed forever, or indeed refounded. McWilliams (1983; 1984; 1987), pre-eminent among others influenced by Strauss, has limned the contribution made by America's Puritan-based religious traditions, especially in their dissent from secular liberalism, to moderating the atomization that haunts modern democracy.[9] Straussian study of the American regime has from the beginning brought to the fore the challenge to the regime's moral self-definition posed by the core problem of race, and has made it a major project to recover African-American theorists, pre-eminently Frederick Douglass, but also theorists of 'Black Nationalism' and 'Black Power', in their dialogue with theorists of assimilation.[10]

Interest groups, civil society, and cultural criticism

The characteristic Straussian approach to the study of interest-group politics and of 'civil society' relies on a new exegesis of Tocqueville's *Democracy in America*. This interpretation, opposing or subordinating more conventional 'sociological' readings, insists on the philosophically inspired, and partially Aristotelian, character of what Tocqueville calls his 'new science of politics' (Ceaser, 1990; Koritansky, 1986; Lawler, 1993; Manent, 1982; Mansfield, 1991: chs 13, 14; McWilliams, 1992). The light cast by this science, so understood, does more than help illuminate how 'associations' in modern democracy can function, in interaction with local government and political party participation, to sublimate private group interest into public interest. More specifically and controversially, what becomes prominent in Straussian–Tocquevillean societal analysis is the vacuum of meaning and sources of dedication that looms as the greatest threat to the human spirit in American democracy. Seen from the Straussian–Tocquevillean perspective, the challenge of filling this vacuum calls for strengthening organized religion as well as organized parties, for preserving as much as can be preserved of traditional family mores and structure, and for the revival of democratic liberal education informed by a concern more characteristic of aristocracy – that is, spiritual deepening and intellectual refinement (as well as character development and civic spirit) (Clor, 1996; McWilliams, 1987; Melzer, Weinberger and Zinman, 1998; Schwartz, 2000; Yarbrough, 1998).

The most dramatic application of this perspective to cultural criticism of contemporary democracy is Alan Bloom's (1987) explosive bestseller, whose impact proved the potential of Straussian political theory to reach out and speak with arresting power to the spiritual perplexities of the broad mass of the reading public in our age. Presenting a dedicated teacher's 'first-person' report on the soulless disintegration of the liberal arts in the university, Bloom offered, as an alternative, a vision of a liberating, erotic encounter with the Great Books, whose deepest unifying theme he explicated through a sustained meditation on the history of political philosophy since Socrates. (What was most original in Bloom's scholarship was his pioneering readings of great works of literature as vehicles for affording vivid access, in our parochially secular-democratic age, to the great alternatives among regimes, among types of human excellence, and among experiences of erotic passion and thought.)[11] Bloom argued that the modern democratic hopes for participating in such a truly liberal, because liberating, education are being washed away by profoundly anti-democratic and anti-rational intellectual trends derived from proto-fascistic distortions of twentieth-century continental philosophy. The scholarly purveyors of these trends, which have come to dominate the liberal arts in the universities, believe themselves to be contributing to democracy while they inadvertently sap its essential moral and mental fibre. That Bloom had struck a nerve became obvious from the thunderous howls of truly febrile indignation that arose from the academic establishment: the 'culture war' (or wars) that Bloom's volcanic eruption ignited have not died out.

Straussian–Tocquevillean concern to shore up or repair the pillars of democratic health may be said to overlap with at least some versions of 'communitarian' critique and analysis [see further Chapter 13]. But the Straussian approach diverges from the 'communitarian' in at least three important (and not necessarily harmonious) ways. In the first place, Straussians are more inclined to respect, and to seek to revitalize, the concern for individual autonomy, responsibility, and hence dignity retrievable from the older Lockean individualist and free enterprise philosophic tradition (Brubaker, 1988; Kautz, 1995; Lerner, 1987: ch. 1; Tarcov, 1984a). In the second place, Straussians (or communitarians influenced by the Straussian approach) are more likely to look to religion and to the religious traditions in America, for counterweights to what are seen as in part excessively secular sources of individualism, materialism, and civic apathy or cynicism (Elazar, 1996–8; Kraynak, 2001; Lawler, 1993; 1999; McWilliams, 1984; 1987). Third, Straussians tend to fault communitarians for neglecting to recognize how much their continental philosophic sources are profoundly anti-liberal, anti-egalitarian, and anti-democratic. Straussians are far from denying that something very important is to be learned from

continental political theory's explicit and implicit critiques of liberal democracy in America, but they tend to insist that the fully discomfiting character of those critiques needs to be confronted, so that we can learn from them what communitarians are prone to overlook – the dangers in the excesses of the democratic spirit itself, and not least in unchecked egalitarianism and egalitarian communalism (Bloom, 1990b; Ceaser, 1997).

FROM CULTURAL CRITICISM TO THE FUNDAMENTAL QUESTIONS

Thus the Straussian critical theory of American civil society draws from and conduces to hermeneutic scholarship aimed at bringing to light the full force and depth of the late modern critique, rooted in Rousseau, of Enlightenment rationalism in theory and in practice. First Rousseau, and then, successively, his more systematic if less intransigent German heirs, diagnosed the imperfections of the Enlightenment – with a view to refurbishing it and thus consummating its deepest (this-worldly) intentions. It was the apparent failure of these magnificent efforts that led Nietzsche to proclaim the need for a shattering transrational departure. But to what extent is this historical dialectic inevitable? And are its results necessarily as crisis-prone as Strauss seems to have concluded? Can we not seriously consider a return to one or another stage of the unfolding drama, there to recover the essential complement that will make a reformed modernity, and perhaps a reformed America, truly defensible? The challenge to modernity that Strauss laid down, in his opposition of ancients to moderns, continues to inspire manifold Straussian interpretive work, on Rousseau (e.g. Bloom, 1993: Part One; Kelly, 1987; Meier, 1984; Melzer, 1990; Orwin and Tarcov, 1997; Schwartz, 1984), Kant (Galston, 1975; Knippenberg, 1993; Shell, 1980; Velkley, 1989), Hegel (Frost, 1999; Maletz, 1983; 1989; Smith, 1989), and Nietzsche (Dannhauser, 1974; Detwiler, 1990; Lampert, 1986; 2001). This scholarship follows with gratitude Strauss's lead, but often seeks, implicitly if not explicitly, to find a way to overcome his profoundly troubling conclusions.

In other words, there is discernible in the work of many of those Strauss has inspired a search, not always explicit (perhaps not even fully self-conscious), for a circumvention of the radical theses that express the core of his thought. This is most apparent in the fissures that have opened up among competing interpretations of the foundations of the American regime and of the Enlightenment rationalism that informs it. Jaffa and his followers go so far as to argue that the American regime, centred on Lincoln, shakes off the contamination of modern philosophy (whose failure Strauss is conceded to have correctly diagnosed) through a quasi-divinatory recovery of Aristotelian *praxis*. Most others among the first generation of Strauss's students (for the best articulation, see Diamond, 1992: ch. 21) have remained more soberly and modestly, if reluctantly, close to Strauss's own judgement – as indicated in his relentless essay on Locke (Strauss, 1971) and in his brief but incisive remarks there and elsewhere on the distinctly modern principles animating the American regime (McWilliams, 1998). Yet is it possible that the living presence of Strauss, and the reverence he naturally aroused, shielded the sober and modest students from facing, paradoxically, the very grave difficulties that his thought teaches must be faced? Strauss not only brought back to life the philosophic quest for final moral truth, he deliberately resuscitated the possibility and the necessity of studying the American regime with genuine, and passionately hopeful, respect for its Founding claim to be grounded on moral 'truths' that are 'self-evident': 'the laws of Nature and of Nature's God'. But Strauss also compelled the recognition that genuine respect for such a claim requires genuine testing of its validity – leading perhaps to the discovery, in the process, of something of the utmost importance regarding one's own soul. Now given Strauss's insistence on 'the lowering of the goals' that comes to sight at the very heart of modern political thought; given Strauss's unmistakable inclination to judge modern rationalism to be ultimately an erroneous if magnificent failure, and to judge classical philosophy to be, in contrast, simply true; given Strauss's much more qualified endorsement of the superiority of ancient to modern practice (his meticulous account of Plato's unvarnished analysis of life in the *polis* at its best: Strauss, 1975b); given these intransigently severe features of Strauss's central contentions, I say, it is understandable that those deeply affected by the serious initial hopes Strauss inspired should encounter, sooner or later, deep perplexity. It is understandable that even or especially those loyally indebted to and respectful of Strauss should find it hard, as dedicated citizens of America or of the West, to accept the detachment from the achievements of modernity, and from the love of one's own, that the logic of Strauss's critique demands. It is not surprising, then, that there has emerged a growing inclination among his followers to depart from Strauss, to challenge his relentless exposure of Locke's Hobbesian individualism and atheism and to seek to discover in Locke, as well as in other early moderns, and thence in the theory and not only the practice of modernity, especially in America, a nobler, and even a more religious, outlook than Strauss's own

analysis allows. By the same token, the question has been pressed whether Strauss's unflattering judgement on modernity, in comparison with antiquity, can stand, once one faces squarely the harshness and inhumanity of the *polis*. Prominent here are the massive though very different books of Paul Rahe (1992) and Michael Zuckert (1994), whose sophisticated historical erudition has greatly enriched, from somewhat divergent perspectives, our understanding of the precise stages in the evolution of republican thought from Machiavelli to the American Founding.[12]

The great question is whether these restive quests, sensible enough on their own terms, for a way out of the Straussian problematic, do not spring from a failure to appreciate what was for Strauss the heart of the matter. That heart is the challenge posed by revelation, and the Socratic dialectical investigation of justice and nobility as the key to meeting that challenge, and thus as the grounding of the truly natural life for man: the contemplative life, consumed by the serene (if mortal and therefore melancholy) joy of the free investigation of the permanent nature of the beings.

Efforts at achieving the appreciation of which I speak, through re-enacting Strauss's confrontation with the Bible and with the capital texts of ancient and medieval rationalism, represent the most profound of the scholarly endeavours that carry forward Strauss's approach to the study of politics.[13] It is fair to wonder, however, whether any of us has yet fully plumbed the existential meaning of that 'permanent human problem' to which Strauss sought to reawaken modern mankind. That problem, I believe Strauss was convinced by Socrates, has gnawed at the marrow, and has propelled the thinking, of every mind genuinely penetrated by the truth of the human condition. It is the lobotomizing of the modern brain's capacity to recognize this problem[14] – it is the 'oblivion of eternity, or, in other words, estrangement from man's deepest desire and therewith from the primary issues' (Strauss, 1959: 55) – that is the soul-destroying consequence which constitutes the decisive inferiority of all modern thought and life to ancient (and medieval) thought and life.

NOTES

1 Plato, *Republic*, 511b (*to anhypotheton*); Aristotle, *Topics*, 101a37–b4; Alfarabi, *The Philosophy of Plato*, s. 12–15.

2 Strauss (1952: introduction and ch. 1; 1959: ch. 9; 1989: ch. 5), Strauss and Kojève (1991: 26–8); see also Ahrensdorf (1994). For detailed Straussian critiques of Quentin Skinner's approach (diametrically opposed to that

of Strauss) to the study of the texts of the history of political philosophy, see Tarcov (1982a; 1982b; 1983) [see further Chapters 2, 30].

3 For what follows, see Storing (1962: esp. 308–11, as well as 124–32 and 317–18), Strauss (1959: ch. 3); also Bartlett (1996a), Ceaser (1990).

4 For other revealing critical comments of Strauss on liberal democracy, see esp. Strauss (1968: 15, 23–5, 263–4, 271–2; 1959: 36–8, 306–11). A very helpful brief characterization and assessment of Strauss's relation to American democracy is McWilliams (1998).

5 The key failing of conventional Soviet studies is stated succinctly by Fairbanks: 'It is impossible to understand the collapse of Soviet Communism without appreciating the role of ideas and convictions in history... [T]he communist system was ... destroyed, in large part because of the contradiction between ideals and reality ... One of the effects of our scholarship's depreciation of ideas and convictions was the expectation that, if there was to be reform in the Soviet Union, it would be made by 'technocrats' or 'pragmatists' such as industrial managers, not by people who were most closely identified with the alien or communist side of the regime, such as the ideological specialists within the Party apparatus, the closely related leadership of the international communist movement, and the political police ... It was thus a surprise to find the 'secret police' intimately involved in the origins of perestroika ... It was also a surprise to find militant reformers within the ideological specialization of the Party apparatus' (1993: 50–1).

6 For Straussian and kindred replies to Fukuyama, see Burns (1994) as well as the responses collected in *The National Interest*, vol. 16 (1989).

7 The most substantial contributions to the Straussian elucidation of the Founding ideas include Diamond (1992), Epstein (1984), Goldwin (1990; 1997), Kurland and Lerner (1986), and Storing (1981; 1995: Part One).

8 Ceaser (1979), Diamond (1992: ch. 11), Milkis (1993), Storing (1995: ch. 21). For an analysis of the mutual benefits of the dialectical struggle between party and bureaucratic influence in American government, see Storing (1995: ch. 15).

9 McWilliams (1998: 242) points us to those brief but pregnant comments with which Strauss indicated his appreciation of biblical religion's role in American public life.

10 Berns (1984: chs 15–17), Brotz (1970; 1992), Jaffa (1965: ch. 7; 1975), Lerner (1987: ch. 5), Mansfield (1991: ch. 7), Storing (1995: chs 7–9 and 11). For explorations of the racial issue as a moral problem in the Founders' thought, see esp. Berns (1984: ch. 14; 1987: ch. 1), Goldwin (1990), Griswold (1991), Lerner (1987: ch. 4), Rahe (1992: Book 3, ch. 2), and Storing (1995: ch. 6).

11 Bloom (1990a; 1993), and, above all, Bloom with Jaffa (1964). Bloom's legacy is seen in studies such as Cantor (1976), Ruderman (1995), Higuera (1995), and Spiekerman (2001).

12 Contrast McWilliams (1998) and Bruell (1991). Zuckert (2001) has recently written in agreement with

Kraynak (2000: 278–9) that 'Mansfield differs from Strauss ... most strikingly in maintaining, as Kraynak has it, that "Locke and Madison are modern Aristotelians" ... [and] that the Lockean theory of rights is better understood in terms of prideful self-assertion than in the Hobbesian terms Strauss attributed to Locke'. While this last characterization of the Lockean theory of rights may reflect Zuckert's own view of that theory, I am not convinced that Kraynak has accurately characterized Mansfield's intention – which may be better understood, I believe, as a supplement to, rather than a disagreement with, Strauss's analysis of Locke's Hobbesian core.

13 Bartlett (1996b; 2001), Bolotin (1979; 1998), Bruell (1994; 1999), Fradkin (1983; 1995), Jang (1997a; 1997b), Stauffer (2001). See also the references to the literature on Thucydides cited earlier in this chapter: Bolotin (1987), Bruell (1974), Orwin (1994), Strauss (1964: ch. 3), Ahrensdorf (1997), Forde (1995), Hassner (1995), Pangle and Ahrensdorf (1999: chs 7, 8), and Shulsky (1991a).

14 The problem, if not classical rationalism's way of grappling with it, has become more visible in the work of theologically inspired Straussians (Lawler, 1999; Manent, 1994) and in the revolution that Meier (1995) has brought about in the understanding of Carl Schmitt, and the latter's lifelong wrestling with Strauss [see further Chapter 29].

REFERENCES

Ahrensdorf, Peter (1994) 'The question of historical context and the study of Plato'. *Polity*, 27: 113–35.

Ahrensdorf, Peter (1997) 'Thucydides' realistic critique of realism'. *Polity*, 30 (2): 231–65.

Baras, Victor (1975) 'Beria's fall and Ulbricht's survival'. *Soviet Studies*, 27 (3): 381–95.

Bartlett, Robert C. (1994) 'The "Realism" of classical political science'. *American Journal of Political Science*, 38 (2): 381–402.

Bartlett, Robert C. (1996a) 'On the decline of contemporary political developmental studies'. *Review of Politics*, 58 (2): 269–98.

Bartlett, Robert C. (1996b) *Xenophon: The Shorter Socratic Writings*. Ithaca, NY: Cornell University Press.

Bartlett, Robert C. (2001) *The Idea of Enlightenment: A Post-Mortem Study*. Toronto: University of Toronto Press.

Berns, Walter (1957) *Freedom, Virtue and the First Amendment*. Baton Rouge, LA: Louisiana State University Press.

Berns, Walter (1984) *In Defense of Liberal Democracy*. Chicago: Regnery Gateway.

Berns, Walter (1987) *Taking the Constitution Seriously*. New York: Simon and Schuster.

Bessette, Joseph M. (1994) *The Mild Voice of Reason: Deliberative Democracy and American National Government*. Chicago: University of Chicago Press.

Bessette, Joseph M. and Jeffrey Tulis, eds (1981) *The Presidency in the Constitutional Order*. Baton Rouge, LA: Louisiana State University Press.

Bloom, Allan (1975) 'Justice: John Rawls vs. the tradition of political philosophy'. *American Political Science Review*, 69 (2): 648–62.

Bloom, Allan (1987) *The Closing of the American Mind*. New York: Simon and Schuster.

Bloom, Allan (1990a) *Giants and Dwarfs: Essays 1960–1990*. New York: Simon and Schuster.

Bloom, Allan (ed.) (1990b) *Confronting the Constitution: The Challenge to Locke, Montesquieu, Jefferson, and The Federalists from Utilitarianism, Historicism, Marxism, Freudianism, Pragmatism, Existentialism …* Washington: AEI Press.

Bloom, Allan (1993) *Love and Friendship*. New York: Simon and Schuster.

Bloom, Allan with Harry V. Jaffa (1964) *Shakespeare's Politics*. New York: Basic Books.

Bolotin, David (1979) *Plato's Dialogue on Friendship*. Ithaca, NY: Cornell University Press.

Bolotin, David (1987) 'Thucydides'. In Leo Strauss and Joseph Cropsey, eds, *History of Political Philosophy*, 3rd edn. Chicago: University of Chicago Press, 7–32.

Bolotin, David (1998) *An Approach to Aristotle's Physics*. Albany, NY: SUNY Press.

Brotz, Howard M. (1970) *The Black Jews of Harlem* (1964). New York: Schocken.

Brotz, Howard M. (1992) *African-American Social and Political Thought 1850–1920* (1966). New Brunswick, NJ: Transaction.

Brubaker, Stanley C. (1987) 'Republican government and judicial restraint'. *Review of Politics*, 49 (4): 570–3.

Brubaker, Stanley C. (1988) 'Can liberals punish?' *American Political Science Review*, 82 (3): 821–36.

Bruell, Christopher (1974) 'Thucydides' view of Athenian imperialism'. *American Political Science Review*, 68 (1): 11–17.

Bruell, Christopher (1991) 'A return to classical political philosophy and the understanding of the American founding'. *Review of Politics*, 53 (1): 173–86.

Bruell, Christopher (1994) 'On Plato's political philosophy'. *Review of Politics*, 56 (2): 261–82.

Bruell, Christopher (1999) *On the Socratic Education*. Lanham, MD: Rowman and Littlefield.

Burns, Timothy (1994) *After History? Francis Fukuyama and His Critics*. Lanham, MD: Rowman and Littlefield.

Canavan, Francis (1971) 'Freedom of speech and press: for what purpose?' *American Journal of Jurisprudence*, 16 (1): 95–142.

Cantor, Paul (1976) *Shakespeare's Rome*. Ithaca, NY: Cornell University Press.

Ceaser, James W. (1979) *Presidential Selection*. Princeton, NJ: Princeton University Press.

Ceaser, James W. (1990) *Liberal Democracy and Political Science*. Baltimore: Johns Hopkins University Press.

Ceaser, James W. (1997) *Reconstructing America*. New Haven, CT: Yale University Press.

Clor, Harry M. (1969) *Obscenity and Public Morality*. Chicago: University of Chicago Press.

Clor, Harry M. (1996) *Public Morality and Liberal Society*. Notre Dame, IN: University of Notre Dame Press.

Danford, John (1980) 'Adam Smith, equality, and the wealth of sympathy'. *American Journal of Political Science*, 24 (4): 674–95.

Dannhauser, Werner (1974) *Nietzsche's View of Socrates*. Ithaca, NY: Cornell University Press.

Detwiler, Bruce (1990) *Nietzsche and the Politics of Aristocratic Radicalism*. Chicago: University of Chicago Press.

Diamond, Martin (1992) *As Far as Republican Principles Will Admit*, ed. William Shambra. Washington, DC: AEI.

Elazar, Daniel J. (1996–8) *The Covenant Tradition in Politics*, 4 vols. New Brunswick, NJ: Transaction.

Epstein, David (1984) *The Political Theory of the Federalist*. Chicago: University of Chicago Press.

Fairbanks, Charles H. Jr (1987) 'Bureaucratic politics in the Soviet Union and in the Ottoman Empire'. *Comparative Strategy*, 6 (3): 333–62.

Fairbanks, Charles H. Jr (1993) 'The nature of the beast'. *The National Interest*, 31: 46–56.

Fairbanks, Charles H. Jr (1995a) 'A tired anarchy'. *The National Interest*, 39: 15–25.

Fairbanks, Charles H. Jr (1995b) 'The postcommunist wars'. *Journal of Democracy*, 6 (4): 18–34.

Fairbanks, Charles H. Jr (1997) 'The public void: antipolitics in the former Soviet Union'. In Andreas Schedler, ed., *The End of Politics? Explorations into Modern Antipolitics*. New York: St Martin's, 146–83.

Faulkner, Robert K. (1968) *The Jurisprudence of John Marshall*. Princeton, NJ: Princeton University Press.

Forbes, H. D. (1985) *Nationalism, Ethnocentrism, and Personality*. Chicago: University of Chicago Press.

Forbes, H. D. (1997) *Ethnic Conflict*. New Haven, CT: Yale University Press.

Forde, Steven (1995) 'International realism: Thucydides, Machiavelli, and neorealism'. *International Studies Quarterly*, 39 (2): 141–60.

Forde, Steven (1998) 'Hugo Grotius' approach to the ethics of war'. *American Political Science Review*, 92 (3): 39–48.

Fradkin, Hillel (1983) 'God's politics: lessons from the beginning'. *This World*, 4: 86–104.

Fradkin, Hillel (1995) 'Poet-kings: a Biblical perspective on heroes'. In M. Palmer and T. Pangle, eds, *Political Philosophy and the Human Soul: Essays in Memory of Allan Bloom*. Lanham, MD: Rowman and Littlefield, 55–66.

Frisch, Morton J. and Richard G. Stevens (1971) *American Political Thought*. New York: Scribner's Sons.

Frost, Bryan-Paul (1999) 'A critical introduction to Alexandre Kojève's *Esquisse d'une phénomenologie du droit*'. *Review of Metaphysics*, 52: 595–640.

Fukuyama, Francis (1992) *The End of History and the Last Man*. New York: Free.

Galston, William (1975) *Kant and the Problem of History*. Chicago: University of Chicago Press.

Goldwin, Robert A. (1990) *Why Blacks, Women, and Jews Are Not Mentioned in the Constitution*. Washington, DC: AEI.

Goldwin, Robert A. (1997) *From Parchment to Power*. Washington, DC: AEI.

Griswold, Charles (1991) 'Rights and wrongs: Jefferson, slavery, and philosophical quandaries'. In Michael J. Lacey and Knud Haakonssen, eds, *A Culture of Rights*. Cambridge: Cambridge University Press, 49–74.

Hassner, Pierre (1961) 'Les concepts de guerre et de paix chez Kant'. *Revue française de science politique*, 11 (3): 642–70.

Hassner, Pierre (1995) *La Violence et la paix*. Paris: Esprit.

Hassner, Pierre (1997) 'Rousseau and the theory and practice of international relations'. In Clifford Orwin and Nathan Tarcov, eds, *The Legacy of Rousseau*. Chicago: University of Chicago Press, 200–19.

Higuera, Henry (1995) *Eros and Empire*. Lanham, MD: Rowman and Littlefield.

Jaffa, Harry V. (1959) *Crisis of the House Divided*. Garden City, NY: Doubleday.

Jaffa, Harry V. (1965) *Equality and Liberty*. Oxford: Oxford University Press.

Jaffa, Harry V. (1975) 'Reflections on Thoreau and Lincoln: civil disobedience and the American tradition'. In *The Conditions of Freedom*. Baltimore: Johns Hopkins University Press, 124–48.

Jang, In Ha (1997a) 'Socrates' refutation of Thrasymachus'. *History of Political Thought*, 18 (2): 189–206.

Jang, In Ha (1997b) 'The problematic character of Socrates' defense of justice in Plato's *Republic*'. In Leslie G. Rubin, ed., *Justice vs. Law in Greek Political Thought (Politikos III)*. Lanham, MD: Rowman and Littlefield, 3–26.

Kautz, Steven (1995) *Liberalism and Community*. Ithaca, NY: Cornell University Press.

Kelly, Christopher (1987) *Rousseau's Exemplary Life*. Ithaca, NY: Cornell University Press.

Knippenberg, Joseph (1989) 'Moving beyond fear: Rousseau and Kant on cosmopolitan education'. *Journal of Politics*, 51 (4): 809–27.

Knippenberg, Joseph (1993) 'The politics of Kant's philosophy'. In Ronald Beiner and William Booth, eds, *Kant and Political Philosophy: The Contemporary Legacy*. New Haven, CT: Yale University Press, 155–72.

Koritansky, John (1986) *Alexis de Tocqueville and the New Science of Politics*. Durham, NC: Carolina Academic Press.

Kraynak, Robert P. (2000) 'The care of souls in a constitutional democracy: some lessons from Harvey Mansfield and Alexander Solzhenitsyn'. In Mark Blitz and William Kristol, eds, *Educating the Prince: Essays in Honor of Harvey Mansfield*. Lanham, MD: Rowman and Littlefield, 270–90.

Kraynak, Robert P. (2001) *Christian Faith and Modern Democracy*. Notre Dame, IN: University of Notre Dame Press.

Kurland, Philip B. and Ralph Lerner, eds (1986) *The Founders' Constitution*, 5 vols. Chicago: University of Chicago Press.

Lampert, Laurence (1986) *Nietzsche's Teaching*. New Haven, CT: Yale University Press.

Lampert, Laurence (2001) *Nietzsche's Task*. New Haven, CT: Yale University Press.

Landy, Marc and Martin Levin, eds (1995) *The New Politics of Public Policy*. Baltimore: Johns Hopkins University Press.

Lawler, Peter Augustine (1993) *The Restless Mind*. Lanham, MD: Rowman and Littlefield.

Lawler, Peter Augustine (1999) *Postmodernism Rightly Understood*. Lanham, MD: Rowman and Littlefield.

Lawler, Peter, Roberta Schaefer and David Schaefer, eds (1997) *Active Duty: Administration as Democratic Statesmanship*. Lanham, MD: Rowman and Littlefield.

Lerner, Ralph (1987) *The Thinking Revolutionary*. Ithaca, NY: Cornell University Press.

Macpherson, C. B. (1962) *The Political Theory of Possessive Individualism*. Oxford: Oxford University Press.

Macpherson, C. B. (1973) 'Hobbes's bourgeois man'. In his *Democratic Theory: Essays in Retrieval*. Oxford: Oxford University Press, 238–50.

Malbin, Michael (1981) *Religion and Politics: The Intention of the Authors of the First Amendment*. Washington, DC: AEI.

Maletz, Donald J. (1983) 'On the revival of Hegelian political thought'. *The Political Science Reviewer*, 13: 155–78.

Maletz, Donald J. (1989) 'Hegel on right as actualized will'. *Political Theory*, 17 (1): 33–50.

Manent, Pierre (1982) *Tocqueville et la nature de la démocratie*. Paris: Julliard.

Manent, Pierre (1994) *La Cité de l'homme*. Paris: Fayard.

Mansfield, Harvey C. (1965a) 'Whether party government is inevitable'. *Political Science Quarterly*, 80 (2): 517–42.

Mansfield, Harvey C. (1965b) *Statesmanship and Party Government*. Chicago: University of Chicago Press.

Mansfield, Harvey C. (1971) 'Hobbes and the science of indirect government'. *American Political Science Review*, 65 (1): 97–110.

Mansfield, Harvey C. (1978) *The Spirit of Liberalism*. Cambridge, MA: Harvard University Press.

Mansfield, Harvey C. (1989) *Taming the Prince*. New York: Free Press.

Mansfield, Harvey C. (1991) *America's Constitutional Soul*. Baltimore: Johns Hopkins University Press.

McNamara, Peter (1999) *The Noblest Minds: Fame, Honor, and the American Founding*. Lanham, MD: Rowman and Littlefield.

McWilliams, Wilson Carey (1983) 'In good faith: on the foundations of American politics'. *Humanities in Society*, 6: 19–40.

McWilliams, Wilson Carey (1984) 'The Bible in the American tradition'. In M. J. Aronoff, ed., *Religion and Politics (Political Anthropology III)*. New Brunswick, NJ: Transaction, 11–46.

McWilliams, Wilson Carey (1987) 'Civil religion in the age of reason: Thomas Paine on liberalism, redemption, and revolution'. *Social Research*, 54 (3): 447–90.

McWilliams, Wilson Carey (1992) 'Tocqueville and responsible parties: Individualism, participation, and citizenship in America'. In *Challenges to Party Government*, John K. White and Jerome Mileur (eds). Carbondale, IL: Southern Illinois University Press, 58–93.

McWilliams, Wilson Carey (1998) 'Leo Strauss and the dignity of American political thought'. *Review of Politics*, 60 (2): 231–46.

McWilliams, Wilson Carey (2000) *Beyond the Politics of Disappointment?* Chatham, NJ: Chatham House.

Meier, Heinrich (1984) *Diskurs über die Ungleichheit*. Paderborn: Schöningh.

Meier, Heinrich (1995) *Carl Schmitt and Leo Strauss: The Hidden Dialogue* (1988), trans. J. Harvey Lomax. Chicago: University of Chicago Press.

Melnick, R. Shep (1983) *Regulation and the Courts: The Case of the Clean Air Act*. Washington, DC: Brookings.

Melnick, R. Shep (1994) *Between the Lines: Interpreting Welfare Rights*. Washington, DC: Brookings.

Melnick, R. Shep (2000) 'Constitutional bureaucracy'. In Mark Blitz and William Kristol, eds, *Educating the Prince: Essays in Honor of Harvey Mansfield*. Lanham, MD: Rowman and Littlefield, 246–63.

Melzer, Arthur (1990) *The Natural Goodness of Man: On the System of Rousseau's Thought*. Chicago: University of Chicago Press.

Melzer, Arthur, Jerry Weinberger and M. Richard Zinman (1998) *Multiculturalism and American Democracy*. Lawrence, KS: University Press of Kansas.

Milkis, Sidney M. (1993) *The President and the Parties: The Transformation of the American Party System Since the New Deal*. New York: Oxford University Press.

Nichols, James H. Jr and Colin Wright, eds (1990) *From Political Economy to Economics – and Back?* San Francisco: Institute for Contemporary Studies.

Orwin, Clifford (1994) *The Humanity of Thucydides*. Princeton, NJ: Princeton University Press.

Orwin, Clifford and Nathan Tarcov (1997) *The Legacy of Rousseau*. Chicago: University of Chicago Press.

Owen, J. Judd (2001) *Religion and the Demise of Liberal Rationalism*. Chicago: University of Chicago Press.

Pangle, Thomas and Peter Ahrensdorf (1999) *Justice among Nations: On the Moral Basis of Power and Peace*. Lawrence, KS: University Press of Kansas.

Plattner, Marc, ed. (1984) *Human Rights in Our Time*. Boulder, CO: Westview.

Rabkin, Jeremy (1989) *Judicial Compulsions: How Public Law Distorts Public Policy*. New York: Basic Books.

Rahe, Paul A. (1992) *Republics Ancient and Modern*. Chapel Hill, NC: University of North Carolina Press.

Rhoads, Steven E. (1985) *The Economist's View of the World*. Cambridge: Cambridge University Press.

Rhoads, Steven E. (1993) *Incomparable Worth: Pay Equity Meets the Market*. Cambridge: Cambridge University Press.

Ruderman, Anne (1995) *The Pleasures of Virtue: Political Thought in the Novels of Jane Austen*. Lanham, MD: Rowman and Littlefield.

Ruderman, Richard (1997a) 'Democracy and the problem of statesmanship'. *Review of Politics*, 59 (4): 759–87.

Ruderman, Richard (1997b) 'Aristotle and the recovery of political judgment'. *American Political Science Review*, 91 (2): 409–20.

Rush, Myron (1958) *The Rise of Khrushchev*. Washington, DC: Public Affairs Press.

Rush, Myron (1965) *Political Succession in the USSR*. New York: Columbia University Press.

Rush, Myron (1974) *How Communist States Change Their Rulers*. Ithaca, NY: Cornell University Press.

Rush, Myron (1993) 'Fortune and fate'. *The National Interest*, 31: 19–25.

Schwartz, Joel (1984) *The Sexual Politics of Jean-Jacques Rousseau*. Chicago: University of Chicago Press.

Schwartz, Joel (2000) *Fighting Poverty with Virtue*. Bloomington, IN: Indiana University Press.

Shell, Susan (1980) *The Rights of Reason*. Toronto: University of Toronto Press.

Shulsky, Abram (1991a) *Silent Warfare: Understanding the World of Intelligence*. Washington, DC: Brassey's/Macmillan.

Shulsky, Abram (1991b) 'The "infrastructure" of Aristotle's *Politics*: Aristotle on economics and politics'. In Carnes Lord and David K. O'Connor, eds, *Essays on the Foundations of Aristotelian Political Science*. Berkeley, CA: University of California Press, 74–111.

Smith, Steven B. (1989) *Hegel's Critique of Liberalism*. Chicago: University of Chicago Press.

Spiekerman, Timothy (2001) *Shakespeare's Political Realism*. Albany, NY: SUNY Press.

Stauffer, Devin (2001) *Plato's Introduction to the Question of Justice*. Albany, NY: SUNY Press.

Storing, Herbert J., ed. (1962) *Essays on the Scientific Study of Politics*. New York: Holt, Rinehart and Winston.

Storing, Herbert J. (1981) *The Complete Anti-Federalist*, 7 vols. Chicago: University of Chicago Press.

Storing, Herbert J. (1995) *Toward a More Perfect Union*, ed. Joseph M. Bessette. Washington, DC: AEI.

Strauss, Leo (1930) *Die Religionskritik Spinozas*. Berlin: Akademie.

Strauss, Leo (1952) *Persecution and the Art of Writing*. Glencoe, IL: Free Press.

Strauss, Leo (1958) *Thoughts on Machiavelli*. Glencoe, IL: Free Press.

Strauss, Leo (1959) *What is Political Philosophy?* Glencoe, IL: Free Press.

Strauss, Leo (1964) *The City and Man*. Chicago: Rand McNally.

Strauss, Leo (1965) 'Autobiographical preface' to *Spinoza's Critique of Religion*. New York: Schocken, 1–31.

Strauss, Leo (1968) *Liberalism Ancient and Modern*. New York: Basic Books.

Strauss, Leo (1971) *Natural Right and History* (1953). Chicago: University of Chicago Press.

Strauss, Leo (1975) *The Argument and the Action of Plato's Laws*. Chicago: University of Chicago Press.

Strauss, Leo (1983) *Studies in Platonic Political Philosophy*. Chicago: University of Chicago Press.

Strauss, Leo (1989) The Rebirth of Classical Political Rationalism: An Introduction to the Thought of Leo Strauss. ed. T. Pangle. Chicago: University of Chicago Press.

Strauss, Leo (1995) *Philosophy and Law* (1935), trans. Eve Adler. Albany, NY: SUNY Press.

Strauss, Leo (1996) 'Vorwort' to *Hobbes' Politische Wissenschaft* (1965). In *Gesammelte Schriften*, 3 vols thus far. Stuttgart: Metzler, vol. 3, 7–10.

Strauss, Leo, and Alexandre Kojève (1991) *On Tyranny* (1948), rev. edn. New York: Free Press.

Tarcov, Nathan (1982a) 'Political thought in early modern Europe II: the Age of Reformation', *Journal of Modern History*, 54 (1): 56–65.

Tarcov, Nathan (1982b) 'Quentin Skinner's method and Machiavelli's *Prince*'. *Ethics*, 92 (4): 692–709.

Tarcov, Nathan (1983) 'Philosophy and history: tradition and interpretation in the work of Leo Strauss'. *Polity*, 16 (1): 5–29.

Tarcov, Nathan (1984a) *Locke's Education for Liberty*. Chicago: University of Chicago Press.

Tarcov, Nathan (1984b) 'Principle and prudence in foreign policy: the Founders' perspective'. *The Public Interest*, 76: 45–60.

Tarcov, Nathan (1989a) Principle and prudence: the use of force from the founders' perspective', in *American Defence Policy and Liberal Democracy*, Fred E. Baumann and Kenneth M. Jensen (eds). Charlottesville: University Press of Virginia, 76–94.

Tarcov, Nathan (1989b) 'If this long war is over', *The National Interest*, 18: 50–53.

Velkley, Richard L. (1989) *Freedom and the End of Reason*. Chicago: University of Chicago Press.

Walzer, Michael (1977) *Just and Unjust Wars*. New York: Basic.

Yarbrough, Jean (1998) *American Virtues: Thomas Jefferson on the Character of a Free People*. Lawrence, KS: University Press of Kansas.

Zuckert, Michael P. (1994) *Natural Rights and the New Republicanism*. Princeton, NJ: Princeton University Press.

Zuckert, Michael P. (2001) 'Pride and political philosophy'. *The Claremont Review of Books*, 1 (4): 17–23.

4

Postmodern Approaches
to Political Theory

JANE BENNETT

The term *postmodernism* has currency in political theory, but also in literary studies, philosophy, anthropology, the arts, and popular discourse, in each case functioning somewhat differently. Its usages can be summarized under three headings: (1) as a sociological designation for an epochal shift in the way collective life is organized (from centralized and hierarchical control towards a network structure); (2) as an aesthetic genre (literature that experiments with non-linear narration, a playful architecture of mixed styles, an appreciation of popular culture that complicates the distinction between high and low); (3) as a set of philosophical critiques of teleological and/or rationalist conceptions of nature, history, power, freedom, and subjectivity. Postmodernism in political theory participates in all three, but perhaps most intensively in the third, which is the emphasis of this chapter.

Judith Butler points out that to use the category 'postmodern theory' is to make an assumption that postmodern theorists find problematic, i.e. that 'theories offer themselves in bundles or in organized totalities, and that ... a set of theories which are structurally similar emerge as the articulation of an historically specific condition of human reflection' (1995: 38). In all arenas, discussions of postmodernism are highly charged; it is routinely denounced as nihilistic, immoral, or politically irresponsible. Indeed, the term is invoked more often by those who oppose postmodernism than by those said to be its practitioners. Many of the latter reject it as a self-description: Gilles Deleuze because he pursued a kind of metaphysics, whereas postmodernism is said to be post-metaphysical, and because he preferred a Kafkaesque humour of sense and

nonsense to the irony more typically associated with postmodernism (Rajchman, 2000: 126); William Connolly (2002) because the term is identified with the theme of the world as text, a theme he takes to underestimate the significance of human corporeality, and because the term's content floats with the concerns of the critic bestowing the name. Drucilla Cornell accepts the designation reluctantly, in part because she rejects 'the very idea that periods of history can be rigidly separated' (1991: 207). Richard Rorty feels 'doomed to be referred to as a "postmodernist"', but acknowledges that 'the people they are bunching me with do share quite a few enemies and attitudes' (1995: 214 n.1). Amidst all this, I will retain the label because it gestures, however imperfectly, toward an innovative body of theoretical work that came of age in the last several decades.

Within political theory, critics from both the right and the left have tended to see postmodernism as a rejection of the quest for an objective truth behind subjective experiences (Cheney, 1996; Dumm and Norton, 1998). Because this quest is thought to set the condition of possibility for *any* affirmative claim, postmodern political theory is charged with being anti-political and unable to take an ethical stand, except that of resistance, disobedience, refusal, or deconstruction for deconstruction's sake. Stephen White offers a subtle version of this criticism: while 'poststructuralist and postmodern thought ... carries a persistent utopian hope of a "not yet"', it too often 'remains blithely unspecific about normative orientation in the here and now' (2000: 90). In response, some postmodernists contend that a positive ethic need not require a universal

God, Reason or some such surrogate, but can be grounded on the cultivation of existential attachment to life rather than on an internal or external authority (Bennett, 2001; Coles, 1997; Foucault, 1988; Kateb, 2000). The complex of epistemological and ontological claims that constitute the distinctive style of thinking called postmodern cannot with justice be reduced to negativism. Nevertheless, the charge has prompted some of its best theorists to articulate more closely the affirmative possibilities within their approach.

I will focus in what follows on the positive themes within postmodernism. My summary is a selective account of what a postmodernist sensibility has to offer in the way of an affirmative political vision. Postmodernism in political theory emerged, and continues to develop, in close relation to other theoretical approaches, including feminism, liberalism, psychoanalytic theory, critical theory, and utopianism. It makes the most sense, then, when understood in dialogue with these other perspectives, as part of a broader discussion about the nature of reality, the degree to which it is knowable or in some way accessible to experience, and the possibilities for its improvement in terms of justice, freedom, or humaneness.

Postmodern theory often takes the form of genealogical studies which reveal how discursive practices and conceptual schemata are embedded with power relations, and how these cultural forms constitute what is experienced as natural or real (Butler, 1993; Brown, 1995; Ferguson, 1991). One of the political insights of postmodern theory is that 'the stakes of a democratic politics ... are as much about the modern crisis of representation as they are about the distribution of other goods' (Dumm, 1999: 60). Deconstructions of madness and criminality, feminist and queer studies of gender and sexuality, postcolonial studies of race and nation – these all seek to uncover the human-madeness of entities formerly considered either natural, universal, or innevitable. Much genealogical work, however, also insists upon the *material recalcitrance* of cultural products. Gender, sexuality, race, and personal identity are viewed as congealed responses to contingent sets of historical circumstances, and yet the mere fact that they are human artifacts does not mean that they yield readily to human understanding or control (Gatens, 1996). A personal identity, for example, is a construction, but one sedimented into bodily movements, instinctive tendencies, linguistic routines, and institutional forms that resist human attempts to redirect or revise them. Everything is acculturated, but cultural forms are themselves material assemblages of natural bodies. Postmodern theory acknowledges the artifice of the natural and the materiality of the cultural. In what follows, I emphasize how its partisans wrestle with this uneasy pair of insights.

THE ELUSIVE AND PRODUCTIVE EXCESS

There always exists – in words, things, bodies, thoughts, artifacts, ways of life – that which is persistently resistant to theoretical capture, or, for that matter, to any fixed form. This indeterminate and never fully determinable dimension of things has been described as difference or *différance* (Jacques Derrida), *the virtual* (Gilles Deleuze), *non-identity* (Theodor Adorno), *the invisible* (Maurice Merleau-Ponty), *the immanent* (William Connolly), *the semiotic* (Julia Kristeva), *sexual difference* (Luce Irigaray), *the real* (Jacques Lacan), *life* (Friedrich Nietzsche), or *negativity* (Diana Coole). Jean-François Lyotard calls it 'that which exceeds every putting into form or object without being anywhere else but within them' (1997: 29).

Whether this restlessness that haunts all positive forms is an ontological necessity or an effect of language is a question answered differently by various postmodern thinkers (Coole, 2000). In all cases, however, it functions as a chastening limit to the projects of political mastery, final moral codes, or normative consensus, reminding us of the capacity for resistance, perhaps even a moment of independence, of life and the world. Postmodern political theory tries to acknowledge this resistance and to resist the urge to expel this disruptive force from politics (Honig, 1993). Difference is important to postmodern theory not only because it 'is' in some sense, and thus ought to be acknowledged, but also because its operation is seen as a condition of positivity or concrete form as such (Corson, 2001). In other words, difference both subsists in the positive *and* helps to produce new positivities; it is 'the principle of generativity itself: that force or movement which ... renders meaning and institutions possible yet menaced' (Coole, 2000: 74). *Différance*, the virtual, non-identity, etc. name, on the one hand, the remainder left out of any theoretical account, and, on the other hand, the creative energy within existing forms out of which new things (identities, rights, social movements) emerge [see further Chapter 20]. That creative process is understood as ever ongoing: any given *being* is seen – if one places it in the appropriate period of duration – as in the process of *becoming*, i.e. becoming otherwise than it is.

A contribution of Lacanian theory to postmodern political theory consists in its identification of these moments of becoming as *political* moments. In contrast to 'politics', or the established, institutional means for organizing collective life, the 'political' here refers to those irruptive events that reveal 'politics' to be a masking of the restless and stubbornly diverse quality of 'the real' or that which always exceeds actuality and eludes symbolic expression. The event of the political provides a glimpse into this real, thus revealing the *fantasmic* character of the image of society as a harmonious whole (Stavrakakis, 1999).

The Lacanian notion of the political functions in a similar way to what Gilles Deleuze and Felix Guattari (1987) call, using a more physicalist vocabulary, the cosmic. The cosmic is that dimension of an entity, an act, or a claim that is energetic and not organized into an object of knowledge or thing with which it is possible to identify. The cosmic consists in unruly and unpredictable 'forces, densities, intensities' that 'are not thinkable in themselves' (1987: 342–3). The cosmic is the virtual world that subsists in the actual and whose presence is signalled by the surprising eruption of an event that no one foresaw or could have foreseen. The cosmic is this 'political' dimension of existence.

Why might postmodern political theorists invoke this turbulent and elusive realm? First, in order to assert the futility of attempts to achieve a final and fixed form of political order – a project which appears as something like an ontological impossibility. And, second, in order to defend democratic culture, with its constitutive tensions between order and disorder, as a form of governance that is, paradoxically, most in harmony with the nature of being. The postmodern story of the world as itself 'political' or having a 'cosmic' dimension is one kind of metanarrative.

A METANARRATIVE OF IMMANENCE

A metanarrative is an overarching theory about the way the world operates, a story about the fundamental character of the natural-social universe. As such, it functions as a frame of reference for judging other theories of more limited scope and aspiration. It may be experienced as a religious truth or as a metaphysical imaginary with a contingent heuristic value, or as occupying one of many positions between these two poles. Metanarratives are used within political theory to help legitimate a theory's claims about authority, the state, citizenship, freedom, rights, etc. For example, Hobbes uses a metanarrative of a world of natural bodies in perpetual motion and a distant, Jobian God to ground his notions of sovereignty, contract, political speech, and civil peace. One distinctive mark of postmodern theory is its rejection of those metanarratives that

present themselves as expressive of a transcendental truth, or that view nature or history as having an intrinsic purpose, or that entail a two-world metaphysic. Examples of the last include Plato's division between the true world of the forms and the deceptive world of sensuous appearances, Augustine's City of God and City of Man, Kant's noumenal and phenomenal realms, and Hegel's implicit Idea as it unfolds in history.

Some postmodern theorists reject any use of metanarrative, but others do not. The second group affirms the psychological utility and ethical power of an ontological imaginary. These theorists, like Hobbes, link their political claims to speculative claims about nature, matter, or being. But their metaphysical views are presented as an *onto-story* whose persuasiveness is always at issue and 'can never be fully disentangled from an interpretation of present historical circumstances' (White, 2000: 10–11). Not all postmodern theorists, then, purport to be post-metaphysical, just as some who purport to be post-metaphysical, such as Rawls and Habermas and those inspired by them, are not postmodern theorists [see Chapters 7 and 12].

Nietzsche is often the inspiration behind the onto-stories affirmed within postmodern theory, in terms of both content and style. He offers a vision of the way the world is. But he also insists that, like all metaphysical orientations, it is a 'conjecture' he is not able to prove:

> do you know what 'the world' is to me? ... a monster of energy ... that does not expend itself but only transforms itself ... [A] play of forces and waves of forces, at the same time one and many ... a sea of forces flowing and rushing together, eternally changing ... with an ebb and a flood of its forms; out of the simplest forms striving toward the most complex, out of the stillest, most rigid, coldest forms toward the hottest, most turbulent ... and then again returning home to the simple out of this abundance, out of the play of contradictions back to the joy of concord. (Nietzsche, 1987: 1067)

The Deleuzean story of a world of protean forces shares Nietzsche's emphasis on open-ended dynamism and flow, as does Lyotard's 'A postmodern fable', a sci-fi tale of humans preparing to escape the earth as the sun is about to burn out. Also like Nietzsche, Lyotard describes a world without the promise of a final or eschatological achievement. If to be modern, says Lyotard, is to long to re-establish a 'full and whole relation with the law of the Other ... as this ... was in the beginning', then to be postmodern is to try to cure thought and action of this eschatological desiring (1997: 96–7). Lyotard discerns this desire not only in Christian political theory but in some Enlightenment narratives, in Romanticist or speculative dialectics, and in Marxism. He is particularly harsh on what he takes to be Habermas's search for universal consensus, a search Lyotard identifies with a terroristic conformity (Docker, 1994). Lacanian political theory, whose relationship to postmodernism is in other ways more complicated, also rejects the desire for fullness discernible in much of political theory (Laclau and Mouffe, 1985). It seeks a democratic polity based not on the vision of a harmonious social whole but upon 'the recognition of the impossibility and the catastrophic consequences of such a dream' (Stavrakakis, 1999: 111).

In more general terms, postmodern theory that does not seek to be post-metaphysical pursues a metaphysics of *immanence*, an onto-story where there is nothing outside of the immensely complex, wondrously diverse, and never fully manifest material world. In the two-world metaphysics of Plato, Augustine, and Kant, immanence is conceived as immanent to something transcendent that is given moral or conceptual primacy (Berg-Sorensen, 2001). The goal of the postmodern metaphysicians, in contrast, is to think immanence without reintroducing transcendence, to narrate what Giorgio Agamben calls 'the vertigo in which outside and inside, immanence and transcendence, are absolutely indistinguishable' (1999: 238–9). The 'outside' is pictured as an evanescent field (of difference, the virtual, etc.) that is nevertheless not 'transcendent' because it is always already folding into the immanent realm of discrete entities. It is a constitutive outside.

There is a materialist energetics in several versions of postmodernism – not the mechanical materialism of classical metaphysics, but an immanent materialism in which the world itself contains the power to metamorphose at unexpected junctures from old forms into new and surprising ones. Deleuze and Guattari speak, for example, of nature as a perpetual machine for generating new and dynamic compositions: nature as 'a pure plane of immanence … upon which everything is given, upon which unformed elements and materials dance' (1987: 255). This onto-story shares Hegel's sense of nature as a fluid field of potentialities, but not Hegel's confidence about the possibility of taming this force or his lack of concern about the violence involved in doing so. For Hegel, the encounter with nature's becoming provokes the desire

> to compel this Proteus to cease its transformations and show itself to us and declare itself to us; so that it may not present us with a variety of ever new forms, but in simpler fashion bring to our consciousness in language what it *is*. (1974: 199)

Postmodern theory affirms Hegel's insight into the protean character of life, but aspires to a different balance between being and becoming in social life.

HUMANS, ANIMALS, CYBORGS

Postmodern theorizing repositions the human in relation to the non-human entities and forces with which it shares the world. Its metaphysics of immanence displaces humans from the centre of the universe. We are viewed instead as a particularly complex and reflexive formation, differing from other forms in significant degree but not in kind. 'Humankind is taken for a complex material system; consciousness, for an effect of language; and language for a highly complex material system' (Lyotard, 1997: 98). Human beings are more complex animals, rather than animals 'with an extra added ingredient called "intellect" or "the rational soul"' (Rorty, 1995: 199). Thought and thinking are not devalued here; they are made part of the natural world in which we are set. The suspicion amongst opponents of postmodern approaches to political theory is that if one denies a two-world metaphysics, one necessarily disparages the importance of thinking. But a variety of postmodern thinkers believe that to give thinking its due as a sophisticated process and creative activity, it is important to address its implication in somatic forces and natural systems.

The human is pictured as a mixture of categories of things against which it has traditionally been defined. We are hybrids of animal and machine, culture and biology, language and affect. We are cyborgs, says Donna Haraway (1989), who examines the advantages and disadvantages of this for democratic politics, feminism, and multicultural coexistence. Bruno Latour says that the human is not one pole to be opposed to another called the non-human, but rather a 'weaver of morphisms': 'The expression "anthropomorphic" considerably underestimates our humanity. We should be talking about … technomorphisms, zoomorphisms, physiomorphisms, ideomorphisms, theomorphisms, sociomorphisms, psychomorphisms … Their alliances and their exchanges, taken together, are what define the *anthropos*' (1993: 137).

Deleuze and Guattari's (1987) discussion of the childhood game of 'becoming animal' explores the positive potential of this mobile hybridity. The game, they say, reveals the child's sense of herself as born from an over-rich field of protean forces and materials, only some of which are tapped by her current, human form. In playing their barking, mooing, chirping, growling games, children bear witness to an 'inhuman contrivance with the animal' within them:

it is as though, independent of the evolution carrying them toward adulthood, there were room in the child for other becomings, 'other contemporaneous possibilities' that are not regressions but creative involutions bearing witness to '*an inhumanity immediately experienced in the body as such*'. (1987: 273)

The postmodern emphasis on the shared material basis of all things – of humans, animals, artifacts and natural objects – also advances an ecological sense of interconnectedness. In its environmentalism, postmodernism competes with other theoretical approaches as a route to a more progressive politics [see further Chapter 14].

THE PHYSICS OF BECOMING

Postmodern theorists picture the human being, like everything else that is, to be engaged in ongoing transitions between being and becoming. For Derrida, becoming is what makes possible any progress or improvement toward an ideal in political life:

If man is a perfectible creature, that is, if the identity of man is something 'to come', then the limits of humanity are not given ... So from that point of view, to be suspicious about the limits of man is not to be anti-humanist, on the contrary, it's a way of respecting what remains 'to come', under the name and the face of what we call 'man'. (2001: 44)

Individuals and states are not, however, fully in charge of this process or best understood as the master agents behind it. Again, humanity is one wondrous material manifestation among others. It has good, though inadequate, resources for intervening in life and inflecting the direction of becoming. The stuff of becoming is conceived as energy, force, affect, intensity, or life. These flows both subsist within intentions, spirituality, morality, culture, identity, and reasoning and help to give them the potential for mobility. None of these traditional entities is denied, but all are taken to be second-order formations emerging out of that which they are not. Within such an onto-story, it would be foolish to attempt to master the world; becomings can be facilitated, shifted, or resisted, but not commanded or ordered completely.

Lyotard's (1997) postmodern fable dramatizes this point. In it 'energy' is engaged in a perpetual and productive struggle between entropic disorder and the development of increasingly complex systems of order. This development

is not an invention made by Humans. Humans are an invention of development. The hero of the fable is not

the human species, but energy. The fable narrates a series of episodes marking now the success of what is most likely, death, and now the success of what is least likely and most precarious, and what is also the most efficient, the complex. (1997: 92)

At the end of the fable, some being is seeking to escape the earth, but whether it is a human and his/her brain, or a brain and its human, 'that, the story does not tell' (1997: 83).

Postmodern theory experiments with the idea that society and nature participate in similar logics, the non-linear ordering of a web of interdependencies. Here cultural theorists have sought to adjust complexity theory, originally developed by scientists to describe the most perplexing physical systems, to describe political and social relations. Lyotard (1997), Deleuze and Guattari (1987), and Michel Serres (1982), for example, draw upon the work of the Nobel laureate in chemistry, Ilya Prigogine. Their postmodern theories do not reject modern science, as some critics contend, but actively endorse one version of modern science, the one that understands nature in terms of turbulent systems where small changes in background conditions can have big effects, where micro-shifts can produce macro-effects.

Prigogine articulates a version of natural science congenial to postmodern cultural theory. He and his collaborator, the philosopher of science Isabelle Stengers, eschew the model of nature implied in classical dynamics, which presents 'a silent world ... a dead, passive nature, a nature that behaves as an automaton which, once programmed, continues to follow the rules inscribed in the program' (Prigogine and Stengers, 1984: 6). Their own model engages a nature where creativity and novelty abound and 'where the possible is richer than the real'. They insist, however, that nature retains a kind of intelligibility, even in its most complex and indeterminate states (Prigogine, 1997). Nature is neither the static world of classical dynamics nor some random set of fluctuations unrecognizable *as* a world: 'a new formulation of the laws of nature is now possible ... in which there is room for both the laws of nature and novelty and creativity' (1997: 16).

Postmodern theory tends, in its various manifestations, to conceive the relationship between social order and change in a similar manner, as an incompletely structured system, an open system susceptible to unpredictable encounters and the periodic emergence of new formations.

REASON AND AFFECT

Postmodern approaches to political theory do not reject reasoning, rationality, or Enlightenment values.

They do call into question Reason, i.e. the Kantian idea of a transcendental field that finds various expressions in the scientific, moral, and aesthetic judgements of human beings. Foucault, for example, believes that 'the central issue of philosophy and critical thought since the eighteenth century has been, still is, and will, I hope, remain the question, *What* is the Reason that we use? What are its historical effects? What are its limits, and what are its dangers?' (1989: 269). To employ reasoning without recourse to Reason, as postmodern theory does, is to develop a heightened sensitivity to the ethical and political dangers of relying upon reasoning outside of its relationship to less cognitive forms of knowing and experiencing.

There is a distinctive set of fears and anxieties that provoke postmodern thinking, including the excessive regulation and normalization of persons, places and experiences. One of the negative effects of societal rationalization and scientific categorization is the marginalization and denigration of people found not to measure up to prevailing criteria of rationality, normality, and responsibility (White, 1998). This element of cruelty within rationality is said to coexist alongside its nobler achievements.

A second liability of rationality concerns its inadequacy as a somatic inspiration for ethical action. Rational principles do not provide their own incentive for enactment. The key claim here is that ethics requires both reasoning and affect, where reasoning refers to acts of representation and systematic thought and affect refers to feeling-imbued thoughts that are not representational. Though affect is in ordinary parlance used as a synonym for emotion, in postmodern theory it is associated with a more protean kind of force, an intensity not yet organized into the distinct shape of emotion (Massumi, 2002). On this model of ethics, ethics entails both a moral code (which condenses moral ideals and metaphysical assumptions into rational principles and reasonable rules) *and* an embodied sensibility (which organizes affects into a style and generates the impetus to enact the code). Moral codes, for example, the Ten Commandments, remain inert without a disposition hospitable to their injunctions, the perceptual refinement necessary to apply them to particular cases, and the affective energy needed to perform them. Foucault puts the point this way:

> for an action to be 'moral', it must not be reducible to an act or a series of acts conforming to a rule, a law, or a value ... There is ... no moral conduct that does not [also] call for the forming of oneself as an ethical subject; and no forming of the ethical subject without ... 'practices of the self' that support them. (1985: 28)

Regardless of whether the ethical code is conceived as divine command or pragmatic rule, if the code is to be transformed into acts, affects must be engaged, orchestrated, and bound to it.

Here postmodern theory adopts and inflects an insight from Romanticism. Its emphasis on the importance of rituals, exercises, drills, and litanies is one example of how postmodern theory attends to the affective and aesthetic dimensions of political and ethical life and thought. In so doing, postmodern theory also connects to religious traditions (see Coles, 1997).

MICROPOLITICS AND MACROPOLITICS

Postmodern theorizing draws attention to the socially transformative potential of micropolitical practices. It insists upon the connections between micropolitics and macropolitics. Deleuze and Guattari use the term *micropolitics* to name a realm of activities that have public effect – that help to shape the tenor of collective life – but which do not fit into the traditional paradigms of political action. Micropolitical activities are not official acts of presidents or parliaments and they are often not aimed directly at elections or legislative agendas. Rather, the key agencies of micropolitics are television shows, films, military training, professional meetings, worship services, clubs, neighbourhood gangs, and Internet mobilizations; and its key targets are bodily affect, social tempers, political moods, and cultural sensibilities. The emphasis upon micropolitics issues from the belief that there is an indispensably somatic and affective dimension to political (and all other human) action, including macropolitical action. Partly a response to Marxist criticisms, the notion of micropolitics is a more intersubjective and collectivist version of Foucault's notion of technologies or practices of the self, which he defined as the means through which humans effect 'a certain number of operations on their own bodies and souls, thoughts, conducts, and way of being, so as to transform themselves' (1988: 18).

Micropolitics aims to reform, refine, intensify, or discipline the emotions, aesthetic impulses, moral and moralistic urges, and diffuse moods that enter into (and make possible) political programmes, party affiliations, ideological commitments, and policy preferences. Why do postmodern theorists advocate working experimentally upon such affections? Because to do so is ultimately, though indirectly and unpredictably, to alter the microsettings in which we participate and to help determine the macropolitical possibilities. Moods and affects are also said to be relevant to public life in that they may provide the motivational energy required to enact intellectual commitments or political priorities – to transform them into actualities. Again, the idea is to give the affective dimension of thought and action its due: politics in the broadest sense – as action that makes a public difference – requires not only intintellectual things (like principles, programmes of reform, visions of the future) but also embodied sensibilities that organize affects into a style and generate the impetus to enact principles, programmes, and visions (Curtis, 1999).

Individualists, iconoclasts, and queer theorists employ micropolitics in order to render themselves resistant to the lure of conformity and the demand for normality. Transcendentalists in the tradition of Henry Thoreau engage in a series of practical exercises – including nature walks, perceptual attentiveness to small details of ordinary things, journal writing – in order to foster a more deliberate life (Bennett, 2002). Ecospiritualists advocate meditation and wilderness excursions as ways of enhancing the experience of the interdependency of all things. Religious activists engage in prayer or church attendance as ways of disciplining the body and developing good character. Deleuze and Guattari use micropolitical techniques to experiment with becoming otherwise and to forestall the reduction of becoming to being. Postmodern political theory acknowledges that micropolitics can be pursued on behalf of different aims and a wide variety of political ideologies.

DISCIPLINARY POWER AND THE POSSIBILITY OF FREEDOM

One influential postmodern insight is that the power exercised over citizens and subjects does not only issue from identifiable loci like the state and its laws. It also operates more diffusely and more insidiously by means of normal, everyday practices which have no particular author and instead present themselves as simply the way things are done. Foucault describes the first as a juridical model of power and the second as disciplinary, normalizing or bio-power. His early genealogies of criminality, madness, and sexuality sensitized readers to the medical, educational, military, and even architectural practices that function to inscribe norms right onto the body (Dumm, 1996). Terry Eagleton describes this second kind of power, which operates primarily not by means of prohibition but rather by constituting the very subjectivity of its objects, when he warns that the Romantic attempt to conjoin reason with sentiment had the effect of inscribing power 'in the minutiae of subjective experience' and thus it participated in the larger historical trend whereby 'power is shifting its location from centralized institutions to the silent, invisible depths of the subject itself (1990: 20, 27).

But this focus on the pervasiveness of power does not mean that there is no such thing, from a postmodern perspective, as freedom. In his later work Foucault, for example, *affirmed* a project of aesthetic self-inscription and suggested that sensibility was susceptible, to some degree, to self-conscious craftsmanship. This craftsmanship is not reducible to those reflexive arcs by which one uses new thoughts to revise old beliefs, though that is part of it. It also folds specific postures, sounds, and images into that process, so as to impinge more actively upon the affective register of being. If the point of Foucault's early genealogies is to expose the normal individual as a ruse of power, and to disrupt our association of self-discipline with freedom, the point of his later work is to enunciate the more complex thesis that there is no self without power and discipline, and no power or discipline that does not also harbour opportunities for freedom in terms of arts of the self.

What kind of freedom can coexist with ubiquitous, productive power? A postmodern notion of freedom is not the Kantian idea of an autonomous rational will; neither is it the Romantic revision of Kant wherein an aesthetic modulation of the psyche allows the rational will to kick in. Freedom is resignified by locating it in a relationship with historically situated rationality and human embodiment. The goal is to find ways to promote a higher degree of self-direction in and against a system of disciplinary power. Freedom is not defined as something that rises above desire, sensibility and feeling; it consists rather in a reflective – and often agonistic – kind of heteronomy. It is the recognition of one's implication in a sticky web of social and physical relations within which *also* reside vital (although unpredictable and contested) opportunities for self-direction. What counts as self-direction depends upon the particularities of what one has become and the sort of obstacles and opportunities culturally available. Sometimes self-direction is direct, by self-command or self-exertion; more often it is pursued through arts, techniques, and strategies applied by the self to a corporeal sensibility below the level of direct intellectual control (Connolly, 1999). The experience of freedom is vibrant; one experiences the exhilaration of making a mark upon what one comes to be. But this sense of liberation does not carry one above the world of sensibility or power. It consists, rather, in tentative explorations of the outer edges of existing regimes of subjectivity and intersubjectivity.

For postmodern political theorists, these engagements with the frontier reveal the possibility of new configurations of identity. These new configurations are still a function of an institutional matrix; they are still implicated in historically contingent practices of power, and they continue to contend with a body that never fully coincides with the subjectivity available to it. The ape in Kafka's story, 'A report to an academy' (1971) makes a similar point. Caught and caged for exhibition, Rotpeter decided to become human, for only then would he be let out: 'Freedom,' he says, 'was not what I wanted. Only a way out; right or left, or in any direction; I made no other demand'(1971: 253–4). The apeman seeks not unconditional freedom, only a way to transform his situation into a place with more room to exercise his potential for self-direction. Kafka here articulates a postmodern conception of freedom.

Postmodern political theorizing typically proceeds, then, on the assumption that moments of critical freedom are internal to a system of power. Power

> pervades the very conceptual apparatus that seeks to negotiate its terms, including the subject position of the critic; and … this implication of the terms of criticism in the field of power is *not* the advent of a nihilistic relativism incapable of furnishing norms but, rather, the very precondition of a politically engaged critique. (Butler, 1995: 38–9; see also Spivak, 1999)

RHIZOMATIC STRUCTURES AND LINES OF FLIGHT

In the onto-story of a world of becoming, things are moving at different speeds and metamorphoses abound; matter is mobile and thus so are humans and their cultural forms. Communitarian political theory tends to view this as a lamentable and dangerous characterization of social life: it undermines the legitimacy of traditional moral codes and dims the prospect of achieving consensus on a basic set of norms and values. The fear is that the postmodern story worsens the postmodern *condition*, characterized as a state of fragmentation plagued by a crisis of meaning. Some postmodern theorists themselves embrace this diagnosis, but others view it as overstated by virtue of the contrast model of harmony it implicitly invokes. The contemporary world will surely appear as fragmented and in crisis if it is compared to a lost, golden age of social coherence, unquestioned morality, and pervasive faith in a single, transcendent God. To question the historical plausibility of this tale of community and cosmological coherence, however, is to see things differently. Postmodern theorists find the nostalgic metanarrative to be inappropriate, even as a regulative ideal, in a world where multicultural societies are the norm, where technological developments increase the speed with which social transformation occurs, and where peoples with diverse onto-stories coexist on the same territory and under the same government.

William Connolly does not, for example, support a world of fragmentation as opposed to unity, but advocates a kind of pluralism where social groups with divergent moral traditions and competing ontological convictions form pragmatic and partial alliances. Attentive to the constitutive tension between the need for order and the value of disruption/ reformation, he moves pluralism away from the image of a cultural centre surrounded by minorities at the margin and toward a vision of public life as populated by multiple minorities with cross-cutting allegiances along 'lines of religion, linguistic habit, economic interest, irreligion, ethnicity, sensuality, gender performances, and moral sources of inspiration' (Connolly, 1999: 92). He calls the relations between and within these minorities rhizomatic rather than fragmenting.

A rhizome is a botanical term for a particular kind of root structure: a non-linear and web-like organization, like that of bulbs, tubers, stems and filaments, in contrast to a single tap-root. A rhizomatic politics does not have as its regulative ideal a general consensus. It is inspired, rather, by the vision of mobile constellations whose members support common policies but not necessarily all for the same reasons, and who attempt to render themselves 'more open to responsive engagement with alternative faiths, sensualities, gender practices, ethnicities, and so on' (1999: 146). Practising a generous 'ethos of engagement', citizens would strive to acknowledge the contestability of any moral source or onto-story, including their own (Connolly, 1995).

Critical theorists, like communitarians, are often wary of postmodern theory and the postmodern condition in so far as the former aggravates the latter and both allow global capital and commodified culture to fill the void left by stable, local ways of life. Postmodern theorists themselves are divided on this issue. Some emphasize the dangers of a world of becoming, e.g. the continual emergence of tensions between a shifting array of social groups, the endless need to renegotiate meanings, and the tendency of power relations to congeal into hegemonic, i.e. capitalist, formations. Others emphasize the liberating potential and marvels of this evolving world. Often the debate exists within theorists as well as between them. The question is to what extent the world of diverse becomings meets its match in a culture where the lifeworld has been colonized by a homogenizing commodity culture.

A good example here is Michael Hardt and Antonio Negri's *Empire* (2000), which attempts to combine Marxist insights about the structural impediments to social justice with those of Deleuze and Guattari about the potential 'lines of flight' within every structure, i.e. the omnipresence of 'paths along which things change or become transformed into something else' (Patton, 2000: 86). Hardt and Negri transform the old notion of the proletariat, defined in terms of industrial wage work, into the more protean and multi-class force called the multitude. Likewise, the logic of capitalism becomes something more flexible and impersonal – and thus both more diabolical and less competent; it is replaced by empire. 'The multitude is the real productive force of our social world, whereas Empire is a mere apparatus of capture that lives only off the vitality of the multitude' (Hardt and Negri, 2000: 62). But industrial, intellectual, aesthetic, and communicative labourers 'cannot be completely subjugated to the laws of capitalist accumulation – at every moment they overflow and shatter the bounds of measure' (2000: 396–7; see also Shapiro, 2000).

Some postmodern theory discerns a limited but real potential for justice and freedom within market and commodity-centred economies. It is unlikely to view capitalism as a closed system, with no way out short of revolutionary violence. It tentatively affirms 'the ambivalent excitement about capitalism's transformative possibilities expressed by Marx himself' (Robbins, 1999: 35). This postmodernism does not necessarily advocate a post-market economy, and it rejects the image of global capital as a monster devouring everything in its path as both empirically inaccurate and politically disabling:

> The impossibility of a global order must be affirmed ... If we can accept that it is impossible to subsume every individual being, place and practice to a universal law ... then it will follow that the local cannot be fully interior to the global, nor can its inventive potential be captured by any singular imagining [of the economy]. (Gibson-Graham, 2003)

Such work aims to deny capitalism quite the degree of efficacy and totalizing power that its critics (and defenders) often attribute to it, and to exploit the positive ethical potential secreted within it (Bennett, 2001). Again, such analyses work with a particular image of power, in which 'there is always something that flows or flees, that escapes ... the overcoding machine' (Deleuze and Guattari, 1987: 216). Though 'capitalists may be the master of surplus value and its distribution ... they do not dominate the flows from which surplus value derives' (1987: 226).

The notion of lines of flight that persist within the densest of networks of power – or of the subsistence of a virtual world within the actual, or of the possibility of forging rhizomatic connections between people who do not share a common moral framework – reveals a link between postmodern theory and the political hopefulness of the cultural revolution of the 1960s. Postmodern theory affirms the value of idealizations, even if they are regulative ideals not fully realizable. Romand Coles, for example, defends a post-secular, non-theistic ethic of generosity even though its practice must always fall 'short of the highest solicitation to give' (1997: 81). Foucault suggests that political freedom is enabled by the impossible desire for self-direction and the dream of a beautifully designed subjectivity. Derrida has faith in a justice that is a 'kind of reserve which is not exhausted by any particular concept of justice':

> On the one hand, you have the law which is deconstructible; that is, the set of legislations ... which are ... deconstructible because we change them, we improve them, we want to improve them, we can improve them ... On the other hand, justice, in the name of which one deconstructs the law, is not deconstructible. (2001: 6, 9)

Like all approaches to political theory, postmodernism has developed a distinctive vocabulary, but perhaps more than other approaches it has refused 'to translate its insights directly into an idiom compatible with the traditional cognitive machinery of political thought' (White, 1991: 19). New modes of political organization seem to require new ways of thinking: the experience of alienation that accompanies the encounter with a foreign language can have positive political effects. If there is a vision of politics common to postmodern theories, it is of a political realm that renegotiates the age-old debate between being and becoming in order to give more room to becoming and to render itself more open to change and democratic in operation.

REFERENCES

Agamben, Giorgio (1999) 'Absolute immanence'. In *Potentialities: Collected Essays in Philosophy.* Stanford, CA: Stanford University Press.

Bennett, Jane (2001) *The Enchantment of Modern Life: Attachments, Crossings, and Ethics.* Princeton, NJ: Princeton University Press.

Bennett, Jane (2002) *Thoreau's Nature: Ethics, Politics, and the Wild.* Lanham, MD: Rowman and Littlefield.

Berg-Sorensen, Anders (2001) 'Paradiso–diaspora: political theologies or critiques of religion'. PhD dissertation, University of Copenhagen.

Brown, Wendy (1995) *States of Injury: Power and Freedom in Late Modernity.* Princeton, NJ: Princeton University Press.

Butler, Judith (1993) *Bodies That Matter: On the Discursive Limits of 'Sex'.* New York: Routledge.

Butler, Judith (1995) 'Contingent foundations'. In Seyla Benhabib, Judith Butler, Drucilla Cornell and Nancy

Fraser, eds, *Feminist Contentions: A Philosophical Exchange*. New York: Routledge, 35–57.

Cheney, Lynne (1996) *Telling the Truth: Why Our Culture and Our Country Have Stopped Making Sense and What We Can Do About It*. New York: Touchstone.

Coles, Romand (1997) *Rethinking Generosity: Critical Theory and the Politics of Caritas*. Ithaca, NY: Cornell University Press.

Connolly, William E. (1995) *The Ethos of Pluralization*. Minneapolis: University of Minnesota Press.

Connolly, William E. (1999) *Why I Am Not a Secularist*. Minneapolis: University of Minnesota Press.

Connolly, William E. (2002) *Neuropolitics: Thinking, Culture, Speed*. Minneapolis: University of Minnesota Press.

Coole, Diana (2000) *Negativity and Politics: Dionysus and Dialectics from Kant to Poststructuralism*. New York: Routledge.

Cornell, Drucilla (1991) *Beyond Accommodation: Ethical Feminism, Deconstruction, and the Law*. New York: Routledge.

Corson, Ben (2001) 'Transcending violence in Derrida: a reply to John McCormack'. *Political Theory*, 29 (December).

Curtis, Kimberley (1999) *Our Sense of the Real: Aesthetic Experience and Arendtian Politics*. Ithaca, NY: Cornell University Press.

Deleuze, Gilles and Guattari, Felix (1987) *A Thousand Plateaus*, trans. Brian Massumi. Minneapolis: University of Minnesota Press.

Derrida, Jacques (2001) 'An interview with Jacques Derrida'. *Theory & Event*, 5 (1).

Docker, John (1994) *Postmodernism and Popular Culture: A Cultural History*. Cambridge: Cambridge University Press.

Dumm, Thomas (1996) *Michel Foucault and the Politics of Freedom*. New York: Rowman and Littlefield.

Dumm, Thomas (1999) 'The problem of the We'. *boundary 2*, 26 (3): 55–61.

Dumm, Thomas and Anne Norton, eds (1998) 'On left conservatism I' and 'On left conservatism II'. *Theory & Event*, 2 (2) and 2 (3).

Eagleton, Terry (1990) *Ideology of the Aesthetic*. London: Blackwell.

Ferguson, Kathy E. (1991) *The Man Question: Visions of Subjectivity in Feminist Theory*. Berkeley, CA: University of California Press.

Foucault, Michel (1985) *The Use of Pleasure: The History of Sexuality, Volume II*. New York: Pantheon.

Foucault, Michel (1988) *Care of the Self: The History of Sexuality, Volume III*. New York: Random House.

Foucault, Michel (1989) 'An ethics of pleasure'. In Sylverer Lotringer, ed., *Foucault Live*, trans. John Johnston. London: Semiotext(e).

Gatens, Moira (1996) *Imaginary Bodies: Ethics, Power and Corporeality*. New York: Routledge.

Gibson-Graham, J. K. (1996) *The End of Capitalism (As We Knew It)*. London: Blackwell.

Gibson-Graham, J. K. (2003) 'An ethics of the local'. *Rethinking Marxism*, 15 (1).

Haraway, Donna (1989) *Primate Visions*. New York: Routledge.

Hardt, Michael and Antonio Negri (2000) *Empire*. Cambridge, MA: Harvard University Press.

Hegel, Friedrich (1974) *Hegel: The Essential Writings*, ed. Frederick Weiss. New York: Harper.

Honig, Bonnie (1993) *Political Theory and the Displacement of Politics*. Ithaca, NY: Cornell University Press.

Kateb, George (2000) 'Aestheticism and morality: their cooperation and hostility'. *Political Theory*, 28 (1): 5–37.

Kafka, Franz (1971) 'A report to an academy'. In *The Complete Stories*. New York: Schocken, 250–62.

Laclau, Ernesto and Chantal Mouffe (1985) *Hegemony and Socialist Strategy*. London: Verso.

Latour, Bruno (1993) *We Have Never Been Modern*. Cambridge, MA: Harvard University Press.

Lyotard, Jean-François (1997) *Postmodern Fables*, trans. Georges van den Abbeele. Minneapolis: University of Minnesota Press.

Massumi, Brian (2002) *Parables for the virtual: Movement, Affect, Sensation*. Durham, NC: Duke University Press.

Nietzsche, Friedrich (1987) *The Will to Power*. New York: Random House.

Patton, Paul (2000) *Deleuze and the Political*. New York: Routledge.

Prigogine, Ilya (1997) *The End of Certainty: Time, Chaos, and the New Laws of Nature*. New York: Free.

Prigogine, Ilya and Isabelle, Stengers (1984) *Order Out of Chaos: Man's New Dialogue with Nature*. New York: Bantam.

Rajchman, John (2000) *The Deleuze Connections*. Cambridge, MA: MIT Press.

Robbins, Bruce (1999) 'Disjoining the Left'. *boundary 2*, 26 (3).

Rorty, Richard (1995) 'Philosophy and the future'. In Herman J. Saatkamp Jr, ed., *Rorty and Pragmatism: The Philosopher Responds to his Critics*. Nashville, TN: Vanderbilt University Press.

Serres, Michel (1982) *Hermes: Literature, Science, Philosophy*. Baltimore: Johns Hopkins University Press.

Shapiro, Kam (2000) 'From dream to desire: at the threshold of old and new utopias'. *Theory & Event*, vol. 4 (4).

Spivak, Gayatri Chakravorty (1999) *A Critique of Postcolonial Reason: Toward a History of the Vanishing Present*. Cambridge, MA: Harvard University Press.

Stavrakakis, Yannis (1999) *Lacan and the Political*. New York: Routledge.

White, Stephen K. (1991) *Political Theory and Postmodernism*. Cambridge: Cambridge University Press.

White, Stephen K. (1998) 'Postmodernism and political theory'. In Edward Craig et al., eds, *Encyclopedia of Philosophy*. New York: Routledge.

White, Stephen K. (2000) *Affirmation in Political Theory: The Strengths of Weak Ontology*. Princeton, NJ: Princeton University Press.

5

Positive Political Theory

H. DONALD FORBES

Positive political theory, narrowly understood, means rational choice theory applied to the study of politics. More broadly understood, as it will be here, it can refer to a much wider array of analytic approaches and final goals. Its limits are set by two familiar contrasts: positive, or what is, is contrasted with normative, or what ought to be; and theory, in the sense of abstraction and explanation, is contrasted with detailed descriptions of particular cases.[1]

The aim of this chapter is to clarify what it can mean, in the academic study of politics, to give simplifying empirical analysis of some kind priority over plain description and explicit prescription. Three main kinds of positive theorizing will be distinguished, which will be called, for want of any better terms, conditional, rational, and intentional. Most of professional political science fits within one or more of these categories, but only a few examples of each can be selected for discussion here.

CONDITIONAL ANALYSIS

The analysis of political facts is often cast in terms of the relations between independent and dependent variables, and when it is, the aim is almost always to isolate some relatively simple functional relationships among the values of the variables. Do any of the independent variables correlate strongly with the dependent dimension? Are any of these correlations more than just correlations – that is, evidence of *causal* connections? What are the necessary and/or sufficient conditions for the outcomes of interest? More generally, which prior conditions make these outcomes more or less likely? In the present context, *conditional* may be better than the standard term *causal* for distinguishing the kind of causal analysis suggested by these questions (cf. King, Keohane and Verba, 1994).

Consider a simple example. Why do some citizens of Detroit vote Democrat and others Republican? Surveys may suggest that Catholics vote significantly more often for the Democrats than do Protestants or Jews. This correlation between religion and vote may be a clear statistical fact, derived by rigorous reasoning from some more elementary (or 'brute') facts about the way a sample of Detroit's residents have answered questions about their race, religion, occupation, education, and so on. Admittedly, it may have almost no relation to what these voters would say if asked to explain why they voted as they did (they might say almost nothing about their religious backgrounds or beliefs), but it may still be an important fact in the context of practically oriented speculation about why voters really vote the way they do and what can be done to make them vote as one would like. In short, it may be part of a 'causal' theory of voting, in Detroit or elsewhere, and the theory may be true or false, regardless of what one thinks 'normatively' about voting for any particular party.

Rigorous statistical reasoning was first widely used in political science to establish and to explain or interpret simple relationships of this kind. The quantitative study of public opinion and voting is now one of the largest subfields of the discipline. Few of its many findings are perhaps of much interest to political theorists, but the methods and overall approach of such 'behavioural' research are another matter. And recently some of their most important applications have had to do with large claims about the causes and effects of democracy, as the following examples will show.

The Democratic Peace Hypothesis

Liberal democracies have rarely or never gone to war with each other. But can we say that democracy is a cause of peace or a sufficient condition for it? The democratic peace hypothesis is essentially the claim that wars have occurred and can occur only between autocracies or between democracies and autocracies. If all countries were democracies, there would be no wars.

The hypothesis can claim a root deep in modern political theory (Doyle, 1983; Cavallar, 2001; Franceschet, 2001). Whether true or false, it may have influenced policy-making at the highest levels. Both theoretically and practically, therefore, it seems important to determine whether it is in fact true or false.

The literature bearing on the hypothesis has grown dramatically in the past 20 years and has gradually become very technical. The earliest statistical studies (Babst, 1972; Small and Singer, 1976) suffered from some obvious shortcomings, but more recent studies have been models of careful conceptualization, assiduous data collection, and sophisticated multivariate data analysis. The basic challenge has been to justify a causal interpretation of a striking statistical regularity. To do so *statistically* one must introduce additional variables and test more complex models. Unfortunately, the more elaborate the statistical models, the more precarious their empirical foundations. War is a rare event, and since most of its causal conditions change only slowly, one cannot easily determine, from the examination of the annual data used in most statistical studies, whether there is any statistically significant relationship between the occurrence of war and particular background conditions, such as the presence or absence of democracy. The choice of an appropriate probability model is evidently a crucial first step in the analysis of the historical record, but it is very difficult to see which model provides the proper benchmark.[2] Moreover, since the relevant cases are so few, the coding of one or two problematic ones (Spain's status as a democracy in 1898, Finland's status as an enemy of the Allied powers from 1941 to 1944) can have a substantial impact on the results of any statistical analysis.[3]

Despite these difficulties, there is now a consensus that empirical research generally supports the hypothesis: joint democracy seems to be a sufficient condition for peaceful relations between states (for reviews of the literature see Chan, 1997; Ray, 1995; 1998; Russett, 1993; Russett and Oneal, 2001). This now widely accepted 'empirical law' about 'democratic dyads' provides an outstanding example of statistically based causal theorizing in political science.

Even strong and well-established statistical relationships invite conflicting causal interpretations, however. Thus Joanne Gowa (1999), using the same historical data as many other studies of democracy and war, suggests that there was a different relationship between these variables before World War I than there has been since World War II. Before World War I, it seems, democracies may have been *more* likely than autocracies to threaten each other militarily and no less likely to be involved in war. Only since World War II do the data support the idea of a 'democratic peace'. In other words, the hypothesis does not hold universally, according to Gowa, but only as a statistical rule in particular circumstances, as a by-product of a particular structure of alliances. Other recent studies have advanced a related critique, suggesting that broad 'cultural variables' (similarities of interest and outlook) are more important than 'structural variables' (forms of government) in explaining the relations between states (Gartzke, 1998; Henderson, 1998; Kacowicz, 1995) or that other political similarities, such as joint republicanism or joint dictatorship, may be as strongly associated with peace between states as joint democracy is (Peceny, Beer and Sanchez-Terry, 2002; Weart, 1998; Werner, 2000).

Democratization and Ethnic Conflict

Controversial hypotheses can sometimes be defended by combining them with others in a more complex theory. Each hypothesis, in isolation, may be vulnerable to damaging objections, but combined with others, it may become part of a much sturdier web of belief. This possibility is nicely illustrated by recent discussions of a practically very important objection to the democratic peace hypothesis.

Mature democracies may not fight wars with each other, and they may have reliable ways of resolving their internal conflicts, but what about countries in transition to a more democratic form of government? The collapse of autocratic authority may mean the end of power-sharing arrangements between ethnic or national rivals. Moreover, the threat of majority rule may give traditional autocratic elites a motive for fostering ethnic or national strife, to block further democratization. Thus democratization, in the context of ethnic diversity and latent ethnic conflicts, may produce not peace, but civil and international war. Examples that seem to fit this pattern come easily to mind, but do they illustrate a general rule?

Attempts to deal with this question in a straightforward way, along the lines suggested by the studies cited above, have yielded inconclusive results

(Ellingsen, 2000; Enterline, 1996; Gleditsch, 2002; Gleditsch and Ward, 2000; Hegre et al., 2001; Mansfield and Snyder, 1995; 1996; 1997; 2002; Mousseau, 2001; Thompson and Tucker, 1997; Ward and Gleditsch, 1998; Weitsman and Shambaugh, 2002). The relationship, assuming it exists, seems to be too weak to stand out clearly from the multitude of other relationships involved in the causes of war and domestic turmoil. In the rigorously quantitative literature, therefore, methodological disputes (about the shortcomings of different data sets, the definition and coding of variables, the treatment of ex-colonial regimes, the calculation of significance levels, and so on) have tended to divert attention from the basic idea that promoting democracy (in China, for example) may actually increase the risks of war. A practically important claim is lost from sight in a blizzard of methodological minutiae.

The merits of the new hypothesis about democratization and war proneness are clearer when it is evaluated in a more 'qualitative' way. Thus Jack Snyder uses a variety of historical case studies to suggest that 'none of the mechanisms that produce the democratic peace among mature democracies operate in the same fashion in newly democratizing states. Indeed, most of them work in reverse' (2000: 55). The sense of security mature democracies feel in dealing with each other, their commercial rather than military preoccupations, the aversion of their peoples to war and their unwillingness to bear its costs: these and other checks on warlike behaviour may all be overridden in semi-democratic regimes, where power elites, threatened by democracy, may foment war as a way of bolstering their power, where wealthy industrialists may profit from the preparations for war, and where ordinary citizens may be neutralized or led astray by unfair constraints on electoral competition, disorganized political parties, and partial media monopolies. Case studies to illustrate these possibilities fall on the 'qualitative' side of the standard quantitative–qualitative divide, but the goal of the qualitative research can remain, as this example shows, 'quantitative', that is, the discovery of simple correlations between background conditions and a dependent variable of interest.

Snyder's basic contention is that traditional autocratic elites create exclusionist ethnic nationalisms when their power is threatened by the spread of democracy. In a quite 'rational' way, they provoke nationalist conflicts to protect their own interests. By claiming to govern in the name of a threatened people, they avoid having to surrender real political authority to the average citizen. 'Nationalist conflicts arise as a byproduct of elites' efforts to persuade the people to accept divisive nationalist ideas' (2000: 32). Nationalism is thus the intervening variable between Snyder's regime variable (democratic, democratizing, etc.) and his dependent variable of internal or external violence. Different varieties of nationalism (three ethnic, one civic) mediate the postulated relationships between mature democracy and peace, on the one hand, and between democratization and war proneness, on the other hand. Snyder's theory lifts these relationships out of their statistical context, one can say, and gives them a more *understandable* meaning, with a 'theoretical logic' illustrated by the case studies.

The resulting theory of nationalism is certainly plausible, and it has a distinguished pedigree, going back to early scientific studies of the deviousness of princes, but a really convincing demonstration of its merits would require a more systematic discussion than Snyder provides of the alternatives to it – the other causal theories that have been abstracted from the vast historical and social scientific literature on nationality and ethnicity. Nonetheless, the rhetorical strategy of the book – supporting a shaky statistical generalization and putative causal law by means of case studies and a 'theoretical logic' loosely related to the idea of rational individual choice – is effective. It resembles the one employed in another recent and very influential theory about the conditions of democracy or good government.

Social Capital and Democracy

Social capital has different meanings in different contexts. Here it will be used for the variable Robert Putnam (1993) argues is a powerful determinant of effective democratic government. This determinant is the number of 'horizontal' linkages between individuals of equivalent status and power in voluntary associations such as choral societies, soccer clubs, hiking clubs, birdwatching clubs, literary circles, and the like. The more such linkages in a region, the better was the performance of that region's government, Putnam found in his celebrated comparative study of the 20 regions of Italy. The relevant correlations were amazingly strong, and they pointed to the conclusion that a dense network of voluntary linkages is a crucial condition for strong, stable, responsive, effective democratic government.

Putnam maintains that 'social trust' (which he also calls social capital) is the variable connecting associational density to democratic performance. Trust is vitally important for a society, he says, because it helps to overcome 'dilemmas of collective action' and thus 'to solve the fundamental Hobbesian dilemma of public order' (1993: 112). Trusting and trustworthy citizens are more able to co-operate with each other, on the basis of voluntary agreements, than are those who lack trust in each other and cannot make credible commitments. A dense (and closed) network of civic engagements sustains generalized trust because it threatens naturally self-interested individuals with realistic punishments for defecting from their commitments (Coleman, 1988; 1990). In looser, more open social networks, individualism or narrow self-interest (opportunism, free riding, etc.) is more likely to flourish, so that all must forgo many opportunities for mutual gain. Trust, and the norm of reciprocity associated with it, serve to reconcile self-interest and solidarity. They 'lubricate' co-operation, not just in politics, but also in economics. In short, 'good government in Italy is a by-product of singing groups and soccer clubs' (Putnam, 1993: 176).

Since its publication, Putnam's remarkably suggestive analysis has been exposed to a great deal of critical scrutiny. Some have objected to his depiction of Italian society and politics; others have challenged the application of his theory to other countries, particularly the United States. Putnam, for example, may not have paid sufficient attention to the role that the Communist Party of Italy played in creating good government (operationalized as pollution controls, daycare centres, responsive bureaucrats, etc.) in those regions where it was strong (Tarrow, 1996). Could the crucial independent variable have been, not singing groups and soccer clubs, but communist cells? And how many regions are there really, from a statistician's standpoint, in Italy? Are there the 20 that are distinguished in law and that are the basis for Putnam's statistics, or are there really just two distinct regions, North and South? The weight of the *statistical* evidence must evidently depend on the answer to this question.

Similar problems appear when the theory is applied to other countries. Some support for its general applicability has been found in studies of the American states, even though the relevant correlations are distinctly weaker (Putnam, 2000; Rice and Sumberg, 1997; Rice and Arnett, 2001). Other comparative studies are not so encouraging, however. Peter Hall's (1999) detailed study of Britain suggests that changes in norms and trust over time may be unrelated to changes in the vibrancy of associational life. Susan Pharr (2000) and Donatella della Porta (2000) make strong cases for attributing high levels of distrust and dissatisfaction with politics in Japan and Italy respectively, not to changes in social capital (in the sense of networks), or to the performance of the economy, but simply to the conduct in office of each nation's politicians (cf. Jackman and Miller, 1998). A number of critics (e.g. Berman, 1997; Fukuyama, 2001; Levi, 1996; Varshney, 2001) have argued that different kinds of social

capital may have different effects, so that democratic political performance may be threatened by its 'bad' or 'uncivic' forms, difficult to distinguish in principle from its more desirable forms. As noted above, a simple horizontal–vertical (or secular–sacred) distinction seems to have worked well for Putnam in Italy, but it may not be so easy to apply and justify elsewhere. (In fact it is silently dropped in Putnam, 2000.) Even if civic norms and trust are consistently related to performance, associational activity may not be (Knack and Keefer, 1997). And heterogeneous communities, where 'bridging' social capital is most needed, may be the least able to develop it (Alesina and La Ferrara, 2000; 2002).

Putnam's chain of correlations (from social networks through trust to democratic performance) gains its aura of causal necessity, not so much from the strength and persistence of the statistical relations he and others have been able to demonstrate, as from the reasoning about collective action problems that accompanies the presentation of the still somewhat scanty evidence. If the chain must hold in theory, one assumes, then surely its links must be observable in the facts.

Some Provisional Generalizations

The studies cited so far illustrate the maturing of the kind of positive science of politics that the partisans of the 'behavioural' movement in political science were calling for 50 years ago.[4] The early behaviouralists could provide only vague outlines and very simple examples of the more scientific research that they thought should replace intellectual history and institutional description as the core political science disciplines (e.g. Easton, 1965; Easton and Dennis, 1968). Their opponents could reasonably argue that nothing coherent or worthwhile would ever come of their attempts to build 'empirical theory'. Impatient critics could wave away the whole enterprise, saying that it might serve to show how Catholics voted in Detroit, but not much else (Taylor, 1968: 90). Such high-handed dismissals are less effective today, where research workers in the social sciences have access to vast archives of machine readable data from scores of countries, and they routinely employ far more powerful methods of statistical analysis than were generally available even a generation ago. The embarrassingly nebulous grand theories of the recent past – systems theory, structural-functional theory, group theory, and the like – have receded from view. Attention now focuses on demonstrable relationships between measurable variables of obvious importance, such as democracy and war, and their analysis does not stop with the establishment of a few simple correlations.

To be sure, studies of the kind cited above remain vulnerable to some common objections. The difficulty of operationalizing key concepts such as democracy, war, nationalism, and good government is obviously a source of serious problems. Such 'essentially contested' political 'variables' do not lend themselves to easy quantification, or even identification, for statistical analysis. In addition, a serious, often insurmountable source of difficulties is the complexity of the background conditions that may have to be untangled before any simple causal connections can be shown. A realistic statistical model of the phenomena of interest may involve many variables whose effects rebound on their causes, making statistical estimation extremely difficult. Nonetheless, statistically based causal analysis does not require for its justification that every statistical study make a major contribution to scientific knowledge or that it be beyond reproach. It requires only that there be rigorous ways of testing hypothesized relationships and untangling the webs of conditioning variables in which they are embedded. The data and methods used in a particular study may be inappropriate, but this will be shown by comparing its assumptions and results with those of other such studies, not by abandoning statistical reasoning altogether for some radically different way of establishing causal conditions. Even case studies, as Gary King, Robert Keohane and Sidney Verba (1994) have argued, can provide grist for the statistical mill.

The trend towards statistical reasoning is even more striking when it is viewed from a longer historical perspective. More than a century and a half ago, John Stuart Mill clearly explained the basic 'logic' of a positive social science in Book VI of his *System of Logic* (1843). He showed that there could be no fundamental differences between social and psychological inquiries ('the moral sciences'), on the one hand, and the natural sciences, on the other, in so far as they were all 'inquiries into the course of nature', that is, attempts to discover the background conditions that produce particular phenomena. Much of contemporary social science is directly descended from his philosophy. But Mill seems to have had no inkling when he wrote that the growth of statistics, not just as data and methods, but as a way of reasoning about cause and effect, would transform the character of the science he projected and narrow its concerns, making it almost indistinguishable from the quantitative analysis of social and economic policy.[5]

Mill saw more clearly that the 'logic' involved in developing and testing scientific hypotheses about sequences of conditions or events is quite different from that required by 'Practice, or Art, including Morality and Policy' (the title of ch. 12 of Book VI). Mill's distinction between 'science' and 'art' is our familiar fact–value distinction: the statements of science are in the indicative mood, he said, while those of art are in the imperative or optative moods. (They have to do with defining and harmonizing our different ends or objects of desire, such as 'health' and 'the happiness of mankind'.) This distinction has always been controversial, but in the present context it is easy to see how the 'scientific' investigation of causal conditions can be separated from the 'ethical' discussion of ends, and also easy, with Mill, to regard the two kinds of inquiry as complementary. Empirically grounded simplifications help political practitioners to know the conditions of the effects they seek and therefore, to some extent, whether they are worth pursuing.

RATIONAL CHOICE THEORY

The rapid development of rational choice theory and research has been the most dramatic change in professional political science since the 1950s. It represents a sharper break from earlier modes of inquiry than the statistically based causal modelling that has also flourished during the same period. Given the training and habits of mind that 'rational choice' requires, it is unlikely ever to win the allegiance of most political scientists or to have much direct impact outside the academy, but it has undeniably had a resounding impact on the more professional strata of the profession. Its root problems – the fairness of games of chance, the unpredictability of strategic interaction, the merits of different voting rules, the peculiarity of spatial competition – have more or less lengthy histories. Around 1960 the techniques that mathematicians and economists had developed to deal with these problems crystallized as a distinctive outlook and set of principles.[6]

The principles can be summarized in three words – individualism, rationalism, and formalism. Rational choice theorists seek to explain collective outcomes by individual choices, which are generally assumed to derive from fixed preferences that are basically self-regarding. Individual actors are assumed to be rational in the limited sense, roughly, of having clear goals (being able to rank the possible outcomes of their choices coherently) and being willing and able to do whatever is necessary (within given constraints) to satisfy them. But there are obviously many situations in which it is difficult to know which choices will in fact best serve one's preferences. These situations may become clear only as the result of a 'formal' mathematical analysis of their elements. Consequently, it is assumed, any satisfactory explanation of what happens in these confusing situations must have the form of a mathematical model that reveals the implications of instrumental rationality.[7]

'Positive political theory', narrowly understood, refers to studies conforming to these principles. Hundreds if not thousands of investigations, by economists and sociologists as well as political scientists, could be cited to illustrate their role in contemporary political science.[8] To ask at this point what contribution they have made to the discipline would be a bit like asking for an assessment of the contribution of probability theory or cross-tabulations. Nonetheless, the legitimacy of the approach, the value of its results, and its future prospects are now matters of heated debate.

Donald Green and Ian Shapiro, after reviewing rational choice studies of American politics up to the early 1990s, concluded that their achievements were 'few, far between, and considerably more modest than the combination of mystique and methodological fanfare surrounding the rational choice movement would lead one to expect' (1994: 179). Elegant as the basic theory may be, they said in effect, it adds nothing to our already large stock of knowledge about American politics and the causal processes at work in it. The cases are very rare, it seems, where an important, distinctive, and falsifiable generalization or prediction derived from the theory has *not* been falsified.[9]

Stephen Walt (1999) offers a similarly harsh assessment of the contributions of game-theoretic models in international relations. After summarizing 11 exemplary studies, he concludes that 'formalization has not led to powerful new explanations of important real-world phenomena' and 'recent formal work generally lacks rigorous empirical support' (1999: 46). He ends his critique with a plea for methodological diversity, but the evidence he has assembled encourages scepticism about formal theory and the empirical research associated with it as sources of new hypotheses or well-verified findings.

Geraldo Munck (2001) makes no attempt to assess the 'substantive contributions' of rational choice theory in the study of comparative politics, but aims only to provide a 'balanced assessment' of the strengths and limitations of formal modelling as practised by comparativists. Its great strength, he suggests, is its focus on *choice*: despite its mathematical complexity and abstractness, it presents actors as *acting*, not just being pushed around by external forces. In Munck's view, this strength is offset by some serious weaknesses, however. The expected utility model may be bad psychology; many game models have multiple equilibria, yielding no clear predictions, and in many studies 'the rules of the game' are treated as givens when in fact, more realistically, they are often what we most want to understand. Because of these limitations, Munck concludes, the 'value added' by formalization may be 'relatively minor' (2001: 191). In short, the reader is not encouraged to think that there are many important 'substantive contributions' attributable to formal modelling in the literature of comparative politics.

A deeper source of the current scepticism may be, as Munck suggests, the research by psychologists and economists on whether people generally choose 'rationally' in simple situations of risk and uncertainty of the kind that decision-theoretic and game-theoretic models are meant to represent. Do they truly want to pursue their own self-interest as it has been defined by their preference orderings and utility functions and are they capable of seeing, despite the confusing situations in which they may find themselves, what they must do in order to achieve this end? The relevant research, much of it experimental, suggests a negative answer.[10] In other words, it seems that people tend to choose cautiously, fairly, trustingly, etc. rather than 'rationally', when dealing with risk, clashes of interest, and uncertainty about how others will behave. Their ordinary conception of reasonableness evidently differs from the 'rationality' favoured by theorists.

One reaction to these and other criticisms has been to retreat from the demanding assumptions about instrumental rationality used in building simple models and to adopt instead more realistic assumptions as a basis for building 'second generation models of empirically grounded, boundedly rational, and moral decision-making' (Ostrom, 1998: 15). Such models may provide a better description of what people actually do. In principle, they could take into account the social norms, emotional reactions, moral inhibitions, limited information, limited computing ability, and cognitive crutches that seem to keep most people from being as instrumentally rational as it is easy to assume they all are. But such models, being more complex, may not yield any useful predictions or insights. The 'folk theorem' of game theorists – roughly that in repeated games no particular outcome can be singled out as more likely or more rational than any other – may apply, or a rule of thumb not unlike it: realism is generally bought at the price of clarity and tractability.

A contrasting reaction would be to maintain the old simplifying assumptions, but to abandon the claim that law-like explanatory generalizations or predictions can routinely be derived from them. One could even say that the simpler theories remain true, even if their predictions are always false, for they define what it is rational for individuals to do (in order to realize their postulated goals), even if nobody in fact behaves as the theories, used predictively, would require. From this perspective, the most important use of rational choice theory (or theories) would be, not as a basis for predictions, but as an aid in understanding more deeply the situations of risk, strategic interaction, and social choice in which people commonly fall into error when pursuing their own interests or advising others, and in which detached observers of their actions can also become confused. Interpreted in this way, rational choice theory remains positive and theoretical, and thus 'scientific', but in quite a different way from the studies of conditioning relationships that provide the standard of comparison for critics like Green, Shapiro, Walt, and (less clearly) Munck.

Some leading rational choice theorists seem to favour this second reaction to the theory's 'mid-life crisis'. Thus Kenneth Shepsle (1995) endorses the combination of 'hard theory and soft assessment' represented by rational choice theory, in contrast to the 'soft (or no) theory with hard assessment' favoured by its critics. The 'hard theory' offers real insight, he maintains, while 'statistical political philosophy' offers only unintelligible correlations. Similarly, Peter Ordeshook (1993; 1995) and Emerson Niou and Ordeshook (1999) make a distinction between science and engineering that amounts to saying that abstract models need not fit any easily observable regularities in order to be illuminating.

In fact, some of the most widely acclaimed contributions of rational choice theory have had little to do with explanation or prediction as usually understood. Thus the theory is sometimes credited with helping to revive interest in institutions, not by providing a rigorous analysis of the conditions that account for institutional differences, but rather by treating 'institutions' as the explanation for an otherwise puzzling fact. Simple rational choice models seem to 'predict' far more political instability than can be observed. Institutions can be understood as ways of constraining individual maximizing behaviour, to reduce this potential instability (Miller, 1997: 1193–8; Weingast, 1996). But how could such constraining institutions develop on the basis of individual self-interest? The recent and much discussed volume on *Analytic Narratives* (Bates et al., 1998) is essentially an offshoot of this 'new institutionalism'. Its authors aim to combine in-depth historical research with formal modelling of co-ordination problems to explain particular institutional or policy developments. Their models and parameters are chosen (and tweaked) to fit particular historical facts – not to make any real predictions, or to explain any common features of all institutions, or to account systematically for differences between them (see also Bates, de Figueiredo and Weingast, 1998).

Rational choice theory thus subordinates conventional ideas about causation to the interpretation of individual intentions and the assumptions about them that underlie institutions. The explanations it provides have a fundamentally different character from those derived from theories about causal conditions. Causal analysis of the kind discussed earlier focuses on rates within classes (the Democratic share of the vote among Catholics in Detroit, and so on). Only at a limit rarely or never reached do its causal laws and statistical generalizations apply, strictly speaking, to individuals. Rational choice theory, by contrast, normally focuses on the choices made by particular individuals – not just individual persons but also other 'individual' actors (firms, states, parties, etc.), each of which is taken individually, so to speak, rather than as belonging to a category and being part of a comparison. The problem is to better understand the decisions these individuals make, given the situations they are in and their preferences or utility functions. They are assumed to be rational and calculating. They may in fact be caught in a vast network of physical causes and effects stretching from the distant past into the remote future – they may be cogs in a complex machine whose behaviour is determined by the past values of its variables – but this is not how rational choice theory deals with them. Whatever their causal entanglements with the past may be, they are treated as agents, not patients. They are pictured looking ahead, as it were, anticipating the consequences of their actions, not with their backs to the future, being swept along by forces beyond their control. They are assumed to be free and reasonable, at least potentially, and not just the victims of blind causation. The situations in which they find themselves may be said to cause their decisions, of course, but these determining situations have their effects, not through fixed laws or statistical generalizations linking independent and dependent variables, but through their being understood rationally (or misunderstood) as situations of choice offering each individual better or worse opportunities to pursue what he or she thinks is good.

Seen from this angle, rational choice theory represents a return to an 'ideographic' mode of inquiry from the currently dominant 'nomothetic' conception of science (Bates et al., 1998: 10). It aims at the right interpretation of individual actions, not the establishment of general laws. And yet, because of its abstractness and generality, its bold simplifications, its affinity with economics, its heavy use of mathematics, and last but not least, its unblinking acceptance of individual self-interest, not as what ought to be but as what is, it stands apart from contemporary 'normative' theorizing and can claim to be the most positively theoretical (or resolutely scientific) approach to the analysis of politics, exceeding in steely-eyed clarity even the most incisive statistical analyses of the hardest possible data.

The conclusion I draw is that the analysis of human behaviour can be both 'positive' and 'theoretical' without being 'causal' in the usual sense.

Rational choice theory shows that one can focus on individuals or single cases, rather than on the statistical differences between groups or classes of individuals or cases, and that one can disregard their conditioning entanglements in order to focus on the logic of voluntary choice, without becoming explicitly normative or merely descriptive. Rational choice theory may thus help to clarify an important kind of positive theoretical inquiry that is often misunderstood today because it is thought to be either essentially normative or simply descriptive.

INTENTIONAL ANALYSIS

Clarifying the purpose or purposes of political institutions and communities is not the same as testing hypotheses about the conditions of their existence, and it may have little to do with providing simple facts about their most obvious features – their sizes, locations, budgets, the names of their officers, and the like. Nor need it have much to do with analysing the interests of individual persons. Institutions may generally serve the interests of their members, but they also shape and define those interests, and it may not be clear what the relevant interests really are. Economic institutions such as firms presumably give priority to economic goals and mainly serve individual economic interests, but it would clearly be cynical to make the same simplifying assumptions about churches and universities: no one seriously maintains that they are primarily *money-making* institutions. Similarly, political institutions obviously have economic functions, but they also claim to promote justice and the good life, and their various ways of understanding these goals and pursuing them raise factual and interpretive questions that invite inquiry.

Alexis de Tocqueville's *Democracy in America* (1835, 1840), particularly its first volume, is an outstanding example of such inquiry. It is a description of American democracy directed to readers unfamiliar with the working of American institutions and their underlying spirit. Its presentation of American democracy may have been governed by a desire to moderate aristocratic fears of modern democracy, and its young author was certainly not shy about offering 'normative' advice, but the book, if it were fresh off the press today, would not be reviewed as a contribution to 'normative political theory'. It is far too 'empirical': Tocqueville's declaration, in his introduction, that he simply wanted to make known what he had seen in America, is too close to the truth. His account of American political institutions involves assumptions about their causes and effects, including their relations to the religious beliefs of Americans, but it would be a distortion of his analysis to say that he wanted to test any general causal hypotheses. Rather, to simplify greatly, he wanted to show, in detail, the affinity between the institutions of a stable democracy and the culture or psychology – the 'social condition' – of its citizens. American political institutions, he thought, expressed the beliefs of a people lacking high aristocratic ambitions and they encouraged those under their authority to pursue practical economic goals.

Another familiar example – a more recent classic of the same kind – is *The Power Elite* (1956) by C. Wright Mills. It too is fundamentally descriptive, but not simply so. It is more quantitative and social scientific in style than Tocqueville's book, but it resembles it in subordinating causal analysis to the elucidation of collective purposes. The overall theme of the book is the transformation of American democracy since the nineteenth century. New social conditions, new institutions (national corporations, mass media, etc.), and a new role in the world have gradually given American democracy a new meaning, by contrast with the meaning it had in Tocqueville's time.

The discussion of a community's purposes can take a variety of forms and need not put a lot of emphasis on formal institutions, as Michael Lind (1995) shows. Indeed, it may look a lot like the analysis of causal conditions. Putnam (2000), for example, is in many ways similar to Putnam (1993), but the two books are directed to different goals. *Making Democracy Work* offers a causal theory based on a quasi-experimental analysis of regional differences. *Bowling Alone* is a more diagnostic and therapeutic investigation of contemporary American political culture. It tries to define a malaise in the way Americans relate to each other and pursue their collective purposes.

The kind of political analysis illustrated by these examples is factual or empirical and thus 'positive', but neither simply 'causal' nor 'rational'. It resembles what we are doing when we try to understand the political outlook and choices of individual persons, famous or obscure. What kind of a citizen is John Doe? What does politics mean for him? What does he think it is about? How does his involvement in it fit within the story of his life? What reasons does he have for voting (assuming he does)? What considerations explain the votes he casts? Questions of this kind can also be raised about loosely organized social groupings – Catholics in Detroit – as well as about organized parties and interest groups. How do they understand their situations? How do they define their identities? What are their concrete objectives? What relation do they see between the interests they wish to promote and the interests of others? How do they justify, publicly and privately, what they are doing or would like to do?

Clarifying collective purposes, particularly those of large, complex, multi-purpose political institutions and whole societies, has always been a challenge for the academic observer of politics. Only in the past century has it gradually been overshadowed by the scientific analysis of causal conditions and, more recently still, by the development of an impressive calculus of individual interests and decisions. Yet the challenge remains, as may be seen in accounts of 'the new institutionalism' (Hall and Taylor, 1996; Immergut, 1998) and in the literature on 'the power of ideas' (Berman, 1998; Blyth, 2002; Hall, 1989; Majone, 1996).

The recent literature on constructivism in international relations and comparative politics (see Adler, 1997; 2002; Checkel, 1998; Finnemore and Sikkink, 2001; Ruggie, 1998; Wendt, 1999) may provide the most revealing discussions of the problem of understanding collective purposes and relating them to the currently dominant forms of political analysis. The approach has developed in opposition to specific academic positions – neorealism and neoliberal institutionalism, for example, in international relations – and it is entangled with confusing theories about the 'social construction' of its objects of study.[11] Nonetheless, it shares with a variety of recent protests against mainstream professional political science a positive analytic purpose and an insistent emphasis on the importance of shared ideas, aspirations, collective identities, and intersubjective meanings.

The common element in these examples and movements is difficult to isolate. 'Interpretation' and 'thick description' are sometimes used to define it. Charles Taylor (1971), the classic plea for interpretation in the social sciences, argued that political phenomena should be regarded as analogous to obscure texts, in need of translation or interpretive explication. As with texts, so with political phenomena: we do not understand them until we understand their meanings. Opinion polls and other surveys (e.g. Almond and Verba, 1963) may be some help, but since the relevant meanings are not just 'subjective' (and more or less widely shared) but also 'intersubjective' (and thus not normally topics for discussion or even reflection), direct answers to direct questions will often be unrevealing. The deeper meanings we seek can be brought to light only by the kind of 'thick description' exemplified in Clifford Geertz's famous (1973) analysis of Balinese cockfighting.

Perhaps the best label today for what Taylor and Geertz represent is the title of this section, 'intentional analysis'. It avoids the unhelpful breadth of 'interpretation', the novelty and obscurity of 'thick description', the distracting associations of 'hermeneutics', and the misleading suggestion, implicit in the old contrast between explanation

and understanding (von Wright, 1971), that the clarification of intentions is not explanatory. It puts the emphasis squarely on the purposive character of individual actions and social institutions and clearly suggests the need for careful analysis, since the relevant purposes may not be obvious or easily stated. They cannot be just postulated, as they are, generally speaking, in rational choice studies, but must be investigated, for they can be complicated and obscure and may even be denied by those to whom they are rightly attributed.

The scientific status of 'intentional analysis' in this restricted sense is admittedly questionable. It may well seem too speculative, subjective, and impractical (too theoretical in the bad sense) as well as too descriptive (not theoretical enough in the sense of abstraction, systematic comparison, and explanation) to merit a place in political *science*. The evidence for its interpretations – its attributions of intentions – will generally come in the form of contestable biographical and historical narratives. Its explanatory inferences, unlike those in statistical studies or rational choice theory, will be more psychological and rhetorical than logical or mathematical. The intentions in question will be entangled with the acceptance and perhaps modification or distortion of 'normative' theories such as Marxism and liberalism which demand the commitment of scientific observers as well as those they observe. It will thus be much harder to maintain the standard fact–value distinction in the study of intentions (because the right description of actions will be the issue) than in the study of 'behaviour' (where actions are already under agreed descriptions). Finally, although an analysis of intentions may be some help to policy-makers (they may benefit from a clearer understanding of their own or others' intentions), it is unlikely to suggest any simple formulas for influencing 'the course of nature'. In short, there is no denying that reasonable objections can be levelled at the idea of a social science dedicated to the elucidation of intentions (cf. Winch, 1958). But there is also no denying its appeal to common sense: political institutions are purposive structures; the collective intentions that sustain them are not simply the conscious purposes of individuals at large; they are often not easily articulated, but come to light only as the result of careful investigation in a 'positive' spirit; and this investigation is necessarily 'theoretical', not just descriptive.

CONCLUSIONS

Positive political theory, broadly understood, embraces most of professional political science, a discipline offering a rich array of competing approaches, methods, models, and theories. The aim of this chapter has been to clarify the current meaning of positive theory among political scientists by focusing on three main forms of it, ignoring all but a few examples of the actual research that could illustrate each type.

The statistical analysis of causal conditions and the formal modelling of rational choices are now clearly the dominant forms. The first is the direct outgrowth of the 'behavioural revolution' of the 1950s and 1960s. It aspires to move from the systematic collection of descriptive facts to well-grounded causal laws about political phenomena. It has shed the grandiose aspirations of earlier years and now strikes, so to speak, at targets of opportunity.[12] It has gradually become very close in methods and spirit to applied policy analysis. Rational choice theory, by contrast, keeps alive larger theoretical ambitions. It has always scorned the vague sociological and psychological concepts, the awkward operational definitions, and the tedious statistical analyses it associates with 'behavioural' research. In developing its explanations, it strives to imitate modern economics, with its elegant, coherent, parsimonious, mathematical models of how people behave.

Sharp as the differences may be between statistical and rational modelling, they nonetheless share some common features. Both rely on mathematical reasoning not accessible to those without special training, and both can be understood to be contributing to causal knowledge as this is generally understood, that is, to objective knowledge of the necessary and sufficient conditions of events. In principle, the statistical analysis of independent and dependent variables goes straight for the goal, while formal modelling of the kind associated with rational choice theory approaches it by a more roundabout route. It tries to isolate and explain basic patterns of social interaction by working out the implications of individualistic assumptions about instrumental rationality.

There is little point denying that progress can be made towards the common goal by following either route. But as the possibility of future advances has become clearer, in the light of past achievements, so too have some of the difficulties to be expected and the reasonableness of some old objections. Thus, despite faster computers, larger data archives, and more powerful statistical methods, it remains true that realistic causal models of political processes often far outrun our ability to test them in any rigorous way. Similarly, findings from the experimental study of individual decision-making and advances in the theoretical analysis of strategic interaction have clarified the difficulty of deriving any solid, interesting generalizations about political behaviour from the basic premises of rational

choice theory. The project of going 'from micromotives to macrobehaviour' in the political realm looks more questionable now than it did a generation ago.

In the long run, the most valuable contribution of rational choice theory to political science may not be its contribution to causal analysis as commonly understood, but rather the light it can throw on the role of thought and ideas in the explanation of the behaviour of individuals. This contribution is close to the original purpose of the theory, which was to guide decision-makers in complicated situations of individual and social choice. It thus demonstrates that the 'normative' analysis of such situations can be closely related to their 'positive' description and 'theoretical' explanation, even when it is unrelated to the testing of any statistical generalizations. In other words, it can show that there is a causality of intentions and reasons as well as one of background conditions, and it can thus open the way for a reconsideration of a classic but now marginalized and frequently misinterpreted form of political analysis.

Alongside or beneath today's two main contenders for the title 'positive political theory', I have suggested that there is a third, 'intentional analysis'. And just as rational choice theory can be positive and theoretical without being causal in the standard sense, so too can the analysis (or interpretation) of the purposes actually pursued by individuals, groups, and political communities. Its rules of procedure may be less easily codified than those for statistical analysis or formal modelling; its criteria of success or failure may be less clear; its assumptions about human motivation may be far less parsimonious than the gross simplifications associated with 'rational choice', but intentional analysis is nonetheless directed to answering factual questions of a theoretical character. It is not just disguised moralizing or devious prescribing – or at least no more so than the currently more reputable forms of positive theorizing. And its descriptions, like theirs, are not just collections of brute facts: they are revealing abstractions from or interpretations of the facts, showing a certain distinctive detachment from practice.

Surveying these three ways of being positive and theoretical in political science, I am struck by the power of conditional analysis to draw both rational choice theory and the study of individual cases into its understanding of the nature and purposes of theory and its relation to practice – and implicitly to exclude intentional analysis from the domain of political *science*. Economics is sometimes said to be a colonizing social science, using its game-theoretic models and concepts like 'social capital' to establish its hegemony over the other social sciences (Fine and Green, 2000). But the broader and more deeply rooted imperial enterprise may be the technological way of thinking about theory, as a roundabout way of improving practical manipulation. It tends to exclude as unscientific the kind of detached observation of collective intentions that should also be called positive, political, and theoretical.

NOTES

1 The primary contrasts here are (1) positive and metaphysical and (2) theory and practice. In the case of *positive*, the derivation of its current meaning from earlier usage is relatively easy to explain: from the assumption that 'normative' propositions are scientifically untestable, it is only a short step to the conclusion that they must be 'metaphysical', unlike the 'empirical' propositions of 'positive' social science, which can be verified by the metaphysically neutral methods of modern science (cf. Ayer, 1936; Easton, 1953; and Robbins, 1935). It is not so easy to explain the meaning of *theory* as used here. Its current meaning derives from the ancient contrast between two ways of life, 'theory' and 'practice'. Gradually its meaning shifted from detached observation (in contrast to political engagement) to abstract thinking (in contrast to the practical application of thought), a trend which is carried further in the distinction now sometimes made in the natural sciences between theorists, who develop mathematical models, and experimenters, who test them in laboratories prior to their application 'in the real world' (Lobkowicz, 1967). In contemporary political science, the praise of theory in manuals of theory construction (e.g. King, Keohane and Verba, 1994; Morton, 1999) is essentially a praise of 'testable' speculative simplifications, in contrast to detailed descriptions of specific phenomena.

2 To see how difficult, the reader should consult Beck and Katz (2001), Beck, King and Zeng (2000), Box-Steffensmeier and Zorn (2001), Green, Kim and Yoon (2001), Oneal and Russett (2001), Russett (1995), and Spiro (1994), which show the investment in statistical training now expected of those preparing to do advanced empirical research in political science.

3 The treatment of Imperial Germany presents especially formidable problems. Oren (1995) has shown that Germany was once widely thought to exemplify the crucial, positively valued characteristics of modern constitutional government (the rule of law, a professional public service, progressive social legislation, academic freedom, etc.). Only as the balance of power and the system of alliances changed, in the 20 years before World War I, did Germany begin to be perceived, to its discredit, as less 'democratic' than the United States and its allies. In short, according to Oren, the description or classification of Germany's system of government by Americans depended on Germany's relations with America. Imperial Germany is now coded as an autocracy, even by most critics of the democratic peace hypothesis, and World War I, rather than counting heavily against the hypothesis, adds

to the evidence favouring it. More generally, Oren suggests, the 'coding rules' used in recent American studies of the democratic peace represent no more than a temporary consensus that will change as American foreign relations change. 'Democracy' is an elastic term, stretched or compressed by practical exigencies, and not the name for a well-defined condition that could have a simple causal relation to war and peace. Countries with similar regimes may never seem to fight each other, but this may be more like an optical illusion than a scientific regularity. Real similarities may not stifle or preclude conflicts, and regime differences may not create them, but violent antagonism may require widespread belief in appropriate political differences.

4 The behavioural movement was in part a reaction against the 'hyperfactualism' of an earlier form of positivism, which identified positive knowledge with solid, practical knowledge of matters of fact, and this in turn, in the social sciences, with scrupulous attention to factual detail. Impressed by the powerful theoretical simplifications of the natural sciences, empiricists in political science began to demand 'empirical theory' – not just more facts, but a new way of ordering and analysing them, more positive and explanatory than the 'historicism' and 'premature' policy prescriptions associated with academic political theory (Easton, 1953).

5 Mill anticipated the creation of a historically based 'general science of society' that would limit and control the conclusions reached in the more specialized branches of social inquiry, such as political economy. Rational choice theory can now claim to be performing that function, but not at all in the way that Mill envisioned. And in the loosely related statistical inquiries of contemporary 'Millian' social science, there is little evidence of any interest in Mill's goal or any movement towards it. Instead, there seems to be an increasingly obsessive concern about proper statistical method.

6 Duncan Luce and Howard Raiffa (1957) provided an influential survey of the development of expected utility theory and game theory. Kenneth Arrow's (1951) 'impossibility theorem' about social welfare functions and Duncan Black's (1958) analysis of voting cycles drew attention to the problem of voting rules and the potential instability of simple majority decision-making [see further Chapter 18]. Anthony Downs (1957) demonstrated that microeconomic reasoning could have interesting applications in the study of electoral politics, James Buchanan and Gordon Tullock (1962) applied it more widely, and Mancur Olson (1965) showed its relevance for understanding interest groups and interest-group politics. Game theory had from the beginning been of interest to those at the cutting edge of international relations research. Anatol Rapoport (1960) and Thomas Schelling (1960) helped to broaden the interest in it.

7 Just as one can say that 'behavioural' political science has more to do with statistics than behaviour, rational choice theory is better defined by its 'formalizations' (the mathematical models it uses) than by its varying

assumptions about rationality. Thus even the most telling objections to the most widely used simplifying assumptions about instrumental rationality become clear only with the help of formal models (e.g. Kahneman and Tversky, 1979; and Tversky and Kahneman, 1981). The current faith in modelling is a version of the formalism analysed by Jeffrey Bergner – 'thoroughgoing concern about the *form* of proper theorizing and about the *form* of evidence which might render the various theories acceptable or unacceptable' (1981: 3) – but it is more directly indebted to the example of economics than to the neo-Kantian philosophy discussed by Bergner. Modern 'formalist' political science has English (Mill, Russell, Ayer) and economic (Marshall, Keynes, Robbins) as well as German (Kant, Cohen, Rickert) and sociological (Weber, Tönnies, Simmel) roots. Broadly speaking, the 'behavioural' political science of the 1950s and 1960s aspired to imitate the econometric model-building of macroeconomists, while the 'rational' political science of more recent times has developed in a close, fertilizing relationship to the new microeconomics of the 1970s and 1980s based on game models (e.g. principal–agent theory).

8 See Mueller (1997) and Shughart and Razzolini (2001) for compendious reviews of the research on many topics. For a digestible survey of the different mathematical models used by rational choice theorists, with simplified examples of their applications, see Shepsle and Bonchek (1997). 'Public choice' and 'rational choice' differ in the emphasis they put on economic motives. The former has closer affinities to economics and is more vulnerable to the objection that human motivation is not exclusively selfish and 'material'. 'Rational choice', by contrast, makes more provision in principle for anger, benevolence, cruelty, duty, envy, and the like. Nonetheless there is a very great overlap between the two varieties of formal modelling, as may be seen from Miller (1997).

9 The simplest example is the familiar 'paradox of voting turnout': a 'rational' analysis of the costs and benefits of voting makes it seem unlikely that very many people would ever go to the polls, but in fact, of course, hundreds of millions of them do so regularly. For recent discussions of this difficulty, see Blais (2000) and Verba, Schlozman and Brady (2000). The problem may be much greater when the discrepancy between 'prediction' and reality is less glaring, as it often is, for then the impressive abstract reasoning can cast an unjustified aura of necessity on hypothesized 'regularities' of doubtful validity. A classic example is Riker's (1962) derivation of a 'size principle' about political coalitions from the assumption that legislative politics can be modelled as a constant-sum co-operative game. Riker appeared to be providing a rigorously 'rational' explanation of a basic law of political behaviour. Only later did it become clear that there was no relevant regularity to be explained 'deductively' (de Swaan, 1973). As suggested above, Putnam (1993) may be an important recent study deserving attention from this perspective.

10 The reviews of experimental research by Camerer (1995), Ledyard (1995), and Roth (1995) show the scope of the problem. For discussions oriented to political science, see Lane (1995), Lee (1997), Levy (1997), and McDermott (2001).

11 It may seem strange to put anything having to do with 'social construction' under the rubric of 'positive theory', but the incongruity disappears if one distinguishes, as John Searle (1995) does, between (a) 'the social construction of reality', with its suggestion that since everything is 'discourse', nothing can be simply true or false, and (b) 'the construction of social reality', which recognizes that the 'ontologically subjective' can be 'epistemologically objective'. See also Hacking (1999).

12 In the spirit of Green and Shapiro: 'Looking for a general theory of politics may be like looking for a general theory of holes; there may be no theory out there waiting to be discovered' (1994: 184). Cf. MacIntyre (1971: 260).

REFERENCES

Adler, Emanuel (1997) 'Seizing the middle ground: constructivism in world politics'. *European Journal of International Relations*, 3: 319–63.

Adler, Emanuel (2002) 'Constructivism in international relations: sources, contributions, debates, and future directions'. In Walter Carlsnaes, Thomas Risse and Beth A. Simmons, eds, *Handbook of International Relations*. London: Sage, 95–118.

Alesina, Alberto and Eliana La Ferrara (2000) 'Participation in heterogeneous communities'. *Quarterly Journal of Economics*, 115: 847–904.

Alesina, Alberto and Eliana La Ferrara (2002) 'Who trusts others?' *Journal of Public Economics*, 85: 207–34.

Almond, Gabriel and Sidney Verba (1963) *The Civic Culture: Political Attitudes and Democracy in Five Nations*. Princeton, NJ: Princeton University Press.

Arrow, Kenneth J. (1951) *Social Choice and Individual Values*. New York: Wiley.

Ayer, Alfred Jules (1936) *Language, Truth and Logic*. London: Gollancz.

Babst, Dean (1972) 'A force for peace'. *Industrial Research*, 4 (4): 55–8.

Bates, Robert H., Rui J. P. de Figueiredo and Barry R. Weingast (1998) 'The politics of interpretation: rationality, culture, and transition'. *Politics and Society*, 26: 603–42.

Bates, Robert H., Avner Greif, Margaret Levi, Jean-Laurent Rosenthal and Barry R. Weingast (1998) *Analytic Narratives*. Princeton, NJ: Princeton University Press.

Beck, Nathaniel and Jonathan N. Katz (2001) 'Throwing out the baby with the bath water: a comment on Green, Kim, and Yoon'. *International Organization*, 55: 487–95.

Beck, Nathaniel, Gary King and Langche Zeng (2000) 'Improving quantitative studies of international conflict: a conjecture'. *American Political Science Review*, 94: 21–35.

Bergner, Jeffrey T. (1981) *The Origin of Formalism in Social Science*. Chicago: University of Chicago Press.

Berman, Sheri (1997) 'Civil society and political institutionalization'. *American Behavioral Scientist*, 40: 562–74.

Berman, Sheri (1998) *The Social Democratic Movement: Ideas and Politics in the Making of Interwar Europe*. Cambridge, MA: Harvard University Press.

Black, Duncan (1958) *The Theory of Committees and Elections*. Cambridge: Cambridge University Press.

Blais, André (2000) *To Vote or Not to Vote: The Merits and Limits of Rational Choice Theory*. Pittsburgh: University of Pittsburgh Press.

Blyth, Mark (2002) *Great Transformations: Economic Ideas and Institutional Change in the Twentieth Century*. Cambridge: Cambridge University Press.

Box-Steffensmeier, Janet M. and Christopher J. W. Zorn (2001) 'Duration models and proportional hazards in political science'. *American Journal of Political Science*, 45: 972–88.

Buchanan, James M. and Gordon Tullock (1962) *The Calculus of Consent*. Ann Arbor, MI: University of Michigan Press.

Camerer, Colin F. (1995) 'Individual decision making'. In John Kagel and Alvin E. Roth, eds, *Handbook of Experimental Economics*. Princeton, NJ: Princeton University Press, 587–704.

Cavallar, Georg (2001) 'Kantian perspectives on democratic peace: alternatives to Doyle'. *Review of International Studies*, 27: 229–48.

Chan, Steve (1997) 'In search of democratic peace: problems and promise'. *Mershon International Studies Review*, 41: 59–91.

Checkel, Jeffrey T. (1998) 'The constructivist turn in international relations theory'. *World Politics*, 50: 324–48.

Coleman, James S. (1988) 'Social capital in the creation of human capital'. *American Journal of Sociology*, 94: S 95–120.

Coleman, James S. (1990) *Foundations of Social Theory*. Cambridge, MA: Harvard University Press.

Della Porta, Donatella (2000) 'Social capital, beliefs in government, and political corruption'. In Susan J. Pharr and Robert D. Putnam, eds, *Disaffected Democracies: What's Troubling the Trilateral Democracies?* Princeton, NJ: Princeton University Press, 587–704.

De Swaan, Abram (1973) *Coalition Theories and Cabinet Formations: A Study of Formal Theories of Coalition Formation Applied to Nine European Parliaments after 1918*. Amsterdam: Elsevier.

Downs, Anthony (1957) *An Economic Theory of Democracy*. New York: Harper and Row.

Doyle, Michael (1983) 'Kant, liberal legacies, and foreign affairs', Parts I and II. *Philosophy and Public Affairs*, 12: 205–35, 323–53.

Easton, David (1953) *The Political System: An Inquiry into the State of Political Science*. New York: Knopf.

Easton, David (1965) *A Systems Analysis of Political Life*. New York: Wiley.

Easton, David and Jack Dennis (1969) *Children in the Political System: Origins of Political Legitimacy*. New York: McGraw-Hill.

Ellingsen, Tanja (2000) 'Colorful community or ethnic witches' brew? Multiethnicity and domestic conflict during and after the Cold War'. *Journal of Conflict Resolution*, 44: 228–49.

Enterline, Andrew J. (1996) 'Driving while democratizing (DWD)'. *International Security*, 20 (4): 183–96.

Fine, Ben and Francis Green (2000) 'Economics, social capital, and the colonization of the social sciences'. In Stephen Baron, John Field and Tom Schuller, eds, *Social Capital: Critical Perspectives*. Oxford: Oxford University Press.

Finnemore, Martha and Kathryn Sikkink (2001) 'Taking stock: the constructivist research program in international relations and comparative politics'. *Annual Review of Political Science*, 4: 391–416.

Franceschet, Antonio (2001) 'Sovereignty and freedom: Immanuel Kant's liberal internationalist "legacy"'. *Review of International Studies*, 27: 209–28.

Fukuyama, Francis (2001) 'Social capital, civil society and development'. *Third World Quarterly*, 22 (1): 7–20.

Gartzke, Erik (1998) 'Kant we all just get along? Opportunity, willingness, and the origins of the democratic peace'. *American Journal of Political Science*, 42: 1–27.

Geertz, Clifford (1973) *The Interpretation of Cultures: Selected Essays*. New York: Basic.

Gleditsch, Kristian S. (2002) *All International Politics Is Local: The Diffusion of Conflict, Integration, and Democratization*. Ann Arbor, MI: University of Michigan Press.

Gleditsch, Kristian S. and Michael D. Ward (2000) 'War and peace in space and time: the role of democratization'. *International Studies Quarterly*, 44: 1–29.

Gowa, Joanne (1999) *Ballots and Bullets: The Elusive Democratic Peace*. Princeton, NJ: Princeton University Press.

Green, Donald P. and Ian Shapiro (1994) *Pathologies of Rational Choice Theory: A Critique of Applications in Political Science*. New Haven, CT: Yale University Press.

Green, Donald P., Soo Yeon Kim and David H. Yoon (2001) 'Dirty pool'. *International Organization*, 55: 441–68.

Hacking, Ian (1999) *The Social Construction of What?* Cambridge, MA: Harvard University Press.

Hall, Peter A., ed. (1989) *The Political Power of Economic Ideas*. Princeton, NJ: Princeton University Press.

Hall, Peter A. (1999) 'Social capital in Britain'. *British Journal of Political Science*, 29: 417–61.

Hall, Peter A. and Rosemary C. R. Taylor (1996) 'Political science and the three new institutionalisms'. *Political Studies*, 44: 936–57.

Hegre, Havard, Tanja Ellingsen, Scott Gates and Nils Peter Gleditsch (2001) 'Toward a democratic civil peace? Democracy, political change, and civil war, 1816–1992'. *American Political Science Review*, 95: 33–48.

Henderson, Errol A. (1998) 'The democratic peace through the lens of culture, 1820–1989'. *International Studies Quarterly*, 42: 461–84.

Immergut, Ellen M. (1998) 'The theoretical core of the new institutionalism'. *Politics and Society*, 26: 5–34.

Jackman, Robert W. and Ross A. Miller (1998) 'Social capital and politics'. *Annual Review of Political Science*, 1: 47–73.

Kacowicz, Arie M. (1995) 'Explaining zones of peace: democracies as satisfied powers?' *Journal of Peace Research*, 32: 265–76.

Kahneman, Daniel and Amos Tversky (1979) 'Prospect theory: an analysis of decision under risk'. *Econometrica*, 47: 263–91.

King, Gary, Robert O. Keohane and Sidney Verba (1994) *Designing Social Inquiry: Scientific Inference in Qualitative Research*. Princeton, NJ: Princeton University Press.

Knack, Stephen and Philip Keefer (1997) 'Does social capital have an economic payoff? A cross-country investigation'. *Quarterly Journal of Economics*, 112: 1251–88.

Lane, Robert E. (1995) 'What rational choice explains'. *Critical Review*, 9 (1–2): 107–26.

Ledyard, John O. (1995) 'Public goods: a survey of experimental research'. In John H. Kagel and Alvin E. Roth, eds, *Handbook of Experimental Economics*. Princeton, NJ: Princeton University Press, 111–94.

Lee, Albert S. (1997) 'Thick rationality and the missing "brute fact": the limits of rationalist incorporation of norms and ideas'. *Journal of Politics*, 59: 1001–39.

Levi, Margaret (1996) 'Social and unsocial capital: a review essay of Robert Putnam's *Making Democracy Work*'. *Politics and Society*, 24: 45–55.

Levy, Jack S. (1997) 'Prospect theory, rational choice, and international relations'. *International Studies Quarterly*, 41: 87–112.

Lind, Michael (1995) *The Next American Nation: The New Nationalism and the Fourth American Revolution*. New York: Free.

Lobkowicz, Nicholas (1967) *Theory and Practice: History of a Concept from Aristotle to Marx*. Notre Dame, IN: University of Notre Dame Press.

Luce, R. Duncan and Howard Raiffa (1957) *Games and Decisions: Introduction and Critical Survey*. New York: Wiley.

MacIntyre, Alasdair (1971) 'Is a science of comparative politics possible?' In his *Against the Self-Images of the Age: Essays on Ideology and Philosophy*. London: Duckworth.

Majone, Giandomenico (1996) 'Public policy and administration: ideas, interests and institutions'. In Robert E. Goodin and Hans-Dieter Klingemann, eds, *A New Handbook of Political Science*. Oxford: Oxford University Press, 610–27.

Mansfield, Edward D. and Jack Snyder (1995) 'Democratization and the danger of war'. *International Security*, 20 (1): 5–38.

Mansfield, Edward D. and Jack Snyder (1996) 'The effects of democratization on war'. *International Security*, 20 (4): 196–207.

Mansfield, Edward D. and Jack Snyder (1997) 'A reply to Thompson and Tucker'. *Journal of Conflict Resolution*, 41: 457–61.

Mansfield, Edward D. and Jack Snyder (2002) 'Democratic transitions, institutional strength, and war'. *International Organization*, 56: 297–337.

McDermott, Rose (2001) 'The psychological ideas of Amos Tversky and their relevance for political science'. *Journal of Theoretical Politics*, 13: 5–33.

Mill, John Stuart (1974 [1843]) *A System of Logic Ratiocinative and Inductive*, 2 vols. In J. M. Robson, ed., *The Collected Works of John Stuart Mill*. Toronto: University of Toronto Press.

Miller, Gary J. (1997) 'The impact of economics on contemporary political science'. *Journal of Economic Literature*, 35: 1173–1204.

Mills, C. Wright (1956) *The Power Elite*. New York: Oxford University Press.

Morton, Rebecca B. (1999) *Methods and Models: A Guide to the Empirical Analysis of Formal Models in Political Science*. New York: Cambridge University Press.

Mousseau, Demet Yelcin (2001) 'Democratizing with ethnic divisions: a source of conflict?' *Journal of Peace Research*, 38: 547–67.

Mueller, Dennis C., ed. (1997) *Perspectives on Public Choice: A Handbook*. New York: Cambridge University Press.

Munck, Geraldo L. (2001) 'Game theory and comparative politics: new perspectives and old concerns'. *World Politics*, 53: 173–204.

Niou, Emerson M. S. and Peter C. Ordeshook (1999) 'Return of the Luddites'. *International Security*, 24 (2): 84–96.

Olson, Mancur (1965) *The Logic of Collective Action: Public Goods and the Theory of Groups*. Cambridge, MA: Harvard University Press.

Oneal, John R. and Bruce Russett (2001) 'Clear and clean: the fixed effects of the liberal peace'. *International Organization*, 55: 469–85.

Ordeshook, Peter C. (1993) 'The development of contemporary political theory'. In William A. Barnett, Melvin J. Hinch and Normal J. Schofield, eds, *Political Economy: Institutions, Competition, and Representation*, Proceedings of the 7th International Symposium in Economic Theory and Econometrics. New York: Cambridge University Press.

Ordeshook, Peter C. (1995) 'Engineering or science: what is the study of politics?' *Critical Review*, 9 (1–2): 175–88.

Oren, Ido (1995) 'The subjectivity of the "democratic" peace: changing U.S. perceptions of imperial Germany'. *International Security*, 20 (2): 147–84.

Ostrom, Elinor (1998) 'A behavioral approach to the rational choice theory of collective action'. *American Political Science Review*, 92: 1–22.

Peceny, Mark, Caroline C. Beer and Shannon Sanchez-Terry (2002) 'Dictatorial peace?' *American Political Science Review*, 96: 15–26.

Pharr, Susan J. (2000) 'Officials' misconduct and public distrust: Japan and the trilateral democracies'. In Susan J. Pharr and Robert D. Putnam, eds, *Disaffected Democracies: What's Troubling the Trilateral Democracies?* Princeton, NJ: Princeton University Press, 173–201.

Putnam, Robert D. (1993) *Making Democracy Work: Civic Traditions in Modern Italy*. Princeton, NJ: Princeton University Press.

Putnam, Robert D. (2000) *Bowling Alone: The Collapse and Revival of American Community*. New York: Simon and Schuster.

Rapoport, Anatol (1960) *Fights, Games, and Debates*. Ann Arbor, MI: University of Michigan Press.

Ray, James Lee (1995) *Democracy and International Conflict: An Evaluation of the Democratic Peace Proposition*. Columbia, SC: University of South Carolina Press.

Ray, James Lee (1998) 'Does democracy cause peace?' *Annual Review of Political Science*, 1: 27–46.

Rice, Tom W. and Marshall Arnett (2001) 'Civic culture and socioeconomic development in the United States: a view from the states, 1880s–1990s'. *Social Science Journal*, 38: 39–51.

Rice, Tom W. and Alexander F. Sumberg (1997) 'Civic culture and government performance in the American states'. *Publius*, 27: 99–114.

Riker, William H. (1962) *The Theory of Political Coalitions*. New Haven, CT: Yale University Press.

Robbins, Lionel (1935) *An Essay on the Nature and Significance of Economic Science*, 2nd edn. London: Macmillan.

Roth, Alvin E. (1995) 'Bargaining experiments'. In John H. Kagel and Alvin E. Roth, eds, *Handbook of Experimental Economics*. Princeton, NJ: Princeton University Press, 253–348.

Ruggie, John Gerard (1998) *Constructing the World Polity: Essays on International Institutionalization*. New York: Routledge.

Russett, Bruce (1993) *Grasping the Democratic Peace: Principles for a Post-Cold War World*. Princeton: Princeton University Press.

Russett, Bruce (1995) 'The democratic peace: "and yet it moves"'. *International Security*, 19 (2): 164–75.

Russett, Bruce and John R. Oneal (2001) *Triangulating Peace: Democracy, Interdependence, and International Organizations*. New York: Norton.

Schelling, Thomas C. (1960) *The Strategy of Conflict*. Cambridge, MA: Harvard University Press.

Searle, John R. (1995) *The Construction of Social Reality*. New York: Free.

Shepsle, Kenneth A. (1995) 'Statistical political philosophy and positive political theory'. *Critical Review*, 9 (1–2): 213–22.

Shepsle, Kenneth A. and Mark S. Bonchek (1997) *Analyzing Politics: Rationality, Behavior, and Institutions*. New York: Norton.

Shughart, William F. and Laura Razzolini, eds (2001) *The Elgar Companion to Public Choice*. Cheltenham: Elgar.

Small, Melvin and J. David Singer (1976) 'The war-proneness of democratic regimes'. *Jerusalem Journal of International Relations*, 1: 50–69.

Snyder, Jack (2000) *From Voting to Violence: Democratization and Nationalist Conflict*. New York: Norton.

Spiro, David E. (1994) 'The insignificance of the liberal peace'. *International Security*, 19 (2): 50–86.

Tarrow, Sidney (1996) 'Making social science work across space and time: a critical reflection on Robert Putnam's *Making Democracy Work*'. *American Political Science Review*, 90: 389–97.

Taylor, Charles (1985 [1968]) 'Neutrality in political science'. In his *Philosophy and the Human Sciences*, Philosophical Papers, vol. 2. Cambridge: Cambridge University Press, 58–90.

Taylor, Charles (1985 [1971]) 'Interpretation and the sciences of man'. In his *Philosophy and the Human Sciences*, Philosophical Papers, vol. 2. Cambridge: Cambridge University Press, 15–57.

Thompson, William R. and Richard Tucker (1997) 'A tale of two democratic peace critiques'. *Journal of Conflict Resolution*, 41: 428–54.

Tocqueville, Alexis de (1966) *Democracy in America* (1835, 1840), trans. George Lawrence, ed. J. P. Mayer. New York: Harper and Row.

Tversky, Amos and Daniel Kahneman (1981) 'The framing of decisions and the psychology of choice'. *Science*, 211: 453–58.

Varshney, Ashutosh (2001) 'Ethnic conflict and civil society: India and beyond'. *World Politics*, 53: 362–98.

Verba, Sidney, Kay L. Schlozman and Henry E. Brady (2000) 'Rational action and political activity'. *Journal of Theoretical Politics*, 12: 243–68.

Von Wright, Georg Henrik (1971) *Explanation and Understanding*. London: Routledge and Kegan Paul.

Walt, Stephen M. (1999) 'Rigor or rigor mortis? Rational choice and security studies'. *International Security*, 23 (4): 5–48.

Ward, Michael D. and Kristian Gleditsch (1998) 'Democratizing for peace'. *American Political Science Review*, 92: 51–61.

Weart, Spencer R. (1998) *Never at War: Why Democracies Will Not Fight One Another*. New Haven, CT: Yale University Press.

Weingast, Barry R. (1996) 'Political institutions: rational choice perspectives'. In Robert E. Goodin and

Hans-Dieter Klingemann, eds, *A New Handbook of Political Science*. Oxford: Oxford University Press, 167–90.

Weitsman, Patricia A. and George E. Shambaugh (2002) 'International systems, domestic structures, and risk'. *Journal of Peace Research*, 39: 289–312.

Wendt, Alexander (1999) *Social Theory of International Politics*. Cambridge: Cambridge University Press.

Werner, Suzanne (2000) 'The effects of political similarity on the onset of militarized disputes, 1816–1985'. *Political Research Quarterly*, 53: 343–74.

Winch, Peter (1958) *The Idea of a Social Science and its Relation to Philosophy*. London: Routledge and Kegan Paul.

Part II

POLITICAL THEORIES

6

A Future for Marxism?

ANDREW LEVINE

Does Marxism have a future? The short answer is 'Yes'. The slightly longer answer is a qualified 'Yes'. What follows elaborates on the slightly longer answer.

What 'Marxism' is has been contentious for as long as the word has been in use. Anyone who would reflect on Marxism's future must therefore address this question. In addition, in light of recent work in Marxist philosophy, the idea that the term designates nothing theoretically distinctive at all must also be taken seriously. I will focus on the latter contention – disputing it by pressing a certain view of Marxism's core theoretical commitments, and by arguing that this core can and should have a role in the political theory of the future. But even those who think differently agree that 'Marxism' designates a body of theoretical work – that of Marx and his closest co-thinkers. In order not to prejudge the question of what, if anything, Marxism is, I will use the term, for now, in this uncontentious sense. The question, then, is whether there are distinctive and defensible views within this tradition that political theorists today ought to make their own.

'Marxism' and 'Marxist' have been used in other ways too – for example, to describe social, political and economic systems like the one in the former Soviet Union, or to characterize political parties and movements that identify with Marx and his successors. However, the connection(s) between these usages and the theoretical work of Karl Marx is tenuous, at best [on Marx, see further Chapter 28]. In the case of Soviet Marxism, it is especially remote. But it does matter for Marxist theory that Marxism, as a political orientation, is now almost extinct in the liberal democratic, capitalist West and in the formerly 'socialist' East. The situation in what was once called the Third World is increasingly tending

in a similar direction. This worldwide phenomenon has caused interest in Marx's thought to lapse. Thus Marxist political theory is nowadays nearly as defunct as Soviet-style regimes and officially Marxist political parties. This is a remarkable development. Rarely has an intellectual tendency faded so rapidly from the scene.

Ironically, Marxism still survives, albeit barely, in universities. Earlier generations of Marxists, even if they could have imagined a period like our own in which Marx's thought is, at best, in eclipse, would hardly have expected that these bastions of 'bourgeois' culture would become its last redoubt. But the irony is more apparent than real. Many, perhaps most, self-described academic Marxists today identify with one or another form of postmodernism [see further Chapters 4, 29]. In doing so, they reject many of the fundamental assumptions that Marx and his closest co-thinkers shared with other intellectual heirs of the Enlightenment tradition [see further Chapter 26], not least among them, a dedication to representing the world as it really is, not just as it seems from particular standpoints or as it might be 'constructed' out of particular 'discursive practices' [see further Chapters 12, 20]. Thus their 'Marxism' has little connection to the letter or spirit of Marx's work. I will therefore have nothing more to say about it here. Instead, I will focus on a very different creature of late-twentieth-century university culture, *analytical Marxism*. Analytical Marxists genuinely were Marxist. And unlike their postmodernist colleagues, they generally exhibited an intellectual seriousness and rigour equal to the best philosophy and social science of their time. Analytical Marxism never achieved the popularity that (self-identified) postmodernist versions of Marxism enjoyed within the academy. But for anyone who would defend a future for Marxism, it is of far greater importance.

To speculate on Marxism's future, it is instructive to tell the story of analytical Marxism. What, after all, could be more in the spirit of Marx's thought than to reflect on the present, and speculate on the future, by understanding the past? The reason to focus on this comparatively inconspicuous swatch of the past will emerge in due course.

The story of analytical Marxism is a short one – beginning in the decade that spanned the years 1968 to 1978, and then continuing for roughly the next decade and a half. The story has a paradoxical aspect. On the one hand, despite the intentions of its founders, analytical Marxism came to reinforce the impression that Marxism is finished as a distinct intellectual current. It did so not just in acquiescence to the spirit of the age, but for reasons grounded in rationally compelling arguments. Work in an analytical Marxist vein therefore poses a challenge to the claim that Marxism has a future. It especially challenges a conviction that lies at the heart of what Marxist political theory maintains – that a regime *beyond* the conceptual horizons of mainstream liberalism is both feasible and desirable. On the other hand, whatever most practitioners of the genre now believe, analytical Marxism uncovered what the living core of the Marxist theoretical tradition is. Thus it would be only slightly facetious to say that this new departure in Marxist theory saved Marxism by destroying it.

But, for all appearances, the analytical turn in Marxist theory resulted in a very different outcome – it collapsed Marxism into liberalism. This feat was achieved with regret. None of the major analytical Marxists became apostates, as so many earlier generations of former Marxists had been. The analytical Marxists saw themselves remaining true to Marxism's spirit, even as they (tacitly) abandoned Marxism. There is nothing disingenuous in this belief. But the analytical Marxists' own assessment(s) of Marxism's fate need not be taken at face value. After analytical Marxism, it is clearer than it ever was what Marxism was about all along. It has therefore become plain that Marx left the world vital theoretical resources, unavailable elsewhere. With respect to political theory specifically, Marx provided means for grasping the difference between forms of societal organization that are humanly feasible and also *politically achievable*, and visions of ideal arrangements that are inaccessible and therefore dangerous to endorse. Marxist socialists have always opposed *utopian* socialisms that envision ideal arrangements apart from accounts of the real course of human history. My suggestion is that this self-representation was basically correct. (Revealingly, one of the foremost analytical Marxists, G. A. Cohen, 2000, has recently argued that the utopian socialists were right, after all.) Only Marxism joins a defensible account of what is historically feasible with a vision of what those who would *complete* the project of the historical left really want.

Analytical Marxism was largely a creature of the Anglo-American university of the 1970s and 1980s. It emerged in consequence of the student movements that came to a head, briefly, in the spring of 1968. But the upheavals of 1968, their short-term political and institutional extensions, and their abrupt subsidence by the mid 1970s, were a worldwide phenomenon. Analytical Marxism was a culturally specific and institutionally structured manifestation of these larger events. To understand analytical Marxism therefore, it is necessary to reflect on Marxism's career in the university culture of the English-speaking world. What follows is not a comprehensive history of the movement.[1] My aim is only to convey a sense of what the analytical Marxists did, with a view to showing, on the one hand, how they contributed to the current dominance of liberal political philosophy and, on the other, how their work can help to restore Marx's vision of a social order beyond liberalism.

THE BACKGROUND

To a degree that is unparalleled elsewhere in the West, the English-speaking world and especially the United States never had significant political or intellectual movements identified with Marxism. Anglophone philosophers and social scientists of the generation of 1968 who were moved to identify with Marxism, whether for reasons of intellectual commitment or out of a sense of solidarity with others in struggle or for some combination of these reasons, therefore had no tradition to continue, in contrast to their counterparts elsewhere. They also had less reason to join political parties identified with Marxism, communist or otherwise. This is why the history of analytical Marxism had more to do with the exigencies of membership in academic communities than with the crises of Marxist political movements at home or abroad. If analytical Marxists were accountable to anyone or anything it was to their own internalized disciplinary standards.

Before analytical Marxism, theoretical work in a Marxist vein was almost always linked to partisan political concerns. In contrast, analytical Marxism was as free-floating as any other academic enterprise. In at least one respect, this situation was advantageous: it left analytical Marxists free to invent themselves and to follow their own course. In this, they were abetted by the fact that they could begin from a nearly clean slate. The English-speaking world had been very little affected by any of the intellectual tendencies we now call Western Marxism,[2] and English-speaking contributions to official communist doctrine were generally marginal and derivative. There were, of course, influential European émigrés on American soil during and after World War II, and also Trotskyists and independent Marxist theorists. In Britain, there was a tradition of Marxist historiography that enjoyed a certain influence by the early 1960s. But, in the main, analytical Marxism represented a fresh start, very little encumbered by what had gone on before.

The kinds of Marxism that were most attractive, at first, to members of the generation of 1968 were varieties of Western Marxism imported from Germany and France [see further Chapter 29]. But Western Marxism proved intractably difficult to integrate into the prevailing intellectual culture, especially as political fervour waned and, along with it, uncritical enthusiasm for *anything* bearing a Marxist pedigree. Just as the earlier emigration of some leading Western Marxists, fleeing Nazism and war, had little lasting influence on the mainstream intellectual culture of the United States or Britain, this later importation of Western Marxism also failed to take hold, except on the fringes of intellectual life. Western Marxism drew on intellectual currents that were, on the whole, unfamiliar in the English-speaking world – neo-Hegelianism, structuralism, phenomenology and existentialism. Unlike logical positivism, another continental import of roughly the same vintage, these doctrines were uncongenial to Anglo-American sensibilities, except on the margins. Western Marxists were proficient at grand theorizing and at programmatic formulations. But they were more inclined to posture than to argue. In the end, they did not do all that much that was recognizably philosophical to philosophers schooled in the analytic tradition, where the reigning inclination was to look on grand theorizing and programmatic pronouncements with suspicion, and to greet the appearance of profundity with derision.

In the 1950s and 1960s, the cutting edge of philosophical work in the English-speaking world consisted in painstaking investigations of ordinary speech, guided by the conviction that most, if not all, long-standing philosophical problems are actually only consequences of linguistic confusions, awaiting dissolution through careful analysis. Ordinary language philosophy had passed from the scene by 1968, but the spirit that motivated it remained in force. Then, as now, mainstream philosophers in the English-speaking world preferred to engage in tasks that look pedestrian from the Olympian vantage-point continental philosophers assumed: discerning conceptual structures, making distinctions (where appropriate), collapsing distinctions (where they are inappropriately drawn), and marshalling clear and sound arguments. To anyone trained in this tradition, continental philosophy seems pretentious and obscure. Because it drew on these currents, Western Marxism courted a similar judgement.

That this understanding took time to register was a consequence of two related phenomena, the one psychological, the other political. By the late 1960s, the *need* for an ideology consonant with prevailing political attitudes was keenly felt by many on the left. Everyone assumed that *some* version of Marxism must fit that description. In those days too, when many student radicals genuinely believed that 'the arm of criticism' was about to pass into 'the criticism of arms', there was little appetite for protracted intellectual undertakings.[3] Novice socialist militants wanted their Marxism ready-made. But desire is the root of denial. Add impressive Franco-German credentials and the possibilities for self-deception become limitless. In retrospect, it seems odd that the intra-Marxist debates of the 1970s between neo-Hegelian Marxists and Althusserians were, in part, debates about which side was more rigorous or scientific. The oddity is partly a consequence of the fact that the intellectual heirs of these tendencies, the postmodernists, characteristically disparage rigour and science – in practice, and often in theory too. But the more astonishing fact is that the obvious answer, *none of the above,* failed to impress itself on the participants. For there was at hand, in the disciplinary standards commonplace in Anglo-American universities, a standard of rigour that none of the parties in these debates began to approach. Everyone should have known this. But so ardent was the desire to assume the mantle of revolutionary Marxism, that hardly anyone acknowledged this incontrovertible fact.

There was also a more political reason why so many welcomed Western Marxism enthusiastically. The student movements of the period were directed, in the first instance, against the institutions in which students found themselves, the universities. In the United States, where radical students were motivated mainly by the struggle for civil rights and by opposition to the Vietnam War, institutional racism and university involvement with the military were therefore the principal arenas of contestation. It was natural, in these circumstances, to oppose the intellectual culture of the institution one was fighting against. For many, this attitude took a nihilistic turn, away from intellectual work altogether, into the realm of an emerging 'counter-culture' or into workerist politics. But, for some, particularly those who looked forward to university careers, the temptation of an alternative intellectual style readily at hand was irresistible. No matter that this alternative was taken from what was, in the end, only a different academy. All the better, in fact, in as much as this alternative was vested with the prestige of German and French culture, a condition that played well against the lingering sense of intellectual insecurity that continued to plague American academics in the humanities. Elsewhere in the English-speaking world, where the underlying political dynamics differed, the theoretical deficit experienced by would-be Marxists was much the same. The temptations of Western Marxism were therefore nearly as lively as in the United States. Thus Western Marxism came to be embraced by student militants in these countries too.

In time, though, the political motivation faded into oblivion and so too did the need of would-be Marxists to deceive themselves about the merits of the Western Marxisms to which they had been drawn. As interest in Marxism generally waned, interest in Western Marxism subsided too. Some descendants of the Frankfurt school continued to enjoy a certain standing among academics with philosophical training. But the figure in that tradition who is taken most seriously, Jürgen Habermas [see further Chapters 12, 20, 29], has come to distance himself from the Marxist past of his intellectual forebears and to ally instead with Anglo-American liberalism. Otherwise, apart from a few vestigial remnants, Western Marxism has passed from the scene.

Contemporaneously, liberal political philosophy underwent a renaissance [see further Chapters 7–9]. In the period immediately preceding the 1960s, after logical positivism and ordinary language philosophy had deflated philosophy's pretensions, political philosophy seemed spent. A cogent statement of this view, registered as late as the early 1960s, was Isaiah Berlin's essay, 'Does political theory still exist?' (1962). Then, in 1971, John Rawls published *A Theory of Justice,* putting that impression definitively to rest. Rawls's masterpiece revived political philosophy and set its subsequent course. The Rawlsian turn in academic political philosophy shaped the course of analytical Marxism from the beginning.

Marxist credentials have never been helpful to Anglophone academics. No one thought Marxism a ticket to academic success. The impulse motivating investigations of Marxist themes in an analytical vein was therefore not academic opportunism. It was to advance Marxism by defending Marx's views; an objective that required, first of all, that they be stated clearly and in a form in which they could be rationally assessed. Thus close reading and, where necessary, imaginative philosophical reconstruction became the order of the day. The guiding conviction was that Marx's positions would survive even the most stringent critical assessments;

in other words, that Marx's views were generally correct. Guided by this conviction, attention focused on a number of issues important in the Marxism of the period preceding the Russian Revolution. Of these, one especially, the problem of justice, coincided with the question that Rawls had made the prime topic in mainstream political philosophy.[4] The coincidence was not accidental. Philosophers working in a field in which Rawls's influence was already paramount cut their teeth on the topic they knew best.

Orthodox Marxists had always denied that justice was a trans-historical 'critical' concept, a standard against which socio-economic structures could be assessed. Their view was that ideas of justice were 'superstructural', that what is just or unjust is relative to the mode of production in place. Injustices can arise *within* capitalism, then, but capitalism itself cannot be unjust. Among the first analytical Marxist ventures were efforts to prove the orthodox view right or, failing that, to show how a suitable trans-historical concept of justice could be integrated into the larger theoretical structure Marx contrived (see Buchanan, 1982; Lukes, 1985: ch. 4). From the outset, then, there was an effort to draw Marx and Rawls together. The connection was not merely topical. It carried over into styles of argumentation too. For the first time, philosophers working on Marxist themes approached their subject in the way that philosophers working on other issues did. In this respect, the debate on Marxist justice anticipated what would follow.

The idea, again, was to interrogate Marx's positions, not Rawls's or any other liberal's, and to debate the question of justice from within a Marxist framework. But in doing so, it was necessary, in the circumstances, to deal with Rawlsian justice too and therefore with liberal political theory generally. Inevitably the engagement took place on the latter's terrain. Analytical Marxism was, after all, in its infancy. Liberal political philosophy was a mature intellectual discipline, undergoing a renaissance. And because it was firmly entrenched in the universities, it had the weight of those embattled but solidly established institutions behind it. If there was to be a Marxist voice in ongoing discussions of justice, it could only be on terms that the institution in which these discussions would take place already acknowledged.

In retrospect, the superior position Rawlsian liberalism enjoyed may have worked to the advantage of the left, at least if it is fair to hold that socialist theory, Marxist or otherwise, was bound to suffer setbacks in the period that ensued. Rawlsian liberalism breathed new life into egalitarian theory and therefore into a core component, arguably *the* core component, of socialist ideology. This fact may seem paradoxical in view of the separate histories of liberalism and socialism. But Rawlsian liberalism upset the conventional wisdom on connections between egalitarianism and liberal theory, and therefore forced a rethinking of the relation between the two (see further Levine, 1998).

The methodological affinity joining early analytical Marxist ventures in the theory of justice to mainstream philosophy was, at first, more accidental than deliberate. Those who engaged Marx on justice knew no other way to do philosophy. Even had they wanted to be Western Marxists, it is not clear how they might have been. The issues involved in the debates of the period were too focused on details and arguments for that grand but obscure style of theorizing to be deployed. Thus Marxism became *one* voice among many in an ecumenical philosophical discussion. In time, it became clear that it was not a different *kind* of voice. Eventually, a virtue was made of this observation. The methodological affinity joining analytical Marxism to mainstream philosophy gave rise to a substantive claim, one to which nearly all analytical Marxists implicitly subscribed.

MARX'S METHOD

That claim is that *there is no distinctive Marxist methodology*. This conviction separated analytical Marxism from other Marxist currents. For if there was a point on which orthodox Marxists and Western Marxists of all stripes agreed, it was that Marx, following Hegel, developed a *dialectical* methodology that distinguishes Marxism from 'bourgeois' science and philosophy. This view is famously associated with a celebrated essay of Georg Lukács, 'What is orthodox Marxism?' (1971: 1–27),[5] though one finds similar claims advanced in the work of nearly all the Western Marxists. It was also commonplace in official and semi-official communist primers on Marxist theory. Indeed, it was assumed throughout the entire intellectual culture. Opponents of Marxism often faulted Marxists on these grounds; they claimed that the method Marxists deployed violated defensible norms of scientific practice. A well-known exponent of this view was Karl Popper (see e.g. Popper, 1958; 1972; 1973). Many less distinguished thinkers agreed with him. But no one took the Marxists' claims to methodological distinctiveness to task. The idea that there is a distinctive Marxist methodology was a dogma of the intellectual culture.

But this claim is ambiguous. If the aim of Marx's investigations of 'the laws of motion of capitalist society' and of his various other explanatory projects was consistent with the aims of modern science generally, as Marx himself maintained (for instance in the preface to the first German edition of *Capital,* vol. 1) – if, in other words, what Marx wanted to do was to discover the real causal determinants of the phenomena he investigated – then the idea would be that Marx contrived or at least deployed a novel and distinctive way of executing this task: of forming concepts, constructing theories, corroborating hypotheses and so on. No one has ever shown this to be the case. On the other hand, if a different sort of objective is supposed, then Marxism's purported methodological distinctiveness would have to be understood in light of this aim, whatever it might be. This is what most believers in Marxism's methodological distinctiveness appear to have had in mind. But the Western Marxists were, at best, unhelpful in identifying an alternative explanatory objective, and so were their orthodox opponents. There are, of course, explanations that social scientists advance that do not involve causal structures. The interpretation of cultural practices is an obvious example. However Marx and the majority of Marxists after him did little that could be construed along these lines, despite the affinity of some latter-day self-identified Marxists with the historicist tradition in social science. There is therefore no reason not to take Marx at his word and to acknowledge that the explanatory aim of Marxist social science is indeed the discovery of real causal determinations. Those who would insist otherwise shoulder the burden of proof. Their first move in discharging this burden must be to identify what alternative explanatory aim Marx might have had in mind. So far, no one has. This is not to deny that the 'dialectical' method has been defended countless times. But the proof lies in the elaboration of the programme, not in its declaration. The analytical Marxists came to realize that dialectical explanations either restate what can be expressed in unexceptionable ways, or else are unintelligible and therefore not explanatory at all. The lesson is plain: if there were a dialectical method that bears constructively on the explanatory aims Marx espoused, it ought by now to have become apparent. That it has not is good reason to conclude that, at most, the dialectic is a way of organizing and directing thinking at a pre-theoretic level. A heuristic device of this sort is not to be despised. But it is not a royal road to knowledge inaccessible to modern science.

Analytical Marxists came to this conclusion reluctantly. Their intent, at first, was only to reconstruct and defend Marxist orthodoxy. That Marx was a 'dialectical materialist' is an orthodox claim. To be sure, Marx never used the expression. But he did identify with the idea. At the same time that he asserted his allegiance to the explanatory objectives of modern science, he represented himself as a dialectician in the Hegelian tradition, faulting his rivals for their shortcomings in this regard.[6] Was this a 'creative tension' or a simple confusion? Perhaps both. In any case, those analytical Marxists who focused on questions of method sought, at first, to rehabilitate dialectical logic, not to debunk it.[7] What transpired as they did so anticipated what would happen in so many other areas: the operation succeeded but the patient died.

For an analytical Marxist, to defend a position is to translate it into terms that bear scrutiny according to the most demanding disciplinary standards in philosophy or in an appropriate social science. Marx's positions have turned out to be remarkably amenable to this kind of treatment (see, for example, Roemer, 1982). Before analytical Marxism, Marx's views were thought to differ qualitatively from mainstream positions, to follow from a different and perhaps incommensurable 'paradigm'. Marxist theoretical work was also thought to imply conclusions that mainstream theorists would, in many cases, reject – not just because of ideological resistance, but on grounds that depend on their own theoretical commitments. These assumptions can no longer be sustained. In making Marx's views acceptable in the way that analytical Marxists did, Marxism became a voice among others in ongoing debates.

THE THEORY OF HISTORY

This conclusion upsets received understandings. But it is not the whole story. For there is a component of Marxist orthodoxy that does lie outside the scope of mainstream thinking – historical materialism, Marx's theory of history. Historical materialism was of nearly as much concern to early analytical Marxism as was justice. But with the publication in 1978 of G. A. Cohen's *Karl Marx's Theory of History: A Defence* the topic assumed a pre-eminent importance (see further Wright, Levine and Sober, 1992; Shaw, 1978). For Marx, the inner workings of capitalism and other modes of production are only intelligible as part of an endogenous process of development and transformation. Historical materialism provides an account of this process. Cohen 'naturalized' this theory, assimilating it into the intellectual mainstream. In doing so, he showed how Marx's theory of history, unlike Hegel's, is not *teleological*. Scientists from at least the seventeenth century on rejected the notion of teleological causality, the idea that to explain a phenomenon is to discover the 'end' or *telos* towards which it tends. Historical materialism, on Cohen's reconstruction, joins the scientific consensus. Cohen made it clear that Marxism is equipped to supply and defend an account of history's structure and direction that in no way compromises modern understandings of causality and explanation.

Contemporary historiography proceeds on the assumption that there are no significant theoretical constraints on what counts as an object of historical inquiry or as a historical explanation, and supposes that there is nothing intelligible to say about history's structure and direction. Past events, no matter how they are individuated or categorized, may be susceptible to causal explanations. But history itself cannot be explained. Historians can, of course, impute structures and directionality to aspects of the past. But, when they do, they are only imposing categories that accord with their own or others' interests or with received understandings – as when American historians identify, say, the Age of Lincoln, or the Progressive Era. Imposing categories in this way is not the same thing as discovering real properties of past events or collections of events. When practising historians deal with trends or when they otherwise generalize over long swatches of time, they are only organizing their data in ways that serve subjective purposes. They are not discovering real properties of human history. One cannot even concoct a trivial account of history's structure and direction by conjoining all particular explanations. To do so, it would be necessary, first, to have a theoretically well-motivated way of marking off events and therefore of identifying discrete explanations to join together. But in the atheoretical view of modern historiography, this is impossible. Even if we allow (almost) anything to count as an explanation, there is no theoretical warrant for dividing the world up into exhaustive and mutually exclusive events and therefore no justification for joining these explanations together.

The idea that history as such is intelligible was advanced first by Christian, Muslim, and eventually secular philosophers whose explanatory objectives were of a piece with neither practising historians nor modern scientists. Instead of looking for causal determinations in history, these philosophers concocted narratives that elaborated theologically prescribed notions of providential design or its secular equivalents in light of which (some) past events take on meanings. Since meanings in this sense are only conceivable from particular vantage-points, to talk of *the* meaning of history is to suppose that there is a definitive perspective, an *end* (*telos*) of history, in light of which everything that comes before is retrospectively intelligible. This is why theories of history, before historical materialism, were teleological – why history was thought to consist in the unfolding of a pre-given end. Among the very first philosophers of history was St Augustine, whose case is exemplary (see Deane, 1963). Augustine sought to make sense of Roman history by situating it in a narrative structured by theological events – the Creation, the Fall, Christ's resurrection and ultimately the Final Judgement, the end, both literally and teleologically, of the historical process. For Augustine, history is the story of the preparation of humankind for the Final Judgement, in which souls are sorted out into two eternal cities – the City of God, where all and only those who are 'saved' reside, and the City of Man, the city of all the reprobate, who will suffer torments for all eternity. For this sorting out to take place in accord with God's will, the sacraments of the Church must be supplied to the elect of all nations. Augustine maintained that Roman institutions and the order they imposed were indispensable in this endeavour. Thus he told the story of Roman history, especially the history of the Empire and its travails, from this perspective, the *telos* but also the final moment of human history. Only one of these senses, the teleological one, survives in the last great teleological philosophy of history, Hegel's [see further Chapter 28]. His was, of course, a secular account. Following developments in Kantian and post-Kantian German philosophy, history for Hegel was the story of the unfolding of the Idea of Freedom, culminating in its realization in the institutions of the *Rechtsstaat*, a state based on universal principles of right (Hegel, 1942). Hegel's 'cunning of reason', therefore, is not quite the same idea as Augustine's providential design. But in its basic structure, Hegel's philosophy of history resembled Augustine's. It too made sense of (part of) the past by telling a story from the vantage-point of history's end.

Hegel's philosophy of history was, of course, the immediate inspiration for Marx's attempt to make sense of history as such. But Marx broke ranks with Hegel and the entire tradition that his work culminated in by rejecting teleology and, with it, the project of discovering what historical events mean. Marx retained Hegel's sense of history's intelligibility; he sought to provide an account of real historical structures and of the direction of historical change. But, for Marx, history is as meaningless as nature is. Like nature too, it has properties that are independent of investigators' interests and that are in principle capable of being known. The philosophers of history, Hegel especially, had grasped aspects of real history, but through the distorting lens of their own teleological convictions. Marx set them right, without succumbing to the atheoreticism of contemporary historians.

Any theory that purports to be part of the larger enterprise of modern science is in principle susceptible to revision. To be sure, the more fundamental it is, the less likely it is to change through the ordinary procedures of 'normal science'. Fundamental theoretical frameworks may sometimes even be recalcitrant to all but thoroughgoing 'scientific revolutions' (Kuhn, 1962). However, even basic theories that are not exactly overthrown undergo revision over time. Historical materialism was no exception. Once it was elaborated in a way that invited scrutiny and assessment, it came under attack and began to fall.

Western Marxisms, for all their differences, were of one mind in distancing themselves from Marx's theory of history. The historical materialist orthodoxy of the Second and Third Internationals was, in the eyes of Western Marxists, too fatalistic to pass muster. It failed to accord human agency its due. Its commitment to historical inevitability even seemed to render the very idea of politics otiose. If the end is already given, one can perhaps hasten its coming, but nothing can fundamentally change the ultimate outcome. This, it seemed to them, was a formula for quiescence, for passively awaiting the revolution. But the historical materialism Western Marxists faulted was not exactly the historical materialism Cohen defended. Cohen's version of historical materialism is, at most, a theory of what *could* happen or, more precisely, of what would happen *ceteris absentibus*, in the absence of countervailing forces. It is not a prophecy of what is bound to come. Its purchase on historical inevitability is therefore more nuanced than anything that can be found in more traditional formulations of Marx's idea.[8] Perhaps for this reason and perhaps also because it was introduced in a period that was already politically quiescent, the Cohen version failed to elicit the kinds of criticisms that earlier accounts had drawn upon themselves. In the discussions it generated, the worries of the Western Marxists were ignored. Attention focused instead on such issues as the adequacy of Cohen's recourse to functional explanations, and on other matters of a generally technical and apolitical nature. Even so, it seemed for a while that Marxist philosophy would revive by returning to its classical roots. But this hope quickly faded. Subject to relentless criticism, some of it from Cohen himself, many historical materialist claims came to seem indefensible. (Cohen's own hesitations about the theory he had reconstructed and defended are evident in Cohen, 1988.) No one maintained that the theory ought to be cast entirely aside. But the historical materialism that emerged in the wake of the scrutiny Cohen's work spawned was a considerably attenuated version of Marx's theory.

Analytical Marxism began with the implicit understanding that Marxism is not methodologically distinctive, a claim it went on to vindicate. It offered the promise, though, of defensible substantive claims that would distinguish Marxism from 'bourgeois' theory. But as historical materialism's explanatory pretensions were progressively retracted, this expectation too diminished. This increasingly evident state of affairs added to an emerging consensus that, to this day, is more tacit than explicit. The idea is not quite that Marxism has suffered a historical defeat in the way that communism did. No analytical Marxist came to the conclusion that Marx's positions were without merit. It was rather that, as *The Communist Manifesto* famously said of 'all that is solid' in bourgeois society, Marxism seemed to have 'melted into air'. What once appeared to be an alternative to 'bourgeois' ways of apprehending the world had vanished, almost without trace. This is analytical Marxism's unintended legacy, or at least the part of it that is apparent for now.

As remarked, the turmoil that attended defections from the Marxist camp in generations past never surfaced in the wake of these developments. Perhaps analytical Marxism was too academic to arouse fundamental passions in the way that earlier strains of Marxist theorizing had. In any case, its internal trajectory gave rise to disappointments, not betrayals. But, for Marxism itself, the effect was even more devastating. For analytical Marxists were driven by ostensibly timeless, rationally compelling arguments, not passing political concerns. If, from this purview, Marxism melts into air, then it is effectively finished.

What happened to historical materialism paralleled developments elsewhere. I have already noted how Marxist political economy, ostensibly an alternative to mainstream, neoclassical economics, collapsed into its putative rival. Marxist sociology suffered a similar fate. If there is no distinctive Marxist methodology in the social sciences, then Marxist sociology is, at most, a framework for generating explanations – one that, following Marx's own example, accords explanatory priority to class structure and class conflict or, more precisely, to the understanding of class structure and conflict that Marx developed.[9] But, then, it is an open question how explanatory class analysis is for the range of phenomena sociologists investigate. There is no doubt that it explains a great deal (see, for example, Wright, 1997). But unless there is a theoretically well-motivated reason to privilege class analysis, one cannot say that it explains the most important or most fundamental things. Historical materialism supplies grounds for according a kind of explanatory pre-eminence to class analysis. But as it came increasingly under attack, this rationale seemed to evaporate and class analysis came to look like nothing more than one explanatory strategy among others. No one denied its importance. But it became difficult to maintain that it is an alternative to mainstream sociology. Thus, in sociology too, the analytical Marxists folded Marxism, unintentionally but inexorably, into its ostensible rival.

INTO LIBERALISM

Eventually, analytical Marxists came to make a case for Marxism's distinctiveness and theoretical integrity on the terrain of normative theory. This stand is doubly ironic. The first irony is a consequence of analytical Marxism's political detachment. Having executed a radical divorce of Marxist theory from its political roots, the analytical Marxists arrived at the conclusion that the one thing that keeps Marxism from melting into air, that keeps it an *ism,* is its valuational commitments. In as much as these commitments imply a dedication to changing the world in the way Marxists have always envisioned, it follows that Marxism is distinguished by its politics, after all. From their apolitical vantage-point, the analytical Marxists brought politics back in, and even placed it at centre-stage.

The second irony arises out of the analytical Marxists' dedication to orthodoxy. Orthodox Marxism derogated normative concerns. Engels, for example, famously insisted that Marx's socialism was 'scientific,' not 'utopian'. By this, he meant that the case for socialism Marx and his followers advanced followed from an analysis of the 'laws of motion' of real history, not from a normative ideal. Orthodox historical materialism took this understanding to heart, and so accordingly did Cohen's reconstruction of it. To be sure, Cohen's defence of historical materialism was friendlier to normative concerns than Marx's own writings generally were. But it was only in the course of *criticizing* the theory he had reconstructed that Cohen and others created a space, within the Marxist fold, for normative theory as such. The idea that Marxism's distinctiveness lies with its normative commitments suggested itself to analytical Marxists because they failed in their original purpose, because they were not able to defend a more orthodox view. It should always have been plain, however, that this was a desperate move. The idea that Marxism is distinguished by its valuational commitments simply does not bear scrutiny, for just the reason that led the orthodox Marxists to disparage morality.

From the time that Marx broke away from Ludwig Feuerbach and the Young Hegelians, from roughly his mid twenties on, he was not much interested in normative theory, except in one respect. He remained a steadfast opponent of applications of moral theory in class divided societies. No doubt, this opposition was partly pragmatic and rhetorical. But there was also, as Marx might have said, a 'rational kernel' contained within the outer, polemical shell of this position.

To begin to extract this kernel, we must first distinguish moral theory from normative theory generally. Let us therefore say, following much precedent, that a moral theory is a normative theory that adopts the moral point of view.[10] This is the point of view implicit in the Golden Rule and epitomized in the categorical imperative, the point of view of generality or universality (see Kant, 1959). (Kant formulated the categorical imperative in several, quite distinct ways. But the guiding idea, already implicit in the Golden Rule, is that, in appropriate contexts, one ought to act according to 'maxims', principles of action, that one could rationally will that all other moral agents act on as well.) The Golden Rule tells us 'to do unto others' as we would have others do unto ourselves. It tells us, in other words, that in deliberating on alternative courses of action, what matters is not what differentiates us from one another, but what we have in common. Thus we are enjoined to deliberate in an impartial or agent-neutral way – from the vantage-point of agency as such, rather than from our own perspectives as particular agents. This point of view is obviously not appropriate in all contexts. In ordering from a menu in a restaurant, where nothing depends on one's order except what food one will be served, it would be pointless to engage in agent-neutral deliberation. One ought simply to order what one prefers to eat; in other words, to deliberate in an agent-specific way. On the other hand, in thinking about whether to pay one's debts or to cultivate one's talents, moral deliberation does seem to have a place. It provides reasons – typically, determinative reasons – governing how agents are to act.

Marx had something to say *about* this deliberative stance – not so much in its applications to individual conduct, however, as in its role in organizing and defending institutional arrangements. He did not take issue with universalizability as such. Indeed, in his early writings, Marx faulted existing social, political and especially economic arrangements from precisely this point of view (see Levine, 1978). Marx's concept of 'alienation', the central normative concept employed throughout his early writings, is essentially the Kantian notion of 'unfreedom' or 'heteronomy' – where heteronomy contrasts with autonomy (freedom), and an action is heteronomously determined when it is determined by the will of another – including, Kant insisted, one's own self, in so far as reason is not in control (Levine, 1978). Marx never rejected this, even as he abandoned Feuerbachian criticism for other explanatory projects. Throughout his life, Marx insisted that claims for universality in class-divided societies are almost always *false* and also *tendentious* in the sense that they promote the particular interests of the economically dominant class. This is why Marx took issue with the idea of *Recht*, of universal principles implemented in social and political institutions, and therefore why he came to fault Hegel's notion of the *Rechtsstaat*. In Marx's view, the *Rechtsstaat*, and the theory that sustains it – moral theory in its definitive, Kantian form – plays a role in the class struggle. It is only under communism, when systemic social divisions generally and class divisions in particular will have disappeared, that institutions can genuinely implement universal ideals. Thus Marx was not a critic of moral theory as such. In his view, a genuinely moral order is a human possibility and an eminently worthy objective. What he denounced was real-world applications of moral theory *in social and political contexts* – not just in particular instances but, this side of communism, in (nearly) all likely cases.

This claim, if sustained, has enormous implications for normative theory. But it does not imply an alternative to moral theory. Rather, Marx was one among a number of nineteenth- and twentieth-century critics of morality, a group that includes Nietzsche, neo-Aristotelian defenders of 'virtue ethics', and some contemporary feminists. The common thread running through their work is the idea that morality itself is problematic. This is a charge worthy of careful attention. But it is hardly a basis for claiming that Marxism is a distinctive and theoretically integral body of thought.

Marx had almost nothing directly to say about the bases of normative evaluation, although he was hardly shy about condemning economic, social and political arrangements in normative and even moralistic terms. Arguably, then, he did have views on the subject, even if they have to be teased out of his various writings. Marx's normative commitments have, in fact, received a great deal of attention in recent years. It is plain that, following Aristotle's lead, but then historicizing Aristotle's idea, Marx valued *self-realization,* the actualization of historically situated human potentialities. He assessed social, political and economic arrangements according to how well they serve this end. It is equally plain that Marx accorded central importance to a particular notion of *community*, evident earlier in the political philosophy of Jean-Jacques Rousseau and, implicitly, in the republican tradition in seventeenth- and eighteenth-century political theory [see further Chapters 13, 26]. Above all, however, Marx valued autonomy. In his view, it was precisely this idea of freedom that took a wrong turn, as it were, into Hegel's philosophy of right; and it is this idea that will finally become feasible under communism, when the *Rechtsstaat*, along with so many other defining institutions of bourgeois society, will have withered away (Levine, 1998; see also Lukes, 1985; Elster, 1985).

But, again, these commitments hardly constitute a distinctive normative theory. The idea that a *Marxism* can be concocted out of Marx's valuational commitments is therefore illusory in the Freudian sense; it is the expression of an (unconscious) wish. Thus the last stand of the analytical Marxists fares no better than the rest. With nowhere else to retreat, some analytical Marxists drew the apparently unavoidable conclusion: that analytical Marxism, despite itself, has brought Marxism itself to its end – not its *telos*, but its final moment.

EGALITARIANISM

The value that has served as the main point of contact between liberalism and Marxism, as liberalism took a Rawlsian turn and as Marxism became ensconced under the broad Rawlsian tent, is *equality*. Therein too lies an irony. For both liberalism and Marxism have, for most of their histories, evinced ambivalence, if not hostility, towards this ideal. The first liberals were concerned mainly to defend property rights – above all, the right to accumulate property privately and without limitation. They were therefore anti-egalitarian, according to the usual understanding of the term. Marxists also have characteristically disparaged egalitarianism, though their views about the distribution of the economic surplus plainly have egalitarian implications. In part, Marxists distanced themselves from egalitarians in order to differentiate their own objectives from those of other socialist traditions. But they had a more substantive reason as well. Marx's goal was communism, a society of a radically new and different kind. In the dialectical language some Marxists still prefer, communism is the 'negation' of capitalism. But income equality or, more generally, resource equality does not imply the negation of capitalism. In principle, it can be realized in capitalist societies through redistributive taxation and other social policies. So too can any other likely egalitarian objective [see further Chapters 16, 17, 30].

More generally, if, by 'socialism', we mean an economic system in which 'social' property replaces private property in society's principal means of production, then, if all socialists want is equality, socialism is, at best, only a means to the desired end. Roemer (1994) is the most ardent defender of the idea that equality is what socialists really want (Levine, 1996). But, then, it is an open question how efficacious this means is. It could turn out that there are better ways to attain the end in view, in some circumstances or perhaps even in all likely cases. Then, paradoxically, socialism would be unnecessary for attaining what socialists want. Marxists could still insist that, in real-world conditions, socialist property relations are useful or perhaps even indispensable for realizing the objectives they and Rawlsian liberals share. But, then, socialism

would be nothing more than a strategy egalitarians might pursue. As with other imaginable strategies, its suitability would depend on circumstances of time and place. This conclusion would mark the end of the Marxists' long-standing commitment to the idea of communism – to a vision of ideal social and political arrangements beyond the purview of liberal political philosophy. This is a high price to pay for joining the liberal camp, and an unnecessary one.

PROFESSIONAL DEFORMATIONS

I would venture that part of the explanation for the fact that the analytical Marxists were so ready to give up on the idea of communism has to do with the professional culture and disciplinary styles to which they held themselves accountable. Analytical Marxism was free from disabling political ties. But analytical Marxists were especially susceptible to certain *déformations professionnelles*.

By far the most influential of the academic disciplines that shaped analytical Marxism was philosophy. In effect, analytical Marxism was just analytical philosophy applied to Marxist themes. Philosophy apart, the academic discipline that, more than any other, influenced analytical Marxism substantively, shaping its explanatory strategies, was economics, the most mathematical of the social sciences and the most self-consciously rigorous in its standards. Analytical Marxism had, on the whole, a beneficial relationship with economic theory. But there are, even so, perennial features of mainstream economics that found their way into analytical Marxism – to its detriment.

Of these, perhaps the most important is a tendency to focus on what can be modelled formally and therefore to emphasize theoretical elegance over substantive insight. This temptation undoubtedly played a role in leading analytical Marxists to focus on equality more than on the values that Marx unambivalently endorsed – self-realization, community and autonomy. Mainstream economics deals with the distribution and redistribution of resources. Equality therefore falls within its purview. Thanks to decades of work on the topic, it is plain that the idea can be modelled in ways that advance understanding. Self-realization, community, and autonomy have received much less attention and are, in any case, less susceptible to formal modelling than equality is. It is not surprising, therefore, that analytical Marxists, prone to internalize the standards of the economics profession, would emphasize this value at the expense of the others.

There is, in addition, a more subtle consequence of the influence of academic economics on analytical Marxism. Professional economists are drawn to rational choice explanations [see further Chapter 5]. They 'deduce' the behaviours of rational agents in idealized accounts of real-world circumstances, and then endeavour to make sense of their various explananda by invoking explanatory principles derived from these idealized cases. In theory, this explanatory strategy can be applied to many aspects of social life, not just to the economy. But, in practice, it only comes into its own in economics itself – in other words, when the explanandum is the behaviours of economic agents, whether individuals or firms. Needless to say, the economic agents the economics profession knows best interact through market arrangements in regimes of private property. It is therefore natural for those who have internalized the norms of the profession, when they investigate equality, to assume, as liberal egalitarians do, that equality enhancing measures involve the *redistribution* of privately owned goods; in other words, that capitalist markets distribute assets that the state then redistributes in accord with one or another egalitarian ideal. Marx's communism is difficult to accommodate within this explanatory programme. So too is any other non-capitalist or non-statist set of institutional arrangements.

Finally, because it is committed to rational choice explanations, mainstream economics is hospitable to *methodological individualism*, a view about explanation that was proposed earlier in this century by philosophers of a deliberately anti-Marxist bent and then revived by the analytical Marxists (see esp. Elster, 1985; Roemer, 1982; for a critical challenge see Wright, Levine and Sober, 1992: ch. 6). In this regard, the irony is extreme. Marx famously inveighed against the 'individualism' of the classical economists and contractarian political philosophers, heaping scorn on their efforts to conceive individuals abstracted from their social relations. In the mid twentieth century, the principal defenders of methodological individualism, Karl Popper and Friedrich von Hayek, took Marx at his word, faulting him on this account. They promoted methodological individualism as an alternative to Marxism. Writers sympathetic to Marxism responded in kind. But for many analytical Marxists, this debate was wrongheaded. What matters, in their view, is just that social scientists risk falling into error when they formulate explanations that fail to take account of the individual-level 'mechanisms', psychological or otherwise, through which social factors become causally efficacious. Elster's methodological individualism, in particular, was motivated by the thought that social scientists are obliged, whenever possible, 'to look under the hood', to identify the micro-foundational means through which social effects are realized. No matter, then, that the older generation of methodological individualists were motivated by a politics inimical to socialism. Their view of explanation was

basically correct, and therefore ought, so far as possible, to be incorporated into the Marxist fold. It had been the conventional wisdom, among Marxists, that Marx set Hegel 'on his feet', putting the dialectical method that Hegel had devised for an 'idealist' metaphysics to good 'materialist' use. Following this precedent, we might say that Elster performed a similar operation on Popper and Hayek. He maintained that it is because many Marxist explanations *are* susceptible to methodological individualist reconstructions that they are generally sound. Elster continued to defend methodological individualism throughout the 1980s and 1990s, even as he turned his attention away from expressly Marxist themes (see e.g. Elster, 1989).

This is not the place to take on Elster's views on explanation (but see Wright, Levine and Sober, 1992: ch. 6). But I would suggest that a penchant for explanations that satisfy methodological individualist constraints encourages a disposition to focus on normative concerns that are compatible with an individualist outlook. The liberal understanding of equality fits this description because it focuses on *individuals'* holdings. In the liberal view, equality is achieved when individuals have equal shares of the right distribuand, whatever it might be. The values that mattered more to Marx accord less well with this sensibility. This is plainly the case for community. Communal interests are irreducible to the interests of individual members of communities (see further Levine, 1993; 1998). But it is also true for self-realization and autonomy, as Marx understood these notions. For Marx as for Aristotle, to self-realize is, among other things, to become a social and political being, an integral part of a political community. For Marx as for Kant, to be autonomous is to act in harmony with other free beings, to become 'self-legislating members of a republic of ends', integral components of a harmonious, internally co-ordinated association of rational beings.

To be sure, methodological individualism, a view about social scientific explanation, is compatible with a wide range of normative commitments. But, psychologically, the doctrine makes it difficult for its adherents to endorse normative commitments that are not individualistic. It is therefore curious that Elster, who did so much to investigate the philosophical implications of such psychological phenomena as cognitive dissonance and denial, generally supports the understanding of Marx's normative commitments set out here (Elster, 1985: esp. ch. 2; for Elster's views on the implications of various psychological phenomena for moral theory, see, for example, Elster, 1983: ch. 2). Unlike Roemer, Elster never claimed, even implicitly, that Marx would have been a liberal egalitarian, if only he had better understood what he and other socialists wanted. Instead, Elster reconstructed and defended

Marx's commitment to self-realization and, to a lesser degree, to autonomy and community as well. He did so, moreover, without suggesting that the normative theory implicit in Marx's work is in any way at odds with sound explanatory practice. But to endorse these values and methodological individualism at the same time is, as it were, to court cognitive dissonance or to invite denial. In Elster's case, the way out was, as he might say, *essentially a by-product* of changes in his intellectual interests. Quietly, Elster abandoned Marxism. Others, like Roemer, buffeted by similar tensions but intent on maintaining continuity with the Marxist political tradition, endeavoured to fit normative concerns that better conform to an individualist world view into a Marxist framework.

IS ANYTHING LEFT?

For more than a century, Marxists led a long march that has only recently fallen into disarray. But that march is likely to resume its forward journey; perhaps, some day, it will successfully conclude. The former prediction, at least, is a good bet, because despite (but also because of) capitalist development, the real-world factors that led so many for so long to yearn for socialism are as much in force as they ever were, albeit on a global scale and in ever changing forms. It is doubtful, though, whether a revived left will ever again march under the banner of 'Marxism'. The burdens of history, especially the taint of the Soviet experience, make this prospect unlikely. Will Marx's work therefore be ignored or, if studied, treated only as a historical artefact? It is not impossible. But it would be unfortunate if this is what the future holds. For it would then be necessary to rediscover what the Marxists already knew. The account I have given of analytical Marxism's trajectory suggests any number of reasons why this is so. I will end by briefly recalling a few of them.

In the 1980s, historical materialism had its day in the sun. Tenets of the orthodox view were challenged, sometimes decisively. Partly in consequence, interest in the topic has waned. But the theory itself remains generally intact. It may not explain all that its defenders once thought that it did, but it still explains a great deal (Wright, Levine and Sober, 1992; Cohen, 1988). It shows what, in the way of real property relations, is materially possible, and therefore what economic structures are on the historical agenda. Suitably qualified, it also shows that 'legal and political superstructures' and 'forms of consciousness' are explained by the nature of the economic base that sustains them. These positions have important implications for political theory. To date, they have been only barely explored.

What historical materialism challenges is nothing less than the central dogma of modern political philosophy after Hobbes: the idea that the state is ultimately a state of its undifferentiated citizenry. On this assumption, social divisions, however trenchant, are of only secondary importance in political life. The state and the individual are the principal players. Class divisions are therefore excluded from the political sphere. This position stands in contrast to the claim, famously articulated in *The Communist Manifesto*, that states are always only 'executive committees' of the economically dominant class. It will be instructive to reflect on the difference.

For political philosophers in the modern era, the point of departure for thinking about political arrangements has always been the individual, conceived atomistically, and the principal problem has been to conceive how the behaviours of such individuals might be co-ordinated, as their interests require. But because Marx was a historical materialist, the fundamental unit of society, for him, was social classes, not individuals. In his view, then, there is no general, inter-individual co-ordination problem for the state to solve. There is, of course, a class co-ordination problem. However, unlike the atomic individuals Hobbes described, classes are not exactly mired in a war of all against all. To be sure, their interests are antagonistic, just as Hobbes thought the interests of individuals in a state of nature are. But a war of all against all presupposes relative equality among the combatants, and, in consequence of the economic structure, classes are too unequal. Among the classes whose interests stand opposed, some (usually one) are powerful enough to dominate the rest. Some (usually one) are in a position to take unfair advantage, to *exploit*, the others. Strictly speaking, then, the inter-class co-ordination problem does not require a solution analogous to the institution of sovereignty in Hobbes's state of nature. Class relations are co-ordinated by the economic structure or mode of production itself. But, for the economic structure to be in place and to reproduce itself, there is an intra-class or, more precisely, an intra-ruling-class co-ordination problem, similar to the one Hobbes identified for subjects generally, that must be solved. Among the exploiters, individuals and coalitions of individuals have conflicting interests. But they also have a common interest, analogous to the interest in peace that individuals in a Hobbesian state of nature share. Everyone in the economically dominant class has an interest in maintaining the system of exploitation itself, for it is only by virtue of this system that they are economically dominant. The state is the means through which they do so. It is what allows the economically dominant class to overcome its own internal co-ordination problem, its intra-class 'war of all against all', the better to wage 'war', class war, against those it dominates. This is why Marx and Engels called the state the 'executive committee' of the entire ruling class. Subordinate classes also face co-ordination problems. These problems are exacerbated by the system of class rule that enforces their subordination. Marx carefully investigated this phenomenon. It was one of the principal concerns of the very subtle analyses of political events that he produced throughout his life. The analytical Marxists had almost nothing to say about this aspect of Marx's thought. It is a treasure trove awaiting philosophical exploration.

It became Marx's view in the 1870s, in the aftermath of the Paris Commune, that different kinds of legislative, administrative and repressive institutions are appropriate for different forms of the state – that, in other words, a proletarian class state would differ institutionally in far-reaching ways from the state that organizes the class power of the bourgeoisie. A proletarian state would be more directly democratic, not just in its manner of rendering collective choices, but also in its system for the administration of justice. Among other things, standing armies would give way to popular militias, and a relatively independent judiciary would be replaced by popular tribunals. In light of what would be done in the Soviet Union and elsewhere in the name of 'the dictatorship of the proletariat', these proposals are plainly problematic. But the extent of Marx's retroactive complicity with what some self-identified Marxists would do is itself a vexed and complicated question. What is clear is that Marx's reflections on institutional forms, and the speculations of some of his co-thinkers, including the Lenin of *The State and Revolution*, provide a rich source of material to reflect upon. Those who would investigate the great political issues of our time – the nature of democracy, the need for liberal constraints on state power, and, ultimately, the relation between liberalism and democracy – cannot afford to ignore what they had to say.

Most of all, though, Marx's political writings provide resources for thinking about the possibility of going beyond the conceptual horizons of mainstream liberalism. Marx was, again, a (small 'c') communist; a proponent of a form of social organization that mainstream liberal political philosophy does not and probably cannot countenance (Levine, 1993; 1998). The model, arguably, was the just state of Rousseau's *Social Contract*. The ideal, as Kant discerned from Rousseau, was a 'kingdom of ends' or, as Marx would have it, in language that resonates back to Kant and Rousseau, a world in which the condition for 'the free development of each' is 'the free development of all'. Historical materialism, however modified and revised it must be, establishes the material possibility of a world of this kind. If the political philosophy of the future is to be true to the most compelling human concerns, it ignores this possibility at its peril.

NOTES

1 There has been to date, very little useful historical analysis of analytical Marxism. An exception is Roberts (1996). The account that follows differs in some respects from the picture Roberts presents and, more importantly, in its assessment of what the analytical Marxist legacy can be.

2 The term *Western Marxism* was introduced by Maurice Merleau-Ponty (1973); see also Perry Anderson (1976). The term denotes the work of a very wide range of thinkers – among others, Georg Lukács, Karl Korsch, Antonio Gramsci, the theorists of the Frankfurt school (Theodor Adorno, Max Horkheimer, Herbert Marcuse, etc.), existentialist Marxists (Jean-Paul Sartre, Maurice Merleau-Ponty), structuralist Marxists (Louis Althusser, Etienne Balibar), and so on. A common thread is hard to find. All Western Marxists opposed the official Marxism of the Soviet Union and the Western European communist parties – though, in some cases, the opposition was *very* tacit, even to the point of maintaining party membership. Another common thread will be noted in the paragraph that follows: Western Marxism drew substantially on twentieth-century 'continental' philosophy, and therefore on the work of such figures as Hegel and Husserl and others whose ideas and methods had little resonance in mainstream, English-speaking academic philosophy.

3 It was these terms – the arm of criticism, the criticism of arms – that the young Marx invoked to describe the unfolding revolutionary dynamic of Germany in the 1840s, a period of ferment that culminated in the revolutionary upheavals of 1848. See 'A contribution to the critique of Hegel's *Philosophy of Right*: introduction' (Marx, 1994: 64).

4 Among others, the journal *Philosophy and Public Affairs*, launched in 1971, opened its pages to these studies, some of which are anthologized in Cohen, Nagel and Scanlon (1980). See also Wood (1981: chs 9 and 10).

5 This collection of essays, written in the wake of the Bolshevik Revolution and the subsequent failure of revolutionary uprisings in Central Europe (including his native Hungary), was first published in 1922.

6 Thus in the same preface to *Capital*, vol. 1 in which Marx declared his scientificity, he also declared his attachment to Hegelian philosophy, even crediting his scientific advances to his Hegelianism.

7 See, for example, Elster (1978, esp. chs 3–5). Elster undertook this investigation of dialectical logic (and a host of related ideas) before he expressly identified with the analytical Marxist camp, though his sympathies with Marxist theory were already evident. For a more considered view, after Elster had become a leading analytical Marxist, see Elster (1985: ch. 1). Perhaps the most ardent defender of the dialectic in a broadly analytical vein has

been Bertell Ollman: see, for example, Ollman (1971; 1993). Ollman would probably resist being described as an analytical Marxist, in part because he finds analytical Marxist writing insufficiently dialectical. But his intellectual style is as 'analytical' as that of any analytical Marxist.

8 Cohen discusses aspects of these issues in a number of articles published after *Karl Marx's Theory of History* (1978). See, especially, 'Historical inevitability and revolutionary agency' in Cohen (1988).

9 For an analytical Marxist account of the Marxist concept of class and its differences from mainstream understandings, see Wright (1985).

10 The more usual distinction is between *ethical* theory, which has to do with that part of normative theory that pertains to individual conduct, and *moral* theory, which is a subset of ethical theory, one that, with respect to individual conduct, proposes, where appropriate, the adoption of the moral point of view. See, for example, Darwall (1998). My suggestion that we view moral theory as a subset of normative, rather than just ethical, theory is motivated by a concern to capture Marx's views not only on how individuals ought to act but also on how institutions ought to be organized.

REFERENCES

Anderson, Perry (1976) *Considerations on Western Marxism*. London: New Left Books.

Berlin, Isaiah (1962) 'Does political theory still exist?' In Peter Laslett, and W. G. Runcimann, eds (1962) *Philosophy, Politics, and Society*, 2nd series. Oxford: Blackwell.

Buchanan, Allen E. (1982) *Marx and Justice: The Radical Critique of Liberalism*. Totawa, NJ: Rowman and Littlefield.

Cohen, G. A. (1978) *Karl Marx's Theory of History: A Defence*. Oxford: Oxford University Press.

Cohen, G. A. (1988) *History, Labour and Freedom: Themes from Marx*. Oxford: Oxford University Press.

Cohen, G. A. (2000) *If You're An Egalitarian, How Come You're So Rich?* Cambridge, MA: Harvard University Press.

Cohen, Marshall, Thomas Nagel and Thomas Scanlon, eds (1980) *Marx, Justice and Utopia*. Princeton, NJ: Princeton University Press.

Darwall, Steven (1998) *Philosophical Ethics*. Boulder, CO: Westview.

Deane, Herbert A. (1963) *The Political and Social Ideas of St. Augustine*. New York: Columbia University Press.

Elster, Jon (1978) *Logic and Society: Contradictions and Possible Worlds*. New York: Wiley.

Elster, Jon (1983) *Sour Grapes: Studies in the Subversion of Rationality*. Cambridge: Cambridge University Press.

Elster, Jon (1985) *Making Sense of Marx*. Cambridge: Cambridge University Press.

Elster, Jon (1989) *Nuts and Bolts: For the Social Sciences*. Cambridge: Cambridge University Press.

Hegel, G. W. F. (1942) *The Philosophy of Right*, trans, T. M. Knox. Oxford: Clarendon.

Kant, Immanuel (1959 [1785]) *Foundations of the Metaphysics of Morals*. New York: Library of Liberal Arts.

Kuhn, Thomas S. (1962) *The Structure of Scientific Revolutions*. Chicago: University of Chicago Press.

Levine, Andrew (1978) 'Alienation as heteronomy'. *The Philosophical Forum*, 8 (2–4): 256–68.

Levine, Andrew (1993) *The General Will: Rousseau, Marx, Communism*. Cambridge: Cambridge University Press.

Levine, Andrew (1996) 'Saving socialism and/or abandoning it'. In Erik Olin Wright, ed., *Equal Shares: Making Market Socialism Work*. London: Verso.

Levine, Andrew (1998) *Rethinking Liberal Equality*. Ithaca, NY: Cornell University Press.

Lukács, Georg (1971) *History and Class Consciousness*, trans. Rodney Livingstone. London: Merlin.

Lukes, Steven (1985) *Marxism and Morality*. Oxford: Oxford University Press.

Marx, Karl (1994) *Early Political Writings*, ed. Joseph O'Malley. Cambridge: Cambridge University Press.

Merleau-Ponty, Maurice (1973) *Adventures in the Dialectic*, trans. Joseph Bien. Evanston, IL: Northwestern University Press.

Ollman, Bertell (1971) *Alienation: Marx's Conception of Man in Capitalist Society* (2nd edn 1977). Cambridge: Cambridge University Press.

Ollman, Bertel (1993) *Dialectical Investigations*. New York: Routledge.

Popper, Karl (1958) *The Poverty of Historicism*. London: Routledge and Kegan Paul.

Popper, Karl (1972) *Objective Knowledge*. Oxford: Oxford University Press.

Popper, Karl (1973) *Conjectures and Refutations*. London: Routledge and Kegan Paul.

Rawls, John (1971) *A Theory of Justice*. Cambridge, MA: Harvard University Press.

Roberts, Marcus (1996) *Analytical Marxism: A Critique*. London: Verso.

Roemer, John (1982) *Analytical Foundations of Marxian Economic Theory*. Cambridge: Cambridge University Press.

Roemer, John (1994) *A Future for Socialism*. Cambridge, MA: Harvard University Press.

Shaw, William H. (1978) *Marx's Theory of History*. Stanford, CA: Stanford University Press.

Wood, Alan (1981) *Karl Marx*. London: Routledge and Kegan Paul.

Wright, Erik Olin (1985) *Classes*. London: Verso.

Wright, Erik Olin (1997) *Class Counts: Comparative Studies in Class Analysis*. Cambridge: Cambridge University Press.

Wright, Erik Olin, Andrew Levine and Elliot Sober (1992) *Reconstructing Marxism: Essays on Explanation and the Theory of History*. London: Verso.

7

Liberalism, Political and Comprehensive

JEREMY WALDRON

THE BACKGROUND DIFFICULTY

The modern distinction between 'political' and 'comprehensive' versions of liberalism arises in connection with a serious problem about the basis of justification for liberal principles in a pluralistic society. The problem arises as follows.

Liberals envisage a tolerant, inclusive society, populated by people adhering to a variety of belief systems. Many modern societies in which liberalism flourishes as a political ideal already have this character: they are religiously pluralist and multicultural societies, in which heritages and ideals of all sorts rub shoulders with one another and compete for adherents, and in which communities of faith and tradition share quarters with groups committed to radical exploration of new ways of living, thinking, and being [see further Chapter 19]. Societies of this sort of course face the same challenges that all human societies face, and they must deal with the questions of justice and order that affect human societies generally. How are property and the economy to be structured? What is the extent of each person's responsibility for the fate of others and for the social fabric as a whole? How are structures of freedom and responsibility, mutual forbearance and mutual aid, co-ordination and co-operation, power and participation to be defined? Those are questions for every society.

But a pluralist society also faces an additional agenda. Where different faiths and cultures rub shoulders, there is likely to be friction and offence: one group's worship or festivities might seem like a reproach or an attack on another group, and as values and philosophies compete in the marketplace of ideas, the competition will often seem disrespectful as each creed tries to discredit its opponents and gain adherents for itself. It is not easy to define the duty of mutual toleration under these circumstances, or to sustain the distinction between harm and offence that a pluralistic regime requires. And that is not the only distinction that pluralism threatens. The line between public and private, between issues of policy and social welfare on the one hand and individual ethics and religious or cultural observance on the other, is always going to be an issue. Certain cultures and religions in a pluralistic society may aspire to be a society unto themselves. A religion, for example, may have its own values with a distinctive bearing on the problems of social life, and it may impose quite particular obligations (for example, dietary laws or rules of religious observance) on its members, which may or may not be compatible with the society's broader social arrangements. To make law and policy for a pluralistic society is thus a greater challenge than for a society that is religiously and culturally homogeneous. The latter just needs to settle on a single set of answers and enforce them. But the former has to deal with the fact that its members are already firmly wedded to disparate answers. The various answers may be incommensurable; but even if they are mutually intelligible, they may not present themselves simply as rival political opinions about how to solve the problems faced by the larger society [see further Chapter 18]. Instead they may present themselves as claims of identity, demanding accommodation as a matter of justice, or as a matter of respect for the persons whose religious and cultural allegiances they represent.

Now these distinctive difficulties associated with pluralism are not in themselves the problem which I mentioned in the opening lines of this chapter. Indeed, the challenge that I have just outlined is one to which liberals respond gamely and enthusiastically.

Since the rise of religious toleration in the West, liberal political philosophy has made a speciality of arguing about structures of order, justice, and liberty for pluralistic societies; it has made a speciality of arguing about the distinctions between harm and offence and between public and private. Though liberals disagree with one another on many of these issues, they pride themselves on their willingness to confront these difficulties and deal with them honestly, straight on, without wishing them away. There is a whole heritage of reflection on the values and principles that may be used to define a fair social and political order under conditions of freedom and diversity. We find it in the canon of liberal theory – in the work of John Locke, Immanuel Kant, the French *philosophes*, the Federalists, John Stuart Mill, as well as the more problematic contributions of Hobbes, Rousseau, Hegel, the utilitarians, and the new liberals who combined with the canon some of the insights of socialism. There may not be consensus among these various liberal thinkers, but there is a wealth of resources to draw on.

But here is the difficulty. The ideas that we draw on in order to elaborate and defend liberal principles and liberal solutions to the problems outlined above are often ideas associated with particular philosophical traditions. The sanctity of life and bodily integrity, the importance of autonomy, consent and individuals' control of their own destiny, the concern we are supposed to have for each other's self-development, the inherent value supposedly attaching to the satisfaction of an individual's preference, the respect accorded to ethical and spiritual thinking at the level of the individual mind and conscience, the key position occupied by reason and rationality, and the principle of equality which associates these values with all human beings, whatever their sex, race, age, or social position – these are artefacts of a particular tradition or cluster of traditions that have grown up in our civilization. Many of us find them compelling. But we cannot be under any illusion that they are features of every culture or tradition that we expect to find represented in a modern pluralistic society. They are features of some world views and not others. So: by elaborating and defending liberal principles and liberal solutions to the problems of social life on this sort of basis, we seem to be *taking sides* in the midst of cultural and ethical plurality. We seem to be picking and choosing among the variety of ethical, philosophical and religious traditions in the world, privileging some as foundational and marginalizing others.

An Example: Locke on Toleration

An example will illustrate the difficulty. John Locke's *Letter Concerning Toleration* (1983) is plainly one of the foundational documents in the early modern liberal tradition of religious freedom and religious plurality. But part of the Lockean defence of religious toleration is built up on religious foundations: 'The toleration of those that differ from others in matters of religion,' says Locke, 'is so agreeable to the Gospel of Jesus Christ, that it seems monstrous for men to be so blind as not to perceive the necessity and advantage of it in so clear a light' (1983: 25). And he goes on to argue that the essence of religion is sincere belief, that Jesus used persuasion rather than force to win adherents to the Gospel, that he did not endow his apostles with earthly power, and that he did not need to because religious heterodoxy by one person is not harmful to the soul or spiritual health of another. Now these are Christian arguments, and there is no reason why they would be convincing to everyone for whom Locke envisaged toleration (let alone for everyone for whom we envisage toleration). True, Locke advanced other more pragmatic arguments for toleration that were not dependent on Christian conceptions in this way. But he evidently thought the Christian foundations were important, and it is arguable that his case would be incomplete or vulnerable to fairly straightforward objections if it were not defended in this way.

So Locke is put to his choice. Either he defends liberal toleration on a basis that is rooted in a particular world view (or a narrow class of world views), and risks diminishing its appeal as something held in common among a variety of faiths. Or he seeks a more pragmatic defence that can appeal to people who start from a genuine variety of religious and ethical assumptions; but it may have to be a shallower and philosophically less sophisticated defence. The second approach may not say, in defence of toleration, everything that John Locke thinks it important to say: maybe what is really important about toleration *is* its agreeability to the Gospel of Jesus Christ. Still this second kind of defence – if it can be concocted – will have the advantage of being more widely appealing. Now I don't think Locke ever in fact faced up to this choice. The politics of his audience was not such that he needed to: though he proposed toleration for Muslims and Jews, and other non-Christians, the success of his proposal did not depend on the acceptability of his argument in their eyes. The mainstream audience he addressed was a Christian audience, and so he could afford to develop a Christian argument. (Indeed the mainstream audience he addressed was a Protestant audience, so he could afford to flirt with grounds for toleration that were unacceptable to Roman Catholics.) In our day, however, the politics of toleration are different: for us, a politically sensible defence of the principle of toleration has to command the allegiance of people of many different faiths (and some with no faith at all). If it cannot be articulated in a way that makes sense to them, it cannot be articulated as part of the shared, public order of the society. And so we face a dilemma. A liberal theory of toleration should try to say what is important about toleration, why it matters, and how values and ideals that seem to point in the other direction can be rebutted. Can this be done in a way that is acceptable to everyone, in a way that does not alienate the adherents of some faith or some philosophy in society? Maybe not. Maybe you cannot see what is really important about toleration except from a perspective that invokes particular values and particular philosophical conceptions. If that is right, then either we opt for a shallow theory of toleration with a broad appeal to diverse groups in society, or in the interest of developing a deeper theory of toleration, we face up to the fact that our liberal commitments will be seen as rooted in the values and conceptions of some particular philosophical outlook.

Defining 'Political' and 'Comprehensive' Liberalism

These two approaches have come to be associated with the labels 'political liberalism' and 'comprehensive liberalism'. Though 'political liberalism' is now associated particularly with the recent work of John Rawls (1993), both labels should be understood in the first instance as referring to *types* of position.

This is partly because 'liberalism' itself is not the name of a determinate set of social and political commitments. There are certain core positions and the various schools of liberal thought may have a family resemblance to one another. But in many areas they offer rival conceptions of the values that are characteristically associated with liberalism, like liberty, equality, democracy, toleration, and the rule of law. Two political liberals may therefore be distinguished from one another by their different positions and their different conceptions. But what they will have in common – as *political* liberals – is their insistence on a distinction between the principles and ideals that (in their respective views) define a liberal order for society, and the deeper values and commitments associated with particular philosophical outlooks. The political liberal insists that the articulation and defence of a given set of liberal commitments for a society should not depend on any particular theory of what gives value or meaning to a human life. A comprehensive liberal denies this. He maintains that it is impossible adequately to defend or elaborate liberal commitments except by invoking the deeper values and commitments associated with some overall or 'comprehensive' philosophy.

There may also be a second layer of difference among political liberals. Whether or not the substance of their liberal commitment is the same, two political liberals may differ in the justificatory strategies they adopt *as political liberals*. One may emphasize the idea of an 'overlapping consensus' – a variety of justificatory paths from disparate philosophical premises to a plateau of liberal principles. (This is Rawls's view, which we shall examine shortly.) Another may opt for a 'lowest common denominator' approach, emphasizing justificatory premises that all members of a pluralist society may be presumed to accept, whatever the differences in their ethics or world view. And the phrase 'may be presumed to accept' may be glossed in various ways, ranging from the idea of universally accessible reasons and reasoning to some fairly aggressive account of basic human interests, like the survivalist account developed by Hobbes (1991).

Obviously there are important differences, also, among comprehensive liberals. A first layer of difference is the same as for political liberals. Two comprehensive liberals may have different liberal commitments: one may be a left liberal and the other a libertarian liberal. A second layer of difference has to do with the content of the comprehensive outlooks on which their liberal commitments are based. John Locke's Christian foundations are not the same as Immanuel Kant's (1991) theory of autonomy, and none of those is the same as the hedonistic foundation of Jeremy Bentham's (1982) utilitarianism. But they all have this in common: they relate liberal commitments in political philosophy to some vision or conception of what matters in life and of the human person and its place in the world. And they are united, too, in their negative conviction that the political liberal cannot complete the assignment that he has taken up. Liberalism, says the comprehensive liberal, is a robust position in political philosophy, a position whose moral partisanship reaches deep into the foundations of our conceptions of person, freedom, and value [see further Chapter 8].

The general difficulty that I have outlined, and the two kinds of response to it, have not always been a staple of discussion in liberal political philosophy. Many of the canonical figures in the liberal tradition are unapologetically 'comprehensive' liberals in the sense that their conceptions of social order and their elaborations and defences of freedom and equality are patently rooted in a deep and extensive vision of the human person and of the ethical significance of human interaction in society.

I have already mentioned John Locke's argument for toleration. Locke's more general theory of politics (his theory of inalienable natural rights, his critique of slavery, his contractarianism, his argument against absolutism) also has a straightforwardly comprehensive character. It rests on the axiom that men are 'all the workmanship of one omnipotent, and infinitely wise maker; all the servants of one sovereign master' – God – 'sent into the world by his order, and about his business', and that 'they are his property, whose workmanship they are, made to last during his, not one another's pleasure' (Locke, 1988: 271). One might also mention the political philosophy of Immanuel Kant. Kant's basic principle of right – 'An action is right if it can coexist with everyone's freedom in accordance with a universal law' (1991: 56) – is presented as part of a metaphysical system that makes rational sense of our ability to distinguish those aspects of force and constraint that are a necessary part of any social order from those that are condemned by the value we attribute to freedom. We proceed in political life as though this distinction were of tremendous importance, and Kant's position is that we cannot explain it without a philosophical theory of the relation between reason, universality, and the harmonization of human wills. And one might cite, too, the work of John Stuart Mill in this regard. A superficial reading of Mill seems to indicate that he was proposing only a political principle: 'the only purpose for which power can be rightfully exercised over any member of a civilized community, against his will, is to prevent harm to others' (1956: 13). But Mill's commitment turns out to depend on a particular vision of human flourishing, in which (as Wilhelm von Humboldt put it, in a passage Mill cited), 'the end of man ... is the highest and most harmonious development of his powers to a complete and consistent whole', and therefore the object 'toward which every human being must ceaselessly direct his efforts ... is the individuality of power of development' (1956: 69).

It does not seem to have occurred to Locke, Kant, and Mill that these foundational positions would pose a problem for the politics of liberalism in a society whose members disagreed about the existence of God, the nature of reason, and the destiny of the human individual. They just took it for granted that liberalism required a philosophical foundation of this kind, and that their task as political philosophers was to articulate that foundation, convince (as Mill put it) 'the intelligent part of the public ... to see its value' (1956: 90), and if necessary argue, as Locke argued in his discussion of atheism (1983: 51), that those who could not subscribe to these foundational positions might have to be regarded as dangerous by the government of a liberal society.

The Principle of Liberal Neutrality

The difficulty I have raised came to the fore in discussions of 'liberal neutrality' in the 1970s and 1980s. A number of theorists attempted to sum up the essence of liberalism in terms of a principle requiring the state to refrain from taking sides on disputed ethical and religious questions. Thus Ronald Dworkin suggested the liberal commitment to treating people as equals meant that

> political decisions must be, so far as possible, independent of any particular conception of the good life or of what gives value to life. Since the citizens of a society differ in their conceptions, the government does not treat them as equals if it prefers one conception to another, either because the officials believe that one is intrinsically superior, or because one is held by the more numerous or more powerful group. (1985: 191)

Dworkin did not suppose that neutrality was a general moral requirement, one that everyone should strive to satisfy. Neutrality was proposed as a principle of specifically *political* morality. It is not wrong for someone to favour a particular conception of what gives value to life, but it is wrong for him to do so in his capacity as a legislator or as a judge. It is not wrong for a church or a firm to pursue some particular spiritual or ethical religion, but it is wrong for the state to do so (Larmore, 1987: 45). The idea had a lot in common with American constitutional doctrines of state action: the First Amendment makes it unconstitutional for the state or the law to favour a religion and the Fourteenth Amendment makes it unconstitutional for the state or the law to discriminate, but neither provision is read as prohibiting religious choice or even racial discrimination by individuals, firms, churches, or clubs (except in cases where their private actions can plausibly be imputed to the state).

Liberal neutrality may be seen as a generalization of religious toleration into the realm of ethical choice generally. The liberal state was no longer required merely to be neutral as between religions; it had to be neutral also between almost all aspects of its citizens' conceptions of the good, whether these were spiritual or secular (the only exceptions being conceptions of the good that themselves denied liberal principles). But therein lay the position's vulnerability. So long as liberalism was read as a principle about religious neutrality, its defence could be rooted in moral ideas. Once it expanded into the ethical realm, it was not clear what it could rest on. It couldn't be based on scepticism about values, for it seemed to represent a particular commitment in the realm of value (Dworkin, 1985: 203). Liberal theorists scrambled to define a distinction within the realm of values between political morality (e.g. moral principles of justice and right, like the neutrality principle itself), on which the state was permitted to act, and ethics (and perhaps the rest of morality besides justice and right), on which it was not permitted to act (Waldron, 1993: 156–63).

But it was always a fine line, and the wider world tended to blur the distinction between ethics and morality and talk generally about the liberal commitment to value neutrality. Once the position was characterized in that way, the defenders of neutrality faced a dilemma: either they left their principle undefended, or they faced accusations of non-neutrality on their own side in respect of the values which they adduced to justify it.

A similar dilemma confronted those who tried to use neutrality as a meta-principle of political justification. Bruce Ackerman (1980) developed a theory of justice in the form of a contractarian dialogue, for which it was laid down as a ground rule that no reason (adduced in conversation to justify any particular distribution of power) 'is a good reason if it requires the power holder to assert … that his conception of the good is better than that asserted by any of his fellow citizens' (1980: 11). Now, why should this be the ground rule? Ackerman said that there were several ways to justify the neutrality principle: it could be justified by reference to the epistemic value of experiments in ethics, or the intrinsic importance of autonomy, or scepticism about ethics, or about the ability of power-holders to reach accurate conclusions about the good (1980: 11–12). The liberal state need not side with any of these justifications in particular. It only needs an assurance that everyone can reach neutrality by at least one of these routes.

Could this strategy work? It might, but only if we were certain that the different paths to neutrality did not make a difference to the meaning or character of the destination. But this seems unlikely. Moral principles are characteristically dependent for their interpretation on some understanding of the point or purpose for which they are imposed. Change the purpose and you provide a different basis for interpreting the principle. So far as neutrality is concerned, one of the main interpretive difficulties concerns the issue of intention: does neutrality forbid only political action motivated by a non-neutral intention or does it forbid also action, however motivated, which is non-neutral in its effects? It turns out that some of Ackerman's paths to neutrality favour the intentionalist interpretation while one, at least, favours the consequentialist interpretation: scepticism about a power-holder's ethical abilities should inhibit only his deliberate attempts to favour one conception of the good. The value of ethical diversity, on the other hand, should make us pause whenever state action actually has a detrimental impact on some conceptions of the good, whether this is intended or not. Ackerman's 'overlapping consensus' is really a recipe for a disordered society, as citizens follow their different paths to an interpretive quarrel and find no common basis to resolve it (see Waldron, 1993: 151–3).

RAWLS'S POLITICAL LIBERALISM

When it was first published in 1971, John Rawls's book *A Theory of Justice* seemed to present itself as a set of more or less universal claims: it was supposed to tell us what justice was and what it required in any society which faced what Rawls called 'the circumstances of justice' – moderate scarcity, mutual disinterest of individuals in one another's ends, and so on (1971: 126). Under these circumstances, Rawls seemed to be implying, it was appropriate for people to use the idea of the 'Original Position' – decision behind a 'veil of ignorance' – as a way of figuring out appropriate principles of justice. And he argued that anyone selecting principles from that perspective would adopt strong principles of equal basic liberty, equal opportunity, and a social framework oriented to the well-being of members of the worst-off group. He seemed prepared to argue for these conclusions and defend them against rival conceptions (like Nozick, 1974) as a conception which could command the support of anyone interested in the subject.

Rawls's Withdrawal from Comprehensive Theory

Through the 1980s, however, Rawls began to offer a more modest characterization than he had in 1971:

[W]e are not trying to find a conception of justice suitable for all societies regardless of their particular social or historical circumstances … We look to ourselves and to our future, and reflect upon our disputes since, let's say, the Declaration of Independence. How far the conclusions we reach are of interest in a wider context is a separate question … What justifies a conception of justice is not its being true to an order antecedent to and given to us, but its congruence with our deeper understanding of ourselves and our aspirations, and our realization that, given our history and the traditions embedded in our public life, it is the most reasonable doctrine for us. (1980: 518–19)

This resonated with a theme emphasized by Walzer (1983) that a well-ordered society is a society true to its own understandings or, if it is to be reproached as unjust, it has to be reproached as having fallen away from values that already have a purchase in the life and practice of its members.

That amounted to a withdrawal from moral universalism in one direction: Rawlsian justice was not a theory for all societies, but a theory for societies like the United States. But it then required us to focus on some of the particular characteristics of societies like the United States, and the most prominent of these – apart from their prosperity and their traditions of political stability – was their religious and cultural diversity. Ethical and religious heterogeneity were no longer to be regarded as a feature that societies governed by justice might or might not have, or might have at one period but not at another. It was to be seen instead as a permanent feature of the societies, one that could not be expected soon to pass away.

By the beginning of the 1990s Rawls had become convinced that his approach in *A Theory of Justice* was disqualified generally on this ground. Though it contained, in the principle governing basic liberties, a robust defence of toleration and mutual accommodation, it grounded that approach in a particular vision of the human individual – 'a thin theory of the good' (1971: 395–9) – according to which individuals have a fundamental interest in forming and following a rational plan of life which enables them to realize and exercise the whole range of their individual capacities. An individual's active engagement with this task, Rawls suggested, is the basis of his or her self-respect. Some commentators (e.g. Barry, 1995) have expressed doubts about Rawls's self-criticism that the adoption of this 'thin theory' means that *A Theory of Justice* was rooted in a particular comprehensive conception. But it is pretty clear that large parts of Rawlsian justice would not work without this thin theory of the good and of the importance of self-respect. The thin theory of the good and the notion of self-respect are implicated in the non-negotiable status that Rawls accords to freedom of conscience, for example, as well as in the general doctrine of the priority of liberty, the doctrine of the priority of opportunity, and his argument to the effect that citizens in a well-ordered society will not be motivated by material envy. Someone who did not regard self-respect as so important, or did not associate it so tightly with individual self-development or the active pursuit of value, might well come up with other conclusions on any or all of these fronts. Moreover, the individualism of Rawls's thin theory drew criticism from communitarian philosophers, who repudiated the implicit assumption that individual plans of life are chosen by persons unencumbered by prior commitments and allegiances. Those who thought of themselves as essentially members of a particular family or community or people might find it hard to accept a theory of justice oriented at foundational level to the well-being of persons conceived as liberated from all such attachments (Sandel, 1982) [see further Chapter 13].

Rawls's Strategy

'[H]ow is it possible,' Rawls asked, 'for there to exist over time a just and stable society of free and equal citizens who remain profoundly divided by reasonable religious, philosophical, and moral doctrines?' (1993: 4). In the introduction to *Political Liberalism*, he argued that this could no longer be achieved by convincing everyone of the ethical and philosophical premises on which a comprehensive liberal theory of justice might be founded. Instead Rawlsian justice would now have to be presented as something that could command support from a variety of ethical perspectives.

The first task in this new Rawlsian agenda was to characterize the array of comprehensive views which needed to be taken into account in our thinking about justice: must a conception of justice be accessible from literally every standpoint that we find represented in society, or are we entitled to ignore or marginalize some as crazy or unreasonable? A second task was to define the appropriate relation between a conception of justice and the various comprehensive doctrines that the political liberal was required to take seriously: should we think of the conception of justice as a *modus vivendi*, or should it be related more robustly to the relevant comprehensive doctrines either by way of minimal shared premises or by way of overlapping consensus? A third task – and this was the substance of the new approach – would involve the detailed reformulation of a conception of justice in a way that was responsive to these specifications: how many of the substantive principles and doctrines of *A Theory of Justice* would survive this new approach? Finally, what would be the implications of this new approach so far as the actual politics of a liberal society were concerned?

All parts of this agenda have proved challenging and controversial, and there has been considerable debate about the ability of Rawlsians and other political liberals to carry through their programme on these four fronts. In what follows I shall outline Rawls's views and explain some of the difficulties they face.

Reasonable Diversity

The starting point of Rawls's new approach was the sheer 'diversity of opposing and irreconcilable religious, philosophical and moral doctrines' (1993: 3–4) flourishing in modern society. Rawls described this diversity as a social fact – a permanent feature of modern society. Some who would agree with him about that might nevertheless regard such diversity as a pathology endemic to the modern or postmodern condition. But Rawls takes no such approach. Human life engages multiple values and it is natural that people will disagree about how to balance or prioritize them. What's more their different positions, perspectives and experiences in life will give them different bases from which to make these delicate judgements. Together factors like these make disagreement in good faith not only possible but predictable.

However, not all dissensus is regarded as reasonable. Some positions, he says, are just crazy and irrational, and those do not in themselves present a compelling case for accommodation. He seems to think that a society will have to exclude aims that are unreasonable in this epistemic sense: 'In their case the problem is to contain them so that they do not undermine the unity and justice of the society' (1993: xvii).

Unfortunately, as Rawls uses it, the term 'reasonable' is ambiguous as between this and another use. Sometimes he uses it in the sense of something that represents a fair use of human reason under modern circumstances. Other times, he uses a more moralized definition: persons are reasonable when

> they are ready to propose principles and standards as fair terms of cooperation and to abide by them willingly, given the assurance that others will likewise do so ... By contrast, people are unreasonable ... when they plan to engage in cooperative schemes but are unwilling to honour, or even to propose, except as a necessary public pretence, any general principles or standards for specifying fair terms of cooperation. They are ready to violate such terms as suits their interests when circumstances allow. (1993: 49–50)

What is crucial on this second definition of reasonableness is one's willingness to share a world with those who accept other conceptions of the good or the holy, one's willingness to submit one's own convictions along with theirs to the governance of neutral principles. Plainly the two senses of reasonableness come apart. There are views which are tolerant but nevertheless irrational, and – this is the greater problem – there are views which are reasonable in the sense of not crazy, but whose orientation to social accommodation with other views is problematic. Militant Islam might provide an example of a comprehensive conception whose claims are (arguably) reasonable in the first (epistemic) sense, but quite unreasonable in the second sense of willingness to live in accommodation with others.

Overlapping Consensus

Assuming we can define, even roughly, the set of conceptions of the good that must be accommodated in the approach that we take to justice and the justification of the basic structure of a liberal society, what is the relation supposed to be between the set of reasonable conceptions and an acceptable theory of justice?

One possibility is to insist on something like a unanimity requirement: i.e. we could say that no

theory of justice is acceptable if members of a given conception of the good are inclined to repudiate it. But this is much too strong, and in a way that misconceives the nature of the difficulty that political liberalism addresses. The problem is not that theories of justice are controversial; the critical reaction that led Rawls to modify the approach he took to the subject of justice was not that people (like Nozick, 1974, for example) disagreed with his principles on justice-related grounds. The problem was that some people would have a particular *kind* of difficulty with his theory, based on the terms in which it was formulated and the approach it took (for the purposes of justice) to the question of what matters in social life. The key, then, is to insist that an acceptable theory of justice, T, must be such that, among whatever reasons there are for rejecting T or disagreeing with T, none turn on T's commitment to a particular conception of value or other comprehensive philosophical conception. Obviously, of course, this is a threshold test only: T may be acceptable in this sense, but still unacceptable overall as a theory of justice. But this would be for justice-related reasons, not because of T's complicity with a particular comprehensive conception.

And there are further questions about how this threshold test should be understood. One possibility is that T represents an acceptable *modus vivendi* for the adherents of the various comprehensive conceptions $\{C_1, C_2, ..., C_n\}$. Like a treaty that puts an end to conflict between previously hostile powers, T may be presented as the best that C_1 can hope for in the way of a theory of justice given that it has to coexist with $C_2, ..., C_n$, and the best that C_2 can hope for given that it has to coexist with $C_1, C_3, ..., C_n$, and so on. Rawls, however, regards this as unsatisfactory as a basis for a conception of justice. It leaves T vulnerable to demographic changes or other changes in the balance of power between rival comprehensive conceptions, a vulnerability that is quite at odds with the steadfast moral force that we usually associate with justice (1993: 148).

Instead Rawls develops the idea that T should represent *an overlapping moral consensus* among $\{C_1, C_2, ..., C_n\}$. By this he means that T could be made acceptable on moral grounds to the adherents of C_1, and acceptable on moral grounds to the adherents of C_2, and so on. The grounds of course would not be the same in each case. But still the adherents of each comprehensive conception would adhere to T for moral reasons. Thus, for example, the proposition that religious toleration is required as a matter of justice may be affirmed by Christians on Lockean grounds having to do with each person's individualized responsibility to God for his own religious beliefs, by secular Lockeans on the grounds of unamenability of belief to coercion, by Kantians on the grounds of the high ethical importance accorded to autonomy, by followers of John Stuart Mill on the basis of the importance of individuality and the free interplay of ideas, and so on. There are different routes to the toleration principle, and adherents of the various conceptions of the good in the society embed toleration in their own overall philosophy in different ways. Still each accepts toleration for moral reasons, of the right sort of weight and stringency, and each knows that all the others do this as well.

Whether this actually works is an issue we considered when we discussed Ackerman's approach to neutrality. The idea of overlapping consensus assumes that there can be many routes to the same destination. Geographically the metaphor is plausible enough, but when the destination is a set of moral principles, and 'routes' is read as reasons for the acceptance of those principles, then the matter is less clear. Unlike legal rules, moral propositions are not just formulas. A principle is perhaps best understood as a normative proposition together with the reasons that are properly adduced in its support. On either of these accounts, the principle of toleration arrived at by the Christian route is different from the principle of toleration arrived at by Mill's route. And this is a difference that may matter, for a theory of justice is not only supposed to provide a set of slogans for a society; it is also supposed to guide the members of that society through the disputes that may break out concerning how these slogans are to be understood and applied.

Justice in Political Liberalism

There are many sources of disagreement about justice, and in the previous section I tried to emphasize that the rivalry among comprehensive conceptions does not account for all of them. Accordingly we should not understand the strategy of the political liberal as a strategy of attempting to suppress all basis for disagreement about justice. Political liberals should think about justice as a topic that naturally evokes disagreement even when the influence of rival comprehensive conceptions is left out of account. The fact that one major source of dissensus is removed should not lead us to assume – what many political theorists mistakenly assume about rights – that what is just and unjust can be determined in some realm of principle that is beyond politics, some arena of philosophical argument where political procedures like voting will not be necessary. Like individual rights, justice remains an intensely contested issue, and though the contestation may be diminished it is not eliminated by the strategies that the political liberal proposes.

A further question is whether political liberalism actually defines a terrain on which disagreements about justice can actually be played out. It is hard to tell from Rawls's later work, for very little of it is concerned with detailed issues of social and economic justice, or with controversies of the level and ferocity that the earlier book evoked. But I suspect the answer is 'No'. Social justice, after all, raises concerns that can hardly be dealt with by the strategy of vagueness or evasion associated with overlapping consensus – putting about a set of anodyne formulas that can mean all things to all people. A theory of social justice has hard, critical work to do, on Rawls's original account: it has to settle complex questions about freedom, equality, desert, and opportunity, and it has to hold its own against rival conceptions (against Nozickian historical entitlement, for example, or against utilitarian or efficiency-based approaches). The actual examples of overlapping consensus for a pluralist society provided in *Political Liberalism* are laughably easy by comparison. Both Kantians and non-Kantians might favour democracy, Rawls says, and both Christians and secularists may well oppose slavery (1993: 122–5). The hard part comes when we try to establish an overlapping consensus among (say) Christian fundamentalists, Hindus, secular humanists, scientific determinists, and members of the dot-com generation on the definition of 'equal opportunity', the use of economic incentives, and the distinction between liberty and the worth of liberty.

Just to give a taste of the difficulty, consider the problem of the relevance of desert to basic social entitlement. This was central in social justice discussions in the 1970s and 1980s, and various approaches to it informed people's views about market success, the problem of the undeserving poor, and so on. Now, it was not hard to see that insistence on a strong theory of desert might mean that a theory of justice would have to buy into social and religious controversies about virtue. But it was much more difficult to know what to *do* with that point, or what would be a fair or a neutral way to move on from it. Does one simply reject desert in this sphere (and the whole view of the person that goes with desert), or does one try to develop a thin theory of desert, or to modify the assumptions, e.g. about freedom and background responsibility for character, that deserving is sometimes thought to presuppose? Can we imagine an overlapping consensus on problems like that between (say) the Protestant work ethic, the notion of apostolic poverty, and ideas of the fundamental solidarity of community? It is easy to despair of answering questions like this under the conditions that Rawls's later work has emphasized.

Public Reason

So far our discussion has been pitched at a rather abstract philosophical level: on what sort of basis is it appropriate to construct a theory of justice? But Rawls is also interested in exploring the consequences of his political liberalism for real-world political arguments. A theory of justice, on his account, is not just some set of esoteric formulas; it is supposed to be something public, something shared among the citizens as a common point of reference for their debates about the allocation of rights and responsibilities. So political liberalism also has implications for what this *sharing a conception of justice* amounts to. We do not share a conception of justice, Rawls argues, and our society is not well ordered by his lights if, when there is argument about the allocation of rights and responsibilities, conceptions of value are invoked which not everybody shares.

Rawls believes this point about public reason is pretty obvious when we think about the way in which some of our political institutions are supposed to operate. For example, the justices of the US Supreme Court cannot invoke 'their own personal morality, nor the ideals and virtues of morality generally' (1993: 236). They must view these as irrelevant to the issues they decide, not just because they are unconnected to the texts and doctrines the courts are supposed to interpret, but because it would be disrespectful to justify the exercise of public power on grounds that they knew many citizens would – quite reasonably – be unable to endorse. Rawls generalizes this to apply also to the other arms of government in their public deliberations and acts and decisions. But he does not leave it there. He also believes it applies to the citizens, who are after all exercising a modicum of public power when they decide how to vote or when they bring pressure to bear on the government or its agencies. At least when they are addressing the fundamentals of justice, Rawls believes that citizens must search their consciences to ensure that they are not voting one way or another under the auspices of principles that they know their fellow citizens cannot accept, and – as a matter of basic civility – when they make arguments in the public realm, they must address these arguuments not just to their co-religionists or those who share their values, but to all their citizens conceived as participants in the just ordering of a society dedicated to the accommodation of all who hold reasonable views about what makes life worth living. So a left liberal like me may not say, for example, to a Social Darwinian that even the feeblest person is entitled to our compassion because he is created in the image of God. I must find some way of putting my point about equality that can be affirmed even by people who do not share my religious convictions. Equally a Christian conservative may not justify laws restricting abortion on the grounds that foetuses have souls, since this too is rooted in a comprehensive conception he cannot expect others to share.

Interestingly some of the discussion in *Political Liberalism* of the abortion example showed how difficult it is to apply this stricture in practice. In a footnote to the original edition Rawls inferred, from the fact that anti-abortion laws usually rest on controversial religious grounds, that liberty in this regard was required (1993: 243n). But he quickly had to concede that that was a mistake (1996: lv), for three reasons. First, we are not entitled to assume liberty in such an area as the default position, any more than we are entitled to conclude that foetuses do not have souls from the fact that political liberalism is unable to countenance religious arguments to the effect that they do. Second, although there might be good neutral arguments for a right to choose abortion in the first trimester, we must not assume that there are no contrary arguments or no way of opposing abortion rights that does not run foul of the strictures of political liberalism. Many opponents of abortion will insist that their arguments for protecting human foetuses are continuous with arguments (that they insist any theory of justice must acknowledge) for protecting all human life, particularly in its most vulnerable forms. They do not accept that a political liberal can casually cut off debate about this and still have a strong doctrine of human dignity and human equality to deploy in other areas of justice where such doctrines are indispensable. Third, the fact that a religious doctrine may not be appealed to in order to justify restrictions on abortion doesn't mean that such doctrines are altogether beyond the pale. Rawls came close to implying that doctrines which might have this consequence are *ipso facto* unreasonable, and so need not even be considered as constituents in the overlapping consensus on which principles of justice are to be based (1993: 243n). It would surely be catastrophic for Rawls's theory if say all or even most religious conceptions were to be excluded from the realm of the reasonable. But if they are not so excluded, then (as we saw in the earlier section on overlapping consensus) there must be a way of reaching the public doctrine of respect for human life from the premises of these religious accounts. And it is not at all clear that that way can be charted if the endpoint is supposed to be a position that the religious adherent cannot but regard as offensively flawed and inconsistent.

The issue illustrates how quickly these arguments can turn into a debate about the whole viability of the political liberal's approach. On the one hand, the political liberal says that the only doctrines of human dignity and human equality we are entitled to deploy are doctrines that are elaborated independently of any comprehensive conception. On the other hand, the political liberal knows that these doctrines have work to do in a theory of justice that requires a considerable amount of moral weight. The doctrine of human dignity and equality deployed in a theory of justice must be able to resist – in more or less the manner of a moral absolute – various pragmatic considerations that might tempt us to sacrifice or neglect the interests of a few weak and vulnerable persons for the sake of the convenience or prosperity of the wealthy or powerful. Justice has to be able to stand up to that, and its constitutive doctrines have to have what it takes to do that heavy moral lifting. Many of the comprehensive conceptions that political liberals want to exclude from the public realm address themselves to exactly this issue: they explain in ethical or transcendent terms why exactly it is that the few weak and vulnerable may not be sacrificed in this way. The political liberal proposes to do this work without help from any such conception, but in a way which nevertheless retains their allegiance in overlapping consensus. It is, I think, a tall order, and the tendency of latter-day Rawlsians to shy away from hard issues of justice – like their masters' own equivocations on the issue of abortion – provides ample reason to think that that tall order cannot be filled.

LIBERALISM AND UNANIMITY

One of the impulses behind the move to political liberalism was the suggestion by some liberal theorists (e.g. Waldron, 1993: 43ff) that social arrangements must be not only justified in the abstract, but justifiable *to* each and every one of persons who have to live under those arrangements and who are (potentially) subject to the force that backs them up. This suggestion is bound up with the basic liberal idea of government by consent, i.e. the principle that the exercise of power can be made legitimate only when those who are subject to it can accept the principles on which its exercise is based. Of course this suggestion might be taken more or less literally: we might talk about principles that everyone actually does accept or we might talk about principles that people would accept if they were well informed, thinking logically, and so on (see Gaus, 1996). Still, the thought was that if political justifications rested on values that derived from religious or ethical conceptions held by some citizens but repudiated by others, then they would not satisfy even the looser versions of this requirement of justifiability to all.

However, the dative element in this requirement – that political justification be understood as justification *to* each and every individual – can be understood in more than one way. It may be understood as a requirement that the justificatation of political arrangements should be directed to the good or interests of each and every one who is subject to those arrangements. I shall call this the 'interest-regarding' interpretation. Or it may be understood as a requirement that the justification of a political decision be plausibly reckoned likely to persuade everyone who is subject to the arrangements. I shall call this the 'premise-regarding' interpretation, because it understands 'justification to X' as justification that seeks to hook up with premises to which X is already committed.

It's pretty clear how the two interpretations may come apart. Suppose I justify the criminalization of prostitution on the ground that this is good for the souls of the prostitutes. A prostitute who is an atheist may find my justification unacceptable, perhaps even unintelligible. Still it does purport to address her interests (only not as she understands them). On the other hand, taking the premise-regarding interpretation, I might justify a law against prostitution on grounds that are perfectly *intelligible* to the prostitute, but they might be grounds that take no account whatever of her interests. I may say, for example, that it is in the interests of the majority of decent citizens that prostitution be banned. The prostitute may *understand* this argument, and if she were submissive and demoralized enough she might even accept this justification. Still the justification would fail my test on the interest-regarding interpretation, because it would not be addressed to her interests.

Clearly Rawls's political liberalism assumes what I have called the 'premise-regarding' interpretation of the requirement that political justification must be justification *to* each and every individual. It may accept the interest-regarding interpretation as well, for the two are not mutually exclusive. Rawls indicates, in his later work, that political liberalism will still have room for the idea of social contract and choice of principles of justice in an original position (1993: 304–10), and these are conceptions which model the idea that principles are acceptable only if they advance the interests of all. A political liberal, however, will have to articulate these ideas carefully so that they do not embody – for example, in the assumptions they make about the motivation of parties in the original position – anything associated with particular conceptions of the good.

However it is also important to see that interest-regarding interpretation of justifiability to all can be maintained even if the premise-regarding interpretation is given up. Our earlier case of the do-gooder's concern for the soul of the prostitute provides one crude example. But even if one felt uneasy about this example, the uneasiness may not be best explained by political liberalism. Someone may reject the salvation-of-the-soul argument for the law against prostitution on the grounds that this makes no sense to the prostitute. But his basis for that may not be political liberalism. It may rather be that the alleged justification fails to connect in the appropriate way with the prostitute's well-being. A case may be made *on comprehensive grounds* for insisting that a justification counts as connecting in the appropriate way with X's interests only if it connects with X's well-being *as X understands it* (or as X would understand it under moderately favourable conditions). And this condition might be argued for, not as a weak version of political liberalism, but on the basis of some affirmative account of what well-being is and of the importance of a person's own conscious engagement with her well-being. For example, the terms of some comprehensive conception may be such that it is implausible to attach moral importance to X's well-being and to insist that others respect it unless X herself already affirms it or could be thought to affirm it under suitable conditions. Liberals have always insisted on paying attention to *how things actually are* for the people they claim to respect, and they have been impatient with political proposals oriented to a person's 'real self', where that self is impossibly distant from the person's occurrent experience. But this is not on account of any metatheoretic requirement of neutrality of the sort maintained by political liberals; it is on the basis of an affirmative focus on the here and now, and on how things actually are for people in their own felt sense of what actually matters to them.

Now here's the point. Some comprehensive conceptions will affirm the moral importance of people's actual experience here and now, while others may sideline or denigrate it. Those that do affirm it will sit more naturally with, and in a way will generate and inspire, the moral and political commitments traditionally associated with liberalism. And that is what the comprehensive liberal wants to remind us of. Liberalism is based on certain ethical commitments, certain propositions about what matters and about the importance of certain kinds of respect for the lives, experiences, and liberty of ordinary men and women. It is not a neutral or nonchalant creed, and its commitments arguably cannot be articulated at a purely political level. Traditional liberals have said that human life, liberty and experience command respect, *period*, not just because of the way we configure our politics but because of what they are. And the same is true of many of the moral absolutes and the stringency and priority associated with justice and rights. These again are not just pragmatic matters established at a political level; instead their application in politics is derivative of deeper truths about the nature of the goods they protect and the moral concerns that they express.

So, although liberals seek a universal application for their principles in a world of many faiths and many philosophies, it may be a mistake to base that universal application on the shallowness of the liberal claims. If liberal positions are to be sustained, certain confrontations at the comprehensive level may be unavoidable. A willingness to face up to these issues and to explore these deeper foundations may be the price one has to pay for robust liberal convictions.

REFERENCES

Ackerman, Bruce (1980) *Social Justice in the Liberal State*. New Haven, CT: Yale University Press.

Barry, Brian (1995) 'John Rawls and the search for stability'. *Ethics*, 105 (4): 874–915.

Bentham, Jeremy (1982 [1780]) *An Introduction to the Principles of Morals and Legislation*, eds, J. H. Burns and H. L. A. Hart. London: Methuen.

Dworkin, Ronald (1985) *A Matter of Principle*. Cambridge, MA: Harvard University Press.

Gaus, Gerald F. (1996) *Justificatory Liberalism: An Essay on Epistemology and Political Theory*. New York: Oxford University Press.

Hobbes, Thomas (1991 [1651]) *Leviathan*, ed. Richard Tuck. Cambridge: Cambridge University Press.

Kant, Immanuel (1991 [1785]) *The Metaphysics of Morals*, trans. Mary Gregor. Cambridge: Cambridge University Press.

Larmore, Charles E. (1987) *Patterns of Moral Complexity*. Cambridge: Cambridge University Press.

Locke, John (1983 [1689]) *A Letter Concerning Toleration*, ed. James H. Tully. Indianapolis: Hackett.

Locke, John (1988 [1688]) *Two Treatises of Government*, ed. Peter Laslett. Cambridge: Cambridge University Press.

Nozick, Robert (1974) *Anarchy, State and Utopia* Oxford: Blackwell.

Mill, John Stuart (1956 [1859]) *On Liberty*, ed. Currin V. Shields. Indianapolis: Hackett.

Rawls, John (1971) *A Theory of Justice*. Cambridge, MA: Harvard University Press.

Rawls, John (1980) 'Kantian constructivism in moral theory'. *Journal of Philosophy*, 77 (9): 515–72.

Rawls, John (1993) *Political Liberalism*. New York: Columbia University Press.

Rawls, John (1996) *Political Liberalism*, new edn. New York: Columbia University Press.

Sandel, Michael (1982) *Liberalism and the Limits of Justice*. Cambridge: Cambridge University Press.

Waldron, Jeremy (1993) *Liberal Rights: Collected Papers 1981–1991*. Cambridge: Cambridge University Press.

Walzer, Michael (1983) *Spheres of Justice: A Defense of Pluralism and Equality*. New York: Basic.

8

The Diversity of Comprehensive Liberalisms

GERALD F. GAUS

COMPREHENSIVE LIBERALISMS

The distinction between 'comprehensive' and 'political' liberalisms, explored in the previous chapter, has become central to contemporary political theory. My aim in this chapter is to examine various 'comprehensive' liberalisms, with particular care to identifying in what sense they are comprehensive. As I have argued elsewhere (Gaus, 2003: ch. 7), the distinction between political and comprehensive liberalisms is elusive. Rawls repeatedly describes as 'comprehensive' 'philosophical', 'moral' and 'religious' 'doctrines' (1996: xxv, 4, 36, 38, 160) or 'beliefs' (1996: 63). Indeed, so often does Rawls characterize comprehensiveness in terms of moral, religious and philosophical doctrines or beliefs that a reader may be tempted to conclude that a doctrine is comprehensive if and only if it is moral, religious or philosophical. But though it is tempting to understand 'comprehensive conceptions' in this way, it would be wrong. Rawls is clear that 'the distinction between the political conception and other moral conceptions is a matter of scope; that is, the range of subjects to which a conception applies and the content a wider range requires' (1996: 13). Comprehensive and general doctrines cover a wide range of topics, values and ideals applicable to various areas of life. Even given the terms of Rawls's own analyses, rather than conceiving of comprehensive liberalisms as all relying on a fully comprehensive doctrine, it is better to conceive of them in terms of a spectrum of theories, from those that rely on something like a fully comprehensive view to those that rely on, say, only a general theory of the right. In this chapter I shall

focus on the following versions of comprehensive liberalism:

- liberalism as a secular philosophy;
- liberalism as a philosophy of the good life;
- liberalism as a political theory derived from a specific moral theory;
- liberalism as itself a distinctive theory of the right or justice.

Liberalism as a secular philosophy is a distinctly radical conception, which in some ways is the paradigmatic 'fully comprehensive' liberalism. On this view, human reason leads to convergence on a theory of human life in society, which includes a metaphysics, an epistemology, as well as theories of morality and politics. On the other hand, liberalism as a theory of right is much more cautious about the extent that human reason converges; its more modest versions shade off into Rawlsian political liberalism. Thus I shall argue that the 'comprehensive' liberalism of *A Theory of Justice* (1971) was a distinctly 'partial' comprehensive view, which was not as comprehensive as many other varieties of liberalism.

LIBERALISM AS A PHILOSOPHICAL SYSTEM

John W. Chapman (1965) argues that all political theories are inherently comprehensive as they combine an account of social reality, epistemology, psychology and ethics to provide political diagnoses and prescriptions. Liberalism certainly has been understood as a political theory in this sense, a truly comprehensive liberalism – an overall theory of inquiry, social life, as well as the good life and political justice. I have argued elsewhere (Gaus, 2000b) that liberal theory over the last hundred years has been characterized by recurring debates about the psychologies, value theories, epistemologies and theories of self and society, as well as principles of justice that must or may form part of a truly liberal comprehensive philosophy. I shall focus here on two core aspects of this debate about liberalism as a comprehensive philosophy: whether there is a distinctively liberal epistemology or social metaphysics.

Liberal Epistemology

We can observe a split between two liberal epistemologies. The rationalistic camp is associated with 'Enlightenment liberalism'; indeed, as Stephen Holmes points out, liberalism's critics often associate it with a 'hyperrationalism' (1993: 247). Thus understood, liberalism not only manifests a faith in reason and science, it is an attack on superstition, custom and, importantly, religion. Thus the secular and anti-religious character of much liberal thought. Here 'liberalism' is 'secular humanism'. This sort of militant, confident rationalism is also associated with great confidence in the ability of humans to understand nature and control their social world.

Liberalism as secular humanism remains important today, though liberalism as a self-confident rationalism has been under attack by pluralists, relativists, postmodernists and pragmatists (see Gaus, 2003: ch. 1) However, in an interesting and surprising sense, the pragmatist liberalism of Richard Rorty (1991) and others, although it depicts itself as rejecting Enlightenment rationalism and epistemology, is nevertheless an inheritor of this conception of liberalism as an overall method for arriving at the truth. To be sure, pragmatism is a reaction to rationalism and representational views of the mind and knowledge; as Rorty stresses, our minds do not mirror nature, and truth is not a correct representation of nature (1979: 176–9). Nonetheless, truth is still the result of convergence in individual reasoning: what is true is what a certain sort of community of inquirers would converge on (Misak, 2000). So, while rejecting the specific view of reason and truth that characterized much Enlightenment thinking, twentieth-century pragmatist liberalism continues to identify liberal democracy with a certain mode of inquiry, and one which, when properly implemented, leads to a convergence of rational belief. Moreover, in the hands of liberals such as Dewey this mode of inquiry allowed society to obtain 'conscious control' – for example, in the form of economic planning – over its collective life (1980: 87).

Thus liberalism is understood as a doctrine about the convergence of rational inquiry that provides for a rationally ordered society.

According to F. A. Hayek, the flaw at the heart of such liberalisms is their faith in the ability of reason to understand and control complex social processes. It is, insists Hayek, 'our ignorance' that makes social rules necessary (1976: 20). Karl Popper (1945) made a similar charge against Plato, Hegel and Marx, namely that they failed to appreciate the limits of knowledge. Hayek and Popper, then, represent the other strain of liberal epistemology: an insistence that reason is limited, and our basic position is one of ignorance. In contrast to liberal rationalism, this cautious, fallibilistic liberalism is less apt to be militantly secular than tolerant of religion; it is more likely to stress the incremental and experimental nature of social policy than to advocate grand social reconstructions. And it is more likely to appreciate the market, as a device for coping with our constitutional ignorance, and less likely to be enamoured with state planning.

The Metaphysics of Liberalism

Throughout the last century, liberalism has been beset by controversies between, on the one hand, those broadly identified as 'individualists' and, on the other, 'collectivists', 'communitarians' or 'organicists' (for scepticism about this, though, see Bird, 1999). These vague and sweeping designations have been applied to a wide array of disputes; I focus here on controversies concerning (1) the nature of society, and (2) the nature of the self.

Liberalism is, of course, usually associated with individualist analyses of society. 'Human beings in society,' Mill claimed, 'have no properties but those which are derived from, and which may be resolved into, the laws of the nature of individual men' (1963b: 879; see also Bentham, 1987: ch. I, s. 4). Spencer agreed: 'the properties of the mass are dependent upon the attributes of its component parts' (1995: 1). In the last years of the nineteenth century this individualist view was increasingly subject to attack, especially by those who were influenced by idealist philosophy [see further Chapter 30]. D. G. Ritchie, criticizing Spencer's philosophy in 1891, explicitly rejected the idea that society is simply a 'heap' of individuals, insisting that it is more akin to an organism, with a complex internal life (1902: 13). Liberals such as L. T. Hobhouse and Dewey refused to adopt radically collectivist views such as those advocated by Bernard Bosanquet (2001), but they too rejected the radical individualism of Bentham, Mill and Spencer. Throughout most of the first half of the twentieth century such 'organic' analyses of society held sway in liberal theory, even in economics (see A. F. Mummery and J. A. Hobson, 1956: 106; J. M. Keynes, 1972: 275).

During and after the Second World War the idea that liberalism was inherently individualist arose again. Karl Popper's *The Open Society and its Enemies* (1945) presented a sustained critique of Hegelian and Marxist theory and its collectivist and historicist, and to Popper *inherently illiberal*, understanding of society. The re-emergence of economic analysis in liberal theory brought to the fore a thoroughgoing methodological individualism. Writing in the early 1960s, James Buchanan and Gordon Tullock adamantly defended the 'individualistic postulate' against all forms of 'organicism': 'This [organicist] approach or theory of the collectivity ... is essentially opposed to the Western philosophical tradition in which the human individual is the primary philosophical entity' (1965: 11–12). Human beings, insisted Buchanan and Tullock, are the only real choosers and decision-makers, and their preferences determine both public and private actions. The renascent individualism of late-twentieth-century liberalism was closely bound up with the induction of Hobbes as a member of the liberal pantheon. Hobbes's relentlessly individualistic account of society, and the manner in which his analysis of the state of nature lent itself to game-theoretic modelling, yielded a highly individualist, formal analysis of the liberal state and liberal morality (see Buchanan, 1975; Hampton, 1986).

Of course, as is widely known, the last 20 years have witnessed a renewed interest in collectivist analyses of liberal society – though the term 'collectivist' is abjured in favour of 'communitarian'. Writing in 1985, Amy Gutmann observed that '[w]e are witnessing a revival of communitarian criticisms of liberal political theory. Like the critics of the 1960s, those of the 1980s fault *liberalism for being mistakenly and irreparably individualistic*' (1985: 308, emphasis added). Starting with Michael Sandel's famous (1982) criticism of Rawls, a number of critics charged that liberalism was necessarily premised on an abstract conception of individual selves as pure choosers, whose commitments, values and concerns are possessions of the self, but never constitute the self. Although the now famous, not to say infamous, 'liberal-communitarian' debate [see further Chapter 13] ultimately involved wide-ranging moral, political and sociological disputes about the nature of communities, and the rights and responsibilities of their members, the heart of the debate was about the nature of liberal selves. For Sandel the flaw at the heart of Rawls's liberalism was its implausibly abstract theory of the self, the pure autonomous chooser. Rawls, he charges, ultimately assumes that it makes sense to identify us with a pure capacity for choice, and that such pure

choosers might reject any or all of their attachments and values and yet retain their identity.

Throughout the 1990s various liberals sought to show how liberalism may consistently advocate a theory of the self which finds room for cultural membership and other non-chosen attachments and commitments which at least partially constitute the self (Kymlicka, 1991). Much of liberal theory has become focused on the issue of how we can be social creatures, members of cultures and raised in various traditions, while also being autonomous choosers who employ our liberty to construct lives of our own. What is important for our purposes is that these debates focus on whether liberalism entails an individualist theory of humans in society, or whether its political and moral commitments can be conjoined with various conceptions of the self and the social order; it is thus a debate about just how 'comprehensive' liberalism really is.

LIBERALISM AS A GENERAL THEORY OF THE GOOD LIFE

The Ideal of the Developed Individual

Over the last century and a half – say, roughly since John Stuart Mill – a great deal of liberal philosophy has been built on a particular view of human excellence. What might be called a perfectionist theory of the good life, or one devoted to self-realization as the end, can be found in Mill, T. H. Green, Bernard Bosanquet, L. T. Hobhouse, John Dewey and even, I would venture, in the third part of John Rawls's *Theory of Justice* – the most distinctly 'comprehensive' element of the book (Gaus, 1983a). The crux of this theory is presented in the third chapter of *On Liberty*, 'Of Individuality, as One of the Elements of Well-Being', where human nature is compared to 'a tree, which requires to grow and develop itself on all sides, according to the tendency of the inward forces that make it a living thing' (Mill, 1963a: ch. 3). Mill closely ties individuality to this growth or development of human nature: 'Individuality is the same thing with development' (1963a: ch. 3). Mill believes that reason reveals our nature and its needs; human nature possesses impulses or energies that try to manifest themselves. Not only do we naturally possess different capacities, but these capacities are sources of energy that seek to express themselves. Consequently, to block a person from developing her capacities is to de-energize her – to make her passive and lethargic (1963a: ch. 3; Gaus, 1983a: ch. 4).

This perfectionist theory of the good life – the good life involves the perfection of human beings in society – has wide appeal in contemporary political theory [see Chapter 30]. It was at the heart of William Galston's earlier (1980; 1991) work and has been employed by Douglas B. Rasmuessen and Douglas J. Den Uyl (1991) as a foundation for a defence of classical liberalism. Although readers are often confused by Ayn Rand's description of her position as 'egoism', some idea of human perfection also seems foundational to Randian-inspired liberalism (Machan, 1989; Smith, 1995: 62ff).

Such perfectionist accounts of the good life are distinctly liberal in two ways. First, and most obviously, they provide the grounds for an argument for liberty. People need room to grow, room to find out which ways of living suit their unique natures and which do not. As Mill puts it, people need freedom to engage in 'experiments in living'. The lack of freedom will constrain growth, thus blocking human impulses and producing passive personalities. Second, such theories tend to place the individual and her choices at the centre of ethical life: liberalism is understood as a theory of *ethical individualism*. This is not to say that such theories see development as asocial; indeed, they often put stress on the way social life is necessary for complete development (Gaus, 1983a, chs 2 and 3; Kymlicka, 1991). Still, it is the individual and her self-realization or flourishing that has ultimate value, and individuals are not so deeply embedded in society as to make their choices a reflection of social history or culture (Sher, 1997: ch. 7).

Loosening the *Telos*: Theories of Personal Autonomy and Project Pursuit

Thus interpreted, Mill advances a quintessential Enlightenment argument: we can know human nature, and the knowledge of human nature provides truths about how we ought to live (Gaus, 2003; ch. 1; cf. Shapiro, 2003). Liberalism becomes identified with the promotion of a certain sort of self-realizing individual, one who develops her nature, is rational and suspicious of custom, experiments with different ways of living and is not prone to conformism. Two worries have been advanced about this as a conception of liberalism. First, its picture of the good life seems too specific and controversial to serve as a basis for liberal politics. Many in liberal societies are not devoted to the cultivation of individual perfection; in the face of this, liberalism seems to be a theory of the elite, which must struggle against the mass, uninterested in perfection. The mass of society, according to Mill, is a 'collective mediocrity': they tend to conform and are not interested in new ideas. The few who do think and invent are 'the salt of the earth: without them, human life would become a stagnant pool' (1963a: ch. 3, para. 10). Second, and following

from this, such perfectionist theories raise the spectre of widespread paternalism. Although Mill argued for a strongly anti-paternalistic morality, it seems that the ideal is so specific and demanding as to open the gates to interferences with liberty, seeking to prod the mediocre mass towards a richer personality. It also becomes less than obvious why they should be granted liberty equal to that of the perfecting elite.

Many have argued that a defence of freedom based on personal autonomy is not subject to these objections [see David Weinstein's discussion in Chapter 30]. According to Joseph Raz, whereas Mill's ideal of '[s]elf-realization consists in the development to their fullest extent of all, or all the valuable capacities a person possesses ... [t]he autonomous person is one who makes his own life and he may choose the path of self-realization or reject it' (1986: 325). The basic thought is that, according to the ideal of autonomy, it is not crucial *that* a person decides to develop her capacities, but that she decides *whether* to develop her capacities and, more generally, how to live her life. The fully autonomous person leads a life of her own choosing – she makes decisions about her life on the basis of the things to which she is committed. The importance of liberty, argue tthe advocates of personal autonomy, is that it makes such a life possible.

The ideal of personal autonomy fractures into a variety of more specific doctrines (Lindley, 1986). Personal autonomy has been understood in terms of project pursuit, self-rule, self-creation and critical reflection on one's projects and values, or consistency between first- and second-order volitions (on this last, see Gill, 2001: 20ff). Most conceptions of personal autonomy draw on several of these ideas.

According to Steven Wall, for example, 'autonomous people need (a) the capacity to choose projects and sustain commitments, (b) the independence necessary to chart their own course though life and to develop their own understanding of what is valuable and worth doing, (c) the self-consciousness and vigor to take control of their affairs' (1998: 132; see also Raz, 1986). And to Gerald Dworkin, '[w]hat makes an individual the particular person he is is his life plan, his projects. In pursuing autonomy, one shapes one's life, one constructs its meaning. The autonomous person gives meaning to his life' (1988: 31). Such visions of autonomy retain much of the structure of nineteenth-century self-realization perfectionism, while making less of the idea of a rich development of one's capacities. The notion of a coherent plan of life was central to nineteenth-century self-realization theory (Gaus, 1983a: 34–44); the idea of a project or a plan points to a coherent and integrated set of ends. To the extent that a conception of personal autonomy presupposes a certain rational structure of ends, or a rationally constructed plan, it invites the elitist and paternalist objections raised against nineteenth-century liberal perfectionism.

These problems are mitigated by conceptions of autonomy according to which 'the fundamental idea in autonomy is that of authoring one's own world without being subject to the will of others' (Young, 1986: 19). An autonomous person employs her critical faculties to evaluate and choose her aims and projects in such a way that they are truly hers, rather than simply imposed by, or unreflectively taken over from, others. Autonomy is thus understood as 'an ideal of self-creation ... Autonomy is opposed to a life of coerced choices. It contrasts with a life of no choices, or of drifting through life without ever exercising one's capacity to choose' (Raz, 1986: 370, 371). This conception of autonomy is thus a much more open-ended, and so less controversial, ideal than the ideals of either self-realization or project pursuit. Autonomy does not tell us what to choose; it only insists on the value of a chosen life. The worry, though, is that nobody really creates himself. Our personalities and choices are deeply influenced by our natural talents and propensities, our culture and our upbringing. What options we consider attractive are strongly affected by our upbringing and culture. As John Stuart Mill pointed out, it is 'mere accident' that decides the traditions into which one is inducted: 'the same causes which make him a Churchman in London, would have made him a Buddhist or a Confucian [or, we might add, a Maoist] in Pekin' (1963a: ch. 2, para. 4).

Given that we necessarily come to adulthood with values and commitments that we did not choose, Stanley Benn argues that an autonomous person is one who is engaged in an ongoing process of 'critical adjustment within a system of beliefs in which it is possible to appraise one sector by canons drawn from another' (1988: 32; but cf. Wall, 1998: 128–9). On this view, a person who leads a self-chosen life is not really one who creates herself, but one who continually evaluates all her commitments and values to ensure that they are ones that she can continue to affirm in light of the other things she accepts. She cannot evaluate everything at once, but she can always be prepared to look critically at her values and projects to ask whether they are really things she is prepared to continue to affirm. Thus understood, a person's life is not a freely chosen, autonomous life, if there are some parts of it she refuses to examine – if she has some commitments that she will not, or cannot, critically reflect upon. If she possesses some such commitments, they are ones that she cannot freely affirm, for her refusal to evaluate them indicates that she can only continue to affirm them so long as she is not free to revise or reject them. Benn recognizes, though, that this renders personal autonomy a character ideal that can be

achieved to various degrees, and that many people fall far short of. Thus, in contrast to most liberal autonomists, Benn refuses to base liberal freedoms on autonomy, seeing it as a personal ideal, but not a foundation for basic liberal justice (1988: ch. 9).

What Makes Personal Autonomy a Liberal Theory of the Good Life?

The theory of personal autonomy, interpreted widely to include Millian self-development, is not simply a view of the good life that has been held by liberals, or even a view of the good life that justifies liberal political institutions. It is a distinctively liberal conception of the good life: the good life is a freely chosen life, and so the good life is a free life. It is, as Raz (1986) says, a morality of freedom; it puts a certain conception of a free life at the centre of morality. This is not to say that the autonomist project succeeds; as I have stressed, freedom *qua* autonomy seems to teeter on the verge of justifying elitism and paternalism, and so invites the sort of critique famously advanced by Berlin in 'Two concepts of liberty'. As Berlin quotes Kant, 'paternalism is the greatest despotism imaginable'(1969: 157). Horacio Spector (1992) provides perhaps the most sophisticated attempt to show that a grounding in autonomy need not lead to such policies, but can justify strong classical liberal rights.

It is a mistake to try to define liberalism; liberal theories are complex clusters of conceptual and value commitments. But surely a crucial criterion for describing a view as 'liberal' is whether freedom is the core conceptual commitment (Freeden, 1996; Gaus, 2000a). Theories of personal autonomy, in insisting both that traditional liberal freedoms are necessary for personal autonomy, and that achieving autonomy is itself a type of freedom, thus have a strong claim to be advancing distinctively liberal moralities. Contrast this to Ronald Dworkin's famous claim that liberalism rests on a basic commitment to equality, not liberty (1978: 115; see also 2000: Part I). According to his egalitarian liberalism, liberties such as freedom of speech and association are ways to achieve equal concern and respect. Their equal distribution is an instance of the general case for an equal distribution of resources and opportunities. The special status attributed to these basic liberties in liberal thought does not derive from the unique importance of freedom, but arises as a way to express equal concern and respect. It must be wondered whether liberalism is rendered more plausible by, first, almost entirely removing its traditional core of liberty and, second, replacing it with equality, a value that has traditionally had a complex and difficult place in liberal theory (Freeden, 1996: 241; Gaus, 2000a: 166–8) [for a sympathetic treatment of egalitarian liberalism, see Chapter 30].

LIBERALISM DERIVED FROM MORAL THEORIES

A moral theory such as that of personal autonomy, I have argued, has a good claim to be a liberal conception of morality as it articulates a view of the good life that has at its core a notion of a free life. Reason should lead us to converge on a liberal understanding of the good life, and in that sense it is a 'comprehensive', though not 'fully comprehensive', view. Now a liberal theory of the good life and morality must be distinguished from a commitment to liberalism built on a moral theory; these two distinct conceptions of liberalism are often lumped together as 'comprehensive' liberalism. Liberal political principles can be derived from moral theories that themselves are not intrinsically liberal. I consider three such theories: utilitarianism, Hobbesian contractualism and value scepticism.

Utilitarian Liberalism

Reason and the principle of utility

Utilitarian moral theories hold that we can possess knowledge of both the good and the right; *pace* Rawls, these are not matters of 'reasonable pluralism'. The most straightforward versions of utilitarianism maintain that the good is either pleasure, happiness or preference satisfaction, and the right is the overall maximization of the good. Bentham, interestingly, did not think that the principle of utility could be proven; he did, though, contend that it could not reasonably be denied (1987: ch. 11, s. 11). Any reasonable person would see that pleasure is the ultimate end: consequently the principle of utility was beyond reasonable dispute. Whether or not the principle of utility could be established by reason was and is, though, a matter of dispute. Mill, famously, advanced a proof (1963c: ch. 4). Sidgwick, in contrast, insists that basic intuitions must be drawn upon in any argument for utilitarianism; in the end, Sidgwick appeared to accept that one could be an egoist and yet not irrational (1962: 418–22). It does seem, though, that if one accepts that (1) I value my own happiness, (2) because happiness is good, and (3) indeed is the only good and (4) more good is better than less good, then (5) assuming that we can interpersonally compare the happiness of different people, (6) one ought to seek the greatest happiness. Each step of this argument is controversial (and remains so regardless of whether 'pleasure' or 'preference satisfaction' is

substituted for 'happiness'); that, however, is a problem in utilitarian ethical theory that need not occupy us here.

Utility and liberty: the orthodox critique

For present purposes the important question is whether, if accepted in ethics, the principle of utility justifies liberal political principles [for more on liberal utilitarianism, see Chapter 30]. Rawls (1971), of course, argued that it was, at best, uncertain whether a principle that aims at maximizing the aggregate amount of utility (happiness, pleasure, etc.) would yield an equal distribution of liberty. If greater happiness for many could be achieved by granting a few a lesser liberty, then the principle of utility would apparently justify illiberal policies. According to this common criticism, the problem is that the principle of utility takes the decision rule for choice by an individual – how he can best maximize his good – as a choice rule for society. While it is perfectly consistent with liberalism for an individual to sacrifice some parts of his life for more good in other parts, this seems illiberal in political decisions about the distribution of benefits between people. Thus the complaint that the principle of utility treats society 'as a sort of single great person' (Chapman, 1964: 163).

This criticism is so common as to be an orthodoxy in contemporary political theory. Utilitarian liberals, though, have advanced a number of replies.

The theory of the market

Rawls's criticism of utilitarianism is so widely accepted that we are apt to forget that liberalism and utilitarianism marched hand-in-hand throughout the nineteenth century. Most of the great classical political economists were utilitarians of some sort (Gaus, 1983b), as probably are most economists today. The theory of the market is, in effect, a sophisticated argument showing that, under certain conditions, the best way to maximize aggregate utility is for each person to act to promote her own welfare. J. R. McCulloch stated the doctrine thus:

> When individuals are left to be guided by their sense of what is best for themselves in the employment of their stock and industry, their interests are identified with those of the public; and those who are most successful in increasing their own wealth, necessarily, also contribute most effectually to increase the wealth of the state to which they belong. (1964: 125)

This supposes, of course, that wealth is a proxy for happiness or utility, an assumption often explicitly made by the liberal political economists (Gaus, 1983b) and indeed by much of economics today (which employs money as an objective utility function). We thus find today that, while most philosophers and political theorists are apt to see a conflict between liberalism and utilitarianism, most economists do not; neoclassical economics reconciles what philosophy draws asunder.

To be sure, it can be pointed out that the conditions under which market transactions maximize preference satisfaction are idealized, and so are not met in the actual world. Thus state action to correct market failures can be justified. Moreover, given the assumption of decreasing marginal utility (or decreasing rates of substitution between goods), utilitarianism can justify an egalitarian redistribution of incomes; P. J. Kelly (1990) argues that even before marginalism, Bentham's utilitarianism endorsed moderate egalitarianism. Given the extent of market failure, utilitarianism can also support a more extensive state. On the other hand, the theory of public choice advances a theory of state failure (Mueller, 2003). If the government action itself suffers from serious failures to promote optimal outcomes, then the market's failure to do so does not establish a case for intervention. Thus even in the face of serious market failures, a utilitarian may endorse relatively free markets.

Whether utilitarianism underwrites liberal politics and economics thus turns on economic theory, public choice, theories of institutional design (Goodin, 1996), and so on. In that sense liberal utilitarianism is indeed a partially comprehensive theory, with various theories of economics and politics being part of the case for liberal utilitarianism. Many philosophers are apt to reject liberal utilitarianism just because it turns on empirical claims; these anti-utilitarians often advance fanciful 'what if' examples, showing that under strange circumstances, utilitarianism might lead to strange results. In contrast, utilitarians typically have high confidence in these theories, and see no reason to suppose that our theory of political right should be independent of our best empirical theories of economics and politics (Goodin, 1982).

Paretian liberalism

Many standard economic utilitarian cases for liberalism presuppose interpersonal comparisons of utility. Although economists are sensitive to problems of comparing the utilities of different people, a great deal of political economy does so (Mueller, 2003: 566ff). If, instead, we suppose that the utilities (or happiness, or pleasure) of different people are incommensurable, we confront the problems of pluralism and social incommensurabilities [explored in Chapter 18]. Even given incommensurable personal utilities, we still can make some minimal overall welfarist judgements. According to the Pareto criterion, (1) social state S_1 is Pareto-superior to S_2 if and only if at least one person is better off in S_1 than in S_2 and no one is worse off in S_1 than in S_2; and (2) if no state is Pareto-superior to S_1, then S_1 is in the set of Pareto-optimal social states. These criteria, of course, may identify a large set of Pareto-optimal states, and so might often be indecisive among the choices open to us.

Even though it may often be indecisive, at least the Pareto criterion avoids the problem identified by Rawls: sacrificing the welfare of the few to benefit the many is excluded. Thus Paretian welfarism would seem at least consistent with liberalism. Amartya Sen, however, has proven this is not necessarily the case. Sen (1970) shows that if rights are understood as conferring individual authority to decide between at least two social states, then if there are two rights holders, liberal rights may conflict with unrestricted Paretian welfarism. Some have contested Sen's characterization of rights as jurisdictions over the selection of social states (for a discussion, see Mueller, 2003: 650–51); recent work on the theory of rights, however, has shown the independent plausibility of such a jurisdictional theory (Mack, 2000; Gaus, 1996: 199–204). Sen's result is important as it shows that *in principle* even a very minimal form of welfarism may be inconsistent with liberalism. More generally, Louis Kaplow and Steven Shavell (2002) have argued recently that almost any non-welfarist principle can conflict with the Pareto criterion.

Utilitarianism and rights

Utilitarians, or more broadly, consequentialists, have spent a good deal of effort investigating in what ways personal rights might enter into a utilitarian system. Sen (1990) offers a version of consequentialism that takes rights satisfaction as part of the utility of a state of affairs (cf. Scanlon, 1977; Nozick, 1974: 166). Mill's complicated utilitarianism – which seems to integrate rules into the concept of a morality – has often been used as a model for utilitarian rights (Lyons, 1978; Frey, 1984) [see further Chapters 17 and 30 on 'indirect' utilitarianism]. Russell Hardin (1988; 1993) has advocated an 'institutional utilitarianism' that takes account of knowledge problems in designing utilitarian institutions, which he offers as an alternative to both act and rule utilitarianism. According to Hardin, '[w]e need an institutional structure of rights or protections because not everyone is utilitarian or otherwise moral and because there are severe limits to our knowledge of others, whose interests are therefore likely to be best fulfilled in many ways if they have substantial control over the fulfillment.'

That, he adds, 'is how traditional rights should be understood' (1988: 78).

L. W. Sumner (1987) presents an especially influential consequentialist case for rights. Sumner recognizes the paradoxical air of a thoroughly consequentialist argument for rights: in so far as the consequentialist seeks to maximize achievement of a certain goal, and rights are a constraint on the ways goals are achieved, it looks as if the consequentialist must argue that the best way to achieve the goal is to constrain our efforts to achieve it. The key to resolving this paradox, says Sumner, is to distinguish consequentialism as a theory of moral justification from the preferred theory of moral decision-making (1987: 179) or, we might say, consequentialism as a theory of evaluation from a theory of deliberation. This argument for rights consequentialism (or, more generally, rule consequentialism) argues that there is no easy transition from the claim that the right action is that which maximizes good consequences to the claim that the best decision procedure is to perform that action which one thinks has the best consequences. Thus, the best decision procedure from a consequential perspective may be to limit the extent to which one engages in consequentialist reasoning by constraining the pursuit of goals through the recognition of rights.

This type of argument was advanced by Sidgwick (1962: 489), who accepted that utilitarianism may be self-effacing, in the sense that it could instruct us not to encourage its use as a theory for making decisions. It may be better, he argued, if many people are guided by common sense morality. Two problems confront such a view. First, it is often not realized that rule utilitarianism puts more, not less, computational burdens on those devising the system of rules. To employ such a rule utilitarian approach, we have to know that following rule *R* is a good way to maximize, or at least promote, utility. But to do so, we need to forecast the utility of large sets of actions, as well as the expected rates at which people will ignore *R* or misapply it, the costs of teaching *R* and the costs of punishments. The problem is highlighted in Sidgwick's own treatment of common sense morality, which makes Herculean assumptions about the tendency of common sense morality to promote the general happiness. Second, by divorcing utilitarianism as a standard of evaluation from its role as a standard of deliberation, we invite the sort of moral elitism that attracted Sidgwick: perhaps *hoi polloi* should be restricted to non-utilitarian reasoning, but the class of excellent calculators may be able to better promote utility by employing utilitarianism as a method of deliberation (1962: 489ff). Drawing inspiration from Sidgwick, Robert E. Goodin (1995: ch. 4) has recently defended 'government

house' utilitarianism, which casts utilitarianism as a 'public philosophy' to be employed by policy-makers, rather than a guide to individual conduct.

Hobbesian Contractualism

As I noted above, the last 20 years has witnessed the induction of Hobbes as a core member of the liberal pantheon. In addition to his relentless individualist analysis on humans in society, the liberalization of Hobbes has been driven by his contractualism, and the way in which it lends itself to game-theoretic modelling, most importantly in the work of Jean Hampton (1986; for a discussion see Kraus, 1993). At first blush one might think that Hobbes did not offer a moral contractualist theory at all: the laws of nature are pre-contractual moral norms, and the contract concerns the institution of a political sovereign, not agreement on moral norms. However, as David Gauthier (1995) has stressed, the Hobbesian contract involves an authorization of the sovereign's use of reason as right reason, including his reasoning about what morality requires; it is thus a political contract that subsumes morality. In any event, recent analyses inspired by Hobbes – most importantly Gauthier (1986) – have converted the Hobbesian approach into an account of justified morality which, in turn, endorses liberal arrangements (for doubts about the Hobbesian pedigree of Gauthier, see Lloyd, 1998).

As is well known, the starting point of neo-Hobbesian theory is a hypothetical analysis of the nature of unstructured interaction among rational individuals who are devoted to maximizing their preferences (Kavka, 1986: 123–4). There is some debate as to whether Hobbesian accounts suppose predominant egoism (Kavka, 1986: 64) or simply non-tuistic preference maximization (Gaus, 1999: 12, 74; Wicksteed, 1946: vol. 1, 180). In such a situation, individuals will confront prisoner's dilemmas, games of chicken and assurance games (Mueller, 2003: ch. 2; Skyrms, 1996); they will generally be unable to secure co-operation, and so the interests of all will suffer. Thus Hobbesian agents have reasons, based on the satisfaction of their own preferences, to agree to rules that structure their interactions and, in particular, that allow them to escape the prisoner's dilemmas in which they find themselves.

Hobbesian contracts confront three main problems (Gaus, 1999; ch. 5; see also Kraus, 1993). First, given that life in the state of nature – the condition of unstructured interaction – is 'nasty, brutish and short' (Hobbes, 1948: ch. 13), it will be relatively easy to show that *some* agreement is better than *no agreement*. However, there are likely to be a large number of social contracts that are

Pareto-optimal: all are better than the state of nature, but none is Pareto-superior to the others. Some contracts will be preferred by some parties, different ones by others. Thus the Hobbesian contract may be indeterminate; if so, then it is doubtful whether it can be seen as a strong justification of substantively liberal principles. Second, given that Hobbesian individuals are single-minded rational maximizers, it seems that they would cheat on any social contract if they would benefit by cheating and their cheating will go undetected. But knowing this is the case, each knows the social contract would not bind anyone to sacrifice their interests, so there is no point in agreeing to it. Lastly, suppose, following James Buchanan (1975), one proposes the following contract: each keeps the holdings that each has in the state of nature, and agrees to call off the war of each against all. This would clearly benefit everyone, since each avoids the cost of protecting her holdings in the state of war. But it also seems *unfair* in the sense that it reflects the bargaining power of parties based on how well they did in the war that characterizes the state of nature. Such a bargain may be a *modus vivendi* – a compromise among competing interests that produces peace – but it hardly seems the basis of morality (for a defence of the Hobbesian contract as a *modus vivendi* see Gray, 2000).

Sophisticated analyses such as David Gauthier's (1986) contractualism seek to solve these problems (for general discussions, see Vallentyne, 1991). Gauthier argues that, in order to best pursue their goals, rational maximizers would agree to stop making maximizing choices. If individuals could adopt a disposition to obey the social contract the second problem, that of compliance, would be solved; once they have this disposition – this tendency to act – they no longer make choices by calculating what would best advance their goals, but on the basis of what would advance their goals in ways allowed for by the contract. If people adopted this disposition, then, somewhat paradoxically, they would do better at maximization, as they could honour the agreement that benefits all. Gauthier calls this 'constrained maximization' (1986: 158).

The obvious problem for Gauthier is that, at least on the face of it, the truly rational thing to do is to *appear* to turn yourself into a constrained maximizer while others *really* turn themselves into constrained maximizers. Gauthier has a two-part response. (1) Constrained maximizers do not adopt an unconditional disposition to constrain themselves no matter with whom they interact. They are only disposed to act in a constrained manner with those who are also constrained maximizers. (2) Gauthier insists that we are not totally opaque to each other; to some extent we can see into others and know their dispositions. As he puts it, we are

'translucent'. People can see through us to some extent. If one is translucent, the conditional co-operators will not act in a constrained way towards one if one is a cheater, and thus one will not achieve the benefits of social co-operation. Thus, concludes Gauthier, a rational agent would not seek to remain an unconstrained maximizer when others turn themselves into constrained maximizers.

It might seem that Gauthier would think that it is always rational to become an unconstrained maximizer when others do so. Not so. In *Morals by Agreement* Gauthier distinguished two dispositions to comply: broad and narrow (1986: 177ff, 225ff). Someone who is broadly compliant will comply with any agreement that benefits her; someone who is narrowly compliant will only comply with a fair and non-coercive agreement. As Gauthier sees it, it is not rational to become a broadly compliant person: you are asking people to take advantage of you, as you will honour any agreement you make regardless of how little you benefit. Thus we can see that Gauthier is addressing the worry about unfair contracts. It is only rational to turn yourself into a narrowly compliant person – someone who will comply with beneficial, fair and non-coercive arrangements.

Rational contractors will only comply with fair and rational bargains, but, as I have said, it is hard to know what is the uniquely best contract, the uniquely rational bargain. Gauthier originally defended a 'minimax relative concession' solution (1986: 226), but has since altered his views (1993: 178ff). Hobbesian accounts of justice thus seem dependent on some bargaining theory, and the complexities such theories involve (see Barry, 1989: Part I).

Value Scepticism

The idea that, somehow, liberalism could be intimately associated with scepticism about values, or some form of subjectivism, is controversial today: many important liberals such as Sher (1997) dispute it. Moreover, opponents of liberalism such as Alasdair MacIntyre (1981) have sought to make just this link, making contemporary defenders of liberalism suspicious about accepting some sort of tie. Nevertheless, scepticism about the interpersonal status of values has long been a part of liberalism. The sceptical camp includes all those liberalisms premised on the supposition that the powers of human reason are insufficient to provide public, definitive answers to the enduring questions concerning what makes life worth living, and to what ends we should devote ourselves. This line of liberal thinking can trace itself back to Hobbes and Locke. According to Locke:

The Mind has a different relish, as well as the Palate; and you will as fruitlessly endeavour to delight all Men with Riches or Glory, (which yet some Men place their Happiness in,) as you would satisfy all Men's Hunger with Cheese or Lobsters; which, though very agreeable and delicious fare to some, are to others extremely nauseous and offensive: And many People would with Reason preferr the griping of a hungry Belly, to those Dishes, which are a feast to others. Hence it was, I think that the Philosophers of old did in vain enquire, whether the *Summum bonum* consisted in Riches, or bodily delights, or Virtue, or Contemplation: And they might have as reasonably disputed, whether the best relish were to be found in Apples, Plumbs or Nuts; and have divided themselves into Sects upon it. (1975: 299)

Such subjectivist theories of value – which equate values with tastes or preferences – have a prominent place in twentieth-century liberal theory. A subjective conception of value was integral to the Austrian school; Carl Menger (1994: ch. 3) and his followers such as Ludwig von Mises (1966) explicitly endeavoured to integrate a subjectivist theory of value into economics. Of course in so far as economic liberalism is based on the supposition that the satisfaction of preferences alone determines value, then it too is subjectivist (for a criticism see Sunstein, 1997: 15ff). Subjectivist accounts of value have been defended by philosophers as well as economists: indeed it may well be that some form of subjectivism – that locates value either in the desires or in the feelings of agents – is the dominant account of value in twentieth-century philosophy (see Gaus, 1990: Part I). The upshot of these subjective accounts is that, by relativizing value to the desires, feelings or preferences of the individual agent, they undermine the proposal that the state should devote itself to pursuing the *summum bonum*. Liberal politics, on this view, cannot be reasonably grounded on pursuit of what is truly valuable, for value is a matter of taste, and our tastes differ. Of course such theories do not themselves lead to liberalism; although they act as 'defeaters' to arguments that seek to establish the justifiability of constructing politics around pursuit of the *summum bonum*, we still require positive arguments for liberal justice, to which we will now turn.

LIBERAL THEORIES OF JUSTICE

The line between a Hobbesian justification of liberal principles and what I shall call a 'liberal theory of justice' is fuzzy and open to challenge. The rationale for the distinction is this: utilitarian, Hobbesian and value subjectivist moralities *may* be employed to justify liberal arrangements, but depending on the details and assumptions, they can also justify

distinctively illiberal policies. They thus require additional premises (say, the theory of the market) to ground liberal political principles. After all, Hobbes's own theory was distinctively illiberal. In contrast, what I shall call 'liberal theories of justice' tie the very idea of justice and moral reasoning to basic liberal principles. On such views, although there may be no liberal theory of the good life or value, there is indeed a liberal theory of right.

Basic Liberal Rights Theories

I note in passing [as they are examined in Chapter 9 at greater length] that Lockean natural right views (Nozick, 1974; Simmons, 1992) are certainly liberal accounts of justice. In general, rights-based theories of justice that give pride of place to individual liberty rights (Lomasky, 1987; Steiner, 1994) are distinctly liberal understandings of justice.

Harm and Liberty

In *On Liberty* J. S. Mill advances his 'one very simple principle ... that the sole end for which mankind are warranted, individually or collectively, in interfering with the liberty of action of any of their number ... is to prevent harm to others' (1963a: ch. 1, para. 9). Mill advances a radical liberal theory of political right: coercion – which includes social pressure intended to discourage any act *A* – must be justified on the grounds that *A* constitutes a harm to others, and the coercion is intended to prevent that harm [see further Chapter 9].

A good deal of recent liberal theory has been devoted to explicating this harm principle, and whether it really can serve as the sole ground for justified coercion. One dispute concerns whether Mill intends the principle to identify a *set of acts* – those that do not directly harm others – that are immune from social coercion (see Riley, 1998: 93ff), or whether the principle is best interpreted as identifying *a set of reasons* – harm to others – that can justify coercion (Ten, 1980: 50–7; Gaus, 1999: 106–13).

The classic work on the harm principle, and more generally on this Millian approach to political justice, is Joel Feinberg's masterful four-volume *The Moral Limits of the Criminal Law* (1984–90). Feinberg's four volumes carefully analyse the main issues in Millian morality. (1) Precisely what is a *harm* (1984)? (2) Does Millian morality allow coercion to prevent acts that, while not harmful to others, are *offensive* to some (1985)? (3) When individuals are unable to make fully voluntary choices, can coercion then be employed to stop them from *harming themselves* (1986)? And (4) are there any conditions under which liberals justify coercion that do not fall into one of the above categories (1990)? Feinberg convincingly shows that, when carefully examined, Mill's radical proposal – that only harm to others can justify social interference – is implausible, but nevertheless is plausibly construed as the core of a liberal social morality (see further Gaus, 1999: Part II).

As Feinberg points out, moralities based on the harm principle are liberal in so far as there is a presumption of liberty: if a person's action does not constitute a harm to others, then she has the right to act as she sees fit (1984: 9). Moreover, fundamental to the harm principle is the principle that where there is consent, there is no harm: thus one may consent to acts that set back one's interests (such as taking drugs); not only does one have the right to harm oneself, but the dealer does not harm you if you have given informed consent to the purchase. However, critics of the harm principle (e.g. de Jasay, 1991) have argued that it is a poor grounding for liberal principles as the concept of harm is so malleable: it can be interpreted to encompass the prevention of psychological and culture harms (see e.g. Kernohan, 1997), thus justifying extensive and intrusive coercive interventions. Moreover, the requirement that the agent give 'informed consent' and that her self-harming acts are 'voluntary' opens the way to paternalistic interventions (Kleinig, 1983). Lastly, although the harm principle might be understood as a free-standing principle of morality that can be endorsed by those with very different views of the good life (Gaus, 1999: ch. 6), Mill and many of his followers have tied it to perfectionist theories, thus making it part of a more comprehensive package.

Kantian Liberalism I: from Respect to Liberal Rights

What Feinberg called the 'presumption in favour of liberty' has been defended by Benn in terms of a principle of non-interference based on respect for persons. Benn (1988) tells the story of Alan the pebble splitter, who is happily splitting pebbles on a public beach, when Betty comes along and demands that he justify himself to her. Benn agrees with Feinberg; he has no burden to justify himself to her. Now suppose she seeks to stop him, and he demands justification from her. Benn insists that a 'tu quoque reply from her that he, on his side, had not offered her a justification for splitting pebbles, would not meet the case, for Alan's pebble splitting had done nothing to interfere with Betty's actions'(1988: 87). There is, argues Benn, a basic asymmetry between you acting and you interfering with the actions of another. Alan does not have to justify his pebble splitting to Betty: he is under no

standing requirement to show Betty that he has good reasons for what he is doing. On the other hand, it is required of Betty that she justify to Alan interfering with his actions, or stopping him for what he is doing.

Benn argues that Betty's recognition of Alan's right to act is required if she is to respect his person: 'One may believe the other's project quite worthless in itself. Its claim to respect rests not on its being valuable and worthy of one's concern ... but simply in its being a person's project' (1988: 107). Because one claims a right to non-interference for oneself, respect for others requires that one grants it to others. In a similar vein, Jeffrey Reiman concludes that 'it is rationally required that we each limit our actions at that point at which all can pursue their sovereign interests to the maximum compatible with the same for everyone. We recognize the truth of the *moral imperative of respect*' (1990: 141–142, emphasis in original). Despite Benn's reference to 'projects', the argument does not presuppose a robust notion of autonomy or a plan of life; as Benn makes clear, the presupposition is that agents possess what he call 'autarchy', the capacity for genuine choice, a condition that is consistent with heteronomy (1988: chs. 8, 9). Thus Benn is advancing a liberal theory of the right that does not presuppose a liberal conception of the good or valuable life: even pebble splitters have a claim to non-interference.

A similar sort of argument was advanced by Alan Gewirth in his important and recently neglected book *Reason and Morality* (1981). Gewirth's argument, like Benn's, starts from a broad conception of agency and holds that, given this conception, individuals are committed to claiming for themselves, and honouring the claims of others to, basic rights to freedom and well-being. Benn and Gewirth thus share the common project of deriving basic liberal rights from the very idea of moral agency. Gewirth's aim, though, is more radical: he argues that the nature of *rational* agency impels one to make a certain prudential claim, which gives rise to *moral* claims on others, which reason requires that one generalize. Moral agency is entailed by rationality. (For a general criticism of this type of argument, see Williams, 1985: 55–64.) In contrast, Benn distinguishes rational agency from moral agency. It is possible, he argues, to be a purely 'natural person' who makes no moral claims: psychopaths, he suggests, may possess rational natural personality – rational agents devoted to securing their goals – but be devoid of moral personality (1988: 101–2). Moral persons are those who see others and themselves in terms of moral relations: it is how we do in fact see ourselves, and it is moral persons who would recognize the basic right of non-interference.

Kantian Liberalism II: from Respect to the Moral Contract and then to Liberal Rights

Despite their differences, Benn and Gewirth both seek a direct route from agency to liberal rights: if we understand the type of agents we are, we see that we must claim certain liberal rights and grant them to others. In contrast, what is often called 'Kantian liberalism' seeks to establish liberal rights via a hypothetical contract, which then generates basic rights. In the words of Sandel, its most famous critic, according to 'deontological' or 'Kantian liberalism', 'society, being composed of a plurality of persons, each with his own aims, interests, and conceptions of the good, is best arranged when it is governed by principles that do not themselves presuppose any particular conception of the good' (1982: 1–7). Because, on this view, each is a chooser of her own ends in life, respect for the person of others demands that we refrain from imposing our view of the good life on her. Only principles that can be justified to all respect the personhood of each. Respect, then, requires a *certain mode of justification*, according to which moral principles are acceptable to all free moral persons in a fair choice situation. Liberal principles are then generated via this mode of justification. 'According to contractualism,' says Thomas Scanlon, 'when we address our minds to a question of right and wrong, what we are trying to decide is, first and foremost, whether certain principles are ones that no one, if suitably motivated, could reasonably reject' (1998: 189; see also Barry, 1995) [see the discussion of contractualism and Barry in Chapter 30].

Notice that Scanlon's test concerns 'reasonable' rejection, not what could be rationally rejected (1998: 191). For Scanlon, '[t]he distinction between what it would be reasonable to do and what it would be rational to do is not a technical one, but a familiar one in ordinary language' (1998: 192). A reasonable person does not make claims that others cannot be expected to live with, or are grossly unfair. Rawls has a similar idea: parties to his original position are 'rational and reasonable', not simply rational: 'Persons are reasonable … when they are ready to propose principles and standards as fair terms of co-operation and to abide by them willingly, given the assurance that others will likewise do so' (1996: 48). In contrast to Hobbesian contractors, Rawlsian contractors seek to respect each other's status as free and equal moral beings (Larmore, 1996: ch. 6).

Kantian contractualism must build into the account some constraint that limits consideration to only justifications that all reasonable people would accept, or that none would reject. One way to do this is, *à la* Rawls, to constrain the choice situation

in such a way that the rational parties are forced to advance only reasonable considerations. The nature of Rawls's argument behind the veil of ignorance (which excludes specific knowledge about a contractor's post-contract life and personality) is such that given the constraints on choice, *the most rational choice for a contractor* will model *a reasonable choice for you and me*. Instead, though, of building into the framework of the choice situation our understanding of the demands of reasonableness, we might, as Scanlon suggests, appeal directly to our intuitions about reasonableness in the contractarian analysis (1998: ch. 5). Alternatively, one could seek to minimize the appeal to intuitions about reasonableness by developing a more systematic theory of justification and reasonable rejection (see Gaus, 1996).

A fruitful project for Kantian liberalism is to integrate the more direct version described above with the contractual argument (Reiman, 1990; Gaus, 1990: Part II). Some basic moral principles may be directly derived from our conceptions of ourselves as moral persons (i.e. a basic right to non-interference), while other moral principles (say, concerning specific schemes of property rights and distributive justice) may be justified via a contractual argument. The rights justified by the direct argument from moral agency would structure and constrain the contractual stage of the justification. In so far as Kantian contractualism supposes that some norms (i.e. concerning what principles are reasonable) are prior to the contract, admitting these additional pre-contractual norms is entirely consistent with the approach.

Kantian contractualism leads to the analysis of 'public reason' (see D'Agostino, 1996), the key element of so-called 'political liberalism'. The line between Kantian contractualism and political liberalism is as thin and uncertain as the line between *A Theory of Justice* and *Political Liberalism*.

CONCLUSION

It should be clear that the label 'comprehensive' liberalism is misleading: it includes everything from truly comprehensive liberalisms as wide-ranging secular philosophies to Kantian liberal theories of political justice that seem consistent with a wide range of notions about value, social knowledge, and selfhood. To be sure, just how wide a range of conceptions of the self are consistent, say, with Kantian liberalism has been one of the hotly disputed issues over the last 20 years; thus just how comprehensive such liberalism must be has been the crux of the debate. For the most part, it seems mistaken to treat Millian and Kantian liberalism as equally comprehensive. Whereas Kantian liberalism makes some claims about the nature of agency and interpersonal rights, Millian liberalism *qua* a theory of individual development seems committed to a rich theory of the good life, while *qua* a utilitarian theory is committed to an overall theory of the good and the right. On the other hand, understood simply as an account of liberalism resting on the harm principle, Millian liberalism may not be any more comprehensive than Kantian liberalism; indeed it may be less comprehensive, adopting a moral principle that can be subject to what Rawls calls overlapping consensus (1996: Lecture 4). All told, it would probably be better to abandon the contrast between 'comprehensive' and 'political' liberalisms in favour of more fine-grained distinctions.

REFERENCES

Barry, Brian (1989) *Theories of Justice.* Berkeley, CA: University of California Press.

Barry, Brian (1995) *Justice as Impartiality.* Oxford: Clarendon.

Benn, Stanley I. (1988) *A Theory of Freedom.* Cambridge: Cambridge University Press.

Bentham, Jeremy (1987) *Introduction to the Principles of Morals and Legislation.* In *Utilitarianism and Other Essays,* ed. Alan Ryan. Harmondsworth: Penguin.

Berlin, Isaiah (1969) 'Two concepts of liberty'. In his *Four Essays on Liberty.* Oxford: Oxford University Press, 118–72.

Bird, Colin (1999) *The Myth of Liberal Individualism.* Cambridge: Cambridge University Press.

Bosanquet, Bernard (2001) *The Philosophical Theory of the States and Related Essays,* eds, Gerald F. Gaus and William Sweet. Indianapolis: St Augustine.

Buchanan, James M. (1975) *The Limits of Liberty: Between Anarchy and Leviathan.* Chicago: University of Chicago Press.

Buchanan, James M. and Gordon Tullock (1965) *The Calculus of Consent: Logical Foundations of Constitutional Democracy.* Ann Arbor, MI: University of Michigan Press.

Chapman, John W. (1964) 'Justice and fairness'. In Carl J. Friedrich and John W. Chapman, eds, *NOMOS VI: Justice.* New York: Atherton.

Chapman, John W. (1965) 'Political theory: logical structure and enduring types'. In *L'Idée de philosophie politique.* Paris: Presses Universitaires de France, 57–96.

D'Agostino, Fred (1996) *Free Public Reason.* Oxford: Oxford University Press.

De Jasay, Anthony (1991) *Choice, Contract and Consent: A Restatement of Liberalism.* London: Institute of Economic Affairs.

Dewey, John (1980) *Liberalism and Social Action.* New York: Putnam's Sons.

Dworkin, Gerald (1988) *The Theory and Practice of Autonomy.* Cambridge: Cambridge University Press.

Dworkin, Ronald (1978) 'Liberalism'. In *Public and Private Morality,* ed. Stuart Hampshire. Cambridge: Cambridge University Press, 115–43.

Dworkin, Ronald (2000) *Sovereign Equality: The Theory and Practice of Equality.* Cambridge, MA: Harvard University Press.

Feinberg, Joel (1984) *The Moral Limits of the Criminal Law.* Vol. I, *Harm to Others.* New York: Oxford University Press.

Feinberg, Joel (1985) *The Moral Limits of the Criminal Law.* Vol. II, *Offense to Others.* New York: Oxford University Press.

Feinberg, Joel (1986) *The Moral Limits of the Criminal Law.* Vol. III, *Harm to Self.* New York: Oxford University Press.

Feinberg, Joel (1990) *The Moral Limits of the Criminal Law.* Vol. IV, *Harmless Wrongdoing.* New York: Oxford University Press.

Freeden, Michael (1996) *Ideologies and Political Theory.* Oxford: Clarendon.

Frey, R. G. (1984) 'Act-utilitarianism, consequentialism and moral rights'. In R. G. Frey, ed., *Utility and Rights.* Oxford: Blackwell, 61–95.

Galston, William (1980) *Justice and the Human Good.* Chicago: Chicago University Press.

Galston, William (1991) *Liberal Purposes: Goods, Virtues and Diversity in the Liberal State.* Cambridge: Cambridge University Press.

Gaus, Gerald F. (1983a) *The Modern Liberal Theory of Man.* New York: St Martin's.

Gaus, Gerald F. (1983b) 'Public and private interests in liberal political economy, old and new'. In S. I. Benn and G. F. Gaus, eds, *Public and Private in Social Life.* New York: St Martins, 183–222.

Gaus, Gerald F. (1990) *Value and Justification: The Foundations of Liberal Theory.* Cambridge: Cambridge University Press.

Gaus, Gerald F. (1996) *Justificatory Liberalism: An Essay in Epistemology and Political Theory.* Oxford: Oxford University Press.

Gaus, Gerald F. (1999) *Social Philosophy.* Armonk, NY: Sharpe.

Gaus, Gerald F. (2000a) *Political Theories and Political Concepts.* Boulder, CO: Westview.

Gaus, Gerald F. (2000b) 'Liberalism at the end of the century'. *Journal of Political Ideologies,* 5 (2): 179–99.

Gaus, Gerald F. (2003) *Contemporary Theories of Liberalism: Public Reason as a Post-Enlightenment Project.* London: Sage.

Gauthier, David (1986) *Morals by Agreement.* Oxford: Clarendon.

Gauthier, David (1993) 'Uniting separate persons'. In David Gauthier and Robert Sugden, eds, *Rationality, Justice and the Social Contract.* New York: Harvester Wheatsheaf.

Gauthier, David (1995) 'Public reason'. *Social Philosophy & Policy,* 12 (Winter): 19–42.

Gewirth, Alan (1981) *Reason and Morality*. Chicago: University of Chicago Press.

Gill, Emily R. (2001) *Becoming Free: Autonomy and Diversity in the Liberal State*. Lawrence, KS: University of Kansas Press.

Goodin, Robert E. (1982) *Political Theory and Public Policy*. Chicago: University of Chicago Press.

Goodin, Robert E. (1995) *Utilitarianism as a Public Philosophy*. Cambridge: Cambridge University Press.

Goodin, Robert E., ed. (1996) *The Theory of Institutional Design*. Cambridge: Cambridge University Press.

Gutmann, Amy (1985) 'Communitarian critics of liberalism'. *Philosophy & Public Affairs*, 14: 308–22.

Hampton, Jean (1986) *Hobbes and the Social Contract Tradition*. Cambridge: Cambridge University Press.

Hardin, Russell (1988) *Morality within the Limits of Reason*. Chicago: University of Chicago Press.

Hardin, Russell (1993) 'Economics of knowledge and utilitarian morality'. In Brad Hooker, ed., *Rationality, Rules and Utility*. Boulder, CO: Westview.

Hayek, F. A. (1976) *The Mirage of Social Justice*. Chicago: University of Chicago Press.

Hobbes, Thomas (1948) *Leviathan*, ed. Michael Oakeshott. Oxford: Blackwell.

Holmes, Stephen (1993) *The Anatomy of Illiberalism*. Cambridge, MA: Harvard University Press.

Kaplow, Louis and Steven Shavell (2002) *Fairness versus Welfare*. Cambridge, MA: Harvard University Press.

Kavka, Gregory (1986) *Hobbesian Moral and Political Theory*. Princeton, NJ: Princeton University Press.

Kelly, P. J. (1990) *Utilitarianism and Distributive Justice*. Oxford: Clarendon.

Kernohan, Andrew (1997) *Liberalism, Equality, and Cultural Oppression*. Cambridge: Cambridge University Press.

Keynes, John Maynard (1972) 'The end of *laissez-faire*'. In his *Essays in Persuasion*. London: Macmillan.

Kleinig, John (1983) *Paternalism*. Totowa, NJ: Rowman and Allenhead.

Kraus, Jody S. (1993) *The Limits of Hobbesian Contractualism*. Cambridge: Cambridge University Press.

Kymlicka, Will (1991) *Liberalism, Community and Culture*. Oxford: Clarendon.

Larmore, Charles (1996) *The Morals of Modernity*. Cambridge: Cambridge University Press.

Lindley, Richard (1986) *Autonomy*. London: Macmillan.

Lloyd, S. A. (1998) 'Contemporary uses of Hobbes's political philosophy'. In Jules S. Coleman and Christopher Morris, eds, *Rational Commitment and Social Justice: Essays for Gregory Kavka*. Cambridge: Cambridge University Press.

Locke, John (1975) *An Essay Concerning Human Understanding*, ed. Peter H. Nidditch. Oxford: Clarendon.

Lomasky, Loren E. (1987) *Persons, Rights, and the Moral Community*. New York: Oxford University Press.

Lyons, David (1978) 'Mill's theory of justice'. In A. I. Goldman and J. Kim, eds, *Values and Morals*. Dordrecht: Reidel, 1–20.

Machan, Tibor (1989) *Individuals and Their Rights*. La Salle, IL: Open Court.

MacIntyre, Alasdair (1981) *After Virtue*. Notre Dame, IN: University of Notre Dame Press.

Mack, Eric (2000) 'In defense of the jurisdiction theory of rights'. *The Journal of Ethics*, 4: 71–98.

McCulloch, J. R. (1964) *Principles of Political Economy*, 5th edn. Edinburgh: Black.

Menger, Carl (1994) *Principles of Economics*, trans. James Dingwall and Bert F. Hoselitz. Grove City, PA: Libertarian.

Mill, John Stuart (1963a) *On Liberty*. In J. M. Robson, ed., *The Collected Works of John Stuart Mill*. Toronto: University of Toronto Press, vol. XVIII, 213–301.

Mill, John Stuart (1963b) *A System of Logic: Ratiocinative and Inductive*. In J. M. Robson, ed., *The Collected Works of John Stuart Mill*. Toronto: University of Toronto Press, vols VII and VIII.

Mill, John Stuart (1963c) *Utilitarianism*. In J. M. Robson, ed., *The Collected Works of John Stuart Mill*. Toronto: University of Toronto Press, vol. X, 203–59.

Misak, Cheryl (2000) *Truth, Politics, Morality: Pragmatism and Deliberation*. London: Routledge.

Mises, Ludwig von (1966) *Human Action: A Treatise on Economics*, 3rd edn. Chicago: Contemporary.

Mueller, Dennis C. (2003) *Public Choice III*. Cambridge: Cambridge University Press.

Mummery, A. F. and J. A. Hobson (1956) *The Physiology of Industry*. New York: Kelly and Millman.

Nozick, Robert (1974) *Anarchy, State and Utopia*. New York: Basic.

Popper, Karl (1945) *The Open Society and Its Enemies*. London: Routledge and Kegan Paul.

Rasmussen, Douglas B. and Douglas J. Den Uyl (1992) *Liberty and Nature: An Aristotelian Defense of Liberal Order*. La Salle, IL: Open Court.

Rawls, John (1971) *A Theory of Justice*. Cambridge, MA: Harvard University Press.

Rawls, John (1996) *Political Liberalism*, paperback edn. New York: Columbia University Press.

Raz, Joseph (1986) *The Morality of Freedom*. Oxford: Clarendon.

Reiman, Jeffrey (1990) *Justice and Modern Moral Philosophy*. New Haven, CT: Yale University Press.

Ritchie, D. G. (1902) *The Principles of State Interference: Four Essays on the Political Philosophy of Mr. Herbert Spencer, J. S. Mill, and T. H. Green*. London: Allen and Unwin.

Riley, Jonathan (1998) *Routledge GuideBook to Mill on Liberty*. London: Routledge.

Rorty, Richard (1979) *Philosophy and the Mirror of Nature*. Princeton, NJ: Princeton University Press.

Rorty, Richard (1991) *Objectivity, Relativism and Truth*. Cambridge: Cambridge University Press.

Sandel, Michael (1982) *Liberalism and the Limits of Justice*. Cambridge: Cambridge University Press.

Scanlon, Thomas (1977) 'Rights, goals and fairness'. *Erkenntnis*, 11 (May): 81–95.

Scanlon, Thomas (1998) *What We Owe Each Other*. Cambridge, MA: Harvard University Press.

Sen, Amartya K. (1970) 'The impossibility of a Paretian liberal'. *Journal of Political Economy*, 78 (Jan./Feb.): 152–7.

Sen, Amartya K. (1990) 'Rights consequentialism'. In Jonathan Glover, ed., *Utilitarianism and its Critics*. London: Macmillan, 111–18.

Shapiro, Ian (2003) *The Moral Foundations of Politics*. New Haven, CT: Yale University Press.

Sher, George (1997) *Beyond Neutrality: Perfectionism and Politics*. Cambridge: Cambridge University Press.

Sidgwick, Henry (1962) *The Methods of Ethics*, 7th edn. Chicago: University of Chicago Press.

Simmons, A. John (1992) *The Lockean Theory of Rights*. Princeton, NJ: Princeton University Press.

Skyrms, Brian (1996) *The Evolution of the Social Contract*. Cambridge: Cambridge University Press.

Smith, Tara (1995) *Moral Rights and Political Freedom*. Lanham, MD: Rowman and Littlefield.

Spector, Horacio (1992) *Autonomy and Rights: The Moral Foundations of Liberalism*. Oxford: Clarendon.

Spencer, William (1995) *Social Statics*. New York: Robert Schalkenback Foundation.

Steiner, Hillel (1994) *An Essay on Rights*. Cambridge, MA: Blackwell.

Sumner, L. W. (1987) *The Moral Foundations of Rights*. Oxford: Oxford University Press.

Sunstein, Cass R. (1997) *Free Markets and Social Justice*. Oxford: Oxford University Press.

Ten, C. L. (1980) *Mill on Liberty*. Oxford: Clarendon.

Vallentyne, Peter, ed. (1991) *Contractarianism and Rational Choice*. Cambridge: Cambridge University Press.

Wall, Steven (1998) *Liberalism, Perfectionism and Restraint*. Cambridge: Cambridge University Press.

Wicksteed, Philip H. (1946) *The Commonsense of Political Economy*, ed. Lionel Robbins. London: Routledge.

Williams, Bernard (1985) *Ethics and the Limits of Philosophy*. London: Fontana/Collins.

Young, Robert (1986) *Personal Autonomy: Beyond Negative and Positive Freedom*. London: Croom-Helm.

9

Classical Liberalism and Libertarianism: The Liberty Tradition

ERIC MACK AND GERALD F. GAUS

THE LIBERTY TRADITION

Alasdair MacIntyre provides a helpful characterization of what constitutes a 'tradition' within moral or political thought. He says that such a tradition is:

an argument extended through time in which certain fundamental agreements are defined and redefined in terms of two kinds of conflict: those with critics and enemies external to the tradition who reject all or at least key parts of those fundamental agreements, and those internal, interpretative debates through which the meaning and rationale of the fundamental agreements come to be expressed and by whose progress a tradition is constituted. (1988:12)

In MacIntyre's sense, libertarianism and classical liberalism constitute a tradition of political thought. Within a tradition the internal debates may be so important to its members that the criteria for genuine membership are tied to one's position on these issues, and so the criteria of membership in the tradition are themselves contested. Some in the tradition will seek to withhold the status of member to others who claim it. For example, some members of the socialist tradition (say Marxists) might not grant that label to other members of that tradition or might themselves insist upon some differentiation between themselves and others (e.g. 'utopian socialists') within the same basic tradition. In the case of the libertarian/classical-liberal tradition, the most radically anti-statist members of this tradition may claim the label 'libertarian' and deny that label to their less anti-statist fellow-travellers, while the least anti-statist members of the tradition may claim

the label 'classical liberal', which they deny to their most hard-core anti-statist comrades. Hence, the hyphenated designation of the tradition that concerns us here. However, despite this hyphenated designation, it is enlightening to understand classical liberalism and libertarianism as comprising a single tradition of political thought. All the positions that we shall place in that tradition share a significant family resemblance, which is acknowledged by *most* members of this tradition by their willingness to accept for themselves and for *most* other members both the designations 'libertarian' and 'classical liberal'. Rather than the awkward phrase 'libertarian/classical-liberal tradition' we shall refer to the more melodious 'liberty tradition'.

The family resemblance among members of the liberty tradition obtains at two related levels. Underlying the tradition is, first, a *doctrinal resemblance*, constituted by a substantial sharing of normative principles and more or less empirical generalizations about how the world works (or fails to work) – principles and generalizations that together yield conclusions about the normative constraints on legitimate states. Second, there is a consequent *political resemblance*, a substantial similarity of conclusions about the way these shared normative constraints are to be applied, and thus what sort of state, if any, *is* justified. As with all traditions in political thought, this commonality of outlook is conjoined with vigorous disagreements. Some members of the liberty tradition accept different versions of the characteristic doctrinal elements. Indeed, some members of the liberty tradition entirely reject some of its characteristic doctrines. Furthermore, members of the tradition accept a range of conclusions about what sort of state, if any, can be justified. This range constitutes a spectrum of political stances which, from the most anti-statist left to its least anti-statist right, encompasses what we shall call Market Anarchism,[1] Minimal Statism, Taxing Minimal Statism and Small Statism.

We begin by explicating the unity of the tradition in terms of the doctrinal family resemblance among its members. Following that explication, the diversity within the tradition is introduced in terms of its internal debate about what sort of state, if any, can be justified. This debate itself, however, reflects and motivates a complex discussion within the tradition about precisely which interpretations of which of the doctrinal elements associated with the liberty tradition ought to be affirmed, and which is central and which is peripheral. Thus, an examination of the diversity of political stances within the liberty tradition quickly brings us back to the doctrinal level of this tradition but, this time, with a focus on internal doctrinal debate. We conclude by considering a recent attempt to extend the liberty tradition far toward statism – so-called 'Left Libertarianism'.

DOCTRINAL UNITY

Let us begin with formulations of a dozen doctrinal elements that unify the liberty tradition. For the sake of including all wings of the liberty tradition, each formulation allows for a range of interpretations. Not all members of the tradition endorse every doctrinal element, let alone all the same interpretations. And behind their endorsement of different combinations of different interpretations of these doctrines, members of the tradition differ in the precedence attributed to various doctrines. Some depend most heavily upon bold versions of the normative doctrines articulated below, while others base their case on bold claims about how the world works, conjoined with more modest versions of the normative doctrines. These dozen doctrinal elements are not independent axioms or theorems entailed by such axioms. Behind the doctrinal unity lies a diversity of deeper philosophical strategies – for example, deontological, contractarian, or consequentialist strategies – for vindicating some set of versions of these normative doctrinal elements. What provides unity at this philosophical level is each member's anticipation that his philosophical strategy best vindicates his interpretation of these doctrinal components which, in turn, supports a political position within the libertarian/classical-liberal spectrum.

(I) The liberty tradition is *normatively individualist*, affirming the separate value of each individual.

Each individual's life, well-being or preference satisfaction is thought of as having supreme importance in and of itself, not merely in so far as it contributes to social life, well-being, or preference satisfaction (Mack, 1999). This normative individualism underlies an insistence on the illegitimacy of actions and policies that impose losses on some individuals in the name of providing more extensive benefits to others (Nozick, 1974: 28–35). It might seem that utilitarian members of the tradition oppose this: utilitarians insist that only the greatest overall happiness is of value, and so it would seem that individuals are normatively important only as a means to aggregate satisfaction. While this might be the crux of utilitarianism in moral theory, it has not been in the liberty tradition. As Samuel Brittan has observed:

> the traditional economist's case for a form of market economy has been based on what might be called *liberal utilitarianism*. This is a belief that individual desires should normally be satisfied to the maximum degree possible without interfering with the desires of others. The utilitarianism involved is a highly qualified one. (1988: 43)

In addition, the liberty tradition is *ontologically* individualist in that it takes individuals, not classes, or races, or nations, to be in the final analysis the only sites of value, the only real agents, the only true bearers of rights and of responsibilities (see Bentham, 1987: ch. 1, s. 4; Buchanan and Tullock, 1965: 11–12). Only individuals make choices; there is, literally, no such thing as 'social choice' (de Jasay, 1991: 57–9).

(II) Normative individualism – the separate importance of each individual's life, well-being or preference satisfaction – is thought to endorse enforceable moral claims held by all individuals against interferences that diminish their lives, well-being or preference satisfaction. A moral claim against interference by others is basic to the liberty tradition (Nozick, 1974: 30ff; Machan, 1989: 7ff). The special importance that each individual's life, well-being or preference satisfaction has for her is an obstacle to justifying moral duties that require an individual to put aside her own concerns to work for the well-being or preference satisfaction of others (Lomasky, 1987: 94ff). At the very least, an additional burden of proof rests upon anyone who asserts that enforceable claims against being interfered with or harmed must be compromised in order to make room for enforceable claims to be assisted (Gaus, 1999: 117–19, 191–4).

(III) The liberty tradition takes individual liberty to be the core *political or legal* norm (Robbins, 1961: 104). Individual liberty is what each individual may *legitimately demand* of each other individual. There may be many other things that are good in life as ends in themselves or as means to those ends, but – at least absent complicating special circumstances – these rarely can be demanded of others as a matter of right. Part of the reason that liberty is the only thing – or at least the primary thing – that may be demanded of others as a political right is that the demand for liberty is uniquely modest; to demand liberty is merely to insist that one be left alone in one's solitary activities or in one's joint activities with other consenting individuals. Liberty as non-interference by others is thus a good that everyone with aims, goals or projects has an interest of demanding from all others, it can only be supplied by others, and it can be universally supplied at modest costs, unlike demands to be benefited or served at the expense of others (Lomasky, 1987: ch. 5).

(IV) According to the liberty tradition, respect for the individual and her liberty requires respect for that individual's control of extra-personal objects – tangible and non-tangible property – that she has acquired in ways that do not infringe upon others' equal liberty (Lomasky, 1987: ch. 6; Mack, 1990). Several related sub-themes are apt to be endorsed by members of the liberty tradition. First, seizing another's peacefully acquired holdings is itself a violation of her liberty. Second, seizing the fruits of another's labour or what a person has acquired through voluntary exchange of his labour or the fruits of his labour violates that person's entitlement or desert (Gaus, 1999: ch. 8). Third, a system that allows such seizures renders all other sorts of liberty insecure; secure private property is a background condition for a general regime of liberty (Gray, 1986: ch. 8). Fourth, secure private property is a background condition for economic prosperity. In general, the liberty tradition insists that freedom is only possible given the institutions of private property and the free market. Indeed, for some members of the tradition 'liberty is property' (Narveson, 1988: 66).

(V) In the liberty tradition, a desirable social order is an association of individuals (and sub-associations), each of whom has and pursues their own legitimate ends in life, but who themselves share no common goals (Oakeshott, 1975). Desirable social order *emerges* through the choices that individuals make when rights are secure. The liberty tradition denies that society is a collective enterprise, in which order is achieved through individual devotion (and subservience) to collective aims. According to the liberty tradition, individuals are able to enter into peaceful and mutually beneficial relations because of their general compliance with certain general rules – rules that are protective of the domains defined by individuals' rights to their lives, liberties, and justly acquired estates. The ideal of the rule of law is that all are subject to the same general rules – rules that do not subordinate them to one another or to some spurious societal end but rather protect and facilitate each person's pursuit of her own projects and ends (Hayek, 1973).

(VI) A social order that emerges out of the choices that individuals make when their rights are secure is more desirable than a centrally planned order because it allows and encourages individuals to bring their highly individualized and dispersed knowledge to bear on their decision-making (Barnett, 1998). When these rights are secure, individuals tend to benefit from their own productive decisions and bear the costs of their own unproductive choices; this provides an economically and socially desirable incentive structure. Moreover, institutions that reflect such decentralized decision-making, such as markets and non-coerced customs, themselves give rise to and convey important information for yet further individual planning and decision-making (Hayek, 1991). The liberty tradition emphasizes the extent to which political decision-makers are and must be ignorant of the knowledge they would have to have in order to engage effectively in the central planning to which they aspire (Hayek, 1944).

(VII) At least as a first approximation, we can say that in the liberty tradition the licit use of coercion is limited to blocking or nullifying infringements upon the rightful claims of individuals. Any use of coercion that infringes upon an individual's control of her person or property (and, thereby, abrogates the basic condition for the emergence of mutually beneficial social interactions) is illicit. To seize another and enslave him is to engage in illegitimate force; to break the slave-catcher's arm to prevent one's capture or to escape from slavery is to engage in legitimate force. Within the liberty tradition, any proposal to expand the list of legitimate uses of force – either by expanding the list of rights for which people can demand coercive protection or by expanding the role of legitimate coercion beyond the protection of rights – bears a heavy burden of proof. And part of what must be proven within the liberty tradition is that the proposed expansion of legitimate coercion still leaves individual liberty, as originally conceived, as the central political norm.

(VIII) The distinctive feature of political institutions in the liberty tradition is that they authorize the use of force and can legitimately threaten and use force against citizens. Because the scope of legitimate force is so limited, political policies and institutions readily fail to be legitimate. As at least a first approximation, we can say that political policies and institutions are legitimate if and only if they restrict their use of force to actions that block or nullify the violation of people's rights to liberty and property. Within the tradition, political institutions that use coercion more extensively must bear an especially heavy burden of justification, one that is too great to justify a state that extensively employs coercion against its citizens.

(IX) The liberty tradition rejects a basic distinction between the morality that applies to individuals generally and the morality that applies to public institutions and officials. To be sure, the special circumstances of public officials – including, perhaps, their possession of political authority – means that they may engage in particular actions, e.g. the punishment of wrongdoers, that is denied to citizens generally. But all sorts of special circumstances can render one individual, e.g. the executor of another's will, free to act in a way that is denied to citizens generally. The recognition of special rights and duties is consistent with the same principles of justice that apply to private individuals applying also to public officials. Illicit coercion is just as criminal when performed by public officials who pretend to be the instruments of justice as when it is engaged in by thieves and murderers. The liberty tradition certainly rejects the idea that there is a 'special distinction and dignity' attaching to the functions of government or the public (von Mises, 1985: 40).

(X) One familiar way of conveying the liberty tradition is to say that individual *A* may rightfully be subject to force by individual or institution *C*, if and only if that force will prevent *A* from harming *B* or will nullify some harm that *A* has already inflicted upon *B*. This formula, deriving from J. S. Mill (1991 [1859]), nicely highlights purposes that do *not* justify the use of force:

(a) *C*'s preventing *A* from harming himself does not justify *C*'s forcible intervention.
(b) *C*'s preventing *A* from acting in some sinful or ignoble way does not justify *C*'s forcible intervention.
(c) *C*'s preventing *A* from offending *B* (in a non-harming way) does not justify *C*'s forcible intervention.
(d) *C*'s causing *A* to bestow a benefit upon *B* does not justify *C*'s forcible intervention.

As is well known, how such a Millian formulation works itself out depends upon such detailed matters as, for example, how one construes harm and what counts as an imposition of harm. The liberty tradition is highly sceptical of proposals that would question (a)–(d) or interpret them in such a way that they provide no real barrier to state coercion. One can remain within the tradition if one chips away at the edges of some of these principles but not if one fractures any of them.

(XI) In contrast to the conventional left and right, members of the liberty tradition reject any fundamental distinction between 'personal' and 'economic' liberties (Machan, 1989: 98), and they certainly deny that there is a strong case only for so-called personal liberty. Because of the tradition's highly generalized endorsement of individual liberty, it is important for members of the tradition to hold that across all the various important dimensions of human life and interaction, desirable order tends to emerge from the exercise of individual liberty rather than from the imposition of some centrally determined structure or arrangement. For some members of the tradition, the fact that secure liberty is the fountainhead of beneficial order will be the generalization about how the world works that stands at the core of their doctrinal stance.

(XII) Members of the liberty tradition believe that most, if not all, political regimes have continuously and grievously infringed upon people's just liberties, and have continuously engaged in extensive acts of unjustified aggression, plunder, and meddlesomeness. The self-image of the liberty tradition is that it *sees through* the common demands and rationalizations for political power to understand the permanent tendency of political power to be oppressive, exploitative, and destructive of harmonious and mutually beneficial social arrangements. Members of this tradition hold that, even though some form of political authority is perhaps necessary and justified, citizens must always be jealous of such power, on their guard against it, be ready to condemn and resist its expansion and misuse.

POLITICAL AND DOCTRINAL DIVERSITY

Let us proceed now to the internal debates within the liberty tradition. We can best articulate these debates by attending to four political positions along the liberty tradition spectrum – (1) Market Anarchism, (2) the Minimal State, (3) the Taxing Minimal State and (4) the Small State – and the intellectual disputes among them. Although one could simply catalogue the doctrinal debates among members of the tradition, the actual structure of and motivation for the tradition's internal doctrinal debate are better captured by seeing how certain key differences about doctrinal elements fit into the contentious dialogue among advocates of these distinct political positions.

Market Anarchism

The liberty tradition's doctrinal commitments easily endorse Market Anarchism (Friedman, 1973). Liberty requires private property and a market order

(IV), desirable order emerges out of individual choices (V), the market uses the dispersed information of individuals (VI), the tradition is deeply sceptical of all coercion (VII) to the extent that most coercion is illegitimate (VIII), and, crucially, because the liberty tradition rejects an important distinction between public and private morality (IX), the grounds for justified coercion must lie in the rights of private individuals. Recall that according to John Locke, in a pre-political condition – a state of nature – individuals would have not only rights to life, liberty and property, but rights to 'punish the offender, and be Executioner of the Law of Nature' (1960: 290). If all rights, including rights to punish and enforce rights, reside in individuals, and if the market order is itself necessary for freedom, there is a strong case to be made that the protection of freedom itself can be left to the market.

Locke himself famously rejected life in anarchy (but see Simmons, 1993). Because each would judge for himself about the proper bounds of his and other rights, and about whether infractions had actually occurred, individuals would end up in conflict. The solution, Locke argued, would be that each would agree to a political society, 'all private judgement of every particular Member being excluded, the Community comes to be Umpire, by settled standing Rules, indifferent and the same to all Parties' and where only some have the authority to interpret and enforce these rules (1960: 342). Market Anarchists, however, do not concede the need for political authority to solve such disagreement. Although people employing their private judgements can come into conflict, Locke himself shows that they seek the good of shared judgement that would resolve the conflict. If so, there is no reason why such a good must be provided by that monopolistic provider we call the state. Against Locke, the market anarchist argues that a market regime of multiple, competing, protective agencies will not produce disorder and strife – so long as there is a strong demand for the orderly, peaceful, and just resolution of disputes. If we suppose that people desire the orderly, peaceful, and just resolution of disputes strongly enough that the powers of a minimal state would be confined to the provision of such resolutions, this very demand for orderly, peaceful, and just resolution of disputes would be strong enough to call forth their market provision.

Members of the liberty tradition attracted to anarchistic solutions thus endorse competitive providers of legal and police services. As in the market generally, competition between providers of judgements and enforcement will tend to produce high-quality goods; in this case, a high-quality good of impartial, efficient umpiring of conflicting rights claims. People will gravitate to impartial judging services for a variety of reasons. Verdicts from partial or unreliable judges will be apt to be resisted by others, and private enforcement agents will not seek to execute them, knowing that they are likely to be biased and, so, opposed by those who are found guilty or liable by them (Barnett, 1998). Market rivalry in the production and sale of protective services will motivate not merely price competition but also the discovery and production of new and better modes of law and rights protection. This is to be contrasted with a monopolistic provider's almost total disinterest in the cost-effective production of good law and good rights protection if it is allowed to maintain its monopoly by suppressing aspiring competitors. Desirable positive law will emerge as the articulated rights and rules that protective agencies will provide in order to satisfy consumer demand. As with other dimensions of desirable social order, claims the market anarchist, desirable positive law is more likely to be the product of market (or market-like) processes than of political processes.

In the world of the market anarchist, politics as we know it – including law that arises through *legislation* – completely withers away. The complete elimination of the political is a better yet alternative to eternal vigilance towards political power (see doctrine XII). The core claim of the market anarchist, then, is that anarchy better respects the very doctrinal elements that motivate the Lockean. All members of the liberty tradition maintain that everyone ought to enjoy the freedom of deploying one's property as one pleases – in any enterprise one pleases – as long as that deployment does not infringe upon anyone's rightful liberty. According to the market anarchist, an aspiring competitor who proposes to sell services very much like those offered by the minimal state is proposing to deploy his resources in ways which the champions of the minimal state cannot honestly claim are impermissible and subject to coercive suppression. The champions of the monopolistic provider called 'government' must themselves recognize that its suppression of these competitive endeavours would be criminal.

Minimal State Views

States as legitimate monopolies

A member of the liberty tradition defending some form of government might reply to this anarchist case in two ways. The first claims that the enterprise of producing and delivering the protection of rightful claims is especially subject to natural monopolies or cartelization.

The argument from natural monopoly, representing a qualification of doctrinal element V, argues that judging and protection are characterized by increasing returns. If it is the case that over the full range of possible outputs, the $(n + 1)$th unit costs less to produce than did the nth unit, then the larger a provider already is, the less its marginal and average costs. This may well be the case with protection services. Suppose a protection agency adjudicates all conflicts among its members peacefully, and typically protects with force the invasion of its members by non-members. If so, the larger an agency is in terms of members, the more conflicts it can adjudicate peacefully, and so its cost per member will decrease. If increasing returns hold, a monopolistic provider is apt to arise in a free market. In two ways this takes the sting out of the anarchist's condemnation of the government's monopoly (Nozick, 1974: 52). First, if markets give rise to monopolistic providers, then the anarchist is wrong to think that his free market case is an anti-monopoly case. Second, if we are stuck with a monopolistic provider, then there seems grounds for following Locke's lead and putting special restrictions on its behaviour. Hence, it might be argued, it must be subject to some other form of public regulation. Perhaps constraining constitutions ought to be thought of as the public regulation of this especially dangerous sort of natural monopoly.

A related argument concerns cartelization (Cowen, 1992). A protective agency will be able to compete effectively in the provision of desired protective services only if it can offer to its clients the enforcement of the rights articulations, rules, procedures, and appeal mechanisms that emerge from agreements among the competing protective agencies. And any particular agency will be able to offer this law enforcement to clients only if it itself is party to those inter-agency agreements. But, once such law-generating agreements are in place, it will be in the interest of the agencies already party to them to exclude further agencies from admission and, thereby, to preclude these agencies from becoming viable competitors to them. Moreover, argues the defender of the state, this exclusion involves no initiation of coercion and, hence, contravenes no liberty tradition norms. Thus, something like a confederation of rights-protecting agencies that enjoys something like a monopoly on the production and sale of defence services can be expected to arise by processes to which the individualist anarchist cannot morally object.

The second response to the anarchistic challenge does involve some explicit refinement, if not weakening, of liberty tradition norms. According to this response, a protective agency or confederation of such agencies that aspires to the status of minimal state can more readily permissibly suppress the putatively rights-protecting activities of its competitors than may at first seem to be the case (Nozick, 1974).

For such an agency or confederation may permissibly suppress activities that pose even a moderate risk of violating rights (at least if it will not be feasible for the boundary crossers to compensate the victims of their violations). Or, to a similar effect, it may be held that such an agency or confederation may permissibly suppress activities of its competitors in the name of the procedural rights of its clients. Thus, considerations of risk or of procedural rights are invoked to refine liberty tradition doctrines in ways that seem to support the minimal statist against the anarchist critique.[2]

The minimal state and revenues

We thus arrive at the endorsement of the minimal state – a monopolistic agency legitimately employing force and the threat of force solely to protect people's lives, limbs, liberties, estates, and contractual rights against both internal and external threats. This minimal state achieves the protection of these rightful claims only in ways that are themselves respectful of people's rightful claims. The effective enforcement of these claims is taken to secure the background conditions out of which mutually beneficial and valued social and economic order is most likely and most extensively to emerge through individuals' own, well-motivated exercise of their protected liberties.

But how can the minimal state acquire the funds to provide protective services without itself violating people's rightful claims? According to its own champions, the minimal state is subject to the same moral strictures that apply to all of us. If it would be criminal for any one of us to seize funds from another, even if that first party proceeded to employ those funds to provide the second party with protection against third parties, then it will also be criminal for the minimal state to seize funds from any of us even if it proceeds to employ those funds to provide us with protection against (other) internal or external threats. One will at least draw this conclusion unless the advocate of the minimal state can bear the burden of showing that, contrary to appearances, the seizures conducted by the minimal state are really distinct from the deprivations conducted by ordinary thieves in morally significant ways (see element XI).

How, consistent with unreconstructed liberty norms, could the minimal state acquire the resources necessary to finance the services it supplies? The key to the minimal statist's answer is that individuals do not have original (pre-contractual) moral claims to the various forms of protection that the state proposes to provide. Whereas individuals have original moral claims not to be interfered with or harmed by others in certain ways, individuals do

	All others	
	Enough others co-operate, so that defence is secured	Not enough others co-operate, so that defence is not secured
Pay my share	Agent gains the public good, but has to pay part of the cost for it	Agent pays the cost, but since others don't co-operate, she doesn't get the public good
Do not pay my share	Agent gets the public good for free	Agent doesn't get the public good, but at least she doesn't pay anything

Figure 9.1   A multi-person prisoner's dilemma

not have original moral claims that other agents protect them against those interferences or harms. If I am shipwrecked on that proverbial island with strangers *A* and *B*, I have a claim that *A* (and *B*) not attack me. But I do not have a claim against *B* that *B* protect me against *A*'s attacks. *B*'s protecting me would be a service and, if I want a claim to that service, I must acquire that claim by paying *B* for it (in cash or kind). Similarly, say the friends of the minimal state, this agency is under no pre-contractual obligation to provide individuals with the protection in which it specializes. It is, therefore, free to offer its presumably highly valued protective services for sale – as is any aspiring supplier of valuable services. The minimal state's acquisition of the resources necessary to provide its services is vindicated as one side of a normal voluntary business transaction. (The minimal state may offer somewhat different packages of services at differing prices to its various potential customers.) Such a minimal state, of course, cannot require that people buy protection. As a monopoly it can charge consumers, and as a constitutionally unregulated monopoly it can charge consumers whatever the market will bear. But it cannot require anyone to purchase its services.

The Taxing Minimal State

Protection as a public good

The market anarchist and the minimal statist share a crucial premise, namely, that the value to individuals of their receipt of protective services will motivate almost everyone to pay for those services. Individuals eager to be protected in their lives, limbs, liberties, and estates will finance the production of protective institutions by patronizing either a range of competing protective agencies or a minimal

state that is the monopoly supplier of those services. Put somewhat differently, the shared premise is that the protection of rightful claims is a standard economic good which people will voluntarily pay for to the extent that they value it. Unfortunately, however, important parts or aspects of the protection of rightful claims are not like standard economic goods; important parts or aspects of the protection of rightful claims are public goods.

The crucial feature of a public good is that, if the good is produced, it will not be feasible to exclude individuals who have not paid for that good from benefiting from it. The usual example of a public good is the protective service of national defence. If a system of national defence is funded and produced, it will not be feasible to exclude occupants of the national territory from its benefits. The non-excludability of these goods provides people with an incentive not to purchase them. Rational individuals confront a multi-person case of the well-known prisoner's dilemma, depicted in Figure 9.1. Defection (not paying her share) is the agent's *dominant strategy*: no matter what the rest of society does, she does best by not paying her share. Thus public goods tend to be undersupplied even if *everyone prefers paying their share for the public good to not having it*. The parties thus end up at a Pareto-inferior result: each orders the north-west over the south-east cell, yet they all end up in the latter. If these special difficulties in soliciting voluntary market payments for public goods cannot cost-effectively be overcome, the public good will not be financed and produced, and every member of the public will be worse off than she would be had she paid her share of the cost of that good and it had been financed and produced. In the case of rights-protective goods, every member of the public will be worse off with respect to the protection of her rightful claims.

It is widely held that these special difficulties of marketing public goods cannot cost-effectively be overcome by voluntary means (but see Schmidtz, 1991; Cowen, 2003), and it is also widely held that public goods can cost-effectively be financed by coercive means. The latter idea is that individuals can be coerced into paying their share of the cost of public goods and this will result in each being a net beneficiary: the direct and indirect costs imposed upon each individual by requiring her to pay her share will be less than the benefits to her of having the relevant public good produced. These views amount to a qualification of the liberty tradition's general endorsement of markets and contractual relationships as the best devices for allocating resources to their most valuable uses (see elements V and VI). Government is justified largely on the grounds of market failure: although the market generally provides for both a free and a prosperous society, it is not perfect (Buchanan, 1975: ch. 3). Thus the classical liberal political economists of the nineteenth century – Adam Smith, J. R. McCulloch, Nassau William Senior, J. B. Say, David Ricardo, Robert Torrens – insisted that the market depended on a political framework that it could not itself provide; the market could not itself provide a coercive public apparatus for the enforcement of property rights and contracts (Robbins, 1961; Gaus, 1983).

Market anarchists and minimal statists may challenge these widely held views. They may argue, first, that coercive state provision of public goods tends to oversupply them, so that it has its own off-setting inefficiencies (Buchanan and Tullock, 1965). And, they may insist, market and contractual arrangements can be envisioned that will yield funding for public goods – especially rights-protective public goods – that is not significantly suboptimal (Buchanan, 1975; Narveson, 1988: 238). Advocates of the minimal state that depict it as a natural monopoly seem better positioned to make this argument than are market anarchists. Such a minimal state will, to a considerable degree, be able to tie its clients' purchase of non-public aspects of rights protection to their also paying for public aspects of rights protection. For instance, it will be able to say, 'We will sell you access to our courts for the settlement of criminal and civil disputes – which you need to purchase *from us* if you are to enjoy it – only if you also agree to buy national defence from us.' Of course the state's monopolist position poses its own problems: in so far as the state is a monopoly it tends to restrict supply and to make consumers pay more for its output than they would under market competition.

If crucial public goods would be significantly underproduced in the absence of individuals being *required* to contribute to their funding (and requiring such contributions would yield a satisfactory level of the production of those public goods), members of the liberty tradition are faced with a hard choice. On the one hand, they may stick with unreconstructed versions of that tradition's basic norms at the cost of precluding the mutual benefits associated with those public goods (while no doubt insisting that the public good characteristics of law enforcement are typically overestimated, and that most of what the state should do is to provide essentially privately consumed protection services). Or, on the other hand, they may legitimate the coercive takings that are, by hypothesis, needed to fund those valuable goods at the cost of weakening at least some of those central norms. The second alternative moves us to the right along the liberty spectrum to the taxing minimal state – a state which funds itself through taxation, but only in so far as is necessary to finance the production of protective services (or, perhaps, the production of these *and* other public goods).

Three justifications for public goods provision

How great will be the *doctrinal* cost of this weakening of liberty tradition norms? That depends upon how much independent reason – reason independent of the felt practical need to allow for the coercive funding of public goods – there is for the adoption of less restrictive versions of these norms. We can identify three approaches to justification: (1) that coercive public goods provision is fully consistent with the basic commitments of the liberty tradition; (2) that the goods at stake justify overriding liberty; and (3) that such provision is benign paternalism.

(1) Many members of the liberty tradition insist that, on the most plausible understanding of its basic norms, they are not violated by coercive public goods provision. According to these defenders of the coercive funding of public goods, to recognize the 'separateness of persons' is to reject the idea that the gains that may accrue to some vindicate the infliction of losses upon others. So the core norm of the tradition is a prohibition on benefiting some individuals at the expense of others. This core, anti-redistributive norm is not offended by the coercive takings involved in financing public goods (which, by hypothesis, would not be voluntarily funded). For, we are assuming, those forced extractions leave everyone better off than they would be were people not subjected to them; *these* forced extractions, inducing Pareto-superior moves, are not redistributive.

This line of argument narrows the scope of the behaviour against which individuals have rightful claims; it says that further reflection upon the basis of liberty and immunity from injury narrows the tradition's prohibitions to treatments by others that, on net, are costly or harmful to the individual. Similar reasoning can be offered for a similar conclusion – but one that is cast in terms of the character, rather than the scope, of the individual's rightful claims. Here it is argued that an individual's rightful claims are justified by the service that those claims provide for her basic interests. People's rightful claims and the correlative constraints upon others' liberty of action ought to be as stringent as necessary to serve the relevant interests of those persons – and no more stringent than that. Rights can be divided by stringency into more stringent rights that straightforwardly prohibit certain interferences with the right holder, and less stringent rights that prohibit certain interferences if (but only if) those interferences leave their subjects injured in her basic interests. One standard way of characterizing these two levels of rights is to say that the more stringent rights are rights protected by a property rule (others simply must not trespass upon the right), while the less stringent rights are protected by a liability rule (others may trespass if and only if the intervention does not on net damage the interests protected by the right) (Calabresi and Melamed, 1972). If the rationale for rights is their service in protecting people's basic interests, the rationale for rights would point to rights of the less stringent sort. In the case of public goods, agents' basic interests are served by possessing rights of the less stringent variety. For this allows the coercive takings that are, by hypothesis, necessary for the public goods to be produced whereas more stringent rights would forbid those takings and leave the agents worse off in their basic interests.

(2) Members of the liberty tradition whose primary philosophical orientation is contractarian or consequentialist will sympathize with more direct vindications of the coercive funding of public goods – vindications that do not focus specifically on the scope or stringency of rights. Contractarians will simply point to the mutual gains which, by hypothesis, the coercive financing of public goods will yield (Buchanan, 1975; Gaus, 1999: ch. 10). Because the consequentialists within the tradition adhere to the core normative commitment (doctrine I), they are highly sceptical of any measure of aggregate societal well-being that would justify harming some to benefit others. They are, instead, apt to hold that the only sound measure of societal improvement is the Pareto criterion: a social change can be said to be an improvement if and only if at least some individuals gain and no individuals lose. Absent special complications, promotions of public goods, if necessary even by coercive means, will be Pareto improvements. Hence, this generally sceptical consequentialism endorses such promotions.

(3) Finally, coercive funding for public goods may be defended within the liberty tradition as involving only a most benign form of paternalism and, hence, as involving little or no weakening of the tradition's strongly anti-paternalist stance (see element X). The problem that exists when individuals are faced with the choice of whether or not to contribute to the funding of a public good is that those individuals will tend to be too clever for their own good as shown by the prisoner's dilemma in Figure 9.1. Rational agents will cleverly refuse to volunteer to pay their share; regardless of what others do – whether enough others contribute or fail to – a rational agent does best by refusing to contribute. But rather than ending up with their most preferred outcome, namely receipt of the good with no payment, each will end up not receiving the good. The actual outcome will be worse, *in terms of the actual values and preferences of the individuals involved*, than the outcome of each individual being required to pay her share. Coercively requiring these payments from individuals merely helps them overcome their indulgence in all-too-clever strategic reasoning, which threatens to harm them.

This appeal to putatively benign paternalism points to a common feature of all these vindications of coercive takings – a feature to which many of the more anti-statist members of the tradition will take exception. From the perspective of these more anti-statist members, these vindications share a failure to take *choice* or *discretionary control* seriously enough (Mack, 2000). These members of the tradition understand its crucial norms as protective of agents' authority (or jurisdiction or sovereignty) over themselves and their personal domains. The primary wrong involved in a coercive intervention consists in the intervener's impairment of the agent's choice and not in the setback to the agent's interests which normally accompanies such an impairment of the agent's discretionary control. Thus, coercive interventions remain wrongful even when they advance the interests of their subjects.

The Small State

If the arguments that support the Taxing Minimal State are extended to legitimize coercive takings for the production of other sorts of public goods (for example, the public good of mosquito abatement) or to correct other types of market failure (say, the regulation of natural monopolies), then we have gone beyond the Minimal State to the Small State. The more types of goods and services that are accepted as significantly public and, hence, as justifiably financed through taxation, the larger the Small State becomes.

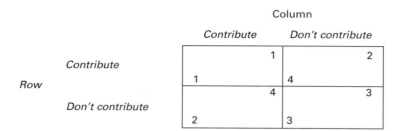

Figure 9.2 An assurance game

The nineteenth-century classical liberal political economists endorsed significant public activity on essentially market failure grounds. Public provision of roads, harbours and canals was generally endorsed, though Adam Smith at least was clear that these were not really public goods (Smith, 1976: 724; O'Brien, 1975: 275–6; Gaus, 1983). Widespread primary and secondary education are also often seen as, if not perfect public goods, goods that possess significant similarities to public goods, and so will be significantly undersupplied by free markets. However, while advocates of the Small State thus endorse taxation to fund general education, this does not justify public provision of that education. 'The strong case for government finance of at least general education,' says Hayek, 'does not however imply that this education should also be managed by the government, and still less that government should acquire a monopoly of it' (1979: 61). Thus advocates of the Small State have endorsed vouchers, by which government compensates for the undersupply of education by additional funding, but leaves provision to the market (Friedman and Friedman, 1980: ch. 6).

The major movement towards the right of the liberty spectrum is driven by the belief that markets will fail to allocate resources efficiently to the production of public goods. Convictions about other sorts of market failure reinforce this rightward movement. For example, a belief in the propensity of unregulated market processes to give rise to monopolies within certain industries will dispose members of the tradition to accept political regulation of those processes or those monopolies – unless it can be argued that the costs of these market failures will, in any case, be less than the costs of the governmental failures associated with this political regulation. Members of the liberty tradition who accept the need and propriety for coercive taxation for the funding of an array of

public goods that go beyond protective services, and the need and propriety for some moderate level of governmental regulation in response to other market failures, are to be located at the Small State position on the liberty spectrum (but see Cowen, 1988).

The social minimum and the liberty tradition

A public goods argument can be advanced for general forced donation to the elimination of poverty. Hayek, for example, suggests that a scheme for assistance against severe deprivation is in the interest of all; indeed, he adds that 'it may be felt a duty of all to assist, within the organized community, those who cannot help themselves' (1976: 87). Now even if we all accept this duty, we may not freely contribute, as Figure 9.2 shows. The numbers in each cell refer to Column's (top right) and Row's (bottom left) preference orderings. In this 'assurance game', each gets his first choice if both contribute; they both prefer contributing to eliminate poverty over not contributing. But neither wants to be played for a 'sucker' in which one contributes but the other does not; not only might such unilateral contribution be less efficient, but the players may think it unfair that one bears the total burden. As can be seen from Figure 9.2, if Row and Column can be assured that the other will contribute, then each gets his best option by also contributing; but if one player thinks that the other will not contribute, then the rational thing to do is also not contribute (thus getting her third rather than fourth option).

It is not at all obvious, though, that charity is a good that must be achieved through joint action of this sort (Narveson, 1988: 258ff). Another difficulty with this argument is that any actual scheme of forced contribution will ensnare individuals who do not much value the amelioration of poverty (who do not have the preference orderings of Row and Column); any actual scheme will, therefore, be a bad for some individuals. Furthermore, members of the tradition will emphasize that benevolent people commonly care not about the general elimination of poverty, but rather about they themselves making a contribution to amelioration of some particular instance or sort of poverty, and this is something individuals can accomplish without the forced co-operation of others.

Nevertheless, the endorsement of state provision of an income floor or safety net remains the most likely and salient route to the Small State. Endorsement of this role for the state most prominently distinguishes advocates of the Small State from advocates of the Taxing Minimal state (and their more anti-statist brethren). Still, the endorsed redistributive role for the state must be modest, if it is not to carry its advocate outside of the liberty tradition. The state's redistributive function must be seen as something of an afterthought or supplement to the primary purpose of the state, namely, the protection of persons' rightful liberties. A further complication is that certain justifications for *transfers* from some individuals to others turn out not to be genuinely *redistributive*. Let us consider two doctrinal refinements that seek to vindicate required *transfers* yet are not genuinely redistributive before proceeding to genuinely redistributive proposals.

The first defends a minimal safety net on the grounds that it is a public good *of the rights-protective sort*. According to this argument, the presence of a safety net enhances the safety of those whose lives, limbs, liberties or estates would otherwise be threatened by those in free fall. If the benefits to non-free-falling individuals of the enhanced safety (in terms of the better protection of their rights) exceed the costs of their contributions to the safety net, there is as strong a justification for taxation to finance the net as there is for such taxation for national defence (Lomasky, 1987). However, such transfers are not genuinely redistributive, and for this reason this endorsement of required transfers does not amount to a move rightward from the Taxing Minimal State to the Small State.

The second non-redistributive doctrinal refinement supporting transfer involves the adoption of a version of the 'Lockean proviso' (a term coined by Nozick, 1974: 178). A Lockean proviso specifies some way in which people's otherwise unobjectionable acquisition, possession, or deployment of private property can have an objectionable net impact upon other individuals, for instance, by making those other individuals worse off than they would be were private property not to exist. An advocate of such a proviso holds that acquisition, possession, or deployment of private property that would have an objectionable impact will, nevertheless, be acceptable if the acquirers, possessors or deployers compensate those individuals so that the net impact is not objectionable (Gaus, 1999: ch. 9). Requiring property holders to make these compensatory payments will *appear* to be taxation for redistributive purposes. But, since the rationale for requiring these payments is much more like the rationale for requiring tort feasors to compensate those they have damaged, it is not actually taxation; requiring such payments is consistent with mere Minimal Statism.

In what ways, then, may a member of the liberty tradition seek to justify genuinely *redistributive* transfers? The ways are as many as the types of underlying philosophical strategies to be found among members of the tradition. Kantian members may argue that whereas the primary way in which we manifest respect for persons is non-interference with their persons and choices, respect for persons also requires that one not gratuitously fail to assist individuals who need assistance merely to sustain their personhood or agency. According to this argument, to fail to assist such persons when that assistance has no significant opportunity cost is to fail to recognize the separate importance or moral standing of these individuals. Contractarian members may argue that reasonable agents bargaining about the basic enforceable norms that will morally govern their interaction will include a modest duty of assistance because, for each individual, the expected costs associated with this duty's enforcement will be less than the expected benefits (Morris, 1998: ch. 5). Consequentialist members may argue that the gains in social welfare generated by this modest level (and extent) of coerced assistance will exceed the losses in social welfare thereby generated.

Of course, advocates of each of these philosophical strategies who favour positions to the left of the small state will dispute their co-strategists' contentions. The more anti-statist Kantian will argue that any coercive taking treats its subject as a means to others' ends, while no failure to assist an individual, no matter how necessitous she is, treats her as a means. The more anti-statist contractarian will argue that reasonable people who have an appropriate level of information about themselves and their prospects will not all sign on to a society-wide mandatory assistance programme. The more anti-statist consequentialist will argue for the greater social value of voluntary philanthropic and mutual aid institutions compared with the actual value of mandatory assistance programmes. Each of these more anti-statist members of the tradition, in response to pro-redistribution arguments offered by advocates of *competing* philosophical strategies, will say that the appearance of those arguments proves that only adherents of her own philosophical strategy will be reliable enemies of the state.

'LEFT LIBERTARIANISM': EXTENDING THE LIBERTY TRADITION INTO STATISM?

We have argued that the liberty tradition, at *its* far right (i.e. statist) wing, accommodates a small state and *perhaps* some small genuinely redistributive transfers. Others, however, have recently attempted to push the liberty tradition to embrace statist conclusions of an egalitarian nature. Although, on our account of the liberty tradition, any movement to more statist positions is a movement to the right, these more statist, egalitarian proposals are generally described as 'leftist' (Steiner and Vallentyne, 2000). We shall follow convention here and speak of this egalitarian push for a more extensive and activist state as 'left libertarianism'. We can identify three strategies that have been pursued by left libertarians: (1) the endorsing of a more positive conception of liberty; (2) the supposition of equal claim to all social resources; and (3) an expansive interpretation of harming others.

Liberty as Effective Opportunity

The liberty tradition's devotion to individual freedom is, of course, a devotion to some version of negative freedom (Berlin, 1969). Now egalitarians have long criticized the liberty tradition for denying that freedom requires resources. Liberty, it has long been argued, is not simply about the absence of interferences with one's actions, but the ability to perform the actions a person desires. In short, a free person can do what she desires to do. As the British socialist R. H. Tawney put it, liberty implies 'the ability to act' (1931: 221).

Phillipe Van Parijs has recently advanced a far more sophisticated version of this so-called left-wing critique of negative liberty (for discussions, see Reeve and Williams, 2003). For Van Parijs, 'real freedom' involves three components: 'security, self-ownership and opportunity – in contrast to formal freedom, which only incorporates the first two' (1995: 22–3). A real libertarian society, Van Parijs argues, meets three conditions:

1 There is some well-enforced structure of rights (*security*).
2 This structure is such that each person owns herself (*self-ownership*).

3 This structure is such that each person has the greatest possible opportunity to do whatever she might want to do (*leximin opportunity*) (1995: 25).

As Van Parijs explains, this last condition requires that 'in a free society, the person with least opportunities has opportunities that are no smaller than those enjoyed by the person with the least opportunities under any other feasible arrangement' (1995: 25). And this in turn leads to the requirement that a society provides the highest sustainable basic income for all, including surfers who spend their days off Malibu (a position rejected by Rawls, 2002: 179).

Van Parijs argues – as he must, given his commitment to self-ownership – that the transfers of income required by such a scheme respect the self-ownership of the industrious and do not exploit them (1995: ch. 5). It is, he argues, the equalization of external endowments that drives redistribution: if someone produces without using resources in scarce supply she has the right to her full product, but because production always requires such resources, his basic income proposal does not lead to exploitation of the industrious.

Van Parijs's case that this proposal is not unfair to the industrious is long, sophisticated and complicated. It is so complex because he is trying to show what seems manifestly false: namely that a scheme in which the productive are required to provide the unproductive with the highest feasible income does not exploit the productive (using them as a mere resource for the surfing pleasure of others). If one has a claim to the fruits of one's labour, removing these fruits so that others can surf certainly appears unjust. Consider a version of an example of Van Parijs (1995: 160), in which the Greens and the Reds live in a society that only produces houses; each person receives a house of equal quality. In their production, the two groups work equally hard but the Reds, alas, are unlucky: their tools break, termites infest their structures, every time they paint it unexpectedly rains, and so on, such that they actually do not produce any houses. Van Parijs takes it as manifest that because the Reds and Greens work equally hard and get the same rewards no exploitation results; indeed he thinks it would be 'embarrassing' to see the Reds as exploiters. Yet for all their (wasted) effort the Reds have not managed to build houses to live in: they only live as well as the Greens because they have taken over some of the fruits of Green labour. Van Parijs's intuition is that luck must be irrelevant to justice (1995: 160): if some have managed to actually produce while others have tried and failed because of bad luck or natural adversities (see also Steiner, 2001), they have a claim on those who do produce. 'It's not our fault,' the Reds appear to claim, 'that we never actually *build* houses; those who succeed must give us houses as good as their own.' This is not an intuition shared by the liberty tradition (Rand, 1957). It violates doctrinal commitment IV of the liberty tradition against seizure of the fruits of another's labour, a commitment that, unsurprisingly, Van Parijs rejects (1995: 145ff). Moreover, Van Parijs's position seems to illustrate how violations of commitment IV also compromise persons' claims to self-sovereignty (doctrinal commitment II).

Equal Ownership of Original Property

In contrast to Van Parijs, the left libertarianism of Hillel Steiner advocates a radical version of negative liberty. Building his theory on a Hobbesian conception of negative liberty, Steiner holds that 'Broadly speaking, it suggests that a person is unfree to do an action if, and only if, his doing that action is rendered impossible by the action of another person' (1994: 8). If, am free to X if and only if I cannot be prevented by another from X-ing, then it follows that I am free to X if and only if none of the locations and objects necessary to X-ing are controlled by others, or would be controlled by others should I attempt to X. Thus 'Freedom is the possession of things' (1994: 39). But to have a right to freedom requires more: it is to have a title to a domain of locations and things: it is to have property rights (1994: 81). Thus all rights to freedom are property rights, and all property rights are rights to freedom, a claim made by many in the liberty tradition (see element IV).

Steiner claims that his account of liberty as property rights has a virtue lacking in competing theories of rights: compossibility. If rights are defined in terms of intentional actions – e.g. I have a right to see a film tomorrow and you have a right to wreck a building tomorrow – they can conflict:

> Whether my seeing a film tomorrow afternoon, and your wrecking a building then, are or are not jointly performable actions depends *inter alia* on whether the building you are to wreck is the cinema I'm to attend. If and only if we each have a duty to do these actions, those two duties are incompossible and so are the respective rights which they correlatively entail. (1994: 91–2)

Steiner thus argues that a system of rights can be guaranteed to be compossible – the performance of all the correlative duties are necessarily jointly possible – only if rights are defined in terms of property over a 'set of extensional elements' (control over objects, locations in time and so on).

Steiner's conception of liberty, rights and the compossibility requirement supports his entitlement account of justice. Justice involves a division of the world into various domains, each person possessing rights over some of it, this defining his sphere of freedom. Since, Steiner insists, rights protect our ability to choose, we are free (while alive) to transfer our holdings to others; the justice of a system of holdings will thus crucially depend on its history – whether it has been brought about by a series of legitimate, non-exploitative, choices.

Thus far all this looks like the liberty tradition, but we still need to know what constitutes a just initial distribution of the world's resources. Only if the initial distribution is just will the subsequent moves be just. And while Steiner insists that we own our bodies (though not our 'germ line genetic information'), he rejects the simple version of Lockean theory, according to which simply by mixing our labour with an unowned resource we appropriate the resource. But if we cannot justly appropriate nature that way, how do we generate just claims over natural resources?

Steiner is attracted to a quick route to egalitarianism. This quick argument for equality requires two premises: (1) justice involves treating equally those who are in relevant respects equal, and treating unequally those who are in relevant respects unequal; and (2) in these matters there are no relevant differences; so (3) justice demands equality. This argument leads Steiner to the claim that everyone is entitled to equal freedom and so to some sort of equal share of natural resources (1994: 216, 235). This equality of ownership may also be depicted as a version of the Lockean theory, in which we originally hold the world in common (Otsuka, 1998). Steiner supports the crucial premise (2) by arguing that rules of justice are intended to adjudicate disputes among those with different moral codes; any attempt to specify the relevant differences between those with different moral codes is sure to draw on those very codes that are being disputed. Consequently it is question-begging to advance any account of relevant differences (1994: 215) and so, from the perspective of justifying a system of justice, we must be completely sceptical that there are any relevant differences. So, in essence, the argument is that formal justice plus thoroughgoing scepticism about public relevant reasons equals equality: if 'no criterion for relevantly differentiating cases can be eligible to serve as a standard of distributive justice, the inference must be that no cases can be regarded as relevantly different; that is, all cases are relevantly alike' (1994: 216).

But the inference is not pellucid. Consider: (1) if justice involves treating equally those who are in relevant respects equal; and (2′) because of thoroughgoing scepticism about public reasons, it cannot be shown that people are equal in any relevant way; then (3′) justice doesn't demand treating everyone equally. As Steiner seems to realize, it is obscure how to apply a doctrine about relevant reasons (formal justice) given the complete absence of relevant reasons; formal justice makes sense in an account of the rule of law against a background of rights and relevant reasons. Although at some points in his *Essay on Rights* Steiner seems to distance himself from this argument, he comes back to its central claim in the same work: that in a world where all reasons are tendentious, only equality is impartial, and so only equality can be accepted by everyone as a 'lexically prior' rule of justice, overriding the rules of their own moral codes.

Steiner, and most left-libertarians, thus uphold some form of substantial income redistribution on the grounds of a claim by each to an equal share in natural resources. Unique to Van Parij's left libertarianism is a 'massive extension' of the scope of resources to be redistributed (taxed) by including job assets as an external resource (Van Parijs, 2003: 206). More specifically, Van Parijs seeks to identify and capture the employment 'rents' associated with jobs. (On the idea of rents, see Mack, 1992.) The core of Van Parijs' argument for treating jobs as assets is that, for a variety of reasons, workers are paid above the market-clearing wage; this constitutes a rent, and should be considered an additional element of their endowment (Van Parijs, 1995: 108). In our economies a worker's endowment can have a value of X (the income she would receive from her job given a market-clearing wage), but she may receive $X+n$; the value of n is a rent which Van Parijs counts as a social resource. Now suppose we are in a situation with a market clearing wage: the marginal entrant gets X and so collects no rent, but given uniform pricing all non-marginal entrants collect a surplus – they would work for $X-m$, but still receive X. Van Parijs, however, explicitly excludes these as rents (1995: 264, n35). His complaint, then, is not that many people get more than they require to do their job; it is that if Marge the marginal worker gets more than she requires, there exists some unemployed person Maggie who would take the job at a lower wage than Marge, but Marge has claimed this scare resource and so effectively denies to it Maggie. Van Parijs sees everyone who gets rent n as having claimed a scarce social resource, and so their rent may be taxed away. However jobs cannot be considered simply as unalloyed resources to be distributed, but as packages of rights and liabilities (Williams, 2003). Given these liabilities, many do not want a job even if it is offered to them: it does not count as a resource to them since they would not take it at any price because since they don't want to work. It looks as if Van Parijs is exploiting those who work to support those who do not want to: those uninterested in actually doing the job receive a sort of compensation for

being excluded from it. Moreover, this is especially odd in a 'libertarian' theory: the benefits of an uncoerced agreement between two free agents employing their labour and property – an employment contract – is said to generate a social resource to which all others have something like an equal claim.

Extending Harmful Action

If equal ownership of resources cannot be established as a default, the egalitarian interpretation of Locke must provide a positive argument as to why we all possess equal claims to external resources. If natural resources are owned in common, how did *that* come about? Far more plausible is the view that natural resources are not originally owned at all – that we all *equally* lack original rights over natural resources – but that any act of acquisition must avoid harming others, which leads to something like the liberty tradition's understanding of the Lockean proviso. Now a third 'leftward' (statist) push comes from attempts to widen the concept of harm, such that almost any economic activity constitutes a harm to others.

Thomas Pogge (2002) has recently argued along these lines. Pogge builds his case on what looks like the liberty tradition's understanding of negative rights, in particular the right not to be harmed (see element X). However, he argues that 'simple libertarianism' is flawed because it fails to appreciate how institutions create harm (2002: 172). In particular, Pogge insists that the imposition of the 'global economic order' causes harm: it 'engenders war, torture and starvation' (2002: 173), and so anyone who participates in that order is contributing to injustice (2002: 211). Indeed, all participants help starve the poor (2002: 214). Thus global redistribution is required to compensate for harms done, as well as to satisfy a version of the Lockean proviso (2002: ch. 8; compare Steiner, 1994: ch. 8).

Note how this argument depends on the idea that there exists an overall global system which is to be the object of our evaluation (rather than, say individual actions), that this system is coercively imposed on the poor, that as a consequence of this system the poor are harmed, and that each one of us is 'deeply implicated' in the harm perpetrated by the system (2002: 142). This is not the place to evaluate these controversial claims about international economics and politics [see further Chapters 17 and 22]. It is important here to note, though, the way that the argument seeks to avoid the normative individualism of the liberty tradition (element I). The idea that there exists an all-encompassing system in which all participate – it is almost impossible to opt out – and so we are all responsible for the results of the system, makes each individual responsible for all the results of 'the global system', which are almost solely the results of other people's actions and decisions.

CONCLUSION

We have characterized the liberty tradition both by its doctrinal commitments and by its internal controversies, and we have criticized attempts to extend it towards statism. The unity of the liberty tradition is comprised by its convergence – not, of course, perfect, but substantial – on the key doctrinal commitments. The tradition's core commitment is a normative individualism that grounds the primary political norm of individual liberty and responsibility; individual liberty is what each individual may *legitimately demand* of each other individual, and individuals are responsible for their own actions and decisions. Respect for the individual and his liberty requires respect for that individual's property rights. The liberty tradition refuses to divide up liberty into the personal and the economic, and it refuses to equate freedom with the power to do what one wants. The market, as well as private property, is fundamental to the tradition. In a market order, desirable social order *emerges* out of the choices that individuals make when their rights are secure. And when these rights are secure, individuals tend to benefit from their own productive decisions and bear the costs of their own activities. In the liberty tradition, coercion is first and foremost justified on the grounds that it is required to block or nullify infringements upon the rightful claims of individuals; use of coercion that infringes upon an individual's control of her person or property is illicit. Or, we might say, justified coercion prevents harms to others, but we must be careful not to stretch the concept of harm so that everything we do always harms others. As the liberty tradition sees it, the state – a mechanism of organized violence – ought to be bound by the morality that applies to all. But, of course, it has not been bound: the state regularly engages in unjustified aggression, plunder, and meddlesomeness.

The liberty tradition's internal disputes focus on the extent of the justified state, from the market anarchist who denies that any monopoly of violence can be justified, to the advocate of the Small State who is willing to countenance not only the state but coercive taxation to promote public goods and correct various 'market failures'. The market anarchist is apt to see the small statist as an ally of the modern expansive state, lending legitimacy to the idea that government's job is to 'fix the market'. The small statist responds that '[classical] liberalism is not anarchism, nor has it anything whatsoever

to do with anarchism' (von Mises, 1985: 37). The classical liberal, said von Mises, is no more an enemy of the state than he is an enemy of sulphuric acid; both can be useful, and both are dangerous (1985: 38). At least about that last part, all members of the liberty tradition will agree.

NOTES

1 Slightly more cumbersome labels for this stance would be 'private property anarchism' and 'anarcho-capitalism'. 'Individualist anarchism' would be fine except for the residue within actual individualist anarchists, such as Benjamin Tucker (1926) and Lysander Spooner (1971), of belief in the labour theory of value. See further Murray Rothbard (2000).

2 See Nozick (1974: chs 4, 5). For Nozick, this greater scope for suppression allows for a legitimate 'ultra-minimal' state, but that legitimacy is only retained if the 'ultra-minimal' state compensates those who are disadvantaged by these prohibitions and, thereby, transforms itself into the 'minimal' state.

REFERENCES

Barnett, Randy E. (1998) *The Structure of Liberty.* Oxford: Clarendon.

Bentham, Jeremy (1987) *Introduction to the Principles of Morals and Legislation.* In Alan Ryan, ed., *Utilitarianism and Other Essays.* Harmondsworth: Penguin.

Berlin, Isaiah (1969) 'Two concepts of liberty'. In his *Four Essays on Liberty.* Oxford: Oxford University Press.

Brittan, Samuel (1988) *A Restatement of Economic Liberalism.* Atlantic Highlands, NJ: Humanities.

Buchanan, James M. (1975) *The Limits of Liberty: Between Anarchy and Leviathan.* Chicago: University of Chicago Press.

Buchanan, James M. and Gordon Tullock (1965) *The Calculus of Consent: Logical Foundations of Constitutional Democracy.* Ann Arbor, MI: University of Michigan Press.

Calabresi, Guido and A. Douglas Melamed (1972) 'Property rights, liability rules and inalienability: one view of the cathedral'. *Harvard Law Review*, 8: 1089–128.

Cowen, Tyler (1988) *The Theory of Market Failure.* Lanham, MD: University Publishing Association.

Cowen, Tyler (1992) 'Law as a public good: the economics of anarchy'. *Economics and Philosophy*, 8: 249–67.

Cowen, Tyler with Gregory Kavka (2003) 'The public goods rationale for government and the circularity problem'. *Politics, Philosophy and Economics*, 2 (June): 265–78.

De Jasay, Anthony (1991) *Choice, Contract, Consent: A Restatement of Liberalism*. London: Institute of Economic Affairs.

Friedman, David (1973) *The Machinery of Freedom*. New York: Harper and Row.

Friedman, Milton and Rose Friedman (1980) *Free to Choose*. London: Secker and Warburg.

Gaus, Gerald F. (1983) 'Public and private interests in liberal political economy, old and new'. In S. I. Benn and G. F. Gaus, eds, *Public and Private in Social Life*. New York: St Martin's, 183–222.

Gaus, Gerald F. (1999) *Social Philosophy*. Armonk, NY: Sharpe.

Gray, John (1986) *Liberalism*. Milton Keynes: Open University Press.

Hayek, F. A. (1944) *The Road to Serfdom*. Chicago: University of Chicago Press.

Hayek, F. A. (1973) *Law, Legislation and Liberty*. Vol. I, *Rules and Order*. London: Routledge.

Hayek, F. A. (1976) *Law, Legislation and Liberty*. Vol. II, *The Mirage of Social Justice*. London: Routledge.

Hayek, F. A. (1979) *Law, Legislation and Liberty*. Vol. III, *The Political Order of a Free People*. London: Routledge.

Hayek, F. A. (1991) 'The use of knowledge'. In Richard M. Ebeling, ed., *Austrian Economics*. Hillsdale, MI: Hillsdale College Press, ch. 14.

Locke, John (1960) Second Treatise of Government. In Peter Laslett, ed., *Two Treatises of Government*. Cambridge: Cambridge University Press.

Lomasky, Loren E. (1987) *Persons, Rights, and the Moral Community*. New York: Oxford University Press.

Machan, Tibor (1989) *Individuals and Their Rights*. La Salle, IL: Open Court.

MacIntyre, Alasdair (1988) *Whose Justice? Which Rationality?* Notre Dame, IN: University of Notre Dame Press.

Mack, Eric (1990) 'Self-ownership and the right of property'. *The Monist*, 73 (October): 519–43.

Mack, Eric (1992) 'Gauthier on rights and economic rents'. *Social Philosophy and Policy*, 9: 171–200.

Mack, Eric (1999) 'In defense of individualism'. *Ethical Theory and Moral Practice*, 2: 87–115.

Mack, Eric (2000) 'In defense of the jurisdiction theory of rights'. *Journal of Ethics*, 4 (January–March): 71–98.

Mill, John Stuart (1991) *On Liberty*. In John Gray, ed., *On Liberty and Other Essays*. New York: Oxford University Press.

Morris, Christopher (1998) *An Essay on the Modern State*. Cambridge: Cambridge University Press.

Narveson, Jan (1988) *The Libertarian Idea*. Philadelphia: Temple University Press.

Nozick, Robert (1974) *Anarchy, State and Utopia*. New York: Basic.

Oakeshott, Michael (1975) *On Human Conduct*. Oxford: Clarendon.

O'Brien, D. P. (1975) *The Classical Political Economists*. Oxford: Clarendon.

Otsuka, Michael (1998) 'Self-ownership and equality: a Lockean reconciliation'. *Philosophy and Public Affairs*, 27 (Winter): 65–92.

Pogge, Thomas (2002) *World Poverty and Human Rights*. Oxford: Polity.

Rand, Ayn (1957) *Atlas Shrugged*. New York: Dutton.

Rawls, John (2002) *Justice as Fairness: A Restatement*, ed. Erin Kelly Cambridge, MA: Belknap.

Reeve, Andrew and Andrew Williams, eds (2003) *Real Libertarianism Assessed: Political Theory after Van Parijs*. New York: Palgrave Macmillan.

Robbins, Lord (1961) *The Theory of Economic Policy in Classical English Political Economy*. London: Macmillan.

Rothbard, Murray (2000) 'The Spooner–Tucker doctrine: an economist's view'. In *Egalitarianism as a Revolt against Nature*, 2nd edn. Auburn, AL: Ludwig von Mises Institute.

Schmidtz, David (1991) *The Limits of Government: An Essay on the Public Goods Argument*. Boulder, CO: Westview.

Simmons, John A. (1993) *On the Edge of Anarchy: Locke, Consent and the Limits of Society*. Princeton, NJ: Princeton University Press.

Smith, Adam (1976) *An Inquiry into the Nature and Causes of the Wealth of Nations*, ed. W. B. Todd. Oxford: Clarendon.

Spooner, Lysander (1971) *The Collected Works of Lysander Spooner*. Weston, MA: M. and S.

Steiner, Hillel (1994) *An Essay on Rights*. Cambridge, MA: Blackwell.

Steiner, Hillel (2001) 'The ethics of redistribution'. *Acta Philosophica Fennica*, 68: 37–45.

Steiner, Hillel and Peter Vallentyne, eds (2000) *Left-Libertarianism and Its Critics: The Contemporary Debate*. Basingstoke: Palgrave.

Tawney, R. H. (1931) *Equality*. New York: Harcourt, Brace.

Tucker, Benjamin (1926) *Individual Liberty*. New York: Vanguard.

Van Parijs, Phillipe (1995) *Real Freedom for All: What (If Anything) Can Justify Capitalism?* Oxford: Clarendon.

Van Parijs, Philippe (2003) 'Hybrid justice, patriotism and democracy'. In *Real Liberterianism Assessed: Political Theory after Van Parijs*, ed. Andrew Reeve and Andrew Williams. Houndsmill, Basingstoke: Palgrave: 201–214.

Von Mises, Ludwig (1985) *Liberalism in the Classical Tradition*. San Francisco: Cobden.

Williams, Andrew (2003) 'Resource egalitarianism and the limits to basic income'. In *Real Libertarianism Assessed: Political Theory after Van Parijs*, ed. Andrew Reeve and Andrew Williams. Houndsmill, Basingstoke: Palgrave: 111–35.

10

Conservative Theories

JOHN KEKES

Conservatism is a political morality. It is political because it aims at political arrangements that make a society good, and it is moral because it holds that a society is good if it enables people living in it to live good lives, that is, lives that are personally satisfying and beneficial for others. Conservatism, like liberalism [see Chapters 7–9] and socialism [see Chapters 6 and 30], has different versions, partly because conservatives often disagree with each other about the particular political arrangements that ought to be conserved.[1] There is no disagreement among them, however, that the reasons for or against those arrangements are to be found in the history of the society whose arrangements they are. This commits conservatives to denying that the reasons are to be derived from a hypothetical contract, or from an imagined ideal order, or from what is supposed to be beneficial for the whole of humanity. In preference to these and other alternatives, conservatives look to the history of their own society because it exerts a formative influence on their present lives and on how it is reasonable for them to want to live in the future. The conservative attitude, however, is not an unexamined prejudice in favour of the historical arrangements of the conservatives' society. They are in favour of conserving only those arrangements that their history has shown to be conducive to good lives.

Another reason for the disagreements among conservatives is that, although they agree in regarding certain questions as basic to political morality and in identifying the range of reasonable answers to them, they nevertheless give answers that fall at different points within that range. The combination of the questions that are thought to be basic and the answers to them that are thought to be reasonable defines different versions of conservatism, explains their differences, and distinguishes between conservative, liberal, socialist, and other theories.

These questions are:

- To what extent should political arrangements be based on history?
- How does the diversity of values affect political arrangements?
- What should be the relation between individual autonomy and social authority?
- How should political arrangements respond to the prevalence of evil?

The discussion will proceed by considering these questions and the different answers conservatives give to them. It will conclude by identifying a version of conservatism that appears to be the most reasonable.

TO WHAT EXTENT SHOULD POLITICAL ARRANGEMENTS BE BASED ON HISTORY?

Conservatives agree that history is the appropriate starting point, but some of them believe that it is not a contingent fact that certain political arrangements have historically fostered good lives, while others have been detrimental to them. Conservatives who believe this think that there is a deeper explanation for the historical success or failure of various arrangements. There is a moral orders in reality. Political arrangements that conform to this order foster good lives, those that conflict with it are bound to make lives worse. These conservatives are committed to a belief about the nature and scope of rational understanding, which, on the one hand, confines it to the promulgation of abstract general propositions and, on the other hand, extends its relevance to the whole of human life – a doctrine which may be called 'rationalism'. And there is as much difference between rational enquiry and 'rationalism' as there is between scientific enquiry and 'scientism', and it is a difference of the same kind. Moreover, it is important that a writer who wishes to contest the excessive claims of 'rationalism' should observe the difference, because if he fails to do so he will not only be liable to self-contradiction (for his argument will itself be nothing if it is not rational), but also he will make himself appear the advocate of irrationality, which is going further than he either needs or intends to go. (Oakeshott, 1993: 99–100)

Rationalistically inclined conservatives are willing to learn from history, but only because history points beyond itself toward more fundamental considerations. That these considerations centre on a moral order is agreed to by all of them. But they nevertheless disagree whether the order is providential, as it is held to be by various religions; or a Platonic chain of being at whose pinnacle is the Form of the Good; or the Hegelian unfolding of the dialectic of clashing forces culminating in the final unity of reason and action; or the one reflected by natural law, which, if adhered to, would remove all obstacles from the path of realizing the purpose inherent in human nature; or some further possibility.

Such disagreements notwithstanding, rationalist conservatives are convinced that the ultimate reasons for or against specific political arrangements are to be found in the moral order of reality. They attribute disagreements to insufficient rationality, and they believe that there is an absolute and eternal truth about these matters. The problem is finding out what it is, or, if it has already been revealed, finding out how the canonical text ought to be interpreted.[2] This belief is held not only by some conservatives, but also by some left-wing and right-wing radicals who otherwise disagree with conservatives. These radicals believe that the laws that govern human affairs have been discovered. Some say that the laws are those of history, others that they are of sociology, psychology, sociobiology, or ethology. Their shared view is, however, that a good society is possible only if its political arrangements reflect the relevant laws. Misery is a consequence of ignorance or wickedness, which leads to arrangements contrary to the laws. History, as they see it, is the painful story of societies banging their collective heads against the wall. They have found the key, however: the door is now open, history has reached its final phase, and from here on all manner of things would be well, if only their prescriptions were followed.

The historical record of societies whose political arrangements were inspired by rationalistic schemes is most alarming. They have tended to impose their certainties on unwilling or indoctrinated people, and they have often made their lives miserable, all the while promising great improvements just after the present crisis, which has usually turned out to be permanent. If the last century has a moral achievement, it is the realization that proceeding in this way is morally and politically dangerous.

Opposed to these rationalistically inclined conservatives and non-conservative utopians are sceptical conservatives. Their scepticism, however, may take either an extreme or a moderate form. The extreme form is fideism. It involves reliance on faith and the repudiation of reason. Fideistic conservatives reject reason as a guide to the political arrangements that a good society ought to have. (It follows from their nature that systematic arguments for fideistic conservatism are rare. One notable exception is Maistre, 1965.) It makes no difference to them whether the reasons are scientific, metaphysical, or merely empirical. They are opposed to relying on reason in whatever form it may take. They believe that all reasoning is ultimately based on assumptions that must be accepted on faith.

Their rejection of the guidance of reason, however, leaves fideistic conservatives with the problem of how to decide what political arrangements they ought to favour. The solution they have historically offered is either to be guided by faith, or to perpetuate the existing arrangements simply because they are familiar. The dangers of these solutions have been made as evident by the historical record as the dangers of the preceding approach. Faith breeds dogmatism, the persecution of those who reject it or who hold other faiths, and it provides no ground for regarding the political arrangements it favours as better than contrary ones. Whereas the perpetuation of the status quo on account of its familiarity makes it impossible to improve the existing political arrangements.

Between the dangerous extremes of rationalistic politics and the fideistic repudiation of reason is scepticism that takes a moderate form. Conservatives who hold this view need not deny that there is a moral order in reality. They are committed only to denying that reliable knowledge of it can be had. Sceptical conservatives are far more impressed by human fallibility than by the success of efforts to overcome it. They think that the claims of revelation, canonical texts, and knowledge of eternal verities stand in need of persuasive evidence. They regard these claims only as credible as the evidence that is available to support them. But the evidence is as questionable as the claims that rest on it. According to sceptical conservatives, it is therefore far more reasonable to look to the historical record of various political arrangements than to endeavour to justify or criticize them by appealing to metaphysical or utopian considerations that are bound to be less reliable than the historical record.[3]

Scepticism, however, does not lead conservatives to deny that it is possible to evaluate political arrangements by adducing reasons for or against them. What they deny is that good reasons must be absolute and universal. The scepticism of these conservatives, therefore, is not a global doubt about it being possible and desirable to be reasonable, to base beliefs on the evidence available in support of them, and to make the strength of beliefs commensurate with the strength of the evidence. Their scepticism is about deducing political arrangements from metaphysical or utopian premises. They want political arrangements to be firmly rooted in the experiences of the people who are subject to them. Since these experiences are unavoidably historical, it is to history that sceptical conservatives look for supporting evidence. They will not try to deduce from metaphysical premises which orifices of the body are suitable for sexual pleasure, or evaluate people's desires on the basis of their conformity to some utopian ideal that the people do not share. Scepticism thus avoids the pitfalls of basing political arrangements on speculation about what lies beyond experience and of suspecting all efforts to make reasonable political arrangements because of a global distrust of reason.

It seems, then, that the most reasonable answer to the question about the extent to which political arrangements should be based on history follows from moderate scepticism. There is a presumption in favour of the arrangements that have endured. Their endurance is a prima facie reason for supposing both that they have been supported by the people subject to them and that they have enhanced the possibility of living lives that are personally satisfying and beneficial for others. If this presumption is justified, then there is a reason against changing the arrangements that have stood the test of time. The presumption, of course, may not be justified. The arrangements may have endured because opposition to them was made too dangerous by powerful interests or because people were manipulated into accepting them. If the case for changing them is based on a cogent claim that the arrangements have endured because of force or manipulation, then it should be seriously considered. But if the case for changing them is inspired by the latest utopian, metaphysical, or revolutionary theory, then much more needs to be said in support of it to represent a reasonable challenge to the presumption.

HOW DOES THE DIVERSITY OF VALUES AFFECT POLITICAL ARRANGEMENTS?

Conservatives are committed to political arrangements that foster good lives, so they must have a view about what lives are good, about what obligations, virtues, and satisfactions are worth valuing. They must have a view, that is, about the values that make lives good. Values, however, appear to be diverse. There are countless obligations, virtues, and satisfactions, countless ways of combining them and evaluating their respective importance, and so there seem to be countless ways in which lives can be good. Conservatives, therefore, must have a view about the diversity of values because it has a fundamental influence on the reasons that can be offered for or against particular political arrangements. The problem is that there are three widely held but mutually exclusive views: absolutism, relativism, and pluralism.

Absolutists believe that the diversity of values is apparent, not real. They concede that there are many values, but they think that there is a universal and objective standard that can be appealed to in evaluating their respective importance. This standard may be a highest value, the *summum bonum*; other values can be ranked on the basis of their contribution to its realization. The highest value may be happiness, duty, God's will, a life of virtue, and so forth. Or the standard may be a principle, such as the categorical imperative, the greatest happiness for the greatest number, the Ten Commandments, or the Golden Rule. If a choice needs to be made between different values, then the principle will determine which value ought to take precedence. Absolutists, then, give as their reason for preferring some political arrangements over others that the preferred ones conform more closely to the universal and objective standard than the alternatives to it.[4]

Absolutism often has a rationalistic basis. For the most frequently offered reason in favour of the universality and objectivity of the standard that absolutists regard as the highest is that it reflects the moral order of reality. This is the inspiration behind the attempts to establish ecclesiastical polities, on the right, and egalitarian, utopian, or millennial ones, on the left. Nevertheless, the connection between absolutism and rationalism is not a necessary one. Standards can be regarded as universal and objective even if they are not metaphysically sanctioned. If, however, their advocates eschew metaphysics, then they must provide some other reason for regarding some particular standard as universal and objective. One such reason will be considered shortly.

It is a considerable embarrassment to absolutists that the candidates for universal and objective standards are also diverse, and thus face the same problems as the values whose diversity is supposed to be diminished by them. Absolutists acknowledge this, and explain it in terms of human shortcomings that prevent people from recognizing the one and true standard. The history of religious wars, revolutions, left-wing and right-wing tyrannies, and persecutions of countless unbelievers, all aiming to rectify human shortcomings, testifies to the dangers inherent in this explanation.

Opposed to absolutism is relativism. Relativists regard the diversity of values as real: there are many values and there are many ways of combining and ranking them. There is no universal and objective standard that could be appealed to in resolving disagreements about the identity and comparative importance of values. A good society, however, requires some consensus about what is accepted as a possibility and what is placed beyond limits. The political arrangements of a good society reflect this consensus, and the arrangements change as the consensus does. What counts as a value and how important it is depends, then, according to relativists, on the consensus of a society. A value is what is valued in a particular context; all values, therefore, are context-dependent.

This is not to say that values and the political arrangements that reflect them cannot be reasonably justified or criticized. They can be, but the reasons that are given for or against them count as reasons only within the context of the society whose values and political arrangements they are. The reasons appeal to the prevailing consensus, and they will not and are not meant to persuade outsiders. The ultimate appeal of relativists is to point at their arrangements and say: this is what we do here. If relativism takes a conservative form, it often results in the romantic celebration of national identity, of the spirit of a people and an age, of the shared landscape, historical milestones, ceremonies, stylistic conventions, manners, and rituals that unite a society.[5]

Just as absolutism is naturally allied to a rationalistic orientation, so relativism is readily combined with fideism. If there is no discernible moral order in reality, then the best guide to good lives and to the political arrangements that foster them is the faith that has prevailed in a society. But the faith of one society is different from the faith of another. It is only to be expected therefore that good lives and political arrangements will correspondingly differ.

Relativism appears to avoid the dangers of dogmatism and repression that so often engulf absolutism, but it does not. Relativism is no less prone to dogmatism and repression than absolutism. From the fact that the political arrangements of the relativist's society are not thought to be binding outside of it, nothing follows about the manner in which they are held within it. If the world is full of people and societies whose values are hostile to the values of the relativist's society, then there is much the more reason to guard jealously those values. If the justification of the political arrangements of a society is the consensus about values that prevails in it, then any political arrangement becomes justifiable just so long as a sufficiently large number of people in the society support the consensus favouring them. Thus slavery, female circumcision, the maltreatment of minorities, child prostitution, the mutilation of criminals, blood feuds, bribery, and a lot of other political arrangements may become sanctioned on the grounds that that is what happens to be valued here.

These pitfalls of the rationalistic aspirations of absolutism and the fideistic orientation of relativism make them unreliable sources of reasons for evaluating political arrangements. It is with some relief then that conservatives may turn to pluralism as an intermediate position between these dangerous extremes. Pluralists are in partial agreement and disagreement with both absolutists and relativists. According to pluralists, there is a universal and objective standard, but it is applicable only to some values. The standard is universal and objective enough to apply to *some* values that must be recognized by all political arrangements that foster good lives, but it is not sufficiently universal and objective to apply to *all* the many diverse values that may contribute to good lives. The standard, in other words, is a minimal one. (For accounts of pluralism in general, see Kekes, 1993; Rescher, 1993.) [See also Chapter 18.][6]

It is possible to establish with reference to it some universal and objective values required by all good lives, but the standard does not specify all the values that good lives require. It regards some political arrangements as necessary for good lives, but it allows for a generous plurality of possible political arrangements beyond the necessary minimum. The standard operates in the realm of moral necessity, and it leaves open what happens in the realm of moral possibility. The standard thus accommodates part of the universal values of absolutism and part of the context-dependent values of relativism. Absolutism prevails in the realm of moral necessity; relativism in the realm of moral possibility.

The source of this standard is human nature. (For a general account of the political significance of human nature for politics, see Berry, 1986. For the specific connection between human nature and conservatism, see Berry, 1983.) To understand human nature sufficiently for the purposes of this standard does not require plumbing the depths of the soul, unravelling the obscure springs of human motivation, or conducting scientific research. It does not call for any metaphysical commitment and it can be held without subscribing to the existence of a natural law. It is enough for it to concentrate on normal people in a commonsensical way. It will then become obvious that good lives depend on the satisfaction of basic physiological, psychological, and social needs: for nutrition, shelter, and rest; for companionship, self-respect, and the hope for a good or better life; for the division of labour, justice, and predictability in human affairs; and so forth. The satisfaction of these needs is a universal and objective requirement of all good lives, whatever the social context may be in which they are lived. If the political arrangements of a society foster their satisfaction, that is a reason for having and conserving them; if the political arrangements hinder their satisfaction, that is a reason for reforming them.

If absolutists merely asserted this, and if relativists merely denied it, then the former would be right and the latter wrong. But both go beyond the mere assertion and denial of this point. Satisfying these minimum requirements of human nature is necessary but not sufficient for good lives. Absolutists go beyond the minimum and think that their universal and objective standard applies all the way up to the achievement of good lives. Relativists deny that there is such a standard. In this respect, pluralists side with relativists and oppose absolutists. Pluralists think that beyond the minimum level there is a plurality of values, of ways of ranking them, and of good lives that embody these values and rankings. According to pluralists, then, the political arrangements of a society ought to protect the minimum requirements of good lives and ought to foster a plurality of good lives beyond the minimum.

If pluralism takes a conservative form, it provides two important possibilities for its defenders. The first is a universal and objective reason in favour of those political arrangements of the conservative's society that protect the minimum requirements and against those political arrangements that violate them. It motivates, gives direction to, and sets the goal of intended reforms. It makes it possible to draw reasonable comparisons among different societies on the basis of how well they protect the conditions on which all good lives depend. Pluralistic conservatism thus avoids the objection to relativism that it sanctions any political arrangement so long as a wide enough consensus supports it. Second, pluralistic conservatism is most receptive to the view that the best guide to the political arrangements that a society ought to have beyond the minimum level is the history of the society. It is that history, rather than any metaphysical or utopian consideration, that is most likely to provide the relevant considerations for or against the political arrangements that present themselves as possibilities in that society. It is thus that pluralistic

conservatism avoids the dangers of dogmatism and repression that beset absolutism.

The most reasonable answer to the question of how the diversity of values should affect political arrangements is that the arrangements that concern the minimum requirements of good lives are not affected at all, but those that concern requirements beyond the minimum are affected. Political arrangements ought to protect the universal and objective conditions that must be met by all good lives. Societies and their arrangements can be reasonably compared and evaluated on the basis of how well they protect them. There are also other conditions that vary with societies. They are particular, not universal, and they reflect the diversity of values. They can also be reasonably evaluated, but only within the context of particular societies. Their evaluation depends on whether or not they have historically enhanced the chances of good lives. If they have, they ought to be protected; if they have not, they ought to be changed.

The political arrangements that pluralistic conservatives favour are committed to a familiar list of values: justice, freedom, the rule of law, order, legal and political equality, prosperity, peace, civility, happiness, and so forth. There is likely to be a significant overlap between the conservative list and those which liberals, socialists, or others may draw up. Nevertheless, there will be also a significant difference between pluralistic conservative politics and the politics of others: this kind of conservatism is genuinely pluralistic, whereas the politics of the alternative approaches are not. Liberals, socialists, and others are committed to regarding some few values as overriding. What makes them liberals, socialists, or whatever is their claim that when the few values they favour conflict with the less favoured ones, then the ones they favour should prevail. If they did not believe this, they would cease to be liberals, socialists, or whatever. Pluralistic conservatives reject this approach. Their commitment is to the conservation of the whole system of values of a society. Its conservation sometimes requires favouring a particular value over another, sometimes the reverse. Pluralistic conservatives hold this to be true of all values. They differ from others in refusing to make the *a priori* commitment that others make to the overridingness of any particular value or small number of values in the prevailing system of values.

WHAT SHOULD BE THE RELATION BETWEEN INDIVIDUAL AUTONOMY AND SOCIAL AUTHORITY?

It is common ground among most political moralities that human beings are essentially social in their nature. In good lives, therefore, the individual and social constituents are inextricably connected. That, however, still leaves the question of which constituent should be dominant. It has far-reaching political consequences in how it is answered. If the individual constituent dominates over the social one, then the desirable political arrangements will foster individual autonomy at the expense of social authority. If, on the other hand, the social constituent is ultimately more important, then the favoured political arrangements will strengthen social authority. The answer that favours individual autonomy over social authority is typically given by many liberals, especially those influenced by Kant. The opposing answer is usually championed by absolutist conservatives, on the right; socialists and Marxists, on the left; and communitarians, somewhere in between [see further Chapter 13]. This leaves room for yet another answer, to be considered shortly, offered by conservatives who are sceptics and pluralists.

Putting individual autonomy before social authority faces two very serious problems. First, it assumes that good lives must be autonomous and cannot involve the acceptance of some form of social authority. If this were so, no military or devoutly religious life, no life in static, traditional, hierarchical societies, no life, that is, that involves the subordination of the individual's will and judgement to what is regarded as a higher purpose, could be good. This would require thinking of the vast majority of lives outside of prosperous Western societies as bad. The mistake is to slide from the reasonable view that autonomous lives may be good to the unreasonable view that a life cannot be good unless it is autonomous. This is not only mistaken in its own right, but also incompatible with the pluralism to which liberals who think this way claim themselves to be committed [see further Chapters 8, 18 and 30].

Second, if a good society is one that fosters the good lives of the individuals who live in it, then giving precedence to autonomy over authority cannot be right, since autonomous lives may be bad. That the will and judgement of individuals take precedence over social authority leaves it open whether the resulting lives will be sufficiently satisfying personally and beneficial for others to be good. Autonomous lives may be frustrating and harmful. The most casual reflection on history shows that social authority must prevail over the individual autonomy of fanatics, criminals, fools, and crazies, if a society is indeed dedicated to fostering good lives.

The problems of letting social authority override individual autonomy are no less serious. What is the reason for thinking that if social authority prevails over individual autonomy, then the resulting lives will be good? Lives cannot just be pronounced good by some social authority. They must actually be satisfying and beneficial, and that must ultimately be judged by the individuals whose will is unavoidably engaged in causing and enjoying the satisfactions and the benefits. Their will and judgement may of course be influenced by the prescriptions of a social authority. But no matter how strong that influence is, it cannot override the ultimate autonomy of individuals in finding what is satisfying or beneficial for them. As the lamentable historical record shows, however, this has not prevented countless religious and ideological authorities from stigmatizing individuals who reject their prescriptions as heretics, infidels, class enemies, maladjusted, or living with false consciousness, in bad faith, or in a state of sin. The result is a repressive society whose dogmatism is reinforced by specious moralizing.

How then is the question to be answered? Which constituent of good lives should be regarded as primary? The answer, as before, is to eschew the two extremes and look for an intermediate position that accommodates the salvageable portions of both. There is no need to insist that either individual autonomy or social authority should systematically prevail over the other. Both are necessary for good lives. Instead of engaging in futile arguments about their comparative importance, it is far more illuminating to understand that they are parts of two interdependent aspects of the same underlying activity. The activity is that of individuals trying to make good lives for themselves. Its two aspects are the individual and the social; autonomy and authority are their respective parts; and the connecting link between them is tradition. The intermediate position that is reasonably favoured by conservatives may therefore be called traditionalism.[7]

A tradition is a set of customary beliefs, practices, and actions that has endured from the past to the present and attracted the allegiance of people so that they wish to perpetuate it. A tradition may be reflective and designed, like the deliberations of the Supreme Court, or unreflective and spontaneous, like sports fans rooting for their teams; it may have a formal institutional framework, like the Catholic Church, or it may be unstructured, like mountain climbing; it may be competitive, like the Olympics; largely passive, like going to the opera; humanitarian, like the Red Cross; self-centred, like jogging; honorific, like the Nobel Prize; or punitive, like criminal proceedings. Traditions may be religious, horticultural, scientific, athletic, political, stylistic, moral, aesthetic, commercial, medical, legal, military, educational, architectural, and so on and so on. They permeate human lives. (For an account of tradition in general, see Shils, 1981; see also Casey, 1978; Kekes, 1998: ch. 6; MacIntyre, 1981: ch. 15; Eliot, 1975.)

When individuals gradually and experimentally form their conceptions of a good life, what they are to a very large extent doing is deciding which traditions they should participate in. This decision may be taken from the inside of the traditions to which they belong, or from the outside by considering other traditions that appeal, repel, bore, or interest them. The decisions may be conscious, deliberate, clear-cut yes-or-no choices, they may be ways of unconsciously, unreflectively falling in with familiar patterns, or they may be at various points in between. The bulk of the activities of individuals concerned with living in ways that strike them as good is composed of participation in the various traditions of their society.

As they participate in them, they exercise their autonomy. They make choices and judgements, their wills are engaged, they learn from the past and plan for the future. But they do so in the frameworks of various traditions which authoritatively provide them with the relevant choices, with the matters that are left to their judgements, and with standards that within a tradition determine what choices and judgements are good or bad, reasonable or unreasonable. Their exercise of autonomy is the individual aspect of their conformity to their tradition's authority, which is the social aspect of what they are doing. They act autonomously *by* following the authoritative patterns of the traditions to which they feel allegiance. When a Catholic goes to confession, a violinist gives a concert, a football player scores a touchdown, a student graduates, a judge sentences a criminal, then the individual and the social, the autonomous and the authoritative, the traditional pattern of doing it and a particular person's doing of it are inextricably mixed. To understand what is going on in terms of individual autonomy is as one-sided as it is to do so in terms of social authority. Both play an essential role, and understanding what is going on requires understanding the roles they play and what makes them essential. Traditionalism rests on this understanding, and it is a political response to it. The response is to have and maintain political arrangements that foster the participation of individuals in the various traditions that have historically endured in their society. The reason for fostering them is that good lives depend on participation in a variety of traditions.

Traditions do not stand independently of each other. They overlap, form parts of each other, and problems or questions occurring in one are often resolved in terms of another. Most traditions have legal, moral, political, aesthetic, stylistic, managerial, and a multitude of other aspects. Furthermore, people participating in one tradition necessarily bring with them the beliefs, values, and practices of many of the other traditions in which they also participate. Changes in one tradition, therefore, are most likely to produce changes in others. Traditions

are intimately connected. That is why changes in one tradition are like waves that reverberate throughout the other traditions of a society.

Some of these changes are for the better, others for the worse. Most of them, however, are complex, have consequences that grow more unpredictable the more distant they are, and thus tend to escape human control. (This is one of the key ideas of Hayek, 1982; see Kukathas, 1989: 174–91 on the complicated connection between Hayek and conservatism.) Since these changes are changes in the traditions upon which good lives depend, the attitude to them of conservative traditionalists will be one of extreme caution. They will want to minimize the changes in so far as it is possible. They will want them to be no greater than what is necessary for remedying some specific defect. They will be opposed to experimental, general, or large changes because of their uncertain effects on good lives.

Changes, of course, are often necessary because traditions may be vicious, destructive, stultifying, nay-saying, and thus not conducive to good lives. It is part of the purpose of the prevailing political arrangements to draw distinctions among traditions that are unacceptable (like slavery), suspect but tolerable (like pornography), and worthy of encouragement (like university education). Traditions that violate the minimum requirements of human nature should be prohibited. Traditions that have shown themselves to make questionable contributions to good lives should be tolerated but not encouraged. Traditions whose historical record testifies to their importance for good lives should be cherished.

The obvious question is *who* should decide which tradition is which and *how* that decision should be made. The answer conservatives give is that the decision should be made by those who are legitimately empowered to do so through the political process of their society and they should make the decisions by reflecting on the historical record of the tradition in question.

From this three corollaries follow. First, the people who are empowered to make the decisions ought to be those who can and do view the prevailing political arrangements from a historical perspective. The political process works well if it ends up empowering these people. They are unlikely to be ill-educated, preoccupied with some single issue, inexperienced, or have qualifications that lie in some other field of endeavour. Conservatives, in a word, are not in favour of populist politics. Second, a society that proceeds in the manner just indicated is pluralistic because it fosters a plurality of traditions. It does so because it sees as the justification of its political arrangements that they foster good lives, and fostering them depends on fostering the traditions in which participation may make lives good. Third, the society is tolerant because it is committed to having as many traditions as possible. Its political arrangements place the burden of proof on those who wish to proscribe a tradition. If a tradition has endured, if it has the allegiance of enough people to perpetuate it, then there is a prima facie case for it. That case may be, and often is, defeated, but the initial presumption is in its favour.

This implies that a conservative society that is sceptical, pluralistic, and traditionalist will be in favour of limited government. The purpose of its political arrangements is not to bring heaven on earth by imposing on people some conception of a good life. No government has a mandate from heaven. The political arrangements of a limited government interfere as little as possible with the indigenous traditions that flourish among people subject to it. The purpose of its arrangements is to enable people to live as they please, rather than to force them to live in a particular way. One of the most important ways of accomplishing this is to have a wide plurality of traditions as a bulwark between individuals and the government that has power over them.

The answer, then, to the question that heads this section is that, as traditionalist conservatives believe, a good society aims to have political arrangements that balance the claims of individual autonomy and social authority. This balance is reached by the mediation of the traditions of a society that make autonomy possible and provide many of the forms that it might take. But conservatives also believe that in a good society it is not assumed that lives cannot be good unless they are autonomous. It is certainly repugnant to force people to live lives that they would not otherwise live. But it is equally certain that many people live satisfying and beneficial lives that are neither autonomous nor forced on them.

HOW SHOULD POLITICAL ARRANGEMENTS RESPOND TO THE PREVALENCE OF EVIL?

One of the safest generalizations is that conservatives tend to be pessimists. In some conservative writings – Montaigne's, Hume's, and Oakeshott's – cheerfulness keeps breaking through, but even then, it does so in spite of their doubts about the possibility of a significant improvement in the human condition. Conservatives take a dim view of progress. They are not so foolish as to deny that great advances have been made in science, technology, medicine, communication, management, education, and so forth, and that they have changed human lives for the better. But they have also changed them for the worse. Advances have been

both beneficial and harmful. They have certainly enlarged the stock of human possibilities, but the possibilities are for both good and evil, and new possibilities are seldom without new evils. Conservatives tend to be pessimistic because they doubt that more possibilities will make lives on the whole better. They believe that there are obstacles that stand in the way of the permanent overall improvement of the human condition.

Conservatism has been called the politics of imperfection (O'Sullivan, 1976: ch. 10; Quinton, 1978). This is in some ways an apt characterization, but it is misleading in others. It rightly suggests that conservatives reject the idea of human perfectibility. (For the history of the idea, see Passmore, 1970; Kekes, 1997.) Yet it is too sanguine because it implies that, apart from some imperfections, the human condition is by and large all right. But it is worse than a bad joke to regard as mere imperfections war, genocide, tyranny, torture, terrorism, the drug trade, concentration camps, racism, the murder of religious and political opponents, easily avoidable epidemics and starvation, and other familiar and widespread evils. Conservatives are much more impressed by the prevalence of evil than this label implies. If evil is understood as serious unjustified harm caused by human beings, then the conservative view is that the prevalence of evil is a permanent condition that cannot be significantly altered.

The politics of imperfection is a misleading label also because it suggests that the imperfection is in human beings. Conservatives certainly think that human beings are responsible for much evil, but to think only that is shallow. The prevalence of evil reflects not just a human propensity for evil, but also a contingency that influences what propensities human beings have and develop independently of human intentions. The human propensity for evil is itself a manifestation of this deeper and more pervasive contingency, which operates through genetic inheritance, environmental factors, the confluence of events that places people at certain places at certain times, the crimes, accidents, pieces of good or bad fortune that happen or do not happen to them, the historical period, society, and family into which they are born, and so forth. The same contingency also affects people because others whom they love and depend on, and with whom their lives are intertwined in other ways, are as subject to it as they are themselves.

The view of thoughtful conservatives is not a hopeless misanthropic pessimism, according to which contingency makes human nature evil rather than good. Their view is rather a realistic pessimism that holds that whether the balance of good and evil propensities and their realization in people tilts one way or another is a contingent matter over which human beings and their political arrangements have insufficient control.[8] This point needs to be stressed. Conservatives do not think that the human condition is devoid of hope. They are, however, realistic about the limited control a society has over its future. Their view is *not* that human beings are corrupt and that their evil propensities are uncontrollable. Their view is rather that human beings have both good and evil propensities and neither they nor their societies can exercise sufficient control to make the realization of good propensities reliably prevail over the realization of evil ones. The right political arrangements help, of course, just as the wrong ones make matters worse. But even under the best political arrangements a great deal of contingency remains, and it places beyond human control much good and evil. The chief reason for this is that human efforts to control contingency are themselves subject to the very contingency they aim to control. And that, of course, is the fundamental reason why conservatives are pessimistic and sceptical about the possibility of significant improvement in the human condition. It is thus that the scepticism and pessimism of conservatives reinforce one another.

It does not follow from this, and conservatives do not believe, that it is a matter of indifference what political arrangements are made. It is true that political arrangements cannot guarantee the victory of good over evil, but they can influence how things go. Whether that is sufficient at a certain time and place is itself a contingent matter insufficiently within human control. The attitude that results from the realization that this is so has a negative and positive component. The negative one is acceptance of the fact that not even the best political arrangements guarantee good lives. The positive one is to strive nevertheless to make the political arrangements as good as possible. The impetus behind the latter is the realization that bad political arrangements worsen the already uncertain human condition.

If the choice of political arrangements is governed by this conservative attitude, it results in arrangements that look both to foster what is taken to be good and to hinder what is regarded as evil. One significant difference between conservative politics and most current alternatives to it is the insistence of conservatives on the importance of political arrangements that hinder evil. This difference is a direct result of the pessimism of conservatives and the optimistic belief of others in human perfectibility. Their optimism rests on the assumption that the prevalence of evil is the result of bad political arrangements. If people were not poor, oppressed, exploited, discriminated against, and so forth, it is optimistically supposed, then they would be naturally inclined to live good lives. The prevalence of evil is thus assumed to be the result of the political corruption of human nature. If political arrangements were good, there would be no corruption. What is needed, therefore, is

to make political arrangements that foster the good. The arrangements that hinder evil are unfortunate and temporary measures needed only until the effects of the good arrangements are generally felt.

Conservatives reject this optimism. They do not think that evil is prevalent merely because of bad political arrangements. It needs to be asked why political arrangements are bad. And the answer must be that political arrangements are made by people, and they are bound to reflect the propensities of their makers. Bad political arrangements are ultimately traceable to the evil propensities of the people who make them. Since the propensities are subject to contingencies over which human control is insufficient, there is no guarantee whatsoever that political arrangements can be made good. Nor that, if they were made good, they would be sufficient to hinder evil.

Conservatives insist, therefore, on the necessity and importance of political arrangements that hinder evil. They stress moral education, the enforcement of morality, the treatment of people according to what they deserve, the importance of swift and severe punishment for serious crimes, and so on. They oppose the prevailing attitudes that lead to agonizing over the criminal and forgetting the crime, to perpetuating the absurd fiction of a fundamental moral equality between habitual evildoers and their victims, to guaranteeing the same freedom and welfare rights to good and evil people, and so forth. Conservatives reject, therefore, the egalitarian view of justice championed by liberals and socialists (inspired and defended by Rawls, 1971), which recommends taking economic resources from people who have more and giving them to those who have less without asking whether the first deserve to have them and the second deserve to receive them. Conservatives think that justice is essentially connected with desert, and its aim is, not equality, but the upholding of the rule of law that assures that people get what they deserve [see also Chapters 7, 17 and 30].

Political arrangements that are meant to hinder evil are liable to abuse. Conservatives know and care about the historical record that testifies to the dreadful things that have been done to people on the many occasions when such arrangements have gone wrong. The remedy, however, cannot be to refuse to make the arrangements; it must be to make them, learn from history, and try hard to avoid their abuse. Conservatives know that in this respect, as in all others, contingency will cause complete success to elude them. But this is precisely the reason why political arrangements are necessary for hindering evil. Their pessimism leads conservatives to face the worst and try to deny scope to it, rather than endeavour to build the City of Man on the illusion of human perfectibility.

CONCLUSION

The central concern of conservatism is with political arrangements that make a society good. Since conservatism takes the goodness of a society to depend on the goodness of the lives of the people who live in it, it is a moral view. Good lives, of course, require much more than what political arrangements can secure. The right political arrangements, however, do secure some of the conditions necessary for them. These arrangements, according to conservatives, are discovered by reflection on the history of the political arrangements that prevail in one's society. This discloses that the society is partly constituted of various enduring traditions in which individuals participate because they conceive of good lives in terms of the beliefs, values, and practices that these traditions embody. The reasons for or against particular political arrangements are then to be found by reflection on their historical success or failure in fostering those traditions and participation in them that is conducive to satisfying and beneficial lives.

As a result of differences in history and circumstances, political arrangements, traditions, and lives that are reasonably regarded as good are likely to vary from society to society. Conservatives, therefore, do not seek to formulate a general theory that provides a blueprint for a good society. There is no such blueprint. This is why the most reasonable version of conservatism is sceptical and pluralistic. The absence of a blueprint, however, does not mean that conservative politics is doomed to arbitrariness. Good reasons in politics, beyond a basic level, are local and historically conditioned. Their concern is with the evaluation of the arrangements and traditions that provide the particular framework in which individuals can try to make good lives for themselves. This is why the most reasonable version of conservatism is traditionalist. But it is also realistically pessimist because it recognizes that the prevalence of evil is created by contingencies over which human control is imperfect, since the attempts at control are affected by the very contingency they aim to control.

Moderate scepticism about general theories in politics; pluralism about traditions, values, and conceptions of a good life; traditionalism; and pessimism about human perfectibility and the eradication of evil; these jointly define the version of conservatism that is the best alternative to its chief contemporary rivals, liberalism and socialism.

NOTES

It is odd but necessary to begin with a note about the notes. In several of the notes below conservative views are attributed to various people. This is not meant to imply that the people who hold these views are conservative. They are conservative in respect to these views, but they also hold other views, which may or may not be conservative. It is often difficult to say whether someone is conservative, especially since few of the people referred to were concerned with formulating an explicit political morality.

1 Reliable accounts of some of these disagreements may be found in O'Sullivan (1976) and Quinton (1978). For general surveys and bibliographies of conservative ideas, see Minogue (1967), O'Hear (1995), Quinton (1993), and Vierhaus (1968). Three useful anthologies of conservatives writings are Kirk (1982), Muller (1997), and Scruton (1991). Some of the classic works that have influenced the development of conservatism are: Plato's *Republic*, Aristotle's *Politics, Nicomachean Ethics*, and *Rhetoric*, Machiavelli's *The Prince* and *Discourses*, Montaigne's *Essays*, Hobbes's *Leviathan*, Hume's *Treatise, Enquiries, Essays*, and *History of England*, Burke's *Reflections on the Revolution in France*, Tocqueville's *Democracy in America* and *The Old Regime and the French Revolution*, Hegel's *Philosophy of Right*, Stephen's *Liberty, Equality, Fraternity*, Bradley's *Ethical Studies*, Santayana's *Dominations and Powers*, Wittgenstein's *Philosophical Investigations* and *On Certainty*, and Oakeshott's *Rationalism in Politics* and *On Human Conduct*.

2 This is the view of many religious conservatives mainly, but not exclusively, in the Catholic tradition. For surveys and bibliographies divided along national lines, see: O'Sullivan (1976), Chapter 2 for France and Chapter 3 for Germany; von Klemperer (1957) for Germany; Quinton (1978) for England; Kirk (2001) for England and America [see also Chapter 30]; Dunn and Woodard (1996), East (1986), Nash (1976), and Rossiter (1982) for America.

3 The roots of sceptical conservatism are to be found scattered in Montaigne's *Essays*, Hobbes's *Leviathan*, Hume's *Treatise, Enquiries, Essays*, and *History of England*, Burke's *Reflections on the Revolution in France*, Tocqueville's *Democracy in America* and *The Old Regime and the French Revolution*, Santayana's *Dominations and Powers*, and Wittgenstein's *Philosophical Investigations* and *On Certainty*. On Montaigne's conservatism, see Kekes (1992: ch. 4); on Hobbes's conservatism, see Oakeshott (1974); on Hume's conservatism, see Letwin (1965: Part I), Livingston (1984: ch. 12), and Wolin (1954); on Tocqueville's conservatism, see Boesche (1987), Frohnen (1993), and Kahan (1986); on Santayana's conservatism, see Gray (1989a) and O'Sullivan (1992); on Wittgenstein's conservatism, see Covell (1986: ch. 1), and Nyiri (1982). Some contemporary sceptical conservative works are Allison (1984), Gray (1989b; 1993a; 1993b), Kekes (1998), Letwin (1982), and Oakeshott (1975; 1991; 1996).

4 For historical surveys of absolutist conservatism, see note 2 above. Some contemporary absolutist conservative works are Finnis (1980; 1983), Grisez (1988), Veatch (1985), and Voegelin (1954–87).

5 The historical origins of relativistic conservatism are to be found in Vico (1970), Herder (1968), Dilthey (1914–77), and, a step removed, Burke (1968). This tradition is most illuminatingly treated by Mannheim (1953) and Berlin (1976; 1980). See also Earmarth (1978).

6 Contemporary works of pluralistic conservatism by and large coincide with those of sceptical conservatism; see note 3 above.

7 Traditionalism is an expression that does not appear in any of the works listed below, but the position defended in them is very close to traditionalism, so it is perhaps justified to claim affinity with them. See Bradley (1927: Essays 5 and 6), Kekes (1989), MacIntyre (1981; 1988; 1990), Oakeshott (1975), Popper (1968), and Scruton (1980). Traditionalism is also embraced by many communitarians [see further Chapter 13]. The relation between communitarianism and conservatism is as obscure as the relation between communitarianism and liberalism. Communitarians tend to be pluralists and traditionalists, so they share much common ground with conservatives. Yet no communitarian claims to be a conservative. For some communitarian works, see Sandel (1982), Taylor (1992a; 1992b), and Walzer (1983).

8 This sort of pessimism may be found in the tragedies of Sophocles, especially in *Oedipus the King* and *Antigone*, Thucydides' *The Peloponnesian War*, Machiavelli's *The Prince* and *The Discourses*, Montaigne's *Essays*, Stephen's *Liberty, Equality, Fraternity*, Bradley's *Ethical Studies*, Essay VII, and Santayana's *Dominations and Powers*. A recent statement of it is Kekes (1990).

REFERENCES

Allison, Lincoln (1984) *Right Principles*. Oxford: Blackwell.

Berlin, Isaiah (1976) *Vico and Herder*. London: Hogarth.

Berlin, Isaiah (1980) 'The counter-Enlightenment'. In Henry Hardy, ed., *Against the Current*. New York: Viking.

Berry, Christopher J. (1983) 'Conservatism and human nature'. In Ian Forbes and Steve Smith, eds, *Politics and Human Nature*. London: Pinter.

Berry, Christopher J. (1986) *Human Nature*. London: Macmillan.

Boesche, Roger (1987) *The Strange Liberalism of Alexis de Tocqueville*. Ithaca, NY: Cornell University Press.

Bradley, Francis Herbert (1927) *Ethical Studies*, Essays 5 and 6, 2nd edn. Oxford: Clarendon.

Burke, Edmund (1968) *Reflections on the Revolution in France*, ed. Conor Cruise O'Brien. Harmondsworth: Penguin.

Casey, John (1978) 'Tradition and authority'. In Maurice Cowling, ed., *Conservative Essays*. London: Cassell.

Covell, Charles (1986) *The Redefinition of Conservatism*. New York: Palgrave Macmillan.

Dilthey, Wilhelm (1914–77) *Gesammelte Schriften*, 18 vols. Stuttgart: Teubner and Gottingen: Vandenhoeck and Ruprecht.

Dunn, Charles W. and J. David Woodard (1996) *The Conservative Tradition in America*. Lanham, MD: Rowman and Littlefield.

Earmarth, Michael (1978) *Wilhelm Dilthey: The Critique of Historical Reason*. Chicago: University of Chicago Press.

East, John P. (1986) *The American Conservative Movement*. Chicago: Regnery.

Eliot, Thomas Stearns (1975) 'Tradition and the individual talent'. In Frank Kermode, ed., *The Selected Prose of T. S. Eliot*. New York: Farrar, Straus and Giroux.

Finnis, John (1980) *Natural Law and Natural Rights*. Oxford: Clarendon.

Finnis, John (1983) *Fundamentals of Ethics*. Oxford: Clarendon.

Frohnen, Bruce (1993) *Virtue and the Promise of Conservatism*. Lawrence, KS: University of Kansas Press.

Gray, John (1989a) 'George Santayana and the critique of liberalism'. *The World and I*, 2, 593–607.

Gray, John (1989b) *Liberalisms*. London: Routledge.

Gray, John (1993a) *Beyond the New Right*. London: Routledge.

Gray, John (1993b) *Post-Liberalism*. New York: Routledge.

Grisez, Germain (1988) *Beyond the New Morality*. Notre Dame, IN: University of Notre Dame Press.

Hayek, Friedrich A. (1982) *Law, Legislation and Liberty*, vols 1–3. Chicago: University of Chicago Press.

Herder, Johann Gottfried von (1968) *Reflections on the Philosophy of the History of Mankind*, trans. by T. O. Churchill. Chicago: University of Chicago Press.

Kahan, Alan S. (1986) *Aristocratic Liberalism*. New York: Oxford University Press.

Kekes, John (1989) *Moral Tradition and Individuality*. Princeton, NJ: Princeton University Press.

Kekes, John (1990) *Facing Evil*. Princeton, NJ: Princeton University Press.

Kekes, John (1992) *The Examined Life*. University Park, PA: Penn State Press.

Kekes, John (1993) *The Morality of Pluralism*. Princeton, NJ: Princeton University Press.

Kekes, John (1997) *Against Liberalism*. Ithaca, NY: Cornell University Press.

Kekes, John (1998) *A Case for Conservatism*. Ithaca, NY: Cornell University Press.

Kirk, Russell, ed. (1982) *Conservative Reader*. Harmondsworth: Penguin.

Kirk, Russell (2001) *The Conservative Mind*. Washington, DC: Regnery.

Kukathas, Chandran (1989) *Hayek and Modern Liberalism*. Oxford: Clarendon.

Letwin, Shirley Robin (1965) *The Pursuit of Certainty*. Cambridge: Cambridge University Press.

Letwin, Shirley Robin (1982) *The Gentleman in Trollope*. Cambridge: Harvard.

Livingston, Donald W. (1984) *Hume's Philosophy of Common Life*. Chicago: University of Chicago Press.

MacIntyre, Alasdair (1981) *After Virtue*. Notre Dame, IN: University of Notre Dame Press.

MacIntyre, Alasdair (1988) *Whose Justice? Which Rationality?* Notre Dame, IN: University of Notre Dame Press.

MacIntyre, Alasdair (1990) *Three Rival Versions of Moral Enquiry*. Notre Dame, IN: University of Notre Dame Press.

Maistre, Joseph de (1965) *Works*, ed., trans. and introduction Jack Lively. London: Macmillan.

Mannheim, Karl (1953) 'Conservative thought'. In Paul Kecskemeti, ed., *Essays on Sociology and Social Psychology*. New York: Oxford University Press.

Minogue, Kenneth (1967) 'Conservatism'. In Paul Edwards, ed., *Encyclopedia of Philosophy*. New York: Macmillan.

Muller, Jerry Z., ed. (1997) *Conservatism*. Princeton, NJ: Princeton University Press.

Nash, George H. (1976) *The Conservative Intellectual Movement in America*. New York: Basic.

Nyiri, J. C. (1982) 'Wittgenstein's later work in relation to Conservatism'. In Brian McGuinness, ed., *Wittgenstein and His Times*. Oxford: Blackwell.

Oakeshott, Michael (1974) *Hobbes on Civil Association*. Oxford: Blackwell.

Oakeshott, Michael (1975) *On Human Conduct*. Oxford: Clarendon.

Oakeshott, Michael (1991) *Rationalism in Politics*. Indianapolis: Liberty.

Oakeshott, Michael (1993) 'Scientific politics'. In Timothy Fuller, ed., *Religion, Politics and the Moral Life*. New Haven, CT: Yale University Press.

Oakeshott, Michael (1996) *The Politics of Faith and the Politics of Scepticism*, ed. Timothy Fuller. New Haven, CT: Yale University Press.

O'Hear, Anthony (1995) 'Conservatism'. In Ted Honderich, ed., *The Oxford Companion to Philosophy*. Oxford: Oxford University Press.

O'Sullivan, Noel (1976) *Conservatism*. New York: St Martin's.

O'Sullivan, Noel (1992) *Santayana*. St Albans: Claridge.

Passmore, John (1970) *The Perfectibility of Man*. London: Duckworth.

Popper, Karl R. (1968) 'Towards a rational theory of tradition'. In *Conjectures and Refutations*. New York: Harper and Row.

Quinton, Anthony (1978) *The Politics of Imperfection*. London: Faber and Faber.

Quinton, Anthony (1993) 'Conservatism'. In Robert E. Goodin and Philip Pettit, eds, *A Companion to Contemporary Political Philosophy*. Oxford: Blackwell.

Rawls, John (1971) *A Theory of Justice*. Cambridge, MA: Harvard University Press.

Rescher, Nicholas (1993) *Pluralism*. Oxford: Clarendon.

Rossiter, Clinton (1982) *Conservatism in America*, 2nd rev. edn. Cambridge, MA: Harvard University Press.

Sandel, Michael J. (1982) *Liberalism and the Limits of Justice*. Cambridge: Cambridge University Press.

Scruton, Roger (1980) *The Meaning of Conservatism*. Harmondsworth: Penguin.

Scruton, Roger, ed. (1991) *Conservative Texts*. New York: St Martin's.

Shils, Edward (1981) *Tradition*. Chicago: University of Chicago Press.

Taylor, Charles (1992a) *Multiculturalism and 'The Politics of Recognition'*. Princeton, NJ: Princeton University Press.

Taylor, Charles (1992b) *The Ethics of Authenticity*. Cambridge, MA: Harvard University Press.

Veatch, Henry B. (1985) *Human Rights*. Baton Rouge, LA: Louisiana State University Press.

Vico, Giambattista (1970) *New Science*, trans. Thomas Goddard Bergin and Max Harold Frisch. Ithaca, NY: Cornell University Press.

Vierhaus, Rudolf (1968) 'Conservatism'. In Philip P. Wiener, ed., *Dictionary of the History of Ideas*. New York: Scribner's.

Voegelin, Eric (1954–87) *Order in History*, 5 vols. Baton Rouge, LA: Louisiana State University Press.

Von Klemperer, Klemens (1957) *Germany's New Conservatism*. Princeton, NJ: Princeton University Press.

Walzer, Michael (1983) *Spheres of Justice*. New York: Basic.

Wolin, Sheldon S. (1954) 'Hume and Conservatism'. *American Political Science Review*, 98: 999–1016.

11

Democratic Political Theory

JOHN S. DRYZEK

A PLETHORA OF DEMOCRACIES

Adversarial, aggregative, associative, capitalist, Christian, classical, communicative, communitarian, consensual, consociational, constitutional, contestatory, corporatist, cosmopolitan, delegative, deliberative, developmental, difference, direct, discursive, ecological, economic, electoral, elitist, epistemic, feminist, global, grassroots, green, juridical, industrial, legal, liberal, local, majoritarian, minimalist, parliamentary, participatory, peoples', pluralist, populist, presidential, procedural, property-owning, protective, push-button, radical, reflective, representative, social, strong, thin, transnational and unitary are all adjectives that can be, and have been, attached to democracy.

One could write an account of the state of democratic theory by elucidating and juxtaposing the meanings of these 54 adjectives. But life is too short, and pages too limited. Let me begin instead with three observations about this list.

The list is a long one; there is a lot of democracy about, at least in theory, and perhaps in practice.

The categories represented by the adjectives are not mutually exclusive. While there are some obvious binary oppositions (aggregative versus deliberative, participatory versus representative), many combinations are plausible and have their advocates and critics.

The categories represented by these adjectives are not collectively exhaustive. The conversation about democratic development shows no signs of closure. (This is no bad thing; arguably the continuation of this conversation is intrinsic to democracy itself, though only for democracy as conceptualized by some of the categories.)

While covering a lot of territory, democratic theory is not completely unbounded. Contributors to the enterprise all address questions pertaining to the collective construction, distribution, application, and limitation of political authority. These questions define the boundaries of the democratic concourse, the sum of communication about democracy. Within these borders may be found a heartland where practitioners consider what rule by the people and the political equality it implies can mean in contemporary complex societies that also value liberty and efficiency. While it would be nice to be able to specify more precisely a common set of problems that democratic theorists try to resolve, along with a set of standards for what constitute adequate solutions, I believe that is not possible. For such standards emerge in the process of dialogue across theorists (and others), and their content may change with time.

Though historically contingent, these standards have real power, as indicated by the number of dead ducks that have fallen victim to them. The most noteworthy dead duck is democracy's long-standing authoritarian opponent. In 1989 Robert Dahl could plausibly organize a major statement and defence of democracy using as a foil guardianship, the idea that some elite both knows what is best for society and has the appropriate expertise to implement that programme. In 2004 that would no longer be worth the effort. Serious advocates of guardianship can no longer be found. For example, in the realm of environmental political thought, in the 1970s eco-authoritarian models were quite popular (for an extreme statement, see Heilbroner, 1974). Come the 1990s, the main flourishing enterprise in ecopolitical thought was green democracy (see for example the essays collected by Mathews, 1996), while advocates of ecological guardianship have almost vanished. Other dead ducks include people's democracy, workplace democracy, community democracy (in the sense of whole-community mobilization), collectives, Theodore Lowi's (1969) juridical democracy, and perhaps democratic socialism. Still, there are only a few dead democratic ducks, and they are always outnumbered by new democratic ducklings. Thus with time democratic theory no less than democracy itself becomes more differentiated and complex.

One might despair in the face of ever increasing variety. So, for example, John Dunn suggests that 'democratic theory is the moral Esperanto of the present nation-state system, the language in which all Nations are truly united, the public cant of the modern world, a dubious currency indeed' (1979: 2). Democracy does indeed sometimes look a bit like a Christmas tree, a positive symbol to which one can attach any good things one likes. Dahl (1971) prefers to use the term 'polyarchy' on the grounds that it provides more in the way of conceptual precision and real-world purchase than 'democracy'. Alternatively, one could try to engage in conceptual clarification when it comes to the term 'democracy' itself, to cut through the confusion in search of the essential meaning. This is the approach of, for example, Giovanni Sartori, who describes his book on democratic theory as 'above all, a housecleaning venture, a task of dispelling sloppiness (in argument) and messiness (in conception)' (1987: xi). Such an approach will not do for two reasons. First, part of what makes democracy interesting in both theory and practice is contestation over its essence. Second, any search for the essential meaning of democracy is undermined by conceptual historians who point to the inevitable historical contingency of key political concepts like democracy (Hanson, 1989), and how democracy's meaning is itself constitutive of politics at particular times and places.

Conceptual history will do for political theory in history of ideas mode. Indeed, Russell Hanson's excellent (1989) history is instructive in that it reminds us that only in the nineteenth century does democracy as a concept cease to be universally reviled, and come to attract positive connotations. In the United States, this comes about largely as a result of the Jacksonian and populist concern for 'The Democracy' – that is, for the ordinary people against the plutocracy. However, while necessary, conceptual history is insufficient for those with critical and evaluative concerns who want to contribute to the continuing conversation of democratic development. Moreover, conceptual history does not equip us to come to terms with radical variety within an era (such as the present), as opposed to change across eras. Hanson himself confronts

present variety only with a lament for the fact that democracy seems to have been emptied of meaning, followed by a plea for the recovery of the class connotations of the term (1989: 85–6).

One way to cope with variety is to isolate and compare the major models of democracy. This is, for example, the approach taken by David Held (1996) in what is the best textbook survey of the field. Held's models are classical, republican, protective, developmental, direct, competitive elitist, pluralist, legal, participatory, democratic autonomy, and cosmopolitan. This set is very helpful in providing a basic vocabulary and identifying some of the main focal points of democratic theory through the ages. Yet Held only has 11 models: at the outset of this essay I listed 54 adjectives. Not all the adjectives can be squeezed into a particular model. For example, deliberative democrats could be classical, republican, developmental, participatory or cosmopolitan, in Held's scheme. Some of the adjectives (for example, associative, difference) find no easy home in any of his models. So while Held's survey is essential reading, it only goes so far in capturing the range of interesting contemporary thinking about democracy.

Just as there are many adjectives to qualify and describe democracy, so there are many axes of contention about what democracy can, ought, and ought not to be. Moreover, different accounts of democracy will dispute the importance of different axes. So how then to proceed, if it is futile to seek a single essence of democracy, if the enumeration of models gets overwhelmed by the complexity of democratic thinking, and if consensus cannot even be found on what constitutes the main lines of contention?

My answer is straightforward. Though democracy comes in many varieties, the dominant current in democratic theory is now a deliberative one. Indeed, it is accurate to say that around 1990 the theory of democracy took a deliberative turn. Thus different accounts of democracy can be appraised in terms of the content, strength, and significance of their relation to the deliberative turn – whether in support, opposition, capture, or qualification.

A second starting point will be the very different view of democracy shared by most of those who study the real world of democracy. Indeed, the depiction of variety when it comes to democracy in theory and practice with which I began will surprise political scientists who study the comparative politics of democracy, as well as more journalistic observers of the recent life and times of democracy. To this latter group, what is striking about contemporary democracy is less its variety than its uniformity. The passing of the Soviet alternative and the contemporaneous withering away of democratic socialism in the West signal to this group the global

- Democratic politics is intrinsically irresponsible because all actors seek benefits for themselves while imposing costs upon others; the result is a negative-sum game where total costs outweigh total benefits.

Now, not all public choice analysts argue all of these points; the most unremittingly anti-state aspects are found only in Virginia-style public choice (see Mitchell and Simmons, 1994, for a statement). The more highly mathematical rational choice treatments of politics found in (say) the pages of the *American Political Science Review* have a less overtly political agenda. Yet it remains true that when such analyses do have implications for democratic politics, the news is usually bad. Thus can Russell Hardin conclude that public choice analyses have 'largely helped to expose flaws – grievous, foundational flaws – in democratic thought and practice' (1993: 170).

However, if, to use the title of Hardin's survey, the conflict is 'Public choice versus democracy', then by the early 2000s democracy was winning. The claims of rational choice as explanatory theory have been severely dented within political science (Green and Shapiro, 1994). Social choice theory in its Rochester-style anti-democratic manifestation has been destroyed by Mackie (2003). Gerry Mackie shows that every real-world example of a voting cycle (*A* beats *B* beats *C* beats *A*) adduced by William Riker or his followers to illustrate the potential for arbitrariness, instability, and manipulation in collective choice is actually inconsistent with the historical evidence.

What, then, remains of public choice as democratic theory? The answer is that it provides a set of warnings about what democratic politics could be like if political actors behaved in *Homo economicus* fashion, and if no mechanisms existed to curb these behavioural proclivities and their consequences. Deliberative democracy provides both a communicative paradigm of personhood and mechanisms to bring *Homo economicus* and his interactions under control (a non-deliberative alternative can be found in Shepsle's 1979 idea of structure-induced equilibrium).

Now, social choice theorists can still try to pour cold water over deliberation because it is easy to demonstrate that the very conditions of free access, equality, and unrestricted communication conducive to authentic deliberation are exactly the conditions conducive to instability, arbitrariness, and so strategic manipulation (van Mill, 1996; see also Grofman, 1993: 1578; Knight and Johnson, 1994). Deliberative democrats can reply that there are mechanisms intrinsic to deliberation that act to structure preferences in ways that solve social choice problems (Dryzek and List, 2003). For

example, deliberation can disaggregate a dimension on which preferences are non-single-peaked (one major cause of cycles across three or more alternatives that are at the root of the kind of instability Riker identifies) into several dimensions on each of which single-peakedness prevails (Miller, 1992). To the extent this deliberative reply succeeds, then the social choice critique undermines only an aggregative account of democracy in which all actors behave strategically, and can actually be deployed to show why deliberation is necessary.

While social choice critics of democracy fear the unmanageable diversity that deliberation can encourage, difference democrats criticize deliberation for exactly the opposite reason: that it represses diversity. To greater or lesser degrees difference democrats take their bearings from the postmodern theory of identity and difference, in which the essence of democracy is seen in terms of the creative encounter of those with disparate identities (for example, Connolly, 1991). Just as for the deliberative democrats, the core of democracy is therefore seen as communication. However, difference democrats problematize communication, and criticize the allegedly neutral forms of communication emphasized by deliberative democrats for their cultural biases. Notably, Iris Young (2000) argues (in a US context) that any main or exclusive emphasis on rational argument further disadvantages minorities who are not well versed in its niceties. Her 'communicative democracy' would feature greeting, rhetoric, and storytelling (or testimony, or narrative) as well as argument – forms of communication she believes are more accessible to disadvantaged minorities. This resonates with Young's earlier (1990) advocacy of guaranteed representation and veto power over policies that affect them for disadvantaged groups.

Deliberative democrats who are not under the sway of an exclusive Rawlsian belief in unitary public reason or an overly narrow Habermasian account of communicative rationality could reply that there is nothing in deliberation that excludes these alternative forms of communication (though they ought to balk at any suggestion of veto power). However, Young's trio should not be accepted uncritically, as she eventually recognizes (2000: 77–80). Instead, they need to be held up to the tests of non-coercion, capacity to induce reflection, and ability to link the particular with the general (Dryzek, 2000: 68–71).

A third group of critics of deliberation, those I style sceptical egalitarians, defend more traditional accounts of democracy against the deliberative turn. In Shapiro's pithy (1999) terms, 'enough about deliberation, politics is about interest and power'. In this light, those interested in improving the quality of democracy should seek the equalization of power; here, issues of democracy become linked to distributive justice. Such sceptics can point to the rather embarrassing fact that deliberation cannot be a complete theory of democracy because its advocates do not specify how collective decisions get made (Saward, 2000). If so, then deliberative democrats might have to retreat to more familiar aggregative mechanisms, and the deliberative/ aggregative dichotomy is proven false, for then democracy is necessarily aggregative, and votes have to be taken (Przeworski, 1998: 140–2). Goodin (2000) points out that deliberation is an activity that can never realistically involve more than a handful of people. Saward (2000) believes that such considerations mean that egalitarians should therefore oppose deliberation's aristocratic leanings that would exclude those with non-deliberative preferences; far better, in this light, to extend democracy in more direct fashion (for example, by greater use of referenda).

Deliberative democrats can reply to the sceptics who charge that deliberation can only be an elite activity in several ways here. In Fishkin's (1995) deliberative opinion polls, participants for a deliberative forum are selected at random from the population, and complete a questionnaire at the end of the process. Citizens' juries too are recruited by random selection, but conclude with a policy recommendation crafted and agreed upon by the jurors rather than a questionnaire (Smith and Wales, 2000). Fishkin argues that a deliberative poll represents what public opinion would be if everyone could deliberate; the same might be said for citizens' juries.

Alternatively, deliberative democrats could allow that deliberation can coexist with a variety of mechanisms for reaching binding decisions, be they voting in referenda, elections, or the legislature, the decisions of courts, consensus among stakeholders in an issue, or even administrative fiat. More radically, they might think about ways in which the deliberative contestation of discourses in the public sphere can generate collective outcomes not only in its indirect influence on public policy, but also via cultural change and paragovernmental action (Dryzek, 2000).

Before leaving the deliberative turn and its critics, one further argument that might weigh against deliberation should be noted. If democracy involves aggregation (however much it is downplayed by deliberative democrats), that can be across judgements and not just across preferences as emphasized in social choice theory. Such judgements can involve disagreement over (say) what is in the common good. This epistemic way of thinking about democracy is associated with Rousseau, according to whom the general will can be ascertained by voting. Bernard Grofman and Scott Feld (1988) argue

that if indeed there is such a thing as the common good, though people differ in their judgements about which option will best serve it, then Condorcet's jury theorem applies. This theorem demonstrates that if each citizen has a better than even chance of being correct in his/her judgement, then the larger the number of voters, the greater the chance of the majority choosing the correct option. The jury theorem therefore justifies the rationality of majoritarian democracy, at least in a republican context of a search for the common good, though only if each citizen reaches and exercises independent judgement. So there should be no factions (which reduce the effective number of voters) and, it might seem, no communication. These, at least, were Rousseau's own views: deliberation should only be a matter of internal reflection, not communication. However, as Robert Goodin (2002: 125) and others point out, discussion is fine so long as people then subsequently exercise their own independent judgements when voting. Goodin then questions an epistemic democracy rooted in Rousseau and the jury theorem by pointing out that in a dynamic context, their implication is that minorities should rationally and immediately cease their opposition when a majority votes against them. Persistent opposition therefore makes sense only when values differ, but not when only factual judgements vary (2002: 144). If only factual judgements are at issue, an epistemic approach threatens to wipe out the contestatory aspect of democracy.

For better or for worse, the deliberative approach sets the agenda for contemporary democratic theory. However, it should be clear that there remains plenty to argue about, both among those who share the deliberative orientation, and those who reject it. Yet there are scholars of democracy who remain untouched by the deliberative approach, and to these I now turn.

LIBERAL MINIMALISM AND ITS ALTERNATIVES

The model of democracy most popular among comparative politics scholars, especially those in the burgeoning field of democratic transition and consolidation, expects far less from democracy than do the deliberative democrats. This model is essentially that proposed long ago by Schumpeter (1942): democracy is no more than competition among elites for popular approval that confers the right to rule. In the 1950s this idea became the foundation for 'empirical' theories of democracy happy with the generally apathetic role of the ignorant and potentially authoritarian masses (Berelson, 1952; Sartori, 1962). Such competitive elitist models have long been discredited among democratic theorists – not least those such as Dahl (1989) who had earlier believed in them as both accurate descriptions of United States politics and desirable states of affairs. Yet they live on among transitologists and consolidologists, who see the hallmark of a consolidated democracy as a set of well-behaved parties representing material interests engaged in electoral competition regulated by constitutional rules (see, for example, Di Palma, 1990; Huntington, 1991; Mueller, 1996; Schedler, 1998). The deliberative democrat's concern with authenticity is nowhere to be seen. Active citizens play no role in such models. There is no outlet for citizen engagement with politics beyond regular elections where the mostly uninformed, uninterested and apathetic masses can register preferences across a limited range of candidates or parties.

What can explain the popularity of this minimalist, electoralist model? Partly it is a matter of the undeniable analytic purchase the model provides for those who study the real world of democracy. To such scholars, the contested character of democracy in political theory is a nuisance when it comes to devising empirical indicators for the comparison of different countries and the tracking of democratic transition and consolidation in particular countries. Acceptance of the minimalist model makes life much easier. It can be applied, for example, in Huntington's (1991: 267) famous two-election test for consolidated democracy, which requires a freely elected government to cede power in a subsequent electoral defeat. Or it can underwrite a temporal scale for assessing the degree to which democracy is consolidated; Lijphart (1984: 38) suggests 30 to 35 years.

Perhaps a more important reason for the popularity of liberal minimalism is its consistency with developments that see capitalist marketization and democratization marching together. Since the mid 1970s, the adoption of liberal democratic systems by ever more countries has gone hand-in-hand with the global expansion of capitalism. It has of course long been noted that there is a correlation between capitalism and liberal democracy. Exactly why such a correlation exists is a matter of dispute. To Lipset (1959) it was a matter of capitalism producing a middle class that had all the right democratic virtues of toleration and moderation. To Rueschemeyer, Stephens and Stephens (1992) the answer lies instead in the fact that capitalism produces a working class with a vested interest in redistribution that is promoted by effective universal franchise. To Adam Przeworski et al. (2000) it is not that capitalism causes democracy, for countries can become democratic at any level of development. However, capitalism produces wealth which in turn provides protection against the overthrow of democracy.

While capitalism facilitates the development or stability of a minimalist liberal democracy, it impedes any strengthening of democracy beyond this minimum. As Lindblom (1982) among others notes, the capitalist market context automatically punishes governments that pursue policies that undermine the confidence of actual or potential investors by causing disinvestment and capital flight. Thus when it comes to public policy, democracy can only operate in what Lindblom calls an 'unimprisoned' zone. The corollary is that too much state democracy means dangerous indeterminacy in public policy (Dryzek, 1996). Democracy may no longer mean, as Plato defined it in the *Republic*, 'a state in which the poor, gaining the upper hand, kill some and banish others, and then divide the offices among the remaining citizens, usually by lot'. But there is a lingering possibility that too much democracy might undermine the inequalities on which effective wealth creation rests. The minimalist model therefore seems uniquely suited to the contemporary liberal capitalist political economy.

This combination of capitalism and liberal minimalist democracy received perhaps its most positive gloss (and a dash of Hegel) in the triumphalism of Francis Fukuyama's (1989; 1992) 'end of history'. Fukuyama's thesis lost plausibility in the ensuing decade, but only in terms of the persistence (or renewal) of challenges such as religious fundamentalisms, ethnic nationalism, and Confucian capitalism. But the basic idea that democracy is globally dominant and that the liberal capitalist model of democracy has few if any plausible challengers that merit the title 'democracy' is still the dominant view among transitologists. Life with this model, and without the kinds of critical questions that democratic theorists are apt to raise, is certainly less complicated for the transitologist. Obviously happy about this state of affairs, Sartori wants to be done with the critics: 'the winner is an entirely liberal democracy, not only popularly elected government, but also, and indivisibly, constitutional government; that is, the hitherto much belittled "formal democracy" that controls the exercise of power' (1991: 437).

The more critical stances that democratic theorists are inclined to take would highlight the limitations on democracy that this global dominance of minimalist liberal democracy plus capitalism entails. But any such critical response is easily countered if it remains devoid of ideas about how such dominance might realistically be challenged (without retreating to ungrounded idealism). Part of the response might involve the strengthening and democratization of international institutions in response to the migration of political power from the state to the transnational political economy. This is, for example, the approach taken by Held and his fellow advocates of a cosmopolitan democracy that would involve a more inclusive United Nations Security Council, a strengthened UN General Assembly, cross-national referenda, and international economic, military and judicial authorities accountable to regional and global parliamentary bodies (Held, 1995; Archibugi, Held and Köhler, 1998). Alternatively, if state democracy can only be minimalist, theorists might explore non-state locations for the pursuit of democracy. Such locations might involve public spheres in both domestic and transnational civil society that remain distant from state power though still oriented to public affairs (Cohen and Arato, 1992; Fraser, 1992; Dryzek, 1996: 46–53), and home to social movements [see further Chapter 20]. Community-based grassroots democracy, collectives, and workplace democracy would also fit here, but today seem to have fallen on hard times. Feminist proposals for democratization of areas of life traditionally considered private, such as the household, remain perhaps more promising (Rowbotham, 1986), but also more tangential, at least in the sense that they do not confront the state and its enmeshment in the transnational capitalist political economy head-on [see further Chapter 21].

A rare normative defence of the minimalist model is provided by Przeworski (1999) who argues that the model at least puts an end to large-scale political violence once those defeated accept that they have a realistic chance to return and win another day (proponents of consensual democracy such as Lijphart, 1999, could respond that power-sharing not majority rule is the best defence against violence in a divided society). Given that the structure of interests in a complex society means that competing interests can never be reconciled, their provisional resolution in electoral competition is about the best we can ever do. Riker's (1982) attempted social-choice-theoretic defence of minimalism is that though voting is meaningless, periodic elections at least provide an opportunity for the removal of tyrannical, incompetent, or corrupt leadership. But Riker's defence fails because his own analysis shows that there is no will of the voters independent of the mechanism that is supposed to measure it – and this has to include the will to dismiss tyrants or incompetents (Coleman and Ferejohn, 1986: 22).

Democratic Theory and Practice

Acceptance of the minimalist model would render most democratic theory unnecessary. But minimalism fails in its own terms, for the following reasons. Democratic theorists are well placed to highlight these failures and move the conversation beyond them.

First, minimalism can allow forms of democracy that are very thin indeed, to the extent they barely merit the description 'democratic'. For example, what Guillermo O'Donnell (1994) calls delegative democracy passes the minimalist test. Under delegative democracy, found especially in Latin America but also in the post-communist world, leaders submit themselves to regular elections, but otherwise govern without accountability, without any sense that election promises need to be remembered and without constitutional constraint (except of course the one specifying regular free elections). Delegative democracy completely misses what Philip Pettit (1999) calls the contestatory as opposed to electoral aspect of democracy. In light of this aspect, the guarantee of freedom (defined as non-domination) is the ability of citizens to contest the content of collective decisions under fair terms, be it via access to courts, legislatures, or administrative review.

Second, minimalism is insensitive to the variety of forms that democracy can take in practice as well as theory, leading to misinterpretation of events and developments, and so undermining the analytical purchase that is one of minimalism's main justifications. For example, under sway of a liberal model of democracy, Juan Linz and Alfred Stepan (1996) fear for democracy in post-communist Poland and the Czech Republic because of the legacy of the kind of politics that characterized their oppositional civil societies in the Soviet era: 'Ethical civil society represents "truth" but political society in a consolidated democracy normally represents "interests"' (1996: 272). However, the kind of politics they criticize is consistent not only with the deeper republican history of these two countries (reaching back to the eighteenth century in Poland), but also with contemporary civic republican political theory (Sandel, 1996). In this light, the practices and discourses bemoaned by Linz and Stepan actually provide resources for those interested in consolidating and deepening democracy (Dryzek and Holmes, 2002: chs 14 and 15).

Such practices and attitudes might also include the civic attributes fostered in associational life that are, according to Robert Putnam (1993; 2000), the key to 'making democracy work'. For Putnam, a widely shared civic orientation that is not reducible to private material interest is necessary to defend state democracy against amoral clientelism (as in southern Italy) or rampant individualism (as in the United States in recent decades).

A variety of democratic systems observable in contemporary nation-states passes the minimalist test: libertarian and social democratic, elitist and pluralist, presidential and parliamentary, nationalist and cosmopolitan, dense and weak civil societies. Uncritical application of liberal minimalism fails to pick up on the importance of these variations. Of course, the minimalist might reply that the variations are unimportant; but he or she should be required to demonstrate this fact rather than merely assert it, and the theorist can at least identify the dimensions along which a response is required.

A third reason why minimalism is inadequate is that it is untrue to democratization as understood by many political actors in transitional systems. The more idealistic, such as Vaclav Havel, President of Czechoslovakia and then the Czech Republic, see continued experimentation with and dialogue about forms of democracy at the centre of the democratic project (Lienesch, 1992: 1012; on the idea of democracy as an open-ended project, see also Downs, 1987: 146). While Havel's idealism may put him in a minority, minimalism fails to do justice to the variety of conceptions that political elites and ordinary people in these societies bring to bear when it comes to their expectations of and hopes for democracy (for evidence for 13 post-communist countries, see Dryzek and Holmes, 2002).

These sorts of considerations might suggest that those who study the real world of democracy (and especially democratic transitions) ought to listen more to democratic theorists. But the converse is also true: democratic theorists should attend more to real-world constraints and possibilities that empirical social science can help to illuminate. In common with many areas of political theory, democratic theory can sometimes lapse into a self-referential dialogue in which connections to real-world events, constraints, and possibilities are lost (Gunnell, 1986). As Jeffrey Isaac (1995) points out, the fall of the Berlin Wall went largely unnoticed by political theory. Whether or not this is a satisfactory state of affairs depends in the end on one's conception of the value and role of political theory. Yet normative democratic theory at least generally looks as though it is developing prescriptions that it has some interest in being followed, or at least attempted, in the real world. It is then problematic when theorists propose schemes that stand little chance of being implemented in the world as it is. For example, Young (1992), picking up on the model of associative democracy proposed by Joshua Cohen and Joel Rogers (1992), wants the first task of the state to be the organization of oppressed minorities into forces capable of exercising real power. This is not a kind of state whose existence it is at all plausible to postulate, especially given the many constraints and imperatives to which real states are subject. The theorist's last line of defence here might be that such abstractions are necessary in order to maintain a critical distance, to present counterfactual ideals that expose the shortcomings of real-world situations in particularly stark form. But does everyone need to do that?

Might not contextually sensitive critique be more productive? And is not a closed, self-referential discourse of democratic theory reflexively undemocratic in cutting itself off from those who struggle to promote, defend, develop, and deepen democracy? (A thoroughly reflexive approach to democratic theory would begin with popular conceptions of democracy; see Dryzek and Berejikian, 1993.)

An additional reason why democratic theorists should attend more to democratic practice is that sometimes problems that concern democratic theorists may actually find solutions in political practice. For example, David Schlosberg (1999) argues that the problem of engagement across deep difference identified by postmodern theorists as the key democratic challenge has been successfully negotiated in the political practice of the environmental justice movement in the United States.

I have argued that the two main poles in contemporary thinking about democracy are the deliberative approach and liberal minimalism. Some schools of thought have engaged both poles. So social choice theory can provide both a defence of minimalism and a critique of deliberation, though it can also be deployed to reach almost the opposite position. Civic republicanism has many synergies with deliberation, and can also be used to criticize liberal minimalism's application to real-world political systems. However, there has yet to be any direct engagement between deliberative democrats and the liberal minimalism of the comparative scholars of democratic transition and consolidation. The two approaches have only connected via intermediaries. This state of affairs might be indicative of the gap between democratic theory and democratic practice, though as I have argued, the minimalists have not got the practice right. And the fact that there are intermediaries shows that the gap can be bridged.

CONCLUSION

One measure of democratic theory's success will be the extent to which it can loosen the grip of liberal minimalism on those who study the comparative politics of democracy and democratization. A second more demanding measure would be found in the degree to which it can contribute to the global conversation about democratic development, in established liberal democracies and the transnational arena, no less than transitional societies and new democracies. These are of course both external tests: the internal conversation currently flourishes without them being passed, though there are sporadic exceptions (for example, in connection with deliberative opinion polls and citizens' juries). The fact that the internal conversation is full of vigour is cause for self-congratulation. But democratic political theory, precisely because it is *democratic* political theory, cannot get off so lightly in this respect as most other areas of political theory.

NOTE

For advice and criticism, I thank Robert Goodin, John Parkinson, and Philip Pettit.

REFERENCES

Ackerman, Bruce (1991) *We the People I: Foundations.* Cambridge, MA: Harvard University Press.

Archibugi, Daniele, David Held and Martin Köhler, eds (1998) *Re-Imagining Political Community: Studies in Cosmopolitan Democracy.* Cambridge: Polity.

Arrow, Kenneth J. (1951) *Social Choice and Individual Values.* New York: Wiley.

Barber, Benjamin (1984) *Strong Democracy: Participatory Politics for a New Age.* Berkeley, CA: University of California Press.

Berelson, Bernard (1952) 'Democratic theory and public opinion'. *Public Opinion Quarterly,* 16: 313–30.

Bessette, Joseph M. (1980) 'Deliberative democracy: the majoritarian principle in republican government'. In Robert A. Goldwin and William A. Shambra, eds, *How Democratic is the Constitution?* Washington, DC: American Enterprise Institute.

Bessette, Joseph M. (1994) *The Mild Voice of Reason: Deliberative Democracy and American National Government.* Chicago: University of Chicago Press.

Bohman, James (1998) 'The coming of age of deliberative democracy'. *Journal of Political Philosophy,* 6: 399–423.

Bohman, James and William Rehg (1997) *Deliberative Democracy: Essays on Reason and Politics.* Cambridge, MA: MIT Press.

Cohen, Jean and Andrew Arato (1992) *Civil Society and Political Theory.* Cambridge, MA: MIT Press.

Cohen, Joshua (1989) 'Deliberation and democratic legitimacy'. In Alan Hamlin and Philip Pettit, eds, *The Good Polity: Normative Analysis of the State.* Oxford: Blackwell.

Cohen, Joshua (1996) 'Procedure and substance in deliberative democracy'. In Seyla Benhabib, ed., *Democracy and Difference: Contesting the Boundaries of the Political.* Princeton, NJ: Princeton University Press.

Cohen, Joshua and Joel Rogers (1992) 'Secondary associations and democratic governance'. *Politics and Society,* 20: 393–472.

Coleman, Jules and John Ferejohn (1986) 'Democracy and social choice'. *Ethics,* 97: 6–25.

Connolly, William E. (1991) *Identity/Difference: Democratic Negotiations of Political Paradox.* Ithaca, NY: Cornell University Press.

Dahl, Robert A. (1971) *Polyarchy: Participation and Opposition.* New Haven, CT: Yale University Press.

Dahl, Robert A. (1989) *Democracy and its Critics.* New Haven, CT: Yale University Press.

Di Palma, Giuseppe (1990) *To Craft Democracies.* Berkeley, CA: University of California Press.

Downs, Anthony (1987) 'The evolution of democracy'. *Daedalus,* 116 (3): 119–48.

Dryzek, John S. (1996) *Democracy in Capitalist Times: Ideals, Limits, and Struggles.* New York: Oxford University Press.

Dryzek, John S. (2000) *Deliberative Democracy and Beyond: Liberals, Critics, Contestations.* Oxford: Oxford University Press.

Dryzek, John S. and Jeffrey Berejikian (1993) 'Reconstructive democratic theory'. *American Political Science Review,* 87: 48–60.

Dryzek, John S. and Leslie Holmes (2002) *Postcommunist Democratization: Political Discourses across Thirteen Countries.* Cambridge: Cambridge University Press.

Dryzek, John S. and Christian List (2003) 'Social choice theory and deliberative democracy: a reconciliation'. *British Journal of Political Science,* 33: 1–28.

Dunn, John (1979) *Western Political Theory in the Face of the Future.* Cambridge: Cambridge University Press.

Estlund, David (1993) 'Who's afraid of deliberative democracy? On the strategic/deliberative dichotomy in recent constitutional jurisprudence'. *Texas Law Review,* 71: 1437–77.

Fishkin, James (1995) *The Voice of the People: Public Opinion and Democracy.* New Haven, CT: Yale University Press.

Fraser, Nancy (1992) 'Rethinking the public sphere: a contribution to the critique of actually existing democracy'. In Craig Calhoun, ed., *Habermas and the Public Sphere.* Cambridge, MA: MIT Press.

Fukuyama, Francis (1989) 'The end of history?' *National Interest,* Summer: 3–18.

Fukuyama, Francis (1992) *The End of History and the Last Man.* New York: Free Press.

Goodin, Robert E. (2000) 'Democratic deliberation within'. *Philosophy and Public Affairs,* 29: 81–109.

Goodin, Robert E. (2002) *Reflective Democracy.* Oxford: Oxford University Press.

Green, Donald P. and Ian Shapiro (1994) *Pathologies of Rational Choice Theory: A Critique of Applications in Political Science.* New Haven, CT: Yale University Press.

Grofman, Bernard (1993) 'Public choice, civic republicanism, and American politics: perspectives of a "reasonable choice" modeler'. *Texas Law Review,* 71: 1541–87.

Grofman, Bernard and Scott Feld (1988) 'Rousseau's general will: a Condorcetian perspective'. *American Political Science Review,* 82: 567–76.

Gunnell, John G. (1986) *Between Philosophy and Politics: The Alienation of Political Theory.* Amherst, MA: University of Massachusetts Press.

Gutmann, Amy and Dennis Thompson (1996) *Democracy and Disagreement*. Cambridge, MA: Harvard University Press.

Habermas, Jürgen (1989) *Structural Transformation of the Public Sphere: An Inquiry into a Category of Bourgeois Society*. Cambridge MA: MIT Press.

Habermas, Jürgen (1996) *Between Facts and Norms: Contributions to a Discourse Theory of Law and Democracy*. Cambridge, MA: MIT Press.

Hanson, Russell L. (1989) 'Democracy'. In Terence Ball, James Farr and Russell L. Hanson, eds, *Political Innovation and Conceptual Change*. Cambridge: Cambridge University Press.

Hardin, Russell (1993) 'Public choice versus democracy'. In David Copp, Jean Hampton and John E. Roemer, eds, *The Idea of Democracy*. Cambridge: Cambridge University Press.

Heilbroner, Robert L. (1974) *An Inquiry Into the Human Prospect*. New York: Norton.

Held, David (1995) *Democracy and the Global Order: From the Nation State to Cosmopolitan Governance*. Cambridge: Polity.

Held, David (1996) *Models of Democracy*, 2nd edn. Cambridge: Polity.

Huntington, Samuel (1991) *The Third Wave*. Norman, OK: University of Oklahoma Press.

Isaac, Jeffrey (1995) 'The strange silence of political theory'. *Political Theory*, 23: 636–52.

Knight, Jack and James Johnson (1994) 'Aggregation and Deliberation: On the possibility of democratic legitimacy'. *Political Theory*, 22: 277–96.

Lienesch, Michael (1992) 'Wo(e)begon(e) democracy'. *American Journal of Political Science*, 36: 1004–14.

Lijphart, Arend (1984) *Democracies: Patterns of Majoritarian and Consensus Government in Twenty-One Countries*. New Haven, CT: Yale University Press.

Lijphart, Arend (1999) *Patterns of Democracy: Governmental Forms and Performance in Thirty-Six Countries*. New Haven, CT: Yale University Press.

Lindblom, Charles E. (1982) 'The market as prison'. *Journal of Politics*, 44: 324–36.

Linz, Juan J. and Alfred E. Stepan (1996) *Problems of Democratic Transition and Consolidation: Southern Europe, South America, and Post-Communist Europe*. Baltimore: Johns Hopkins University Press.

Lipset, Seymour Martin (1959) 'Some social prerequisites of democracy: economic development and political legitimacy'. *American Political Science Review*, 53: 69–105.

Lowi, Theodore J. (1969) *The End of Liberalism*. New York: Norton.

Mackie, Gerry (2003) *Democracy Defended*. Cambridge: Cambridge University Press.

Manin, Bernard (1987) 'On legitimacy and political deliberation'. *Political Theory*, 15: 338–68.

Mathews, Freya, ed. (1996) *Ecology and Democracy*. London: Cass.

Miller, David (1992) 'Deliberative democracy and social choice'. *Political Studies*, 40 (special issue): 54–67.

Mitchell, William C. and Randy T. Simmons (1994) *Beyond Politics: Markets, Welfare, and the Failure of Bureaucracy*. Boulder, CO: Westview.

Mueller, John (1996) 'Democracy, capitalism and the end of transition'. In Michael Mandelbaum, ed., *Postcommunism: Four Perspectives*. New York: Council on Foreign Relations.

O'Donnell, Guillermo (1994) 'Delegative democracy'. *Journal of Democracy*, 5: 55–69.

Pateman, Carole (1970) *Participation and Democratic Theory*. Cambridge: Cambridge University Press.

Pettit, Philip (1999) 'Republican freedom and contestatory democratization'. In Ian Shapiro and Casiano Hacker-Cordón, eds, *Democracy's Value*. Cambridge: Cambridge University Press, 163–90.

Przeworski, Adam (1998) 'Deliberation and ideological domination'. In Jon Elster, ed., *Deliberative Democracy*. Cambridge: Cambridge University Press, 140–60.

Przeworski, Adam (1999) 'Minimalist conception of democracy: a defense'. In Ian Shapiro and Casiano Hacker-Cordón, eds, *Democracy's Value*. Cambridge: Cambridge University Press, 23–55.

Przeworski, Adam, Michael E. Alvarez, Jose Antonio Cheibub and Fernando Limongi (2000) *Democracy and Development: Political Institutions and Well-Being in the World, 1950–1990*. Cambridge: Cambridge University Press.

Putnam, Robert D. (1993) *Making Democracy Work: Civic Traditions in Modern Italy*. Princeton, NJ: Princeton University Press.

Putnam, Robert D. (2000) *Bowling Alone: The Collapse and Revival of American Community*. New York: Simon and Schuster.

Rawls, John (1993) *Political Liberalism*. New York: Columbia University Press.

Rawls, John (1997) 'The idea of public reason revisited'. *University of Chicago Law Review*, 94: 765–807.

Riker, William H. (1982) *Liberalism against Populism: A Confrontation between the Theory of Democracy and the Theory of Social Choice*. San Francisco: Freeman.

Rowbotham, Sheila (1986) 'Feminism and democracy'. In David Held and Christopher Pollitt, eds, *New Forms of Democracy*. Beverly Hills, CA: Sage, 78–109.

Rueschemeyer, Dietrich, Evelyn Huber Stephens and John D. Stephens (1992) *Capitalist Development and Democracy*. Chicago: University of Chicago Press.

Sandel, Michael (1996) *Democracy's Discontent*. Cambridge, MA: Harvard University Press.

Sartori, Giovanni (1962) *Democratic Theory*. Detroit: Wayne State University Press.

Sartori, Giovanni (1987) *The Theory of Democracy Revisited*. Chatham, NJ: Chatham House.

Sartori, Giovanni (1991) 'Rethinking democracy: bad polity and bad politics'. *International Social Science Journal*, 129: 437–50.

Saward, Michael (2000) 'Less than meets the eye: democratic legitimacy and deliberative theory'. In Michael

Saward, ed., *Democratic Innovation: Deliberation, Association and Representation*. London: Routledge, 66–77.

Schedler, A. (1998) 'What is democratic consolidation?' *Journal of Democracy*, 9: 91–107.

Schlosberg, David (1999) *Environmental Justice and the New Pluralism: The Challenge of Difference for Environmentalism*. Oxford: Oxford University Press.

Schumpeter, Joseph A. (1942) *Capitalism, Socialism, and Democracy*. New York: Harper.

Shapiro, Ian (1999) 'Enough of deliberation: politics is about interest and power'. In Stephen Macedo, ed., *Deliberative Politics: Essays on Democracy and Disagreement*. New York: Oxford University Press, 28–38.

Shepsle, Kenneth (1979) 'Institutional arrangements and equilibrium in multidimensional voting models'. *American Journal of Political Science*, 23: 27–60.

Smith, Graham and Corinne Wales (2000) 'Citizens' juries and deliberative democracy'. *Political Studies*, 48: 51–65.

Van Mill, David (1996) 'The possibility of rational outcomes from democratic discourse and procedures'. *Journal of Politics*, 58: 734–52.

Young, Iris Marion (1990) *Justice and the Politics of Difference*. Princeton, NJ: Princeton University Press.

Young, Iris Marion (1992) 'Social groups in associative democracy'. *Politics and Society*, 20: 529–34.

Young, Iris Marion (2000) *Inclusion and Democracy*. Oxford: Oxford University Press.

12

Discourse Theory

JAMES BOHMAN

'Discourse theory' may be used in a broad and in a narrow sense. In the broad sense it refers to any theoretical enterprise that considers language in use, that is, language as it is used in practices and performances, from the analysis of ordinary conversation or public argumentation to formal scientific papers or parliamentary discussion. It can also be used in the narrow sense of a particular sort of normative ethical and political theory derived from the work of Jürgen Habermas (1984; 1996) [see also Chapters 20 and 29]. This theory provides an account of those social practices in which dialogue, reason giving and argumentation play a central role and which thus may be called 'discursive'. It is also a theory of rationality based on the practical know-how of speaking and acting subjects that is a social scientific alternative to instrumental or strategic conceptions dominant in rational choice and game theory. Discourse theory in both senses has already found wide application from argumentation theory (Crosswhite, 1996) to the sociology of scientific knowledge (Lynch, 1993). It has also become significant in political theory, especially in constructive approaches to the public sphere and democracy on the one hand (Habermas, 1996; Calhoun, 1989) and in critical analyses of race and gender on the other (Goldberg, 1990; Butler, 1993). While the former figures prominently in normative theories, the latter sort of discourse theory is often the basis for showing the inadequacies of normative claims to reason and justification.

Discourse in the broad sense includes 'talk', 'writing', and 'discussion'. Social scientists use discourse theory to analyse how people talk about politics and social problems (Gamson, 1992). Discourse theory may also attempt to uncover shared assumptions and assumed capabilities, such

as the ways in which specific policy issues (such as nuclear power or international trade) are framed in terms of the extent of expert authority. Such assumptions can shift to a more publicly oriented frame (Gamson, 1988). Political discourses also emerge around institutions, as when constitutions and constitutional courts produce an evolving discourse on the nature of rights and obligations in liberal democracies (Dryzek, 2000), or Orientalism around European colonialism (Said, 1978), or when various international financial institutions give loans and create policies to promote 'development' based on specific models of 'baskets' of human goods as commodities (Sen, 1999). These discourses themselves can become the subject of second-order public debate and discussion, as critics and citizens become dissatisfied with such policies and the assumptions that guide them. In this case, discourse becomes a means not merely for conveying information or for public discussion, but rather for the contestation and challenge of policies and practices.

How can discourse do all these things? When applied to politics, discourse theory focuses on practices that have features that go beyond mere talk. Discourse in political practices and in the public sphere seems to be directed to an implied audience or 'unseen gallery' and thus goes beyond 'sociable' interaction among friends (Gamson, 1992: 20). Thus, discourse is communication directed to an indefinite audience, and an extension of face-to-face interaction that is made possible by technologies of writing, mass media or computer assisted communication and by formal political institutions (Thompson, 1995). Second, discourse that has the property of being public is also reflexive or second-order communication; it must at least include the possibility of communication about the mode and assumptions of communication itself, for example, whether it is really public or not (Habermas, 1984). This reflexivity is apparent especially when communication fails, when the assumptions that we make for practical purposes 'until further notice' in Garfinkel's (1969: 33) phrase are no longer successful in producing mutual understanding or co-ordination of action. In this case, speakers must make explicit the basis of communication itself by providing reasons and arguments that others might be able to accept. Just how far the demand for justification can be pursued by speakers and institutionalized in practices is subject to dispute among the proponents of various theories of discourse. For some, the linguistic medium makes reflexivity possible, while for others it imposes insuperable limits on reflection (Hoy and McCarthy, 1994).

For these reasons, discourse theory emerges at the intersection between philosophy, social science and political theory. On the one hand, various disciplines in philosophy underwent the 'linguistic turn', especially in the philosophy of language where the slogan 'meaning as use' replaced less socially informed theories. This emphasis on use focuses attention on 'how we do things with words' and thus also on the conditions of success for various sorts of speech acts (Austin, 1962; Searle, 1969; Habermas, 1979). At the same time, the philosophy of social science attempted an 'interpretive turn', in which agents' own self-interpretations become central to making actions intelligible to us, rather than explaining actions in light of causal laws or mechanisms available to the observer. In interpretive social science, texts and discourse become central objects for interpretation (Geertz, 1973; Taylor, 1985), while the focus on shared meaning led to the rejection of the emphasis on individual preferences and aggregation common to rational choice theorists. In social theory, then, these turns gave new importance to the potential generative role of communication and the structuring role of language and linguistic practices.

Political theory has experienced a similar set of turns. The role of discourse highlights the differences between the 'market' and the 'forum', between the aggregation of given preferences in social choice mechanisms and the formation and transformation of preferences in public discourse (Elster, 1997; Cohen, 1997). Nowhere was the shift to discourse more important than in democratic theory. This distinction allows political theory to take a 'deliberative turn' in emphasizing discursive and communicative practices in which participants attempt to convince each other by offering reasons in public discussion and debate. Not only does this open up a space for giving and asking for reasons in

the public sphere or in various forums, but reason giving is also a particularly non-coercive form of political integration and a potentially effective method for solving problems and settling conflicts [see further Chapter 11]. All of these various 'turns' in philosophy, social science and political theory together make discourse central to normative and empirical theorizing and mark a watershed in thinking about the form of democratic politics and social integration specific to modern societies.

The focus of this chapter is on the various uses of discourse theory that are now common in political theory. First, several approaches to discourse theory need to be distinguished along three important dimensions: whether they are normative, empirical, or both. Next, the usefulness of discourse theory will be illustrated with respect to normative democratic theory, with respect to institutional design and to democratic deliberation. Third, the critical uses of discourse theory will be developed in terms of problems of ideology and toleration that are not merely limited to 'non-ideal theory' in Rawls's (1999) sense. Finally, I consider the limits of discourse theory and suggest that the issue is properly epistemic rather than linguistic, a matter of the precise nature of the critical know-how necessary to participate in discursive practices. The proper goal of such a discursive political theory is to avoid the impasses of past debates: the Scylla of an empty idealization of discourse and the Charybdis of a blind scepticism that offers no guide to the practices in which discourse is employed.

APPROACHES TO DISCOURSE THEORY: NORMATIVE AND EMPIRICAL

Discourse theory has been developed through three competing approaches. The first and broadly 'constructive' approach is fundamentally normative, where the practical know-how of speaking and acting subjects is developed into a theory of communicative rationality that has implications for how we ought to think of political and legal institutions (Habermas, 1984; Rawls, 1999). It construes discourse as a rule-governed activity, the rules of which may be reconstructed as procedural idealizations (such as giving all the opportunity to speak, to engage in all forms of speech and so on). Such a theory permits political theorists to develop explicit rules for governing discourses, rules that may have either a role in criticizing existing discursive practices or a constructive role in evaluating and designing institutions. Since not all assumptions of discourse can be made fully explicit in rules, such an account can no more be a complete account of democratic political life than a written constitution can describe all of its derivative practices. If such a theory is too idealizing, there may be a wide gap between the norms and ideals it proscribes and the existing practices. Faced with this gap, other theories of discourse try to capture deeper, more structural assumptions and presuppositions that shape actual discussion and practices (Foucault, 1977; Bourdieu, 1991; Butler, 1993). This approach identifies deep linguistic structures and thus eschews explicit rules, aiming instead to uncover deep practical constraints operating through norms. It alerts us to relations of power within discourses.

These two conflicting approaches are not the only available theoretical options. The third, broadly 'reconstructive' and critical approach combines the best features of both (Bohman, 1996; Hoy and McCarthy, 1994). It seeks a theory that is normative without relying solely on idealizations and counter-factual ideals, and empirical without becoming skeptical of all attempts to institutionalize discursive practices of justification. Such an approach is operative in some proponents of the deliberative turn in democratic theory [see Chapter 11]. A defensible discourse theory thus provides a test case for normative theory that is informed by social science but still seeks to develop robust and practical norms for guiding institutions and practices.

CONSTRUCTING IDEAL DISCURSIVE PROCEDURES

As the leading proponent of the normative theory of discourse, Habermas proposes that the development of norms of discourse is the task of a theory of communicative or discursive rationality, where rationality is defined as 'how speaking and acting subjects acquire and use knowledge' (1984: 11). Such a broad definition suggests that the theory could be developed through explicating the conditions for reaching understanding through language, and this task falls primarily on 'formal pragmatics'. 'Formal pragmatics' is Habermas's term for a general account of the capacity of a speaker to use and understand speech acts correctly: 'the know-how of subjects who are capable of speech and action, who are attributed the capacity to produce valid utterances, and who consider themselves capable of distinguishing (at least intuitively) between valid and invalid expressions' (1990: 31). The focus of formal pragmatics is on the know-how necessary for producing and evaluating correct and incorrect expressions or valid and invalid utterances, or for producing well-formed utterances that meet the conditions of successful communication.

What might such a formal pragmatic analysis contribute to a theory of discourse? The intuitive knowledge of a competent speaker permits them to engage in second-order evaluation in asking for justification or reasons for various sorts of validity claims that are implicit in utterances; to understand an utterance is to know its 'acceptability conditions'. While validity claims may remain implicit so long as communication is unproblematic and ongoing, competent speakers may also demand that the implied warrant be redeemed and demand explicit justification in second-order communication (communication about communication, or 'discourse' proper) in order to reach an understanding. Habermas locates the rational potential of communication in discourse in the explicit and second-order capacities of actors to provide reasons for their own claims and evaluate the reasons offered by others; they thereby engage in argumentation, through which the implicit basis of ongoing communication is suspended and made the basis of explicit testing, judgement and assent. Such second-order communication is *discourse* when it takes the form of acts of communication that suspend the constraints of action and co-ordination and examine the validity claims implicit in the utterances made by speakers.

Such a reconstruction of implicit know-how may have a critical function in so far as it can specify when speakers violate the conditions of rationality implicit in communicatively successful utterances. For Habermas, reconstruction also has a constructive role to the extent that these conditions can be explicated and then formulated as explicit rules or principles. A formal pragmatic theory could then reconstruct discursive justification in a general way, through what Habermas calls 'the principle of discourse'. When applied to normative statements, this principle offers a proceduralist justification of any norm in the form of a principle of universalization: 'Only those norms of actions are valid to which all those affected could agree as participants in rational discourses' (Habermas, 1996: 138; Baynes, 1995: 208). The general principle of discourse is then specified in a principle for the justification of norms or rules. Second-level principles of discursive justification can then be applied in various more specific principles tailored to specific domains of discourses, such as moral or legal argumentation or the variety of forms of political deliberation (Alexy, 1989). These explicit principles guide practice, and institutions in various domains ought to approximate them in justifying their rules or actions.

Habermas's explicit rule for democratic legitimacy is analogous to Kant's 'general principle of right', in that the principle of democracy is a general principle of legitimate law making: 'Only those laws are legitimate that can meet with the agreement of all legal consociates in a discursive process of law making that in turn has been legally constituted' (1996: 141). The democratic principle is then an application of discursive justification applied to the law making process. Laws are valid as norms to the extent that those subject to law also formulate and agree to them as participants in rational discourse. In this discursive process, citizens are the authors of the laws to which they are subjected; they are legally guaranteed certain rights that ensure public and private autonomy. Discourse theory not only permits us to recast general normative principles in terms of discursive procedures, thus enriching Kant's principle of right or Rawls's first principle of justice as equal freedom; it also has a constructive role in formulating principles that guide or regulate the very practices it reconstructs. The principle is both ideal and proceduralist: the conditions of legitimacy are counterfactual. Under such ideal conditions of assertibility, all participants in the discourse would not only agree, but would agree for the same reason, so that all disagreement must be due to the ways in which the actual conditions fall short of the ideally rational procedure. This abstraction from actual discourse leads some to propose a historically contingent and context-specific theory rather than a theory of discursive rationality.

EMPIRICAL AND SOMETIMES SCEPTICAL APPROACHES

The second set of approaches start from a less idealized and more empirical view of discourse, finding in it a constraining and limiting rather than an enabling condition for reflection and deliberation as essential aspects of social practices. Social scientific approaches look closely at the specific features of discursive contexts, noting for example the role of social status in the emergence of the scientific discourse (Shapin, 1994) or the role that slavery and racial categories play in the discourse on citizenship in American history (Smith, 1997). Here we find that the closer we look at actual discourses, the more they depart from the ideal procedural conditions that constitute their rationality. Moreover, ethnomethodological discourse analysis tied to specific situations shows that norms and rules are highly flexible and contingent in their application in informal contexts, even if they are crucial to the act of making others intelligible (Heritage, 1984). The critical legal studies movement has shown that many legal and constitutional norms are indeterminate, and even capable of justifying decisions that now seem to contradict them (Unger, 1986). Indeed, empirical studies demonstrate how rules shape practices (when they do) and are useful in

closing the gap between ideal counterfactual analysis and its application to social and political practices, as well as in showing why procedures may fail to realize the discursive principles on which they are purportedly based (Hoy and McCarthy, 1994). However, some empirical analyses of discourse attempt to underwrite more sceptical challenges to normative theories. There are two main critics who take these empirically informed challenges a step further in language related to social power: Michel Foucault and his theory of 'discursive formations' as regimes of truth, and Pierre Bourdieu and his conception of symbolic power.

Michel Foucault argues discourses can be analysed as 'regimes of rationality' which are not independent of power and its effects but rather are constitutive of a 'general politics of truth'. It is on the basis of such a regime rather than ideal discursive conditions that speakers accept that something is a 'truth candidate' (Hacking, 1986). In this way, validity is not independent of social context but is relative to a regime of truth that shapes what is possibly true, normatively correct or practically feasible. Moreover, the human sciences are themselves inscribed in a regime of truth that is also implicated in social technologies that establish the normal and the abnormal, the distribution of bodies in social space. Foucault (1977) argues that the effects of power discourses are connected to 'disciplinary practices' that cannot be dissolved by democracy. Here the issue is one of agency: whether or not discourse is something so deeply constitutive that it is no longer under the control of speakers [see further Chapters 4, 20 and 29].

By contrast, Bourdieu's challenge is more epistemic, relativizing linguistic activities and practices to a background habitus, a set of dispositions inculcated in socialization. The object here is to appeal to 'generative and implicit schemata' rather than explicit or consciously sanctioned rules. Practices are regular and reproducible patterns of action 'without being the product of rules and without presupposing a conscious aim or the express mastery of them' (Bourdieu, 1977: 55). He criticizes ideal theories for their 'linguistic communism', as blind to the forms of status and inequalities that make it possible for speakers to be authoritative and persuasive. The capacity to produce comprehensible utterances 'may be quite inadequate to produce sentences that are likely to be listened to, likely to be recognized as acceptable in all situations in which there is occasion to speak' (Bourdieu, 1991: 55). Normative discourse theories leave out social relations among speakers, their different social positions and their capacities to garner linguistic authority. Bourdieu thinks that because habitus is not a matter of rules, its limitations are not in principle accessible to speakers at the level of second-order communication, when speakers must offer explicit justification for their actions and practices. Both challenges see power as operating within discourse itself, not merely as an external constraint upon it. These same sorts of constraints on discourse may also operate in the ways that deeply historically embedded inequalities such as race and gender shape discourse and restrict its reflexivity (Butler, 1993: 232).

These challenges to normative theories of discourse raise important questions about the epistemic constraints on speakers and social limitations on the linguistic medium. This sort of limitation may in part be overcome by the formal organization of speech in institutional settings, such as in courts of law or democratic institutions of parliamentary debate. They also must be answered at the same level at which they are raised: the analysis of the restrictions on communication and more importantly on discourse as the second-order communication in which justification of practices and policies occur. Normative theories of discourse discuss these same issues in terms of the theory of ideology and the critical attitude of toleration in communication. Before turning to these problems as limitations on democratic practices, let me turn first to the discursive reconstruction of democratic theory, including questions of institutional design.

DISCOURSE AND DEMOCRACY

Any discursive account of democracy is not merely an account of democratic discourse, however idealized it may be. Rather, it must itself be a complete account of democracy, in the sense of offering a reconstruction of its usual elements while giving them novel interpretations. In what follows, I will discuss the main lines of a reconstruction of democracy as a discursive practice, guided to a large extent (although not exclusively) by Habermas's normative political theory. Although Habermas, Dryzek and some others use the terms 'discursive' or 'communicative' democracy or offer a 'discursive theory of democratic legitimacy', almost all theories of deliberative democracy have to a large degree been shaped by discourse theory proper or offer an implied theory of discourse themselves. This discursive component defines what deliberation is to be; for example, 'reasoned argumentation', or discussion guided only by 'the force of the better argument', where decision making must be based on reasons that 'all may accept as free and equal citizens'. Indeed, John Dewey already argued that democracy itself is not a feasible idea unless there exists 'full publicity', or free and open communication necessary for deliberation as a form

of social inquiry. Whatever obstructs or restricts publicity, he argued, 'limits and distorts public opinion and checks and distorts thinking on social affairs' (Dewey, 1988: 339). How might institutions approximate this ideal and promote full publicity?

Discursive Designs

Discourse theory has a properly constructive role in providing the basis for various forms of institutions designed with the aim of creating opportunities for wide and effective participation in discursive processes of public discussion, deliberation and argumentation. Constitutions are in part discursively designed, so as to establish not only the separation of powers and thus discursive competence, but also a division of labour in communication and deliberation. Broadly speaking, the framers of the United States Constitution had deliberation in mind, in designing institutions that would produce the 'mild voice of reason' that would overcome narrow self-interestedness, the passions, and the mischief of factions (Bessette, 1994). More recent discussions of the deliberative or discursive design of democratic institutions reflect a three-level distinction of various aspects of political life in a complex and pluralistic modern society. Such a society is differentiated in a number of ways, with distinctions between the state and the market, civil society and its associations, and the political public sphere of citizens and various sub-public spheres. In general, discourse and deliberation can go on both within and outside various formal institutions, in civil society and the public sphere as well as in the formal institutions of the modern state with its law making powers and authority (Habermas, 1996; Dryzek, 1996).

The discursive approach to democracy leads to an institutional design that is based on a 'two-track model', in which on the one hand formal institutions generate effective decisions through the medium of law and thus are 'jurisgenerative' (Michelman, 1988; Habermas, 1996), and on the other hand robust public sphere and civil society allow citizens to engage in deliberation with each other from a variety of perspectives. Deliberative politics then takes place in both tracks at once, in a complex discursive network that includes argumentation, discussion, bargaining and compromise. Formal institutions must be designed to be open to influence from the wider and more informal public sphere and civil society, with various mechanisms such as representation and elections that ensure not only access to influence but also that a variety of perspectives emerge in deliberation and debate. Formal institutions require at least the widespread perception of legitimacy, and in this way 'cannot operate without an associated and supportive discourse (or discourses)' (Dryzek, 1996: 204). This includes the discourse of rights and citizenship for liberal institutions or the discourse of scientific authority and expertise for many administrative institutions.

A main issue separating various proponents of deliberative designs is whether or not and in what ways public deliberation actually shapes or should influence decisions. Such influence may be direct or indirect. Others want a more direct role for deliberation, seeing institutional reform of law or administration as necessary in order to make them more open to citizens' deliberation; this would require new forms of decision making, including deliberative planning or citizen juries. Thus, there is a conflict between a view of public discourse as providing challenges to formal legal and political authority and, as such, being indirectly deliberative (Dryzek, 2000; Pettit, 1998) and subject to discursive challenge from the outside; and the view of those who see it as more directly deliberative in the decision making process itself (Habermas, 1996: ch. 8; Dorf and Sabel, 1998). This is not as much of a forced choice as some make it out to be, since in some instances challenge may be the best or indeed the only effective means for influence given the way in which political authority is constituted; or there may be cases in which more directly deliberative approaches are necessary to preserve the reality of popular sovereignty and accountability to citizens. Scientific or expert authority that is delegated public power provides an example of the first; the planning process in public administration provides an example of the second. Indeed, there seems to be a continuum from direct to indirect deliberation, depending on the sort of institutions and supportive discourses involved.

Democracy and Administration: Designing Non-Democratic Institutions Discursively

The discursive design of democratic institutions seeks to open the policies and decisions of powerful institutions to discursive testing. Newer forms of political authority such as expertise and the media seem to operate outside the potentially discursively designed constitutional state and are less open to discursive influence. Administrative institutions act for the common good, a use of public power authorized by legislative mandates to achieve certain ends. For that reason, philosophers from Locke to Hegel and Weber see administrators as engaged only in 'neutral' means/ends reasoning, a necessity for the exercise of effective political power. Foucault and others have analysed the way in which this power is exercised in part via discursive means,

in the way that people and things are named, classified and disciplined in a 'symbolic order' (Foucault, 1977; Bourdieu, 1991; Flyvbjerg, 1998). Social scientists also have long recognized the ambiguous relationship between democracy and bureaucracy: Weber saw that democracy helps produce more bureaucracy, even as bureaucracy tends to undermine democracy as the former becomes an efficient 'social machine' (Weber, 1946; Hummel, 1994), open only indirectly to deliberative influence.

The alternative is to put deliberative mechanisms and interaction with the public within the design of administrative institutions themselves, and this sort of design has taken the form of 'deliberative planning' (Fischer and Forester, 1994; Forester, 1993). As Habermas puts it, administrators 'cannot avoid appealing to normative reasons when implementing legal imperatives', so these processes must occur within procedures that pass the test of constitutional legitimacy and lead to the 'democratization of administration' (1996: 440) by discursive means. Similar sorts of considerations might apply to other forms of non-democratic social authority, such as the authority of medical researchers that has been recently challenged by AIDS activists who sought to directly influence the practice of medical experimentation (Epstein, 1996).

These collaborative processes could certainly be fruitfully applied to deliberative processes within other institutions of the constitutional state, making them all potentially more 'directly deliberative' than the two-track solution to size and complexity permits (Dorf and Sabel, 1998). Discursive modes of decision making are more feasible if decision making power is dispersed, where implementation is not subject to the requirement of uniform solutions and thus open to local variations and concerns. In fact, such decentralized and directly deliberative processes seem appropriate in supranational contexts that go beyond the representative institutions of the modern state, such as the emerging post-sovereign polity of the European Union.

Democratic Discourse: Restricted or Plural in Form?

For some proponents of deliberative democracy, a strong distinction between reasoned argumentation and mere discussion provides the basis for the claim that deliberation must be oriented to consensus (Habermas, 1996; Cohen, 1997). Deliberation is not merely discourse or dialogue, Cohen argues, because it must be 'reasoned', that is based on 'public argument and reasoning among equal citizens' that yield the single best answer (1997: 74). Critics often charge that both of these claims are exclusionary and lead to undemocratic consequences under the circumstance of background injustice and pervasive inequalities. It might seem that an orientation to consensus is not a requirement of deliberation, even if it may function as a regulative ideal. Deliberation must at least resemble argumentation to the extent that it is a matter of giving and asking for reasons. The reasons that make a decision acceptable ought to be distinguished from modes by which they are communicated. Democratic standards demanded for decisions need not apply to the medium of communication as such, and not all formal public spheres need to be ideally inclusive. This means that formal theories of communication and rationality cannot decide in advance precisely what modes and forms of communication are empirically appropriate in various settings.

The first tension between the empirical and normative dimensions of a theory of democratic deliberation concerns whether or not there is a specific type of discourse that characterizes democratic deliberation in general, as Habermas and Cohen hold for argumentation. Once again, it appears that the choice is between a theory of deliberative democracy that takes deliberation to be highly constrained and thus potentially exclusionary, and one that takes deliberation to have no normative constraints in the informal public sphere. The rejection of the former may be motivated by the attempt to see public deliberation as broader than the confines of formal institutions of the constitutional state (Dryzek, 2000). Any specific form of discourse may privilege certain citizens over others, as when argumentation favours articulate and dispassionate speakers and thus the better-educated elites (Young, 2000; Sanders, 1997). It seems an empirical question whether argument favours the privileged. Regardless of how this debate about acceptable forms of discourse is settled, even more important for political equality is the fact that some differences in competence and abilities among participants will remain. Assuming that both formal and informal settings are necessary for robust deliberation, how could formal and informal discourses interact so that unjust privilege and unequal influence may be avoided?

Is argumentation really a formal mode of discourse? If discourse is to be distinguished from acts of communication as a second-order and reflective activity, then argumentation in a general sense is the mode of critical self-reflection, of making claims and justifications explicit. Furthermore, if utterances make validity claims and these claims are supported by reasons, then argumentation is precisely the process by which speakers' claims can be tested and made explicit (Habermas, 1984: 42). Even here, however, there remains an irreducible empirical diversity of types of argumentation, from the strict arguments made in the context of scientific disciplines or the regulated context of a court with rules of evidence, to arguments that attempt to convince 'anyone'. Rather than being merely formal, argumentation can be seen rhetorically as a way to settle conflicts over reasons and assumptions that inform practices, although less than in the conception of persuasion through oratory favoured by some critics of deliberative democracy (Remer, 1999). As opposed to both formal and rhetorical models, such an account conceives of arguments dialogically, as the giving of reasons and the answering of objections raised by one's fellow citizens. Rather than as a means of reaching a conclusive agreement, argumentation is better seen as an ongoing means of resolving conflict that is successful only if each perspective is taken into account and each objection given a hearing (Crosswhite, 1996: 102ff).

Similar criticisms emerge when reason giving is thought of by critics in an overly cognitivist and consensualist way. With regard to the first, reasoned argumentation is often construed logically as linking premises to a conclusion in a complex series of statements that is not enthymematic. While some reason giving may be guided by institutionalized, strict requirements such as in a court of law, reasons are better construed as discursive responses to challenges to claims: 'A claim is not an argument; a claim with a reason is' (Crosswhite, 1996: 79). Reason giving and argumentation may be seen not only in a more dialogical way, but also as operating in the specific context of disagreement and conflict and their resolution. Argumentation makes the conflict explicit and mutual, establishing an exchange of challenges and reasons between the claimant and respondent (1996: 102ff). On this view, there are special features of all 'public' reasons; if all participants may raise challenges, this responsiveness must be oriented to an indefinite audience and is still possible even given persistent disagreement. Indeed, disagreement is precisely what makes democratic deliberation not only necessary, but also fruitful and productive when tested through the variety of perspectives typical of a diverse and pluralistic audience. Argumentative discourse need not presuppose unanimity, or seek consensus, but rather places conflicts within a mutually constructed space of reasons.

This fact of disagreement raises the issue of whether or not public deliberation is 'oriented to consensus'. Consensus is meant here to contrast with mere aggregation of preferences in voting and with bargaining or compromise. Certainly, if democracy were only voting and bargaining, it would lack the self-critical testing and responsiveness of reason giving and discourse; the problems of the tyranny of the majority and aggregation problems of social choice would undermine the effectiveness of democracy and its claims to legitimacy. However, if we demand too much agreement and an overly strong conception of consensus, then we lose the advantages of resolving conflict through argumentative means. Habermas thinks that participants in argumentation must be guided by the ideal of a single right answer to which all agree 'for the same reasons' (1996: ch. 8; Bohman and Rehg, 1996). He may well be correct that an overly agonistic conception of public discourse would undermine the epistemic basis for claims to democratic legitimacy, that is, that democratic deliberation is legitimate and not only is a fair process, but is more likely to find the most equitable and true outcome (Estlund, 1997). For all its attractions to critics of deliberation, agonistic debate is no less open to the charge of elitism (Benhabib, 1991), and even less based on the sort of co-operation needed to resolve conflict mutually. At the same time, the demand that all agree for the same reasons is overly strong and reduces the epistemic benefits of argumentation and challenge. If participants agree for different reasons, the epistemic gains that result from testing any agreement from a plurality of perspectives would arguably be superior to the gains of any orientation to consensus as a regulative norm.

Besides issues related to the emphasis on argumentation and consensus as overly narrow, other critics of deliberative democracy argue that it has too narrow a conception of the range of discursive possibilities within the public forum, leading to the exclusion of rhetoric, testimony, and other important modes of speech that do not seem to be forms of reason giving. The wider notion of argumentation as involving claims, challenges and reasons as responses vitiates these criticisms to some degree. If 'all speech acts must be open to all participants' in free and open communication, then perhaps the most important deliberative speech act is related to the opening of a discursive exchange or the proposing of a topic or theme for public deliberation (Bohman, 1996). Indeed, to make a claim is to invite a response, and with this kind of invitation comes an implicit obligation to be responsive to those who reply. Indeed, the discursive obligations of citizenship involve not only the willingness to engage in the special mutual conflict distinctive of argumentative practices but also obligations of responsiveness and answerability to others. Listening is thus just as important an obligation as speaking, and it is here that asymmetries are likely to emerge rather than on the expressive side, however formally restrictive some public spheres may be in permissible modes of expression. What if such collaborative perspective taking is blocked, and communication remains unsuccessful in resolving conflict? This raises issues of ideology and toleration, of putting the current and sometimes unnoticed limits of discourse up for democratic debate and challenge.

IDEOLOGY AND DEMOCRACY: TOLERATION AND THE LIMITS OF DISCOURSE

Democracy traditionally refers to a specific set of institutions that assure citizens' self-rule via procedural mechanisms that, at the very least, permit equal access to political influence. For example, making decisions according to voting rules such as the formal principle of 'one person, one vote' is also an attempt to assure political equality by distributing political power widely. Other decision rules would require different forms of equality: in 'deliberative politics' in the constitutional state, equal chances to participate in deliberation might be conjoined with mechanisms of decision making by majority rule (Habermas, 1996: ch. 8). However important they may be, the necessary conditions for deliberative politics are not exhausted by explicit rules of justification or the distribution of power in decision making. Besides the background of common knowledge of such rules and of a shared political culture, democracy in general and deliberative democracy in particular require a particular communicative infrastructure. Without the effective operation of implicit norms of communicative success as a resource available to all, formal procedures and institutions, no matter how well designed, will not succeed in distributing power in accordance with explicit norms of political freedom, equality and publicity (Bohman, 1996: ch. 3). The lack of consideration of the relation between implicit norms of communicative success and explicit norms for the distribution of power has led to practical deficits in normative theories of discursive politics. Here we can incorporate the insights of sceptical-empirical theories and apply them to the existing structures of communication and deliberation in particular institutions. If they are to be made grounds for deepening democratic practices, these should be formulated not as theoretical claims about the limits of language or reflection in general, but as the efficacy of citizens who currently lack effective voice and address their criticisms to other citizens as claims to justice. Is democratic discourse a means of overcoming the implicit restrictions of political discourses informed by social categories of racist and sexist speech?

Rather than only being a set of explicit principles of justification and institutional decision rules, *democracy* is also a particular structure of communication. It is a structure of communication among free and equal citizens. By contrast, *ideology* restricts or limits social processes of communication and the conditions of success within them [see further Chapter 1]. As a reconstruction of the correct insights of the Marxian critique of liberal ideology, the theory of distorted communication is therefore especially suited to the ways in which meanings are used to reproduce power even under explicit rules of equality and freedom. This is not to say that explicit rules are unimportant: they make it possible for overt forms of coercion and power to be constrained, the illegitimacy of which requires no appeal to norms implicit in practices. For example, violations of communicative freedom may remain implicit: the success of a deliberation may simply not be a matter of putting one's reasons up for evaluation by others when one avoids communication altogether. Under conditions of great inequality, contested topics may simply be avoided at the agenda setting stage that reflects organizational bias.

In any actual democracy, both strategic and communicative action may be present. For example, large advantages in the agency freedom of one group over all others may be due to the possession of vastly greater resources or other forms of social power; the achievement of their goals may not depend upon the consensual resolution of a conflict with groups with less social power. If Przeworski and Wallerstein (1988) are right, for example, powerful economic groups have historically been able to attain their agency goals not by explicitly excluding topics from democratic discussion but rather by implied threats and other non-deliberative means (Bohman, 1996). We can see the differences between such strategic forms of interaction to the extent that they reflect differences in bargaining power, regardless of the democratic means used to reach this equilibrium. Threats of declining investments block redistributive schemes, such as those that would burden well-off groups with higher tax rates; these credible threats circumvent the need to convince others of the reasons for such policies or to put some issue under democratic control. Similar discursive effects occur when institutions operate with implicit discursive frames, as did the Nuclear Regulatory Agency when it considered the 1966 partial meltdown of the Detroit Edison reactor to be a mere 'engineering mishap' (Gamson, 1992). The excessive agency freedom of some and the lack of social power of others means that some dissenting reasons will not become topics to be recognized or respected. However, it is possible to shift the framework of justification in both these cases, where the meanings of policies are changed and new agendas formed. In these cases, strategic actions by social movements are used to open up communication where it is blocked, to move discourse and deliberation beyond a bargaining equilibrium asymmetrical negotiating power [see further Chapter 20].

By looking at such cases, we can better see the division of labour in reconstructive theories of discourse. Explicit rules function to create the frameworks in which institutions operate to the extent that they can be embodied in deliberative procedures. But this constructive role for the theory is not sufficient, since implicit social norms can undermine communicative success within an institutional framework of explicit rules. Civil rights, for example, may be interpreted legally so as to establish and guarantee a minimum threshold and the fair value of communicative liberties. They can be interpreted, for example, to assure that voting power is more equitably distributed, permitting greater access to representative forums, or they may open up regulations of political speech to diminish the effects of discrepancies in campaign financing. The emergence of new norms or the reinterpretation of old ones may require a period of what Ackerman (1991) calls 'constitutional politics' within an existing democracy. Ackerman thus sees the constitution as an open-ended discursive project subject to paradigm shifts at historical junctures such as Reconstruction after the Civil War and the Great Depression. These changes reflect 'discourse moments', to use Gamson's (1992: Part I) term, in which the people, the courts, or the executive respond to historical circumstance by reinterpreting and recreating the Constitution.

Besides constitutional reform, limitations on expression may demand the formation of alternative public spheres, the developed forms of expression of which expand the pool of reasons and the styles of acceptable public communication in the larger public sphere. In all of these cases, the critic is equipped with the reflective abilities of a participant in a communicative process, not the least of which entails the ability to challenge the correctness of the communicative process itself. But in this case, circularity is avoided because the critic does not have to start from scratch: bootstrapping of new communicative possibilities begins with the ability to participate in those areas of everyday communication, no matter how small, which are not distorted by power. At the very least, reflection produces gains in freedom by permitting speakers to become aware of the ways in which implicit violations of norms limit public functioning and inhibit those very corrective and transformative performances that might change the conditions of communication.

This possibility of self-critical communication requires that the virtue of toleration be given a discursive reconstruction and brought to bear on the problem of ideological restrictions on deliberation and communication. In a context of a high degree of social and cultural pluralism and the conflicts that it might engender, proper responsiveness would require toleration among citizens, even if such toleration were extended to taking their perspectives seriously while challenging their claims in public deliberation. In this way, toleration is required in order that we treat others as political equals, as having equal entitlement to contribute to the definition of the society in which they live (Scanlon, 1996). In order to capture the obligations of public deliberation, Onora O'Neill (1990) correctly argues that it is communication itself that is 'the proper object of toleration' in a democracy. In deliberative settings, citizens manifest their equality with each other not only by refraining from interfering with their acts of expression, but also by sustaining the conditions for communication. How do they do this? They do this reflexively, in their communication with each other in public deliberation and in their attitudes towards others as participants in a public process (Bohman, 1999). Toleration in this sense is discursive openness.

If publicity is the more general norm and attitude of concern for the structures and processes of communication in a democracy, then toleration demands that citizens be concerned with the structural features of public debate and discussion through which deliberation takes place. Toleration in a weak sense is directed towards the reasons that others offer in communication: they must be taken seriously and not disqualified *ex ante* (either in principle or in fact). Toleration is needed in the public process aimed at discovering whether a reason is a publicly acceptable one or not. Publicity in this sense is practical and historical rather than merely a formal ideal. If the public character of a reason in this sense is better seen as an outcome of an actual process of discussion, then it is not necessarily significant if the reason is religious or secular (Rawls, 1999). However, taking reasons seriously is not all that deliberation requires. Toleration in the strong sense extends not directly to *reasons* as such but to the *perspectives* that inform these reasons and give them their cogency. Before a reason can first be seen as a reason and then potentially as one that passes the critical scrutiny of all citizens, the perspectives of others and the experiences that inform them must be recognized as legitimate; in light of this inclusion of their perspective, groups recognize themselves as contributing to democratic decisions. The toleration of others' perspectives is then part of recognizing them as equal members of a political community, despite the potential for persistent disagreements and deep conflicts. As Scanlon (1996) puts it, what toleration expresses is recognition of common membership that is deeper than these conflicts, recognition of others as just as discursively 'entitled as we are to contribute to the definition of our society'.

These two features of toleration – as perspective taking and as normative attitude in communication – take up the sceptical challenge of putative limits of discourse. A regime of toleration is illegitimate if it denies discursive entitlements by falsely generalizing the perspective of the tolerating group so that they can reject the claims and reasons of the tolerated group. A regime of toleration is just if it permits citizens to fulfil their obligations of justification to all if they are to respect the equal entitlement of each to contribute to the definition of their society. The toleration of perspectives is a matter not only of first-order communication, but of the second-order properties of the regime that aims at protecting the integrity of communication and deliberation (Young, 1997; 2000). In this respect, toleration is a second-order property of the framework that creates a deliberative community. It is also a property of citizens, who are obligated to exhibit concern for democratic communication. When coupled with critical reflection on the conditions of successful communication, toleration acts as a form of antipower to overcome the restrictions of ideology on the structure of communication in democratic processes. Those who make these criticisms may act as the 'generalized other' in Mead's sense, the other whose claims test the limits of the supposedly free and open discursive community of citizens. The limits on discourse are then limits on the regime of toleration and its implied generalized other to whom the regime must be justified.

CONCLUSION: EXTENDING THE DISCURSIVE COMMUNITY

Besides these applications to democratic practices and institutions, discourse has properties that make it a unique medium. It is certainly reflexive and self-referential, since it is primarily through discourse that we can challenge discourses and their implicit restrictions. This reflexivity makes discourse uniquely suited to extending democracy. By permitting indefinitely large and indirect social relations, discourses are not confined to specific linguistic communities but may extend beyond their historical, social and cultural origins. As Mead (1934) put it, 'the universe of discourse' is the most inclusive and extensive of all human communities, if that term may be applied to any grouping determined by participation in intensive communicative interaction. The universe of discourse then enables 'the largest conceivable number of individuals to enter into some social relationship to each other, however indirect and abstract that may be' (1934: 158). Mead asks further political questions of organizing discourse in institutions: 'Can we carry on a conversation in international terms? It is largely a question of social organization' (1934: 271). With global communications, interaction, and media, the global public sphere seems to be a new reality to be reckoned with politically (Bohman, 1999; Habermas, 2000). This provides at least the potential for democratic innovation and for new cosmopolitan discourses, both made possible at least in part by the extension of communicative interaction in the emerging global public sphere.

The emergence of a transnational civil society and a global public sphere provides the countervailing global infrastructure for the same sort of contestation that is the basis for the democratic accountability of the media and technoscience. Cosmopolitan democrats must foster the conditions for communication that make this contestation effective. Their goal has already been formulated in deliberative theories of democracy: to support a communicative infrastructure needed to expand the possibilities of democratic politics to the global arena where asymmetries are now prevalent. Given the scale of such a democracy, influence on decision making may be highly mediated and often indirect. The political structure of this higher-level democracy is yet to be determined, but its demands of scale make it unlikely that it will institutionalize the discursive principle in the same way as it has been in the modern state. For now, cosmopolitan democracy consists mostly of discursive challenges to the current international order from transnational civil society and public spheres, since it is not yet organized institutionally as to permit deliberative authorization or equal opportunities for effective participation rather than contestation. The cosmopolitan ideal is thus another potential target for discursive reconstruction, since in discourse all speakers become the potential addressee of claims made by others to whom we have the rational obligation to be open and responsive. If politics is the means by which a society acts upon itself, then increasing interdependence may lead to the expansion of politics. Since discourse remains the means by which politics becomes deliberative, the question is then to come up with a feasible institutional design to organize discursive exchange in the international political community [see further Chapter 22].

REFERENCES

Ackerman, Bruce (1991) *We the People*, vol. I. Cambridge: Harvard University Press.

Alexy, Robert (1989) *A Theory of Legal Argumentation: The Theory of Rational Discourse as a Theory of Legal Justification*. Oxford: Oxford University Press.

Austin, J. L. (1962) *How to Do Things with Words*. Oxford: Oxford University Press.

Baynes, Kenneth (1995) 'Democracy and the *Rechtsstaat*'. In S. White, ed., *The Cambridge Companion to Habermas*. Cambridge: Cambridge University Press.

Benhabib, Seyla (1991) *Situating the Self*. London: Routledge.

Bessette, Joseph (1994) *The Mild Voice of Reason*. Chicago: University of Chicago Press.

Bohman, James (1996) *Public Deliberation*. Cambridge, MA: MIT Press.

Bohman, James (1999) 'Citizenship and norms of publicity: wide public reason in cosmopolitan societies'. *Political Theory*, 27: 176–202.

Bohman, James and William Rehg (1996) 'Discourse and democracy: the formal and informal bases of democratic legitimacy'. *The Journal of Political Philosophy*, 4 (1): 79–99.

Bourdieu, Pierre (1977) *Outline of a Theory of Practice*. Cambridge: Cambridge University Press.

Bourdieu, Pierre (1991) *Language and Symbolic Power*. Cambridge: Polity.

Butler, Judith (1993) *Bodies that Matter: On the Discursive Limits of Sex*. London: Routledge.

Calhoun, Craig, ed. (1989) *Habermas and the Public Sphere*. Cambridge, MA: MIT Press.

Cohen, Joshua (1997) 'Deliberation and democratic legitimacy'. In J. Bohman and W. Rehg, eds, *Deliberative Democracy*. Cambridge, MA: MIT Press.

Crosswhite, James (1996) *The Rhetoric of Reason*. Madison, WI: University of Wisconsin Press.

Dewey, John (1988) *The Public and Its Problems*. In *The Later Works*, vol. 2. Carbondale, IL: Southern Illinois University Press.

Dorf, Michael and Charles Sabel (1998) 'Democratic experimentalism'. *Columbia University Law Review*, 26: 270–472.

Dryzek, John (1996) 'The informal logic of institutional design'. In R. Goodin, ed., *Theories of Institutional Design*. Cambridge: Cambridge University Press.

Dryzek, John (2000) *Deliberative Democracy and Beyond*. Oxford: Oxford University Press.

Elster, Jon (1997) 'The market and the forum'. In J. Bohman and W. Rehg, eds, *Deliberative Democracy: Essays on Reason and Politics*. Cambridge, MA: MIT Press.

Epstein, Stephen (1996) *Impure Science: AIDS, Activism and the Politics of Knowledge*. Berkeley, CA: University of California Press.

Estlund, David (1997) 'Beyond fairness and deliberation: the epistemic dimension of democratic authority'. In J. Bohman and W. Rehg, eds, *Deliberative Democracy: Essays on Reason and Politics*. Cambridge, MA: MIT Press.

Fischer, Frank and John Forester, eds (1994) *The Argumentative Turn in Policy Analysis and Planning*. Durham, NC: Duke University Press.

Flyvbjerg, Bent (1998) *Rationality and Power*. Chicago: University of Chicago Press.

Forester, John (1993) *Critical Theory, Public Policy, and Planning Practice*. Albany, NY: State University of New York Press.

Foucault, Michel (1977) *Discipline and Punish*. New York: Vantage.

Gamson, William (1988) 'Political discourses and collective action'. *International Social Movement Research*, 1: 219–44.

Gamson, William (1992) *Talking Politics*. Cambridge: Cambridge University Press.

Garfinkel, Harold (1969) *Studies in Ethnomethodology*. Englewood Cliffs, NJ: Prentice Hall.

Geertz, Clifford (1973) *Interpretation of Cultures*. New York: Basic.

Goldberg, David Theo (1990) 'The social formation of racist discourse'. In *Anatomy of Racism*. Minneapolis: University of Minnesota Press.

Habermas, Jürgen (1979) 'What is universal pragmatics?' In his *Communication and the Evolution of Society*. Boston: Beacon.

Habermas, Jürgen (1984) *The Theory of Communicative Action*, vol. I. Boston: Beacon.

Habermas, Jürgen (1990) *Moral Consciousness and Communicative Action*. Cambridge, MA: MIT Press.

Habermas, Jürgen (1996) *Between Facts and Norms*. Cambridge, MA: MIT Press.

Habermas, Jürgen (2000) *The Postnational Constellation*. Cambridge: Polity.

Hacking, Ian (1986) 'Language, truth and reason'. In S. Lukes and M. Hollis, eds, *Rationality and Relativism*. Cambridge, MA: MIT Press.

Heritage, John (1984) *Garfinkel and Ethnomethodology*. Cambridge: Polity.

Hoy, David and Thomas, McCarthy (1994) *Critical Theory*. London: Blackwell.

Hummel, R. P. (1994) *The Bureaucratic Experience: A Critique of Life in the Modern Organization*. New York: St Martin's.

Lynch, Michael (1993) *Scientific Practice and Ordinary Action*. Cambridge: Cambridge University Press.

Mead, George Herbert (1934) *Mind, Self and Society*. Chicago: University of Chicago Press.

Michelman, Frank (1988) 'Law's republic'. *Yale Law Review*, 97: 1493–537.

O'Neill, Onora (1990) 'Practices of toleration'. In J. Lichtenberg, ed., *Democracy and the Mass Media*. Cambridge: Cambridge University Press.

Pettit, Philip (1998) *Republicanism*. Oxford: Oxford University Press.

Przeworski, Adam and Michael Wallerstein (1988) 'The structural dependence of the state on capital'. *American Political Science Review*, 82: 11–29.

Rawls, John (1999) 'The idea of public reason revisited'. In Samuel Freeman, ed., *John Rawls: Collected Papers*. Cambridge, MA: Harvard University Press: 573–615.

Remer, Gary (1999) 'Political oratory and conversation: Cicero versus deliberative democracy'. *Political Theory*, 27: 39–64.

Said, Edward (1978) *Orientalism*. New York: Pantheon.

Sanders, Lynn (1997) 'Against deliberation'. *Political Theory*, 25: 347–76.

Scanlon, T. M. (1996) 'The difficulty of toleration'. In D. Heyd, ed., *Toleration: An Elusive Virtue*. Princeton, NJ: Princeton University Press.

Searle, John (1969) *Speech Acts*. Cambridge: Cambridge University Press.

Sen, Amartya (1999) *Development as Freedom*. New York: Knopf.

Shapin, Stephen (1994) *A Social History of Truth*. Chicago, IL: University of Chicago Press.

Smith, Rogers (1997) *Civic Ideals*. New Haven: Yale University Press.

Taylor, Charles (1985) 'Interpretation and the sciences of man'. In his *Collected Papers: Volume 2*. Cambridge: Cambridge University Press.

Thompson, John (1995) *The Media and Modernity*. Stanford, CA: Stanford University Press.

Unger, Roberto (1986) *The Critical Legal Studies Movement*. Cambridge, MA: Harvard University Press.

Weber, Max (1946) *From Max Weber*, eds, H. H. Gerth and C. Wright Mills. Oxford: Oxford University Press.

Young, Iris (1997) 'Difference as a resource for democratic communication'. In James Bohman and William Rehg, eds. *Deliberative Democracy*. Cambridge, MA: MIT Press.

Young, Iris (2000) *Democracy and Inclusion*. Oxford: Oxford University Press.

13

Communitarianism and Republicanism

RICHARD DAGGER

Communitarianism and republicanism are closely related schools of thought – so closely related that friend and foe alike sometimes conflate them. The relationship is evident in their Latin roots: communitarians are concerned with *communitas*, the common life of people who form a community, and republicans are devoted to the *res publica*, the good of the public. Of the two, however, only republicanism traces its lineage as well as its name to ancient Rome. Indeed, scholars often look beyond Rome to the philosophers and city-states of ancient Greece, particularly Aristotle and Sparta, for the origins of republicanism. For the origins of communitarianism, though, one need look no farther back than the nineteenth century, and it is only since the 1980s that the term 'communitarian' has gained its present currency as a result of the so-called liberal–communitarian debate.

This debate points to another way in which communitarianism and republicanism are related. Both the emergence of communitarianism and the revival of republicanism in recent years stem from an uneasiness with liberalism. In both cases the fundamental complaint is that liberalism is guilty of an excessive or misguided emphasis on the rights and liberties of the individual that 'nurtures a socially corrosive form of individualism' (Newman, 1989: 254). But exactly how liberalism has gone wrong and what should be done to set matters right are points on which communitarians and republicans disagree – not only with each other but among themselves. Some communitarians and republicans advance their theories as alternatives to liberalism, while others take themselves to be restoring or reviving the concern for community or civic life that once informed liberal theory and practice. For contemporary communitarians and republicans alike, then, the abiding challenge is to define their position in relation to liberalism.

This challenge is especially daunting for communitarians, who seem to be joined more by a common impulse or longing than by agreement on shared principles. As a result, as I shall explain below, communitarians have been vulnerable to three charges: first, that their objections to liberal theory are largely misconceived; second, that they have no clear alternative to offer, largely because they fail to define 'community' in a precise or useful way; and third, that the vague alternative they do offer runs the risk of imposing stifling conformity, or worse, on society. There is, in addition, the embarrassment that some of the most prominent scholars to wear the communitarian label have either abandoned communitarianism or denied that the label ever truly fitted them.

Contemporary republicans face similar charges, but they have more resources with which to meet them. To understand what these resources are, however, and to appreciate the superiority of republicanism to communitarianism, we shall need to begin at the beginning – before the liberal–communitarian debate and before the republican revival of the last 30 years or so – with a brief account of the republican tradition in the history of political thought. With that and an even briefer account of the development of communitarianism lending the necessary background, we shall be in a position to assess the merits and prospects of contemporary communitarianism and republicanism.

REPUBLICANISM, CLASSICAL AND MODERN

According to the standard dictionary definition, a republic is a political system with a representative government and an elected executive officer rather than a monarch. In places where the presence or vestiges of monarchy are not a concern, the stress is likely to fall on the representative aspect of republicanism, as it did when James Madison distinguished a 'republic' from a 'pure democracy' in *Federalist* 10 (Rossiter, 1961: 81–2). Where the real or symbolic power of monarchy is still a political force, the anti-monarchical aspect of republicanism will be primary – as the statements of the Australian Republican Movement and similar groups in other Commonwealth countries indicate.[1] The same is true of France and other countries in which the struggle between pro- and anti-monarchical forces became a defining feature of the political culture.[2] Setting these differences of emphasis aside, however, it seems safe to say that a republican is someone who favours representative government and opposes hereditary monarchy.

Safe, perhaps, but neither entirely accurate nor especially enlightening. Whether they were Greeks or Romans, the original republicans did not think of the republic as a form of *representative* government. The ideal, at least, was that the republic would be a form of self-government in which citizens would act and speak for themselves. Historically, moreover, republicans have been concerned less with the elimination of monarchy than with preventing the abuse of power by anyone holding public office. Cicero does ask in his *Republic*, 'So who would call that a republic, i.e., the property of the public, when everyone was oppressed by the cruelty of a single man?' (1998: 72 [Book III, 43]). But the subsequent discussion reveals that Cicero believed that rule by the few and rule by the many could also be tyrannical – and therefore not republican. Like Polybius, Aristotle, and Plato, he held that there are both just and tyrannical forms of rule by one, by the few, and by the many, and he agreed with Polybius when he insisted that the surest way to prevent tyranny is through 'a carefully proportioned mixture' (1998: 21 [Book I, 45]) of these forms of rule. If Cicero and other republicans have often opposed monarchy, it is because hereditary monarchs tend to regard the state or body politic as their property, to be disposed of as they wish, rather than as the *res publica* – the public's property or affair. The core of republicanism, in short, is neither a desire for representation nor opposition to monarchy as such; it is the belief that government is a public matter to be directed by the members of the public themselves.[3]

This is to say that *publicity* and *self-government* are the cornerstones of republicanism. By 'publicity' I mean the condition of being open and public rather than private or personal. This is the sense in which John Stuart Mill uses the word when he argues in *Considerations on Representative Government* that the vote is not a right to be exercised

in secret but a trust or duty that 'should be performed under the eye and criticism of the public' (1991: 355). But what, then, is 'the public'? And how are its members to govern themselves? There is no single republican answer to these questions. Republicans long assumed that only citizens counted as members of the public and only property-owning, arms-bearing men could be citizens. Contemporary republicans define the public and citizenship more expansively, however, to include women and people without substantial property. Similar shifts have occurred with regard to self-government. When they designed representative institutions for the new republic, for example, the men who drafted the US Constitution knew they were departing from the classical conception of self-government as direct participation in rule; yet they saw representation as an improvement within, not an abandonment of, republican practice. Whether they were right to think so, or whether they sacrificed too much participation and relied too heavily on representation, remains a point of contention. But it is the commitment to publicity and self-government that generates this and other intramural disputes among republicans. For republicans, the question is not whether publicity and self-government are good things, but how best to achieve them.

One could say the same, of course, about liberals, conservatives, socialists, and others who claim to promote government of, by, and for the people. To the extent that they stress the importance of publicity and self-government, however, modern political theories draw upon the legacy of classical republicanism. To the extent that they differ from one another – and from republicanism – it is because they pursue the implications of publicity and self-government in different ways. To understand what is distinctive about republicanism, then, we must examine the implications republicans draw from publicity and self-government.

In the case of publicity, the implications are twofold. The first is that politics, as the public's business, must be conducted openly, *in public*. The second is that 'the public' is more than a group of people; it is an aspect or sphere of life with its own claims and considerations, even if it is not easily distinguished from the private. Something is public when it involves people who share common concerns that take them out of their private lives and beyond: as Tocqueville put it in *Democracy in America*, 'the circle of family and friends' (1969: 506). No matter how desirable they may seem to others, neither a life of unfettered self-indulgence nor one devoted exclusively to family and friends will appeal to a republican.

From these aspects of publicity follow the republican emphases on the *rule of law* and, perhaps most distinctively, *civic virtue*. The public business must be conducted in public not only for reasons of convenience – literally, of coming together – but also to guard against *corruption*. As citizens, people must be prepared to overcome their personal inclinations and set aside their private interests when necessary to do what is best for the public as a whole. The public-spirited citizens who act in this way display public or civic virtue. If they are to manifest this virtue, furthermore, the public must be bound by the rule of law. Because it is the public's business, politics requires public debate and decisions, which in turn require rules establishing who may speak, when they may speak, and how decisions are to be reached. Decisions must then take the form of promulgated rules or decrees that guide the conduct of the members of the public. From the insistence on publicity, the rule of law quickly follows.[4]

The connection of self-government to the rule of law is at least as strong and immediate. Self-governing citizens cannot be subject to absolute or arbitrary rule, whether it proceeds from external or internal forces. If the citizen is to be *self*-governing, that is, he or she must be free from the absolute or arbitrary rule of others, which means that citizens must be subject to the rule of law – the government or empire of laws, not of men, according to the old formula.[5] Moreover, self-government requires self-*governing*. The republican citizen is someone who acts not arbitrarily, impulsively, or recklessly, but according to laws he or she has a voice in making. 'For the impulse of appetite alone is slavery', as Rousseau declared in the *Social Contract* (1978: 56 [Book I, ch. 8]), 'and obedience to the law one has prescribed for oneself is freedom'.[6] Again, the need for the rule of law is evident.

As with publicity, the republican commitment to self-government leads to characteristic republican themes, such as concern for freedom, equality, and, again, civic virtue. Self-government is, of course, a form of freedom. For republicans, it is the most important form, for other kinds of individual freedom are secure only in a free state, under law. Freedom thus requires dependence upon the law so that citizens may be independent of the arbitrary will of others. As Rousseau said in *Émile*:

> Dependence on men ... engenders all the vices, and by it, master and slave are mutually corrupted. If there is any means of remedying this ill in society, it is to substitute law for man and to arm the general wills with a real strength superior to the action of every particular will. (1979: 85)

Rousseau also knew, as he makes plain in the *Discourse on the Origin of Inequality* and *Political Economy*, that the law itself could be corrupted. That is why he ends Book I of the *Social Contract* with this note: 'laws are always useful to those who

have possessions and harmful to those who have nothing. It follows from this that the social state is only advantageous to men insofar as they all have something and none of them has anything superfluous' (1978: 58). Equality under law is only possible, in other words, when wealth and property are distributed in a way that prevents some people from bending the law to their will. Republicans, including Rousseau, have typically endorsed private ownership of property because they see in it a means of fostering independence. They have been less interested in an equal opportunity to become rich, however, than in equal protection under the law and equal opportunities to participate in public life. That is why they have sometimes called for limits on the accumulation of wealth, as James Harrington did in *Oceana* when he advocated an 'agrarian' law 'fixing the balance in lands' (1992: 13). (For similar views in contemporary republicanism, see Sandel, 1996: 329–33 and Pettit, 1997: 135.) It also explains Mary Wollstonecraft's complaint that the inferior status of women often compels them to eat 'the bitter bread of dependence' (1985: 158).

The law only ensures the citizen's freedom, however, when it is responsive to the citizenry and when the republic itself is secure and stable enough for its laws to be effective. Sustaining freedom under the rule of law thus requires not only public-spirited participation in public affairs and a willingness to bear the burdens of a common life – the civic virtue of the republican citizen – but also the proper form of government. This usually has been some version of *mixed* or *balanced* government, so called because it mixes and balances elements of rule by one, by the few, and by the many. As J. G. A. Pocock (1975) and others have noted, writers from Polybius and Cicero to Machiavelli and the American Founders celebrated the mixed constitution for its ability to stave off corruption and tyranny [see further Chapter 26]. Monarchy, aristocracy, and democracy, according to these writers, are prone to degenerate into tyranny, oligarchy, and mob rule, respectively; but a government that disperses power among the three elements could prevent either the one, the few, or the many from pursuing its own interest at the expense of the common good. With each element holding enough power to check the others, the result should be a free, stable, and long-lasting government. To be sure, republicans have sometimes struggled to reconcile their faith in mixed government with their distrust or even hatred of hereditary monarchy and aristocracy. But this struggle, as in the case of the American Founders, has led to a reinterpretation of balanced government as one that relies upon the *checks and balances* of separated powers or functions of government. Whether mixed in the older sense or balanced in the newer, though, the point is to resist the corruption of power by preventing its concentration.

If the balanced constitution is the characteristic form of the republic, civic virtue is its lifeblood. Without citizens who are willing to defend the republic against foreign threats and to take an active part in government, even the mixed constitution will fail. Republics must thus engage in what Michael Sandel calls 'a formative politics ... that cultivates in citizens the qualities of character that self-government requires' (1996: 6). Constitutional safeguards may be necessary to resist avarice, ambition, luxury, idleness, and other forms of corruption, but they will not be enough to sustain freedom under the rule of law. Replenishing the supply of civic virtue through education and other means will thus be one of the principal concerns of a prudent republic – a concern manifest in the works of writers as different in other respects as Aristotle and Wollstonecraft.

A prudent republic will also be a small one. That, at least, has been the conclusion – or presumption – of many republicans throughout the centuries. 'In a large republic,' Montesquieu explained in *The Spirit of the Laws*, 'the common good is sacrificed to a thousand considerations; it is subordinated to exceptions; it depends upon accidents. In a small one, the public good is better felt, better known, lies nearer to each citizen; abuses are less extensive and consequently less protected' (1989: 124 [Book VIII, ch. 16]). So widespread was this view in the late eighteenth century that the American authors of the *Federalist* found it necessary to point out that Montesquieu had also allowed for the possibility of a 'federal' or 'CONFEDERATE' (*Federalist* 9) republic. Even then, the debate over the proposed Constitution often turned on the question of whether the United States would become a 'federal' or a 'compound' republic – that is, a republic comprising 13 or more smaller republics – or whether it would become a 'consolidated' republic that could not long preserve its republican character.

Some scholars have taken disagreements about the proper size of a republic to mark one way in which modern republicans have diverged from the path of classical republicanism. According to this view (Pangle, 1988; Rahe, 1992; Zuckert, 1994), the truly *classical* republicans of ancient Greece saw civic virtue as desirable because it protected and preserved the *polis* in which the highest virtues could be cultivated: 'Wherever the genuine classical republican tradition still lives, there is some kind of agreement as to the supreme value of the intellectual virtues, and of a life spent in leisured meditation on the nature of justice, the soul, and divinity' (Pangle, 1988: 61). By contrast, modern republicans, who stem from Machiavelli, are willing to accept representative government and large polities

because of their conception of virtue, which allows for commerce and acquisitiveness, and their concern for natural rights [see also Chapters 3 and 26].

Other scholars are more impressed by the continuity of the republican tradition. Some of these, such as Pocock (1975), trace the line of development from the 'Atlantic republicans' of the seventeenth and eighteenth centuries back through Machiavelli to Polybius and Aristotle, while Quentin Skinner (1998) and others hold that modern republicanism derives primarily from Roman theory and practice (see e.g. Sellers, 1998). Those who look back to Aristotle tend to stress the side of republicanism that calls for a life of public-spirited political participation; those who look to Rome stress the republican commitment to independence as freedom under the law. (See Honohan, 2002, for an analysis that stresses the distinction between participatory and rule-of-law republicanism.) In neither case, however, is there an attempt to draw a sharp or significant distinction between classical and modern republicanism. To the contrary, these scholars take the historical consciousness of modern republicans – a consciousness reflected in their tendency to look to the ancient world for exemplars – as evidence of the continuity of the classical republican tradition.

Whether the camp that insists on distinguishing modern from classical republicanism or the camp that resists that distinction is right is, of course, a contested matter. But there is no doubt that it is the latter group that is largely responsible for the republican revival of recent years. Before turning to that revival, however, we should step back for a brief survey of communitarianism, with special attention to the liberal–communitarian debate [see further Chapters 8 and 30].

COMMUNITARIANISM

Longing for community is no doubt to be found in political thought at least as far back as the republican concern for publicity and self-government. But that longing did not find expression in the word 'communitarian' until the 1840s, when it and *communautaire* appeared almost simultaneously in the writings of English and French socialists [see further Chapters 28 and 29]. French dictionaries point to Étienne Cabet and Pierre-Joseph Proudhon as the first to use *communautaire*, but the *Oxford English Dictionary* gives the credit for 'communitarian' to one Goodwyn Barmby, who founded the Universal Communitarian Association in 1841 and edited a magazine he called *The Promethean, or Communitarian Apostle*. According to Ralph Waldo Emerson's essay on 'English reformers', Barmby advertised his publication as 'the cheapest of all magazines, and the paper most devoted of any to the cause of the people; consecrated to Pantheism in Religion, and Communism in Politics' (1842: 239).

In the beginning, then, 'communitarian' seems to have been a rough synonym of 'socialist' and 'communist'. While those words gradually acquired a more precise sense in the ideological battles of the nineteenth and twentieth centuries, 'communitarian', when it was used at all, remained a vague, general term. To be a communitarian was simply to believe that community is somehow vital to a worthwhile life and is therefore to be protected against various threats. Socialists and communists were leftists, but a communitarian could as easily be to the right as the left of centre politically (Miller, 2000c) [see further Chapter 10].

Communitarianism in this sense began to take shape as a self-conscious way of thinking about society and politics in the late nineteenth century [see Chapters 28 and 29]. According to one line of thought that developed at the time, the primary threat to community is the centrifugal force of modern life. That is, people who moved from the settled, family-focused life of villages and small towns to the unsettled, individualistic life of commerce and cities might gain affluence and personal freedom, but they paid the price of alienation, isolation, and rootlessness. Ferdinand Tönnies (2001), with his distinction between *Gemeinschaft* (community) and *Gesellschaft* (association or civil society), has been especially influential in this regard. As Tönnies defines the terms, *Gemeinschaft* is an intimate, organic, and traditional form of human association; *Gesellschaft* is impersonal, mechanical, and rational. To exchange the former for the latter, then, is to trade warmth and support for coldness and calculation.

Concern for community took another direction in the twentieth century as some writers began to see the centripetal force of the modern state as the principal threat to community. This turn is evident, for instance, in José Ortega y Gasset's warnings in *The Revolt of the Masses* against 'the gravest danger that today threatens civilisation: State intervention; the absorption of all spontaneous social effort by the State' (1932: 120). Robert Nisbet's *The Quest for Community* (1953) provides an especially clear statement of this position, which draws more on Tocqueville's insistence on the importance of voluntary associations of citizens than on a longing for *Gemeinschaft*. Community, on Nisbet's account, is a form of association in which people more or less spontaneously work together to solve common problems and live under codes of authority they have generated themselves. But the free and healthy life of community is increasingly difficult to sustain, he argues, in the face of constant pressure from the modern state, with its impulses toward centralized power and bureaucratic regulation.

In the nineteenth and twentieth centuries, in short, the longing for community took the form of a reaction against both the atomizing, anomic tendencies of modern, urban society and the use of the centripetal force of the modern state to check these tendencies. Moreover, modernity was often linked with liberalism, a theory that many took to rest on and encourage atomistic and even 'possessive' individualism (Macpherson, 1962). Against this background, communitaria*nism* developed in the late twentieth century in the course of a debate with – or perhaps within – liberalism. This debate occasionally took an overtly political form as various political figures insisted on the need to defend community standards and cohesion against the onslaught of relentless individualism. Most notably, Bill Clinton in the United States and Tony Blair in Britain appealed to communitarian concerns as they advocated policies meant to give as much weight to individual responsibilities as to individual rights. The terms of the liberal–communitarian debate, however, were set not so much by politicians as by political philosophers.

Four books published in rapid succession in the 1980s – Alasdair MacIntyre's *After Virtue* (1981), Michael Sandel's *Liberalism and the Limits of Justice* (1982), Michael Walzer's *Spheres of Justice* (1983), and Charles Taylor's *Philosophical Papers* (1985) – marked the emergence of this philosophical form of communitarianism.[7] Different as they are from one another, all of these books express dissatisfaction with liberalism, especially in the form of theories of justice and rights. The main target here was John Rawls's *A Theory of Justice* (1971), but Robert Nozick's *Anarchy, State, and Utopia* (1974), Ronald Dworkin's *Taking Rights Seriously* (1977), and Bruce Ackerman's *Social Justice in the Liberal State* (1980) also came in for criticism. A typical complaint was, and is, that these theories are too abstract and universalistic. In opposing them, Walzer proposes a 'radically particularist' approach that attends to 'history, culture, and membership' by asking not what 'rational individuals … under universalizing conditions of such-and-such a sort' would choose, but what would 'individuals like us choose, who are situated as we are, who share a culture and are determined to go on sharing it?' (1983: xiv, 5). Walzer thus calls attention to the importance of community, which he and others writing in the early 1980s took to be suffering from both philosophical and political neglect.

Nor do Walzer and the others who came to be known as 'communitarians' believe that theoretical indifference has merely coincided with the erosion of community that they see in the world around them. In various ways Walzer, MacIntyre, Sandel, and Taylor, among others, have all charged that the liberal emphasis on distributive justice and individual rights works to divide the citizens of the modern state against one another, thereby fostering isolation, alienation, and apathy rather than commitment to a common civic enterprise. Liberals responded, of course, and the liberal–communitarian debate was on.

Those enlisted on the communitarian side of the debate have pressed four major objections against their 'liberal' or 'individualist' opponents. The first is the complaint, already noted in Walzer, that abstract reason will not bear the weight philosophers have placed on it in their attempts to ground justice and morality. This 'Enlightenment project' (MacIntyre, 1981) is doomed by its failure to recognize that reasoning about these matters cannot proceed apart from shared traditions and practices, each with its own set of roles, responsibilities, and virtues. Second, the liberal emphasis on individual rights and justice comes at the expense of civic duty and the common good. In Sandel's words, 'justice finds its limits in those forms of community that engage the identity as well as the interests of the participants. … [T]o some I owe more than justice requires or even permits … in virtue of those more or less enduring attachments and commitments which taken together partly define the person I am' (1982: 179, 182). Contemporary liberals are blind to these enduring attachments and commitments, according to the third charge, because they too often rely on an atomistic conception of the self – an 'unencumbered self', in Sandel's terms – that is supposedly prior to its ends and attachments. Such a conception is both false and pernicious, for individual selves are largely constituted by the communities that nurture and sustain them. When Rawls and other 'deontological liberals' teach individuals to think of themselves as somehow prior to and apart from these communities, they are engaged quite literally in a *self*-defeating enterprise. The fourth objection, then, is that these abstract and universalistic theories of justice and rights have contributed to the withdrawal into private life and the intransigent insistence on one's rights against others that threaten modern societies. There is little sense of a common good or even a common ground on which citizens can meet. In MacIntyre's words, the conflict between the advocates of incommensurable moral positions has so riven modern societies that politics now 'is civil war carried on by other means' (1981: 253). The best we can do in these circumstances is to agree to disagree while we try to fashion 'local forms of community within which civility and the intellectual and moral life can be sustained through the new dark ages which are already upon us' (1981: 263).

The communitarians have not all pressed all of these objections with equal force, nor have they all

understood themselves to be criticizing liberalism from the outside. Taylor (1989), for instance, has argued that reasonable liberals and communitarians share a commitment to 'holist individualism' – a view that rejects ontological atomism and affirms that individuals are somehow socially constituted, on the one hand, yet also recognizes, on the other, the importance of individual rights and liberties. Other theorists with communitarian leanings continue to regard themselves as liberals (Galston, 1991; Spragens, 1995). From their point of view the fundamental worry is that *other* liberals are so preoccupied with the rights and liberties of the abstract individual that they put the survival of liberal societies at risk. Whether this worry is well founded is a question that the 'liberal' side of the debate has raised in response to the 'communitarians'. (For a valuable, full-length survey of this debate, see Mulhall and Swift, 1996.)

Here we may distinguish three interlocking responses. The first is that the communitarians' criticisms are misplaced because they have misconceived liberalism (Caney, 1992). In particular, the communitarians have misunderstood the abstractness of the theories they criticize. Thus Rawls maintains (1993: Lecture I) that his 'political' conception of the self as prior to its ends is not a metaphysical claim about the nature of the self, as Sandel believes, but simply a way of representing the parties who are choosing principles of justice from behind the 'veil of ignorance'. Nor does this conception of the individual as a self capable of choosing its ends require liberals to deny that individual identity is in many ways the product of unchosen attachments and social circumstances. 'What is central to the liberal view,' according to Will Kymlicka, 'is not that we can *perceive* a self prior to its ends, but that we understand ourselves to be prior to our ends, *in the sense that no end or goal is exempt from possible re-examination*' (1989: 52, emphasis in original). With this understood, a second response is to grant, as Kymlicka, Dworkin (1986; 1992), Gewirth (1996), and Mason (2000) do, that liberals should pay more attention to belonging, identity, and community, but to insist that they can do this perfectly well within their existing theories. The third response, finally, is to point to the dangers of the critics' appeal to community norms. Communities have their virtues, but they have their vices, too – smugness, intolerance, and various forms of oppression and exploitation among them. The fact that communitarians do not embrace these vices simply reveals the perversity of their criticism: they 'want us to live in Salem, but not to believe in witches' (Gutmann, 1992: 133; Friedman, 1992). If liberals rely on abstractions and universal considerations in their theories of justice and rights, that is because they must do so to rise above – and critically assess – local prejudices that communitarians must simply accept.

Communitarian rejoinders have indicated their sensitivity to this last point. Sandel, as we shall see, has decided that 'republican' better defines his position than 'communitarian', and MacIntyre has denied, quite forcefully, that he is or ever was a communitarian.[8] Others have embraced the communitarian label, but their rejoinders to 'liberal' criticisms stress their desire to strike a balance between individual rights and civic responsibilities (Etzioni, 1996) in order to 'move closer to the *ideal of community life*' – a life in which 'we learn the value of integrating what we seek individually with the needs and aspirations of other people' (Tam, 1998: 220, emphasis added). In contrast to MacIntyre, Sandel, Walzer, and Taylor, these 'political communitarians' (Frazer, 1999) are less concerned with philosophical criticism of liberalism or individualism than with moving closer to the ideal of community life by reviving civil society. They hope to do this, in particular, by calling attention to shared values and beliefs, encouraging active and widespread participation in civic life, and bringing politics down to the local, properly 'human' level (Frazer, 1999: 41–2).

The key question for these 'political' communitarians is whether 'the ideal of community life' is precise and powerful enough to do the work they want it to do. To the 'political' communitarian, appealing to the 'spirit' of community holds the promise of uniting people of various political inclinations – left, right, and centre. To others, however, it seems that 'the communitarian political movement, avoiding controversial political issues in order to appeal to as wide a range of constituents as possible, ends up as little more than a moral appeal to us all to behave better: take more responsibility for our social environment, avoid corruption, etc., etc.' (Miller, 2000c: 109). Communitarianism of this sort may be useful as exhortation, but it is too vague and accommodating to succeed as a political philosophy.

REPUBLICANISM REVIVED

Whether 'philosophical' or 'political', communitarianism is too vague to be helpful and too accommodating to be acceptable. Communities take a great many forms, including some – such as fascist or Nazi communes – that communitarians themselves must find unpalatable or intolerable. Sandel acknowledges the point when he says, in his review of Rawls's *Political Liberalism*, that the 'term "communitarianism" is misleading ... insofar as it implies that rights should rest on the values or preferences that prevail in any given community at any given time' (1994: 1767). He has, accordingly, abandoned this misleading term in favour of 'republicanism'. He persists in his criticism of liberalism, to be sure, but he apparently believes that he is in a better position to criticize as a republican committed to 'a formative politics ... that cultivates in citizens the qualities of character self-government requires' (1996: 6) than as a communitarian committed to the prevailing values and preferences in a given community at a given time. What counts for the republican is not community *per se*, but the community of self-governing, public-spirited citizens.

Sandel's profession of republicanism has contributed to a revival of republican political theory that has been under way since at least 1975, when Pocock's *Machiavellian Moment* called attention to the 'Atlantic republican tradition'. Pocock himself drew on the work of other historians, such as Zera Fink (1945), Caroline Robbins (1959), Bernard Bailyn (1967), and Gordon Wood (1969), who had stressed the importance of republican or 'commonwealth' themes in the political controversies and upheavals of England and America in the seventeenth and eighteenth centuries [see further Chapter 26]. Another source of inspiration was the political theorist Hannah Arendt: 'In terms borrowed from or suggested by the language of Hannah Arendt, [*The Machiavellian Moment*] has told part of the story of the revival in the early modern West of the ancient ideal of *homo politicus* (the *zōon politikon* of Aristotle), who affirms his being and his virtue by the medium of political action' (1975: 550) [see further Chapter 23].

It would be unwise to say that a thinker as multifarious as Arendt was first, last, and above all a republican, but there is certainly a strong streak of republicanism in her writings (Canovan, 1992, esp. ch. 6). This streak is most evident in her recurring concern for what I have called the cornerstones of republicanism – publicity and self-government. To some commentators this concern seems little more than misplaced nostalgia for the ancient *polis* (e.g. O'Sullivan, 1975). But Arendt's complaint is not so much that civic life in modern democracies has declined dramatically from some golden age, as that it has failed to realize the promise of republican citizenship. Technology has eased the burdens of labour and freed us to act as citizens in the public realm, she argued in *The Human Condition* (1958), yet we forsake public life in favour of private consumption. We want government to provide for the welfare of the citizenry, she declared in *On Revolution*, but we 'deny the very existence of public happiness and public freedom' as we 'insist that politics is a burden' (1965: 273). We are, in short, squandering an opportunity to achieve what the republicans of ancient Greece and Rome thought to be impossible – a polity in which the freedom of republican self-government is available not only to the well-to-do few but to almost the entire people.

Similar worries about 'the erosion of the distinctively political' animated Sheldon Wolin's influential *Politics and Vision* (1960: 290). Like Arendt, Wolin's complaint is that 'the political' has been displaced by 'the social' in the modern world. What we call 'politics' is little more than the squabbling of groups seeking to protect and promote their interests, with devastating consequences for civic life. 'There is substantial evidence,' Wolin remarks, that

> participation in public affairs is regarded with indifference by vast numbers of members. The average citizen seems to find the exercise of political rights burdensome, boring, and often lacking in significance. To be a citizen does not appear an important role nor political participation an intrinsic good ... By reducing citizenship to a cheap commodity, democracy has seemingly contributed to the dilution of politics. (1960: 353)

In retrospect, then, Pocock's *Machiavellian Moment* appears to have brought together and supplied a name for two previously distinct bodies of scholarship: the efforts of historians to recover a form of political thought that seemed to be all but lost; and the efforts of political theorists, notably Arendt and Wolin, to remind their contemporaries of the value of the public life of the self-governing citizen. Those scholars who have subsequently seen themselves as engaged in the republican revival have tried, for the most part, to combine these tasks by dedicating themselves to the historical retrieval and reconstruction of republicanism (e.g. Sullivan, 1986; Boyte, 1989; Oldfield, 1990). So much is necessary, it seems, if they are to show that the republican concepts and idioms of earlier eras still speak to present concerns. Thus Sandel tries in *Democracy's Discontent* to devise a 'public philosophy' for the United States by reclaiming the republicanism of the American Founding and the 'political economy of citizenship' that governed American thinking about economic relationships, he argues, into the late nineteenth century.

But that is not to say that neorepublican theorists have shied away from prescription as they have explored the implications of republicanism for contemporary politics. To the contrary, their recommendations range from the specific – national or civic service programmes (Barber, 1984: 298–303), campaign finance reform (Sunstein, 1988: 1576–8), and compulsory voting (Dagger, 1997: 145–51), for example – to such general issues as national identity (Miller, 1995), economic arrangements that foster citizenship and strong communities (Sandel, 1996: Part II; Sullivan, 1986; ch. 7), and the justification of

punishment (Braithwaite and Pettit, 1990). They are not so united on any of these points as to warrant the claim that there is a neorepublican programme for political change, but it is possible to discern four broad themes on which they do agree. These are the interrelated themes of political equality, freedom as self-government, deliberative politics, and civic virtue (cf. Sunstein, 1988: 1548).

The commitment to equality is hardly distinctive of neorepublicanism, for it is a commitment shared, if Dworkin (1977: 179–83) and Kymlicka (1990: 4–5 and *passim*) are correct, by every plausible political theory. It does distinguish them, of course, from their classical forebears, whose praise of the equal rule (*isonomia*) of citizens sometimes went hand-in-hand with a defence of slavery. What makes the neorepublican position truly distinctive, however, is the combination of a belief in the equal moral worth of persons with the traditional republican emphasis on the importance of *political* equality. Everyone, that is, should have the opportunity to become a citizen, and every citizen should stand on an equal footing, under law and in the political arena, with every other citizen. Republicanism may thus require steps to be taken to relieve women from subjection to men, workers from subjection to employers, and the members of some racial, ethnic, or cultural groups from subjection to others. In the traditional idiom, these steps may be necessary to free some people from dependence on others. They may also require some redistribution of wealth and limits on the use of money to obtain or exercise political influence. Even so, neorepublicans typically take the Aristotelian view of property – private ownership for the public good – and see no point in 'material egalitarianism' for its own sake (Pettit, 1997: 161).

The connection of political equality to the second theme, freedom as self-government, is a close one. Both involve what Philip Pettit calls 'the frankness of intersubjective equality' (1997: 64). On the republican view, as we have seen, freedom is not so much a matter of being left alone as it is of living under the rule of laws that one has a voice in making. Republicans differ from liberals in this regard, according to Pettit, because 'the supreme political value' (1997: 80) of republicanism is freedom understood not as non-interference – the liberal view – but as non-domination or, in Skinner's terms, 'absence of dependence' (2002: 18). It is not interference as such that is objectionable, on this view, but its arbitrariness. The slave and the citizen may both suffer interference when one must bow to the will of the master and the other must bow to the law, but it is a mistake to say that they both suffer the loss of freedom. The master need not be concerned for the slave's desires or interests, but the law, at least in the ideal, must attend to the interests of the citizen *qua* citizen even when it interferes with his or her activities. By protecting the citizen against arbitrary power, the law is 'the non-mastering interferer' (Pettit, 1997: 41) that ensures the citizen's freedom. So valuable is this independence from arbitrary power, Pettit insists, that it is a 'primary good' in the Rawlsian sense. Whatever else people may want, they will want to be free from domination because they then will have the ability to make plans, to speak with independent voices, and simply to be *persons*: 'everyone – or at least everyone who has to make his or her way in a pluralistic society – will want to be treated properly as a person, as a voice that cannot be generally ignored' (1997: 91).

Republican political institutions, then, must ensure the political equality of self-governing citizens. To this end, neorepublicans call for a more *deliberative* form of politics [see further Chapters 11 and 12]. As Cass Sunstein puts it, 'republicans will attempt to design political institutions that promote discussion and debate among the citizenry; they will be hostile to systems that promote lawmaking as "deals" or bargains among self-interested private groups' (1988: 1549). This is not to say that republicans believe that citizens would easily or quickly come to agreement about what the common good requires if only government could be freed from the stranglehold of interest groups. The point, instead, is that reviving the republican conception of politics as the public business means rejecting the 'economic model' of politics, according to which individuals and groups bring their preferences, already fixed, to the political marketplace, where they use their political capital and bargaining power to strike the best deals for themselves. On the republican view, politics of this sort is a form of *corruption* that reduces the citizen to a consumer seeking to promote his or her personal interests. Steps must be taken, then, to limit the power of private interests, to prepare people through civic education to take the part of the public-spirited citizen, and to provide them with arenas or forums in which they may engage in debate and deliberation on the public business.

Deliberative politics will succeed, however, only if there is a sufficient supply of civic virtue; otherwise debate and deliberation will be little more than a vain display that distracts attention from the 'real' politics of bargaining for personal advantage. This is the fourth theme of the neorepublicans: civic virtue is necessary if self-government is to be sustained. But the neorepublicans also tend to believe that civic virtue is either in decline or in jeopardy, and they frequently place the blame on liberalism. As Sandel says, 'the civic or formative aspect of our [American] politics has largely given way to the liberalism that conceives persons as free and

independent selves, unencumbered by moral or civic ties they have not chosen' (1996: 6). This 'voluntarist' or 'procedural' liberalism, as found in the works of liberal philosophers such as Rawls and the decisions of liberal jurists, has fostered a society in which individuals fail to understand how much they owe to the community. The chief purpose of the state is thus taken to be the arbitration of conflicting claims of individuals in pursuit of their disparate conceptions of the good life. Such a society will be self-subverting, Sandel insists, for it 'fails to capture those loyalties and responsibilities whose moral force consists partly in the fact that living by them is inseparable from understanding ourselves as the particular persons we are – as members of this family or city or nation or people, as bearers of that history, as citizens of this republic' (1996: 14). Where such loyalties and responsibilities cannot be sustained, self-government cannot survive. Hence the need for a republican revival.

Taken together, these four themes suggest that republicans today have a powerful and coherent political theory – more powerful and coherent, in my view, than communitarianism. But there is a fifth theme running through the writings of the new republicans, and on this point they seem to divide. This theme is the relationship of republicanism to liberalism. In general, neorepublicans share the communitarian conviction that many liberals give too much attention to individual rights and too little to civic duties. This is particularly true, they hold, of libertarians and those who maintain that liberalism must be strictly neutral with regard to competing conceptions of the good [see further Chapter 9]. In response, some scholars with republican sympathies see a need to recall the 'civic' or 'republican' elements in liberalism (e.g. Holmes, 1995; Terchek, 1997; Spragens, 1999) or otherwise argue for the adoption of republican liberalism or liberal republicanism (Sunstein, 1988; Burtt, 1993; Dagger, 1997). But others insist, with Pettit and Sandel, that republicanism is different enough from liberalism to justify thinking of them as rival theories. By doing so, however, they open themselves to the objection that Sandel has brought against those liberals who have embraced the ideals of political neutrality and the unencumbered self: that they are engaged in a self-subverting enterprise. Just as a liberal society must be able to count on a sense of community and civic engagement, so a republican polity must be able to count on a commitment to principles generally associated with liberalism, such as tolerance, fair play, and respect for the rights of others. If their zeal for individual rights and liberty sometimes leads liberals to undercut their position by threatening the communal or republican underpinnings of a liberal society, so Pettit, Sandel, and others who oppose republicanism to liberalism are in danger of undercutting their position by threatening the liberal principles upon which they implicitly rely. (See Dagger, 1999 and 2000, for elaboration of this criticism of Sandel and Pettit, respectively.)

CONCLUSION

Two conclusions follow from this survey of communitarianism and republicanism. One is that republicanism is superior to communitarianism; the other is that neither historical considerations (Banning, 1986; Isaac, 1988) nor theoretical prudence warrant a sharp distinction between republicanism and liberalism. In developing their theory, though, neorepublicans continue to face difficulties and challenges – two of which I shall briefly discuss by way of conclusion.

The first challenge is to respond to those who hold that neorepublicans can never escape the biases implicit in the traditional republican ideal of the citizen as a property-owning, arms-bearing man. This objection is put forcefully by Iris Marion Young, who detects a denial of 'difference' in republican attempts to establish a 'civic public' in which citizens devote themselves to the common good. 'This ideal of the civic public,' Young charges, 'excludes women and other groups defined as different, because its rational and universal status derives only from its opposition to affectivity, particularity, and the body' (1990: 117).

The second challenge is to demonstrate the relevance of republicanism in an age of globalization. In the face of the rapid spread of global communications, the rise of the global economy, and threats to the environment that respect no boundaries, political theorists must think in cosmopolitan terms. To a critical eye, however, republicanism may seem to be a nostalgic form of political thinking that is so fixed on the small-scale polities of years long past – on the Italian city-states, the Roman *civitas*, and the Greek *polis* – as to be incapable of responding to the challenges of globalization.

These are challenges that republicans must take seriously. Indeed, they are taking them seriously, as recent republican or 'civic liberal' responses to the challenges of 'difference' and of globalism indicate.[9] These responses engage the four themes mentioned above, and they rely ultimately on the republican commitment to publicity and self-government – a commitment that cannot be met if too much is conceded to either the politics of difference or cosmopolitanism. There will be disagreement, no doubt, as to the adequacy of these responses. There should be no doubt, however, that neorepublicans are capable of responding to challenges that

their classical forebears neither faced nor anticipated. That their theory contains such resources is, in the end, the best testimony to the importance of reviving republicanism.

NOTES

I am grateful to Terence Ball, Iseult Honohan, and David Miller for helpful comments on earlier drafts of this chapter.

1 The website of the Australian Republican Movement quotes a dictionary definition of a republic as a system in which the people elect representatives, then adds this statement: 'In particular, a republic refers to a system of government that has no hereditary monarch – a person who holds political or constitutional office purely as a birthright' (www.republic.org.au, 18 July 2002).

2 Even Sudhir Hazareesingh, who identifies the leading characteristics of French republicanism as '[p]articipationism, perfectionism, universalism, nationalism, and revolutionism' (1994: 68–9), assumes that opposition to monarchy is a defining feature of republicanism: 'None of the central figures of the revolution was a self-confessed republican, and France was declared a Republic only in September 1792, after the experiment of a constitutional monarchy had been deemed a failure. The proclamation of the Republic was itself accelerated by popular pressure, emanating particularly from such grass-roots organizations as the anti-monarchical *clubs de quartiers*' (1994: 69).

3 Cf. Everdell in a book entitled *The End of Kings*: 'The essential republican principle is that no one person shall rule the community, that everyone shall have a part in the public's business' (1983: 297).

4 Cicero again is apposite: 'a public is not every kind of human gathering, congregating in any manner, but a numerous gathering brought together by legal consent and community of interest' (1998: 19 [Book I, 39]). See also Book III, 45 (1998: 73): 'there is no public except when it is held together by a legal agreement'; and for analysis and assessment, see Schofield (1995).

5 Historians (Wirszubski, 1960: 9; Skinner, 1998: 45) trace this formula to the Roman writers Sallust, Livy, and Cicero.

6 Note also the challenge Rousseau sets himself in the *Social Contract*: 'Find a form of association that defends and protects the person and goods of each associate with all the common force, and by means of which each one, uniting with all, nevertheless obeys only himself and remains as free as before' (1978: 53 [Book I, ch. 6]).

7 A fifth book, Bellah et al. (1985), invoked communitarian themes in the course of a sociological analysis of the American middle class.

8 Note Bell (1993: 4 and n. 14) on the reluctance of MacIntyre, Walzer, Taylor, and Sandel to admit to being

communitarians. See also MacIntyre: 'Contemporary communitarians, from whom I have strongly dissociated myself whenever I have had an opportunity to do so, advance their proposals as a contribution to the politics of the nation-state' (1994: 302); 'Liberals … mistakenly suppose that those [totalitarian and other] evils arise from any form of political community which embodies substantive practical agreement upon some strong conception of the human good. I by contrast take them to arise from the specific character of the nation-state, thus agreeing with liberals in this at least, that modern nation-states which masquerade as embodiments of community are always to be resisted' (1994: 303); 'In any case the liberal critique of those nation-states which pretend to embody the values of community has little to say to those Aristotelians, such as myself, for whom the nation-state is not and cannot be the locus of community' (1994: 303). See further MacIntyre (1998: 243–50).

9 For responses to 'difference', see Dagger (1997: 176–81), Spragens (1999: ch. 4), and Miller (2000b). For responses to the global or cosmopolitan challenge, see Sandel (1996: 338–51), Miller (2000a), and Dagger (2001).

REFERENCES

Ackerman, Bruce (1980) *Social Justice in the Liberal State*. New Haven, CT: Yale University Press.

Arendt, Hannah (1958) *The Human Condition*. Chicago: University of Chicago Press.

Arendt, Hannah (1965) *On Revolution*. New York: Viking.

Bailyn, Bernard (1967) *The Ideological Origins of the American Revolution*. Cambridge, MA: Harvard University Press.

Banning, Lance (1986) 'Jeffersonian ideology revisited: liberal and classical ideas in the new American republic'. *William and Mary Quarterly*, 43 (January): 3–19.

Barber, Benjamin (1984) *Strong Democracy: Participatory Politics for a New Age*. Berkeley, CA: University of California Press.

Bell, Daniel (1993) *Communitarianism and Its Critics*. Oxford: Clarendon.

Bellah, R., R. Madsen, W. Sullivan, A. Swidler and S. Tipton (1985) *Habits of the Heart: Individualism and Commitment in American Life*. New York: Harper and Row.

Boyte, Harry (1989) *CommonWealth: A Return to Citizen Politics*. New York: Free Press.

Braithwaite, John and Philip Pettit (1990) *Not Just Deserts: A Republican Theory of Criminal Justice*. Oxford: Clarendon.

Burtt, Shelley (1993) 'The politics of virtue today: a critique and a proposal'. *American Political Science Review*, 87 (June): 360–8.

Caney, Simon (1992) 'Liberalism and communitarianism: a misconceived debate'. *Political Studies*, 40 (June): 273–89.

Canovan, Margaret (1992) *Hannah Arendt: A Reinterpretation of Her Political Thought*. Cambridge: Cambridge University Press.

Cicero (1998) *The Republic and The Laws*, eds, J. Powell and N. Rudd, trans. N. Rudd. Oxford: Oxford University Press.

Dagger, Richard (1997) *Civic Virtues: Rights, Citizenship, and Republican Liberalism*. New York: Oxford University Press.

Dagger, Richard (1999) 'The Sandelian republic and the encumbered self'. *The Review of Politics*, 61 (Spring): 181–217.

Dagger, Richard (2000) 'Republicanism refashioned: comments on Pettit's theory of freedom and government'. *The Good Society*, 9 (3): 50–3.

Dagger, Richard (2001) 'Republicanism and the politics of place'. *Philosophical Explorations*, 4 (3): 157–73.

Dworkin, Ronald (1977) *Taking Rights Seriously*. Cambridge, MA: Harvard University Press.

Dworkin, Ronald (1986) *Law's Empire*. Cambridge, MA: Harvard University Press.

Dworkin, Ronald (1992) 'Liberal community'. In S. Avineri and A. de-Shalit, eds, *Communitarianism and Individualism*. Oxford: Oxford University Press.

Emerson, R. W. (1842) 'English reformers'. *The Dial*, 3 (2).

Etzioni, Amitai (1996) *The New Golden Rule: Community and Morality in Democratic Society*. New York: Basic.

Everdell, William (1983) *The End of Kings: A History of Republics and Republicanism*. New York: Free.

Fink, Zera (1945) *The Classical Republicans: An Essay in the Recovery of a Pattern of Thought in Seventeenth Century England*. Evanston, IL: Northwestern University Press.

Frazer, Elizabeth (1999) *The Problems of Communitarian Politics: Unity and Conflict*. Oxford: Oxford University Press.

Friedman, Marilyn (1992) 'Feminism and modern friendship: dislocating the community'. In S. Avineri and A. de-Shalit, eds, *Communitarianism and Individualism*. Oxford: Oxford University Press.

Galston, William (1991) *Liberal Purposes: Goods, Virtues, and Diversity in the Liberal State*. Cambridge: Cambridge University Press.

Gewirth, Alan (1996) *The Community of Rights*. Chicago: University of Chicago Press.

Gutmann, Amy (1992) 'Communitarian critics of liberalism'. In S. Avineri and A. de-Shalit, eds, *Communitarianism and Individualism*. Oxford: Oxford University Press.

Harrington, James (1992 [1656]) *The Commonwealth of Oceana and A System of Politics*, ed., J. G. A. Pocock. Cambridge: Cambridge University Press.

Hazareesingh, Sudhir (1994) *Political Traditions in Modern France*. Oxford: Oxford University Press.

Holmes, Stephen (1995) *Passions and Constraint: On the Theory of Liberal Democracy*. Chicago: University of Chicago Press.

Honohan, Iseult (2002) *Civic Republicanism*. London: Routledge.

Isaac, Jeffrey (1988) 'Republicanism vs. liberalism? A reconsideration'. *History of Political Thought*, 9 (Summer): 349–77.

Kymlicka, Will (1989) *Liberalism, Community, and Culture*. Oxford: Clarendon.

Kymlicka, Will (1990) *Contemporary Political Philosophy: An Introduction*. Oxford: Clarendon.

MacIntyre, Alasdair (1981) *After Virtue: A Study in Moral Theory*. Notre Dame, IN: University of Notre Dame Press.

MacIntyre, Alasdair (1994) 'A partial response to my critics'. In J. Horton and S. Mendus, eds, *After MacIntyre: Critical Perspectives on the Work of Alasdair MacIntyre*. Cambridge: Polity.

MacIntyre, Alasdair (1998) 'Politics, philosophy and the common good'. In K. Knight, ed., *The MacIntyre Reader*. Cambridge: Polity.

Macpherson, C. B. (1962) *The Political Theory of Possessive Individualism: Hobbes to Locke*. Oxford: Clarendon.

Mason, Andrew (2000) *Community, Solidarity, and Belonging: Levels of Community and Their Normative Significance*. Cambridge: Cambridge University Press.

Mill, J. S. (1991 [1861]) *Considerations on Representative Government*. In John Gray, ed., *On Liberty and Other Essays*. Oxford: Oxford University Press.

Miller, David (1995) *On Nationality*. Oxford: Clarendon.

Miller, David (2000a) 'Bounded citizenship'. In his *Citizenship and National Identity*. Cambridge: Polity.

Miller, David (2000b) 'Citizenship and pluralism'. In his *Citizenship and National Identity*. Cambridge: Polity.

Miller, David (2000c) 'Communitarianism: left, right and centre'. In his *Citizenship and National Identity*. Cambridge: Polity.

Montesquieu, C. (1989 [1748]) *The Spirit of the Laws*, eds and trans. A. Cohler, B. Miller and H. Stone. Cambridge: Cambridge University Press.

Mulhall, Stephen and Adam Swift (1996) *Liberals and Communitarians*, 2nd edn. Oxford: Blackwell.

Newman, Stephen (1989) 'Challenging the liberal individualist tradition in America: "community" as a critical ideal in recent political theory'. In A. C. Hutchinson and L. J. M. Green, eds, *Law and the Community: The End of Individualism?* Toronto: Carswell.

Nisbet, Robert (1953) *The Quest for Community*. Oxford: Oxford University Press.

Nozick, Robert (1974) *Anarchy, State, and Utopia*. New York: Basic.

Oldfield, Adrian (1990) *Citizenship and Community: Civic Republicanism and the Modern World*. London: Routledge.

Ortega y Gasset, José (1932) *The Revolt of the Masses*. New York: Norton.

O'Sullivan, Noel (1975) 'Hannah Arendt: Hellenic nostalgia and industrial society'. In A. de Crespigny and K. Minogue, eds, *Contemporary Political Philosophers*. New York: Dodd, Mead.

Pangle, Thomas (1988) *The Spirit of Modern Republicanism: The Moral Vision of the American Founders and the Philosophy of Locke*. Chicago: University of Chicago Press.

Pettit, Philip (1997) *Republicanism: A Theory of Freedom and Government*. Oxford: Clarendon.

Pocock, J. G. A. (1975) *The Machiavellian Moment: Florentine Political Thought and the Atlantic Republican Tradition*. Princeton, NJ: Princeton University Press.

Rahe, Paul (1992) *Republics Ancient and Modern: Classical Republicanism and the American Revolution*. Chapel Hill, NC: University of North Carolina Press.

Rawls, John (1971) *A Theory of Justice*. Cambridge, MA: Harvard University Press.

Rawls, John (1993) *Political Liberalism*. New York: Columbia University Press.

Robbins, Caroline (1959) *The Eighteenth-Century Commonwealthman*. Cambridge, MA: Harvard University Press.

Rossiter, Clinton, ed. (1961 [1787]) *The Federalist Papers*. New York: New American Library.

Rousseau, Jean-Jacques (1978 [1762]) *On the Social Contract*, ed. R. D. Masters, trans. J. R. Masters. New York: St Martin's.

Rousseau, Jean-Jacques (1979 [1762]) *Émile*, trans. A. Bloom. New York: Free Press.

Sandel, Michael (1982) *Liberalism and the Limits of Justice*. Cambridge: Cambridge University Press.

Sandel, Michael (1994) 'Political Liberalism'. *Harvard Law Review*, 107 (May): 1765–94.

Sandel, Michael (1996) *Democracy's Discontent: America in Search of a Public Philosophy*. Cambridge, MA: Harvard University Press.

Schofield, Malcolm (1995) 'Cicero's definition of *res publica*'. In J. G. F. Powell, ed., *Cicero the Philosopher: Twelve Papers*. Oxford: Clarendon.

Sellers, M. N. S. (1998) *The Sacred Fire of Liberty: Republicanism, Liberalism and the Law*. London: Macmillan.

Skinner, Quentin (1998) *Liberty before Liberalism*. Cambridge: Cambridge University Press.

Skinner, Quentin (2002) 'A third concept of liberty'. *London Review of Books*, 4 April: 16–18.

Spragens, Thomas Jr (1995) 'Communitarian liberalism'. In A. Etzioni, ed., *New Communitarian Thinking: Persons, Virtues, Institutions, and Communities*. Charlottesville, VA: University of Virginia Press.

Spragens, Thomas Jr (1999) *Civic Liberalism: Reflections on Our Democratic Ideals*. Lanham, MD: Rowman and Littlefield.

Sullivan, William (1986) *Reconstructing Public Philosophy*. Berkeley, CA: University of California Press.

Sunstein, Cass (1988) 'Beyond the republican revival'. *Yale Law Journal*, 97 (July): 1539–89.

Tam, Henry (1998) *Communitarianism: A New Agenda for Politics and Citizenship*. Basingstoke: Macmillan.

Taylor, Charles (1985) *Philosophical Papers*, 2 vols. Cambridge: Cambridge University Press.

Taylor, Charles (1989) 'Cross-purposes: the liberal–communitarian debate'. In N. Rosenblum, ed., *Liberalism and the Moral Life*. Cambridge, MA: Harvard University Press.

Terchek, Ronald (1997) *Republican Paradoxes and Liberal Anxieties*. Lanham, MD: Rowman and Littlefield.

Tocqueville, Alexis de (1969 [1835, 1840]) *Democracy in America*, ed. J. P. Mayer, trans. G. Lawrence. Garden City, NY: Doubleday Anchor.

Tönnies, Ferdinand (2001 [1887]) *Community and Civil Society*, trans. J. Harris and M. Hollis. Cambridge: Cambridge University Press.

Walzer, Michael (1983) *Spheres of Justice: A Defense of Pluralism and Equality*. New York: Basic.

Wirszubski, Ch. (1960) *Libertas as a Political Idea at Rome during the Late Republic and Early Principate*. Cambridge: Cambridge University Press.

Wolin, Sheldon (1960) *Politics and Vision: Continuity and Innovation in Western Political Thought*. Boston: Little, Brown.

Wollstonecraft, Mary (1985 [1792]) *Vindication of the Rights of Woman*, ed. M. Brody. London: Penguin.

Wood, Gordon (1969) *The Creation of the American Republic, 1776–1787*. Chapel Hill, NC: University of North Carolina Press.

Young, Iris Marion (1990) *Justice and the Politics of Difference*. Princeton, NJ: Princeton University Press.

Zuckert, Michael (1994) *Natural Rights and the New Republicanism*. Princeton, NJ: Princeton University Press.

14

Green Political Theory: A Report

JOHN BARRY AND ANDREW DOBSON

In 1983 the United Nations undertook a little-reported series of 'time-lapse' experiments on selected individuals to try to calibrate the effect of ever-accelerating social and intellectual change. The fear that underlay these experiments was that humans are ill-adapted to rapid change, and that if the rate of change continued to accelerate to the degree observed throughout the twentieth century, humanity's non-adaptive reactions could become pathological, with potentially disastrous consequences.

The experiment required that individuals from various walks of life be isolated from developments occurring in their fields of endeavour for a period of 20 years from 1 January 1983. Although cryogenic technology would have been the perfect way of achieving the required 'deep sleep', ethical and technical difficulties counted decisively against it. In the end, the UN's Time-Lapse Secretariat (TLS) decided on geographical rather than strictly diachronic isolation. Advertisements went out in specialist journals for volunteers for the experiment, and after a vigorous selection process including tests to determine individuals' representativeness of their occupation or station in life, as well as their ability to stand up to the rigours of 20 years of isolation, 500 individuals were sent to an uninhabited atoll in the Pacific Ocean to begin their period of isolation. Thereafter the only contact they had with the outside world was with the service craft and personnel charged with maintaining, on a periodic basis, the atoll's life support systems. Contact between the experiment's subjects and service personnel was strictly regulated to prevent the transfer of information of any sort in either direction.

Twenty years later, on 1 January 2003, the isolation phase of the experiment ended with the return of the subjects to their families and communities. Subjects were returned, too, to their former occupations or stations in life and asked, simply, to record the changes they observed in them, and to try, impressionistically, to calibrate the rate of change.

In general, the conclusions reached at the end of the time-lapse experiments were encouraging and comforting. The experimental subjects proved capable of assimilating the changes that had occurred in their fields and occupations during their isolation, even in areas where change had been extremely rapid, such as information technology and breakfast cereal development. Apart from these broad conclusions, no more concrete results for the time-lapse experiment are due for release until 2005 when detailed assessment will be complete. By a circuitous route, however, one experimental subject's complete account has come into our hands, and what follows is an abridged version of one part of it.

The subject in question was a normative political theorist, well known to his colleagues and peers in the early 1980s as a researcher across a formidably wide range of topics in his subdiscipline – just the qualities that spurred the TLS to select him to represent his field of endeavour in the time-lapse experiment. The part of the report that concerns us here is that which deals with what the subject (let's call him 'Z') variously calls 'green', 'environmental' or 'ecological' political theory. What follows are verbatim extracts from Z's report.

* * *

I never thought I'd suffer so much from book and article deprivation during my time in the Pacific Ocean. When they let me loose on 2 January 2003 in my old university library I felt like a kid in a candy store. Where was the best place to look to get an overview of the previous 20 years of political theory? Predictably, I made a beeline for the textbooks on political ideologies, and there I made my first discovery. Before I left for the Pacific the last chapter in every textbook of this sort was on feminism [see further Chapter 21]. Now the last chapter seemed to be called 'ecologism' or 'environmentalism'. What was this? What had happened? And should I pay it any attention? The key theme running through the various interpretations of ecologism – indeed *the* key theme, I was to discover, running through everything I came to understand as 'green political theory' – is that while we have known since Aristotle that 'human beings are political animals', political theory has generally focused more on the 'political' than on the 'animal'. Green political theory asks us, in effect, to invert this prospectus. We are invited to ask what it means for politics when the public and private spaces it inhabits include the 'natural' world.

LIMITS TO GROWTH

One way of couching the question, I discovered after reading my way through several 'ecologism' chapters, is in terms of 'the limits to growth' (Meadows et al., 1972). This is not only the title of a book that I remember well myself and that made a massive public impact – referred to by some as signalling the beginning of the modern environmental movement – but also a phrase that has become a pervasive trope in green political literature. I had a dim memory of the 'doom and gloom', 'eco-catastrophic' character of the limits to growth argument, which complemented the plethora of post-apocalyptic movies of the 1970s, and also coincided with the oil shortages of 1972. Commentators regard it as one kind of expression of the embeddedness of the human condition, an embeddedness that constitutes the context within which political projects must be written. Reflecting on this in the context of other chapters in the textbooks on modern ideologies, it occurred to me that the closest cousin of this sort of idea is conservatism [see further Chapter 10]. Yet ecologism is more often politically and analytically presented as a progressive ideology, an heir to the Enlightenment tradition of equality, closely related to the 'new social movements' (another category I've had to learn about since my return from the Pacific) [see Chapter 20] and aligned with (sometimes in fraternal competition with, indeed) social democratic and labour parties. Is this an ideology that manages to lean left and bear right at the same time? Or is it just – in the immortal phrase – over the rainbow? I'll come back to this.

Limits to growth is, it seems, in part a descriptive commentary on the metabolistic relationship between human beings and their environment, regarded in terms of its capacity to provide services for the production and reproduction of human life. The stock and flow of these services is the context for any human project. None of the other ideologies in the textbooks on my 1983–2003 shelf talks quite like this. 'Stock' refers to resources such as coal that are to all intents and purposes finite, and 'flow' refers to resources that are in principle renewable, such as fish and energy from the sun, and the capacity of the earth's systems to absorb waste and pollution. Stock resources run down as they are accessed and converted into useful material for the reproduction of human life, and flow resources, while to all intents and purposes infinite in quantity, may be difficult to capture effectively (the sun's energy, for example), or easy to run down if not carefully looked after (fish in the sea, for example).

As a critical commentary, limits to growth suggests that 'industrialism' – broadly, the productive path followed by all so-called advanced industrial countries since the industrial revolution, and regarded by most developing countries as the right development path to follow – cannot continue indefinitely because it fails to take account of the resources context in which it is inscribed. Stock resources are used up as if they had no limit, and no attempt is made to seek substitutes to enable the services they provide to continue. Flow resources are over-exploited, sometimes to the point where they are unable to recover. Ecologism presents itself as unique among modern political ideologies in pointing to this metabolistic context for political projects, and it self-consciously criticizes other ideologies for not doing so.

Reading more, I found out that two of the most significant examples of this metabolistic relationship going wrong are global warming or climate change, and biodiversity loss. While obviously I was alarmed at the rate and extent of human-induced changes to the earth's climate and depletion of the variety of species on the planet, the phenomenon of global warming did at least explain why I noticed that the atoll we lived on in the Pacific did indeed get smaller as the years went by, and it was not due (as some of my island companions intimated) to my taste for home-brewed coconut beer.

It didn't take me long to discover that the limits to growth thesis has its detractors. Some suggest that the model on which its conclusions were based is fragile. How can one accurately model such a vast range of complex inputs and outputs, simultaneously taking full and appropriate account of the variables that constitute the weft and warp of the metabolistic relationship of individuals and societies with their environment? Some pointed to the obvious issue of how we tell 'environmental degradation' (bad) from 'environmental change' (neutral)?

Others focused on the variables themselves. The report dwells on population growth as a key factor in resource use, but without discriminating between different rates of resource use among poorer and wealthier populations. Not everyone is equally culpable, surely, of exceeding the limits set by a finite environment. I wondered, then, to what extent this could be called a *politics*, so bereft of analyses of power does it seem to be? However, upon further reading, it was clear that as green political theory evolved, the analysis of power and how it is directly related to responsibility for environmental damage also developed. Impoverished people clear-cutting a forest to survive is in quite a different moral and political category to the environmental damage caused by affluent consumer lifestyles, which are energy and resource intensive. The emergence of a discourse of 'environmental justice' (both local and global) and green political economy, both of which focused on inequalities in power, wealth and environmental quality, were important here (Dobson, 1998; Dower, 1998; Schlosberg, 1999; Martinez Alier, 2002; J. Barry, 1999a).

I also wondered about the politics of the language of 'limits' itself. I recalled Karl Marx's devastating critique of Thomas Malthus which pointed out that limits are not 'given', but that nature is, rather, in a dialectical relationship with humanity (Benton, 1996; Hayward, 1992; J. Barry, 1999c; Dobson, 1994). Humans transform nature as nature transforms humans, and this means that limits are a function of humans' metabolistic relationship with nature rather than set in some predetermined way.

But does this do terminal damage to the green case? Marx's is an acknowledgement that nature – 'man's inorganic body' – is a political category, a notion entirely absent from all the other chapters in the ideologies textbook I have in front of me, but which is ecologism's central point. Political ecologists don't seem to deny that human beings can shape the contours of environmental limits (Benton, 1993; J. Barry, 1999b), but they do claim that modern ideological unwillingness to regard the environment as a political category has led to local, regional and now global breakdowns in the environment's capacity to offer a more or less predictable and sustainable set of services to human beings. I have discovered some evidence to suggest that political parties of both left and right – if not the ideologies from which they seek their inspiration – regard this as a message worth listening to. 'The environment' is now clearly a category through which many party manifestos speak, and it constitutes a major policy area that cuts across other policy issues such as energy, housing, transport, agriculture and food. One of the biggest surprises on my return from the Pacific was to find green parties not only with parliamentary representation, but also sharing power in national governments (Müller-Rommel and Poguntke, 2002).

THE ETHICAL STATUS OF THE NON-HUMAN WORLD

I came to regard the 'limits to growth' reasons for care for the environment as 'pragmatic' responses to observable deteriorations in the environment. However, they do not exhaust the range of reasons that ecologism has to offer. I was struck by the way in which ecologism is part of a broader remoralization of politics, according to which people do the right thing because it is morally the right thing to do, not because of some financial incentive or other prudential set of reasons. In this context the striking suggestion made by some political ecologists – in its most general form – is that the non-human natural world has moral standing. The meaning and implications of this took some time for me to digest. A suggestive letter to the national press in the UK that I came across as I trawled through back numbers of newspapers soon after my return from the Pacific captures the 'foot-in-the-door' approach that characterizes green attempts to make inroads into our scepticism. The letter was written in response to news that scientists had implanted an alien gene in a monkey, with a view to creating transgenic monkeys that perfectly mimic human diseases so as to road test cures for them. The letter ran as follows:

> If the rhesus monkey really is 'so similar' to human beings then shouldn't we resist experimenting on it for the same reasons we resist experimenting on human beings? And if it's dissimilar enough for us not to have such ethical qualms, then why are we experimenting on it at all? (*The Guardian*, 13 January 2001)

Scientists insist on the necessity of experimenting on our close species relatives precisely because they are close relatives. The claim is that they can learn more from animals that are physiologically similar to human beings than from those that are distant. This makes scientific sense. But it also tweaks a moral tail in the way captured in the first question of the letter. The characteristic that makes the rhesus monkey such an ideal pharmacological subject – i.e. similarity with the human species – is the very same characteristic that suggests a moral prohibition against experimentation. Note that this prohibition would not turn on prudential arguments, but would take the same form as arguments for human rights. If humans have a right not to be experimented upon this is because they should be treated as ends in themselves and not as means only. The letter writer points out that if this is true for humans it must be true for other beings similar in relevant respects to humans.

Ah! There's the phrase that rings throughout green political theory: 'similar in relevant respects'. Litres of green ink have been spilt arguing over what 'relevant respects' means, in particular. What, exactly, is the 'X factor' that makes for moral considerability? Jeremy Bentham alerted us to the massive difference that alternative answers can make when he said that, 'The day may come when the rest of the animal creation may acquire those rights which could never have been withholden from them but by the hand of tyranny ... The question is not, Can they *reason*?, nor Can they *talk*?, but Can they *suffer*?' (1970: 311). If reason and/or verbal communication are the X factor then the charmed moral circle is restricted to human beings. (Or at least it is restricted to those who can reason and/or talk. But what about those in a persistent vegetative state, for example? Are they now on the same level as the rhesus monkey, and legitimately liable to the same treatment?) If the capacity to suffer pain is the X factor, on the other hand, then the moral circle is widened considerably. And there are ways of widening it even further. We could, it seems, render the X factor as 'autopoiesis' (Eckersley, 1992: 60–1), or the capacity for self-reproduction, and then the circle is even bigger.

And so, it seems, the debate goes on, ever more arcane and insecure, taking in collections of beings as well as individuals until the circle of moral considerability includes, in principle, the whole of the non-human natural world.[1] It is easy to lose sight of the key point on this side of ecologism's equation: that the environment should be protected not (only) for prudential reasons but because it has (something akin to) a right to protection. From either point of view – the moral or the prudential – ecologism politicizes the environment by opening up the question of its use and abuse as a *political* question. I'll come back to this, but there's one other interesting aspect of the motivational question ('Why protect the environment?') on which I ought to report. There is evident dissatisfaction with the Byzantine and politically unconvincing arguments that the 'similar in relevant respects' debate has spawned. I was intrigued to see an argument that cuts the Gordian knot by politicizing the environment indirectly.

FUTURE GENERATIONS AND THE ENVIRONMENT

This is done by broadening the political community in a different kind of direction – but again quite unlike anything else I came across in the political ideologies textbook. Before my Pacific exile I had grown used to thinking of progressive politics as about the recognition of the political claims of ever-increasing numbers of previously marginalized social groups. Most obviously, for example, women are now recognized in a way that would have been unthinkable even 100 years ago. As befits the last chapter in the ideologies textbook, ecologism has its own novel take on the 'recognition question'. Think, for a moment, of 'the environment' as a diverse range of resources of all types. Not just the kinds of resources that are required for physiological survival but also those that are a necessary condition for conceiving life plans of all sorts. This, in other words, is the environment conceived as the 'stuff' through which life plans are formed and carried out. Put differently again, the environment constitutes a range of options for life-plan conception and execution.

Think, now, of all this in terms of justice. What is the fairest way of distributing this thing (the environment) that constitutes a range of options for life plans? And, crucially for ecologism, who should be recognized as legitimate recipients of the fruits of this distribution? For political ecology, the answer includes, among others, future generations of human beings. For ecologism, there is no reason in justice why the present generation of human beings should be entitled to deprive future generations of the 'stuff' through which and from which plans for life are conceived and executed.

It is not hard to see how all of this amounts to the indirect protection of the environment. It is protected, in effect, by doing justice to future generations of human beings. Any degradation of the environment amounts to intergenerational injustice in that it constitutes a reduction in the options available to them. Bryan Norton, for example, has developed a 'convergence hypothesis' (1991: 188–203), which he proposes as a way to advance environmental protection politically as well as to heal the division within ecologism between 'ecocentrism' and 'anthropocentrism'. Couching the reasons for protecting or being concerned about the environment in terms of obligations to future generations involves using anthropocentric means to achieve ecocentric ends. Of equal significance is the fact that focusing on intergenerational justice amounts to the building of a bridge between green political theory and mainstream contemporary political theory, as Brian Barry's forays into environmental issues demonstrate (B. Barry, 1978; 1989; 1999). As well as being of intellectual interest, this argument also has some political merit. My political-ecological investigations have led to me to believe that one of ecologism's biggest political disadvantages is the suspension of disbelief required when you land on some of its wildest shores. As a political idea, the great ape project, for example, might make some headway on the 'similar in relevant respects' platform, but species extensions much beyond this are difficult to make stick politically. Justice, however, is a well-established discourse both in normative political theory and in civil society, and its extension to future generations, while by no means universally accepted as legitimate among commentators, is a bridge less far than extending moral recognition to louseworts. Justice is also related to the discourse of rights, which is the dominant ethical and political normative grammar within modern liberal theory and practice. I shall come back to the issue of future generations later.

One thing I noticed by this point in my investigation was that ecologism as an ideology was heading out of ideologies textbooks and into the broader territory of political theory. I have come to think that the best way of capturing this is to think of ecologism as expressing a political objective, which we might call 'sustainability'. Sustainability, in turn, is best thought of as a 'concept' – as the sustaining of some X into the future – which has many competing 'conceptions'. These conceptions will all offer different answers to some basic sustainability questions, like: how long should X be sustainable into the future? For whom or what should X be sustainable? And what is X anyway?

Once we think of sustainability as a political objective, the rather traditional question arises of how it stands in relation to other political objectives. The form of this question is one with which political theorists are well acquainted. The history of political theory itself can be seen in terms of arguments of priority and compatibility between liberty and equality, democracy and order, justice and liberty, and so on. My reading of what has taken place over the past 20 years – the period of my exile from the development of political theory – is that ecologism has added another political objective to the list of competitors.

This is borne out by a survey of the development of green political theory over the past 10 years or so. It is as though so-called 'green theorists' are working their way through the list of political desiderata and working out the relationship between them and sustainability in a normative sense. This move from ideology to theory seems also to have had the effect of taking green political theory out of what might have been regarded as a ghetto in its early days. My reading of the environmental ethical literature, for example, reveals a vicious downwards spiral of debate of ever-decreasing size and political relevance (between ecocentrism and anthropocentrism, deep and shallow ecology, light and dark greens) that would have been the envy of medieval theologians trying to work out how many angels can fit on a pinhead.

The move outwards occasioned by debates over conflict and compatibility between sustainability and other political objectives, on the other hand, has drawn mainstream theorists into the green political theory debate. From my vantage point of 20 years absence from political theory, I would judge this as good for both sides.

Before I try to make good this claim, though, let me return briefly to the conundrum of whether green politics – a.k.a. ecologism – is a progressive or a conservative ideology. One way of groping for an answer is to think of it in terms of the discourse of utopianism. We are inclined to think of progressive ideologies as having a utopian 'moment', in that their prescriptive dimension contains a picture of the world as we have never seen it before. This contrasts with conservative prescriptions that tend to paint an idealized picture of some valued moment in the past which conservatives would like to see restored in the present, typically coupled with a negative/realistic view of human nature which sets clear limits to political change. Ecologism, I think, occupies a place somewhere in between these two positions. It shares the progressive view that what is usually referred to as 'human nature' is malleable, so we are not condemned to 'selfish' or any other determined sort of behaviour, but it also nods in the direction of conservative thoughts by suggesting that the human condition sets limits on our projects. This distinction between human *nature* and the human *condition* allows ecologism to claim elasticity for the former, and a degree of fixity for the latter. The outcome is a kind of progressive politics whose utopian element firmly accepts limits, which is another distinctive feature of the ideology of ecologism.

SCIENCE, TECHNOLOGY AND VULNERABILITY

The notion of limits is extremely important within ecologism, and the role of science in identifying such limits gives it a unique place within ecologism. Unlike all other ideologies and political theories I was familiar with (with the notable exception of the flawed attempts to develop a 'scientific Marxism'), ecologism is firmly based on science. From its relationship to ecological science in the nineteenth century, to more recent scientific discoveries of global climate change and scientific debate over genetically modified crops, ecologism is the first political theory to be so firmly involved with scientific knowledge. After all, without scientific knowledge, most of the ecological problems that concern green political theory would not be 'problems'. Science thus plays a vital role in ecologism by providing it with the 'facts' and 'problems' relating to our metabolic dependence upon the non-human world and its natural systems.

However, my reading of green literature suggests that a positive relationship to and attitude towards science is not universally shared. For some political ecologists, science (and more particularly techno-logical developments and innovations) is a major part of the cause of ecological damage, that is, it is part of the problem not the solution. Such views point to scientific and technological developments such as nuclear power, the internal combustion engine, biotechnology and generally the way science and technology have been harnessed to produce more effective ways of consuming the planet's resources as evidence in their case against science. This critique of science and technology moves ecol-ogism in the direction of Ulrich Beck's (1992; 1995) critique of the 'risk society' and the dangers 'mega technologies' can pose to modern societies in terms of both actual harm and dangers to demo-cratic practices, especially in terms of the anti-democratic dangers of rule by experts (J. Barry, 1999a: 202–6). It is thus no surprise that many green theorists have integrated the concepts and discourses around risk society into the green perspective (Blühdorn, 2000; Achterberg, 2001).

Equally, a well-established argument within green political theory concerns the 'techno-fix' mentality of industrialism. The 'techno-fix' view is most closely associated with those who, while they may agree with political ecologists that there are definite ecological problems, remain absolutely confident that there are technological solutions, and that science and technological innovation will find these solutions. The main import of this techno-fix perspective is that finding solutions to ecological problems does not require major changes to current political and economic systems, or consumption and production patterns. John Dryzek points to the close association between this techno-fix view and the 'cornucopian discourse' which denies the 'limits to growth' view so central to green political theory (1997: 45–61). Here, green views identify another limit in terms of human scientific knowledge, questioning that we can or ought to proceed on the basis that we will (at some future stage) have complete knowledge (and thus control and power) over the natural world (O'Neill, 1993: 146–67).

Finally, for many political ecologists an over-reliance on science and technology as the only or dominant 'frame' to understand the ecological crisis tends to both 'depoliticize' and 'demoralize' that crisis. That is, adopting a purely technological or scientific approach to the ecological crisis tends to reduce it to a 'technical' matter (often best left to 'experts' to sort out), thus denying the profound ethical and political character of the ecological crisis in terms of what it says about our ethical obligations to the natural world and its place in our moral thinking and action (J. Barry, 1999a: 109; O'Neill, 1996).

In the main, however, political ecologism does not reject science and technology, despite what crit-ics of ecologism from both left and right may think in terms of ecologism as espousing a 'Luddite' world view (Holmes, 1993: 122–41) or as a conser-vative, backward looking, anti-modernist ideology (Giddens, 1994; J. Barry, 1999c: 94–104), seeking a return to some premodern 'ecological Golden Age'.[2] Ecologism accepts science and technology, but does so knowing that they are intrinsically polit-ical and not 'neutral' instruments, that they have ethical implications, but nevertheless will (where appropriate) be part of the solution to many ecolog-ical problems. In this way ecologism is firmly within rather than outside the Enlightenment and modernity, though sharing with other political per-spectives such as socialism and feminism a 'critical insider' status.

The scientific identification of ecological limits and measurement of ecological degradation also highlights human dependency upon the natural world, and shows up the flaws in an arrogant assumption of human control and power over the non-human world. In keeping with its stress on limits, notions of vulnerability, dependence and asso-ciated ideas of care and responsibility are common features of green discourse. Greens stress the mutual vulnerability of the non-human world and humanity (J. Barry, 2002). They offer, in the increasingly technologically driven globalizing world, a cautionary voice which stresses the dan-gers of the underlying assumption or aim of human technological control over the natural world based on complete knowledge of its workings generated by science. In response to the limits to human knowledge, limits to growth, the ethical consider-ability of the non-human world, and the mutual dependence of human and non-human worlds, greens speak of caution, prudence and care. The growing significance (ethically, politically, eco-nomically and epistemologically) of the precaution-ary principle within green political theory is evidence of this (O'Riordan and Jordan, 1995; O'Riordan, Cameron and Jordan, 2001). In the con-text of the irreducible ignorance (Faber, Manstetten and Proops, 1992) and complexity of the metabo-lism between humans and the non-human world, we are, according to greens, foolhardy to rush head-long with irreversible and large-scale alterations to the natural world, the long-term effects of which we simply do not know. The green perspective is nicely captured in Aquinas' view that 'It is better that a blind horse be slow.'

SUSTAINABILITY, DEMOCRACY AND SOCIAL JUSTICE

Returning to the issue of the conversation with the broader themes of political theory that 'greens' have initiated, two political concepts, in particular, have occasioned a great deal of comment in connection with sustainability: social justice and democracy. The former has been an especially rich source of cross-fertilization between green political theorists and their mainstream colleagues, but 'democracy and sustainability' came onto the scene first, so let me make one or two comments about democracy here. A brief journey back to the 'limits to growth' idea will serve to show why democracy has been so closely examined from a green point of view.

Two characteristics of the limits to growth idea stand out. First, there is the urgency which supporters of the idea try to impress upon us. Certain characteristics of resource use – its supposedly exponential nature, for example – add up to the thought that limits of extraction and use can be reached very quickly. Collapse will only be avoided, therefore, if rapid action is taken. Second, and connected, there is the point that sustainability will only be possible if major changes in lifestyles – particularly those of high consumption individuals – take place. Most people, it has been suggested, will not do this voluntarily, and so sustainability will involve coercion. Both of the positions point away from democracy, of course. This is because, first, democracy takes time, and time is as scarce a resource as oil for limits to growth enthusiasts. Second, democracy as a way of making decisions is founded on the autonomy of individuals. But what if autonomous individuals make the wrong choices? What if they do not want to make the changes required to live a sustainable life? They may, then, have to be 'forced to be free'. I remember these arguments being put, indeed, before I volunteered for the time-lapse study, so I was especially intrigued to see them having been debated so thoroughly during my time away.

The environmental movement, as distinct from green political theory, has been self-consciously democratic in orientation. Its most visible successes have been in parliamentary and local or municipal elections, while green parties have long been noted for their extremely open, transparent and democratic internal structures, making them the most internally democratic parties within modern electoral politics (Doherty, 2002). This may be the reason why the relationship between democracy and sustainability has been so thoroughly explored (Doherty and de Geus, 1996; Lafferty and Meadowcroft, 1996; Mathews, 1996). The debate is of considerable interest to theorists of democracy in general, and not only those who come at it from the sustainability end, as it were. Sustainability as an objective has a number of general characteristics that make it a 'test bed' for whether political objectives of this type are compatible with democracy. Two aspects of sustainability in the previous paragraph seemed to point away from democracy. But it has other features that point towards compatibility too. I have already pointed up the indeterminate nature of sustainability, for example. The 'limits' argument for imposed solutions to unsustainability depends, it seems, on there being a determinate answer to the question 'What is to be done?' But precisely because sustainability is a normative notion there can be no fixed idea of what it is, and therefore no clearly defined route map for how to get to it. I have come to find it useful to interrogate that classical sustainability concept, 'threshold', from this point of view. A threshold designates the point beyond which further disturbance to a natural process or further exploitation of a natural resource will tip it into unsustainability. This point might seem scientifically determinate but we only have to ask ourselves the question 'Unsustainable for whom or for what?' to see that while science can provide us with information on which to base a decision, we cannot expect a computer to crunch out a complete answer for us.

Two examples come to mind. First, do we count future generations of human beings as a legitimate answer to our 'For whom?' question? If we do, then we have to be much more careful with what we do with finite resources such as coal, oil and gas than if we believe that sustainability is only an issue for the present generation. Given that there are sufficient of these resources to satisfy the needs and wants of the present generation, there is no need to think in terms of 'thresholds' at all as far as this generation is concerned. Thresholds for finite resources only become relevant if we envisage users of these resources sometime after the point at which their running-down endangers their effective use and exploitation.

A second example throws into relief the possibility that sustainability might have interspecies ramifications too. Some species are much more resilient to disturbance than others, so a threshold for one species might not be a threshold for others. Human beings are adaptable to an extraordinary degree and have proved themselves adept at occupying ecological niches for which they are singularly unsuitable. We are the species nature did not specialize in many respects, making the whole planet our 'ecological niche' as it were. Humans seem almost infinitely capable, then, of transgressing whatever thresholds are designated for them. Yet even this tremendous capacity for adaptation pales against that of creatures such as spiders and cockroaches which, as I recall from debates around the 'nuclear winter' that would have resulted from an exchange of atomic weapons between the USA and the USSR, would have survived even this kind of cataclysmic event. The 'nuclear threshold', then, would have been more critical to human beings than to cockroaches. The decision as to whether to include only cockroaches or human beings – or both – in threshold calculations is clearly a normative one.

So if sustainability is a normative notion, how do we determine what it is? Democracy is one answer to this question [see further Chapter 11]. We find out what it is, in an appropriately provisional and temporary sense, by debating it, allowing many perspectives and voices to be heard. And at this point, epistemology and political pragmatism seem to be happily coincidental. From the epistemological point of view, if there is anything like a 'truth' of sustainability then it is more likely to emerge from an open-ended democratic conversation than from the deliberations of a closed epistemic community of 'experts'. And from the pragmatic point of view, measures for sustainability are more likely to be endorsed and supported by people if they have had the opportunity to decide upon and design them than if they have not. The latter is especially important in terms of ensuring popular legitimacy for sustainability policies that will require changes in the lifestyles of many people – especially in the 'developed' countries.

So while democracy and sustainability seem to be in tension, sustainability as a policy objective has enough in common with other objectives to be regarded as a late addition to the list rather than something entirely new. In this regard, sustainability requires both some kind of definition and an acceptance of the legitimacy of the definition – even if both definition and legitimacy are provisional. *Especially* if they are provisional, indeed. Democracy as a form of decision-making seems ideally suited to both of these requirements.

What it cannot guarantee, though, is sustainable outcomes. The green engagement with democracy brings into sharp relief the fact that the *procedural* nature of democracy means that it cannot be expected to deliver any specific *outcomes*. This is a lesson worth learning, recognizing and applying in other contexts, and it raises interesting wider questions regarding decisions 'produced' by democracies. The fact that democracies cannot guarantee outcomes to any extent prompts the question of whether decisions that undermine democracy itself can be regarded as legitimate. The idea that a democracy might take a series of decisions leading to systematically unsustainable policies, thereby undermining the conditions for its own existence, is structurally similar to a democratic election producing a government determined to end the democratic process. How should democracies react to this possibility?

A related issue, which I see emerging from the later stages of the literature with which I was presented, is that of 'green citizenship' (Dobson, 2003; Smith, 1998; J. Barry, 1999a; 2002; Christoff, 1996). Part of the idea here is that citizens are the 'raw material' of democracy, the ones who make the decisions – at least in principle. If one wants sustainable outcomes from the democratic process, then, one way of maximizing the possibility is to 'ecologize' citizens. This is what 'greening' citizenship consists in. 'Green' or 'ecological' citizenship demands that we think of citizenship in rather novel ways. First, we must think of the rights and obligations of citizenship as existing outside the usual citizenship context of the nation-state. There are those who will argue that this cannot be done, and that citizenship is definitionally about the rights and responsibilities of individuals in relation to the states of which they are members. I see an interesting debate developing here between supporters of so-called cosmopolitan citizenship (e.g. Linklater 1998) and their ecological counterparts [see further Chapters 15, 19 and 22]. Second, the rights and duties of citizens in traditional conceptions are usually regarded as reciprocal, but what sense can this make in a global context in which ecological damage is asymmetrically inflicted? Ecological citizenship suggests that while my duty as a causer of damage to reduce it is generated by the reciprocal right of those on the receiving end to a liveable environment, they have no reciprocal and corresponding duty towards me. Third, ecological citizenship seems to revive the idea of virtue – pretty much absent from citizenship talk since the heyday of civic republicanism [see further Chapter 13]. Yet it talks about citizenship virtue in rather novel ways, and asks whether the virtues we more normally associate with the private realm – compassion and care, for example – ought not to be brought into the discursive fold of citizenship. This is part, fourth and finally, of the transgressive move to associate citizenship with the private realm itself, on the grounds that 'private' acts of consumption and (re)production have 'public' effects. Citizenship, some ecological theory seems to suggest, begins at home.

The other key democracy issue raised by the sustainability debate is that of representation. There are at least three types of constituency in the green context that are unfamiliar to democratic theory and practice – in terms of boundaries in space, time and the species barrier. First, we know that environmental problems, such as pollution, cannot be restricted to one country, so decisions with an environmental dimension made in any given country may – indeed probably will – affect people in other countries.

Do these people have a right to be democratically represented, on something like a 'principle of affected interests'? Second, the discussion above indicated that future generations of human beings form a key part of the sustainability equation. They are evidently not actually present (and could not be present) when environmental decisions are taken, but should they be 'present' surrogately – for democratic reasons – in some way? Representation in democratic theory has always been about making the absent present, so if there are objections to the idea of representing future generations democratically, this is likely to be for practical rather than normative reasons. Finally, we saw earlier that one aspect of the green normative agenda revolves around expanding the moral and – perhaps – the political community to include (some) species other than the human one. The interests of other species are evidently affected by human actions, so should these interests be represented in some way in the democratic process?[3]

The ecologism–democracy debate, then, is interesting for reasons internal to green politics, but democratic theorists in general have reason to think about the implications of the environmental problematic for democratic theory and practice too. The same goes for social justice [see further Chapter 17]. As we know, social justice is about the fair distribution of benefits and burdens in society. Sustainability makes us think about this general prospectus in a number of different ways. First of all, there is the question of whether the 'environment' can and should be regarded in terms of 'benefits and burdens'. No theory of justice has made this a central question, but the presuppositional nature of 'the environment' for leading meaningful lives would suggest that it should be. The fact that the environment has been ignored as a potential feature of theories of justice speaks volumes for the disembodied and disembedded nature of much modern political theory. It is curious, yet significant, to recognize that that which makes social justice possible at all, as theory and as practice, has no place in the considerations of social justice theorists. It is part of the significance of green political theory, indeed, that this stricture might be applied to political theory in general (Baxter, 1996).

But of course social justice theorists are not only interested in the 'What?' of distribution, but also in the 'According to what principle?' question. Typical candidates are equality, merit, and historical right. In other words, what does 'fair' mean? My readings over the past few weeks suggest that thinking of the environment as something that can be distributed provides us with an interesting case against which to test Michael Walzer's (1983) 'spheres of justice' notion. It will be remembered that Walzer resists the standard view that a universal metric of distribution can be applied across all distributable goods and bads. He argues that specific goods and bads (or 'spheres') have a principle of distribution 'attached' to them. One of his points is that goods with a preconditional quality should be distributed equally. This is something of a challenge to those who believe that a more universal metric should be applied – such as merit, for example. On this reading, goods of all sorts should be distributed on the basis of what people deserve, with the rider, perhaps, that they should begin in conditions of equal opportunity. Walzer provides an alternative view to this, and 'the environment' constitutes a test case for this alternative view. Green political theory suggests that the environment is a preconditional good *par excellence*, so if Walzer's variable metric for distribution cannot be made to work in this context, then that may indicate a flaw in the theory itself. It occurs to me that this is an excellent example of the way in which issues raised in green political theory have a wider salience. In this case, I am persuaded that 'mainstream' political theorists are doing themselves a disservice if they regard environmental issues as unconnected with their interests. On the contrary, environmental issues constitute a rich context within which standard political theoretical enquiries take on new inflections and generate new implications.

This is true of another dimension of social justice theory, too – that which concerns the 'community of justice', or the issue of who can be appropriately regarded as potential recipients of justice. It is a measure of the boundary-pushing nature of green political theory that it also raises the unusual question of whether beings other than human beings can be regarded as recipients of justice (Dobson, 1998; Low and Gleeson, 1998). A less exotic but nevertheless instructive and challenging possibility suggested by the environmental problematic is that future generations of human beings should be included in the community of justice. The idea of intergenerational justice hardly figures in most theories of justice, and I can't help thinking that this is a missed opportunity for social justice theory. The possibility that future generations might be regarded as legitimate recipients of justice raises some standard social justice questions in the starkest form, such as: how much sacrifice can be demanded of one group in order to do justice to other groups? The general shape of this question is familiar to us in the context, for example, of redistributive taxation policies: how much is it legitimate to ask those that have to forgo for the sake of doing justice to those that have not? In the intergenerational context this becomes a question of how much the present generation should be asked to forgo for the sake of leaving future generations with the opportunities (in environmental terms) to live full

CONCLUSIONS

and meaningful lives. It is something of a mystery why questions such as this have not been broached in social justice theory before, and my exposure to the justice/environment debate that took place while I was away has led me to the conclusion that social justice theorists are not doing their job properly if they fail to take seriously and fully Walzer's stricture that membership of the community of justice is the most important thing to be distributed – and that this community may well include generations of people yet to be born (as well as non-humans and non-nationals).

CONCLUSIONS

Twenty years was a long time to be away. I had no idea what to expect when I returned to home and hearth but I certainly had plenty of time to think about it. One recurring thought I had was that returning would be like being born again, in the sense that changes would have taken place over which I had had no control and in regard of which I had had no input. It worried me that decisions would be made without taking account of the needs and potential wants of people 20 years hence – i.e. me when I returned from the Pacific. Imagine my surprise, then, when I discovered that this 'worry' had become a central concern of this new branch of political theory that had developed while I was away – green political theory. Sitting in splendid isolation on my Pacific island, I was clearly a member of the global political community but my actual absence meant that I played no part in it, even though my interests were being affected by decisions taken in it. This is the lived experience both of the many people marginalized from global decision-making today, and an accurate surrogate portrayal of the 'absence' of future generations from the decision-making process even though their interests are clearly harmed or enhanced by it.

Green political theory, then, challenges us to expand the political community, and to grapple with the implications of imagining the interests of future generations as our own, at least in the first instance. One dimension of this involves understanding the embeddedness of human beings in their 'natural' environment. Future generations cannot live without the skein of life support that starts just below the surface of the earth and ends at the stratosphere. I 'knew' this in my mind when I first went to the Pacific island, but I 'lived' it during my feeble yet ultimately more or less successful attempts to grow indigenous crops during my time there. And my relationship with my surroundings underwent a more subtle change too. Physically isolated from the rest of the world, the island was – and

is – the home of species of animal and plant that are found nowhere else in the world. It was a source of great joy to me and to some of my companions on the experiment to live with this flora and fauna and to observe its rare rhymes and rhythms. As it happened I was the very last person to leave the island, having volunteered to do some clearing up and closing down. During that final day on the island I felt like the last person on earth.[4] The island was there to do with as I wished; everything on it was at my mercy and in my gift. Almost the last thing I saw before boarding the boat that would take me home was a nest containing one egg belonging to what we believed was the last breeding pair of a bird known only to this island. I briefly considered taking the egg as a memento of my 20 years' isolation from the world – and then realized in flash of blinding clarity that this was the wrong thing to do, not for any reason relating to human beings (there were none left) but because, simply, it might have been the last egg of all.

I never thought I would see that experience turned into a key aspect of a 'new politics' during my time away, yet politicizing and moralizing our relationship with the non-human natural world is indeed the leitmotif of green political theory. I am not a green political theorist myself, but I am firmly of the belief that the future of political theory should contain – and would be enriched by – a systematic engagement with its themes and challenges. Like its general subject – the multifaceted relationship, both physical/metabolic and ethical-political, between humans and the non-human world – there are few issues that green political theory does not touch upon. Given the range of problems and issues that we face in the twenty-first century (the democratic and social justice consequences of corporate led globalization, biotechnology and the commercial application of genetic knowledge; energy and resource shortages; and conflicts based on resource scarcity, world poverty and global inequality) it is clear that green political theory will continue to evolve as a key aspect of political theory to help us critically understand these developments and offer alternatives to them.

NOTES

1 Within green political theory (and the wider environmental movement), this issue as to the ethical status of the non-human world (or parts of it) and the weight to be attached to this status/value has led to debates between 'ecocentric' and 'anthropocentric' schools of thought (Dobson, 2001; J. Barry, 2001).

2 Like all forms of political theory, ecologism includes a range of perspectives; thus there are some self-professed

political ecologists who do come close to a Luddite, anti-technological perspective such as Sale (1995).

3 One recent direction in which this has led green political theory is exploring legal and constitutional provisions and means for representing these constituencies and enshrining environmental protection. See Hayward (2001).

4 Thinking about the value of the environment or one's reasons for valuing the environment via the thought experiment of being the last person on earth is interesting and can reveal support for arguments as to the intrinsic value of the non-human world. Most people in this position do not endorse the view that the earth or parts of it should be destroyed or harmed just because there will be or are no humans around to appreciate it. That is, there is no good reason that can support the wanton destruction of the non-human world in this case. For a critical account of this see Lee (1993).

REFERENCES

Achterberg, W. (2001) 'Democracy, justice and risk society: the meaning and shape of ecological democracy'. In J. Barry and M. Wissenburg, eds, *Sustaining Liberal Democracy: Ecological Challenges and Opportunities*. New York: Palgrave Macmillan.

Barry, B. (1978) 'Circumstances of justice and future generations'. In R. I. Sikora and B. Barry, eds, *Obligations to Future Generations*. Philadelphia: Temple University Press.

Barry, B. (1989) 'The ethics of resource depletion'. In B. Barry, *Democracy, Power and Justice*. Oxford: Clarendon.

Barry, B. (1999) 'Sustainability and intergenerational justice'. In A. Dobson, ed., *Fairness and Futurity: Essays on Environmental Sustainability and Social Justice*. Oxford: Oxford University Press.

Barry, J. (1999a) *Rethinking Green Politics: Nature, Virtue and Progress*. London: Sage.

Barry, J. (1999b) 'Marxism and ecology'. In A. Gamble, D. Marsh and T. Tant, eds, *Marxism and Social Science*. Basingstoke: Macmillan.

Barry, J. (1999c) *Environment and Social Theory*. London: Routledge.

Barry, J. (2001) 'Green political theory'. In J. Barry and E. Gene Frankland, eds, *International Encyclopedia of Environmental Politics*. London: Routledge.

Barry, J. (2002) 'Vulnerability and virtue: democracy, dependency and ecological stewardship'. In B. Pepperman-Taylor and B. Minteer, eds, *Democracy and the Claims of Nature: Critical Perspectives for a New Century*. New York: Rowman and Littlefield.

Baxter, B. (1996) 'Must political theory now be green?' In I. Hampshire-Monk and J. Stanyer, eds, *Contemporary Political Studies*. Belfast: Political Studies Association.

Beck, U. (1992) *Risk Society: Towards a New Modernity*. London: Sage.

Beck, U. (1995) *Ecological Politics in an Age of Risk*. Cambridge: Polity.

Bentham, J. (1970 [1823]) *The Principles of Morals and Legislation*. Darien, CT: Hafner.

Benton, T. (1993) *Natural Relations: Ecology, Animal Rights and Social Justice*. London: Verso.

Benton, T., ed. (1996) *The Greening of Marxism*. New York: Guilford.

Blühdorn, I. (2000) *Post-Ecologist Politics: Social Theory and the Abdication of the Ecologist Paradigm*. London: Routledge.

Christoff, P. (1996) 'Ecological citizens and ecologically guided democracy'. In B. Doherty and M. de Geus, eds, *Democracy and Green Political Thought: Sustainability, Rights and Citizenship*. London: Routledge.

Dobson, A. (1994) 'Ecologism and the Relegitimation of Socialism'. *Radical Philosophy*, 67: 13–19.

Dobson, A. (1998) *Justice and the Environment: Conceptions of Environmental Sustainability and Dimensions of Justice*. Oxford: Oxford University Press.

Dobson, A. (2001) 'Environmentalism and ecologism'. In J. Barry and E. Gene Frankland, eds, *International Encyclopedia of Environmental Politics*. London: Routledge.

Dobson, A. (2003) *Citizenship and the Environment*. Oxford: Oxford University Press.

Doherty, B. (2002) *Ideas and Action in One Green Movement*. London: Routledge.

Doherty, B. and M. de Geus, eds (1996) *Democracy and Green Political Thought: Sustainability, Rights and Citizenship*. London: Routledge.

Dower, N. (1998) *World Ethics: The New Agenda*. Edinburgh: Edinburgh University Press.

Dryzek, J. (1997) *The Politics of the Earth: Environmental Discourses*. Oxford: Oxford University Press.

Eckersley, R. (1992) *Environmentalism and Political Theory: Toward an Ecocentric Approach*. London: University College London Press.

Faber, M., R. Manstetten and J. Proops (1992) 'Humankind and the environment: an anatomy of surprise and ignorance'. *Environmental Values*, 1 (3): 217–41.

Giddens, A. (1994) *Beyond Left and Right: The Future of Radical Politics*. Cambridge: Polity.

Hayward, T. (1992) 'Ecology and Human Emancipation'. *Radical Philosophy*, 62: 3–13.

Hayward, T. (2001) 'Constitutional environmental rights and liberal democracy'. In J. Barry and M. Wissenburg, eds, *Sustaining Liberal Democracy: Ecological Challenges and Opportunities*. New York: Palgrave Macmillan.

Hayward, T. (forthcoming) 'Greening the constitutional state: environmental rights in the European Union'.

In J. Barry and R. Eckersley, eds, *The Global Ecological Crisis and the Nation-State*. Cambridge, MA: MIT Press.

Holmes, S. (1993) *The Anatomy of Anti-Liberalism*. Cambridge, MA: Harvard University Press.

Lafferty, W. and J. Meadowcroft, eds (1996) *Democracy and the Environment*. Cheltenham: Elgar.

Lee, K. (1993) 'Instrumentalism and the last person argument'. *Environmental Ethics*, 14 (4): 333–44.

Linklater, A. (1998) *The Transformation of Political Community: Ethical Foundations of the Post-Westphalian Era*. Cambridge: Polity.

Low, N. and B. Gleeson (1998) *Justice, Society and Nature: An Exploration of Political Ecology*. London: Routledge.

Martinez-Alier, J. (2002) *The Environmentalism of the Poor*. Cheltenham: Elgar.

Mathews, F., ed. (1996) *Ecology and Democracy*. London: Cass.

Meadows, D. H., D. L. Meadows, J. Randers and W. W. Brehens III (1972) *The Limits to Growth*. New York: New American Library.

Müller-Rommel, F. and T. Poguntke (2002) 'Green parties in national governments'. *Environmental Politics*, Special Issue, 11 (Spring).

Norton, B. (1991) *Toward Unity among Environmentalists*. Oxford: Oxford University Press.

O'Neill, J. (1993) *Ecology, Politics and Policy: Human Well-Being and the Natural World*. London: Routledge.

O'Neill, O. (1996) *Towards Justice and Virtue: A Constructive Account of Practical Reasoning*. Cambridge: Cambridge University Press.

O'Riordan, T., J. Cameron and A. Jordan, eds (2001) *Reinterpreting the Precautionary Principle*. London: Cameron May.

O'Riordan, T. and A. Jordan, (1995) 'The precautionary principle in contemporary environmental politics'. *Environmental Values*, 4 (3): 191–212.

Sale, K. (1995) *Rebels against the Future: The Luddites and Their War on the Industrial Revolution: Lessons for the Computer Age*. Reading, MA: Addison-Wesley.

Schlosberg, D. (1999) *Environmental Justice and the New Pluralism*. Oxford: Oxford University Press.

Smith, M. (1998) *Ecologism: Towards Ecological Citizenship*. Milton Keynes: Open University Press.

Walzer, M. (1983) *Spheres of Justice: A Defence of Pluralism and Equality*. Oxford: Robertson.

Part III

THE MODERN STATE

15

The Modern State

CHRISTOPHER W. MORRIS

Modern political philosophy takes its principal object of study to be the state. How to understand it? How should it be organized? What is its justification? It is hard to teach a course in modern political philosophy that does not focus on the state – it is what preoccupies Hobbes, Locke, Rousseau, and Hegel – and a discussion of contemporary political theory cannot ignore it. While few political thinkers today go so far as to accept Hegel's conception of political science which would have us 'attempt to comprehend and portray the state as an inherently rational entity' (1821: 21), most take the state to be the central feature of the political landscape and the task of determining its justification to be central to political philosophy. A few thinkers question our acceptance of the state and take seriously the challenge of anarchism, but most think states in some form or another are justifiable.

It is hard to ignore the state or government – 'You may not be interested in the state, but the state is certainly interested in you', to adapt Trotsky's quip about war. Almost wherever we find ourselves today we find government. Some have urged that the state be kept out of our lives, or at least our bedrooms, but to little avail. The state is omnipresent.

States appear as much in our dreams and nightmares as in our lives. Movements of 'national liberation' typically aspire to a state of their own; secessionists seek independence in order to found a new state. Only states are accorded the privilege of a seat at the (misnamed) United Nations. The European Union is feared by some lest it become a superstate, just as the United Nations was opposed long ago by opponents of 'world government'. Those sceptical about the possibility of world government often conclude that international affairs must be anarchic in the absence of a world state, as if state and anarchy exhaust the possibilities [see further Chapter 22].

It may be hard to ignore the state, and as theorists of politics we cannot do so. But does it deserve the central place it has been given in our thought and action? Might anarchists be right in thinking that we can do without the state or that it is not justified? Is the only alternative to the current system of states world government or a single suprastate?

To answer questions like these we need to know more about what we are talking about in the first place. Casual reference to 'the state' may suggest that we are relatively clear about the object of our inquiry. But this may be an illusion as it turns out to be very difficult to determine what exactly it is that we are talking about when referring to 'the state'.

WHAT IS THE STATE?

At an early stage in most discussions of the state a 'definition' is trotted out. Most often it is an abbreviated version of Max Weber's well-known characterization of the state as 'a human community that (successfully) claims the monopoly of the legitimate use of physical force within a given territory' (1919: 78). Weber says that 'the right to use physical force is ascribed to other institutions or to individuals only to the extent to which the state permits it. The state is considered the sole source of the "right" to use violence.'

This oft-cited definition, however, is problematic for a number of reasons. In the section that follows I shall question the centrality it accords to force and coercion. The first thing to note about it now is its simplicity. A human community is a state if and only if it successfully claims to possess two things: a monopoly of force and the sole right to determine who may legitimately use force. Could an organized criminal organization or one of Nozick's protective agencies be a state? One might have thought something more would be required. States are rather large and complex sorts of things, with legal systems, administrative agencies, and a number of other important features. In fact Weber himself, as one might expect, thought there was much more to the matter. Elsewhere he offered a much more complete characterization:

> Since the concept of the state has only in modern times reached its full development, it is best to define it in terms appropriate to the modern type of state, but at the same time, in terms which abstract from the values of the present day, since these are particularly subject to change. The primary formal characteristics of the modern state are as follows: It possesses an administrative and legal order subject to change by legislation, to which the organized corporate activity of the administrative staff, which is also regulated by legislation, is oriented. This system of order claims binding authority, not only over the members of the state, the citizens ... but also to a very large extent, over all actions taking place in the area of its jurisdiction. It is thus a compulsory association with a territorial basis. Furthermore, today, the use of force is regarded as legitimate only so far as it is either permitted by the state or prescribed by it. (1947: 156)

A number of additional features or attributes are singled out by Weber in this passage: the existence of an administrative and legal order subject to change by legislation, maintained by a substantial administrative staff, itself regulated by legislation, a claim to 'binding authority, not only over the members of the state, the citizens ... but also to a very large extent, over all actions taking place in the area of its jurisdiction ... a compulsory association with a territorial basis'.

Simple definitions like the one customarily attributed to Weber are inadequate; at the very least they require supplementation. I shall argue later that these definitions make force or coercion too central and draw our attention away from other important features. What are some of the other features of states?

A theme of this chapter is that political theorists take states too much for granted. The world was not always organized as a system of states, and it is helpful to recall the ways the world was before the development of states. We can appreciate better the nature of states by contrasting them with the orders they replaced. As states originate in early modern Europe, the contrast that is most revealing is the world of late medieval Europe [see further Chapter 25].

Philosophers raised on a diet of classical Greek and modern philosophy, without much attention to the long period of thought that lies between the two, often assume that the discussions and concerns of Hobbes and other early modern political theorists are continuous with the work of Greek and Roman thinkers. There is some continuity, of course, and the works of the latter were certainly used by late medieval and early modern theorists, as well as developers, of the state. But it is a mistake to identify the Greek *polis* and the Roman *civitas* with our modern state as if nothing had changed. There are some structural resemblances, but significant differences. Although certain features of the *polis* and of Roman law were adapted to late medieval and early modern governance, the Greek *poleis* and the Empire had disappeared by the time modern states were emerging. The historical context for the emergence of the modern European state has only traces of the classical world of Greece and Rome. The distinctiveness of the modern state is most noticeable when contrasted with the complex forms of political organization of medieval Europe.

'Europe' from the end of the Roman Empire to the end of the feudal period or the thirteenth century was a complicated social order in which political power is decentralized and highly fragmented.[1] Political relations between people were multifaceted, allegiances varied and overlapping, and the resulting political orders complex. Social order was not secured by centralized, hierarchical institutions, as in our societies; power and authority were decentralized. Broadly speaking, medieval Europe consisted of complex, crosscutting jurisdictions of towns, lords, kings, emperors, popes and bishops. While all were unified as part of Christendom, power was fragmented and shared by many different parties, allegiances were multiple, and there was no clearly defined hierarchy of authority. Allegiances could, and frequently did, overlap. Different lords, monarchs, and emperors could each have some claim over someone, and bishops and popes as well. Governance was typically mediated. No single agency controlled, or could possibly control, political life in the ways now routine for modern states. Given the largely customary nature of law, there is no single legal system, with an unambiguous hierarchy of juridical authorities. Several features are important to note. Not only was power fragmented and control of territory denied any one group or institution, but relations of authority overlapped and were not exclusive, and no clear hierarchy was discernible. In addition, feudal rule was essentially personal. Rule was based on particular (voluntary or involuntary) relations between individuals, governance was essentially over people rather than land, and power was treated as a private possession: 'It can be divided among heirs, given as a marriage portion, mortgaged, bought and sold. Private contracts and the rules of family law determine the possessors of judicial and administrative authority' (Strayer, 1965: 12). Relations between particular persons, many essentially promissory, laid the basis for the complex obligations between lords and vassals. Governance was not territorial. It is not so much that control of particular geographical areas was incomplete or insecure (though this was the case), it is that allegiances were not territorially determined: '[I]nclusion in the feudal structure was not defined by physical location ... One's specific obligations or rights depended on one's place in the matrix of personal ties, not on one's location in a particular area' (Spruyt, 1994: 35, 40). In these important ways, certain characteristic features of modern governance were not to be found.

Christendom was a unifying force and as such could be thought to be analogous in some ways to our polities. But, as noted, the Church's authority was (and still is) over believers and not territorial, and there were no geographical limits to its jurisdiction. The importance of customary law, and the local nature of important political allegiances, limit its power. It is not that the Church's power was contested by 'secular' rulers (though it was); rather, it is that its control was never intended to be as complete as with modern polities. The instruments of power did not, of course, permit this. But the different elements of medieval governance coexisted, in principle, with Christendom and its agents. Pope, bishops, monks, monarchs, lords, vassals, serfs, all were part of a single order, or better, an order of orders. Further, though we speak about political authority and organization in the Middle Ages, there is no clear distinction between the political and the rest of life. It is said that 'the very term "political" did not enter the vocabulary of governments and writers before the thirteenth century' (Ullmann, 1965: 17). There was only one normative world, so to speak, and all – Christians at least – were part of it. Not only does this mean that the various realms of Christendom were not separate, self-sufficient juridical domains. It means that all, including monarchs and 'sovereigns', were subject to law, both customary and natural.

'Political' organization in medieval Europe, in summary, was complex, and 'political' power highly fragmented and decentralized. Allegiances were multiple and largely personal, and no clear hierarchy of political authority was discernible. Governance was not territorial; it was largely rule over persons, *qua* individuals or *qua* Christians. The complexity of relations of authority meant that rule was mediated and not, for the most part, 'direct' and institutions did not 'penetrate' society in the ways characteristic of our states. There were no 'self-sufficient' polities and consequently no 'international relations'. The modern state did not yet exist.

In the modern world, governance is territorial. Modern polities for the most part have definite and distinct territories. The colours and lines on modern maps have a particular and familiar sense: within the boundaries of a state, there is a single system of governance, distinct from others, operating 'outside' or 'externally'. Today, virtually all inhabitable parts of the globe are the territory of some state. Governance is territorial in another sense, namely, that law applies to (virtually) all who find themselves within these boundaries. Geography acquires a new significance, the territorialization of political obligation. By virtue of being in a place, circumscribed by lines or markers, people acquire obligations, independently of personal relations, vows, faith, or origin.

The territorialization of governance is not compatible with the personal nature of political relations. And it is not compatible with power being understood as the personal possession of rulers. One of the features distinguishing modern polities from earlier kingships is the distinction between the persons of the rulers and the office and institutions they occupy. But it is not just that there emerges a distinction between a person and roles and institutions. It is that the polity, that is, the state, comes to be understood as an order distinct from its agents and institutions, something reflected in the linguistic distinctions discussed earlier between 'state' and 'government'. The modern use of 'state' to refer to a public order distinct from both ruled and ruler, with highly centralized institutions wielding power over inhabitants of a defined territory, seems to date back no earlier than the sixteenth century (see Skinner, 1978: vol. 2, 352ff; 1989: 90–131; Dyson, 1980: 25ff; Vincent, 1987: 16–19). The word derives from the Latin *stare*, to stand, and *status*, standing or position. *Status* also connotes stability or permanence, which is carried over into 'estate', the immediate ancestor of 'state'. But the modern use of the word is new:

> Before the sixteenth century, the term *status* was only used by political writers to refer to one of two things: either the state or condition in which a ruler finds himself (the *status principis*); or else the general 'state of the nation' or condition of the realm as a whole (the *status regni*). What was lacking in these usages was the distinctively modern idea of the State as a form of public power separate from both the ruler and the ruled, and constituting the supreme political authority within a certain defined territory. (Skinner, 1978: 353)

The development of a new vocabulary signals a new conception of the polity, that of an order which is separate from ruler and ruled (or citizen), separate from other polities like it, and operating in a distinct territory.

The territoriality of modern rule means that all who find themselves within the polity's boundaries are, by that fact, governed. Territory becomes a jurisdictional domain. Rule also becomes direct in a particular sense. In empires rule is typically indirect: considerable power is left to local governors and administrators, and governance is largely through intermediaries. In medieval Christendom, popes for the most part governed believers indirectly through clergy and kings. In the modern world rule comes to be direct; each and every subject is governed by the sovereign or the state, without mediation (see especially Tilly, 1990). The development of direct rule in this sense is a late development, and it is related to the 'penetration' of society by the state stressed by Michael Mann and others: 'the modern state added routine, formalised, rationalised institutions of wider scope over citizens and territories. It penetrates its territories with both law and administration ... as earlier states did not' (1986: vol. II, 56–7).

Direct rule and 'penetration' presuppose not only territoriality of the state but also its extensive authority. The boundaries of the state – its borders – create an 'inside' and an 'outside'. What happens 'inside' is the concern of the state; no 'external' authority has jurisdiction here, at least without the state's acquiescence. Not only is the state's authority exclusive within its realm, it is increasingly far-reaching. States – initially, sovereigns – come to claim to be the ultimate sources of political power within their realms. That is, they come to claim sovereignty. And this becomes a significant and distinguishing feature of modern states.

It is always important to have established means of resolving conflict and disagreement. In medieval societies, as in most, there were many such means, some more formal and institutional than others. But, as I noted, allegiances were multiple, jurisdictions frequently overlapped, and there often were significant disagreements and conflicts among the governing bodies and persons. In the absence of an unambiguous and widely acknowledged hierarchy of authorities, resolutions might be ineffective. Without a single, ultimate source of political power within a domain, many have thought, disagreements could not be 'decided', except by force. This possibility may be looked upon with alarm, especially given the ferocity of much human conflict. The more serious the conflicts between people, the more pressing the question 'who decides?' is likely to be. 'To decide' a matter, in this sense, is frequently understood to mean to be 'the final arbiter'. In Christendom this could only be God and, in the event that His word would require frequent interpretation, the Church. Indeed, the very notion of a final arbiter seemed to presuppose a cosmological hierarchy like that provided by Christian monotheism. The state's answer to the question 'who decides?' is to put itself in the Church's place, or

rather, God's place – 'le prince est image de Dieu' (Bodin, 1583: Book I, ch. VIII, 137).[2] It, and only it, is the final arbiter, at least locally, on matters that pertain to it. To assert this, states had to contest the Church's authority. They had, as well, to contest the power of 'internal' rivals, namely, feudal lords. Emerging from these contests is the modern notion of sovereignty: the state is the ultimate source of political power within its realm.

It is a mistake to think that modern sovereignty is merely a restatement of old ideas about power and authority. The elements may be present in different forms, especially in Roman law and in certain theological accounts of God's power. But the conception of political power that is thereby attached to a new type of political order is novel: 'at the beginning, the idea of sovereignty was the idea that there is a final and absolute political authority in the political community ... and no final and absolute authority exists elsewhere' (Hinsley, 1986: 25–6). The concept of the modern state in fact develops along with that of sovereignty. This is evident in the work of the master theorist of the modern state, where sovereignty is the 'Artificiall Soul' of 'that great LEVIATHAN called a COMMON-WEALTH, or STATE, (in latine CIVITAS)' (Hobbes, 1651: introduction, 9).

States not only claim ultimate power within their realms ('internal sovereignty'), they also claim independence of one another ('external sovereignty'). In rejecting the authority of popes and emperors, sovereigns asserted the state's autonomy of other states. Not only is the state the author of its own laws – the etymological meaning of *autonomos* – but the laws of others have no claim on it. With the advent of the sovereign state, relations between states or 'international relations' become possible. Prior to this, there were no 'foreign affairs' or distinction between 'internal' and 'external', and the modern conception of the nature of world politics as 'anarchical' or unregulated was not yet possible. Once the sovereignty of states is admitted, their relations are thought to constitute a 'state of nature', one which, for most early modern theorists, was beyond law. For some, to such a condition, 'this also is consequent; that nothing can be Unjust. The notions of Right and Wrong, Justice and Injustice have there no place. Where there is no common Power, there is no Law: where no Law, no Injustice' (Hobbes, 1651: ch. 13, 90).[3]

States claim sovereignty. In the early modern quarrel between monarchs and lords on the one side, and popes on the other, the kings won. The core idea of sovereignty is the notion of the ultimate source of political authority within a realm. We distinguish between 'internal' and 'external' sovereignty, the first pertaining to the structure or constitution of a state, the second to the relations between states. Internal sovereignty thus conceived has to do with the state's authority over its subjects, while the second notion refers to the independence or autonomy of states. The two conceptions are closely linked in early modern conceptions of sovereignty. In the writings of Bodin, Hobbes, and Rousseau, internal and external sovereignty are tightly connected. These thinkers thought sovereignty to be absolute (legally unconstrained or unlimited), indivisible (unique and undivided), and inalienable (cannot be delegated or 'represented'). If absolute sovereignty is attributed to states, then their authority cannot be constrained by international law or possibly even by the rights of individuals. Conceiving of sovereignty as absolute thus requires granting states a certain autonomy or liberty in their 'international relations'.

The core idea of sovereignty is that of the ultimate source of political authority within a realm. This is the power that monarchs claimed in their battles against lords and princes on the one hand and popes on the other. Their realm (or kingdom) was theirs, and their authority over it was to be shared with no one. The core notion of sovereignty – the ultimate source of political authority within a realm – requires unpacking. Sovereignty is associated with modern kingdoms and states; the 'realms' in question are the well-defined territories of such states. The relevant notion of political authority is more controversial. Something is an authority, in the sense relevant here, only if its directives are (and are intended to be) action-guiding. For instance, consider the law. It forbids us from doing certain things, and it intends these prohibitions to guide our behaviour; specifically, these prohibitions are reason-providing. Authorities, then, mean to guide behaviour by providing reasons for action to their subjects. On this view, political authority is not to be understood simply as justified force; something is a genuine authority only in so far as its directives are reasons for action. Sanctions or force may frequently be necessary as a means to make effective this authority, but the two are not to be conflated.

The key to the notion of sovereignty lies in the idea of ultimate authority. What is it for a source of authority to be ultimate? An authority may be ultimate if it is the highest in a hierarchy of authorities. Such an authority may also be final: there is no further appeal after it has spoken (it has 'the last word'). Lastly, an ultimate authority may be one which is supreme in a particular sense: it has authority over all other authorities in its realm. The state's authority is sovereign in this sense; it takes precedence over competing authorities (e.g. corporate, syndicate, church, conscience). Summarizing, then, sovereignty is the highest, final, and supreme political authority within a modern territorial realm.

States claim sovereignty and demand considerable loyalty from their subjects and citizens. Their power is considerable, and they frequently appear to resort to the use of force in securing their will. Presumably this is the source for the common characterization of states in terms of their concentrated power and their control over the use of force, and specifically, the source of the appeal of Weberian characterizations.

The social order – or orders – from which the modern state emerged were ones in which governance was decentralized, fragmented, varied, overlapping and non-exclusive, mediated, and personal. These social orders were also part of Christendom, and its practical unity was less than claimed. Governance in the modern state is, by contrast, relatively centralized, unified, uniform, hierarchical and exclusive, non-mediated or direct, penetrating, impersonal and territorial. The concept of the modern state, then, as it emerges in medieval and early modern history, is that of a new and complex form of political organization. To summarize, we may think of the state in terms of a number of interrelated features (Morris, 1998: ch. 2):

1 *Continuity in time and space.* (a) The modern state is a form of political organization whose institutions endure over time; in particular, they survive changes in leadership or government. (b) It is the form of political organization of a definite and distinct territory.

2 *Transcendence.* The modern state is a particular form of political organization that constitutes a unitary public order distinct from and superior to both ruled and rulers, one capable of agency. The institutions that are associated with modern states – in particular, the government, the judiciary, the bureaucracy, standing armies – do not themselves constitute the state; they are its agents.

3 *Political organization.* The institutions through which the state acts – in particular, the government, the judiciary, the bureaucracy, the police – are differentiated from other political organizations and associations; they are formally co-ordinated one with another, and they are relatively centralized. Relations of authority are hierarchical. Rule is direct and territorial; it is relatively pervasive and penetrates society legally and administratively.

4 *Authority.* The state is sovereign, that is, the ultimate source of political authority in its territory, and it claims a monopoly on the use of legitimate force within its territory. The jurisdiction of its institutions extends directly to all residents or members of that territory. In its relations to other public orders, the state is autonomous.

5 *Allegiance*. The state expects and receives the loyalty of its members and of the permanent inhabitants of its territory. The loyalty that it typically expects and receives assumes precedence over that loyalty formerly owed to family, clan, commune, lord, bishop, pope, or emperor. Members of a state are the primary subjects of its laws and have a general obligation to obey by virtue of their membership.

Modern states, then, are distinctive territorial forms of political organization that claim sovereignty over their realms and independence from other states. A state system can be thought of simply as a group of states interacting in ways, often hostile, that significantly affect the fate of each.

This general characterization of the state may not be suitable for all purposes, and I do not wish to say that all other characterizations of the state are straightforwardly mistaken. Some are, but many others are not. Different characteristics of related forms of political organization may be emphasized, depending on one's explanatory or evaluative purposes. For some purposes it may be useful to distinguish less sharply between modern and premodern forms of political organization. (For instance, differences between state, empire, principality, or *polis* may not be important for many anthropological research projects.) By contrast, my characterization is helpful for raising certain normative questions about distinctively modern forms of political organization and considering alternative ways of arranging our world. The world of states appears to be changing – the effects of the demise of the Soviet Union, various trends clustered under the label of 'globalization', the threats of Islamist terrorism or insurgency – and evaluating these changes requires understanding the modern state.

COERCION AND AUTHORITY

State power is closely associated with force, as we see from the popularity of the Weberian definition. Many theorists think states are necessarily or essentially coercive. 'States are "grounded" in force in the sense that, by definition, they are coercive: they coordinate behavior through the use or threat of force' (Levine, 1987: 176); 'State-power is in the last analysis coercive power' (Geuss, 2001: 12); 'political power is always coercive power backed up by the government's use of sanctions, for government alone has the authority to use force in upholding its laws' (Rawls, 1996: 136). The view that governments must wield force or that their power is necessarily coercive is widespread in contemporary political thought.

The incompleteness of Weberian definitions of the state is only part of my objection to them. The second concern is about understanding coercion or force to be part of the concept of the state. One might have thought, to the contrary, that states without coercion or force are conceivable; if so, state and coercion and force cannot be conceptually connected. Consider a 'state' without law, or one whose jurisdiction was not territorial. We would not consider it to be a genuine state. Law and territoriality are essential properties of states, part of the concept of a state. Contrast these properties with coercion or force. We can conceive of a state which does not employ coercion or force. Imagine a state that is legitimate; its basic structure and its laws are just, and those subject to its laws are obligated to obey them. Suppose that the latter are always motivated to comply with just laws; they do not, for instance, suffer from any weakness of the will or any other problem which might lead them to fail to do what they ought to do. Then, coercion and force would not be needed to enforce the law. This possibility, admittedly fantastic and utopian, seems perfectly coherent. There is nothing in the nature of a law which requires that compliance be assured coercively. It does not seem to be, then, a conceptual truth that states are coercive.

Why might we think, with Rawls, that 'political power is always coercive power backed up by the government's use of sanctions'? Perhaps because of the conjunction of law and sanction. But that connection is not necessary. Some laws are not enforced by sanctions (for instance, laws governing the obligations of officials, laws establishing powers, constitutional laws). Attempts to understand the law in terms of the coercive commands of a sovereign are implausible (see Austin, 1885, for the classic formulation of this position; and Hart, 1994, for the classic refutation). There does not seem to be a conceptual connection between states and coercion.

It is hard to imagine a state in our world which did not coerce. Even if sanctions are not always in place or necessary, we should ask why most laws are in fact backed by sanctions and why coercion often is needed. Why must compliance sometimes be assured by coercion? At least on occasion, most of us will not do as we are required to do unless prodded. Presumably virtually all of us will always refrain from intentional homicide, but we do not always put coins in parking meters or adhere to speeding limits or pay all of our taxes in the absence of the threat of sanctions. Legal systems provide for sanctions in order to offer special incentives when people are not otherwise motivated to comply. Why exactly might people fail to comply? There are a number of circumstances which contribute to disobedience. Sometimes we violate laws because of ignorance or stupidity. Other times we may fail to obey out of weakness of the will or some other form of irrationality. We may sometimes simply wish to defy authority. Or we may be fanatics, in the grip of beliefs recommending disobedience. Of course, if our state is illegitimate there may be additional reasons not to obey its laws.[4]

What is crucial to note about these rationales is that they implicitly understand sanctions to be secondary. Coercion and force are thus rationalized but only as supplementary measures. And this is as it should be: the law's primary appeal is to its authority. Hart notes this early in his discussion of command theories of law: 'To command is characteristically to exercise authority over men, not power to inflict harm, and though it may be combined with threats of harm a command is primarily an appeal not to fear but to respect for authority' (1994: 20). Authorities guide behaviour by providing reasons for action to their subjects. Something is an authority in this sense only if its directives are meant to be reasons for action (see: Raz, 1979; 1986; Green, 1988). One does not understand law and, more generally, states if one does not see coercion and force as supplementary to authority. Coercion and force are needed when the state's authority is unappreciated, defective, or absent.

We should, of course, expect that laws will be backed by the threat of sanctions and that force may be needed. One of the reasons, after all, for wanting to have a legal system is to ensure compliance on the part of those otherwise inclined or tempted to behave in the ways required by social order. But recourse to sanctions and force, it must be stressed, does not mean that laws cannot provide reasons or motivate without such sanctions or that they must presuppose them. The law claims authority, and that claim may often be valid. Unless one assumes that norms *per se* cannot be reasons, then there should be no reason to insist that legal rules must necessarily be backed up with sanctions. But given human nature we should expect them to be an important part of virtually all legal and political orders.

Most governmental activities of liberal states do not require the deployment of force, many that involve the threatening of sanctions do not customarily involve force, and much compliance with law is secured by other means. It may still be claimed that the state's influence is 'ultimately based on' force. In the end, 'in the final instance', we may say, its power is based on force. 'State-power is in the last analysis coercive power' (Geuss, 2001: 14). This is not an uncommon view.

What does it mean to say that law is ultimately backed by sanctions or ultimately a matter of force? The term 'ultimate' is one of the most opaque in philosophy and social theory and should be used with care. In some contexts the term has a clear sense. An authority, for instance, may be ultimate if it is the highest authority. This idea presupposes that authorities constitute an ordering (often a strict ordering),

and that the highest authority is the last one in a certain chain or continuum of authorities. Legal systems are usually thought to have such a hierarchical structure, so that we can talk of the highest or ultimate authority for any such legal order – the notion of sovereignty presupposes such a hierarchy. Even if we were able to find in every legal system a hierarchical ordering of authorities, it is very unlikely that powers generally will be so ordered. That is, it is very unlikely that we can order power relations in this way, so that for any pair of powers one is greater than the other and the set of all powers is an ordering (i.e. transitive). If this is right, it means that the concept of an ultimate power will be ill-defined. This means that it is unclear and likely misleading to talk of 'ultimate' powers, for there may never be one power that is so placed that it is 'ultimate' or 'final' (see Morris, 1998: ch. 8).

One may argue that force is fundamental to maintaining social order. That is, it may be thought to be more important than any other factor in maintaining the state. The proof is that no state can do without it. Remove force (and sanctions), and the legal order collapses. But this argument, common as it is, is too swift. Why do we obey the law or, for that matter, do almost anything? Usually our reasons are multiple, and very often our actions are overdetermined. Consider the case of overdetermined actions. Removing one consideration favouring the action in question may not change the balance of reasons. (I am supposing that we act, and should act, in most circumstances on the balance of reasons.) The metaphor here is that of weights and measures. The rationality of an act is determined by the relative 'weight' of reasons favouring it over alternatives. If an act is overdetermined by reasons, then removing one reason (e.g. the threat of sanctions) may not affect our rational choice. Consider next acts that are not overdetermined. Suppose, for instance, that I decide to put money in a parking meter or not to hide some of my income from the tax authorities, and that I would not have taken these decisions had there been no credible threat of sanctions. Does this show that coercion is decisive in determining my action? We could say that it does but only in the sense that any number of things are equally decisive. After all, if the act is not overdetermined and is favoured by the balance of reasons, virtually any change will alter the balance; anything that 'tips the balance' will, on this account, be decisive.

Coercion and force may be important and even indispensable, but that does not mean they are more important than anything else. A political order which may not hold together without force may also collapse if numerous other factors are not present – for instance, if subjects cease to be patriotic, if they become less prudent, if they become literate, if they act together, if they sober up. Even tyrannical regimes require something more than force to remain in place; they cannot maintain themselves only with force.

An overemphasis on the role of coercion and force in contemporary discussions of the state contributes as well to the neglect in contemporary political theory – but not in legal theory – of the importance and centrality of the state's authority. Theorists put the state's coercive powers at centre stage, but these are less puzzling or problematic than their claims to authority. Indeed, what's puzzling about the state's coercive powers is not its justification for its use of sanctions or force; rather it is the justification for its claim to monopolize legitimate force. The authority claimed by states – typically, sovereignty – is extraordinary. In a certain respect, states are both easier and harder to justify. In my view their use of force may be much less problematic than is usually assumed. It is not hard to justify the use of force against killers and bullies. What is hard to justify are the extraordinarily sweeping normative powers claimed by states.

LEGITIMACY

Modern states claim sweeping normative powers. On my analysis they claim sovereignty. Citizens and other subjects of states are held to be obligated to obey the law and to have no greater loyalty to any other country or cause. We may think that states can and often do serve important interests and that life in their absence would very often be very bad. Suppose that some states – those that serve our interests, that behave justly, and so on – are such that they are justified and that they are thereby legitimated. Do they then possess all of the normative powers they claim? We need to investigate legitimacy. When are states legitimate? What is the basis of their legitimacy? And what exactly does legitimacy entail?

'Legitimacy' is derived from *lex* and has the same root as 'legislation'. One sense of 'legitimate' is being in accordance with law or lawful (legality). Any lawful or 'legal' state is legitimate in this sense. Closely related would be the more general notion of being in accordance with the established rules or procedures relevant to the matter at issue (e.g. a legitimate move in chess, the legitimate heir to the throne). These senses of 'legitimate', largely procedural and similar to the primary sense of 'legal' (being in accordance with the law), are not very useful for our normative inquiry.

Often in politics and especially international affairs a state is thought to be legitimate if it is recognized or accepted by others. There is considerable unclarity as to what this means. Sometimes the suggestion seems to be merely that a legitimate state is a genuine state. Legitimacy in this sense is uninteresting. Sometimes the idea of acceptance or recognition suggests that being a legitimate state requires being so recognized by other states, as if legitimacy were a kind of membership in an organization or club. Even if the members of this club are not all corrupt, this notion also seems uninteresting. The question is what conditions ought to be imposed for membership.

In the social sciences, accounts derived from Weber would have us understand the state's legitimacy in terms of the attitudes of subjects. The crudest would say that a state is legitimate in so far as it is so regarded by its subjects, which is not very illuminating until we understand what it is for someone so to regard a state. People may regard their state as legitimate when they believe it to be lawful or justified. But given that it is possible that they may be mistaken, the interesting question would concern the conditions of lawfulness or justification. Legitimacy may depend on people's attitudes, but the first question is what attitudes ought we to have.

What is it then for a state to be legitimate in a more substantive sense? If a state is legitimate it has a certain status. At the least, its existence is permissible. It may also have a (claim-)right to exist. A state exists to the extent that a territory and its inhabitants are organized politically (as we described above) and when many of the state's powers related to governance are acknowledged by significant bodies of people. States are forms of governance, and they also claim certain powers, liberties, and rights related to governance. Legitimacy may also confer these. A legitimate state, we shall say, is minimally one which has a liberty, presumably a (claim-)right, to exist. It would presumably also possess the liberty or the right to establish laws and to adjudicate and enforce these as necessary for the maintenance of order and other ends. Legitimacy in this minimal sense would be the right to exist and to rule.

The right to rule is often thought of as entailing obligations to obedience. Trivially we have an obligation to obey any valid (obligation-creating) law.[5] If an obligation-creating law is valid and applies to us, then we are obligated. Often it is said that this obligation is merely 'legal' and not necessarily 'moral'. A more than minimal conception of legitimacy would construe the right to rule as entailing a moral obligation to obey the law. If a state is legitimate in this stronger sense then it would be wrong or unjust for a citizen to violate a valid law (except in special circumstances).

It is useful at this point to distinguish weaker and stronger conceptions of legitimacy. A legitimate state possesses a (claim-)right to exist and to rule. The right to exist entails obligations on the part of others not to threaten its existence in certain ways (e.g. not to attack or to conquer it). A state is minimally legitimate, I shall say, if its right to rule entails that others are obligated not to undermine it but are not necessarily obligated to obey it. By contrast, a state is fully legitimate if its right to rule entails an obligation of subjects, or at least citizens, to obey (each valid law). This obligation may be thought of as a general obligation to obey the law, one which requires compliance with every law that applies to one except in circumstances indicated by the law (e.g. justified or excused disobedience). The second, stronger understanding of legitimacy may be the most common one in contemporary discussions.[6] But I think it illuminating to invoke the weaker conception too.

What establishes minimal legitimacy? Suppose a state to be just.[7] That is, suppose that it respects the constraints of justice and does not act unjustly. In addition, suppose that it provides justice to those subject to its rule; it makes and enforces laws, adjudicates disputes, and provides mechanisms for collective decisions (e.g. contracts, corporate law, local governments, parliaments). Some of the laws as well as a number of social programmes seek to effect distributive justice [see further Chapters 16 and 17]. Government in general is responsive to the just interests or wishes of the governed. A state like this would be just. Suppose in addition that it is relatively efficient in its activities. Elsewhere I have argued that a relatively just and efficient state is one that is justified, and that justification confers minimal legitimacy (Morris, 1998: chs 4 and 6).

It may, however, be thought that there is too much disagreement about justice to make justice the basis of legitimacy. Some have thought that one of the main reasons for states is the absence of agreement about justice or right. And positions like this are popular today both in North America and in Europe. Sovereign states, on this view, may be needed for social order in large part because people have incompatible views about justice. The thought is that where there is little agreement about justice and other moral values, these standards cannot be the basis for legitimation. 'Realist' accounts of legitimacy may be understood thus (see, for instance, Morgenthau, 1978). This sort of position may be most plausible if it is seen as derived from some kind of scepticism about morality or 'right reason'. Hobbes can be read as one of the originators of this idea. His Sovereign can be understood to be an arbitrator made necessary by disagreement and conflict:

> as when there is controversy in an account, the parties must by their own accord, set up for right Reason, the Reason of some Arbitrator, or Judge, to whose sentence they will both stand, or their controversie must either come to blowes, or be undecided, for want of a right Reason constituted by Nature. (Hobbes, 1651: ch. 5, 32–3)

If moral disagreement renders justice an inappropriate standard for legitimacy, then the question is what alternative to use. Elsewhere I have considered what I called 'rational justification' (Morris, 1998: 114–15, 122–7, 134–6, 160–1). A rational justification of a state, we may say, is provided when the relevant people have reasons to respect its laws and to support it in various ways. More broadly, they may have reasons to do their part in supporting and maintaining the state. Such a state might be thought to be minimally legitimate. Now it is very unlikely that many states are such as to provide (virtually) all subjects with reasons to obey (virtually) all laws, even if we take sanctions to provide reasons of the relevant sort. It may also be that many states that do offer most subjects reasons are tyrannical or capable of committing various evils. It is doubtful, therefore, that rational justification is the sort we should seek. It would seem that some species of moral justification is what is needed.[8]

There certainly is considerable disagreement about justice, as well as about many other things. But surely to say that there is no agreement about justice is hyperbolic. While there is considerable disagreement about distributive justice, the rights of property, the death penalty, and the like, there is striking consensus today about a number of matters – for instance, that slavery is (very) wrong and that persons have certain basic rights not to be killed or not to be restricted in their liberties without cause, that torture is rarely, if ever, to be used, that it is wrong to threaten or to harm the innocent. Often disagreement about justice concerns the specification of widely accepted principles. For instance, all parties to the contemporary controversies about abortion, assisted suicide, and the death penalty presuppose that killing generally is wrong. There is considerable disagreement at the margins, but a significant core agreement seems to exist. Even if many norms require determination or specification – for instance, norms prohibiting theft or trespass will always require application to new and puzzling cases – there are some norms of justice which seem to be widely acceptable and applicable prior to the establishment of familiar legislative and judicial institutions. It seems that we might very well be able to evaluate our states by many of the norms of justice.

What must a state do to be just? A just state presumably is first of all one that respects the constraints of justice. Justice imposes constraints on the behaviour (and intentions) of persons and, presumably, institutions. We may suppose that many of these constraints take the form of (moral) rights and duties. States, then, must respect the (moral) rights of individuals and fulfil duties owed to individuals. We may suppose that we each have moral rights to our lives, liberty, and possessions, though, as I said, the difficult questions concern their nature and scope. It is not particularly controversial to say of the regimes of Nazi Germany, the former Soviet Union, China, Iraq, etc. that they violated the rights to life, liberty, and possessions of many.

States typically claim sovereignty and exclusive rights to use force. Individuals are not supposed to use force without the state's permission. It is often argued that states have the particular task of ensuring that we do not individually need to use force (e.g. to protect ourselves). If this is true then states may consequently have the provision of justice as one of their main tasks. Restrictions on one's capacity to use force might not be advantageous or justified except as part of a package that offered one better protection. Justice may then require of states not only that they respect the constraints of justice but also that they provide justice. What might be involved in a state's provision of justice? Typically states create and enforce laws, adjudicate disputes, and provide mechanisms for collective decisions; they also seek to effect distributive justice.

We may then require of states that they respect and provide justice. Suppose that we say that a state is justified in so far as it is just (and efficient). Now it may be that no state is, or could be, thereby justified. 'Individuals have rights ... So strong and far-reaching are these rights that they raise the question of what, if anything, the state and its officials may do. How much room do individual rights leave for the states?' (Nozick, 1974: ix). It may be that the constraints of justice are such as to fill up all of moral space or at least leave no room for the state's exercise of its functions or even for its existence. For instance, should we possess indefeasible (or 'virtually indefeasible') natural rights to (our) life, (our) liberty, and (our) possessions, then it is doubtful that the state may do very much, if anything, without violating our (moral) rights.

Natural rights – rights which are held by virtue of the possessor's nature – seem to constrain states by requiring them to secure the consent of the governed. This is, in effect, to assume that rights protect choices. It is now common in the literature on rights to distinguish between choice (or will) accounts and interest (or benefit) accounts. The latter understand rights to be protected interests or benefits, where the former conceive of them as protecting choices. In one case, the correlative duties protect interests or guarantee benefits, in the other the duties (and accompanying powers) protect choices. Consent would effect (limited) alienation or suspension of our rights and thus be a condition of justified state interference. However, it may be that our fundamental rights are best construed as protecting interests or benefits. On this interpretation they would not block states, at least as easily as choice-protecting

rights. We could then argue that 'to secure these rights, governments are instituted amongst men' and that (the) people may alter or abolish governments that become 'destructive of these rights', without endorsing Jefferson's principle that governments derive 'their just powers from the consent of the governed'.

Consent can be a necessary condition for legitimacy or merely a sufficient one (or both). Assuming that consent could suffice to legitimate only (reasonably) just governments or states, we should think of consent theory as affirming both the necessity and the sufficiency of consent to legitimacy. The claim that consent is sufficient is the less controversial of the two (see Simmons, 1979: 57; 1993: 197–8; Green, 1988: 161–2; Beran, 1987). It is the claim of its necessity that is of greater concern, and I take it to constitute the core of consent theory or political consentualism. Many partisans of consent have as well affirmed the consensual legitimacy of some states or types of states (e.g. republics or democracies), but this need not be part of the theory. Consent theory is a normative account, and it is possible that all actual states fail to satisfy its conditions for legitimacy. This is what many contemporary consent theorists in fact claim.

Consent is to be distinguished from consensus or general agreement. Most forms of political organization depend to some degree on consensus or agreement. But the latter have to do largely with shared beliefs (or values). Sometimes terms like these are used to suggest more, but they essentially refer to agreement in belief or thought (or value).[9] Consent, by contrast, involves the engagement of the will or commitment. Something counts as consent only if it is a deliberate undertaking. Ideally, an act is one of consent if it is the deliberate and effective communication of an intention to bring about a change in one's normative situation (i.e. one's rights or obligations). It must be voluntary and, to some degree, informed. Consent can be express (direct), or it can be tacit or implied (indirect). Both are forms of actual consent. By contrast, (non-actual) 'hypothetical consent' is not consent.

Consent theory should be seen as a distinctive philosophical position, one standing in opposition to other traditions which find the polity or political rule to be natural or would see government and law as justified by their benefits. The mutual advantage, Paretian tradition and different types of consequentialism seek to base full legitimacy in what the polity does for its subjects and others (for the former see J. Buchanan, 1975; Gauthier, 1986). Other, more 'participatory' traditions might require active involvement by citizenry for legitimacy. Political consentualism should not be conflated with these other traditions, however closely associated they may be historically, and it should certainly not be confused with other allegedly 'consensual' theories that base legitimacy on consensus or agreement.

The conclusion of contemporary consent theorists seems to be that virtually no states satisfy the account's conditions for full legitimacy. It is simply that few people, 'naturalized' citizens and officials aside, have explicitly or tacitly consented to their state. It is implausible to interpret voting in democratic elections as expressing the requisite consent, and mere residence and the like do not seem to be the sort of engagements of the will required by consent theorists for obligation. Consequently, most people may not have the general obligation to obey the laws of their states that they are commonly thought to have.

The adjudication of the challenge posed to state legitimacy by consentualism is a complicated matter and cannot be taken up here. For now let me summarize some of the implications of our discussion. Supposing reasonably just and efficient states to be justified and thus to be minimally legitimate, something more seems required for full legitimacy and obligations to obey the law. The literature on this question is substantial (see Edmundson, 1999), and the debates cannot be adequately explored here. Many have argued that the conditions for what I have called full legitimacy are hard to realize even in states that are justified or minimally legitimate. This position is one defended by me (in Morris, 1998) and, in different terms, by John Simmons (1979; 1993). If a state is minimally but not fully legitimate, then the obligations of citizens and other subjects are similar to those of foreigners. The latter, even when not in the territory of a legitimate state, are obligated not to undermine its institutions and possibly to support or assist it in certain circumstances. Noncitizens have no general obligation to obey the laws of legitimate states to which they do not belong or in whose territories they do not find themselves. Citizens of a merely minimally legitimate state have the same kinds of obligations: obligations not to undermine its institutions, and to support or assist it in certain circumstances, but no general obligation to obey every law (in the absence of a special relation, for instance, of taking an oath to obey).

Full legitimacy is required for a general obligation to obey the law. But we can ask what follows from such an obligation. As I have said, a general obligation to obey the law requires compliance with every law that applies to one except in circumstances indicated by the law (e.g. justified or excused disobedience). It is commonly assumed that someone so obligated always has a reason (of a stringent or pre-emptive kind) to comply. But it is possible to deny this and to assume that obligations do not always entail reasons to comply. The first position is often labelled a kind of 'internalism' in moral theory and the latter 'externalism'. So the questions about legitimacy, obligation, and action are more complicated than we may have thought. It is possible to think that states can be fully legitimate but that citizens lack reasons to comply, in which case they would not necessarily have more reasons to comply with the law than they would if the state in question were merely minimally legitimate. Without the assumption that obligations always provide stringent or pre-emptive reasons, full legitimacy is not much more demanding than minimal legitimacy.

NATIONS AND NATION-STATES

What I have called states are often spoken of as 'nations'. This is confusing but understandable. In everyday settings we don't make distinctions unless necessary, and often 'nation' doesn't mean anything more than 'country'. In addition, the term 'state' in American English is already reserved for the subunits of the US federal system and is also sometimes used to refer to government. (The United Nations could not have been called the 'United States of the World'.) States in the sense we have been discussing are also referred to as 'nation-states', perhaps to distinguish them from Greek *poleis* or Renaissance city-republics. If we think of states and nations as different things, an interesting question is whether states must be nation-states. To raise this question we need to distinguish states and nations.

In the sense that interests us here, a nation is a society whose members are linked by sentiments of solidarity and self-conscious identity based on a number of other bonds (e.g. history, territory, culture, race, 'ethnicity', language, religion, customs) [see further Chapter 19]. A group of humans will constitute a nation in this sense in so far as the members share certain properties and in so far as they are conscious of this shared condition and recognize one another by virtue of these common properties. Nations, then, will be collections of individuals with common histories, cultures, languages, and the like, and whose members recognize other members by virtue of their possession of these attributes (see Morris, 1998: ch. 8). This characterization may be incomplete; for instance, many nationalities seem based on 'ethnic' attributes (e.g. Japan), and the common history may be thought to involve common ancestry (see below). But this way of characterizing nations will help in explaining and evaluating certain significant ways humans have of understanding themselves.

Once states and nations are distinguished, a number of possible relations become obvious. Since the entire land mass of the globe is now the territory of some state, we do not find any nation that does not overlap with a state. We can then eliminate the possible 'one nation, no state' relation. The main remaining possibilities are:

- one nation + one state (e.g. Japan, Germany)
- one nation + several states (e.g. the Basques, the Kurds)
- several nations + one state (e.g. Canada, Switzerland, Belgium).

The first possibility is the salient one as it is that adopted by nationalists and defenders of the view that national peoples are entitled to their own state. Some have claimed that nationalism, the principle 'which holds that the political and the national unit should be congruent', 'determines the norm for the legitimacy of political units in the modern world' (Gellner, 1983: 1, 49). A related thesis is that nationality is a basis for the legitimacy of states: 'Nationalism ... holds that the only legitimate type of government is national self-determination' (Kedourie, 1993: 1).

It is a mistake, albeit an understandable one, to characterize nationalism as Gellner does; some nationalists do not seek statehood for their people, and characterizing nationalism in terms of statehood begs the question against 'liberal' or anarchist nationalism and other moderate positions. We might expect that most contemporary nationalist movements would claim a state for their nation, but one can be a nationalist without being a statist.

The best cases for the claim that nations are entitled to become states are heavily qualified and will not accord a right to statehood to every nation.[10] Defences of the national principle based on self-rule have to answer the questions why self-rule must take the form of statehood (as opposed to democratic federalism) and why nations are the appropriate unit of self-rule.

We may think of nation-states as the combination 'a single nation + a single state'. If it is not the case that every nation is entitled to become or ought to become a distinct state, and if consequently not every state will be the state of a single nation, what then are nation-states? Most states today and throughout the last two centuries have been multinational states – in this respect multiculturalism is not a new invention. Consider France: the existence of Basques, Bretons and Catalans seems to make it a multinational country. Similarly the United States is multinational, and many Americans explicitly identify themselves in multicultural 'hyphenated' ways (e.g. Italian-American). These two countries are interesting as they are comparatively old states. In addition, both share an Enlightenment tradition which is hostile to nationalism; each was born of an eighteenth-century revolution fought in the name of universal principles. Even if they are multinational as well as somewhat hostile to nationalism, they both seem in

certain senses to be nation-states of a kind. Each is a state which has developed a 'national' culture, easily recognizable to outsiders, whose members are readily moved by sentiments of patriotic allegiance. In terms of the characterization of nation that I have invoked, there is a way in which we can say that France and the US have become in their distinct ways multinational nations and thus nation-states.

An interesting question is then whether there are tendencies for states to become, over time, nation-states of sorts, at least to the extent of coming to have a common culture and of their members developing sentiments of patriotic allegiance. Perhaps states, that is, modern societies organized politically as states, even if multinational, tend to become nation-states. Even if nations need not and may not always be entitled to become states, states nevertheless tend to become nation-states.

ALTERNATIVES

There is a tendency in political philosophy to think of the state in opposition to 'the state of nature' or to anarchy. It is important not to think of these concepts as exhausting the possible forms of political organization. Hobbes, of course, understood these alternatives to be exhaustive: either asocial anarchy or a sovereign state. It is important, especially at this time, to consider more carefully the variety of forms of political organization that may be available to us. The tendency of many philosophers and of some social scientists, in particular anthropologists, to think of 'state' expansively to include all forms of political organization is an error, one which hides the diversity of ways of arranging our lives.

The state, as the fundamental form of political organization, has swept the world. Today virtually all of the land masses of the globe are territorial states. The state system, once European, now includes China and Japan, as well as the former colonies of all the modern empires. But the global spread of the state system does not convey the full extent of the state's victory over alternative forms of political organization. The state has conquered our imaginations as well. It is not just that we tend to dismiss anarchism. It is that we do not easily imagine many alternatives to states. We have trouble, for instance, understanding the status of various 'international' bodies and often instinctively categorize institutional attempts to regulate states as themselves proto-states; for instance, the United Nations was once thought of as a step towards 'World Government' (more threatening if capitalized), and now the European Union is feared as a potential federal state, a 'United States of Europe'. Consider as well our understanding of the remnants of pre-statist European polities, such as Luxembourg (a grand duchy), Liechtenstein and Monaco (principalities), San Marino (a republic), or Andorra (under the joint suzerainty of the President of France and the Bishop of Urgel, Spain). We commonly take these to be states. It is not thought an absurdity to consider the Vatican a state, though it has no citizenry (see Shaw, 1991: 167–8). It is as if our minds, as well as the categories of our systems of law, had room only for one sort of entity or unit.

Normatively, the state's victory is equally complete. It is common in political philosophy to assume that our societies are and must be states, the difficult questions revolving over what shape they should take, what policies governments should implement, what ideals they should serve, if any, and the like. I referred in my opening remarks to the common tendency to take the state to be the subject matter of modern political philosophy.

Consider the case of Rawls, who understands 'the primary subject of justice [to be] the basic structure of society, or more exactly, the way in which the major social institutions distribute fundamental rights and duties and determine the division of advantages from social cooperation'. These major institutions are 'the political constitution and the principal economic and social arrangements' (1971: 7). In *Political Liberalism* Rawls specifies the basic structure as 'a society's main political, social, and economic institutions, and how they fit together into one unified system of social co-operation from one generation to the next' (1996: 11). And he indicates that he takes the basic structure to be 'a modern constitutional democracy'. It is certainly possible to think of non-statist political, social, and economic institutions that might be thought to be a basic structure, but it is not clear that they would necessarily constitute a single, unitary system. Rawls seems simply to assume that modern states are the setting for his account of justice.[11]

We considered earlier how modern states emerged from the political orders of late medieval Europe. The world replaced by the modern state system had many alternative arrangements. Charles Tilly reminds of the possibilities offered by these alternatives when he argues that the victory of the modern state was not inevitable:

> In the thirteenth century, then, five outcomes may still have been open: (1) the form of national state which actually emerged; (2) a political federation or empire controlled, if only loosely, from a single centre; (3) a theocratic federation – a commonwealth – held together by the structure of the Catholic Church; (4) an intensive trading network without large-scale, central political organization; (5) the persistence of the 'feudal' structure which prevailed in the thirteenth century. (1975: 25–6)

Tilly notes that the Roman Empire was followed by the Holy Roman Empire and reminds us not to forget about the Habsburgs' Empire or federation. The city-republics of northern Italy and the cities of northern Europe were also, for some time, viable alternatives to states.

Even if the various political orders of late medieval Europe are not viable models for our world, certain features of these older forms of political organization represent alternatives. Hedley Bull speculates that it is 'conceivable that sovereign states might disappear and be replaced not by world government but by a modern and secular equivalent of the kind of universal political organization that existed in Western Christendom in the Middle Ages' (1997: 254). It is hard to say, however, what forms a viable alternative to the state system may take. Presumably the growth and development of international law will figure prominently in a new world order. But it is too soon to tell what alterations the state system may undergo. In the last decade of the twentieth century there was considerable enthusiasm about globalization and a new world order, one which limited the sovereign powers of states. But the security fears caused by international terrorism at the start of the new century may serve only to reinforce the old state system. It may be too early for Minerva's owl to take flight.

NOTES

1 For accessible accounts of the development of the modern state, see van Creveld (1999), Tilly (1990), Spruyt (1994), Pogge (1978), Mann (1986), and Dyson (1980). See also Hall and Ikenberry (1989), Hinsley (1966) and Strayer (1970). Less historical and more theoretical accounts are provided by Oakshotte (1975), Mairet (1997), Beaud (1994). See also Morris (2001).

2 'All significant concepts of the modern theory of the state are secularized theological concepts' (Schmitt, 1985: ch. 3, 36).

3 Hegel's view is similar: 'since the sovereignty of states is the principle governing their mutual relations, they exist to that extent in a state of nature in relation to one another' (1821: para. 333). Varying accounts of this state of nature are the hallmark of the 'realist' tradition of international relations.

4 If there are circumstances in which others will not, in the absence of sanctions, be adequately motivated to comply with laws, then an important additional reason for sanctions is *assurance*. To threaten to impose sanctions for disobedience will assure those who are otherwise disposed to comply that they will not be taken advantage of by the violators. In situations where compliance with certain laws is thought to be conditional on the like compliance

of others, enforcement may have as its main purpose the provision of assurance [see further Chapter 9].

5 My cumbersome formulation is due to the fact that many laws do not create or recognize obligations (e.g. power-creating laws).

6 'A state's legitimacy … is its exclusive right to impose new duties on subjects by initiating legally binding directives, to have those directives obeyed, and to coerce noncompliers' (Simmons, 1999: 137). '"Justifying the state" is normally thought to mean showing that there are universal obligations to obey the law … [T]he goal of justification of the state is to show that, in principle, everyone within its territories is morally bound to follow its laws and edicts' (Wolff, 1996: 42).

7 'Without justice, what are kingdoms but great robber bands?' (Augustine, 1984: 30). 'Justice is the first virtue of social institutions, as truth is of systems of thought' (Rawls, 1971: 3).

8 A number of contemporary theorists have defended democracy as a procedurally fair way to make decisions in the face of serious disagreement about justice. These thinkers argue that democratic institutions are essential to the legitimation of states (see Christiano, 1996). See also A. Buchanan (2002) for a similar claim about democratic legitimacy and for a conception of legitimacy similar to Morris (1998).

9 Consent in this sense should also be distinguished from 'endorsement consent' in Hampton (1997: 94–7).

10 One of the very best cases is that offered by Margalit and Raz (1990).

11 Consider also the influential characterization of equality expressed by Will Kymlicka: 'A theory is egalitarian in this sense if it accepts that the interests of each member of the community matter, and matter equally. Put another way, egalitarian theories require that the government treat its citizens with equal consideration' (1990: 4–5). In much of contemporary political philosophy, the state is taken for granted to such an extent that it is no longer visible.

REFERENCES

Augustine (1994 [425]) *Political Writings*, eds E. Fortin and D. Kries, trans. M. Tracz and D. Kries. Indianapolis: Hackett.

Austin, John (1995 [1885]) *The Province of Jurisprudence Determined*. Cambridge: Cambridge University Press.

Beaud, Olivier (1994) *La Puissance de l'État*. Paris: Presses Universitaires de France.

Beran, Harry (1987) *The Consent Theory of Political Obligation*. Beckenham: Croom Helm.

Bodin, Jean (1993 [1583]) *Les Six Livres de la République*, ed. G. Mairet. Paris: Livres de Poche.

Buchanan, Allen (2002) 'Political legitimacy and democracy'. *Ethics*, 112 (July): 689–719.

Buchanan, James (1975) *The Limits of Liberty: Between Anarchy and Leviathan*. Chicago: University of Chicago Press.

Bull, Hedley (1997) *The Anarchical Society: A Study of Order in World Politics*. New York: Columbia University Press.

Christiano, Thomas (1996) *The Rule of Many: Fundamental Issues in Democratic Theory*. Boulder, CO: Westview.

Dyson, Kenneth H. F. (1980) *The State Tradition in Western Europe*. New York: Oxford University Press.

Edmundson, William A., ed. (1999) *The Duty to Obey the Law: Selected Philosophical Readings*. Lanham, MD: Rowman and Littlefield.

Gauthier, David (1986) *Morals by Agreement*. Oxford: Clarendon.

Gellner, Ernest (1983) *Nations and Nationalism*. Ithaca, NY: Cornell University Press.

Geuss, Raymond (2001) *History and Illusion in Politics*. Cambridge: Cambridge University Press.

Green, Leslie (1988) *The Authority of the State*. Oxford: Clarendon.

Hall, John A. and G. John Ikenberry (1989) *The State*. Milton Keynes: Open University Press.

Hampton, Jean (1997) *Political Philosophy*. Boulder, CO: Westview.

Hart, H. L. A. (1994) *The Concept of Law*, 2nd edn. Oxford: Oxford University Press.

Hegel, G. W. F. (1991 [1821]) *Elements of the Philosophy of Right*, ed. A. Wood, trans. H. Nisbet. Cambridge: Cambridge University Press.

Hinsley, F. H. (1986) *Sovereignty*, 2nd edn. Cambridge: Cambridge University Press.

Hobbes, Thomas (1991 [1651]) *Leviathan*, ed. Richard Tuck. Cambridge: Cambridge University Press.

Kedourie, Elie (1993 [1960]) *Nationalism*, 4th edn. Oxford: Blackwell.

Kymlicka, Will (1990) *Contemporary Political Philosophy*. Oxford: Clarendon.

Levine, Andrew (1987) *The End of the State*. London: Verso.

Mairet, Gérard (1997) *Le Principe de souveraineté: Histoires et fondements du pouvoir moderne*. Paris: Gallimard.

Mann, Michael (1986) *The Sources of Social Power*, 2 vols. Cambridge: Cambridge University Press.

Margalit, Avishai and Joseph Raz, (1990) 'National self-determination'. *Journal of Philosophy*, 87 (September): 439–461.

Morgenthau, Hans J. (1978) *Politics among Nations*, 5th edn rev. New York: Knopf.

Morris, Christopher W. (1998) *An Essay on the Modern State*. Cambridge: Cambridge University Press.

Morris, Christopher W. (2001) 'Peoples, nations, and the unity of societies'. In C. Gould and P. Pasquino, eds, *Cultural Identity and Nation-State*. Lanham, MD: Rowman and Littlefield, 19–29.

Nozick, Robert (1974) *Anarchy, State, and Utopia.* New York: Basic.

Oakeshott, Michael (1975) 'On the character of a modern European state'. In his *On Human Conduct.* Oxford: Clarendon.

Poggi, Gianfranco (1978) *The Development of the Modern State.* Stanford, CA: Stanford University Press.

Rawls, John (1971) *A Theory of Justice.* Cambridge, MA: Harvard University Press.

Rawls, John (1996) *Political Liberalism.* New York: Columbia University Press.

Raz, Joseph (1979) *The Authority of Law.* Oxford: Clarendon.

Raz, Joseph (1986) *The Morality of Freedom.* Oxford: Clarendon.

Schmitt, Carl (1985 [1922]) *Political Theology*, trans. G. Schwab. Cambridge, MA: MIT Press.

Shaw, Malcolm N. (1991) *International Law*, 3rd edn. Cambridge: Grotius.

Simmons, A. John (1979) *Moral Principles and Political Obligations.* Princeton, NJ: Princeton University Press.

Simmons, A. John (1993) *On the Edge of Anarchy: Locke, Consent, and the Limits of Society.* Princeton, NJ: Princeton University Press.

Simmons, A. John (1999) 'Justification and legitimacy'. In his *Justification and Legitimacy: Essays on Rights and Obligations.* Cambridge: Cambridge University Press, 122–57.

Skinner, Quentin (1978) *The Foundations of Modern Political Thought*, 2 vols. Cambridge: Cambridge University Press.

Skinner, Quentin (1989) 'The state'. In T. Ball, J. Farr and R. Hanson, eds, *Political Innovation and Conceptual Change.* Cambridge: Cambridge University Press, 90–131.

Spruyt, Hendrik (1994) *The Sovereign State and Its Competitors.* Princeton, NJ: Princeton University Press.

Strayer, Joseph (1965) *Feudalism.* Princeton, NJ: Van Nostrand.

Strayer, Joseph (1970) *On the Medieval Origins of the Modern State.* Princeton, NJ: Princeton University Press.

Tilly, Charles (1975) 'Reflections on the history of European state-making'. In his *The Formation of National States in Western Europe.* Princeton, NJ: Princeton University Press, 3–83.

Tilly, Charles (1990) *Coercion, Capital, and European States, AD 990–1990.* Oxford: Blackwell.

Ullmann, Walter (1965) *Medieval Political Thought.* Harmondsworth: Penguin.

Van Creveld, Martin (1999) *The Rise and Decline of the State.* Cambridge: Cambridge University Press.

Vincent, Andrew (1987) *Theories of the State.* Oxford: Blackwell.

Weber, Max (1946 [1919]) 'Politics as a vocation'. In *From Max Weber: Essays in Sociology*, eds and trans. H. Gerth and C. Wright Mills. New York: Oxford University Press.

Weber, Max (1947) *The Theory of Social and Economic Organization* (Part I of *Wirtschaft und Gesellschaft*), trans. A. M. Henderson and T. Parsons. New York: Oxford University Press.

Wolff, Jonathan (1996) *An Introduction to Political Philosophy.* Oxford: Oxford University Press.

16

The Political Theory of the Welfare State

J. DONALD MOON

The term 'the welfare state' came into common usage in the middle of the twentieth century. Its use reflected the growth in Western democracies of governmental responsibility for, and programmes addressing, an extensive range of human needs, such as education, health care, housing, child care, and economic security for the elderly, the unemployed, and the disabled. Some of the programmes of the welfare state, such as public schools and old age pensions, were first developed in the nineteenth century, but what might be called the 'institutional' welfare state did not fully emerge until after World War II, when most democratic countries adopted a more or less integrated range of programmes of welfare provision and policies of economic management. The institutional welfare state is characterized by a range of programmes designed to meet different needs and to provide security against various contingencies. Depending upon what 'category' one falls into, one would be eligible for different types of benefits. Thus, elderly people would be eligible for pensions, sick people for sickness benefits and health care, unemployed people for unemployment compensation, young people and those without marketable skills for education or job training, etc. At least as an ideal, as Brian Barry (1990) points out, the institutional welfare state would not even require a general safety net, since specialized programmes would cover all of the different conditions that prevent people from meeting their needs. In reality, of course, there will always be some who fall between the cracks, and so the welfare state must have a programme of 'social assistance' to cover residual cases. The emergence of the institutional welfare state is reflected in the enormous growth of government expenditures to finance its programmes, both in absolute terms and in relation to national income. In the UK, for example, social expenditure increased from less than 6 percent of GNP in 1920 to 25 percent in 1996–7 (Barr, 1998: 171).

There is no standard definition of the welfare state, and there are major national variations in the forms it has taken, reflecting the different sequences through which welfare states emerged, the social forces that advanced or resisted their creation, and the various political cultures and institutional frameworks. Students of the welfare state have offered a variety of classifications of welfare regimes, and disagree among themselves even about whether particular countries (notably, the US) even qualify as welfare states. Some students of welfare politics emphasize the difference between selective and universal welfare states (e.g. Rothstein, 1998); others discern liberal, corporatist, and social democratic regimes (e.g. Esping-Andersen, 1990); while yet others distinguish among social democratic, Christian democratic, liberal, and wage-earner welfare states (Huber and Stephens, 2001). More philosophically oriented theorists place the welfare state in the context of different traditions of political thought, and different ideals and/or patterns of justification. Thus, some discuss the minimal state and the arguments for and against it (e.g. Nozick, 1974; Schmidtz and Goodin, 1998); others consider the 'residual' versus the 'institutional' welfare state (e.g. Barry, 1999); yet others find four distinct strands, *laissez-faire*, feminism, socialism, and Fabianism (Clarke, Cochrane and Smart, 1987). While most recognize that class is a major concern of the welfare state, an increasing number of theorists see that gender is at least as important (Gordon, 1990; Fraser, 1997).

As a political formation the welfare state tends to divide theorists who in other respects share a view of politics. Thus, defenders and critics of the welfare state include people who identify themselves as (*inter alia*) conservatives, liberals, communitarians, socialists, and postmodernists, and so both its critics and its defenders find themselves with strange allies and opponents. There is certainly no single, unified theory of the welfare state setting out its fundamental principles and institutions. In the untidy field of political theory, theorizing of the welfare state is particularly untidy, and any general survey – including this one – must be highly selective not only in the issues it covers, but also in the way in which it constructs the topic itself.

One natural way of conceptualizing the welfare state is to view it in instrumental terms, as the organization of society to promote 'welfare' or well-being. The roots of this view can be found in Jeremy Bentham's political thinking, particularly his insistence on rationalizing law and political institutions to make them maximally effective in realizing the interests of the community, which is to say, in his words, 'the sum of the interests of the members who compose it' (1948: 126). Different accounts of the welfare state on this view would project different accounts of what constitutes 'welfare' or 'well-being', how the welfare of different individuals should be aggregated, and what policies and institutions are most effective in promoting welfare so understood. Although this instrumental approach captures many important issues, particularly justifications of the welfare state in terms of 'efficiency', it sits uncomfortably with other important theories of the welfare state, particularly those that see it as 'expressing' or embodying the requirements of social solidarity and democratic citizenship.[1]

In this chapter I will proceed nominalistically so to speak. In spite of the great variability mentioned above, welfare states share important features; four of the most important are a democratic political system, a largely private market economy, a wide range of public programmes that provide monetary support or services as a matter of right, and an active role for the state in managing the economy to dampen the business cycle and to regulate economic activities. It is important to emphasize the third feature, since it distinguishes the welfare state from an earlier tradition of relief for the poor. In the welfare state, receiving benefits does not undermine one's citizenship; social provision is not an act of charity or a mere exercise of the state's police powers.

Theorizing about the welfare state has tended to develop in response to its emergence, and the political conflicts and unanticipated consequences it had, rather than being the object of a particular political programme or philosophy. In an earlier time the welfare state may have provided a clearer target for study and criticism. Some may have bemoaned it for its role in shoring up capitalism. Others may have envisioned it as a possible road to a socialism, gradually contributing to the decommodification of labour and the collectivization of consumption and, eventually, investment. In this age of muted expectations, few see the welfare state as having such power, and attention has shifted to the different forms it has taken, and to the ongoing dilemmas with which it struggles. The hopeful visions of a T. H. Marshall or a R. H. Tawney, who imagined that the institutionalization of the social rights of citizenship would pave the way for a genuinely inclusive, democratic society, have given way to agonizing struggles over what appear to be permanent dilemmas of social policy. The very institutions that make the relief of destitution possible, at the same time create new forms of marginalization; the promise of freedom is accompanied by the reality of new and not so new forms of discipline, measures to increase efficiency and responsiveness at the same time raise troubling questions of equity and access. In the next section, I will set out a line of argument, appealing to the value of 'efficiency', justifying one of the welfare state's principal features – the collective, mandatory organization and provision of certain services. I will then address the 'redistributive' function of the welfare state, which is justified by appeal to values such as rights, solidarity, and social justice. In the last section I will discuss some of the ways in which both left-wing and right-wing critiques of the welfare state have converged in recent years.

EFFICIENCY-BASED ACCOUNTS

The task of meeting our needs in areas such as education, health, and old age security is obviously not uniquely assigned to the state. Even in countries with extensive social programmes, most of the 'labour' involved in providing welfare services, such as care for the young, the elderly, and the ill, is provided informally in households, through kinship networks, and by volunteers in religious and other organizations in civil society.[2] In addition, many welfare services are provided through market transactions, such as the purchase of life or medical insurance. Why, then, should the state be involved in providing welfare, either directly in the form of specific services (such as health care or education) or in the form of resources or income to enable people to meet their own needs? Government programmes, after all, both involve an element of coercion and impose uniformity. Social insurance for unemployment or pensions, for example, is based on mandatory 'contributions' – i.e. taxes – and sets uniform benefit schedules, retirement ages, and other requirements.[3] Allowing people to meet their own needs permits people to shape their lives according to their own priorities.

The alternative to state provision is often taken to be the market, where profit-seeking firms provide consumers with goods and services. But this is an oversimplification, as families and voluntary associations also play key roles. Prior to the rise of the welfare state, at least in Britain and America, people formed voluntary organizations to cover contingencies such as illness, disability, death, and old age. Individuals and families, wishing to insure themselves against various contingencies, could often choose among a variety of groups, or in some cases commercial firms, offering protection on different terms, and could make arrangements that were more or less tailored to their own circumstances and aspirations. The rise of the welfare state with its compulsory programmes has led to the demise of many of these voluntary associations and private firms, reducing citizens' autonomy and imposing uniformity on them. The more extensive the welfare state, the more it has displaced other welfare institutions.[4]

One reason for substituting state for private provision is that state provision (either of services or of resources) can sometimes be more effective than private provision, either because it can provide services or resources more cheaply, or because private provision is incapable of providing an optimal (or even adequate) level of services. In such cases, public provision may be justified on the grounds that it corrects some form of what is called 'market failure'. A standard example of market failure is public goods, such as national defence. In such cases, providing the good for one member of the group is impossible without providing it for all. It is difficult for a group to provide public goods for itself voluntarily, because each member has an incentive to free ride on the efforts of others, with the result that the good in question is not provided at all (or is provided only at a less than optimal level) [see further Chapter 9].

But are typical welfare goods public goods in that sense? To some degree, perhaps. If we all wanted to live in a society where no one suffered from destitution, and were willing to pay something to see that achieved, then we would all be better off if the government provided a safety net. Reasoning along these lines, Milton Friedman (1962: 191) has argued for a minimal welfare state, in which a 'negative income tax' would be employed to provide a subsistence income to people without other means of support. The minimal welfare state would not, however, be an 'institutional welfare state', since its main concern would be to ensure that everyone had enough income to avoid destitution. Presumably, it would also provide other public goods such as public health and sanitation, for each of us is better off if others are inoculated against infectious diseases, or if the town disposes of every household's sewage and garbage in a sanitary manner. But many welfare programmes do not seem to provide public goods: the principal beneficiary of an old age pension is the pensioner, the principal beneficiary of a high school or college education is the student whose skills are improved and whose life is enriched, the principal beneficiary of open heart surgery is the patient whose life is saved, and so forth.

Even when the institutional welfare state does not provide public goods, strictly speaking, there are other limitations of the voluntary model it can overcome. For example, private firms and voluntary organizations are poorly equipped to protect individuals from income loss due to unemployment. Non-governmental risk-pooling schemes work best when the chances that one person will suffer a given condition – say disability or death – are more or less independent of anyone else's chances, and when the overall risks facing the group are known. Under these conditions, each individual can pay into the fund, which can accumulate enough to provide benefits to the unfortunate. But if the risks in question are not independent, if one person's suffering increases the likelihood that others will suffer as well, then a private scheme may collapse, as more and more people shift from being contributors to being claimants, and the group's reserves are depleted. Unemployment is (in part) cyclical, which means that in a downturn some people lose their jobs, and as a result reduce their consumption, thereby leading other firms to lay off workers, in an expanding cycle. Thus, a private firm or voluntary association offering unemployment insurance would run the risk of going out of business as fewer and fewer people held jobs (and so paid into the fund) and more and more people lost their jobs, and so became claimants. Because state-sponsored schemes, unlike private associations, are able to run deficits, and to the extent that these deficits actually contribute to expanding demand and so reducing unemployment and stabilizing the economy, they can deal with problems that non-state schemes cannot.

Voluntary welfare provision may also be unable to cover everyone in a society. Many people in the heyday of mutual aid societies were not members, and non-members were often among the least advantaged, those without steady jobs and a secure place within the community. And it is easy to understand why. Organizations offering protection recognize that those most likely to need protection have the greatest incentive to seek it, and so to join a mutual aid society or to purchase insurance, while those facing the lowest risks have an incentive to stay out. As a result of this process of 'adverse selection', risks tend to be spread over a smaller and smaller part of the population, and premiums must rise accordingly. This process of adverse selection can continue to the point where most of those in need of protection are unable to afford it, because premiums have to rise so high that all but the most vulnerable drop out. The welfare state can combat the problem of adverse selection by making membership compulsory: 'because low risks cannot opt out, it makes possible a pooling solution' (Barr, 1992: 755).

Adverse selection is reinforced by a second process or condition, called 'moral hazard'. People who are insured against a certain risk may be more willing to take chances than they would be in the absence of insurance. Knowing that if I get sick or injured, my medical bills will be covered, may make me more willing to engage in risky behaviour, such as downhill skiing. To the extent that this occurs, organizations may face higher claims, thereby forcing them to raise their charges, and discouraging others from purchasing protection. More obviously, unemployment insurance schemes are subject to moral hazard, for knowing that I will be covered in the event that I am unemployed, I have an incentive to quit (or arrange to be fired) and/or not to seek or accept employment. Of course, state schemes are subject to moral hazard as well, but the key point is that if the genuine risk of losing one's job is to be covered at all, it must be covered through a public programme (see Barr, 1998: 190–2).

A related problem is a tendency for people to overuse services when they are free at the point of delivery. If my purchasing an insurance policy or joining a mutual aid society gives me the right to a free service, I may be tempted to take advantage of that opportunity to a greater extent than I would be if I had to pay for it each time I used it. In that case, costs would tend to escalate and the group as a whole may end up paying more for the protection than would be optimal from their own point of view.

For all of these reasons organizations offering protection will try to limit use, to prevent too many high risk people from joining, and to charge them more in order to hang on to their other members. In the case of voluntary groups, such as neighbourhood-, work- or craft-based mutual aid societies, informal patterns of social surveillance and affinity may function to exclude outsiders and others who are thought to be especially likely to need benefits. Similarly, private firms may use various underwriting mechanisms to screen out high risk individuals or groups. The overall result may well be that certain groups may receive no or inadequate coverage, and the cost of services may be much greater than

they would be if they were provided through a compulsory plan that spread risks more widely and rationed services to avoid overuse.[5]

It is important to stress that state provision is not necessarily superior to private provision. Even if there are clear examples of 'market failures', areas in which voluntary provision is incapable of providing an optimal level of services of one sort or another, it does not follow that government action will be superior. Just as real-world markets are subject to market failure, so real-world governments are subject to non-market failure. For example, while mandatory programmes can avoid the problem of adverse selection, by requiring low risk individuals to participate in the risk-sharing scheme, they may exacerbate the problem of moral hazard, by giving individuals incentives not to provide for themselves (e.g. by reducing their savings rate, or not taking a job) and relying upon the public programme of pensions or unemployment compensation to meet their needs. And government provision is subject to its own limitations. For example, government programmes can be run for the benefit of the bureaucrats who administer them, at the expense of the clients they are supposed to serve, or may be captured by special interest groups, who succeed in diverting resources to their own ends. Moreover, markets are often able to provide public goods or deal with externalities in effective ways. What is required, then, is a balancing of the relative costs and benefits of different forms of provision for different kinds of contingencies, and in different settings.[6]

The recognition that public provision can involve greater costs than voluntary programmes has led to calls for 'privatization' of some welfare state activities during the past 20 or 25 years. Different groups have advocated devolving to private parties those activities once performed by the state, ranging from the sale of nationalized industries to contracting with private firms to provide public services, such as running schools or supplying cleaning services to a government bureaucracy. In a similar vein, recent years have seen efforts to increase choice and simulate market processes within public programmes, such as the use of vouchers in public education, or the 'internal market' in Britain's National Health Service. In all of these initiatives, the hope is to increase efficiency, to make service providers more responsive to clients, and to enable people to receive more individualized services, reflecting their specific needs and interests. On the other hand, these developments raise the concern that even 'quasi-market' choice in areas such as pensions or education will adversely affect disadvantaged groups. For example, when the successful school in a system relying upon vouchers or other 'parental choice' mechanisms is able to attract more students than it has space for, the fear is that it may respond by excluding 'problem' children, possibly leaving them even worse off than before. Whether the issue is pensions, education, health care, or other areas of the welfare state, efficiency arguments for public versus private provision involve a balancing of their relative costs.[7]

THE WELFARE STATE AND REDISTRIBUTION

A second line of argument supporting the welfare state appeals to the idea of justice rather than efficiency. The policies of the welfare state do not simply make it possible for individuals to realize their own interests more effectively, but generally redistribute income [see further Chapter 17]. Efficiency-based arguments normally take the outcome produced by market exchange, prior to governmental taxation and transfers, as their baseline, and show that a particular policy can at least in principle make everyone better off than they would be given that baseline. But to the extent that welfare policies deliberately redistribute income, those whose income goes down would normally (though not necessarily) be worse off; such policies could be justified, then, only by invoking values other than efficiency.[8]

More important, the appeal to efficiency is itself problematic, in as much as the pretax/pretransfer baseline it takes for granted must be justified. There are some risks which we face, when we think of our lives taken as a whole, that cannot be covered by any form of private provision, because they reflect conditions into which we are born, such as congenital handicaps, genetic predispositions to certain diseases, and the cultural and economic disadvantages one's parents may suffer. Because of these conditions, those who are fortunate have no incentive to join a risk-sharing scheme to compensate those who are not. Any private system of provision is limited to pooling the shared risks that people face in the future, and so presupposes a 'baseline' of a given distribution of advantages and disadvantages. But from a larger point of view, this restriction to a given status quo is arbitrary.

Even using the term 'redistribution' may be misleading to the extent that it seems to presuppose that the initial 'distribution' is somehow morally privileged, so that deviations from it – redistributions – must be 'justified'. But a moment's reflection should be sufficient to see that this presupposition is false, and that any distribution of 'the advantages of social co-operation' must be justified, whether it results from market transactions or from welfare state policies specifically designed to redistribute income.

The presumption that distributions that result from 'government' action must be justified, and

that pretax and pretransfer distributions are presumptively just, appears to be widespread at least in America, leading to hostility on the part of some towards the welfare state. Strong libertarians like Nozick hold that taxation to redistribute resources from some taxpayers to others is not only presumptively but actually unjust because it violates citizens' property rights [see further Chapter 9]. This critique obviously presupposes that the right we have to our property, including income from employment or business activity, is not created by the state, but exists in some sense 'prior' to political life, and so limits what governments may legitimately do. If such a theory of natural or prepolitical rights could be vindicated, it would block redistributive welfare state programmes.

Welfare Rights

It goes beyond the scope of this chapter to examine the case for natural or prepolitical property rights, but it is worth pointing out that many of the considerations that can be invoked to support strong property rights also support welfare or 'positive' rights, and so can be used to justify the redistributive activities of a welfare state. When we think about why we are attracted to the idea that humans have rights at all, including a (defeasible) right not to be coerced by others, the reasons we are likely to come up with will support the idea that people ought to be accorded certain basic welfare rights, rights to goods and services necessary for human functioning. For example, Nozick refers to the idea that people are capable of leading meaningful lives, and so they have (or should have) a right against being coerced by others because such a right is necessary to protect that fundamental human capacity. I can only create projects for myself, and organize my life to realize those projects, and thus find meaning in my life, if I am free from coercion by others: they can't force me to do their bidding rather than fulfil my own aspirations.

This is a powerful argument, but it is equally true that to live my own life requires not only protection against interference from others, but also access to the resources necessary to life itself. If those resources can be appropriated as private property, then a person could be deprived of anything resembling a decent life, or even life itself, because she lacked the necessary resources. Jeremy Waldron (1993: 309–38) gives the example of a homeless person, in a setting in which all land and other amenities, such as toilets or sleeping places, are privately owned. Under those circumstances, she would not be able to live, or at least to live without violating someone's 'rights'. But what reason would she have to acknowledge a duty not to take what she needed, when her life depended on it? It is hard to see why people, recognizing the possibility that they might become impoverished, would have reason to accept a system of property rights that could leave them in such desperate straits. As Waldron (1993: ch. 1 and *passim*) argues, the only system of property rights that all have a reason to endorse would be one that ensured that no one need be deprived of essential resources, and the obvious way of achieving that would be to make property holdings subject to taxation, so that the state could provide essential goods and services, or at least a minimum income, when necessary.[9]

This line of argument supports what might be called a social minimum state, not necessarily an institutional welfare state. The core argument is that some fundamental human values – the idea of a meaningful life, personal autonomy, or life itself – can be realized (or at least guaranteed) only if there are government programmes providing enough income at least for subsistence. F. A. Hayek, for example, is renowned as a critic of the welfare state, but he accepts the idea of a social minimum, arguing that citizens may feel that there is 'a clear moral duty of all to assist, within the organized community, those who cannot help themselves', and so the society could provide 'a uniform minimum income ... outside the market' to those who are indigent (1976: 87).[10]

Others have argued that people have prepolitical welfare rights, on all fours with the 'negative' rights to non-interference such as the right to bodily integrity, and that it is the government's responsibility to secure those rights. A just society, then, could only be a society in which those rights are secured, and so only a welfare state could be a just state. To the extent that welfare rights are rights to specific resources, such as health care, education, and housing, fulfilling them may require or at least justify an institutional welfare state, not just a redistributive tax and transfer system. More plausibly, arguments from positive or welfare rights might be combined with the efficiency-based arguments surveyed above to justify an institutional welfare state.

The view that we have welfare rights that are, in some sense, prepolitical, which require that the state provide various goods and services, is subject to well known difficulties. The standards defining the scope of such rights claims are notoriously vague. Raymond Plant et al. (1980), for example, base positive rights claims in 'needs', but what are the boundaries of need? I may 'need' an enormously expensive kind of medical treatment in order to prolong my life, if only for a few days, but is it plausible to say that I have a right to such treatment? Ronald Dworkin argues the traditional practice of medicine may be based on the 'rescue principle', which answers that question affirmatively: 'it says

we should spend all we can [on health care] until the next dollar would buy no gain in health or life expectancy at all', but he insists that 'No sane society would try to meet that standard' (2000: 309): it would require sacrificing too many competing goods, including other rights claims, like the right to an education or a minimal standard of living.

Alan Gewirth views positive rights claims as implicit in the commitment to human agency, a commitment one necessarily undertakes in performing any intentional action, because doing so presupposes that one views oneself as an agent, and so is implicitly committed to those conditions necessary for the exercise of agency, which include access to certain resources. But who is responsible for ensuring that I have access to the resources necessary to exercise agency in my own case? Gewirth holds that when I cannot meet my needs through my own efforts, others have an obligation 'positively to assist' me (1978: 134). But what standards are they to use to determine what constitutes a reasonable effort on my part?

These concerns may not be decisive to reject the idea of basic welfare rights, but they do mean that specifying them is impossible in the absence of some political process through which the standards governing responsibility and trade-offs among conflicting uses can be determined (see Holmes and Sunstein, 1999). And because these rights cannot be specified except through a political process, it is implausible to view them as establishing a prepolitical standard of justice to which that political process must conform.

Equality of Opportunity

A second justice-based argument for the welfare state appeals to the idea of 'fair equality of opportunity', to use Rawls's phrase. Fair equality of opportunity requires not only that there be no 'arbitrary' barriers to the life choices one may make, such as restrictions on occupational or educational opportunity based on race or gender, but that everyone has access to the resources and experiences necessary to qualify for the different positions and careers that exist in society. To the extent that one's chances in life are determined by the class position into which one is born, then fair equality of opportunity is denied. Arguably, fair equality of opportunity supports not only a social minimum state, but an institutional welfare state, in which education, including perhaps early childhood education, and medical care are provided on a common basis for all. But, like welfare rights generally, the requirements of fair equality of opportunity cannot be specified except in specific social contexts; the kind of educational opportunities necessary in a largely agrarian society, to take an obvious example, are very different from those required in a postindustrial setting. And once again it is necessary to make trade-offs between equal opportunity and other values, such as the privacy and autonomy of families.

Membership and Solidarity

Because concepts of positive rights and equal opportunity are not well defined outside of specific social contexts, they are often combined with arguments appealing to ideals of citizenship and social solidarity. The basic argument is that the welfare state should guarantee the inclusion of all citizens as full members of a democratic society, which requires that an extensive range of social rights be provided. The reasoning is fairly straightforward: just as citizens must have civil and political rights, they must be guaranteed certain social rights if they are to be full members of a society, and specifically if they are to participate in democratic politics. The key premise in this argument is that citizenship must be universal. All who are capable of intentional or responsible action must be full citizens. The only legitimate basis for exclusion is incapacity for responsible action.

T. H. Marshall (1977) offers a classical account of the welfare state as the necessary result of the universal extension of citizenship. He traces the emergence of universal citizenship by observing three successive phases, the first involving the general extension of civil rights, the second the universalization of the suffrage, and the third the growth of the welfare state and the creation of the 'social rights of citizenship'.[11] Social citizenship is essential for democratic equality; people who are destitute, or who lack access to essential resources such as medical care, or who do not have at least a basic education, cannot stand with others on an equal plane. If citizenship is to be universal, the state must guarantee that everyone has access to these essential goods. The democratic state must thus be a welfare state.

There are a number of variants of this argument, but a common theme is a deep suspicion of the market and at least certain forms of individualism. Whereas arguments from efficiency take the market as a baseline, and justify social policies on the ground that they can correct market failures, arguments from solidarity begin with something close to the opposite assumption – projecting an ideal in which all activities are organized through collective associations, in which individuals are oriented principally towards common needs and aspirations. Richard Titmuss (1972) extols the 'gift relationship', and David Harris (1987) speaks of the family

as a model for social life. More concretely, Claus Offe (1984) and Gosta Esping-Andersen (1985) once expressed the hope that the growth of collective consumption and other forms of decommodification will eventually displace capitalism, leading to a socialist order of society.

Harris offers a communitarian version of the argument from solidarity. He argues that 'full membership' in a society requires that each person be able to enjoy 'a certain style of life' and 'certain life chances' (1987: 147). Although he recognizes that modern societies include a plurality of different groups, he insists that there are more or less common standards of what an individual must be able to do and how one must be able to live if one is not to be excluded or socially marginalized. These standards determine the needs of members of that society, and should be equally available to all citizens as a matter of right, for only in that way can the equal status of members be recognized and respected (1987: 154–7). This line of argument supports the institutional welfare state in which services are provided in kind in part because 'citizens have a right to that specific resource', such as 'education', rather than a right 'to income which may or may not be spent on education' (1987: 150). Further, the universal provision of certain services is expressive of, and may contribute to, a sense of community and equal citizenship. Finally, providing services in kind may be a form of 'justified paternalism' to the extent that 'some persons may be imprudent or wasteful or be unable to make adequate use of cash' (1987: 150–1).

Harris's account relies upon an analogy between political society and the family: just as we have obligations towards, and rights against, members of our family, irrespective of what they may have done for us individually, so we have obligations towards, and rights against, our fellow citizens. The stress on obligations is crucial, for the possibility of enjoying one's rights depends upon the willing support of social policies on the part of the citizenry, and to claim one's rights one must be prepared to fulfil the 'system of duties' that 'underlies the structure of citizen rights' (1987: 160). Thus, a person 'who is genuinely and personally responsible for his condition' has no rights-based claim to assistance, for he has not fulfilled his 'duty to maintain himself as an independent member of society' (1987: 160). However, Harris goes on to argue that the pragmatic difficulties involved in determining whether someone's unfulfilled needs are a result of his own choices are so great that we should presume that there are no such cases, and should rely upon a 'sense of duty or community ... to prevent or minimize abuse of the system' (1987: 161). Of course, this same sense of community is necessary if those relatively advantaged citizens, who are net contributors to welfare schemes, are to be willing participants in the process.

These arguments are subject to a number of obvious reservations. In the first place, the founding of rights and obligations on 'membership' is deeply problematic, in as much as it begs the question of whether the social order of which we are to be members is just. To say that we are all equally members, and so should be equally entitled to the resources necessary to be full members, is not to say that as members we are equal, as Harris seems to suppose. In a caste or feudal society, everyone might equally be a member, and membership may well carry with it certain welfare (and other) rights, but these rights are not equal but differentiated by status, and the distribution may be deeply unjust. The general argument from membership does little to support a modern welfare state in the absence of a larger theory of justice. I will return to this point below.

Second, and ironically, welfare states have a systematic tendency to undermine the very communitarian sentiments and relationships that would support the values of solidarity and equality. Although participating in a common programme, such as a national health service or medicare, may give rise to feelings of solidarity with others, what people actually experience may often be quite different. In many cases it is more like being reduced to the status of a client, attempting to meet one's needs through an impersonal and unresponsive bureaucracy. Far from contributing to a sense of community, public provision (which is almost inevitably bureaucratic provision) may disrupt the communitarian forms through which needs may have been met in the past, replacing personal relationships which engender obligations and mutual identification with legally prescribed associations of strangers.[12]

Further, the commitment to equality can sometimes sit uneasily with the commitment to democracy. Consider, for example, Albert Weale's argument for earnings-related welfare state schemes, such as social security in the US. Weale argues that such schemes increase the total volume of government transfers, thus leading to greater 'egalitarian effectiveness'. Weale explains this egalitarian effectiveness in part as follows:

> Of course, there is no necessary incentive to redistribute savings in the public earnings-related system, but equally there is little practical opportunity to resist any modest redistribution that managers of the public scheme determine. Denied the 'exit' option of shopping around, the typical citizen is confronted merely with the costly 'voice' option of changing the terms of the public scheme. Since people are often highly ignorant of the details of pension schemes, participation to change their terms is extremely costly. (1990: 481)

In short, because democratic control is difficult, popular opposition to redistribution will be ineffective, allowing elites to achieve greater 'egalitarian effectiveness' than citizens would be willing to support directly.

Solidaristic Conceptions of Justice

An adequate account of the welfare state, one that can justify its redistributive aims, must ultimately be based upon a theory of justice, and the most promising theories are those which Phillipe Van Parijs calls 'solidaristic conceptions of justice' (1995: 28), such as those offered by Rawls, Dworkin, Amartya Sen, and Van Parijs himself. Solidaristic conceptions of justice are based upon a commitment to 'equal concern' for the interests of all, and to 'equal respect, that is, the view that what counts as a just society should not be determined on the basis of some particular substantive conception of the good life' (1995: 28). The 'liberal' commitment to equal respect in solidaristic theories of justice underlies their support for the standard 'negative' and democratic rights characteristic of the welfare state, and the commitment to equal concern underlies their accounts of social justice and so the redistributive elements of the welfare state.

Different solidaristic theories provide different accounts of social justice, and support different institutions. No theory, by itself, directly supports the institutional welfare state. Van Parijs, for example, rejects it in favour of a system providing the highest possible basic income for all, and Rawls explicitly rejects the welfare state on the grounds that it tolerates the highly unequal distribution of wealth produced by a capitalist society, and so undermines democracy by concentrating too much economic and political power in a wealthy elite. Still, solidaristic theories can supply the deficiencies, noted above, in justifications of the welfare state that appeal to membership and solidarity, and to the baseline problem in efficiency-based arguments. With regard to the appeal to membership, solidaristic theories of justice provide grounds for the value of social inclusion on a principle of equality. And they address the serious lacunae in efficiency-based arguments, specifically the fact that they take a market generated outcome as their starting point, and ask whether that outcome could be improved through some government policy. But because there is nothing privileged about market generated outcomes, market institutions and the 'initial' distribution of resources must themselves be morally justified, and solidaristic theories of justice address that problem.

While solidaristic arguments do not necessarily justify the welfare state as the ideal regime, they do provide grounds for central welfare state policies. Rawls's ideal regimes, a property-owning democracy or market socialism, would have to be welfare states in the sense I have used the term here: that is, they would have to have social policies that would collectively provide for certain needs, justified in terms of efficiency and their redistributive consequences. And Van Parijs allows significant scope for collective provision including the area of medical care.[13]

PARADOXES OF THE WELFARE STATE

I have asserted that the justification of the welfare state rests upon arguments invoking both efficiency and justice. Arguments for redistribution or equality do not necessarily support the collective provision of services or categorical forms of income support characteristic of the welfare state, but must be supplemented by other considerations. These can include the 'expressive' value of common provision stressed in some social democratic and communitarian accounts, with their direct appeals to solidarity and membership, or to analyses that show that collective provision of services (e.g. medical care) or social insurance is superior to voluntary and market provision in terms of enabling individuals to meet their needs.

A common theme in justifications for the welfare state is the need for social provision if freedom is to be effectively realized for all citizens. Ironically, this very commitment to freedom and solidarity is subject to a certain inner tension. One way to think about this is to see that the effort to empower individuals and to promote social inclusion also leads to new forms of marginalization and control. One major reason for this is that the goal of social inclusion cannot be achieved merely by providing people with resources, for what is ultimately required is that people be able to participate effectively in the social and political 'life of the community' (Sen, 1992: 5). Thus, we must be concerned not simply with citizens' command of external resources, but with what they can do with them, as Amartya Sen argues. He distinguishes between 'functionings', which 'represent parts of the state of a person – in particular, the various things that he or she manages to do or be in leading a life', and a person's 'capability', which 'reflects the alternative combinations of functionings the person can achieve' (Sen, 1993: 31). Functionings can be very complex performances or states of being, or ensembles of performances and states of being, such as 'being in good health' or 'achieving self respect or being socially integrated' (1993: 31).

In spite of the importance of functioning as opposed to possessing, most evaluations of welfare state performance focus on what people have, rather than on what they can do. One common measure, for example, is 'percentage of poor households lifted out of poverty as a result of taxes and transfers', where poverty is defined as having an income below 50 percent of adjusted median household income of the country in which one lives (Rothstein, 1998: 183–4). But if the objective of the welfare state is to enable citizens to participate effectively, this measure is problematic because income, or income alone, does not provide the capability to achieve many of the most important functionings. In a recent study aptly titled *What Money Can't Buy* (1997), Susan Mayer has examined the 'functionings' of children, adolescents, and young adults, and correlated them with family income. Her findings, consistent with Sen's general argument about the relationship between resources and functionings, are that, above a basic level, in most cases 'additional parental income does not improve children's chances for success' (1997: 2). Mayer hypothesizes that the reason that income has such a limited effect is that other parental characteristics, such as 'skills, diligence, honesty, good health, and reliability, also improve children's life chances, independent of their effect on parents' income. Children of parents with these attributes do well even when their parents do not have much income' (1997: 3). The more general point here is that functionings that are important for full membership or citizenship depend upon internalized dispositions and skills and not merely on access to external resources. Thus, it might be concluded, ensuring equal citizenship requires programmes that go beyond the provision of external resources.

Welfare and Work

The argument about the necessity for effective functioning, as opposed simply to having access to resources, has been most heated in the area of work. If democratic citizenship requires that all be enabled to participate fully in society, then people must have not only certain resources, but also certain capacities, skills, and dispositions. Recently, however, the issue of duties of citizens has become more urgent, as all welfare states have seen the emergence of a class of citizens who are dependent on the state's welfare programmes for their survival, and who do not provide for themselves and their families through their own labour, or through benefit programmes such as social security in which benefits reflect their previous efforts and earnings. In much popular discourse, the welfare-dependent population is stigmatized as exploitative, irresponsibly taking advantage of the social safety net to avoid work and provide themselves with more leisure than they could otherwise afford, giving rise to demands for punitive measures to limit access to such benefits. But even people who are sympathetic to the plight of those who more or less permanently rely upon public assistance have cause for concern. One can acknowledge that people rely upon 'welfare' because their options are so limited, and so their condition represents an indictment of the society rather than the individuals concerned, but the fact remains that receipt of social assistance does not enable one to attain full citizenship or membership in society. It simply sustains one in a marginalized condition. Social inclusion requires more than receiving benefits.

This line of argument has been advanced by a number of 'conservative' critics of the welfare state. Lawrence Mead (1992), for example, argues that the character of poverty at least in America has changed in the past several decades, and that the social exclusion represented by poverty reflects the inability of poor people to act as rational agents in pursuit even of their own interests.[14] The key to overcoming this exclusion is to inculcate in the passive poor the capacities for agency, for acting to promote their own interests and to control their own lives, by imposing adequate disciplinary controls on them. If poverty creates social exclusion, and so is a barrier to citizenship, then the state must ensure that its citizens develop the capacities that enable them to escape poverty. The key policy, in Mead's view, is workfare; the poor must be required to work as a condition of support, for unless they develop the discipline and sense of accomplishment that work involves, they will be unable to escape the conditions of dependency. Social policy must take on an explicitly 'paternalistic' character, and the state self-consciously assume a tutelary role. Mead holds out the possibility that 'public paternalism might help regenerate … informal [social] controls, by involving community organizations in directive programs' (1997: 27–8). In that case, 'paternalism in its public sense might not have to be permanent', but only because the necessary disciplines are imposed through other social agencies.

Nikolas Rose has pointed out that the emphasis on paid employment is not a monopoly of the right: 'From the "social democratic left", too, work [is] now seen as the [principal] mode of inclusion, and absence from the labour market the most potent source of exclusion' (1999, 163). In some solidaristic accounts, the emphasis on work invokes an older language of duties. In Harris's account, for example, the duties correlative to our welfare rights are 'strict obligations' and may be enforced by 'coercion' (1987: 161). In this, he echoes Marshall, who looked beyond the social rights of citizenship to

consider the duties of the enriched and inclusive model of citizenship he advocated, including 'the duty to work', which he thought was of 'paramount importance'. Similarly, Amy Gutmann and Dennis Thompson offer a justification for enforcing work obligations that draws on the idea of citizenship, arguing that 'work should be seen as a necessary part of citizenship' (1996: 293), because it is 'essential to social dignity'. Since 'earning is not only a means of making a living but also a mark of equal citizenship', paid employment has a 'political dimension' that 'provides a further justification for the obligation to work' (1996: 302).

But this obligation to work is not, or is not merely, a demand to be made on the individual, one which he might reasonably wish to resist, for ultimately it is rooted in an ideal of social inclusion and active citizenship through which the individual's own interests and needs can be realized. Anthony Giddens sounds this theme in his call for 'the positive welfare society', in which 'the contract between individual and government shifts, since autonomy and the development of self – the medium of expanding individual responsibility – become the prime focus' (1998: 128). Replacing the traditional 'welfare state' with the 'social investment state', the task of government would be to invest in 'human capital' rather than 'the direct provision of economic maintenance' (1998: 117). Although he allows that full employment might not be realized, he calls for the redistribution of work to include as many as possible, and various forms of payment for participation in the 'social economy', the sphere of civil society traditionally maintained by voluntary work. As Rose puts it, the contemporary 'organization of freedom' views individuals as best able to 'fulfil their political obligations in relation to the wealth, health and happiness of the nation not when they are bound into relations of dependency and obligation, but when they seek to fulfil themselves as free individuals', which depends 'upon the activation of the powers of the citizen' (1999: 166).

There is a certain irony in this development. It is not just that the welfare state's commitment to providing the resources necessary for everyone, including the most disadvantaged, to make their formal freedom effective comes with new forms of social control. That could hardly be avoided. Rather, the irony is to be found in the way in which this current in thinking about the welfare state appropriates and reverses the emphasis of those who first resisted it. Long before the development of the welfare state, von Humboldt argued that 'The true end of Man … is the highest and most harmonious development of his powers to a complete and consistent whole' (1969: 16), a condition which can be realized only if the authority and action of the state are limited to protecting individuals against violations of their rights, for any effort on the part of the state to advance the 'positive welfare of the citizen is harmful' (von Humboldt, 1969: 3). State action 'invariably produces national uniformity' (von Humboldt, 1969: 23), and leads to the 'deterioration of the moral character' of citizens because they are deprived of the opportunity and need to manage their own concerns, and the stimulus to intellectual and moral development that such management provides. Von Humboldt's argument inspired important strands in John Stuart Mill's thinking, and his ideas are reflected in the work of many nineteenth-century liberals, who often defended the elimination of outdoor relief and similar policies on the grounds that welfare undermines capacity for autonomy and other virtues of its intended beneficiaries.[15] Today, in the focus on social inclusion and the recognition that this involves not just having rights and resources, but fulfilling duties and exercising capacities, the welfare state is being reshaped (or at least readvertised) as a device for shaping citizens and inculcating virtue, including the virtues necessary to 'fulfil themselves as free individuals' (Rose, 1999: 166). That is not, I hasten to add, a reason to reject the welfare state, but only a reason to recognize both the causes of its persistence in the face of continual 'crises', and its limitations.

NOTES

1 For an introduction to the political theory of the welfare state that takes 'welfare' as its point of departure, see Barry (1999). For a critique of the welfare state conceived in instrumental terms, focusing on the major (and in the author's view, unrealizable) epistemic demands it makes, see Gaus (1998).

2 In general, the economic value of unpaid 'work' in modern market economies rivals that of paid employment. Kaufman reports that in West Germany in 1992 the amount of paid work consisted of 60 billion hours, while unpaid work (including 'time for household production, network assistance and volunteer activities') amounted to 95.5 billion hours, and its value was 'only 9% less than the total of all gross wages and salaries in the West German economy' (2001: 20).

3 For example, unemployment benefits are usually available only to people who are actively seeking work.

4 See Paul (1997), particularly the articles by Beito, Davies, and the references cited therein for an account of non-state forms of welfare.

5 An example of how a system dominated by private provision both is more expensive, *and* provides protection to a smaller proportion of the population, may be medical

care in the US. The US spends a far higher proportion of its GDP (12.9 percent in 1998 compared with Germany's 10.3 or the UK's 6.8) on medical care than other rich countries, but fails to provide coverage for over 20 percent of its population. Ironically, public provision of medical care in the US is larger than that of the UK (5.8 versus 5.7 percent of GDP), not even counting the implicit subsidy represented by the favourable tax treatment of employer-provided health insurance (OECD health statistics).

6 See Cowen (1988) for analyses of how markets can provide public goods and handle externalities; see Tullock, Seldon and Brady (2002) for sustained critiques of the capacity of government to correct market failures.

7 For an excellent range of studies of the 'revolution in social policy' created by the move to 'quasi-markets' in a variety of policy areas and countries, see Bartlett, Roberts and Le Grand (1998).

8 The argument that the alleviation of poverty is a public good, discussed above, would be an example of justifying redistribution on efficiency grounds.

9 See Lomasky (1987) for a rights-based defence of a minimal welfare state, which taxes people to provide for a minimum standard of living for all.

10 Although generally critical of the welfare state, Hayek seems to allow for certain forms of public provision and compulsory insurance (1960: 285–394).

11 Like so much of social science, Marshall's account is blind to issues of gender, as he depicts these phases as a historical succession, the completion or virtual completion of one laying the basis for the realization of the next. His stages describe the gradual extension of the rights associated with citizenship for men, but they ignore the experience of women (and, I might add, other non-class-based exclusions), who often were able to claim various welfare rights (e.g. widows' pensions) before they were entitled to political or even full civil rights.

12 This is an important theme in Wolfe's analysis and critique of state provision (see 1989: esp. chs 4 and 5).

13 See Rawls (2001: 135–40) and the preface to the revised edition of his *Theory of Justice* (1999) for his discussion of politico-economic regimes; and see Van Parijs (1995: 41–5).

14 It should be noted that Mead would reject the characterization of his position as 'conservative', arguing that at least in America the conservative position shares the liberal assumption that the poor are 'competent', and believes that the problem of poverty is caused by the way in which welfare programmes distort the incentives poor people face. The solution, then, is not to reform the poor, but to abolish welfare programmes. No doubt this view reflects the thinking of some conservatives, but other self-identified conservatives do view the issue in terms similar to Mead's.

15 Collini points out that 'one of the most distinctive features of the political argument of this period (in the late 19th century) seems ... to be the independent and overriding value assigned to the fostering of "character" as a primary aim of politics' (1979: 28). See also Friedman's (1990: ch. 3)

contrast of the nineteenth- and twentieth-century conceptions of freedom and individualism.

REFERENCES

Barr, Nicholas (1992) 'Economic theory and the welfare state'. *Journal of Economic Literature*, 30 (2): 741–803.

Barr, Nicholas (1998) *The Economics of the Welfare State*, 3rd edn. Stanford, CA: Stanford University Press.

Barry, Brian (1990) 'The welfare state versus the relief of poverty'. *Ethics*, 100 (June): 503–29.

Barry, Norman (1999) *Welfare*, 2nd edn. Minneapolis: University of Minnesota Press.

Bartlett, Will, Jennifer Roberts and Julian Le Grand, eds (1998) *A Revolution in Social Policy: Quasi-Market Reforms in the 1990s*. Bristol: Policy.

Bentham, Jeremy (1948 [1823]) *An Introduction to the Principles of Morals and Legislation*. Oxford: Blackwell.

Clarke, John, Allan Cochrane and Carol Smart (1987) *Ideologies of Welfare*. London: Hutchinson.

Collini, Stefan (1979) *Liberalism and Sociology*. Cambridge: Cambridge University Press.

Cowen, Tyler, ed. (1988) *The Theory of Market Failure*. Fairfax, VA: George Mason University Press.

Dworkin, Ronald (2000) *Sovereign Virtue*. Cambridge, MA: Harvard University Press.

Esping-Andersen, Gosta (1985) *Politics against Markets*. Princeton, NJ: Princeton University Press.

Esping-Andersen, Gosta (1990) *Three Worlds of Welfare Capitalism*. Princeton, NJ: Princeton University Press.

Fraser, Nancy (1997) *Justice Interruptus*. New York: Routledge.

Friedman, Lawrence M. (1990) *The Republic of Choice*. Cambridge, MA: Harvard University Press.

Friedman, Milton (1962) *Capitalism and Freedom*. Chicago: University of Chicago Press.

Gaus, Gerald (1998) 'Why all welfare states (including *laissez-faire* ones) are unreasonable'. *Social Philosophy and Policy*, 15 (2): 1–33.

Gewirth, Alan (1978) *Reason and Morality*. Chicago: University of Chicago Press.

Giddens, Anthony (1998) *The Third Way: The Renewal of Social Democracy*. Cambridge: Polity.

Gordon, Linda, ed. (1990) *Women, State, and Welfare*. Madison, WI: University of Wisconsin Press.

Gutmann, Amy, ed. (1988) *Democracy and the Welfare State*. Princeton, NJ: Princeton University Press.

Gutmann, Amy and Dennis Thompson (1996) *Democracy and Disagreement*. Cambridge, MA: Harvard University Press.

Harris, David (1987) *Justifying State Welfare*. Oxford: Blackwell.

Hayek, Friedrich (1960) *The Constitution of Liberty*. Chicago: University of Chicago Press.

Hayek, Friedrich (1976). *The Mirage of Social Justice*. Chicago: University of Chicago Press.

Holmes, Stephen and Cass Sunstein (1999) *The Cost of Rights*. New York: Norton.

Huber, Evelyne and John D. Stephens (2001) *Development and Crisis of the Welfare State*. Chicago: University of Chicago Press.

Kaufman, Franz-Xavier (2001) 'Towards a theory of the welfare state'. In Stephan Leibfried, ed., *Welfare State Futures*. Cambridge: Cambridge University Press.

Lomasky, Loren (1987) *Persons, Rights, and the Moral Community*. New York: Oxford University Press.

Marshall, T. H. (1977 [1950]) 'Citizenship and social class'. In his *Class, Citizenship, and Social Development*. Chicago: University of Chicago Press.

Mayer, Susan (1997) *What Money Can't Buy*. Cambridge, MA: Harvard University Press.

Mead, Lawrence M. (1992) *The New Politics of Poverty*. New York: Basic.

Mead, Lawrence M., ed. (1997) *The New Paternalism*. Washington: Brookings Institution.

Nozick, Robert (1974) *Anarchy, State, and Utopia*. Oxford: Blackwell.

Offe, Claus (1984) *Contradictions of the Welfare State*. Cambridge, MA: MIT Press.

Paul, Ellen, ed. (1997) *The Welfare State*. Cambridge: Cambridge University Press.

Plant, Raymond, H. Lesser and P. Taylor-Gooby (1980) *Political Philosophy and Social Welfare: Essays on the Normative Basis of Welfare Provision*. London: Routledge and Kegan Paul.

Rawls, John (1999) *A Theory of Justice*, rev. edn. Cambridge, MA: Harvard University Press.

Rawls, John (2001) *Justice as Fairness: A Restatement*. Cambridge, MA: Harvard University Press.

Rose, Nikolas (1999) *Powers of Freedom*. Cambridge: Cambridge University Press.

Rothstein, Bo (1998) *Just Institutions Matter*. Cambridge: Cambridge University Press.

Schmidtz, David and Robert Goodin (1998) *Social Welfare and Individual Responsibility*. Cambridge: Cambridge University Press.

Sen, Amartya (1992) *Inequality Reexamined*. Cambridge, MA: Harvard University Press.

Sen, Amartya (1993) 'Capability and well-being'. In Martha Nussbaum and Amartya Sen, eds, *The Quality of Life*. Oxford: Oxford University Press.

Solow, Robert (1998) *Work and Welfare*. Princeton, NJ: Princeton University Press.

Tullock, Gordon, Arthur Seldon and Gordon Brady (2002) *Government Failure: A Primer in Public Choice*. Washington, DC: Cato Institute.

Titmuss, Richard (1972) *The Gift Relationship: From Human Blood to Social Policy*. New York: Random House.

Von Humboldt, Wilhelm (1969) *The Limits of State Action*, ed. and trans. J. W. Burrow. Cambridge: Cambridge University Press.

Van Parijs, Philippe (1995) *Real Freedom for All*. Oxford: Oxford University Press.

Waldron, Jeremy (1993) *Liberal Rights*. Cambridge: Cambridge University Press.

Weale, Albert (1990) 'Equality, social solidarity, and the welfare state'. *Ethics*, 100: 473–88.

Wolfe, Alan (1989) *Whose Keeper? Social Science and Moral Obligation*. Berkeley, CA: University of California Press.

17

Distributive Justice

JULIAN LAMONT

The conceptual terrain produced by modern theories of distributive justice is multi-dimensional. It can be conceived and categorized in many ways. One way to gain insights is to view the different theories according to the importance they afford the competing considerations of welfare (or utility) and responsibility, since the relative importance of these considerations is a constant theme in political discussion throughout the world. At one end of the spectrum, a utilitarian approach to the distributive problem would identify welfare as the only morally relevant consideration in the design of distributive systems, with other moral considerations, including responsibility, entering the calculation not at all, or only in so far as they increase welfare. Alternatively, an approach with responsibility as the primary moral consideration would endeavour to allocate goods and services only on the basis of factors for which individuals are fully responsible. So, for instance, the fact that giving goods to a group would increase their welfare would not be a relevant consideration, but whether that group produced such goods would be. Such an approach would not consider the various levels of welfare different people derive from their goods – that is something for which people themselves are responsible. Furthermore, the distributive institutions under such an approach would be designed to reduce the influence of factors that are the converse of responsibility, those over which people have little or no control (sometimes called luck).

Before examining the different theories of distributive justice, it is important to reflect for a moment on the purpose of developing such theories in the first place. The various positions on offer usually describe idealized distributive systems, which often attract the criticism that such systems could never

be realized – 'they don't apply to the real world' is how the complaint is expressed. This criticism is misguided, as it misconstrues the practical influence of normative theories of distributive justice. These theories should be viewed not as holding out a utopian dream, but as proposing ideals against which the messiness of real-world systems can be understood and evaluated. No society can avoid assessment of its distributive systems, since even the choice not to change the current distributive system is to make the *de facto* evaluation that it is preferable to any available alternative. In fact, though, all real-world distributive systems are in a constant state of change. Changes in the distribution of goods, services, wealth and opportunities are effected by most legislative decisions, at all levels. While there never will be a pure utilitarian, pure Rawlsian, or pure libertarian state, the advocates for these and the other theories of justice surveyed here have a significant role to play in informing the constant changes made to distributive systems: they provide the evaluative tools to assess current systems, with each theorist an advocate for moving current distributive systems in a particular direction for the reasons provided in their theory.

UTILITARIANISM

Over the last couple of centuries, one traditional answer to the question of how the goods and services of a society should be distributed has been that they should be distributed in a way that increases the welfare of the poor. The most common suggestion for achieving this has been through the provision of adequate food, shelter, health and education services. Utilitarianism extends this traditional answer, so that welfare is not simply to be increased, but must be maximized, and for the whole population, not just for the poor. Under utilitarianism, the right distribution is that which maximizes overall welfare, or 'utility', variously interpreted as net positive happiness, preference satisfaction, pleasure, or well-being (Bayles, 1978; Kelly, 1990; Smart and Williams, 1973) [see further Chapters 8 and 30].

Unfortunately, through such extension, the theory makes the requirement to benefit the poor a contingent matter, according to the degree such help will maximize overall welfare. Utilitarians, who tend to accept the diminishing marginal utility of resources, believe resources will tend to produce more good when redistributed to the poor than to the rich. Nevertheless, there are easily describable conditions, such as in the case of a poor but satisfied person and a non-satiated rich person, under which utilitarianism would prescribe forcibly transferring goods from the poor to the rich person. Because of prescriptions such as this, and others, which systematically violate common sense morality (Scheffler, 1988; 1994), the ongoing movement in utilitarian theory, in the last two decades, has been towards variations of 'indirect' and 'institutional' utilitarianism (Bailey, 1997; Goodin, 1988; 1995; Pettit, 1997). The most forceful idea of these theories is to restrict the application of utilitarianism to guide the choice of practices, institutions or public policies rather than to guide individual actions. Such a move ameliorates some of the force of the criticisms from common sense morality. In the case above, for example, even if satisfied poor and non-satiated rich individuals do exist, it is very hard to describe conditions where a general policy of redistributing goods from the poor to the wealthy will definitely increase utility.

The move to indirect and institutional utilitarianism has breathed new life into utilitarian theory, but at a high price. Under institutional utilitarianism, the theoretical criterion for accepting an institution or policy is straightforward: does it maximize the aggregate utility of the population? The problem arises at the practical level, where the information requirements needed to determine which institutions or policies maximize aggregate utility are almost always too great (Gaus, 1998). For example, consider the question of whether institutional utilitarianism would recommend welfare payments to the poor unemployed. This question would be more easily answered if all people obtained the same amount of welfare from all the goods and services available, and if the amount of welfare obtained from a good declined as more of the good is received (that is, if all people had identical diminishing marginal utility functions). Under these conditions we would have some reason to believe that taking goods from the rich and giving them to the poor would increase overall utility. However, every individual has a different utility function and, of course, nobody knows what these functions are. The informational requirements for determining whether utilitarianism recommends welfare payments seem impossible to meet. Unfortunately, the same situation arises for the full range of policies. This problem is compounded by analogues to the common sense morality objections that plagued earlier versions of utilitarianism. For instance, most people in modern liberal democracies strongly believe some policies, such as those that discriminate against racial minorities, are abhorrent, yet even these policies cannot be absolutely ruled out by utilitarianism. While many utilitarians claim that economic or legal discrimination against ethnic minorities will not maximize overall utility, they do not provide the evidence required to support their claims against the populist politicians advocating such policies. Partly, this is due to the complexity of the required evidence, but a further counterintuitive element of the theory is that the consequences, for overall welfare, of discriminatory practices include such contingencies as the size of the ethnic minority and whether the majority has racist beliefs and preferences. Few reasonable people, outside academia, are willing to embrace a theory according to which racist policies and institutions are morally right so long as the ethnic minority is small enough. So substantial stumbling blocks have been encountered in the utilitarian justification for expanding the government's role from improving the welfare of the poor to maximizing overall welfare.

RAWLS

The most influential theory of distributive justice over the last half century has been John Rawls's theory, termed 'justice as fairness'. Rawls develops a rival to utilitarianism, what he saw as the dominant theory of his time (Daniels, 1975; Kukathas and Pettit, 1992; Pogge, 1989; Rawls, 1972; 1993; 2001). Rawls proposes two principles of justice, the first of which guarantees equal basic liberties. His second principle, composed of two parts, governs the distribution of social and economic goods:

Social and economic inequalities are to satisfy two conditions: (a) The Principle of Fair Equality of Opportunity: They are to be attached to positions and offices open to all under conditions of fair equality of opportunity; and (b) The Difference Principle: They are to be to the greatest benefit of the least advantaged members of society. (1993: 5–6)

Though Rawls permits some inequality, he falls clearly on the egalitarian side of the political spectrum. That inequality is permitted under the difference principle at all is a recognition that the *absolute* position of the poor is important, and can sometimes be improved, when greater rewards to some serve as an incentive for increasing the overall social product. When such inequalities are justified, however, the competition for these positions is governed by a substantive, not merely formal, equal opportunity, requiring that 'those equally talented and motivated have the same chances for success' (1972: s.12). Even when this strong version of equal opportunity is achieved, social and economic inequalities are permitted only when they benefit the least advantaged.

Of Rawls's many arguments for his distributive principles, the most interesting is his argument from luck (Rawls, 1972; 2001). The role of the principles of justice in the Rawlsian framework is to constrain the operation of major social and political institutions, such as the system of political rights and obligations, the provision of education and health, the market, and the family. His argument for this is that these institutions significantly affect people's chances in life. These institutions contain inequalities that are present from the start, and hence are not the predictable or deserved consequences of people's actions. So Rawls defends the substantial redistributive measures required by fair equality of opportunity and the difference principle by appeal to elements over which we have no control, which otherwise would be permitted in large part to determine our outcomes. Since Rawls's version of equal opportunity requires that those similarly talented and motivated have the same chances of success, it ideally removes the influence of such social circumstances as economic class and gender or racial discrimination. If redistributive matters ended here, the result would be that not only people's choices, but also the social value of their natural talents and their motivation to work, would still influence their expectations of goods (1972: 72). But Rawls goes on to argue that since one does nothing to deserve one's natural talents or their value to society, and since one's motivation to work is largely determined by family upbringing, these factors can provide no justification for unequal distributive shares: 'Once we are troubled by the influence of either social contingencies or natural chance on the determination of distributive shares, we are bound, on reflection, to be bothered by the influence of the other' (1972: 75).

For these reasons Rawls argues that equality in the distribution of basic liberties, and fair equality of opportunity, are insufficient to constrain morally arbitrary influences in people's starting positions. Therefore, the difference principle is also required

(Barry, 1988; Hill, 1985). The logical progression of Rawls's argument is straightforward. Begin with formal equality of opportunity because nobody should have their life chances fundamentally affected by factors over which they have no control, such as race and gender. Then observe that factors, such as family wealth or access to education, over which people have no control, would still fundamentally affect their life chances. This justifies the move from merely formal to the more substantive fair equality of opportunity, whereby those similarly talented and motivated have the same life chances. Observe, though, that people's life chances are still greatly influenced by factors over which they have little or no control, such as their degree of natural talent or intelligence, and the type of family support they are given. Since these impediments to equal opportunity are practically impossible to overcome, an additional governing principle is required, the difference principle. It does not eliminate the influence of luck on life chances, but it does provide compensation for those least advantaged: the basic structure of society is organized so that, in absolute terms, their life prospects are maximized relative to any alternative structure. In Rawls's theory, then, we get one of the most powerful arguments, based on luck, for aiding the poorest in a society.

REFLECTIVE EQUILIBRIUM AND EMPIRICAL BELIEFS

It is worthwhile to digress briefly from considering substantive theories of distributive justice to consider one of the most common methodologies for evaluating different theories. The method of reflective equilibrium in moral and political philosophy has strong analogies with the scientific method of theory evaluation. The main differences are that instead of observations and experiments, we have moral judgements and thought experiments. The idea is to develop moral principles that cohere with our considered 'lower level' moral judgements (Rawls, 1993: 8). Under the methodology, when proposed principles do not cohere with our moral judgements, we may modify or reject the principles, or choose to give up some of our moral judgements in favour of those principles with especially good explanatory power for our other judgements. Also, thought experiments can be used to decide between two theories that have similar recommendations over everyday domains. The ideal is that these adjustments are made until eventually our theories and our considered moral judgements are in equilibrium (Daniels, 1996).

This methodology can be understood as operating both at the personal level and at the level of the wider community. Theorists, the general population, and hopefully politicians, engage in a collective cognitive process through discussion and debate in order to come up with principles and policies to better cohere with the moral judgements and beliefs of the people. Of course, theorists can achieve such an equilibrium only by finding out what people believe (Miller, 1999: chs 3–4; Swift et al., 1995). Fortunately, over the last couple of decades, there has been a sustained effort to collect the data necessary to this project (Elster, 1995; Hochschild, 1981; Kluegel and Smith, 1986; Miller, 1999).

David Miller (1999: ch. 4) has surveyed the empirical studies, partly summarizing the findings as follows:

> in people's thinking about social distribution, [there is] a tendency to favour more equality than presently exists in liberal democracies. This is partly to be explained by considerations of desert and need: people do not regard income inequalities of the size that currently obtain as deserved, and at the bottom of the scale they think it unfair that people cannot earn enough to meet their needs. (1999: 91)

In a series of experiments conducted to see what distributive principles people would choose, Frohlich and Oppenheimer (1992) presented the subjects with four principles for distributing income: (1) maximizing the average income, (2) maximizing the minimum income, (3) maximizing the average subject to a floor constraint (no income to fall below x), and (4) maximizing the average subject to a range constraint (the gap between top and bottom incomes not to exceed y). Maximizing the average subject to a floor constraint (or safety net) was chosen by the vast majority of individuals, while maximizing the average was a distant second. The alternative used to gauge support for the difference principle – maximizing the minimum income – had very little support. So while Rawls (1993: 8) popularized the theory of reflective equilibrium, his own theory of distributive justice gains little support from it. Some critics of his difference principle provide one reason for this. Although the argument, outlined above, for the difference principle gives moral weight to reducing the influence of factors over which people have no control, it gives little positive weight to choice and responsibility. Under the difference principle, the social structure is designed to maximize the position of the least advantaged group (characterized by Rawls, 1972: 97, as the bottom socio-economic quartile), no matter what choices individual members of that group have made. If the general public has a stronger view of the moral weight that should be given to responsibility, as Samuel Scheffler (1992) has argued they do, then the degree of support the public believes is owed to the disadvantaged will depend on whether the disadvantage is due to a disability, a lack of motivation, or an individual lifestyle choice. Such considerations have influenced resource egalitarians and desert theorists, whose theories we consider next.

RESOURCE EGALITARIANISM

Influenced by Rawls's natural arbitrariness argument, but even more sensitive than Rawls to what is and what is not a matter of luck, are the resource egalitarians. Since the rejection of slavery, feudalism, and aristocracy, one point of agreement among contemporary theorists has been that equality, in some sense, is a necessary part of any plausible theory of justice. Disagreements arise, however, in articulating the sense in which equality matters, or in specifying what is to be distributed equally (Sen, 1980). In answer to this question, a number of thinkers have promoted equality of resources, usually because they believe in both equality and in responsibility, seeking to hold individuals responsible for the choices they make in using their resources (Cohen, 1989; Dworkin, 2000; Sen, 1980). By the same token, however, they believe that social institutions should be designed to prevent inequalities resulting from factors beyond individuals' control. They also recognize that an equal distribution of material goods does not achieve equality of resources, because people's unequal genetic endowments are also important resources. Thus, they tend to argue for some kind of compensation to individuals who are unlucky in the natural lottery, to achieve a genuinely equal distribution of resources (Roemer, 1985).

An important question for any theory of distributive justice is how to measure or compare individuals' positions or shares of goods. A key insight of the resource theorist is that individuals' overall positions relative to others depend not only on their shares of social or economic goods, but on their natural endowments. One with severe disabilities, for example, may need more money or more educational opportunity to reach the same level of well-being as others. Thus, even if egalitarian in its motivation, a theory which fails to take into account people's natural endowments in the measurement of distributive shares will not, according to the resource theorist, achieve a genuinely egalitarian result. The key question for resource theorists, and what determines differences among them, is which endowments are natural, and which are the result of one's own choices. A paraplegic injured in an unavoidable accident is disadvantaged relative to others even with the same social and economic goods, so a resource theorist would favour their having a larger share. However, a lack of skill resulting from the preference to play rather than work does not entitle one to any compensation in economic resources. The resource theorist's aim is to include natural endowments as resources, and distribute the social and economic goods in such a way as to ensure that people are compensated only for bad luck, not for the consequences of their own choices.

The most prominent resource-based theory, developed by Ronald Dworkin (2000), proposes that people begin with equal resources but end up with unequal economic benefits as a result of exercising their capacity to choose [see further Chapter 30]. Dworkin's method is to determine justice in material distributions by way of imagining the behaviour of reasonable people at a hypothetical auction. He asks us to suppose that everyone is given equal purchasing power with which to bid, in a fair auction, for resources best suited to their life plans. They are then permitted to use those resources as they see fit. In addition, Dworkin supposes that before bidding, people do not know their own natural endowments or the value and distribution of these in society. They can, however, contribute payments to an insurance pool to compensate those who are unlucky in the 'natural lottery', thereby protecting themselves from this sort of disadvantage. Although people are likely to finish with different economic benefits, they have been treated equally, since they began with equal resources and total freedom to bid for other resource bundles had they wished.

The hope of Dworkin and other resource theorists is that institutions can be designed with this hypothetical ideal in mind: individuals enjoy the fruit of, or bear the burden of, their choices, but the negative impact of luck is shared by society, unless individuals choose to face the risk alone. Though this ideal is plausible, its full implementation in a real economy requires what now seems impossible: the measurement of differences in people's natural talents. There is no philosophical or empirical agreement about which talents are natural, the result of individuals' choices, or largely influenced by social factors beyond an individual's control. A system of special assistance to the physically and mentally handicapped and to the ill would be a partial implementation of Dworkin's compensation system, but most natural inequalities would be untouched by these measures. Despite its theoretical advantages, therefore, it is difficult to see 'equality of resources' as a practical improvement on the difference principle, at least until there are answers to these implementation questions.

As Allen Buchanan argues, however, the theoretical aims of the resource theorist movement may become more practically relevant as scientific knowledge and technological advancement in the area of genetics grow. The human genome project is likely to affect our ideals regarding distributive justice in a number of fundamental ways. First, as we gain more knowledge of people's genetic probabilities, we are more likely to pass judgement about what is and what is not a matter of choice or luck. We may also expect others to make responsible choices in light of this information. Second, much of what is now seen as one's 'natural' endowments may come to be seen as subject to human intervention and so part of the social institutions to which principles of justice apply. If our likelihood of facing certain illnesses or disabilities depends not entirely on luck or genetic makeup, but also on the way in which access to and use of appropriate technologies is regulated, and whether we choose to make use of these, then this changes the scope of what is natural and what is social. Thus, advances in genetic technology have the potential to change where the line is drawn between what is a matter of luck, what is a matter of choice, and what is a matter of social responsibility, so that the previous array of theoretical positions may have very different implications in the social context of the coming century (Buchanan et al., 2001).

DESERT THEORIES

Like resource egalitarians, desert theorists (Pojman and McLeod, 1998) emphasize responsibility and the minimization of the influence of factors over which people have little control. Their primary moral notion is not equality, however, as it is in resource egalitarianism, but the notion of deserving (though desert theories normally require a background of equal opportunity). Desert theorists seek to correct Rawls's failure to appreciate the extent to which individuals are responsible for, and hence deserving of, the fruits of their labour (Miller, 1976; 1989; 1999; Sher, 1987; Sterba, 1980). They argue that the role of luck in determining our success is not significant enough to undermine a legitimate class of claims to deserve greater distributive shares on the basis of greater effort or a more valuable contribution towards the social product (Lamont, 1994; McLeod, 1996; Miller, 1999; Richards, 1986; Sher, 1987). Central to the theories is the ideal of people as agents who have the capacity to choose responsibly for themselves. People exercise this capacity to influence others' treatment of them and to act in ways that bring into the world goods and services that others find valuable.

Desert theories differ about what should be the basis for desert claims. The three main categories are:

1 *Productivity*. People should be rewarded for their work activity with the product of their labour or value thereof (Gaus, 1990: 410–16, 485–9; Miller, 1976; 1989; 1999; Riley, 1989).
2 *Effort*. People should be rewarded according to the effort they expend in contributing to the social product (Sadurski, 1985).
3 *Compensation*. People should be rewarded according to the costs they voluntarily incur in contributing to the social product (Carens, 1981; Dick, 1975; Feinberg, 1970; Lamont, 1997).

Desert theorists in each category also differ about the relationship between luck and desert. All desert theorists hold that there are reasons to design institutions so that many of the gross vagaries of luck are reduced, but theorists diverge with respect to luck in the genetic lottery. For instance, advocates of effort or compensation reject productivity as a desert basis on the grounds that people's productivity is too influenced by luck in the genetic lottery.

Desert theories have been relatively less prominent, over the last 40 years, than other theories discussed in this chapter. This is peculiar given the frequent usage of the notion of deserving in everyday language. As noted earlier, over the last two decades there has been an enormous increase in empirical data regarding people's beliefs about justice. The data reveal that desert is one of the most common moral notions that people, across many societies, use to justify and/or criticize economic distributions, but many contemporary theories ignore or dismiss the concept (Miller, 1999: ch. 4). The reason for this can most easily be illustrated by comparing desert and utilitarian theories of distribution. Desert theorists, because of their emphasis on outcomes being tied to people's responsibility rather than their luck, view with concern how much people's level of economic benefits still depends significantly on factors beyond their control. By contrast, utilitarians consider this of no moral consequence since, for them, the only morally relevant characteristic of any distribution is the utility resulting from it. This gap between the desert and utilitarian theorists, and hence between the general public and utilitarian theorists, is partly attributable to differences in empirical views. Desert theorists are much more likely to view people as significantly responsible for their actions and want to give effect to that responsibility by reducing the degree to which people's life prospects are influenced by factors beyond their control. Utilitarians are more likely to see people as largely the products of their natural and social environment, and so not responsible for many of their actions in the first place. On the latter view, the point of reducing the effect of luck is less attractive. But, as Scheffler (1992) points out, the general population has a noticeably more robust view of the responsibility of people than many academic theorists. For this reason, he thinks certain theories of distributive justice, such as utilitarianism, have, over recent decades, been seen by the population as irrelevant. In contrast, the ability of desert theorists to give direct recommendations about contemporary institutional design, and the general public's receptiveness to appeals to desert, are combining to effect a resurgence in this area of distributive justice research.

LIBERTARIANISM

In contrast to the theories so far presented, libertarian theories deny the relevance, for distributive justice, of both luck and utility. In terms of the political institutions affecting distributive justice, libertarians (also known as classical liberals or right libertarians) typically recommend that in ideally just conditions goods and services be distributed in a free market with minimal state intervention, redistributive measures and protectionism [see further Chapter 9]. These recommendations are usually based on what libertarians see as the normative implications of property rights and liberty (Kukathas, 2003; Lomasky, 1987; Machan, 1989; Machan and Rasmussen, 1995; Narveson, 1989; Nozick, 1974). The starting point for libertarians' strong interpretation of property rights is commonly self-ownership. The most influential libertarian, Robert Nozick (1974), argues that since people own their natural endowments and their labour power, and since they freely exercise these in various ways, they are entitled to the fruits of their labour. Even though outcomes are not justified according to desert (and hence may be the result of luck), Nozick rejects Rawls's description of them as morally arbitrary, since self-ownership gives rise to entitlements (1974; ch. 7). Compensation for the influence of luck has no place in the Nozickean conception of justice, nor do any government measures to improve the lives of people or to relieve human suffering. Aid to the less fortunate must result from the individual voluntary actions of others.

Libertarian theories proposing minimal states on the basis of self-ownership have generally encountered two stumbling blocks internal to the theories themselves (Haworth, 1994). One is in defending the argument that self-ownership implies unequal and nearly absolute property rights. Critics of libertarianism are more disturbed with the unequal ownership of material goods and natural resources than with self-ownership *per se*. The problem of how ownership of oneself extends out to ownership of natural resources has plagued all ownership-based libertarian theories. Nozick tried unsuccessfully to justify the acquisition of natural resources with a version of the 'first come, first served' principle. Such principles, whereby people can acquire unequal natural resources to the detriment of, and against the will of, others, including future generations, are implausible for determining the use of natural resources. The issue of how to solve this problem continues to be a fertile area for research and has been the source of a resurgence in 'left libertarianism' with its emphasis on material guarantees for the disadvantaged (Cohen, 1995; Reeve and Williams, 2003; Steiner, 1994; Steiner and Vallentyne, 2000a; 2000b; Van Parijs, 1995), but the most plausible suggestions regarding ownership of natural resources appear unlikely to yield the minimal state political systems normally associated with libertarianism.

The second problem internal to ownership-based libertarianism is what to do about past injustices. Libertarianism is widely interpreted as advocating a change to a *laissez-faire* system with government functions limited to minimal taxes for police, defence, and a court system. This interpretation, however, is a mistake for the majority of libertarian theories. Although right libertarians do believe such minimal government is ideal when there has been no injustice, current holdings of goods and land are not morally legitimate under libertarianism if they have come about as a result of past injustices. Given that such past injustices are systemic to any current society, libertarians have difficulty justifying any move towards a more minimal state, unless they can specify some way of recognizing and rectifying past injustices first. As Nozick noted with his own theory:

> In the absence of [a full treatment of the principle of rectification] applied to a particular society, one cannot use the analysis and theory presented here to condemn any particular scheme of transfer payments, unless it is clear that no considerations of rectification of injustice could apply to justify it. (1974: 231)

The treatment Nozick requires, however, is simply beyond our capabilities. We know every existing society is systematically infected with past injustice including theft and forcible seizure of natural resources. So, for instance, even if we could discover all the ways in which the majority of natural resources were unjustly acquired, we have no way of knowing what the distribution would look like if the injustices had not occurred. A theory can make a serious contribution to ongoing debate and policy only if it can offer a realistic proposal for rectifying past injustice, or if there are other resources in the theory for recommending distributive principles which do not depend on an entirely clean slate. The problem seems particularly damning to ownership or property rights versions of right libertarianism,

though, because the theory recommends a near absolute respect for property rights over all other moral considerations. These strong property rights are implausible if infected with past injustice, but the theory has little to offer for addressing the past injustice problem.

The more fruitful arguments for libertarianism are based on the value of liberty itself. The most famous twentieth-century champion of such arguments was Friedrich Hayek (1944; 1976a; 1976b), though there are many varieties, often inspired by John Stuart Mill's essay *On Liberty* (1982). This group of libertarians have responded to critics with greater depth. To see this, consider two of the more general criticisms of libertarianism (Haworth, 1994). First, critics complain that libertarianism excludes state measures to improve the lives of the people, including the provision of public goods (Morris, 1998: ch. 9; Van Parijs, 1995). Second, libertarianism is also charged with preventing state measures to alleviate deprivation and suffering. Most ownership-based libertarian theories have failed to respond to the first criticism, parting company at this point with neoclassical economists, who have generally taken the public goods problem more seriously than political libertarians. The most common responses to the second criticism have been various versions of 'tough luck': while it might be nice if individuals transfer some of their property rights to others in order to relieve suffering, people cannot justly be coerced to do so. Nozick's view, for instance, is that respect for people's absolute property rights is more important than improving the lot of the least fortunate. The harshness of this reply has been unappealing to the majority in liberal democracies.

Millean and Hayekian versions of libertarianism have been able to provide more fruitful replies, by appealing more directly to the values of liberty and autonomy (Lomasky, 1987). People's optimism about the government's ability to aid and empower people grew in the first 60 years of the twentieth century, but stalled in the late 1960s and the 1970s. Greater government intervention in the economy, particularly to increase welfare in the general population rather than just for the most needy, proved considerably less successful than preceding interventions targeted only to the poor. Hayek's explanation for this failure was that governments do not, and never will, have the information required for successful intervention to help the majority of the population. In agreement, Mill's view was that individuals themselves are in the best informational position for improving their own situation, so the government should allow them the liberty to act upon it. To suppose that governments improve the lives of the destitute by providing adequate food and shelter is a much simpler and more plausible matter than to suppose governments improve the lives of the middle class by taxing and spending for their own good. These forms of libertarianism do not in principle oppose state measures to alleviate suffering or to provide public goods, but are merely sceptical of governments' ability successfully to carry out such functions. They differ about the income level at which governments no longer have sufficient information to intervene effectively in people's lives, and they differ on what level and type of public goods governments have enough knowledge to provide efficiently.

A related contribution of Millean and Hayekian libertarianism is to highlight the costs of government intervention. While the increase in government intervention in liberal democracies in the first half of the twentieth century enjoyed widespread support and success, the increase in the size of government was not without costs. With the increase in government size came an increase in regulation, only some of which was beneficial. Much regulation primarily served the interests of bureaucracies, while decreasing individuals' autonomy. Public choice theorists, inspired by libertarians such as James Buchanan (Brennan and Buchanan, 1985; Buchanan and Tullock, 1962; Buchanan, 1975; Rowley et al., 1988), also argued forcefully that increasing government size substantially increases rent-seeking by lobby groups, professions, and other powerful groups, distorting economic distribution in their favour. Once these and other consequences are taken into account, the success of government interventions in realizing their intended benefits is quite uncertain, compared with the clear and demonstrable detrimental effects these interventions have on people's liberty and autonomy. Hence, as one of their most important ongoing contributions, libertarians have argued the possible benefits need to be very large, or their realization very certain, for the policies to be justified.

The third ongoing contribution of libertarian-inspired theories is in the area of relations between nations. The economic success of both the North American Free Trade Agreement and the European Economic Union have increased the momentum towards global free trade. Although various other liberal theorists have also supported free trade, libertarians have usually been its most vocal advocates. One of the main areas for discussion and research arises from the fact that a reduction in barriers to trade or immigration typically causes upward pressure on the wages/employment of workers in Third World countries and downward pressure on the wages/employment of workers in equivalent First World industries. Moreover, the effect is most pronounced with respect to low wage occupations such as agricultural and labour-intensive manufacturing workers in First World countries.

Libertarians argue that keeping trade barriers up in order to protect low wage workers in First World countries makes much poorer people in Third World countries worse off. The poorer people's liberty to engage in consensual trade with consumers in First World countries is restricted, thereby denying them an important means of improving their economic well-being (Lomasky, 2001).

This issue arises as a result of technological advances that have overcome distance, leading to economic globalization and with it the capacity of countries and corporations, through their policies and actions, dramatically to influence the freedom and well-being of people around the globe. So far, the question has been framed in the libertarian context in terms of restricted liberty. However, the same question can instead be framed in terms of who is the proper subject of distributive justice concerns: is restricting the economic liberties of much poorer people in other societies a legitimate means to increasing the economic well-being of the poor at home? Indeed, put this way, the question is crucial to all the theories discussed so far. Whether the justification for distributive institutions in a society is based on beneficence, the arbitrariness of luck, egalitarian concerns, self-ownership, or freedom, theorists need to address whether the scope of the theory should be local, national, or global. Peter Singer (2002), for example, asks whether political leaders should see their role as promoting the interests of their own citizens or whether they should be concerned with the welfare of people everywhere. This question is connected to the more general problem of partiality/impartiality in moral theory: are we morally permitted or even sometimes required to give priority to the interests of one's own citizens, or indeed to one's own family (Barry, 1995; Friedman, 1989; 1991)? Thomas Pogge argues from a position of moral universalism to the conclusion that the standard attitude of recognizing greater obligations to alleviate the conditions of the poor or oppressed at home than those of the poor abroad counts as arbitrary discrimination (Pogge, 2001a; 2001b; Jones, 1999). In one form or another, this question is crucial for all distributive justice theories. Ever increasing globalization will require greater attention to this area of research in each of the theories [see further Chapter 22].

ALTERNATIVE CHARACTERIZATIONS

So far the major theories discussed have been characterized mainly according to the content of their approach to the moral demands of welfare (or luck) and responsibility. It is important to note here some of the complications of these characterizations and also other ways of conceptualizing the distributive justice literature. Most theorists are accurately described by a number of non-equivalent labels. The classifications used here are widespread in the contemporary literature, but there are nevertheless subtle differences in the ways different authors use these labels.

One important distinction is between the content of a distributive principle, and its justification. 'Content' refers to the distribution ideally recommended by a principle, whereas 'justification' refers to the reasons given in support of the principle. Theorists can be distinguished and labelled according to the content of their theory or according to the justification they give. The classifications used in this chapter have been divided according to the content but they could have been divided, though somewhat more messily, according to their justifications.

The messiness comes from two sources. First, the common labels used here refer sometimes to the content and other times to the justifications for various positions. Second, most groups of theories have justifications from a number of different sources and single writers even will sometimes use more than one source of justification for their theory. Most combinations of content and justification, in fact, have been tried. For instance, different libertarians use natural rights, desert, utilitarianism or contractarianism in the justification of their theories; different desert theorists use natural rights, contractarianism and even utilitarianism (Mill, 1877; Sidgwick, 1890). Partly this comes about because there are different versions of justifications which nevertheless, due to some similarity, share the same broad label. For instance, contractarianism features in the justifications of many theories, and covers both Hobbesian and Kantian contractarians, after Thomas Hobbes and Immanuel Kant (Hampton, 1991). Hobbesian contractarians, such as David Gauthier, attempt to justify morality in terms of the *self-interested* reasons individuals have for agreeing to certain terms of social co-operation. Kantian contractarians, such as John Rawls, appeal to *moral* reasons to justify the terms of social co-operation that would be worthy of consent, usually arguing for distributions on the egalitarian end of the spectrum. A Hobbesian contractarian, as you might suspect, is more likely to argue for libertarian oriented systems (Buchanan, 1982; Gauthier, 1987; Levin, 1982). However, there are also followers of Hobbes who insist his contractarianism is better read to justify some important aspects of the welfare state, rather than a merely minimalist government (Kavka, 1986; Morris, 1998: ch. 9; Vallentyne, 1991). So theorists who share the 'contractarian' label may also be characterized by a libertarian rejection of redistribution or an egalitarian

insistence on widespread distribution [see further Chapter 8].

The most common alternatives to characterizing distributive justice theories along the dimensions of welfare and responsibility have been to characterize them either along the related dimension of equality, or according to the degree of egalitarianism the theories prescribe. So each of the theories already surveyed here could alternatively be categorized according to its treatment, or approach, to equality (Joseph and Sumption, 1979; Rakowski, 1991). In his influential lecture 'Equality of what?' (1980), Amartya Sen addresses the question of what metric egalitarians should use to determine the degree to which a society realizes the ideal of equality. In his lecture, Sen was addressing a debate over two candidate metrics, welfare (or utility) on the one hand, and Rawlsian primary goods on the other. At issue between these were questions about the extent to which the welfare metric unfairly caters to morally wrongful preferences or expensive tastes. Between these extremes, Sen introduced 'capability equality', where capabilities refer to what various goods do for people, apart from the welfare they achieve (Sen, 1985; 1987). This introduced another variable into the 'equality of what' literature which had been dominated by arguments between equality of outcome and equality of opportunity advocates (for more recent contributions see Bowie, 1988). A range of alternative variables for what should be equalized have since been introduced (Daniels, 1990) and refined, including the resource egalitarians discussed above (Dworkin, 2000), equal opportunity for welfare (Arneson, 1989; 1990; 1991), equal access to advantage (Cohen, 1989), and equal political status (Anderson, 1999).

In arguing for equal political status, Elizabeth Anderson (1999), in contrast to Rawls, resource egalitarians, and desert theorists, criticizes the prominence placed on luck and choice in the contemporary distributive justice literature. Even though she supports egalitarian ideals, the point of equality, in her view, is not to compensate for different amounts of luck, but to express an ideal of political equality in which all members of the citizenry are publicly recognized as equally valuable and of equal status. Redistribution might be required to ensure public institutions effectively express political equality, but equality in the distribution of resources, whether to rule out luck or to hold people responsible for their choices, is not, according to Anderson, the primary or even legitimate aim of liberal redistributive institutions. Anderson's arguments align her to a significant degree with a number of other political theorists, including communitarians and some feminists, who argue for the primacy of political recognition and equality over the more directly material policies of many other theorists. One of the challenges for this group is to give the details of the policies designed to give effect to their theories. Once this is done, others will be in a much better position to evaluate the substance of their proposals. For instance, if the material policies designed to give effect to political recognition and equality turned out to be substantially similar to the theories with which they were supposed to contrast, then they would be considerably less interesting. If, however, they rejected the distributive policies of many other theories, then that would be an interesting contrast likely to provoke ground-breaking debate. But until such detail is given, proper evaluation is difficult.

Another approach not canvassed in detail here has been to explore the notion of fairness more fully. Some of the earliest discussions of distributive justice involved claims of fairness with respect to the division of profits between labour and capital. This work has continued as an important part of the political economy literature on distributive justice. In recent times it has moved away from Marxist theories with state controlled socialism to market socialism (Le Grand and Estrin, 1989; Ollman, Lawler and Ticktin, 1998; Pranab, Bardhan and Roemer, 1997; Roemer and Wright, 1996). For socialists the motivation for this move has been to embrace the virtues of the market mechanism for the allocation of resources while avoiding the vices of capitalism (Arnold, 1995).

Another approach to fairness, favoured by economists, has developed in the context of modern game theory. The most common strategy is to introduce an 'envy-free' requirement: a distribution is deemed fair when none of the relevant parties to the distribution are envious of others' allocations. This and related notions of fairness are commonly applied to 'microjustice' issues which arise in more everyday or localized situations rather than distribution for the whole society (Baumol, 1986; Brams and Taylor, 1996; Le Grand, 1991; Varian, 1975; Young, 1994). The difficulties these theories face is to specify real allocations satisfying the envy-free criterion, but which do not achieve this by unreasonable extensions of our everyday notion of being envy-free. Despite these difficulties, some theorists have extended the analysis within the broader context of bargaining theory to deal with the traditional problems of distributive justice (Barry, 1989; Binmore, 1994; 1998; Zajac, 1995). This trend is likely to continue in the future with more engagement between economists, political theorists and philosophers.

Another complication worth noting, in presenting a comprehensive classification of theories, comes from differences in how the very topic of distributive justice itself is conceived, with some theorists emphasizing process rather than content or justification. For the most part, the theories discussed so far address the question of distributive justice by recommending principles intended as normative ideals for institutions, which themselves will significantly determine the distribution of resources. These theories reflect progress and a growing consensus throughout most of the twentieth century about what is not acceptable. For example, all of the theories on offer reject the inequalities characteristic in feudal, aristocratic, and slave societies, as well as the inequalities inherent in systems that restrict access to goods, services, jobs or positions on the basis of race, gender, ethnicity or religion. However, there remains a large area of reasonable disagreement about which is the best theory, with all theories offering some good reasons and some problematic consequences. In the context of such disagreement, philosophical argument can continue to guide reasoned public debate and democratic decision-making towards building public institutions which instantiate one or some combination of the proposed theories.

On the other hand, some theorists believe that the ongoing existence of reasonable disagreement reflects importantly on the very nature of distributive justice. They argue that, within the area of *reasonable* disagreement about what are the best distributive ideals, the additional questions to examine are whether the processes for deciding distributive questions are just. So, some argue that certain distributive justice issues should be dealt with at the constitutional level, variously described, while other issues are properly decided at the legislative level. A subgroup of these theorists also take the view that some decisions about distributive justice issues can be partly or fully justified because they are the result of a just process (Christiano, 1996; Gaus, 1996). Rational argument alone may be able to exclude some systems as unjust, but others will be justified not simply on the grounds of their content, but also by the process by which they were reached. This view does not exclude content-based argument but adds that process-based arguments will also be essential for the ongoing project of distributive justice in contemporary society.

CHALLENGES TO LIBERAL DISTRIBUTIVE THEORIES

Most of the theories of distributive justice discussed so far are properly seen as embedded in liberal theories that also answer questions broader than the concerns of distributive justice. So, for instance, Rawls's difference principle and equality of opportunity principle have their place in a broader theory in which the first principle is equal basic liberty for all. 'Liberalism' or a 'liberal position' usually indicates an emphasis on individual liberty. That is, government institutions are thought by liberal philosophers to work in the interests of individuals, as opposed to groups defined by ethnicity, geographic location, community identity, gender, or class. The rights and obligations defended by liberals are held by individuals. Usually, these include political institutions which protect a set of civil liberties, such as free speech, freedom of thought and of religion, freedom of association, a free press, due process under the law, etc. Liberals usually also believe that the freedom of individuals entails that government institutions be 'neutral', in the sense that the government is not in the business of promoting or discouraging particular views, religions, lifestyles, or conceptions of the good, except where this is required to protect the basic liberties of individuals (Hampton, 1997: 170–81; Nussbaum, 1999).

Within this framework, as we have seen, liberals divide on questions of distribution. Classical liberals generally favour minimal government involvement in the marketplace, or in other distributive institutions, such as those that distribute education or health care. These theorists commonly argue for their positions by reference to the value of individual liberty, and they see government interference as a threat to, rather than a protector of, liberty. Welfare liberals, at the other end of the spectrum, view markedly unequal distributive outcomes as, among other things, a threat to individual liberty. They argue for government involvement in the marketplace and in the delivery of important resources such as health care or education, in order to limit the degree of inequality that might emerge from the unhampered pursuit of individual liberty (Hampton, 1997: 172).

In addition to these content positions, 'liberalism' sometimes refers to a kind of methodology whereby arguments are crafted largely *a priori*, abstracting away from the particular history, culture, or empirical conditions associated with a particular society. Such arguments might appeal to human nature, universal characteristics of persons, or *a priori* reasons, and might even idealize, referring to ideal conditions or ideal persons which are only hypothetical but nevertheless generate an ideal principle to guide our necessarily imperfect institutions (Buchanan et al., 2000: 371–82). 'Contractarianism', 'rights-based' theories, and 'utilitarianism' are all, in different ways, examples of justifications of this type.

The ideals that liberals specify are proposed as constraints on the development and operation of cultures; they are viewed as a way to ensure that cultures develop freely and justly. They do not, for the most part, employ a methodology that takes distributive ideals to arise from specific cultural practices, or historical struggles specific to a community. In this respect, communitarians and postmodern theorists have objected to the methodology of liberalism as abstract, individualistic, universalistic, and anti-democratic (MacIntyre, 1984; Mulhall and Swift, 1996; Sandel, 1982; Walzer, 1983). Communitarians and feminists have also questioned the nature of persons and autonomy that is the celebrated core of liberalism. Communitarians see individuals as largely the products of culture, rather than as autonomous individuals who choose freely by exercising an objective capacity to reason (Mulhall and Swift, 1996; Taylor, 1985a; 1985b). The dialogue growing out of the communitarian critique, along with the response of Rawls and other liberals, has coincided with political movements in Western democracies to respond to the myriad of issues raised by the realities of multiculturalism and feminism [see further Chapter 19]. This body of literature discusses justice as much in terms of cultural recognition as in terms of resource distribution (Taylor, 1994; Willet, 1998).

Communitarians oppose the methodology, but not necessarily the content, of liberalism. They represent a range of positions that specify a methodology, a style of justification, and a theory of the nature of persons. Communitarians, along with Marxists, emphasize the relevance of the particular history, culture, class struggles, and community interests to the content and justification of distributive principles. Hence, they tend to be moral relativists. A communitarian liberal, then, such as Michael Walzer (1983), is someone who, for some particular society, will argue for liberal institutions on communitarian grounds. One clear strand in the communitarian critique is the claim that whatever principles are proposed from a liberal-style methodology will be too vague and abstract to be of any practical use, and at the same time, that they will tend to be oppressive in so far as they ignore the ideals actually arising from real political and cultural histories (Fisk, 1989; Walzer, 1983; Willet, 1998; Young, 2000). Theorizing about distributive justice, for these thinkers, must be largely empirical and relativistic.

Of the communitarian philosophers, Michael Walzer (1983) is perhaps the most specific in proposing a methodology for arriving at just distributive principles. For Walzer, criteria for the just distribution of goods in a society are relative both to the particular goods in question and to the particular society's values and understandings of those goods. Walzer argues that goods such as political membership, market commodities, education, health care, prestige, political office, professional expertise, or income are always understood and interpreted in a social context. Different societies have different meanings, understandings, and values associated with these goods. The particular meanings of the goods, moreover, determine their proper distribution. So social meanings of goods give rise to distributive principles valid only in a given society, within the sphere of those goods. Injustice occurs when the distributive criteria for one good are allowed to encroach on the sphere of another (Walzer, 1983). For example, if a given society's interpretation of health care is that it should be distributed according to need, then injustice occurs when health care becomes inaccessible to the needy ill and available only to those who have money, or talent, or fame. Similarly, if a particular society's interpretation of education is that it should be distributed equally or according to merit, then injustice occurs when it is in fact distributed according to wealth or social connection (Gutmann, 1980).

However, no argument for the injustice of such distributions of health care or education can be given independently of a particular society's views, histories, and culture. Walzer's claim is that the philosopher's attempt to derive distributive criteria for abstract goods from abstract reasons is 'undemocratic'. Democracy, for Walzer, requires that real people base principles on their actual views, whatever they are, in deliberation with others. The outcome of the deliberation and democratic struggle will be principles reflecting compromises arising from the actual historical processes of each society, and there is no reason to expect much similarity from culture to culture in the resulting ideals (Fisk, 1989). The right way to distribute the goods will depend only on the requirement that all members of the society actually participate in a manner free of dominance in the development of the principles. Thus, Walzer himself goes so far as to say that even a caste system, where people's positions of birth determine their access to a whole range of social goods, is permissible, so long as the social meanings inherent in the caste system are genuinely shared by the society (Mulhall and Swift, 1996: 140). Of course, no such systems in the real world are genuinely embraced by everyone in society, raising questions as to what constitutes a 'shared' culture or community, and how to resolve disagreements within them. Walzer recognizes the reality of disagreement in communities, but insists the resolution of disagreements must take place within the specific historical and shared cultural context. The consequence of this, he argues, is that there can be no reference to hypothetical or objective abstract ideals, independent of the particular community's standards, in resolving the disagreements or in determining the institutional methods and procedures for resolving disagreements [see further Chapters 13 and 30].

Where there is genuine disagreement within a culture, what within the communitarian theory ensures that voices of criticism and dissent will not be drowned by the dominant, possibly oppressive, culture? If there are no independent normative standards for defining oppression, and if even the points of view of dissenting individuals are secondary to the normative primacy of cultures, how can any cultures be shown oppressive on the communitarian view? Jean Hampton is one liberal theorist who believes communitarian theories lack the theoretical resources needed to answer these questions: in her words, communitarian theories lack 'critical moral distance' (1997: 188). Whether communitarians can answer this complaint in a distinctive way will determine the success of communitarian theory as a viable alternative to liberalism, and will also determine, more broadly, the success of cultural relativism for distributive justice.

Perhaps the most significant distributive change of the twentieth century has occurred as a result of the feminist movement, yet it is surprisingly unclear whether this movement is best classified as an extension of, or a rejection of, liberalism. Certainly the so-called first wave of feminism, in which the focus was primarily on securing for women equal rights in the areas of education, work, pay, and political participation, seemed to extend liberal rights. The theoretical underpinnings of this movement were largely liberal in character, as evidenced in such classic works as Mary Wollstonecraft's *A Vindication of the Rights of Women* (1995) and John Stuart Mill's *The Subjection of Women* (1979), in which feminism is presented as a natural implication of liberalism. However, feminists have also developed their views under Marxist, socialist, communitarian, postmodern, or radical frameworks, and have proposed creative and novel positions modelled on the distinctive reasoning and nurturing associated with relationships, especially the relationship between mother and child (Jaggar, 1983; Tong, 1989; 1993).

The feminist field has been unprecedented in its diversity, yet remarkably a common theme has emerged, usually expressed under the motto 'the personal is political'. These feminists argue that liberal theories of distributive justice are unable to address oppression which surfaces in the so-called private sphere of government non-interference. There are many versions of this criticism, but perhaps the best developed is Susan Moller Okin's (1989: 128–30), which documents the effects of the institution of the nuclear family. She argues that the consequence of this institution is a position of systematic material and political inequality for women. Okin demonstrates, for example, that women have substantial disadvantages competing in the market because of childrearing responsibilities which are not equally shared with men. As a consequence, any theory relying on market mechanisms, including most liberal theories, will yield systems which result in women systematically having less income and wealth than men. The theoretical trouble for liberalism is that in its respect for individual liberty, and in its insistence on government neutrality, it cannot even recognize the inequalities in the economic or political positions of women as unjust, since these inequalities result from the combined effect of many individual choices (Hampton, 1997: 200–8; MacKinnon, 1987: 36). In the distribution of domestic labour, for example, classical liberal philosophers would view these decisions as largely non-political, to be made by individuals. So long as government laws do not dictate unequal roles for men and women – if men and women in their particular cultural contexts choose roles that in the long run create unequal economic positions for men and women – the liberal view would ordinarily permit the outcome as not unjust. The feminist point is that the choices are not necessarily free, and do not preserve equality, but a liberal government is powerless to change the situation. Similar points can be made about the unequal impact of other cultural views, such as those that are racist or in other ways work against minorities [see further Chapter 21].

Despite these important challenges, there is as yet no consensus among feminists or communitarians about what alternatives are needed. Thus, the distinctive issues raised by cultural diversity or the political effects of the personal sphere are likely to be addressed via refinements, rather than wholesale rejections, of the liberal frameworks inherited from Locke and Mill.

NOTE

Thanks to Christi Dawn Favor for a great deal of help in conceptualizing all the different theories and to Pauline Long for research assistance.

REFERENCES

Anderson, Elizabeth (1999) 'What is the point of equality?' *Ethics*, 109 (2): 287–337.

Arneson, Richard (1989) 'Equality and equal opportunity for welfare', *Philosophical Studies*, 56: 77–93.

Arneson, Richard (1990) 'Liberalism, Distributive Subjectivism and equal opportunity for welfare', *Philosophy and Public Affairs*, 19: 159–94.

Arneson, Richard (1991) 'Lockean self-ownership: towards a demolition', *Political Studies*, 39 (1): 36–54.

Arnold, N. Scott (1995) *The Philosophy and Economics of Market Socialism: A Critical Study*. Oxford: Oxford University Press.

Bailey, James Wood (1997) *Utilitarianism, Institutions, and Justice*. Oxford: Oxford University Press.

Barry, Brian (1988) 'Equal opportunity and moral arbitrariness'. In Norman Bowie, ed., *Equal Opportunity*. Boulder, CO: Westview, 23–44.

Barry, Brian (1989) *Theories of Justice*. Berkeley, CA: University of California Press.

Barry, Brian (1995) *Justice as Impartiality*. Oxford: Clarendon.

Baumol, William J. (1986) *Superfairness: Applications and Theory*. Cambridge, MA: MIT Press.

Bayles, Michael D., ed. (1978) *Contemporary Utilitarianism*. Gloucester, MA: Smith.

Binmore, Ken (1994) *Game Theory and the Social Contract*. Vol. 1, *Playing Fair*. Cambridge, MA: MIT Press.

Binmore, Ken (1998) *Game Theory and the Social Contract*. Vol. 2, *Just Playing (Economic Learning and Social Evolution)*. Cambridge, MA: MIT Press.

Bowie, Norman (1988) *Equal Opportunity*. Boulder, CO: Westview.

Brams, Steven J. and Alan D. Taylor (1996) *Fair Division: From Cake-Cutting to Dispute Resolution*. Cambridge: Cambridge University Press.

Brennan, Geoffrey and James M. Buchanan (1985) *The Reason of Rules: Constitutional Political Economy*. New York: Cambridge University Press.

Buchanan, A., D. Brock, N. Daniels, and D. Wikler, eds (2001) *From Chance to Choice: Genetics and Justice*. Cambridge: Cambridge University Press.

Buchanan, Allen (1982) 'A critical introduction to Rawls' theory of justice'. In H. Gene Blocker and Elizabeth H. Smith, eds, *John Rawls' Theory of Social Justice: An Introduction*. Athens, OH: Ohio University Press.

Buchanan, Allen, et al. (2000) *From Chance to Choice*. Cambridge: Cambridge University Press.

Buchanan, James M. (1975) *The Limits of Liberty: Between Anarchy and Leviathan*. Chicago: University of Chicago Press.

Buchanan, James M. and Gordon Tullock (1962) *The Calculus of Consent*. Ann Arbor, MI: University of Michigan Press.

Carens, Joseph (1981) *Equality, Moral Incentives and the Market*. Chicago: University of Chicago Press.

Christiano, Thomas (1996) *The Rule of the Many: Fundamental Issues in Democratic Theory*. Boulder, CO: Westview.

Cohen, G. A. (1989) 'On the currency of egalitarian justice'. *Ethics*, 99 (4): 906–44.

Cohen, G. A. (1995) *Self-Ownership, Freedom, and Equality*. New York: Cambridge University Press.

Daniels, Norman, ed. (1975) *Reading Rawls: Critical Studies of A Theory of Justice*. Oxford: Blackwell.

Daniels, Norman (1990) 'Equality of what: welfare, resources, or capabilities?' *Philosophy and Phenomenological Research*, 50 (Fall): 273–96.

Daniels, Norman (1996) *Justice and Justification: Reflective Equilibrium in Theory and Practice*. Cambridge: Cambridge University Press.

Dick, James C. (1975) 'How to justify a distribution of earnings'. *Philosophy and Public Affairs*, 4: 248–72.

Dworkin, Ronald (2000) *Sovereign Virtue: The Theory and Practice of Equality*. Cambridge, MA: Harvard University Press.

Elster, Jon (1995) 'The empirical study of justice'. In David Miller and Michael Walzer, eds, *Pluralism, Justice, and Equality*. New York: Oxford University Press, 81–98.

Feinberg, Joel (1970) *Doing and Deserving*. Princeton, NJ: Princeton University Press.

Fisk, Milton (1989) *The State and Justice: An Essay in Political Theory*. Cambridge: Cambridge University Press.

Friedman, Marilyn (1989) 'The impracticality of impartiality'. *Journal of Philosophy*, 86 (11): 645–56.

Friedman, Marilyn (1991) 'The practice of partiality'. *Ethics*, 101 (4): 818–35.

Frohlich, N. and J. Oppenheimer (1992) *Choosing Justice: An Experimental Approach to Ethical Theory*. Berkeley, CA: University of California Press.

Gaus, Gerald F. (1990) *Value and Identification*. Cambridge: Cambridge University Press.

Gaus, Gerald (1996) *Justificatory Liberalism*. New York: Oxford University Press.

Gaus, Gerald (1998) 'Why all welfare states (including *laissez-faire* ones) are unreasonable'. *Social Philosophy and Policy*, 15 (2): 1–33.

Gauthier, David Peter (1987) *Morals by Agreement*. Oxford: Clarendon.

Goodin, Robert E. (1988) *Reasons for Welfare: The Political Theory of the Welfare State*. Princeton, NJ: Princeton University Press.

Goodin, Robert E. (1995) *Utilitarianism as a Public Philosophy*. New York: Cambridge University Press.

Gutmann, Amy (1980) *Liberal Equality*. London: Cambridge University Press.

Hampton, Jean (1991) 'Two faces of contractarian thought'. In Peter Vallentyne, ed., *Contractarianism and Rational Choice: Essays on David Gauthier's Morals by Agreement*. New York: Oxford University Press, 31–55.

Hampton, Jean (1997) *Political Philosophy*. Oxford: Westview.

Haworth, Alan (1994) *Anti-Libertarianism*. London: Routledge.

Hayek, Friedrich A. (1944) *The Road to Serfdom*. London: Routledge.

Hayek, Friedrich A. (1976a) *Law, Legislation, and Liberty*. Vol. 2, *The Mirage of Social Justice*. London: Routledge.

Hayek, Friedrich A. (1976b) *The Constitution of Liberty*. London: Routledge.

Hill, Christopher (1985) 'Desert and the moral arbitrariness of the natural lottery'. *Philosophical Forum*, 16: 207–22.

Hochschild, Jennifer L. (1981) *What's Fair: American Beliefs about Distributive Justice*. Cambridge, MA: Harvard University Press.

Jaggar, Alison (1983) *Feminist Politics and Human Nature*. Totowa, NJ: Rowman and Littlefield.

Jones, Charles (1999) *Global Justice: Defending Cosmopolitanism*. Oxford: Oxford University Press.

Joseph, Keith and Jonathan Sumption (1979) *Equality*. London: Murray.

Kavka, Gregory S. (1986) *Hobbesian Moral and Political Theory*. Princeton, NJ: Princeton University Press.

Kelly, P. J. (1990) *Utilitarianism and Distributive Justice*. Oxford: Clarendon.

Kluegel, James R. and Eliot R. Smith (1986) *Beliefs about Inequality*. Hawthorne, NY: Aldine De Gruyter.

Kukathas, Chandran (2003) *The Liberal Archipelago: A Theory of Diversity and Freedom*. Oxford: Oxford University Press.

Kukathas, Chandran and Philip Pettit (1992) *Rawls: A Theory of Justice and its Critics*. Cambridge: Polity.

Lamont, Julian (1994) 'The concept of desert in distributive justice'. *Philosophical Quarterly*, 44: 45–64.

Lamont, Julian (1997) 'Incentive income, deserved income, and economic rents'. *Journal of Political Philosophy*, 5 (1): 26–46.

Le Grand, Julian (1991) *Equity and Choice: An Essay in Economics and Applied Philosophy*. London: Harper Collins.

Le Grand, Julian and Saul Estrin, eds (1989) *Market Socialism*. Oxford: Oxford University Press.

Levin, Michael (1982) 'A Hobbesian minimal state'. *Philosophy and Public Affairs*, 11 (4): 338–53.

Lomasky, Loren E. (1987) *Persons, Rights, and the Moral Community*. New York: Oxford University Press.

Lomasky, Loren (2001) 'Toward a liberal theory of national boundaries'. In David Miller and Sohail Hashmi, eds, *Boundaries and Justice*. Princeton, NJ: Princeton University Press, 55–78.

Machan, Tibor R. (1989) *Individuals and their Rights*. La Salle, IL: Open Court.

Machan, Tibor R. and Douglas B. Rasmussen eds (1995) *Liberty for the Twenty-First Century: Contemporary Libertarian Thought*. Lanham, MD: Rowman and Littlefield.

MacIntyre, Alasdair (1984) *After Virtue: A Study in Moral Theory*, 2nd edn. Notre Dame, IN: University of Notre Dame Press.

MacKinnon, Catherine A. (1987) *Feminism Unmodified: Discourses of Life and Law*. Cambridge, MA: Harvard University Press.

McLeod, Owen (1996) 'Desert and wages'. *Utilitas*, 8: 205–21.

Mill, John S. (1877) *Utilitarianism*, 6th edn. London: Longmans, Green.

Mill, John S. (1892) *On Liberty*. London: Longmans, Green.

Mill, John S. (1970) *The Subjection of Women*. Cambridge, MA: MIT Press.

Mill, John Stuart (1979) *Three Essays: On Liberty, Representative Government, the Subjection of Women*. Oxford: Oxford University Press.

Miller, David (1976) *Social Justice*. Oxford: Clarendon.

Miller, David (1989) *Market, State, and Community*. Oxford: Clarendon.

Miller, David (1999) *Principles of Social Justice*. Cambridge, MA: Harvard University Press.

Morris, Christopher (1998) *An Essay on the Modern State*. Cambridge: Cambridge University Press.

Mulhall, Stephen and Adam Swift, eds (1996) *Liberals and Communitarians*. Cambridge: Blackwell.

Narveson, Jan (1989) *The Libertarian Idea*. Philadelphia: Temple University Press.

Nozick, Robert (1974) *Anarchy, State and Utopia*. New York: Basic.

Nussbaum, Martha C. (1999) *Sex and Social Justice*. Oxford: Oxford University Press.

Okin, Susan Moller (1989) *Justice, Gender, and the Family*. New York: Harper Collins.

Ollman, Bertell, James Lawler and Hillel Ticktin eds (1998) *Market Socialism: The Debate Among Socialists*. London: Routledge.

Pettit, Philip (1997) *Republicanism: A Theory of Freedom and Government*. Oxford: Oxford University Press.

Pogge, Thomas (1989) *Realizing Rawls*. Ithaca, NY: Cornell University Press.

Pogge, Thomas (2001a) 'Priorities of global justice'. *Metaphilosophy*, 32 (1 and 2): 6–24.

Pogge, Thomas (2001b) 'Global justice'. *Metaphilosophy*, 32 (1 and 2): 1–5.

Pojman, Louis P. and Owen McLeod, eds (1998) *What Do We Deserve? A Reader on Justice and Desert*. Oxford: Oxford University Press.

Pranab, K., J. Bardhan and John E. Roemer eds (1997) *Market Socialism: The Current Debate*. Oxford: Oxford University Press.

Rakowski, Eric (1991) *Equal Justice*. Oxford: Clarendon.

Rawls, John (1972) *A Theory of Justice*. Oxford: Oxford University Press.

Rawls, John (1993) *Political Liberalism*. New York: Columbia University Press.

Rawls, John (2001) *Justice as Fairness: A Restatement*. Cambridge, MA: Harvard University Press.

Reeve, Andrew and Andrew Williams, eds (2003) *Real Libertarianism Assessed: Political Theory after Van Parijs*. New York: Palgrave Macmillan.

Richards, Norvin (1986) 'Luck and desert'. *Mind*, 95: 198–209.

Riley, Jonathan (1989) 'Justice under capitalism'. In John H. Chapman, ed., *NOMOS XXXI: Markets and Justice*. New York: New York University Press, 122–62.

Roemer, John (1985) 'Equality of talent'. *Economics and Philosophy*, 1: 151–86.

Roemer, John E. and Erik Olin Wright, eds (1996) *Equal Shares: Making Market Socialism Work*. New York: Verso.

Rowley, C. K., R. D. Tollison and G. Tullock, eds (1988) *The Political Economy of Rent-Seeking*. Boston: Kluwer.

Sadurski, Wojciech (1985) *Giving Desert Its Due*. Dordrecht: Reidel.

Sandel, Michael J. (1982) *Liberalism and the Limits of Justice*. Cambridge: Cambridge University Press.

Scheffler, Samuel, ed. (1988) *Consequentialism and its Critics*. Oxford: Oxford University Press.

Scheffler, Samuel (1992) 'Responsibility, reactive attitudes, and liberalism in philosophy and politics'. *Philosophy and Public Affairs*, 21 (4): 299–323.

Scheffler, Samuel (1994) *The Rejection of Consequentialism*, rev. edn. Oxford: Clarendon.

Sen, Amartya (1980) 'Equality of what?' In Sterling M. McMurrin, ed., *Tanner Lectures on Human Values*, vol. 1. Cambridge: Cambridge University Press, 195–220.

Sen, Amartya (1985) *Commodities and Capabilities*. Oxford: Elsevier Science.

Sen, Amartya (1987) *On Ethics and Economics*. Cambridge, MA: Blackwell.

Sher, George A. (1987) *Desert*. Princeton, NJ: Princeton University Press.

Sidgwick, Henry (1890) *The Methods of Ethics*, 4th edn. London: Macmillan.

Singer, Peter (2002) *One World: The Ethics of Globalisation*. Melbourne: Text.

Smart, J. J. C. and Bernard Williams (1973) *Utilitarianism For and Against*. Cambridge: Cambridge University Press.

Steiner, Hillel (1994) *An Essay on Rights*. Oxford: Blackwell.

Steiner, Hillel and Peter Vallentyne, eds (2000a) *Left-Libertarianism and Its Critics: The Contemporary Debate*. Basingstoke: Palgrave.

Steiner, Hillel and Peter Vallentyne, eds (2000b) *The Origins of Left-Libertarianism: An Anthology of Historical Writings*. Basingstoke: Palgrave.

Sterba, James (1980) *The Demands of Justice*. Notre Dame, IN: University of Notre Dame Press.

Swift, A., G. Marshall, C. Burgoyne and D. Routh, (1995) 'Distributive justice: does it matter what the people think?' In James R. Kluegel, David S. Mason and Bernard Wegener, eds, *Social Justice and Political Change*. New York: Aldine De Gruyter, 15–47.

Taylor, Charles (1994) *Multiculturalism and the Politics of Recognition*. Princeton, NJ: Princeton Universtiy Press.

Taylor, Charles (1985a) *Human Agency and Language*. New York: Cambridge University Press.

Taylor, Charles (1985b) *Philosophy and the Human Sciences*. New York: Cambridge University Press.

Tong, Rosemarie Putnam (1993) *Feminine and Feminist Ethics*. Belmont, CA: Wadsworth.

Tong, Rosemarie (1989) *Feminist Thought: A Comprehensive Introduction*. Boulder, CO: Westview Press.

Tong, Rosemarie (1993) *Feminine and Feminist Ethics*. London: Wadsworth.

Vallentyne, Peter (1991) *Contractarianism and Rational Choice: Essays on David Gauthier's Morals by Agreement*. New York: Cambridge University Press.

Van Parijs, Philippe (1995) *Real Freedom for All: What (If Anything) Can Justify Capitalism?* Oxford: Oxford University Press.

Varian, Hal R. (1975) 'Distributive justice, welfare economics, and the theory of fairness'. *Philosophy and Public Affairs*, 4: 223–47.

Walzer, Michael (1983) *Spheres of Justice*. Oxford: Martin Robertson.

Willet, Cynthia, ed. (1998) *Theorizing Multiculturalism*. Oxford: Blackwell.

Wollstonecraft, Mary (1995) *A Vindication of the Rights of Man and Vindication of the Rights of Woman and Hints*. ed. Sylvanna Tomaselli. Cambridge: Cambridge University Press.

Young, H. Peyton (1994) *Equity: In Theory and Practice*. Princeton, NJ: Princeton University Press.

Young, Iris Marion (2000) *Inclusion and Democracy*. Oxford: Oxford University Press.

Zajac, Edward E. (1995) *Political Economy of Fairness*. Cambridge, MA: MIT Press.

18

Pluralism and Liberalism

FRED D'AGOSTINO

In this chapter I consider the relation between liberalism and pluralism. I show, first, how pluralism is related to the phenomenon of evaluative diversity that is everywhere evident in our individual and collective activities. I distinguish a weak version of pluralism, associated with the work of John Rawls, and a strong version, largely stemming from the work of Isaiah Berlin, and perhaps more closely associated with British than with American political thought [see further Chapter 30]. I next give a brief account of a famous result in social choice theory, Arrow's Theorem, in order to develop a way of modelling what is potentially at issue in articulating a theoretical relationship between pluralism and liberalism. I then identify two devices – one theoretical, one institutional – for managing diversity consistently with specifically liberal ethical commitments. I finally consider how the issue of liberalism's relation to pluralism might look from other theoretical perspectives, including especially those of Jürgen Habermas and Michel Foucault, who have, largely unnoticed by contemporary liberal theorists, articulated a powerful and mainly immanent critique of liberalism's response to diversity, and hence of its compatibility with pluralism.

DIVERSITY AND PLURALISM

It will be useful, at the outset, to distinguish *the fact of diversity* from the thesis of pluralism, or, more accurately, from various pluralist doctrines and arguments.

The fact of diversity is evident everywhere in our social worlds. Individuals express different preferences, perhaps even different 'reflective' (i.e. well-informed, carefully considered and suitably 'impartial') judgements, when it comes to the ways in which their personal and collective lives are to be organized. Of particular political relevance, as John Rawls recognized, is the fact that people 'disagree about which principles should define the basic terms of their association' (1973: 5). Different standards for the assessment of options are current in different social domains as well (Walzer, 1983), meaning, *inter alia*, that even a given individual's attitudes may not be stable across those domains in which she may have occasion to enact roles. Of particular political relevance is the fact, as Thomas Nagel noted, that '[c]onflicts between personal and impersonal [ethical] claims are ubiquitous' and cannot 'be resolved by subsuming either of the points of view under the other, or both under a third' (1979: 134). Even within a single domain, there may be multiple standards, relevant to choice in that domain, that favour different options.

Obviously, the fact of diversity poses prima facie problems. Suppose that *A* prefers *X* to *Y* and that *B* prefers *Y* to *X*, but that *A* and *B* must make a collectively binding choice between these two options. Or consider what might happen if *A*, perhaps acting as an agent for some collectivity, finds himself in a situation in which, according to one criterion relevant to his choice, *X* is preferable to *Y*, whereas, according to another such criterion, also relevant, *Y* is preferable to *X*. In some cases, as when the choice-relevant criteria are from different domains and are constituted as 'side-constraints' on action (Nozick, 1974) rather than as values to be maximized subject to 'trade-offs', *A* may face a 'tragic dilemma', of the kind analysed by theorists such as Stanley Benn (1988) and Martha Nussbaum (1986). In other cases the choice may be little easier, phenomenologically, even if it doesn't exhibit hallmark characteristics of a specifically 'tragic' choice. As Philip

Tetlock noted, 'people are reluctant decision makers who do their damnedest to minimize cognitive effort, emotional dissonance, and moral angst by denying that important values conflict' (2000: 240). He continues:

> People … will be slow to recognize that core values clash; they will rely on mental shortcuts that eliminate direct comparisons between clashing values; they will engage in the dissonance-reduction strategy of bolstering to reduce the stress of those value conflicts they are forced to acknowledge; and they will resort to decision-evasion tactics, such as buck-passing, procrastination, and obfuscation, to escape responsibility for making choices. (2000: 240)

(The psychic tendencies that Tetlock refers to can make it hard to achieve political compromise, an important mechanism in the liberal repertoire.)

Diversity, then, is a familiar phenomenon, of some potential relevance to political theory and practice. *Pluralism*, on the other hand, is embodied in theses and arguments about this phenomenon. At the most general level, pluralism is simply the proposition that the fact of diversity must be acknowledged as of fundamental ethico-political significance, or more pointedly, as George Crowder put it, that 'such diversity is desirable' (1994: 293). In particular, it cannot be assumed, according to pluralism, that diversity is legitimately eliminable in all cases – that it always, for instance, reflects corrigible epistemic or motivational deficiencies. If diversity of assessments creates difficulties for individual or collective choice, then, in at least some cases, according to pluralism, these difficulties have to be addressed on terms which recognize the significance of the diversity which engenders them.

Pluralism, in this sense, stands in opposition to evaluative monism, which holds, on the contrary, that difficulties for choosing posed by prima facie diversity of evaluations are to be addressed, precisely, by the elimination of diversity. (The model here is, in effect, that of 'realist' epistemology, according to which, if *A* asserts and *B* denies that *p*, this diversity in their doxastic commitments must in the limit be eliminated, resulting, as it must on this account, from error in the assessment of evidence or the drawing of inferences.) Just, then, as the appeal of realism rests on the consistency in truth (and hence unity in belief) which it posits, the appeal of monism rests, as R. M. Hare (1981: 26), for instance insisted, on a point tellingly made by John Stuart Mill in *A System of Logic* and quoted by Brian Barry:

> There must be some standard by which to determine the goodness or badness, absolute and comparative, of ends or objects of desire. And whatever that standard is, *there can be but one*: for if there are several ultimate

principles of conduct, the same conduct might be approved by one of those principles and condemned by another; and there would be needed some more general principles as umpire between them. (1990: 4, emphasis added)

The notion of *incommensurability* is therefore crucially important in the debate between monists and pluralists (see, especially, Chang, 1997; Raz, 1986: ch. 13). Pluralists needn't, of course, insist on across-the-board incommensurability. As Barry already argued in 1965, with his use of economists' 'indifference curves' (1990: ch. I, s. 2), and as James Griffin (1986: 89–90) and others have reaffirmed subsequently, a single, unequivocal ranking of options is possible, even with multiple underlying bases of assessment, so long as these values 'trade off' against one another. Indeed, pluralism and incommensurability are logically independent; even a pluralist who believes that trade-offs are *always* possible does not thereby become a monist (see Dancy, 1993: 121). She has a basis, for instance, which the genuine monist seems to lack, for conceptualizing the regret that we frequently experience even when we choose the best option (see Stocker, 1997: 199). Rhetorically, it is nevertheless understandable that pluralists have tended to focus on cases where, because trade-offs seem impossible or inappropriate, incommensurability is evident. For pluralists identify their position at least partly in opposition to monism, and incommensurability *is* incompatible with full-blooded monism. (This is the significance, for utilitarianism, of the debate about 'interpersonal comparability' of welfare. Without such comparability, utilitarianism becomes a pluralist approach, lacking the single overall normative standard whose importance Mill stressed. See, for instance, Elster and Roemer, 1991.)

There are, of course, a variety of *pluralisms*, of stances towards and arguments about the purported political relevance of diversity.

We might believe, for instance, that, 'in the limit', diversity of evaluations would be eliminated by the progressive correction of epistemic and/or motivational deficiencies, much as monism presupposes. We might nevertheless also believe that, given human finitude (Cherniak, 1986), such a 'limit' is unapproachable (to any very great degree) without forms of corrective action that would themselves be manifestly indefensible, ethico-politically, and, hence, that it cannot be demanded, as monism does demand, that we actually aim at the elimination of such diversity. This seems to have been John Rawls's view in the book *Political Liberalism* and he grounds such *weak pluralism*, as I will call it, in his analysis of the so-called 'burdens of judgment' (1993: ch. II, s. 2). These are, specifically, those 'hazards involved in the correct (and conscientious) exercise of our powers of reason and judgement in the ordinary course of political life', which make it improbable that 'conscientious persons with full powers of reason, even after free discussion, will all arrive at the same conclusion' (1993: 56, 58). Rawls himself characterizes this doctrine in terms of 'the practical impossibility of reaching reasonable and workable political agreement' (1993: 63), and says that it expresses 'a political conception [that] tries to avoid, so far as possible, disputed philosophical theses and to give an account ... that rests on plain facts open to all' (1993: 57, n. 10) [see further Chapter 7].

We might believe, instead, and as Isaiah Berlin influentially claimed, that diversity in valuations is a reflection, empirically, of a deep and objective fact about values *per se*, and not about the limitations, however profound, of human reasoning about them. We might hold, as John Gray put it, that such values

> are many, [that] they often come into conflict with one another and are uncombinable in a single human being or a single society, and that in many of such conflicts there is no overarching standard whereby the competing claims of such ultimate values are rationally arbitratable. (1993: 65)

Here, monism is rejected not on 'practical' grounds, as in Rawls's weak version of pluralism, but rather on the basis, precisely, of 'disputed philosophical theses' [see further Chapter 30]. In particular, monism is rejected on ontological grounds – values *are* plural – and on ethical grounds – the elimination of apparent diversity can slight values that ought to be honoured (and not merely, as in Rawls's 'weak pluralism', because the elimination of diversity would itself require impermissible forms of behaviour). As Berlin said,

> it is better to face [the] intellectually uncomfortable fact [of 'objective' diversity] than to ignore it, or automatically attribute it to some deficiency on our part which could be eliminated by an increase in skill or knowledge; or, what is worse still, suppress one of the competing values altogether by pretending it is identical with its rival – and so end by distorting both. (1969: 1)

Such a *strong pluralism* is no longer merely 'practical', though Rawls's own analysis alludes to some of the argumentation supporting such a stance. Three points are worthy of notice.

(1) Rawls points out that '[e]ven where we fully agree about the kinds of considerations that are relevant [to assessment and choice], we may disagree about their weight, and so arrive at different [overall] judgments' (1993: 56). Rawls himself of course treats this phenomenon in purely 'practical' terms: reduction of such diversity would require the deployment of morally impermissible tactics. Some observations of Thomas Kuhn (1977: 330ff) provide the basis, however, for an argument in favour of precisely this kind of diversity.

Suppose that the disagreement between *A* and *B* about the relative merits of *X* and *Y* reflects the fact that *A* weights some *X*-favourable standard of assessment more heavily than *B* does. If a reduction of diversity is not demanded, *A* and *B* will make different choices and thus be in a position to collect different information, that may not have been available antecedently, about the *consequences* of choosing. But this can lead, and in suitable institutional settings will lead, to an improved basis for choosing for both *A* and *B* (and for others). (This point doesn't presuppose any eventual 'convergence' of attitudes. *A* and *B* can improve their *different* bases for judgement by observing one another's judgements without having to come to agreement about how to judge.) There are, in other words, positive grounds for refusing the monist's demands for the elimination of diversity in weighting. (See D'Agostino, 2000. The monist might, of course, say of this argument that it establishes, not that values *are* plural, but rather that it is better, consequentially, to behave *as if* they were plural.)

(2) Rawls points out that 'all our [choice-relevant] concepts ... are vague and subject to hard cases [and that] this indeterminacy means that we must rely on judgement and interpretation ... where reasonable persons may differ' (1993: 56). This might mean, schematically, that *A* considers *X* superior to *Y* whereas *B* does not because he, *A*, does judge that some choice-relevant concept (e.g. 'is just') applies to *X* whereas, because of indeterminacy or vagueness, she, *B*, does not. (*A* and *B* agree about 'core cases' for the application of the term but disagree about 'peripheral cases', which may, of course, still be important, ethico-politically.)

There is, of course, a weak reading of this claim and, in so far as Rawls is committed to avoiding 'disputed philosophical theses', he must have such a reading in mind. He must mean, on this weak reading, merely that there is some 'practical impossibility' associated with the reduction of those conceptual indeterminacies associated with evaluation and choice. Still, there are also strong readings of this claim, of which H. L. A. Hart provided a well-known and influential example, in terms, specifically, of the 'open texture' of (specifically normative and evaluative) language.

In particular, the sort of abstract and general terminology that unavoidably figures in the assessment of options always represents a compromise between two factors. On the one hand, such terminology must provide for the unsupervised co-ordination of people's attitudes and actions – both *A* and *B* forgo Φ-ing because each understands, independently of the other, that Φ-ing is unjust. On the other hand, such terminology must, as Hart put it, 'leave open, for later settlement by an informed [deliberative] choice, issues which can only be properly appreciated and settled when they arise in a concrete case' (1962: 127). Any choice-relevant general idea that is sensitive to these two demands will be sufficiently vague in its applications to specific cases to admit, at least 'at the margins', of multiple interpretations consistent with previous usage. (The *moral particularism* of such theorists as Jonathan Dancy, 1993, provides the basis for an analogous argument, as does the *finitism* which Barry Barnes, 1982, detects in the work of Mary Hesse and Thomas Kuhn.)

(3) Rawls notes, finally, that 'any system of social institutions is limited in the values it can admit so that some selection must be made from the full range of moral and political values that might be realized' (1993: 57). This idea is better expressed, perhaps, in terms of Stuart Hampshire's notion of 'the inexhaustibility of description'. According to Hampshire, '[a]ny situation which confronts me, and which is not a situation in a game, has an inexhaustible set of discriminable features over and above ... those which are mentionable within the vocabulary that I possess and use' (1983: 106). From this it follows, presumably, that whatever *A*'s basis, in the description of options, for preferring *X* to *Y*, there are potentially choice-relevant features of these options which he has not considered but which might be considerable by *B*, and which might, being considered by *B*, lead her to favour *Y* instead of *X*. On this account, as with (2) above, diversity of judgements about options is given 'in the nature of things', and not merely as a practical consequence of corrigible human limitations. (Practically speaking, different individuals may find different choice-relevant features 'considerable' on account of occupying different social roles. This will be particularly important in societies recognizing or, more strongly, valorizing a complex division of labour.)

In Rawls's terminology, diversity in individuals' evaluations 'rests on plain facts open to all'. And, indeed, there may even, as Rawls himself believes, be versions of the diversity-endorsing doctrine of pluralism which manage to avoid 'disputed philosophical theses'. But there are also versions of pluralism which are more robust philosophically (than Rawls's weak pluralism), and which are argued for on quite different bases.

DIVERSITY AND 'CHAOS'

Barry said: 'On the face of it, the claim made by value monism is an extremely implausible one, and

I think the only reason for its having been adhered to so tenaciously by philosophers is the fear that *the only alternative is chaos*' (1990: xxxix, emphasis added). (Compare Berlin: unless monism is true, 'the universe is not a cosmos, not a harmony (1969: 168).) In considering the implications for liberalism of diversity and hence of such pluralist doctrines and arguments which endorse it, it may be helpful, though it is certainly not customary, to begin with Arrow's Theorem. I tried elsewhere (D'Agostino, 1996) to show that this result provides a model for theorizing about ideals, such as 'public reason', that are, at least nowadays, directly associated with liberalism *per se* (see also Gaus, 1996; and D'Agostino and Gaus, 1998). I invoke it here, however, entirely tactically – to provide a parable, if you will. I think, in other words, that the theorem can provide a particularly vivid basis for exploring the relations between diversity and such problems of collective decision-making as liberalism is certainly concerned with, even if it is not concerned with those problems in exactly the (rather restricted) way that social choice theory is.

What is Arrow's Theorem? Consider a collection of individuals, each of whom has well-behaved preferences (or judgements) over a domain of alternative social arrangements. The *problem of collective choice* is to specify a procedure, meeting (at least) minimal conditions of fairness, that will deliver a rating of these alternative arrangements, based on individuals' assessments, that is sufficiently determinate to warrant the selection of one of them as the collectively binding arrangement for this group. What Arrow shows, and what much subsequent tinkering has confirmed, is that there is no formal procedure of amalgamation that can be *relied on* for this purpose (see Arrow, 1979; and, for helpful commentary, see Mueller, 1989, and Sen, 1970). In so far as a procedure fairly recognizes the antecedent assessments of the various individuals, it will, on certain profiles of assessments, fail to achieve determinacy, and, hence, will fail to identify a collectively binding social arrangement. (Even an unreliable procedure will, of course, sometimes identify a collectively binding arrangement, subject to conditions of fairness.) The point of Arrow's Theorem is not that formal procedures never work, but rather that they don't always work. And this point is ethico-politically significant for two reasons. (1) When we apply a procedure in concrete circumstances, we typically will not be able to tell, antecedently, whether or not it will work in these circumstances. (2) Even if we can determine that it will not work in these circumstances, we have, according to Arrow's Theorem, no alternative procedure (of the same type) to use instead, except, of course, another that also will not work.

A brief (and crude) illustration may be helpful. Suppose that we have three individuals (*A*, *B*, *C*)

Table 18.1

	A	B	C
S1	1st	3rd	2nd
S2	2nd	1st	3rd
S3	3rd	2nd	1st

Table 18.2

Procedure	S1/S2 then S3	S1/S3 then S2	S2/S3 then S1
Winner	S3	S2	S1

Table 18.3

	A	B	C
S1	1st	1st	1st
S2	2nd	3rd	3rd
S3	3rd	2nd	2nd

and three possible social arrangements (*S1, S2, S3*), and that individuals' assessments of these arrangements are as shown in Table 18.1. Given this 'profile' of preferences (or deliberative judgements), no merely 'mechanical' procedure of combination will produce a non-arbitrary (and hence legitimately collectively binding) ranking of the alternative social arrangements. (Since rankings by individuals are just that, rank *orderings*, it does not follow, from the fact that each option has the same profile of rankings as the others, that the three options are collectively of equivalent standing and, hence, that the group could for instance simply pick one stochastically to play a collectively binding role.)

Consider, for instance, what happens if the individuals involved propose voting, pairwise, on the alternatives in a two-stage process. In this case, *any* of the three options could be selected, depending on the particular procedure that was employed, as shown in Table 18.2. If *S1* is compared initially with *S2*, then, since both *A* and *C* prefer *S1* to *S2*, *S1* emerges as the first-stage winner. When it is subsequently compared with *S3*, *S3* is, according to this scheme of comparison, the overall best since both *B* and *C* prefer *S3* to *S1*. Because we could, by exactly parallel reasoning, derive *S2* or *S1* as best overall for the group, it is clear that, on this profile of preferences, a collectively binding choice can be determined mechanically only on an ethico-politically arbitrary basis – e.g. by fixing the order in which alternatives are compared. (The alternative to such arbitrariness is simple indeterminacy: none of the options can be identified as the collectively binding best for the group.)

In fact, unless there are strong constraints on 'profiles', it is possible to establish a very general result, known in the literature of social choice as the *chaos theorem*, according to which, as Melvin Hinich and Michael Munger put it, 'it is possible to construct an agenda, or sequence of comparisons of pairs of alternatives, that leads to any alternative … Choosing an agenda implies a choice of an outcome' (1997: 160–1). The situation is 'chaotic', in

particular, because the procedure fails to provide any legitimate basis for distinguishing the alternatives among which individuals are imagined as choosing. This situation is also, of course, chaotic *dynamically*, in the sense that any coalition to fix a particular procedure, and thus a particular outcome, can be destabilized. (This is called 'cycling' in the social choice literature.) Consider Table 18.1. Both *B* and *C* prefer *S3* to *S1*, and hence could form a coalition against *A* to fix the agenda (*S1/S2* then *S3*) that will deliver *S3* as the overall result. But both *A* and *B* prefer *S2* to *S3* and, indeed, since *B* ranks *S2* first, *A* could plausibly appeal to *B* to abandon her coalition with *C* and join him in a coalition against *C*; and so on *ad nauseam* (see Mueller, 1989: ch. II.5).

When it comes to the mechanical aggregation of assessments, even as much diversity among individuals' assessments as is exhibited in Table 18.1 is 'too much': no collectively best alternative can be identified except on a basis which is arbitrary and unstable. It is equally significant, of course, that, *conversely*, once such diversity among individuals' assessments is 'managed', exactly the indeterminacy of such formal procedures as voting (and other modes of amalgamation) disappears. Suppose, for instance, that through some programme of socialization and education, individuals' assessments are sufficiently 'homogenized' that one of the alternative social arrangements that individuals are assessing is 'dominant' in the sense that it is best from all relevant points of view. In this case, we might have the configuration in Table 18.3. Given this configuration, there would be no difficulty with collective choice, either statically or dynamically. There is a unique collectively best option whose identification as such is not dependent on arbitrary factors and whose selection as such cannot be destabilized (so long as individuals' assessments themselves remain constant).

I said that Arrow's Theorem might be considered a parable; that it might suggest something, vividly, for liberalism about the implications of diversity (and hence pluralism). What, to this effect, does it actually show? Albert Weale (1992) provides a helpful analysis whose upshot also applies to specifically liberal modalities of collective deliberation. He notes, in particular, that the conditions which Arrow imposes on formalistic procedures for collective choice should be understood as involving two distinct requirements – 'of coherence and representativeness', which, as he says, 'come into conflict'. He continues: 'Coherence requires decision-makers to know their own mind all things considered, but representativeness pushes towards the inclusion of considerations that may make knowing one's own mind impossible' (1992: 213).

Representativeness, in other words, requires, of any approach to collective decision-making, that it make adequate provision for reasonable antecedent diversity of preferences or judgements. Coherence, on the other hand, requires of such an approach that it make adequate provision for the identification of collectively binding social arrangements. What Arrow's Theorem itself *shows* is that the specifically formalistic approaches to collective decision-making that are illustrated, for instance, in systems of voting cannot, in fact, satisfy both these desiderata reliably. What, treated as a parable, Arrow's Theorem *suggests* is a conundrum: how can we reconcile the demand for coherence in social arrangements with the fact of evaluative diversity?

Of course, Arrow's Theorem, and its extensions, can be read as an argument for monism. Arrow courts chaos in providing, as pluralists would insist, for the recognition of diversity. If the price for the avoidance of chaos is the abandonment of pluralism, this is anyway warranted by the fact that all apparent diversity is ethico-politically insignificant and merely conceals a deeper uniformity of assessments that sustains coherence in social arrangements. This reading is implicit, for instance, in John Harsanyi's (1977) attempt to show that, even when they differ in their assessments of options, individuals can be brought to share the same '*extended preferences*' about social arrangements, and that coherent collective choice procedures can be defined on the basis of such ('extended') assessments. And, of course, it has indeed been suggested, more pertinently, that specifically *liberal* doctrines and institutions are incompatible with pluralism and, hence, with the evaluative diversity which this family of doctrines and arguments sanctions (see Kekes, 1992; Crowder, 1994). Much recent liberal political theory can, however, profitably be interpreted, I submit, as an attempt to find a principled basis for acknowledging the demands both of diversity and of coherence.

LIBERAL RESPONSES TO DIVERSITY

According to pluralism, there are good reasons for recognizing, ethico-politically, at least some of the diversity of attitudes that are characteristic of societies such as ours. On the other hand, if we tolerate 'too much' diversity in individuals' cognitive and evaluative attitudes, it cannot be ruled out that we will be unable to identify a collectively best system of social arrangements. Of course, neither pluralism nor representativeness requires the recognition of *all* empirically given diversity of attitudes (see, especially, Gaus, 1996). Some attitudes can reasonably be 'filtered out' or *normalized* as part of any reasonable procedure for the identification of collectively binding social arrangements. If this can be done compatibly with specifically liberal principles, then liberalism *can* acknowledge diversity without abandoning a commitment to coherence in theory and in its institutional embodiments. (The idea of normalization is associated with Michel Foucault, 1977, and I will return later to its specifically Foucauldian associations.)

John Rawls's *original position* (1973: ch. III) represents the most influential attempt to identify a device of normalization that meets specifically liberal requirements. Bruce Ackerman's (1980) 'neutral dialogue' and Jürgen Habermas's (1990) 'ideal speech situation' are other examples [see further Chapter 13]. On Rawls's analysis, the members of a society have to decide, in a way that will be collectively binding, how to rank proposals about the so-called 'basic structure of society' which determines their relations with one another, at least in certain institutionally fundamental ways. Of course, if we take individual diversity as we find it, convergence on a ranking of proposals is unlikely. Each individual will prefer a basic structure in which she fares well. But structures in which some individuals do fare well are, in the 'circumstances of justice' (especially scarcity of resources relative to total demand), structures in which other individuals do not. A profile of rankings much like that in Table 18.1 above is likely, and non-arbitrary identification of a collectively best basic structure will therefore be difficult.

Rawls addresses this problem by considering how diversity of individuals' antecedent judgements might be reduced compatibly with specifically liberal ideals and principles. His task is twofold: (1) to find a *basis* for reduction, and (2) to find a specifically liberal *rationale* for reduction. Without (1), the coherence requirement cannot be satisfied; there is 'too much' antecedent diversity for a collectively best structure to be identified. Without (2), representativeness is not adequately acknowledged, for, absent a rationale, any reduction will be arbitrary from an ethical point of view – i.e. will arbitrarily fail adequately to represent decision-relevant diversity of assessments.

Rawls's solution is embodied, specifically, in the *veil of ignorance*. When individuals deliberate about the basic structure, they do so subject to a restriction on their knowledge. No individual knows, for instance, 'his place in society, his class position or social status ... his fortune in the distribution of natural assets and abilities, his intelligence and strength, and the like' (Rawls, 1973: 137). Accordingly, no individual can, in his own deliberations about the basic structure, rank proposals about it in accordance with how well he is likely to fare if these proposals are implemented. How is he to rank them, then? In accordance with how *any* person is likely to fare if they are implemented. And, according to Rawls, when individuals deliberate in this way, how one person ranks proposals is the same as how any other person ranks them, and coherence is therefore achieved. (A dominant option is available, as in Table 18.3 above.) This is how Rawls's original position argument seeks to provide an adequate *basis* for reduction. (There is, of course, considerable controversy about whether this argument succeeds: see the articles in Daniels, 1975.)

Notice, furthermore, that a specifically liberal *rationale* might indeed be provided for the use of this device. What the veil of ignorance prevents the use of is, precisely, information that it would be morally improper to use as a basis for the assessment of alternative basic structures. It prevents the use of information that people would, characteristically, use in a self-interested way. As Rawls says, '[o]ne excludes knowledge of those contingencies which set men at odds and allows them to be guided by their prejudices' (1973: 19). Blocking the use of such information forces individuals to think impartially, i.e. ethically, about the terms of their association with one another. On the other hand, the information about themselves that *is* available to individuals deliberating about the basic structure does, according to Rawls (1993: ch. II, s. 6), represent them as (potential) citizens of a specifically liberal state, especially in acknowledging their identities as free and equal moral agents. There is, then, nothing arbitrary, according to this reasoning, about the reductions of diversity effected by deployment of the veil of ignorance.

Such normalizing devices are, then, one liberal response to the conundrum which is posed by the fact of diversity and by the endorsement of this fact by various pluralist doctrines and arguments. These kinds of devices achieve coherence by tweaking our understanding of what representativeness requires. It is interesting, then, that other characteristically liberal devices work, in effect, by tweaking our understanding of what coherence requires.

It will be helpful to consider, again, Table 18.1. A problem of coherence results, in fact, precisely in so far as we demand, of a solution to the problem of collective choice, that it identify a particular *option* as one which will be binding on all the individuals involved. There is, however, another possibility, and it has been widely exploited in specifically liberal institutions. It is, in effect, to see the profile of preferences represented in Table 18.1 as the end-point, not the starting-point, of a process of collective deliberation. Perhaps the individuals involved agree to *devolve* decision-making about these options to the individual level. In so far as they do agree to this, we have a collective solution to a problem of choice. Each of the individuals agrees, with all the others, not about what preference should collectively be honoured, but rather that that *distribution* of preferences over individuals is to be preferred to any other in which each individual has the preferences which he antecedently has (or which he would have, subject to specifically liberal normalization of his attitudes). And there are, of course, numerous, specifically liberal grounds for reaching such an agreement. (I draw, ironically, on Crowder, 1994: 296ff.) When decision-making is devolved in this way:

- Tolerance of diversity is institutionally recognized.
- Individuals' freedom of choice is protected, especially since individuals' relations with one another must, with devolved responsibility, be constituted on the basis of joint consent and reciprocal advantage.
- Each individual has opportunities to develop and to exercise her individuality and her uniqueness and irreplaceability are socially recognized.
- Each individual has opportunities to develop and to exercise her autonomy as a moral agent.

Exactly this device of devolution is embodied, of course, in such familiar, specifically liberal institutions as the market and the system of individual rights (e.g. of conscience).

Consider the question 'What should we believe?', meaning, in particular, 'What beliefs should we adopt as a moral or spiritual framework for our lives?' (Call these 'basic beliefs'.) This is a question that *could* be considered collectivistically and, if it were, the assessment of the various options – Christian fundamentalism, new age spiritualism, secular humanism, historical materialism, etc. – might require techniques of normalization if a collectively binding best option were to be discoverable. (Without this, we might easily have a profile over options like those in Table 18.1.) That the very idea of treating the matter in this way is preposterous is, of course, a fundamental commitment of specifically liberal approaches. Rather than viewing the question 'What should we believe?' collectivistically as requiring a substantively singular answer that would be binding on all, we view it in liberal contexts individualistically, or more properly, distributionally. In effect, we say that in a society with *n* individual members, there are *n* separate spheres in which an answer to this question might be sought, each of which is, in theory, inviolable and particular to the individual who, in effect, occupies it. *A* decides for himself what he should believe, *B* for herself, and so on.

The matter is similar in many ways (but not all) with the market. Of course, in so-called 'command economies', as in the former Soviet bloc, the question 'What should be produced and how should it be distributed?' was thought to require a collective solution, in a special, and specifically anti-liberal, sense. Although, empirically, individuals might differ in their requirements for commodities, it must be assumed – and not just to ease calculational difficulties but also, of course, as a reflection of specifically socialist assumptions about the person and her relation to society – that there is a 'normal' level of demand for each of these products and that production and distribution should be aligned to this norm. That such an approach seems absurd, and perhaps too difficult computationally even when implausible normalizing assumptions *are* made, simply reflects, of course, our own disinclination, in specifically liberal societies, to see the matter in this way.

Just as each individual, under liberty of conscience, can decide for herself what 'basic beliefs' she adopts as a framework for living, so too, under liberty of exchange, can each individual decide for himself what kinds and quantities of goods he is willing to pay for. Of course, there is some co-ordination of individuals' demand for commodities in a market economy, as there arguably is not in relation to 'basic beliefs'. How easy an individual will find it to satisfy his various requirements will depend, in part, on how these articulate with those of other consumers and with the abilities of suppliers to produce objects satisfying these requirements, given other demands for the various factors of production which enter into the manufacture of these objects. It is not, in particular, that every individual can have as much of every commodity as he might, in the abstract, want to possess. (Since he can, under liberty of conscience, believe what it is right for him specifically to believe, this is a disanalogy between the market and civil society.) It is, rather, that each individual can have as much of every commodity as he is able and willing, concretely, to pay for at the price that it commands given the demand for it collectively among all consumers, and the availability of substitutes for it and for its input factors of production. Again, and this time analogously with the case of civil society, we achieve coherence via devolution.

In particular, we don't approach the matter of production and distribution of commodities as one which, impossibly (?), requires that individuals' judgements about this matter be aggregated (perhaps after normalization). (This is one of Friedrich Hayek's most strongly emphasized points in favour of the market. He says, for instance: '[T]he cosmos of the market neither is nor could be governed by such a single scale of ends; it serves the multiplicity of separate and incommensurable ends of all its separate members' (1976: 108).) We see it, rather, as a question which is devolved to individuals and mediated by the price mechanism. The answer to the question 'What should be produced and how should it be distributed?' is, then, simply the result, via market mechanisms, of individuals' answers to the question 'What do *I* want and how willing am *I* to pay for it?' That (social) option is best, in effect, in which each individual holds as her share of the commodities produced in her society those that she is willing and able to pay for. Other options, in which all individuals, regardless of their own assessments, hold the some 'normal' share of basic commodities or in which individuals' holdings differ but are not 'aligned' to individuals' own payments, are ranked below this particular option by the system which is defined by the principles of liberty of exchange. (This is the rationale, relative to the ideology of the market, for the principle of 'user pays' which has recently been much applied in commodities, including services, which have traditionally been produced by public sector organizations.)

The conundrum involving coherence and representativeness is addressed in these cases, then, by reinterpreting what is required for coherence. While one form of coherence is to be obtained by identifying an option as collectively best for all, another form of coherence, and emphatically a specifically *liberal* form of coherence, is to be obtained, on the contrary, by identifying a *distribution* of options as collectively best for all.

ALTERNATIVE PERSPECTIVES

On the account developed here, the market is a (specifically liberal) device for achieving coherence without sacrificing diversity. As Hayek said, 'it is the great advantage of ... the market that ... it makes agreement on ends unnecessary [representativeness] and a reconciliation of divergent purposes possible [coherence]' (1976: 112). To be sure, some theorists, across a range of theoretical perspectives, suspect and argue that the sort of 'reconciliation of divergent purposes' which specifically market mechanisms of devolution facilitate in fact works via a covert (and illegitimate) normalization of subjects, and hence does depend, contrary to Hayekian ideology, on a (manipulated) 'agreement on ends'.

Working within a pragmatist tradition, Elizabeth Anderson and Margaret Radin notably complain, for instance, of the way in which economistic modes of assessment increasingly supplant others, with a consequent reduction in the diversity of ways of evaluating options. According to Radin, 'universal commodification implies that all value can be expressed in terms of price [and hence] ... "reduces" all values to sums of money' (1996: 8). Anderson carries the argument to an overtly pluralist conclusion:

> To attempt to reduce the plurality of standards to a single standard, ground, or good-constituting property threatens to obliterate the self-understandings in terms of which we make sense of and differentiate our emotions, attitudes, and concerns [and hence] ... to hopelessly impoverish our responsive capacities. (1993: 5)

On this account, even though individuals need not, when acting in the market, agree on substantive ends, they will, as a result of conducting their transactions under the banner of 'economic exchange', increasingly come to resemble one another in their impoverished bases for choice. The point is twofold, of course. (1) Populations of individuals become less diverse – because all individuals tend, increasingly, to prioritize economistic modes of evaluation. (2) For many an individual, her specific mode of evaluation becomes less complex, being increasingly based on market values, rather than the 'use values' and other evaluative features that are 'overwritten' by the narrowly economic considerations that come to predominate in her thinking.

That the increasing dominance of economistic modes of evaluation and co-ordination may be implicitly normalizing is also, of course, urged by Habermas, who has long excoriated the tendency of money and of its institutionalization in markets to supplant, as a basis for the co-ordination of social behaviour, that kind of free discussion based on a variety of explicitly normative principles that, in his view, facilitates a genuinely consensual basis for social relations. (This is, in effect, one of the forms of 'colonization of the lifeworld' that Habermas and his interpreters have been keenest to expose.) Habermas says, for instance:

> The point is to protect areas of life that are functionally dependent on social integration through values, norms, and consensus formation, to preserve them from falling prey to the systemic imperatives of economic and administrative subsystems growing with dynamics of their own, and to defend them from becoming converted over, through the steering mechanism of the law, to a principle of sociation that is, for them, dysfunction. (1987: 372–3)

On this account, (monetarily mediated) exchange increasingly superintends the distribution of resources in a wide variety of contexts in which distribution might, previously, have been subject to collective deliberation according to context-specific norms and standards. Again, there is normalization. Again, it is twofold. (1) Each of a number of previously differentiated evaluative contexts becomes, as a result of 'colonization', a context in which economistic considerations are primary. (2) Each individual's evaluative repertoire is reduced in its complexity. Where once she had multiple, context-specific bases for evaluation, now she has the one, generic basis that is provided by the economistic model. (On Stanley Benn's account, this results in a degradation of the individual's autonomy. She can no longer, in these circumstances, use the standards 'native' to one context to assess options in other, unrelated contexts, a capacity which, according to Benn, 1988: 182, is crucial to her autonomy as a deliberator and chooser.)

Devolution (in the form of marketization) can work to normalize as well, according to these claims. Of course, from a purely liberal perspective, no issue is settled even if this observation is correct. For normalization is, in principle, itself a legitimately liberal device for balancing the demands of representativeness and coherence. (This is the significance of my discussion of the Rawlsian mechanism of normalization – i.e. the original position.)

This is, of course, the relevance of specifically Foucauldian perspectives to the relation between liberalism and pluralism [see further Chapter 4]. For what Foucault and his followers have argued quite vigorously is, of course, that some of the characteristic forms of normalization in contemporary societies are, in fact, hostile, not merely to the prospects for diversity of values and attitudes, but to the moral bases of liberalism itself. Nikolas Rose is eloquent (and representative). He says:

> [O]ne central feature of the emergence of this contemporary regime of the free individual, and the political rationalities of liberalism to which freedom is so dear, has been the invention of a range of ... technologies for governing individuals in terms of their freedom. The importance of liberalism as an ethos of governments, rather than as political philosophy, is thus not that it first recognized, defined, or defended freedom as a right of all citizens. Rather, its significance is that for the first time the arts of government were systematically linked to the practice of freedom and hence to the characteristics of human beings as potentially subjects of freedom ... The forms of freedom we inhabit today are intrinsically bound to a regime of subjectification in which subjects are not merely 'free to choose', but obliged to be free, to understand and enact their lives in terms of choice under conditions that systematically limit the capacities of so many to shape their own destiny. Human beings must interpret their past, and dream their future, as outcomes of personal choices made or choices still to make yet within a narrow range of

possibilities whose restrictions are hard to discern because they form the horizon of what is thinkable. (1996: 16–17)

There is, on this account, a liberal rationale for the sorts of normalization that are characteristic of liberal societies, but that rationale falls far short of providing the kinds of protections with which liberalism is especially associated. In particular, on this account, individuals can be recognized in liberal societies as 'free and equal moral persons' only after they have been submitted to a great deal of 'disciplinary' shaping (*à la* Foucault), specifically to ensure that these individuals act in sufficiently *self*-disciplined way to make their freedom compatible with social coherence. As Jon Simons put it:

We are given the impression that society functions because of a social contract, whereas it is discipline that constitutes the social fabric. While 'philosophers and jurists' had a 'dream of a perfect society' based on a 'primal social contract', there was also 'a military dream of society' based on national discipline … In so far as sovereignty theory legitimizes power by referring to the willingness of subjects to obey, *it is dependent on the practices that have already rendered them obedient*. (1995: 56, 58, emphasis added)

Perhaps, then, as John Gray seems to suggest 'cultural pluralism … advocated, but everywhere discouraged by modern liberalism' (1993: 27) plays a primarily ideological role in contemporary societies. While formally liberal societies purport to provide protections for diversity, their primary mechanisms for the mediation of diversity (and hence for the recognition of plural*ism*) are in fact hostile to diversity and perhaps even inconsistent with liberalism's own core commitment – e.g. to tolerance of difference, to individual autonomy, and so on.

REFERENCES

Ackerman, Bruce (1980) *Social Justice in the Liberal State*. New Haven, CT: Yale University Press.

Anderson, Elizabeth (1993) *Value in Ethics and Economics*. Cambridge, MA: Harvard University Press.

Arrow, Kenneth (1979) 'Values and collective decision making'. In Frank Hahn and Martin Hollis, eds, *Philosophy and Economic Theory*. Oxford: Oxford University Press.

Barnes, Barry (1982) *T. S. Kuhn and Social Science*. London: Macmillan.

Barry, Brian (1990) *Political Argument: A Reissue with a New Introduction*. Berkeley, CA: University of California Press.

Benn, Stanley (1988) *A Theory of Freedom*. Cambridge: Cambridge University Press.

Berlin, Isaiah (1969) *Four Essays on Liberty*. London: Oxford University Press.

Chang, Ruth, ed. (1997) *Incommensurability, Incomparability, and Practical Reason*. Cambridge , MA: Harvard University Press.

Cherniak, Christopher (1986) *Minimal Rationality*. Cambridge, MA: MIT Press.

Crowder, George (1994) 'Pluralism and liberalism'. *Political Studies*, 42: 293–305.

D'Agostino, Fred (1996) *Free Public Reason*. Oxford: Oxford University Press.

D'Agostino, Fred (2000) 'Incommensurability and commensuration'. *Studies in the History and Philosophy of Science*, 31: 429–47.

D'Agostino, Fred and Gerald Gaus, eds (1998) *Public Reason*. Aldershot: Dartmouth.

Dancy, Jonathan (1993) *Moral Reasons*. Oxford: Blackwell.

Daniels, Norman, ed. (1975) *Reading Rawls*. Oxford: Blackwell.

Elster, Jon and John Roemer, eds (1991) *Interpersonal Comparisons of Well-Being*. Cambridge: Cambridge University Press.

Foucault, Michel (1977) *Discipline and Punish: The Birth of the Prison*, trans. A. Sheridan. London: Allen Lane.

Gaus, Gerald (1996) *Justificatory Liberalism*. Oxford: Oxford University Press.

Gray, John (1993) *Post-Liberalism*. New York: Routledge.

Griffin, James (1986) *Well-Being*. Oxford: Clarendon.

Habermas, Jürgen (1987) *The Theory of Communicative Action*, trans. Thomas McCarthy. Boston: Beacon.

Habermas, Jürgen (1990) *Moral Consciousness and Communicative Action*, trans. Christian Lenhart and Shierry Weber Nicholson. Cambridge: Polity.

Hampshire, Stuart (1983) *Morality and Conflict*. Oxford: Blackwell.

Hare, R. M. (1981) *Moral Thinking*. Oxford: Clarendon.

Harsanyi, John (1977) 'Cardinal welfare, individualistic ethics, and interpersonal comparisons of utility'. In his *Essays on Ethics, Social Behaviour and Scientific Explanation*. Dordrecht: Reidel.

Hart, H. L. A. (1962) *The Concept of Law*. Oxford: Clarendon.

Hayek, Friedrich (1976) *Law, Legislation and Liberty*. Vol. 2, *The Mirage of Social Justice*. Chicago: University of Chicago Press.

Hinich, Melvin and Michael Munger (1997) *Analytical Politics*. Cambridge: Cambridge University Press.

Kekes, John (1992) 'The incompatibility of liberalism and pluralism'. *American Philosophical Quarterly*, 29: 141–51.

Kuhn, Thomas (1977) *The Essential Tension*. Chicago: University of Chicago Press.

Mueller, Dennis (1989) *Public Choice II*. Cambridge: Cambridge University Press.

Nagel, Thomas (1979) 'The fragmentation of value'. In Alan Ryan, ed., *The Idea of Freedom*. Oxford: Oxford University Press.

Nozick, Robert (1974) *Anarchy, State and Utopia*. Oxford: Blackwell.

Nussbaum, Martha (1986) *The Fragility of Goodness*. Cambridge: Cambridge University Press.

Radin, Margaret (1996) *Contested Commodities*. Cambridge, MA: Harvard University Press.

Rawls, John (1973) *A Theory of Justice*. Oxford: Oxford University Press.

Rawls, John (1993) *Political Liberalism*. New York: Columbia University Press.

Raz, Joseph (1986) *The Morality of Freedom*. Oxford: Clarendon.

Rose, Nikolas (1996) *Inventing Our Selves*. Cambridge: Cambridge University Press.

Sen, Amartya (1970) *Collective Choice and Social Welfare*. San Francisco: Holden-Day.

Simons, Jon (1995) *Foucault and the Political*. London: Routledge.

Stocker, Michael (1997) 'Abstract and concrete value: plurality, conflict, and maximization'. In Ruth Chang, ed., *Incommensurability, Incomparability, and Practical Reason*. Cambridge, MA: Harvard University Press.

Tetlock, Philip (2000) 'Coping with trade-offs: psychological constraints and political implications'. In Arthur Lupia, Mathew McCubbins and Samuel Popkin, eds, *Elements of Reason*. Cambridge: Cambridge University Press.

Walzer, Michael (1983) *Spheres of Justice: A Defense of Pluralism and Equality*. Oxford: Blackwell.

Weale, Albert (1992) 'Social choice'. In Shaun Hargreaves Heap, Martin Hollis, Bruce Lyons, Robert Sugden and Albert Weale, eds, *The Theory of Choice: A Critical Guide*. Oxford: Blackwell.

19

Nationalism and Multiculturalism

CHANDRAN KUKATHAS

DIVERSITY AND CONTEMPORARY POLITICAL THEORY

If any issue dominates contemporary political theory, it is how to deal with cultural diversity and the claims – moral, legal, and political – made in the name of ethnic, religious, linguistic, or national allegiance (Kymlicka, 2001: 17). Today, governments are confronted by demands from cultural minorities for recognition, protection, preferential treatment, and political autonomy within the boundaries of the state. Equally, international society and its political institutions, as well as states themselves, have had to deal with demands from various peoples for political recognition as independent nations, and for national self-determination. The turbulent politics of the contemporary world may account in part for this development: the collapse of communist Eastern Europe led to an upsurge of nationalist demands from peoples aspiring to statehood; the challenges to the legitimacy of rulers in such places as Kashmir, Burma, East Timor, and Bougainville have fed demands for national independence as well as attempts at secession; the emergence of an indigenous peoples' movement gave further encouragement to aboriginal groups calling for affirmative action, or compensation for past injustice, as well as rights of self-government; and the mass migrations of peoples, fleeing war or simply seeking better opportunities in new countries, have seen the emergence of substantial cultural minorities in states unprepared for the problems this could bring.

Political theory had, until recent times, said relatively little about these matters (exceptions include Plamenatz, 1960; Van Dyke, 1977; 1982; 1985).

But the issues raised by cultural diversity and nationalist claims could not be ignored for long, since they posed a challenge to the prevailing political theories – and to liberal and democratic theory in particular. Indeed, the challenge of multiculturalism and nationalism has provoked a re-examination of a great number of issues in political theory, from the role of the state, the limits of toleration and the rights of women, to the proper scope of public education and the nature of citizenship. It has brought about a reconsideration of the basis of political order.

This chapter surveys the literature of nationalism and multiculturalism as it has grown and developed over the past 15 years. Its aim, however, is not simply to summarize that body of writing but to draw attention to the problems that have confronted contemporary political theory – and liberal theory in particular – as it has struggled to embrace diversity. How can the many live as one? That is an old question in political theory, and the theorists of nationalism and multiculturalism have, in different ways, tried to offer an answer.

WHAT IS MULTICULTURALISM?

The term 'multiculturalism' predates its use in political theory, but not by very long. Although nationalism is an old concept which has been much discussed in the past century (Kedourie, 1967; Minogue, 1967), multiculturalism did not appear until the 1960s and 1970s, when it was used to describe a new public policy, first in Canada and then in Australia. In both of these cases, this development marked an explicit movement by federal governments away from policies of assimilation of ethnic minorities, and immigrants in particular, toward policies of acceptance and integration of diverse cultures (Lopez, 2000: 2–3). The term did not enter the American (or British) lexicon until the 1980s (Glazer, 1997: 8). When it did enter American debates, however, it did so in the first instance, in discussions about public education. 'Multiculturalism,' according to Nathan Glazer, 'is just the latest in [a] sequence of terms describing how American society, particularly American education, should respond to diversity' (1997: 8).

Multiculturalism, then, is a term that describes one particular way of responding to ethnic diversity. 'It is a position that rejects assimilation and the "melting pot" image as an imposition of the dominant culture, and instead prefers such metaphors as the "salad bowl" or the "glorious mosaic", in which each ethnic and racial element in the population maintains its distinctiveness' (1997: 10). Yet in reality there is no single multiculturalist position but rather a range of views of what multiculturalism requires. For some, multiculturalism requires moderate changes to social and political institutions to enable cultural minorities to preserve their languages and their distinctive customs or practices. For others, however, multiculturalism requires much greater social transformation to turn modern society into one in which racism has been eliminated and 'difference' is nurtured rather than repudiated, or simply tolerated.

But if multiculturalism is a way of embracing diversity, this still leaves open the question of how diversity is to be embraced. If a multicultural society is one in which different religions, cultures, languages, and peoples can coexist without some being subordinated to others, or to a single, dominant group, how can this be achieved, and what principles would describe such a society? This issue arises because even if there is diversity, there must surely be some kind of unity for a society to exist. Unless we aspire to a borderless world, in which people could move freely unimpeded by national (and other) boundaries, even a multicultural society would have to settle on some basic institutions, decide what it would accept as official languages, and define itself as a nation, membership of which it controls by determining who (and how many) may join it. The real question, in other words, is what does multiculturalism mean in practice?

This question, however, was not addressed systematically until the 1990s when political theorists began to consider what might be the principled basis of a multicultural society. It was only then that the case for multiculturalism began to receive any kind of sustained defence – and criticism.

MULTICULTURALISM DEFENDED

Kymlicka's Theory

The first systematic theory of multiculturalism was developed by Will Kymlicka in two major works: *Liberalism, Community and Culture* (1989) and *Multicultural Citizenship* (1995a). This field of inquiry has also been shaped by Kymlicka's other writings (Kymlicka, 2000) and edited collections (Kymlicka, 1995b; Kymlicka and Shapiro, 1997; Kymlicka and Norman, 2000b). Kymlicka's work was born out of a dissatisfaction with the political theory of post-war liberalism which, in his view, had wrongly assumed that the problem of national minorities could be resolved by ensuring the provision of basic individual rights. Just as religious minorities were protected by the separation of church from state, and the entrenching of freedom of religion, so would ethnic identity be protected by freedom to express in private life those cultural attachments that were no business of the state. The state would neither oppose nor nurture the freedom people enjoyed to express their attachments to their particular cultures, but respond with what Glazer called 'benign neglect' (1975: 25; 1983: 124; Kymlicka, 1995a: 3). But benign neglect, in Kymlicka's view, was not a plausible option. The question is, why?

According to Kymlicka, minority rights could not simply be subsumed under human rights because 'human rights standards are simply unable to resolve some of the most important and controversial questions relating to cultural minorities' (1995a: 4). These included questions about which languages should be recognized in the parliaments, bureaucracies and courts; whether any ethnic or national groups should have publicly funded education in their mother tongue; whether internal boundaries should be drawn so that cultural minorities form majorities in local regions; whether traditional homelands of indigenous peoples should be reserved for their benefit; and what degree of cultural integration might be required of immigrants seeking citizenship (1995a: 4–5). Traditional human rights doctrines, Kymlicka suggests, simply give us no guidance on these questions. And unless they are supplemented with a theory of minority rights, human rights theory will not enable us to address some of the most pressing issues confronting us in places like Eastern Europe, where disputes over local autonomy, language, and naturalization threaten to leave those regions mired in violent conflict. Kymlicka's ambition, therefore, has been to develop a liberal theory of minority rights that explains 'how minority rights coexist with human rights, and how minority rights are limited by principles of individual liberty, democracy, and social justice' (1995a: 6).

The theory ultimately advanced by Kymlicka distinguished three kinds of minority or group-differentiated rights that were to be accorded to ethnic and national groups: self-government rights, poly-ethnic rights, and special representation rights. Self-government rights require the delegation of powers to national minorities, such as indigenous peoples, but these rights would not be available to other cultural minorities who had immigrated into the country. The latter would be eligible for polyethnic rights, which guarantee financial support and legal protection for practices peculiar to some ethnic or religious groups. Both indigenous peoples and immigrant minorities might also be eligible for special representation rights which guarantee places for minority representatives on state bodies or insti-tutions. Central to Kymlicka's account of group-differentiated rights is a distinction between two kinds of minorities: national minorities and ethnic minorities. National minorities are peoples whose previously self-governing, territorially concentrated cultures have been incorporated into a larger state. Examples include 'American Indians', Puerto Ricans, Chicanos, and native Hawaiians in the United States; the Quebecois and various aboriginal communities in Canada; and the Australian Aborigines. Ethnic minorities, however, are peoples who have immigrated to a new society and do not wish to govern themselves, but nonetheless wish to hold on to their ethnic identities and traditions. A modern state may be 'multicultural' in one (or both) of two senses: either because it is 'multinational', since its members belong to different nations; or because it is 'polyethnic', since its members emigrated from different nations (1995a: 18). In Kymlicka's theory, these two kinds of groups have very different legitimate claims to make, and under-standing this should make clear that national minorities need not fear that policies of multicultur-alism would reduce them to the status of migrants, just as other citizens need not fear that multicultur-alism implied that immigrants had a legitimate claim to self-government.

At the heart of Kymlicka's theory of multicultur-alism is a form of nationalism – or liberal national-ism, to be precise. It is his contention that the liberal tradition has a history of recognizing group-differentiated rights. This is most evident, in his view, in the fact that most liberal theorists accept that the world is made up of separate states. These states are normally assumed to have the right to decide who may enter their jurisdictions to visit, reside, or acquire citizenship. Kymlicka's view is that 'the orthodox liberal view about the right of states to determine who has citizenship rests on the same princi-ples which justify group-differentiated citizenship within states, and that accepting the former leads logically to the latter' (1995a: 124). That is to say, citizenship or state membership is itself a group-differentiated notion, and liberalism is a view that recognizes the rights of individuals *as members of states*. It therefore makes perfect sense for liberals to be willing to recognize groups within states, for groups, like states, exist to protect people's cultural membership. What liberals defend is individual freedom. Yet this is 'not primarily the freedom to move beyond one's language and history, but rather the freedom to move around within one's societal culture, to distance oneself from particular cultural roles, to choose which features of the culture are most worth developing, and which are without value' (1995a: 90–1). National cultures are 'soci-etal cultures', and the modern world is divided into such groupings. They provide their members with meaningful ways of life across the range of human activities – from the economic to the educational and religious. 'These cultures tend to be territorially concentrated, and based on a shared language' (1995a: 76). These are 'societal' cultures because they comprise not just shared memories or values but also common institutions and practices. A 'soci-etal culture' is *embodied* in schools, in the media, in the economy, and in government.

For Kymlicka, national minorities are, typically, groups with societal cultures – albeit cultures that have struggled against conquest, colonization, and forced assimilation. Immigrants, however, have no societal culture (though tthey may have left their own societal cultures). Societal cultures tend to be national cultures, and nations are almost invariably societal cultures (1995a: 80). In the modern world, cultures which are not societal cultures are not likely to prosper, given the pressures towards the creation of a single common culture in each country. His theory of group-differentiated rights accordingly focuses on enabling national minorities to sustain their societal cultures, while protecting immigrants with polyethnic rights that would 'help ethnic groups and religious minorities express their cul-tural particularity and pride without it hampering their success in the economic and political institu-tions of the dominant society' (1995a: 31). Nonetheless, both kinds of group-differentiated rights have something in common: they afford groups protection against the impact of *external* decisions without granting the group any right to make *internal* restrictions on their members as it sees fit. His argument is that 'liberals can and should endorse certain external protections, where they promote fairness between groups, but should reject internal restrictions which limit the right of group members to question and revise traditional authorities and practices' (1995a: 37). What group-differentiated rights are granted, then, depends on whether the particular multinational, polyethnic, or special representation rights in question provide 'external protections', or enforce 'internal restrictions'.

Problems of Liberal Multiculturalism

Kymlicka's defence of group-differentiated rights immediately raised a range of questions and problems, and the literature on multiculturalism over the past decade has tackled many of them. The first issue to be addressed was the question of whether groups could properly be the bearers of rights. To some it was plain that they could not: only individuals could have rights (Narveson, 1991; Hartney, 1991). According to one view, groups were fictitious entities – and fictitious entities could not be rights bearers (Graf, 1994: 194). Yet in spite of such reservations, political theory has in recent years (with the rise of multiculturalism) become much more sympathetic to the idea of group rights.

Even before multiculturalism acquired its current prominence, however, some philosophers had already advanced accounts of group rights. Joseph Raz (1986: 207–8), for example, in his influential account of rights leaves space for collective rights. Larry May (1987: 180), while remaining cautious about the extent to which groups should be recognized as rights holders, argued that moral theorists needed to examine more closely the actions and interests of social groups as possible bearers of rights and responsibilities. And Frances Svensson (1979) had earlier suggested that group rights were needed to do justice to the claims of native peoples. Nonetheless, theorists (or critics) of multiculturalism did not always mean the same thing when they invoked group rights or 'cultural' rights. The most helpful elucidation of the different kinds of rights claims made on behalf of cultural groups was offered by Jacob Levy (1997: 24–5), who distinguished eight categories of rights. These include exemption rights (exempting groups from laws that burden their cultural practices), assistance rights (to do those things the majority can do unassisted), self-government rights, rights to impose external rules (say, restricting non-members' rights to buy property or restricting their right to use their own language), rights to enforce internal rules (even if they violate other rights), rights of recognition of the group's legal code, rights of representation in government, and rights to symbolic claims to acknowledge the worth, status, or existence of the group (1997: 25).

The consensus of opinion is that it is quite possible for groups to have rights, or for rights to be accorded both to groups and to individuals on the basis of identity. A group may hold a right as an independently recognized entity; and individuals may hold particular rights because they are members of particular collectivities. Nonetheless, this issue has remained controversial because of the implications of granting rights on the basis of group membership. As Peter Jones put it, 'Group rights are often articulated as demands for group freedom, but they are also feared as vehicles for group oppression' (1999: 354). Thus Raz's view of group rights, though widely accepted (Brett, 1991; Freeman, 1995; Margalit and Halbertal, 1994), has been criticized for being too capacious in as much as it identifies groups as no more than collectivities of individuals who share nothing more enduring than an interest in a matter (Réaume, 1988; 1994; Jones, 1999: 359). Yet even if we draw a distinction between collective rights and corporate rights (Jones, 1999) there remain other concerns about the need for, or wisdom of, granting rights to groups. For one thing, it is not clear that the identity of the group is readily established, since groups are not only changeable but also often composed of other, smaller groups. To recognize groups is often to reify or entrench formations that might otherwise be temporary, and also to empower those who have authority to speak for the group (Kukathas, 1992a; 1992b; 2003a). Equally, the way in which boundaries distinguishing groups are drawn may be contentious because people may not be happy about being excluded, or included, within a designated collective (Offe, 1998).

Further issues arise, however, once we begin to consider the content of group rights. The demands of some groups for rights in the form of exemptions, for example, have generated a substantial debate about the implications of such special rights. This debate becomes especially vigorous, however, when particular issues become salient: religion, education, and children. While most liberal defenders of multiculturalism have been ready to grant cultural minorities the right to live by their own beliefs, children and education have raised special problems. For many, the limits of multiculturalism are set by the need to protect the interests of children, which override even the rights of parents or communities to inculcate their own religious beliefs. There is considerable tension here within liberal theories of minority rights in particular, as liberals have sought both to respect cultural minorities and to demand of those minorities that they abide by certain liberal strictures.

Kymlicka (1995a :163), for example, recognizes the dilemma liberals face here, but suggests that in the end children need to be educated so that they choose for themselves the paths they will take. Others, however, have been more insistent that the education of children is without doubt of fundamental importance, both from the perspective of the individual child and from the perspective of the liberal state – and should take priority over religious or other claims. Education is education for citizenship. Stephen Macedo, for example, argues that those who embrace multiculturalism should not forget that 'liberal citizens do not come into existence naturally', that diversity 'must be constituted for liberal democratic purposes'. Children, in his view, must be educated so that they become liberal citizens (Macedo, 1995a: 68; and also Macedo, 1995b; 2000). A similar view is advanced by Amy Gutmann, even as she is at pains to emphasize the importance of a multicultural education and the dangers of a schooling that ignores the diversity of traditions found in a society. Education must, in the end, be education for democratic citizenship, even if not only for citizenship (Gutmann, 1996). That it will also tend to assimilate minorities, and work toward the transformation of religious communities, cannot be denied, and so must be accepted (Walzer, 1995: 29). As Eamonn Callan observes, 'schools must somehow honour both the interest in identity formation that rightly belongs to parents and the interest we all share as members of a civic community' (2000: 66; see also Callan, 1997).

The tension between the claims of state and religious community when the treatment and education of children are at issue has surfaced on numerous occasions in legal cases, which have in turn generated considerable debate in political theory. In 1972, in the case of *Wisconsin* v. *Yoder*, the United States Supreme Court decided in favour of Old Order Amish parents who wished to withdraw their children from Wisconsin state schools after eighth grade, two years earlier than statutory requirements for compulsory education permitted. A number of theorists have argued that this was a poor decision, either because it neglects the interests of the child, though this should not be exaggerated since only two additional years of education were at issue (Feinberg, 1980; Gutmann, 1980), or because it fails to recognize the importance of education for citizenship (Arneson and Shapiro, 1996). Others, however, have argued that the liberal state should resist usurping parental authority in order to impose its opinion on what is the best way of life for the child (Burt, 1996: 432).

An equally significant amount of ink has been spilt discussing the somewhat different case of *Mozert* v. *Hawkins*, which involved an (unsuccessful) attempt by Christian fundamentalist parents to win an exemption from Tennessee state regulations requiring public school children to be taught from textbooks that exposed them to a variety of values. Once again, liberal theorists have been divided on the limits of parental authority and the scope for exemptions based on religious or cultural beliefs (compare Callan, 1997 and Tomasi, 2001). One of the dilemmas posed by such circumstances is

whether to bear the costs of granting exemptions or the costs of refusing them. If the cost of granting parents exemptions is that their children will not be exposed to a diversity of views (which, presumably, would make them better citizens), the cost of denying parents exemptions might be that more parents decide to home school their children, thereby cutting them off even more seriously from the democratic mainstream (Reich, 2002).

The conflict between state and religion or culture surfaced in a different, though no less controversial, form in France in 1989 in the so-called 'headscarves affair'. In this instance, a problem arose because three North African immigrant women in a French public secondary school chose to wear their headscarves in class, in a gesture that was interpreted as a challenge to the national policy of secularism in schools. The headscarves were regarded as a form of (Muslim) religious dress, and when the French education minister insisted that the pupils be readmitted to class many objected that this amounted to buckling before the power of religious fanaticism. As Bhikhu Parekh notes, this issue 'went to the heart of the French conceptions of citizenship and national identity and divided the country' (2000: 250). But it also divided political theorists (Galeotti, 1993; 1994; Moruzzi, 1994a; 1994b). In this, as with other controversies surrounding the matter of dress, the problem is that dress is not unambiguously a private matter. It is complex enough when turbaned Sikhs seek exemption from laws mandating the use of motorcycle helmets. In the headscarves case, however, the problem was deepened by the French educational system and its philosophical principle, *laïcité*, which demands state neutrality towards 'all kinds of religious practices, institutionalized through a vigilant removal of sectarian religious symbols, signs, icons, and items of clothing from official public spheres' (Benhabib, 2002: 95–6). How this was to be squared with other public commitments to freedom of religion and liberty of conscience, as well as personal liberty, became entirely obscure.

On this, as on many other occasions, the liberal contention that individuals should be left free to live by their own lights in matters that are of private and not public concern does not help to resolve things. Even the matter of what one eats has a public dimension since there are laws governing the treatment of animals, and in particular the slaughtering of animals for human consumption. Religious demands for kosher or halal meat go against laws providing for the humane slaughter of animals in Europe. And to the extent that religious and cultural groups can gain exemptions to allow ritual slaughter or killing for sport, multiculturalism turns out not only to be bad for animals but problematic for political theory (Casal, 2003). What is to be regarded as a public issue and what as private itself becomes a matter of political and philosophical disagreement. This is even more evidently the case when disputes centre on state symbols, the official status of languages, and the timing of holidays.

One of the reasons such issues become problematic is that diversity is sometimes sustained by continuing immigration which, in many countries, has led to the growth of significant ethnic or cultural minorities within a host society. Immigration might thus further complicate the cultural landscape when a society is already composed of a settler population and an indigenous minority, and perhaps a significant minority population among the settler society. Canada is an obvious example, as a polity dominated by the descendants of English-speaking settlers, with a substantial French minority, various indigenous peoples and a significant immigrant community of people from across the world. But most of Europe and North America is now marked by a similar diversity, accentuated by immigration by peoples from the Third World. While Kymlicka's philosophical response to this has been a theory of group-differentiated citizenship, with specific rights for immigrant and indigenous minorities, others have responded with calls for a slowing or halting of immigration from culturally different people (Brimelow, 1995) or restricting the granting of citizenship to those who have more completely assimilated into the ways of their new society (Pickus, 1998). For some, the nation-state is indeed the expression of a specific ethno-cultural group, and to try to create a multicultural state is therefore a mistake (Auster, 1992).

Conservative reservations about immigration notwithstanding, immigration policy is unlikely to change substantially enough to alter the fact that migrants will continue to add to cultural and ethnic diversity, particularly in the developed West. Immigration will therefore continue to shape multicultural policy, and so multicultural theory (Kukathas, 2003c). At this point, the strains in multicultural policy also start to become evident in political theory, and in liberal political theory in particular. In part, this is because immigration is itself problematic from a liberal point of view and political theorists are divided on the question of how free people should be to move from country to country. While some favour open borders (Dowty, 1987; Carens, 1987; 1992; 2000; Goodin, 1988; 1992), others are less sure of the wisdom of letting the liberal state throw open its society to all-comers, particularly if that might threaten to undermine the liberal state (Buchanan, 1995).

Unsurprisingly, then, much of the debate about multiculturalism has been a debate about citizenship. The question is, how can it be possible to admit a diversity of people into a society, and allow (or even encourage) them to retain their own cultural traditions or customs, and still preserve a polity governed by, and respectful of the rights of, citizens united by a common allegiance? The dilemma is that the more robust the conception of citizenship, the less accommodating must the polity be of cultural diversity, to the extent that it cannot tolerate cultural traditions that do not value citizenship. The greater the diversity it wishes to admit, the weaker must be the demands of citizenship the polity imposes upon its members (Kukathas, 1993; 2003d: 72–5). Or citizenship may have to be rethought completely (Kymlicka and Norman, 1994; 2000a).

Alternative Theories

While Kymlicka's work has dominated the landscape of the political theory of multiculturalism, this is not for any lack of other contributors. On the contrary, a number of other theorists have offered their own accounts of multiculturalism, some agreeing with Kymlicka's general standpoint while disagreeing on particular questions, others offering entirely independent theories of multiculturalism, or rejecting Kymlicka's ideas altogether.

Among the most important of these alternative theories is that offered by Charles Taylor, in his political writings generally but, more particularly, in his influential essay 'The politics of recognition' (1994). Taylor rejects as inadequate what might be called the liberal theory of multiculturalism, for liberalism, in his view, is incapable of giving culture the recognition it requires. Liberalism offers to recognize individuals as the bearers of rights and the possessors of dignity as equal citizens, regarding each person as essentially the same. But what many cultural groups want is recognition not of their sameness, but of their distinctness. Out of such desires, according to Taylor, grew a philosophical alternative to liberalism: the politics of difference. This view is sceptical about the pretensions of liberalism to offer neutral or difference-blind principles that are more than simply reflections of the standards of the dominant culture. Taylor thus rejects the efforts of Kymlicka to develop a liberalism that might accommodate difference by granting individuals differential rights to enable them to pursue their particular cultural ends. For him, the problem with this solution is that it works only 'for existing people who find themselves trapped within a culture under pressure, and can flourish within it or not at all. But it does not justify measures designed to ensure survival through indefinite future generations' (1994: 62). It cannot, for example, justify the collective goals of the Québecois, whose aim is the long-term survival of the French-speaking community in Canada.

A number of other theorists have developed arguments about how cultural diversity might be accommodated by giving greater recognition to 'difference' rather than extending the scope or range of liberal rights (Baumeister, 2000). James Tully's *Strange Multiplicity* (1995), for example, offers a reconstruction of modern constitutionalism that is able to accommodate a greater variety of cultural traditions, and adapt elements from some of them to enhance the quality of liberal constitutional arrangements. In many of these cases, defenders of the politics of difference present an approach to cultural diversity which not only criticizes liberal individualism but also advocates a greater emphasis on the extension of democratic processes to give greater scope to the participation of cultural minorities in the shaping and governing of the polity (see Young, 1990; 2000; Phillips, 1995; Devaux, 2000; Williams, 1998; Tully, 2003).

Yet divisions exist not only between liberal defenders of multiculturalism and their critics but also among liberal theorists themselves. Two major interrelated issues have shaped debate among them: the extent to which diversity ought to be tolerated by liberals when minorities turn out to be illiberal in character, and the principled basis of liberal acceptance of cultural diversity. For some, the limits of liberal toleration are clear: toleration is not extended to illiberal minorities. For Kymlicka, for example, liberalism endorses group-differentiated rights which provide for external protection for groups, but does not permit 'internal restrictions': groups may not curb the basic civil rights of their members. Indeed, for Kymlicka (1989; 1995a) what liberalism protects, above all, is the individual's capacity for autonomous choice; culture is important because it is the context within which individuals learn how to choose, but its value diminishes when it ceases to enable individuals to choose their lives for themselves. A number of other liberal theorists concur with Kymlicka in this matter, arguing that liberalism protects autonomy, and that cultures that do not value or promote autonomy are less deserving of toleration or, at best, should be tolerated on pragmatic rather than principled grounds (Fitzmaurice, 1993; Levey, 1997; Gill 2001) [see further Chapter 8].

Other liberals, however, are less enamoured of autonomy. Some, like Jeff Spinner-Halev, consider autonomy to be valuable, but are critical of those who over emphasize its importance or define autonomy so strictly that many ways of living do not qualify (Spinner-Halev, 2000: 62–7; Spinner, 1994). Others, however, have been more critical still of autonomy, suggesting that toleration or respect for diversity are much more important considerations for liberals (Galston, 1995; Kukathas, 1992a; 1999; 2003a; for an analysis of this liberal divide see Levy, 2003). Kukathas (1997; 2001; 2003b), in particular, has argued vigorously that toleration is so important a liberal virtue that a liberal order will tolerate a diversity of cultures even if some of them are highly illiberal. What a good society protects is freedom of association, not autonomy. And for as long as individuals are free to exit the arrangements or communities or groups within which they find themselves, that order is legitimate – even if it might be one in which many groups or communities are highly illiberal in as much as they are themselves intolerant of diversity. This view, however, gives no particular rights to groups as such, and denies them the external protections advocated by Kymlicka and others; though it also denies outside authorities any right to intervene to lift internal restrictions imposed by such communities upon their members.

This issue of the treatment of minorities within minorities has itself become the subject of considerable debate, many arguing that respect for minorities cannot become grounds for accepting the mistreatment of internal minorities (Green, 1994). Levy, in particular, has offered a treatment of this matter which is sensitive to the claims of minorities seeking to live by their own cultural traditions but nevertheless robust in its rejection of claims to perpetuate practices that are cruel or hateful. *The Multiculturalism of Fear*, borrowing from Judith Shklar's reading of the liberal tradition emphasizing the significance of Montesquieu, insists that a political theory of multiculturalism must be 'centrally concerned neither with preserving and celebrating ethnic identities nor with overcoming them' but with 'mitigating the recurrent dangers such as state violence toward cultural minorities, interethnic warfare, and intra-communal attacks on those who try to alter or leave their cultural communities' (Levy, 2000: 12–13). This theory tries to steer a course between condemning cultural identification and insisting that all minorities become good Millian liberals, and condemning liberalism for failing to be sufficiently hospitable to diversity.

MULTICULTURALISM UNDER FIRE

Not all theories, however, have been entirely sympathetic to multiculturalism, particularly when the price of cultural diversity has looked like being acceptance of illiberal or tyrannical practice. According to Stanley Fish (1998: 73–5), no one could genuinely advocate multiculturalism because that would require tolerating all cultures, including those determined to stamp out tolerance. Most multiculturalists are thus not 'real' but 'boutique' multiculturalists, prepared to tolerate difference for as long as differences are trivial. But regardless of whether Fish's argument is sound – and it is at least debatable, in light of the long history of debate over the question of the toleration of the intolerant (Heyd, 1996) – some theorists have concluded that when multiculturalism comes into conflict with more important fundamental values, multiculturalism will have to yield. Two critiques of multiculturalism are particularly worthy of note, the first coming from the liberal egalitarian perspective and the second from a feminist point of view. A third, coming from an aboriginal perspective, is perhaps also worth considering.

The Liberal Egalitarian Critique

The most comprehensive liberal egalitarian critique of multiculturalism has been offered by Brian Barry in his book *Culture and Equality* (2001). According to Barry, multiculturalism is inconsistent with liberalism and a respect for liberal values and should therefore be rejected. Attempts to show that it is consistent with liberalism are, in his view, implausible. In this regard, he rejects what William Galston has termed 'Reformation liberalism'. Unlike 'Enlightenment liberalism', which emphasizes the importance of individual autonomy, 'Reformation liberalism', Galston maintains, values diversity and sees the importance of 'differences among individuals and groups over such matters as the nature of the good life, sources of moral authority, reason versus faith, and the like' (1995: 521). Barry rejects this distinction, but is especially critical nonetheless of those who are members of the diversity-promoting liberalism camp.

Barry rejects three major arguments advanced in support of Reformation liberalism. The first is that liberal theory values respect for persons and this implies respect for the cultures to which individuals belong. To this Barry replies that illiberal cultures often violate the requirement of equal respect and to that extent they do not deserve respect (2001: 128). The second argument is that liberalism values diversity because it increases the range of options available to individuals. To this Barry responds that liberals prize individuality rather than diversity (2001: 129). The third argument is that liberalism attaches great importance to the public/private distinction, and so should be committed to non-intervention in the private realm. To this Barry replies that liberalism has historically challenged the sanctity of parental and paternal authority, and sought to protect individuals from the groups to which they belong. This does not mean that, for Barry, liberalism requires every group to conform to liberal principles. Individuals must be free to associate in any way they like (consistent with the law protecting the interests of those outside the association). But there are two important conditions: all participants in the association should be sane adults, and their participation should be voluntary (2001: 148). Groups may then do as they please, provided those who do not like the way a group's affairs are run are able to exit without facing excessive costs (2001: 150).

Barry's view imposes serious constraints, then, on the operation of groups. In the end, what it tolerates is only what Fish calls 'boutique multiculturalism'. It requires that illiberal practices not be condoned, that parents be required to send their children to school, and that generally the state ensures that children are appropriately educated and not made the victims of creationists and religious zealots – even if they are their parents. Equally, multiculturalism provides no warrant, in Barry's view, for allowing religious groups to be exempt from the legal requirements for the humane treatment of animals. Jewish and Muslim demands for kosher or halal meat are indefensible, and diversity provides no warrant for making an exception (2001: 40–6). In the end, Barry's view amounts to a reassertion of liberal egalitarianism as a doctrine that is simply incompatible with multiculturalism. (For criticisms of Barry see the papers in Kelly, 2002; for another defence of liberal egalitarianism see Kernohan, 1998.)

The Feminist Critique

If multiculturalism is inconsistent with liberal egalitarianism, it is perhaps even more at odds with contemporary feminism. One of the most important objections to multiculturalism is that, in seeking exemptions or special rights for cultural groups or religious communities and organizations, it in effect seeks protection for groups whose practices are sexist and highly disadvantageous – if not altogether harmful – to women. This view has been put most forcefully by Susan Okin (1998; 1999a; 1999b; 2002), who has taken issue with almost all of the most prominent defenders of multiculturalism, and found their commitment to women's rights and interests wanting.

Multiculturalism is in tension with feminism because the two ideas represent political visions that stand some way apart. As Katha Pollit puts it, 'In its demand for equality for women, feminism sets itself in opposition to virtually every culture on earth … multiculturalism demands respect for all cultural traditions, while feminism interrogates and challenges all cultural traditions' (1999: 27). Feminist critics of multiculturalism thus not only ask why groups which do not accord women equal opportunity, or even equal dignity, should be given special rights or protections, but also why the liberal state fails to intervene in such cultural communities to ensure that women are not denied education, forced into marriage or made the victims of bodily mutilation. Why should a cultural group be entitled to try to live by its ways if these ways violate the individual rights of their members? 'Why shouldn't the liberal state, instead, make it clear to members of such groups, preferably by education but where necessary by punishment, that such practices are not to be tolerated?' (Okin, 1998: 676). Thus when writers such as Margalit and Halbertal (1994) defend public funding of religious education for ultra-orthodox Jews on the basis of the right to culture, feminists like Okin (1999b: 131) ask how this can be defensible when the corollary of this practice is an education for girls that is oriented towards facilitating the religious life of boys.

There is no doubt that feminism and multiculturalism come into conflict, for precisely the reasons that Okin has identified. But the fact of this conflict does not establish whether one philosophical stance or the other ought to prevail (Kukathas, 2001). Some writers, however, have tried to argue that multicultural accommodation need not be incompatible with feminist concerns. The most notable contribution to this position has come from Ayelet Shachar, who argues that it is a mistake to think of multiculturalism simply in terms of the granting of 'external protections' to cultural groups. Since individuals are typically members of many groups, the question is how to 'allocate jurisdiction to identity groups in certain legal arenas while simultaneously respecting group members' rights as citizens' (Shachar, 2001: 27–8). The fact that individuals are members of multiple groups holds out the hope that power might be divided among a number of jurisdictions, enabling women both to secure protection against the power of particular groups and to retain the capacity to participate in the cultural traditions they cherish.

Other writers have also sought ways to reach some solution to the tension between feminism and multiculturalism. Some have concluded that some form of differentiated citizenship will need to be developed if the claims of women and the claims of culture are to be mediated (Benhabib, 2002: 82–104). Others have suggested that a dialogic solution, forswearing the appeal to individual rights or procedural justice, offers a better prospect of reaching an accommodation of cultural values and women's interests (Eisenberg, 2003).

The Aboriginal Critique

Generally, multiculturalism is assumed to speak not only for the interests of immigrant cultural minorities but also for the aboriginal peoples who are minorities in modern states. Canada, Australia, New Zealand, and the United States, no less than Fiji, Malaysia, Indonesia, India and most of South and Central America, are home to peoples whose ancestry may be traced back to premodern times, and their interests are sometimes thought to be addressed by the development of the institutions of a multicultural society. Yet for many indigenous peoples multiculturalism is less than welcome, for its implication is the further marginalization of their communities and culture in a modern state more attuned to the needs of migrants than to those of aborigines.

The recognition of this issue has shaped the development of Kymlicka's theory, which is particularly aware of the distinctive concerns of indigenous peoples. His model of group-differentiated rights deliberately makes space for national minorities, as distinct from polyethnic groups. Whether or not Kymlicka's theory is defensible, however, aboriginal groups around the world have pressed the case for the rights of indigenous minorities. (For a sceptical assessment of the notion of indigenous rights see Mulgan, 1989a. Mulgan, 1989b also suggests that, in the case of New Zealand, the land is occupied by two indigenous peoples: the Maori and Pakeha, or descendants of white settlers.) Moreover, many indigenous groups have insisted that, unlike immigrant peoples, what they need is not only recognition of their independent status but also rectification for past injustice.

Extended treatments of the problem of incorporating aboriginal peoples into modern liberal democratic society, in a way that respects the integrity of aboriginal traditions, have been offered by Tully (1995) and, more recently, Ivison (2002). Both suggest that a viable liberal order requires the establishment of a constitutional *modus vivendi* that incorporates recognition of aboriginal custom and culture. However, as Ivison argues, mere incorporation of indigenous law may not be enough given that circumstances vary and both society and indigenous societies are themselves changing (2002: 141–62).

The problem of rectification for past injustice, however, remains a serious difficulty, particularly when the effluxion of time has made the matter of ascribing to present generations responsibility for past injustice a difficult one, morally, legally, and politically. Jeremy Waldron (1992), for one, has suggested that public policy should focus on future welfare rather than past injustice if the aim is to do justice to the concerns of aboriginal people (see also Sher, 1981; Goodin, 2001). Though others have offered theories of rectification that might do justice to the demands of aboriginal peoples (Kukathas, 2003a; Hill, 2002), it seems unlikely that those demands will ever be met philosophically, let alone politically. In this regard, the distinctive position of aboriginal peoples may not survive the advance of multiculturalism, even if aboriginal peoples remain reluctant to be content with the status of one minority among many.

NATIONALISM

The emergence of multiculturalism over the past three decades has been coterminous with the re-emergence of nationalism, both as a political phenomenon and as a topic for historical and philosophical investigation. Multiculturalism as a public policy has been, at least in part, a response to nationalist demands of a sort – at least to the extent that cultural groups have begun to demand some form of recognition of their distinctive identity, even if they have not always demanded rights of self-government or independence. Unsurprisingly, then, concerns about culture have prompted a rethinking of theories of nationalism, no less than have concerns about nationality helped to shape theories of multiculturalism. (The literature on nationalism is vast, but the focus here is on normative theories of nationalism.)

Defining and Defending Nationalism

Nationalism, according to Margaret Moore, is 'a normative argument that confers moral value on national membership, and on the past and future existence of the nation, and identifies the nation with a particular homeland or part of the globe' (2002: 5). In her account, nations are moral communities characterized by bonds of solidarity and mutual trust, and the attachment people feel to such communities is reason enough to recognize national identity. This very recent account of nationalism takes issue with a number of prominent theories – such as Ernest Gellner's, which argued famously that 'nationalism is primarily a political principle, which holds that the political and national unit should be congruent' (1983: 1). The problem with this view is that it implies that every nationalist movement seeks independence and political separation. Yet there are many groups which are nationalist in character but do not demand statehood, and would be content with greater freedom from external control within the existing state (Moore, 2001: 4) [see further Chapter 15].

In Moore's view, nations are moral communities marked by bonds of solidarity and mutual trust. Thus they are not grounded in culture, for national identity should not be confounded with a common culture. While nationalists seek to preserve political communities, this does not mean that they seek to preserve their cultures. In this regard, Moore's account is at odds with the arguments of liberal nationalists such as Kymlicka, Margalit, Raz, and Yael Tamir, who see nationality as grounded in culture (Kymlicka, 1995a; Raz, 1994; Margalit and Raz, 1990; Tamir, 1993). It has perhaps more in common with Goodin's (1997) suggestion that group attachment is best explained in Bayesian terms, as conventions arising out of an unwillingness of people to expend scarce resources to question the prejudices and presuppositions they grow up with inside their own groups (for a similar analysis see Kukathas, 2002).

The definition, and also the sources, of nationalism are much disputed, some seeing it as the product of modernity and others as its cause. (See the differing historical accounts of Gellner, 1983; Greenfeld, 1992; and Anderson, 1993.) Similarly, the question of the justifiability of nationalism has been much argued about among political theorists. Among liberal theorists in particular, nationalism is viewed with suspicion, since its emphasis on community and belonging puts it at odds with liberal commitments to individual rights and to freedom and equality as universal values. Often, they are inclined to give it only a qualified endorsement (see McMahan, 1997; Hurka, 1997; Lichtenberg, 1997). Increasingly, however, liberal theorists (though not only liberal theorists) have begun to look more sympathetically at nationalist aspirations (Tamir, 1993; Kymlicka, 1995a; Kymlicka, 2001: 203–89). This has led to a reconsideration of the claims of nationality in two respects. First, there is the claim for national self-determination, often associated with demands for independence or secession. And second, there is the claim for the importance of the principle of nationality for the coherence of the state and the pursuit of liberal values in particular. Both kinds of arguments in defence of nationality reveal important conflicts of value with which political theory – and liberal theory in particular – continues to grapple.

National Self-Determination and Secession

National self-determination has re-emerged as an important issue in part because the 1990s saw the break-up of an Eastern European empire as well as the rise of secessionist movements around the world, from Kashmir to East Timor. But the question is an old one, not only in the politics of the twentieth century (which saw the redrawing of the maps of Africa, the Middle East and South East Asia to accommodate nationalist demands for independence), but also in liberal thought. In the nineteenth century, nationalism was allied with liberalism as the principle of nationality was invoked as a principle of freedom – and against alien rule. The liberalism of Mazzini, for example, advocated the unification of Italy as a national republic from which French, Austrian and Papal power was expelled. [see further Chapter 28]. And John Stuart Mill saw a common nationality as a prerequisite for (liberal) representative government.

In this light, national self-determination might seem unproblematic, as an ideal both liberals and non-liberals alike might readily accept: liberals because they favour self-determination, and non-liberals because they favour national community. Yet matters are not so straightforward. In the first instance, what is always, and inescapably, controversial is the issue of who is the 'self' that is entitled to self-determination. Even if people within a boundary are entitled to govern themselves, how is the boundary to be drawn: who is to be included and who is to be excluded (Barry, 1991; 2001: 137)?

Theorists such as Raz and Margalit (1990) look to resolve the problem by tying group membership to culture, suggesting that 'encompassing groups' have a number of characteristics that give them a unity which enables them to mount claims to selfhood and therefore self-determination. Central to such groups is a common culture, but no less important is the fact that people within them recognize each other as members and regard their membership as important for their own self-identification. It is also important to recognize, however, that the right of self-determination can be enjoyed only by a group that is a majority in a territory (1990: 441). What Raz and Margalit reject, as an undesirable illusion, is the individualist principle of consent: 'It is undesirable since ... the more important human groupings need to be based on shared history, and on criteria of nonvoluntaristic (or at least not wholly contractarian) membership to have the value they have' (1990: 456).

Yet it is difficult to see how consent can fail to play a significant role in any account of self-determination if self-determination is to mean something more than the determination of the lives of some by the will of others. And many other theories of self-determination give a substantial role to consent as central to any account of political legitimacy. Among the most sustained defences of the importance of consent is that offered in the writings of Harry Beran, particularly in his defence of the right of secession as central to the legitimacy of the liberal state (Beran, 1984; 1987; but see also Green, 1988; and Simmons, 2001) [see further Chapter 15].

Secession has attracted considerable attention from political theorists since Beran revived the issue, not least because of its pertinence whenever the question of nationality is raised. The most influential work is Allen Buchanan's *Secession: The Morality of Political Divorce* (1991), which explicitly rejected consent as a sufficient condition for the justification of secession, and suggested that, while groups could have the right to secede, this was very much a limited right. In the literature that has developed in the debates that followed Buchanan's original contribution, three main categories of theories of secession have emerged: just-cause theories (Buchanan, 1991; 1997; Norman, 1998), choice theories (Philpott, 1995; 1998), and nationalist theories (Raz and Margalit, 1990; Nielsen, 1998). Of the three, only just-cause theories have come close to developing justifications with any prospect of being codified in a way that might influence or shape secessionist politics (Norman, 1998). However, the reality of political power and its operation in the world makes one suspect that no theory of secession is likely to provide the basis for a workable, constitutionally guaranteed, right of secession (Norman, 2003: 609).

Nationalism and Multiculturalism

Clearly national sentiment sometimes leads to calls for some consideration to be given to the case for secession. On other occasions, however, it pushes in the other direction. While the principle of nationality is sympathetic to the interests or claims of groups, and particularly to their claims to the protection of their identity, by definition it must also be wary of group claims that might undermine a national identity.

This issue arises in particular when nationalism runs up against the question of multiculturalism. To the extent that multiculturalism advocates the accommodation of a plurality of identities holding to divergent values within a polity, it is inconsistent with any form of nationalism. And yet, in another sense, multiculturalism is the theory of nationalism *par excellence*, at least if one takes Moore's view that nationalism implies not separatism, but only a measure of independence. To reconcile multiculturalism, or indeed any form of pluralism, with nationalism has been an important concern for a number of theorists who wish to hold on to the principle of nationality without jettisoning cultural diversity and the toleration of difference.

Of particular significance here is the work of David Miller (1995; 2000; 2001), who considers that nations have good reason for wanting to be self-determining, but also thinks that we can recognize the claims of nationality without suppressing other sources of identity, such as ethnicity. A major reason why nationality is important for Miller is that it is a precondition of the pursuit of social justice, which cannot plausibly be pursued globally (Miller, 1999). The pursuit of social justice requires, in particular, that a measure of social solidarity is necessary if citizens are to go along with institutions which perform a redistributive function. Indeed, as others have argued, the workings of legal and political institutions may depend to a significant degree on a substantial willingness on the part of the population of a state to view themselves as members of the same group, who owe something to each other in a way which they do not owe to outsiders (Patten, 2001). For this reason, it may be necessary for the state to take an interest in the fostering of a sense of citizenship and belonging.

This, however, brings us back to the problems with which our discussion began. The desire of each to be recognized as different and distinctive gives rise to a demand for a politics of multiculturalism – one that recognizes and tolerates, or even encourages and honours, diversity. Yet the politics of diversity in turn may give rise to a demand for political separation, and the emergence of communities in which diversity has no place. How the many can live as one remains a salient question in political theory.

REFERENCES

Anderson, Benedict (1993) *Imagined Communities: Reflections on the Origin and Spread of Nationalism*. New York: Verso.

Arneson, Richard and Ian Shapiro (1996) 'Democratic autonomy and religious freedom: a critique of *Wisconsin* v. *Yoder*'. In Ian Shapiro and Russell Hardin, eds, *Political Order: NOMOS XXXVIII*. New York: New York University Press, 365–411.

Auster, Lawrence (1992) 'The forbidden topic: the link between multiculturalism and immigration'. *National Review*, 27 (April).

Barry, Brian (1991) 'Self-government revisited'. *Democracy and Power*. Oxford: Clarendon, 156–86.

Barry, Brian (2001) *Culture and Equality: An Egalitarian Critique of Multiculturalism*. Oxford: Polity.

Baumeister, Andrea T. (2000) *Liberalism and the 'Politics of Difference'*. Edinburgh: Edinburgh University Press.

Benhabib, Seyla (2002) *The Claims of Culture: Equality and Diversity in the Global Era*. Princeton, NJ: Princeton University Press.

Beran, Harry (1984) 'A liberal theory of secession'. *Political Studies*, 32: 21–31.

Beran, Harry (1987) *The Consent Theory of Political Obligation*. London: Croom Helm.

Brett, Nathan (1991) 'Language laws and collective rights'. *Canadian Journal of Law and Jurisprudence*, 4: 347–60.

Brimelow, Peter (1995) *Alien Nation: Common Sense about America's Immigration Disaster*. New York: Random House.

Buchanan, Allen (1991) *Secession: The Morality of Political Divorce from Fort Sumter to Lithuania and Quebec*. Boulder, CO: Westview.

Buchanan, Allen (1997) 'Theories of secession'. *Philosophy and Public Affairs*, 26 (1): 30–61.

Buchanan, James (1995) 'A two-country parable'. In Warren F. Schwartz, ed., *Justice in Immigration*. Cambridge: Cambridge University Press, 63–6.

Burt, Shelley (1996) 'In defense of *Yoder*: parental authority and the public schools'. In Ian Shapiro and Russell Hardin, eds, *Political Order: NOMOS XXXVIII*. New York: New York University Press, 412–37.

Callan, Eamonn (1997) *Creating Citizens: Political Education and Liberal Democracy*. Oxford: Oxford University Press.

Callan, Eamonn (2000) 'Discrimination and religious schooling'. In Will Kymlicka and Wayne Norman, eds, *Citizenship in Diverse Societies*. Oxford: Oxford University Press, 45–67.

Carens, Joseph H. (1987) 'Aliens and citizens: the case for open borders'. *Review of Politics*, 49 (2): 251–73.

Carens, Joseph H. (1992) 'Migration and morality: a liberal egalitarian perspective'. In Brian Barry and Robert E. Goodin, eds, *Free Movement: Ethical Issues in the Transnational Migration of People and Money*. University Park, PA: Pennsylvania State University Press, 25–47.

Carens, Joseph H. (2000) *Culture, Citizenship and Community: A Contextual Examination of Justice and Evenhandedness*. Oxford: Oxford University Press.

Casal, Paula (2003) 'Is multiculturalism bad for animals?' *Journal of Political Philosophy*, 11 (1): 1–22.

Devaux, Monique (2000) *Cultural Pluralism and Dilemmas of Justice*. Ithaca, NY: Cornell University Press.

Dowty, Alan (1987) *Closed Borders: The Contemporary Assault on Freedom of Movement*. New Haven, CT: Yale University Press.

Eisenberg, Avigail (2003) 'Diversity and equality: three approaches to cultural and sexual difference'. *Journal of Political Philosophy*, 11 (1): 41–64.

Feinberg, Joel (1980) 'The child's right to an open future'. In William Aiken and Hugh LaFollette, eds, *Whose Child? Children's Rights, Parental Authority, and State Power*. Totowa, NJ: Littlefield Adams.

Fish, Stanley (1998) 'Boutique multiculturalism'. In Arthur Melzer, Jerry Weinberger and M. Richard Zinman, eds, *Multiculturalism and American Democracy*. Lawrence, KS: University of Kansas Press, 69–88.

Fitzmaurice, Deborah (1993) 'Autonomy as a good: liberalism, autonomy and toleration'. *Journal of Political Philosophy*, 1 (1): 1–16.

Freeman, Michael (1995) 'Are there collective human rights?' *Political Studies*, Special Issue, 43: 25–40.

Galeotti, Anna Elisabetta (1993) 'Citizenship and equality: the place for toleration'. *Political Theory*, 21 (4): 585–605.

Galeotti, Anna Elisabetta (1994) 'A problem with theory: a rejoinder to Moruzzi'. *Political Theory*, 22 (4): 673–7.

Galston, William (1995) 'Two concepts of Liberalism', *Ethics*, 105(3): 516–34.

Gellner, Ernest (1983) *Nations and Nationalism*. Ithaca, NY: Cornell University Press.

Gill, Emily R. (2001) *Becoming Free: Autonomy and Diversity in the Liberal Polity*. Lawrence, KS: University of Kansas Press.

Glazer, Nathan (1975) *Affirmative Discrimination: Ethnic Inequality and Public Policy*. New York: Basic.

Glazer, Nathan (1983) *Ethnic Dilemmas: 1964–1982*. Cambridge, MA: Harvard University Press.

Glazer, Nathan (1997) *We Are All Multiculturalists Now*. Cambridge, MA: Harvard University Press.

Goodin, Robert E. (1988) 'What's so special about our fellow countrymen?' *Ethics*, 98: 663–86.

Goodin, Robert E. (1992) 'If people were money? …'. In Brian Barry and Robert E. Goodin, eds, *Free Movement: Ethical Issues in the Transnational Migration of People and Money*. University Park, PA: Pennsylvania State University Press, 6–22.

Goodin, Robert E. (1997) 'Conventions and conversions, or why is nationalism sometimes so nasty?' In Robert McKim and Jeff McMahan, eds, *The Morality of Nationalism*. Oxford: Oxford University Press, 88–106.

Goodin, Robert E. (2001) 'Waitangi tales'. *Australasian Journal of Philosophy*, 78 (3): 309–33.

Graf, James A. (1994) 'Human rights, peoples, and the right to self-determination'. In Judith Baker, ed., *Group Rights*. Toronto: University of Toronto Press, 186–214.

Green, Leslie (1988) *The Authority of the State*. Oxford: Oxford University Press.

Green, Leslie (1994) 'Internal minorities and their rights'. In Judith Baker, ed., *Group Rights*. Toronto: University of Toronto Press, 100–17.

Greenfeld, Liah (1992) *Nationalism: Five Roads to Modernity*. Cambridge, MA: Harvard University Press.

Gutmann, Amy (1980) 'Children, paternalism and education'. *Philosophy and Public Affairs*, 9 (4): 338–58.

Gutmann, Amy (1996) 'Challenges of multiculturalism in democratic education'. In Robert K. Fullinwider, ed., *Public Education in a Multicultural Society: Policy, Theory, Critique*. Cambridge: Cambridge University Press, 156–79.

Hartney, Michael (1991) 'Some confusions concerning collective rights'. *Canadian Journal of Law and Jurisprudence*, 4: 293–314.

Heyd, David, ed. (1996) *Toleration: An Elusive Virtue*. Princeton, NJ: Princeton University Press.

Hill, Renée A. (2002) 'Compensatory Justice: Over Time and Between Groups'. *Journal of Political Philosophy*, 10 (4): 392–415.

Hurka, Thomas (1997) 'The justification of national partiality'. In Robert McKim and Jeff McMahan, eds, *The Morality of Nationalism*. Oxford: Oxford University Press, 139–57.

Ivison, Duncan (2002) *Postcolonial Liberalism*. Cambridge: Cambridge University Press.

Jones, Peter (1999) 'Group rights and group oppression'. *Journal of Political Philosophy*, 7 (4): 353–77.

Kedourie, Elie (1967) *Nationalism*. London: Hutchinson.

Kelly, Paul, ed. (2002) *Multiculturalism Reconsidered: Culture and Equality and Its Critics*. Oxford: Polity.

Kernohan, Andrew (1998) *Liberalism, Equality, and Cultural Oppression*. Cambridge: Cambridge University Press.

Kukathas, Chandran (1992a) 'Are there any cultural rights?' *Political Theory*, 20 (1): 105–39.

Kukathas, Chandran (1992b) 'Cultural rights again: a rejoinder to Kymlicka'. *Political Theory*, 20 (4): 674–80.

Kukathas, Chandran (1993) 'The idea of a multicultural society'. In Chandran Kukathas, ed., *Multicultural Citizens: The Philosophy and Politics of Identity*. St Leonards, NSW: Centre for Independent Studies, 19–30.

Kukathas, Chandran (1997) 'Cultural toleration'. In Will Kymlicka and Ian Shapiro, eds, *Ethnicity and Group Rights: NOMOS XXXIX*. New York: New York University Press, 69–104.

Kukathas, Chandran (1999) 'Tolerating the intolerable'. *Papers on Parliament*, 33: 67–81.

Kukathas, Chandran (2001) 'Is Feminism Bad for Multiculturalism?' *Public Affairs Quarterly*, 15 (2): 83–98.

Kukathas, Chandran (2002) 'Equality and diversity'. *Politics, Philosophy and Economics*, 1 (2): 185–212.

Kukathas, Chandran (2003a) 'Responsibility for past injustice: how to shift the burden'. *Politics, Philosophy and Economics*, 2 (2): 165–88.

Kukathas, Chandran (2003b) *The Liberal Archipelago: A Theory of Diversity and Freedom*. Oxford: Oxford University Press.

Kukathas, Chandran (2003c) 'Immigration'. In Hugh LaFollette, ed., *The Oxford Handbook of Practical Ethics*. New York: Oxford University Press, 567–90.

Kukathas, Chandran (2003d) 'Ethical pluralism from a classical liberal perspective'. In Richard Madsen and Tracy B. Strong, eds, *The Many and the One: Religious and Secular Perspectives on Ethical Pluralism in the Modern World*. Princeton, NJ: Princeton University Press, 55–77.

Kymlicka, Will (1989) *Liberalism, Community and Culture*. Oxford: Oxford University Press.

Kymlicka, Will (1995a) *Multicultural Citizenship: A Liberal Theory of Minority Rights*. Oxford: Oxford University Press.

Kymlicka, Will, ed. (1995b) *The Rights of Minority Cultures*. Oxford: Oxford University Press.

Kymlicka, Will (2000) *Finding Our Way: Rethinking Ethnocultural Relations in Canada*. Don Mills, Ontario: Oxford University Press.

Kymlicka, Will (2001) *Politics in the Vernacular: Nationalism, Multiculturalism, and Citizenship*. Oxford: Oxford University Press.

Kymlicka, Will and Wayne Norman (1994) 'The return of the citizen'. *Ethics*, 104 (2): 352–81.

Kymlicka, Will and Wayne Norman (2000a) 'Citizenship in culturally diverse societies: issues, contexts, concepts'. In Will Kymlicka and Wayne Norman, eds, *Citizenship in Diverse Societies*. Oxford: Oxford University Press, 1–41.

Kymlicka, Will and Wayne Norman, eds (2000b) *Citizenship in Diverse Societies*. Oxford: Oxford University Press.

Kymlicka, Will and Ian Shapiro, eds (1997) *Ethnicity and Group Rights*: *NOMOS XXXIX*. New York: New York University Press.

Levey, Geoffrey Brahm (1997) 'Equality, autonomy and cultural rights'. *Political Theory*, 25 (2): 215–48.

Levy, Jacob (1997) 'Classifying cultural rights'. In Will Kymlicka and Ian Shapiro, eds, *Ethnicity and Group Rights*: *NOMOS XXXIX*. New York: New York University Press, 22–66.

Levy, Jacob (2000) *The Multiculturalism of Fear*. Oxford: Oxford University Press.

Levy, Jacob (2003) 'Liberalism's divide, after socialism and before'. *Social Philosophy and Policy*, 20 (1): 278–97.

Lichtenberg, Judith (1997) 'Nationalism, for and (mainly) against'. In Robert McKim and Jeff McMahan, eds, *The Morality of Nationalism*. Oxford: Oxford University Press, 158–75.

Lopez, Mark (2000) *The Origins of Multiculturalism in Australian Politics*. Melbourne: Melbourne University Press.

Macedo, Stephen (1995a) 'Multiculturalism for the religious right? Defending liberal civic education'. In Yael Tamir, ed., *Democratic Education in a Multicultural State*. Oxford: Blackwell, 65–80.

Macedo, Stephen (1995b) 'Liberal civic education and religious fundamentalism: the case of God v. John Rawls'. *Ethics*, 105: 468–96.

Macedo, Stephen (2000) *Democracy and Distrust: Civic Education in a Multicultural Democracy*. Cambridge, MA: Harvard University Press.

McMahan, Jeff (1997) 'The limits of national partiality'. In Robert McKim and Jeff McMahan, eds, *The Morality of Nationalism*. Oxford: Oxford University Press, 107–38.

Margalit, Avishai and Moshe Halbertal (1994) 'Liberalism and the right to culture'. *Social Research*, 61: 491–510.

Margalit, Avishai and Joseph Raz (1990) 'National self-determination'. *Journal of Philosophy*, 87: 439–61.

May, Larry (1987) *The Morality of Groups: Collective Responsibility, Group-Based Harm, and Corporate Rights*. Notre Dame, IN: University of Notre Dame Press.

Miller, David (1995) *On Nationality*. Oxford: Clarendon.

Miller, David (1999) 'Justice and global inequality'. In Andrew Hurrell and Ngaire Woods, eds, *Inequality,*

Globalization and World Politics. Oxford: Oxford University Press, 187–210.

Miller, David (2000) *Citizenship and National Identity*. Oxford: Polity.

Miller, David (2001) 'Nationality in divided societies'. In Alain-G. Gagnon and James Tully, eds, *Multinational Democracies*. Cambridge: Cambridge University Press, 299–318.

Minogue, Kenneth (1967) *Nationalism*. London: Batsford.

Moore, Margaret (2002) *The Ethics of Nationalism*. Oxford: Oxford University Press.

Moruzzi, Norma Claire (1994a) 'A problem with headscarves: contemporary complexities of political and social identity'. *Political Theory*, 22 (4): 653–72.

Moruzzi, Norma Claire (1994b) 'A response to Galeotti'. *Political Theory*, 22 (4): 678–9.

Mulgan, Richard (1989a) 'Should indigenous peoples have special rights?' *Orbis*, 33 (3): 375–88.

Mulgan, Richard (1989b) *Maori, Pakeha and Democracy*. Auckland: Oxford University Press.

Narveson, Jan (1991) 'Collective rights?' *Canadian Journal of Law and Jurisprudence*, 4: 329–45.

Nielsen, Kai (1998) 'Liberal nationalism and secession'. In Margaret Moore, ed., *National Self-Determination and Secession*. Oxford: Oxford University Press, 103–33.

Norman, Wayne (1998) 'The ethics of secession as the regulation of secessionist politics'. In Margaret Moore, ed., *National Self-determination and Secession*. Oxford: Oxford University Press, 34–61.

Norman, Wayne (2003) 'National autonomy'. In Hugh LaFollette, ed., *The Oxford Handbook of Practical Ethics*. Oxford: Oxford University Press, 591–619.

Offe, Claus (1998) ' "Homogeneity" and constitutional democracy: coping with identity conflicts through group rights'. *Journal of Political Philosophy*, 6 (2): 113–41.

Okin, Susan Moller (1998) 'Feminism and multiculturalism: some tensions'. *Ethics*, 108: 661–84.

Okin, Susan Moller (1999a) 'Is multiculturalism bad for women?'. In Joshua Cohen, Matthew Howard and Martha C. Nussbaum, eds, *Is Multiculturalism Bad for Women?* Princeton, NJ: Princeton University Press, 7–24.

Okin, Susan Moller (1999b) 'Reply'. In Joshua Cohen, Matthew Howard and Martha C. Nussbaum, eds, *Is Multiculturalism Bad for Women?* Princeton, NJ: Princeton University Press, 115–31.

Okin, Susan Moller (2002) ' "Mistresses of their own destiny": group rights, gender, and realistic rights of exit'. *Ethics*, 112: 205–30.

Parekh, Bhikhu (2000) *Rethinking Multiculturalism: Cultural Diversity and Political Theory*. London: Macmillan.

Patten, Alan (2001) 'Liberal citizenship in multinational societies'. In Alain-G. Gagnon and James Tully, eds,

Multinational Democracies. Cambridge: Cambridge University Press, 279–98.

Phillips, Anne (1995) *The Politics of Presence*. Oxford: Clarendon.

Philpott, Daniel (1995) 'In defence of self-determination'. *Ethics*, 105 (2): 352–85.

Philpott, Daniel (1998) 'Self-determination in practice'. In Margaret Moore, ed., *National Self-Determination and Secession*. Oxford: Oxford University Press, 79–102.

Pickus, Noah M. J. (1998) 'To make natural: creating citizens for the twenty-first century'. In Noah M. J. Pickus, ed., *Immigration and Citizenship in the Twenty-First Century*. Lanham, MD: Rowman and Littlefield, 107–40.

Plamenatz, John (1960) *On Alien Rule and Self-Government*. London: Longmans.

Pollit, Katha (1999) 'Whose culture?' In Joshua Cohen, Matthew Howard and Martha C. Nussbaum, eds, *Is Multiculturalism Bad for Women?* Princeton, NJ: Princeton University Press, 27–30.

Raz, Joseph (1986) *The Morality of Freedom*. Oxford: Clarendon.

Raz, Joseph (1994) 'Multiculturalism: a liberal perspective'. In his *Ethics in the Public Domain*. Oxford: Clarendon, 155–76.

Réaume, Denise G. (1988) 'Individuals, groups, and rights to public goods'. *University of Toronto Law Journal*, 38: 1–27.

Réaume, Denise G. (1994) 'The group right to linguistic security: Whose right? What duties?' In Judith Baker, ed., *Group Rights*. Toronto: University of Toronto Press, 118–41.

Reich, Rob (2002) *Bridging Liberalism and Multiculturalism in American Education*. Chicago: University of Chicago Press.

Sher, George (1981) 'Ancient wrongs and modern rights'. *Philosophy and Public Affairs*, 10 (1): 3–17.

Shachar, Ayelet (2001) *Multicultural Jurisdictions*. Cambridge: Cambridge University Press.

Simmons, A. John (2001) *Justification and Legitimacy: Essays on Rights and Obligations*. Cambridge: Cambridge University Press.

Spinner, Jeff (1994) *The Boundaries of Citizenship: Race, Ethnicity and Nationality in the Liberal State*. Baltimore: Johns Hopkins University Press.

Spinner-Halev, Jeff (2000) *Surviving Diversity: Religion and Democratic Citizenship*. Baltimore: Johns Hopkins University Press.

Svensson, Frances (1979) 'Liberal democracy and group rights: the legacy of individualism and its impact on American Indian tribes'. *Political Studies*, 23 (3): 421–39.

Tamir, Yael (1993) *Liberal Nationalism*. Princeton, NJ: Princeton University Press.

Taylor, Charles (1994) 'The politics of recognition'. In Amy Gutmann, ed., *Multiculturalism: Examining the Politics of Recognition*. Princeton, NJ: Princeton University Press.

Tomasi, John (2001) *Liberalism Beyond Justice*. Princeton, NJ: Princeton University Press.

Tully, James (1995) *Strange Multiplicity: Constitutionalism in an Age of Diversity*. Cambridge: Cambridge University Press.

Tully, James (2003) 'Ethical pluralism and classical liberalism'. In Richard Madsen and Tracy B. Strong, eds, *The Many and the One: Religious and Secular Perspectives on Ethical Pluralism in the Modern World*. Princeton, NJ: Princeton University Press, 78–85.

Van Dyke, Vernon (1977) 'The individual, the state, and ethnic communities in political theory'. *World Politics*, 29 (3): 343–69.

Van Dyke, Vernon (1982) 'Collective rights and moral rights: problems in liberal-democratic thought'. *Journal of Politics*, 44: 21–40.

Van Dyke, Vernon (1985) *Human Rights, Ethnicity, and Discrimination*. Westport, CT: Greenwood.

Waldron, Jeremy (1992) 'Superseding historic injustice'. *Ethics*, 103: 4–28.

Walzer, Michael (1995) 'Education, democratic citizenship, and multiculturalism'. In Yeal Tamir, ed., *Democratic Education in a Multicultural State*. Oxford: Blackwell, 23–32.

Williams, Melissa (1998) *Voice, Trust, and Memory: Marginalized Groups and the Failings of Liberal Representation*. Princeton, NJ: Princeton University Press.

Young, Iris Marion (1990) *Justice and the Politics of Difference*. Princeton, NJ: Princeton University Press.

Young, Iris Marion (2000) *Democracy and Inclusion*. Oxford: Oxford University Press.

20

New Social Movements

DAVID WEST

New social movements (NSMs) are both a major phenomenon of recent Western history and an important topic within contemporary social and political studies. The study of these movements extends from straightforward empirical description to more theoretical attempts to explain their rise, activities and ultimate fate. However, the category of NSMs has proved contentious almost from its first use. In fact, the newness of new social movements is best understood in the context of an unfolding set of theoretical debates rather than simply as a reflection of a particular stage of Western society. The focus, in what follows, is on the theoretical context or, more precisely, the intersections and interactions between both theoretical and historical contexts, in order to identify the 'nub' of the problematic concept 'new social movement'. As a result, there will be no attempt either to provide an exhaustive overview of theories or commentaries on NSMs (impossible within the scope of the present chapter) or to discuss the range of broadly similar social movement activity in other regional contexts such as the 'Second' or communist and 'Third' or developing worlds.

HISTORICAL CONTEXT: THE EMERGENCE OF NEW SOCIAL MOVEMENTS

A Preliminary Definition

Although there is no straightforward answer to the question 'What are new social movements?', a provisional definition will help to locate the problem. Social movements, then, are less organized, partially extra- or anti-institutional forms of collective activity aiming, over an extended period, to bring about (and sometimes prevent) social change. Social movements interact with, influence and sometimes succeed in transforming the institutionalized political structures of a society. The term '*new social movements*' refers to a group of contemporary (or recent) social movements that have played a significant and, for most commentators, largely progressive role in Western societies from the late 1960s. The identification of these waves of activism as 'new' typically refers to their concern with issues other than class. The category normally includes peace and anti-nuclear movements, environmental, ecological or green movements, lesbian and gay liberation, second-wave feminism, anti-racist and alternative lifestyle movements.

After Stability: the Emergence of New Social Movements

The emergence of new social movements in the West came as a surprise to most commentators. The 'long economic boom' and 'social democratic consensus' after World War II corresponded to a period of political stability and even apathy, marked by academic pronouncements of the 'end of ideology' (Lipset, 1960: 403–17; Vincent, 1995: 9–13). The conflict between capital and labour was tamed by the class-compromising structures of the welfare state with its progressive taxation, social security and welfare provision, policies of full employment, and 'neocorporatist' consultation between employers, trade unions and government (Berger, 1981; Offe, 1984). A state of permanent Cold War with the communist East helped to contain social conflicts in the capitalist West, cementing consensus under US hegemony around a security policy based on the nuclear deterrence of 'mutually assured destruction'. Liberal democrats and 'elitist pluralists' celebrated the stability of Western societies as the permanent achievement of an 'open' political system, which functioned as a political market mediating the conflicting demands of organized political interests (Schumpeter, 1950; Bachrach, 1967). Even Herbert Marcuse, a left-wing critic of liberal capitalism, portrayed the prevailing social order in substantially similar terms – albeit negatively – as a 'one-dimensional society' that had outgrown the polar opposition of capitalists and workers (Marcuse, 1964).

But although Marcuse was pessimistic about the proletariat's immediate revolutionary potential, he was alert to other cracks in the façade of liberal democratic stability. From the 1950s in the USA, the black Civil Rights movement spoke for 'outcasts and outsiders', who were excluded not just from most of the material benefits of the 'affluent society' but also from civil and democratic rights (1964: 199–200). During the 1960s further cracks appeared. Protests against the USA's war in Vietnam were both products and catalysts of an emerging student radicalism, giving rise to organizations like Students for a Democratic Society (SDS) at Berkeley (Cockburn and Blackburn, 1969). Student radicalism was itself inseparable from a more diffuse 'counterculture' of 'sex, drugs and rock 'n' roll'. Students and 'hippies' chose to 'drop out', rejecting their parents' commitments to work and consumerism (Roszak, 1969). Others sought to channel these developments into a reconstructed movement for socialism. Horrified by the failures and crimes of Stalinism but equally dissatisfied with the compromise and bureaucratic paternalism of social democracy, New Left intellectuals fashioned a more democratic, even more hedonistic version of socialism (Thompson et al., 1960; Oglesby, 1969). These diverse strands of dissent and activism reached their public and symbolic apogee in the 'May Events' of Paris in 1968, when a combination of students and workers seemed on the point of toppling the French state. Although prospects of revolution were soon averted, the dramatic nature of these events shattered complacent belief in the inevitable stability of Western democracies (Touraine, 1971; Urwin, 1989: 229–55).

It is in the aftermath of the Paris Events that the origins of new social movements can be located. The 1969 riots at the Stonewall Bar in New York were the spark for the formation of the Gay Liberation Front, the vanguard of the contemporary gay and lesbian movements (Jagose, 1996: 30–43; Weeks, 1977: 185–206). Likewise, partly driven by disillusionment with the 'sexism' of their New Left comrades in the students' and anti-war movements, 'second-wave feminism' flourished from the beginning of the 1970s [see further Chapter 21]. This

period also saw a strong revival of peace and anti-nuclear activism, and the upsurge throughout Western societies of the environmental or 'green' movements [see further Chapter 14]. In the former West Germany, the 'extra-parliamentary opposition' was overtaken by a proliferation of large- and small-scale protests against nuclear power stations and military bases and other 'citizens' initiatives' (*Bürgerinitiativen*). Peace and environmental activism cross-fertilized with a broad array of feminist, gay and lesbian, alternative lifestyle, countercultural and 'alternative' groups (Hülsberg, 1988: 36–63), culminating in 1980 with the formation of the German Green Party (*Die Grünen*) – the 'anti-party' party of NSMs.

What Was *New* about New Social Movements?

The new social movements of the 1970s displayed a number of seemingly novel characteristics and/or displayed certain characteristics to a novel degree. In contrast to the 'old politics' dominated by class and distributional issues, new social movements addressed issues of gender, sexuality, race, nature and security. Although they still made material demands (for equal pay and opportunities, social justice, fair trade, etc.), the new movements insisted on their independence from class-based divisions. In contrast to the centralist and bureaucratic electoral and revolutionary organizations of the old left, new forms of political practice and collective action were also in evidence. Alongside more conventional organizations, there was a flourishing of more fluid, participatory and even anarchistic groups. Loosely organized 'affinity' and 'consciousness-raising' groups practised a different kind of politics, which included the transformation of personal consciousness and identity as well as direct action, moral and symbolic protest. The activists of the new movements also differed from the traditionally working-class stalwarts of the labour movement: they were mainly younger, tertiary educated, from middle or 'new middle' class backgrounds and less preponderantly male (Dalton and Kuechler, 1990; Melucci, 1989: 5–6; Pakulski, 1991: 39–42).

On the other hand, of course, neither agents and issues, nor forms of political practice and collective action, were absolutely new. The wish to protect nature from industrial civilization can be traced to William Blake and the Romantic movement (Eder, 1990: 28–32). The isolated feminist protests of Mary Wollstonecraft and Abigail Adams in the eighteenth century were followed by the more organized campaigning of anti-slavery, temperance, moral revival movements and suffragettes in the nineteenth and twentieth centuries (Evans, 1977). An energetic homosexual rights movement was founded in Germany by Magnus Hirschfeld in 1897 (Steakley, 1993). Nineteenth-century anarchists and some early socialists (dismissed by Marx and Engels as 'utopian') already warned of the dangers of state socialism. They advocated measures later familiar from the movements of the 1960s and 1970s, such as direct democracy, rotation of offices and the recall of delegates, designed to prevent the re-emergence of tyrannical elites. Individual moral renewal and even 'free love' within alternative communities should anticipate or 'prefigure' the ideal society (Gray, 1947; Lichtheim, 1968). As E. P. Thompson (1968) has shown, even the 'making' of the English working class during the industrial revolution was less a matter of economic determination than a *self*-making born of moral and cultural creativity.

In fact, it was in large part the New Left and NSM activists of the 1960s and 1970s who themselves, through the rediscovery of previously 'hidden' histories of women, homosexuals, utopian socialists, slaves and indigenous peoples, most effectively contradicted claims of the absolute novelty of new social movements (Duberman, Vicinus and Chauncey, 1989; Rowbotham, 1974). If the scale of the new movements and the prominence of their distinctive traits nevertheless begin to establish their relative historical significance, their novelty ultimately depends as much on the theoretical and ideological context of their emergence.

THEORETICAL AND IDEOLOGICAL CONTEXT I: FROM COLLECTIVE BEHAVIOUR TO COLLECTIVE ACTION

The 'Collective Behaviour' Tradition

The novelty of new social movements derives, in large part, from their challenge to the state of theory and ideology at the time of their emergence. Thus new social movements challenged not only the stability but, at the level of *normative political theory*, also the legitimacy of liberal democratic societies. Political developments from the 1960s made clear that liberal democracies did not, as their apologists had claimed, successfully represent all significant political interests (cf. Bachrach, 1967). African-Americans, women, lesbians and gays, and environmentalists could all claim to be excluded from the social democratic consensus. Changes such as the Civil Rights Acts in the USA, equal opportunities, equal pay and anti-discrimination legislation regarding gender, race and sexuality, and the decriminalization of homosexuality, amounted to obvious extensions of liberal values, but many

liberals ignored these issues at the time. Rawls is typical in this regard for his initial failure to consider the justice of women's position in society (Rawls, 1971; Okin, 1989). Long-lasting controversies were also sparked over issues such as affirmative action (Dworkin, 1978: 223–39). Furthermore, the campaigns that led to these changes transgressed the conventional boundaries of acceptable or 'institutionalized' political activity, which included voting, lobbying and standing for office, but not civil disobedience, direct action and the ever-expanding repertoire of protest. Accordingly, normative theorists were inspired to reconsider the legitimacy of these and other extra-institutional forms of social movement activity (Dworkin, 1978: 206–22; Rawls, 1971: 363–91; Singer, 1973; Walzer, 1970).

The normative reappraisal of social movement activities also contributed to significant *methodological* developments in empirical social science, summed up in the very term 'social movement'. Social movement activity had previously been studied mainly as 'collective behaviour'. Continuing a long tradition of suspicion towards unruly 'rabbles', 'mobs' and 'masses', classic studies from this perspective examined instances of collective irrationality from the riots, rumours and panics of the French Revolution to the mass hysteria of National Socialism and the Stalinist cult of personality (Le Bon, 1947; Killian, 1964; Pakulski, 1991: 3–31). Mainstream sociology and political science after World War II, particularly in the USA, retained this emphasis, typically regarding collective behaviour as a threat to the rational, ordered, organized collective action enabled by liberal democratic institutions. One representative example of this approach, Kornhauser's *Politics of Mass Society*, noted the 'widespread readiness to abandon constitutional modes of political activity in favor of uncontrolled mass action', contrasting 'mass society' with the 'pluralist society' of diverse but organized interests required for a healthy liberal democracy (1959: 5, 13). Smelser's classic study similarly treats collective behaviour as the disruptive consequence of 'structural strain', which is characterized in terms of 'quasi-magical' belief systems, 'exaggerations, crudeness and eccentricity' and 'impatient' and 'intolerant' actions 'based on rumors, ideology and superstitions' (1962: 8, 67–130). This sociological disposition to denigrate social movement activity corresponded to the almost complete absence of the topic from political science. Political scientists, who devoted considerable attention to the quasi-institutional relationships between core political institutions and organized interest and pressure groups, relegated the extra-institutional activities of social movements to a sphere beyond politics altogether – as merely social rather than properly political behaviour.

The Political and Social Science
of 'Social Movement'

The methodological shift to the more neutral term 'social movement', which now spans the disciplines of sociology and political science, reflects the ideological impact of the civil rights, anti-war and student activism of the 1960s (Brand, Büsser and Rucht, 1986: 35–7; Gamson, 1975; Oberschall, 1973; Piven and Cloward, 1977). Social movements, according to Pakulski's useful definition, are 'recurrent patterns of collective activities which are partially institutionalized, value oriented and antisystemic in their form and symbolism' (1991: xiv). In effect, the non-, anti- or partially institutionalized activities of social movements are no longer equated with the irrational collective behaviour of mobs, riots and panics. Social movement activity involves potentially *rational collective actions*. Social movements can be recognized as significant achievements on the part of previously isolated and powerless social groups. In other words, social movements solve the 'problem of collective action'; for a particular constituency they achieve the collective good of political action (Taylor, 1987).

By implication, the concept of social movement extends the scope of political studies by recognizing political actions beyond the sphere of institutionalized politics. Since social movement activity significantly influences and may serve to transform institutionalized political forms, it must be acknowledged as a proper element of the political field. Accordingly, political scientists need to understand how social movements function, how they relate to government, parties and other political organizations. They need to study how contemporary social movements are in the process of transforming existing political institutions, just as the institutionalized activities of twentieth-century labour organizations (a long-time staple of political studies) emerged from the extra-institutional and often illegal activities of the working class. What is more, social movements can be seen to exert political influence not only through existing institutions but also directly within 'civil society' (Keane, 1984; 1988). This possibility is even a self-conscious feature of the political practice of new social movements in the form of 'personal' and 'identity politics', direct action, inventive use of mass media and determined resistance to institutional co-option. New social movements directly attack intrinsically political features of civil society, such as patriarchy, homophobia and racism (Eisenstein, 1984). They seek changes independently of, as well as through, state action. Social movements are, in sum, both an important determinant of institutionalized politics and a crucial constituent of the relatively autonomous politics of civil society.

Recognition of the potential rationality of collective action is also reflected in theoretical attempts to explain social movement activity. In the USA, in particular, the influential paradigm of 'rational choice theory' has applied the methods of neoclassical economics to the explanation of social behaviour, giving rise to 'resource mobilization theory' (RMT) [see further Chapter 5]. RMT treats social movements as more or less successful attempts by individuals to mobilize human and other resources for the sake of collective goals. The availability of resources, the capacity of 'political entrepreneurs' to mobilize these resources and the 'political opportunity structure' of the surrounding political system, all contribute to the distinctive trajectory of success and failure, growth and decline – or 'life cycle' – of movements (Oberschall, 1973; Tilly, 1978; Zald and McCarthy, 1987).

However, although resource mobilization theory was, to a significant degree, a response to new social movements, there are limits to its ability to address what is distinctive about these movements. In the first place, RMT addresses the *formal* properties of social movements in general, rather than the *substantive* characteristics of new social movements in particular. It considers general preconditions, problems and determinants of collective action. But like other rational choice theories, it has nothing to say about the particular goals, values or ideology of new social movement agents (Piven and Cloward, 1992). Rational choice theories may be able to deduce theorems predicting the 'rational' choices that agents make on the basis of particular 'preferences', but they are notoriously unable to cast light on the formation of these preferences or their possible replacement by others (Hindess, 1988). A second limitation of RMT derives more directly from its individualistic assumptions. Although it is certainly worthwhile examining the incentives of individual participants in social movement activity, it seems unlikely that a theory modelled on the egoistic materialism and narrow sympathies of *homo economicus* will ever provide an adequate explanation of social movement activity. Rational choice approaches have, for example, been much engaged by the 'problem of voting' – the apparent irrationality of exerting even minimal effort when the chances of influencing the outcome of elections are infinitesimally small (Brennan and Lomasky, 1993). They must surely have difficulty, then, in understanding why people expend considerable long-term effort and even undergo serious (sometimes mortal) risk for the sake of political goals. Rational choice approaches can surely only explain such actions to the extent that they are prepared to consider the role of integrity, commitment and identity, culture, community and solidarity, in accounting for the otherwise inexplicable element of self-sacrifice that they involve. Recently, indeed, there has been consideration of such concepts (Johnston and Klandermans, 1995). But such evidently crucial determinants of social movement activity are not obviously susceptible to rational choice explanations, which are better equipped to explain actions within, rather than transitions between, social value systems, identities and cultures (Eyerman and Jamison, 1991).

The revaluation of social movement activity is reflected, finally, in the flourishing from the 1970s of more straightforwardly empirical studies within both sociology and political science. Within both English-speaking and European social science, there has been a plethora of descriptive and quantitative studies of contemporary social movements of all kinds, both 'new' and 'old', progressive, conservative and reactionary (Kriesi et al., 1995; Rucht, 1991). These studies provide much of the empirical basis for what has been called new social movement theory.

THEORETICAL AND IDEOLOGICAL CONTEXT II: NEW SOCIAL MOVEMENT THEORY

Farewell to the Working Class

Associated more with continental Europe than with the English-speaking world, NSM theory seeks to provide a substantive, as opposed to merely formal, explanation of the rise, role and prospects of NSMs. In contrast to the individualistic or agent-centred approach of rational choice approaches, NSM theorists pursue a 'structural' approach, explaining the rise of new social movements in terms of the systemic tensions or 'contradictions' of contemporary Western societies. In addition, like Marxism, which pioneered a similarly substantive, structural account of the politics of capitalist society, NSM theory is a variety of 'critical theory' (Geuss, 1981). In other words, the attempt to understand the fundamental conflicts of Western society is designed to contribute to its progressive transformation. The normatively engaged stance of NSM theory is apparent straight away in the designation of a particular category of movements as 'new' rather than merely contemporary. The term 'new' evidently belongs to the family of normative, philosophico-historical or developmental concepts inherited from the Enlightenment and closely related ever since to Western claims of modernity (Williams, 1976). NSMs are conceived as 'radical' or 'progressive', because they are expected to contribute to the further development of Western societies. This also explains the exclusion of nationalist movements and

religious revivals as well as more straightforwardly 'reactionary' racist, sexist and homophobic movements from the category of NSMs.

Within the normative and theoretical domain so defined, it is, however, the exclusion of class-based social movements as 'old' that provides the most direct entry into NSM theory. For many intellectuals and activists already disillusioned with what Rudolf Bahro dubbed 'actually existing socialism', the failure of the New Left in the late 1960s was more than an event at the social and political level. It was the occasion of a final loss of faith in the proletariat as the agent of an imminent, or even distant, socialist revolution. A working class integrated into the institutional structures and 'reward mechanisms' of welfare state capitalism seemed an unlikely agent of revolution. In contrast to mainly middle-class and student draft evaders and protesters, workers had largely supported the Vietnam War. Again, although trade unions eventually played a major role in the Paris Events of 1968, the traditional organizations of the left were seen to lag behind, and then to seek to exploit the apparently spontaneous eruption of protest. The scene was set for a shift of theoretical paradigm, heralding NSMs as the latest challengers to the existing order (Brand, Büsser and Rucht, 1986; Jennett and Stewart, 1989).

From Advanced Capitalism to Modernity

But, if NSMs are set to replace the working class as agents of social advance, what transformations of capitalist society account for this change? New social movement theorists relate the emergence of NSMs to basic structural features of contemporary Western societies. Although these societies are variously portrayed as 'late', 'advanced', 'organized' or 'welfare state' forms of capitalism, as 'postindustrial' or 'programmed' societies, as the culmination of 'modernity' or in transition to 'postmodernity', these different theoretical constructions in fact belie considerable continuity of sociological and political analysis.

Closest to the Marxist paradigm – indeed almost continuous with schools of Western and neo-Marxism, which acknowledge the changing nature of capitalism and corresponding decline of working-class activism – are theories of new social movements as a response to the crises of 'welfare state' capitalism (WSC) (Offe, 1984; 1985). A starting-point for such theories is the neocorporatist inclusion of the working class into the institutional structures of capitalist society through trade union and party political representation. The social democratic legal order characteristic of WSC supplements civil and political rights (cherished by liberal democracy) with 'social welfare rights' realized through provision of social welfare (health, education, housing), social security (unemployment, sickness and retirement benefits), measures of economic redistribution (progressive taxation) and Keynesian economic policies (full employment, demand management) (Marshall, 1963: 74–126; Offe, 1985: 821–5). These developments involve a considerable expansion of the state's activities in comparison with liberal capitalism [see further Chapters 16 and 17]. The associated decline of working-class activism is reinforced by the changing nature of production in the transition from 'Fordism' or 'Taylorism' to 'post-Fordism' and 'post-Taylorism' (Lash and Urry, 1987). This involves, in the first place, the decline of traditional manufacturing and the rise of the service sector, which is geographically more dispersed and industrially less organized. But, second, the Fordist model – of mass, assembly-line production of a relatively small range of products for mass consumption – is gradually replaced by more diversified and decentralized forms of production and consumption. Both developments undermine traditional forms of working-class solidarity and organization and tend to support a multiplication and diversification of forms of identity apart from class.

But if the post-Fordist welfare state pacifies the working class by partially satisfying its demands whilst disrupting traditional forms of class identity and solidarity, it is also subject to crisis tendencies of its own. Although the welfare state performs certain essential functions for capitalism (securing social stability, infrastructure and other public goods), its ever-expanding financial requirements ultimately threaten the profitability of capital. If the welfare state denies the escalating demands of citizens, then it risks a loss of authority or legitimacy (Offe, 1985: 818–20; Habermas, 1976). But the demands of citizens must inevitably grow, because the expansion of the state's responsibilities erodes such 'uncontested and non-contingent premises … of politics' as the family, religion and the work ethic (Offe, 1985: 819). It is, of course, precisely this 'crisis of governability' (Huntington, 1975; O'Connor, 1973) that has motivated neoliberal attempts to revive the less expansive state of liberal capitalism. To the extent, however, that WSC emerged as the necessary solution to the systemic failures and crisis tendencies of liberal capitalism, the neoliberal agenda must prove futile.

However, WSC has also given rise to new forms of identity and activism associated with NSMs, who promise a more satisfactory resolution of its crisis tendencies. The new movements raise issues and concerns excluded from the social democratic class compromise. Women have been excluded or devalued not only by employers but also by trade unions and welfare structures committed to a man's right to the 'family wage'. WSC has institutionalized the shared interest of capital and labour in continued economic growth and industrial expansion without regard to longer-term damage to the environment. The politics of nuclear deterrence and the burgeoning 'military-industrial complex' accommodate the interests of capital and labour within a largely shared understanding of security. The changing nature of capitalism is thus related not only to diminishing activism of the traditional working class but also to the rise of the women's, peace and environmental movements (Offe, 1985: 825–32). For Offe, NSMs offer a potentially more promising response to the crisis of the welfare state in the form of a reconstituted civil society independent of the state. This possibility is more systematically explored in the work of Habermas.

Habermas and the Incomplete Project of Modernity

But the welfare state does not operate simply as a manager of capitalist crisis tendencies. Shifting the focus more decisively from capitalism to modernity, Jürgen Habermas draws on Weber's account of societal rationalization to provide an account of the bureaucratic state as a relatively independent source of domination [see also Chapters 12 and 29].[1] The purely 'formal' or, in Habermas's terms, 'instrumental' rationalization characteristic of Western processes of modernization manifests itself in the development of both capitalism and the state. In Habermas's terms, both capitalism ('money') and the state ('power') represent developed forms of 'systems rationality' (1984: 143–399; 1987: 113–97). As Pusey puts it, the 'system refers to those vast tracts of modern society that are "uncoupled" from communicatively shared experience in ordinary language and *co-ordinated, instead, through the media of money and power*' (1987: 107). The development of both capitalism and the state corresponds to the gradual 'uncoupling' and expansion of social systems, which co-ordinate the consequences of economic and political actions quasi-mechanically and, as it were, behind the back of participants. As these systems develop further, they begin to invade or 'colonize' the intersubjective perspective of participants anchored in what Habermas terms the 'lifeworld' (1987: 301–73).

The systems' invasion of the lifeworld explains what Habermas sees as the ambivalent potential of modernity. As Weber's notion of 'disenchantment' also implied, the formal or instrumental rationalization of society disrupts the substantive value systems of tradition and religion. In Habermas's more optimistic terms, the disruption of tradition opens the way for the critical reassessment of what were often oppressive norms, institutions and practices. Then, through an unconstrained and self-critical process of discourse, more universally acceptable norms can emerge in what amounts to a 'communicative' rationalization of the lifeworld. On the other hand, the expansion of state and capitalist systems increasingly organizes human life according to the instrumental logic of money and power, overwhelming any possibility of communicatively achieved consensus and reducing the lifeworld to a lifeless shell.

New social movements are understood in these terms as an embryonic counterattack from the lifeworld against the colonizing force of instrumentally rationalized systems (Habermas, 1981; 1987: 391–6). The new conflicts are displaced from economic and state systems to the lifeworld or, more precisely, the 'seam' between system and lifeworld: 'the new conflicts arise in areas of cultural reproduction, social integration and socialization ... the new conflicts are not sparked by *problems of distribution*, but concern the *grammar of forms of life*'. NSMs respond to the disruption and 'colonization' of the lifeworld in either 'defensive' or 'offensive' ways according to whether it is a question of 'how to defend or reinstate endangered life styles, or how to put reformed life styles into practice' (1981: 32). However, the women's movement is

> the only movement that follows the tradition of bourgeois-socialist liberation movements. The struggle against patriarchal oppression and for the realization of a promise that is deeply rooted in the acknowledged universalist foundations of morality and legality lends feminism the impetus of an offensive movement, whereas all other movements are more defensive in character. (1981: 34)

Environmental and peace movements – usual paradigms of new social movements – represent a more 'defensive' reaction, albeit one 'which already operates on the basis of a rationalized lifeworld and tries out new forms of co-operation and community' (1981: 35).

Touraine on Programmed or Postindustrial Society

Although the work of Alain Touraine applies a quite different vocabulary to the task of understanding new social movements, there are strong parallels with the Weberian approach of Habermas and even, more distantly, echoes of Marx. Touraine, like Habermas, emphasizes the reflexive, self-critical potential of modernity. Although human beings have always made history, they have previously done so only unconsciously. This is because in premodern societies, society's 'self-production' was restricted and obscured by 'meta-social guarantees' – metaphysical and religious systems that represented certain values as absolute limits on social action and development. Modernity has eroded these limits and so enhanced society's 'historicity', which refers to society's 'capacity to produce its own social and cultural field, its own historical environment' (Touraine, 1977: 16). For Touraine the ultimate bearer of this potential is social movements: 'Men make their own history: social life is produced by cultural achievement and social conflicts, and at the heart of society burns the fire of social movements' (1981: 1).

But modernity's promise of autonomy and social creativity is, once again, threatened by the increasing pervasiveness of technical knowledge and bureaucratic structures of management within what Touraine calls 'postindustrial' or 'programmed' societies. This 'technocracy' extends beyond economy and state to institutions concerned with communication (media), production and transmission of knowledge (education) and creation of symbolic and cultural contents (media, entertainment industry, marketing, design, etc.). By implication, the fundamental contradiction of industrial society, that between capital and labour, is being superseded by new conflicts. The fundamental opposition of programmed society is between 'those who manage the apparatus of knowledge and economic transformation, and those who are caught up in change and are trying to regain control over it' (1977: 156). The student activism of May 1968 in Paris was an early symptom of new patterns of conflict (1971: 347); anti-nuclear and environmental protesters represent subsequent waves of resistance to the new form of domination.

Evidently, although Touraine updates the Marxist theory of class conflict, he retains its binary structure. Despite the apparent plurality and diversity of new social movements, ultimately

> [A] society is formed by two opposing movements: one which changes historicity into *organization*, to the point of transforming it into *order* and power, and another which breaks down this order so as to rediscover the orientations and conflicts through *cultural innovation* and through *social movements*. (1981: 31)

Less radical forms of political activism are relegated to lesser categories of collective action in accordance with Touraine's aim 'to extract the social movement from the admixture in which it is compounded with other types of collective behaviour' (1981: 24; 1985).[2] The genuine social movement is identified by its relation to the progressive option of resistance to technocratic domination in the crisis of programmed society. Like Habermas's analysis in its focus on reflexive modernity and on the role of technocratic or instrumental reason, and, above all, in its commitment to the schemata of Marxian critical theory, Touraine's approach differs mainly in what he regards as the alternative to an increasingly technocratic society. As Touraine puts it:

> Some, like myself, think it necessary to re-introduce the concept of the subject, not in a Cartesian or religious sense, but as the effort of the individual to act as a person, to select, organize and control his individual life against all kinds of pressures. Others, like Habermas, oppose to the instrumentalist view of modernity the idea of intersubjectivity, communicative action and, in more practical terms, democracy. (1991: 390–1)

Theorists of Postmodernity

Touraine and Habermas, with their commitment to classically modern values like autonomy and rationality and variations on the Marxian schema of critical theory, are both evidently theorists of modernity. What has been described as the 'mood of postmodernity', on the other hand, involves scepticism about precisely such universal values and 'grand metanarratives', and an enthusiastic celebration of diversity and 'difference'. In this spirit, postmodernist theorists frequently refer to NSMs as proof of the irreducible plurality of 'subject positions' and 'voices' characteristic of postmodern Western societies in the aftermath of the unifying (universalizing and 'essentializing') project of Marxism (Laclau and Mouffe, 1985; Lyotard, 1984).

However, although postmodernists are sceptical of any attempt to impose unifying or 'totalizing' theoretical constructions on the irreducible diversity of social life, a number of theorists nevertheless seek a more general understanding of NSMs as responses to the arrival of postmodernity.[3] What is more, postmodernity is characterized in terms of social and economic developments that are already familiar from theorists of modernity. Characteristic in this respect is Lash and Urry's (1987) theory of 'disorganized capitalism'. Their notion of disorganized capitalism refers to a series of social and economic developments – the replacement of 'Fordism' by 'post-Fordism', the internationalization of production and finance, the relative decline of manufacturing and rise of the service sector, and the related decline of the traditional working class and the rise of 'new middle classes'. Like other theorists of NSMs, Lash and Urry associate these developments with the shift from the organized class politics of industrialized societies to the new politics of NSMs (1987: 311). An important further consequence of these economic, social and political

developments is the increasing importance of culture as a site of domination and resistance: 'domination through cultural forms takes on significance in disorganized capitalism which is comparable in importance to domination in the sphere of production itself' (1987: 14).

What differentiates Lash and Urry most clearly as theorists of *post*modernity is their distinctively postmodernist view of contemporary culture. Disorganized capitalism is associated with the 'appearance and mass distribution of a cultural-ideological configuration of "postmodernism" [which] affects high culture, popular culture and the symbols and discourse of everyday life' (1987: 7). Accordingly, philosophical postmodernism can be regarded as a symptom of broader cultural developments, which can, in their turn, be characterized in terms of postmodern philosophy. Postmodern culture is 'transgressive' both of intellectual boundaries between 'rational' and 'non-rational' and of aesthetic boundaries between 'high' and 'low' culture. It is suspicious of the distinction (so important for Habermas) between ethical, scientific and aesthetic discourse. Drawing on the work of Walter Benjamin, Lash and Urry describe postmodern culture as 'post-auratic' (1987: 286): the work of art is no longer an eternal object of contemplative, almost religious reverence, just another constituent of an 'economy of pleasure', a means of distraction like any other. By implication, postmodern culture is particularly resistant to the discursive forms characteristic of modernity. Communication now occurs more through images, sounds and impulses than through the spoken or written word. Culture, finally, is an increasingly important medium of political struggle. It is the potential site for the imposition of an 'authoritarian populism' closely identified with the politics of the new right and Thatcherism. On the other hand, developments like the counterculture, popular music and film testify to the alternative possibility of an 'anti-authoritarian radical democracy'. Less clear from Lash and Urry's analysis are the details of this progressive alternative: they offer little guidance beyond the need for a 'genuine dialogue' between 'new social movements' and the old left (1987: 312).

Laclau and Mouffe (1985), in their largely parallel account of contemporary society and culture, offer a similarly abstract vision of 'radical and plural democracy'. Radical and plural democracy is said to imply radicalization of the liberal tradition to include a deeper commitment to 'autonomy' and 'pluralism' as well as an ongoing commitment to socialism, albeit only as 'one of the components' [see further Chapter 18]. The abstraction of these postmodernist recommendations is, however, not so much coincidence as unavoidable consequence of postmodern principles:

This point is decisive: there is no radical and plural democracy without renouncing the discourse of the universal and its implicit assumption of a privileged point of access to 'the truth', which can be reached only by a limited number of subjects. (1985: 191–2)

There is no predetermined logic of revolutionary transformation such as to place either the working class or even new social movements at the heart of political struggle: 'There is no unique privileged position from which a uniform continuity of effects will follow, concluding with the transformation of society as a whole' (1985: 169). Neither particular social interests nor possible alliances between them are given in advance, in the way Marxist and other 'essentialist' theories have assumed. Laclau and Mouffe reject any notion of 'representation' that posits pre-existing interests. Rather, both the unity that constitutes a particular social interest (or 'subject position') and any possible alliance between interests are the contingent and unpredictable results of 'articulation', which refers to 'any practice establishing a relation among elements such that their identity is modified as a result of the articulatory practice' (1985: 105). Unity is never 'the expression of a common underlying essence but the result of political construction and struggle' (1985: 65).

Limitations of New Social Movement Theory

New social movement theory typically regards NSMs as the bearer of political tasks peculiar to the present stage of Western history. By the same token, it rehearses a figure of thought familiar from Marxian critical theories, which seek to avoid the futility of utopian moralizing by basing normative critique on a 'crisis' theory of society (Habermas, 1976: 1–31). A first problem with this species of theory is its unhelpful abstraction. Thus, for example, although Touraine's critique of technocracy resonates with some goals of NSMs, his insistence that 'the' social movement must be defined in terms of a single social choice or alternative relegates most social movement activity to the indecisive margin of politics. In a similar way, the universalistic ambition of Habermas's ideal of communicative rationality fails to do justice to the more substantive and specific insights of particular movements. As a result, as we have seen, Habermas has difficulty identifying most NSMs with his progressive ideal. In both cases, undoubted insights about prevailing structures of domination fail to connect convincingly with the actual, practical politics of NSMs, which seem as unlikely to live up to the world-historical expectations of their theorists as was the proletariat to Marx.

The detachment of NSM theory from the actual politics of NSMs is related to a second problem

familiar from Marxism, namely the tension between the pessimistic demonstration of the bondage of contemporary society and the hoped-for escape into a future realm of freedom. Thus, both Habermas and Touraine locate the progressive potential of modernity in a possible escape from the 'burden of history' into a future of communicatively rational or individually autonomous self-determination. Marx too, after all, had envisaged communist revolution as an escape from a prehistory constrained by economic scarcity and class domination into a history made, in Habermas's words, 'with will and consciousness'. But the more systematically the present state of unfreedom is described and explained, the more implausible appears the anticipated leap into a realm of freedom (Connerton, 1980: 88–9). This implausibility is increased when, for the sake of presenting a single, unifying prospectus of social change, critical theories abstract from the specific and intractably complex activities of social movements. The universalistic construction of a *single* social contradiction and choice effectively denies the concrete social creativity of actual social movements which, according to the theory, have failed to discern their true political task.

At the opposite end of the theoretical spectrum from these totalizing theories, postmodern approaches are scarcely more helpful. Certainly, Laclau and Mouffe resist the temptation to impose any totalizing logic of binary struggle on the irreducibly diverse social creativity of NSMs. But at the same time, they risk making no useful theoretical contribution at all to the politics of contemporary societies. Certainly, their emphasis on the always constructed and contingent nature of political constituencies and alliances is a salutary antidote to both fatalism and voluntarism, opposing pitfalls of the Marxist tradition of politics. What is more, the commitment to difference is not, as critics of postmodernism have repeatedly alleged, simply equivalent to a vacuous relativism without political import. Laclau and Mouffe's (1985) advocacy of radical and plural democracy implies, at least, the positive normative commitment to tolerance of diversity. But understood in this way, their postmodernist approach differs little from Habermas's commitment to communicative rationality, which also recommends a normative framework ensuring the greatest possible coexistence of individual differences compatible with social harmony.

CONCLUSION: CRITICAL THEORY OF NEW SOCIAL MOVEMENTS

The outcome of the foregoing discussion can best be presented in terms of the earlier distinction between 'substantive' and 'formal' approaches. Rational choice approaches undoubtedly offer important insights into the nature of social movements considered as a distinctive *form* of political activity. These approaches also represent an important methodological advance over earlier studies, which were unduly preoccupied with instances of irrational, 'mass' behaviour. But at the same time, rational choice approaches are, as we have seen, limited in two ways. First, the atomism of rational choice approaches seems ill-equipped to illuminate notions of identity, value and cultural change, which are both fundamental to the distinctive form of social movement activity and irreducibly social or collective. Second, by definition formal approaches do not illuminate the substantive goals, values and culture of new social movements in contemporary Western societies. The two problems are mutually reinforcing to the extent that the role of identity and culture is particularly prominent in NSMs.

On the other hand, during recent decades sociologists and political scientists have gathered much information concerning *substantive* characteristics – the emergence, structures, strategies, tactics, political opportunities, agents, goals, evolution or 'life cycle', successes, failures and sometimes decline – of contemporary social movements (Della Porta and Diani, 1999). But purely descriptive empirical theories cannot, indeed do not aim to, provide theoretical guidance for the political practice of NSMs. the same time, such empirical findings have been incorporated into new social movement theory, which presents a *substantive* account of the current state, crises and possible transformation of contemporary Western societies. However, understood in this way as a crisis theory in the tradition of Marxian critical theory, NSM theory also presents two basic problems. First, it reduces the complexity of concrete practice and discourse to a single choice between what amount to some variants of 'socialism' or 'barbarism'. Second, and relatedly, this abstraction from the concrete political practice and experience of NSMs converts their actual, demonstrable social creativity into a projected, but highly implausible leap into a predefined realm of freedom and justice. Not surprisingly, NSM activists have only exceptionally been inspired by such theoretical constructions.

In fact, the best substantive explanation of the nature, directions and possibilities of NSMs is to be gained from their own concrete discourse and experience – including ideologies, values and theories, but also histories, literature, music and art, individual narratives and so on. In these terms, the flourishing discourses of women, lesbians and gays, ethnic minorities and indigenous people, greens and peace activists, have undoubtedly served to enrich the political, cultural and moral universe of Western societies over the last decades. Furthermore, feminism, queer theory, postcolonialism and green theory can be recognized, in these terms, as so many critical theories combining empirical observation, theoretical analysis, normative critique and political engagement. Approaches like those of Habermas, Touraine and the postmodernists should be understood as supplements rather than substitutes for such theories, canvassing additional concerns for deliberative democracy, personal autonomy and toleration of difference. What is more, at the level of the socially embodied and concrete critical discourse of NSMs, the mutual relations between oppression, experience, identity, communication, theory and practice are less problematic. Recognizing the concrete critical discourses of actual social movements promises to resolve the tension, otherwise endemic to the broadly Marxian tradition, between critical theory and emancipatory practice.

Finally, is any role left for the idea of a critical theory of society that has general rather than merely movement-specific pretensions? Briefly, a more productive relationship both to the actual experience, discourse and practice of NSMs and to future possibilities for the transformation of society can arguably be sustained by means of a formal rather than substantive approach to a critical theory of society. A clue to the nature of such an approach is provided by Foucault and Deleuze (1977). Against the totalizing theories associated with modernism and modernity, they present theory as a 'local and regional practice' committed to multiplying rather than unifying perspectives, experiences and voices; theorists should aim to provide a 'political toolbox' for social movements (1977: 208). Such an approach is formal, since it asks the critical theorist to provide general political means or 'tools' of political action rather than prescribing substantive goals or utopian blueprints for social movements. The critical theorist who is engaged on behalf of the exploited and oppressed may yet avoid the 'representative' and totalizing pretensions of the radical intellectual of Marxian provenance (1977: 205–9).

NOTES

1 Offe (1985: 850) also understands the issues of NSMs in terms of a 'modern' critique of modernization.

2 Melucci (1985; 1989) follows Touraine's approach but, in a spirit closer to postmodernism (see below), attempts to avoid such 'totalizing' tendencies.

3 Some like Lyotard (1984), who understands the 'mood' of postmodernity as a feature of 'postindustrial' societies, effectively attempt to do both.

REFERENCES

Bachrach, P. (1967) *The Theory of Democratic Elitism.* Boston: Little, Brown.

Berger, S., ed. (1981) *Organizing Interests in Western Europe: Pluralism, Corporatism and the Transformation of Politics.* Cambridge: Cambridge University Press.

Brand, K.-W., D. Büsser and D. Rucht (1986) *Aufbruch in eine andere Gesellschaft: Neue soziale Bewegungen in der Bundesrepublik,* 3rd rev. edn. Frankfurt and New York: Campus.

Brennan, Geoffrey and Loren Lomasky (1993) *Democracy and Decision: The Pure Theory of Electoral Preference.* Cambridge: Cambridge University Press.

Cockburn, A. and R. Blackburn, eds (1969) *Student Power: Problems, Diagnosis, Action.* Harmondsworth: Penguin.

Connerton, Paul (1980) *The Tragedy of Enlightenment: An Essay on the Frankfurt School.* Cambridge: Cambridge University Press.

Della Porta, Donatella and Mario Diani (1999) *Social Movements: An Introduction.* Oxford: Blackwell.

Dalton, R. J. and M. Kuechler, eds (1990) *Challenging the Political Order: New Social and Political Movements in Western Democracies.* Oxford: Oxford University Press.

Duberman, M. B., M. Vicinus and G. Chauncey, eds (1989) *Hidden from History: Reclaiming the Gay and Lesbian Past.* New York: New American Library.

Dworkin, Ronald (1978) *Taking Rights Seriously.* Cambridge, MA: Harvard University Press.

Eder, Klaus (1990) 'The rise of counter-culture movements against modernity: nature as a new field of class struggle'. *Culture and Society,* 7 (4): 21–47.

Eisenstein, Hester (1984) *Contemporary Feminist Thought.* London: Allen and Unwin.

Evans, R. J. (1977) *The Feminists: Women's Emancipation Movements in Europe, America and Australasia, 1840–1920.* London: Croom Helm.

Eyerman, Ron and Andrew Jamison (1991) *Social Movements: A Cognitive Approach.* Cambridge: Polity.

Foucault, M. and G. Deleuze (1977) 'Intellectuals and power'. In *Language, Counter-Memory, Practice,* trans. D. F. Bouchard and S. Simon. Ithaca, NY: Cornell University Press.

Gamson, William A. (1975) *The Strategy of Social Protest.* Homewood, IL: Dorsey.

Geuss, Raymond (1981) *The Idea of Critical Theory: Habermas and the Frankfurt School.* Cambridge: Cambridge University Press.

Gray, Alexander (1947) *The Socialist Tradition: Moses to Lenin.* London: Longmans.

Habermas, Jürgen (1976) *Legitimation Crisis,* trans. T. McCarthy. London: Heinemann.

Habermas, Jürgen (1981) 'New social movements'. *Telos,* 49: 33–7.

Habermas, Jürgen (1984) *The Theory of Communicative Action.* Vol. I, *Reason and the Rationalization of Society,* trans. T. McCarthy. Cambridge: Polity.

Habermas, Jürgen (1987) *The Theory of Communicative Action.* Vol. II, *Lifeworld and System: A Critique of Functionalist Reason,* trans. T. McCarthy. Cambridge: Polity.

Hindess, Barry (1988) *Choice, Rationality and Social Theory.* London: Unwin Hyman.

Hülsberg, Werner (1988) *The German Greens: A Social and Political Profile.* London: Verso.

Huntington, S. P. (1975) 'The United States'. In M. Crozier et al., eds, *The Crisis of Democracy.* New York: New York University Press.

Jagose, Annamarie (1996) *Queer Theory: An Introduction.* New York: New York University Press.

Jennett, Christine and Randal G. Stewart (1989) *Politics of the Future: The Role of Social Movements.* Melbourne: Macmillan.

Johnston, Hank and Bert Klandermans, eds (1995) *Social Movements and Culture.* Minneapolis: University of Minnesota Press.

Keane, John (1984) *Public Life and Late Capitalism.* Cambridge: Cambridge University Press.

Keane, John, ed. (1988) *Civil Society and the State.* London: Verso.

Killian, Lewis M. (1964) 'Social movements'. In Robert E. L. Faris, ed., *Handbook of Modern Sociology.* Chicago: Rand McNally.

Kornhauser, William (1959) *The Politics of Mass Society.* Glencoe, IL: Free.

Kriesi, H., R. Koopmans, J. W. Dyvendak and M. G. Giugni (1995) *New Social Movements in Western Europe: A Comparative Analysis.* Minneapolis: University of Minnesota Press.

Laclau, Ernesto and Chantal Mouffe (1985) *Hegemony and Socialist Strategy: Towards a Radical Democratic Politics.* London: Verso.

Lash, Scott and John Urry (1987) *The End of Organized Capitalism.* Cambridge: Polity.

Le Bon, Gustave (1947) *The Crowd: A Study of the Popular Mind.* London: Benn.

Lichtheim, George (1968) *The Origins of Socialism.* New York: Praeger.

Lipset, Seymour Martin (1960) *Political Man.* London: Heinemann.

Lyotard, J. F. (1984) *The Postmodern Condition: A Report on Knowledge,* trans. G. Bennington and B. Massumi. Manchester: Manchester University Press.

Marcuse, Herbert (1964) *One Dimensional Man.* London: Routledge and Kegan Paul.

Marshall, T. H. (1963) *Sociology at the Crossroads and Other Essays.* London: Heinemann.

Melucci, A. (1985) 'The symbolic challenge of contemporary movements'. *Social Research,* 52 (4): 789–815.

Melucci, A. (1989) *Nomads of the Present: Social Movements and Individual Needs in Contemporary Society,* eds J. Keane and P. Mier. London: Hutchinson Radius.

Oberschall, Anthony (1973) *Social Conflict and Social Movements*. Englewood Cliffs, NJ: Prentice Hall.

O'Connor, J. (1973) *The Fiscal Crisis of the State*. New York: St Martin's.

Oglesby, Carl, ed. (1969) *The New Left Reader*. New York: Grove.

Offe, Claus (1984) *Contradictions of the Welfare State*, ed. John Keane. Cambridge, MA: MIT Press.

Offe, Claus (1985) 'New social movements: challenging the boundaries of institutional politics'. *Social Research*, 52 (4): 817–68.

Okin, Susan Moller (1989) *Justice, Gender, and the Family*. New York: Basic.

Pakulski, Jan (1991) *Social Movements: The Politics of Moral Protest*. Melbourne: Longman Cheshire.

Piven, F. F. and R. A. Cloward (1977) *Poor People's Movements: Why They Succeed, How They Fail*. New York: Pantheon.

Piven, F. F. and R. A. Cloward (1992) 'Normalizing collective protest'. In A. Morris and C. M. Mueller, eds, *Frontiers in Social Movement Theory*. New Haven, CT: Yale University Press.

Pusey, Michael (1987) *Jürgen Habermas*. London: Tavistock.

Rawls, John (1971) *A Theory of Justice*. Cambridge, MA: Harvard University Press.

Roszak, Theodore (1969) *The Making of a Counter Culture*. London: Faber and Faber.

Rowbotham, Sheila (1974) *Hidden from History: 300 Years of Women's Oppression and the Fight Against It*, 2nd edn. London: Pluto.

Rucht, Dieter, ed. (1991) *Research on Social Movements: The State of the Art in Western Europe and the USA*. Boulder, CO: Westview.

Schumpeter, Joseph (1950) *Capitalism, Socialism, and Democracy*, 3rd edn. New York: Harper.

Singer, Peter (1973) *Democracy and Disobedience*. Oxford: Clarendon.

Smelser, Neil J. (1962) *Theory of Collective Behavior*. London: Routledge and Kegan Paul.

Steakley, J. D. (1993) *The Homosexual Emancipation Movement in Germany*. Salem, NH: Ayer.

Taylor, Michael (1987) *The Possibility of Co-operation*. Cambridge: Cambridge University Press.

Thompson, E. P. (1968) *The Making of the English Working Class*. Harmondsworth: Penguin.

Thompson, E. P., K. Alexander, S. Hall, A. MacIntyre, R. Samuel and P. Worsley (1960) *Out of Apathy*. London: Stevens.

Tilly, Charles (1978) *From Mobilization to Revolution*. Reading, MA: Addison-Wesley.

Touraine, Alain (1971) *The May Movement: Revolt and Reform*. New York: Random House.

Touraine, Alain (1977) *The Self-Production of Society*, trans. D. Coltman. Chicago: University of Chicago Press.

Touraine, Alain (1981) *The Voice and the Eye: An Analysis of Social Movements*. Cambridge: Cambridge University Press.

Touraine, Alain (1985) 'An introduction to the study of social movements'. *Social Research*, 52 (4): 749–87.

Urwin, Derek W. (1989) *Western Europe since 1945: A Political History*, 4th edn. London: Longman.

Vincent, Andrew (1995) *Modern Political Ideologies*, 2nd edn. Oxford: Blackwell.

Walzer, Michael (1970) *Obligations: Essays on Disobedience, War, and Citizenship*. Cambridge, MA: Harvard University Press.

Weeks, Jeffrey (1977) *Coming Out: Homosexual Politics in Britain, from the Nineteenth Century to the Present*. London: Quartet.

Williams, Raymond (1976) *Keywords: A Vocabulary of Culture and Society*. Glasgow: Fontana.

Zald, Mayer N. and John McCarthy (1987) *Social Movements in an Organizational Society*. New Brunswick, NJ: Transaction.

21

Feminism and Gender Theory:
The Return of the State

VÉRONIQUE MOTTIER

Early feminist perspectives within political science have tended to focus primarily on issues such as gender differentials in political representation and participation. Feminist critiques of mainstream political theory have been slower to develop. This could be explained by the dominance of universalistic liberal thought, especially within the Anglo-Saxon, German and French traditions, which leaves little theoretical space for the conceptualization of identity differences. The past two decades however have seen the development of an extensive feminist perspective within political theory, which has set out to rethink fundamental issues such as the nature of power, the boundaries of the political, and the democratization of citizenship and the public sphere. This is not to suggest that feminist political theory constitutes in any way a homogeneous field. Within feminist theory, there are debates and disagreements about most of the above issues, and even about the concept of gender itself.

The analytical distinction between sex and gender has been the subject of much discussion within feminist theory. The concept of gender (understood as the social meanings around 'natural' sex differences) has been the focus of an old and now rather tired debate between essentialist and anti-essentialist views, somewhat resuscitated by the recent repopularization of evolutionist and genetic explanations. Essentialist approaches to gender consider that women are fundamentally different from men, in particular for biological reasons – although the label of essentialism has become so unpopular today that few feminists seem comfortable with describing their own position in these terms. Anti-essentialists, often inspired by postmodern ideas, consider gender to be a social and political construction. They insist on the cultural and historical variations and multidimensionality of gender identities, and their imbrication with institutionalized relations of power. Both essentialist and anti-essentialist feminists recognize the importance of sex differences, but the political consequences that the respective theorists draw from these diverge. For essentialists, the fundamental differences between men and women need to be addressed by political action, aiming to reduce inequalities between the genders. For anti-essentialists, on the contrary, the social construction of gender identities itself is identified as 'the problem' and object of study. Consequently, not just sexual inequality, but also sexual differentiation are considered social constructions (Okin, 1991: 67).

However, inequalities of power can neither be reduced to, nor explained by, gender differences alone. Gender is not just about difference between the sexes, but about power. Any convincing analysis of the gender order will therefore need to combine the analysis of gender difference with an account of gender power. The focus of the theorization of links between gender and politics thus shifts to the social and political institutionalization of sex differences. The state has played a central role in this process by regulating the relations between the public and private spheres of social life, as well as the access of citizens to social and political rights and to democratic decision-making. Theorizing the relations between gender and the state is consequently a central aspect of the feminist critique of mainstream political theory. The following sections will explore the feminist rethinking of the state, of the relations between the public and the private spheres, and of citizenship and democratic theory.

GENDER THEORY AND THE STATE

For a long time, feminist theory paid scant attention to the role of the state in gender relations. There are obvious historical reasons for this initial 'state-blindness' of gender analysis. At its inception in the 1970s, the new women's movement was deeply suspicious of mainstream politics and the state, which were seen as fundamentally patriarchic in nature. Many feminists intended to avoid conventional strategies and power games in favour of anti-hierarchical action within new social movements outside of the formal political arena [see further Chapter 20]. At the level of practical political action, this critical stance was nevertheless often combined with an appeal to the state, in key areas of feminist struggles such as abortion, pornography, or anti-rape legislation (Petchesky, 1986; Randall, 1998). The analytical consequence of the movement's distrust of mainstream politics was an under-theorization of the role of the state. Since the mid 1980s, there has been a revaluation of the central role of the state in the structuration and insti-tutionalization of relations between men and women, and in establishing and policing the frontiers between public and private spheres. Somewhat paradoxically, at a time when the importance of the state itself is eroded by supranational processes, the state has been brought back into feminist theory.

Initially, as Waylen (1998) points out, gender theorists tended to view the state in primarily negative terms. Socialist feminists in particular integrated the oppression of women within the Marxist perspective. They consequently saw the state as an instrument of domination in the hands of the ruling class, and emphasized the importance of the role of women in the reproduction of the workforce within the family for the development of capitalism. Like socialist feminists, radical feminists such as Catharine MacKinnon also conceptualized the liberal state as a monolithic entity which institutional-izes the interests of dominant groups, particularly through the law; only this time the latter were not the bourgeois classes described by Marxist theorists but the category of male citizens. The liberal legal system, mainstream politics and the state were seen as instruments of the subordination of women to men, and of the legitimization of male interests as the general interest. As MacKinnon put it, 'liberal legalism is thus a medium for making male dominance both invisible and legitimate by adopting the male point of view in law at the same time as it enforces that view on society' (1989: 237). Within

these approaches, the state was perceived above all as a patriarchal instrument which institutionalizes and reproduces male domination. From the late 1980s, such an understanding of the state has been challenged by a number of alternative perspectives. The latter question, first, whether the impact of the state on gender relations should be conceptualized in negative terms only; and second, whether the state is adequately theorized as a homogeneous actor.

Concerning the first question, a number of analyses of the welfare state promote a far more positive vision of the state. Scandinavian authors such as Drude Dahlerup (1987), Birte Siim (1988), and Helga Hernes (1984; 1987) argue that the welfare state has a positive effect on gender relations, in that it makes for a lessening of financial dependency of women towards men. Liberal authors defend a simi-larly more benign view, in that they conceptualize the liberal state as a neutral arbiter between groups rather than as an instrument of male domination (see also Waylen, 1998). Other analyses, developed par-ticularly in the Australian, Dutch and Scandinavian context, argue that the state offers scope for the subversion and transformation of gendered power relations. They emphasize the possibilities of insti-tutionalization – and therefore of promotion – of women's interests within the state, either through the action of 'femocrats' (feminist bureaucrats) working from *within* the state system to empower women, or when the state itself acts in a way to fur-ther women's status (Stetson and Mazur, 1995). In this context, an important policy tool has been *gen-der mainstreaming*, by which is meant the system-atic incorporation of gender concerns into policies rather than as an 'afterthought' or, alternatively, the emphasis on gender issues in specific policies.

The second issue, that of the homogeneous nature of the state, is challenged particularly by poststructuralist research. Feminists who draw on poststructuralist (especially Foucauldian) theories argue that it is problematic to consider the state as an homogeneous, unitary entity which pursues specific interests. They consider the state as a plurality of arenas of struggle, rather than as unified actors [see further Chapter 18]. Consequently, poststructuralist analyses of the state introduce less dichotomous perspectives which take into account the local, diverse and dispersed nature of sites of gender power (see, for example, Pringle and Watson, 1992). They consider feminist attempts to define what 'women's interests' might be by authors such as Virginia Sapiro (1981) and Irene Diamond and Nancy Hartsock (1981) as problematic, since these treat as pre-given both the state and the notion of interests. Drawing on poststructuralist theory, R. Pringle and S. Watson point out that the analytical focus needs to shift instead to the discursive prac-tices which construct specific interests, including those by femocrats. Comparative research has similarly led to scepticism towards a vision of the state and its role in structuring gender relations that is too unilateral. Comparative analyses of welfare states suggest that the impact of the state on gender relations varies greatly from one welfare regime to another, and importantly allow for the universalizing of the experience of individual states to be avoided (Sainsbury, 1994; Lewis, 1997; Fraser and Gordon, 1994).

Influenced by poststructuralist, postmodern, and comparative perspectives, current feminist analyses of the state thus usefully challenge the *a priori* assumption that the state (always or necessarily) acts as an agent of male domination. They increasingly turn away from the theorization of relations between gender and the state in general terms, to focus instead on the construction of gender within specific state discourses and practices.[1] It is important to recognize that relations between the state and gender are not *intrinsically* positive or negative. Feminist analyses of the state need to take into account its historical complexity, its variations within different political contexts such as liberal democracy, colonialism or state socialism, and its dynamic relationship to gendered power relations (Waylen, 1998: 7). It is important for feminist analysis to develop instead more sophisticated models which consider the complex, multidimensional and differentiated relations between the state and gender. Such models should recognize that the state can be a positive as well as a negative resource for feminists, and they should emphasize the gendered nature of concepts such as the welfare state or citizenship while also taking into account historical and spatial national variations [see further Chapters 16 and 19].

PUBLIC AND PRIVATE SPHERES

Whereas feminist theory has increasingly turned towards the state, there is considerable disagreement as to how precisely to conceptualize the boundaries of the state. As Susan Moller Okin (1991) points out, political science tends to confuse different usages of the terms 'public' and 'private': first, to refer to the distinction between state and society; and second, to refer to the distinction between domestic and non-domestic spheres. The first distinction between state and family is particularly problematic from a feminist point of view: this dichotomy, where everything that relates to the family is considered as private, leads to the exclusion from the conceptual field of political science of a whole series of themes that are, in fact, essential, such as the problem of justice in everyday life, the political dimension of the family, or inequalities

between men and women (Okin, 1991). The majority of classic and modern political thinkers (with the exception of Held, Walzer and Sandel) consequently exclude the family from their analyses of political power either explicitly, as do Rousseau, Locke or Hegel, or implicitly, as does John Rawls (Pateman, 1989; Okin, 1991). As Okin notes, this omission is somewhat ironic since the revitalization of modern political theory has in fact coincided with major changes in the family, as well as in wider social relations of gender and their challenge by feminist theory and practice.

The new feminist movement of the 1970s made the contestation of the traditional separation between the spheres into a central issue of struggle, represented in the slogan 'the personal is political'. There have been many controversies about the exact meaning of this slogan. It was originally directed mainly at male socialist or radical activists, reminding them that the theoretical focus on capital and labour and the extension of the notion of politics ignored the gender inequalities at home (Phillips, 1998). For some feminists at the time, it referred to the desire to free women by suppressing the family, since the family was considered to be the source of the oppression of women. Nowadays, most feminists reject this extreme position, while recognizing the important impact of unequal power relations within the family. However, their 'solution' is not to abolish the family but rather to democratize it. In so doing, they recognize the relevancy of the existence of two separate spheres. The disagreements bear on the nature of these spheres, as well as on the relations between them. In Okin's (1991) work for example, the numerous inequalities of the private sphere are attributed to the structuration, by the state, of the relations between men and women within the family. The labour market and the economic market have been profoundly gendered and cannot be understood adequately without taking into account their grounding in male domination and the female responsibility for the domestic sphere. Consequently, she argues that the democratization of the public sphere is not possible without the prior democratization of the private sphere. In order to render possible the democratization of the private sphere, we need to acquire a better grasp of the ways in which the private sphere is shaped by the public sphere. Despite her critical view on the interdependency of the spheres, Okin thinks that it is important to maintain the distinction between the private and the public. Quite a few women's rights such as the right to abortion, for example, require a right to 'privacy' in order to be exercised; that is, the respect of a sphere within which the individual has the right to decide freely, Okin (1991) argues. Anne Phillips (1991) similarly conceptualizes the public and private spheres as interdependent, but nevertheless distinct. For her, 'the private is political' means primarily that it is necessary to extend the notion of 'the political'. For political science in particular, this means that it is necessary to integrate the private sphere into the analysis, rather than to restrict the analytical focus to the public sphere, as traditional political scientists tend to do.

In order to show the necessity of taking into account the private sphere, Phillips focuses on the concept of democracy. She argues that to conceptualize democratic participation without taking into account the constraints of the private sphere entails too narrow a view of democracy. She criticizes the traditional approaches to democracy for neglecting the gendered nature of power relations around love, sex and economics within the family. The inequalities within the family are as relevant to issues of social justice as inequalities in the public sphere, Phillips argues. Similarly to Okin, but also to arguments about the private sphere developed by theorists of participative democracy such as Carole Pateman (1989), Phillips contends that the democratization of the public sphere – understood as the higher participation of women in this sphere – is impossible without the prior democratization of the private sphere. In this sense, the democratization of the private sphere is not only a means for achieving the goals of active political citizenship, but also a value in itself. Phillips thus argues for a conceptualization of democracy which includes power relations in the private sphere.

Whereas feminists agree on the necessity of democratizing the private sphere, they disagree as to the political solutions. Pateman, for example, argues for the abandoning of the distinction between public and private spheres in favour of more politicization of the private sphere. Other authors think that it is essential to maintain clear boundaries between the two spheres. Jean Bethke Elshtain (1981), in particular, vehemently rejects Pateman's position. She considers the assimilation of both spheres to be 'totalitarian' since it would not leave any areas of life outside of politics. According to Elshtain, the liberalist rigid separation of the spheres leads to the removal from the political sphere of family values, solidarity and care. The public sphere becomes a space regulated only by the principle of individualistic, rational pursuit of egoistic self-interests. Consequently, the political sphere becomes emptied of its more central values. Elshtain thus argues that the application of principles of the public sphere to the private sphere let loose the most negative tendencies of the modern world. The family, she argues, should be protected against the destructive effects of politicization by rigorous maintenance of clear boundaries between the two spheres.

For Phillips (1991), on the contrary, the idea of a private sphere independent from the political sphere is meaningless. She points out that relations within the private sphere are regulated by the state, economics, and the subordination of women. Consequently, 'these relations are already politicized, whether we want it or not' (1991: 106). Despite this disagreement, Phillips rejoins Elshtain in arguing for maintaining a separation between the public and the private, but for different reasons: whereas Elshtain argues for the protection of family values from the intervention of the state, Phillips bases her argument on the necessity to preserve areas within which the principle of individual decision and privacy is maintained, and she uses here the example of abortion. On this point, Phillips's position is close to that of Okin and Iris Marion Young (1987; see also Petchesky, 1986: 108). However, Phillips goes one step further than Okin in arguing for the degendering of the distinction public/private: she argues for detachment of the definition of the spheres from the definition of gender roles. In other words, the distinction between public and private spheres should be detached from gender differences, and based instead on the criterion of the right to privacy.

Both Phillips and Young build on Habermasian, deliberative theories to advocate retaining the concept of the public sphere, where personal identities are shed to arrive at democratic decision-making through rational deliberation [see further Chapters 11 and 12]. Most feminist theory has currently moved towards similar arguments for maintaining some sort of demarcation between the two spheres while recognizing that the boundaries are relevant to mechanisms of exclusion of women from politics, and that normative political theory can bring questions of justice and freedom to the domestic sphere. However, in contrast to Pateman's, Phillips's, Young's or Okin's positions on this point, the question of whether these spheres are separate, interdependent, or identical needs to be problematized in itself. As Terrell Carver (1996) points out, these two spheres are not simply pre-given, and the task of political theory is not just to theorize their relations. These are sociopolitical constructs, the frontiers of which are regulated by the state. Joining others such as Robert Connell (1990), Judith Squires (1994b), or Chantal Mouffe (1992), Carver draws the conclusion that it is precisely the process of construction of these spheres and their respective frontiers that needs examining since it is there that power issues operate.

Carver (1996) further emphasizes that the traditional structuration of the two spheres also has consequences for men – a point which feminist theorists tend to neglect. As he puts it somewhat provocatively, 'gender is not a synonym for women'.

Feminists have routinely criticized traditional political theory for marginalizing themes conventionally associated with femininity – such as sexuality, the care of children, or reproduction – to the private sphere. As Carver points out, issues such as male sexualities, the reproductive functions of men, or the role of men in the education and care-giving of children have also been excluded both from political theory and from political debate.

CITIZENSHIP AND DEMOCRATIC THEORY

Much of feminist theory has focused on the absence of women from political theory. This theme was first addressed by authors such as Okin (1979), Elshtain (1981), Pateman (1983) and Arlene Saxonhouse (1985; see also Mottier, Sgier and Ballmer-Cao, 2000). Their pioneering work demonstrated that modern political theory neglects to address the subordinated position attributed to women in classical theories of democracy. The emergence of modern liberal democracy introduced a universalistic political discourse which claimed to be indifferent to gender or other identity differences. Mainstream political theory consequently considers citizenship as a universal concept. Democratic rights of social and political participation apply to each citizen without regard for his or her race, religion or gender. Feminist authors have shown the central premises of universalistic conceptions of citizenship to be flawed due to gender bias. As the work of Vicky Randall (1998), Ruth Lister (1997) and Sylvia Walby (1994) illustrates, women have been either excluded, or differentially included, in citizenship.

Walby's historical analysis, for example, demonstrates the gendered nature of citizenship through a critical assessment of the work of T. H. Marshall (1950), which is often taken to be the starting point for modern debates on the question [see further Chapter 16]. According to Marshall, different types of citizenship developed successively, with civic rights in the eighteenth century, political rights in the nineteenth and social rights in the twentieth. Analysing the history of citizenship in the United Kingdom and the US, Walby questions Marshall's thesis. For example, up to the 1920s, in contrast to men, British and American women had not yet acquired the majority of civic and political rights. In addition, the political rights were acquired by women before the civic rights, contradicting Marhall's sequential model. In other words, as Walby demonstrates, the three types of citizenship rights described by Marshall have followed different historical trajectories for different social groups. The conception of a unique model of citizenship

therefore reveals a gender bias which is also present in the work of later authors who built on Marshall's work, such as Turner and Mann. As Walby points out, these authors similarly put the emphasis on the importance of social class in the history of citizenship and the formation of the nation-state, but neglect other factors such as gender or race.

In this respect Walby joins other feminist critics of the concept of citizenship, such as Lister (1990) and Pateman (1989), for whom the fact that women have not been treated in any democracy as full and equal citizens means that 'democracy has never existed' (1989: 372). However, Walby also points out an important contradiction in their work: on the one hand, authors such as Lister and Pateman question the gendered nature of the frontiers between the public and the private while insisting on the importance of female values and roles (Pateman, 1991) and on the recognition by the public sphere of the work done by women in the private sphere (Lister, 1990). On the other hand, these authors propose as a solution to the domestic exploitation of women their entry into the public sphere, particularly in the labour market. Feminist theorists have been instrumental in demonstrating the particularistic rather than universal nature of citizenship. They reveal that liberal democratic theory has been based on the implicit assumption that 'political action and masculinity were congruent, whereas political action and femininity were antithetical', as K. Jones and A. G. Jonasdottir (1988: 2) put it. They also take issue with the liberalist claim to universality for asking subordinated social groups such as women to subordinate their own 'partial' needs to the 'general' interest (Young, 1990). Feminist perspectives on citizenship diverge, however, as to the ways in which they conceptualize citizenship, the theoretical foundations of these conceptualizations, and the conclusions to be drawn from the questioning of the universality of citizenship. Perhaps most importantly, they diverge in their relationship to liberalist thought. There has been an important move over the last two decades within feminist theories of citizenship 'to recuperate the liberal project' (Squires, 1994a: 62). Authors such as Pateman (1989), Susan James (1992), Phillips (1993) and Mouffe (1992) explore the affinities between liberal and feminist conceptions of citizenship. Feminist theorizations of political citizenship and the democratization of the public sphere have consequently been dominated by debates between liberal feminist theorists and their critics. Amongst the latter, maternalist and Marxist perspectives have been particularly prominent in the 1980s, but more recently the focus of debate has shifted to poststructuralist and postmodern critiques of liberal understandings of citizenship.

For feminist Marxists, the notion of individual rights is an illusion which serves to mask the capitalist and patriarchal foundations of the liberal state, as well as its domination by a male elite. They insist particularly on the necessity of recognizing the value of 'reproductive work' accomplished by women. However, as Mary Dietz (1992) points out, the theme of citizenship is highly underdeveloped in the Marxist critique of capitalism and representative democracy. Marxist theorists tend to reduce feminist politics to the revolutionary struggle against the state – seen as the principal source of the oppression of women – and to reduce women to their reproductive functions.

'Maternalist' thinkers also reject the liberal contractual conception of citizenship. They place the emphasis on the relational dimension of social life. Drawing on the work of Nancy Chodorow (1978) and Carol Gilligan (1982), maternalists argue that the private sphere, in particular the family, is ruled by a relational morality, an 'ethics of care' anchored in mothering activities. As Sara Ruddick (1980) argues, women who are mothers have developed capacities, values and moral judgements that are both little recognized and contrast with the dominant bureaucratic and technological rationality of the modern public sphere. According to maternalists, women bring to the public sphere these relational capacities, including a respect for others and a care for their well-being. They also bring a different use of power since the aim of ethics of care is to empower others, not to control them. The public sphere, on the contrary, is seen to be ruled by a masculinist ethics of justice, founded on individual rights.

For maternalist theorists, the ethics of care is morally superior to the individualist values that dominate the public sphere. They see in the ethics of care of the private sphere a possible source for rethinking both morality in the public sphere and the model of liberal citizenship. Consequently, maternalist theorists such as Ruddick (1980; 1989) and Elshtain (1982) argue for an integration into the public sphere of relational skills such as listening skills, emotions, and recognition of others' needs and vulnerability as a basis for democratic deliberation (Ruddick, 1980; 1989; Elshtain, 1982; Held, 1990). Women's experiences from the private sphere are thus taken as a normative model for behaviour in the public sphere, where women's capacities for love and care for others come to be seen as a model to be emulated by others, and as a potential basis for public morality. Elshtain (1982) calls for a 'social feminism' as an alternative to the 'amoral statecraft' of the modern bureaucratic state. In her critical development of maternalist theory, Selma Sevenhuijsen (1998: 20) shares this emphasis on the revaluation of caring activities. However, she emphasizes that social practices of care do not always spring from worthy motives but can also be

driven by the desire for control over others, or from 'Christian guilt'. As Sevenhuijsen points out, 'bad' motives can lead to 'good' care, while a 'good' motive, such as attentiveness to vulnerability, is no guarantee of good care but can lead to paternalism or undue protection.

Maternal thinking has been the object of violent disagreements within feminist theory. MacKinnon (1989), for example, rejects its basic premise, arguing that women's caring 'instincts' are in fact the consequences of the socialization of women into their subordinate roles, and serve to sustain male domination. Martha Nussbaum, while sympathetic to the emphasis on care and the possible role of trust and understanding in our lives, warns that 'women are often valued as creatures of care and sympathy. Often they are devalued for the same characteristics' (1999: 13). The most systematic and influential critique of maternal thinking has been formulated by Dietz (1992). Dietz criticizes maternalists for committing the same errors as liberal thinkers: first, by transforming a historical model of female identity into a universal and ahistorical one; and second, by reproducing the same rigid distinction between the public and the private as liberal approaches to citizenship. As Dietz points out, there is no reason to think that the experience of mothering leads necessarily to democratic practices. Values that are virtues when taking care of vulnerable children in the private sphere are not necessarily a good model for political interactions between equal citizens in the public sphere. She consequently pleads in favour of a conception of citizenship that would resist the 'temptation of womanism' which attributes a superior moral nature to women (1992: 393). As Dietz puts it, 'such a premise would posit as a starting-point precisely what a democratic attitude must deny – that one group of citizens' voices is generally better, more deserving of attention, more worthy of emulation, more moral, than another's' (1992: 393). Rather than a withdrawal into the assumed values of the private sphere or interest-group politics, Dietz emphasizes the active engagement of women in the public sphere.

Forceful as these criticisms have been, it would be premature to assume the demise of maternal thinking within feminist theory. Despite its contested nature, its influence remains felt, particularly in feminist analyses of the welfare state and in ecofeminist thought.[2] However, current feminist critiques of citizenship tend to engage more explicitly with liberal thought, and to reappropriate critically some of its key elements.

Pateman's critical rethinking of citizenship operates through a critique of theories of liberal democracy on the one hand and of theories of participatory democracy on the other. 'Feminism, liberalism and democracy (that is, a political order in which citizenship is universal, the right of each adult individual member of the community) share a common origin,' Pateman argues.

> Feminism, a general critique of social relationships of sexual domination and subordination and a vision of a sexually egalitarian future, like liberalism and democracy, emerges only when individualism, or the idea that individuals are by nature free and equal to each other, has developed as a universal theory of social organization. (1989: 373ff)

Similarly to Walby, Pateman (1983; 1989) emphasizes the necessity for feminist theories of citizenship to rethink the links between the private and public spheres. She develops this argument through a rereading of classical and contemporary theories of democracy, in which citizenship is assumed to be universal. The problem with classical political theories of democracy is, in her view, that only individuals of male gender are considered to have individual rights and liberties. Social contract theories such as those of Locke and Rousseau, for example, are founded on the subordination of women to men. As Pateman notes, contemporary democratic theory sees no contradiction between universal citizenship on the one hand and the exclusion of women from equal political participation, their relegation to the private sphere, and their subordination to men on the other. For theories of liberal democracy, social inequalities are in any case irrelevant to democratic citizenship. Such a view predominates in analyses of citizenship, including in those that recognize that democracy does not concern only the state, but also the organization of society (for example, Barber, 1984). However, most authors continue to consider relations between men and women in society as part of private life, and consequently do not integrate a gender dimension in their theories. Pateman argues that it is important to reconceptualize the division between the private and the public sphere and to raise questions about the implications of that division for democratic theory. In her view, it is impossible to democratize the public sphere – whether through equality of chances as promoted by liberalism or through participative citizenship which includes all citizens – without a radical transformation of the links between men and women in the private sphere. 'Democratic ideals and politics have to be put into practice in the kitchen, the nursery and the bedroom,' Pateman writes (1989: 382).

Other authors such as Young and Seyla Benhabib draw on liberalist thought to develop deliberative models of democracy. Benhabib (1992) builds on Habermas's and Hannah Arendt's analyses of the public sphere to emphasize the necessity of democratizing public debate and opening access to it, while at the same time criticizing these authors for paying little attention to the exclusion of women from that sphere. Although Benhabib is in favour of maintaining some division between the spheres, she takes issue with Arendt for conceptualizing this separation in overly rigid terms. She also criticizes Habermas for operating a distinction between public norms of justice and private values, thereby running the risk of reinstating the separation between the two that has been at the origin of the exclusion of women. Benhabib (1992), similarly to Joan Landes (1995), argues for a Habermasian model of public debate while rejecting the idea of an abstract universal public, a rejection that allows 'differences' between men's and women's experiences to be taken into account instead.

Like Pateman, Young and Benhabib, Dietz (1992) also founds her critique of the gendered nature of citizenship on a critical reading of liberal theories, based especially on the American political context. She is, however, more hostile towards liberal perspectives. Whereas Pateman reproaches liberal theories for their relative indifference towards social inequalities, including those between men and women, Dietz's critique is more radical: she argues that liberalism and gendered concepts of citizenship are fundamentally incompatible. She thus joins other feminist critics for whom the central themes of liberalism – the citizen who has rights and pursues his own interests in a capitalist and competitive society – do not allow for the adequate conceptualization of interrelations or relations of dependency between individuals, either in the political or in the family spheres. Dietz shares the views of Pateman and Walby concerning the necessity of reconceptualizing the links between the public and the private, and of rethinking the distinction between the spheres. She also emphasizes the importance of citizenship as 'a continuous activity and a good in itself, not as a momentary engagement (or a socialist revolution) with an eye to a final goal or a societal arrangement', calling for a 'feminist revitalization' of citizenship (1992: 392).

Mouffe (1992) similarly founds her conception of citizenship on a critique as well as a critical reappropriation of liberalism. However, Mouffe's project of 'plural democracy' also draws strongly on postmodern and poststructuralist arguments [see further Chapter 4]. Indeed, Mouffe adopts an anti-essentialist position towards citizenship, emphasizing the social and political construction of gender identities. Certain feminists fear that anti-essentialist positions limit the possibilities for political action and mobilization around women's identity. For Mouffe, on the contrary, the critique of essentialist identities is in fact a precondition for a truly feminist politics. The most urgent task in her view is to recognize the process of social construction through which sex difference has acquired such importance as a structuring factor of social relations of subordination. According to Mouffe, it is precisely within these processes that the real power relations operate in society. Therefore, a perspective that focuses only on the consequences of sex difference – whether 'equality of treatment' means that women and men should be treated differently or the same – is meaningless in her eyes.

Mouffe's anti-essentialism leads her to criticize feminists who primarily promote the revalorization of female values, such as (although coming from different perspectives) Pateman or Elshtain. For Mouffe, as for Judith Butler (1990), such a position is problematic, as it assumes the existence of homogeneous identities such as 'men' and 'women'. Mouffe does not criticize only the essentialist outlook of such a position; she also shares the scepticism of Dietz towards the assumed link – especially by maternalist thinkers – between maternal values and democratic practices. Mouffe also criticizes both Pateman's project of a 'sexually differentiated citizenship', which argues for the revalorization through the public sphere of typically female activities that are usually relegated to the private sphere, and Young's 'group-differentiated citizenship'. Contrary to Pateman and Young, Mouffe thinks that the solution is not to make gender or other group characteristics relevant to the concept of citizenship, but on the contrary, to decrease their importance. The project of radical and democratic citizenship that she proposes implies a conception of citizenship which is neither gendered nor gender-neutral, based on a real equality and liberty of all citizens. She proposes, on the contrary, to focus on political issues and claims and not on presumably fixed and essential gender identities. Accordingly, the distinction between the private and the public spheres needs to be redefined from case to case, according to the type of political demands, and not in a fixed and permanent way. Similarly to Nancy Fraser (1998), Mouffe argues for the importance of coalition building. Rather than seeking to define the interests of 'women', the feminist movement should seek strategic alliances with other social groups to defend together their political claims regarding specific issues.

From an anti-essentialist perspective, the *a priori* categorization of certain issues as relevant to *either* gender – men or women – is in fact problematic. While emphasizing an anti-essentialist understanding of the category of women, feminist political theory has at times been guilty of essentializing the category of men. As Carver (1996) points out, the theorization of masculinity is crucial not only for understanding the origins of gender inequalities but also for identifying the possibilities for change, which would be minimal if we stop at the idea that men are always and necessarily only oppressors. Feminist authors tend to conceptualize the citizen within traditional political theory as simultaneously degendered and male. Although Carver agrees that the subject of traditional political theory is certainly 'not a woman', he points out that what is degendered cannot at the same time be male. He further criticizes feminist theorists for being inconsistent. With respect to female identity, theorists such as Susan Mendus and Phillips share his anti-essentialist view (contrary to others such as Walby and the maternalist thinkers, who consider the female body as an essential component of gender identity). But when it comes to theorizing masculinity, Carver argues, even anti-essentialist feminist theorists fall back upon a 'crypto-biological' and homogenizing essentialist perspective. Indeed, men are defined primarily through their lack of capacity to bear children. As Carver points out, recent writings on masculinity show how problematic it is to treat the dominant and stereotypical representations of masculinity as a universal model of gender identity. Such writings also indicate the need to analyse the construction of masculinity critically. Drawing on the postmodern theories of Donna Haraway and Butler, Carver thus defends a multidimensional theorization of gender identities – both female and male. An adequate theorization needs to take into account the multiple component parts and forms of these identities, including those aspects that are marginalized with respect to dominant gender identity constructions (such as sexual orientation, race, or ethnicity), he argues.

The postmodern theoretical move towards the dissolution of essentialist understandings of identity, as exemplified by Mouffe and Carver, has been challenged by black and postcolonial feminist analyses. These take issue with this move for also dissolving race and therefore analytically marginalizing racism (Mohanty, 1992). However, a false universalism of gender is also problematic. As Butler puts it, 'identity categories are never merely descriptive, but always normative, and as such, exclusionary' (1992: 15ff). The very category of the universal is grounded in an ethnocentric bias. As Chandra Talpade Mohanty (1992) points out, in order to make gender visible, feminist theory again runs the risk of making categories of race and class invisible (see also Crenshaw, 1989). While placing similar stress on difference and the centrality of coalition building, Mohanty (1992) importantly emphasizes the need to think through the issue of 'difference' in feminist cross-cultural analyses, and to contextualize and historicize relations of gender power and political agency.

CONCLUDING REMARKS

Feminist perspectives have importantly exposed the false universalism of much of contemporary political theory. In doing so, they have operated a theoretical shift from an initial emphasis on politics of identity towards the affirmation of a politics of difference, especially since the 1990s. Whereas much of feminist activism has aimed to increase the inclusion of women and 'women's issues' into the sphere of practical politics, the theoretical move away from essentialist understandings of the identity category of 'women' and 'women's issues', as well as the increasing recognition of the need for cross-cultural and historicized understandings of 'women's experience', has produced suspicion towards the universality inherent in feminist political theory itself, especially of the categories of gender and gender oppression. Black and postcolonial feminist perspectives have been instrumental in questioning the universality of gender struggles, while poststructuralist and postmodern perspectives have offered theoretical tools for critically rethinking feminist politics. On a more critical note, despite an awareness of the need to avoid over-universalizing Western political experiences and institutions, it should be recognized that feminist political theory is still paying too little attention to postcolonial contexts and states (Rai and Lievesley, 1996).[3]

As Phillips puts it, the recent shift from an emphasis on identity to difference has 'moved feminism beyond the question of women's exclusion/inclusion to a less gender-specific set of issues associated with homogeneity/heterogeneity, sameness/diversity, and universality/difference' (1998: 15). Against this backdrop, identity differences come to be seen in positive terms, rather than as impediments towards political mobilization. Indeed, the affirmation of group difference acts as a possible platform for political action (Young, 1990; Mendus, 1992). However, feminist theory is not limited to providing tools for rethinking 'women's issues' or the role of women in practical politics, important though these tasks are. More fundamentally, feminist political theory transforms the ways in which we think about central issues within political theory, including the state, the relations between public and private spheres, citizenship, and other core aspects of democratic theory.

In particular, feminist theory has expanded the notions of power and the political. On this point, feminist political theory has operated a double move over the past few decades. First, it has extended the notion of the political to sites of power outside of the formal arena of politics and key institutions of the public sphere such as the state, to include family life and sexuality as sites of gender inequality and construction of gender identities. Recent feminist political theory has thus renewed earlier concerns with sexuality and gender. Early feminist theorists such as Kate Millett (1970) and Shulamith Firestone (1970) emphasized the central role of sexuality and reproduction in gender relations of power, thereby extending the boundaries of the political. At the level of practical politics, the politicization of sexuality was correspondingly central to an important part of feminist political claims, such as the issues of contraception, sexual violence, pornography, incest and sexual harassment. Thus, feminist discourse endeavoured to introduce the politics of sex in the political arena – and often succeeded (see Carver and Mottier, 1998). Later feminist theorists have tended to shift the focus to relations of power around the economy and the state. Feminist debate on relations between the public and the private have, as we have seen, tended to move in recent years towards an argument for maintaining some separation between the two spheres. Current trends in the area of biotechnologies and reproductive technologies, combined with the increasing influence of poststructuralist and postmodern theories, have again put sexuality at the centre of feminist analysis and practice. The broadening of the concept of democracy and power to include relations in the private sphere, promoted by many feminist theorists, is amongst the major contributions of gender theory.

This is not to say that conventional sites of politics are of secondary importance to feminist theorists. Rather, the emphasis placed upon them varies depending on the different theoretical strands. Liberal feminists such as Pateman, Phillips and Young in particular argue for what Phillips (1995) has termed a 'politics of presence', involving greater representation of women in conventional political sites. In contrast, postmodern authors such as Mouffe tend to privilege instead a broader notion of politics, aiming to make gender *less* significant to models of citizenship (see also Nash, 1998).

The second key move in recent feminist political theory is a renewed interest in the role of the state in regulating gender relations. As we have seen, feminist theorizations of the state have in recent years tended to move away from generalizing theories of the state to an increasing focus on the analysis of discursive practices which construct gender within specific state policies. They explore the ways in which politics produces gendered subjects and institutionalizes gender relations, as well as the ways in which gender produces politics. Feminist analyses of such discursive processes importantly explore struggles over meanings, without reducing politics to its discursive aspects only.

There is a certain irony in the return of the state within feminist theory just as its importance in the structuration of gender relations may currently be decreasing as a result of transnational processes. This is not to say that the state does not remain a crucial actor in the structuration of gender relations.

Rather, the effects of current changes in the role of the state resulting from processes of globalization signal the need to take into account the importance of alternative agents for understanding the reproduction as well as transformation of current gender relations. From the focus on the effects of states on gender relations, current feminist research is therefore increasingly exploring the impact of global arenas such as the global political economy and international relations on gender relations, gender identifications, and gender mobilizations (for example, Elshtain, 1987; Enloe, 1989; Peterson, 1992; Sylvester, 1994; Steans, 1998). The feminist rethinking of the relations between states and the international arena further contributes to the move away from what Christine Sylvester (1993) terms 'Western feminist narcissism' [see further Chapter 22].

In his much-quoted outline of the future of political theory, John Dunn (1996) recently argued that political theory needs to be more historical and more contextualized; it needs to be more engaged with the world, with issues of oppression and human misery; it needs to become more cosmopolitan, to consider consequences of growing global interdependence and to propose a moral vision. Beyond the disagreements and debates between different feminist perspectives, given its emphasis on historicized and contextualized analysis, its focus on 'real-world' inequalities, its intensifying dialogue with black and postcolonial critiques, its increasing attention to supranational processes, and its moral critique of universalistic models of democratic representation, justice and redistribution, feminist political theory has much to offer to political theory as a whole.

NOTES

I wish to thank Max Bergman, Lea Sgier and Judith Squires for extremely helpful comments on all or parts of earlier drafts, and the editors, Jerry Gaus and Chandran Kukathas, for encouragement as well as stoic patience. Thanks are also due to Catherine O'Brien and Jon Grossman for linguistic improvements of the text.

1 See, for example, Carol Bacchi's (1999) discursive analysis of the ways in which gender issues such as 'women's inequality' are constructed in policy debates, drawing on Foucault and the notion of 'frames'.

2 Ecofeminism similarly draws upon the idea of women having different dispositions, which can serve as a basis for public morality – in this case, the care for nature with which women have conventionally been associated. In the same way that it is rare nowadays to find feminists who feel comfortable with the much-derided label of essentialism, most ecofeminists also argue that women's traditional association with 'nature' rather than 'culture' can be evaluated positively, while routinely rejecting the

charge that this necessarily entails an essentialist position (for example, Sturgeon, 1997).

3 Phillips (2001) has in this context importantly warned against the temptation of 'substitutionism', when certain groups present themselves as spokespeople for all.

REFERENCES

Bacchi, Carol Lee (1999) *Women, Policy and Politics: The Construction of Policy Problems*. London: Sage.

Barber, Benjamin (1984) *Strong Democracy: Participatory Politics for a New Age*. Berkeley, CA: University of California Press.

Benhabib, Seyla (1992) *Situating the Self: Gender, Community and Postmodernism in Contemporary Ethics*. New York: Routledge.

Butler, Judith (1990) *Gender Trouble: Feminism and the Subversion of Identity*. New York: Routledge.

Butler, Judith (1992) 'Contingent foundations'. In Judith Butler and Joan W. Scott, eds, *Feminists Theorize the Political*. New York: Routledge, 3–21.

Carver, Terrell (1996) *Gender Is Not a Synonym for Women*. Boulder, CO: Lynne Rienner.

Carver, Terrell and Véronique Mottier, eds (1998) *Politics of Sexuality: Identity, Gender, Citizenship*. London: Routledge.

Chodorow, Nancy (1978) *The Reproduction of Mothering*. Berkeley, CA: University of California Press.

Connell, Robert (1990) 'The state, gender and sexual politics'. *Theory and Society*, 19: 507–44.

Crenshaw, Kimberle (1989) 'Demarginalising the intersection of race and sex: a black feminist critique of antidiscrimination doctrine, feminist theory, and antiracist politics'. *The University of Chicago Legal Forum*, 139: 139–67.

Dahlerup, Drude (1987) 'Confusing concepts – confusing reality: a theoretical discussion of the patriarchal state'. In A. Showstack Sassoon, ed., *Women and the State*. London: Routledge, 93–127.

Diamond, Irene and Nancy Hartsock (1981) 'Beyond interests in politics: a comment on Virginia Sapiro's "When are interests interesting? The problem of political representation of women"'. *The American Political Science Review*, 75: 717–21.

Dietz, Mary (1992) 'Context is all: feminism and theories of citizenship'. In Chantal Mouffe, ed., *Dimensions of Radical Democracy*. London: Verso, 63–85.

Dunn, John (1996) *The History of Political Theory and Other Essays*. Cambridge: Cambridge University Press.

Elshtain, Jean Bethke (1981) *Public Man, Private Women: Women in Social and Political Thought*. Princeton, NJ: Princeton University Press.

Elshtain, Jean Bethke (1982) 'Antigone's daughters'. *Democracy in the World*, 2: 48–59.

Elshtain, Jean Bethke (1987) *Women and War*. New York: Basic.

Enloe, Cynthia (1989) *Bananas, Beaches and Bases: Making Feminist Sense of International Relations.* London: Pandora.

Firestone, Shulamith (1970) *The Dialectic of Sex.* New York: Bantam.

Fraser, Nancy (1998) 'From redistribution to recognition? Dilemmas of justice in a "post-socialist" age'. In Anne Phillips, ed., *Feminism and Politics.* Oxford: Oxford University Press, 430–60.

Fraser, Nancy and Linda Gordon (1994) 'A genealogy of dependency: tracing a keyword of the U.S. welfare state'. *Signs,* 19 (2, Winter): 309–36.

Gilligan, Carol (1982) *In a Different Voice: Psychological Theory and Woman's Development.* Cambridge, MA: Harvard University Press.

Held, Virginia (1990) 'Mothering versus contract'. In Jane Mansbridge, ed., *Beyond Self-Interest.* University of Chicago Press, 288–304.

Hernes, Helga (1984) 'Women and the welfare state: the transition from private to public dependence'. In H. Holter, ed., *Patriarchy in a Welfare Society.* Oslo: Universitetsvorlag, 26–44.

Hernes, Helga (1987) *Welfare State and Woman Power.* Oslo: Norwegian University Press.

James, Susan (1992) 'The good-enough citizen: female citizenship and independence'. In G. Bock and S. James, eds, *Beyond Equality and Difference.* London: Routledge, 48–65.

Jones, K. and A. G. Jonasdottir (1988) 'Gender as an analytic category in political theory'. In K. Jones and A. G. Jonasdottir, eds, *The Political Interests of Gender.* London: Sage.

Landes, Joan (1995) 'The public and the private sphere: a feminist reconsideration'. In Johanna Meehan, ed., *Feminists Read Habermas: Gendering the Subject of Discourse.* London: Routledge, 91–116.

Lewis, Jane (1997) 'Gender and welfare regimes: further thoughts'. *Social Politics,* 4 (2): 160–77.

Lister, Ruth (1990) 'Women, economic dependency and citizenship'. *Journal of Social Policy,* 19 (4): 445–67.

Lister, Ruth (1997) *Citizenship: Feminist Perspectives.* Basingstoke: Macmillan.

MacKinnon, Catharine (1989) *Toward a Feminist Theory of the State.* Cambridge, MA: Harvard University Press.

Marshall, T. H. (1950) *Class, Citizenship and Social Development.* Chicago: University of Chicago Press.

Mendus, Susan (1992) 'Losing the faith: feminism and democracy'. In John Dunn, ed., *Democracy: The Unfinished Journey 508 BC to AD 1993.* Oxford: Oxford University Press, 207–19.

Millett, Kate (1970) *Sexual Politics.* New York: Doubleday.

Mohanty, Chandra Talpade (1992) 'Feminist encounters: locating the politics of experience'. In Michèle Barrett and Anne Phillips, eds, *Destabilizing Theory: Contemporary Feminist Debates.* Stanford, CA: Stanford University Press, 254–72.

Mottier, Véronique, Lea Sgier and Than-Huyen Ballmer-Cao (2000) 'Les rapports entre le genre et la politique'.

In Thanh-Huyen Ballmer-Cao, Véronique Mottier and Lea Sgier, eds, *Genre et politique: Débats et perspectives.* Paris: Gallimard.

Mouffe, Chantal (1992) 'Feminism, citizenship and radical democratic politics'. In Judith Butler and Joan Scott, eds, *Feminists Theorise the Political.* New York: Routledge, 22–40.

Nash, Kate (1998) 'Beyond liberalism? Feminist theories of democracy'. In Vicky Randall and Georgina Waylen, eds, *Gender, Politics and the State.* London: Routledge, 45–57.

Nussbaum, Martha (1999) *Sex and Social Justice.* Oxford: Oxford University Press.

Okin, Susan Moller (1979) *Women in Western Political Thought.* Princeton, NJ: Princeton University Press.

Okin, Susan Moller (1991) 'Gender, the public, the private'. In David Held, ed., *Political Theory Today.* Cambridge: Polity, 67–90.

Pateman, Carole (1983) 'Feminist critiques of the public/private dichotomy'. In S. I. Benn and G. F. Gaus, eds, *Public and Private in Social Life.* London: Croom Helm, 281–303.

Pateman, Carole (1989) *The Disorder of Women: Democracy, Feminism and Political Theory.* Cambridge: Polity.

Pateman, Carole (1991) *The Disorder of Women.* Stanford: Stanford University Press.

Petchesky, Rosalind (1986) *Abortion and Woman's Choice: The State, Sexuality and Reproductive Freedom.* London: Verso.

Peterson, Spike V., ed. (1992) *Gendered States: Feminist (Re-) Visions of International Relations Theory.* Boulder, CO: Lynne Reinner.

Phillips, Anne (1991) *Engendering Democracy.* Cambridge: Polity.

Phillips, Anne (1993) *Democracy and Difference.* Cambridge: Polity.

Phillips, Anne (1995) *The Politics of Presence.* Oxford: Clarendon.

Phillips, Anne (1998) 'Introduction'. In Anne Phillips, ed., *Feminism and Politics.* Oxford: Oxford University Press, 67–90.

Phillips, Anne (2001) *Multiculturalism, Universalism and the Claims of Democracy.* UNRISD Programme on Democracy, Governance and Human Rights. Programme Paper no. 7. Geneva: UNRISD.

Pringle, R. and S. Watson (1992) '"Women's interests" and the poststructuralist state'. In Michele Barrett and Anne Phillips, eds, *Destabilising Theory: Contemporary Feminist Debates.* Cambridge: Polity, 53–73.

Rai, S. and G. Lievesley, eds (1996) *Women and the State: International Perspectives.* London: Taylor and Francis.

Randall, Vicky (1998) 'Gender and power: women engage the state'. In Vicky Randall and Georgina Waylen, eds, *Gender, Politics and the State.* London: Routledge, 185–205.

Ruddick, Sara (1980) 'Maternal thinking'. *Feminist Studies,* 6 (Summer): 342–67.

Ruddick, Sara (1989) *Maternal Thinking: Towards a Politics of Peace*. Boston: Beacon.

Sainsbury, Diane (1994) 'Women's and men's social rights: gendering dimensions of welfare states'. In Diane Sainsbury, ed., *Gendering Welfare States*. London: Sage, 150–69.

Sapiro, Virginia (1981) 'When are women's interests interesting? The problem of political representation of women'. *The American Political Science Review*, 75 (3): 701–16.

Saxonhouse, Arlene (1985) *Women in the History of Political Thought*. New York: Praeger.

Sevenhuijsen, Selma (1998) *Citizenship and the Ethics of Care: Feminist Considerations on Justice, Morality and Politics*. London: Routledge.

Siim, Birte (1988) 'Towards a feminist rethinking of the welfate state'. In Kathleen B. Jones and Anna G. Jonasdottir, eds, *The Political Interests of Gender*. London: Sage, 160–86.

Squires, Judith (1994a) 'Citizenship: androgynous or engendered participation'. *Annuaire Suisse de Science Politique*, 34: 51–62.

Squires, Judith (1994b) 'Private lives, secluded places: privacy as political possibility'. *Environment and Planning D: Society and Space*, 12.

Steans, Jill (1998) *Gender and International Relations*. Cambridge: Polity.

Stetson, D. and A. Mazur, eds (1995) *Comparative State Feminism*. London: Sage.

Sturgeon, Noel (1997) *Ecofeminist Natures*. New York: Routledge.

Sylvester, Christine (1993) 'Homeless in international relations? "Women's" place in canonical texts and feminist reimaginings'. In M. Ringrose and A. J. Lerner, eds, *Reimagining the Nation*. Milton Keynes: Open University Press, 76–97.

Sylvester, Christine (1994) *Feminist Theory and International Relations in a Postmodern Era*. Cambridge: Cambridge University Press.

Walby, Sylvia (1994) 'Is citizenship gendered?' *Sociology*, 28 (2): 379–95.

Waylen, Georgina (1998) 'Gender, feminism and the state: an overview'. In Vicky Randall and Georgina Waylen, eds, *Gender, Politics and the State*. London: Routledge, 1–17.

Young, Iris Marion (1987) 'Impartiality and the civic public'. In Seyla Benhabib and Drucilla Cornell, eds, *Feminism as Critique*. Cambridge: Polity, 56–76.

Young, Iris Marion (1990) *Justice and the Politics of Difference*. Princeton, NJ: Princeton University Press.

22

Political Theory and International Relations

CHRIS BROWN

For much of the last century, 'international relations' and 'political theory' inhabited separate, clearly demarcated, intellectual spaces. In the academic discourse of international relations, 'theory' referred to linked sets of cause-and-effect propositions that purported to explain patterns of behaviour discernible in the international system, on the model of the natural sciences and, closer to home, economics. Non-explanatory theory – that is, theory that addressed normative issues or interpreted the underlying nature of the international order – was undervalued. 'Realism', the dominant international relations theory, rested on a refusal to ask questions that looked beyond the workings of the system, characterizing theory that attempted this task as 'utopian' and 'idealist' – terms of abuse in the realist lexicon (it should be noted that realism and idealism here are terms of art, bearing no relationship to their eponymous philosophical traditions). Meanwhile, the dominant approaches to political theory, within at least the Anglo-American world, implicitly endorsed this refusal. Analytical political theorists asked normative questions within the context of bounded communities; they examined the nature of the state [see Chapter 15], but rarely focused on interstate relations. In this they followed in the footsteps of earlier liberal, Anglo-American, 'social contract' theorists, although it should be noted that pre-twentieth-century continental theorists (and English-speaking followers such as the British idealists) had been more willing to theorize the 'international' (Boucher, 1998; Brown, Nardin and Rengger, 2002). The gap here between the continental and the Anglo-American traditions is given added significance by the fact that the academic

discipline of international relations has been, and remains, dominated by the 'Anglo-Saxons', or, more accurately nowadays, by academics employing the English language.

In any event, the mutual neglect of international relations and political theory has changed over the last two decades; although mainstream international relations theory remains explanatory and positivist in approach, and much political theory still ignores the international, there now exists a substantial community of 'international political theorists'. Some have entered this community as a result of dissatisfaction with conventional international relations theory's neglect of the normative and issues of interpretation, while others are analytical theorists who have become equally dissatisfied by accounts of justice and rights that ignored or sidestepped the international dimension to these topics. International political theorists have also emerged from non-analytical traditions; adherents to discourse ethics, constructivism, radical feminism, poststructuralism, postmodernism and many other varieties of late modern thought have found it necessary, in an age of globalization, to encompass the international. From being one of the most staid of academic disciplines, conservatively locked into a position that specifically and explicitly undervalued speculative thought, international relations has become one of the most open-minded fields in the modern academy. Indeed, it could well be argued, it has become rather too open-minded: the rigidity of the old discipline has been replaced by an 'anything goes' attitude that, while undoubtedly entertaining, is perhaps a little too indiscriminate in its affection for the new. Most of the rest of this chapter will be devoted to 'international political theory', focusing on both analytical theory and, in much less detail, constructivist and late modern thought; but first some attention will be given to unreconstructed international relations theory, and in particular to realism.

REALISM AND POLITICAL THEORY

The genealogy of realist international relations theory is interesting, and somewhat counter-intuitive. Realists take the state to be the key international actor, assume that states pursue interests defined in terms of power and, thus, hypothesize a world which can be characterized as a 'struggle for power and peace', the subtitle of Hans J. Morgenthau's influential *Politics among Nations* (1948). Presented with this thumbnail sketch, a political theorist might reasonably assume this doctrine to be connected with nineteenth-century German power politics of the school of Heinrich von Treitschke or, perhaps, at a higher level of sophistication, with the twentieth-century, right-wing, political philosopher and legal theorist Carl Schmitt, whose 'friend–enemy' distinction seem highly relevant here (Schmitt, 1996; Treitschke, 2002). As will become apparent, nothing could be further from the truth.

Augustinian Realism

Classic American realism emerged in the 1930s and 1940s. Its three most influential figures were the radical theologian Reinhold Niebuhr, the diplomat George Kennan, and the *émigré* international lawyer, political theorist and, from 1943 onwards, University of Chicago professor Morgenthau; their work is well described in a number of modern studies (Smith, 1986; Rosenthal, 1991; Murray, 1996). In 1919 an attempt had been made to bring international relations under the rule of law and the League of Nations was established, largely at the instigation of US President Woodrow Wilson, although the US Senate refused to ratify the Treaty of Versailles which contained the Covenant of the League. By the early 1930s it was clear that the hopes resting on the League were to be disappointed and realist thought developed on the back of this disappointment, explaining what had gone wrong and proposing an alternative account of international relations. Niebuhr was one of the first to undertake this task; his message is conveyed in shorthand by the title of his most influential work, *Moral Man and Immoral Society* (1932); his point was that the liberals who created the League wildly exaggerated the capacity of collectivities of humans to behave in ways that

were truly moral. Niebuhr held that 'men' had the capacity to be good, but that this capacity was always in conflict with the sinful acquisitive and aggressive drives that are also present in human nature. These drives are given full scope in society and it is unrealistic to think that they can be harnessed to the goal of international peace and understanding in bodies such as the League of Nations. Niebuhr's approach is essentially Augustinian, resting on Augustine's account of the coexistence of the two cities: the community of believers which encompasses past, present and future and all that is good in humanity, and the world as it is, fallen and imperfect. The liberal internationalists of 1919 made the mistake of assuming that a world of reason and justice could be erected while these cities coexist; instead this coexistence requires a politics based on a clear-headed understanding of power.

The diplomat, Kennan, reinforced this message – arguing that the moralizing tendencies of US foreign policy were damaging to the real interests of the United States – but it was the professor, Morgenthau, who turned it into a coherent doctrine both in his philosophical works and in his influential text (Morgenthau, 1947; 1948; Kennan, 1951). Morgenthau was a German-Jewish refugee who had studied jurisprudence in Berlin in the 1920s; he was well aware of Schmitt's work, and despised both its amoralism and its author's engagement with the Nazis. Instead, what runs through Morgenthau's work is an awareness of the greed and violence of which human beings are capable, and his belief that to neglect questions of power is to court the kind of disaster that he and his co-religionists faced after 1933. Out of this position, Morgenthau shaped a kind of secularized Augustinianism, a sense of original sin that did not have overt theological roots; to neglect this feature of human nature was to repeat the errors of 1919, when well-meaning liberals took their wishes for reality, and in so doing undermined the balance of world power, the only basis there could be for an orderly world.

Liberal Realism and Rational Choice Theory

On the other hand, for E. H. Carr (2001 [1939]), the most influential British realist, the dilemmas of international relations are created by the human condition not by human nature. Scarcity, not sin, is at the root of realism; there are not enough of the good things to go around, and thus the liberal internationalist assumption of a natural harmony of interests is wrong. Rather, the privileged, whether states or individuals, will seek to defend the status quo, dressing up this defence in legalistic and moralistic terms, while the disadvantaged will, equally understandably, seek to overturn it. International politics is about this conflict, and the mistake of 1919 was to attempt to assign a moral status to the outcome of the First World War that it did not deserve. In the first edition of his book, Carr makes it clear that the correct way to deal with the challenge posed by figures such as Hitler and Mussolini in the 1930s was to buy them off in the general interest, if necessary with other people's property; this position somehow failed to appear in the second edition, published in 1945 (Fox, 1985; Cox, introduction to Carr, 2001).

Carr's politics were quasi-Marxist and his opponents were liberal internationalists, yet there is much about his account of the world that is consistent with at least one variety of liberalism. Carr presents an essentially Hobbesian account of the human condition. For Carr, states and individuals have interests which they pursue rationally, using whatever means are at their disposal, and this inevitably leads to conflict, which the international system is unable to resolve because there is no international Leviathan. Instead, and here Carr's realism and American realism can agree, the only check on the exercise of power by one state (or coalition) is the power of another.

It is for this reason that the balance of power is the *Theory of International Politics*: the reference is to the most important recent realist (or neorealist) work, in which the argument from the human condition is recast in terms which are explicitly oriented towards contemporary social choice theory (Waltz, 1979). Kenneth Waltz assumes that there are two kinds of political systems: hierarchical, in which the constituent units are functionally differentiated; and anarchical, in which units are differentiated only in terms of capabilities. The former characterizes domestic politics, the latter international. States are assumed to be unitary, rational, egotistic actors; Waltz is aware that states are not actually unitary bodies and that their behaviour is not always rational, but the working assumption is that non-rational, non-egotistic behaviour will tend to be punished one way or another. The imperatives imposed by a self-help system will drive states to behave rationally and selfishly: states are obliged to treat each other as potential enemies, although, if a balance of power can be sustained, a degree of stability may emerge. The beauty of this approach is that by marginally recasting its assumptions, a version of liberal internationalism can also be defended. Neorealists argue that rational egoists cannot co-operate under anarchy, while neoliberals argue that, given a degree of institutionalization and improved information flows, co-operation is possible, albeit at suboptimal levels (Axelrod and Keohane, 1985; Keohane, 1989; Mearsheimer, 2001).

The shift from Augustinian to 'rational choice realism' has had important consequences. On the positive side, it has undermined the assumption that international relations theory is, in some strong sense, *sui generis*, unconnected with the other social sciences and based on a kind of ethnomethodology of diplomatic practice to which social theory more generally cannot contribute. On the other hand, the dominance of neorealist/neoliberal thought has significantly narrowed the range of questions that theorists of international relations deem appropriate or answerable. Whether states pursue relative gains or absolute gains (one way of distinguishing between neorealist and neoliberal assumptions) is an interesting question, but can hardly form a satisfactory basis for an examination of the foundations of the current international order (Grieco, 1988). Older realists were more willing to criticize these foundations, and at least made some attempt to engage with issues such as the ethics of force, or the justice of a world characterized by great material inequalities. Morgenthau himself was a forceful opponent of America's war in Vietnam, and, as befits a close friend of Hannah Arendt, wrote movingly on the importance of speaking 'truth to power' (Morgenthau, 1970). Classical realists such as Stanley Hoffman, influenced by the French thinker Raymond Aron, and the English school's Hedley Bull at least attempted to engage with the Third World's 1970s demand for a new international economic order (Aron, 1967; Hoffman, 1981; Bull, 1984). By way of contrast, neither neorealism nor neoliberalism make any attempt to consider, much less defend, the justice of the existing international order; anarchy is simply a given, an assumption that cannot be questioned, and concern with the internal characteristics of states, such as their poverty, is misdirected since states are posited to be similar in their behaviour, relevantly differentiated only by their capabilities. In contrast to the practical realism of Morgenthau, the realism of the 'anarchy problematic' rests on a theoretical construct, but, perhaps paradoxically, its very limitations have actually opened up a space which, over the last two decades or so, a different kind of theory has attempted to fill.

INTERNATIONAL POLITICAL THEORY

International political theory covers a wide range of issues, but there is one central question that recurs, namely that of establishing the right relationship between the universal and the particular in international relations. More concretely, contemporary international relations can be seen as the site of a clash between two conflicting sets of norms: the 'sovereignty' norms associated with the so-called Westphalia system, which endorse notions such as national self-determination and non-intervention and focus on the rights of states and/or political communities, and the 'human rights' norms, established post-1945, which lay down universal standards of behaviour that all sovereigns are expected to respect. This clash takes a number of different forms, obviously coming into play when issues such as humanitarian intervention and universal criminal jurisdiction are involved, but also lying behind the current discourse on global inequality and international social justice. It is also present, although less obviously, in much of the discourse on cultural diversity and international political theory.

The Rights of States, Communities and Individuals

Richard Tuck (1999) has traced the way in which humanist, Roman and republican notions of politics contested with medieval, scholastic universalism in the sixteenth and seventeenth centuries. As Friedrich Kratochwil (1995) has argued, the origin of the Westphalian notion of sovereignty is best understood in terms of the successful assertion by seventeenth-century rulers of the Roman notion of *dominium* with respect to their territories. In other words, these rulers established that their princedoms were their property, in the absolute, Roman, sense of the term; what they did within their lands was their own business, subject only to the requirement that they do not discomfort their fellow property-holders, other sovereigns. There, in a nutshell, is the doctrine of non-intervention, fundamental to traditional international law. Originally, sovereigns were – with one or two minor exceptions – actual individuals, but with the coming of nationalism in the nineteenth century, the system adapted to accommodate the idea of popular sovereignty, with the same rights and privileges assigned to the sovereign people as has been claimed by kings and princes. More, the doctrine of popular sovereignty became associated with the right to national self-determination, which, although initially subversive of multinational empires, ultimately strengthened the norm of non-intervention, by assigning a moral status to national autonomy. Thus were set in place the Westphalian norms that were challenged by the development of a human rights regime post-1945 [see further Chapter 19].

What intellectual rationale, if any, can be given for the Westphalian order? Why should states as opposed to individuals be assumed to be the normative focus of the system? Theorists of 'international society' offer two, conflicting rationales: that Westphalian norms allow for pluralism, the coexistence of competing conceptions of the good; and, conversely and from a solidarist viewpoint, that states are, in Hedley Bull's phrase, 'local agents of the common good' (1984: 14; Wheeler, 1992). The first of these ideas is best represented today by Terry Nardin's (1983) Oakeshottian account of international society as a 'practical association', the international equivalent of Oakeshott's (1975) 'civic association'. States are committed to the practices of conventional international law and diplomacy because they have no common projects; they simply desire to coexist under conditions of peace and (procedural) justice. The norm of non-intervention protects the ability of states to be different, to develop their own sense of the good. This position is not, strictly speaking, anti-universalist, because it applies to all states, but it clearly stands in opposition to the substantive universalism of the international human rights regime. Partly for this reason Nardin (1989) has recently somewhat distanced himself from his earlier work, but the latter still stands as the best defence of the conventional Westphalian norms currently available.

The notion that states are local agents of the common good can be expressed in simple, utilitarian terms: a common good can be identified, but the world is simply too big and complex to allow for global government, and the interests of all are served by a plurality of governments. However, such a position does not require that states be sovereign, as opposed, for example, to being members of a global federation. A better defence of state sovereignty on these lines might be Hegelian: the rights of individuals are actually established by the state and therefore the sovereignty of the latter is not in conflict with the rights of the former. Mervyn Frost (1996) provides a modern version of this argument. However, the most influential contemporary defence of the rights of states, to be found in the work of Michael Walzer, takes a different form. For Walzer, the rights of political communities derive from the rights of their members and '[t]he moral standing of any particular state depends on the reality of the common life it protects and the extent to which the sacrifices required by that protection are willingly accepted and thought worthwhile' (1992: 54). What distinguishes this position from that of the human rights regime is that it is up to the members of a political community to determine what kind of 'common life' they wish to live, and it cannot be assumed that their choice will be based on the rights of the individual; thus the universal element in this position does not concern what the community chooses, but rather its right to choose for itself the arrangements under which it is governed. For Walzer (1992: 90), communal autonomy should be respected, and outsiders may only intervene when it is clear that the common life of a community does not exist or has broken down, for instance into slavery, massacre or genocide. This position, which Walzer initially established in the context of a discussion of the ethics of warfare, has been defended in a series of books over the last two decades, and is consistent with the general account of justice presented in his major work of 'domestic' political theory, *Spheres of Justice* (1983; see also Walzer, 1987; 1994).

One obvious objection to Walzer's position – and to Nardin's and Frost's – is that the picture these writers paint of the state does not seem to be drawn from life. Even if one accepts that communities should have the right to choose their form of government, overriding thereby the putative rights of individuals – and many would deny this, arguing that there is no intrinsic value to diversity – it is by no means clear that the 'fit' between existing states and political communities allows this communal right to be activated under the Westphalian system. How many actual states are based on a collectively chosen 'common life'? More to the point, perhaps, how could we know the answer to this question in the absence of democracy and individual rights? Walzer assumes that regimes are legitimate unless their populations have delegitimated them by resorting to open revolt, but while giving the state the benefit of the doubt in this way may be sensible practice in an international order based on sovereign states, it is more difficult to see it as normatively compelling. Walzer's position on this matter is similar to that of John Stuart Mill (2002), who argued that freedom could not be given to a people, only taken by them, but the techniques of control available to modern tyrants are rather more effective than in Mill's day and the suppression of popular discontent by the security forces easier. Walzer's position makes sense on the assumption that once the people have reached a settled adverse verdict on a regime, the security forces will step aside, which seems unduly optimistic.

In any event, in response to the atrocities committed by the Nazi regime in Germany – and as an ideological stand against the rising power of the USSR – an account of universal principles based on the rights of individuals rather than on the rights of collectivities was instituted by the UN Charter of 1945, and, more specifically, by the Universal Declaration of Human Rights adopted by the UN General Assembly in 1948. There is, as might be expected, a very large literature on the international human rights regime; here, the focus will be on economic rights and the theory of justice, and on cultural critiques of the rights regime (Dunne and Wheeler, 1999). Before moving on, however, it is worth noting one important feature of the human rights regime; although it purports to impose universal standards upon states, it has been, until very recently, itself statist in origin and modes of operation. It comprises declarations made by states, covenants signed and ratified by them, and institutions subordinated to them. Only in one case, that of the European Convention on Human Rights, can it be said that effective mechanisms exist for ensuring that states live up to their treaty obligations.

In the last decade or so practices have emerged that have challenged this situation. In the first place, groups of states have, on occasion, taken it upon themselves to intervene forcibly in the internal affairs of another state, in the interests of its inhabitants; second, more radically, developments in international law have begun to undermine the principle of sovereign immunity. As to the first of these changes – humanitarian intervention – the record of the 1990s has been mixed (Mayall, 1996; Moore, 1998). There was no effective intervention in the case of the worst atrocity of the decade – the Rwanda genocide – and the results of external interventions in Somalia, Bosnia, Kosovo, East Timor and Sierra Leone have been ambiguous. In each case the motives of the interveners have been impugned, and, rather more serious because the importance of motive is contestable, it is by no means clear that these actions have actually improved the position of those they were designed to assist. In short, although there have been developments of international law in this area, it may be premature to talk of an emerging norm of humanitarian intervention, as Nicholas Wheeler does (2000) in the best book on the subject.

Developments in international law have been more unambiguously radical. The final ruling in the Pinochet case in Britain (1998–2000) established that the doctrine of 'sovereign immunity' could not be allowed to cover acts banned under the international Torture Convention of 1984. War crimes tribunals established by the UN Security Council in the wake of the Rwanda genocide and the wars of the former Yugoslavia have brought in some high level convictions, and a former head of state is currently on trial, Milosevic of Yugoslavia. The International Criminal Court, established by the 1998 Rome Statute which was ratified by the necessary 60 states in April 2002 and came into existence on 1 July 2002, represents an even greater challenge to Westphalian sovereignty norms. In principle, under the Rome Statute individuals up to and including heads of state and government can be held personally responsible for crimes against humanity and against the laws of war. In practice the powers of the ICC are strictly circumscribed but even so, a number of influential states, including China, India, Russia and the US, regard this as a step too far. American 'new sovereigntists' have argued that the ICC and the Pinochet judgement have taken international law far beyond its proper function, which is to promote coexistence between sovereigns (Spiro, 2000; Rivkin and Casey, 2000–1). The key issue here, to be returned to at the end of this chapter, is whether there exists a sufficiently deep sense of community at the global level to support a legal system based on individuals as opposed to states. In this connection, it should be noted that the bedfellows of the new sovereigntists include all the major Asian powers, few of whom have signed, let alone ratified, the Rome Statute.

Global Inequality and International Social Justice

The international human rights regime initially stressed a political conception of rights, but economic and social rights have never been far from the agenda. The most influential account here has been that of Henry Shue (1983), who argues the focus should be on basic rights seen as 'everyone's minimum reasonable demand upon the rest of humanity'. Basic rights can be broken down into two components: security rights, that is, the right not to be subjected to murder, torture, mayhem, rape or assault; and subsistence rights, that is, the right to minimal economic security, 'unpolluted air, unpolluted water, adequate food, adequate clothing, adequate shelter and minimum preventive public health care' (1983: 19, 23). An obvious question is whether these are 'rights' in the full sense of the term, as opposed to desiderata. Are there correlative duties to these rights? Can the 'rest of humanity' be seen as the kind of entity that could deliver on such duties? These are difficult questions to answer in a satisfactory way, and the notion of basic rights is probably best seen as a rhetorical device to draw attention to the great inequalities that characterize the contemporary international order; such inequalities are the subject of theories of global social justice.

The reinvigoration of theories of justice begun by John Rawls's A Theory of Justice is examined elsewhere in this Handbook [Chapters 6, 7, 17 and 18]; here, the technicalities of Rawls's scheme will be taken for granted, and the focus will be on their international implications (Brown, 1997; 2002a; 2002b). Notoriously, Rawls himself believes that these implications are very limited; on his account the principle of political equality has an international analogue in terms of the sovereign equality of states and the principles of non-aggression and non-intervention, but there is no international equivalent of the 'difference principle'. International society is not a 'co-operative venture for mutual advantage'; individual societies are assumed to be bounded and self-sufficient, and so there is nothing that could provide the basic materials for redistribution required by the notion of international distributive justice.

Few have agreed with this position. For a theory of social justice to have nothing to say about the extraordinary inequalities that exist between societies appears perverse. For Brian Barry this is symptomatic of wider problems with Rawls's project. International justice poses problems that are structurally similar to those posed by, for example, intergenerational justice and environmental justice; in each case the central notion of a contract based, at least in part, on the search for mutual advantage by the contractors, cannot easily respond to the interests of those who cannot be present as contractors, which category includes foreigners. Moreover, the requirement that arrangements be, in some sense, based on reciprocity is equally if not more limiting (Barry, 1989). Barry's alternative account of 'justice as impartiality' has substantial international implications; impartiality requires that the vital interests of each be put before the non-vital interests of anyone, which means that the existing distribution of wealth, and the environmental degradation characteristic of contemporary capitalism, must be regarded as unreasonable and unjust. The inescapable conclusion is that the advanced industrial world should slow down, or put into reverse, its growth and transfer resources to the poor via a system of 'progressive' global taxation (Barry, 1994; 1998).

Others have been more Rawlsian, but reach not dissimilar conclusions. The most important text here is the first, Charles Beitz's pioneering study Political Theory and International Relations (1979); many of the key arguments first see the light of day here. Beitz offers two reasons why Rawls is wrong. First, even if we accept that states are separate self-contained societies, their representatives would insist on a more wide-ranging contract than Rawls envisages. But, second, since states are not self-contained there is no reason to look for a second contract between them; instead Rawls's full account of justice should be applied worldwide, including a global 'difference principle'.

Beitz's first argument concerns the treatment of 'natural' resources. He argues contra Rawls that the representatives of states meeting in the second original position would not agree to a rule that confirmed that natural resources belong to the states whose territory encompasses them; risk-averse representatives would introduce a rule that distributed the world's resources equally, via some kind of global wealth tax. This is, on the face of it, a rather strong and widely supported argument; as noted above, Barry also argues for a global tax system, though without employing the veil of ignorance or a second original position, while Hillel Steiner

(1999) derives a similar idea for a redistributive global fund from libertarian foundations. The main problem with these proposals is that they could produce unintended and counter-intuitive results; as Rawls (1999) points out in his later defence of his position, the wealth of a state is only very loosely, if at all, correlated with its material resource base.

Beitz's second position is that, as a result of interdependence, the world must now be treated as a single society, which means that Rawls's full account of social justice applies, with no necessity for a second contract between state representatives. The problem here is that, however interdependent the present world order may be, it can hardly be seen as a co-operative venture for mutual advantage given the gross inequalities it generates. The international economy is certainly based on the idea that everyone benefits from economic exchange, but it would be a particularly enthusiastic neoliberal who argued that this applies across the board to all interactions between rich and poor. Beitz has now acknowledged the strength of this criticism and effectively abandoned much of the Rawlsian justification for his cosmopolitanism in a later article – but not the cosmopolitanism itself, which he now grounds in a Kantian account of the moral equality of persons (Beitz, 1983). To some extent, Beitz's original position is restated by Thomas Pogge in his *Realizing Rawls* (1989). Pogge suggests that it is legitimate to have separate societies only if they can be seen as the product of a decision that emerges from a kind of meta-original position in which all the inhabitants of the world are represented. The latter may well decide to create separate societies but they are unlikely to endorse Westphalian-style sovereignty norms. Instead, the units created through this meta-contract will acknowledge responsibilities towards one another. Pogge, like Barry, favours a scheme of global taxation (a global resources dividend) and, like Beitz, sees it as best based on natural resources; but in order to meet environmental goals he suggests it should be based on the value of natural resources actually used, rather than on those left in the ground.

This position conveniently raises the issue of borders and international political theory. Since existing boundaries are clearly not the result of any kind of contract – nor are they 'natural' – what, if any, justification can be given for the norm which assigns to state authorities the right to control such borders, and thus creates categories such as 'political refugee' and 'economic migrant'? Pogge suggests none, and the majority of cosmopolitan liberals agree (Barry and Goodin, 1992; O'Neill, 1994). However, as most cosmopolitans also agree, there are obviously practical problems with such a position, and liberal nationalists such as Michael Walzer and David Miller argue that Rawls was

essentially correct to assume that distributive justice can only be a feature of bounded communities (Miller and Walzer, 1995). A socially just society will involve redistribution of resources, and the willingness of citizens to redistribute depends crucially on the existence of a sense of community (Miller, 1995). A community is a mutual aid association, membership of which will confer benefits and duties; such benefits cannot be made global given the current state of the world, and it is reasonable that such an association should have the right to determine its own membership. It should be noted that this position is compatible with an acknowledgement of the essentially arbitrary nature of borders; it is not how a community came to be defined that is crucial for its legitimacy, but rather its conduct in the here and now, its commitment to social justice. Even so, from this perspective, a world of socially just communities might still be a radically unequal world. Can such a state of affairs truly be just?

There is an impasse here which is symptomatic of a wider set of problems for contemporary cosmopolitan liberalism (Brown, 2000a). The distinction between 'insiders' and 'outsiders' is difficult to justify rationally, but a politics without this distinction, a politics without borders, is, in the world as it is, unattainable and undesirable, unless a libertarian conception of liberalism be taken to its limits, as Hillel Steiner (1992) advocates. [see further Chapter 9]. This dilemma is built into Westphalian politics; it may also reflect a certain utopianism in contemporary analytical normative theory, where the theoretical possibility of a proposal such as 'open borders' is given greater importance than its practical implausibility.

Cultural Diversity and International Political Theory

Economic and social rights are often described as 'second generation', political rights being 'first'. 'Third-generation' rights are the rights of peoples, which include such general notions as a right to self-determination, but also more specific sets of rights such as those of indigenous peoples (Crawford, 1988). There is a conceptual problem here; the notion of human rights is associated with the promotion of universal standards and equality of treatment, but the rights of peoples can only be meaningful if they endorse a right to be different. Indigenous peoples, for example, demand the right to be governed in terms of their own customs and mores, which may well not sit easily with universal norms; this is a well-recognized issue in the politics of multiculturalism (Kymlicka, 1995; Parekh, 2000) [see further Chapter 19]. However, in international relations, the most striking manifestation of this problem arises in the context of a wider challenge to the notion of human rights: the argument that the international human rights regime is based on specifically Western values, an argument most clearly articulated by a number of East Asian states, hence often referred to as the 'Asian values' debate (Bauer and Bell, 1999; Bell, 2000).

The core argument is that the human rights identified in the 1948 Declaration and subsequently are related to a specifically Western conception of the individual and the public sphere; Asian values, it is argued, are oriented towards the family and the collectivity, stress duties and responsibilities rather than rights, and place a greater emphasis on religion. The argument here is structurally similar to the feminist critique of the notion of rights as patriarchal, based on a specifically masculine conception of political life, although since advocates of Asian values usually deplore the modern liberal emphasis on gender equality there is no real meeting of minds here (Peters and Volper, 1995). The East Asian critique emerged in the early 1990s, and is perhaps best seen as a foreign policy response to the 'democracy promotion' that was characteristic of the immediate post-Cold-War era. There was then a widespread and understandable resentment that, after several hundred years of imperialism and exploitation, the West should now, once again, be telling the rest of the world what to do, and the notion of Asian values was developed as part of a strategy of resistance to this pressure. Of course, another way of expressing the last point would be to say that this argument was developed in order to protect the positions of undemocratic Asian leaders – although it is worth noting in passing that the argument could only perform this task domestically if it actually struck a chord with ordinary Asians.

Democracy promotion is a less prominent feature of contemporary US policy than it was in 1993, and the debate over human rights and Asian values is less salient today than it once was, but the general issue of cultural diversity and international political theory remains on the agenda (Brown, 2000b). The central point here is that both the Westphalian values of sovereignty, and the values of the international human rights regime, originate in one particular region and political order – the classical Western European international system – and are now applied on a world stage, regulating relations between states many of which developed out of very different contexts. This need not present a problem – it is noticeable that the states whose rulers have criticized Western notions of human rights have enthusiastically adopted the even more Western notion of the sovereign state – but in the longer run, as the impact of colonialism becomes more distant, it seems likely that there will be some shift in the normative foundations of the system.

It is unlikely that this shift will take the dramatic form of a 'clash of civilizations', civilizations not being the kind of discrete physical entities that could 'clash', even though Al-Qaeda's attack on the US on 11 September 2001 and the subsequent 'war on terrorism' have given a certain superficial plausibility to Samuel Huntington's (1993) thesis. Just as 'Western civilization' covers a multitude of viewpoints, so the idea that a coherent Islamic world view can be identified is patently false; all 'civilizations' have been influencing each other for thousands of years, and the self-presentation of a figure such as Osama Bin Laden draws on a great many diverse sources, from Ibn Khaldoun to Madison Avenue. Still, the fact that so many people throughout the non-Western world – including many non-Muslims – have been prepared to applaud Al-Qaeda's crimes suggests a certain resistance to Western notions of universal values, as well, of course, as resentment at the power of the United States. It seems quite plausible that in the interests of intercultural relations a renewed ethics of coexistence based on older notions of international society will come to challenge the universal standards promoted by the human rights regime.

The question then arises, coexistence with whom? Are all positions entitled to be treated equally simply because they are associated with particular religions or cultures, which could easily lead to absurdities? If not, how are we to discriminate? John Rawls in his *Law of Peoples* (1999) attempts this task, identifying a potential category of 'decent' well-ordered societies – characterized by their adherence to basic rights even though they privilege one particular comprehensive account of the good – who form with liberal societies the membership of a confederation of peoples, and who are entitled to the protection of a norm of non-intervention designed to promote coexistence. Many critics, such as Allen Buchanan (2000), adhere to a stronger account of liberalism and doubt the legitimacy of any non-liberal society, but from the perspective of international political theory Rawls's limited openness to diversity has much to commend it (Brown, 2002a).

Constructivism and Late Modern Thought

Difference, cultural and otherwise, is also one of the major themes of late modern thought as applied to international relations, with postcolonialist and radical feminist literatures rubbing shoulders with Levinasian accounts of ethics as an encounter with 'otherness', and Lacanian readings of subjectivity (George, 1994; Shapiro and Alker, 1996; Edkins, 1999; Edkins, Persram and Pin-Fat, 1999). As will be immediately apparent, there is more on offer here than can be discussed within the limits of this chapter, and readers are referred to the above general texts and collections for further references and critical discussions. There are, however, two aspects of this thought that do deserve further, albeit brief, consideration, namely the 'constructivist' turn in international theory of the past decade, and the increasing, but perhaps unwise, interest in epistemological and ontological issues shown by many theorists of international relations.

In the late 1980s, as noted above, dissatisfaction with the limits imposed by the neorealist–neoliberal debate led to a revival of international political theory, but it also led to critiques of orthodoxy that explicitly attacked the methodological foundations of social choice theory. Influential works on the philosophy and methodology of international relations drew a sharp distinction between 'explanation' and 'understanding' (Hollis and Smith, 1991). Most notably, writers employing a somewhat uneasy mix of Husserlian social psychology, Giddensian 'structuration' theory, and a Wittgensteinian interest in languages and rules, developed a 'constructivist' critique of orthodoxy which denied that the 'anarchy' that formed the basis of neorealist–neoliberal thought had a reality independent of the theories which purported to explain its characteristics; instead, we live in a 'world of our making', and 'anarchy is what states make of it' (Kratochwil, 1989; Onuf, 1989; Wendt, 1992). During the course of the 1990s constructivism grew in importance, albeit aided perhaps by a certain lack of definition which enabled a great many varieties of nominally constructivist thought to flourish. The publication of Alexander Wendt's *Social Theory of International Politics* in 1999 – a text explicitly designed to play the same kind of role for constructivism as that played by Waltz's *Theory of International Politics* for neorealism – marked a kind of coming of age for the new approach [see further Chapter 5].

Wendt's achievement is to combine a high level of epistemological sophistication with insights drawn from older traditions of international thought, especially the work of the so-called 'English school' (Dunne, 1998). He develops three different and competing accounts of 'anarchy' – broadly, Hobbesian, Lockean and Kantian – and works through the different kinds of international system that could be expected to emerge under these different accounts and their implications for the kinds of questions addressed elsewhere in this chapter. Wendt's statism has been criticized, and he has been accused of attempting to construct a new orthodoxy by means of a Faustian bargain, producing a critique of conventional international thought that buys acceptance from the mainstream by toning

down its criticism of the latter (Kratochwil, 2000). This is harsh, although, as a recent forum on Wendt's work demonstrates, it is certainly the case that mainstream writers have been more favourably disposed to its positions than late modernists (*Review of International Studies*, 2000). In fact, these criticisms, even if accurate, miss the real point: the value of Wendt's work is precisely the promise it offers of bringing the concerns of international political theory and mainstream international relations theory back together, to the advantage of both discourses.

What is less praiseworthy is the way in which constructivist thought, and late modern thought more generally, has emphasized the importance of metatheoretical issues at the expense of a more practically minded approach to international political theory. Paralleling the emphasis on quantitative and qualitative methods at the expense of substance in the mainstream discipline of international relations, late modern thought seems at times rather more interested in displaying its philosophical sophistication than in contributing to the exploration of the real-world problems and dilemmas towards which its theories are nominally directed. There are, of course, numerous exceptions to this narcissism – such as David Campbell's (1998) Levinasian work on Bosnia, William Connolly's (2000) global extensions of America's 'culture wars', Cynthia Enloe's (1989; 1993) feminist explorations of political economy and post-Cold-War politics – but, overall, the self-absorption and inappropriate abstraction of international relations theory have been increased rather than diminished by the late modern turn. To adapt some terminology of Stephen White's (1991: 25), the 'world-disclosing' aspect of late modern thought in international relations may, sometimes, be admirable, but a greater focus on language that can help us to co-ordinate action in the world would also be helpful.

CONCLUSION: GLOBALIZATION AND INTERNATIONAL POLITICAL THEORY

Inevitably, this chapter has only had space to cover a selection of possible topics raised by the juxtaposition of political theory and international relations, but one final issue cannot be avoided (Brown, 2002b). Are the social and economic changes conveniently summarized by the shorthand term 'globalization' undermining the relevance of the debates outlined and discussed above? It is possible to argue that the economic significance of these changes has, at times, been overstated, but the sober work of David Held and his colleagues (1999) leaves little doubt as to the scope of recent changes, or the increasing pace of change in the 'runaway world' (Hirst and Thompson, 1999; Giddens, 1999). On the face of it, the clash between the universal and the particular may be in the process of being decided in favour of the former, not because universal ideas have suddenly become compelling, but because the material basis for an international political theory that stresses the autonomy and rights of collectivities is being undermined on the ground.

This kind of argument is at the heart of Held's school of 'cosmopolitan democracy' (Held, 1995; Archibugi, Held and Köhler, 1998) and is the basis for Andrew Linklater's (1998) critical-theoretical, Habermasian account of the transformation of political community. For Held and his colleagues, democracy is about self-rule, and if local jurisdictions no longer have the capacity to govern themselves then democratic global institutions must be created by the reform of existing bodies such as the UN and the creation of new representative organs. Linklater acknowledges the inevitability of systems of inclusion and exclusion, but holds that such systems will have to be renegotiated as a result of immanent features of the current transformation of the global politics, and the costs of exclusion lowered.

The heart of the matter here – and, as noted above, this relates also to issues as broad as cultural diversity and international relations, and as narrow as the jurisdiction of the new International Criminal Court – is whether the material changes summed up by the term 'globalization' have actually created the kind of minimal sense of global community that would be required if global governance is to be democratized. Democracy ultimately rests on the willingness of minorities to accept majority decisions, and it is optimistic to assume that such a willingness is currently being created on a global scale, especially since globalization is busily creating its own anti-bodies, stimulating nationalist reactions to the processes it has set in train. On the other hand, democracy itself can be creative of a sense of community; there is a dialectical relationship here that makes it excessively pessimistic to require that community exists before democracy can function.

The intellectual debate here may be unresolved, but the glacial pace at which global institutions are actually being democratized suggests that, for the foreseeable future, we will inhabit a world in which increasingly globalized social and economic forces will be obliged to coexist with political authorities that remain locally based, and where political loyalties will be uneasily divided between competing local, regional and global bodies. Equally uncomfortably, it often seems that no one actually controls this world, although corporate capitalism certainly exercises more influence than any hypothetical

global *demos*; indeed, perhaps we now live in an 'empire' characterized precisely by diffuse networks of power that no one controls (Hardt and Negri, 2000). In short, the inherent conflict between the universal and the particular will continue, albeit shaped differently and in more complex ways; the Westphalian nature of international relations seems fated to remain ever under challenge from competing ways of organizing political life without actually succumbing, and the dilemmas posed by this stalemate seem unlikely to disappear within any timescale relevant to this *Handbook*.

NOTE

I am grateful to David Owen and Andrew Mason for comments on an earlier draft of this chapter; the usual disclaimers apply.

REFERENCES

Archibugi, D., D. Held and D. Köhler, eds (1998) *Re-Imagining Political Community: Studies in Cosmopolitan Democracy*. Cambridge: Polity.

Aron, R. (1967) *Peace and War: A Theory of International Relations*. London: Weidenfeld and Nicolson.

Axelrod, R. and R. O. Keohane (1985) 'Achieving cooperation under anarchy: strategies and institutions'. *World Politics*, 38: 226–54.

Barry, B. (1989) 'Humanity and justice in global perspective'. In B. Barry, *Democracy, Power and Justice*. Oxford: Clarendon.

Barry, B. (1994) *Justice as Impartiality*. Oxford: Oxford University Press.

Barry, B. (1998) 'International society from a cosmopolitan perspective'. In D. Mapel and T. Nardin, eds, *International Society*. Princeton, NJ: Princeton University Press, 144–63.

Barry, B. and R. E. Goodin, eds (1992) *Free Movement*. Hemel Hempstead: Harvester Wheatsheaf.

Bauer, J. and D. A. Bell, eds (1999) *The East Asian Challenge for Human Rights*. Cambridge: Cambridge University Press.

Beitz, C. R. (1983) 'Cosmopolitan ideas and national sovereignty'. *Journal of Philosophy*, 80: 591–600.

Beitz, C. R. (2000) *Political Theory and International Relations* (1979), 2nd edn. Princeton, NJ: Princeton University Press.

Bell, D. (2000) *East Meets West: Human Rights and Democracy in East Asia*. Princeton, NJ: Princeton University Press.

Boucher, D. (1998) *Political Theories of International Relations*. Oxford: Oxford University Press.

Brown, C. (1997) 'Review essay: theories of international justice'. *British Journal of Political Science*, 27: 273–9.

Brown, C. (2000a) 'On the borders of (international) political theory'. In N. O'Sullivan, ed., *Political Theory in Transition*. London: Routledge.

Brown, C. (2000b) 'Cultural diversity and international political theory'. *Review of International Studies*, 26: 199–213.

Brown, C. (2002a) 'The construction of a realistic utopia: John Rawls and international political theory'. *Review of International Studies*, 28: 5–21.

Brown, C. (2002b) *Sovereignty, Rights and Justice*. Cambridge: Polity.

Brown, C., T. Nardin and N. J. Rengger, eds (2002) *International Relations in Political Thought: Texts in International Relations*. Cambridge: Cambridge University Press.

Buchanan, A. (2000) 'Rawls's *Law of Peoples*: rules for a vanished Westphalian world'. *Ethics*, 110: 697–721.

Bull, H. (1984) *Justice in International Relations: The Hagey Lectures*. Waterloo, ON: University of Waterloo.

Campbell, D. (1998) *National Deconstruction: Violence, Identity and Justice in Bosnia*. Minneapolis: University of Minnesota Press.

Carr, E. H. (2001 [1939]) *The Twenty Years Crisis*, ed. and introduction Michael Cox. London: Palgrave.

Connolly, W. E. (2000) 'Speed, concentric circles and cosmopolitanism'. *Political Theory*, 28: 596–618.

Crawford, J., ed. (1988) *The Rights of Peoples*. Oxford: Clarendon.

Dunne, T. (1998) *Inventing International Society*. London: Macmillan.

Dunne, T. and N. Wheeler, eds (1999) *Human Rights in Global Politics*. Cambridge: Cambridge University Press.

Edkins, J. (1999) *Poststructuralism and International Relations*. Boulder, CO: Lynne Rienner.

Edkins, J., N. Persram and V. Pin-Fat, eds (1999) *Sovereignty and Subjectivity*. Boulder, CO: Lynne Rienner.

Enloe, C. (1989) *Bananas, Beaches and Bases*. London: Pandora.

Enloe, C. (1993) *The Morning After: Sexual Politics at the End of the Cold War*. Berkeley, CA: University of California Press.

Fox, W. R. T. (1985) 'E. H. Carr and political realism: vision and revision'. *Review of International Studies*, 11: 1–16.

Frost, M. (1996) *Ethics in International Relations*. Cambridge: Cambridge University Press.

George, J. (1994) *Discourses of Global Politics: A Critical (Re) Introduction to International Relations*. Boulder, CO: Lynne Rienner.

Giddens, A. (1999) *The Runaway World*. Cambridge: Polity.

Grieco, J. M. (1988) 'Anarchy and the limits of cooperation: a realist critique of the newest liberal institutionalism'. *International Organisation*, 42: 485–508.

Hardt, M. and A. Negri (2000) *Empire*. Cambridge, MA: Harvard University Press.

Held, D. (1995) *Democracy and the Global Order*. Cambridge: Polity.

Held, D., A. G., McGrew, D. Goldblatt and J. Perraton (1999) *Global Transformations: Politics, Economics and Culture*. Cambridge: Polity.

Hirst, P. and G. Thompson (1999) *Globalisation in Question: The International Economy and the Possibilities of Governance*. Cambridge: Polity.

Hoffmann, S. (1981) *Duties beyond Borders*. Syracuse, NY: Syracuse University Press.

Hollis, M. and S. Smith (1991) *Explaining and Understanding International Relations*. Oxford: Clarendon.

Huntington, S. (1993) 'The clash of civilisations'. *Foreign Affairs*, 72: 22–49.

Kennan, G. (1951) *American Diplomacy 1900–1950*. Chicago: University of Chicago Press.

Keohane, R. O. (1989) *International Institutions and State Power*. Boulder, CO: Westview.

Kratochwil, F. (1989) *Rules, Norms and Decisions*. Cambridge: Cambridge University Press.

Kratochwil, F. (1995) 'Sovereignty as dominion: is there a right of humanitarian intervention?' In G. Lyons and M. Mastanduno, eds, *Beyond Westphalia?* Baltimore: Johns Hopkins University Press, 21–42.

Kratochwil, F. (2000) 'Constructing a new orthodoxy? Wendt's *Social Theory of International Politics* and the constructivist challenge'. *Millennium: Journal of International Studies*, 29: 73–101.

Kymlicka, W., ed. (1995) *The Rights of Minority Cultures*. Oxford: Oxford University Press.

Linklater, A. (1998) *The Transformation of Political Community*. Cambridge: Polity.

Mayall, J., ed. (1996) *The New Interventionism*. Cambridge: Cambridge University Press.

Mearsheimer, J. (2001) *The Tragedy of Great Power Politics*. New York: Norton.

Mill, J. S. (2002) 'A few words on non-intervention'. In C. Brown, T. Nardin and N. Rengger, eds, *International Relations in Political Thought*. Cambridge: Cambridge University Press.

Miller, D. (1995) *On Nationality*. Oxford: Oxford University Press, 486–93.

Miller, D. and M. Walzer, eds (1995) *Pluralism, Justice and Equality*. Oxford: Oxford University Press.

Moore, J., ed. (1998) *Hard Choices: Moral Dilemmas in Humanitarian Intervention*. Lanham, MD: Rowman and Littlefield.

Morgenthau, H. J. (1947) *Scientific Man and Power Politics*. Chicago: University of Chicago Press.

Morgenthau, H. J. (1948) *Politics among Nations*. New York: Knopf.

Morgenthau, H. J. (1970) *Truth and Power*. London: Pall Mall.

Murray, Alastair (1996) *Reconstructing Realism*. Edinburgh: Keele University Press.

Nardin, T. (1983) *Law, Morality and the Relations of States*. Princeton, NJ: Princeton University Press.

Nardin, T. (1989) 'The problem of relativism in international ethics'. *Millennium: Journal of International Studies*, 18: 140–61.

Niebuhr, R. (1932) *Moral Man and Immoral Society*. New York: Scribner.

Oakeshott, M. (1975) *On Human Conduct*. Oxford: Clarendon.

O'Neill, O. (1994) 'Justice and boundaries'. In C. Brown, ed., *Political Restructuring in Europe*. London: Routledge, 69–88.

Onuf, N. (1989) *World of Our Making*. Columbia, SC: University of South Carolina Press.

Parekh, B. (2000) *Rethinking Multiculturalism*. Basingstoke: Palgrave.

Peters, J. S. and A. Wolper, eds (1995) *Women's Rights, Human Rights: International Feminist Perspectives*. New York: Routledge.

Pogge, T. (1989) *Realizing Rawls*. Ithaca, NY: Cornell University Press.

Rawls, J. (1999) *The Law of Peoples*. Cambridge, MA: Harvard University Press.

Review of International Studies (2000) 'Forum on Alexander Wendt's *Social Theory of International Politics*', 26: 123–80.

Rivkin, D. B. and L. A. Casey (2000–1) 'The rocky shoals of international law'. *The National Interest*, 2: 35–46.

Rosenthal, J. (1991) *Righteous Realists*. Baton Rouge, LA: University of Louisiana Press.

Schmitt, C. (1996 [1932]) *The Concept of the Political*. Chicago: University of Chicago Press.

Shapiro, M. and H. Alker, eds (1996) *Challenging Boundaries: Global Flows, Territorial Identities*. Minneapolis: University of Minnesota Press.

Shue, H. (1983) *Basic Rights: Famine, Affluence and United States Foreign Policy*. Princeton, NJ: Princeton University Press.

Smith, M. J. (1986) *Realist Thought from Weber to Kissinger*. Baton Rouge, LA: University of Louisiana Press.

Spiro, P. J. (2000) 'The new sovereigntists'. *Foreign Affairs*, 79: 9–15.

Steiner, H. (1992) 'Libertarianism and the transnational migration of people'. In B. Barry and R. E. Goodin, eds, *Free Movement*. Hemel Hempstead: Harvester Wheatsheaf.

Steiner, H. (1999) 'Just taxation and international redistribution'. In I. Shapiro and L. Brilmayer, eds, *Global Justice: NOMOS XLI*. New York: New York University Press, 171–91.

Treitschke, H. von (2002) *Politics*. Extracts in C. Brown, T. Nardin and N. J. Rengger, eds, *International Relations in Political Thought*. Cambridge: Cambridge University Press.

Tuck, R. (1999) *The Rights of War and Peace*. Cambridge: Cambridge University Press.

Walzer, M. (1983) *Spheres of Justice*. London: Martin Robertson.

Walzer, M. (1987) *Interpretation and Social Criticism*. Cambridge, MA: Harvard University Press.

Walzer, M. (1992) *Just and Unjust Wars* (1977), 2nd edn. New York: Basic.

Walzer, M. (1994) *Thick and Thin: Moral Argument at Home and Abroad*. Notre Dame, IN: University of Notre Dame Press.

Waltz, K. (1979) *Theory of International Politics*. Reading, MA: Addison-Wesley.

Wendt, A. (1992) 'Anarchy is what states make of it: the social construction of power politics'. *International Organisation*, 46: 391–426.

Wendt, A. (1999) *Social Theory of International Politics*. Cambridge: Cambridge University Press.

Wheeler, N. J. (1992) 'Pluralist and solidarist conceptions of international society: Bull and Vincent on humanitarian intervention'. *Millennium: Journal of International Studies*, 21: 463–87.

Wheeler, N. J. (2000) *Saving Strangers*. Oxford: Oxford University Press.

White, S. (1991) *Political Theory and Postmodernism*. Cambridge: Cambridge University Press.

Part IV

THE HISTORY OF POLITICAL THOUGHT

23

Ancient Greek Political Thought

DAVID KEYT AND FRED D. MILLER, JR

This chapter covers the classical period of Greek civilization (fifth and fourth centuries BC). It is organized by theory rather than by philosopher. We consider in turn relativism, contractualism, Platonism, naturalism, and anarchism. Since theories arise in reaction to other theories, the five we consider form, to a considerable extent, a logical as well as a chronological progression. The focus on theories rather than philosophers has several advantages. First of all, it allows us to highlight the different ways the five theories are grounded, as their names suggest. Second, it allows us to skirt the problem of the authorship of several of the theories. Plato is the chief source for three of them, and it is often a matter of controversy whether an idea expressed by a character in a Platonic dialogue is to be attributed to Plato or to the historical figure after whom the character is named. Finally, it allows the reader to judge the extent to which Greek political thought foreshadows later political philosophy in the West.

Two recent books on the entire period deserve mention right at the beginning: Rowe and Schofield (2000) – a mammoth history by many hands – and Coleman (2000) – a shorter introduction by a single author.

'NO BETTER THAN SLAVES'

In the *Memorabilia* (I.2.40–6) Xenophon relates a (possibly apocryphal) conversation between the Athenian statesman Pericles and his teenage nephew Alcibiades over the nature of law. Pericles advances the thesis that law (*nomos*) is whatever the rulers in a city, or *polis*, enact. But what, Alcibiades asks, about enactments imposed by the strong upon the weak by force rather than by persuasion – imposed, say, by a tyrant upon the citizens or by the few upon the many in an oligarchy? Pericles agrees that these are the negation of law (*anomia*). But what happens, Alcibiades continues, when the mass imposes rules upon the property owners in a democracy? Surely these are also examples of force rather than law. Pericles (the leader of the Athenian democracy) can only respond that when he was young he too used to devise such clever conundrums. This draws from Alcibiades a lament at not knowing him at his cleverest. This humorous interchange sets the stage for the rest of our chapter. It raises the question of the proper relation of ruler and ruled, expresses the widely held assumption in the ancient world that rule by force is illegitimate, and implicitly challenges the legitimacy of every existing government (assuming that rule by one, few, or many, exhausts the possibilities).

The prime relation in the Greek world based on force was that of master to slave (Aristotle, *Pol.* I.3.1253b20–3). The dread of slavery, which sprang from a very real fear, was a prominent feature of Greek life and thought. Greek cities were frequently at war, and it was a common practice to kill the soldiers and enslave the wives and children of a captured city (Thucydides III.62.2, V.32.1, V.116.3, and elsewhere). The Greeks regarded any relation of ruler to ruled based on force as akin to that of master to slave. Their word for such a relation was 'despotic' (*despotikê*, literally, 'of a master'). To be forcibly subjected to another was in their eyes to be no better than a slave. This idea seems to be the driving force behind the evolution of Greek democracy, the most important political innovation of the Greeks. Freedom and equality were (as they still are) the defining marks of democracy (Plato, *Rep.* VIII.557a2–b6; Aristotle, *Pol.* V.9.1310a25–34, VI.1318a3–10). Freedom was popularly defined as living as one wishes (Herodotus III.83.3; Thucydides II.37.2; Plato, *Rep.* VIII.557b4–6; Isocrates, *Areop.* 20; Aristotle, *Pol.* V.9.1310a31–2, VI.2.1317b10–12). By this popular definition, to be forced to do something against one's will is to lose one's freedom, and to lose one's freedom is to be enslaved. Thus, to be forced by a ruler to do something one does not want to do is to be treated as a slave. The Greek democrat, in consequence, was loath to be ruled at all. Wishing, however, to live in a political community, he sought to avoid the despotism inherent in the unequal power of ruler and ruled. Without equality there is, in his view, no freedom (Plato, *Menex.* 238e1–239a4). So he invented a number of clever devices for eliminating or minimizing inequalities of political power: self-rule (every free man is a member of the assembly), rotation of office, short tenure of office, and the use of the lot. Ironically, Athenian democracy under Pericles was denounced by its enemies for trying to enslave all the other Greeks by establishing a universal empire (Thucydides I.124.3).

The two major political thinkers of antiquity, Plato and Aristotle, though no less hostile to despotic rule over free men than Athenian democrats (Aristotle, *Pol.* III.6.1279a19–21; Plato, *Laws* VIII.832c), travel a different road. They are unimpressed by the democratic argument for two reasons. First of all, they understand freedom differently. Following Socrates' lead (Xenophon, *Mem.* I.3.11), they define it as rational, rather than unimpeded, agency: a man who is enslaved to a passion but whose activity is unimpeded is free in one sense of the word but not in the other (Plato, *Rep.* IX.577d, 579d–e; Aristotle, *Metaph.* XII.10.1075a18–23). Second, they think that Athenian democracy, being in practice if not in theory the rule by force of the mass over the wealthy, is itself despotic (Plato, *Laws* VIII.832c; Aristotle, *Pol.* III.6.1279a19–21 together with 7.1279b4–6). Wishing to maintain rather than to minimize or eliminate the distance between ruler and ruled, they are led to distinguish different sorts of rule and in particular to distinguish the rule of the wise and the virtuous from despotic rule (Plato, *Laws* III.689e–690d; Aristotle, *Pol.* III.4.1277a33–b11). (The response of Greek intellectuals to Athenian democracy is the theme of Ober, 1996 and 1998; Saxonhouse, 1996; and Veyne, 1983.)

VOCABULARY

The modern term 'political' derives from the Greek word *polis* (plural *poleis*), which originally referred

to a citadel or high stronghold. (The acropolis of Athens was still called the *polis* in the late fifth century: Thucydides II.15.6.) The polis came to include the households and businesses gathered around the citadel and later the surrounding territory, and thus evolved by the sixth and fifth centuries into the classical Greek city-state: for example, Attica with Athens as its urban centre (*astu*), and Laconia with Sparta as its urban centre. There were as many as 800 Greek poleis, and Aristotle and his students composed descriptions of 158 different constitutions. Despite important similarities, the poleis varied considerably in size, location (on the coast, inland, or on an island), economic activity (agricultural or mercantile in varying degrees), customs, and temperament. Each polis was a microcosm, geographically distinct, and, to a significant extent, economically self-sufficient and politically independent. Although its members remained tightly intertwined by relationships of kinship, economic exchange, custom, and religious practice, a polis was often subject to powerful revolutionary forces. Moreover, as the Greeks continued to found new colonies around the Mediterranean and Black Sea, they had to address basic constitutional issues: for example, what laws and political institutions should be established? Who should be recognized as citizens? It is understandable, then, that the polis was the object of reflection by Greek philosophers. A broad historical investigation of the Greek polis is currently being conducted by a team of scholars under the auspices of the Copenhagen Polis Center and its director, Mogens Herman Hansen.

The rise of Greek political thought was facilitated by the existence in the ancient Greek language of an elaborate political vocabulary based on the word *polis*. The following terms occur frequently:

polis	city, state, city-state, polis
politês	citizen
politis	female citizen
politeia	constitution, regime
politeuma	governing class
politeuesthai	participate in government
politik-	of or pertaining to the polis or to a citizen

The adjective with the stem *politik-* (the ancestor of the modern term 'political') has masculine (*politikos*), feminine (*politikê*), and neuter (*politikon*) forms. For example,

ho politikos (sc. *anêr*)	the politician or statesman
politikê archê	political office or political rule
politika (sc. *pragmata*)	political things (title of Aristotle's *Politics*)

Finally, the feminine *politikê* is applied in various ways to the discipline of political thought:

politikê technê	political art
politikê epistêmê	political science
politikê philosophia	political philosophy
hê politikê	politics

The political vocabulary of English and many other modern languages is based on *polis* and partly on *civis*, the Latin word for 'citizen'. Consequently, and as the above list of equivalents shows, English does not mark out the special field of politics as vividly as Greek. It is especially difficult to render the word *polis* in English. It is variously translated as 'city', 'state', or 'city-state', or else simply transliterated as 'polis'. Each rendering has disadvantages, and none of them suggests the interconnections among, for example, 'citizen', 'statesman', 'constitution', and 'politician'.

The unity of Greek political terminology lends the polis enough substantiality to be the subject of literary as well as philosophical works. According to some recent scholars, the polis was enough of a concrete entity in Thucydides' eyes to displace individual men and women as the subject of his history. Thus, the eminent classicist Hugh Lloyd-Jones writes that Thucydides' *History of the Peloponnesian War* 'is not the tragedy of Pericles, or of Alcibiades, or of any man or men, but the tragedy of Athens' (1971: 144).

ANTITHESES

In addition to the strictly political vocabulary there are a number of related pairs of opposites that set the parameters and provide the universal themes of Greek political thought. Two of them have been noted already: ruler and subject, and free and slave. Some others are concord (*homonoia*, literally 'like-mindedness') and faction (*stasis*), persuasion and force, justice and injustice, and nature (*phusis*) and convention (*nomos*).

Two stories from Aesop illustrate the Greek attitude toward concord and faction, and persuasion and force. The first is about a farmer and his factious sons. When arguments were insufficient to get his sons to stop fighting with each other, the farmer turned to action and asked them to bring him a bundle of sticks. He ordered them to break the bundle, which try as they might they couldn't do. He then untied the bundle and gave his sons the sticks one at a time, which they now broke easily. This illustrates, he told them, their invincibility while in concord and their weakness while engaged in faction (*Aesopica* 53). (On *homonoia* see also Democritus, DK 250, and Xenophon, *Mem.* IV.4.16.) The

second story concerns a quarrel between the Sun and the North Wind over who was the more powerful. They decided that the quarrel would be won by whichever of the two could strip the clothes off a passer-by. The North Wind went first and blew hard, thinking by the sheer force of his blast to blow the man's clothes off. The man responded by pulling his clothes more tightly around himself. The Sun, taking his turn, shone down upon the man and brought him relief from the cold, raw wind. When the Sun shone more brightly still, the man threw off his clothes. The moral of this story is that persuasion is often more effective than force (*Aesopica* 46).

Justice and injustice are among the themes of the earliest works of Greek civilization that have come down to us. The wrath of Achilles of which Homer writes in the *Iliad* is caused by Agamemnon's unjust commandeering of the beautiful girl Briseis, the portion of the plunder awarded Achilles after a raid. The loss of the girl, representing as it does a loss of honour (*Iliad* I.171), touches his ego, his *thumos*, as much as his id. But Achilles too is in the wrong for not properly honouring Agamemnon (*Iliad* I.275–9). The *Iliad* is, thus, among other things, about a dispute over the just distribution of honour, the honour due to a great warrior and the honour due to a king (see, for example, *Iliad* IX.158–61, IX.318–36). As distributive justice is a theme of the *Iliad*, retributive justice is a theme of the *Odyssey* – retribution for the injustice of Penelope's suitors in their courtship of her, in their conduct in Odysseus's house, and in their treatment of a stranger (Odysseus in disguise) (for the injustice of the suitors see *Odyssey* II.282, XIV.90). Lloyd-Jones (1971) argues that the justice of the gods is a major theme of Homer's epics and that it continues to be a theme of Greek poetry, historiography, and philosophy until traditional ideas about the morality of the gods succumb to Plato's destructive criticism. (Balot, 2001, is a valuable discussion of *injustice* in classical Athens.)

The crucial distinction among these pairs of opposites for the philosopher or theorist interested in the foundations of political thought is that between nature and convention, *phusis* and *nomos*. *Nomos* stands to *phusis* as the artificial, the man-made, stands to the real, and as common opinion stands to truth (Aristotle, *Sophistici Elenchi* 12.173a7–18). Two stock examples of the conventional are money (Aristotle, *Pol.* I.9.1257b10–17) and the names of things – one's own name, for example (Plato, *Crat.* 384d). The idea that *nomos* and *phusis* are antithetical seems to have originated in the fifth century BC. Once it gained currency it set the terms for the discussion of ethical and political ideas. A favourite way of undermining the validity of something was to argue that it existed only by *nomos* and not by *phusis* (Plato, *Laws* X.889e–890a).

Thus, when Antigone in Sophocles' play invokes the eternal unwritten law calling upon her to bury her brother in the face of the law of Creon demanding that her brother remain unburied, her appeal to the eternal law (Sophocles, *Antigone* 456–8) is taken by Aristotle to be an appeal to nature in spite of the fact that her speech does not mention *phusis* (*Rhet*. I.13.1373b1–18, I.15.1375a25–b4). (There is a large literature on this distinction. One of the major works on the *nomos-phusis* distinction is Heinimann, 1945. On the evolution of ancient legal thought from earliest times see Miller, 2004.)

RELATIVISM

Given the antithesis between *nomos* and *phusis*, it is natural to wonder, once one becomes acquainted with the variety of *nomoi* among different peoples, whether any action, law, or custom is fine or just by *phusis*. Herodotus notes that all men think their own customs, or *nomoi*, are the finest (*kallistoi*, 'most beautiful', 'noblest'), offering in illustration the following anecdote. When Darius, the Persian king, asked some Greeks who were with him if they could be persuaded by a sum of money to eat their fathers' corpses, they replied that no amount of money would induce them to do that. He then turned to some Indians whose custom it is to do just that, asked them what they would charge to cremate their parents (the custom of the Greeks), and received in reply a cry of horror (Herodotus III.38). What follows from this anecdote, strictly speaking, is only that the Indians and the Greeks cannot both be right in thinking their own custom for dealing with their parents' remains is the finest; it does not follow that they are both wrong or that the two customs stand on an equal footing with respect to fineness. On the other hand, it seems like narrow-minded prejudice to affirm, in the face of cultural diversity, the superiority of one's own customs. Thus, Aristotle remarks that 'fine and just actions ... exhibit much variation and fluctuation, so that they *seem* to exist by *nomos* only, not by *phusis*' (*EN* I.3.1094b14–16). It is but a short (though invalid) step from cultural diversity to moral relativism.

There are other paths to moral relativism. Protagoras, the most prominent advocate of moral relativism in antiquity, derived it from a more general ontological relativism. In the opening and only surviving sentence of his work on *Truth*, Protagoras famously proclaimed that 'man is the measure of all things, of things that are, that they are, and of things that are not, that they are not'. Plato takes Protagoras to mean that 'things are to me as they appear to me, and are to you as they appear to you' (*Crat*. 386a) and in general that 'what *seems* true to

each [man] *is* true for each [man]' (*Crat*. 386c). Moral relativism is just one application of this universal relativism. In Socrates' elaborate account of Protagoras in Plato's *Theaetetus*, ontological and moral relativism are discussed in tandem. By the man–measure principle, if the wind *feels* cold to me but not to you, then the wind *is* cold for me but not cold for you (*Tht*. 152b); and by the same principle, 'whatever things *appear* just and fine to each polis *are* so for it as long as it holds by them' (*Tht*. 167c4–5). As the latter passage makes plain, the man–measure formula in Plato's view applies to collections of men as well as to individual men. In one passage Protagoras is even made to apply his formula to individuals and poleis indifferently: 'what seems to each private person and to each polis actually is [for them]' (*Tht*. 168b5–6). Since by the man–measure formula '*seems F* to *a*' entails '*is F* for *a*', there is for Protagoras nothing more ultimate than appearances, nothing deeper than convention. In particular, as Socrates duly notes, on Protagorean principles no polis is just by nature (*Tht*. 172b).

The extent to which Socrates' account of Protagoras can safely be attributed to the historical Protagoras remains an open question. The very fact that Protagoras does not speak for himself in the dialogue but only through Socrates should put the reader on his guard; it may be Plato's way of disclaiming historical accuracy. Some scholars think, nevertheless, that there are clues within the speeches of Socrates that allow a careful reader to distinguish the ideas that are authentically Protagorean from those that are Plato's own invention. When Socrates refers to the 'secret doctrine' of Protagoras at *Theaetetus* 152c10, for example, this is taken by such scholars to indicate that Plato is shifting from an account of Protagoras' explicit doctrine to an implication that in Plato's view can be reasonably drawn from the explicit doctrine (see, for example, McDowell, 1973: 121–2). Whatever the truth of the matter, it is a mark of Plato's genius that relativism, very much as Socrates explains it in the *Theaetetus*, has taken on a life of its own unmoored from both Plato and Protagoras.

Socrates' account of Protagoras is combined with spirited criticism. One question that arises about Protagoras' universal relativism is whether it is self-refuting (*Tht*. 170a–171c). Applied to itself the Protagorean formula asserts that 'man is the measure' is true for those for whom it seems true. But to most men the Protagorean formula seems false. Thus, the formula is more false than true. (For more on self-refutation see Burnyeat, 1976.) A second problem, a problem in the political realm, relates to Protagoras' claim to be wiser than others and on that basis to deserve his high fees (*Tht*. 167c–d). What role can there be for a wise man, a sophist, one might wonder, if truth is relative? Speaking through Socrates, Protagoras has an interesting answer to this question. He claims not access to truth that is denied to lesser mortals but rather an ability to change the way things appear to poleis: when harmful things seem just to a given polis the wise man can make beneficial things seem and be just to that polis. This response leads directly to a third problem over which Protagorean relativism seems to break down (*Tht.* 177c–179b). The laws of a polis, Socrates claims, aim at what is advantageous for the polis in the future. According to the man–measure formula, what *seems* to a lawmaker to be to the future advantage of his polis *is* to the future advantage of his polis; but when the future arrives, it may *seem to be* (and hence *actually be*) to his polis's disadvantage. What *seemed* true may not *be* true.

The Platonic dialogue bearing Protagoras' name contains a long passage (*Prot.* 320c–328d), customarily referred to as Protagoras' 'Great Speech', filled with ideas relating to political philosophy. Since the Great Speech and Socrates' account of relativism in the *Theaetetus* are associated with the same philosopher, it is natural to wonder if the two are connected and to wonder, in particular, if the relativism expounded in the *Theaetetus* has any bearing on the political thought of the Great Speech. This is primarily an issue of the relation of the two fore-mentioned passages; whether it is also an issue concerning the historical Protagoras depends upon their authenticity. The authenticity of the Great Speech is difficult to gauge since the work or works of Protagoras on which it might be based are lost. (For a recent defence of its authenticity see Nill, 1985: 5–22.)

The Great Speech is an answer to two Socratic arguments that the political art (*hê politikê technê*), which Protagoras claims to teach, cannot in fact be taught. The answer is given first in myth (*muthos*) (*Prot.* 320c–324d) – not to be taken literally, given Protagoras' well-known agnosticism about the gods (DK 4 and *Tht.* 162e) – and then in argument (*logos*) (*Prot.* 324d–328d). The mythological answer is that the gifts of Zeus, justice and shame (*aidôs*) and the rest of political virtue (*politikê aretê*), unlike the technical skills such as metallurgy, spinning, and weaving distributed by Prometheus, are given to everyone. Demythologized, the gifts of the gods are the gifts of teachers, and the point of the myth is that political virtue is taught to everybody by everybody.

The Great Speech touches upon most of the antitheses that structure Greek political philosophy. Persuasion and force are the means by which justice and shame are taught (*Prot.* 325d5). Plato's Protagoras, supposedly an advocate of the art of persuasion, is a surprisingly strong believer in the efficacy of the use of force. The child who resists his teachers' admonitions about the unjust, impious, and base, 'is straightened by threats and blows, like a piece of bent or warped wood' (*Prot.* 325d; see also 322d, 325ab, 327d). Although *nomos* and *phusis* are not explicitly distinguished until later in the dialogue (*Prot.* 337d), one of the themes of the Great Speech is that justice and shame come not by nature but by teaching (*Prot.* 323c–d). Since these virtues make possible 'the bonds of friendship' (*Prot.* 322c3) – the Protagorean version of *homonoia* – these bonds and the poleis they hold together do not exist by nature either.

The prime interpretive issue concerning the Great Speech is its connection with the universal relativism of Socrates' account of Protagoras in the *Theaetetus*. Some scholars such as Gregory Vlastos (1956: xvii) believe that Protagoras' Great Speech presupposes his relativism, whereas others such as S. Moser and G. L. Kustas (1966) deny any connection with relativism. In any case a strong argument can be made that the Great Speech is inconsistent with a thoroughgoing relativism. In the Great Speech justice is given to man by Zeus to serve a particular purpose, namely, to create the bonds of friendship that hold a polis together. This end, or goal, would seem to limit the range of conceptions of justice. A notion that falls outside this range, that does not promote the bonds of friendship, would seem, by the theory of the Great Speech, not to be a notion of justice at all.

Another hotly debated issue concerning the Great Speech is whether it is a defence of democracy. The Great Speech does contain a defence of the democratic practice of the Athenian assembly of allowing every citizen a voice about issues of justice and temperance (*Prot.* 322d–323a). This has led one scholar to claim that Protagoras 'has produced for the first time in human history a theoretical basis for participatory democracy' (Kerferd, 1981: 144) and another to say that Protagoras is 'the first democratic political theorist in the history of the world' (Farrar, 1988: 77). Furthermore, there does seem to be a natural alliance between Protagorean relativism and democracy if the locus of relativism is the individual (Taylor, 1976: 83–4). By such relativism whatever seems good to citizen *A* is good for *A*, and whatever seems good to citizen *B* is good for *B* (*Tht.* 166c–d). But *A* and *B* cannot be friends if they thwart each other's good. Thus, if there are to be the bonds of friendship, without which a polis cannot exist, *A* must take account of what seems good to *B*, and *B* of what seems good to *A*, and in general each citizen must take account of what seems good to every other citizen. Otherwise *stasis* results. But this 'live and let live' philosophy is one of the defining features of democracy. On the other hand, when the locus of relativity is shifted from the individual to the polis, Protagorean relativism does not seem to favour democracy over any other form of government: if oligarchy or monarchy seems just to the citizens of a polis, oligarchy or monarchy is just for them. (Rosen, 1994, is a useful survey of the extensive literature on both sides of this issue.)

A final issue of debate is whether a theory of the social contract can be found in the Great Speech. There are scholars on both sides of this issue. Although political relativism is consistent with a social contract, the elimination argument usually used to attribute a social contract theory to Protagoras – not by nature or by the gods, therefore by a social contract (see, for example, Guthrie, 1969: 137) – tacitly assumes a false disjunction. Another possibility, noted in passing by Plato, is that laws are due to chance in the guise of war, poverty, and disease (*Laws* IV.709a–b).

Schiappa (1991) is a recent book-length study of Protagoras.

CONTRACTUALISM

The Greek word for a compact or a covenant is *sunthêkê*. There are four passages spread among Plato, Aristotle, and Epicurus in which the word is used to express a view identifiable as a kind of social contract theory. In the *Crito* Socrates imagines what the Laws of Athens might say to him if he attempted to escape from prison: they would, he says, remind him of the covenants (*sunthêkas*) and agreements (*homologias*) through which he contracted with them to live as a citizen (*Cr.* 52d). In the *Republic* Glaucon, posing as devil's advocate, asserts that the origin of justice lies in laws and covenants (*sunthêkas*) (*Rep.* II.359a). In the *Politics* Aristotle rejects the idea associated with the sophist Lycophron that law is a covenant (*sunthêkê*, 'a surety to one another of just actions') (*Pol.* III.9.1280a34–b12; for Lycophron see Mulgan, 1979). And, finally, in his *Key Doctrines* Epicurus says that 'there never was a justice in itself, but only [a justice] in dealing with one another in whatever places there used always to be a covenant [*sunthêkê*] about neither harming nor being harmed' (*KD* XXXI–XXXV = D.L. X.150–1). For the origins of social contract theory see Chroust (1946) and Kahn (1981).

These four passages share two ideas but differ on another. The two ideas that are shared are connected with the basic antitheses underlying Greek political thought. The first of these is that covenants are man-made, not gifts of the gods or of nature. The second is that the covenant to live as a citizen is also a compact to be of one mind (*homonoein*). This idea rises to the surface in an interchange between Socrates and the sophist Hippias

in Xenophon's *Memorabilia* (IV.4). Hippias challenges Socrates to say what justice is, and Socrates responds like a contractarian by identifying the just with the lawful (*Mem.* IV.4.12). He goes on to connect obedience to the laws with concord, or *homonoia*, and to note that such *homonoia* is consistent with sharp disagreement on particular issues (*Mem.* IV.4.16).

The passages above differ over the relation of an original covenant to justice. In the *Crito* the personified Laws of Athens point out to Socrates that he has had 70 years to leave Athens 'if his agreements [to live as a citizen under them] did not seem just to him' (*Cr.* 52e). But if an agreement can be just or unjust, justice must be logically prior to the agreement; the agreement cannot be the origin of justice. This is what may be called 'shallow contractualism'. Deep contractualism, on the other hand, is the view that a covenant or an agreement is the origin of the distinction between justice and injustice. Glaucon and Epicurus in the passages cited above are deep contractualists. (Aristotle does not provide us with enough information about Lycophron to classify him one way or the other.) In modern philosophy Hobbes is a deep contractualist, Locke a shallow.

The shallow contractualism of the *Crito* raises at once the problem of principled disobedience. Since the covenant that Socrates, according to the Laws of Athens, tacitly consented to 'by deeds, not by words' (*Cr.* 52d) is not the origin of justice, nothing in the covenant prevents laws and lawful orders from being unjust. Indeed, the Laws concede that Socrates' lawful execution is unjust (*Cr.* 54bc). It is a Socratic principle, moreover, that one should never do anything unjust (*Cr.* 49b). Suppose, now, that the man ordered to administer the hemlock to Socrates realized that Socrates' execution was unjust. Would the personified Laws of Athens allow him to disobey the lawful order? They insist, after all, that they do not issue savage commands, but offer two alternatives: persuade or obey (*Cr.* 52a). (Those who do neither are guilty of using force, the antithesis of persuasion, against Athens: *Cr.* 51c2.) The interpretation of the 'persuade or obey' doctrine is the central interpretive issue concerning the *Crito*, and it has generated a mountain of commentary. Interpretations range from authoritarian at one end of the spectrum – 'Change the law if you can; if you cannot, do what it commands or else emigrate' – to liberal at the other end – 'You can disobey as long as you act justly and render a persuasive account of your action'. Every aspect of 'persuade or obey' raises a question. What is the nature of the disjunction? To whom is the persuasion addressed – the assembly or the popular courts? To what is obedience owed – an official's command, a particular law or decree, or the legal system? What is it to persuade? Is it to try to convince or to succeed in convincing? Does it count as persuasion if one renders a reasonable account of a just action, whether one convinces anyone or not? The interpretation of the *Crito* is further complicated by the fact that in Plato's *Apology* Socrates mentions several cases where he disobeyed or would disobey those in authority (*Ap*. 29c–d, 32a–e). (Five lengthy studies of these matters are: Allen, 1980; Brickhouse and Smith, 1994; Kraut, 1984; Santas, 1979; and Woozley, 1979.)

The Laws of Athens tell Socrates that he must do what his polis commands or persuade it 'as to what is just by nature' (*hê(i) to dikaion pephuke*) (*Cr*. 51c1). This seems to be an appeal to a higher standard than the laws themselves, the sort of standard needed by a person who thinks a law is unjust. The shallow contractualist will need to give an account of the ontological status of such a standard, an account missing from the *Crito* and from all of Plato's early dialogues. This issue is bequeathed to the *Republic* and other middle dialogues.

Glaucon's deep contractualism is based on views of human motivation, of human rationality, and of relative human equality (*Rep*. II.358e–359c). He supposes that people desire to get more and more, grabbing it from others if they can. But, being relatively equal, they lack the power to act unjustly and to avoid unjust treatment. Lacking such power but possessing what has come to be called 'strategic rationality', they decide that it is in their interest to make a covenant with each other neither to act nor to be treated unjustly and 'begin to make laws and covenants, and to call what the law commands "lawful" and "just"' (*Rep*. II.359a3–4). Glaucon's description of their situation before they make laws and covenants is not strictly accurate. Since their laws and covenants call into existence the just and the unjust, it is inconsistent to describe anything they do before they make their original covenants as unjust. To be consistent, Glaucon should have spoken of actions 'that will come to be called "unjust"'.

On Glaucon's view of justice as a necessary evil and a shackle of natural desires, no one is just willingly: people practise justice 'as something necessary, not as something good' (*Rep*. II.358c16–17). This is the point of the story of Gyges' ring, the ring that gives its possessor 'equal to a god among men' (*Rep*. II.360c3) by giving him the power of invisibility. Glaucon claims that the possessor of such a ring would exploit its power to satisfy his natural desires unrestrained by justice. Antiphon in *On Truth* makes a similar point: if justice consists of obeying the laws of one's polis, 'a person would best use justice to his own advantage if he considered the laws [*nomoi*] important when witnesses are present, but the consequences of nature [*phusis*]

important in the absence of witnesses' (DK 44 col. 1; see also Caizz, 1999). The story of Gyges' ring poses the problem that Plato addresses in the rest of the *Republic*, and echoes through the history of Western philosophy. Contemporary contractualists like Gauthier (1986: ch. 10) continue to worry about it, and Hobbes' Foole seems to be a descendant of Gyges.

PLATONISM

By 'Platonism' we refer to the rule of reason as Plato construes this idea in the four political dialogues *Gorgias*, *Republic*, *Statesman*, and *Laws*.

After 2,400 years there is still no settled interpretive strategy for reading Plato. Since he writes dialogues rather than treatises, the extent to which his characters speak for their author is bound to remain problematic. The major divide is between interpreters who respect Platonic anonymity and those who do not (see D.L. III.50–1). The former are impressed by the literary 'distancing' that Plato creates between himself and his readers. (The ideas attributed to Protagoras in the *Theaetetus*, for example, are thrice removed from Plato: they are expressed by Socrates, whose speeches are read in turn by Euclides, the narrator of the dialogue.) Interpreters who take such distancing seriously might be called 'characterologists' since they hold that the characters in the dialogues are literary characters who speak for themselves, not for Plato. Characterologists take the dialogues to be 'sceptical', or aporetic, rather than 'dogmatic', or doctrinal, and emphasize their dramatic and literary elements. Thus, Leo Strauss, a particularly fervent characterologist, claims that the dialogues must be read as dramas: 'We cannot,' he says, 'ascribe to Plato any utterance of any of his characters without having taken great precautions' (1964: 59) [see further Chapter 3]. The opposing group of interpreters suppose that in each dialogue Plato has an identifiable spokesman: Socrates in the *Gorgias* and the *Republic*, the Eleatic Stranger in the *Statesman*, and the Athenian Stranger in the *Laws* (D.L. III.52). Such interpreters fall into three camps (1) Unitarians suppose that Plato's spokesmen present a consistent doctrine in all four dialogues. (2) Developmentalists believe that the doctrine expressed by Plato's spokesmen evolves from one dialogue to the next. They believe, of course, that the order of composition of our four dialogues can be established, the order usually favoured being, from earliest to latest, *Gorgias*, *Republic*, *Statesman*, *Laws*. (3) Particularists interpret each dialogue on its own. Though they allow that there may be thematic links among the four dialogues, they do not worry overly much about the relation of one dialogue in the group to the others. Griswold (1988) and Smith (1998: vol. I) are two useful collections of essays on interpretive strategies, and Tarrant (2000) is a major new work on Platonic interpretation.

The four great political dialogues form a connected series, the connecting link being the pre-eminent role assigned to reason and knowledge in politics. In the *Laws* the Athenian Stranger enumerates seven claims to rule – the claim of the well-born to rule the base-born, the strong to rule the weak, and so forth – and concludes that the greatest claim of all is that of the wise to rule the ignorant (*Laws* III.690a–d). This conclusion is the animating idea of the four political dialogues. (We shall assume the current consensus on their order of composition.) In the *Gorgias* Socrates maintains that true statesmanship (*politikê*) differs from public speaking (*rhetorikê*) in being an art (*technê*) rather than an empirical knack (*empeiria*) – where an art, unlike an empirical knack, has a rational principle (*logos*) and can give the cause (*aitia*) of each thing (*Gorg.* 465a). He argues that none of the men reputed to be great Athenian statesmen practised true statesmanship (*Gorg.* 503b–c, 517a), and claims to be himself the only true statesman in Athens (*Gorg.* 521d6–9). In the *Republic* the role of reason and knowledge in politics is neatly encapsulated in the simile of the ship of state: just as a steersman must pay attention to sky, stars and wind if he is to be really qualified to rule a ship, so a statesman must have knowledge of the realm of Forms, a realm of incorporeal paradigms that exist beyond space and time, if he is to be really qualified to rule a polis (*Rep.* VI.488a7–489a6). Whether the theory of Forms was radically revised before the *Statesman* and *Laws* were written is a matter of great controversy. But, however that may be, the theme of the rule of reason is never abandoned or weakened. In the *Statesman* the Eleatic Stranger asserts that the only correct constitution is the one in which the rulers possess true statesmanship, all other constitutions being better or worse imitations of this one (*Plt.* 293c–294a, 296e4–297a5); and in the *Laws* the Athenian Stranger affirms the same principle (IX.875c3–d5). (The relations among these dialogues are discussed by Owen, 1953; Klosko, 1986; Laks, 1990; Gill, 1995; Kahn, 1995; and Kahn, 1996.)

The *Gorgias* is a forerunner of the *Republic*. The challenge of amoralism posed by Callicles and Polus in the *Gorgias* is reiterated by Thrasymachus and Glaucon in the *Republic*; but the response in the *Republic* outstrips that in the *Gorgias* by as much as a nuclear eclipses a chemical explosion. The challenge of Gyges' ring is to show that justice pays, that it is not a necessary evil but an intrinsic good.

The response requires a definition of justice in the soul, or *psychê*. But instead of defining it directly Socrates first defines social justice, and then, assuming the analogy of polis and psyche, constructs a corresponding definition of psychic justice. The definition of social justice, as Socrates notes himself (*Rep.* IV.433a), is simply the principle of the natural division of labour, which was introduced to explain the origin of the polis. (According to Socrates, it is mutual need that gives rise to the polis rather than, as Glaucon hypothesized, fear of harm.) This is not the economic principle championed by Adam Smith and modern economists but an implicitly anti-democratic affirmation of human inequality and implasticity. Socrates' principle has three parts: that a person has a natural aptitude for one sort of work, that he should devote his life to it, and that he should pursue no other (*Rep.* II.370a5–c6, 374b6–c2). The three great natural aptitudes (in terms of the myth of the metals) are for ruling (gold), for guarding (silver), and for working (iron and bronze), which by an application of the principle of the natural division of labour give rise to the three-tiered political structure of rulers, warriors, and workers (*Rep.* III.415a–c). The just polis is the one in which each person does the one job for which he is suited by nature and no other: rulers rule, warriors defend, and workers provision the polis (*Rep.* IV.432b–434c). By an independent argument Socrates infers that the psyche has three parts analogous to the three parts of the just polis, and then, following a principle of isomorphism, defines a just psyche as one with the same structure as a just polis. Thus, in a just psyche each of the psychic elements sticks to its own work: reason rules the psyche; spirit, or *thumos*, defends it from insult; and the appetites provide for its bodily support (*Rep.* IV.441d–442b). Psychic justice turns out to be something like mental health, an intrinsic good no one wants to be without, so the challenge of Thrasymachus and Glaucon is answered (*Rep.* IV.444c–445b). There is an ongoing controversy, however, over the cogency of Socrates' response. For it is unclear that the Platonically 'just' man is just in the sense of the problem of Gyges' ring. What prevents the Platonically just man from harming others? (The controversy, stoked by Sachs, 1963, has generated an enormous literature. Dahl, 1991, is a good representative of the current state of the debate.)

The absolute power of the rulers in Socrates' just polis is justified by their knowledge, especially their knowledge of what is really good. As all the world knows, they are philosophers as well as rulers, not run-of-the-mill philosophers (like you and me) but brilliant individuals whose extraordinary talents and rigorous education have gained them access to a realm of Forms existing outside time and space – the realm of reality and nature (*Rep.* VI.501b2, X.597b6–598a3). At the apex of the realm of Forms stands the Form of the Good, the source of the being and truth of all other Forms and of the psyche's knowledge of them (*Rep.* VI.506d–509c). Given the metaphysics and epistemology of the *Republic*, the argument for the rule of philosopher-kings is straightforward: only true philosophers know what is really good and how to achieve it; everyone seeks what is really good, not what merely seems good (*Rep.* VI.505d5–10); whoever seeks an end seeks the means to that end; consequently, everyone (whether they realize it or not) really seeks to be ruled by a philosopher-king. (Santas, 2001, is a ground-breaking study of the central concepts of the *Republic*.)

The *Republic* is the most controversial work in Greek philosophy. There is no settled interpretation of the dialogue as a whole, of any of its parts, or even of its characters. Of the current controversies surrounding its political ideas the most notable concern its communism, its view of women, and its hostility toward Athenian democracy, and its utopianism. Plato's rejection of private, or separate, families and of private property (at least for the rulers and warriors of his ideal polis) is usually examined through the lens of Aristotle's critique of Platonic communism in *Politics* II.1–5. T. H. Irwin (1991) and Robert Mayhew (1997) reach opposite conclusions about the cogency of Aristotle's critique. Whether Plato was a feminist and whether he masculinized women are hotly debated issues, especially among feminist philosophers. Tuana (1994) is a collection of diverse essays on this topic. Plato vents his hostility toward Athenian democracy not only in his sarcastic description of democracy in Book VIII but throughout the dialogue. His unfavourable view of Athenian democracy is implicit already in the principle of the natural division of labour introduced in Book II, one target of which is the pretension of the typical Athenian citizen to play multiple roles, to be at different times throughout the year worker, warrior, and ruler. Plato's advocacy of intellectual aristocracy and caustic criticism of democracy were vigorously attacked in Popper (1971), the most provocative book published on Plato in the twentieth century. Though the intense controversy that erupted when the book was originally published in 1945 has abated, the issue is by no means dead. Monoson (2000), for example, disputes the canonical view of Plato as virulent antidemocrat. The controversy turns to some extent on one's interpretation of Plato's utopianism. Is the ideally just polis in Plato's view a revolutionary goal, a guide for reform, a standard for evaluating existing constitutions, or something else entirely? A case can be made for each of these alternatives. The fact that the standard for being a true philosopher is set so high that even Socrates, by his own admission (*Rep.* VI.506b2–e5), fails to qualify strongly suggests that the ideal polis is not intended as an attainable ideal. (New books on the *Republic* appear regularly. Among the most notable are Cross and Woozley, 1964; Annas, 1981; White, 1979; and Reeve, 1988. Three recent collections of essays are particularly helpful: Fine, 1999: vol. II; Kraut, 1997b; and Höffe, 1997.)

In the *Statesman* the Eleatic Stranger pursues the idea of the rule of reason to its logical terminus and draws a conclusion that in the *Republic* remains tacit – that knowledge by itself provides sufficient warrant for the application of force, even deadly force, when persuasion fails (for the antithesis see *Plt.* 296b1, 304d4). It is within the bounds of justice, according to the Eleatic Stranger, for the true statesman, the man who possesses the political art and is 'truly and not merely apparently a knower', to purge his polis, with or without law, with or without the consent of his subjects, by killing or banishing some of its members (*Plt.* 293a2–e2). The only true constitution is the one ruled by such a person. Since such persons are exceedingly rare (*Plt.* 292e1–293a4, 297b7–c2), a central question is how a polis bereft of a true statesman can share in reason. The answer of the Eleatic Stranger is that it can share through law, law being an imitation of the truth apprehended by the true statesman (*Plt.* 300c5–7, 300e11–301a4). Since the true statesman rules without law, there is a better and a worse way of imitating him. The rulers of a polis can imitate reason's rule by ruling according to reason's reflection in law, or they can imitate reason's lawlessness by ruling contrary to law (*Plt.* 300e7–301c5). Given that the rulers are one, few, or many, there are three good and three bad imitations of the one true constitution. Since the fewer the rulers the stronger the rule, the six imitations form a hierarchy, fewer rulers being better when rule is according to law but worse when it is contrary (*Plt.* 302b5–303b5). The rulers under these imitative constitutions, we learn, are not statesmen at all but factionists (*stasiastikoi*); concord (*homonoia*) and friendship (*philia*), each an antithesis of faction, are within the purview only of the ruler of the one true constitution (*Plt.* 303c2, 311b9). One matter of controversy is the extent to which this latter ruler is a reprise of the philosopher-king of the *Republic*. (After long neglect the *Statesman* has recently come into the spotlight. Lane, 1998, is a study of its political philosophy; and Rowe, 1995, is an extensive collection of papers on all aspects of the dialogue.)

The *Laws* reaffirms the ideal of reason ruling without law but devotes itself entirely to the second best, order and law, since, as the Athenian Stranger explains, such ideal rule exists nowhere 'except to a small extent' (*Laws* IX.875c3–d5). In line with the change in focus the status of law subtly improves. The Athenian Stranger differs from the Eleatic Stranger in regarding law as an embodiment, rather than as merely an imitation, of reason. The various pairs of antitheses that structure Greek political philosophy provide a convenient framework for understanding the Athenian Stranger's concept of law and his view of the mixed constitution developed in tandem with it. The important distinction between numerical and proportionate equality underlies the Stranger's account of justice and its antithesis (*Laws* VI.756e–758a). Numerical equality, the equality of measure, weight, and number, counts each citizen the equal of any other; proportionate (or true) equality distributes honours in proportion to the virtue of the recipients, equals to equals, unequals to unequals. The Athenian Stranger calls proportionate equality 'political justice' and claims that it should be the guide in making laws and establishing poleis, though he reluctantly concedes that numerical equality must also play a role if *stasis* is to be avoided. Constitutions are divided into those that aim at the advantage of the stronger – at the continuation of the rule of those in power – and those that aim at what is common to the whole polis. The former are not constitutions at all strictly speaking, and those who live under them are factionists (*stasiôtai*) rather than citizens (*politai*). Only true constitutions have correct laws (*orthoi nomoi*) (*Laws* IV.714b–715b; see also III.697d). Which are the true constitutions? In the view of the Athenian Stranger only those that combine the principles of monarchy and democracy by distributing their offices on the basis of both proportionate and numerical equality (*Laws* III.693d2–e3). No pure, or unmixed, constitution, not even aristocracy or kingship, is a true constitution (*Laws* IV.712c–713a, VIII.832b10–c3). In framing correct laws the lawgiver aims at three things: freedom (the antithesis of slavery), friendship (the antithesis of faction), and wisdom (*Laws* III.693b3–5, 693d7–e1, 701d7–9). Through a strange paradox freedom is achieved through its antithesis. Enslavement to the laws is a major theme of the *Laws* (*Laws* III.698c1, 699c3, VI.762e4–5). When the rulers are slaves of the laws, safety and good things abound; when they enslave the laws, they destroy the polis by creating faction (*Laws* IV.715d, IX.856b). Similarly, persuasion and its antithesis are both elements of law (*Laws* IV.722b6). Persuasion is better than force, and statutes are to be accompanied by persuasive prefaces designed to motivate obedience; but sanctions must be attached to laws to rein in those who cannot be persuaded. One interpretive issue concerns the nature of this persuasion: is it manipulative persuasion or rational persuasion? Bobonich

(1991) is a vigorous defence of the latter alternative. The third and most important instance of the union of antitheses is the uniting of law and nature, of *nomos* and *phusis*. The correctness of law, we are led to understand, is founded in nature (*Laws* I.627d3–4, 636b4–5, III.690c1–3, VIII.836c1–2), where nature is divine reason (*Laws* X.890d6–7). (Until recently the *Laws* has been a lonely field of research. Morrow, 1960, is still after 40 years the most important work in English on the dialogue. Pangle, 1980; Stalley, 1983; Saunders, 1991; Benardete, 2000; and Bobonich, 2002, represent the increasing interest in it.)

NATURALISM

We discuss Aristotle's political philosophy under the banner of 'naturalism' because of the prominent role played by nature in the *Politics* and because of the continuity between his concept of nature and the modern concept. Plato had already attempted to combat Protagorean relativism and conventionalism by an appeal to nature, but the nature to which he appealed was either divine reason (in the *Laws*) or a realm of incorporeal and changeless Forms existing beyond time and space (in the *Republic*). Though Aristotle too wishes to combat relativism by an appeal to nature, he wishes to do so without invoking a suprasensible standard or a supernatural being: his aim is to avoid Platonism as well as relativism. As Raphael's famous painting *The School of Athens* so beautifully illustrates, Aristotle, by identifying nature with the realm of sensible objects and of change (*Metaph.* XII.1.1069a30–b2), brings it down to earth. Aristotle's concept of nature, unlike Plato's, would be recognizable to a modern physicist or biologist.

Aristotle regards the *Ethics* (in either its *Eudemian* or *Nicomachean* incarnation) as well as the *Politics* as a political treatise (*EN* I.2.1094b10–11; *Rhet.* I.2.1356a25–7; [*MM* I.1.1181a24–8, b24–8]). The two works are so closely intertwined that neither can be understood in isolation from the other. The ideal political community sketched in *Politics* VII–VIII has as its aim the life of virtue and happiness described in the *Ethics*; and the fundamental virtue in the *Politics* – namely, justice (III.13.1283a38–40) – is the topic of *Nicomachean Ethics* V (= *Eudemian Ethics* IV). By the same token, many of the virtues studied in the *Ethics* such as bravery, munificence, and justice relate in one way or another to a political community; the life of moral virtue is for Aristotle a political life; and the theory of the *Ethics* cannot be put into practice without the aid of statesmen and lawgivers. (For more on the relation of the two treatises see

Newman, 1887–1902: vol. II, 385–401 and Bodéüs, 1993.)

Nature makes its first appearance in three basic theorems that stand as the portal to the *Politics*: (1) the polis exists by nature, (2) man is by nature a political animal, and (3) the polis is prior by nature to the individual (*Pol.* I.2). These statements are referred to as theorems because they are not simply asserted but argued for. Nothing concerning them or the arguments supporting them is uncontroversial. The very content of the theorems is contested, for it is unclear what 'nature' means in each of them. Aristotle distinguishes several senses of 'nature' (*Phys.* II.1; *Metaph.* V.4), the most important of which correspond to his four causes (final, formal, efficient, and material); but he usually relies on the context to indicate the intended sense of a particular occurrence of the term. It has even been suggested that 'nature' has an entirely different sense in the *Politics* than it has in the physical and metaphysical treatises. The controversy over the content of the theorems leads naturally to controversy over the arguments for them. What is Aristotle tacitly assuming? Are the arguments valid or invalid? How plausible are his premises? The tenability of Aristotle's naturalism depends upon the answer to these questions. (For the controversy see Ambler, 1985; Keyt, 1991b; Depew, 1995; Miller, 1995: 27–66; and Saunders, 1995: 59–71.)

Aristotle's analysis of nature leads to a complex treatment of the antithesis between *phusis* and *nomos*. *Nomos* (law) is 'a kind of order', in that it organizes human conduct through its commands and prohibitions (*Pol.* VII.4.1326a29–30). The legal is a product of human reason (legislative science) and is thus opposed to the 'natural', in the sense of what has a natural efficient cause (see *EN* V.7.1134b18–1135a4). But Aristotle implies that law can (and should) be 'natural', in the sense of having a natural final cause, that is, of promoting natural human ends (see *Pol.* I.2.1253a29–39). It is only in the *Rhetoric* that Aristotle explicitly discusses natural law (I.10.1368b7–9, 13.1373b2–18, and 15.1375a25–b26). How this discussion relates to his discussion of natural justice in the *Ethics* and *Politics* is unclear, and this has generated controversy over whether Aristotle is 'the father of natural law' (for the controversy see: Shellens, 1959; Miller, 1991; Burns, 1998).

The concept of natural existence paves the way for the notion of an *unnatural* condition, and along with it an account of the opposition between force and persuasion. Only a natural entity can be in a natural or an unnatural condition: a horse can be blind and deaf, but not a statue of a horse (see *Pol.* I.5.1254a34–b9). Furthermore, Aristotle identifies what is contrary to nature with what is forced (*Cael.* I.2.300a23). He also thinks that natural entities,

unlike artifacts, are unified wholes by nature and not by force (*Metaph.* X.1.1052a22–5). It follows, then, that it is unnatural for a polis, which in Aristotle's view is a natural entity, to be a unified whole by force. This means that coercion and brute force are alien to a polis in a natural condition (the ramifications of this point are explored in Keyt, 1996). In a political setting the alternative to force is its antithesis, persuasion, the source of willing obedience (for the opposition see *EE* II.8.1224a39). Aristotle devotes an entire treatise to this subject, and addresses the question of political persuasion specifically (*Rhet.* I.4, 8). One central issue is whether persuasion in Aristotle's view is essentially concerned with truth (compare *Rhet.* I.1.1355a29–33 and I.2.1356a19–20). Scholars are found on both sides of this issue and in the middle as well. (Three works that span the spectrum are Oates, 1963; Engberg-Pederson, 1996; Wörner, 1990.)

Aristotle's account of justice and injustice is one expression of his naturalism. The prime justificatory principle in the *Politics* is that everything within the sphere of social conduct that is (un)natural is (un)just (*Pol.* I.3.1253b20–3, 5.1254a17–20, 1255a1–3, 10.1258a40–b2; III.16.1287a8–18, 17.1287b37–9; VII.3.1325b7–10, 9.1329a13–17). In the *Ethics* Aristotle distinguishes universal justice (or lawfulness) from particular justice (or fairness) and divides the latter into distributive and corrective justice (*EN* V.1-4). His theory of distributive justice consists in the combination of his justice-of-nature principle with the Platonic principle of proportional equality. By this theory a just constitution is one under which political power is distributed in proportion to worth, where worth is assessed according to the standard of nature – the standard of a polis with a completely natural social and political structure. Aristotle describes such a polis in *Politics* VII–VIII, and virtue, rather than wealth or freedom, turns out to be nature's standard (for details see Keyt, 1991a).

Since the perception of injustice often leads to *stasis*, or faction, the opposition between *homonoia* and *stasis* is closely tied to that between justice and injustice. Aristotle discusses *stasis* in *Politics* V and *homonoia*, or like-mindedness, in *Eudemian Ethics* VII.7 and *Nicomachean Ethics* IX.6. Poleis of one mind, Aristotle says, 'when their citizens agree about what is advantageous, choose the same things, and do that which is decided upon in common', whereas when each of two rivals wishes himself to rule, they engage in *stasis* (*EN* IX.6.1167a26–34). The rulers under correct constitutions cultivate *homonoia* by aiming at the common advantage, whereas those under deviant constitutions generate *stasis* by aiming solely at their own advantage (*Pol.* III.6.1279a 17–20). Scholars disagree over whether Aristotle

understands the common advantage as the overall
advantage (holism) or the mutual advantage
(individualism). If the latter, then Aristotle's theory
of justice supports rights, or just claims, in an interesting sense. (For varying views see Miller, 1995
and 1996; Cooper, 1996; Kraut, 1996; Schofield,
1996. For Aristotle's account of *stasis* see Yack,
1993, and the commentary on *Politics* V in Keyt,
1999.)

Aristotle's treatment of slavery and its antithesis
is also rooted in his naturalism. Aristotle's defence
of natural slavery in *Politics* I.3–7 is the most noto-
rious passage in ancient philosophy. Aristotle
argues that any person whose deliberative capacity
is too enfeebled to provide for his own preservation
is by nature a slave and, hence, can be justly
enslaved. But who are these people? Are any of
them Greeks? How strong is Aristotle's argument
and are its premises consistent with Aristotle's own
principles (see Newman, 1887–1902: vol. II, 146)?
In Aristotle's ideal polis the farmers are slaves (*Pol.*
VII.9.1329a26, 10.1330a25–8). Are they slaves by
nature or slaves by law only? Aristotle's idea that
freedom should be held out to them as a reward
(*Pol.* VII.10.1330a32–3) seems inconsistent with
their being natural slaves (and hence in need of a
master); but if they are slaves by law only, his ideal
polis, supposedly a paradigm of justice, rests on a
grave injustice. (For discussion of some of these
issues see Charles, 1990: 191, 196; Smith, 1991.)

The idea of slavery is not exhausted by Aristotle's
much pilloried defence of natural slavery; it enters
his analysis of constitutions, and runs as an under-
current through the entire *Politics*. According to this
analysis constitutions that are based on force (*Pol.*
III.3.1276a12–13, 10.1281a23–4) and are contrary
to nature (*Pol.* III.17.1287b37–41) are despotic
(*despotikai*) (*Pol.* III.7.1279a21). *Despotikê* is the
adjective of *despotês*, 'master (of slaves)'. The subjects under despotic constitutions (democracy,
oligarchy, and tyranny in Aristotle's view) are thus
taken to be virtual slaves. Since most constitutions in
the fourth century BC were democracies, oligarchies,
or tyrannies, it is implied that almost everyone outside a ruling circle was a virtual slave.

The antithesis between rulers and subjects is a
major topic in the *Politics*. Aristotle articulates a
principle tacitly assumed in most of Greek political
thought – that political communities must divide into
rulers and ruled (*Pol.* VII.14.1332b12–13). This
principle of rulership is an instance of a broader
Aristotelian principle applicable to all of nature – that
in every unified entity there is ruler and ruled (*Pol.*
I.5.1254a28–33). What this broader principle denies
is that order ever arises spontaneously by an 'invisible
hand' (as in a free economy) without some governing
power. (For discussion see Miller, 1995: 366–73.)

The difference of political rule from regal and
despotic rule, the key question of the *Politics* introduced in its opening chapter, is part of the same topic.
Political rule is rule over people who are free and
equal where each one rules and is ruled in turn (*Pol.*
I.7.1255b20, III.6.1279a8–10). Such rule is characteristic of democracy (*Pol.* VI.2.1317a40–b17). Aristotle
is more favourable to democracy than Plato, and in
his famous 'summation' argument, which applies his
favoured standard for distributing political power to
men taken collectively as well as individually (*Pol.*
III.11), he even offers an 'aristocratic' justification (for
which see Keyt, 1991a: 270–2; Waldron, 1995).
Political rule in Aristotle's view is also the proper
form of rule of a husband over his wife – as long as
the husband is permanently ensconced as ruler (*Pol.*
I.12.1259a37–b10). The rule is political since women
have the same deliberative capacity as men, but it
should be permanently in the hands of the husband
since woman's reason in Aristotle's view is *akuron*
'without authority' (*Pol.* I.13.1260a13). This raises
one question about Aristotle's concept of political
rule and another about his views of women. How can
rule be political if one person is permanently ruled by
another? And in justifying such permanent rule of
husband over wife, what can Aristotle mean when he
says that woman's reason is 'without authority'?
Without authority over what – over her emotions
(the intrapersonal interpretation) or over men (the
interpersonal interpretation)? (Not surprisingly
there is a large literature on Aristotle's treatment of
women. For a sample see Fortenbaugh, 1977;
Saxonhouse, 1982; Smith, 1983; Swanson, 1992; Bar
On, 1994.)

(After 100 years Newman, 1887–1902, is still the
most important work on Aristotle's *Politics*. Two
recent commentaries are the unfinished series
Schütrumpf, 1991a; 1991b; Schütrumpf and Gehrke,
1996; and the four volumes of the Clarendon
Aristotle Series: Saunders, 1995; Robinson, 1995;
Kraut, 1997a; and Keyt, 1999. Miller, 1995, and
Kraut, 2002, are major studies of Aristotle's political philosophy. Lord, 1982, and Curren, 2000,
are studies of Aristotle's views on education. Six
collections of essays should be noted: Barnes,
Schofield and Sorabji, 1977; Patzig, 1990; Keyt and
Miller, 1991; Lord, O'Connor and Bodéüs, 1991;
Aubenque, 1993; Höffe, 2001. Galston, 1980, is an
example of neo-Aristotelianism.)

ANARCHISM

Whereas Aristotle appeals to nature to vindicate the
polis, at least one philosopher appeals to nature to
undermine it and everything conventional. That

philosopher is Diogenes the Cynic (*kuôn*, 'dog'), a contemporary of Plato and Aristotle.

As a champion of (primitive) nature (*phusis*), Diogenes led a life as free as possible from the bondage of material goods, possessing only a single cloak, a staff, and a beggar's wallet, and dwelling in a wine-jar. As a foe of convention (*nomos*), he made a point of performing all bodily functions including urinating, defecating, and masturbating in public.

A full-blown anarchism is implied by some of the sayings attributed to this 'Socrates gone mad' (D.L. VI.54). He claimed to be without a polis (*apolis*) (D.L. VI.38), said that 'the only correct constitution is that in the cosmos' (D.L. VI.72), and declared himself to be a citizen of the cosmos (*kosmopolitês*) (D.L. VI.63). The second of these sayings entails that no constitution in a polis is correct (and hence just) whereas the first and third may be taken, consonant with this, to disavow citizenship in any polis. In the same spirit the famous anecdote of Diogenes' encounter with Alexander the Great illustrates among other things his scorn for political power. Coming upon Diogenes sunning himself, Alexander asks what he can do for him and draws the reply, 'Stand out of my light' (D.L. VI.38; see also VI.32, 60, and 68). Diogenes had similar anarchistic ideas about slavery and marriage. 'To those who advised him to pursue his runaway slave, he said, "It would be absurd if Manes can live without Diogenes, but Diogenes cannot without Manes"' (D.L. VI.55). Diogenes implies in this saying that slavery should be a voluntary relation resting on the need of the slave for a master. 'He also said that wives should be held in common, recognizing no marriage except the joining together of him who persuades with her who is persuaded' (D.L. VI.72). In this saying Diogenes advocates free cohabitation and disavows marriage based on coercion.

(Navia, 1995, is an annotated bibliography of over 700 items on the Cynics. Two books on Cynicism that appeared subsequent to the bibliography are Branham and Goulet-Cazé, 1996, an extensive collection of essays, and Navia, 1996, an important new study.)

Controversy over Diogenes' political ideas concerns the nature of his anarchism and cosmopolitanism. Is Diogenes a nihilistic or an idealistic anarchist? Is he 'the saboteur of his civilization, the nihilist of Hellenism, the parasite of his culture' or the apostle of a higher law and a higher authority (Navia, 1996: 102–3)? In a similar vein, is his cosmopolitanism positive or negative? When he refers to himself as a *kosmopolitês*, a citizen of the cosmos, is he denying all bonds of citizenship or affirming a universal bond?

The latter is the Stoic interpretation. Claiming to be a follower of Diogenes, the first Stoic, Zeno of Citium (335–263 BC), wrote in his *Republic* that 'we should regard all men as our fellow-citizens and local residents, and there should be one way of life and order, like that of a herd grazing together and nurtured by a common law' (Plutarch, *LA* 329a). Like Diogenes, Zeno challenged conventions, holding that 'men and women should wear the same clothes and keep no part of the body completely covered' (D. L. VII.33); and his follower Chrysippus (*c.* 280–207 BC) claimed 'that sexual intercourse with mothers or daughters or sisters, and eating certain food ... have been discredited without reason' (Plutarch, *CS* 1044f–1045a).

Ironically for a philosophy stemming from Diogenes, Stoicism became the *de facto* official philosophy of the Roman Empire through its popularization by Cicero (106–43 BC), Seneca (*c.* AD 1–65), Epictetus (*c.* AD 55–135), and the emperor Marcus Aurelius (AD 121–180). These later Stoics developed Zeno's idea that all humans are governed by a 'common law'. Marcus Aurelius expounds a more explicit concept of natural law, the common law governing the cosmic polis (*Med.* III.11, IV.4, VII.9). Following Cicero, he thought the Stoic principle that natural law is the rule of reason justified Rome, acting as an agent of reason, in imposing its imperium over the barbarians. Although the later Stoics lavished praise on Diogenes, they subverted his anarchism, as the following argument of Marcus Aurelius makes clear: 'That is advantageous to each person which accords with his constitution and nature. But my nature is rational and political. As Antoninus [familiar name of Aurelius] my polis and country is Rome, and as a human being it is the cosmos. The things that benefit these poleis are the only things good for me' (*Med.* VI.44). (Erskine, 1990, and Schofield, 1991, are two recent studies of Stoic political philosophy. For Stoic theories of justice and rights see Schofield, 1995; and Mitsis, 1999.)

NOTE

At every stage of the composition of this chapter we were helped by our research assistants Jason Gatliff and Khalil S. Khan, whose perceptive comments and criticisms led to many improvements in expression and in thought. Gatliff was also extremely helpful in the preparation of the references. Richard Mulgan reviewed the manuscript for the editors and offered a number of valuable suggestions. We are especially grateful to the Social Philosophy and Policy Center for providing the visiting fellowship that allowed David Keyt to spend a fruitful autumn in Bowling Green collaborating with its Executive Director.

ABBREVIATIONS

DK	Diels and Kranz (1951–2)

Marcus Aurelius
Med.	*Meditations*

Aristotle
Cael.	*de Caelo*
EE	*Eudemian Ethics*
EN	*Nicomachean Ethics*
Metaph.	*Metaphysics*
MM	*Magna Moralia*
Phys.	*Physics*
Pol.	*Politics*
Rhet.	*Rhetoric*

Diogenes Laertius
D.L.	*Philosophers' Lives*

Epicurus
KD	*Key Doctrines*

Isocrates
Areop.	*Areopagiticus*

Plato
Ap.	*Apology*
Cr.	*Crito*
Crat.	*Cratylus*
Gorg.	*Gorgias*
Menex.	*Menexenus*
Plt.	*Politicus (Statesman)*
Prot.	*Protagoras*
Rep.	*Republic*
Tht.	*Theaetetus*

Plutarch
LA	*Luck of Alexander*
CS	*Confusion of the Stoics*

Xenophon
Mem.	*Memorabilia*

REFERENCES

Allen, Reginald E. (1980) *Socrates and Legal Obligation*. Minneapolis: University of Minnesota Press.

Ambler, Wayne (1985) 'Aristotle's understanding of the naturalness of the city'. *Review of Politics*, 47: 163–85.

Annas, Julia (1981) *An Introduction to Plato's Republic*. Oxford: Clarendon.

Aubenque, Pierre, ed. (1993) *Aristote Politique: Études sur la Politique d'Aristote*. Paris: Presses Universitaires de France.

Balot, Ryan K. (2001) *Greed and Injustice in Classical Athens*. Princeton, NJ: Princeton University Press.

Barnes, Jonathan, Malcolm Schofield and Richard Sorabji, eds (1977) *Articles on Aristotle*. Vol. II, *Ethics and Politics*. London: Duckworth.

Bar On, Bat-Ami, ed. (1994) *Engendering Origins: Critical Feminist Readings in Plato and Aristotle*. Albany, NY: State University of New York Press.

Benardete, Seth (2000) *Plato's 'Laws': The Discovery of Being*. Chicago: University of Chicago Press.

Bobonich, Christopher (1991) 'Persuasion, compulsion, and freedom in Plato's *Laws*'. *Classical Quarterly*, 41: 365–87.

Bobonich, Christopher (2002) *Utopia Recast: Plato's Later Ethics and Politics*. Oxford: Oxford University Press.

Bodéüs, Richard (1993) *The Political Dimensions of Aristotle's Ethics*. Albany, NY: State University of New York Press.

Branham, Robert Bracht and Marie-Odile Goulet-Cazc, eds (1996) *The Cynics: The Cynic Movement in Antiquity and Its Legacy for Europe*. Berkeley, CA: University of California Press.

Brickhouse, Thomas C. and Nicholas D. Smith (1994) *Plato's Socrates*. Oxford: Oxford University Press.

Burns, Tony (1998) 'Aristotle and natural law'. *History of Political Thought*, 19: 142–66.

Burnyeat, Myles (1976) 'Protagoras and self-refutation in Plato's Theaetetus'. *Philosophical Review*, 85: 172–85.

Caizz, Fernanda Decleva (1999) 'Protagoras and Antiphon: Sophistic debates on justice'. In A. A. Long, ed., *The Cambridge Companion to Early Greek Philosophy*. Cambridge: Cambridge University Press.

Charles, David (1990) 'Comments on M. Nussbaum'. In Günther Patzig, ed., *Aristoteles' 'Politik': Akten des XI Symposium Aristotelicum*. Göttingen: Vandenhoeck and Ruprecht.

Chroust, Anton-Hermann (1946) 'The origin and meaning of the social compact doctrine'. *Ethics*, 57: 38–56.

Coleman, Janet (2000) *A History of Political Thought from Ancient Greece to Early Christianity*. Oxford: Blackwell.

Cooper, John M. (1996) 'Justice and rights in Aristotle's *Politics*'. *Review of Metaphysics*, 49: 859–72.

Cross, R. C. and A. D. Woozley (1964) *Plato's Republic: A Philosophical Commentary*. New York: St Martin's.

Curren, Randall R. (2000) *Aristotle on the Necessity of Public Education*. Lanham, MD: Rowman and Littlefield.

Dahl, Norman O. (1991) 'Plato's defense of justice'. *Philosophy and Phenomenological Research*, 51: 809–34.

Depew, David J. (1995) 'Humans and other political animals in Aristotle's *History of Animals*'. *Phronesis*, 40: 159–81.

Diels, H. and W. Kranz (1951–2) *Die Fragmente der Vorsokratiker*, 2 vols, 6th edn. Berlin: Weidmann.

Engberg-Pederson, Troels (1996) 'Is there an ethical dimension to Aristotelian rhetoric?' In Amélie

Oksenberg Rorty, ed., *Aristotle's Rhetoric*. Berkeley, CA: University of California Press.

Erskine, Andrew (1990) *The Hellenistic Stoa: Political Thought and Action*. Ithaca, NY: Cornell University Press.

Farrar, Cynthia (1988) *The Origins of Democratic Thinking: The Invention of Politics in Classical Athens*. Cambridge: Cambridge University Press.

Fine, Gail (1999) *Plato 2: Ethics, Politics, Religion, and the Soul*. Oxford: Oxford University Press.

Fortenbaugh, William (1977) 'Aristotle on slaves and women'. In Jonathan Barnes, Malcolm Schofield and Richard Sorabji, eds, *Articles on Aristotle*. Vol. II, *Ethics and Politics*. London: Duckworth.

Galston, William A. (1980) *Justice and the Human Good*. Chicago: University of Chicago Press.

Gauthier, David (1986) *Morals by Agreement*. Oxford: Oxford University Press.

Gill, Christopher (1995) 'Rethinking constitutionalism in *Statesman* 291–303'. In C. J. Rowe, ed., *Reading the Statesman: Proceedings of the III Symposium Platonicum*. Sankt Augustin: Academia.

Griswold, Charles L. (1988) *Platonic Writings/Platonic Readings*. New York: Routledge.

Guthrie, W. K. C. (1969) *A History of Greek Philosophy*. Vol. 3, *The Fifth-Century Enlightenment*. Cambridge: Cambridge University Press.

Heinimann, Felix (1945) *Nomos und Physis: Herkunft und Bedeutung einer Antithese im Griechischen Denken Des 5 Jahrhunderts*. Basel: Reinhardt.

Höffe, Otfried, ed. (1997) *Platon Politeia*. Berlin: Akademie.

Höffe, Otfried, ed. (2001) *Aristoteles Politik*. Berlin: Akademie.

Irwin, T. H. (1991) 'Aristotle's defense of private property'. In David Keyt and Fred D. Miller, eds, *A Companion to Aristotle's Politics*. Oxford: Blackwell.

Kahn, Charles H. (1981) 'The origins of social contract theory'. In G. B. Kerferd, ed., *The Sophists and Their Legacy: Proceedings of the Fourth International Colloquium on Ancient Philosophy*. Wiesbaden: Steiner.

Kahn, Charles H. (1995) 'The place of the *Statesman* in Plato's later work'. In C. J. Rowe, ed., *Reading the Statesman: Proceedings of the III Symposium Platonicum*. Sankt Augustin: Academia.

Kahn, Charles H. (1996) *Plato and the Socratic Dialogue: The Philosophical Use of a Literary Form*. Cambridge: Cambridge University Press.

Kerferd, G. B. (1981) *The Sophistic Movement*. Cambridge: Cambridge University Press.

Keyt, David (1991a) 'Aristotle's theory of distributive justice'. In David Keyt and Fred D. Miller, eds, *A Companion to Aristotle's Politics*. Oxford: Blackwell.

Keyt, David (1991b) 'Three basic theorems in Aristotle's *Politics*'. In David Keyt and Fred D. Miller, eds, *A Companion to Aristotle's Politics*. Oxford: Blackwell.

Keyt, David (1996) 'Aristotle and the ancient roots of anarchism'. *Topoi*, 15: 129–42.

Keyt, David (1999) *Aristotle Politics Books V and VI*. Oxford: Clarendon.

Keyt, David and Fred D. Miller, eds (1991) *A Companion to Aristotle's Politics*. Oxford: Blackwell.

Klosko, George (1986) *The Development of Plato's Political Theory*. New York: Methuen.

Kraut, Richard (1984) *Socrates and the State*. Princeton, NJ: Princeton University Press.

Kraut, Richard (1996) 'Are there natural rights in Aristotle?' *Review of Metaphysics*, 49: 755–74.

Kraut, Richard (1997a) *Aristotle Politics Books VII and VIII*. Oxford: Clarendon.

Kraut, Richard, ed. (1997b) *Plato's Republic: Critical Essays*. Lanham, MD: Rowman and Littlefield.

Kraut, Richard (2002) *Aristotle: Political Philosophy*. Oxford: Oxford University Press.

Laks, André (1990) 'Legislation and demiurgy: on the relationship between Plato's *Republic* and *Laws*'. *Classical Antiquity*, 9: 209–29.

Lane, M. S. (1998) *Method and Politics in Plato's Statesman*. Cambridge: Cambridge University Press.

Lloyd-Jones, Hugh (1971) *The Justice of Zeus*. Berkeley, CA: University of California Press.

Lord, Carnes (1982) *Education and Culture in the Political Thought of Aristotle*. Ithaca, NY: Cornell University Press.

Lord, Carnes, David K. O'Connor and Richard Bodéüs, eds (1991) *Essays on the Foundations of Aristotelian Political Science*. Berkeley, CA: University of California Press.

Mayhew, Robert (1997) *Aristotle's Criticism of Plato's Republic*. Lanham, MD: Rowman and Littlefield.

McDowell, John (1973) *Plato Theaetetus*. Oxford: Clarendon.

Miller, Fred D. (1991) 'Aristotle on natural law and justice'. In David Keyt and Fred D. Miller, eds, *A Companion to Aristotle's Politics*. Oxford: Blackwell.

Miller, Fred D. (1995) *Nature, Justice, and Rights in Aristotle's Politics*. Oxford: Claredon.

Miller, Fred D. (1996) 'Aristotle and the origin of natural rights'. *Review of Metaphysics*, 49: 873–907.

Miller, Fred D., (ed.) (2004) *A History of the Philosophy of Law from the Ancient Greeks to the Scholastics*. Dordrecht: Kluwer.

Mitsis, Phillip (1999) 'The Stoic origin of natural rights'. In Katerina Ierodiakonou, ed., *Topics in Stoic Philosophy*. Oxford: Oxford University Press.

Monoson, S. Sara (2000) *Plato's Democratic Entanglements: Athenian Politics and the Practice of Philosophy*. Princeton, NJ: Princeton University Press.

Morrow, Glenn R. (1960) *Plato's Cretan City: A Historical Interpretation of the Laws*. Princeton, NJ: Princeton University Press (reprinted 1993).

Moser, S. and G. L. Kustas (1966) 'A comment on the relativism of the "Protagoras"'. *Phoenix*, 20: 111–15.

Mulgan, R. G. (1979) 'Lycophron and Greek theories of social contract'. *Journal of the History of Ideas*, 40: 121–8.

Navia, Luis E. (1995) *The Philosophy of Cynicism: An Annotated Bibliography*. Westport, CT: Greenwood.

Navia, Luis E. (1996) *Classical Cynicism: A Critical Study*. Westport, CT: Greenwood.

Newman, W. L. (1887–1902) *The Politics of Aristotle*, 4 vols. Oxford: Clarendon.

Nill, Michael (1985) *Morality and Self-Interest in Protagoras, Antiphon, and Democritus*. Leiden: Brill.

Oates, Whitney J. (1963) *Aristotle and the Problem of Values*. Princeton, NJ: Princeton University Press.

Ober, Josiah, ed. (1996) *The Athenian Revolution: Essays on Ancient Greek Democracy and Political Theory*. Princeton, NJ: Princeton University Press.

Ober, Josiah (1998) *Political Dissent in Democratic Athens: Intellectual Critics of Popular Rule*. Princeton, NJ: Princeton University Press.

Owen, G. E. L. (1953) 'The place of the *Timaeus* in Plato's dialogues'. *Classical Quarterly*, 3: 79–95.

Pangle, Thomas L., trans. (1980) *The Laws of Plato*. New York: Basic.

Patzig, Günther, ed. (1990) *Aristoteles' 'Politik': Akten des XI Symposium Aristotelicum*. Göttingen: Vandenhoeck und Ruprecht.

Popper, Karl Raimund (1971) *The Open Society and Its Enemies* (1945), 5th rev. edn. Princeton, NJ: Princeton University Press.

Reeve, C. D. C. (1988) *Philosopher-Kings: The Argument of Plato's Republic*. Princeton, NJ: Princeton University Press.

Robinson, Richard (1995) *Aristotle Politics Books III and IV with a Supplementary Essay by David Keyt* (1st edn 1962). Oxford: Clarendon.

Rosen, F. (1994) 'Did Protagoras justify democracy?' *Polis*, 13: 12–30.

Rowe, C. J. (1995) *Reading the Statesman: Proceedings of the III Symposium Platonicum*. Sankt Augustin: Academia.

Rowe, C. J. and Malcolm Schofield, eds (2000) *The Cambridge History of Greek and Roman Political Thought*. Cambridge: Cambridge University Press.

Sachs, David (1963) 'A fallacy in Plato's *Republic*'. *Philosophical Review*, 72: 141–58.

Santas, Gerasimos (1979) *Socrates: Philosophy in Plato's Early Dialogues*. London: Routledge and Kegan Paul.

Santas, Gerasimos (2001) *Goodness and Justice: Plato, Aristotle, and the Moderns*. Oxford: Blackwell.

Saunders, Trevor J. (1991) *Plato's Penal Code: Tradition, Controversy, and Reform in Greek Penology*. New York: Oxford University Press.

Saunders, Trevor J. (1995) *Aristotle Politics Books I and II*. Oxford: Clarendon.

Saxonhouse, Arlene W. (1982) 'Family, polity, and unity: Aristotle on Socrates' community of wives'. *Polity*, 15: 202–19.

Saxonhouse, Arlene W. (1996) *Athenian Democracy: Modern Mythmakers and Ancient Theorists*. Notre Dame, IN: University of Notre Dame Press.

Schiappa, Edward (1991) *Protagoras and Logos: A Study in Greek Philosophy and Rhetoric*. Columbia, SC: University of South Carolina Press.

Schofield, Malcolm (1991) *The Stoic Idea of the City*. Cambridge: Cambridge University Press (reprinted 1999).

Schofield, Malcolm (1995) 'Two Stoic approaches to justice'. In André Laks and Malcolm Schofield, eds, *Justice and Generosity: Studies in Hellenistic Social and Political Philosophy: Proceedings of the Sixth Symposium Hellenisticum*. Cambridge: Cambridge University Press.

Schofield, Malcolm (1996) 'Sharing in the constitution'. *Review of Metaphysics*, 49: 83–58.

Schütrumpf, Eckart (1991a) *Aristoteles Politik*, Buch I. Berlin: Akademie.

Schütrumpf, Eckart (1991b) *Aristoteles Politik*, Bücher II und III. Berlin: Akademie.

Schütrumpf, Eckart and Hans-Joachim Gehrke (1996) *Aristoteles Politik*, Bücher IV–VI. Berlin: Akademie.

Shellens, M. Salomon (1959) 'Aristotle on natural law'. *Natural Law Forum*, 4: 72–100.

Smith, Nicholas D. (1983) 'Plato and Aristotle on the nature of women'. *Journal of the History of Philosophy*, 21: 467–78.

Smith, Nicholas D. (1991) 'Aristotle's theory of natural slavery'. In David Keyt and Fred D. Miller, eds, *A Companion to Aristotle's Politics*. Oxford: Blackwell.

Smith, Nicholas D., ed. (1998) *Plato: Critical Assessments*. Vol. 1, *General Issues of Interpretation*. London: Routledge.

Stalley, R. F. (1983) *An Introduction to Plato's Laws*. Indianapolis: Hackett.

Strauss, Leo (1964) *The City and Man*. Chicago: Rand McNally.

Swanson, Judith A. (1992) *The Public and the Private in Aristotle's Political Philosophy*. Ithaca, NY: Cornell University Press.

Tarrant, Harold (2000) *Plato's First Interpreters*. London: Duckworth.

Taylor, C. C. W. (1976) *Plato Protagoras*. Oxford: Oxford University Press.

Tuana, Nancy (1994) *Feminist Interpretations of Plato: Re-Reading the Canon*. University Park, PA: Pennsylvania State University Press.

Veyne, Paul (1983) 'Did the Greeks invent democracy?' *Diogenes*, 124: 1–32.

Vlastos, Gregory (1956) 'Introduction' to *Plato's Protagoras*. Indianapolis: Bobbs-Merrill.

Waldron, Jeremy (1995) 'The wisdom of the multitude: some reflections on Book 3, Chapter 11 of Aristotle's *Politics*'. *Political Theory*, 23: 563–84.

White, Nicholas P. (1979) *A Companion to Plato's Republic*. Indianapolis: Hackett.

Wood, Neal (1991) *Cicero's Social and Political Thought.* Berkeley, CA: University of California Press.

Woozley, A. D. (1979) *Law and Obedience: The Arguments of Plato's Crito.* Chapel Hill, NC: University of North Carolina Press.

Wörner, Markus H. (1990) *Das Ethische in Der rhetorik des Aristoteles.* Munchen: Alber.

Yack, Bernard (1993) *The Problems of a Political Animal: Community, Justice, and Conflict in Aristotelian Political Thought.* Berkeley, CA: University of California Press.

24

Premodern Chinese Political Thought

HELEN DUNSTAN

Political thought in ancient and imperial China could be studied from two opposite perspectives. An 'externalist' agenda would reflect the preoccupations of political theorists outside the Chinese tradition. Given the persistence of Western hegemony in scholarship, the preoccupations of the European heritage would doubtless be privileged, the questions those that would occur to Western intellectual historians. The aim of an 'internalist' approach, by contrast, is to see the development of Chinese political thought from the inside. This may mean operating in a conceptual world that is opaque and not necessarily interesting to historians of Western thought. The codes are different, the allusions obscure; one seems to encounter a perversely enduring fixation with the hermeneutics of scraps of ancient text. Yet much premodern Chinese political thought indeed took place within such scriptural and backward-looking frameworks. To understand it, one must attempt to sojourn in Chinese cognitive structures. 'Internalist' perspectives are essential.

The dichotomy between the two approaches need not be absolute. While Eurocentrism is perhaps betrayed by utterances that begin 'What was the nearest Chinese equivalent of ...' (cf. L. Liu, 1995: 7), 'externalist' questions are more likely to spring from curiosity than arrogance. As stimulants to enquiry, they usefully complement sinologists' research agendas. Indeed, sinologists may ask them. The following discussion, intended for both non-sinologists with basic knowledge of the main schools of Chinese philosophy, and sinologists interested in English-language scholarly developments outside their own fields, draws on both approaches. Where the 'externalist' approach predominates – as in the discussion of Chinese

ideas on (1) the origin of the state and civil society, and (2) provision for popular participation in government – the findings illustrate both its heuristic value and its limitations.

THE NEW TEXTUAL SCHOLARSHIP ON ANCIENT CHINESE POLITICAL THEORY (LATE ZHOU TO EARLY HAN, *c.* 500 TO *c.* 180 BC)

Scholarship on ancient Chinese political theory has been transformed since 1980 through investigation of recently discovered texts and radical rethinking of the concepts of author, book and text as applied to pre-Qin (antiquity to 221 BC) writing. The silk manuscript versions of the *Dao de jing* (*Tao te ching*, hereafter 'the *Laozi*') and the previously unknown 'Yellow Emperor' texts found with them in 1973 are only the most famous of the archaeological discoveries that repeatedly jolt our understanding of ancient China's intellectual vitality.[1] Recent inventories of known texts reveal a diverse corpus, some of it reflecting the cultural background to the emergence of philosophy, some of it explicitly political or governmental (e.g. Loewe, 1993; Giele, 1998–9: 306–37). Meanwhile, attention to the physical characteristics of ancient Chinese books has stimulated both experimentation with the received arrangement of surviving text and a displacement of authors. The surveys of ancient Chinese philosophy thought standard in the early 1980s (Fung, 1952; Hsiao, 1979) now serve as rich statements of the conventional understanding that was the point of departure for more recent scholarship.

The New Approach to Ancient Text

In the English-speaking world, the harbinger of the new scholarship was Angus Graham, whose supremely perceptive *Disputers of the Tao* (1989) is priority reading. Perhaps more influential among specialists was his retranslation of the *Zhuangzi* (*Chuang-tzu*, fourth to second centuries BC), one of the two great classics of what became known as the Daoist (Taoist) school (Graham, 1981). Graham's translation was distinguished from earlier attempts by his greater attention both to the work's generically variegated content and to the probability that parts of the received text are out of sequence. Ancient Chinese philosophical texts were usually written on bamboo strips that were linked with thongs and bundled. Strips usually outlasted thongs. Later editors inherited disintegrating bundles and, where necessary, rearranged the contents into chapters. This might involve juxtaposing generically disparate material, both verse and prose, perhaps including unmarked quotations. Recognizing the range of material in the *Zhuangzi's* core chapters, Graham made a point of adopting appropriate diction and layout for the different types of text. He transposed passages that seemed out of place and rearranged much of the material in the later chapters by theme or philosophical tendency (1981: 31–2). His reconstructed *Zhuangzi* is a miscellany of work by multiple authors and of different dates. It represents at least three other tendencies besides the 'school' of Zhuangzi and his followers.

Parts of the *Zhuangzi* are important for the study of ancient Chinese political thought. Graham identified two groups of utopian writings, including a chapter that represents 'the first documented instance of a true anarchist in China' (1981: 170) and a set of chapters by a radical anti-moralist whom he called 'the Primitivist' (1981: 170–5, 195–217). He clarified the political significance of the 'egoist' doctrines of the school of Yang Zhu (Chu), writings from which constitute another section of the *Zhuangzi* (1981: 223, 219–53). However, Graham's *Zhuangzi* is relevant here mainly because of its methodological influence on work on other texts. Consensus seems to have emerged that to treat thematic collocations of material like unitary essays is to misrepresent the thought of the original. While it has long been recognized that many ancient works include writings by several hands, there is a new interest in breaking received textual units into their component parts, the dating and authorship of which are the next challenge.

A deeper rationale for this new 'deconstructionism' is supplied by Mark Lewis (1999), who draws radical implications from the 'fluidity' of texts written on bamboo strips. For at least two centuries from the age of Confucius (*fl. c.* 500 BC), he suggests, text strips were media through which philosophical schools elaborated and transmitted their doctrines. Possession, custodianship and ongoing creation of the texts helped to define the schools; the doctrines were attributed to a founding 'master', but the texts grew by accretion as successive generations added new material and rearranged the old. To give their pronouncements authority, the later-generation disciples represented them as sayings of the master, a quasi-fiction whose own authority came from the fact that he addressed disciples (or rulers in disciple role). Historical masters, such as Confucius, presumably existed, but the masters whom we perceive through texts were constructs of disciples with their own agendas (1999: 54–8).

The views of Lewis and those on whose work he draws profoundly challenge previous understandings, including some of Graham's. The clearest illustration of this is the fragmentation of Confucius by E. Bruce Brooks and Taeko Brooks (1998).

The Confucian 'Analects' of Brooks and Brooks

In his attempt to reconstruct Confucius's intellectual personality, Graham (1989) was unperturbed by the existing consensus that not every dictum preserved in the *Analects* transcribes the master's words. It was enough that the *Analects* is 'a book homogeneous in thought, marked by a strong and individual mind'; one could assume that it represented 'the earliest stage of Confucianism' without worrying about its literal authenticity (1989: 10). Graham convincingly portrayed a unitary Confucius, believer in the full efficacy for government of an ethicized tradition of aristocratic 'ceremony', and advocate of rulership through *de* (*te*), conventionally translated 'virtue'. *De* had previously meant 'the power ... to move others without exerting physical force', but for Confucius it became 'the capacity [or 'Potency', Graham's preferred rendering] to act according to and bring others to the [moral] Way' (1989: 13–15). If the Brookses are right, this reconstruction is untenable.

In their recent translation, Brooks and Brooks (1998) rearrange the *Analects* dicta by suggested order of accretion. For them, out of the entire *Analects*, only 16 of the 26 short utterances in Chapter 4 possibly represent the authentic voice of 'the historical Confucius': a 'mentor' advising 'protégés' on the importance, for would-be courtiers, of maintaining a morality befitting the hereditary nobility (1998: 1, 11, 13–16, 203–4, 208–9). The famous sayings taken to epitomize Confucius's approach to government are typically late additions to a work that took over two centuries to reach its final form. Some of these dicta are from chapters added in the late fourth century BC, in the days of Mencius (Confucian doctrine's most influential ancient expositor). From Chapter 12, which Brooks and Brooks date to *c*. 326, comes the proposition that rulers, vassals, fathers and sons should all be what their names imply, and the analogy between the influence of the 'virtue' (Potency) of the gentleman in government and wind blowing over grass. The even later Chapter 2 includes the declaration that rule by 'virtue' and 'ritual' has superior effects to that by 'government' and punishments, and the analogy between the efficacy of governing 'by virtue' and the still force of the 'North [polar] Star'. The paradoxical claim that the prehistoric sage-emperor Shun did nothing but respectfully face south is from Chapter 15, whose core Brooks and Brooks date to the very end of the fourth century (1998: 89, 92–4, 109–10, 131, 226–30, 234). The Brookses suggest that much in these later chapters reflects, or reacts to, the ideas or concerns of rival schools – the Legalist preoccupation with order, the Daoist promotion of non-action, the Mohist belief in undifferentiating love for others, and a new interest in theorizing the cosmos (1998: 95, 97, 109–10, 137, 226–31).

Many assumptions will have to be rethought if Brooks and Brooks are right. They and others in the Warring States Working Group (a network centred on the University of Massachusetts, Amherst) have proposed yet further conjectures. *Prima facie*, their reading makes exciting sense, but their methodology is debatable. The scholarly community needs time to reach mature consensus as to the value of their work. The overall approach, already enshrined in *The Cambridge History of Ancient China*, may win more widespread approval than the details of the Brooks interpretation (compare Nivison, 1999: 745–6, 755–9, with Makeham, 1999: 1–15).

The Xunzi of John Knoblock

Especially important for studies of ancient Chinese political thought is the late John Knoblock's three-volume study-cum-translation of the works of Xunzi (Hsün-tzu: Knoblock, 1988; 1990; 1994). The Confucian Xunzi (*c*. 310 to *c*. 215 BC) arouses Western curiosity because some of his ideas seem reminiscent of Hobbes and Locke. Knoblock's integral translation shows how limited the resemblance is. Perusal of the most obviously 'political' chapters (9–16) reveals Xunzi as, above all, a relentless moralist. His concern was with urging better ways upon contemporary rulers and refuting the errors of rival schools and some fellow-Confucians. Western readers will escape disappointment with Xunzi only if they accept him on these terms.

Knoblock's study features close textual analysis and reconstruction, explications of content, context and allusions, and a biography of the presumed primary author. The translation's layout reflects the discontinuous structure of a work that may, in part, have been reconstituted from Xunzi's jottings or disciples' notes. Sometimes 'Xunzi' himself is editor, commentator or transmitter of earlier writing (1988: 6, 127–8). Knoblock nonetheless took the historical Xun Kuang as the main intelligence behind the book. His study clarifies how one of China's major political thinkers used pre-existing historical and rhetorical traditions to discuss what it meant to posit morality and ceremony as the only sound bases for government. It also shows Xunzi responding (not always negatively) to the *realpolitik* concerns and doctrines of the turbulent third century.

Concerns about the translation's accuracy have been raised (Harbsmeier, 1997: 183–95). Indeed, the rendering of key terms, such as *fen* (basically 'to divide'), is sometimes overdetermined. For Graham, *fen* could represent the concept of 'allot[ting] portions', while in another school's usage, *fen* ('portion') as a noun could signify the duties incurred through one's position relative to others. It is troubling that where Graham understands *fen* as 'apportion', Knoblock has 'divide society into classes', while Knoblock renders *fen zhi* ('divide them') as 'create proper social class divisions' (1990: 96, 104; cf. Graham, 1978: 46, 255–6; 1989: 255ff). Without dogmatically endorsing Graham's reading, one should warn against uncritical reliance upon Knoblock.

Legalism, Syncretism and the Political Wing of Daoism

The retranslation of the writings of the ancient Legalists (political realists) is still in progress. J. J. L. Duyvendak's (1928) pre-war translation of the *Shang jun* (*Shang-chün*) *shu* (Book of Lord Shang) has not been superseded, but a new, annotated translation of the *Han Feizi* (*Han Fei Tzu*) by Christoph Harbsmeier is forthcoming with Yale University Press, and Allyn Rickett (1985; 1998) has completed his translation of that partially Legalist miscellany, the *Guanzi* (*Kuan-tzu*). Meanwhile, archaeological discoveries have stimulated new work on the syncretism of the late Warring States and early Han, especially the *rapprochement* between the *Laozi* (*Lao-tzu*) wing of Daoism and the Legalists.

The *Laozi* has itself come under scrutiny. Until recently there was no proof of its existence before the mid-third century BC, but in 1993 bamboo strips with an earlier version of parts of the received text were found in a late-fourth-century (BC) tomb at

Guodian in central China. Experts differ as to both the likely 'date of composition' of the Guodian text, and the transmission processes through which the familiar version emerged not later than the early second century BC (Allan and Williams, 2000: 118–20, 142–6). The new material may help decide where the truth lies between Graham's intuition of a single authorial personality behind this 'long philosophical poem or poem cycle', and the subsequent hypothesis of a multi-authored work that took 'almost a century' from the mid fourth to gain its present length (Graham, 1989: 216–19; Brooks, 1994: 64–6). Such issues of textual chronology are crucial for speculation about inter-school influences. The discovery that 'about a third' of the material in the received *Laozi* existed, in a different sequence, in the late fourth century (Allan and Williams, 2000: 128) makes it completely possible that the most sophisticated Legalist, Han Fei (died 233 BC), was influenced substantially by this text.

Graham (1989) found it 'debatable' whether Han Fei wrote those *Han Feizi* chapters that discuss the *Laozi* or blend its ideas with Legalism. However, if indeed the *Laozi* 'presents itself as another guide to the art of rulership', there is nothing incongruous about its 'mystical statecraft' appealing to a pragmatist with no time for Confucian moral gestures (1989: 170, 285). Both Graham (1989: 286–9) and Wang Hsiao-po and Leo Chang (1986: *passim*) convincingly portrayed a synthesis in which metaphysical and meditational ideas from the *Laozi* underpin the ideal of the impartial, non-assertive monarch. Neither imposing his will on reality nor taking personal initiatives, this monarch conducts government as personnel management, administering rewards and punishments according to objective facts and standards. The poetic expositions of this view in the *Han Feizi* are expressions, whoever wrote them, of a synthetic philosophy that was fashionable by the late third century BC.

Somewhat similar texts, newly accessible through Rickett's translation, appear in the *Guanzi* in chapters, one of which Rickett dates to the early third century. Despite its title, 'Clearing the mind' has more political than meditational content. It expounds the approach of a sage ruler, who is receptive to forces outside himself, such as a mysterious 'Great Brilliance', but otherwise does little but maintain a constant set of laws, name things correctly (to create order), and verify subordinates' accomplishments. Importantly, however, he does engage in warfare (Rickett, 1998: 85–97). Rickett associates this text with a strain of thought that is loosely called 'Huang-Lao', a Han-dynasty term projected back into the Warring States because Sima Qian (Ssu-ma Ch'ien, 145 to *c.* 86 BC) identified several Warring States thinkers, including Han Fei, as students of Huang-Lao doctrines. 'Huang' refers

to the Yellow Emperor, mythical 'inventor of the state and of war', and through him to 'the Legalist strand' within the synthesis (Graham, 1989: 170–1). This culture hero fittingly represents an intellectual tradition centred on advising rulers on the socio-political preconditions of military conquest.

Four texts, discovered in 1973 and identified by some as the lost 'The Four Scriptures of the Yellow Emperor', lend plausibility to the notion of a pre-Qin Huang-Lao movement. Only the second text features the Yellow Emperor, shown consulting his advisers, whose purported replies are reproduced at length. The texts, disparate in content, format and, probably, authorship, are addressed to rulers and reflect a fusion of 'Daoist' and 'Legalist' ideas, plus elements from other traditions. Particularly intriguing is the advice to adopt 'feminine [or 'soft' or 'weak'] conduct' (humility and yielding, coupled with a benevolent disposition) rather than the assertive 'masculine' counterpart. However, the ideal is not pacifism but military success (L. Chang and Feng, 1998: 67–70, 163–5, 177–8). Another theme is that the ruler should model his government on the operations of Heaven and Earth, complementing civil governance with resort to force, just as Heaven has seasons for life-giving and life-taking. As the cosmological references suggest imperial pretensions, it is no surprise to find passages envisaging a universal sovereign – a uniquely informed autocrat who values educated men who 'understand [the] *Dao* [Way]' (1998: 33–7, 42, 46–7, 104, 111, 116–20).

Two translators of the four texts opine that they were probably written 'around 290' BC (1998: 214). Other scholars argue for a date between the mid-third century and early Han, pointing out, for example, that the breadth of the syncretism resembles that of the 'philosophical encyclopedia' *Lüshi chunqiu* (The Spring and Autumn Annals of Lü Buwei) (Peerenboom, 1993: 18–19; Puett, 2001: 239–40, n. 111). The eclectic *Lüshi chunqiu* was compiled about two decades before the Qin unification (221 BC). A plea for morality in government that draws little from the *Laozi* (Graham, 1989: 373–4), it is newly accessible through a bilingual translation volume (Knoblock and Riegel, 2000). Understanding of the four syncretist texts is less definitive. Unreadable in places, the manuscripts are riddled with 'loan' characters. Alternative translations remain desirable.

THE ORIGIN OF CIVIL SOCIETY AND THE STATE

Xunzi: Civilization as the Sages' 'Artifice'

The best-known premodern Chinese theorist of how political organization arose was Xunzi. Xunzi's best-known proposition (that human nature is bad) seems too inconsistent with much else that he wrote to be considered the foundation of his political philosophy, although it is commonly taken as such. For Xunzi, it was the introduction of 'ceremony' (Graham's translation) and morality that marked the emergence of civil society. The 'Former Kings' (sage monarchs of antiquity) had established ceremony and morality to institute principles of allocation, thus ending the chaos that had prevailed when the people were left to compete for means of satisfying their innate desires without attention to 'measures' and 'boundaries' (Graham, 1989: 257; Knoblock, 1994: 55). Crediting sages with the invention of specific aspects of culture was a convention in the Warring States, but Xunzi almost dispensed with sages. Elsewhere he located the origin of civil society in that ability, indeed lifelong compulsion, to 'associat[e]', that is the secret of man's dominion over physically superior animals. Sage founders appear here only in the definition of a 'lord' as 'one who is accomplished at causing men to form societies'. Doing without the myth of sagely 'artifice', Xunzi ascribed moral sense to humankind's distinctively 'exalted' nature (translations variously from Knoblock, 1990: 103–5; Graham, 1989: 244, 255; Lewis, 1990: 171–2). He further identified the human emotions, senses and intellect as 'Heavenly', the sage being one who trains to perfection that which Heaven has implanted in him (Puett, 2001: 67–9).

The claim that human nature is bad is consistent with, but not necessarily entailed by, Xunzi's assumption of primeval chaos. The pertinent fact about human nature is that, 'born with desires', man is incapable of not pursuing them. However, the desires need not lead to chaos if controlled through civilization's artifices. Graham wisely suggested that Xunzi's oversimplifying 'slogan' about human nature was adopted for debating purposes and should not be mistaken for a fundamental tenet (1989: 250–1). Knoblock's efforts to date the separate chapters of the *Xunzi* might have clarified the relationship between the 'slogan' and the account of man's need for culture. Unfortunately, he changed his views on a key question while producing his three-volume translation (compare Knoblock, 1988: 9–11 with 1994: vii). At present, one can only note that his attempt to date the various materials in the *Xunzi* raised for the first time the possibility of tracing the chronological development of an ancient Chinese intellectual's political philosophy.

Whether the historical Xunzi really thought human nature bad is less important than how he elaborated the notion that principled apportionment is fundamental to civil society. Knoblock's retranslation of Xunzi's chapter on ceremony shows how inappropriate it would be to see him as a contractarian *manqué*. His central interest was in the rationale for ritual and ceremony, subjects he discussed in celebratory detail. This was reasonable, as he considered ceremony ultimately more important than military might for enabling rulers to extend their sway while remaining secure at home. Ceremony, embodying differential entitlements and graduated expressions of respect and love, safeguarded order from the lurking threat of 'anarchy' (1994: 57–61, 70–1).

The Yellow Emperor and the Origin of the Martial State

Mark Lewis (1990), by contrast, has drawn attention to the martial characteristics of the pre-unification Chinese states as a problem in ancient Chinese political thought. Using disparate texts, he reconstructed the Yellow Emperor myth as an ancient rationalization of the emergence of 'sanctioned [governmental] violence'. The Yellow Emperor brought order to a chaotic age by subduing warring nobles, an oppressive Fiery Emperor, and that savage, bestial-looking rebel, Chi You. Thereafter, he ruled as a travelling order-keeper, instituting other prerequisites of civilization such as the calendar. Sima Qian represented him as civilization's original founder (Lewis, 1990: 174–6).

To Lewis, the precedence that Sima gave the Yellow Emperor over more pacific culture heroes reflects elite espousal of a doctrine of legitimate and necessary force. Probing of other layers of the myth reveals that the Yellow Emperor was also lord of storms. Chi You was a rival lord of storms, weapons and warfare. Uncontrolled, he represented brute, anarchic violence. The Yellow Emperor was the originator of organized, cosmically sanctioned, strategically guided warfare, as well as due judicial process. His story, emerging (through elite reinterpretation) in the Warring States, was a mythological representation of those social, political and military transformations whose theorists were the Legalists and Strategists. It eventually 'became a charter myth for the absolutist state' (1990: 176–84, 195–212).

Michael Puett (2001) criticizes Lewis's presumption of a single myth complex. For Puett, the rewritings of the Yellow Emperor story by exponents of rival Warring States philosophies should be analysed as conflicting accounts of the origin of punishment, warfare and the force-using state. Puett posits the establishment of three narrative patterns and associated messages before the Yellow Emperor entered the debate in the third century BC. Pattern One, first found in a Confucian text, displaces the responsibility for creating punishments (or weapons) onto barbarians or reprobates, and has the civilizing powers to 'appropriate' these tools. In Pattern Two, there is nothing ethically problematic about the invention of weapons and punishments; the issue is how they are used. Pattern Three evades the problem of creation by envisaging the sage as 'organizer'. Rather than imposing novelty on nature, the organizing sage brings out the order inherent therein (2001: 101–11).

In Warring States stories that include the Yellow Emperor and/or Chi You, the assignment of characters to roles reflects the author's favoured pattern. The rebel figure is not always Chi You, who may be minister, not rebel. Chi You as rebel originator of violence is paired with an 'appropriating' and/or 'organizing' Yellow Emperor, Chi You as minister with a 'creating' Yellow Emperor (2001: 120–7, 131–3). Chi You's multivalency illustrates the richness not of ancient Chinese myth but of the rhetorical strategies used to debate the morality of government's coercive aspects. The issue of origins is, after all, not central: origins feature as symbols of moral status.

Other Ideas about the Origin of Culture and the State

Puett (2001) relocates Xunzi's speculations in the context of the Warring States assumption that civilization's material, organizational and ceremonial constituents began as the creations of specific individuals (although the establishment of rulers might be attributed to Heaven). Opining that whether sages should 'create' was a contentious issue in pre-Qin times; he discusses references to acts of cultural creation as reiterations, variants or hybrids of three basic positions. The Confucian view, adumbrated in the *Analects* and developed by Xunzi, was that the sages' innovations had been 'patterned' upon Heaven; the sages had only 'brought forth' the constituents of culture, thereby completing the generative processes of the natural world. Mohists validated cultural creation – for them, the invention of useful techniques and artefacts – as having imitated Heaven's creative acts; Daoistic texts reject it as 'transgress[ive]' against nature (2001: 44–55, 62–3, 68–73). Thus the (Confucian) 'Xici' (Hsi-tz'u) appendix to the *Book of Changes* represents institutions, techniques and implements as having been derived, at one remove, from nature. These innovations of the sages were inspired by the trigrams and hexagrams, which were themselves sage-made abstractions from nature's patterns (2001: 86–90). In partial contrast, three *Lüshi chunqiu* chapters combine the Mohist appreciation of useful inventions with the Daoist viewpoint that the sage does not impose himself on nature. Past sages had succeeded by leaving creation to their able ministers, thus freeing themselves to cultivate the stillness through which they identified with Heaven (2001: 81–6).

The Legalist *Shang jun shu* represents the state's emergence in secular, developmental terms, positing

a sequence of approaches to the problem of disorder. While accepting the sagely origin of mankind's means of quelling chaos, it grounds the need for sagely intervention in population growth. Ancient people started quarrelling because population was outstripping resources. Impartiality and disinterestedness began as society's response to its first age of disorder, when the old kin-based groups learned the disadvantages of pursuing self-interest by force. Unfortunately, instituting the norms of justice meant 'elevating' men of superior ability, and this, combined with further population growth, engendered a new phase of disorder, marked by competition among the able. Sages then moved to establish the state, instituting demarcations of landed property and between the sexes, 'prohibitions', 'officials', and, finally, 'a ruler'. Only now was hierarchy established as the fundamental principle of order. While this account was offered to justify the principle of institutional and legislative innovation, it created a prototype for historicizing explanations of contemporary political arrangements (Fung, 1952: 315; Graham, 1989: 271–2; Y. Liu, 1998: 177–80).

How was the legacy of pre-Qin thought about the early history of human institutions developed in the imperial period (221 BC to 1911)? Hoyt Tillman's (1994) work on the mid-imperial 'utilitarian' Confucian Chen Liang (1143–94) illustrates the interest of this under-researched question. Influenced by Xunzi, Chen diverged from him on the origin of rites and ceremony, tracing the latter to norms implanted in human hearts by Heaven (1994: 32). Chen had his own theory both of the origin of civil society, and of the emergence and morality of hereditary monarchy, which he discussed in terms of the polarity between public spirit, *gong* (*kung*), and self-interest, *si* (*ssu*). In the earliest times of greatest public spirit, the non-hereditary rulers were chosen by the communities they ruled. Moral deterioration led to formalization in the governmental structure; thus the Confucian culture heroes Yao and Shun selected their successors (while refraining from appointing their own sons). By the time of the fully historical dynasties, the hereditary principle had long been established, but public spirit remained necessary for dynastic success. It was just that the founders of successful dynasties could not match the superb public spirit of the prehistoric rulers (1994: 34–7).

POPULAR PARTICIPATION IN GOVERNMENT, ELITE CRITICISM, AND THE NOTION OF A CHINESE 'LIBERALISM'

That Chen could imagine a utopian antiquity in which communities chose their rulers suggests that it need not be Eurocentric to adopt 'Chinese ideas on popular political participation' as a research topic. Admittedly, there remains the danger of reading Western concepts into Chinese writings – as illustrated by the treatment of Mencius in a long-influential textbook. Here, the notion of a popular 'right of revolution' is discerned in Mencius's claims that a righteous conqueror will be welcomed as liberator by entire peoples, that a vassal who kills a reprobate ruler need not be said to have murdered his lord, and that the legitimacy of a new overlord is manifested through popular acceptance (de Bary, Chan and Watson, 1960: 87, 95–7). As Graham pointed out, however, in Mencius it is Heaven and distinguished nobles who appoint and depose rulers, the people being little more than Heaven's mouthpieces (1989: 115–17). The Chinese rebel commoner could appeal for justification only to the righteousness of Heaven, not the rights of man; he could legitimately expect government *for* the people, but sovereignty was a matter between Heaven and the ruler. The new edition of this textbook sets the record straight (de Bary and Bloom, 1999: 124).

Some ancient Chinese authors did nonetheless rhetorically envisage an autonomous political role for commoners. This was as junior members of remonstrance hierarchies: schematically defined sets of people from whom wise rulers accepted feedback on their governance. These hierarchies – expounded in speeches recorded in the pre-Qin works *Zuo zhuan* (*Tso chuan*) and *Guo yu* (*Kuo yü*) – probably reflect fourth-century (BC) political ideas. They are conveniently assembled in David Schaberg's study of the rhetorical structure of remonstrance speeches, texts that took the past as principal source of authority and used 'inherited' material to make their point effectively (1997: 135–7, 140–2; cf. Schaberg, 2001).

One speech claims that Heaven, having created the people and established rulers for them, gave the rulers helpers 'to serve as [their] teachers and protectors and to keep [them] from exceeding proper measures' (1997: 144). The rulers' helpers (loyal critics) comprise the entire social order. Scribes and blind musicians give criticisms literary clothing, performers 'recite their remonstrances', senior administrators 'correct and instruct', knights 'pass on words', and ordinary people murmur in the marketplace or work criticisms into their manufactures. Another speech warns that, after perfecting their moral potency, the ancient kings 'listened to the people', soliciting remonstrances and poems from their officers. They heeded popular ditties, the gossip of the marketplace, and evaluations of their governance 'along the roads'. A third text likens the people's words to flowing water: blocked, either may burst out disastrously, but prudently drawn forth, either can enrich the kingdom (1997: 143–8).

The ideal of remonstrance, supposedly endorsed by Confucius, found institutional embodiment in later Chinese history in the form of the censorate, a branch of government whose functions included loyal criticism of the ruler. However, institutional provision for the upward flow of popular opinion was usually confined to token gestures. Similarly, later discussion of public opinion's importance generally focused on the contribution that members of the Confucian-educated elite could make from outside the bureaucracy, if granted a respectful hearing. Thus, when the private intellectual Fang Dongshu (1772–1851) alluded to the admonition about the people's words resembling water, the context was his vindication of political debate by educated men of principle who did not currently hold power. There was a continuum between *jiangxue* (seminar-style) exploration of issues in moral philosophy and morally inspired discussion of 'the evils of the day'. Both were necessary, both could enlighten the ruler, and the natural home of both was the academy (de Bary, 1991: 80–5).

Huang Zongxi and Confucian 'Liberalism'

The intellectual best known for his supposed advocacy of *jiangxue*-style political debate is Huang Zongxi (Huang Tsung-hsi, 1610–95), whose loyalty to the Ming dynasty (1368–1644) precluded his taking office under the succeeding Qing (Ch'ing, 1644–1911). Huang's status in modern Chinese nationalist historiography, as China's greatest proto-democrat, rests on passages in his rhetorical critique of despotism, the *Mingyi daifang lu* (1663). Lynn Struve has warned against overestimating this work's significance, for many of Huang's ideas had been anticipated in the critical writings, reform proposals and scholarly practice of the previous generation of Confucian dissidents (1988: 475–9). However, the recent publication of Wm. Theodore de Bary's (1993a) book-length study and translation of Huang's tract presumably represents a claim for its importance. Its centrality in de Bary's earlier (1983) attempt to delineate a 'Confucian liberalism' raises interesting issues.

Two passages in particular encourage the view of Huang as proto-democrat. In one, Huang deplored the role reversal that he claimed had taken place since the ancient era when 'the [people of the] empire' had been recognized as the realm's proprietors, and their rulers merely as retainers. Elsewhere, Huang suggested that in antiquity, schools had provided moral guidance to the ruler, for in those days 'even the Son of Heaven [emperor] did not dare to decide right and wrong for himself, but shared with the schools the determination of right and wrong'

(1993a: 104). Huang proposed the restoration of this ancient ideal through adaptation of more recent institutions. The emperor and key high officials should attend monthly seminars conducted by the Chancellor of the Imperial Academy, who would be empowered to address the emperor frankly on flaws in his governance. In the provinces, the renowned scholars appointed, after public discussion, as directors of education would hold twice-monthly seminars, with the local officials in studential role. Thus could minor flaws in the officials' governance be reproved, and major flaws denounced to the beating of drums. The local degree candidates would be empowered to repudiate collectively a director whose morality had provoked adverse discussion, and the assembled elders to give the local officials feedback and advice at periodic drinking ceremonies (Z. Huang, 1663: 2, 11–13; de Bary, 1993a: 92, 106–8).

This is less than a blueprint for democracy. While the metaphor of society as proprietor (literally, 'host') is powerful, the context is mere polemic against the historical emperors' usurpation of the people's role. Huang does not say explicitly that current governmental policies would be subject to open seminar-style discussion, or that local literati would have powers beyond participation in denunciations. If, then, the notion of Huang as a proto-democrat is problematic, what of de Bary's 'Confucian liberalism' thesis as applied to Huang? De Bary adopted the word 'liberal' to posit continuity between the great Neo-Confucians of the Song (Sung) dynasty (960–1279) and Huang. This 'liberalism' featured both rejection of conservative rigidity in favour of humanist political reformism, and an 'individualism' that stressed personal responsibility for internalizing moral doctrine (1983: 5–9). The intellectual independence achieved through broad learning would give one a basis for reformist activism (or criticism) in the political sphere.

In suggesting that, in the *Mingyi daifang lu*, Huang 'advanced Neo-Confucian liberal thought', de Bary (1983: 85) probably referred both to the potential of Huang's proposed educational reforms to nurture larger numbers of independent-minded moral persons, and to his ideas for change in governmental institutions. These themes were linked, for institutional change would be required to liberate the full political potential of the moral individual. The 'unlawful laws' of despotism must yield to a more fundamental kind of law intended 'to protect and promote impartially the general interests of mankind'; the reformed schools would be 'institutions through which a broader, more informed public could participate in the political process'; the seminars would 'provide a firm institutional basis' for 'open discussion of public and intellectual issues', thereby '[bringing] to a climax' the Neo-Confucian

tradition of discussion as a pedagogical technique (1983: 81–8). Huang was, however, distinctly illiberal on such issues as whether others might dress as they liked, enjoy fiction and drama, buy 'useless' objects, or embrace un-Confucian doctrines (de Bary, 1993a: 106–7, 109–10, 159–60). Could 'something like' Huang's positive concept of law 'have provided a framework for what we call today "human rights"' (1983: 85, 89)? Huang's discussion of law (1993a: 97–9) is largely polemical and shows no interest in procedure. Where were the rights to 'due process' of educational directors whose private lives upset some local people, or county officials whose controversial actions could be dubbed major flaws, fit for denunciation to the sound of drums?

The claims advanced in de Bary's (1993a) study of the *Mingyi daifang lu* are bolder yet. Huang 'intends that [schools] should perform much the same purpose as political parties or parliaments'; he 'can reasonably qualify as a constitutionalist, albeit a Confucian one'; the constructive proposals in the *Mingyi daifang lu* arguably comprise 'a kind of Confucian constitution' (1993a: 56, 63, 68). De Bary both expounds the differences between Huang's 'constitutionalism' and the Western liberal-democratic type, and draws inspiring lessons from the *Mingyi daifang lu* for a contemporary China that has left Maoism behind but not embraced democracy (1993a: 69–71). It is nonetheless hard to discern the careful prescriptiveness of modern constitutions in the rhetoric of the *Mingyi daifang lu*. The work is better viewed as a provocative attempt to rethink the design of China's polity, including its military and economic systems. Huang's institutional proposals are better compared with those in other seventeenth-century works, whether 'utopias' such as Wang Yuan's *Pingshu*, or essay collections such as Tang Zhen's and Gu Yanwu's.

A Chinese Constitutionalism at the Dawn of China's Modern Age?

More convincing, yet claiming less, is Philip Kuhn's (2002) discussion of the thought of Wei Yuan (1794–1857) in terms of constitutionalism. Wei's collected essays date from the transitional period before the collapse of the imperial system, but after the First Opium War. His political thought (as represented by Kuhn) borrows an ancient format – comment on the pre-Confucian *Book of Odes* – to advocate remedies for the ineffective autocracy established by late eighteenth-century misrule. In advocating broader political participation to strengthen the state, he inadvertently foreshadowed a key difference between much modern Chinese democratic thought and the Western preoccupation with limiting the power of the executive (2002: 32, 47–53; cf. Nathan, 1986: 45–66).

Politically conscious literati of Wei's day were frustrated by the undersupply of bureaucratic posts relative to the numbers qualified to fill them, the inherited tendency to view private political associations as unprincipled factions, and the lack of openness to outsiders' suggestions for improving government. Wei's 'constitutional' opinions reflected his position as a graduate inhabiting the margins of the political establishment, although exceptionally knowledgeable on public affairs. Concerned to redraw the 'boundary' delineating 'that part of the community that properly participates in national politics', Wei resembled Huang in advocating some role for the Confucian-educated elite and envisaging urban academic institutions as fit venues for 'discussions of ideas' (2002: 27, 42). Wei, however, would have had consultation confined to those non-office-holding literati with solid academic qualifications. He interpreted an image of deer calling to each other as referring to the need for elite political discussion, and read the line 'I shall seek everywhere for information and advice' as encouraging 'a broad search for policy opinion'. He recognized the importance of rulers having divergent views from which to choose (2002: 39–44). Kuhn's study indicates the need for an annotated translation of Wei's political essays, permitting his 'constitutionalist' remarks to be assessed in context.

Scholarship as Ersatz Political Participation

Even granted that the *Odes* had canonical status for Confucians, how could Wei read 'constitutional' lessons into these diverse poems? Wei was affiliated with the New Text school, a revived Han-dynasty hermeneutic tradition that sought hidden messages in texts whose surface meaning suggested no particular moral or political intent. For Wei, interpreting the *Odes* should transcend mere scholasticism to inspire reformist moral action (Kuhn, 2002: 34–9). Better known for their reinterpretations by New Text adherents are the ultra-concise *Chunqiu* (*Ch'un ch'iu*, Spring and Autumn) annals covering the years 722–481 BC from the perspective of the ducal court of Lu (Confucius's native state). Confucius, the supposed compiler, was thought to have conveyed judgements on the events recorded through subtle vocabulary choices. One more radical interpretation, exemplified in the Yuan dynasty (1272–1368), was to read the *Chunqiu* as a manual of statecraft, or even penal law (Langlois, 1982). Another – the New Text school's – approached the *Chunqiu* through its most visionary

early commentary, the *Gongyang* (*Kung-yang*) *Tradition*.

The *Gongyang* understanding of Confucius is best known through its reshaping by Kang Youwei (K'ang Yu-wei, 1858–1927). Kang represented Confucius as an 'institutional reformer' who would have recognized the need for constitutional monarchy had he lived in Kang's day. Kang took a Han-dynasty *Gongyang*-ite three-stage theory of history, originally intended to apply to the era covered by the *Chunqiu*, and elevated it into a doctrine of global political development. The world was passing from an 'age of disorder', heyday of absolute monarchy, to one of 'approaching peace' and constitutional monarchy, whence it would eventually enter an age of 'universal peace' and republicanism (H. Chang, 1980: 287–8; Fung, 1953: 81–5).

Benjamin Elman (1990) has investigated Kang's intellectual precursors in the late-eighteenth-century New Text school of Changzhou, Jiangsu province. The first was Zhuang Cunyu (1719–88), an educational official and Grand Secretariat academician who briefly held vice-ministerial office at the time when the emperor's favourite Heshen (Ho-shen) was consolidating his infamous ascendancy. Elman views Zhuang's *Gongyang*-style interpretation of the *Chunqiu* as an oblique lamentation of Heshen's rise. In advocating the revival of a moralistic reading of the *Chunqiu*, Zhuang expressed his opposition to changes that he could not fight directly (1990: 108–16, 171–85).

It was Zhuang's grandson Liu Fenglu (1776–1829) who, with his followers, supplies the missing link between Zhuang's turn to the *Gongyang* commentary and Kang's invention of Confucius as utopian reformer. Several years before attaining governmental office, Liu was working to restore the interpretations of He Xiu (Ho Hsiu, AD 129–82), exponent of the three-stage periodization of the *Chunqiu* era and other *Gongyang*-inspired notions. For He, as explicated by Liu, the 'uncrowned king' Confucius had a 'mandate to establish institutions' in Lu, the putative future springboard for a new dynastic order. To avoid presumptuousness, Confucius worked his governmental 'models' into the Lu court annals, thereby 'provid[ing] lessons for ten thousand generations'. His historiography offered inspiration for 'epochal change' – ultimately, 'great unification', a concept echoed in the name of Kang Youwei's utopia (1990: 233–4, 240, 255; H. Chang, 1980: 288–9).

Elman rightly stresses the Confucian scriptures' importance as the ideological mainstay of the imperial government establishment (1990: 74–5). However, it was the tragedy of both Kang and the so-called historical Confucius to be political outsiders. Liu's notion of Confucius as a Heaven-appointed prophet (Elman, 1990: 231) seems fundamentally an outsider's fantasy. Would systematic study of the sociology of Qing New Text Confucianism confirm that the image of Confucius as prophet and reformer appealed chiefly to politically powerless and disempowered literati? New Text Confucianism may have been most significant as an ideology of scholars who did not hold office or had little power within it – although adherents who joined the bureaucracy might apply New Text perspectives to official business (1990: 215–18).

MAINSTREAM CONFUCIANISM AND THE IMPERIAL STATE

What of Confucianism in power: the main overt ideology of government for most of the imperial age? What, in particular, of the Song reinterpretations and elaborations that are conventionally regarded, under the name 'Neo-Confucianism', as the official orthodoxy of the remaining dynasties? For James Liu, the introspective self-cultivation urged by Neo-Confucian moralism implied a retreat from engagement with external reality that was partially responsible for the lack of dynamism and creative change in China's subsequent development (1988: 9–11, 149–53). In Ray Huang's brilliant critique of the Confucian political order in Ming China, the thought of the great synthesizer Zhu Xi (Chu Hsi, 1130–1200) is lampooned for 'committ[ing] every literate person within the empire to a lifetime of study whose only purpose was to affirm that the world is organic and that he was bound by law of nature to perform his assigned duties in society' (1981: 204). Other Chinese scholars, however, affirm Neo-Confucianism's continuing validity and positive role in modernized East Asia. Tu Wei-ming has even tentatively anticipated a 'third epoch of the Confucian Way' (1993: 214–22).

Acceptance that a long-established ideology of moral governance and social (or socio-cosmic) harmony has lessons for the modern age inspires volumes with such titles as *Confucianism and Human Rights* or *Confucianism and Ecology* (de Bary and Tu, 1998; Tucker and Berthrong, 1998). Thoughtful, rewarding essays have been written on these themes (e.g. W. Chang, 1998; Twiss, 1998). Yet the scholarly priority remains accurate understanding of the content, scope and functions of Confucian ideology while it still underpinned the Chinese polity (until about 1905). It would be an outrageous exaggeration to call the Confucian tradition itself stagnant over two millennia. The major changes and subtle refinements are explored in numerous publications, of which Peter Bol's (1992) study of the early evolution of Neo-Confucian moral doctrine is a magisterial example.

Neo-Confucianism as Call for the Rule of the Moral Mind

Neo-Confucianism is indeed best known for its Buddhist-influenced emphasis on self-cultivation and the systematic metaphysical and cosmological speculation of some of its founders (Fung, 1953: chs 10–14). However, self-cultivation within the governing elite was to serve a larger purpose. The concept of moral self-development was central to a reasserted political idealism reflected in the chapters on government in the Neo-Confucian anthology of Zhu Xi and Lü Zuqian (1137–81) (Chan, 1967: 202–59). Here we find Cheng Yi (Ch'eng I, 1033–1107) asserting that, fundamentally, the 'way of government' is 'nothing but "rectifying what is wrong in the ruler's mind" and "rectifying one's mind in order to rectify the minds of"' other officials, starting with those at court (1967: 213). Still more revealing is Cheng's ideal of the sage's mirror-like heart-mind that objectively identifies the good and evil confronting it, responds with the appropriate emotion and action, and yet remains detached (Fung, 1953: 525). A Neo-Confucian paragon would conduct administration in precisely such a spirit.

For a sympathetic exploration of Neo-Confucian political moralism, one may consult de Bary's studies of the thought of Zhen Dexiu (Chen Te-hsiu, 1178–1235) (de Bary, 1981: 67–126; de Bary, 1993b). De Bary analysed Zhen's *Canonical Writings on the Heart-Mind* and *Extended Meaning of the Great Learning* as culminations of the Neo-Confucian insistence, articulated in an earlier Song didactic tradition called the 'Learning of the Emperors and Kings', on the ruler's self-cultivation as key to sound government. Zhen's *Extended Meaning*, an elaboration of his lectures as court scriptural expositor, was reportedly accepted as 'a guide and model for the ruler' (1981: 87). Its subject, the 'Great Learning' (a chapter of the ancient *Book of Rites*), contains the *locus classicus* for the doctrine that attaining governmental order begins with the ruler's moral and intellectual self-discipline (Graham, 1989: 132–4). Together with the *Canonical Writings*, which took an extreme position against human desires, the *Extended Meaning* offered the emperor learned advice on rectifying his thoughts and conducting his personal life. Supported by quotations from other authoritative texts and reinforced by historical examples, the central message was: 'Though the four seas are vast, if the ruler's mind-and-heart are rectified, there is order; if not, there is disorder' (de Bary, 1981: 115–16).

James Liu and Peter Bol have proposed different explanations for Neo-Confucian moralism's success in implanting itself in China's intellectual culture. Liu (1988) related the process by which Cheng Yi's and Zhu Xi's thought became state orthodoxy to Southern Song (1127–1279) dynastic politics, arguing that the espousal of Neo-Confucianism was a matter initially of political convenience, later of national defence. He represented the focus on the ruler's mind, from Zhu Xi on, as a rational response to the strengthening of imperial autocracy that he saw as a key trend in the early Southern Song (1988: 104, 146–8). This reverses the conventional assumption that Neo-Confucianism fostered autocracy, a view further challenged by Alan Wood in his (1995) study of Northern Song (960–1126) commentaries on the *Chunqiu*. But the Neo-Confucian call to perfect the self in order to transform society was not intended for rulers alone. Bol (1992) has considered Neo-Confucian self-cultivation's appeal to a large literati class, many of whom might never reach bureaucratic office, still less political power. As the growth of the civil service examination system progressively weakened the links between birth and government position, the educated elite needed a new source of esteem with which to validate their status and identity as *shi* (*shih*, scholars) (1992: 330–42). Neo-Confucian study and practice thus achieved a broadly based tenacity.

Neo-Confucianism Displaced: Indigenous and Manchu Challenges

Pamela Crossley and Benjamin Elman have highlighted the inadequacy of the assumption that 'Cheng-Zhu orthodoxy' provided the ideological framework of all post-Song imperial government. Crossley (1999) has emphasized constructed notions of ethnic identity in the changing political ideology of the Qing-dynasty Manchu rulers, who governed a growing multi-ethnic empire of which the Chinese world was only part. She discerns a transition from the 'transformationalist' ethos of the early Qing reigns, whose emperors increasingly represented themselves as aliens qualified to rule by their conversion to Confucian values and techniques, to a 'universalist' phase during the Qianlong reign (1735–96). Universalist ideology elevated the emperor as transcendent source of wisdom and authority; complementing his 'culturally null' 'capacity to contain worlds' were the 'essentialist identities' assigned to the peoples of his realm, who were to be controlled through definition (1999: 28, 38, 221 and Part 3).

This universalism, which borrowed the Buddhist symbol of the 'wheel-turning king', deployed Confucianism without being Confucian. While the supplanted 'transformationalism' was not specifically *Neo*-Confucian, a central prop of the newly

elevated emperorship affirmed a Han-dynasty contention that Zhu Xi had opposed. For Zheng Xuan (Cheng Hsüan, 127–200), only the ruler could attain the heights of moral efficacy, thus becoming Heaven and Earth's associate in exercising 'transforming and nurturing powers'. To Zhu, the scriptural passage that Zheng had so interpreted referred to sages, a category that Zhu considered open to all who cultivated moral prowess. Under Qianlong, Zhu and his chosen scriptures remained enshrined in the examination curriculum and much imperial rhetoric, but the court preferred Zheng's position as to who could fully embody 'moral mind' (1999: 225, 229–32).

Elman (1994) has argued that the Cheng-Zhu hold on the Qing examination system was compromised by the philological research on the Confucian scriptures known as 'Han learning' or *kaozheng* (*k'ao-cheng*, 'evidential') scholarship. If texts on which Song Neo-Confucian moralism had relied could be exposed as forgeries, what justified the requirement that candidates reproduce the orthodox interpretations? The system adjusted slowly to such challenges, but from *c.* 1770 on, examiners began to include questions on the problems that the new research had raised. Questions reflecting Cheng-Zhu orthodoxy still predominated, and the incorporation of Han learning into the examinations perhaps blunted its challenge. Nonetheless, 'the straitjacket of Neo-Confucian orthodoxy' is now a contested concept (1994: 133–43).

Confucian Statecraft and Political Economy

The notion of Confucianism as straitjacket has been further undermined with respect to Chinese statecraft and political economy. 'Statecraft' is the standard translation of *jingshi* (*ching-shih*), a term that can embrace what Chang Hao has termed 'moral statesmanship' – Neo-Confucian self-perfection as the means to ordering society (1974: 38–46). In English-language scholarship, however, 'statecraft' commonly refers to writing about practical approaches. Such writing characteristically propounds schemes for institutional, administrative, or fiscal improvement, theoretical rationales being relegated to the preambles. One can use such documents as source materials for Chinese political thought by analysing the authors' assumptions and their allusions to classic texts. However, seekers of explicit political theory may find the conscientious thinking-through of practicalities that typifies these documents an unfruitful distraction.

Statecraft writings are nonetheless often valuable sources for opinions on ultimately political issues, such as social inequality and the stance of government towards it. The researcher must know some codes. For example, discussions about restoration of the ancient 'well-field' system are probably about agrarian inequality and reflect views on the state–society relationship. Below, I introduce recent scholarship on selected topics in which the state's role is an important theme. However, a prerequisite for discussion of Confucian statecraft is an introduction to the ancient *Guanzi* book on which it sometimes drew.

The *Guanzi* as a manual of statecraft

The *Guanzi* reflects the sophistication of ancient Chinese ideas of political economy. Its governmental sections had the Legalist virtue of being about method but lacked the taint of close association with the state of Qin. The work purported to be by Guan Zhong (Kuan Chung), a seventh-century chief minister of Qi supposedly praised by Confucius. While its advice to rulers seems largely pragmatic, it is not devoid of notions that Confucians could have welcomed. In Graham's view, the *Guanzi* 'gives both morality and law places in the organization of the state, in proportions not very different from the Confucian [Xunzi]'s' (1989: 268).

A key set of statecraft chapters in the *Guanzi* is that on '[The Art of] Light and Heavy' (*qing zhong*), or economic management. Political morality, *pace* Graham, seems conspicuous by its absence from these chapters. They provide the theoretical rationale for that classic form of state economic intervention in premodern China, the maintenance of 'ever-normal' granaries for stabilizing grain prices in times of glut or shortage. This practice was usually represented as an expression of Confucian paternalism towards both growers (after harvest) and consumers (in the lean pre-harvest season). However, so redolent was the *Guanzi* account of cynical manipulation that it was the sanitized version in the Former Han dynastic history that became the *locus classicus*.

The tone of the 'Qing zhong' section probably reflects the context of its composition. *Guanzi* chapters may date from any century from the fourth to the first BC. Among various suggestions regarding the 'Qing zhong' section's date of composition, Rickett (1998) favours the view that its schemes for state enrichment are linked with the economic policies of the expansionist Han emperor, Wudi (Wu-ti, reigned 141–87 BC). Fiscal problems drove Wudi's court into a controversial series of government monopolies and other state trading operations. Rickett endorses the hypothesis that the 'Qing zhong' texts provided blueprints for these experiments. However, he qualifies previous findings

through careful attention to the dating of separate chapters as well as differences of style, format and authorship throughout the section (1998: 345–57). He does not raise the possibility that those dialogues that propose gross or far-fetched schemes for exploiting society are not 'promonopolistic propaganda' (1998: 360), but caricatures intended to discredit unprincipled fiscality.

The 'light' and 'heavy' of 'Qing zhong' refer to value. The ruler should be able to change the value of commodities or means of exchange by manipulating supply and demand. The classic *qing zhong* operation involved playing the speculator's game in order to quell private profiteering. State agents bought grain while it was 'light' (cheap) and sold it when it became 'heavy' (dear). Although this technique later became a tool of public welfare policy, the major *Guanzi* exposition mentions three goals: price stabilization, 'tenfold' profit for the ruler, and the curbing of private accumulations of commercial wealth, which sap the ruler's influence. The 'Qing zhong' section advocates rural credit schemes that exploit seasonal price fluctuations to the treasury's advantage, suggests government monopolies and other trading operations as ways of introducing indirect taxation, and explains how to manipulate the relative value of money and commodities so that all types of transaction between state and subjects benefit the former. Set in the multi-state world of Guan Zhong's day, it warns against market forces emanating from rival states. It even advocates a kind of mercantilism, with grain, rather than bullion, as the object of interstate competition (1998: 338–44, 378–84 and e.g. 362–75, 390–8, 411).

One 'Qing zhong' passage observes that 'When the prince's demands are pressing, the value of gold increases. When they are relaxed, it decreases' (1998: 425). Another mentions the legend that the founders of the ancient Xia and Shang dynasties cast coin from mountain ores to relieve famine (1998: 397). Such notions are frequently invoked in later statecraft writings. What issues do they raise about Chinese monetary theory and ideas of sovereignty?

Chinese monetary theory: the political implications of cartalism

Once a state provides means of exchange, discussions of what money is reflect particular conceptions of state power. Richard von Glahn (1996) has argued that the story of money's creation as a famine relief tool contributed to the establishment of a form of cartalism as the dominant strand in Chinese monetary theory. Cartalism is the doctrine that money is deliberately created by a 'monetary authority' (here, the sovereign or state), it being this authority that determines money's nominal value, which in principle is arbitrary. The notion of money as a consciously created thing fitted well with the ancient Chinese tendency to conceive of the constituents of civilization as the inventions of sages (1996: 23, 25–8). Although the *Guanzi* 'Qing zhong' section introduced a quantity theory of money by which the (real) value of money was determined by its supply relative to that of commodities, the section's emphasis was on techniques for manipulating exchange values. The ruler could enhance the value of money by restricting its supply, or affect the value of specific currencies by adjusting his demand for them. He should be aware of the impact of his fiscal practice on the value of money, 'arrogate to himself sole authority over the ratios of exchange', and deploy consummate skill in managing those ratios (1996: 29–33).

In imperial times, monetary thought and practice perforce recognized the limitations on the sovereign's power to determine the value of money by fiat. Premodern discussions reflect a 'compromise between theoretical cartalism and practical metalism', the latter meaning a pragmatic understanding that the market value of monetary metals could not be ignored (1996: 34). Von Glahn traces the interplay of cartalism, practical metalism and occasional 'catallacticism' (a monetary theory stressing exchange) in an important survey of premodern Chinese 'monetary analysis' (1996: ch. 1). However, fundamentalist cartalist rhetoric survived into the seventeenth century, when an advocate of token coins declaimed: 'The power of the ruler over men is such that he transforms the myriad things. If in an instant he can change the value of a man, can he not also in an instant change the value of a thing?' (Gao Heng in He and Wei, 1827: ch. 53, pp. 21a–b). The increasing monetary use, beginning in the fifteenth century, of unminted, generally imported silver, and the resulting development of an asymmetrical bimetallism meanwhile created a new context for the *Guanzi*'s advice that rulers manipulate exchange values. *Guanzi*-inspired arguments that the state should increase popular esteem for coin by demanding it in tax payments gained a new, anti-silver, meaning. Silver was an affront to cartalism: not instituted, as currency should be, by the sovereign, it weakened the ruler's grasp on the controls of the economy (e.g. Ren Yuanxiang in He and Wei, 1827: ch. 29, p. 12a; ch. 53, p. 12a).

The Tang poet Bo Juyi (Po Chü-i, 772–846) wrote in an examination essay that 'One who reigns as king will level dear and cheap and adjust light and heavy, causing the hundred commodities to flow in every part, the people of the four directions to know mutuality of interest' (quoted in He and Wei, 1827: ch. 53, p. 13b). The slogans of Chinese cartalism did not belong to an isolated realm of discourse, but should be addressed in the historiography of premodern Chinese conceptions of sovereignty.

The debate over the statist policies of Wang Anshi

Premodern China's bitterest debate about how large and activist the state should be was that provoked by the 'New Policies' (1069–73) of the chief minister Wang Anshi (An-shih, 1021–86). Confronting high defence expenditures, Wang proceeded on the unconventional assumption that one could 'create wealth'. The prerequisite to enriching the state was to help society enrich itself, using a necessarily expanded civil service. State and society should indeed form a single body. Key parts of the economic programme would involve displacing private interests. Schemes to combat 'engrossers', conceived in *Guanzi*-derived terms, were justified by invoking a dubious Confucian scripture called *The Rites of Zhou* (or *The Officers of Zhou*). This text contains detailed prescriptions for a highly complex, interventionist bureaucracy (Smith, 1993: 82–8; Bol, 1993: 144–5).

Robert Hartwell and Peter Bol have linked the New Policies with Wang's distinctive approach to the Confucian canon. Hartwell (1971) dubbed him a 'classicist', referring to his belief in certain scriptures, including *The Rites of Zhou*, as depicting the hallowed governance of antiquity. Although Wang advocated the revival only of the intentions behind the ancient system, he singled these texts out for emphasis in the examinations, commissioning official commentaries to the three he valued most. What he discouraged, and his followers rejected, was the study of history as moral guide or source of statecraft lessons (1971: 690–4, 712–17). Hartwell focused on the historicist alternative to classicism, especially the tradition of 'historical analogism' developed by Wang's foremost adversary, Sima Guang (Ssu-ma Kuang, 1019–86). This was a sophisticated discipline, supported (since the eighth century) by classified encyclopaedias of historical policy precedents that, Hartwell suggested, could have contributed to the emergence of a science of political economy (1971: 701, 708–12, 717–27).

Hartwell's study delineates an opposition between fundamentalism (classicism) and realism (historical analogism). This opposition re-emerges, differently clad, in Bol's comparisons of Wang and Sima (1992: ch. 7; 1993). In Bol's view, Wang thought there was a unitary moral-political system underlying the diverse Confucian scriptures. Close study would reveal the coherence of the system and thus provide optimal training for prospective civil servants. Perhaps surprisingly, given Paul Smith's (1993) insistence that Wang wanted entrepreneurially minded bureaucrats, the goal of education was to produce not intellectual independence but uniformity of viewpoint. Only thus could society's leaders revert to antiquity's unitary standards. The *shi* should become identified with the government, and 'divergent opinion' should be recognized as undesirable in principle. The disaffected could be expected to mellow, if only the court held fast to 'moral principles' (Bol, 1993: 142–6, 160–3, 170–3; Smith, 1993: 87–8). To Sima, Wang's proposed dictatorship of *dirigisme* and virtue betrayed ignorance of, and jeopardized, the normal workings of society. It was preferable to have intermediaries between state and common people: the rich, on whom the poor depended, and the moral-intellectual elite – the *shi* – who emerged from society and were its natural leaders. Rather than presuming to mould new *shi*, the state must earn the support, and attract the service, of those who already existed (Bol, 1993: 159, 178–80).

Song discussions of the state and private wealth

Zhihong Liang Oberst (1996) puts the Wang–Sima controversy in broader perspective by surveying Song writings on the well-field system – the ancient tenurial regime whereby equal-sized squares of land were supposedly arranged in groups of nine, loosely imitating the character for 'well'. Eight squares were individual household allotments; the ninth, central square was tilled by all eight households for the local lord. It was a cliché in imperial China that the well-field system could not be restored, although constraints on latifundia might be feasible. As Oberst notes, however, a system of state-allocated landholdings ('equal fields') had been implemented in north China between the fifth and eighth centuries AD (1996: 34). For eleventh-century writers, a theoretically egalitarian land tenure system was not necessarily a utopian ideal from remote antiquity, but a historical reality.

Oberst's account of Northern Song discussions of the well-field system is based largely on examination essays. Her material suggests that for junior intellectuals of this period, the well-field system could represent a number of ideals: socio-economic equality, diligence and thrift, a rational balance between production and consumption, a rationally planned society, public security, local harmony, famine preparedness, fair taxation, universal education, and a sustainable military system. Shang Yang's putative abolition of well-fields in the state of Qin was blamed for evils such as agrarian inequality and exploitation, vagrancy, and the abandonment of land, many of which caused concern during the Northern Song. While Oberst's essayists might lament the usurpation of the sovereign's role as patron of the poor, they generally stopped short of advocating restoration of the well-fields (1996: 42–9). She groups their proposals under two headings: the 'land ownership' and the 'market' approaches.

Representatives of the 'land ownership approach' – measures to restrict landholdings without major social upheaval – included Li Gou (Kou, 1009–59) and Zhang Zai (Chang Tsai, 1020–77). The former advocated limiting landholdings as a means to fuller exploitation of the empire's agricultural potential; the latter suggested use of non-hereditary tax-collection rights to compensate rich landowners whose land would be absorbed in well-field units (1996: 52–7). 'Market approach' refers to the *Guanzi*-inspired strategy of helping poor farmers by substituting state grain trading and agricultural credit for the depredations of 'engrossers'. Oberst shows that Wang Anshi was not eccentric in his animus against 'engrossers'. Neither Zhang Fangping (Chang Fang-p'ing, 1007–91) nor Su Che (Ch'e, 1039–1112) was aligned with Wang's reform party, but the former blamed 'engrossers' for much of the agrarian misery that made peasants desert the land. He advocated that the state squeeze 'engrossers' out of the grain business, using sumptuary laws to remove the incentive for unconscionable profiteering. Su Che proposed state loans to the needy to undermine rich usurers in 1061, eight years before Wang launched a controversial rural credit scheme. Su represented usurers as oppressors of the poor and a potential challenge to the state (1996: 58–60). Wang acted on preoccupations that others left in the realm of academic exercises, while his schemes betrayed stronger fiscal concerns than are discernible in some of his contemporaries.

Wang's 'market approach' literalism provoked a backlash. Oberst documents the emergence of a counter-discourse stressing the social functions of the rich. Several writers responded to Wang's bureaucratic credit scheme with vindications of the private lender. Sima Guang's role was to broaden the defence of private credit into a doctrine of mutual reliance between rich and poor, and between the state and the rich (1996: 122–8, 134–5). His lead was followed by several Southern Song scholar-officials, such as Chen Liang and Ye Shi (Yeh Shih, 1150–1223). The pro-wealth discourse included arguments that the rich contributed to the polity's stability and local government effectiveness; that social inequality was natural; that resourceless people depended on the rich for land, employment, patronage and charity; that as the state could not supply the folk with livelihoods, it should not ruin those who did; and that the rich made manifold payments to the government and generally deserved their wealth. Government's proper role was to ensure that rich and poor remained harmonious and contented with their stations. This might require action to protect the poor, but not coercively except in cases of extreme recalcitrance (1996: 135–40; Lo, 1974: 117–20; Tillman, 1994: 53–4, 56).

A 'liberal' tendency in Chinese political economy?

The notion that society's own arrangements can be trusted to provide a certain level of security was reflected, under Song and Qing, in an economic discourse in many ways opposed to the *Guanzi* tradition. This discourse combined expressions of awareness of the functioning of market forces with suggestions that these forces were best left unimpeded. Such expressions – found particularly in discussions of state intervention in the grain trade – have been uncovered by historians combing administrative documents to determine the concepts of political economy reflected therein. One result has been a cautious use of the term 'economic liberalism' to refer to certain tendencies in public policy discussion in specific periods, especially the mid-eighteenth century.

Exemplifying the methodology of such research is the close reading of a 1763 memorial on grain brokers by Pierre-Étienne Will, who pioneered the application of the terms 'liberalism' and *laissez-faire* to mid-Qing imperial grain-trade policy (1980: 186; cf. Will, 1990: 213). Will shows that the 1763 document expresses understanding both of the discipline spontaneously imposed by competition, and of the need for a continuous flow of trade, undisrupted by blind action against 'hoarders' (1999: 335–49). This documentary approach is used extensively by Helen Dunstan, who has translated mid-Qing texts reflecting belief in self-correcting mechanisms, the social utility of grain speculation, and the functioning of price incentives and the profit motive (1996: esp. 97–9, 276–8, 324–6). She argues that the term 'economic liberalism' has a place in the analysis of indigenous Chinese political economy if used restrictively, and if the persistence of competing interventionist tendencies is recognized and no unwarranted assumptions are imported from European history. The emergence of a rudimentary economic liberalism did not depend upon the ideology of the Enlightenment (1996: 7–8, 327–30).

This research could be developed, first, by extending its temporal scope. Robert Hymes has shown that the argument that high grain prices trigger a self-correcting mechanism was made already in a famine relief manual dated *c.* 1200 (1993: 295–6). We know little about how such ideas fared between then and the eighteenth century, or later in the eighteenth century. Second, attempts should be made to relate the economic thought of individual civil servants to their philosophical and scholastic allegiances within the broader Confucian tradition. William Rowe's (2001) portrait of the eighteenth-century statesman Chen Hongmou constitutes a promising beginning. Finally, systematic comparison between Chinese economic liberalism and that of the French physiocrats and Adam Smith remains to be undertaken.

CONCLUSION

What can scholars of premodern Chinese political thought offer to those who see it as a 'legacy', important for its presumed influences on modern Chinese political development and/or presumed potential contribution to the future evolution of East Asian political forms? Perhaps the most responsible answer is to warn against superficial judgements and teleological assumptions. To be sure, the tradition offers precedents, some less convincing than others, for various political styles and forms that different groups may advocate. Justification by indigenous precedent is a time-honoured Chinese technique for rendering the alien acceptable. Such justification may come at a price, if it tends to perpetuate essentialist ethno-cultural criteria for evaluating institutions. It is one thing explicitly to argue ethno-cultural particularism as a political principle, another to admit it unexamined.

As to influences, indigenous political culture was but one of many factors shaping modern Chinese political development; the premodern intellectual tradition (itself not monolithic) was but one factor shaping indigenous political culture. Perhaps the most responsible statements to be made about the Chinese intellectual tradition's influence are negative. 'The Chinese' are not doomed by their heritage to totalitarian forms of government requiring mindless intellectual conformity. The tradition offered precedents both for super-elevation of the ruler and for the promotion of rigid orthodoxy, but these precedents were neither dominant nor necessarily esteemed. However, it is not surprising in view of the tradition that, since the late nineteenth century, authoritarianism has generally prevailed over moves towards multi-party democracy in China, and that the principles and values of Western political and social liberalism have been thought problematic. Nor is it surprising that hierarchical principles have displaced radical egalitarianism, that moralism and paternalism have featured in Chinese communist political culture, or that some advocacy of popular political participation has had an elitist tone. What may be found intriguing is that the post-Mao combination of continuing political authoritarianism with trust in market forces is not the radical departure from premodern tradition that might have been assumed.

And yet the premodern intellectual tradition need not even be invoked in a convincing explanation of contemporary developments in Chinese political economy. It probably 'caused' few, if any, of the phenomena listed above. The value of studying it lies elsewhere: in its intrinsic interest and in the potential for accurate knowledge and responsible interpretation to combat ill-informed assumptions.

NOTES

I thank Peter Bol, Derek Herforth and Edmund Ryden for bibliographical advice.

1 *Pinyin* romanization is used in this chapter. For key names and terms, the older Wade–Giles versions are supplied in brackets if significantly different.

REFERENCES

Allan, Sarah and Crispin Williams (2000) 'An account of the discussion'. In Sarah Allan and Crispin Williams, eds, *The Guodian Laozi: Proceedings of the International Conference, Dartmouth College, May 1998.* Berkeley, CA: Society for the Study of Early China and Institute of East Asian Studies, University of California, 117–83.

Bol, Peter K. (1992) *'This Culture of Ours': Intellectual Transitions in T'ang and Sung China.* Stanford, CA: Stanford University Press.

Bol, Peter K. (1993) 'Government, society, and state: on the political visions of Ssu-ma Kuang and Wang An-shih'. In Robert P. Hymes and Conrad Schirokauer, eds, *Ordering the World: Approaches to State and Society in Sung Dynasty China.* Berkeley, CA: University of California Press, 128–92.

Brooks, E. Bruce (1994) 'The present state and future prospects of pre-Hàn text studies'. *Sino-Platonic Papers* (University of Pennsylvania), 46: 1–74.

Brooks, E. Bruce and A. Taeko Brooks (1998) *The Original Analects: Sayings of Confucius and His Successors: A New Translation and Commentary.* New York: Columbia University Press.

Chan, Wing-tsit, trans. (1967) *Reflections on Things at Hand: The Neo-Confucian Anthology Compiled by Chu Hsi and Lü Tsu-ch'ien.* New York: Columbia University Press.

Chang, Hao (1974) 'On the "ching-shih" ideal in Neo-Confucianism'. *Ch'ing-shih wen-t'i*, 3 (1): 36–61.

Chang, Hao (1980) 'Intellectual change and the Reform Movement'. In John K. Fairbank and Kwang-ching Liu, eds, *The Cambridge History of China.* Vol. 11, *Late Ch'ing, 1800–1911, Part 2.* Cambridge: Cambridge University Press, 274–338.

Chang, Leo S. and Yu Feng (1998) *The Four Political Treatises of the Yellow Emperor: Original Mawangdui Texts with Complete English Translations and an Introduction.* Honolulu: University of Hawaii Press.

Chang, Wejen (1998) 'The Confucian theory of norms and human rights'. In Wm. Theodore de Bary and Tu

Weiming, eds, *Confucianism and Human Rights.* New York: Columbia University Press, 117–41.

Crossley, Pamela Kyle (1999) *A Translucent Mirror: History and Identity in Qing Imperial Ideology.* Berkeley, CA: University of California Press.

De Bary, Wm. Theodore (1981) *Neo-Confucian Orthodoxy and the Learning of the Mind-and-Heart.* New York: Columbia University Press.

De Bary, Wm. Theodore (1983) *The Liberal Tradition in China.* Hong Kong and New York: Chinese University Press and Columbia University Press.

De Bary, Wm. Theodore (1991) *The Trouble with Confucianism.* Cambridge, MA: Harvard University Press.

De Bary, Wm. Theodore (1993a) *Waiting for the Dawn: A Plan for the Prince. Huang Tsung-hsi's Ming-i tai-fang lu.* New York: Columbia University Press.

De Bary, Wm. Theodore (1993b) 'Chen Te-hsiu and statecraft'. In Robert P. Hymes and Conrad Schirokauer, eds, *Ordering the World: Approaches to State and Society in Sung Dynasty China.* Berkeley, CA: University of California Press, 349–79.

De Bary, Wm. Theodore and Irene Bloom, comps (1999, 2000) *Sources of Chinese Tradition,* 2nd edn, vols 1 (1999) and 2 (2000). New York: Columbia University Press.

De Bary, Wm. Theodore, Wing-tsit Chan and Burton Watson, comps (1960) *Sources of Chinese Tradition,* vol. 1. New York: Columbia University Press.

De Bary, Wm. Theodore and Tu Weiming (1998) *Confucianism and Human Rights.* New York: Columbia University Press.

Dunstan, Helen (1996) *Conflicting Counsels to Confuse the Age: A Documentary Study of Political Economy in Qing China, 1644–1840.* Ann Arbor, MI: The University of Michigan, Center for Chinese Studies.

Duyvendak, J. J. L. (1928) *The Book of Lord Shang: A Classic of the Chinese School of Law.* London: Probsthain.

Elman, Benjamin A. (1990) *Classicism, Politics, and Kinship: The Ch'ang-chou School of New Text Confucianism in Late Imperial China.* Berkeley, CA: University of California Press.

Elman, Benjamin A. (1994) 'Changes in Confucian civil service examinations from the Ming to the Ch'ing dynasty'. In Benjamin A. Elman and Alexander Woodside, eds, *Education and Society in Late Imperial China, 1600–1900.* Berkeley, CA: University of California Press, 111–49.

Fung, Yu-lan (1952, 1953) *A History of Chinese Philosophy,* trans. Derk Bodde, vols 1 (1952) and 2 (1953). Princeton, NJ: Princeton University Press (first Chinese edn 1931–4).

Giele, Enno (1998–9) 'Early Chinese manuscripts: including addenda and corrigenda to *New Sources of Early Chinese History: An Introduction to the Reading of Inscriptions and Manuscripts'. Early China,* 23–4: 247–337.

Graham, A. C. (1978) *Later Mohist Logic, Ethics and Science*. Hong Kong and London: Chinese University Press and School of Oriental and African Studies.

Graham, A. C. (1981) *Chuang-tzǔ: The Seven Inner Chapters and Other Writings from the Book* Chuang-tzǔ London: George Allen and Unwin.

Graham, A. C. (1989) *Disputers of the Tao: Philosophical Argument in Ancient China*. La Salle, IL: Open Court.

Harbsmeier, Christoph (1997) 'Xunzi and the problem of impersonal first person pronouns'. *Early China*, 22: 181–220.

Hartwell, Robert M. (1971) 'Historical analogism, public policy, and social science in eleventh- and twelfth-century China'. *American Historical Review*, 76 (3): 690–727.

He, Changling and Wei Yuan, comps (1827) *Huangchao jingshi wenbian*, 1873 edn, reprint 1964. Taibei: Shijie shuju.

Hsiao, Kung-chuan (1979) *A History of Chinese Political Thought*. Vol. 1, *From the Beginnings to the Sixth Century AD*, trans. F. W. Mote. Princeton, NJ: Princeton University Press (first Chinese edn 1945–6).

Huang, Ray (1981) *1587, A Year of No Significance: The Ming Dynasty in Decline*. New Haven: Yale University Press.

Huang, Zongxi (1663) *Mingyi daifang lu*. Beijing: Zhonghua shuju (reprint 1981).

Hymes, Robert P. (1993) 'Moral duty and self-regulating process in Southern Sung views of famine relief'. In Robert P. Hymes and Conrad Schirokauer, eds, *Ordering the World: Approaches to State and Society in Sung Dynasty China*. Berkeley, CA: University of California Press, 280–309.

Knoblock, John (1988, 1990, 1994) *Xunzi: A Translation and Study of the Complete Works*, vols 1 (1988), 2 (1990) and 3 (1994). Stanford, CA: Stanford University Press.

Knoblock, John and Jeffrey Riegel (2000) *The Annals of Lü Buwei: A Complete Translation and Study*. Stanford, CA: Stanford University Press.

Kuhn, Philip A. (2002) *Origins of the Modern Chinese State*. Stanford, CA: Stanford University Press.

Langlois, John D. (1982) 'Law, statecraft, and the *Spring and Autumn Annals* in Yüan political thought'. In Hok-lam Chan and Wm. Theodore de Bary, eds, *Yüan Thought: Chinese Thought and Religion under the Mongols*. New York: Columbia University Press, 89–152.

Lewis, Mark Edward (1990) *Sanctioned Violence in Early China*. Albany, NY: State University of New York Press.

Lewis, Mark Edward (1999) *Writing and Authority in Early China*. Albany, NY: State University of New York Press.

Liu, James T. C. (1988) *China Turning Inward: Intellectual-Political Changes in the Early Twelfth Century*. Cambridge, MA: Harvard University, Council on East Asian Studies.

Liu, Lydia H. (1995) *Translingual Practice: Literature, National Culture, and Translated Modernity – China, 1900–1937*. Stanford, CA: Stanford University Press.

Liu, Yongping (1998) *Origins of Chinese Law: Penal and Administrative Law in its Early Development*. Hong Kong: Oxford University Press.

Lo, Winston Wan (1974) *The Life and Thought of Yeh Shih*. Gainesville, FL and Hong Kong: University Presses of Florida and the Chinese University of Hong Kong.

Loewe, Michael, ed. (1993) *Early Chinese Texts: A Bibliographical Guide*. Berkeley, CA: Society for the Study of Early China and Institute of East Asian Studies, University of California.

Makeham, John (1999) 'Review of E. Bruce Brooks and A. Taeko Brooks, translators and commentators, *The Original Analects: Sayings of Confucius and His Successors*; Roger T. Ames and Henry Rosemont, Jr, translators and commentators, *The Analects of Confucius: A Philosophical Translation*'. *China Review International*, 6 (1): 1–33.

Nathan, Andrew J. (1986) *Chinese Democracy*. Berkeley, CA: University of California Press.

Nivison, David Shepherd (1999) 'The classical philosophical writings'. In Michael Loewe and Edward L. Shaughnessy, eds, *The Cambridge History of Ancient China from the Origins of Civilization to 221 BC*. Cambridge: Cambridge University Press, 745–812.

Oberst, Zhihong Liang (1996) 'Chinese economic statecraft ideas in the Song period (960–1279)'. PhD dissertation, Columbia University.

Peerenboom, R. P. (1993) *Law and Morality in Ancient China: The Silk Manuscripts of Huang-Lao*. Albany, NY: State University of New York Press.

Puett, Michael J. (2001) *The Ambivalence of Creation: Debates Concerning Innovation and Artifice in Early China*. Stanford, CA: Stanford University Press.

Rickett, W. Allyn (1985, 1998) *Guanzi: Political, Economic, and Philosophical Essays from Early China: A Study and Translation*, vols 1 (1985) and 2 (1998). Princeton, NJ: Princeton University Press.

Rowe, William T. (2001) *Saving the World: Chen Hongmou and Elite Consciousness in Eighteenth-Century China*. Stanford, CA: Stanford University Press.

Schaberg, David (1997) 'Remonstrance in Eastern Zhou historiography'. *Early China*, 22: 133–79.

Schaberg, David (2001) *A Patterned Past: Form and Thought in Early Chinese Historiography*. Cambridge, MA: Harvard University Asia Center.

Smith, Paul J. (1993) 'State power and economic activism during the New Policies, 1068–1085: the tea and horse trade and the "Green Sprouts" loan policy'. In Robert P. Hymes and Conrad Schirokauer, eds, *Ordering the World: Approaches to State and Society in Sung Dynasty China*. Berkeley, CA: University of California Press, 76–127.

Struve, Lynn A. (1988) 'Huang Zongxi in context: a reappraisal of his major writings'. *Journal of Asian Studies*, 47 (3): 474–502.

Tillman, Hoyt Cleveland (1994) *Ch'en Liang on Public Interest and the Law*. Honolulu: University of Hawaii Press.

Tu, Wei-ming (1993) 'Confucianism'. In Arvind Sharma, ed., *Our Religions*. New York: HarperCollins, 139–227.

Tucker, Mary Evelyn and John Berthrong eds (1998) *Confucianism and Ecology: The Interrelation of Heaven, Earth, and Humans*. Cambridge, MA: Harvard University, Center for the Study of World Religions.

Twiss, Sumner B. (1998) 'A constructive framework for discussing Confucianism and human rights'. In Wm. Theodore de Bary and Tu Weiming, eds, *Confucianism and Human Rights*. New York: Columbia University Press, 27–53.

Von Glahn, Richard (1996) *Fountain of Fortune: Money and Monetary Policy in China, 1000–1700*. Berkeley, CA: University of California Press.

Wang, Hsiao-po and Leo S. Chang (1986) *The Philosophical Foundations of Han Fei's Political Theory*. Honolulu: University of Hawaii Press.

Will, Pierre-Étienne (1980, 1990) *Bureaucratie et famine en Chine au 18ᵉ siècle*. Paris: Mouton. Trans. Elborg Forster as *Bureaucracy and Famine in Eighteenth-Century China*. Stanford, CA: Stanford University Press.

Will, Pierre-Étienne (1999) 'Discussions about the market-place and the market principle in eighteenth-century Guangdong'. In Tang Xiyong, ed., *Zhongguo haiyang fazhan shi lunwen ji*, vol. 7. Taibei: Academia Sinica, Sun Yat-sen Institute of Humanities and Social Sciences, 323–89.

Wood, Alan T. (1995) *Limits to Autocracy: From Sung Neo-Confucianism to a Doctrine of Political Rights*. Honolulu: University of Hawaii Press.

25

Medieval Political Theory

JOHN KILCULLEN

Every intellectual discipline constructs and reconstructs its own history, as writings not previously regarded as important get into reading lists and others fall out. Until recently students of political theory were urged to read Plato and Aristotle, and then Hobbes and Locke, but nothing, or very little, between the Greeks and the early moderns. Those who have ventured into this gap have found that, at least from the thirteenth century, there was a good deal of political theory and clear links with the theories of the seventeenth century. The seventeenth-century writers are better understood if we are also familiar with the work of their predecessors, who are in any case as much worth reading as they are. An interesting task for historians of political theory, and for political theorists, is to integrate the study of medieval thought into the discipline.

As with many of the seventeenth-century classics, the medieval contributions to political theory were works 'of occasion'. They were produced by academics for academically trained readers, but their authors did not produce them as part of their teaching duties. They were written in an attempt to intervene in the public affairs of the time, especially in controversies within the Church and between churchmen and lay rulers. Given the relatively slow reproduction of manuscripts before the introduction of printing, these writings probably had little impact on the public events that prompted them (except perhaps so far as their arguments circulated orally), but they were collected and studied by university-educated professionals in law and government, ecclesiastical and secular, and over time they occupied the libraries and the minds of institutions and individuals likely to be involved in similar events in the future. (On the dissemination of political writings and the social position of people interested in

them, see Miethke, 1980; Oui, 1979; Miethke, 2000b.) Some of these medieval writings were produced in the early days of printing, and in the seventeenth century there were several major printed collections (notably Goldast, 1611–114; Dupuy, 1655). Protestants as well as Catholics read these works (Goldast was a Protestant), and they exercised an influence throughout Europe (see Oakley, 1962; 1969; 1996). The parallels between, for example, Hobbes and Marsilius, and Locke and Ockham, are striking.

One of the main tasks set itself by the reformed papacy of the eleventh century was to free Church offices from the control of the aristocratic families who also held military and political power, and beyond that to make Christianity the effective conscience of rulers. This was indeed a 'papal revolution', and it led to a 'crisis of Church and state' that lasted into modern times (see Berman, 1983; Tierney, 1980). Its early stage is called the 'Investiture Contest', which included Pope Gregory VII's deposition of the Emperor Henry IV. During the thirteenth century there were conflicts between popes and emperors, including Pope Innocent IV's deposition of the Emperor Frederick II. There were disagreements over the constitution of the Empire – whether election by the electoral princes gave the emperor-elect his power, or whether this required approval by the pope – and over the relationship between the Empire and the Kingdoms of France, England and Spain. The increasing wealth of the Church attracted careerists, and also provoked critics who advocated a return to the poverty of the Apostles. The rise of the mendicant orders, especially the Franciscans, prompted controversy about poverty as a religious ideal, which led to works about property which are among the sources of seventeenth-century theories of property (see Lambertini, 2000; Kilcullen, 2001b). The support which the popes gave to the mendicant orders provoked opposition from bishops and parish clergy, which led to controversy about the powers of the pope within the Church (see Congar, 1961). There were disputes between Church authorities and secular rulers about whether the clergy should be exempt from taxation and from the ordinary criminal courts, and whether money collected by the local churches should be used by the papacy to finance not only crusades against the Saracens but also military campaigns in Europe. A number of these disputes moved toward a climax in the late thirteenth century, when studies in philosophy, law, and theology were at a high level of activity in the universities. From near the end of the thirteenth century until the middle of the fourteenth there was a complicated and connected series of debates involving Pope Boniface VIII, King Philip the Fair of France, Pope John XXII, the 'Roman Emperor' Ludwig of Bavaria, the Franciscan order and the University of Paris, in the course of which theologians produced many treatises concerning the relationship between religion and secular government, the constitution of the Church, and the constitution of secular government, drawing on the resources not only of theology but also of the law and Aristotelian philosophy. The writings produced during this period became relevant again at the end of the century with the 'Great Schism' (1378–1417), which prompted the 'conciliar' movement. The Council of Constance resolved the schism by removing three rival popes and appointing another.[1]

Since the nineteenth-century revival of interest in medieval intellectual history, all these matters have been closely studied. Libraries have been searched for manuscripts and new editions have been made, many important writings have been translated from Latin, interpretive studies have been produced in many languages. There is not enough room to survey in this chapter more than part of the field. I will concentrate on what I see as a central theme, the relationship between religion and secular government, restricting myself to the crucial period between Thomas Aquinas and William of Ockham.[2]

THE SPIRITUAL AND TEMPORAL POWERS

Separation

In the classical world there was no separation between religion and politics. Aristotle included religion among the functions of a state (Aristotle, *Politics*, VII.8, 1328 b4–15); the Roman Emperor

was called by the religious title 'Pontifex' (a title later assumed by the pope), and the Roman law attributed religious powers to the state (see Ullmann, 1974: 7). But during the early middle ages in Western Europe a separation developed between Church and state, or – in the language of the time – between priesthood and kingship. The classic expression of this separation was in a letter sent in 494 by Pope Gelasius I to the Emperor Anastasius:

> Two there are, august emperor, by which this world is chiefly ruled, the sacred authority of the priesthood and the royal power. Of these the responsibility of the priests is more weighty, in so far as they will answer for the kings of men themselves at the divine judgment … [I]n the order of religion … you ought to submit yourselves [to priests] rather than rule … [T]he bishops themselves … obey your law so far as the sphere of public order is concerned. (translated Tierney, 1980: 13–14)

This document was later incorporated (in part and in association with material from Pope Gregory VII) into Gratian's *Decretum*[3] as the canon *Duo sunt* (dist. 96, c. 10, Friedberg, 1879: I, 340; translated Tierney, 1980: 13–14).[4] The separation of powers may have developed in fact simply because the earliest exponents of the Christian religion did not possess political power. However, another canon, *Cum ad verum* (also based on a letter of Gelasius, as quoted by Pope Nicholas I), suggested deeper reasons for it, namely that mutual limitation of their powers would restrain the pride of priest and emperor, and that those on God's service (the clergy) should be kept free of worldly entanglements (dist. 96, c. 6, Friedberg, 1879: I, 339; translated Tierney, 1980: 14–15; on the materials from Gelasius in the *Decretum* see Watt, 1965: 12–33).

From these and other passages handed down by Gratian, medieval lawyers and theologians arrived at a view of their world as containing two orders of power, the priesthood culminating in the pope, and the lay government culminating in king or emperor. These two kinds of power were unequal in dignity, the spiritual being superior. Although they were separate, there was no 'wall of separation'. (The phrase seems to have been used first by Hooker, 1989: 131, who rejected the idea.) They were expected to co-operate with one another. In particular, the temporal power was required by the spiritual, on pain of spiritual sanctions (excommunication, interdict, etc.), to support its spiritual authority, for example, by eradicating heresy. From time to time kings or emperors acted to reform and purify the Church. At the time it was not assumed that in one territory there would be just one agency with a monopoly of the legitimate use of force (an idea first proposed by Marsilius). It was tacitly assumed that the Church had an inherent right to coerce – in fact, some theologians, perhaps under the influence of the Aristotelian idea of a 'perfect' (i.e. self-sufficient) society, explicitly held that the Church, being self-sufficient, could coerce its members; thus a cleric might be imprisoned as a punishment by his bishop, without needing the permission of the secular ruler. It was thought that the clergy should not engage in any cruel coercion, 'judgements of blood', but it was not thought that the influence of severe punishment could always be dispensed with. Hence the requirement of aid from the secular ruler, who would use methods of coercion which the clergy could not use. Gratian quotes Isidore of Seville, according to whom princely power exists within the Church 'so that what priests are not strong enough to effect by word of teaching, this power might command by terror of discipline' (C. 23, q. 5, c. 20, *Principes*, Friedberg, 1879: I, 936). When John of Paris points out that with reference to heretics Paul said 'avoid', not 'burn', and suggests that beyond such spiritual penalties as avoidance the spiritual power cannot go (1971: 161), he is supposing that the spiritual power may well require the temporal power to go further (1971: 143). (In practice the wielders of the material sword seem to have kept control: see Watt, 1988: 387–99, on practice in England and France.)

Subjection

Another key idea handed down by Gratian was that the pope enjoyed *plenitudo potestatis*, 'fullness of power' (C. 3, q. 6, c. 8, Friedberg, 1879: I, 739; see Rivière, 1925). This meant, not that the pope had every conceivable power, but that the pope was the source of all ecclesiastical jurisdiction, having authority to intervene directly in any matter anywhere within the Church; thus within a diocese the pope could do directly anything the local bishop could do. (As Giles of Rome explained (see below), a cause that can do directly whatever it can also do through secondary causes has 'fullness of power'.) By virtue of 'fullness of power', the thirteenth-century popes insisted that the mendicants (Franciscans, Dominicans and others) should be permitted to preach and minister anywhere, with or without the support of the local bishop. The idea that the pope can exercise directly any of the powers that Christ has given to the Church does not infringe the principle of separation of spiritual and temporal power, as long as it is accepted that Christ did not give temporal power to the Church.

However, during the thirteenth century the papal claim to fullness of power came to be extended to temporal matters. Pope Innocent III wrote: 'Paul … writing to the Corinthians to explain the plenitude of power, said, "Know you not that we shall judge angels? How much more the things of this world?" Accordingly [the papacy] is accustomed to *exercise the office of secular power* sometimes and in some things *by itself*, sometimes and in some things *through others*'[5] – the 'others' being the kings and emperors. The popes were thinking of the Church as coextensive with the human community in Christian parts of the world, with the pope as its head on earth, the secular rulers being his agents in temporal matters and the clergy his agents in spiritual matters. The two powers, often referred to as the 'two swords', were generally said both to belong to the pope, though it was said that he had the 'exercise' of the spiritual sword only. He was said to entrust the exercise or 'administration' of the temporal sword to the secular ruler, while he kept its 'authority', meaning that the secular ruler used his sword 'at the command' (*ad nutum*) of the pope (Tierney, 1980: 93–4, 120–4). The withholding from the pope of the exercise of the temporal sword signified some restriction upon papal intervention in secular affairs, namely that he could not act directly; but the claim that the temporal sword 'belonged to' the pope and that he had its 'authority' implied a power to give binding directions to the temporal ruler, leaving no autonomous sphere of temporal power.

The principle of *Duo sunt*, the separation of powers, was not simply abandoned. The popes presented their interventions in temporal matters as exceptional. Canon lawyers, including Pope Innocent IV himself in his capacity as lawyer commenting on the decretals, drew up lists of the exceptional circumstances in which the spiritual power might intervene in temporal affairs (Tierney, 1980: 153–4; cf. Watt, 1965: 68–9). The most comprehensive rubric for intervention was *ratione peccati*, 'by reason of sin': if a secular ruler's actions are unjust, then this is a sin against which the spiritual power may act. As the pro-papal writer Giles of Rome remarked, this rubric 'is so broad and ample that it may embrace all temporal disputes whatsoever' (1986: 167–8). It began to look as if very little, if any, sphere of autonomy was being left for the temporal power. This especially seemed so from the main line of argument underlying papal claims: the pope is Christ's vicar (place-holder, substitute) on earth, Christ is God, and God is lord of all; therefore the pope is lord of all (see, for example, the passage from Innocent IV in Watt, 1965: 66–7).

The claim to ultimate papal supremacy will no doubt seem objectionable to the modern reader, but there are elements in it with which we should sympathize. We can agree, I assume, that everything governments do is subject to moral assessment – there is no 'autonomous sphere' of government action exempt from moral assessment; and we can perhaps agree that citizens and others make their moral assessment of government and other social institutions by applying moral values or principles that are independent of government and popular opinion ('natural law'). We can also agree that there may be people whose opinion on moral matters is especially worth considering, either because they are factually well informed or because they have thought much about ethical issues (and among these we may include the clergy, unless we think that Christianity is actually misleading); that such people should speak out when they believe government is doing wrong; that in extreme cases they might be justified in calling on people to reject a government, either by electing another, or by disobeying, or by rebellion. The popes went beyond all this, however, in claiming that their moral assessments of government should be accepted without dispute and acted on obediently.[6] It was not supposed that in such matters papal judgements were infallible. Indeed, it was envisaged that a pope might fall into heresy or into serious and persistent sin, and in such cases the pope could be judged and deposed (Gratian, *Decretum*, dist. 40, c. 6; Tierney, 1980: 124–6). But a pope still in the papal office must be obeyed, apparently without any possibility of objection or resistance: the pope 'judges all and is judged by none' (cf. Hugh of St Victor, Tierney, 1980: 94–5). There was in fact a good deal of resistance but at the risk of excommunication or worse; perhaps the safest form of resistance was to accuse the pope of heresy, as Philip IV did Pope Boniface.

THE DEBATE ON THE POWER OF THE POPE

Toward the end of his life William of Ockham expressed the opinion that zeal for Christianity required that 'in these dangerous times' all the learned should investigate the basis and extent of papal power, because of the infinite evils that ignorance of it has brought about among Christians from ancient times (1998: 136). Ockham had been active in this investigation for some 20 years, and debate on the extent of papal power had already been in progress since the time of Boniface and earlier. In this chapter it is not possible to do more than sketch the contributions of a few writers. Five must suffice: two of them, namely Thomas Aquinas and Giles of Rome, extended papal power to temporal matters; three, namely John of Paris, Marsilius of Padua and William of Ockham, opposed this extension.

Thomas Aquinas

Thomas Aquinas gives two significantly different accounts of the relationship between the two powers, though in both accounts the secular power is subjected to the spiritual. In an early writing, *Scriptum super libros sententiarum*, he asks, 'When two authorities conflict, how should we decide which to obey?' He answers that if one authority originates totally from the other (as, he says, the authority of a bishop derives from the pope), greater obedience in all matters is due to the originating authority. If, however, both of the authorities in conflict originate from a higher authority, the higher authority will determine which of them takes precedence on which occasion. Spiritual and secular power, he says, both come from God, so we should obey the spiritual over the secular only in matters which God has specified, namely matters concerning the salvation of the soul; in civic matters we should obey the secular power – 'unless,' Thomas immediately adds, 'spiritual and secular power are joined in one person, as they are in the Pope, who by God's arrangement holds the apex of both spiritual and secular powers' (the relevant passage of the *Scriptum* is translated in Phelan and Eschmann, 1978: 106–7). This seriously restricts the application of the doctrine of *Duo sunt*: at the lower levels the spiritual and temporal powers are held by different individuals, but at the highest level they are both held by the same man.

In another writing of uncertain date, *De regno*,[7] Thomas applies Aristotle's teleological thinking to politics. A polity has an end, purpose or goal, which may be sought in a variety of ways, effectively or not, and it is a composite entity consisting of many individuals with their own individual purposes. For both reasons there is needed some directing or steering agency or government (*gubernatio* in Latin means literally 'steering', as of a ship) to guide the potentially conflicting individuals effectively to their common goal. The goal is in some way single – otherwise the polity will disintegrate. Every being is in some way one; a composite entity has a unity of order, i.e. of direction to a single end. In preserving its being, therefore, the steering agency has to preserve the polity in peace and unity by ordering it to a common goal. There is a hierarchy of goals, that is, there are intermediate ends which are also means to higher ends. A polity exists to secure its citizens' lives, but above living there is living well, i.e. virtuously, and above that there is living so as to attain the 'beatific vision' of God (the Christian heaven). If all these ordered ends were attainable simply by human effort, the one supreme directing agency would be concerned with them all; however, to attain the beatific vision requires 'grace', i.e. God's special help, which natural human activity cannot earn. God's Church is a human agency that God has established as a means to grace, especially through the sacraments. Hence there is a distinction between secular government using naturally available means to guide citizens to their final goal, and ecclesiastical government using supernatural means, the sacraments. This provides a theological rationale for the separation called for by *Duo sunt*: the distinction between the two powers is based upon a distinction between natural and supernatural means of attaining the goals of human existence. Secular government has the task of leading citizens toward the beatific vision, by way of the lower goals of securing the essentials of physical life and, above that, of virtuous living; but it cannot attain the highest goal, the beatific vision, because natural human means are not adequate. On this view also the secular power is subordinated to the spiritual. Secular rulers must be subject to the pope, 'for those to whom pertains the care of intermediate ends should be subject to him to whom pertains the care of the ultimate end' (Thomas Aquinas, 1978: 3–13, 58–67).[8]

Giles of Rome

In his *On Ecclesiastical Power* (1302), Giles of Rome[9] argues that all *dominium* (lordship), including ownership of property as well as governmental power or jurisdiction, belongs primarily to the Church, and in particular to the pope, though the 'busyness' (*sollicitudo*) of administering temporalities is allotted to the laity, so as to leave the clergy free for spiritual matters. To establish the primary lordship of the pope Giles gives many arguments. The following are the more significant.

(1) Whether bodily health is served by bodily goods does not depend on whether they are lawfully possessed, but spiritual health does depend upon whether bodily goods are lawfully possessed. Hence the bodily physician has no concern with rightful possession, and hence does not have lordship over his patient's bodily goods, but the spiritual physician does have. The spiritual physician has such power over temporal goods that he must be called their lord. 'For he who judges a thing is always lord of the thing judged' (Giles of Rome, 1986: 86, 87, 97–8).

(2) According to Augustine in *De civitate dei* IV.4 (1998: 147), without justice, kingdoms and empires are great bands of robbers; and in *De civitate dei* II.21 (1998: 80) Augustine says that there is no true justice except in the commonwealth whose founder and ruler is Christ. In *De civitate dei* XIX.21 (1998: 950–2) Augustine argues that the commonwealth of the Romans was not a true commonwealth because it did not attain true justice, since the Romans did not worship the true God.[10] Similarly, Giles of Rome maintains that non-Christians cannot justly have lordship: 'Since you are unjustly withdrawn from Christ your Lord, everything is justly withdrawn from your own

lordship' (1986: 69; cf. 1986: 92). As far as just and worthy possession is concerned, then, lordship is conferred by membership of the Church, which (Giles assumes) implies that the Church has pre-eminent lordship (1986: 65–95).

(3) The Church has power to excommunicate, but possessions are held by virtue of laws which rest upon pact, which rests upon the communion of men with one another. If the Church can cause a man to be excluded from the community of the faithful – and Giles supposes that there is no genuine community of men apart from the community of the faithful – then the Church can cause him to be deprived of the foundation upon which all legal transactions are grounded, and he will not be able to claim lordship over anything (1986: 98–102).

In the last part of his book Giles undertakes to answer objections. Christ says, 'Render to Caesar the things that are Caesar's and to God the things that are God's' (Matthew 22.21), implying that some things are Caesar's. Giles answers that just as God normally leaves things to take their own course under the 'common law' (i.e. the ordinary laws of physics), although he has power to intervene by miracle at any time, so the pope normally allows secular lords to act under the common laws, although he has the power to intervene directly at any time by virtue of his 'fullness of power'. A cause that can do directly whatever it can also do through secondary causes has 'fullness of power' (1986: 187–8). The pope has fullness of power in the sense that he can do directly anything that can be done by any agency within the Church (1986: 188); this includes secular government, because, as the arguments above have shown, outside the Church there can be no lordship.[11] However, just as God normally allows secondary causes to take their course and only occasionally intervenes directly (i.e. miraculously), so the pope normally leaves secular government to laymen (1986: 189). Thus, even if ultimate temporal authority belongs to the pope, a dualism of a sort is still possible: the pope may relate to secular government in the same way as in modern times a state (provincial or national) government relates to city government, normally leaving city affairs to the lower level of government, but being able to intervene with full constitutional right when it sees fit.

John of Paris

On Royal and Papal Power (1302) by John of Paris is also concerned with lordship (see: Rivière, 1926; Leclercq, 1942; John of Paris, 1971; Tierney, 1998). John denies that the pope is the supreme lord on earth in both spirituals and temporals. He rejects the argument that since the pope is Christ's vicar, and Christ is God, and God is lord of all, therefore the pope is lord of all (1971: 100). According to John, this argument breaks down twice. First, the pope is the vicar of Christ as man (not as God), and Christ as man was not lord of all. Second, even if Christ as man had been lord of all, Christ did not give all of his own powers to his vicar: in particular there is no evidence that he gave him universal *dominium* on earth (1971: 106–10, 115–16; William of Ockham, 1992: 66–7, makes the same reply). God is supreme lord in both spirituals and temporals, but on earth there is no individual who is God's vicar in both at once. The secular ruler is God's vicar in temporals, and the pope is Christ's vicar in spirituals.

John reasserts the long-standing distinction between the two senses of *dominium* that Giles had run together, namely ownership of property and jurisdiction; a ruler's jurisdiction in property disputes does not mean that he has superior ownership over his subjects' property (1971: 106; cf. Giles of Rome, 1986: 86, 'For he who judges a thing is always lord of the thing judged'). John argues that the pope has jurisdiction in spiritual matters but does not have ownership even of Church property, let alone of the property of laymen. Property is in the first instance acquired by individuals,[12] not by communities; a community acquires its property by donations from individuals, who make their gifts to the community, not to its officers as individuals, and the donors' intentions must be respected. Church property belongs to some religious community (a monastery, the diocese, the Church as a whole, etc.), and the head of such a community is only an administrator, not an owner. (These points were commonplace: see Leclercq, 1942: 134.) He ought not manage property negligently or corruptly, and if he does he can be deposed. In emergencies the pope may call on individuals and communities to supply resources to assist the common good (1971: 104), and the prince may do likewise (1971: 210). The power to do this does not constitute ownership of their subject's things.

As for *dominium* in the sense of jurisdiction, John argues (1) that among Christians the spiritual and temporal powers should be physically distinct, and (2) that the temporal power does not owe its existence to the spiritual power. On the first point, he says that among Christians the temporal and spiritual jurisdictions should be distinct *subiecto* (i.e. distinct in the persons in whom they are located), which would mean that the pope cannot be both spiritual and temporal ruler. This is the traditional tenet of *Duo sunt*, and John gives the traditional reasons, emphasizing the argument that the priest should be exclusively devoted to spiritual affairs (1971: 115–18; Hooker, 1989: 129–31, argues against the view that between Church and

commonwealth there must be a 'personal' separation, a separation 'in subsistence'). In pre-Christian times there were priests, or persons with priestly functions, who also had temporal power, but under Christianity priests are exclusively priests (1971: 200). (There are echoes here of the canon *Cum ad verum*, dist. 96, c. 6, and of canonist comment; see Tierney, 1980: 121–2.) His opponents accepted that *in respect of their exercise* the spiritual and temporal powers are distinct *subiecto*, but said that the pope 'possesses' and 'has the authority of' the temporal sword, which must be exercised on his direction. Against this John argues that it would have been a notable lack of wisdom on God's part to have given the pope power he was permanently debarred from exercising (1971: 123–6, 129).

On the second point, he says that the temporal power is not established by, or in any way caused by, the spiritual power; both come from God, but neither through the other. The spiritual is in some sense superior, but not as being the cause of the temporal power (1971: 93, 96, 192).

Thus there are separate spheres of jurisdiction, with prince superior to pope in temporal matters and pope to prince in spiritual matters. Both powers have been established by a higher power, God, who has appointed their limits, and the spiritual power is limited to spiritual matters (1971: 93). However, the two powers have some common concerns. The temporal power is not merely corporeal (1971: 182), but exists to further virtuous living as the way to eternal beatitude, so far as this can be done by natural means. At the same time, the spiritual power is concerned for the physical well-being, the survival at least, of the Christian community. Further, John accepts the principle stated in Gratian in a text from Isidore (see above), that sin should be physically punished in this world, which John expects to be done by the temporal power (1971: 143); he also holds that heretics should be compelled to return to the Church (1971: 204). Hence he does not advocate the modern 'wall of separation' but distinction and co-operation. Either power may on occasion intervene in the sphere of the other, but each power must use only its own appropriate means of action: this is the basis of the distinction between the two powers. The secular ruler can use only temporal penalties (e.g. seizure of goods, corporeal punishment), and the Church can use only spiritual penalties (e.g. excommunication, interdict).

Indirectly prince and pope may coerce one other. If a pope does wrong spiritually, correction is primarily the business of the cardinals; if a prince does wrong temporally, correction is primarily the business of his barons or peers. The first step in correction is advice and exhortation, but coercive measures may follow, and the other power may intervene (perhaps at the request of cardinals or barons). John distinguishes various cases. If a prince does wrong in spirituals, the pope can use spiritual penalties (e.g. excommunication of those who obey the prince) to influence the people to depose him. If a pope does wrong in spirituals the prince can use temporal penalties (e.g. sequestration of goods of those who obey him) to induce the pope to resign or to induce the people to depose him. (Note that John supposes that the people can depose a pope.) If the prince is delinquent in temporals the barons can call on the Church to support them by spiritual penalties (e.g. excommunication) against those who continue to obey the prince. If the pope is delinquent in temporals, the emperor can directly punish him (unless, as some say, he is exempt not only by privilege granted by the emperor but by divine law; John does not decide this question). In each of these cases pope and prince use only their respective kinds of penalties, spiritual and temporal (1971: 156–61).

The coercion and deposition of a pope was a topical matter, since Philip's response to Boniface's apparent claim to temporal power was to propose a General Council to depose him. John implicitly supported this. Gratian had said that a pope cannot be judged 'unless he is found straying from the faith', i.e. had become a heretic. To heresy commentators had added other serious sins (Tierney, 1980: 124–5). John adds age, illness, insanity, uselessness and abuse of Church property as justifying deposition (1971: 101, 241). But with Boniface heresy was the main issue. John asks, what if a pope were to introduce a 'new teaching' without proper discussion among the learned or a general council; for example, what if the pope were to teach the heresy that it is heresy to deny that the king of France is subject in temporals to the pope? John answers that, if possible, papal teaching should be given a traditional, orthodox meaning, but if the pope insists on a new and injurious meaning and the Church is in danger, then the prince should resist by force and the Church should move to depose the heretic pope (1971: 231–4). 'The prince is permitted to withstand the abuse of the spiritual sword as best he may, even by the use of the material sword' (1971: 212). In deposing a pope the Church can be represented by the College of Cardinals, though a General Council would be better (1971: 241–3, 250).

On Royal and Papal Power contains a section that lists and then refutes arguments for the temporal supremacy of the pope. John's list is very comprehensive, but we will look only at his discussion of some arguments used by Giles of Rome and Thomas Aquinas. One of Giles's recurrent themes is the superiority of the spiritual over the corporeal (1971: 133). John replies that it is not true that the royal power is corporeal and not spiritual and is in charge of bodies and not souls; its end is life according to virtue. Also, it is not true that every spiritual function as such has authority over every corporeal function as such: in a household the tutor does not appoint the physician, but both are appointed by the head of the household (1971: 182–3). Another of Giles's arguments was drawn from Augustine's *City of God*, to the effect that there cannot be a true republic except among Christians (1971: 135). John replies that natural moral virtue, including justice, can exist without supernatural faith, and that this is enough for true government, which is concerned with the good life so far as it can be lived by natural human power.[13]

John's disagreement with Thomas Aquinas is of particular interest. Many passages in John's book are taken almost verbatim from Thomas Aquinas,[14] and John has been regarded as a follower of Thomas. Yet he mounts an effective criticism against the argument Thomas used in *De regno* to support papal lordship over temporals, namely the argument from the subordination of ends – that 'those to whom pertains the care of intermediate ends should be subject to him to whom pertains the care of the ultimate end' (compare Thomas Aquinas, 1978: 62, with John of Paris, 1971: 134). John offers a number of points in reply. The higher art uses the lower only in relation to its own end. It does guide, but not always with authority: in a household the physician guides the pharmacist but cannot give authoritative directions or dismiss the pharmacist, since they are both under the authority of the householder, and similarly both pope and prince derive their authority from God.[15] The lower art may have something good or desirable in itself, and indeed life in accordance with naturally acquired virtue is something good in itself. Finally, the lower end may be related to the higher in more than one way (e.g. a tyrant's oppression may also lead people to God), so the higher art cannot uniquely direct the lower (1971: 184–6; the subordination of arts is discussed in several other places, 1971: 93, 182, 201).

Marsilius of Padua

Marsilius wrote his *Defensor pacis* (1324)[16] to counter a cause of strife that Aristotle had not included in his discussion of revolutions (*Politics*, V) because it arose long after his time, namely a 'certain perverted opinion' among Christians (Marsilius of Padua, 1980: 5). Marsilius is in no hurry to tell us what that revolutionary opinion is, but eventually it transpires that it is the doctrine that the pope has fullness of power (1980: 361–2). An explicit attack on this doctrine occupies II.xxiii–xxvi, after the ground has been well prepared. All coercive power comes from the people (the 'legislator') and is entrusted to a ruler who rules in accordance with the law established by the people or by a subordinate legislator authorized by the people (1980: 44–9, 61–3).[17] No community can have more than one supreme ruler, who must be the source of all coercive power in the community – otherwise strife will break out (1980: 80–6).[18] This is the first of the four main points of Marsilius's argument against papal fullness of power: unless the pope is the supreme ruler,[19] pope and clergy can have coercive power only if they derive it from the supreme ruler. The second point is theological: that Christ excluded the clergy from the exercise of coercive rulership (1980: 113–40). This rules out the possibility that the pope or any cleric might be the supreme ruler. The third main point is also theological, a rejection of the view of Isidore and most churchmen, that the ruler must punish sin. According to Marsilius God wills that divine law should be enforced by sanctions only in the next world to give every opportunity for repentance (1980: 164; the contrast between 'this world' and 'the next world' was later the basis of Locke's main argument in his *Letter of Toleration*). Marsilius does not advocate toleration: for secular ends the secular ruler may enforce religious uniformity, that is, he may enforce the divine law, but not the divine law as such (1980: 136, 175–9). So there is only one supreme ruler, not a member of the clergy, who does not enforce divine law as such and therefore does not coerce in any sense on behalf of the clergy. Fourth, Christ gave Peter no special authority among the apostles, and Peter never was in Rome (1980: 44–9).[20] The Roman bishop therefore has no special Christ-appointed role in shepherding the whole Church. From these four points it follows that the doctrine of papal fullness of power is false in all its senses; in particular, the claim that the pope has supreme coercive jurisdiction over all secular rulers is false, for the pope and the clergy have no coercive jurisdiction at all, direct or indirect. As for ownership of property, Marsilius sides with the Franciscans against Pope John XXII's thesis that no one can use consumable property without ownership, and argues that, in accordance with Christ's will, the pope and the clergy should all live in poverty like the Franciscans (1980: 183–4, 196–215; see Tierney, 1997: 108–18). On his view, then, the clergy should have no lordship at all, either in the sense of coercive jurisdiction or in the sense of ownership of property. In the management of the externals of Church life, Marsilius argues that the only source of coercive authority is the secular ruler (if he is a Christian), who decides how many churches and clergy there will be, distributes Church jurisdictions, makes or approves appointments, and enforces canon law (1980: 65–6, 254–67),

and only he can authorize excommunication (1980: 147–52). The only sources of doctrinal authority in the Church are the Bible and general councils: he argues that general councils are infallible (1980: 274–9). (William of Ockham, 1995: 207–19, opposed Marsilius on this point, and argued that no part of the Church is infallible; see also Kilcullen, 1991.) However, only the ruler can assemble a council, and its decisions can be enforced only by the secular ruler (1980: 287–98).

Marsilius does not deny the truth of Christianity, does not deny that Christ gave spiritual powers to the clergy (their 'essential' or 'inseparable' powers, in contrast to the 'non-essential'; 1980: 235–6, 239–40), and does not deny that the clergy are the expert judges and teachers of Christian doctrine. What he denies is that Christ gave the clergy any coercive power and that Christ gave the pope any special power not possessed by other priests. Marsilius does not advocate the separation of Church and state, but (once the people have become Christians) something more like subordination of Church to state; more exactly, he maintains that coercion in Church life is then exclusively the business of the secular ruler. Marsilius gives different accounts of the relationship between Christian communities and secular government before and after the conversion of the peoples (1980: 256–9, 263–4). Before conversion the Church managed the externals of Church life autonomously, but afterwards its affairs are regulated by 'the faithful human legislator which lacks a superior' or by the ruler authorized by the legislator (1980: 272–3). After conversion the community and the Church are one, the 'legislator' has become 'the faithful legislator' and the ruler authorized by the faithful legislator has become the source of all enforcement within the Church.[21]

William of Ockham

Ockham (see McGrade, 1974; Knysh, 1996) disagreed with Marsilius at many points, though he seems to have taken over from him the idea that the doctrine of fullness of power (or a certain version of it) was the root of much of the trouble in the Church. Ockham's earliest political writing was the *Work of Ninety Days* (*c.* 1332), in which he defends the Franciscan theory of voluntary poverty as a religious ideal against Pope John XXII's thesis that no one can justly consume without owning (William of Ockham, 2001). Part I of his *Dialogus* (*c.* 1334) discusses heresy and heretics, suggesting that to show that someone is a heretic it is not enough to show that what that person believes is heresy; it is necessary also to show that he or she believes it 'pertinaciously', and to show this it is necessary to enter into discussion to discover whether the person is ready to abandon the error when it is shown to be such. On the other hand, a pope who tries to impose a false doctrine on others is known to be pertinacious precisely from the fact that he is trying to impose false doctrine on others, and a pope who becomes a heretic automatically ceases to be pope. Thus ordinary Christians (or a pope arguing as a theologian and not purporting to exercise papal authority) can argue for a heresy in discussion as long as they make no attempt to impose it on others, whereas a pope who tries to impose a heresy ceases to be pope and loses all authority. This is an argument for freedom of discussion within the Church, though not for toleration in general (see McGrade, 1974: 47–77; McGrade, Kilcullen and Kempshall, 2001: 484–95).

In his *Contra benedictum* (*c*. 1335) Ockham began his preoccupation with the Marsilian theme of fullness of power, which he continued in other works written in the later part of his life. Ockham rejects two versions of the doctrine of fullness of power. He denies that the pope has power from Christ to do whatever is not contrary to divine or natural law: against this he argues that a pope must respect not only rights and liberties under natural law, but also rights and liberties existing under human law, including those conferred on rulers by the law of nations and the civil law and custom, and that he must refrain from imposing excessive burdens (1992: 23–4, 51–8).[22] He also rejects a weaker version of the doctrine of fullness of power, according to which the pope has all power necessary to secure the good government of the Christian people. Against this he maintains that securing good government in temporal matters is the concern of the laity, not of the clergy (1974: 70–1). However, there is some sense in which Ockham agrees that the pope has fullness of power: in spiritual matters (i.e. matters relating to eternal salvation and peculiar to the Christian religion) that are of necessity (not just useful), the pope regularly has full authority over believers (not unbelievers); in temporal matters he regularly has no authority, but on occasion, in a situation of necessity, the pope may do, even in temporal matters, whatever is necessary if it is not being done by whoever is normally responsible to do it (1992: 62–3; Kilcullen, 1999: 313–14). (Note the distinction between what is regularly or ordinarily true and what is true on occasion or extraordinarily: see Bayley, 1949.)

If Marsilius was the first exponent of the doctrine, later held by many others, notably Hobbes, that in any well-ordered community there must be a single locus of coercive power, Ockham was its first opponent. Ockham argues, as Locke would argue later, that if the community were subjected to one supreme judge in every case, then the supreme judge could do wrong with impunity. To prevent tyranny, it must on occasion be possible for the regularly supreme judge to be coerced by others. At the same time, it does no harm if there are some (for example pope and clergy, or cities or princes) who are regularly exempt from the jurisdiction of the supreme judge provided they can be coerced on occasion, and it does no harm if there are some who have coercive power that they have not received from the supreme judge – again, provided they can be coerced when they do wrong. To prevent tyranny some plurality of centres of power is needed, and how exactly those centres relate to one another does not matter, provided no one can do wrong with impunity. On various occasions, each of pope and prince may become subject to one another 'by reason of wrongdoing', and in this way the pope might even become subject to the jurisdiction of a non-Christian emperor.[23] An emperor coercing a pope for temporal wrongdoing would be exercising his ordinary power, whereas a pope coercing an emperor for temporal wrongdoing would be acting extraordinarily (William of Ockham, 1995: 310–31).

In his political writings Ockham makes much use of the theory of natural law,[24] which originated in ancient philosophy[25] and had been taken up again by medieval theologians and lawyers. The essential idea of the theory, as Thomas Aquinas and Ockham hold it, is that the human mind, reflecting on and analysing human experience, can 'see' the truth of various fundamental moral norms, which are thus 'self-evident', not in need of proof, and too fundamental to be capable of proof (Thomas Aquinas, *Summa*, 1–2, q. 91, a. 3, and q. 94, a. 2).[26] Ockham distinguishes several kinds of natural law (1995: 286–93), including natural laws 'on supposition': supposing certain contingent facts, natural reason sees intuitively that certain kinds of action are on that supposition morally right or wrong. Given the consequences of Original Sin, human communities have a natural right[27] to establish institutions of government and property; given the establishment of those institutions, individuals have a natural right to acquire property (or to live without property, relying on the generosity of those who have property); given that some thing has become some person's property, others have a natural duty not to use the thing without that person's permission; and so on. The Christian community's right to depose a heretic pope and choose a replacement is, for Ockham, such a natural right, in the same category as the right of any 'people' to depose a tyrant and establish a just regime.[28] 'Natural' rights belong to human beings as such, to pagans as well as to Christians; thus the powers of the pope and clergy are limited by lay rights that pre-exist Christianity

(1992: 51–8; not only natural rights but also rights under human positive law limit the pope's power).

There has been a tendency in Christian thought to say that after Adam's fall into sin, the human mind is too depraved to be capable of genuine moral insight; indeed, that since the Fall no human being can do anything but sin and can have no rights, without God's special grace.[29] Ockham, Thomas Aquinas and the medieval Church strongly rejected this opinion and attributed to 'fallen' human nature, even apart from grace, the ability to distinguish right from wrong, to possess rights, and to direct human action to ends that are legitimate (though without grace it is impossible to attain the very highest end of 'beatitude'). This optimistic view of the moral capacities of even unregenerate nature is at the root of Ockham's contention that non-Christians are capable of genuine 'lordship' in both senses, i.e. of governmental power and of property rights. Later theologians inspired by this conception of natural rights defended the property and governmental rights of the natives of America against European aggressors, some of whom argued that unregenerate savages could have no rights (see Muldoon, 1966; 1980). Luther and Calvin, despite their emphasis on the corruption of human nature by Original Sin, and despite their maxims *sola scriptura* and *sola fide*, still found a place for natural law (see McNeill, 1946). Hooker continued this natural law tradition, arguing (as Ockham and the conciliarists had done) that natural reason can be a source of principles even in regard to Church polity (see Kirby, 1999).

Natural law was, of course, a leading political idea in the seventeenth and eighteenth centuries. Hobbes's egoism was a radical departure, but Locke was clearly in the medieval tradition. Hume's 'invented' natural laws were close to Ockham's natural laws 'on supposition'. (On the continuity of the tradition see Buckle, 1991. For references to laws of nature being 'invented', see Hume, 1975: 520, 543.) There continued into the eighteenth century a common conception, derived from medieval writers, of natural reason, i.e. reason unaided by Christian revelation, as a source of fundamental ethical principles. According to Bayle, the natural light of reason must guide interpretation of revelation itself: if God seems to have commanded in the Bible anything clearly contrary to natural morality, then we must have misunderstood his command (1708: 43–57, Part 1, ch. 1).

CONCLUSION

On the central question of the relationship between spiritual and temporal power, Thomas Aquinas endorsed papal claims to supremacy, Giles maintained that all legitimate power on earth belongs primarily to the pope, and Marsilius that all legitimate coercive power belongs to the secular ruler. John of Paris argued for a restriction of the spiritual power to spiritual methods of action, and of the temporal power to temporal methods of action, but allowed each to use its appropriate methods to achieve indirectly some effects in the other's sphere. William of Ockham argued that the pope has fullness of power in spiritual matters and may on occasion intervene in temporal affairs, but only in situations of necessity when the laity will not or cannot act. James of Viterbo argued a position like that of Giles (see Dyson, 1995); so did Augustine of Ancona (see McGrade, Kilcullen and Kempshall, 2001: 418–83). John Wyclif continued Giles's argument that lordship cannot belong to unbelievers, or, as Wyclif argued, to anyone in sin (2001: 587–654). Several short works akin to John of Paris, *On Royal and Papal Power*, were produced at about the same time (see Dyson, 1999a; 1999b; on the circumstances of these writings see Saenger, 1981). There were other contributors to the debate whose works are not available in English (for these see Miethke, 2000a). No medieval writer, as far as I know, argued that secular power should as a matter of principle not be used to benefit true religion and discourage religious error. To my knowledge the first persuasive argument[30] for such a degree of separation of the two powers was Bayle's in the *Philosophical Commentary*.

It may seem remarkable that such active and free-ranging debate should have taken place during the middle ages on such a central topic of religious belief as the role of the religious head. Why did not piety and faith repress discussion and demand unquestioned deference to God's representative on earth? The theologians who debated the power of the pope sometimes felt called on to justify debating the topic; both John of Paris (1971: 229–35) and William of Ockham (1992: 5–12) offered justifications, but so did one of the strongest advocates of papal power, Augustine of Ancona (William of Ockham, 1992: 6, n. 10). Justification was easy enough, because it was already the established tradition in the medieval universities to allow, indeed encourage and require, students and academics to debate both sides of every question from the existence of God and the creation of the universe to the details of grammar. Even heretical opinions were supposed to be presented in university debate, though they were not supposed to win. Ockham also did not want heresy to win: in fact his 'political writings' are a campaign against papal heresy. But his discussion of 'heresy and heretics', making the point that one can maintain a heretical opinion without being a heretic as long as one remains open to correction and does not try to impose one's opinion on others, made it easier to argue freely.

Medieval academic debate was more formal than we are accustomed to, and the conventions required that a teacher state and explicitly answer a fair number of arguments, as strong as possible, for the thesis the teacher wanted to reject. This formal dialectical style is exemplified by most medieval writings on political theory.[31] The literature of Christianity, for example the works of Augustine, already embodied a tradition of theological questioning, a continuation of the philosophical and literary culture of the ancient world. In the medieval universities this was strongly reinforced by the study of logic and the practice of formal dialectical discussion, and by the example and precept of Aristotle:

> For those who wish to get clear of difficulties it is advantageous to discuss the difficulties well; for … it is not possible to untie a knot of which one does not know … Hence one should have surveyed all the difficulties beforehand … Further, he who has heard all the contending arguments, as if they were the parties to a case, must be in a better position to judge. (*Metaphysics*, III.1, 995 a23–b5)

Aristotle here follows Plato and Socrates. The medieval universities handed down to modern times the Socratic tradition of free discussion of important and sensitive topics. Although political theory was not an ordinary subject of instruction, the involvement of university people in writing on political questions for a university-educated readership carried into politics the academic practice of free argument on both sides of fundamental questions.

NOTES

1 On the conciliar movement see Tierney (1998), Black (1979), and Burns and Izbicki (1997). Part of the text of the decree of deposition, *Haec sancta*, is translated online at http://www.fordham.edu/halsall/source/constance1. html. On the reconciliation of this decree with later orthodoxy see Tierney (1998: xxii–xxvii). It would be a nice irony if the decree on which the succession of modern popes depends were heretical.

2 For a comprehensive account of the findings of recent scholarship, including work not in English, the reader should consult Miethke (2000a). My essay covers a selection of the topics and authors covered by Miethke's book, to which I refer readers for historical and bibliographical information and analysis of argument. They should also consult the introductions to the translations cited, and Dyson (2003). For treatment of my topic by the canon lawyers see Watt (1988) and Muldoon (1971). For a comprehensive history of medieval political thought see Burns (1988). On medieval ideas of the corporation see Tierney (1998; 1982). Certain areas of medieval political thought not previously much explored are investigated in Blythe (1992) and Kempshall (1999).

3 Gratian's *Decretum* (*c.* 1140) was an anthology of extracts from writings of popes, bishops and theologians of late antiquity and the earlier middle ages arranged and connected with commentary by Gratian himself. It became the textbook used in schools of canon law. For a specimen in translation see Thompson and Gordley (1993). In 1234 Pope Gregory IX issued a book of *Decretals*, which was also received as a textbook by the canon law schools. Other collections of decretals were added later.

4 During the middle ages documents were often referred to by their opening words.

5 *Per venerabilem*, Decretales 4.17.13 (Friedberg, 1879: II, 714f; translated Tierney, 1980: 138, emphasis added). Compare the document *Eger cui levia*, attributed (doubtfully) to Innocent IV (Tierney, 1980: 147).

6 'If the pope decided that the exercise of his *plenitudo potestatis* was called for, his judgement should be accepted unquestioningly and obeyed implicitly because he was the vicar of Christ' (Watt, 1965: 133).

7 For differing views on date and circumstances of composition, see Eschmann (1949) and Dondaine (1979).

8 Eschmann (1958: 178–9) points out the difference between the theory of the *Scriptum* and that of *De regno*. He seems to suspect the text of *De regno*. I would be inclined to suspect the authenticity of the final comment of the *Scriptum* ('nisi forte potestati spirituali etiam saecularis potestas coniungatur, sicut in papa …'), but according to Fr Bataillon of the Leonine edition it is well attested in the manuscript tradition.

9 On his life and other writings, see Lambertini (2001).

10 Augustine uses this as an *argumentum ad hominem*. He says elsewhere that 'according to a more practicable definition' the Romans had 'a commonwealth of a sort' (Augustine, 1998: 80; cf. 1998: 960). Augustine was not a 'black and white' thinker. Perhaps under the influence of neo-Platonism with its many-levelled universe, he was ready to recognize many levels of virtue, of peace, of happiness, etc., and corresponding degrees of perfection in commonwealths. The earthly state has a value of its own, and members of the two mystical cities belong to it intermingled.

11 The doctrine that only believers can have lordship was supported by some writers, including Pope Innocent IV in the (possibly inauthentic) decretal *Eger cui levia* (Tierney, 1980: 148), and opposed by others, including Innocent IV again (1980: 155) and William of Ockham (1992: 86–7). Later, Wyclif claimed that only those 'in grace' can have lordship, and that everything others do is sinful (McGrade, Kilcullen and Kempshall, 2001: 587ff). The Council of Constance condemned Wyclif's doctrines.

12 The underlying assumption seems to be that an original act of appropriation cannot be done by a corporation but only by an individual. John's remarks on original appropriation (1971: 103) have been interpreted by Janet Coleman (1983) as an anticipation of Locke, and she has since traced John's appropriation theory to Thomas Aquinas's account of individuation: 'Hence John presents a theory of human acquisition that is natural and which, in effect, is the means by which men not only survive, but are

individually who they are, as a consequence of their actions, while being essentially one species' (1991: 204–5). I do not find this interpretation persuasive. Aquinas does not hold that I became me by labouring to acquire other things. John does say that things are acquired 'by skill, labour and diligence', but he does not say *by virtue of what rule* this occurs – by natural law, or by convention and human law. From other passages (1971: 154, 225–6) it is clear that he meant by convention and human law. John accepted the theory common among medieval theologians that property is based not on natural law but on human conventions and laws made in view of the usefulness to humanity of the practice of appropriation, the theory later held by Hume and the Utilitarians (see Kilcullen, 2001b).

13 John says that the acquired moral virtues can be 'perfect' without the theological virtues (Christian faith, hope and supernatural love of God), and that the theological virtues perfect the acquired moral virtues only by an accidental perfection. This language is contrary to that used by Thomas Aquinas (cf. *Summa*, 2-2, q. 23, a. 7; see Griesbach, 1959: 41), but perhaps there is agreement on the relevant point. Thomas says: 'If the particular good [to which the moral virtue is ordered] is a true good, for example the preservation of the commonwealth or the like, it will indeed be a true virtue' (though not a 'simply true' virtue); that is, a moral virtue, e.g. political justice, may be truly such though the person lacks Christian faith or is in sin.

14 For John's sources see Leclercq (1942: 31, 35–6). Griesbach (1959), suggests that John often distorts the material he borrows from Thomas.

15 Here John uses Thomas's argument from the *Scriptum super libros sententiarum*, except for Thomas's final remark, 'unless spiritual and secular power are joined in one person, as they are in the Pope' – a union ruled out by Johnn's argument that the temporal and spiritual jurisdictions should be distinct *subiecto*.

16 On Marsilius see Gewirth (1951–6), Nederman (1995), and Dyson (2003).

17 Note that the legislator's 'will' is not arbitrary, but informed by discussion of what furthers the common good. That political power comes from the people was a commonplace at the time. It does not imply any commitment to democracy. Marsilius's references to 'the weightier part' (Marsilius of Padua, 1980: 45) are reminiscent of the canon lawyers' phrase *sanior pars* (Tierney, 1982: 23). When Marsilius mentions 'election' he means simply choice, and he is not imagining that the choices of different individuals will all be given equal weight. When in *Defensor minor* Marsilius says that the correction of rulers pertains 'preferably to the workmen or craftsmen' (1993: 6), he means in preference *to priests*.

18 To illustrate this point Marsilius asks what would happen if two mutually independent rulers called the same person to two different places at the same time – an allusion to the dilemma of the French clergy when Pope Boniface and King Philip called them to separate meetings at the same time. This problem of being called to two places at once is mentioned by William of Ockham (1995: 325) and also by Hooker (1989: 152). Since there seems to be nothing as durable in philosophy as an example, this example is perhaps an index of Marsilian influence – though since examples circulate easily, it may not indicate first-hand acquaintance.

19 This possibility is envisaged in William of Ockham's version of a Marsilian theory, *Octo quaestiones*, III.i, answered in III.xii (1995: 305–7, 326–7). As Ockham acknowledges, there is no philosophical reason why spiritual and temporal power cannot be held by the one person – the reason is theological (1974: 21–7).

20 It was generally agreed that Christ had given all the Apostles the same power of holy orders, but most held that Christ had in addition given Peter supreme jurisdiction, so as to distribute jurisdictions to the other apostles, bishops and priests. Marsilius denies that Christ gave Peter this supreme jurisdiction. (William of Ockham defends the common opinion against Marsilius in 3.1 *Dialogus* 3, 4; 1995: 219–29; 2002.) In the controversy over the pope's intervention in favour of the mendicants (Congar, 1961) it seems to have been agreed on all sides that the other apostles were Peter's equal in the power of holy orders, though Peter had superior jurisdiction (see Tierney, 1982: 60–5; cf. John of Paris, 1971: 119, 125, 147).

21 Hooker's (1989) theses in defence of Elizabeth's governorship of the Church are Marsilian – namely, that when the people are Christians there is no 'personal separation' between Church and state, and that the secular ruler is then (in some sense) the head of the Church, with sole authority to call church assemblies and a veto over their legislation, with authority to appoint bishops and other officials, with exemption from excommunication. The Marsilian themes are balanced by the notion of an ecclesiastical 'law of nations' (1989: 150–1, 156–7). But perhaps this is Marsilian too, since Hooker suggests that such law may need to be settled by a General Council (a 'peaceable and true consultation' of the Christian world; 1989: 157). Hooker's acquaintance with Marsilius may have been at second hand, and there were many other influences on his thinking (see Piaia, 1977: 213–18). Marsilius's book had been translated (with alterations) to support Henry VIII's ecclesiastical supremacy; see Lockwood (1991).

22 As Tierney points out (1997: 119–20), Ockham did not address the distinction between the subjective sense and other senses of 'right', but like many of his contemporaries he sometimes used the term in its subjective sense (the rights of a person), without confusion with other senses. John of Paris does not use the term, but he uses the concept (1971: 102, 213), also to say that the pope must respect the rights of lay people.

23 'And before an unbelieving emperor a case of faith could be treated … insofar as it could touch upon morals and detract from the commonwealth and bring injury upon the common good or upon any person' (William of Ockham, 1995: 330).

24 This has sometimes been regarded as an inconsistency on Ockham's part, in the belief that his non-political writings advance a 'divine command' theory of morality. For a rejection of this interpretation see Kilcullen (2001a).

25 It underlies Aristotle's discussion of slavery (*Politics*, I.6) and is explicit in the Roman law texts (e.g. Justinian, *Institutes*, 1.2.2: 'according to natural law, all men were originally born free'). Cicero gave clear expression to the idea of natural law, e.g. in *Republic*, III.xxii.33. [See further Chapter 23.]

26 The argument in the latter text is not meant to prove laws of nature, but to order them. For Ockham see the quotations in Kilcullen (2001a). (According to Ockham some natural laws are not fundamental but derived; 1995: 273–4.) The theory as held by Aquinas and Ockham is a species of what Sidgwick called 'intuitionism' (1930, Book 1, ch. 8, esp. 101).

27 That is, a right implied by natural law. The concept of a right is not found in the work of Thomas Aquinas, but it was common in the works of other medieval lawyers and theologians. On the history of the notion of natural rights, see Tierney (1997).

28 In reaction against conciliarist parallels between Church and political society, Cajetan emphasized that the Church is not a 'free community' with the power to erect its own government, but is subject to Christ's commands (see Burns, 1991; Burns and Izbicki, 1997). Ockham also recognized that Christ's commands had established a papal monarchy, but nevertheless held that the Christian community could vary the constitution of the Church at least for a time, arguing that necessity and utility may make exceptions even to Christ's commands (see 1995: 171–203, especially 181–90). The decree *Haec sancta* of the Council of Constance can be interpreted as relating to a situation of necessity.

29 See above, note 11. Hooker was opposed by Calvinists who, unlike Calvin himself, rejected the idea of natural law; see Kirby (1999). Karl Barth (1946) also rejected natural law on theological grounds.

30 The arguments of Locke's first *Letter of Toleration* were not strong enough to persuade those who needed persuading: it is not self-evident that the state exists to serve this-worldly purposes only. In his fourth letter Locke used arguments like Bayle's.

31 The medieval dialectical style survived into the seventeenth century in controversial writings not often read these days, for example in the controversies between Hobbes and Bramhall, Chillingworth and Knott, Locke and Proast, and in various works of Arnauld, Leibniz and Bayle.

REFERENCES

Augustine (1998) *The City of God against the Pagans*, ed. and trans. Robert W. Dyson. Cambridge: Cambridge University Press.

Barth, Karl (1946) 'No! Answer to Emil Brunner'. In *Natural Theology*, trans. P. Fraenkel. London: Bles.

Bayle, Pierre (1708) *A Philosophical Commentary on These Words of the Gospel, Luke xiv.23, 'Compel them to come in, that my house may be full'*. London: Darby.

Bayley, C. C. (1949) 'Pivotal concepts in the political philosophy of William of Ockham'. *Journal of the History of Ideas*, 10: 199–218.

Berman, Harold J. (1983) *Law and Revolution: The Formation of the Western Legal Tradition*. Cambridge, MA: Harvard University Press.

Black, Anthony (1979) *Council and Commune: The Conciliar Movement and the Fifteenth Century*. London: Burns and Oates.

Blythe, James (1992) *Ideal Government and the Mixed Constitution in the Middle Ages*. Princeton, NJ: Princeton University Press.

Buckle, Stephen (1991) *Natural Law and the Theory of Property: Grotius to Hume*. Oxford: Clarendon.

Burns, J. H., ed. (1988) *The Cambridge History of Medieval Political Thought c. 350–c. 1450*. Cambridge: Cambridge University Press.

Burns, J. H. (1991) 'Conciliarism, papalism, and power, 1511–1518'. In Diana Wood, ed., *The Church and Sovereignty c. 590–1918: Essays in Honour of Michael Wilks*. Oxford: Blackwell for the Ecclesiastical History Society.

Burns, J. H. and Thomas M. Izbicki, eds (1997) *Conciliarism and Papalism*. Cambridge: Cambridge University Press.

Coleman, Janet (1983) 'Medieval discussions of property: *Ratio* and *Dominium* according to John of Paris and Marsilius of Padua'. *History of Political Thought*, 4: 209–28.

Coleman, Janet (1991) 'The Dominican political theory of John of Paris in its context'. In Diana Wood, ed., *The Church and Sovereignty c. 590–1918*. Oxford: Blackwell, 187–223.

Congar, Yves (1961) 'Aspects ecclésiologiques de la querelle entre mendiants et séculiers dans la seconde moitié du XIIIe siècle et le début du XIVe'. *Archives d'histoire doctrinale et littéraire du moyen âge*, 36: 35–151.

Dondaine, F. (1979) 'Introductio' to *De regno ad regem Cypri*. In Thomas Aquinas, *Opera Omnia*, vol. 42, 421–44. Rome: Editori di San Tommaso.

Dupuy, Pierre, ed. (1655) *Histoire du différend d'entre le Pape Boniface VIII et Philippe le Bel Roy de France*. Paris.

Dyson, Robert W., trans. (1995) James of Viterbo, *On Christian Government*. Woodbridge: Boydell.

Dyson, Robert W., ed. and trans. (1999a) *Three Royalist Tracts, 1296–1302: Antequam essent clerici; Disputatio inter clericum et militem; Quaestio in utramque partem*. Bristol: Thoemmes.

Dyson, Robert W., ed. and trans. (1999b) *Quaestio de potestate papae (Rex pacificus): An Enquiry into the Power of the Pope*. Lewiston: Mellen.

Dyson, Robert W. (2003) *Nature, Morality and Politics, 400–1450: Normative Theories of Society and Government in Five Medieval Political Thinkers*. Lewiston: Mellen.

Eschmann, Ignatius (1949) 'Introduction and notes'. In Gerald Phelan and Ignatius Eschmann, trans., Thomas Aquinas, *On Kingship: To the King of Cyprus*. Toronto: Pontifical Institute of Medieval Studies, 1978.

Eschmann, Ignatius (1958) 'St Thomas Aquinas on the Two Powers'. *Mediaeval Studies*, 20: 177–205.

Friedberg, Aemilius (1879) *Corpus iuris canonici*. Leipzig: Tauchnitz.

Gewirth, Alan (1951–56) *Marsilius of Padua, the Defender of Peace*. New York: Columbia University Press.

Giles of Rome (1986) *On Ecclesiastical Power*, trans. Robert W. Dyson. Woodbridge: Boydell.

Goldast, Melchior, ed. (1611–14) *Monarchia sacri Romani imperii, sive tractatus de jurisdictione imperiali seu regia et pontificia seu sacerdotali*. Hanau, Frankfurt am Main.

Griesbach, Marc F. (1959) 'John of Paris as a representative of Thomistic political philosophy'. In Charles O'Neil, ed., *An Étienne Gilson Tribute*. Milwaukee: Marquette University Press, 33–50.

Hooker, Richard (1989) *Of the Laws of Ecclesiastical Polity*, ed. Arthur Stephen McGrade. Cambridge: Cambridge University Press.

Hume, David (1975) *Treatise of Human Nature*, ed. L. A. Selby-Bigge, rev. edn P. H. Nidditch. Oxford: Clarendon.

John of Paris (1971) *On Royal and Papal Power*, trans. John Watt. Toronto: Pontifical Institute of Medieval Studies.

Kempshall, Matthew (1999) *The Common Good in Late Medieval Political Thought*. Oxford: Oxford University Press.

Kilcullen, John (1991) 'Ockham and infallibility'. *The Journal of Religious History*, 16: 387–409.

Kilcullen, John (1999) 'The political writings'. In Paul Vincent Spade, ed., *The Cambridge Companion to Ockham*. Cambridge: Cambridge University Press.

Kilcullen, John (2001a) 'Natural law and will in Ockham'. In John Kilcullen and John Scott, trans., *William of Ockham, Work of Ninety Days*. Lewiston: Mellen, 851–82.

Kilcullen, John (2001b) 'The origin of property: Ockham, Grotius, Pufendorf and some others'. In John Kilcullen and John Scott, trans., *William of Ockham, Work of Ninety Days*. Lewiston: Mellen, 883–932.

Kirby, W. J. Torrance (1999) 'The theology of Richard Hooker in the context of the Magisterial Reformation.' Online at http://www.mun.ca/animus/1998vol3/kirby3.htm#N_1_. Also in his *The Theology of Richard Hooker in the Context of the Magisterial Reformation*. Princeton, NJ: Princeton Seminary Press.

Knysh, George (1996) *Political Ockhamism*. Winnipeg: WCU Council of Learned Societies.

Lambertini, Roberto (2000) *La povertà pensata: Evoluzione storica della definizione dell' identità minoritica da Bonaventura ad Ockham*. Modena: Mucchi.

Lambertini, Roberto (2001) 'Giles of Rome'. Online at http://plato.stanford.edu/entries/giles/.

Leclercq, Jean (1942) *Jean de Paris et l'ecclésiologie du XIIIe siècle*. Paris: Vrin.

Lockwood, Shelley (1991) 'Marsilius of Padua and the case for the Royal Ecclesiastical Supremacy'. *Transactions of the Royal Historical Society*, sixth series, 1: 89–119.

McGrade, Arthur Stephen (1974) *The Political Thought of William of Ockham*. Cambridge: Cambridge University Press.

McGrade, Arthur Stephen, John Kilcullen and Matthew Kempshall (2001) *The Cambridge Translations of Medieval Philosophical Texts. Vol. 2, Ethics and Political Philosophy*. Cambridge: Cambridge University Press.

McNeill, John (1946) 'Natural law in the teaching of the reformers'. *Journal of Religion*, 26: 168–82.

Marsilius of Padua (1980) *Defensor Pacis*, trans. Alan Gewirth. Toronto: University of Toronto Press.

Marsilius of Padua (1993) Marsiglio of Padua, *Defensor Minor and De Translatione Imperii*, trans. Cary Nederman. Cambridge: Cambridge University Press.

Miethke, Jürgen (1980) 'Marsilius und Ockham: Publikum und Leser ihrer politischen Schriften im späteren Mittelalter'. *Medioevo*, 6: 534–58.

Miethke, Jürgen (2000a) *De potestate papae: Die päpstliche Amtskompetenz im Widerstreit der politischen Theorie von Thomas von Aquin bis Wilhelm von Ockham*. Tübingen: Mohr Siebeck.

Miethke, Jürgen (2000b) 'Practical intentions of scholasticism: the example of political theory'. In William J. Courtenay and Jürgen Miethke, eds, *Universities and Schooling in Medieval Society*. Leiden: Brill.

Muldoon, James (1966) '*Extra ecclesiam non est imperium*: the canonists and the legitimacy of secular power'. *Studia Gratiana*, 9: 533–80. Reprinted in James Muldoon, *Canon Law, the Expansion of Europe, and World Order*. London: Variorum, 1998.

Muldoon, James (1971) 'Boniface VIII's forty years of experience in the law'. *The Jurist*, 31: 449–77.

Muldoon, James (1980) 'John Wyclif and the rights of the infidels: the *Requerimiento* re-examined'. *The Americas*, 36: 301–16. Reprinted in James Muldoon, *Canon Law, the Expansion of Europe, and World Order*. London: Variorum, 1998.

Nederman, Cary (1995) *Community and Consent: The Secular Political Theory of Marsiglio of Padua's Defensor Pacis*. Lanham, MD: Rowman and Littlefield.

Oakley, Francis (1962) 'On the road from Constance to 1688'. *Journal of British Studies*, 1:1–32. Reprinted in Francis Oakley, *Natural Law, Conciliarism and Consent in the Late Middle Ages*. London: Variorum, 1984.

Oakley, Francis (1969) 'Figgis, Constance and the divines of Paris'. *American Historical Review*, 75: 368–86. Reprinted in Francis Oakley, *Natural Law, Conciliarism and Consent in the Late Middle Ages*. London: Variorum, 1984.

Oakley, Francis (1996) '"Anxieties of influence": Skinner, Figgis, Conciliarism and early modern constitutionalism'. *Past and Present*, 151: 60–110. Reprinted in Francis Oakley, *Politics and Eternity: Studies in the History of Medieval and Early-Modern Political Thought*. Leiden: Brill, 1999.

Oui, G. (1979) 'Simon de Plumetot (1371–1443) et sa bibliothèque'. In *Miscellanea codicologica F. Masai dicata MCMLXXIX*, ed. P. Crockshaw. Gent: Scriptorium 81, 353–81.

Phelan, Gerald and Ignatius Eschmann, trans. (1978) Thomas Aquinas, *On Kingship: To the King of Cyprus*. Toronto: Pontifical Institute of Medieval Studies.

Piaia, Gregorio (1977) *Marsilio di Padova nella riforma e nella controriforma: Fortuna ed interpretazione*. Padua: Antenore.

Rivière, Jean (1925) 'In partem sollicitudinis … : évolution d'une formule pontificale'. *Revue des sciences religieuses*, 5: 210–31.

Rivière, Jean (1926) *Le problème de l'église et de l'état au temps de Philippe le Bel*. Louvain: Spicilegium sacrum Lovaniense.

Saenger, Paul (1981) 'John of Paris, principal author of the *Quaestio de potestate papae* (*Rex pacificus*)'. *Speculum*, 56: 41–55.

Sidgwick, Henry (1930) *The Methods of Ethics*, 7th edn. London: Macmillan.

Thomas Aquinas (1978) *On Kingship: To the King of Cyprus*, trans. Gerald Phelan and Ignatuis Eschmann, Toronto: Pontifical Institute of Medieval Studies.

Thompson, Augustine and James Gordley, trans. (1993) Gratian, *The Treatise on Laws: (Decretum DD. 1-20) with the Ordinary Gloss*. Washington: Catholic University of America Press.

Tierney, Brian (1980) *The Crisis of Church and State 1050–1300*. Englewood Cliffs, NJ: Prentice-Hall.

Tierney, Brian (1982) *Religion, Law and the Growth of Constitutional Thought, 1150–1650*. Cambridge: Cambridge University Press.

Tierney, Brian (1997) *The Idea of Natural Rights: Studies on Natural Rights, Natural Law and Church Law 1150–1625*. Atlanta: Scholars.

Tierney, Brian (1998) *Foundations of the Conciliar Theory: The Contributions of the Medieval Canonists from Gratian to the Great Schism*, enlarged edn. Leiden: Brill. Original edn 1955, Cambridge University Press.

Ullmann, Walter (1974) *A Short History of the Papacy in the Middle Ages*. London: Methuen.

Watt, John (1965) *The Theory of Papal Monarchy in the Thirteenth Century: The Contribution of the Canonists*. London: Burns and Oates.

Watt, John (1988) 'Spiritual and temporal powers'. In J. H. Burns, ed., *The Cambridge History of Medieval Political Thought c. 350–c. 1450*. Cambridge: Cambridge University Press, 367–423.

William of Ockham (1974) Guillelmi de Ockham, *Opera politica*, vol. 1, 2nd edn, ed. H. S. Offler. Manchester: Manchester University Press.

William of Ockham (1992) *A Short Discourse on the Tyrannical Government Usurped by Some Who Are Called Highest Pontiffs*, ed. Arthur Stephen McGrade, trans. John Kilcullen. Cambridge: Cambridge University Press.

William of Ockham (1995) *A Letter to the Friars Minor and Other Writings*, ed. Arthur Stephen McGrade, ed. and trans. John Kilcullen. Cambridge: Cambridge University Press.

William of Ockham (1998) *On The Power of Emperors and Popes: William of Ockham*, trans. Annabel S. Brett. Durham: Thoemmes.

William of Ockham (2001) *Work of Ninety Days*, trans. John Kilcullen and John Scott. Lewiston: Mellen.

William of Ockham (2002) *Dialogus*, eds and trans. John Kilcullen, George Knysh, Volker Leppin, Jan Ballweg and John Scott. Online at http://www.britac.ac.uk/pubs/dialogus/.

26

Political Theory of the Renaissance and Enlightenment

FREDERICK G. WHELAN

APPROACHES

The period covered by this chapter extends through three centuries from the time of Machiavelli to that of Burke. The unit as a whole may be thought of as the 'early modern' period of European history, post-medieval and yet premodern, if such developments as the Industrial Revolution and effectual movements towards mass democracy are taken to have brought about decisively 'modern' social and political change. One must immediately acknowledge the ambiguity of these categories, however. Recent research, for example, has set Machiavelli's thought in a tradition of Italian civic humanism and republicanism that extends back a century or more before the conventional medieval–modern dividing line of 1500, while it is now recognized that Thomistic or scholastic modes of political philosophy remained robust in some parts of Europe for a century or more after that date. Montesquieu and Burke, for that matter, stressed the medieval (feudal or Christian) origins of modern liberty and civil life in their own 'enlightened' theories. On the other hand, contemporary 'postmodern' theorists usually take the thought of the eighteenth-century Enlightenment to be distinctively modern, displaying the essential philosophical (or ideological) features that have allegedly been superseded or at least subjected to severe criticism by the postmodern sensibility [see further Chapter 4].

The conventional temporal units nevertheless remain useful for surveys such as this, as well as for pedagogical purposes. It remains, then, to note that the three-century period covered in this chapter is rich in subperiods of intellectual and political history that provide elements of the background for political thought: the Renaissance, the Reformation, the Counter-Reformation and religious conflicts, state-building and the emergence of absolutism, the evolution of the European state system and its enshrinement in the modern law of nations and in reason of state doctrine, the scientific revolution, economic modernization and the emergence of 'commercial society' or what was later to be termed 'capitalism', overseas explorations and empires, the civil conflicts of seventeenth-century England, the Enlightenment, the aristocratic resurgence of the eighteenth century, and the American and French Revolutions. All these episodes, along with the political theories in which they are reflected, have left their mark on the political heritage of the modern Western world.

The study of historical political theory continues to be healthily eclectic in methodology, just as it continues to be a discipline that, while primarily located (in the United States) in political science departments, has long enjoyed interdisciplinary contributions from scholars in philosophy, history, and law. An additional recent trend is for scholars in literary and cultural studies, using approaches developed in literary theory for the interpretation of texts, to scrutinize the works of classic political theorists.

The traditional enterprise of scholarly commentary on and interpretation of the works of classic authors continues, both because these works continue to provide the indispensable canon or common core of concepts for political studies, and because each generation inevitably rereads the classics, with novel results, from the vantage point of its own political and intellectual concerns. One may distinguish three approaches that, singly or in combination, guide the study of classic texts [see Chapter 2]. They may be analysed, without too much worry about anachronism, as containing the intrinsically valuable ideas of great thinkers, who can be compared with one another and mined for insights of timeless importance. They may be read in a strictly historical fashion, along the lines defended over the past few decades by Quentin Skinner (Tully, 1988), in relation to their political and intellectual context and the debates being carried on by their contemporaries. Or they may be viewed as key contributors to the development of modern political science or political philosophy and accordingly (re)read as precursors of or as valuable contributors to contemporary developments in these fields. A noteworthy recent publishing venture, the Cambridge Texts in the History of Political Thought, most of whose volumes are devoted to individual authors, testifies to the ongoing vitality of the field conceived in this manner, as do recent surveys of 'great political thinkers' (Hampsher-Monk, 1992).

A prominent alternative to studying the ideas of particular thinkers is to take the ideas or concepts themselves, or the languages in which they are expressed, as the objects of study. The method of studying the history of political thought that has been elaborated and self-consciously applied by Skinner (now often referred to as the 'Cambridge approach') aims to recover an author's intention in issuing (or 'uttering') a given text regarded as a linguistic act. The intention is inferred by examining not only the precise political circumstances in which the author was situated, but also how the author deployed and perhaps altered the received vocabularies and assumptions of political argumentation. The latter project requires comparison of the text in question with texts of the author's contemporaries and predecessors on similar themes. The result is a showing that the author should be understood as standing within a definite tradition of discourse or, more interestingly, as deviating from it or building on it in innovative ways and for his own political purposes (Skinner, 1978). Since this approach requires the reconstruction of what may variously be termed intellectual traditions, languages, language games, idioms, discourses, or paradigms as they have been employed by theorists in different periods and as they have evolved over time, it is a short step to taking the latter phenomena as the primary objects of investigation. This approach may diverge from Skinner's in so far as it downplays the role of any particular author and eschews any aim of recovering intentions. In viewing particular authors and texts as vehicles for the transmission of ideas as expressed in distinctive languages or, more interestingly, of entire discourses over time, this approach has affinities with some branches of contemporary literary theory and, as in the case of Skinner as well, has been influenced by the 'linguistic turn' in modern philosophy.

J. G. A. Pocock, a practitioner of this method, explains that it involves a shift from the 'history of political thought' to the 'history of discourse', making reference or alluding to methodologists such as Saussure, Gadamer, and Kuhn, as well as Skinner, who have influenced his work (1985: ch. 1; cf. Pocock, 1987). The objective, he argues, is 'the recovery of an author's language no less than of his intentions, toward treating him as inhabiting a universe of *langues* that give meaning to the *paroles* he performs in them'. It should be borne in mind that in any period a number of different discourses, with their conventional modes of understanding and judging, will exist simultaneously and interact in complex ways. Thus a given thinker may draw upon several distinct languages, shifting from one to the other or combining them in creative ways. The research of Pocock and various associates on the Anglophone eighteenth century, for example, has touched upon the distinctive discourses of republicanism, 'ancient constitutionalism', 'politeness', natural and common law jurisprudence, Anglicanism, and political economy, among others. This approach is exemplified by – and indicated in the very titles of – works such as Nicholas Phillipson and Quentin Skinner (1993) and Anthony Pagden (1987). Although a few individual writers are mentioned, the titles of the essays included in the latter volume indicate that the objects of study are such matters as the 'history of the word *politicus*', the 'language of Spanish Thomism', the 'language of Renaissance humanism', the languages of republicanism, and the 'language of sociability and commerce', among others. Well-known or canonical figures such as More, Harrington, and Rousseau are treated not as solitary theoretical geniuses but as exemplars of traditions. Under close historical scrutiny, it may be said, no idea is entirely new and no one's body of thought as original as it may seem at a distance.

It is important, however, not to lose sight of the fact that discourses in political theory, like other cultural artefacts, change, incrementally or sometimes dramatically, and the contributions of creative figures to this process should not be underestimated. Closely related to the study of discourses as such, therefore, are investigations into 'conceptual change' or 'innovation', the study of which Terence Ball terms 'critical conceptual history' (Ball, 1988; Ball and Pocock, 1988; and Ball, Farr and Hanson, 1989). All these approaches to studying political thought, however, remain deeply historical. Political theorists who are not primarily historians can certainly learn much from the applications of these methods, while not being committed to them as the exclusive manner of reading historical texts. Certainly the classic texts continue to invite interpretation and appropriation in ways that reflect timeless or contemporary concerns of political theory (and contemporary political life) – which is, of course, why they are considered 'classics'.

MACHIAVELLI AND HIS TIMES

The most prominent interpretation of Machiavelli's political theory in recent decades, that associated especially with the work of Skinner and Pocock (1975), has situated it in the civic humanist tradition of Florence and Renaissance Italy more generally and has focused on its republican themes. Machiavelli's *Discourses*, his debt to classical theory, his commitments as a citizen, and his experience of the crises that overtook republican regimes in Italy (except in Venice) have been emphasized to the near exclusion of Machiavelli's traditional reputation (Bock, Skinner and Viroli, 1990). However, a recent study largely in this vein also recognizes Machiavelli's practice of the anti-classical and more cynical 'art of the state', a precursor of reason of state teaching (Viroli, 1998). The study of Machiavelli in his historical context requires access to texts of his contemporaries for comparison. A noteworthy contribution here is a new English edition of a work by Guicciardini that contains the first mention of 'reason of state' (Brown, 1994).

The more venerable view of Machiavelli as a political realist and an advocate of amoral power politics was reasserted several decades ago by Leo Strauss, who regarded Machiavelli as a key founder of modernity and its problems [see further Chapter 3]. As such, Machiavelli was shown to have repudiated key elements of the classical and Biblical traditions (including natural law), distorting classic texts for his purposes, sometimes by esoteric methods, in the process. This reading has been continued, most notably by Harvey C. Mansfield, who has examined Machiavelli's contributions to the modern political science of executive power (Mansfield, 1993) and what is presented as his deliberate and pervasive, if disguised, assault on Christianity and its political teachings (Mansfield, 1996). Mansfield and his associates have also provided accurate translations of all three of Machiavelli's major political works, thus making the *Florentine Histories* available to students as well as *The Prince* and the *Discourses*.

Two recent studies that fall in neither of these opposing camps are Fischer (1997), who offers a valuable analysis of Machiavelli's psychology, and Coby (1999), who examines Machiavelli's treatment of ancient Rome. These studies, along with the interpretive controversies indicated above, suggest that Machiavelli remains a challenging and ambiguous figure.

THE LATER RENAISSANCE

The period between Machiavelli and Hobbes produced no single political theorist of their stature and therefore has been comparatively neglected by students of political thought. Montaigne has been invoked appreciatively by Judith N. Shklar (1984) as an inspiration for her distinctive approach to liberalism, but she grants that Montaigne himself was neither a liberal nor primarily a political thinker. Montaigne was, however, an important contributor to the sixteenth-century revivals of stoicism and scepticism and to the sensibility that supported both subjective individualism and religious toleration, and thus to a rich literary culture in which many political themes can be traced. Bodin, the author of a major political work of acknowledged importance for the emergent conception of sovereignty, seems to have attracted few Anglophone specialists other than Julian H. Franklin, whose earlier research is continued in Franklin (1991).

Francis Bacon is another important figure from this period who has attracted a steady stream of interest but has never quite been accepted into the first rank of political theorists. Traditionally, work on Bacon's political theory related this to his extensive writings promoting the advancement of science and focused on *The New Atlantis* as an ambiguous prophecy of modern society in which science provided the political authorities with technologies of control as a facet of power more broadly (Faulkner, 1993). More recent scholarship has explored Bacon's debts to civic humanist themes and to the discourse, prevalent in his lifetime, of reason of state (Peltonen, 1996). Bacon's long career as a royalist statesman close to the centre of power in England undoubtedly shaped the practical, even openly Machiavellian, orientation of his political writings. Bacon's insights into the machinations of courtly politics and his concern with the sources of the 'greatness' or power of the state relative to its rivals reflect the diplomatic intrigues and growing absolutism of the period.

An important theme in this period was the rise of the reason of state discourse that has been studied recently by Richard Tuck (1993) and Maurizo Viroli (1992). This research involves, in effect, a reconsideration of material that was last treated by Meinecke in his *Die Idee der Staatsrason* of 1924.

Reason of state has no single definitive text but was propounded in a number of influential writings, mainly by Italians and Spaniards associated with the Habsburg Empire in the sixteenth century and French writers associated with Richelieu in the seventeenth. Bacon, as mentioned above, may count as an English adherent. Reason of state refers both to a theory about politics and the state and to a practical orientation that became increasingly common and explicit among statesmen in the service of the emergent monarchies of the period. It focused on what Viroli identifies as the 'art of the state', which displaced the older emphasis on 'civic life' and participatory 'politics' that were upheld in the older civic humanist tradition as republican life gave way to absolutism in most European countries. The 'art of the state' included practical doctrines regarding the strengthening of the central government, administration, and economic and military resources of the state, as well as strategies for advancing the state's well-being in what was coming to be seen as a permanent international system of competing states. Its central analytic concept for understanding politics was interest, as its basic value or objective was the state's interest. As a derivative of Machiavellianism (although deliberately formulated so as to be compatible with Christianity), reason of state upheld a double standard with respect to the problems of political morality; that is, statesmen or state officials, by virtue of their role or office, were permitted (or required), by special 'reasons', to act in ways that violated ordinary moral principles when doing so was necessary for the good of the state. More than just a chapter in the intellectual and political history of Europe, reason of state is thus an important source for ideas of continuing interest in political realism and the practical ethics of real-world politics.

Another important (and understudied) current in the political thought and culture of the late sixteenth and early seventeenth centuries is Tacitism. The earlier 'civic' humanism of the Renaissance was dominated by Cicero, who supplied arguments and rhetoric in praise of the virtues of a good ruler, the civic virtues of good citizens, and a life dedicated to the service of one's state or republic. Ciceronian moralism was partially displaced, or supplemented, later in the sixteenth century by the influence of another classical model, the Roman historian Tacitus, who was best known for detailing the unscrupulous high politics and tyranny of the early Roman Empire. Tacitus could be viewed as teaching the arts of absolutist rule (*arcana imperii*, in his famous phrase), along with all the stratagems and intrigues of political manoeuvre in an absolutist court, increasingly the dominant setting for affairs of state in early modern Europe; or alternatively he could be read as warning against these methods by exposing them. Either way, Tacitism implied a politics of interest, conflict, and deception as the standard modes of operating, a view that fitted the mood of moral scepticism and political cynicism in the wake of the religious wars, as well as the evident permanence of conflict in the emergent European international system. The assumptions and teachings associated with Tacitism resembled those of both Machiavellianism (as usually understood) and reason of state; all three of these traditions may thus be said to have reinforced one another in promoting an attitude of political realism in the writers of this period and beyond (Burke, 1991).

This period, finally, is of course that of the Reformation and its aftermath of religious-political conflict in much of Europe for the following century and a half. The political writings of Luther and Calvin do not seem to have retained the place they once had in the canon of political theory, although scholarly interest in the political aspects of the Reformation of course continues (Oakley, 1991; Kingdon, 1991). This may be due in part to a decline in confidence in the theses, once so prominent in Protestant historiography, regarding the decisive contributions of early Protestantism to both capitalism and liberal democracy – though these claims may be due for re-examination. It may also reflect an extension of attention to a wider array of figures in varying national contexts; the Cambridge Texts series, for example, has made available works not only of Luther and Calvin, but the 'Radical Reformation', the Dutch Revolt, Knox, Baxter, and, for the Counter-Reformation, Bossuet, as well. One theme of continuing interest is the religious sources, in contexts where religious dissidents were able to assert themselves, of resistance theory and, by extension, theories maintaining the limited authority and putatively contractual basis of a legitimate state. Traditionally, this theme was associated mainly with French, Dutch, English, and Scottish Calvinists. In earlier work that continues to be decisive, Skinner drew attention to Catholic versions of resistance theory rooted in continuing traditions of scholastic philosophy. Similarly, sixteenth-century Anglican political thought, as reflected in the Aristotelianism of Hooker, like other variants of Protestant Aristotelianism, seems not to have attracted a major new study in the period covered in this survey.

HOBBES

Hobbes continues to be a major presence in political theory, both historically and analytically. Important trends in contemporary social science and political philosophy acknowledge Hobbes as an intellectual precursor and sometimes even a figure whose work can be profitably reassessed and systematized to bring out its contributions to contemporary research. These include most notably the revival of interest in the logic of social contract theories (Hampton, 1986; Krauss, 1993) and the development of rational choice or game theory (Kavka, 1986). Such contemporary uses of Hobbes take him to have been a founder of economistic approaches to political theory through his postulation of a strict form of rational egoism in combination with methodological individualism. Although passages in *Leviathan* can clearly be cited to support this interpretation, it relies on a process of abstraction that falls short of a full appreciation of Hobbes's social and psychological thought in relation to the culture of his time (Holmes, 1990).

A principal contribution to Hobbes scholarship in the past decade (Skinner, 1996) presents an approach and conclusions that are strikingly at variance with efforts to recruit Hobbes to contemporary issues. Skinner attempts to situate Hobbes's aspiration to found a new 'civil science' or political theory, always a central concern of his, in the complex intellectual context of its time. According to Skinner, Hobbes stood at the juncture of two major cultural forces, the continuing, classically inspired humanism of the Renaissance, with its attention to the uses of rhetoric in moral discourse, and the increasingly influential methods and culture, generally anti-classical, of the natural scientists, who held that scientific demonstration compelled intellectual assent without recourse to persuasive techniques. Hobbes, who sought to create a novel 'science' of the state in a modern sense, rejected the humanist legacy (with which he was of course fully conversant) in his earlier political works, the *Elements* and *De Cive*. In *Leviathan*, however, a work whose rhetorical qualities are readily apparent, as others have noticed, he returned to a mixed position in which eloquence is recognized as indispensable to the persuasive enterprises of political life. This study brings out previously underestimated links between Hobbes's thought and that of the previous century, thus making Hobbes a less isolated intellectual figure than he has sometimes appeared. At the same time, his close affinity to the scientific revolution is reaffirmed, although with qualifications. In this work Skinner reaffirms his well-known method of studying political texts, one that regards them as linguistic actions performed within a determinate historical setting: 'The essence of my method consists in trying to place such texts within such contexts as enable us in turn to identify what their authors were *doing* in writing them' (1996: 7). Not surprisingly, this book has revived debates and controversies about the method and its success when applied to Hobbes (Goodhart, 2000).

Several other recent studies of Hobbes may be mentioned. The unresolved issues of Hobbes's religious belief and the religious basis of his political theory, especially his account of obligation, is addressed by Martinich (1992), which examines Hobbes's theology at face value. In contrast to Skinner, Flathman (1993: xxi) sets out to 'wrench [Hobbes] out of his context' and into ours, finding in his theory a programme of self-creative individuality that informs Flathman's own conception of a highly voluntarist or 'willful' form of liberalism. A valuable collection of essays (Dietz, 1990) comprises a wide range of recent scholarly interests in Hobbes, both historical and contemporary.

THE REPUBLICAN TRADITION

Thanks in large part to earlier work by Pocock, it is now recognized that a tradition or discourse of republicanism subsisted as an important current in early modern Europe and America alongside the previously more familiar liberal tradition with its constituent elements and precursors. Indeed, republican thought, a derivative of civic humanism extending back to the Renaissance, was arguably a more self-conscious phenomenon, and less purely a construction (however useful) of scholars, than 'liberalism', a term that is anachronistic prior to the nineteenth century. Pocock emphasized the role of Machiavelli in transmitting republican ideals from the ancient world to his own, and the role of Harrington in transmitting this body of political analysis and values from Machiavelli to mid-seventeenth-century England and beyond. More recent work has found evidence of civic humanism in pre-Civil War England (Peltonen, 1995). This republicanism is described as 'classical' because it drew on ancient political theory and relied on ancient models, especially an idealized picture of the Roman republic. A central theme, acccordingly, was a concern with the civic virtue or public-spiritedness of self-governing citizens and its constant susceptibility to various corrupting influences. Classical republicanism also emphasized the importance of a balanced constitution, the independent-mindedness of citizens sustained by widespread landed property-holding, and a martial capacity that would enable arms-bearing citizens to resist tyranny as well as external enemies.

So conceived, classical republicanism may have accorded with the political aims and self-conception of the parliamentary gentry in the era of the English interregnum. As an essentially anti-modern doctrine, however, deeply distrustful of commerce and finance as factors that would undermine the landed interest and corrupt both virtue and the constitutional balance, it came to seem increasingly archaic by the eighteenth century. In England it survived as the outlook of an ongoing but marginal 'commonwealth' tradition and of the 'country' opposition to the dominant Whig oligarchy, with its ties to the modern economic sector. In France it was praised (though not embraced) by Montesquieu and asserted powerfully by Rousseau in conjunction with his attacks on the modern world. In eighteenth-century Britain, however, republicanism seems to have assumed a more modern form that coexisted with, perhaps gradually displacing, the classical version. Modern republicanism had to accommodate both a society marked by the increasing pursuit of wealth through commerce and a world of power politics and imperial aspirations among states that relied on professional armies rather than old-fashioned civic militias. Hopes for civic virtue seemed misplaced in this context, where the interests (and self-interest) of both individuals and states predominated, but the possibility of balanced constitutional government and the rule of law could be reasserted, as by Hume, both drawing on and checking the competition of interests. Recent studies of Harrington himself have downplayed the role of civic virtue, and emphasized more the role of institutional design, in his thought (Wootton, 1994; Worden, 1994), and republicanism in this post-classical form is arguably that most often found among the American founders (Rahe, 1992). Such 'modern' republicanism merges with 'classical' (i.e. early modern) liberalism, to which it adds confidence regarding people's capacity for self-government – though in representative rather than direct fashion.

Republicanism, like other themes and writers in the period covered by this chapter, has been studied not only as a historical phenomenon but as a rich source of contributions to contemporary political philosophy and public debates [see further Chapter 13]. Pettit (1997) analyses the 'republican' conception of liberty as 'non-domination' or freedom from arbitrary power, with numerous historical references. It may be questioned, however, whether republicanism so conceived is adequately distinguished from liberalism, especially when Locke and the *Federalist* authors are located in the former camp. It is not simply that historical authors have sometimes drawn upon and mingled two or more different discourses, but that 'republicanism' and 'liberalism' as plausible organizing constructs or concepts of political philosophy appear to overlap considerably, particularly if the former is meant to embrace modern as well as 'classical' forms of the doctrine. Thomas L. Pangle (1988) likewise points to Locke's influence on the republicanism of the American founding, but his Straussian framework accentuates the important differences between modern and classical republicanism [see further Chapter 3].

NATURAL JURISPRUDENCE

Another major tradition of thought in the seventeenth and eighteenth centuries was natural law, which was often pursued (outside England) in close connection with Roman or civil law jurisprudence. The depth of the rupture between modern and ancient or medieval systems of natural law has long been a matter of dispute. The emphasis in modern versions on individual rights draws on the Roman law of property and contract, but in the modern context this theme seems to be associated with distinctively modern forms of individualism and thus to constitute one of the strands that contributed (via Locke, for example) to the emergence of liberalism. The centrality of the concept of rights in jurisprudence also seems to mark a clear differentiation between this tradition and that of civic humanism or republicanism, with their focus on virtue and the public good, although these discourses were sometimes combined, for example in some eighteenth-century Scottish thinkers. Civil law also provided the materials for the modern theory of state sovereignty in seventeenth-century thinkers like Hobbes, to which corresponded what has been termed the 'neo-Roman' understanding of the civil liberty of the subject of the modern state (Skinner, 1998).

The most important figures in seventeenth-century natural jurisprudence in Protestant Europe were Grotius and Pufendorf, who have been neglected in Anglophone scholarship. Two new editions of some of his writings suggest that this situation may be changing at least with respect to Pufendorf (Tully, 1991; Carr, 1994; also Tuck, 1991). Pufendorf's theory responded to what he viewed as the excessive egoism of Hobbes; his own understanding of individualism and sociability was influential in later doctrines of property and the evolution of society (Hont, 1987). Haakonssen (1996) offers a survey of the (largely Protestant) tradition of modern natural law and explores its impact on the Scottish Enlightenment, while Hochstrasser (2000) concentrates more intensively on the German tradition. In Catholic Europe, on the other hand, a more explicitly Aristotelian or Thomist form of natural law survived into the modern period. A particularly interesting chapter in the history of early modern political thought is the application, in Spain, of this neoscholastic jurisprudence to questions arising from the Spanish conquests in America – the justifiability of the empire and the status and treatment of the Indians. The most important figure in this setting is Vitoria, whose writings are accessible in a new edition (Pagden and Lawrence, 1991).

Natural jurisprudence, finally, as enunciated by Vitoria, Grotius, Pufendorf and others, both

Protestant and Catholic, formed the basis for the early development of the law of nations. The need for agreement on principles of international law reflected the emergence of the modern European state system, which was generally recognized by 1648 and which rested, along with modern diplomatic practice, on the notion of formally equal and independent sovereign states. This conception was formally enshrined in the work of Vattel, the principal eighteenth-century exponent of the law of nations, whose doctrine indicates the complementarity in Enlightenment thought of liberal principles (internally) and the right of the sovereign state (externally) to pursue its interests as it sees fit (Whelan, 1999).

VARIETIES OF ENLIGHTENMENT

Use of 'the Enlightenment' as a term to cover much of the liberal, progressive, or revolutionary thought of the eighteenth century continues to be inescapable, even though it is now recognized that thinkers considered to be 'or who understood themselves to be' 'enlightened' did not monopolize the thought of the period. Moreover, sweeping criticisms of the Enlightenment go back to the succeeding Romantic period or indeed back to the Enlightenment itself in thinkers as diverse as Rousseau and Burke. For a generation after World War II the liberal aspects of eighteenth-century thought enjoyed an enthusiastic revival, although misgivings about the 'Enlightenment project' that had been expressed earlier continued to be pursued by scholars of the Frankfurt School. Recent years have seen a renewal of criticisms, some new and some amounting to variations on older themes. Conservatives deplore the Enlightenment's overconfident utopianism or reformism, communitarians its individualism, multiculturalists its universalism, feminists its patriarchalism, Foucauldians and critical theorists its legacy of technologies of social control and manipulation, postcolonial theorists its endorsement of Eurocentrism and imperialism, and postmodernists its earnest embrace of foundationalism (e.g. MacIntyre, 1984; 1988; Rorty, 1989; Gray, 1995). To actual scholars of the period, however, it seems that the very concept of 'the Enlightenment', and especially the notion of a unitary 'Enlightenment project', have often been constructed by the critics and bear little relation to what is found in the texts of the period (Schmidt, 2000). Certainly the moral and political theories of the Enlightenment are far more complex and diverse than the criticisms imply, with such key figures as Montesquieu, Rousseau, and Hume scarcely fitting such stereotypes as 'rationalism' or disregard of history and context.

Nevertheless, each age rewrites history from its own perspective, including the history of political thought, and new questions have and will continue to provoke new research into what will doubtless continue to be referred to by many, if sometimes obscurely, as the Enlightenment.

A noteworthy feature of recent Anglophone political philosophy has been a relative decline in the stature accorded to Locke, for two unrelated reasons. The increased attention to the republican tradition has involved a downgrading of the place of Lockean 'liberalism' in eighteenth-century thought; concurrently, the revitalization of liberal philosophy has brought with it an increase in attention to Kant as the key figure among the classical liberal antecedents of contemporary doctrines. The latter development reflects a general acceptance of Rawls's claim that Kantianism furnishes the essential philosophical basis for his liberal theory of justice and, by extension, an assumption that Kant is decisive for the entire liberal tradition. Closer attention to Locke, however, might reveal substantive similarities, in the relevant respects, between these two major figures, standing as they do towards the beginning and end of the eighteenth century. Locke as well as Kant grounds his political theory in an objective moral law, knowable by the practical reason of autonomous individuals conceived as responsible moral agents, that prescribes equality, equal liberty, and the reciprocity of rights and duties properly understood. In any event, neither the Kantian nor the republican turn in political philosophy has discouraged significant ongoing research into the political thought of Locke.

James Tully (1993) offers a methodologically mixed set of studies of Locke. As a historian in the Cambridge tradition he seeks to understand Locke in the 'discursive and practical contexts' in which he wrote and criticizes projections of more modern frames of reference (such as capitalism) back onto Locke's accounts of property and citizenship – though Locke is credited with a theory of 'popular sovereignty' that was radical for its time. At the same time Tully maintains that an enhanced historical understanding of a theory as influential as Locke's can illuminate such contemporary issues as aboriginal rights. Expanding on this latter theme, Barbara Arneil (1996) interprets the *Two Treatises*, and especially Locke's theory of property, as providing a justification of the dispossession of the Amerindians and a defence of English colonization, an enterprise in which Locke was involved. A non-historical approach to the texts is embodied in John A. Simmons (1992), who examines Locke's theory of rights in light of recent philosophical analysis of rights, obligations, property, punishment, and related matters. A political concern with contemporary rights controversies animates Kirstie M. McClure's inquiry into the 'problematic of judgement' (1996: 8) and what is seen as the premodern world view that underlies Locke's notion of consent to authority. The unmistakable differences in style, method, and research questions in this small sampling of recent books indicate something of the diversity of approaches to the acquisition of political understanding, to all of which the study of a historical theorist like Locke may contribute.

Of the handful of indisputably major Enlightenment figures, Montesquieu has attracted less attention than others from political theorists, at least in the English-speaking world, evidently because his digressive, descriptive, and sometimes aphoristic style does not readily yield the elements of a clear normative theory. The complexity or 'non-linear' composition of the comparative analysis of regimes in *The Spirit of the Laws* is the point of departure for Anne M. Cohler (1988), who also considers the affinity between Montesquieu's thought and that of the *Federalist Papers* and Tocqueville. A very different approach (Macfarlane, 2000) looks to Montesquieu and others for clues about the sources of the great transformations of 'modernity' that took hold in eighteenth-century Europe.

The complexity of Rousseau's thought, reflecting his own passionate and troubled personality, has long attracted astonishingly diverse interpreters and continues to do so (Gourevitch, 1998). Scholars who turn to Rousseau do so, it seems, less in a strictly historical spirit (in the Skinnerian mode) than in search of anticipations or the inspiration of any number of contemporary concerns – problems of the self, authenticity, alienation, community, egalitarianism, feminism, and other critical (and postmodern) inquiries. Conceding Rousseau's complexity, as well as his great and variegated impact on modern sensibilities, Arthur M. Melzer (1990) attempts to explicate his philosophy as a systematic whole. Mira Morgenstern (1996) is a recent addition to a series of studies of Rousseau's controversial views on women and gender issues. A somewhat more historical study, but one that is germane to the problem of the 'Enlightenment project' mentioned above, treats Rousseau in relation to the *philosophes* and sees in him the Enlightenment's capacity for self-criticism (Hulliung, 1994). Attention to the *philosophes*, as to the venerable question of their responsibility for the French Revolution, has not been prominent in Anglophone scholarship, but a recent study of Helvetius may be cited as an exception (Wootton, 2000).

As mentioned above, research into Kant's political thought, scarce a generation ago, has enjoyed a resurgence. This is true despite the fact that its study, like that of other major philosophers who wrote on politics, presupposes mastery of a formidable system of thought. Kant's essentially liberal theory of 'right' or law is thoroughly integrated with his theory of 'pure practical reason', or ethics, with its conception of self-legislated principles of action. His theory of the gradual realization of a regime of individual freedom within a constitutional state is associated with a teleological philosophy of history, in which progress is conceived as the collective development or emancipation of the rational and moral capacity of humanity (for an overview see Kersting, 1992). These themes comprise what is often taken today to be central to the Enlightenment and its 'project'. In this regard, it is noteworthy that Kant (like others in Germany as well as France) was quite self-conscious about being a participant in a process of enlightenment or *Aufklaerung* and sought to articulate the historical significance as well as the political implications of intellectual efforts (Schmidt, 1996). Two recent collections of essays contain contributions by many of the political theorists and philosophers who have been elucidating Kant's politics in recent years (Williams, 1992; Beiner and Booth, 1993). The latter collection especially contains studies not only of Kant's thought as such but of the contemporary impact of 'Kantian liberalism' that has stimulated much of the interest in him, including essays by Rawls and Habermas. It is useful to assess this entire subject in light of the criticisms of modern appropriations of Kant offered by a scholar who was among the first to make Kant's political writings widely accessible in English (Reiss, 1999).

Consideration of Enlightenment political thought must, finally, acknowledge Pocock's studies, in progress, of the intellectual formation of Gibbon and of the text of his *Decline and Fall of the Roman Empire* (1999a; 1999b; with forthcoming volumes expected to focus on Gibbon's treatment of Christianity and the influence of Tacitus). As a study of a historical classic, Pocock's work is concerned with problems of eighteenth-century historiography, but, as is shown in his previous work as well as in this, historiography was a common and important mode of expressing political theories in the early modern period. Perceived tensions among civic virtue, commercial society, and the Christian religion formed an important part of the background of the problems Gibbon addressed in his history, just as they engaged many of the political theorists of the period. Of special interest is the second volume, titled *Narratives of Civil Government*, which surveys several 'enlightened' constructions of European history, including those of Voltaire, Hume, Smith, and Ferguson, as the frameworks of these writers' own assessments of modern politics as well as of Gibbon's thought. Methodologically, Pocock's aim is to establish the intellectual 'contexts' in which Gibbon should be read. In addition to the various political and philosophical discourses available to him, the notion of 'contexts' here refers to the claim that there were in fact a number of 'Enlightenments' among which the cosmopolitan Gibbon moved, varying in their preoccupations and tone from one country to another, especially with respect to religious issues. Gibbon reflects, among other things, Protestant and English forms of Enlightenment that, though sceptical about religion and its political impact, were more conservative than the Enlightenment of the French *philosophes*.

THE SCOTTISH ENLIGHTENMENT

The political thought of eighteenth-century Scotland deserves separate treatment because the exceptional richness of the Enlightenment in that country has attracted notable scholarly attention in recent years. Scottish writers of the period seem to have been uniquely situated to address important problems with a variety of intellectual resources. As inheritors of well-established intellectual links to the continent, they were in a position to combine European philosophy and jurisprudence with modes of thought emanating from England. As members of a peripheral nation that had been united (in 1707) with a more powerful and advanced one, they confronted issues of economic development in a modern commercial society that led to decisive contributions to political economy. And as members of a nation with a strong historical identity that was now joined politically to England, with its own distinctive constitutional traditions, the Scots pioneered historical approaches to an understanding of social development and comparative government. Christopher J. Berry (1997) provides a useful overview of the themes of eighteenth-century Scottish social thought. An older volume (Hont and Ignatieff, 1983), however, remains indispensable for its more specialized articles, particularly for a focus on the creative tensions between the legacy of civic, republican, and patriotic commitments and the inexorable growth of commerce, which forced a rethinking of the possibilities of virtue in the modern world. Many of the contributors to this book continue to be active in research on aspects of this branch of political theory.

Eighteenth-century Scotland produced a number of writers of interest in the area of moral, social, and political thought. Among the less well-known ones who have attracted recent scholarly attention are the philosophers Francis Hutcheson and Thomas Reid, the jurist Lord Kames, the social theorists John Millar and Adam Ferguson, and the historian William Robertson. In Hutcheson and Reid one can observe the movement from natural law modes of thought to the more peculiarly Scottish 'moral sense' and 'common sense' approaches to moral life. In Ferguson one finds strong traces of the 'republican' outlook, marked by its concern with civic virtue and corruption, combined with an apprehensive sense of the special qualities of modern life. Some of these figures (especially Kames and Millar) were instrumental in formulating or applying the distinctive Scottish 'four-stage' theory of social development, from hunter-gatherer and pastoral ways of life through agricultural predominance to the commercial society that was the principal contemporaneous concern. The historical mode of understanding societies and social development, in which complexes of customs, manners, laws, forms of government and other institutions are viewed as forming functional systems, suggests the influence of (or convergence with) Montesquieu's approach to political theory; the emphasis on changing forms of property and modes of production has been seen as influencing Marx's as well as Smith's historical approach to political economy. Others (including Robertson), in keeping with the Scottish historical perspective, sought to describe the transition from the feudal institutions and manners of the middle ages to the emergence of a more modern society and state system over the previous two centuries.

The major figures of the Scottish Enlightenment, however, continue to be Hume and Smith, whose traditionally high reputations have been enhanced by recent work. Hume's political theory has received less attention (and is less often taught) than that of other major thinkers because it is not presented in a single, easily accessible work. An abstract account of justice and government is presented in his *Treatise of Human Nature* as an adjunct to extensive investigations of the philosophy of mind and moral psychology; more concrete political and economic topics, such as parties, commerce, the British constitution, the theory of the 'original contract', and a scheme for a 'perfect commonwealth', are discussed in a large number of lucid essays. Hume's once-famous *History of England* (which, like the *Essays*, is now readily available in a Liberty Classics edition) is also attracting attention as a source of political ideas, which Hume, like the other Scottish thinkers, often treats in a historical context. Frederick Whelan (1985) offers an analysis of Hume's political theory based largely on the *Treatise*, emphasizing Hume's account of how social order is created through rules prescribed by 'artifices' such as justice (with their attendant 'artificial virtues' of compliance with rules), and paralleling his sceptical account of how cognitive order is created through the application of rules of inferential reasoning. Although on many key issues, such as civil and economic liberty and constitutional government, Hume is a central figure in the classical liberal tradition, his emphasis on rules and order leads Whelan, with others, to characterize his philosophy as 'conservative'. In response, John B. Stewart (1992) argues that Hume's aim was to influence public opinion in a 'reform'-oriented direction in relation to the more practical political issues of his time. More specific facets of Hume's wide-ranging political thought have been explored in articles, including his constitutionalism (Manzer, 1996), his critique of contractarianism (Whelan, 1994), his account of the balance of power in relation to British foreign policy (Robertson, 1993; Whelan, 1995a), and his version of a doctrine of 'prescriptive right' – an idea more often associated with Burke – as the basis of regime legitimacy (Whelan, 1995b).

Renewed attention to Smith, finally, has followed in the wake of a new edition of his works. The old 'Adam Smith problem' of reconciling the sentiment- and sympathy-based ethics of the *Theory of Moral Sentiments* and the self-interest of the *Wealth of Nations* continues to serve as a starting point. One approach might involve the view that in both works Smith portrays people as sociable beings motivated by the desire for recognition and the esteem of their peers rather than by the simple desire for economic gain. Another holds that Smith's doctrine is a version of classical liberalism in which moral and economic individualism, grounded in equal dignity and independence, reinforce each other (Darwall, 1999) [see also Chapter 9].

Work on Smith must now attend to the fact that Smith left three, not two, major works on 'moral philosophy', broadly construed to include political matters. His *Lectures on Jurisprudence*, now readily available, link Smith to the natural and civil law tradition mentioned above as well as to the Scottish school of historical sociology, which also figures prominently in *The Wealth of Nations*. Adding these to political economy and moral sentiments, one can say that Smith was a key participant in at least four of the major discourses of Enlightenment political thought. It is also apparent that a theory of justice figures in all three works – a theory whose emphasis on property and contract derives from jurisprudence, whose psychological basis is the resentment an impartial spectator would experience in the face of oppressive actions, and that indicates the necessary legal framework that the 'sovereign' must provide in order for a market economy to function.

Interest in Smith as with other thinkers considered here is often not strictly historical but reflects contemporary intellectual issues. Inquiry into the philosophical sources of (neo)classical economics naturally turns to Smith (as well as Hume) and

reveals that the moral foundations of this doctrine were more complex than simplistic modern accounts, whether friendly or hostile, might suggest (Minovitz, 1993). Charles L. Griswold (1999) presents Smith's moral philosophy not only as embodying central Enlightenment ideals such as liberty and equality, but also as anticipating and responding to contemporary criticisms of Enlightenment liberalism through his concern with virtue and sociability. Samuel Fleischacker (1999), finally, not only pursues similarities between the moral philosophies of Smith and Kant, but relates these to a subsequent tradition of liberalism centring on the development of the individual's capacity for judgement, to Rawls, and to contemporary justifications of the welfare state.

ENGLISH RADICALS AND BURKE

Burke and a group of writers who were often his critics or adversaries may be treated together, in the conventional manner, in this final section, although this conjuncture would doubtless have irritated all of them. The writers in question, usually termed the English radicals, include Richard Price, Joseph Priestley, Thomas Paine, William Godwin, and Mary Wollstonecraft. As religious dissenters or free-thinkers, they were excluded from the major establishments of eighteenth-century English life, a fact that did not preclude economic prosperity and high levels of intellectual vigour in the communities to which they belonged. Not surprisingly, their central political cause was the anti-establishmentarian one of regularizing and extending the parliamentary franchise in a democratic direction, a programme which, along with the removal of religious disabilities, Burke opposed. They also espoused and developed some of the self-consciously progressive and egalitarian elements of philosophical radicalism more characteristic of the French than of the British Enlightenment; these included both natural rights (or Paine's 'rights of man') and utilitarianism (or appeals to the 'principle of utility'), both of which – sometimes in combination – were deployed in such a way as to attack traditional institutions and social privilege of all sorts. They were of course favourably disposed to (and in Paine's case, took part in) the American and French Revolutions. This latter issue led to dramatic clashes in the 1790s with Burke, whose attack on the French Revolution was denounced by the radicals (and some of his fellow Whigs) as inconsistent with his earlier sympathetic response to American grievances.

In the end, the war with France and the general reaction against the revolution terminated radical agitation in England and set the radicals' causes back for a full generation. Nevertheless, the works of these writers remain well worth reading as expressions of Enlightenment and as a chapter in the history of political theory; recent editions of all of them have facilitated their study and teaching, though scholarly work in this area is sparse. The major exception is Isaac Kramnick (1990), which studies the political theories of Price, Priestley, Paine and others, as well as the dissenting political culture that produced this current of middle-class radicalism. Kramnick unabashedly reasserts the primacy of Locke and of Lockean, individualistic liberalism, with its call for equal opportunity and its valuation of productive work over privileged leisure, among these thinkers and in the later eighteenth-century Anglo-American world more generally. His primary target is Pocock and his followers, who have challenged the earlier thesis of Lockean hegemony in eighteenth-century British thought by documenting the prevalence of classical republicanism, and who have also sometimes suggested that the emphasis on Locke has been per-petrated by (Straussian) critics of modernity and (Marxist) critics of 'bourgeois' society in need of a theoretical personification of the (liberal) values they oppose. Kramnick's secondary target is con-temporary communitarians who have embraced the 'classical republican' idea as providing historical and moral support for their programme of reviving a public-spirited civic culture in the United States today. Thus do the 'politics of scholarship' (1990: 35) animate the study of political theory, joining contemporary debate and historical research.

The 'politics of scholarship' is a concept that may be applied to Burke as well. The still unan-swered question is whether the ideological uses (or dismissals) of Burke as a stereotyped 'conserva-tive' will subside with the passing of the Cold War, and the almost exclusive focus on his *Reflections on the Revolution in France* give way to broader study of his thought (Whelan, 2001). A new edition of Burke's writings and speeches (Oxford) is replacing the century-old versions that have been used until now, and a detailed new biography (Lock, 1998), of which the first of two volumes has appeared, will provide political theorists with valu-able background information on a thinker whose ideas are closely tied to an active political career. Conor Cruise O'Brien (1992) and James Conniff (1994) are two recent interpretive studies of Burke's political thought as a whole, the former arguing that its major components were inspired by Burke's sympathy for those suffering various forms of oppression, and the latter associating Burke with the reformist politics of his time. Burke's views on Great Britain's Indian Empire and his role in the impeachment of Warren Hastings (one of Burke's reformist causes) in relation

to his general political theory were until recently the major gap in Burke scholarship. This topic has now been treated by Whelan (1996), which, in addition to an analysis of Burke's views on the practical problems of administering an empire, attempts to square Burke's appreciation for the integrity of traditional Indian civilization with his commitment to the norms of an evidently universal moral law. Political theorists should note that Burke, especially his rhetoric and his ambivalent position in relation to British imperialism, is a frequent subject for scholars in literature and cultural studies departments, where theoretically driven studies of political issues and texts are very much in vogue.

REFERENCES

Arneil, Barbara (1996) *John Locke and America: The Defence of English Colonialism*. Oxford: Clarendon.

Ball, Terence (1988) *Transforming Political Discourse: Political Theory and Critical Conceptual History*. Oxford: Blackwell.

Ball, Terence and J. G. A. Pocock (1988) *Conceptual Change and the Constitution*. Lawrence, US: University Press of Kansas.

Ball, Terence, James Farr and Russell L. Hanson (1989) *Political Innovation and Conceptual Change*. Cambridge: Cambridge University Press.

Beiner, Ronald and William James Booth, eds (1993) *Kant and Political Philosophy: The Contemporary Legacy*. New Haven, CT: Yale University Press.

Berry, Christopher J. (1997) *The Social Thought of the Scottish Enlightenment*. Edinburgh: Edinburgh University Press.

Bock, Gisela, Quentin Skinner and Maurizio Viroli, eds (1990) *Machiavelli and Republicanism*. Cambridge: Cambridge University Press.

Brown, Alison, ed. (1994) Francesco Guicciardini, *Dialogue on the Government of Florence*. Cambridge: Cambridge University Press.

Burke, Peter (1991) 'Tacitism, scepticism, and reason of state'. In J. H. Burns, ed., *The Cambridge History of Political Thought 1450–1700*. Cambridge: Cambridge University Press.

Carr, Craig L., ed. (1994) *The Political Writings of Samuel Pufendorf*. New York: Oxford University Press.

Coby, Patrick (1999) *Machiavelli's Romans: Liberty and Greatness in the Discourses on Livy*. Lanham, MD: Lexington.

Cohler, Anne M. (1988) *Montesquieu's Comparative Politics and the Spirit of American Constitutionalism*. Lawrence, US: University Press of Kansas.

Conniff, James (1994) *The Useful Cobbler: Edmund Burke and the Politics of Progress*. Albany, NY: State University of New York Press.

Darwall, Stephen (1999) 'Sympathetic liberalism: recent work on Adam Smith'. *Philosophy and Public Affairs*, 28 (2): 139–64.

Dietz, Mary G., ed. (1990) *Thomas Hobbes and Political Theory*. Lawrence, KS: University Press of Kansas.

Faulkner, Robert K. (1993) *Francis Bacon and the Project of Progress*. Lanham, MD: Rowman and Littlefield.

Fischer, Markus (1997) 'Machiavelli's political psychology'. *Review of Politics*, 59 (4): 789–829.

Flathman, Richard E. (1993) *Thomas Hobbes: Skepticism, Individuality and Chastened Politics*. Newbury Park, CA: Sage.

Fleischacker, Samuel (1999) *A Third Concept of Liberty: Judgment and Freedom in Kant and Adam Smith*. Princeton, NJ: Princeton University Press.

Franklin, Julian H. (1991) 'Sovereignty and the mixed constitution: Bodin and his critics'. In J. H. Burns, ed., *The Cambridge History of Political Thought 1450–1700*. Cambridge: Cambridge University Press.

Goodhart, Michael (2000) 'Theory in practice: Quentin Skinner's Hobbes, reconsidered'. *Review of Politics*, 62 (Summer): 531–61.

Gourevitch, Victor (1998) 'Recent work on Rousseau'. *Political Theory*, 26 (4): 536–56.

Gray, John (1995) *Enlightenment's Wake*. London: Routledge.

Griswold, Charles L., Jr (1999) *Adam Smith and the Virtues of Enlightenment*. Cambridge: Cambridge University Press.

Haakonssen, Knud (1996) *Natural Law and Moral Philosophy: From Grotius to the Scottish Enlightenment*. Cambridge: Cambridge University Press.

Hampsher-Monk, Iain (1992) *A History of Modern Political Thought: Major Political Thinkers from Hobbes to Marx*. Oxford: Blackwell.

Hampton, Jean (1986) *Hobbes and the Social Contract Tradition*. Cambridge: Cambridge University Press.

Hochstrasser, T. J. (2000) *Natural Law Theories in the Early Enlightenment*. Cambridge: Cambridge University Press.

Holmes, Stephen (1990) 'Political psychology in Hobbes's *Behemoth*'. In Mary G. Dietz, ed., *Thomas Hobbes and Political Theory*. Lawrence, KS: University Press of Kansas.

Hont, Istvan (1987) 'The language of sociability and commerce: Samuel Pufendorf and the theoretical foundations of the "Four-Stages Theory"'. In Anthony Pagden, ed., *The Languages of Political Theory in Early-Modern Europe*. Cambridge: Cambridge University Press.

Hont, Istvan and Michael Ignatieff, eds (1983) *Wealth and Virtue: The Shaping of Political Economy in the Scottish Enlightenment*. Cambridge: Cambridge University Press.

Hulliung, Mark (1994) *The Autocritique of Enlightenment: Rousseau and the Philosophes*. Cambridge, MA: Harvard University Press.

Kavka, Gregory S. (1986) *Hobbesian Moral and Political Theory*. Princeton, NJ: Princeton University Press.

Kersting, Wolfgang (1992) 'Politics, freedom, and order: Kant's political philosophy'. In Paul Guyer, ed., *The Cambridge Companion to Kant*. Cambridge: Cambridge University Press.

Kingdon, Robert M. (1991) 'Calvinism and resistance theory, 1550–1580'. In J. H. Burns, ed., *The Cambridge History of Political Thought 1450–1700*. Cambridge: Cambridge University Press.

Kramnick, Isaac (1990) *Republicanism and Bourgeois Radicalism*. Ithaca, NY: Cornell University Press.

Krauss, Jody S. (1993) *The Limits of Hobbesian Contractarianism*. Cambridge: Cambridge University Press.

Lock, F. P. (1998) *Edmund Burke*, vol. I. Oxford: Clarendon.

Macfarlane, Alan (2000) *The Riddle of the Modern World: Of Liberty, Wealth and Equality*. London: Macmillan.

MacIntyre, Alasdair (1984) *After Virtue*. Notre Dame, IN: University of Notre Dame Press.

MacIntyre, Alasdair (1988) *Whose Justice? Which Rationality?*. Notre Dame, IN: University of Notre Dame Press.

Mansfield, Harvey C., Jr (1993) *Taming the Prince: The Ambivalence of Modern Executive Power*. Baltimore: Johns Hopkins University Press.

Mansfield, Harvey C. (1996) *Machiavelli's Virtue*. Chicago: University of Chicago Press.

Manzer, Robert A. (1996) 'Hume's constitutionalism and the identity of constitutional democracy'. *American Political Science Review*, 90: 488–96.

Martinich, A. P. (1992) *The Two Gods of Leviathan: Thomas Hobbes on Religion and Politics*. Cambridge: Cambridge University Press.

McClure, Kirstie M. (1996) *Judging Rights: Lockean Politics and the Limits of Consent*. Ithaca, NY: Cornell University Press.

Melzer, Arthur M. (1990) *The Natural Goodness of Man: On the System of Rousseau's Thought*. Chicago: University of Chicago Press.

Minovitz, Peter (1993) *Profits, Priests, and Princes: Adam Smith's Emancipation of Economics from Politics and Religion*. Stanford, CA: Stanford University Press.

Morgenstern, Mira (1996) *Rousseau and the Politics of Ambiguity: Self, Culture, and Society*. University Park, PA: Pennsylvania State University Press.

Oakley, Francis (1991) 'Christian obedience and authority, 1520–1550'. In J. H. Burns, ed., *The Cambridge History of Political Thought 1450–1700*. Cambridge: Cambridge University Press.

O'Brien, Conor Cruise (1992) *The Great Melody: A Thematic Biography and Commented Anthology of*

Edmund Burke. Chicago: University of Chicago Press.

Pagden, Anthony, ed. (1987) *The Languages of Political Theory in Early-Modern Europe*. Cambridge: Cambridge University Press.

Pagden, Anthony and Jeremy Lawrence, eds (1991) Francisco de Vitoria, *Political Writings*. Cambridge: Cambridge University Press.

Pangle, Thomas L. (1988) *The Spirit of Modern Republicanism: The Moral Vision of the American Founders and the Philosophy of Locke*. Chicago: University of Chicago Press.

Peltonen, Markku (1995) *Classical Humanism and Republicanism in English Political Thought 1570–1640*. Cambridge: Cambridge University Press.

Peltonen, Markku (1996) 'Bacon's political philosophy'. In M. Peltonen, ed., *The Cambridge Companion to Bacon*. Cambridge: Cambridge University Press.

Pettit, Philip (1997) *Republicanism: A Theory of Freedom and Government*. Oxford: Clarendon.

Phillipson, Nicholas and Quentin Skinner, eds (1993) *Political Discourse in Early Modern Britain*. Cambridge: Cambridge University Press.

Pocock, J. G. A. (1975) *The Machiavellian Moment: Florentine Political Thought and the Atlantic Political Tradition*. Princeton, NY: Princeton University Press.

Pocock, J. G. A. (1985) *Virtue, Commerce, and History: Essays on Political Thought and History, Chiefly in the Eighteenth Century*. Cambridge: Cambridge University Press.

Pocock, J. G. A. (1987) 'The concept of a language and the *métier d'historien*: some considerations on practice'. In Anthony Pagden, ed., *The Languages of Political Theory in Early-Modern Europe*. Cambridge: Cambridge University Press.

Pocock, J. G. A. (1999a) *Barbarism and Religion*. Vol. I, *The Enlightenments of Edward Gibbon, 1737–1764*. Cambridge: Cambridge University Press.

Pocock, J. G. A. (1999b) *Barbarism and Religion*. Vol. II, *Narratives of Civil Government*. Cambridge: Cambridge University Press.

Rahe, Paul A. (1992) *Republics Ancient and Modern: Classical Republicanism and the American Revolution*. Chapel Hill, NC: University of North Carolina Press.

Reiss, Hans (1999) 'Kant's politics and the Enlightenment: reflections on some recent studies'. *Political Theory*, 27 (2): 236–73.

Robertson, John (1993) 'Universal monarchy and the liberties of Europe: David Hume's critique of an English Whig doctrine'. In Nicholas Phillipsons and Quentin Skinner, eds, *Political Discourse in Early Modern Britain*. Cambridge: Cambridge University Press.

Rorty, Richard (1989) *Contingency, Irony, and Solidarity*. Cambridge: Cambridge University Press.

Schmidt, James, ed. (1996) *What Is Enlightenment? Eighteenth-Century Answers and Twentieth-Century Questions*. Berkeley, CA: University of California Press.

Schmidt, James (2000) 'What Enlightenment project?' *Political Theory*, 28 (6): 734–57.

Shklar, Judith N. (1984) *Ordinary Vices*. Cambridge, MA: Harvard University Press.

Simmons, A. John (1992) *The Lockean Theory of Rights*. Princeton, NJ: Princeton University Press.

Skinner, Quentin (1978) *Foundations of Modern Political Thought*, 2 vols. Cambridge: Cambridge University Press.

Skinner, Quentin (1996) *Reason and Rhetoric in the Philosophy of Hobbes*. Cambridge: Cambridge University Press.

Skinner, Quentin (1998) *Liberty before Liberalism*. Cambridge: Cambridge University Press.

Stewart, John B. (1992) *Opinion and Reform in Hume's Political Philosophy*. Princeton, NJ: Princeton University Press.

Tuck, Richard (1991) 'Grotius and Selden'. In J. H. Burns, ed., *The Cambridge History of Political Thought 1450–1700*. Cambridge: Cambridge University Press.

Tuck, Richard (1993) *Philosophy and Government 1572–1651*. Cambridge: Cambridge University Press.

Tully, James, ed. (1988) *Meaning and Context: Quentin Skinner and His Critics*. Princeton, NJ: Princeton University Press.

Tully, James, ed. (1991) Samuel Pufendorf, *On the Duty of Man and Citizen According to Natural Law*. Cambridge: Cambridge University Press.

Tully, James (1993) *An Approach to Political Philosophy: Locke in Contexts*. Cambridge: Cambridge University Press.

Viroli, Maurizio (1992) *From Politics to Reason of State*. Cambridge: Cambridge University Press.

Viroli, Maurizio (1998) *Machiavelli*. Oxford: Oxford University Press.

Whelan, Frederick G. (1985) *Order and Artifice in Hume's Political Philosophy*. Princeton, NJ: Princeton University Press.

Whelan, Frederick G. (1994) 'Hume and contractarianism'. *Polity*, 27: 201–24.

Whelan, Frederick G. (1995a) 'Robertson, Hume, and the balance of power'. *Hume Studies*, 21: 315–32.

Whelan, Frederick G. (1995b) 'Time, revolution, and prescriptive right in Hume's theory of government'. *Utilitas*, 7: 97–119.

Whelan, Frederick G. (1996) *Edmund Burke and India: Political Morality and Empire*. Pittsburgh: University of Pittsburgh Press.

Whelan, Frederick G. (1999) 'Vattel's doctrine of the state'. In Knud Haakonssen, ed., *Grotius, Pufendorf and Modern Natural Law*. Aldershot: Ashgate.

Whelan, Frederick G. (2001) 'Taking Burke seriously'. In Aleksandar Jokic, ed., *Essays in Honor of Burleigh Wilkins: From History to Justice*. New York: Lang.

Williams, Howard Lloyd, ed. (1992) *Essays on Kant's Political Philosophy*. Chicago: University of Chicago Press.

Wootton, David, ed. (1994) *Republicanism, Liberty, and Commercial Society, 1649–1776*. Stanford, CA: Stanford University Press.

Wootton, David (2000) 'Helvetius: from radical enlightenment to revolution'. *Political Theory*, vol. 28 (3): 307–36.

Worden, Blair (1994) 'James Harrington and *The Commonwealth of Oceana*'. In David Wootton, ed., *Republicanism, Liberty, and Commercial Society, 1649–1776*. Stanford, CA: Stanford University Press.

27

Modern Islamic Political Thought

MICHAELLE BROWERS

When, for the first time in their history, Muslims found themselves dominated – militarily, politically, and economically – by a colonizing Christian West, they began to raise questions such as:

What are the causes that led to the general degradation of the modern Muslims?

If Islam is a faith that unifies, why this numerous diversity among Muslims?

Is Muslim unity a reasonable hope capable of realization?

Is it possible for one of us to be a loyal nationalist and a sincere Muslim, at one and the same time?

How did it happen that the modern states came into existence only in Christendom?

Does Islam tolerate free, liberal institutions [and] [i]s it able to adapt itself to the demands of such institutions?

Why have we become such deniers of science and enemies of wisdom?

Who would have imagined that Islam – which based itself on reason and thinking – would be deprived of the freedom of *ijtihad* [rational religious interpretation] and would be left under the yoke of *taqlid* [imitation of great scholars]?

What is to be done?[1]

It was in the confrontation with these questions that we see the beginnings of modern Islamic thought.

This chapter examines the transformations that have occurred over the last two centuries in Islamic political thought. Thinkers working in the Islamic tradition during this period shared the common concerns of renewal in the face of decline, the fact of Western supremacy and modernization, and the abiding role of the Islamic heritage (*turath*) in modern society. Islamic modernists first took up these issues at the beginning of the nineteenth century when 'several Islamic states adopted European military and technical organization, and various Muslim travelers to Europe brought back influential tales of progress and enlightenment' (Kurzman, 2002: 4). In terms of political reform, Islamic modernists sought to adopt aspects of European political systems on the one hand, and to reassert Islam as a socio-political system in perfect harmony with modernity on the other. Islamic modernists' failure to fully meet that challenge contributed to the rise of Islamic revivalist forces in the latter half of the twentieth century. While modernist Islamic thought continues until the present, in the contemporary period the modernists share discursive space with competing trends – Islamists, traditionalists, and Islamic liberals – each of which offers their own vision of reform. In contemporarary writings, the means of dealing with problems facing Islamic societies have expanded and transformed such that Islamic political thought, which has always been diverse, has become increasingly multi-vocal and fractured, and the interactions among intellectuals working *within* the tradition of Islam thought are increasingly characterized by tension, hostility, and even violence. There is also a sense, articulated by non-Islamic observers and even on the part of Islamic thinkers themselves, that Islamic political thought today seems to have reached an impasse on at least three issues: how to deal with the Islamic tradition, the function of religion in society, and the basis of political organization. It is true that these issues have consistently re-emerged in each of the three trends of Islamic political theorizing discussed here: Islamic modernism, Islamism, and Islamic liberalism. Yet this common focus, despite the vast differences between thinkers, suggests a common project, as old questions and old answers are re-evaluated anew and each of the three trends has increasingly adopted a similar political focus: the amelioration of arbitrary rule and the establishment of more populist forms of governance.

ISLAMIC MODERNISM

The emergence of modernism[2] in Islamic thought corresponds with what has come to be called the Arab *Nahda* (renaissance or awakening), 'a vast political and cultural movement that dominate[d] the period of 1850–1914 ... [that] sought through translation and vulgarization to assimilate the great achievements of modern European civilization, while reviving the classical Arab culture that ante-dates the centuries of decadence and foreign domi-nation' (Laroui, 1976: vii).[3] Muslims working in this tradition sought to revive Islamic thought both by affirming continuity with the past and by assim-ilating what they saw as the achievements of modern Europe – specifically, modern material technology, modern techniques of social organiza-tion and mobilization, and modern political institu-tions such as parliaments. They also sought to give Islamic thought a more rationalist, futuristic, and universalistic orientation.

Certainly Islamic modernism was not the first movement calling for revival, renewal and reform of the tradition in Islamic history. As early as the eighth and ninth centuries, Muslim thinkers had been involved in disputes over how Islamic socio-political life could best be structured as the chal-lenges of Shi'i, Sufi, Mu'tazila, and Kharijite movements emerged alongside the formation of an Islamic orthodoxy. In the thirteenth and fourteenth centuries, reformists sought to revive Islam amidst a waning Caliphate. Fazlur Rahman (Pakistan–US, 1919–88) cites a number of 'premodernist' refor-mation movements that 'swept over the larger part of the Muslim World in the seventeenth, eighteenth, and nineteenth centuries' and shared characteristics of a 'consciousness of degeneration, and of the cor-responding need to remedy social evils and raise moral standards' (1970: 641). However, the differ-ence between the 'premodern' and 'modern' reform movements is that whereas the former owed little – Rahman goes so far as to say 'nothing whatsoever' – to foreign inspiration, the latter is as much a reaction to the West as it is a continuation of the thought and activism of the premodernist Islamic reformers. As Charles Kurzman rightly notes, the movement that begins in the first half of the nineteenth century

was not simply 'modern' (a feature of modernity) but also 'modernist' (a proponent of modernity). Activists [of modernist Islam] describe themselves and their goals by the Arabic terms *jadid* (new) and *mu'asir* (con-temporary), [and] the Turkish terms *yeni* (new) and *genç* (young), and similar words in other languages. (2002: 4)

Muslims often contend that, while Christianity is primarily a faith, Islam is complete and holistic in the sense of being a way of life as well as a religion (*dunya wa din*). Islamic law (*shari'a*) is understood as a comprehensive system containing principles regulating both mankind's relationship to God (*'ibadat*) and relationships among human beings (*mu'amalat*). Islamic modernists had to combat the orthodoxy which claimed that not only is there no need to look outside of the Islamic tradition (*turath*) in organizing the social and political affairs of the community, but to do so is anti-Islamic.

Many Islamic thinkers justified their use of mod-ern values by arguing that Europe's current status was an outgrowth of the accomplishments of medieval Islamic thinkers, and thus they were only retrieving their own lost heritage. For example, Khayr al-Din al-Tunisi (Tunisia, 1822–90) claims that

there is no reason to reject or ignore something which is correct and demonstrable simply because it comes from others, especially if we had formerly possessed it and it had been taken from us. On the contrary, there is an obligation to restore it and put it to use. (in Kurzman, 2002: 42)

Others, like Sayyid Jamal al-Din al-Afghani (Iran, 1838–97), asserted that 'the Islamic religion is the closest of all religions to science and knowledge, and there is no incompatibility between science and knowledge and the foundation of the Islamic faith' (in Donohue and Esposito, 1982: 19). Most Islamic modernists believed that the tension between Islam and modern values was 'a historical accident, not an inherent feature of Islam' (Kurzman, 2002: 4). However, the extent to which particular modernists were willing to borrow from the West ranged from those who argued, in the words of Mirza Malkom Khan (Iran, 1833–1908), that 'in all the new institu-tions which Europe offers us there is nothing, absolutely nothing, which is contrary to the spirit of our religion' (in Bakhash, 1978: 15); to those like Rashid Rida (Syria–Egypt, 1865–1935) who claimed Muslims need only to acquire Europe's 'scientific achievements, technical skill and advanced industries' (in Shahin, 1993: 49); to those who, like Afghani, look no more fondly on the blind imitation of the West than of the past, in that 'expe-rience and past evidence have taught us that imita-tors in every nation, and those who copy foreign customs, constitute the very chinks and loopholes through which foreign domination penetrates a country' (in Awwad, 1986: 84).

In the political discourse of modernist Islam, the primary concern was to articulate a tenable understanding of the relationship between religion and the state. One of the early strands of modernist Islamic thought gave Islam a nationalistic understanding, focused on building a strong state that could compete with the West. We see this, for example, in the work of Rifa'a Badawi Rafi al-Tahtawi (Egypt, 1801–1873):

> The love of religion and the passion to protect, which the people of Islam hold so tenaciously and which give them an advantage over other nations in power and force, [people in the West] call love of fatherland. However, among us, the people of Islam, love of the fatherland is just one branch of the faith, and the defense of religion is its capstone. Every kingdom is a fatherland for all those in it who belong to Islam, it combines religion and patriotism. (in Donohue and Esposito, 1982: 13)

Tahtawi sees no conflict between religion and patriotism and, in fact, views Islam as the basis of Arab nationalism, in general, and the foundation of Egyptian nationalism, in particular. In contrast, Rida claims that 'one of the imperatives of Islam is its prohibition of partisanship in wrong for the sake of relatives, people, or fatherland. It prohibits enmity and divisions among Muslims' (in Donohue and Esposito, 1982: 58). In the works of thinkers such as Afghani, 'Abduh and Rida, Islam took on a more pan-Islamic character and the aim was to reinstate the Muslim *umma* (community) in the image of the Ottoman Empire. This understanding of Islam and renewal became an important inspiration for later Islamists, discussed in the next section.

Others sought to incorporate modern political values with Islamic notions of the state. The Islamic tradition had formulated general principles governing authority, but there were few checks on absolute authority provided by that tradition. Many modernist Muslims sought to limit the traditional authoritarian powers of rulers originally derived from Islamic sources, but no longer deemed compatible with Muslim interests, by claiming a principle of equivalence between various aspects of the *shari'a* (Islamic law) and the ideals of constitutionalism. According to Sunni orthodoxy, a leader was to be chosen by an elite class referred to as *ahl al-hall wa al-'aqd* (literally, those who loose and bind), people of authority and stature in the community such as tribal chieftains, governors of provinces, state dignitaries. However, modernist Islamic thinkers claimed that this privilege should now fall to representative assemblies whose members

have become the effective 'people of authority'. Khayr al-Din al-Tunisi asks, 'Is it fitting that the physicians of the *umma* should be ignorant of its ailments?' (1967: 72), thus suggesting that matters that affect the public should involve consulting the public in some form.

In advancing their claims, some Islamic modernists turned to a passage in the Qur'an which advised Muhammad to 'seek their council in the matter' (Sura 3, Verse 159), interpreting it to mean, as Musa Kazin (Turkey, 1858–1920) does, that leaders are required to 'consult with the *umma* in every matter' (in Kurzman, 2002: 176). In an essay that bears the verse as its title, Namik Kemal (Turkey, 1840–88) argues that in order to 'keep the state within the limits of justice' Muslims must undertake two reforms: (1) making government operations public and open to scrutiny, that is, 'emancipat[ing] the fundamental principles of the administration from the domain of implicit interpretation and mak[ing] them public', and (2) exercising 'the method of consultation [*al-shura*], which takes the legislative power out of the hands of the members of the government' and places it in those of the larger Islamic community (*umma*) (in Kurzman, 2002: 145).

'Abd al-Hamid Ibn Badis (Algeria, 1889–1940) bases his argument that 'it is the people that have the right to delegate authority to the leaders and depose them' on a well-known speech by Abu Bakr al-Siddiq, delivered in 632 when, after the death of the Prophet Muhammad, he was sworn in as the first caliph:

> O People, I was entrusted as your ruler, although I am not better than any one of you.
>
> Support me as long as you see me following the right path, and correct me when you see me going astray. Obey me as long as I observe God in your affairs. If I disobey Him, you owe me no obedience. The weak among you are powerful [in my eyes] until I get them their due. The powerful among you are weak [in my eyes] until I take away from them what is due to others. I say this and seek God's forgiveness for myself and for you. (in Kurzman, 2002: 93–4)

Based upon this speech, Ibn Badis identifies 13 principles that should govern Islamic polities, including: 'no one can rule without the consent of the people'; 'assuming the affairs of the people does not make the ruler better than anyone else'; the people have the right and responsibility to 'monitor', 'advise', 'correct', and 'question' the ruler; the ruler must 'declare the plan he is going to follow, so that the people become aware of and agree to it'; the law emanates from the 'will of the people'; and 'all are equal before the law' (in Kurzman, 2002: 94–5).

The Moroccan thinker Muhammad 'Abd al-Jabiri
(b. 1936) points out how the generation that
included Afghani and Abduh often attempted to
bridge the Arab-Islamic tradition and the European
Enlightenment by correlating Islamic concepts with
European ones. According to al-Jabiri, they suggested an equation between democracy and *al-
shura* 'not because they were congruent, or because
they were ignorant of the differences that separated
them', but rather because 'they acted in a framework which called for an ideological action aimed
at the pacifying of the rigid ideologues among the
"religious scholars" and perhaps also the rulers, by
assuring them that the invocation of democracy
does not mean the insertion of a heretical doctrine
into the stronghold of Islam' (1994: 41). The equiva-
lences asserted, for example, between *maslaha* and
general will, *ijma'* and public opinion, and *shura*
and parliamentary democracy, cannot be explained
as merely an attempt to give foreign ideas an
Islamic colouring, any more than they can be
described as simply a defensive action aimed at
asserting Islamic values in the face of the West's
onslaught. It is an example of thinkers working in a
defensive manner, but also evidence that Islamic
thinkers in this period were guided by a faith that
Islam contained universal elements that are available to anyone who employs their reason and which
could provide the foundation for moving the *umma*
forward toward the creation of a better future.

Kurzman points out that, although one does find
discussions of democracy during this period, most
Islamic modernists 'did not necessarily intend constitutionalism to mean democracy, as it came to be
understood over the course of the twentieth
century: universal adult suffrage, reduction of
monarchs to symbolic offices, and constitutional
protection of a growing lists of rights' (2002: 20).
Rather, their concern was the rule of law and limits
on political power, within the conceptual framework of Islam. As such, constitutional reforms often
retain a distinct concern with a sense of justice
(*'adala*), which denotes a harmonious arrangement,
and unity (*tawhid*), in addition to the concern with
providing legal protections. Shaykh Muhammad
Husayn Na'ini (Iran, 1860–1936) defines constitutionalism in a manner typical among modernist
Islamic thinkers that captures both the rights and
responsibilities of political power: 'bound, limited,
just, conditioned, responsible and authoritative' (in
Donohue and Esposito, 1982: 289).

Certainly in this period there were also traditionalist or orthodox Islamic thinkers who rejected
modern values. So too, there were considerable differences among Islamic modernists themselves over
many questions of methodology and aim. One can
distinguish, for example, between reformist thinkers
who sought reform primarily through a reconstruction

and modernization of Islamic culture and education
on the one hand, and modernist thinkers who were
more Western in orientation and borrowed more
freely and widely from various aspects of modern
Europe on the other. But their common project – of
reconciling the demands of the modern age with the
Islamic faith – spurred a proliferation of modern
forms of writing and publishing, including the
novel and the periodical press, and contributed to
anti-colonial movements in North Africa and South
Asia. Modernist ideas also inspired the reformation
of religious educational institutions and the secular
schools, which had the effect of displacing or reducing the significance of the *'ulama* (doctors of
Islamic sciences) from their traditional roles as civil
servants in the field of education.

However, in general, Islamic modernists failed to
transform their ideas into mass movements or a
fundamental transformation of Islamic society.
Although constitutional movements took up many
of the ideas of the modernists and religious groups
supported the constitutional experiments undertaken in Tunisia (1860), Turkey (1876), Egypt
(1881), and Persia (1905), as Majid Khadduri
points out, the constitutions that were ultimately
implemented

> took no notice of Islamic principles save for reference
> to Islam as the official religion of the state. They were
> framed under the exclusive influence of European mod-
> els and thereby lost touch with religious groups whose
> support was essential for the operation of those novel
> institutions. (1970: 30–1)

As such, in the view of many, the institutions that
emerged in this period represented less an authentic
reformation of Islamic political thought and more
an indication of continued Western domination.

A change in Islamic political thought began to
emerge by the 1930s, as faith in liberal nationalism
began to decline in the region, exacerbated by economic problems, political corruption, two world
wars, and the creation of the state of Israel (in
1948). The emergence of competing discourses of
secular nationalism, socialism, and fascism sapped
the energy and divided the ranks of modernist
Islamic thinkers. 'A series of military *coups d'état*
brought to power regimes that were disillusioned
with the liberal West and attracted by the progress
of socialism in Russia and Eastern Europe'
(Donohue and Esposito, 1982: 98). Successors
tended either to emphasize the modernist values of
the earlier thinkers while overlooking or rejecting
their Islamic points of reference (secularists), or to
downplay or dismiss appropriating from the West
and modernity while emphasizing a 'return' to
the fundamentals of Islam (Islamic revivalists and
traditionalists).

ISLAMIC AWAKENING

According to Yusuf al-Qaradawi (Egypt, b. 1926) (1982; 1988), the 'Islamic awakening' (*al-sahwa al-Islamiyya*) is directly related to the *nakba* (disaster) of the expulsion of Palestinians from their homeland in 1948, and the *naksa* (fall), which occurred when during the Six Day War of 1967, instead of recapturing Palestine, the Arab forces led by Gamal Abd al-Nasser of Egypt lost further territory. Both events shook the credibility of the Arab nationalist regimes and provided fertile soil later tilled by Islamist forces.[4] The *naksa* (fall) signalled the end of the *Nahda* (renaissance). By the latter half of the 1970s the corrupt and inefficient nature of a number of existing (Arab nationalist and socialist) states in the region became apparent to all, and Islamists, who rejected the Western model of the state – yet also seem to have appropriated Western socialist models aimed at seizing state power, as is discussed below – had become a force to be reckoned with in a number of Muslim countries. One of the early Islamist works, by Abu al-Hasan al-Nadwi's (India, 1913–99), offers the following explanation of decline: 'Dazzled by the power and progress of the Western nations, Muslims began to imitate Western social and economic institutions regardless of the consequences ... The prestige of religion was diminished. The teachings of the Prophet were forgotten.' The solution to the moral degeneration and spiritual malaise, according to al-Nadwi, lies in a renewal of Islamic thought: 'The Qur'an and the *Sunnah* can still revitalize the withered arteries of the Islamic world' (in Abu-Rabi', 1996: 19, 20).

One must distinguish between Islamic revivalists – often referred to as 'Islamic fundamentalists' – who seek to return to authoritative sources in the Islamic tradition with the aim of legitimizing changes in the present, and Islamic traditionalists, who resist changes and seek to preserve an Islamic orthodoxy. Revivalists share with the modernists that preceded them a belief that Islam can and should be adapted to modern conditions. *Ijtihad* (independent reasoning) is permitted in adapting the *Shari'a*. However, unlike modernists, they strongly emphasize the distinctiveness of Islam and reject the adoption of Western political ideals. Traditionalist Muslims tend to eschew *ijtihad* in favour of *taqlid* (imitation) of time-honoured understandings of the Islamic tradition. A central concern of revivalists is the introduction of more Islamic law in order to clearly establish the Islamic character of the state. The traditionalists, among whom number many of the *'ulama* (traditional Islamic scholars), in many cases have a vested interest in maintaining the status quo. Traditionalists, or those who suggest that the Islamic *turath* (heritage) – the Qur'an and the *Sunna* (prophetic tradition) – are not affected by changing circumstances and point to the existence of an institutionalized juridical tradition (*'ilm al-fiqh*) as the protector of the religion, have always existed in the Islamic tradition. Islamists tend more toward political activism than theology and are also more selective in emphasizing segments of the Qur'an that serve their purposes. For our purposes here, the revivalists and their response to both modernist Islam and the problems confronting contemporary Islamic society are more relevant, since they are a distinctly modern trend in Islamic political thought.

This new movement arose under the slogan 'Islam is the solution' (*al-Islam huwa al-hall* or *al-hall al-islami*) and called for a 'return to the forefathers' (*al-salaf*) – from whence comes the name of the *Salafiyya* movement, which advocated a return to a *shari'a*-minded orthodoxy that would purify Islam of foreign accretions. The most important historical source for this trend in Islam is the Syrian jurist Taqiy al-Din Ibn Taymiyya (1263–1328), a staunch defender of Sunni Islam based on strict adherence to the Qur'an and the authentic *Sunna*. Writing amidst the strife brought about by external aggression from Christian crusaders and the Mongols, as well as internal struggles, Ibn Taymiyya believed that these two sources contained all the religious and spiritual guidance necessary for Muslims and the revival of the Islamic world. In his most famous work, *al-Siyasa al-shar'iyya* (*Governance According to Islamic Law*) Ibn Taymiyya emphasizes the necessity of government and leadership in all societies, as a way of avoiding strife and enforcing religious commandments, and of *jihad* (holy struggle) against infidels. In his *Fatawa* (juridical rulings), Ibn Taymiyya considers the specific case of the invading Mongols, as well as the cases of local rulers who gave allegiance to these Mongols, and rules that all such people were infidels who should be fought against by true Muslims, because they failed to apply the *Shari'a* (1966: vol. 4, 332–58).

Among the leaders of the Islamic revival is Abu al-'Ala Mawdudi (1903–79), founder of the Jama'at-i Islami in still-united India (in 1941), who called for a return to the Qur'an and a purified Sunna as a means of revitalizing Islam. Mawdudi describes Islam as an ideology and the Islamic state as an ideological state: 'It is clear from a careful consideration of the Qur'an and the Sunna that the state in Islam is based on an ideology and its objective is to establish that ideology' (in Donohue and Esposito, 1982: 256–7). The central theme in Mawdudi's thought is the concept of God's sovereignty (*hakimiyya*), which entails the idea that human beings can only exercise power in the name of God

and in pursuit of God's commands. He argued that
the only way this could truly be carried out was
though an Islamic state that is in 'all respects ...
founded upon the law laid down by God through
His Prophet' (in Moaddel and Talattof, 2002: 271)
and this was the political goal he worked toward in
Pakistan.

In Egypt, Sayyid Qutb (1906–66) became the
intellectual spokesperson for the Muslim
Brotherhood. Among Qutb's contributions to
Islamism is his elaboration of the idea of *jahiliyya*,
the time of 'ignorance' that existed prior to God's
message to the Prophet Muhammad, to describe a
condition that can exist at any time when human
beings do not live up to God's plan. In Qutb's
assessment, the contemporary age is one of ignorance, godlessness, and perplexity – summed up by
the notion of *jahiliyya* – and Muslims must withdraw from *jahili* society, establish a truly Islamic
social order (*al-nizam al-islami*) and, ultimately,
(re)conquer the existing ignorant order (*al-nizam
al-jahili*). According to this perspective, Islam is
incompatible with the modern 'secular' reality and
the Islamic *umma* can only grow and flourish at the
expense of this reality. The only antidote to the current state of *jahiliyya* – especially Western materialism which he saw as the chief contaminant – was
the *hakimiyya* of God: a total Islamic view of life
and a divinely ordained Islamic system. The harbinger of this new order is a body of believers Qutb
refers to as a 'vanguard': 'A vanguard must resolve
to set it in motion in the midst of the *jahiliyya* that
now reigns over the entire earth' (in Kepel, 1986:
45). It is this vanguard that undertakes the task of
purging themselves of corruption – a sort of *hijra* in
the manner undertaken by the Prophet Muhammad
when he left for Medina after facing opposition
from Meccan authorities, only to return a few years
later to conquer Mecca – and then returns to engage
in *jihad* against the forces of *jahiliyya*.

Both Qutb and Mawdudi articulate a notion of
political struggle aimed at gaining political power,
before all other considerations, in order to establish
an Islamic state. Mawdudi sees Islam as a 'revolutionary ideology which seeks to alter the social
order of the entire world and rebuild it in conformity with its own tenets'. In pursuing that aim he
calls for the establishment of an 'International
Revolutionary Party' aimed at waging *jihad* against
tyrannical governments (1976: 3, 17–18). '*Jihad*',
Mawdudi claims:

is part of this overall defense of Islam. *Jihad* means
struggle to the utmost of one's capacity. A man who
exerts himself physically or mentally or spends his
wealth in the way of *Allah* is indeed engaged in *Jihad*.
But in the language of *Shari'ah* this word is used particularly for the war that is waged solely in the name of

Allah and against those who perpetrate oppression as
enemies of Islam. (1960: 150)

Qutb divides the world into two spheres: *dar al-
Islam* and *dar al-harb*. The first sphere includes
every country in which the legal judgements of
Islam are applied, regardless of whether Muslims,
Christians, or Jews form the majority of citizens, so
long as those who wield power are Muslim and
adhere to the injunctions of their religion. The
second sphere consists of every territory in which
Islamic rules are not applied, irrespective of
whether its rulers claim to be Muslim (in Moaddel
and Talattof, 2002: 241–2). Although Mawdudi
refers to *jihad* as a 'defense of Islam', in the context
of these conflicting spheres, Qutb is quite clear that
jihad is a duty incumbent on all true Muslims. In
order to bring about the desired end – an Islamic
state – 'Islamic Jihad' must provide Muslims 'with
a free atmosphere to exercise their choice of faith. It
either completely dynamites the reigning political
systems or, subjugating them, forces them into sub-
mission to and acceptance of Jizyah [tax paid by
non-Muslims in an Islamic state]. Thus it does not
allow any impediment to remain in the way of
accepting the belief. Thereafter it allows complete
freedom to people to accept or reject belief' (in
Moaddel and Talattof, 2002: 226).

Qutb's thought containeds two innovations
which proved to be of particular significance for the
Islamists he inspired. First, in declaring that not
only non-Islamic governments but also governments led by Muslims could be considered to be
existing in a state of *jahiliyya*, he gave Islamic sanction to Muslims' opposition to and overthrow of the
governments that ruled them. Up until this time,
Islamists in Egypt viewed the British as the enemy,
though occasionally also the Egyptian monarchy
and capitalism. However, Qutb's last and most
influential work, *Milestones* (*Ma'alim fi al-tariq*,
literally 'signposts along the road') (1990), constituted a harsh critique of the *jahiliyya* and, hence,
illegitimacy of the Nasser regime. Second, Qutb not
only opened the door to fighting against corrupt or
insufficiently Islamic governments, but also introduced the ability to excommunicate individuals:
'This absolute command also lies in the Quran, that
no link should be had with a person who turns his
face from the remembrance of God and world-seeking
alone is his objective and outlook' (in Moaddel and
Talattof, 2002: 205). Qutb personally played a role
in criticizing and opposing Egyptian modernists
such as Taha Hussayn (1889–1973).

However, the primary target of Islamists is the
secular nation-state in Islamic countries, and their
ultimate aim is the establishment of an Islamic state.
The state they envision has the Qur'an as its constitution, the ruler implements the *shari'a*, to which

he is also bound, and the ruler engages in *shura* (consultation). As Qutb writes, 'political theory in Islam rests on the basis of justice on the part of the rulers, obedience on the part of the ruled, and collaboration between ruler and ruled' (1980: 93). Most Islamists are quick to resist equations of *shura* with democracy. Democracy, which is based on the idea of popular sovereignty, not the sovereignty of God, is considered a *jahiliyya* form of government. According to Qutb, those Muslims who argue for human sovereignty in politics confuse the exercise of power with its source. In his view, the people do not possess, and thus cannot delegate, sovereignty. Rather, they must implement what God, the sovereign, has legislated. Since Islamic law provides a complete legal and moral system, no further legislation is either possible or necessary. Similarly, Mawdudi claims that 'it is quite clear that Islam, speaking from the viewpoint of political philosophy, is the very antithesis of secular Western democracy' (in Donohue and Esposito, 1982: 254).

Another blueprint for an Islamic order is found in Khomeini's *vilayat-i faqih* (the guardianship or rule of the jurists), which constituted the official ideology of the Islamic Republic of Iran that he helped establish in 1979. This vision of Islamic government, achieved under the guardianship of the jurists, represents a significant innovation in Shi'i political thought which was traditionally based on a waiting for the return of the 'hidden Imam'. *Vilayat-i faqih* is founded on the existence of an institutionalized and hierarchical Shi'a 'clergy' (something absent to the Sunni tradition). While this aspect of Khomeini's thought remained largely confined to Iran, other aspects had a wider influence on contemporary Islamism elsewhere, such as his use of Qur'anic notions to draw a picture of Muslims as 'the downtrodden (*mustad'afun*) of the earth', who have been dominated and ruled over by the 'arrogant' (*mustakburun*) (1982: 106), his critique of Western 'materialism' and his populism.

These latter ideas illustrate the extent to which Islamists appeal directly to those who are hurt most when economic, social, and political conditions are dire. The end of the twentieth century offered them many opportunities to make such appeals: enduring unemployment and declining public services, the lack of response to continued Israeli occupation and military actions (such as the 1993 bombardment of villages in southern Lebanon), the increasing repression of the Muslim Brotherhood in Egypt during the 1980s and 1990s, the annulment of elections in Algeria after the balloting success of the Islamic Salvation Front in December 1991 and the ensuing civil war, the outlawing of the Tunisian Renaissance Party led by Rashid al-Ghannushi and of the Syrian Muslim Brethren. However, some Islamist movements and parties, such as the Muslim Brethren of Jordan, have officially accepted the means and practices of secular institutions and have been integrated into the political process. Most of the attention and energy of Islamists has continued to focus on problems internal to states and societies with predominantly or exclusively Muslim populations. However, military strikes and economic sanctions by a US-led coalition against the regime in Iraq has led some to speculate that the Islamist challenge was refocusing against the contemporary international order. Nonetheless, even this newest dimension to Islamic political thought confirms Robert Hefner's assessment that the real 'clash of civilizations' or 'world views' in the contemporary period is not so much 'between the West and some homogeneous "other" but between rival carriers of tradition within the same nations and civilizations' (1998: 92). Although much of the focus in the West has been on Islamism, this trend is only one of many that are now vying for space in contemporary Islamic discourse.

LIBERAL ISLAM

Islamism's visibility and power have waxed and waned throughout the middle and latter part of the twentieth century. Late in the twentieth century modernist discourses were revived and strengthened, alongside what has been termed 'Islamic liberalism'.[5] According to Kurzman, Islamic liberals 'sought to resuscitate the reputation and accomplishments of earlier modernists' (2002: 4). Certainly, one finds liberal elements in the thought of those earlier modernists and, in some respects, Islamic liberalism dates back to the very beginning of the *Nahda*. However, a distinct trend emerged around the 1970s, on the heels of the Islamic revival, and became more prevalent in the mid 1980s with Gorbachev's launching of *perestroika* and as elections were held in a number of Islamic countries and governments seemed to be transformed, or on the verge of being transformed, by forces of civil society. Contemporary Islamic liberalism is distinct from both Islamic modernists and Islamists in three respects.

First, against Islamist slogans that 'Islam is the solution', and secularist claims that Islam is the problem, Islamic liberals attribute most social and political ills to a lack of democracy and basic rights, especially freedom of thought. Although in some cases the focus on democracy might be interpreted as merely a strategic compromise on the part of Islamists to protest against secular states that exclude Islamist parties from participation, among liberal Islamic thinkers the argument is consistently aimed at both secular and theocratic states.

Responding to those who argue for secularism, Muhammad Shahrour (Syria, b. 1938) argues:

> Since religion has an important normative role in the Middle East societies, it is impossible to ignore it. Liberals tried to do so, and they failed in their attempt to transport a Western political formula to the Arab/Muslim states. Marxists wanted to impose a secularization, to deconstruct religion, and also failed. Anyhow, there could be secularism in the Arab or Islamic states, but it would not solve anything. The Middle East problem is not secularism, but democracy. The secular state has been there for seventy years, it was imposed upon society and it did not work. (1999: 2)

In response to Islamists, Sadek J. Sulaiman (Oman, b. 1933) maintains that 'as a concept and as a principle, *shura* in Islam does not differ from democracy', and 'the relationship between democracy and *shura* touches the essence of our national existence (*qawmiyya*). It determines the quality of our civic experience and the world we would like to leave for future generations. For this reason the subject merits our full attention' (in Kurzman, 1998: 98, 10). Rahman argues specifically against Mawdudi's and Qutb's dismissals of democracy as in violation of God's sovereignty, claiming that their view is based on a confusion of religio-moral and political issues. 'Sovereignty', Rahman argues,

> is a political term of relatively recent coinage and denotes that definite and defined factor (or factors) in a society to which rightfully belongs *coercive force* in order to obtain obedience to its will. It is obvious that God is not sovereign in this sense and that only people can be and are sovereign. (in Donohue and Esposito, 1982: 264)

Accepting the sovereignty of God, in Rahman's view, involves accepting 'the principles enunciated in the Qur'an [which] are justice and fair play'.

Liberal Islamic thinkers maintain that a democratic system best codifies and preserves rights and duties that can curtail arbitrariness and authoritarianism on the part of the state. Among the most important values attributed to democracy in liberal Islamic thought is tolerance, and among the most important rights are the freedoms of thought and speech. Rahman argues that 'difference of opinion, provided it is meaningful, has to be assigned a high positive value' (in Kurzman, 1998: 317). Nurcholish Madjid (Indonesia, b. 1939) ranks the freedoms of thought and expression as the most important of individual liberties and argues that even ideas that appear strange or incorrect must be protected:

> It is by no means rare that such ideas and thoughts, initially regarded as generally wrong, are [later] found to be right ... Furthermore, in the confrontation of ideas

and thoughts, even error can be of considerable benefit, because it will induce truth to express itself and grow as a strong force. Perhaps it was not entirely small talk when our Prophet said that differences of opinion among his *umma* were a mercy [from God]. (in Kurzman, 1998: 287)

Mohamed Talbi (Tunisia, b. 1921) analyses several Qur'anic verses, including Sura 5, Verse 51 – 'To each among you, have We prescribed a Law and an Open Way. And if God had enforced His Will, He would have made of you all one people' – to argue that Islam supports religious liberty and that the traditional death penalty for apostasy is based upon a misreading of the divine text (in Kurzman, 1998: 164).

Further, in national contexts where Muslims comprise a minority or are only a marginal majority, liberal Islamic thinkers have expressed a particular interest in the protection of religious rights and minorities. A number of thinkers have pointed to what has become known as the 'Constitution of Medina', a treaty signed by the Prophet Muhammad under which the various clans in Medina, including Jews and polytheists, formed an alliance or federation. According to 'Ali Bula (Turkey, b. 1951): 'The urgent problem of the day was to end the conflicts and to find a formulation for the co-existence of all sides according to the principles of justice and righteousness. In this respect, the Document is epochal' (in Kurzman, 1998: 173). Bula characterizes the society set up under this agreement as 'righteous and just, law respecting', as well as democratic, and he claims it manages to achieve 'a rich diversity within unity, or a real pluralism', since 'each religious and ethnic group enjoys complete cultural and legal autonomy' (in Kurzman, 1998: 174). Others quote Qur'anic passages to support an ideal of a society respectful of religious differences. Chandra Muzaffar (Malaysia, b. 1947) quotes Sura 49, Verse 13 – 'O mankind! We created you from a single pair of a male and a female, and made you into nations and tribes, that ye may know each other, not that ye may despise each other' – to support arguments for tolerance in Malaysia, a diverse country where Muslims enjoy only a slight majority (in Kurzman, 1998: 157).

The second distinct aspect of liberal Islamic thinkers is that they eschew efforts to seize state power, or even to Islamicize the state, and focus instead on reviving an Islamic ethos at the societal level. In this context, many Islamic liberals have argued for a reconsideration of a thesis put forth by Shaykh 'Ali 'Abd al-Raziq (Egypt, 1888–1966) in the 1920s, that 'Muhammad, peace be upon him, was a Messenger of a religious call, full of religiosity, untainted by a tendency to kingship or a call to government' (in Kurzman, 1998: 29). According to 'Abd al-Raziq, government 'is a worldly aim, and

God, may He be elevated, has rendered it a matter to be resolved by our minds, and has left people free to manage it in the manner that their minds, knowledge, interests, desires, and tendencies would guide them' (in Kurzman, 1998: 35). The book generated considerable controversy when it was published and 'Abd al-Raziq was widely criticized and suffered the loss of his academic and juridical positions.

Muhammad Khalaf-Allah (Egypt, 1916–97), an Islamic liberal and similarly controversial figure, takes 'Abd al-Raziq's argument one step further by suggesting that not only does the Qur'an allow human beings to manage the affairs of government, but it requires them to do so and in a democratic manner. Like earlier thinkers, Khalaf-Allah advocates *shura*, which he interprets as democracy. However he interprets the second part of Sura 3, Verse 159 – 'And seek their counsel in affairs. And when you have come to a decision, place your trust in God alone' – to claim that when Muslims have come to a decision about a matter, they should 'execute this decision without waiting for divine opinion', either in the form of revelation, or even of the religious scholars' (*'ulama*) explanation in light of religious texts (in Kurzman, 1998: 39). According to Khalaf-Allah, God has delegated to Muslims the responsibility to establish a system of consultation so that they can decide upon political matters for themselves.

As with Islamic writings on democracy, it is sometimes difficult to assess the extent to which some statements critical of projects aimed at Islamicizing the state indicate a realist strategy, as opposed to a liberalist conviction. For example, the International Forum for Islamic Dialogue (IFID) is one of many modern, liberal Islamic organizations that currently exist throughout the world.[6] The IFID publishes a newsletter in English and Arabic entitled *Islam21* and provides an interactive website for exchanging and developing ideas among Muslims. According to the IFID charter, the organization explicitly sees itself as occupying and developing a new realm in a period that is witnessing 'the advancement of civil society and the retreat of state control'. The Forum distinguishes its dialogue from earlier Islamist movements which 'were chasing state power', a strategy that the Forum's organizers describe as not only 'very costly and rarely achievable', but also unlikely to 'solve problems' and potentially a 'liability to the Islamic project as a whole'. 'The options for socio-political activism must not be confined to an all-out opposition to the State. In fact, Islamists can be more effective through pursuing the advancement of civil society' (IFID, 1999: 1).

However, in general, liberal Islamic thinkers demonstrate a significant shift toward replacing theocratic arguments with those aimed at instilling or protecting an Islamic ethos. Some, like Khalaf-Allah, argue that 'if any government is to be described as Islamic, it should be in the sense of "Islam-the-culture" (*al-Islam al-hadara*) and not of "Islam-the-religion" (*al-Islam al-din*)' (Ayoubi, 1991: 302). The Egyptian jurist Shaykh Muhammad Sa'id al-'Ashmawy (b. 1932) argues for the same conclusion, based on different premises:

> The principle of separating politics from religion, that is, civic rule, the so-called secularism, is needed. Politics should be practiced unfettered by religion but on the basis of civil code. At the same time religion needs to be protected from political distortion or corruption and unimpeded by early disputes or conflicts of power. When religion is meshed with politics it becomes an ideology, not a religion, and its followers become politicians or party members. To succeed, religion must recognize that it is a faith of profound power instilled in mankind's conscience to connect the individual with his faith, society, humanity and the cosmos at large. (1998: 71)

In al-'Ashmawy's assessment, Islamists are guilty of ideologizing Islam, that is, denigrating and exploiting the faith for temporal ends and separating and dividing Muslims. 'True religion,' according to al-'Ashmawy, 'is open to all humankind, requiring each individual to refine him or herself and elevate his or her conscience to co-operate with all humankind' (1998: 72).

A third element that distinguishes at least some of the Islamic liberals from modernists, Islamists, and traditionalists has to do with the way they approach the issue of interpreting the religious tradition or *ijtihad*. Islamic modernists had already taken on the Sunni orthodoxy which claimed that the 'gates of *ijtihad*' had been shut in the early centuries of Islam and that later Muslims need to follow the practice of *taqlid*, the imitation of established traditions. For example, at the turn of the century Mahmud Shukri al-Alusi (Iraq, 1857–1924) declared the 'thesis concerning the closing of the gate of *ijtihad*' put forth by his contemporary, the 'miserable', 'ignoramus' Yusuf al-Nabhani's (Palestine–Lebanon, 1850–1932), to be 'false and heretical' (in Kurzman, 2002: 171). Subhi Mahmasani (Lebanon, b. 1911) writes that 'the door of *ijtihad* should be thrown wide open for anyone juristically qualified. The error, all of the error, lies in blind imitation and restraint of thought' (in Donohue and Esposito, 1982: 182). Afghani maintained that Muslims must 'not be content with mere *taqlid* of their ancestors' (in Keddie, 1968: 171). Shaykh Na'ini argued that '*taqlid* of religious leaders who pretend to present true religion is no different from obedience to political tyrants' (in Kurzman, 2002: 122). In fighting against the practice of *taqlid*, Islamic modernists sought to rehabilitate and expand the right to engage in *ijtihad* in order to reinterpret the Islamic tradition to meet the needs of the modern age.

Wael Hallaq distinguishes between two strands of contemporary Islamic legal thought that offer competing visions of *ijtihad*. The first he terms 'religious utilitarianism', the second – in his view a 'new phenomenon' in Islam – he terms 'religious liberals' (1997: 214). Among the religious utilitarians he includes earlier modernist figures such as Rashid Rida, the Egyptian jurist 'Abd al-Wahhab Khallaf (1888–1956), and 'Allal al-Fasi (Morocco, 1910–74), as well as Hasan Turabi (Sudan, b. 1932). Among the religious liberals he includes al-'Ashmawy, the Pakistani scholar Fazlur Rahman, the Sudanese professor of law 'Abdullahi Ahmed an-Na'im (b. 1946), as well as Muhammad Shahrour, Muhammad Arkoun (Algeria–France, b. 1928), and Hassan Hanafi (Egypt, b. 1935). Although Turabi might merit inclusion among the Islamic liberals, by virtue of his emphasis on democracy and pluralism, Hallaq's distinction captures a dominant and unique facet of contemporary Islamic liberals. Both the liberal and the utilitarian, according to Hallaq, share the same goal: 'the reformulation of legal theory in a manner that brings into successful synthesis the basic religious values of Islam, on the one hand, and a substantive law that is suitable to the needs of a modern and changing society, on the other'. But what most divides these two trends are the methods they have devised to pursue this end. Whereas religious utilitarians place the public interest [*maslaha*] at the centre of their interpretive approach as a sort of guiding principle, religious liberals seek to develop a hermeneutic that departs from traditional literalist interpretations altogether. The 'main thrust of the liberalist approach', according to Hallaq, is 'understanding revelation as both text and context' (1997: 231).

In 1982, Rahman noted that it is

something of an irony to pit the so-called Muslim fundamentalists against the Muslim modernists, since, so far as their acclaimed procedure goes, the Muslim modernists say exactly the same thing as the so-called Muslim fundamentalists say: That Muslims must go back to the original and definitive sources of Islam and perform *ijtihad* on that basis. (1982: 142)

Both modernists and Islamists 'come up with radically different answers to some basic issues according to their respective environments', but the problem, as Rahman sees it, is not their different conclusions, but their lack of 'method' in interpreting the Islamic tradition so that it would provide for sound and reliable interpretations and eliminate

'vagrant' ones. Liberal Islamic thinkers revise the orthodox understanding of the Islamic law, stressing, as Shaykh al-'Ashmawy does, that 'the true meaning of *shari'a* is the path, the method the way' (1999: 97). While not denying the binding character of the *shari'a*, al-'Ashmawy does deny its character as a comprehensive legal system or detailed legal code. He suggests that the form of obedience required by this understanding of the *Shari'a* is more demanding because it requires active efforts of interpretation (*ijtihad*) by the faithful to discover the essential normative requirements of Islam.

Other Islamic liberals take the task of *ijtihad* even further by subjecting aspects of the Islamic *turath* to a more critical approach. An-Na'im seeks to 'criticize Shari'a and oppose its application today' by demonstrating that it was '*constructed* by Muslim jurists over the first three centuries of Islam' as they interpreted the Qur'an and Sunna (1996: 185). Thus, contemporary Muslims must engage in their own process of interpretation to develop a system of law appropriate for implementation today. In approaching the Qur'an, an-Na'im follows the traditional method of exegesis in distinguishing between those verses revealed to the Prophet Muhammad in Mecca and those revealed in Medina. However, following his teacher Mahmoud Muhammad Taha (Sudan, 1909–85), an-Na'im maintains that whereas the Suras of the Mecca period contain the eternal theological message of Islam, the Medina Suras refer to the particular needs of the first Muslim community in the context of war, and at a time when society lacked equal consideration of persons regardless of status and, thus, cannot be immediately applied to modern circumstances (1996: 52–8). According to this approach, the Mecca verses would be established as the basis of Muslim law abrogating the Medina verses.

In contrast, Shahrour (1990) employs a linguistic approach to delineate various meanings of the words found in the Qur'an. It is on this basis that Shahrour distinguishes between that which is 'divinely sanctioned (*halal*) and the divinely prohibited (*haram*) and the humanly forbidden (*mamnu'*)', maintaining that 'the basic tenet of Islam is that everything not specifically prohibited is permitted' (1990: 141). Shahrour's method illustrates a methodological tack common to Islamic liberals. Whereas modernist Muslims located various liberal ideas in the Islamic heritage, Islamic liberals maintain that the heritage is silent on certain issues. Al-'Ashmawy, for example, notes that 'of some 6000 Qur'anic verses, only 200 have a legal aspect, that is, approximately one-thirtieth of the Qur'an, including the verses which were abrogated by subsequent ones' (in Kurzman, 1998: 51).

According to Shahrour, consultation (*shura*) is required to work out the legislative questions for a modern polity within the limits set by God, to determine what sort of laws will govern those aspects of life God left to human regulation, relative to the particular social, economic and political circumstances of each political community. The idea that there is room for interpretation, that Islam can encompass myriad viewpoints, is another common trope of Islamic liberalism. Ayatollah Syed Mohammad Bahrul Uloom (Iraq, b. 1927) cites two Qur'anic verses to support diversity: 'The right to differ in ideas, positions, and methods is acknowledged so that one does not deprive others of their convictions. Had your Lord please, He would have made mankind a single nation' (Sura 11, Verse 118); 'There was a time when men were one nation. They disagreed among themselves' (Sura 10, Verse 19) (1994: 26). Some Islamic liberals go so far as to argue that disagreement over the interpretation of the Islamic tradition is what keeps Islam vibrant. 'In our time,' Shahrour argues, 'genuine *shura* means genuine pluralism of points of view, *and* democracy' (1997: 8).

FRACTURED DIALOGUE

Rather than resolving the fundamental conflicts within modern Islamic thought, the current focus on method seems to have only added a new level to the debate. In the contemporary period one sees not only 'radically different' interpretations of the Islamic tradition, but also some radically divergent methods of interpretation. Yet, it is possible to identify at least two important transformations in Islamic political thought. The first is that the increasing plurality of interpretive strategies employed by liberal Islamic thinkers has further opened the door to a wide sector of the *umma* to return to the original texts of their heritage and offer new interpretations. Mohammed Arkoun has referred to the Qur'an as a closed official corpus (*le fait coranique*): '*official*' in the sense that it 'resulted from a set of decisions taken by "authorities" recognized by the community'; '*closed*' on account of the fact that it is no longer permissible 'to add or subtract a word, to modify a reading in the Corpus now declared authentic' (1994: 33). However, any monopoly the *'ulama* might have once had seems to have been broken.

Although, like Islamic modernists, liberal Islamic thinkers seem to offer a promising way of negotiating the conflict between and meeting the demands of both modernization and the Islamic heritage, they have also faced serious challenges. They are under attack from both sides: they are criticized both for being too liberal and for being too Islamic. Secularists see liberal Islam (as well as modernist Islam) as an oxymoron and argue either that Islam is too inflexible to be transformed or that it should be relegated to the private sphere. Both revivalist and traditional Islamists argue that Islamic liberals are no more than secularists in Islamic guise, and either deny that modern values have a place in Islam's lexicon or cite them for taking their liberalism too far at the expense of the Islamic heritage. Quite often their works have garnered a considerable readership, but they have also been accused of treason and heresy, and been subject to censorship, loss of position, and violence – all of which tend to result in the unintended consequence of further increasing interest in their ideas. In a 1979 article that has been reprinted a number of times, the liberal Islamic thinker Hassan Hanafi attributes the 'historical roots of the impasse with regard to freedom and democracy in the general contemporary trend of our thought' to a lost ability to listen, discuss, and, thus, move forward. Hanafi's assessment is perhaps a bit too harsh. Islamic political thought has transformed considerably over the last two centuries and there does seem to be evidence of a growing reading public. Further, despite Hanafi's claims to the contrary, there are some common meeting points in divergent discussions of political reform. Even the least tolerant of the Islamists – even some of Hanafi's own worst critics and detractors – are in some sense sharing the same discursive space and at least partially assimilating the discourse of liberal and modernist thought.

NOTES

1 Questions quoted are from Amir Shakib Arslan (Lebanon, 1869–1946) (in Donohue and Esposito, 1982: 60), Muhammad 'Abduh (Egypt, 1849–1905) (in Kurzman, 2002: 59), Sati al-Hursi (Syria, 1880–1964) (in Donohue and Esposito, 1982: 66), 'Abd al-Rahman al-Bazzaz (Iraq, 1913–71) (in Donohue and Esposito, 1982: 84), Ziya Gökalp (Turkey, 1876–1924) (in Kurzman, 2002: 196), Ahmed Aghayev (Azerbaijan, 1869–1939) (in Kurzman, 2002: 229), Mirza Malkum Khan (Iran, 1833–1908) (in Kurzman, 2002: 113), Abdullah Bubi (Tatarstan, 1871–1922) (in Kurzman, 2002: 232), and Mahmud Tarzi (Afghanistan, 1865–1933) (Tarzi, 1912). The sourcebooks edited by Kurzman (2002), Donohue and Esposito (1982), and Moaddel and Talattof (2002) each offer excellent selections of representative texts by modern Islamic thinkers.

2 I am using 'modernism' in a manner articulated by Derek Hopwood: 'Modernity (modernism) is a general term for the political and cultural processes set in motion by integrating new ideas, an economic system, or education into society. It is a way of thought, of living in the contemporary world, and of accepting change' (2000: 2).

3 Dating of this period varies, though most take Islamic modernism to have begun at some point in the nineteenth century and to have ceased to be a predominant trend by the middle of the twentieth century (Rippin, 1990; Moussalli, 1999). According to Black (2001), the 'age of modernism' starts around 1830 with the Ottoman *Tanzimat* (Reform) and the writings of various Muslim thinkers, most notably those of Khayr al-Din al-Tunis (Tunisia, 1822/3–90), and ends around 1920 with the onset of what he terms the 'age of fundamentalism' (*c.* 1920–2000). Kurzman uses 1840 as 'a rough marker' of when this period of Islamic modernization began and maintains that 'by the 1930s the movement was in serious decline' (2002: 26). Moaddel and Talattof (2002) date the period a bit later, between the late nineteenth and the early twentieth century. In contrast, Albert Hourani's (1983) pioneering work examines Arab thought during what he terms 'the liberal age' (referring more to the liberal trend in Europe during the period than to a general characterization of the Arab intellectuals he discusses who were interacting with the West), which begins with Napoleon's Egyptian campaign in 1798, the first major colonial penetration in the region, and ends in 1939 when World War II breaks out.

4 The architects of the Islamic awakening have been described by terms such as 'revivalist', 'fundamentalist', 'Wahhabist', 'Salafiyya', and 'Islamist', among others. I opt for the last term, both because I find it to be the least problematic, albeit not perfect, of the alternatives ('revivalist' is too broad, encompassing both traditionalists and Islamists; 'fundamentalist' has origins in Protestant Christianity; and 'Wahhabist' and 'Salafiyya' tie Islamists too closely to specific – albeit related – movements), and because it captures the activist and ideological character of this trend. 'Islamist' refers here to those who see Islam as a self-sufficient system providing for all aspects of modern life. Islamism is a modern political ideology aimed at increasing the role of Islam in society and at establishing an Islamic state based on the *shari'a*. As such, one must distinguish Islamists from thinkers who are 'Islamic' (consciously organize their thinking within the conceptual framework of Islam, but do not actively seek to create an Islamic state or implement Islamic law).

5 This chapter uses 'Islamic liberalism' in a more limited sense than both Binder (1989) and Kurzman (1998). Binder includes in his study a number of thinkers who are significantly more liberal than Islamic and some who are more socialist than liberal. For example, although a number of the Islamic liberals are secularists, they argue for secularism on the basis of what they believe is called for by the religion. It is on that basis that I try to maintain a distinction between secular Muslims and secular Islamic thinkers. Although I share Kurzman's delineation of Islamic liberalism in his *Sourcebook*, I focus on the more recent formulation of this trend.

6 The IFID is a non-profit organization founded in 1994 and based in London. Some of the other organizations

include the Freedom Movement of Iran, the International Institute of Islamic Thought in Herndon, Virginia and Malaysia, and the Ibn Khaldun Society in London.

REFERENCES

Abu Rabi', Ibrahim M. (1996) *Intellectual Origins of the Islamic Resurgence in the Modern Arab World*. Albany, NY: State University of New York Press.

al-'Ashmawy, Muhammad Sa'id (1998) *Against Islamic Extremism*, ed. and trans. Carolyn Fluehr-Lobban. Gainesville, FL: University Press of Florida.

al-Jabiri, Muhammad 'Abd (1994) *al-Dimuqratiyya wa huquq al-insan (Democracy and Human Rights)*. Beirut: Center for Arab Unity Studies.

al-Qaradawi, Yusuf (1982) *al-Sahwa al-islamiyya bayn al-juhud wa al-tatarruf (The Islamic Awakening between the Limits and the Extremes)*. Qatar: Mataba'at al-dawha al-haditha.

al-Qaradawi, Yusuf (1988) 'al-'Itar al-'amm lil-sahwa al-islamiyya al-mu'asira' ('The general framework of the contemporary Islamic awakening'). In Saad Eddin Ibrahim, ed., *al-Sahwa al-Islamiyya wa humum al-watan al-'arabi*. Amman: Muntada al-fikr al-'arabi.

al-Tunisi, Khayr al-Din (1967) *The Surest Path: The Political Treatise of a Nineteenth-Century Muslim*, trans. and ed. Leon Carl Brown. Cambridge, MA: Harvard University Press.

An-Na'im, Abdallahi Ahmed (1996) *Toward an Islamic Reformation: Civil Liberties, Human Rights, and International Law*. Syracuse, NY: Syracuse University Press.

Arkoun, Mohammed (1994) *Rethinking Islam*. Boulder, CO: Westview.

Awwad, Louis (1986) *The Literature of Ideas in Egypt*. Atlanta: Scholars.

Ayoubi, Nazih (1991) *Political Islam: Religion and Politics in the Arab World*. London: Routledge.

Bakhash, Shaul (1978) *Iran, Monarchy, Bureaucracy, and Reform under the Qajars, 1858–1896*. London: Ithaca Press for the Middle East Centre, St Antony's College.

Binder, Leonard (1989) *Islamic Liberalism*. Chicago: University of Chicago Press.

Black, Antony (2001) *The History of Islamic Political Thought: From the Prophet to the Present*. London: Routledge.

Donohue, John J. and John L. Esposito (1982) *Islam in Transition: Muslim Perspectives*. Oxford: Oxford University Press.

Hallaq, Wael B. (1997) *A History of Islamic Legal Theories: An Introduction to Sunni Usul al-Fiqh*. New York: Cambridge University Press.

Hanafi, Hassan (1979) 'al-Juzur al-tarikhiyya li-azimat-al-hurriyya wa al-dimukraia fi wujdanuna al-mu'asir'

(The Historical Roots of the Crisis of freedom and democracy in our Zeitgeist.). *al-Mustaqbal al-'arabi.*

Hefner, Robert W. (1998) 'Multiple modernities: Christianity, Islam and Hinduism in a globalizing age'. *Annual Review of Anthropology*, 27.

Hopwood, Derek (2000) 'Introduction: the culture of modernity in Islam and the Middle East'. In John Cooper, Ronald Netter and Mohamed Mahmoud, eds, *Islam and Modernity: Muslim Intellectuals Respond.* London: Tauris.

Hourani, Albert (1983) *Arabic Thought in the Liberal Age, 1798–1939* (1962). Cambridge: Cambridge University Press.

Ibn Taymiyya, Taqiy al-Din (1966) *al-Fatawa al-Kubra,* 5 vols. Cairo: Dar al-kutub al-hadithah.

Ibn Taymiyya, Taqiy al-Din (1985) *al-Siyasa al-shar'iyya* (*Governance According to Islamic Law*). Beirut: al-Afaq al-Jadid. English trans. in Omar A. Farrukh, *Ibn Taimiya on Public and Private Law in Islam.* Beirut: Khayat, 1966.

IFID (1999) International Forum for Islamic Dialogue, 'The need for a charter'. *Islam21*, 15 (February).

Keddie, Nikki R. (1968) *An Islamic Response to Imperialism: Political and Religious Writings of Sayyid Jamal ad-Din al-Afghani.* Berkeley, CA: University of California Press.

Kepel, Gilles (1986) *Muslim Extremism in Egypt.* Berkeley, CA: University of California Press.

Khadduri, Majid (1970) *Political Trends in the Arab World.* Baltimore: Johns Hopkins University Press.

Khomeini, Ruhollah (1982) *Light of the Path: Selected Messages of Imam Khomeini.* Tehran: Jihad-e-Sazandegi (Jihad for Construction).

Kurzman, Charles (1998) *Liberal Islam: A Sourcebook.* New York: Oxford.

Kurzman, Charles (2002) *Modernist Islam, 1840–1940: A Sourcebook.* New York: Oxford.

Laroui, Abdallah (1976) *The Crisis of the Arab Intellectual: Traditionalism or Historicism?* Berkeley, CA: University of California Press.

Mawdudi, Syed Abul A'la (1960) *Towards Understanding Islam.* Lahore: Islamic.

Mawdudi, Syed Abul 'Ala (1976) *Jihad in Islam.* Lahore: Islamic.

Moaddel, Mansoor and Kamran Talattof (2002) *Modernist and Fundamentalist Debates in Islam.* New York: Palgrave.

Moussalli, Ahmad (1999) *Moderate and Radical Islamic Fundamentalism.* Gainesville, FL: University Press of Florida.

Qutb, Sayyid (Kotb, Sayed) (1980) *Social Justice in Islam*, trans. John B. Hardie. New York: Octagon.

Qutb, Sayyid (1990) *Milestones.* Indianapolis: American Trust.

Rahman, Fazlur (1970) 'Revival and reform in Islam'. In P. M. Lambton Holt, Ann Katharine Swynford and Bernard Lewis, eds, *The Cambridge History of Islam.* Cambridge: Cambridge University Press.

Rahman, Fazlur (1982) *Islam and Modernity: Transformation of an Intellectual Tradition.* Chicago: University of Chicago Press.

Rippin, Andrew (1990) *Muslims: Their Religious Beliefs and Practices.* Vol. 2, *The Contemporary Period.* London: Routledge.

Shahin, Emad Eldin (1993) *Through Muslim Eyes: M. Rashid Rida and the West.* Herndon, VA: International Institute of Islamic Thought.

Shahrour, Muhammad (1990) *al-Kitab wa al-qur'an: qira'a mu'asira* (*The Book and the Quran: A Contemporary Reading*). Damascus: al-Ahli lil-taba'a wa al-nashr wa al-tawzi.

Shahrour, Muhammad (1997) 'The divine text and pluralism in Muslim societies'. *Muslim Politics Report of the Council on Foreign Relations*, 14 (July–August).

Shahrour, Muhammad (1999) 'Reading the religious text: a new approach'. *Islam 21*, 20.

Tarzi, Mahmud (1912) *Chih Bayad Kard?* (What is to be Done?). Kabul: Siraj ak-akhbar.

Uloom, Ayatollah Syed Mohammad (1994) 'Islam, democracy, and the future of Iraq'. In Richard W. Bulliet, ed., *Under Siege: Islam and Democracy.* New York: Middle East Institute of Columbia University.

28

European Political Thought in the Nineteenth Century

RAYMOND PLANT

Political thought in the nineteenth century developed against the background of momentous events and intellectual developments in the spheres of science, sociology, theology and history, and we need first of all to understand in broad terms the nature of some of these themes.

THE FRENCH REVOLUTION

The French Revolution still exercised an enormous influence on both progressive and self-consciously reactionary thinkers. Many revolutions and insurrections took place in Europe during this period (Hobsbawm, 1975). The post-Napoleonic period had been a very great disappointment to many radical thinkers and groups. In the immediate aftermath of the defeat by Napoleon of the forces of the Holy Roman Empire of the German nation at Jena in 1806 there had been some political and social progress, particularly in Prussia where the reforms of Stein and Hardenberg were well on their way to producing a more liberal form of constitutional monarchy. Following the final defeat of Napoleon however, the Holy Alliance of Austria, Prussia and Russia came into existence with a self-consciously reactionary agenda, which led to greater censorship and political persecution. Nevertheless in Russia in December 1825 there had been an attempted coup against the new Tsar Nicholas I and some of the Decembrist leaders were unexpectedly and rather incompetently executed. In France the Orleanist monarchy was overthrown in February 1848 as the result of popular insurrection. This set off something of a chain reaction. By early March the

south-western German states were affected, as was Bavaria by 6 March and Berlin by 11 March, and a National Parliament representing all the German states was set up in the Paulskirche in Frankfurt am Main. By 13 March the uprisings reached Vienna, followed by Hungary, and Metternich, the architect of post-Napoleonic Europe, was forced to flee. The tide of revolution reached Italy by 18 March with rebellions or the perceived threat of rebellions in Sicily, Piedmont, Tuscany, Rome and, indeed, the papal states. These led rulers of what was not then a united nation (Metternich had called Italy a 'geographical expression' only, and Italian nationality a 'meaningless word': Mack Smith, 1994: 51) to promise some degree of representative government. Switzerland too was not immune to these developments and had in fact had a civil war in 1847. So these years were seen as a pivotal moment in European history, and both the possibility and the fear of revolution dominated political thought and practice for most of the century.

While a good deal of the motivating force for revolution came from general democratic ideals of republican self-government, these were also revolutions in which a self-conscious form of socialism and communism played a leading role. Marx and Engels, of course, at this time wrote *The Communist Manifesto*. The first German edition of the *Manifesto* was published in London on about 24 February with words which within a few days were going to sound prophetic:

A spectre is haunting Europe – the spectre of communism. All of the Powers of old Europe have entered into a holy alliance to exorcise this spectre: Pope and Tsar,

Metternich and Guizot, French Radicals and German police spies. (Marx, 1978: 473)

Many of Europe's leading political thinkers were involved in the events of 1847–9 as activists, protagonists and commentators. Frequently they knew one another even though relationships were often fraught. Indeed Alexander Herzen, the leading Russian liberal thinker, often acted as a banker and frequently unpaid money lender to a group which included Marx, Engels, Mikhail Bakunin, Pierre Proudhon, Giuseppi Mazzini, and George Herwegh (Carr, 1998). Others involved in the events of this period were Ludwig Feuerbach and the great historian Theodor Mommsen. Later in the century other thinkers were involved in direct political struggle including Ferdinand Lasalle, Peter Kropotkin and Eduard Bernstein.

It has frequently been said that this period sees the emergence of a genuine European intelligentsia involved both in theorizing about the nature of society and politics and in trying to change society in a socialist, communist, or in the case of Bakunin and Kropotkin, anarchist direction. In their different ways and in some cases for different reasons they were committed to Marx's dictum in his eleventh *Thesis on Feuerbach*: 'The philosophers have only interpreted the world in various ways; the point however is to change it' (1978: 145). *Praxis* – the unity of theory and practice – is what they aimed for, but they did differ in terms of both theory and prescription.

COUNTER-REVOLUTIONARY THOUGHT

Other centrally important thinkers were, however, engaged in a very different enterprise, namely that of formulating a response to the experience of the French Revolution and to the prospect of more to come in Europe. These counter-revolutionary themes are central to the writings of Joseph Arthur Gobineau (Biddiss, 1970), the Christian conservatism of Joseph de Maistre (1994), and Louis Gabriel Ambrois Bonald (1859; Menczer, 1952), Taine le Bon and later Maurice Barrès and Charles Maurras (all in McClelland, 1970). Other major thinkers who cannot be so easily classified nevertheless had the French Revolution and its aftermath at the centre of their thought: this is true for example of Alexis de Tocqueville and François Auguste René Chateaubriand (1884).

These revolutionary events were also closely related to the rise of nationalism as a force in European states. In the earlier part of the century the demand for revolutionary change was often linked to the idea of democratic self-government

and nationalism. Nationalism for Mazzini, to take an example, embodied the idea of a democratic self-governing republic. So in this sense, it was a kind of liberal nationalism. In Mazzini's thought, it was also linked to the idea that a nation could develop the idea of a particular national mission. This was not understood by Mazzini to be part of national self-aggrandisement. It was only that different nations had different characters and it was perfectly possible to think that these could contribute in different ways to the achievement of a rich common humanity, rather than a sense of national identity being taken as involving the devaluation of others. Indeed, Mazzini developed the idea of a common economic market in Europe within which nation-states would contribute their respective strengths to something that would be to the benefit of all (Mack Smith, 1994).

CULTURAL AND RACIAL NATIONALISM

There were, however, other forms of nationalism which were conceived by their intellectual supporters in much more specific cultural, ethnic and exclusionary terms. This strand of thinking in France runs from de Maistre and Gobineau through to Barrès and Maurras, and in Germany from Johann Gottlieb Fichte's *Addresses to the German Nation*, delivered following the defeat of the German states by Napoleon at the Battle of Jena, through to some of the ideas which formed part of Richard Wagner's circle and which informed his operas. Fichte's addresses are predicated on the idea that the German nation has a special mission, particularly in the context of European culture. The German nation is part of what he regards as the *Urvolk* – the primal people, the people of creativity, imagination and insight. Given the late-eighteenth-century flowering of German culture in Weimar and Jena where Fichte had been a professor and where Goethe, Friedrich Schiller, the Schlegels, Ludwig Tieck, Friedrich Hölderlin, Friedrich Schelling and Hegel were to be found (Beiser, 1992), one can perhaps understand this assessment. Nevertheless, the idea of a special national mission, which Mazzini also held, was in the hands of Fichte far more aggrandizing and exclusionary than anything entertained by Mazzini. Of those who are not part of the German sensibility Fichte says:

> All who believe in arrested being, in retrogression, in eternal cycles … in inanimate nature, and put her at the helm of the world, whatever be their native country, whatever be their language, they are not Germans, they are strangers to us, and one would hope that one day

they would be wholly cut off from our people. (Berlin, 1999: 96)

This linking of nationalism with the idea of the spirit of a people, with its national mission and the exclusion of those who do not share in that spirit, embodies quite a shift away from Fichte's own earlier reformist liberalism and individualism as embodied, for example, in his *Zuruckforderung der Denkfreiheit von den Fursten Europas* (Reiss, 1955). This abandonment is evident in his *Reden an die deutsche Nation* and theorized in great and somewhat tedious detail in his posthumous *Staatslehre*. The position he held at this stage of his life also led him to be committed to the idea of a patriotic education. The new citizen of the German nation was to be the product of a state educational system (*Nationalerziehung*) which would foster the establishment of a specific German character. At this time many of Fichte's ideas were shared by the philosopher and theologian Friedrich Schleiermacher, and a whole raft of German intellectuals in the early part of the nineteenth century, including Hegel, Schelling and Hölderlin, took the view that the philosopher had a cultural and pedagogical task in terms of trying to create a nation, even though they did not share Fichte's conception of exactly how this was to be done. This approach marks quite a shift from the understanding of the role of reason during the Enlightenment. During the period of the Enlightenment it was assumed that reason was universal and that a rational state and political order would reflect that universality, and would focus more on the demands of on the one hand cosmopolitanism and on the other the rights of the individual rather than on the cultural particularity of the nation and how this should be sustained in a rational way.

NATIONALISM AND ROMANTICISM

Fichte's nationalism is heavily indebted to his philosophical origins in the German Romantic movement (Berlin, 1999; Beiser, 1992; 2002). The movement perhaps most focused in Jena consisted of the writers, thinkers, poets and belletrists mentioned above, although it also included the philosopher Friedrich Jacobi, the statesman William von Humbolt (Beiser, 1992), and the historian and philosopher Johann Gottfried Herder who had lived in Weimar and exercised a profound influence (Berlin, 1999). For many of these thinkers the idea of the spirit of a people and its embodiment in a culture, politics, and religion specific to that people was one with great attractions. For many of them, particularly Herder, Schiller, Holderlin and Hegel (Plant, 1983), a society with a pervading ethos or spirit would be able to embody a strong sense of

belonging, of community and of being at home in the world. Partly as a reflection of such an integrated culture it was possible to envisage the ideal of the whole person – an integrated and whole personality. At this time in Germany the ideal for both man and society was drawn from ancient Greece in which it was believed politics, culture, religion and private life were woven together in an indissoluble manner, and this vision finds its way very strongly into the poetry and prose of Schiller, particularly *Die Gotter Griechenlands* and the sixth *Letter on the Aesthetic Education of Man*. This idea of an integrated person in a harmonious society was also an immense influence on Herder, Holderlin and Hegel (Plant, 1983). It was also a vision which Marx inherited and indeed held onto while he sought to delineate the kind of social and economic order which could actually embody such an ideal [see further Chapter 6]. In the writings of others, as we shall see, medieval society rather than Attic Greece provided the counterweight to the more fragmenting aspects of modernity. But it can be seen that this Romantic emphasis on personal and social integration could be consistent with, if not actually demanding, a strong sense of national identity; and it also involved an implicit and frequently explicit critique of liberal individualism and many aspects of modernity, particularly the growing market economy and the division of labour which were held to militate against the idea of the wholeness of the personality. These are still very strong themes in Marx and Engel's *The German Ideology* (Marx, 1978), published in 1846.

GERMAN ROMANTICISM AND ENLIGHTENMENT

This Romantic emphasis on the sense of integration of life could take a much wider course too. It could first of all be taken as a critique of the Enlightenment, as for example by Herder, and this perspective was developed in a much fuller way as the century wore on. Counter-Enlightenment thinkers stress the value of community rather than the individual; the local over the general; a traditional way of life rather than the moral demands of universal reason; the value of existing cultures against an ideal kingdom of ends; an emphasis on the idea of history and situatedness against the idea that the proper form of human society could be deduced from some ahistorical account of human nature; and an emphasis on virtue and obligation over individual rights and interests.

In Germany this led to a particular emphasis upon culture and language as constituting the unity of society and as a vehicle for national identity. The researches of the Grimm brothers into folklore are a good example of an attempt to retrieve a set of premodern understandings of German life which could contribute to a new sense of national solidarity built upon a shared culture and shared narratives. Jacob Grimm was a pupil of Friedrich Savigny, whose work on jurisprudence is discussed below. As Savigny sought to locate the authority of a post-Napoleonic form of law in Germany in the culture of small communities, particularly of pre-Reformation Germany, so the Grimm brothers' collection of stories was seen by them as a patriotic task and as an essential contribution to a sense of cultural identity which would underwrite national identity, as was Wilhelm Grimm's *German Heroic Tales* of 1829 (Habermas, 2001). The identity of a state and a nation was to be found in narrative and the ethos sustained by that narrative, not by resting institutions and identities upon claimed universal rational features of individuals. In this they were true disciples of Herder who was one of the main representative Romantic political and social thinkers of the last third of the previous century. Herder had argued in favour of a 'Patriotic Institute to foster a common spirit in Germany' and this would involve the institute in the collection and observance of folklore. The unity of society would occur not through the rights of individuals or through the social contract, but through shared culture and history. These were the genuine forms of legitimation, not reason and autonomy.

For Herder and the Grimm brothers it is also true that language is the key to national identity. The boundaries of the *Volk* are not primarily geographical but linguistic. In 1846 the *Germanistenversammlung* (the Germanists' Assembly) took place in Frankfurt and the idea was to bring together scholars in German law, language and history. The aim of the assembly, as Jürgen Habermas (2001) has pointed out, was the unification of a politically disunited fatherland. At the assembly Jacob Grimm argued that 'the borders of those peoples, who have expanded beyond mountains and rivers, can be defined exclusively by virtue of their language'. Similar themes run through his monumental *German Grammar* which was designed to exhibit the profound spirit of the language. As Habermas wryly remarks, it has often been argued that the Frankfurt meeting which took place in the *Kaisersaal* where the Holy Roman Emperor had previously been elected did not in fact amount to a coherent political force since, when the Frankfurt Parliament was set up in 1848 in the Paulskirche just a stone's throw away, the 10 percent of the Germanists who were its members clearly failed in their attempts to interpret the will of the people. This may point to quite a profound issue, namely the extent to which liberal style institutions and practices such as freedom of the press and freedom of speech can in fact grow out of

a strong sense of cultural identity [see further Chapters 13, 19 and 30]. It also raises the issue to which reference was made earlier, namely the emergence of an intelligentsia that was politically committed. In the earlier reference this was in respect of radical thinkers such as Herzen, Marx, Engels, Bakunin and others, and it is to this group that Isaiah Berlin (1978: 114) refers when he talks about the emergence of the intelligentsia in the nineteenth century. It is however equally true that there was a Romantic, nationalistic and Counter-Enlightenment intelligentsia which sought to articulate the spirit of the people, the spirit of its laws and the nature of its politics. The claims these thinkers made to legitimacy were not to universal rational principles but to historical circumstance and a habitual way of life, whether in *La France profonde*, or the medieval *marks* of Germany (Collini, Winch and Burrows, 1983), or the still existing *mirs* of Russia (Hare, 1964). This made the task of the Counter-Enlightenment intelligentsia more interpretive than constructive, as was the case for the radical intellectuals.

FRANCE: CULTURE, COMMUNITY AND NATIONALISM

These ideas became very strong in nineteenth-century Counter-Enlightenment and counter-revolutionary thinkers, for example, de Maistre when he argues in *The Study of Sovereignty* that: 'Every question about the nature of man must be resolved by history. The philosopher who wants to show us by *a priori* reasoning what man must be does not deserve an audience' (McClelland, 1970: 41). It was also a central theme in Hippolyte Taine's critical study of the French Revolution, particularly in its Jacobin form, as the following ironic passage from *The Origins of Contemporary France* makes clear:

> At length the rule of right is to begin. Of all that the past has founded and transmitted nothing is legitimate. Overlaying the natural man it has created an artificial man, either ecclesiastic or laic, noble or plebeian, sovereign or subject, proprietor or proletarian, ignorant or cultivated, peasant or citizen, slave or master, all being factitious qualities which we are not to heed, as their origin is tainted with violence and robbery. Strip off these superadded garments; let us take man in himself, the same under all conditions, in all situations, in all countries, in all ages, and strive to ascertain what sort of association is the best adapted to him. The problem thus stated the rest follows. (McClelland, 1970: 61)

This theme of the falsity of a political and social philosophy built upon some idea of the nature of the individual stripped of all sorts of identity, loyalty and obligation becomes a major theme of French thought in the nineteenth century, although it does have its origins in German Romantic thought of an earlier generation. It is the distinctive motif of right-wing counter-revolutionary thought; however, it is important to recognize that in so far as such thought might be called a bit anachronistically 'communitarian' there is, as we shall see, a communitarianism of both the right and the left during this period, and it would be a mistake to see the critique of liberal individualism as being just a feature of right-wing thought. A good example of its deployment in the writings of a self-conscious counter-revolutionary would be Barrès's essay with the rather unpromising title *Hegel and the Working Mens' Canteens of the North*, published in *Scènes et doctrines du nationalisme*, in which he draws attention to his central idea of the *déraciné* – rootless, cosmopolitan, rationalistic and universalistic in outlook, almost the potential hero of an Enlightenment thinker like Condorcet. For Barrès such an individual cannot live a satisfactory life and in fact can only find his salvation in a sense of strong identification with a nation, understood not in Mazzini's rather liberal sense, but as one with a strong and thick form of cultural and indeed racial identity. Against the ideal of cosmopolitanism he says:

> the varied influences of race, custom and climate would soon come into their own and real differences would reassert themselves. It is essential that these aspects of human development should be given free reign, so that humanity can affirm the life giving nature of diversity, of variety, of difference. No single one contains the truth. Only the total diversity approaches the truth. (McClelland, 1970: 156)

For Barrès the paradigm of society lies not in Attic Greece or in the *marks* and *mirs* of medieval Europe but in the *fermières* of Lorraine – almost a mythical place to him. Barres's thick nationalism took the Jews to be prime examples of the rootless cosmopolitan, and his view of the Jews at least up to the time of the Great War was an exclusionary one – a race antagonistic to my own, as he called it in one of his paeans to Lorraine, which also contains a discussion of the Dreyfus affair. Against the universalist demands of liberal individualism have to be set the demands of identity, loyalty and obligation and the way in which these are necessarily rooted not in reason but in the emotional and affective ties of national identity. This is a view widely shared by counter-revolutionary thinkers during this period.

TAKING STOCK OF THE FRENCH REVOLUTION

Other thinkers without this specific political agenda were also concerned one way or another with how

we are to understand politics, society and personal psychology after the French Revolution. During the Revolution, ostensibly under the impact of Rousseau's *Social Contract* and the critique of sectional interests and intermediate forms of identity which he believed would detract from individual identification with the General Will, many ancient mediating institutions and practices which embodied dispersed forms of social authority had been proscribed or undermined: Church, guild, locality as a locus for obligation and service, aristocracy, and the estates. In place of this diverse distributed power we witness the growth of the power of the centralized state and state sovereignty which displaces more pluralistic forms of sovereignty. This is the central theme of Tocqueville's *The Old Regime and the French Revolution* (1955) and his first book *Democracy in America* (1945). These books are a very profound study of the impact of democracy, individualism and the ideas of equality and human rights on traditional institutions and ways of life. In his view the salience of democracy and its power has emerged as the result of pressure from two sources: the historic growth of central power in the hands of monarchs in old states, which consolidated this monarchical rule over more diverse medieval forms of power in favour of strong national government, and the growth in the equality of status. Far from democracy decentralizing and dispersing power, equality of status, which seems to be a core idea of democracy, has undermined intermediate institutions that could stand between the individual and central power, which could be exercized in a tyrannical way whether in a monarchy or a democracy:

> I perceive that we have destroyed these individual powers which were able, single handed, to cope with tyranny; but it is the government alone that has inherited all the privileges of which families, guilds and individuals have been deprived; to the power of a small number of persons, which if it was sometimes oppressive, was often conservative, has succeeded the weakness of the whole community. (1945: 10)

So equality, democracy and centralization have gone together for Tocqueville since the Revolution, but at the same time those forces, accumulating in his estimation for over 700 years, are clearly now almost impossible to reverse or modify. Other thinkers shared this view. As we have seen, from the counter-revolutionary perspective there are cultural critics such as Barrès but also figures such as Lammenais who, while he started as an *ultramontane* Catholic, nevertheless ended his life preoccupied with co-operatives and labour unions and who argued in an arresting image in favour of decentralization, because centralized societies lead to apoplexy at the centre and anaemia in the extremities. P. G. T. Le Play in *La Reforme sociale* (1864) took a similar view, as did Bonald in *Théorie du pouvoir* (1966). Equally, though, so did Proudhon and Bakunin who as anarchists were clearly opposed to the centralized state and saw the political future in terms of decentralization and localism while not, of course, endorsing antique types of localism.

One of the more complex responses to the French Revolution was to be found in the writings of Auguste Comte, the positivist philosopher. He took the view that the Revolution was a destructive force and that it did not have the capacity to construct anything out of what it had destroyed. His account of the Revolution was embedded within his overall theory or philosophy of history for which he claimed scientific sanction. His view was that history passed through three stages: the theological, the metaphysical, and the scientific or positivist age which we are now entering. Morality and politics would be emancipated from theology and metaphysics and would be grounded in physical science. This would form the basis of a common educational system and would also constitute a new religion of humanity that, because it was based on the universality of science, could be shared by all (Comte, 1998). By putting man, the *grand être,* at the centre of his thought, he ensured that other Counter-Enlightenment French Catholic thinkers regarded his work as satanic.

THE CULTURE OF COMMUNITY

Whereas Voltaire and Condorcet, as paradigmatic Enlightenment thinkers, despised the middle ages, the growing interest among Counter-Enlightenment thinkers in dispersed social and political power led to a renewed interest in medieval social and political organization. Modern societies seemed to be developing a culture of individualism influenced by all sorts of factors, including Roman Law, the Christian religion, particularly in its Protestant form, the growth of the market economy, Kantian moral philosophy and rationalistic universalism, whilst major thinkers such as Fustel de Coulanges, Savigny, Otto von Gierke and Rudolf Stammler sought to retrieve for modern thought the medieval emphasis on locality, status, and community. A parallel investigation was going on in Britain at the hands of Henry Maine and Frederic Maitland. Very important in this development both in the United Kingdom and on the continent was the development of the school of historical jurisprudence, which Savigny had developed initially. This was taken to a very high level of sophistication by Gierke in his monumental *Das deutsche Genossenschaftsrecht*

(*The German Law of Association*) (1868–1913), which traced the origins, practices and constitutions of guilds and fellowships, marked by co-proprietorship through the middle ages. He chronicled the ways in which the monopolies of guild were eroded by the economic market, by the ideology of economic liberalism and by the antagonism of Enlightenment thinkers, particularly Rousseau. In this book he stresses the extent to which these bodies had a legal personality of their own and stood as an important source of power, loyalty, obligation and identity between the individual and the state. In his heyday Gierke welcomed the development of bodies which he felt could step into the void left by the erosion of the guilds: co-operatives, labour unions, banking co-operatives, and vocational and religious groups. However, as time passed, Gierke became increasingly conservative and nationalistic and he lost his enthusiasm for some forms of successors to guilds such as trade unions.

These issues were not only a matter of social and political philosophy in the narrow sense but also because these theories of association and community recognized, at least implicitly, the point made by Maine that the transition from medieval to modern societies also marked the transition from relationships based upon *status* to those based upon *contract*. From the feudal order to bourgeois society was a transition which Marx was also to trace, as we shall see, in terms of his historical materialism. By 1887 this contrast between different types of human society and the different character of human relationships within them had been definitively theorized by Ferdinand Tönnies in his *Gemeinschaft und Gesellschaft* (*Community and Civil Society*) (2001), with the main contrasts between the general forms of these two types of social organization and the human relationships which they presuppose being drawn in Sections 1 and 2 of that work [see further Chapter 13].

It would, however, be wrong to think that this emphasis upon community was entirely backward-looking – a nostalgic rejection of liberal individualism and the market economy – since some communitarian thinkers were anxious to develop socialist or anarchist approaches to the idea of community and its reinstatement in the modern world. They were unlike the German Romantics looking back with nostalgia to ancient Greece, and unlike French counter-revolutionaries evoking *l'ancien régime*; rather than endorsing ancient forms of community, they were busy devising blueprints for new socialist/ anarchist ones. The best example here among several including Proudhon and Bakunin is probably Kropotkin in *The Conquest of Bread* (1995). Kropotkin argued for the anarchist position in terms of the abolition of the state and its replacement by a decentralized network of small self-sufficient communities based upon voluntary agreement (thus recognizing that the growth of individualism and choice to that extent is irreversible) and marked by distributive or social justice. Similar ideas were held by Herzen who believed that such co-operatives could be created in the *mirs* of Russia. Kropotkin argued that the achievement of such a society could not come by socialists or communists taking over the state and then seeking to decentralize it into a collection of self governing co-operative communities. The state would not wither away once it was taken over by a communist revolution. The dictatorship of the proletariat would remain and it would just be another state as centralized and potentially tyrannical as any other. Kropotkin had a strong belief in the importance of the co-operative and altruistic features of the human personality, and he argued in *Mutual Aid* that co-operation is a vital force in human evolution which turns not upon competition and the survival of the fittest.

COMMUNITY AND THE ROLE OF LAW

We need to revert to the role of historical jurisprudence, not just in giving a kind of theoretical underpinning to the rediscovery of the importance of the idea of community but also in terms of its account of the nature of law and its relation to the overall culture of society. There is an interesting debate here between Anton Thibaut and Savigny – two early-nineteenth-century jurists. This has come to be called the *Kodifikationsstreit* – a dispute about the extent to which the law should be codified and the relationship of this question to that of nationalism and national identity. The debate took place around 1814 in the context of the issue of drafting a new legal code for the German states in a post-Napoleonic era. Deep theoretical questions were raised to do with the authority of law, the sources of the normativity of law and the relationship between the law and political institutions (Whitman, 1990; Thompson, 2001). The Code Napoléon had been rejected for the future of Germany because in the view of the particularists who were party to this debate the Code, through its guarantee of the rights of individuals, would eradicate the historically rooted differences among the very many German peoples. The dilemma was what was to replace it, and one popular view was that it should be replaced by Roman Law codified at the time of Justinian. This was, for example, the view taken by Gustav Hugo in *Beitrage zur Civilistischen Bucherkenntnis* and *Uber die Institutionen des heutigen romischen Recht* and Karl Ernst Schmidt in *Deutschlands Wiedergeburt*.

Thibaut, who was close to Hegel, in his *Uber die Notwendigkeit eines allgemeinen burgerlichen Rechts für Deutschland* was sympathetic to the others in their rejection of the Code Napoléon, but he was very sceptical about overlaying the diversity of German society with Roman Law, not least because social and economic circumstances had changed so fundamentally over the centuries. He shared the Romantic idea, discussed earlier, of the reunification of Germany, but this could not be achieved by the imposition of an alien code. This required going back to pre-revolutionary, pre-Reformation, pre-Enlightenment forms of law, and it was this law that should be codified with the backing of an educated citizenry. Thibaut's view was that the principles of universal law could be discerned by an educated person reflecting on nature, and this would allow an educated citizenry to understand the types of historical law which could be incorporated into a set of universal laws. In his view the codification of ancient statutes would allow the emergence of a universal body of law rooted in the practices and culture of German society and would unite the country.

Savigny, in his *Vom Beruf unser Zeit für Gesetzgebung und Rechtswissenschaft*, disagreed with this position. He thought that there had to be a kind of reconciliation between particularism and Roman Law and this could be achieved by a legal professoriate of jurisprudents who would be able to relate Roman and German legal concepts to one another and who would also be learned in the particularistic legal structures of German states and communities. In this way law would be both systematic (in the sense that it would relate one set of concepts, the Roman, to another, the historical German) and historical, and its normativity would arise from its embodiment of these two features. This was linked to the idea that the presence of this jurisprudential professoriate, who would be able to publish their legal treatises without censorship, would allow judges who would base their decisions on these treatises also to be free from political pressure.

So it can be seen how a Romantic concern with community, culture, history and national identity could come together in what otherwise would be a rather dry academic dispute but which was in reality a deep issue about where the normative principles were to be found in modern society. Do they lie in history and a systematic working with that history, as Savigny thought? Or are they to be found in some general principles of quasi-natural law which can be discerned by the reason of an educated mind, as Thibaut thought? This debate, as we shall see, carries over into Hegel's thinking about politics. Before discussing Hegel, however, we shall look briefly at the work of constitutional liberals whose stance also is taken account of by Hegel.

CONSTITUTIONALISM AND LIBERALISM

It would be wrong to think that the French Revolution occasioned only responses of a strongly counter-revolutionary and Counter-Enlightenment sort, emphasizing as we have seen culturally or ethnically based forms of nationalism, or responses based upon a kind of pre-revolutionary nostalgia, emphasizing the charms of either the medieval or the Attic Greek social and political experience. There was also in the work of Tocqueville and Benjamin Constant a distinctive form of constitutionalism and liberalism that emerged from the impact of the Revolution, and for Tocqueville there was the impact of the new nation of the United States of America, 'the land of the future' as Hegel called it. Constant and Tocqueville are very different thinkers and it will be best to give a necessarily brief sketch of the thought of each of them.

Constant experienced the French Revolution from first hand. He lived to become Napoleon's constitutional adviser during the Hundred Days (having been threatened with prison by Napoleon for his critique of his exercise of power before his exile on Elba – indeed, he had compared him to Attila the Hun) and he died during the fall of the Orléanist Monarchy in 1830. He was educated, in part, in Scotland at Edinburgh University where he studied the work of both political economists such as Adam Smith and common sense philosophers such as Dugald Stewart, an experience that was to play a major role in his account of liberty.

In 1803–4 he also spent time in Weimar, which is only a very short distance from Jena, the centre of German Romantic thought, although by then past its greatest days. He had very little time for the political ideas of the Romantics, particularly in relation to Fichte's *Closed Commercial State* which did not endear itself to someone who had studied the Scottish political economists, and he regarded the Romantics' ideas on economics as lunacy. His ideas on liberty reflect the contrast that he draws between the liberty of the ancients and that of the moderns, the theme of a speech given in Paris in 1820. Although it was given in his last decade it does reflect in a more systematic way many of the preoccupations of his life and education. The emphasis on the word *systematic* should not mislead us, however, since Constant is not a metaphysician and his views on freedom are based upon what he sees as practical observations about the nature of ancient societies and modern commercial societies. In this sense, to borrow from Rawls's distinction, it is a political rather than a metaphysical conception of freedom. His argument about ancient liberty is straightforward.

The size of the Greek city-state, its cultural homogeneity and the fact that work was undertaken by slaves meant that each citizen could be fully involved in the political life of the society. Freedom was understood in terms of this participation and involvement. It also had as a cost the downgrading of the importance of private life and private taste. Because of the unity of the society (which had been lauded by Romantic thinkers), while sovereignty was held in common nevertheless each individual was subject to a very wide degree of authority by the state. There was no sense of a sacrosanct private sphere. Indeed the assumption was that since the society was culturally and religiously homogeneous there would be no proper role for such a private sphere. The growth of commercial societies had changed all of this. Most citizens are now involved in work to sustain life. The division of labour had led to a much greater differentiation of function and social experience, and culture and taste are now much more varied from individual to individual. There is therefore a demand for a private sphere within which individuals will be able to follow their own interests and indulge their own tastes free of state interference.

In Constant's view the Jacobin period of the French Revolution had led to an attempt to recreate some of the ideas of the city-state as a republic of virtue in which all aspects of life were to be under political jurisdiction and in which there was to be a direct participatory democracy. The Terror, for Constant, was a natural outgrowth in this attempt at political nostalgia. Part of the task for the constitutional lawyer and thinker was to devise ways in which this anachronistic form of politics could not prevail. At the same time, however, Constant was clear that modern forms of politics do involve a kind of crisis in representation. In the Attic city-state there were no representatives, for each citizen directly participated; in a modern commercial society, however, the division of labour and the need for most to work in the productive part of the economy now means that representation has become inevitable, but at the same time it is problematic. In so far as the representative is a delegate from a political grouping like a constituency, political negotiation in a parliament or an assembly becomes impossible because the mandate will prevent it; alternatively if the representative is to be regarded as autonomous, then it may well be that this is effective in terms of *realpolitik* but the representative function will have declined to vanishing point. So there is a basic problem of representative legitimacy in the modern world, and part of the solution of course lies in many areas of life not being subject to political control and interference so that the issue of representativeness covers a narrow area. Nevertheless for Constant (1988) this did pose one of the major challenges of the modern world.

Constant also believed that a politics of liberty did have to be underpinned by a set of values. These were however neither metaphysically grounded nor heroic. What he wanted was a regime of liberty that would leave people in a commercial society free in their private lives to follow their own tastes and interests. He had learned from the Scottish economists that market societies undermine heroic virtues but nevertheless liberty does depend on virtue, although not that of a Pericles or a Cato. This point comes out particularly in his novel *Adolphe*. In Constant's view we need to rely on virtues such as strength of will, commitment, human sympathy and an unwillingness to injure others. These virtues, domestic as they are, can underpin a culture and politics of liberty.

It is in the writings of Tocqueville that we encounter a more developed set of ideas about the values that underpin liberty. Tocqueville's position falls somewhere between Constant's highly practical account of freedom and a more metaphysically based one, or in modern parlance one based upon a comprehensive doctrine. Tocqueville had a strong commitment to the necessary link as he saw it between religion and the maintenance of liberty, and within religion he approved of the idea of natural law. It is certainly true, as we have already seen, that Tocqueville approves of the role of intermediate institutions in society as a guarantee of liberty, since they stand between the individual and a state whose power grows in a democratic era, and to that extent community life and what falls under what he calls *mores* or customs are part of what sustains liberty. Religion, however, comes into this because he wants to distinguish between arbitrary *mores*, conventions and the institutions on which they depend, and those that grow up from religiously and natural law sanctioned habits and forms of character. For Tocqueville, these include the innate idea of freedom and its importance in human life, the recognition of the soul and that the human person is more than a body and mind, and sentiments of honesty and common sense. When these things pervade character they can sustain the 'habits of the heart' that are essential to freedom and a free society. Constitutional arrangements and legislation have to be sustained by these *mores* for, as he argues in his *Conversations with Nassau Senior*: 'Liberty depends on the manners and beliefs of the people who are to enjoy it.' These manners and beliefs are more sustaining to liberty if they are held to be true and not just arbitrary or convenient inventions or historical accretions. So what Tocqueville argues for is a regulated liberty held in check by religion, custom and law. He is however certain that constitutions and legislation have to be rooted in ideas of this sort that are pervasive in the population and cannot be brought into being by legislation.

THE PLACE OF HEGEL

It is difficult to overestimate the importance of Hegel in nineteenth-century political thought. His thought influenced significant thinkers in Germany, such as David Friedrich Strauss, Otto Bauer, Feuerbach, Arnold Ruge, Marx, Engels, Lasalle; in France, as the title of Barrès's essay *Hegel and the Working Mens' Canteens of the North* makes clear; in Italy, in the politically committed writing of the Neapolitan Hegelians such as Bertrando Spaventa (Bellamy, 1992) as well as the vitally important figure of Mazzini; and in Russia, in the writings of Bakunin, Visarión Belinsky and (by way of reaction) Herzen (Berlin, 1978). One explanation for this pervasive influence lies in the fact that in Hegel's philosophy we can see a treatment of all the themes that dominated political writing in this period, accentuated by the fact that these themes are dealt with in a systematic way. Hegel's work has been called a project of reconciliation (Plant, 1983; Hardimon, 1994). That is to say, Hegel's work was animated by a desire to produce a deep and interconnected account of the whole range of human experience and practice – moral, legal, political, artistic, religious and philosophical – together with a philosophical history of these such that the philosophy would demonstrate the rational structure of the thought and practice of the modern world in its most mature form in Western European societies and nation-states. The understanding of this rational structure would create a sense of reconciliation with the world or, as Hegel puts the point in *The Philosophy of Right* (1952): 'I am at home in the world when I have understood it – even more so when I have a full conceptual grasp of it.' This meant that for Hegel philosophy had to be:

- *Systematic*: it had to deal with the interconnectedness of all the central forms of human experience.
- *Historical*: it had to deal with what he saw as the rational development through history of these basic forms of experience.
- *Dialectical*: there is a rational structure both to the character and to the history of experience which will exhibit a dialectical form which can be uncovered by the philosopher.

By 'dialectical' Hegel meant that the different forms of life in history and the different forms that our experience takes as we seek to categorize it will reach certain kinds of limits, and the recognition of these limits will lead to a transformation in the historical process and in our conceptual understanding. Lying at the heart of this process, which for Hegel gives it a kind of metaphysical underpinning, is a secularized form of Christianity (Plant, 2001). This sees the Biblical account of creation, incarnation, resurrection and eternal life not as a once-and-for-all set of events but as a kind of symbolic narrative of the deep structure of human existence which can ultimately be laid bare in philosophical and non-symbolic/religious or narrative terms, in a way that shows that the God of the Bible can be understood as the Absolute Idea which embodies itself in the created world and in the world of human history and eventually becomes progressively conscious of itself in the processes of human thought and human history. In this process it becomes transformed from the Idea to Spirit and dwells in the consciousness of human beings when they understand the world aright. Hence history and the processes of human thought are not arbitrary but have this dialectical necessity. We experience the Good Friday of alienation and fragmentation through history to arrive at a kind of analogue to Easter Day in which reconciliation is achieved. Hegel held as much as any Romantic thinker to the ideal of the integrated personality in an integrated society, but he saw the possibility of this if we understood human history and human freedom aright in the politics of post-Napoleonic Europe and in the nation-states, which were continuing to develop in the period after the French Revolution.

In the process of this integrated account Hegel gives an important historical place to many of the themes we have seen so far. One such was the ideals of the Revolution, which Hegel had celebrated as a young man, and which after the Golgotha of the Terror was gradually being transformed into a form of politics and statehood which could recognize rights and equality. Another was Romanticism, with its emphasis on the integration of the human personality and the integration of society within a nation-state, but an integration to be achieved not by the exercise of the Romantic imagination and its inwardness, or by the celebration of historical particularity which failed as with Herder in providing a conceptual grasp of the place of the particularities of specific societies in the context of an overall rational historical order and thus lapsed into relativism. This was also the basis of his critique of Savigny and the historical school of jurisprudence. Unlike Hegel's friend Thibaut, Savigny and his followers could not exhibit the rationality implicit in the historically specific forms of law which they made central to their study without the anachronistic appeal to Roman Law (Thompson, 2001). The idea of freedom was central to Hegel, but this freedom was not the antinomian freedom of the exercise of pure will and choice but rather rational freedom, that is to say, one that is exercised within a normative structure which has a historical reality (what he called *Sittlichkeit* or ethical life) and whose rationality can be understood. This normative

structure is not a set of formal moral rules, as it was for example for Kant with his doctrines of the categorical imperative and the principle of universalizability; but is rather a comprehensible world of norms and values into which we are born and which we can make our own by deliberating on the rationality embodied in that normative structure. However, the development of this idea of freedom is what it says, namely a process of development, and many things have contributed towards its diverse forms in history: the ancient oriental world; the world of Attic Greece; the medieval world; Roman Law; the growth of Protestant and more personalized forms of Christianity; the development of the market economy; and Romanticism in art, literature and philosophy. Freedom for Hegel is not something which individuals have in terms of some kind of pre-social state of nature, or purely in terms of their metaphysical standing. It has, like all concepts, as he makes clear in the preface to *The Philosophy of Right*, to be understood in terms of its history. The circumstances and movements listed have all contributed in necessary ways to the achievement of freedom. As such freedom is not a *status*, it is an *achievement*, and one with many forms of horror and estrangement on the way.

For Hegel the nation-state was central to the achievement of freedom in his understanding of it because it is within the nation-state that we find the normative structure that can give meaning and salience to freedom. We do not find freedom in a kind of general cosmopolitanism because that would have to be guided by general rules of the sort that Kant espoused, nor do we find freedom in a wholly private and voluntary existence withdrawn from the public world of politics and nationhood. It is found through belonging to a modern nation, which he believed was evolving from about 1812 (with a good many disappointments subsequently, not least in Prussia where his chair at the University of Berlin was situated).

Characteristic of these modern nations would, however, be a rich private life, as for example to be found in Romanticism and in Protestantism but equally importantly in civil society (*Burgerliche Gesellschaft*), which included for Hegel the market economy (he was a keen student of Adam Smith, James Steuart and other Scottish political economists: Plant, 1983) and the institutions which go along with it, particularly corporations through which again the citizen learns about a structure of values and interests which are outside the particular private interests of the individual. He sees in civil society not the fragmentation of society and the general will by sectional interests which Rousseauians see, but rather in its institutions a school for civic virtue. At the same time, however, he does not accept, as many subsequent anarchists did, that with a sufficient degree of decentralization a modern society could be self-equilibrating. The state was required for Hegel to resolve some of the tensions to which the institutions of civil society will nevertheless lead and also to be a kind of articulation or embodiment of the nation, particularly in the figure of the constitutional monarch which he favoured. At the same time, however, for Hegel the state was to be a universal in two important senses of that word. It was to provide the necessary framework within which all the important forms of human experience could take place, including what he calls the forms of Absolute Spirit (art, religion and philosophy). For Hegel these forms of Absolute Spirit are universal in their resonance and should not be seen in a historicist or particularistic way, although the ways in which they are achieved will depend very importantly on political and economic conditions. The state is also universal in the sense that it does not favour any particular group within civil society; indeed it is independent of civil society and seeks, where necessary, to regulate it, particularly via its police functions. In respect of the economy Hegel argues that, thus understood, the modern state is able to reconcile the individual and the community, the citizen and the state. This will no longer be the unmediated and sensuous kind of identification of citizen and state that might have been found in the Greek city-state and which many German intellectuals (including Hegel in his youth) had sought to re-establish in modern Europe and which they thought that the French Revolution might be in the process of establishing. It will, rather, be a highly mediated, differentiated and complex form of identity because the modern state has to reconcile the demands of the social and political order with a great sense of subjectivity and individuality on the part of citizens. It will be what Schiller – one of the Romantic political heroes – called a moral (*moralische*) harmony, in contrast to the more direct and immediate harmony of earlier forms. Hegel puts the point in *The Philosophy of Right* (1952) in the following way:

> The principle of the modern state has prodigious depth and strength because it allows the principle of subjectivity to progress to its culmination and yet at the same time brings it back to the substantive unity and so maintains this unity as the principle of subjectivity itself.

The principle of subjectivity is embodied in ideas like rights, Protestantism, conscience and the market economy together with forms of individualism in art, religion and philosophy. In Hegel's view the modern nation-state is able to accommodate this kind of subjectivity while maintaining a sense of social and political unity within which freedom in his understanding of it can be secure. It is this

capacity for reconciliation and assimilation of different features of social life (and indeed different religious and cultural practices, as with the Jews) that gives the modern state its strength. It also explains why Hegel was so hostile in the last few months of his life to the liberal and radically democratic assault on Restoration regimes post-1815, particularly after the fall of the restored French monarchy in 1830. In his view this kind of radical liberalism misunderstood the nature of freedom and the way in which freedom was contingent upon a shared ethical life. Such radicalism was a further exemplar of subjective political Romanticism which he had earlier criticized in the German student movement which had culminated in the famous rally at the Wartburg near Eisenach in 1817.

THE INFLUENCE OF HEGEL

After Hegel's death in 1831 his influence was pervasive in the fields of philosophy, political science, theology, aesthetics and law, and until at least the middle of the century most European thinkers, however much they may have disagreed with Hegel, for example Kierkegaard and Nietzsche, felt the need to define their own position in relation to his. However, it would not be correct to say that just one interpretation of Hegel's work held sway. Hegel had left a rather ambiguous legacy, particularly in relation to his account of Christianity and its sublated role within his system. It was this type of ambiguity that led to different responses to Hegel with very important ramifications for political thought (Toews, 1980). Almost immediately after his death there developed a right-wing and a left-wing or radical form of Hegelianism, along with what might be seen as a kind of middle-of-the-road form associated with Eduard Gans, one of Hegel's former pupils and co-professor at Berlin University. The right-wing form of Hegelianism emphasized both its compatibility with Protestant Christianity and the reconciling power of Hegel's thought, which had led Hegel to say in *The Philosophy of Right* that 'what is rational is actual and what is actual is rational.' The exegesis of this claim is more complex than it looks but an easy emphasis on the second part of the formulation could lead to a strong sense of reconciliation with the social and political world wherever it is to be found. This sort of interpretation of Hegel was followed by his successor in Berlin, Georg Gabler (whose appointment, given his accommodationist view of Hegel, was influenced by royal alarm at revolutionary events in France and Belgium where the actual had quite clearly not been seen as the rational), by Leopold Henning and by Judge Karl Friedrich Göschel. For

Göschel Hegel's political philosophy was best seen as a justification for a traditional Lutheran authoritarian state, and he interpreted Hegel's complex arguments about the role of corporations and estates in the role of the state as a re-emphasis on the social organization of feudal life, which was far from Hegel's own idea. It was this accommodationist form of Hegelianism which had an impact in Russia, particularly via the teaching of Nicholas Stankevich (who appears in Ivan Turgenev's novel *Rudin* in the person of Pokorsky: Berlin, 1978) and the influence that this had on Bakunin, T. N. Granovsky and Belinsky. Nicholas Stankevich's interpretation of Hegel was accommodationist and also one that saw Hegelianism as a kind of metaphysical religion which could replace faith in the Orthodox Church which was, of course, one of the mainstays of the prevailing Tsarist regime.

Eduard Gans occupied a position to the left of this and probably should be regarded as the godfather of left Hegelianism, although he is frequently not cited in the list that usually includes Strauss, Ruge, Feuerbach, Max Stirner, and Marx (Toews, 1980). Gans was in fact articulating his own stance on Hegel's thought while still a colleague of Hegel's in 1830. He disagreed with what seemed to be Hegel's position on the dialectic of history – that we now stand in Prussia (or perhaps Western Europe more generally) at the end of a history in which, at least implicitly, the modern state will be able to reconcile subject and object, citizen and state. For Gans the dialectic does not come to this abrupt end. The philosophical comprehension of history coupled with the idea that we are not yet at the end can justify progressive political activity and he regarded the modern Prussian state as a tutelary state, but one in which the idea of subjectivity had a central place, as Hegel's thought had shown. The need for Gans was to ensure that all were included in the ethical life of the modern state and not just the better situated. So in this sense he saw the possibility of an ideal of emancipation emerging from within Hegel's own thought. He did not see himself as a revolutionary, but rather held that the possibility of inclusion for all in the ethical community was implicit or intimated in the modern state and in Hegel's thought, as the best conceptual account of that – all this while believing that he was loyal to the idea of the Prussian state as embodying the principle of reason and ethical life.

There was however a much more radical interpretation becoming available at this time. In the hands of Strauss and Feuerbach, two of Hegel's students (although in the case of Strauss only for the briefest time), this reinterpretation took on a religious rather than a directly political form. But this transformation was perhaps a necessary precursor to the more radical political interpretation of Hegel, since Hegel's own thought incorporated at its heart both metaphysical and religious assumptions. In his *Life of Jesus* Strauss treated Jesus in a wholly non-supernatural way, opening up what he believed was at least implicit in Hegel's treatment, namely the idea of a religion of humanity – not in a God and a world beyond (Plant, 2001). This idea is taken much further and much more systematically by Feuerbach. He adopts a similarly demythologizing view of Christianity and sees the supernatural idea of the divine as a kind of projection of the human mind and imagination, a projection which can be understood in the sense of a place where longing and need may be fulfilled in a way they are not in this world. Feuerbach situates his account of Christianity in *The Essence of Christianity* into a materialist metaphysic that takes things much further than Strauss (at least at this time). Although Feuerbach's work was essentially in the philosophy of religion, such was the link seen by continental radicals between the critique of religion and the possibility of radical politics that, in 1848, a somewhat bemused Feuerbach found himself feted by student revolutionaries and giving lectures to them. It was, however, Marx and Engels who together, more than any others, engaged in this critique of religion and Hegel's philosophy of the state as a way of developing an account of history and politics that they believed would aid emancipation.

MARX AND ENGELS

In a series of books and articles – for example *The German Ideology, Contribution to the Critique of Hegel's Philosophy of Right*, and *Theses on Feuerbach* (all in Marx, 1978) – Marx and Engels positioned their evolving work in relation to Hegel's philosophy. They were in agreement with Strauss's and Feuerbach's attempts to demystify Hegel but argued that they had not gone far enough. There is not space here to do justice to the subtleties of this rapidly evolving position in the early 1840s, but it is worth noting that Marx did start out as a Hegelian of sorts and did initially at least believe that the state could be a universal mediator between different social and political interests. His journalistic experiences on the *Rheinische Zeitung* (Plant, 1983), however, came to disabuse him of this view. Seeing the state in action led him to believe that it was the instrument of the dominant class in civil society, not something that stood as a universal over and above society regulating it in a disinterested manner. This loss of faith in Hegel's approach betokened a more general critique of Hegel. He still adopted some distinctively Hegelian positions, particularly as these were understood by the left or new Hegelians. So, for example, as he makes clear in the *Economic and Philosophical Manuscripts of 1844,* Marx (1978) was concerned with Hegelian sorts of questions about the alienation of the person in modern society, the fragmentation of modern society, and the lack of a sense of wholeness within the individual personality [see further Chapter 6]. Unlike Hegel, however, he saw these as having ultimately economic causes and that they could have only an economic resolution following a complete transformation of the social, political and economic order. However, unlike utopian socialists, who defined socialist aims in ethical terms and sought to devise forms of social organization such as Bakunin's (1990) anarchist communities or Herzen's self-sufficient *mirs* to realize their aims, Marx and Engels saw the prospects for radical social change as being rooted in historical, social and economic circumstance. To this extent they adopted Hegel's dialectic of history, but instead of the dialectic being pushed along by the workings of a metaphysical *Geist* they saw the motor of historical change in economic terms. They distinguished between the means of production (labour tools and raw materials) and the relations of production (the types of relationship both legal and social which facilitated the use and application of the means of production). These two things taken together form the economic base of society, which is the driver of dialectical historical change. At any epoch in history, given a particular pattern of means and relationships of production, there will correspond particular forms of consciousness expressed in terms of ideas about politics, morality, law, religion, art, philosophy, etc. For Hegel, art, religion and philosophy are the modes of Absolute Spirit, the most universal achievements of the human mind; for Marx and Engels they are ideological forms of consciousness, that is to say, forms of thought and feeling whose nature and objects are ultimately to be understood in terms of their relationship to the dominant social interests embodied in the relations of production. These forms of consciousness are not autonomous but have a social and indeed political function and a socio-economic explanation. This explanation can be exhibited in the materialist theory of history, which looks in detail at the ways in which forms of consciousness relate to dominant economic interests.

For Marx and Engels these interests are basically to do with class. Class is not defined so much in sociological terms – in terms, that is to say, of consumption patterns or values since these belong to the ideological superstructure of society. Rather, class is seen in economic terms: who does and who does not own the means of production? The possibility of a progressive renewal of society, whether it

was from feudalism to capitalism or from capitalism to socialism and ultimately to communism, depends upon a growing mismatch between the relations of production and the means of production. That is to say that technological and scientific change will produce new tools, new raw materials and different demands for labour. As this process accelerates, the prevailing relations of production – that is, class relations – will become more and more of a constraint on the productive use that can be made of these new technologies. At some point the clash between social relations and productive forces ushers in a revolutionary period of social change. So in the case of the transition from feudalism to capitalism, it was not that this was a matter of choice. Feudal relations of production had become totally counterproductive in respect of the exploitation of technological change. Hence on this account social, political and economic revolution go together and there is no way that socialism or even social democracy can be built from within capitalism if the appropriate stage of conflict between the means of production and the relations of production has not been reached. So for Marx and Engels, while it is possible to think in terms of the ideals of socialism – a principle of justice like 'from each according to his ability, to each according to his needs', or the aim of human fulfilment through a life in which alienation from economic activity, as in industrial capitalism, can be overcome – they were always clear that these goals would be mere *sollen* (oughts) without the historical circumstances favouring such a revolutionary change in society.

In this context it is worth looking briefly at Marx's critique of social democracy in his biting *Critique of the Gotha Programme* (1978). The programme was an attempt to unify the then two existing workers' organizations in Germany – the Social Democratic Workers' Party and the Lassallean Organization (a group inspired by Lassalle, who was of a Hegelian cast of mind and who believed that it was possible to use the state within a capitalist society to achieve real gains in social justice via redistribution of income, wealth and power). For the reasons already given Marx regards this as wholly futile. At best the pursuit of social justice can alleviate only the symptoms of the problems of capitalist society, which are caused by the maldistribution of the ownership of the means of production in that society. While this pattern of distribution of the means of production prevails, the social injustices of capitalism in terms of income and wealth will continue. Social democracy, which is essentially what the *Gotha Programme* was about, cannot address the ownership of the means of production in political terms. It requires a basic social revolution to do that, which in turn requires the right historical circumstances. So Marx says:

> What is 'fair' distribution?
>
> Do not the bourgeois assert that the present-day distribution is fair? And is it not, in fact, fair distribution on the basis of the present-day mode of production? Are economic relations regulated by legal conceptions or do not, on the contrary, legal relations arise from economic ones? Right can never be higher than the economic structure of society and its cultural development conditioned thereby. (1978: 528)

Lassalle's Hegelian idea that the state can be autonomous in relation to the dominant interests in civil society is false on this view and the idea of social democracy is false with it. Taken in its strict sense, therefore, Marx's *political* theory is rather limited in that politics and political values are part of the ideological superstructure of society, and values and ideas of themselves cannot produce social change in the way that Hegel and Lassalle thought.

The social democratic tradition reasserted itself in the writings of Bernstein, particularly in his *The Preconditions of Socialism* which was first published in 1899 (Bernstein, 1993). Bernstein rejected several of the major tenets of Marx's historical materialism and with it the claim to have a scientific basis for socialism. Along with the rejection of the methodology of Marx's theory there was also a rejection of some of the predictions which Marx had based upon this methodology, in particular his claim about the growing immiseration of the working class and his argument that as capitalism would develop then classes would polarize. Neither of these had happened in Bernstein's view. He defined socialism or social democracy in terms of values which were to be pursued by political and parliamentary means and in so doing set off a debate which was to be continued with dramatic consequences in the next century by, amongst others, Lenin and Rosa Luxemburg.

REFERENCES

Bakunin, M. (1990) *Statism and Anarchy.* Cambridge: Cambridge University Press.

Beiser, F. (1992) *Enlightenment, Revolution and Romanticism: The Genesis of Modern German Political Thought 1790–1800.* Cambridge, MA: Harvard University Press.

Beiser, F. (2002) *German Idealism: The Struggle against Subjectivism 1781–1801.* Cambridge, MA: Harvard University Press.

Bellamy, Richard (1992) *Liberalism and Modern Society.* State College, PA: Pennsylvania State University Press.

Berlin, I. (1978) *Russian Thinkers.* London: Penguin.

Berlin, I. (1999) *The Roots of Romanticism.* London: Chatto and Windus.

Bernstein, E. (1993) *The Preconditions of Socialism.* Cambridge: Cambridge University Press.

Biddiss, M. (1970) *Father of Racial Ideology: The Social and Political Thought of Count Gobineau.* London: Weidenfeld and Nicolson.

Bonald, L. G. A. (1859) *Oeuvres.* Petit-Montrouge: Migne.

Bonald, L. G. A. (1966) *Théorie du pouvoir politique et religieux.* Paris: Union générale d'éditions.

Carr, E. H. (1998) *The Romantic Exiles.* London: Serif.

Chateaubriand, F. A. R. (1884) *The Genius of Christianity,* trans. C. I. White. Baltimore: Murphy.

Collini, S., D. Winch and J. Burrows (1983) *That Noble Science of Politics: A Study of Nineteenth Century Intellectual History.* Cambridge: Cambridge University Press.

Comte, A. (1998) *Early Political Writings.* Cambridge: Cambridge University Press.

Constant, B. (1988) *Political Writings.* Cambridge: Cambridge University Press.

De Maistre, J. (1994) *Considerations on France.* Cambridge: Cambridge University Press.

Gierke, O. von (1868–1913) *Das deutsche Genossenschaftsrecht.* Berlin: Weidmann.

Habermas, J. (2001) *The Postnational Constellation.* Cambridge: Polity.

Hardimon, M. O. (1994) *Hegel's Social Philosophy: The Project of Reconciliation.* Cambridge: Cambridge University Press.

Hare, R. (1964) *Pioneers of Russian Social Thought.* New York.

Hegel, G. W. F. (1952) *The Philosophy of Right.* Oxford: Clarendon.

Hobsbawm, E. (1975) *The Age of Capital 1848–1875.* London: Weidenfeld and Nicholson.

Kropotkin, P. (1995) *The Conquest of Bread.* Cambridge: Cambridge University Press.

Le Play, P. G. F. (1864) *La Reforme sociale.* Paris.

Mack Smith, D. (1994) *Mazzini.* New Haven, CT: Yale University Press.

Marx, K. (1978) *The Marx–Engels Reader,* 2nd edn, ed. R. Tucker New York: Norton.

McClelland, J. S. (1970) *The French Right from Maistre to Maurras.* London: Cape.

Menczer, B. (1952) *Catholic Political Thought 1789–1848.* London: Burns and Oates.

Plant, R. (1983) *Hegel: An Introduction.* Oxford: Blackwell.

Plant, R. (2001) *Politics, Theology and History.* Cambridge: Cambridge University Press.

Reiss, Hans (1955) *The Political Thought of the German Romantics.* Oxford: Blackwell.

Thompson, K. (2001) 'Institutional normativity: the positivity of right'. In R. R. Williams, ed., *On Beyond Liberalism and Communitarianism: Studies in Hegel's*

Philosophy of Right. Albany, NY: State University Press of New York.

Tocqueville, A. de (1945) *Democracy in America*. New York: Knopf.

Tocqueville, A. de (1955) *The Old Regime and the French Revolution*. Garden City, NY: Anchor.

Toews, J. E. (1980) *Hegelianism: The Path toward Dialectical Humanism*. Cambridge: Cambridge University Press.

Tönnies, F. (2001) *Community and Civil Society*. Cambridge: Cambridge University Press.

Whitman, J. Q. (1990) *The Legacy of Roman Law in the German Romantic Era*. Princeton, NJ: Princeton University Press.

29

Political Thought in Continental Europe during the Twentieth Century

RICHARD BELLAMY, JEREMY JENNINGS AND PETER LASSMAN

The alleged divide between the 'Anglo-American' and 'continental' traditions of political thought is largely a mid-twentieth-century construction. Like the fault line between the West and East Europe, it grew out of the Cold War and a series of studies tracing the intellectual origins of fascism and Stalinism to the continental fascination with post-Hegelian, anti-Enlightenment, anti-modern, anti-individualist, and anti-empiricist metaphysics. Though such polemics occasionally resurface in debates on postmodernism or multiculturalism, they now seem best relegated to the intellectual history of the 1950s and 1960s. What substance this division does possess has more to do with philosophical styles than geography or ideology. After all, continental thinkers as diverse as Frege, Wittgenstein and the Vienna Circle influenced the supposed Anglo-American analytical tradition, which in its turn always had a following on the continent, while the putative continental school spawned numerous epigone across the channel and the Atlantic. Likewise, every ideology has been associated at some point with every available epistemological, ontological and metaphysical position. For example, there have been analytical Marxists [see Chapter 6], structuralist and neo-Hegelian liberals [see Chapter 30], and vice versa. Indeed, even the differences of philosophical approach are breaking down. Increasingly, North American and European scholars engage equally with both traditions, using 'analytical' and 'continental' thinkers, such as Rawls and Foucault respectively, to illuminate each other.

If political thought as practised on the continent possesses any distinctive characteristics, they derive from other and much wider cultural sources – including political culture. Why certain of the various ideological and philosophical positions found in all continental countries predominated over others can only be understood by referring to the political, social, academic, intellectual and other contexts within which individual thinkers were engaged, and their personal, albeit contextually shaped, preferences. This chapter explores three of these contexts: Germany, France and Italy. As we shall see, in all these cases it is grossly distorting to talk of a single tradition of political thought. Nevertheless, national political thinking was invariably shaped by certain general characteristics of their respective political cultures broadly conceived.

GERMANY

The development of political thought in Germany during the twentieth century can be analysed in terms of several recurring themes. Central among these are the problems of the nation-state and national identity, the nature of democracy, liberalism, and the rule of law. All of these themes are themselves debated, most directly, at least before 1933, within the context of a generally pessimistic critique of the culture of modernity. This critique can take either a radical or a conservative direction. Therefore, a marked feature of the German tradition is to be found in its concern with the nature of modernity. This highly contested question, in turn, cannot be separated from deep disagreement about the nature and value of politics. It is not surprising, therefore, that much German political thought during this period exists within an intellectual field that is constituted through a conjuncture of political analysis and cultural criticism.

It cannot be denied that late unification as a nation-state had a profound effect upon the development of political thought in Germany. According to some accounts, in order to understand the political thought of twentieth-century Germany it is necessary to look further back into the peculiarities of its intellectual history. For example, it can be argued that during the eighteenth century a division between intellectual perceptions that looked either towards Roman or Greek antiquity for a model of culture and politics was to have profound implications. The Roman model was taken to provide an image that emphasized politics in terms of the relations of power and *realpolitik* [see further Chapter 22]. During the same period the Greek image that focused upon the Athenian *polis* was taken as the model within which politics ought to be understood as a component of a cultural ideal. Significantly, prior to the unification of the German state the Greek model provided a means for imagining cultural strength as a compensation for political weakness. According to this account the survival into the twentieth century of a much-noted apolitical tradition within the educated middle class (*Bildungsburgertum*) is understandable. Furthermore, it provides an explanation for the way in which much German political thought during this period has often had a tendency to oscillate between two extremes in its philosophical understanding of the nature of politics. On one side is a dominant tendency that perceives and often celebrates the identification of politics with the state, power, and the apparatus of ruling (*Herrschaft* and *Macht*). This vision is easily vulgarized into a crude form of political realism in which politics is understood as nothing more than the play of power. The other tendency focuses upon a view of politics that stresses the aim of creating or presupposing an ideal polity of universal reason and culture. This too can easily develop into a vision of political conduct that aims for the creation of a utopian and non-coercive community of freely associating individuals. The essential point is that these two outlooks continue to coexist in an antagonistic and complementary relationship throughout the twentieth century (Vollrath, 1987; 1990).

At the beginning of the twentieth century the dominant tradition of political reflection was one in which the identification of the realm of politics with the state was clear. Political thought in Germany at this time was predominantly academic in its location and style. It reflected to a large degree an earlier history in which political thought is addressed to those in power, fellow academics and students. It also directed itself towards an abstract idea of the state rather than to a virtually non-existent politically active public realm. A further peculiarity of the history of German normative political thought is that the academic discipline in which much of it was expressed during the nineteenth and early twentieth century was that of a particular form of legal theory concerned with the state and public law (*Staatsrechtlehre*). Political philosophy, understood as a subdiscipline of philosophy, has generally been regarded as a form of practical or moral philosophy [see further Chapter 1]. As a result it is probably correct to say that the claim that political philosophy was dead, made in the context of America and Britain in the mid twentieth century, did not apply to Germany. However, it also true to say that the idea of an autonomous form of political theorizing has found it difficult to find a secure intellectual or institutional location.

Max Weber and Georg Jellinek, two of the most important political thinkers of the early twentieth century, were both trained in law and much of their work was produced from within this intellectual context. Jellinek, in his highly influential *Allgemeine Staatslehre* (*General Theory of the State*), first published in 1900, marked a break with an older tradition of purely legalistic and formal analysis. Jellinek argued for a new form of *Allgemeine Soziallehre des Staates* (general social theory of states) which did not recognize any clear separation between state and society. Nevertheless, this analysis of politics is clearly focused upon the form, function, and organization of the state in both historical and legal terms. Max Weber's political thought, much influenced by Jellinek, developed these themes but with a greater clarity of conceptual development and a much sharper conception of impending cultural crisis. It is true that Weber introduced a more sophisticated level of analysis in making the *Verband* ('association') rather than the state as such a central political concept. Nevertheless, it is still clear that Weber's general anthropological starting point is the idea, adapted in part from Jellinek, that social relations ought to be understood, essentially, in terms of relations of rule (*Herrschaft*) and struggle (Hübinger, 1988; Breuer, 1999; Weber, 1994).

For Weber and his colleagues, as Tocqueville had claimed in an earlier period, a new political reality requires the creation of a new political science. The older form of political theory that relied upon largely Aristotelian notions of the forms and purposes of the state was now totally outmoded. In its place, Weber promoted a view of the state that totally bypassed the classical idea that it ought to be analysed in terms of its serving some moral purpose or *telos*. This idea was replaced with a concept of the modern state defined in terms of the means rather than the ends that are specific to it. These means are force and violence. The state is no more or less than an association of the rule of human beings over human beings. It is the institution that is able to successfully claim the monopoly of legitimate violence over a given territory. Although both Jellinek and Weber expressed extreme scepticism concerning any essentialist or racial understanding of the state, both agreed the modern state is typically a nation-state. Indeed, throughout his life Weber had insisted that the supreme aim of German state policy must be to serve the national interest (Weber, 1994).

This understanding of the state and politics takes on a particular pathos in so far as it is framed by a general criticism of the culture of modernity. Max Weber presents a particularly dramatic picture that is compounded from a range of currently available ideas. Echoing Nietzsche's (1974) claims concerning the 'death of God', he saw modernity as centrally an age of disenchantment and loss of meaning. For Weber, the disenchantment of the world by the spirit of rational scientific inquiry (*Wissenschaft*) has had the paradoxical effect of undermining its own intellectual and moral foundations. The consequences for politics are potentially disastrous. Facing the spectre of 'the new serfdom', Weber and many of his contemporaries despaired of the possibility of finding a political form for a democratic modern Europe that would preserve the limited sphere of personal freedom that had been achieved (Weber, 1994). [See further Chapter 15].

In keeping with this general diagnosis, the emergence of democracy in the Wilhelmine period and its realization in the Weimar Republic met with little genuine enthusiasm. For Weber, democracy was to be regarded, objectively, as no more than a particularly useful method for the possible selection of a genuinely political leadership. At best, representative parliamentary democracy was a necessary guard against the stultifying effects of bureaucratic rule either from within a capitalist market economy or, more threateningly, by a centrally planned socialism. At the same time, the socialist and communist left had no faith in either constitutional democracy or liberalism.

A notable feature of German political thought in the first half of the twentieth century is the way in which it questions the relationship between democracy and liberalism. The most extreme expression of this view is found in the writings of the legal scholar Carl Schmitt. Schmitt's rejection of liberalism and democracy, along with the idea that the relationship between them is no more than historically contingent, belongs to a general pattern of anti-democratic thought that was vociferous in its opposition to the Weimar Republic (Schmitt, 1996; 1985; 1963). The thinkers of the 'Conservative Revolution', among whom Schmitt can be numbered as a prominent representative, were as one in their cultural pessimism, nationalist resentment following defeat in the war of 1914–18, opposition to democracy, liberalism, constitutionalism, and what they considered to be the soulless character of modernity. The opposition between 'the ideas of 1914' and the alien 'ideas of 1789' is a common theme.

Carl Schmitt expressed in an acute form the opposition to the liberal constitution of the Weimar Republic. His open and public support for the Nazi regime after it came to power in 1933 was the outcome of an attempt to resolve what was perceived to be a crisis in the tradition of *Staatslehre*. This problem coexisted with a mood of cultural despair common among the proponents of the Conservative Revolution. The significance of the crisis that Schmitt identified in legal theory was that it threatened to destroy the underpinnings of the liberal idea of the rule of law. As early as 1912, Schmitt had argued that the application of the law to particular cases is always, under current conditions, permeated by ambiguity. The implication, for Schmitt, is that the liberal view, maintained since the Enlightenment, that political power could be restrained by the rule of law was a fiction. The answer that Schmitt arrived at was that the only way in which this crisis of legal indeterminacy could be overcome was by rejecting the universalistic premises upon which the idea of the rule of law is based. Schmitt's response was to replace liberalism and the ideals of the Enlightenment with an image of a homogeneous nation (*Volk*) united by a common purpose. This account of the legal crisis is at one with Schmitt's (1985) understanding of the decay of parliamentary democracy and the tension that exists between it and liberalism.

Schmitt's political thought presents a clear illustration of a tendency amongst German theorists to stress a particularly extreme version of the nature of politics in the modern world. Indeed, in his *The Concept of the Political* first published in 1927 Schmitt's starting point is a rejection of the unsatisfactory circularity of the conventional depiction of the conceptual relationship between the state and politics (Schmitt, 1985; 1996). For Schmitt, before we can talk about politics we require an understanding of the defining characteristic of 'the political'. This is to be found in the antithesis between friend and enemy. Any genuine politics presupposes an understanding of 'the political' in this sense. 'The political' refers to the most extreme and intense antagonism in human relations. Who counts as 'the enemy' at any particular moment is based upon a decision made by a political state. Clearly, for Schmitt and other like-minded thinkers of the Conservative Revolution, this vision of 'the political' must be intensely hostile to liberalism in all of its forms. Liberalism is taken to be a clear example of the 'neutralizing' and 'depoliticizing' tendencies of the modern age. Furthermore, Schmitt (1996) argues that the political state, as 'friend', must express the political unity of a people.

Political thinkers and philosophers such as Schmitt, Ernst Jünger, Oswald Spengler, Hans Freyer and Martin Heidegger combined their opposition to the politics of the Weimar Republic with a general distaste for the culture of the 'age of technology'. Schmitt and Heidegger, in particular, were supporters of the National Socialist dictatorship, although the precise nature and manner of that support have been the subject of seemingly endless debate. At the same time, political thinkers of the left, and in particular those associated with the Frankfurt school, rejected the Republic and the culture of modernity on similar lines. The interconnection between these themes is especially marked in the biographies of some of Heidegger's more influential (and Jewish) students who became intellectual and political refugees during the period of the Nazi dictatorship. Here Hannah Arendt, Karl Löwith, Herbert Marcuse, and Leo Strauss are among the most significant (Wolin, 2001; Arendt, 1951; Löwith, 1989; 1994; Marcuse, 1964; Strauss, 1950) [on Strauss, see Chapter 3].

The roots of the neo-Marxism of the Frankfurt school can be found in the early work of Georg Lukács, a former student of Max Weber. In his *History and Class Consciousness* (1924) Lukács had proposed a reinterpretation of the philosophical foundations of Marxism in direct response to the challenge set out by Weber in his account of the antinomies of modern rationality. The stress upon the role of the concepts of consciousness, reification and totality in the revitalization of Marxism was taken up by the intellectual founders of what has come to be known as critical theory. Max Horkheimer (1972) formulated the concept of 'critical theory' in direct opposition to 'traditional theory'. The two founders of critical theory, Max Horkheimer and Theodor Adorno, situated initially in the Institute for Social Research in Frankfurt, set out a programme of research that was meant to fulfil the promise of critique in the true sense. The method was to be one of immanent criticism: to reveal the contradictions within the social order and point the way towards an emancipated and rational society. However, by the time Horkheimer and Adorno had composed their highly influential work on the *Dialectic of Enlightenment* (1947) they had returned to a familiar theme in twentieth-century political thought and cultural criticism in Germany. The establishment of dictatorships in the Soviet

Union and National Socialist Germany, along with the triumph of 'instrumental reason' in the West, now led to a general pessimism with regard to any possible attempt to escape from the totally administered to the rational society. Dialectical theory became a critique of ideology in the form of 'negative dialectics'. Herbert Marcuse's *One Dimensional Man* (1964) was a much-simplified and popular version of this thesis.

The work of Jürgen Habermas represents an attempt, initially, to work within and at the same time to escape from the intellectual dead end in which the critical theory of Adorno and Horkheimer seemed to have found itself [see further Chapters 12 and 20]. Habermas, while continuing in the tradition of the earlier generation of critical theory in turning his attention primarily away from the relations of production and towards the relations of communication, still found himself facing the legacy of Max Weber's account of the rationalization and disenchantment of the modern world (Habermas, 1976; 1984). Also in the spirit of the interdisciplinary approach of the original critical theorists, Habermas drew upon diverse resources to reconstruct a viable form of critical theory. Most noticeable in Habermas's work, and this is indicative of much post-1945 political thought in Germany, is an opening towards the central concerns and concepts of Anglo-American political theory. This is a deliberate strategy to counter those intellectual currents from the past that could be associated with the catastrophic years of the National Socialist regime. Throughout his work there is an attempt to counter the claims of Carl Schmitt and his contemporary followers. Habermas is notable for his attempt to reclaim the legitimacy of the role of public intellectual in a country where, it is claimed, the concept of the intellectual has been treated as a 'swearword'. This is evident in his interventions in several public debates. Habermas has been an important instigator or participant in the 'historians' dispute' concerning 'coming to terms with the (National Socialist) past', and debates concerning the political implications of postmodernism, the Gulf War, political asylum, German unification, the future of the European Union, and the prospects for global peace (Habermas, 1989; 1994; 2001b).

Habermas's work, which began as an attempt to transcend the impasse of critical theory, has now reached beyond those confines. In his most recent theoretical work on the elaboration of his 'discourse ethics' Habermas (1999) has engaged in a debate with the American philosophers John Rawls and Robert Brandom in an attempt to find the necessary philosophical grounding for a political theory that can combine universalist claims with a practical purpose. In that sense, it can be argued that Habermas has remained faithful to his roots in critical theory. However, despite its universal scope, Habermas's theory cannot entirely escape the tension that exists between that claim and the particularity of its national context of origin.

Attempting to survey or summarize the history of political thought over more than a hundred years, even in one country, is a risky business. Much has to be left out and much has to be simplified. However, it is possible to discern some continuities. With the collapse of communism and the unification of the German state it appears that some traditional themes have reappeared or, at least, have become more openly discussed. The emergence of the 'Berlin Republic' has become the occasion for reflection upon the nature of the modern state, the global position of Germany (too big for Europe and too small for the world), and the nature of citizenship or membership in that state (Habermas, 1998a, 1998b). On a more general or philosophical level, there has been a return to the fundamental question of the nature of 'the political'. Therefore, in order to complete the picture, we ought not to be too surprised to find the renewal of interest in the work of one of 'Heidegger's children', Hannah Arendt (Wolin, 2001; Kemper, 1993). Although Arendt did not speak of 'the political' as such, her accounts of modernity, totalitarianism, republicanism and the nature of politics have been seized upon by many who do not accept what they see as the potentially utopian and apolitical character of Habermas's version of critical theory. At the same time, interpretations of Arendt serve as an antidote to Carl Schmitt's concept of 'the political' while reviving a view of political theory that restores the traditional question of the relationship of theory to practice to its central place [see further Chapter 13].

FRANCE

If the dominant theme of much German political thought was the restricted possibilities for politics in a disenchanted world characterized by the empty formalities of the bureaucratic state, in France modern politics was defined by the Revolution of 1789 and its subsequent decline into revolutionary terror and dictatorship. French theorists divided over how far the revolution could realize its republican promise without degenerating into anarchy or despotism. On the one hand, republicans were accused of undermining the moral bonds of Church and crown, forcing republican intellectuals to take on the role of secular priests and to fashion a lay morality. On the other hand, this debate focused attention on republicanism's ambiguous relationship to liberalism, pointing up the potential tensions between the republican emphasis on popular sovereignty and its commitment to the rights of man [see further Chapter 13].

The nineteenth (and, indeed, much of the twentieth) century is littered with accounts and analyses of the Revolution and its aftermath by such eminent writers as Jules Michelet, Alexis de Tocqueville, Edgar Quinet, Louis Blanc, and Hippolyte Taine, each of which sought to gauge their significance and meaning. If, for some, the Revolution marked the dawn of a new age of enlightenment and the rights of man, for others it denoted, at best, a divine punishment upon a sinful France. Either way, the events of the revolutionary decade which came to a close with the rise to power of Napoleon Bonaparte serve to give structure to French political thought in ways which it has only succeeded in escaping from in recent decades. Curiously, political thinking in France became both insular and parochial, the universalist ambitions of her eighteenth-century *philosophes* being replaced by the pious pretensions of those who continued, despite evidence to the contrary, to believe that France and her history had a special meaning which could provide lessons of relevance to all the nations of the world. As this world ceased to speak and think in French, so political thought in France, if it looked beyond its own national boundaries, did so largely only with a mind to discover the ways in which English, German or American experience might help, if at all, to resolve France's own internal problems. Consequently, few political thinkers in France between 1815 and the end of the Second World War achieved anything like an international audience. Auguste Comte (regrettably) and Henri Bergson (improbably) are exceptions, but their fame rested upon their reputations, respectively, as the philosophers of positivism and intuition rather than upon whatever they might have written about politics.

As revolution followed revolution, and political regime followed political regime, this propensity towards national introspection was only further accentuated during the nineteenth century. Upon what basis could political stability and order be restored to France? And upon what foundations could her political culture be refashioned? These became the abiding preoccupations. If by the early 1870s there was an emerging consensus that it was a moderate form of republican government that divided the French least (a view articulated by politicians and political thinkers alike), this should not disguise either the ferocity or the longevity of anti-republican political thinking. Given substance and coherence in the wake of the 1789 Revolution by Joseph de Maistre and Louis de Bonald, the calls of anti-democratic, Catholic reactionary thought for a return to the *ancien régime* continued to be articulated well into the twentieth century, not least by Charles Maurras for whom democracy would always be tainted by the stains of Judaism, Protestantism and Freemasonry. Few indeed were those who, like Felicité de Lamennais in the 1840s, sought to reconcile the Church with the forces of progress or who, like Charles Péguy at the beginning of the twentieth century, sought to embrace the *mystiques* of both republicanism and Catholicism.

Hostility to the Republic had other, perhaps more surprising forms, especially when it came from the left. From Pierre-Joseph Proudhon onwards there existed an anti-statist tradition that saw little to admire in the rhetoric of republican citizenship and which accordingly counselled abstention from the practices of parliamentary democracy. This perspective was no better exemplified than by Georges Sorel who, in his *Réflexions sur la violence* (1908), advised the French proletariat to utilize the tactic of the general strike to bring down what he characterized as a corrupt and decadent bourgeois republic. The same writer subsequently rallied to the support of Lenin and the Bolshevik Revolution, thereby setting a pattern for many later writers (including Jean-Paul Sartre) who would clothe their distaste for the everyday realities of France's republican institutions and politics with an admiration for the Soviet Union.

France's institutional instability and political uncertainties made themselves felt upon political thought in other ways. Internal dissent rendered suspect all calls for decentralization, local self-government or federalism, thus strengthening the position of the advocates of Jacobin centralization and rule from Paris. It also convinced republicans that the battle had to be taken to their enemies, producing a form of republican militantism that exists in French political thought to this day. Most spectacular of all was the removal of liberalism to the margins of French political thinking. The failure of François Guizot to establish both the political and intellectual supremacy of a bourgeois-dominated *juste milieu* meant that, with the fall of the July Monarchy in 1848, the liberal voice found it difficult to be heard. The neglect displayed towards the writings of Benjamin Constant, arguably the most perceptive of French political thinkers of the last 200 years, was matched by the near-contempt visited upon Raymond Aron until shortly before his death in 1983. Albert Camus fared no better at the hands of the Sartrian supporters of Algerian terrorism.

The France of Napoleon III's Second Empire had both an official philosophy – Victor Cousin's 'spiritualism' – and an official religion – Roman Catholicism. The surprise (and humiliating) defeat at the hands of Prussia in 1870 invited their wholesale rejection and in part took the form of what Claude Dignon (1992) termed 'the German crisis of French thought'. If Prussia symbolized both militarism and barbarism, then equally Germany could be characterized as the land of philosophy and science. The frivolous luxury and lax morals associated with Bonapartism needed to be replaced by a new doctrine of individual liberty and responsibility, and where better could this be found than in Kantianism. The appointment of Jules Lachelier to teach philosophy at the prestigious École Normale Supérieur in 1864, followed by that of Emile Boutroux in 1877, led to a situation where Kantianism became the *de facto* official philosophy of the French educational establishment. If this had its critics – most famously in the shape of nationalist writer Maurice Barrès, for whom the products of this education were nothing more than an 'uprooted' generation – it also meant that Kantianism found its way very powerfully into the emerging political culture and discourse of the newly established Third Republic. Two key figures here were Charles Renouvier and Jules Barni. If Renouvier's *Science de la Morale* (1869) provided the philosophical basis for the stream of articles on politics that were to be at the heart of his journal *La Critique philosophique, politique, scientifique et littéraire* from 1872 onwards (Blais, 2000), then similarly Barni's *La Morale dans la démocratie* (1868) provided the foundations of his *Manuel républicain* of 1872. The ambition, as Renouvier phrased it, was 'to transport ethics into politics' to create a 'public morality'. For Barni, the 'form' of the Republic was to be transposed into a 'moral democracy'. The latter therefore summarized his understanding of the republican principles of 'liberty, equality and fraternity' as a system where 'there was no longer a master, king or emperor, and subjects, but rather citizens subject equally to a common law which they have given to themselves in the interests of all'. 'Without civic virtue,' he continued, 'there is no republic.'

For the Kantian republicans, therefore, liberty quite definitely did not mean licence. Both made much of the need for personal dignity and laid great emphasis upon the importance of the family as a moral unit. Both also shared the preoccupation that the Republic as a set of political institutions must endure and not fall foul of the dictatorial and personal power that had brought down its predecessor in 1851. Accordingly, republican political thought in the early years of the Third Republic sought to sketch out a set of constitutional arrangements which would thwart demands for either monarchical restoration, a strong executive or direct democracy. Universal suffrage (which excluded women) was to be matched by a separation of powers designed to check 'despotism', 'caesarism' and what moderate republicans described as 'the dictatorship of an assembly'. The same programme also sought to codify a range of personal and civil liberties (for example, freedom of the press, equality before the law, the right to join a trade union) as part of a 'message' which Philip Nord (1995) recently summarized as 'the emancipation of conscience from the structures of philosophical and clerical orthodoxy, the emancipation of civil society from the intrusions of state or corporate authority'.

Much has been made of the Third Republic's failure to live up to this emancipatory political programme – Jean-Pierre Machelon has famously referred to *La République contre les libertés* (1976) – and there can be no doubt that the desire not to alienate conservative forces produced a republican practice which simultaneously integrated established elites and excluded the industrial working class. Republican political thought, however, did not waver from its commitment to emancipate the citizens of the fledgling Republic. Specifically, they recognized that there could not be a 'true' republic which was not established upon the republican education of its members. This in turn necessitated the separation of Church and state and the provision of a free, obligatory and secular education system as the first duty of the state. As Barni expressed it, all citizens must understand 'their rights, their duties and their real interests'.

Herein lay what François Furet (1985) has described as 'the touchstone' of republicanism: the principle of *laïcité*. At its simplest, *laïcité* denoted a straightforward demand for public neutrality on the part of the state: the individual existed as a citizen bearing rights rather than as a member of an ascribed community. In its more militant form, however, it commended the existence of a secular ethic, grounded in science and philosophy, that would act as both a civil religion and a social bond. As the nineteenth century came to a close, *laïcité* produced its own ideology, 'solidarism', articulated at a philosophical level by Célestin Bouglé and Alfred Fouillée amongst others and popularized by Léon Bourgeois in his work *Solidarité* (1896). The 'law of solidarity,' Bourgeois proclaimed, 'is universal' and rested upon the convergence of 'scientific method' and 'the moral idea.'

Laïcité also produced one of the most important and enduring particularities of French political life, the intellectual (Jennings, 1999). In his *L'Avenir de la science* Ernest Renan had written that 'enlightenment, morality, art, will always be represented among mankind by a magistracy, by a minority, preserving the traditions of the true, the good and the beautiful'. To combat the forces of reaction and Catholicism, the Republic sought to produce its own magistracy in its universities, and it was these men (and sometimes women) who came to the defence of the Republic when it was threatened by the events that came to be known as the Dreyfus Affair. From the outset there were those – for example,

Ferdinand Brunetière – who challenged the legitimacy of interventions by intellectuals into public debate, but the Dreyfus Affair nevertheless established a pattern of political behaviour that marked French political thought throughout the entire twentieth century. Intellectuals – as Emile Zola had demonstrated when he proclaimed the innocence of Captain Dreyfus – spoke out in the names of Truth and Justice and did so in the cause of Humanity.

The example was repeated during the First World War when France's philosophers, writers and artists again had little difficulty contrasting the vices of a barbaric and authoritarian Prussia with the virtues of a democratic and egalitarian France (Soulez, 1988). Emile Boutroux's *L'Idée de la liberté en France et en Allemagne* (1916) is a classic example of the genre. After the war, different themes – Bolshevism, colonialism and, later, the rise of fascism – galvanized intellectuals into action, forcing them time and time again to reassess the virtues of a Third Republic which lurched from crisis to crisis, only to implode with the fall of France in 1940. The mood of the 1930s was one of a crisis of civilization and many of those who were critical of Marxism and who saw little of attraction in the Soviet Union nevertheless sought an alternative to capitalism and to parliamentary democracy. Recognizing the growing malaise, Julien Benda penned his *La Trahison des clercs* (1927), calling for intellectuals to abandon their new-found enthusiasm for 'political passions' and to fulfil their proper function by defending the 'abstract values' associated conveniently with the Republic and democracy. The damning response came from the young Marxist Paul Nizan. Intellectuals – and specifically France's Kantian philosophers – were nothing more than the representatives of 'the official ideology of the state'. The function of 'bourgeois philosophy', he went on, was 'to obscure the miseries of contemporary reality'.

For Nizan, to defend Dreyfus was to defend the bourgeoisie. To attempt to stand above the political and economic conflicts of the day was the real treason. Everyone had to decide whether they stood by the side of the oppressed or the oppressors. We were all – like it or not – participants in 'the impure reality of the age'. The intellectual, siding with humanity against the bourgeoisie, was to become a 'technician of revolutionary philosophy'.

Such was the argument of Nizan's *Les Chiens de garde* (1932) and here was the first full formulation of what, after the Second World, War was to become the fashionable doctrine of 'commitment'. Its principal advocates – Jean-Paul Sartre and Simone de Beauvoir – seem to have spent the 1930s blithely unaware of the revolutionary causes that so agitated Nizan, as indeed they spent most of the Second

World War far from the Resistance. Nevertheless, it was they who benefited from the post-war *épuration* in order to establish a political and philosophical dominance which lasted into the 1960s. Following in the footsteps of Raymond Aron, Sartre had studied in Berlin, there becoming familiar with the phenomenology of Husserl and Heidegger. His early philosophical essays and literary works set out the themes that were to inform his great existentialist masterpiece *L'Être et le néant* (1943). 'Our point of departure,' Sartre wrote, 'is in fact the subjectivity of the individual and this for strictly philosophical reasons … because we want a doctrine based on the truth.' But what, for example, did the imperative to avoid 'bad faith' tell us about politics? Sartre's first response was to argue that existentialism was a form of humanism, but given the implausibility of this suggestion he was obliged to begin the ultimately unsatisfactory philosophical quest of marrying existentialism to Marxism, culminating in his *Critique de la raison dialectique* (1960). He condemned American imperialism, turned a blind eye to oppression in the Soviet bloc, and supported a whole series of revolutionary regimes in the Third World.

The tide turned philosophically, if not politically, in the early 1960s with the rise to prominence of structuralism. In the concluding chapter of *La Pensée sauvage* (1962) Lévi-Strauss answered Sartre's espousal of an existential Marxism by proclaiming: 'I believe the ultimate goal of the human sciences to be not to constitute but to dissolve man.' The goal was to break with the inheritance of humanism, an aim fully articulated in Foucault's *Les Mots et les choses* (1966) where we are told that man will disappear 'like a face drawn in sand at the edge of the sea'. In political terms, structuralism represented a decisive rejection of the ideology of bourgeois society and the supposed superiority of the categories of Western reason. As Roland Barthes (1957) was to comment, the world of the bourgeoisie had succeeded in describing itself as the world of Eternal Man.

Sartre secured his political revenge with the student protests of May 1968. The philosophical decline of structuralism followed shortly afterwards, as did a move away from the Marxism that had cast a shadow over French political thought for the previous 30 years. What followed was a recuperation of the subject and the rejection of the anti-humanism and determinism, rightly or wrongly, attributed to structuralism. This took various forms: the return to philosophy associated with *les nouveaux philosophes* (such as André Glucksman and Bernard-Henri Lévy); the formulation of a 'post-metaphysical humanism' inspired by Kant; and the prominence given to a religiously inspired ethics in the thought of Emmanuel Levinas and Paul Ricoeur.

There were other important outcomes. The role of the intellectual was put under serious scrutiny, with virtually everyone accepting that the days of the Sartrian 'universal' intellectual were now over. Next, French political thought began for the first time to engage with liberalism, seeking first to rediscover its own neglected liberal heritage and then to engage with the Anglo-American tradition. Mark Lilla, prefacing a volume exploring *New French Thought* (1994), went so far as to talk of the 'legitimacy of the liberal age'.

Crucially, however, there also took place an enthusiastic return to the hallowed principles of republicanism, aided by the bicentenary celebrations of the French Revolution in 1989. With the hopes of the left in tatters after the failure of François Mitterrand's first socialist government, the transcendent and universal goals of liberty and equality seemed still to offer an emancipatory vision of the future. Republican political thought therefore renewed its commitment to civic virtue and social solidarity, to the creation of what Dominique Schnapper (1994) defined as 'a community of citizens'. But was this ideal, forged in the nineteenth century, still of relevance? In particular, could its conception of the abstract individual divested of cultural, ethnic or religious particularisms be sustained in a society increasingly characterized by multicultural diversity? For some, like Régis Debray, there could be no compromise with these demands. For others, the principles of republicanism could be adapted to suit new realities. A minority believe that it represents an oppressive form of Western universalism that should be abandoned for good. The point, however, is that after two centuries French political thought still remains focused upon the founding principles of the French Revolution and the republican tradition that they produced. There is every indication that this will remain so for the foreseeable future.

ITALY

Although the Risorgimento produced both a self-conscious search for a distinctively Italian political and philosophical tradition and an important body of original work focused on the struggle for national unity by thinkers such as Giuseppe Mazzini, Carlo Cattaneo and Vincenzo Gioberti, Italian political philosophers were profoundly influenced by the writings of British, French and German scholars. However, though the first had been hugely important during the eighteenth and nineteenth centuries, it was the second and especially the third that proved the most influential for much of the twentieth century. Even so, followers of these foreign schools offered deliberately Italian variations on their ideas. Three characteristically Italian themes proved particularly salient. The first concerned the competing attractions of the two Romes (Emperor versus Pope, active versus contemplative life, social emancipation versus heavenly contemplation, politics versus morality). The second related to the respective strengths and weaknesses of authoritarian and democratic rule – a contrast that went back to the rivalry between *signorie* and *communes*. The third theme arose from the struggles in which these polarized conceptions of politics partook and which they partly generated, namely, a recurrent linking of the idea of Italian political unity with ethical order and an end both to sectarian and interstate strife and to the foreign domination that often accompanied them – as the unification of the two Romes, of authority and democracy. Throughout the twentieth century, Italian political theorists of diverse philosophical and ideological stripes were to bemoan the failure of the unified Italian state to live up to this expectation. Not only had unification failed to 'make Italians', as a famous phrase put it, but also Italy remained the least of the great powers, comparatively weak both economically and militarily. This disappointment led in turn to discussion of the role of philosophy in moulding such unity, either in conjunction with state power or as an alternative to it, and the degree to which such philosophical engagement was possible without committing *la trahison des clercs* by betraying the intellectuals' role as the guardians of truth and justice.

The importance of these themes can be illustrated by considering two of the most distinctive contributions of twentieth-century Italian political thought: the analysis of liberal democracy in terms of the elite manipulation of the electorate, and the reconceptualization of state and society in terms of the relations of force and consent. The two theses were related, with the second providing the background for the first. They were also elaborated in different ways by thinkers from across the philosophical and ideological spectrum, with opposed positions drawing on as well as criticizing each other. What structured these discussions were common cultural assumptions about the central issues in Italian politics.

The elitist view of liberal democracy originated in the positivist political sociologies of Vilfredo Pareto and Gaetano Mosca. Initially developed as a critique of socialism, it not only led to various criticisms of liberal democracy and reformulations of its working, but also prompted reflections on the strategy to be adopted by both socialist and fascist parties operating within liberal democratic regimes. Though Mosca claimed to have developed the elitist argument first, his and Pareto's versions arose independently from each other and emphasize different aspects of this phenomenon. Pareto (1848–1923) was born in Paris, where his father had been exiled, and pursued his early career in Florence prior to taking up the chair of political economy at Lausanne University in 1893. A classic liberal deeply influenced by Herbert Spencer and more particularly J. S. Mill, he had initially supported the extension of liberal democracy as an appropriate mechanism for representing the interests of society as a whole. During the early 1890s he expressed support for the cause of organized labour, regarding 'popular socialism' as a legitimate reaction to the 'bourgeois socialism' practised by the Italian political class gathered around Francesco Crispi and his successors, which employed state monopolies and economically disastrous protectionist tariffs to buy votes and adopted increasingly coercive measures to dampen unrest. He also sympathized with individual socialists, such as Napoleone Colajanni, sharing many of their progressive hopes. However, a convinced economic liberal, he had never accepted either the efficiency or the legitimacy of state intervention in the economy, regarding it as merely increasing political power and patronage. His deconstruction of *Socialist Systems* (1902) and his later fascist sympathies arose largely because he felt that from 1900 the pendulum had swung the other way. Instead of counterbalancing 'bourgeois socialism' in ways that might have established a liberal economic system, 'popular socialism' simply threatened to take its place. Its apparent democratic credentials notwithstanding, socialist ideology, particularly its reformist variant, was simply a mechanism for promoting the interests of a particular group of politicians (Finer, 1968; Bellamy, 1987: ch. 2; 1990).

A rigorous mathematical economist, who pioneered modern welfare economics, Pareto believed the prime question confronting the social scientist was why individuals were invariably moved by 'nonlogical' motivations, rather than self-interested 'logico-experimental' instrumental reasoning. He thought the answer lay in humans being motivated by a number of basic emotional 'residues' which could then be manipulated by certain sorts of argumentation, which he called 'derivations'. Though his *Treatise of General Sociology* of 1916 (Pareto, 1964) enumerated some 52 residues, the most important were 'the instinct of combinations' and the 'persistence of aggregates'. Updating Machiavelli, Pareto contended the rise and fall of governing classes reflected altering balances of these two residues within the elite, with the first favouring the cunning needed to rule through consent and the latter a more conservative desire for strength. He argued societies tended to alternate between periods of prosperity, when the skills of persuasion were at a premium, and austerity when policies of law and order were demanded. He linked the reformist governments of Giovanni Giolitti that, with the exception of the First World War, dominated the period 1900–22, with the former, suitably situated between the periods of coercive rule of Crispi and Mussolini (Pareto, 1921). Reformist socialism, on this account, was simply an ideology or 'derivation' employed by the prevailing ruling class to maintain their power. Like democracy, with which it had an affinity, it was well suited to elites employing the consensual methods of the 'instinct of combinations', giving their rule a veneer of popular legitimacy. In common with other anti-democrats, Pareto was more sympathetic to revolutionary syndicalism, which in his view reflected the forceful 'persistence of aggregates'. However, he believed its claims were just as illusory, amounting to little more than rhetorical gestures to legitimize a counter-elite's bid for power. Though he initially welcomed fascism, it was as a confirmation of his social theory rather than because of agreement with its ideals. He remained an economic liberal and had no sympathy with the syndicalist strand in fascist ideology. However, his disillusionment with democracy had led him to the paradoxical belief that a free market involving minimal state intervention could only be maintained by an authoritarian state that did not have to bargain with democratically entrenched vested interests. Had he lived, Mussolini would soon have disabused him in this regard and he would undoubtedly have been as critical of the fascist regime as he had been of Giolitti.

By contrast, Gaetano Mosca (1858–1941), who was born in Palermo, belonged to the conservative southern intelligentsia. Unlike Pareto, he doubted the capacity of the lower classes to participate in politics and had little insight into the plight of northern workers. Though Mosca shared Pareto's doubts about both popular sovereignty and socialism, his account of the ascendancy of a political class was more truly sociological (Bellamy, 1987: ch. 3). Minorities always rule because they form a more coherent group, able to act with greater consistency and coherence and to organize themselves better than the necessarily more diffuse and inchoate majority (Mosca, 1939: vol. 1, ch. 2). He agreed with Pareto that universal suffrage promoted the corrupt and devious political skills of the flatterer, the wheeler-dealer and the populist demagogue. He also thought that terms such as 'popular sovereignty' and the 'common good' were simply ideological 'political formulae' whereby a ruling class legitimized its position and obtained the consent of the governed. However, he departed from Pareto in believing that ideally the elite should be, and in fact often was, the most capable. However, the qualities making the group the best altered as

societies evolved. Thus, the rulers of the industrial age required rather different talents to those of the feudal era, when military prowess was at a premium (1939: vol. 1, chs 3–4). A deputy from 1909 to 1919, he opposed the introduction of universal suffrage in 1912 but ultimately accepted the need to come to terms with mass democracy and to concentrate not on its debunking so much as its reworking so that it would produce a democratic meritocracy committed to liberal values and possessing the administrative skills essential for the efficient and just government of contemporary societies. Crucial to this scheme was his doctrine of 'juridical defence'. Mosca argued that a political system had to be so designed as to mix the 'aristocratic' and the 'democratic' tendencies within any society, producing in the process a balance between the 'autocratic' and 'liberal' principles of government (1939: vol. 1, ch. 5; vol. 2, ch. 4). Unlike Pareto, he saw electoral competition between elites and an openness to the demands of and recruitment from the lower strata as mechanisms for reducing rather than exacerbating corruption. For they ensured rulers could further their own interests in governing only by taking account of the interests of the ruled in good government.

If one compares Pareto's and Mosca's arguments with those of Max Weber (1978) and Roberto Michels (1959) (who later joined Mosca at Turin University), who developed parallel theses that were in part influenced by them, then two differences are noticeable (Beetham, 1977; 1987). First, there is the emphasis on clientalistic politics and Machiavellian manipulation rather than bureaucracy – the distinguishing feature of Michels's account in particular. This contrast clearly reflects the different political cultures of the two countries, and can be compared in turn with the emphasis on crowd and mass behaviour found in the work of French elite theorists such as Le Bon (1895). Second, there is the propensity to treat elite theory as a universal psychological or social 'law' rather than a historically specific phenomenon. Here the difference can partly be attributed to the tendency for the Italians to seek explanatory models reflecting those of the natural sciences compared with the Germanic tradition of *Kulturwissenschaft*. However, it is noticeable that the same emphasis emerges even in thinkers clearly influenced by the German historical school – notably Benedetto Croce (1866–1952) and, via him, Antonio Gramsci (1891–1937).

Both Croce and Gramsci shared the Machiavellianism of the elitists, but even more than Mosca they saw the elite use of consent and force as linked to the way power relations were structured within the political system as a whole. A fellow southerner from a wealthy family, Croce shared many of Mosca's political prejudices. However, he had made his name as a philosopher criticizing the very positivist methodology Mosca employed. His first philosophical essay, 'History subsumed under the general concept of art' (1893), had drawn on the contemporary German debate between Windelbrand and Dilthey over the identity of the human sciences to attack the Italian positivist Pasquale Villari's claim that history was a science. From 1900 to 1917, Croce progressively developed his own idealist philosophy of spirit (Croce, 1902; 1909a; 1909b; 1917). Croce argued that thought always preceded action, with individuals reconceiving their present circumstances as a preliminary to seeking to change them. He also maintained that human activity was orientated towards the concepts of Beauty, Truth, the Useful and the Good. These were 'pure concepts', the specific content of which had altered through history as individuals reworked these ideas according to the various conceptions they held of the world. Most importantly, they were also distinct concepts. He believed that a grave error of earlier positivist and idealist philosophers was to confuse them. Finally, Croce's philosophy was aggressively anti-transcendental and metaphysical. There was no other reality than the human history of individual thoughts and actions – a doctrine he termed absolute historicism. Even the natural sciences were but the historical practices through which humans have understood and acted upon the world. Notions of the world in itself were meaningless.

Croce thought politics was orientated towards the useful, by which he meant instrumental, practical reasoning to achieve whatever goals we might have. However, the ethical evaluation of any given act had to be sharply distinguished from practical success. Such evaluation resulted from reflection on what others and oneself had achieved, producing in its turn a spur to action in the future (Croce, 1900; 1909b; 1930). At one level, therefore, politics was about force – possessing the strength of purpose and the means to realize one's ends. At another level, however, it concerned consent and the capacity for politicians to get people to identify with the state as realizing their ends (Bellamy, 1991). In his early writings, Croce tended to insist on the primacy of the first level. This was motivated by a frustration with what he then regarded as the ineffectiveness of contemporary politicians which he thought often went with an empty utopian rhetoric. Thus, unrealistic plans for an ideal world were substituted by concrete programmes for political action, without offering either a grounded critique of present problems or a plausible moral orientation for future action. He levelled this criticism at socialism in particular, but also against the Giolittian liberals. Though he saw Marxism as an entirely appropriate ideology for the proletariat to

adopt – praising Georges Sorel and the syndicalists in particular in this regard – he disputed Marxism's pretension to offer a philosophy based on historical materialism. Croce placed economics alongside politics in the realm of the useful, and charged Marxism with grossly reducing the other three aspects of human endeavour to this one.

Like Pareto, Croce initially supported Mussolini, albeit reluctantly, as a needed source of law and order. He soon changed his mind. For fascism made a parallel error to Marxism, in this case collapsing morality and everything else into politics and the coercive force of the fascist state. This argument was most notoriously made by Croce's erstwhile collaborator, Giovanni Gentile, who identified the moral force of fascism in the persuasive power of the blackjack (Gentile, 1925: 50–1). As the self-styled philosopher of fascism, he argued that the fascist state derived its authority from offering a 'totalitarian' order that organized every part of social life. In response, Croce reiterated his distinction between politics and morals, but now underlined the qualifications that this imposed on the political realist. We rightly desired efficacy from a state, but we also could question the purposes it served. The tensions between state and civil society, government and opposition, force and consent reflected at a systemic level the dialectic between thought and action in the individual. Each effective act was both the product and the subject of theoretical criticism of the circumstances in which agents found themselves (Croce, 1924a). Adapting Mosca's theory, Croce now saw the history of the product of rival political classes inspired by competing ethico-political conceptions. The purpose of liberal political institutions was to allow this rivalry to freely play itself out (Croce, 1923; 1924b).

Gramsci was greatly influenced by Croce, but redeployed his ideas within a Marxist context (Bellamy, 2001). A Sardinian by birth, he moved to Turin to study in 1911 where he became involved in the labour movement – providing intellectual leadership for the occupation of the factories in 1920. A founder member of the Communist Party of Italy in 1921, he was arrested by Mussolini in 1926 and spent the next decade in jail, dying shortly after his release in 1937. He shared much of Croce's criticisms of 'scientific Marxism', disputing the then conventional Marxist view that revolution was determined by changes in the economic base alone. He claimed it also required mobilizing the revolutionary will amongst the working class to exploit favourable social and economic circumstances. Reflecting on Lenin's success in Russia relative to the failure of revolutionary movements in the more developed West, he noted how revolution was in fact far harder to organize in advanced industrial and liberal democratic societies (Gramsci, 1994).

Gramsci explored the reasons for these difficulties most profoundly in his posthumous *Prison Notebooks* (1977), written during the early part of his incarceration, where he developed the notion of hegemony or 'ideological' power. There are both Italian and Russian sources for this term, but Gramsci's argument largely adapts the Machiavellian theme of force and consent as interpreted by Croce. Advanced democracies, he argued, ruled not simply on the basis of state force but also through winning social consent. They achieved this result by buttressing the state in the narrow sense of the government, bureaucracy and army with a broader set of institutions based in civil society, ranging from semi-public organizations such as schools and political parties to private bodies such as churches and the media. By working through civil society as well as the state, liberal democracies were able to legitimize the bourgeoisie's rule by creating a popular consensus around their values and self-image. Consequently, people failed to recognize the exploitative and inefficient character of the capitalist economy. He then employed elitist arguments to elaborate a socialist strategy to counter this circumstance. The party's leadership represented the new Machiavelli. Working through intellectuals, the leadership had to develop a counter-hegemony amongst the masses, gradually winning a foothold in various positions within civil society. Only then would the party be in a position to employ force for a revolutionary assault on the state. However, Gramsci saw the new communist order not simply as an alternative to liberal democracy, but as the mirror image of the fascist state: namely a society without a state, united by a 'total' moral vision that was fully in accord with the real needs of the people.

Though both Croce and especially Gramsci drew on non-Italian sources and had an important non-Italian following, the distinctiveness of their thinking derives once again from its Italian colouring. Thus Croce's divide between politics and morals reflects the theme of the two Romes, with his attack on transcendence getting its peculiar force from its anti-clerical connotations, just as the balance between force and consent has a pronounced Machiavellian flavour linked to the opposition between principalities and republics. Similar attitudes surface in Gramsci and even in Gentile, with both also seeking to overcome these tensions in a social and political unity that they explicitly associated with realizing the hoped-for benefits of a 'true' unification of Italy.

With post-war Italian politics dominated by the two 'religions' represented by the Catholic Christian Democrats (DC) and the Gramsci-inspired Italian Communist Party, political theorists continued to address the tensions between the two

Romes, particularly the difficulties of reconciling the pragmatic concessions of politics with a broader cultural and moral aspiration for social unity. Unsurprisingly, dissenters on both sides typically accused their parties of sacrificing the latter to the former. Significantly, the main political thinker to emerge in this period, Norberto Bobbio (1909–), though aligned to neither camp as a member of the 'lay' Italian Socialist Party (PSI), led a return to the neo-Machiavellian tradition of Pareto and Mosca (Bobbio, 1977).

Bobbio started out as a legal theorist, and his earliest writings were inspired by the legal positivist tradition of Hans Kelsen – a distinctive position in the Italian context that proved highly influential. Bobbio shared Kelsen's deep commitment to the liberal ideal of the *Rechtsstaat*, sharply criticizing the right and especially the Marxist left for overlooking the importance of the rule of law for the defence of individual liberty. However, he had a more realist view of the nature of law than Kelsen, regarding it as institutionalized power. This approach led him to a series of path-breaking studies of Hobbes and ultimately to political theory. In 1972 he exchanged his chair in law at Turin University for one in the newly created politics faculty. He now embarked on a series of essays exploring the nature of the state and democracy. These pieces were often motivated by his own engagement with the peace movement (Bobbio, 1979) on the one hand, and his critique of the radical new left (Bobbio, 1987a) on the other. Deeply opposed to nuclear weapons, he became a pioneering advocate of some form of cosmopolitan democracy as the only plausible way to institutionalize international law. Yet he remained deeply sceptical of radical schemes for participatory democracy at any level. Returning to Pareto and especially Mosca, Bobbio (1987b) defined democracy as simply a means for formalizing the rules whereby elites compete for and exercise power. Though modest by comparison with the hopes of radical democrats, it offers the only available mechanism whereby 'force' can be limited by 'consent'.

CONCLUSION

As Europe becomes more closely integrated, with the adoption of the euro and the proposed enlargement of the European Union to Central and East European countries, the question arises of whether the twenty-first century will see the different national political cultures explored in this chapter being amalgamated within, or made redundant by, an emerging pan-European public sphere. Germany, Italy, and France were amongst the initiators of the integration process and their populations have remained predominantly pro-European. Nevertheless, the EU has usually been defended as being congruent with and even reinforcing the member states. Increasingly, however, intellectuals and citizens have expressed concern that the EU might be subverting domestic democratic and constitutional arrangements. As a result, debate for and against extending and deepening the EU has typically developed arguments stemming from national political traditions.

For example, Habermas (2001a; 2001b) has probably offered the most sophisticated and influential theoretical argument for the creation of a European political culture. Yet his appeal to rights as the basis of a European 'constitutional patriotism' reflects a typically post-war (West) German preoccupation to find an alternative to the *Volk* as the foundation of the state and to ground democracy in a robust defence of the rule of law (Habermas, 1996). Within Germany, however, his arguments have aroused opposition from critics who fear that depatriating the constitution will weaken their compatriots' identification with such ideals and its role within the national democratic process (Grimm, 1997; Habermas, 1997). In France there has been a parallel debate, but this time expressed in the language of republicanism and the peculiar place of popular and state sovereignty within that tradition (Ferry and Thibaud, 1992). Finally, the widespread Italian enthusiasm for Europe has been largely motivated by the belief that it rectifies supposed weaknesses of the national political system. Yet a resurgent movement for regional autonomy in the north has prompted worries that the EU could undermine national unity without offering as deep an alternative source of social and political cohesion (Rusconi, 2001).

Even amongst Europhiles, therefore, it seems premature to talk of the displacement of a national by a European political culture. However, there is an emerging consensus that on certain issues continental Europe has become distinct from the United States and, in certain respects, albeit to a lesser degree, Britain too – notably opposition to the death penalty and less draconian criminal policies, a commitment to humanitarian intervention and international human rights, an approach to multiculturalism shaped by the legacy of colonialism, and a commitment to defend the social market economy against global capitalism, all of which were to some degree reflected in the recently declared Charter of Fundamental European Rights (Habermas, 2001a: ch. 4; 2001b; Cerutti and Rudolph, 2001). How far, if at all, these perceived differences in political culture will translate into distinctive theoretical positions remains to be seen.

REFERENCES

Arendt, H. (1951) *The Origins of Totalitarianism*. New York: Harcourt, Brace.

Barni, J. (1868) *La Morale dans la démocratie*. Paris: Baillière.

Barni, J. (1872) *Manuel républicain*. Paris: Bailliére.

Barthes, R. (1957) *Mythologies*. Paris: Seuil.

Beetham, D. (1977) 'From socialism to fascism: the relation between theory and practice in the work of Robert Michels. I. From Marxist revolutionary to political sociologist' and 'II. The fascist ideologue', *Political Studies*, 25: 3–24, 161–81.

Beetham, D. (1987) 'Mosca, Pareto and Weber: a historical comparison'. In W. Mommsen and J. Osterhammel, eds, *Max Weber and His Contemporaries*. London: Unwin Hyman, 139–58.

Bellamy, R. (1987) *Modern Italian Social Theory: Ideology and Politics from Pareto to the Present*. Cambridge: Polity.

Bellamy, R. (1990) 'From ethical to economic liberalism: the sociology of Pareto's politics'. *Economy and Society*, 19 (4): 431–55.

Bellamy, R. (1991) 'Between economic and ethical liberalism: Benedetto Croce and the dilemmas of liberal politics'. *History of the Human Sciences*, 4: 175–95.

Bellamy, R. (2001) 'A Crocean critique of Gramsci on historicism, hegemony and intellectuals'. *Journal of Modern Italian Studies*, 6 (2): 209–29.

Benda, J. (1927) *La Trahison des clercs*. Paris: Grasset.

Blais, M.-C. (2000) *Au principe de la République: Le cas Renouvier*. Paris: Gallimard.

Bobbio, N. (1977) *Saggi sulla scienza politica in Italia*. Bari: Laterza.

Bobbio, N. (1979) *Il problema della guerra e le vie della pace*. Bologna: Il Mulino.

Bobbio, N. (1987a) *Which Socialism? Marxism, Socialism and Democracy*, ed. Richard Bellamy. Cambridge: Polity (first Italian edn 1976).

Bobbio, N. (1987b) *The Future of Democracy: A Defence of the Rules of the Game*, ed. Richard Bellamy. Cambridge: Polity (first Italian edn 1984).

Bourgeois, E. (1896) *Solidarité*. Paris: Colin.

Boutroux, E. (1916) *L'Idée de la liberté en France et en Allemagne*. Paris: Éditions de Foi et de Vie.

Breuer, S. (1999) *Georg Jellinek und Max Weber: Von der sozialen zur soziologischen Staatslehre*. Wiesbaden: Nomos.

Cerutti, Furio and Enno, Rudolph (2001) *A Soul for Europe: On the Political and Cultural Identity of Europeans*. Leuven: Peeters Publishing.

Croce, B. (1893) 'La storia ridotto sotto il concetto generale dell'arte'. *Atti dell'Accademia Pontaniana*, XXIV: 1–32.

Croce, B. (1900) *Materialism storico ed economia marxista*. Palermo: Sandron.

Croce, B. (1902) *Estetica come scienza dell'espressione e linguistica generale*. Milan: Sandron.

Croce, B. (1909a) *Logica come scienza del concetto puro*, 2nd edn. Bari: Laterza.

Croce, B. (1909b) *Filosofia della pratica, economia ed etica*. Bari: Laterza.

Croce, B. (1917) *Teoria e storia della storiografia*. Bari: Laterza.

Croce, B. (1923) 'Review of G. Mosca, *Elementi di scienza politica*, 2nd edn'. *La critica*, 21: 374–8.

Croce, B. (1924a) 'Lo stato e l'etica'. In his *Etica e politica, economica*, 2nd edn 1973. Bari: Laterza, 183–8.

Croce, B. (1924b) 'I partiti politici'. In his *Etica e politica, economica*, 2nd edn 1973. Bari: Laterza, 189–95.

Croce, B. (1930) *Etica e politica, economica*. Bari: Laterza. 2nd edn 1973.

Dignon, C. (1992) *La Crise allemande de la pensée française*. Paris: PUF.

Ferry, J.-H. and Thibaud, P. (1992) *Discussion sur l'Europe*. Paris: Calmann-Levy.

Finer, S. (1968) 'Pareto and pluto-democracy'. *American Political Science Review*, LXII: 440–50.

Foucault, M. (1966) *Les Mots et les choses*. Paris: Gallimard.

Furet, F. (1985) 'Préface' to *Jules Ferry: Fondateur de la République*. Paris: EHESS.

Gentile, G. (1925) *Che cosa è il fascismo?* Florence: Valecchi.

Gramsci, A. (1977) *Quaderni del carcere*, ed. V. Gerratana. Turin: Einaudi.

Gramsci, A. (1994) *Pre-Prison Writings*, ed. Richard Bellamy. Cambridge: Cambridge University Press.

Grimm, D. (1997) 'Does Europe need a constitution?'. In P. Gowan and P. Anderson, eds, *The Question of Europe* (1995). London: Verso, 239–58.

Habermas, J. (1976) *Legitimation Crisis*. London: Heinemann.

Habermas, J. (1984) *The Theory of Communicative Action*. London: Heinemann.

Habermas, J. (1989) *The New Conservatism*. Cambridge: Polity.

Habermas, J. (1994) *The Past as Future*. Cambridge: Polity.

Habermas, J. (1996) 'Citizenship and national identity'. Appendix II to *Between Facts and Norms: Contributions to a Discourse Theory of Law and Democracy* (1990), trans. W. Rehg. Cambridge: Polity, 491–515.

Habermas, J. (1997) 'Reply to Grimm'. In P. Gowan and P. Anderson, eds, *The Question of Europe* (1995). London: Verso.

Habermas, J. (1998a) *The Inclusion of the Other*. Cambridge, MA: MIT Press.

Habermas, J. (1998b) *A Berlin Republic*. Cambridge: Polity.

Habermas, J. (1999) *Wahrheit und Rechtfertigung*. Frankfurt am Main: Suhrkamp.

Habermas, J. (2001a) *The Postnational constellation: Political Essays*. Cambridge: Polity.

Habermas, J. (2001b) 'Why Europe needs a constitution'. *New Left Review*, 11 (Sept/Oct): 5–26.

Horkheimer, M. (1972) *Critical Theory*. New York: Herder and Herder.

Horkheimer, M. and T. Adorno (1947) *Dialectic of Enlightenment*. New York: Herder and Herder, 1972.

Hübinger, G. (1988) 'Staatstheorie und Politik als Wissenschaft im Kaiserreich: Georg Jellinek, Otto Hintze, Max Weber'. In H. Maier et al., eds, *Politik, Philosophie, Praxis: Festschrift für Wilhelm Hennis*. Stuttgart: Klett-Kotta.

Jellinek, G. (1900) *Allgemeine Staatslehre*. Berlin: Springer.

Jennings, J. (1999) 'The clash of ideas: political thought, intellectuals and the meanings of "France"'. In M. Alexander, ed., *French History since Napoleon*. London: Arnold, 203–21.

Kemper, P., ed. (1993) *Die Zukunft des Politischen: Theoretische Ausblicke auf Hannah Arendt*. Frankfurt am Main: Fischer.

Le Bon, G. (1895) *La Psychologie des foules*. Paris: Alcan.

Lévi-Strauss, C. (1962) *La Pensée sauvage*. Paris: Plon.

Lilla, M. (1994) *New French Thought*. Princeton, NJ: Princeton University Press.

Löwith, K. (1989) *From Hegel to Nietzsche: The Revolution in Nineteenth-Century German Thought*. New York: Columbia University Press.

Löwith, K. (1994) *My Life in Germany before and after 1933*. Urbana, IL: University of Illinois Press.

Lukács, G. (1924) *History and Class Consciousness*. Cambridge, MA: MIT, 1971.

Machelon, J.-P. (1976) *La République contre les libertés*. Paris: Presses de la Fondation Nationale des Sciences Politiques.

Marcuse, H. (1964) *One Dimensional Man*. London: Routledge.

Michels, R. (1959) *Political Parties: A Sociological Study of the Oligarchical Tendencies of Modern Democracy* (1921). New York: Free.

Mosca, G. (1939 [1896]) *Elementi di scienza politica*, 3rd edn, 2 vols. Bari: Laterza (vol. 1, 1st edn 1896; vol. 2 added to 2nd edn 1923).

Nietzsche, F. (1974) *The Gay Science* (1887). New York: Random House.

Nizan, P. (1932) *Les Chiens de garde*. Paris: Maspero, 1976.

Nord, P. (1995) *The Republican Moment: Struggles for Democracy in Nineteenth-Century France*. Cambridge, MA: Harvard University Press.

Pareto, V. (1902) *Les Systèmes socialistes*, 2 vols. Paris: Giard et Briere.

Pareto, V. (1921) *La Trasformazione della democrazia*. Milan: Corbaccio.

Pareto, V. (1964) *Trattato di sociologia generale*, 2 vols, 2nd Italian edn, ed. N. Bobbio. Milan: Communità (1st edn 1916, 2nd edn 1923).

Renouvier, Charles (1869) *Science de la Morale*, 2 vols. Paris: LOD Rank.

Rusconi, G. (2001) 'Appartenenza e cittidinanza tra dimesione nazionale e dimensione europea'. In A. Loretoni, ed., *Interviste sull'Europa: Integrazione e identità nella globalizzazione*. Rome: Carocci.

Sartre, J.-P. (1943) *L'Être et le néant*. Paris: Gallimard.

Sartre, J.-P. (1960) *Critique de la raison dialectique*. Paris: Gallimard.

Schmitt, C. (1963) *Der Begriff des Politischen: Text von 1932 mit einem Vorwart und drei Corollarien*. Berlin: Duncker und Humblot.

Schmitt, C. (1985) *The Crisis of Parliamentary Democracy* (1923). Cambridge, MA: MIT Press.

Schmitt, C. (1996) *The Concept of the Political*. Chicago: University of Chicago Press.

Schnapper, D. (1994) *La Communauté des citoyens: sur l'idée moderne de nation*. Paris: Gallimard.

Sorel, G. (1908) *Réflexions sur la violence*. Paris: Rivière.

Soulez, P., ed. (1988) *Les Philosophes et la guerre de 14*. Paris: Presses Universitaires de Vincennes.

Strauss, L. (1950) *Natural Right and History*. Chicago: University of Chicago Press.

Vollrath, E. (1987) *Grundlegung einer philosophischen Theorie des Politischen*. Würzburg: Königshausen und Neumann.

Vollrath, E. (1990) 'Die Kultur des Politischen: Konzepte politischer Wahrnehmung in Deutschland'. In V. Gerhardt, ed., *Der Begriff der Politik*. Stuttgart: Metzler.

Weber, M. (1978) 'Parliament and government in a reconstructed Germany' (1918). In G. Roth and C. Wittich, eds, *Economy and Society*, 2 vols. Berkeley, CA: University of California Press, Appendix 2, 1381–1469.

Weber, M. (1994) *Political Writings*, eds P. Lassman and R. Speirs. Cambridge: Cambridge University Press.

Wolin, R. (2001) *Heidegger's Children*. Princeton, NJ: Princeton University Press.

30

English Political Theory in the Nineteenth and Twentieth Centuries

DAVID WEINSTEIN

ANALYTICAL PHILOSOPHY'S LEGACY

The converging currents of Anglo-American political theory have swept away much of English political theory's distinctiveness. Nevertheless, the latter has been sufficiently distinctive and influential, warranting our concern as intellectual historians. Indeed, as it has become less Anglo and more American, English political theory has become more rigorously analytical and, consequently, increasingly insensitive to its own historical past. For all its many virtues, contemporary Anglo-American political theory is an impoverished history of ideas, having substituted a truncated eulogized canon for the richness of its predominantly English historical tradition.

This historical amnesia stems, in large part, from the legacy of logico-positivism, which discredited normative political theorizing as just another variety of emotive venting and unmeaning metaphysical gibberish. Fortunately, H. L. A. Hart's *The Concept of Law* (1961) and Brian Barry's *Political Argument* (1965) resurrected normative political theory. John Rawls followed with *A Theory of Justice* (1971) which, in turn, unleashed an industry of criticism that shows no signs of abating.[1] Ironically, then, English analytical philosophy eviscerated English-speaking political theory at the beginning of the last century, only to redeem it 50 years later. And what it redeemed quickly spread elsewhere, becoming what we now know as Anglo-American political theory [see further Chapter 1].

Whereas English political theory may have lost much of its identity in the confluence of Anglo-American political theory, the latter remains

robustly at odds with the continental philosophical tradition. Whatever English political theory has become, its analytical rigour and empiricism extensively immunized it from the Counter-Enlightenment preoccupations of continental theory. This is not to say that Anglo-American political theory has been uninfluenced by continental theorizing, especially recently. As we shall see, continental motifs informed late-nineteenth-century English idealism, Isaiah Berlin's value pluralism and the Cambridge school of textual interpretation.

THE HISTORY OF POLITICAL THOUGHT

Despite Anglo-American political theory's homogenizing interpolation, English theorists have resisted forsaking intellectual history more than their American counterparts. The triumph of conceptual analysis caused American political theorists to lose interest in the history of political thought except as a way of certifying their current theoretical positions. Canonical theorists were typically invoked (Nozick's 1974 use of Locke) as remarkably prescient in anticipating – or at least identifying – solutions to current conceptual disputes.

By the 1970s, the Cambridge school of political thought, led by Quentin Skinner, J. G. A. Pocock, John Dunn and Richard Tuck, began challenging such interpretive strategies, countering that the meanings of past political philosophical texts could only be recovered with difficulty by historically contextualizing them [see further Chapter 2]. According to Skinner, we should first ascertain the range of possible meanings available to an author when writing a piece of text, and next deploy 'this wider *linguistic* context as a means of decoding the actual intention of the given writer' (1969: 49).

For his part, Pocock (1985) insists that proper interpretation depends more on discovering the discourse paradigms that inform political philosophical texts than on trying to discover their authors' intentions. In his view, discourse paradigms function hegemonically, *structurally* infusing texts with often-contested yet related core meanings. Hence, we must first sensitize ourselves to the debates and secondary literature contextualizing any text and then map these core meanings back into them. Moreover, discourse paradigms are dynamic, evolving with each new 'spin' that canonical works impart to their inheritance. And subsequent readings of these texts spin them again, making each reader, in part, a new author. Interpretation is inherently open-ended and unstable. Language paradigms 'impose upon actors in subsequent contexts the constraints to which innovation and modification are the necessary but unpredictable responses' (1985: 7).

Contemporary English political theory has struggled to resist marginalizing the history of political thought in the face of the ascendancy of philosophical analysis. Indeed, the parochialism of analysis has rejuvenated the former, which has, in turn, rebounded to the practice of analysis itself. For the Cambridge school, intellectual history remains a veiled analytic exercise. Both its method and its purpose are fundamentally linguistic. What words formerly meant can help us refine our own meanings and consequently improve our own philosophical thinking. Intellectual history, when not rational reconstruction, can be analytically provocative and therefore 'educationally mandatory' (Dunn, 1996: 1).

Pocock is less vexed than Skinner about the dangers of parochialism, which may partially account for the similarities between his method of doing intellectual history and continental political theory. For instance, his emphasis on the determining role played by discursive paradigms makes his interpretive methodology structuralist. Yet, his interpretive methodology is equally poststructuralist in so far as meanings are unstable since subsequent interpretive spins recast and multiply meanings in ways unintended by the author. As poststructuralists insist, 'language, as "writing", inevitably harbors the possibility of ... an indefinite multiplicity of recontextualizations and reinterpretations' (McCarthy, 1989–90: 148) [see further Chapter 4].

Contemporary Oxford political theory hasn't been entirely swept aside by the vogue of philosophical analysis either. Berlin early on abandoned analytical theorizing for a Herderian-inspired history of ideas. Like Pocock, he affirms that intellectual history 'is to a large degree a history of dominant

models'. In examining any civilization, 'you will find that its most characteristic writings ... reflect a particular pattern of life which those who are responsible for these writings ... are dominated by' (Berlin, 1999: 2). Echoing Skinner, he writes that 'unless you try by some act of imagination to reconstruct within yourself the form of life which these people led ... your chances of truly understanding ... their writings and really knowing what Plato meant ... are small (1999: 62).

More recently, Oxford's Michael Freeden (1996) has championed conceptual political theory but also without forsaking the value of the history of political thought [see Chapter 1]. Following W. B. Gallie, Freeden agrees that conceptual disputes are unavoidable but locates the source of these disputes in the underlying ideological structure of political theorizing. For Freeden, political ideologies are distinct systems of interrelated conceptual interpretations. Liberalism's and socialism's disagreements about liberty are tethered, for example, to their respective disagreements about the meaning of equality. Hence, conceptual disputes are always disputes about a host of interconnected political ideas. Political ideas come in distinctive conceptual packages. Diligent intellectual history is crucial in sensitizing us to the nuanced variety of these conceptual packages, reminding us of the contested nature of all normative political concepts and thus commemorating the always-unfinished nature of political theory.

In sum, analytical English political theory has never forsworn the history of political thought as much as its American counterpart. For it, the ascendance of Anglo-American philosophical analysis has not relegated intellectual history to the margins of scholarship. And in taking intellectual history seriously, English political theory has been less historically near-sighted and less prone to mistake its purported discoveries for unwitting duplications of past debates.[2]

VARIETIES OF ENGLISH POLITICAL THEORY

Nineteenth- and twentieth-century English political theory comes in distinct varieties: liberal utilitarianism, egalitarian liberalism, socialism, and conservatism. This list is not exclusive and is perhaps somewhat arbitrary. Moreover, as I have been suggesting, these varieties are no longer distinctively English; they are now becoming distinctively Anglo-American. Consequently, my history spins them with inescapable Anglo-American prejudice. And since I am interested in how the history of these varieties exposes contemporary Anglo-American political theory's inflated sense of novelty and conceit, my interpretive strategy unavoidably spins them further, replicating some of contemporary theorizing's insensitivity to its own past.

Liberal Utilitarianism

Utilitarianism, modern English political theory's most venerable legacy, holds that morally right actions are those that maximize utility. Utilitarian theories are therefore typically welfarist, consequentialist, and aggregative (see Scarre, 1996: introduction, for a concise, nuanced account of utilitarianism's basic features) [see further Chapter 8 on liberalism and utilitarianism].

Utilitarianism is welfarist in so far as it identifies good with human welfare. Whereas early-nineteenth-century utilitarians such as Bentham and James Mill construed welfare more hedonically in terms of pleasure and pain, J. S. Mill construed welfare more subtly as consisting in higher (mental) and lower (sensual) pleasures. But by regarding the former as more valuable, Mill arguably corrupted his version of utilitarianism by infusing it with another criterion of value besides happiness. Contemporary Anglo-American utilitarians have worked hard to salvage utilitarianism from such inconsistencies by offering preference, informed preference and objectivist accounts of welfare. However, objectivist accounts of welfare are problematic because they presuppose that individuals can be mistaken about their own happiness. John Harsanyi concludes that we have no choice but to rely on actual preferences. But preferences must be *informed* preferences, namely those that individuals would have after rational reflection on all relevant information (Harsanyi, 1976: 31–2). However, informed preference accounts of individual welfare are susceptible to the criticism that they are surreptitiously objectivist in so far as they invoke rationality as a criterion.

Utilitarianism is also a form of consequentialism because it holds that general welfare should always be promoted. Hence, moral rightness is a function of whatever best promotes universal welfare. Like all forms of consequentialism, then, utilitarianism prioritizes the good over the right. Consequentialism also comes in egoistic varieties, which stipulate that agents should always promote their own welfare exclusively. Whether Jeremy Bentham's utilitarianism was purely universalistic (about maximizing general welfare) or egoistic (about maximizing individual welfare) is a matter of some dispute. For Elie Halévy, Bentham's and James Mill's versions of utilitarianism were essentially egoistic (1972: 66–8, 474–8); others have held that

Bentham's utilitarianism was a species of universal hedonism (Harrison, 1983: ch. 5).

Lastly, utilitarianism is aggregative in so far as it assumes that welfare is measurable and therefore can be summed. However, some critics have denied that utilities can be intrapersonally or interpersonally compared. According to them, utilitarian calculations are illusory, making utilitarian moral judgements impossible. Others, following William Hazlitt and Thomas Carlyle, have condemned utilitarianism for being too rational and 'philistine' for endeavouring to reduce morality to spiritless calculations, assuming that such calculations could nevertheless be made. But utilitarians from Bentham to Harsanyi have responded, insisting: (1) that utilitarianism incorporates feelings, especially pleasure and pain; (2) that rough ordinal calculations *can* usually be made, particularly when the welfare stakes are high; and (3) that they *must* be made.

Utilitarianism's purported willingness to sacrifice some for the sake of the greatest aggregate happiness has always been its Achilles' heel. According to Rawls, it fails to take 'seriously the distinction between persons'. But Mill's utilitarianism wasn't so unsophisticated; nor was Bentham's, according to recent interpreters. For Frederick Rosen, Bentham was the 'first liberal utilitarian' because he successfully integrated a robust theory of individual liberty with his principle of utility, thereby precluding sacrificing some in the name of the rest (1990: 64; also see Kelly, 1990). According to Jonathan Riley, Mill likewise successfully infused his utilitarianism with a powerful commitment to liberty, insisting that generous self-regarding freedom of action was necessary to maximizing welfare. We maximize individual happiness by cultivating our talents, which, in turn, requires that we freely experiment with our lives. Hence, individuals flourish and general welfare is maximized wherever societies live by the liberty principle, which stipulates that citizens may be coerced solely 'to prevent harm to others' (Mill, 1963: 223).

Mill's utilitarianism seems more immune to traditional criticisms than Bentham's because it also incorporates a spirited defence of stringent moral rights. As Mill says in the much undervalued last chapter of *Utilitarianism*:

> Justice is a name for certain classes of *moral rules*, which concern the essentials of human well-being more nearly, and are therefore of more *absolute obligation* ... and the notion which we have found to be of the essence of the idea of justice, that of a *right* residing in an individual, implies ... this more binding obligation. (1969: 255, emphasis added)

'Utility in the largest sense' flourishes wherever citizens cultivate their individualities subject to respecting each other's rights-protected interests in security and freedom. Moreover, the sanctity of basic rights encourages continued moral self-development that, in turn, promotes greater respect for rights. As Riley observes, rights and moralized individuality reinforce each other symbiotically, accelerating the growth of general welfare (1988: chs 8–9).[3] Compared with Bentham's indirect utilitarianism, then, Mill's is more traditionally liberal because it is so thoroughly rights-oriented. His two seminal essays, *Utilitarianism* and *On Liberty*, work hand in glove; the former's last chapter bridges their respective, seemingly irreconcilable principles of utility versus liberty.

Now many critics, from James Fitzjames Stephen and F. H. Bradley in the nineteenth century to John Gray more recently, have faulted Mill's attempt to accommodate utilitarianism and liberalism as illogical. As Stephen asks rhetorically, 'Why should [anyone] prefer obedience to a rule to a specific calculation in a specific case, when ... the only reason for obeying the rule is the advantage to be got by it, which by the hypothesis is ... a loss in the particular case?' (1991: 277).

Notwithstanding Mill's efforts to accommodate utility and liberty, we shouldn't ignore Henry Sidgwick's and Herbert Spencer's sophisticated versions of nineteenth-century liberal utilitarianism either. Although their reputations have declined, recent scholarship has resurrected their importance (see: Schneewind, 1977; Schultz, 1992; Weinstein, 1998).

Sidgwick's significance for contemporary political theory has been enormously undervalued. John Rawls's *Theory of Justice* is, to a considerable extent, a critical response to Sidgwick. When Rawls says we 'often seem forced to choose between utilitarianism and intuitionism', the utilitarianism he has in mind is Sidgwick's (1971: viii). Like the English nineteenth-century utilitarians, Rawls sees intuitionism as an unsystematic and therefore unsatisfactory rival. But, unlike them, he rejects utilitarianism as a credible alternative.

Contemporary political theorists must take Sidgwick seriously if they take Rawls seriously [on Rawls's theory, see Chapter 7]. If Barry is right in insisting that we live in a 'post-Rawlsian' world, then navigating this world requires that we take better account of Sidgwick. How ironic it is that the rise of analytical political philosophy has blinded contemporary Anglo-American political theorists from properly appreciating their historical debts.

Sidgwick's 'classical' utilitarianism was also a form of liberal utilitarianism in so far as Sidgwick held, like Mill, that utility was best promoted *indirectly* via intermediary moral principles. Hence, Rawls's attack on 'classical' utilitarianism is warfare against a straw man. For Sidgwick, the 'middle axioms' of common sense morality generally constituted appropriate happiness-maximizing guides and therefore needed modest critical refinement. Sidgwick nevertheless held, like Mill, that 'as this actual moral order is admittedly imperfect, it will be the Utilitarian's duty to aid in improving it' (1981: 476).

More recently, Rawls has embraced Sidgwick's healthy reverence for common sense. Following Sidgwick, Rawls holds that our moral intuitions play a critical role in *justifying* and *systematizing* our political principles. Whereas Sidgwick justifies and systematizes common sense by appealing to utility, Rawls deploys the veil of ignorance as a justificatory and systematizing filtering device [see also Chapter 18]. According to Rawls's reflective equilibrium, the principles we choose behind the veil of ignorance should match more or less our existing moral convictions; otherwise we risk trying to construct political morality *de novo*, as Sidgwick would say. We risk making our political morality unrealistic. For Sidgwick as well as Rawls, common sense tames radical reform. The utilitarian reformer

> will naturally contemplate [established morality] with reverence and wonder, as a marvelous product of nature, the result of long centuries of growth ... he will handle it with respectful delicacy as a mechanism, constructed of the fluid element of opinions and dispositions, by the indispensable aid of which the actual *quantum* of human happiness is continually being produced. (1981: 475)[4]

In sum, for Sidgwick, utility was best maximized indirectly via healthy but not uncritical deference to the 'middle axioms' of common sense morality. Hence, his liberal utilitarianism was closer to Hume's and thus more conservative than Mill's. But it looked back not only to Hume but also ahead to Rawls because common sense needs systematizing, but not without abandoning its justificatory role.

Sidgwick's indirect utilitarianism also resembled Spencer's liberal utilitarianism despite Sidgwick's protestations to the contrary (see Weinstein, 2000). Spencer agreed with Sidgwick that established morality was the 'marvelous product of nature, the result of long centuries of growth' with modern liberal societies converging on the same array of utility-promoting moral rules. And he agreed with Mill, though not Sidgwick, that we have reformulated our most fundamental moral rules as stringent rights.

Spencer was therefore as much a liberal utilitarian as Mill in so far as he combined a rights-constrained, maximizing theory of right with a hedonic conception of good. For Spencer, rights were *indefeasible* logical 'corollaries' of his principle of equal freedom, which stipulated that: 'Every man is free to do that which he will provided he infringes not the equal freedom of any other man' (1978: I, 62).

General happiness was best promoted wherever basic liberal rights to life, personal integrity and property were unconditionally enforced, making Spencer's liberal utilitarianism more uncompromising than Mill's. While Spencer and Mill acknowledged the extensive similarities between them, Spencer distanced himself markedly from Bentham, disparaging the latter's utilitarianism as merely 'empirical', or unconstrained, and therefore as morally inferior. Being 'empirical', Benthamism allegedly justified sacrificing individuals in the name of maximizing utility even marginally. By contrast, he characterized his own brand of utilitarianism as 'rational' precisely because it purported to derive basic rights from the principle of equal freedom and because these putative logical derivations were indefeasible. But Spencer exaggerates his differences with Bentham, if Rosen and Paul Kelly have interpreted Bentham correctly.

Contemporary English utilitarians have championed liberal utilitarianism with increasing subtlety and sophistication. Rule utilitarians stress utilitarianism's compatibility with accepted moral rules and intuitions (Hare, 1981; Harsanyi, 1985; Hooker, 2000), whereas liberal utilitarians marry utilitarianism with strong liberal rights (Gray, 1983; Riley, 1988). All such accounts nevertheless constitute different versions of what is now commonly known as *indirect* utilitarianism. For indirect utilitarians, according to James Griffin, the principle of utility serves as a 'criterion' for assessing classes of actions. By contrast, established moral rules and/or basic liberal rights function as sources of direct obligation (or 'decision procedures') for guiding individual actions (Griffin, 1994: 179). Actions are morally wrong if they violate these decision procedures. Indirect utilitarians hold that respecting such decision procedures will best maximize general utility overall, though not necessarily in short-term individual cases. In other words, sometimes *acting* rightly is *doing* wrong. But why should I act rightly if acting rightly happens not to be for the utilitarian best in a given situation? Why should I be a mindless, rule-worshipping sucker?[5]

As just suggested, for liberal utilitarianism, fundamental rights function as critical decision procedures, making it more juridical than rule utilitarianism. Rights indirectly steer our actions along inviolable channels of acceptable behaviour that purportedly generate overall general utility. But liberal utilitarianism is not simply a more juridical version of indirect utilitarianism. Following Mill, it also champions individuality in so far as individual flourishing also constitutes happiness. For liberal utilitarians, wherever citizens can meaningfully cultivate their personalities by their own lights within the limits proscribed by equal basic rights, individuality thrives and society is happier.

Contemporary liberal utilitarianism is often criticized in the same way as Mill's contemporary opponents assailed him for trying to reconcile the irreconcilable. For instance, John Gray (1989: 218–24) has recanted his earlier enthusiasm for liberal utilitarianism, agreeing with liberal utilitarianism's critics that it futilely seeks to join multiple *ultimate* normative criteria, namely utility and indefeasible moral rights. For Gray, either maximizing utility logically trumps rights, or rights (in so far as they possess authentic moral weight) trump maximizing utility. Liberal utilitarianism fails logically because it pulls in opposite normative directions, instructing us to maximize utility when doing so violates rights and to respect rights when doing so fails to maximize utility. We sometimes must choose between our liberalism and our utilitarianism.

Liberal utilitarianism strains to combine the systematizing efficiency of utility with liberal ethical appeal by sanctifying individuality. It gallantly seeks to systematize liberalism and liberalize utilitarianism. All forms of utilitarianism (though not all forms of consequentialism) are necessarily monistic for better and for worse, but liberal utilitarianism is surely utilitarian monism at its moderated – though problematic – best.

Egalitarian Liberalism

Utilitarianism reigned in England during the nineteenth century, gradually giving way to analytical egalitarian liberalism during the twentieth. As English political theory lost its distinctively utilitarian identity, it also lost its distinctively English identity, becoming just another voice in the homogenizing discourse of Anglo-American, egalitarian liberalism.

Egalitarian liberals, in contrast to utilitarians, feature equality over utility as their overriding normative concern. Still, utilitarians are not indifferent to equality and distributive justice. As we have just seen, indirect utilitarians take these values seriously, though not so seriously that they trump maximizing utility as the ultimate normative standard. Utilitarians also prize equality in the sense that impartiality is constitutive of the principle of utility. Each person's 'happiness ... is counted for exactly as much as another's' (Mill, 1969: 257).[6] For egalitarian liberals, however, equality plays a more commanding role because many of them favour internalist arguments for equality.[7] And because equality matters for them up front, they also tend to be more preoccupied with questions about equality of *what* rather than *why*.

Egalitarian liberalism's pedigree emerged in the late nineteenth and early twentieth centuries via new liberals like T. H. Green, L. T. Hobhouse,

J. A. Hobson and D. G. Ritchie who were, in turn, powerfully influenced by the British idealists.[8] Idealists combined a coherence theory of truth with neo-Hegelian historical teleology. For them, thinking partially constitutes whatever we describe, explain or interpret. Facts are never simply discovered or just speak for themselves but are mediated by cognition. When we theorize, we make and organize facts according to our systems of value, interpretive perspectives and preoccupations. Hence, the more coherently we theoretically mediate and organize the world, the more truthful our understanding becomes. And as we theorize the world with increasing sophistication, we realize universal history more completely.

Now, English idealists like F. H. Bradley and Bernard Bosanquet were as much indebted to Hegel for their social ontology and moral and political theory as for their conception of history [on Hegel, see Chapter 28]. Bradley argues that individuals are socially constituted, making morality fundamentally social in the sense that acting morally requires acting *for* others rather than simply leaving them alone. Hence, in so far as good is self-realization, acting morally means promoting everyone's self-realization, not merely one's own. Being so interdependently constituted, we best promote our own self-realization by simultaneously promoting our fellow citizens' and they best promote theirs by promoting ours (Bradley, 1988: 116). Moreover, because our identities are socially encumbered, rationalistic moral theories like utilitarianism and Kantianism are misconceived and self-defeating. Both theories share the misguided pre-Hegelian delusion that we can somehow detach ourselves from our social milieu when determining how to act. Acting morally primarily entails embracing one's socially constituted identity and fulfilling 'one's station and its duties'. Nonetheless, fulfilling the duties of one's station isn't the whole of morality since the kind of society in which one lives also matters. Conventional morality must not be taken uncritically.

Bosanquet's *The Philosophical Theory of the State* (1899) takes up politically where Bradley's *Ethical Studies* (1876) leaves off morally. Bosanquet agrees with Bradley that, in so far as our identities are socially constituted, others are not merely external constraints on our self-realization. Societies are free according to how well they manipulate social relations so that everyone flourishes. For Bosanquet, and new liberals, freedom consists in being empowered by meaningful opportunities ('positive or political ... liberty') as well as being left alone ('negative or juristic liberty'). Thus, '"higher" liberty is also ... the "larger" liberty, presenting ... the more extensive choice to self-determination' (Bosanquet, 2001: 147). In addition, for Bosanquet, higher freedom *also*

entails mastering oneself in the sense of giving 'effect to the self as a whole, or remov[ing] its contradictions and so mak[ing] it most fully what it is able to be' (2001: 149–50).[9]

Moreover, being positively free entails juridical security: Our 'liberty ... may be identified with such a system [of rights] considered as the condition and guarantee of our becoming the best that we have it in us to be' (2001: 139). Self-realization is most effectively promoted indirectly by a system of strong, though not indefeasible, rights. As with liberal utilitarianism, rights function as ready-made decision procedures. Like habitual bodily activities such as walking, acting justly by respecting others' rights usually demands 'no effort of attention', enabling citizens to devote themselves to 'problems which demand ... intenser efforts' (2001: 201–2). And whenever citizens lose their justice habit, liberal states swiftly re-educate them through punishment. While states can never make citizens just, they can encourage just behaviour by maintaining a system of rights. By hindering 'hindrances of the good life', they warrant our loyalty (2001: 21).

New liberals joined Bosanquet in combining a moralized theory of freedom and strong rights with a communitarian social ontology. For Green, Ritchie, Hobhouse and Hobson, moral self-realization was unconditionally good. Realizing oneself morally meant being fully free by being both 'outward[ly]' and 'inward[ly]' free (Green, 1986: 234–5). It meant having the enabling 'positive power or capacity of doing ... something worth doing' *and* actually 'doing ... something worth doing' (1986: 199). As Hobhouse put it, self-realization consists in 'social' as well as 'moral' freedom. Whereas the former concerns external harmony between citizens or 'freedom of man in society', the latter is 'proportionate to the [self's] internal harmony' (Hobhouse, 1949: 51, 57).[10]

For new liberals as well, rights indirectly promoted everyone's self-realization by enabling each to flourish. And to the extent that each flourished morally, each, in turn, promoted common good by respecting the rights of others. Thus, for Hobhouse, common good was 'the foundation of all personal rights' (1968: 198). In Green's words, rights realize our moral capacity negatively by 'securing the treatment of one man by another as equally free with himself, but they do not realise positively, because their possession does not imply that ... the individual makes a common good his own' (1986: 26).

However, new liberals favoured a more robust threshold of equalizing opportunity rights. Although they concurred with Bosanquet that possessing property was a potent means of 'self-utterance' and therefore crucial to successfully externalizing and realizing ourselves, they also stipulated that private property was legitimate only in so far as it did not subvert equal opportunity. In Hobson's words, 'A man is not really free for purposes of self-development ... who is not adequately provided' with equal and easy access to land, a home, capital and credit. Hobson concludes that although liberalism is not state socialism, it nevertheless implies considerably 'increased public ownership and control of industry' (1974: xii).[11] New liberals, then, transformed English liberalism by making social welfare, and the state's role in promoting it, pivotal. They crafted welfare liberalism into a sophisticated theoretical alternative.[12]

Regrettably, contemporary Anglo-American political theory has underappreciated the new liberalism because it constitutes an idiosyncratic medley of neo-Kantianism, consequentialism, communitarianism and perfectionism (see Weinstein, 2001). Hence, contemporary liberals and communitarians have disabled themselves, due to their historical insensitivity, in their struggle for theoretical accommodation (see Simhony and Weinstein, 2001).

Contemporary political theory's historical myopia has consequently made Joseph Raz's perfectionist liberalism seem more anomalous than, in fact, it is. Though Stephen Mulhall and Adam Swift are correct in concluding that Raz 'transcends' the rivalry between liberalism and communitarianism, they overemphasize his originality (1996: 250). Raz's perfectionist liberalism is refurbished new liberalism but with some differences. For instance, Raz distinguishes autonomy, a seminal value requiring serious political attention, from self-realization, which he holds is merely one variety of autonomy. Whereas a self-realizing person develops all of his capacities to their full potential, an autonomous person merely develops 'a conception of himself, and his actions are sensitive to his past'. In 'embracing goals and commitments, in coming to care about one thing or another', such persons 'give shape' to their lives, though not necessarily according to a unified plan as with Hobhouse (Raz, 1986: 375, 387) [see further Chapter 8].

Moreover for Raz, unlike new liberals, autonomy entails value pluralism because goods and virtues are incommensurable, often forcing us to trade them off, 'relinquishing one good for the sake of another' (1986: 398–9).[13] And, tragically, we have to make trade-offs because (though Raz fails to argue why) the menu of goods and virtues available to us is largely socially determined (1986: 366, 398–9) [see further Chapter 18].

Notwithstanding these differences, for Raz autonomous agents nevertheless 'identify' with their choices and remain 'loyal' to them, just like new liberal self-realizing agents. Second, in shaping their lives, autonomous agents, like self-realizing agents, don't arbitrarily recreate themselves in spite of their social circumstances. Brute Nietzschean self-creation

is impossible, for we are all born into communities presupposing our values. At best, acting autonomously transforms slightly, or reconfirms, these values selectively (1986: 382, 387–8).

More than anything, what makes new liberals Raz's predecessors is the thoroughly liberal nature of his perfectionism. For Raz, following the new liberals, rights equalize opportunities for acting autonomously. Rights are necessary though insufficient conditions for achieving autonomy. Furthermore, these conditions must be redistributively robust if citizens are to enjoy *meaningful* opportunities to make the best of themselves. Hence, as with new liberals (and liberal utilitarians), rights indirectly promote good. Governments can't make citizens good but governments should indirectly encourage them to make themselves good by providing appropriate opportunities. Hence, politics can, and should be, perfectionist:

> The autonomy principle permits and even requires governments to create morally valuable opportunities, and to eliminate repugnant ones. Does not that show that it is incompatible with [Mill's] harm principle? ... Perfectionist goals need not be pursued by the use of coercion. A government that subsidizes certain activities, rewards their pursuit, and advertises their availability encourages those activities without using coercion. (1986: 417)

In other words, we are duty bound to provide fellow citizens with the conditions of autonomy as long as we don't harm them. Coercing citizens into leading valuable lives harms them whereas providing valuable options for all harms no one.

David Miller's egalitarian liberalism also resuscitates unawares the kind of liberal communitarianism earlier championed by new liberals. According to Miller, justice is (1) pluralistic, in so far as desert, need and equality comprise its threefold criteria, and (2) contextual, in so far as the strength of these criteria varies according to the goods and social practices at issue. Miller's justificatory strategy on behalf of these three criteria owes much to Sidgwick, though he trades on Sidgwick largely via Rawls's reflective equilibrium. Miller hopes to 'show that a theory of justice rooted in popular beliefs can retain a sharp critical edge' (1999: xi). We first try to discover the principles of justice embodied in our everyday beliefs. We next hone them philosophically before reapplying them as guides to the distributive social dilemmas facing us. But we never forgo the moorings of common sense justice lest our theory become either so abstract or so controversial as to prove irrelevant [see further Chapter 17].

Miller prefers Rawls's later writings where the original position becomes little more than a heuristic device for impartially systematizing and clarifying our common sense notions of justice. Consequently,

It ... merely highlights his preferred method of proceeding, which is to move back and forth between our particular beliefs about justice and the general principles that might be used to systematize them, always bearing in mind that these principles ... must be publicly justifiable'. (1999: 58)

But given this shift towards public justifiability, Rawls ought to have been more sensitive to empirical evidence about how we, in fact, understand justice. Miller, then, evokes Sidgwick unawares, and empirical social science, to rehabilitate Rawls in the name of egalitarian communitarianism.

Miller would resist being characterized as an egalitarian liberal; he would view this label as conflating 'simple' distributive equality with the 'complex' market socialist equality he favours.[14] The former stipulates that people should be equal with regard to some X and thus limits debates about equality to disputes about 'equality of what?'. Following Michael Walzer, complex equality is not about distributing some X. Rather, it is a 'social ideal' about how we should *treat* each other as equals. But Miller remains an egalitarian liberal nevertheless: 'An egalitarian society must be one which recognizes a number of distinct goods', ensuring that each 'is distributed according to its own proper criterion [desert, need and equality]'. As long as no distributive sphere dominates others, complex equality is secured. The real 'enemy of equality is *dominance*', which must be politically regulated (1995: 203). And dominance is nefarious because it is so harmful to individual self-development.

Miller readily concedes that his political theory draws on two political traditions: 'distributive equality from the tradition of liberalism, social equality from social democracy and socialism' (1999: 244). Consequently, Miller is a true heir to the new liberals. Equally for them, no justice principle is sovereign. Equality and need temper desert *qua* individual choice and responsibility, allowing all citizens real equal opportunity to develop their talents according to their own lights.

Ronald Dworkin, Amartya Sen and Barry recall the new liberalism much less. Dworkin and Sen feature the sovereignty of equality (though, for Sen, equality is 'consequence-based') while Barry prefers the justificatory logic of social contract. By contrast, new liberals and their heirs have balked at fetishizing the first, while rejecting the *modus vivendi* of the latter. Dworkin's, Sen's and Barry's versions of egalitarian liberalism are nevertheless compelling.[15] As already noted, Dworkin's and Sen's versions are egalitarian in what Miller pejoratively labels the 'simple' sense. Whereas Dworkin prefers equalizing resources, Sen prefers equalizing capabilities. In his recent *Sovereign Virtue*, Dworkin presses hard his familiar defence of equality of resources, appealing to what he calls the 'challenge model' of ethical value, which he insists is non-consequentialist. For Dworkin, lives go better when they are lived from the *inside* with 'ethical integrity', meaning when they are not lived mechanically from the *outside* in accordance with rote habit. Ethically honest lives are skilful performances exhibiting ongoing, critical self-reflection. For such lives, choice is constitutive of living well. Welfarism and utilitarianism are immoral since they instrumentalize choice in the name of promoting states of affairs.[16]

For Dworkin, equality of basic resources 'flows from' the challenge view. If living well means meeting the challenges we assign ourselves, then having sufficient basic resources is ethically imperative. And if it is 'equally important how each person lives', then everyone ought to have *equal* basic resources. Hence, 'ethical liberals begin with a strong ethical reason for insisting on an egalitarian distribution of resources' (Dworkin, 2000a: 279). In other words, equal concern and respect somehow entail resource egalitarianism since equality 'must be measured in resources and opportunities' (2000a: 237; also see Dworkin, 1985: 192–3). Notwithstanding the circularity of arguing that equal concern and respect entail treating people equally along some separately identified domain, Dworkin never stipulates precisely what he means by equality of resources also 'flow[ing] from' the challenge model.[17] But if the latter is meant to be a source of justification, then Dworkin's egalitarian liberalism begins to look like Sen's more than Dworkin realizes.

Sen's egalitarian liberalism testifies to liberalism's conceptual flexibility by combining an 'inclusive' form of consequentialism with basic 'capability equality'. For Sen, morality is 'consequence-based' though it is not more narrowly consequentialist. Consequentialism is narrower because it is arbitrarily evaluator-neutral. 'Consequence-based evaluation', by contrast, includes non-utility information such as agent relativity. In Sen's words, 'deontological values can, in fact, be accommodated within consequence-based evaluation through evaluator-relative outcome moralities' (1982: 38).[18] More recently, Sen refers to his version of practical reasoning as 'deontic-value inclusive consequential reasoning' (2001: 64). Such reasoning forbids prioritizing either the right or the good. Rather, these concepts are linked, thus requiring that we consider them simultaneously: 'While considerations of freedoms, rights and duties are not the only ones that matter (for example, well-being does too), they are nevertheless *part* of the contentions that we have reason to take into account in deciding on what would be best ... to do' (2001: 61).

Sen concedes that his modified consequentialism turns even Williams into a consequentialist (though Williams would likely respond that, with Sen, we have an unholy hodgepodge that is no longer remotely consequentialist). Perhaps Sen's theory of equality can assist us here. Sen rejects Rawlsian primary goods equality and Dworkin's resource equality as well as welfare equality in favour of capability equality. Capability equality is a modified needs account of equality similar to Miller's. For Sen, functionings and capability functionings determine well-being. That is, a person's life goes well when she not only manages to do various things (functions) but *also* possesses the wherewithal (capabilities) to choose to do these things from many alternatives. Moreover, certain functionings are more elementary, such as being adequately nourished, and are therefore the purview of the principle of equality. Other functionings, such as being happy, are important although they are not basic. Everyone deserves equal basic nourishment but not equal happiness. Freedom itself is elementary, too, and therefore everyone also deserves equal basic freedom or capability equality.

In sum, morality is complex though fundamentally 'consequence-based'. Moral evaluation measures how effectively freedom and rights are promoted, duties are honoured and well-being is maximized. And these metrics are premised, in turn, on all enjoying the basic capability equality of 'being adequately nourished, having mobility' and 'taking part in the life of the community' (Sen, 1993: 36–7). Notwithstanding the intricacies of measuring behaviour according to such diverse consequences, we still might insist that Sen's consequentialism is consequentialist in name only.

With Barry, however, we clearly have unadulterated liberalism, which is nevertheless deeply informed by English utilitarianism. As Kelly recently notes, 'there is a very real sense in which most of Barry's work … has involved an engagement with … utilitarianism' (1998: 44). These debts aside, Barry has emerged as one of the leading champions of Anglo-American contractualism.[19] Like Thomas Nagel, Rawls and Thomas Scanlon, Barry holds that the existence of incompatible conceptions of the good necessarily prioritizes the right over the good. Justice as impartiality adjudicates 'between the conflicting demands that arise from the pursuit of those conceptions of the good' by giving citizens a 'veto over proposals [principles of justice] that they could not reasonably be expected to accept' (Barry, 1998: 229, 223).[20] The sieve of disapproval makes surviving principles impartial: nobody is unreasonably privileged by what survives in pursuing his respective conceptions of the good. Utilitarian justice is precluded because reasonable citizens would purportedly veto it. Few would be

prepared to bear the self-sacrificing burdens of agent neutrality. Justice as impartiality is therefore self-limiting, excluding utilitarian impartiality as too extreme. In the name of impartiality, it constrains impartiality. Being impartial about competing conceptions of good does not entail such indifference towards them that one is always prepared to sacrifice one's own interests for the general interest.[21]

Justice as impartiality thus preserves the liberal public versus private goods distinction that feminists have claimed reinforces patriarchy. Barry nevertheless concedes that domestic violence and marital rape are public concerns. The personal is indeed largely political. But as Susan Mendus perceptively worries, 'what is to block the move to the kind of society which Barry fears – one in which very little is left to private judgement and almost everything to public scrutiny and censure?' (1998: 183). In short, Barry's feminism risks collapsing the private into the public, imperilling his liberalism. Barry responds, accusing Mendus of 'alarmism' and denying that prohibiting domestic violence and marital rape would 'open the floodgates' to tyrannizing (utilitarian) impartiality. He insists that rightful public intervention in some cases won't lead 'inexorably to public intervention in other cases where that is wrong' (Barry, 1998: 256).[22] Surely this begs the question.

Like Rawls and Scanlon, Barry's debts to Sidgwick are palpable, stemming no doubt from his complex engagement with utilitarianism. For Barry, as for Scanlon, justice as impartiality is merely a 'device for focusing our thoughts' about justice. It simply helps us in 'thinking for ourselves in a more structured way' (1998: 194–5). In short, following Sidgwick, it systematizes our considered views of justice though not through the lens of utilitarian good for, with Barry, good is pluralistic.

Good is famously pluralistic for Berlin as well. In his case, however, value pluralism precludes systematizing justice because values are so clearly irreconcilable, making Berlin's liberalism difficult to classify. Berlin has lately become an academic industry, leading Barry to criticize Berlin's literary executor of publishing every bit of trivia Berlin wrote as though it was reputable philosophy (see Barry, 2001: 7). Berlin's reputation initially rested on his analysis of negative versus positive freedom, which has overdetermined much theorizing ever since. Berlin defends negative freedom, condemning positive freedom as historically, if not logically, anti-liberal. For Berlin, the problem goes back to Green's unfortunate appropriation of Hegel (for Berlin's misreading of Green, see Simhony, 1991). But Berlin's defence of negative freedom, and hence his liberalism, is problematic in so far as the more he clarifies what he means by negative freedom, the more negative freedom resembles positive freedom. For instance, in the original 1958 'Two concepts of liberty', Berlin reconceptualizes negative freedom in a much-ignored footnote. Being free is not simply having options to do what one wants. Rather, the

> extent of my freedom seems to depend on (a) how many possibilities are open to me ... (b) *how easy or difficult* each of these possibilities is *to actualize*; (c) *how important* in my plan of life ... these possibilities are ... (d) how far they are closed and opened by deliberate human acts; (e) *what value* not merely the agent, but the general sentiment of the society in which he lives, puts on the various possibilities. (Berlin, 1969: 130, emphasis added)

Hence, being free is also being empowered to realize worthwhile aims. (But see Berlin's 1969 Introduction to *Four Essays on Liberty*, where he omits (b) and (e).)

More recently, scholarly attention has shifted to Berlin's value pluralism because of its congruence with postmodern scepticism [see further Chapter 18]. In 'Political judgment', Berlin asserts unequivocally that there is 'no natural science of politics' or 'natural science of ethics' but only political judgement (1996: 49, 52). Attempts to substitute the former for the latter can too often result in disaster, especially wherever political science and revolutionary theory converge. Such theorizing lacks a 'sense of reality' in naively assuming that politics is scientifically generalizable and therefore predictable. For Berlin, such scientific conceit is the Enlightenment's most unfortunate legacy. We simply can't anticipate all the important consequences of public policies. Justice, whether utilitarian, contractarian or socialist, is always controvertible in practice.

Berlin holds that Herderian Romanticism cured political theory of this conceit [see further Chapter 28]. A double-edged alloy of expressivism and irreconcilable ideals, this 'new romantic transvaluation of values substituted the morality of motive for that of consequence, that of the inner life for that of effectiveness in the external world' (1996: 191). But the cure became its own disease, degenerating into emotivism and aestheticism, causing Berlin to eschew subjectivism while embracing pluralism:

> I am not a relativist; I do not say 'I like my coffee with milk and you like it without; I am in favour of kindness and you prefer concentration camps' – each of us with his own values, which cannot be overcome or integrated. Pluralism is not relativism because multiple values are objective ... rather than arbitrary creations of men's subjective fancies. (2000: 11–12)[23]

And crucially, because objective values are incompatible, pluralism privileges freedom (2000: 23).

Gray has recently defended Berlin, agreeing that freedom should be privileged because it allows us to 'negotiate' our way among incommensurable values. Negative freedom is *pre-eminently* valuable because it 'facilitates' unavoidable radical choice-making between incommensurables (Gray, 1996: 143–4). Though Berlin's 'agonistic' liberalism purportedly unmasks the rationalistic pretensions of 'legalistic' liberalisms like Mill's, Dworkin's and Barry's, Gray nevertheless views Berlin's justification of negative freedom's priority as incomplete.[24] For Gray, Berlin's 'historicist turn' suggests that 'there can be, and need be, no universal justification for liberalism'. Rather, liberalism 'is instead best understood as a particular form of life, practiced by people who have a certain self-conception, in which the activity of unfettered choice is central' (1996: 161). And given what Gray has written most recently, this self-conception flourishes in value-pluralistic sensitive cultures that, as a matter of prudence, embrace the politics of *modus vivendi* in order to survive (2000: ch. 4). (However, Alan Ryan, 2001: 56, argues that Gray's *modus vivendi* liberalism is much closer to Rawls's political liberalism than Gray realizes.) Gray's Berlin combines intimations, which Gray now sees as his task to make explicit, of a communitarian theory of identity with a postmodern theory of value. However, Gray exaggerates Berlin's abandonment of Enlightenment rationalism.[25]

Socialism

Nineteenth- and twentieth-century English socialism is a medley of currents, not all of which are philosophically systematic: Fabianism, ethical socialism, labour Marxism and, more recently, analytical Marxism, new left socialism and new labourism. (For an overview of English socialist thought, see Foote, 1997.) I examine some of these varieties more extensively than others because I want to underscore English socialism's distinctiveness.

For Fabians like G. Bernard Shaw and the Webbs, unearned increments on land and capital caused poverty which redistributive taxation could solve. But only democracy coupled with collectivist professionalism could manage class struggle and capitalism away. C. A. R. Crosland's and Richard Titmuss's post-war revisionism inherited Fabianism's enthusiasm for managerial gradualism, though neither viewed public ownership as a panacea. In *The Future of Socialism* (1956) and *Socialism Now* (1974), Crosland argued that while welfarism had nearly eliminated poverty, only tempered socialism could eradicate class without eroding democracy.

Ethical socialists like Edward Caird, W. J. M. Mackenzie and R. H. Tawney likewise favoured gradualism in advocating a 'heroic' moralized socialism that derived much from the new liberals.[26] They valorized moral autonomy and citizenship, arguing that neither could flourish unless capitalism was radically reformed, providing all citizens with meaningful equal opportunities.[27] Moreover, ethical socialists contrasted themselves to 'scientific' socialists whom they denounced as mechanistic, dogmatic and corporatist.

Tawney seems to have been the only English socialist Berlin admired, mostly because his commitment to socialism was both ethically grounded and historically erudite (see Ignatieff, 1998: 235). Christian values emphasizing our common humanity and dignity informed Tawney's socialism, causing him to stress duties over rights. Capitalism regrettably eviscerated our common humanity by generating enormous economic inequalities and privileging polarizing rights over duties. Educational and health care inequalities particularly crippled the working class from making their lives meaningful.

Tawney's 'higher' socialism both mimics Hobson's 'liberal socialism' and anticipates contemporary egalitarian liberalisms like Dworkin's. Although his theorizing lacks Dworkin's rigour, it likewise begins with our common dignity and regards liberty and equality as compatible (Tawney, 1964: 46–7). Liberty and equality are fully commensurate, especially where greater economic equality protects all citizens from undue economic coercion. Greater economic equality is 'essential' to greater liberty (1964: 168). Tawney thus follows new liberals in insisting that extreme economic inequalities are no less constraining than physical threats.

In the 1952 edition of *Equality*, Tawney clarifies why liberty and equality are compatible. He insists that political liberties are more 'fundamental' than 'secondary' economic liberties. Hence, while redistributive justice plainly compromises the freedom to acquire and exchange property (a 'secondary' liberty), it enhances political liberties by making them more than merely nominal for the poor. In short, greater economic equality frees us by opening our political 'range of alternatives' and fortifies our 'capacity' to choose between them. Liberty and equality 'can live as friends' (1964: 227–9).

English socialism includes modified Marxism too. From guild socialists like G. D. H. Cole and Harold Laski through Ralph Miliband more recently, Marxists have championed varied combinations of industrial democracy and nationalization, although Cole and Laski became increasingly less enthused about both. Cole and Laski also became more statist, despite Laski never relinquishing his affection for Mill and Hobhouse.

More recently, G. A. Cohen and Steven Lukes have taken up Tawney's challenge, insisting that Marxists need to defend equality philosophically rather than take it for granted. Because capitalism has failed to dig its own grave and because we seem fated to perpetual scarcity, we need to engage in greater 'moral advocacy'. We need to *argue* for egalitarian justice (Cohen, 1995: 7–12; 2000b: 103–9).[28] Marxists need to resolve their paradoxical commitment to both adopting and rejecting moral criticism, for otherwise they will disable Marxism from 'offering moral resistance to measures taken in its name' (Lukes, 1985: 141). Arguing for equality means arguing analytically, which means arguing anti-dialectically and anti-holistically. Analytical Marxists are anti-dialectical because they refuse to substitute dogma for rigorous argument. They refuse to 'bullshit' because ideological 'bullshit[ting]' leaves too many conceptual misapprehensions (say, about freedom) intact, reinforcing the status quo [on analytical Marxism see Chapter 6]. Traditional Marxist theses that fail to survive the 'corrosive acid of analysis' should be abandoned. Analytical Marxists are also anti-holistic because they reject economic historicism (Cohen, 1981: 7; 2000a: xvii–xxvii).[29]

As Dworkin rightly points out, Cohen agrees with Sen that citizens should be equal not in welfare or resources but in *opportunities* to achieve welfare. As Cohen recently claims, injustice prevails not when different distributions of goods reflect differences in people's choices but when these differences stem from sundry lucky and unlucky circumstances (2000b: 130). Socialist justice neutralizes these circumstances with the aim of making different distributions exclusively a function of people's socially unencumbered choices. But for Dworkin, Cohen's attempt to distinguish between choice and circumstance breaks down because unvarnished choosing doesn't exist. All choosing is circumstantial, making inexpensive preferences no less unlucky than expensive ones. Equality of welfare opportunity thus collapses into simple equality of welfare. Consequently, if we are

> not responsible for the upshot of some of our 'expensive' tastes, on the ground that we did not choose those tastes, then we are not responsible for any of them, and the community is obliged ... to see that we suffer no comparative financial disadvantage in virtue of any of them. (Dworkin, 2000a: 289)

Cohen, in short, is just a left utilitarian in disguise.

Cohen has tried to separate himself from what he regards as Sen's less demanding egalitarianism, no doubt, in part, because he is keen *not* to be mistaken for some sort of disguised welfarist. In particular, he criticizes Sen for advocating an 'athletic' notion of capability which makes freedom and well-being entirely a function of actively choosing between functionings. Hence, well-nourished infants could not experience well-being. Indeed, adults couldn't experience well-being either unless they were actively meeting challenges (Cohen, 1993: 16–32). And this seems to entail aggressively perfectionist politics, which Cohen presumably finds distasteful. But Sen rejects Cohen's interpretation as a mischaracterization, arguing that a person's ability to 'achieve various valuable functionings [well-being] may be greatly enhanced by public action and policy' (1993: 44). Well-being depends upon being economically empowered, which depends upon considerable wealth redistribution. Cohen has also tried to distance himself from Miller's market socialism, arguing that it is neither consistent with Miller's emphasis on desert nor just. Desert is little more than a bourgeois principle that treats talents as a 'natural privilege' (Cohen, 1995: 259; for the reply see Miller, 1999: 327, endnote 1).

Left-wing feminists have, in turn, criticized Marxists for stubbornly holding on to maleness as a 'natural privilege'. For Sheila Rowbotham, Marxists have failed to appreciate how capitalism reproduces itself through patriarchy.[30] Because working-class women suffer both class and gender exploitation, they are the true vanguard of working-class consciousness. Women's oppression is unique in that unlike 'the working class, who have no need for the capitalist under socialism, the liberation of women does not mean that men will be eliminated' (Rowbotham, 1973: 117). Recent socialist feminists have expanded upon Rowbotham's anxieties, attacking radical feminists for their parochial women-centred analysis: 'Although affirming an identity creates a refuge for marginalized women, a transformative politics is required if that refuge is not to become a ghetto' (Lovenduski and Randall, 1993: 91).[31]

Despite these nuances, English socialism has mostly become left-wing egalitarian liberalism. Indeed, classifying left new liberals, as well as market socialists like Miller as egalitarian liberals rather than socialists, seems arbitrary. We could just as easily classify ethical socialists, and even some analytical Marxists, as left egalitarian liberals.[32] But however much English socialism and liberal egalitarianism have converged, neither have forsworn English political theory's concern with class, which still distinguishes it from its American counterpart.

Conservatism

Even more so, conservatism has served to retard English political theory's shrinking distinctiveness [see further Chapter 10]. More properly a philosophical mood, it has eschewed the sustained argumentative rigour typifying Sidgwick through Cohen. According to Anthony Quinton (1993),

conservatism is a continuous tradition stretching back to Burke and culminating in Michael Oakeshott, whom Quinton considers the only philosophically interesting twentieth-century English conservative. For Quinton, three doctrines characterize this tradition. First, conservatives fear precipitous change, preferring continuity in existing political practices and institutions. Second, they are deeply sceptical about the possibilities of political *knowledge*, preferring the purported political *wisdom* accumulated in established laws, institutions and moral conventions. Third, conservatives view individuals as organically constituted by the societies in which they live. Universal human nature does not exist, making systematic political theory illusory and self-defeating (1993: 244–5, 252).

Exemplifying Quinton's doctrinal anxieties, nineteenth-century conservatives like Samuel Coleridge, Thomas Carlyle and James Fitzjames Stephen excoriated utilitarianism for its super-charged, community-subverting rationalism. For instance, Stephen condemned Mill's liberty principle as morally subversive in so far as it authorized all acts short of harm to life and liberty. The liberty principle thus circumscribed moral obligation, undermining community (Stephen, 1991: 58–9). Notwithstanding his disingenuous account of Mill's theory of obligation (for Mill also maintained that we owe each other imperfect as well as perfect obligations), Stephen's fears have resurfaced in Patrick Devlin's *The Enforcement of Morals* (1959). Devlin follows Stephen, condemning Millian liberalism for vitiating society's organic, moral integrity. Hart has responded by reformulating Mill's distinction between merely offensive and harmful acts. For Hart, Devlin errs by agreeing with Stephen against Mill that 'law might justifiably enforce morality as such' (Hart, 1963: 16). In conventional utilitarian fashion, Hart denies that positive morality carries independent moral force simply by virtue of its existence. Moreover, while *distressing* others does not constitute harm, publicly *shocking* them is 'another matter', possibly justifying legal prohibition. Though he concedes that the distinction remains a 'fine one', Hart provides no criterion for making it. Presumably, general utility serves this function. But Hart must show just how much general disutility transforms mere distress into harmful shock. This dilemma merely exemplifies the larger one plaguing liberal utilitarianism discussed previously, namely what is our *supplemental* criterion for determining *how much* threatened disutility warrants violating basic rights?

Quinton's assessment that Oakeshott is the only theoretically interesting twentieth-century English conservative is compelling. Michael Oakeshott's appeal stems from his sophisticated rehabilitation of idealism combined with his willingness to take utilitarianism and socialism as worthy philosophical opponents. As one of his sympathetic interpreters urges, Oakeshott forcefully challenges the 'commonsensical' or 'liberal utilitarian' view of freedom, which regards laws purely instrumentally. Whereas liberal utilitarians hold that law necessarily restricts freedom, Oakeshott claims that only certain types of laws do. That is, liberal utilitarians follow Berlin in thinking that *how much* government interferes with its citizens determines the extent of their political freedom, while Oakeshott thinks that political freedom is just as significantly a function of government's *mode* (Liddington, 1984: 308–9). 'Enterprise' government 'runs' citizens' lives, compromising their freedom, by instrumentalizing law in the name of promoting some substantive goal such as general utility, equality or distributive justice. 'Enterprise' politics is therefore naively rationalistic. By contrast, 'civil' government merely 'rules' citizens without determining their ends. Reason is incapable of delivering up new Jerusalems. And whenever we mistakenly convince ourselves otherwise, we risk creating what Karl Popper called 'closed' societies.[33] Rationalistic insolence is the enemy of *civitas*.[34]

Since Oakeshott, conservatism has been mostly lamentation. Shirley Letwin's (1978) 'conservative individualism' is little more than simplified Oakeshott. Kenneth Minogue's 'conservative realism' berates political theorists for 'grinding their concepts into a finer and finer powder'. Conservative realists reject 'rationalist ways of thinking' exemplified by 'Dworkinian believers in social justice'. They follow Oakeshott, condemning rationalism as the misguided belief that the 'conditions of any activity could be exhaustively formulated in precepts' (Minogue, 1996: 4, 160).[35]

No contemporary conservative, however, surpasses Roger Scruton for moodiness over carefully crafted argument. Scruton concedes as much when he says that his 'concern is with dogma' and that 'argument is not the favourite pursuit of conservatives'. A conservative is '"for" certain things … not because he has arguments in their favour, but because he knows them, lives with them, and finds his identity threatened … by the attempt to interfere with their operation' (Scruton, 1980: 12–13).[36] In short, conservative political theory is not so much theory but pathos and profession.

CONCLUSION

Every intellectual history is a narrative. My intellectual history of nineteenth- and twentieth- century English political theory privileges liberal utilitarianism and the new liberalism because I firmly believe that both constitute English political theory's most significant contribution to modern Anglo-American political theory as well as to modern political theory in general. In my view, contemporary American political theorists, for whom Anglo-American political theory begins with Rawls, haven't taken either seriously enough. But those who fetishize Rawls should at least read Sidgwick, since *A Theory of Justice* was written largely in response to him.

Contemporary English political theory is less historically myopic, not only because liberal utilitarianism has long been an English preoccupation, but also because English political theory largely avoided falling under the ideological spell of German *émigré* intellectuals like Hannah Arendt, Leo Strauss and Eric Voegelin, who found refuge in the US academy in the 1930s and 1940s, and who read their anxieties about fascism into their depictions of liberalism. They infused American political theory with intoxicating fevers and fascinations. No wonder Rawls's analytical liberalism seemed so bracing and therefore proved so historically numbing in turn. And no wonder American political theory unwittingly reinvented communitarianism since it knew next to nothing about the new liberalism. English political theory has fared somewhat better. From Bentham on, it has simultaneously maintained its analytical rigour without losing its historical memory.

NOTES

I would like to thank Peter Nicholson, Fred Rosen, Avital Simhony, Susan Mendus, Gale Sigal and an anonymous reviewer for their helpful comments on earlier drafts.

1 I am following Pettit (1993), who provides a compelling account of the impact of analytical philosophy on modern political theory. Also see Tuck (1993).

2 For how recent efforts by contemporary liberals and communitarians to achieve accommodation replay unknowingly new liberal political theory, see Simhony and Weinstein (2001: introduction).

3 This symbiotic consolidation also informs Mill's feminism in *The Subjection of Women*. According to Susan Mendus (1994), Mill's essay and his wife's earlier *Enfranchisement of Women* also anticipated efforts by later radical feminists to expose patriarchy's debilitating false consciousness.

4 Rawls's later writings elevate the justificatory role of common sense at the expense of Kantian constructivism.

5 For critics of contemporary indirect utilitarianism, rule-worshipping suckers are irrational because rule utilitarianism is not merely paradoxical, but illogical. *Acting* rightly can never sometimes entail *doing* wrong as if *acting* and *doing* mean different things. Rule utilitarians have

responded by distinguishing between idealistic rule utilitarianism, actual state rule utilitarianism and conditional rule utilitarianism. Ideal rule utilitarianism holds that actions are right if they comport with rules whose general acceptance *would* promote utility. Actual state rule utilitarianism adds the condition that these rules must, *in fact*, be generally accepted. Conditional rule utilitarianism is weaker still as it further stipulates that actions are right if they conform to rules that *always* maximize utility.

6 Mill continues, 'The equal claim of everybody to happiness … involves an equal claim to all the means to happiness …' (1969: 257). In a revealing footnote about Spencer, Mill adds that 'perfect impartiality between persons' supposes that 'equal amounts of happiness are equally desirable, whether felt by the same or by different persons'. These egalitarian implications of impartiality are not identical and entail vastly different redistributive strategies.

7 For Gerald Gaus (2000: 136–45), utilitarian arguments for equality are external because they endorse equal treatment for the sake of advancing some external value, namely happiness. Arguments from fundamental human equality justify equal treatment on the basis of some (internal) attribute according to which people are purportedly equal in fact.

8 For Nicholson (1990), Green is a quintessential idealist as much as Bradley and Bosanquet. For Boucher and Vincent (2000), Green, Bosanquet and Ritchie are idealists, in addition to Bradley, Caird, Jones, Haldane, Collingwood and Oakeshott. By contrast, Hobhouse and Hobson are new liberals. But Boucher calls Green, Caird, Ritchie, Bosanquet, Jones and Haldane 'Idealist New Liberals' (1997: xxiii).

9 Bosanquet's theory of freedom anticipates MacCallum's (1972) celebrated analysis of the overinflated distinction between negative and positive freedom. See Bosanquet (2001: 148).

10 Also see Ritchie (1895: 430). Ritchie's new liberalism eclectically blends utilitarianism, neo-Hegelianism and Darwinism.

11 In his celebrated *Liberalism* (1964: 87), Hobhouse calls his new liberalism 'Liberal Socialism'.

12 Idealists, like Jones and Collingwood, similarly favoured vigorously expanding equal opportunities through government.

13 But trading off goods and virtues implies commensurability.

14 For Miller, there is 'no profound antagonism between meritocracy' and a suitably regulated market because the more egalitarian a market economy is, the more likely it allocates rewards according to merit (1999: 179). Also see Miller's defence of market socialism in *Market, State and Community* (1989) and Cohen (1995: ch. 11) for a critical response. [For a further discussion of Miller's conception of social justice, see Chapter 17.]

15 I include Dworkin in my English pantheon because he epitomizes the kind of cross-fertilization that characterizes so much of contemporary Anglo-American political theory. Barry and Sen typify this cross-fertilization from the direction of England.

16 Following Sen, Dworkin (2000a: ch. 1) considers utilitarianism a form of welfarism. For Sen's rejection of utilitarianism though not consequentialism, see Sen (1979). Also see Dworkin (2000a: ch. 7) for his criticisms of Sen's and Cohen's conceptions of equality.

17 In Dworkin's recent response to Miller's review of *Sovereign Virtue*, he says that by equal resources 'flow[ing] from' equal concern and respect, he means 'consistent with'. He also says that his book aims to 'find attractive conceptions of democracy, liberty, community and individual responsibility that are consistent with or flow from' equal resources in order to 'protect' these values 'from subordination' to equality (Dworkin, 2000b: 15). Now this meaning of 'flow[ing] from' merely requires that distributive justice be compatible with equal concern and respect and not that it is entailed by it.

18 For Sen (1979), welfarism is a narrower form of consequentialism while utilitarianism is a narrower form of welfarism. Whereas consequentialism evaluates actions according to the goodness of the state of affairs they produce, welfarism judges the goodness of a state of affairs by the goodness of its utilities. Utilitarianism judges the goodness of a state's utilities by their sum total.

19 Dunn perceptively argues that contractualism has recently 'recaptured a considerable degree of attention, especially in North America'. But unlike seventeenth-century versions, which focused on political obligation, contemporary versions concentrate on distributive justice (1996: 60).

20 For Scanlon, principles of justice must pass the test of reasonable rejectability. And like Barry, reasonable rejectability endorses principles favouring the worst-off.

21 See especially Barry (1991: ch. 2). For Barry's full treatment of justice as impartiality, see Barry (1995).

22 Also see Phillips (1999a) for a liberal feminist account of the dangers of radically overpoliticizing the personal.

23 Berlin adds that values are objective because we naturally pursue them. But the fact that we happen to pursue them doesn't establish them as true.

24 Gray has recently defended Mill as an anti-rationalist pluralist (2000: 12–13). But he views Raz's value-pluralist liberalism as coming closest to Berlin's, despite the former's perfectionism (Gray, 1996: chs 1 and 6).

25 I concur with Riley that Berlin is a 'humble' rationalist (2001: 284). In my view, Berlin's uneasy marriage of Romantic radical choice and minimal rationalism stems from his Jewishness and Zionism. Fetishizing Romanticism alone invariably encourages 'intolerable choices', while fetishizing rationalism invites final solutions.

26 They also followed Morris, condemning capitalism for degrading labour and community.

27 See Dennis and Halsey (1988) for the history of ethical socialism.

28 But non-Marxist socialists have never hesitated to argue for equality (see Crosland, 1963: ch. VII).

29 Other analytical Marxists include Elster, Roemer and van Parijs. Analytical Marxism again testifies to the converging discourse of Anglo-American political theory, but from the left.

30 Also see Mitchell (1966) for her criticism of Marxists for making women's emancipation an 'adjunct' of critical theory. But see Cohen (2000b: ch. 9) for a recent contrary example.

31 Lovenduski and Randall also provide an excellent account of the rise and contraction of English socialist feminism. Also see Phillips (1999b) where she criticizes radical feminism's 'retreat' from economic egalitarianism, and Phillip's (1999a) contribution to the Horton and Mendus volume.

32 Hence, analytical Marxism's battle with liberal egalitarianism seems more like a sustained skirmish.

33 I eschew discussing Popper and Hayek because neither was arguably English or essentially a political theorist.

34 See especially Oakeshott (1975). Crick argues that Oakeshott's 'enterprise' association is a philosophical caricature 'made of straw' (1973: 130). But note that, for Oakeshott, 'civil' and 'enterprise' associations are archetypes, whereas *societas* and *universitas* are their respective historical manifestations. For the relationship between Oakeshott's two paradigms of political association and his idealism, see Boucher and Vincent (2000: ch. 7).

35 Minogue concedes that his 'conservative realism' is anti-foundational and is thus 'curiously similar' to postmodernism (in Minogue, 1996: 156). Also see O'Sullivan (1992) for more anti-foundationalist conservatism.

36 Hence, conservatism does 'not readily translate itself in universal principles' (Scruton, 1980: 36). A conservative is equally against certain things like Marxism (see Scruton, 1985). See Coates (1996) for a Marxist response.

REFERENCES

Barry, B. (1965) *Political Argument*. London: Routledge and Kegan Paul.

Barry, Brian (1991) *Liberty and Justice*. Oxford: Oxford University Press.

Barry, Brian (1995) *Justice as Impartiality*. Oxford: Oxford University Press.

Barry, Brian (1998) 'Something in the disputation not unpleasant'. In P. Kelly, ed., *Impartiality, Neutrality and Justice*. Edinburgh: Edinburgh University Press, 186–257.

Barry, Brian (2001) 'Isaiah, Israel and tribal realism'. *Times Literary Supplement* (London), 9 November: 7–8.

Berlin, Isaiah (1969) *Four Essays on Liberty*. Oxford: Oxford University Press.

Berlin, Isaiah (1996) *The Sense of Reality*. New York: Farrar, Straus and Giroux.

Berlin, Isaiah (1999) *The Roots of Romanticism*. Princeton, NJ: Princeton University Press.

Berlin, Isaiah (2000) *The Power of Ideas*. Princeton, NJ: Princeton University Press.

Bosanquet, Bernard (2001 [1899]) *The Philosophical Theory of the State*, eds Gerald F. Gaus and William Sweet. South Bend, IL: St Augustine's.

Boucher, David (1997) *The British Idealists*. Cambridge: Cambridge University Press.

Boucher, David and Andrew Vincent (2000) *British Idealism and Political Theory*. Edinburgh: Edinburgh University Press.

Bradley, F. H. (1988 [1927]) *Ethical Studies* (1876). Oxford: Oxford University Press.

Coates, David (1996) 'Roger Scruton and the New Left'. In Neville Kirk, ed., *Social Class and Marxism*. Aldershot: Scolas, 194–213.

Cohen, G. A. (1981) 'Freedom, justice and capitalism'. *The New Left Review*, 126: 3–16.

Cohen, G. A. (1993) 'Equality of what?' In Martha Nussbaum and Amartya Sen, eds, *The Quality of Life*. Oxford: Oxford University Press, 9–29.

Cohen, G. A. (1995) *Self-Ownership, Freedom and Equality*. Cambridge: Cambridge University Press.

Cohen, G. A. (2000a) *Karl Marx's Theory of History*. Princeton, NJ: Princeton University Press.

Cohen, G. A. (2000b) *If You're an Egalitarian, How Come You're So Rich?* Cambridge, MA: Harvard University Press.

Crick, Bernard (1973) *Political Theory and Practice*. New York: Basic.

Crosland, C. A. R. (1963 [1956]) *The Future of Socialism*. New York: Schocken.

Crosland, C. A. R. (1974) *Socialism Now*. London: Cape.

Dennis, Norman and A. H. Halsey (1988) *English Ethical Socialism*. Oxford: Oxford University Press.

Devlin, Patrick (1959) *The Enforcement of Morals*. Oxford: Oxford University Press.

Dunn, John (1996) *The History of Political Theory*. Cambridge: Cambridge University Press.

Dworkin, Ronald (1985) *A Matter of Principle*. Cambridge, MA: Harvard University Press.

Dworkin, Ronald (2000a) *Sovereign Virtue*. Cambridge, MA: Harvard University Press.

Dworkin, Ronald (2000b) 'Equality – an exchange'. *Times Literary Supplement* (London), 1 December: 15–16.

Foote, Geoffrey (1997) *The Labour Party's Political Thought*. New York: St Martin's.

Freeden, Michael (1996) *Ideologies and Political Theory*. Oxford: Oxford University Press.

Gaus, Gerald (2000) *Political Concepts and Political Theories*. Boulder, CO: Westview.

Gray, John (1983) *Mill on Liberty: A Defence*. London: Routledge.

Gray, John (1989) *Liberalisms*. London: Routledge.

Gray, John (1996) *Isaiah Berlin*. Princeton, NJ: Princeton University Press.

Gray, John (2000) *Two Faces of Liberalism*. New York: New Press.

Green, T. H. (1986 [1895]) *Lectures on the Principles of Political Obligation and Other Essays*, eds Paul Harris and John Morrow. Cambridge: Cambridge University Press, 194–212.

Griffin, James (1994) 'The distinction between a criterion and a decision procedure', *Utilitas*, 6: 177–82.

Halévy, Elie (1972) *The Growth of Philosophic Radicalism* (1928). London: Faber and Faber.

Hare, R. M. (1981) *Moral Thinking*. Oxford: Oxford University Press.

Harrison, Ross (1983) *Bentham*. London: Routledge.

Harsanyi, John (1976) *Essays on Ethics, Social Behavior, and Scientific Explanation*. Dordrecht: Reidel.

Harsanyi, John (1985) 'Rule utilitarianism, equality and justice'. *Social Philosophy and Policy*, 2: 115–27.

Hart, H. L. A. (1961) *The Concept of Law*. Oxford: Clarendon.

Hart, H. L. A. (1963) *Law, Liberty, and Morality*. Stanford, CA: Stanford University Press.

Hobhouse, L. T. (1949 [1922]) *The Elements of Social Justice*. London: Allen and Unwin.

Hobhouse, L. T. (1964 [1911]) *Liberalism*. Oxford: Oxford University Press.

Hobhouse, L. T. (1968 [1911]) *Social Evolution and Political Thought*. Port Washington: Kennikat.

Hobson, J. A. (1974 [1909]) *The Crisis of Liberalism*. Brighton: Barnes and Noble.

Hooker, Brad (2000) *Ideal Code, Real World*. Oxford: Oxford University Press.

Ignatieff, Michael (1998) *Isaiah Berlin*. New York: Holt.

Kelly, P. (1990) *Utilitarianism and Distributive Justice*. Oxford: Oxford University Press.

Kelly, P. (1998) 'Taking utilitarianism seriously'. In P. Kelly, ed., *Impartiality, Neutrality and Justice*. Edinburgh: Edinburgh University Press, 44–59.

Letwin, Shirley (1978) 'On conservative individualism'. In Maurice Cowling, ed., *Conservative Essays*. London: Cassell, 52–68.

Liddington, John (1984) 'Oakeshott: freedom in a modern European state'. In Z. Pelczynski and John Gray, eds, *Conceptions of Liberty in Political Philosophy*. New York: St Martin's, 289–329.

Lovenduski, Joni and Vicky Randall (1993) *Contemporary Feminist Politics*. Oxford: Oxford University Press.

Lukes, Steven (1985) *Marxism and Morality*. Oxford: Oxford University Press.

MacCallum, Gerald C. (1972) 'Negative and positive freedom'. In Peter Laslett, W. G. Runciman and Quentin Skinner, eds, *Philosophy, Politics and Society*, fourth series. Oxford: Blackwell, 174–93.

McCarthy, T. (1989–90) 'The politics of the ineffable'. *Philosophical Forum*, 21: 146–68.

Mendus, Susan (1994) 'John Stuart Mill and Harriet Taylor on women and marriage'. *Utilitas*, 6: 287–99.

Mendus, Susan (1998) 'Some mistakes about impartiality'. In P. Kelly, ed., *Impartiality, Neutrality and Justice*. Edinburgh: Edinburgh University Press, 176–85.

Mill, J. S. (1963) *On Liberty*. In J. M. Robson, ed., *The Collected Works of J. S. Mill*, vol. 18. Toronto: University of Toronto Press.

Mill, J. S. (1969) *Utilitarianism*. In J. M. Robson, ed., *The Collected Works of J. S. Mill*, vol. 10. Toronto: University of Toronto Press.

Miller, David (1989) *Market, State and Community*. Oxford: Oxford University Press.

Miller, David (1995) 'Complex equality'. In David Miller and Michael Walzer, eds, *Pluralism, Justice and Equality*. Oxford: Oxford University Press, 197–225.

Miller, David (1999) *Social Justice*. Cambridge, MA: Harvard University Press.

Minogue, Kenneth (1996) 'Introduction' and 'Three conservative realists'. In Kenneth Minogue, ed., *Conservative Realism*. London: Harper Collins, 1–7, 157–71.

Mitchell, Juliet (1966) 'Women: the longest revolution'. *New Left Review*, 40: 11–37.

Mulhall, Stephen and Adam Swift (1996) *Liberals and Communitarians*. Oxford: Blackwell.

Nicholson, Peter (1990) *The Political Philosophy of the British Idealists*. Cambridge: Cambridge University Press.

Nozick, Robert (1974) *Anarchy, State and Utopia*. New York: Basic.

O'Sullivan, Noel (1992) 'Conservatism: a reply to Ted Honderich'. *Utilitas*, 4: 133–43.

Oakeshott, Michael (1975) *On Human Conduct*. Oxford: Oxford University Press.

Pettit, Philip (1993) 'The contribution of analytical political philosophy'. In Robert Goodin and Philip Pettit, eds, *A Companion to Contemporary Political Philosophy*. Oxford: Blackwell, 7–38.

Phillips, Anne (1999a) 'The politicisation of difference'. In John Horton and Susan Mendus, eds, *Toleration, Identity and Difference*. London: Macmillan, 126–45.

Phillips, Anne (1999b) *Which Equalities Matter?* Cambridge: Polity.

Pocock, J. G. A. (1985) *Virtue, Commerce, and History*. Cambridge: Cambridge University Press.

Quinton, Anthony (1993) 'Conservatism'. In Robert Goodin and Philip Pettit, eds, *A Companion to Contemporary Political Philosophy*. Oxford: Blackwell, 244–68.

Rawls, John (1971) *A Theory of Justice*. Cambridge, MA: Harvard University Press.

Raz, Joseph (1986) *The Morality of Freedom*. Oxford: Oxford University Press.

Riley, Jonathan (1988) *Liberal Utilitarianism*. Cambridge: Cambridge University Press.

Riley, Jonathan (2001) 'Interpreting Berlin's liberalism'. *American Political Science Review*, 95: 283–95.

Ritchie, D. G. (1895) 'Free-will and responsibility'. *International Journal of Ethics*, 5: 409–31.

Rosen, Frederick (1990) 'The origin of liberal utilitarianism'. In Richard Bellamy, ed., *Victorian Liberalism*. London: Routledge, 58–70.

Rowbotham, Sheila (1973) *Woman's Consciousness, Man's World*. Harmondsworth: Penguin.

Ryan, Alan (2001) 'Live and let live'. *The New York Review of Books*, 17 May: 54–6.

Scarre, Geoffrey (1996) *Utilitarianism*. London: Routledge.

Schneewind, Jerome (1977) *Sidgwick's Ethics and Victorian Moral Philosophy*. Cambridge: Cambridge University Press.

Schultz, Bart (1992) *Essays on Henry Sidgwick*. Cambridge: Cambridge University Press.

Scruton, Roger (1980) *The Meaning of Conservatism*. London: Macmillan.

Scruton, Roger (1985) *Thinkers of the New Left*. London: Longman.

Sen, Amartya (1979) 'Utilitarianism and welfarism'. *The Journal of Philosophy*, LXXVI: 463–89.

Sen, Amartya (1982) 'Rights and agency'. *Philosophy and Public Affairs*, 11: 3–39.

Sen, Amartya (1993) 'Capability and well-being'. In Martha Nussbaum and Amartya Sen, eds, *The Quality of Life*. Oxford: Oxford University Press, 30–53.

Sen, Amartya (2001) 'Reply'. *Economics and Philosophy*, 17: 51–65.

Sidgwick, Henry (1981 [1907]) *The Methods of Ethics*. Indianapolis: Hackett.

Simhony, Avital (1991) 'On forcing individuals to be free'. *Political Studies*, 49: 303–20.

Simhony, Avital and D. Weinstein, eds (2001) *The New Liberalism*. Cambridge: Cambridge University Press.

Skinner, Quentin (1969) 'Meaning and understanding in the history of ideas'. *History and Theory*, VII: 3–53.

Spencer, Herbert (1978 [1879–93]) *The Principles of Ethics*, 2 vols. Indianapolis: Liberty.

Stephen, James Fitzjames (1991 [1874]) *Liberty, Equality and Fraternity*. Chicago: University of Chicago Press.

Tawney, R. H. (1964 [1952]) *Equality*. London: Unwin.

Tuck, Richard (1993) 'The contribution of history'. In Robert Goodin and Philip Pettit, eds, *A Companion to Contemporary Political Philosophy*. Oxford: Blackwell, 72–89.

Weinstein, D. (1998) *Equal Freedom and Utility*. Cambridge: Cambridge University Press.

Weinstein, D. (2000) 'Deductive hedonism and the anxiety of influence'. *Utilitas*, 12: 329–46.

Weinstein, D. (2001) 'The New Liberalism and the rejection of utilitarianism'. In Avital Simhony and D. Weinstein, eds, *The New Liberalism*. Cambridge: Cambridge University Press, 159–83.

Index

Library
01254 292120

Please return this book on or before the last date below